Morocco

Footprint

Justin McGuinness

D0393677

Over every treasure there stands a genie

Moroccan proverb

4th edition

Morocco Highlights

See colour maps at back of book

1 Tanger
City of the straits. Shades of Burroughs' Interzone in the Kasbah, decaying charms of the Boulevard, beaches

2 Larache and Roman Lixus
Roman site with Atlantic views

3 Rabat
Médina and ville nouvelle, a gentle introduction to Morocco's contrasts

4 Casablanca
Go-getting and grind-you-down , the capital of one-time 'French California'. Art Deco buildings and the world's third largest mosque. (Setting for a Bonfire of the Vanities, Moorish version)

5 Safi
Working fishing port, pottery and phosphates capital. Gritty but real

6 Essaouira
'The windy one', surf centre, a Moroccan St Malo?

7 The Tizi-n-Tichka routes
Switch-back turns over the Atlas, gentle Ouirgane, the remote austerity of Tin Mal mosque

8 Marrakech
The Red City, pleasure capital. Jewel-box guesthouses, souks teeming with must-buy crafts, mountain excursions

9 Sidi Ifni
Once an obscure Spanish colony. Surf beaches and cliff arches at Lagzira

10 Tata and Akka
Chleuh villages and prehistoric carvings in the desert

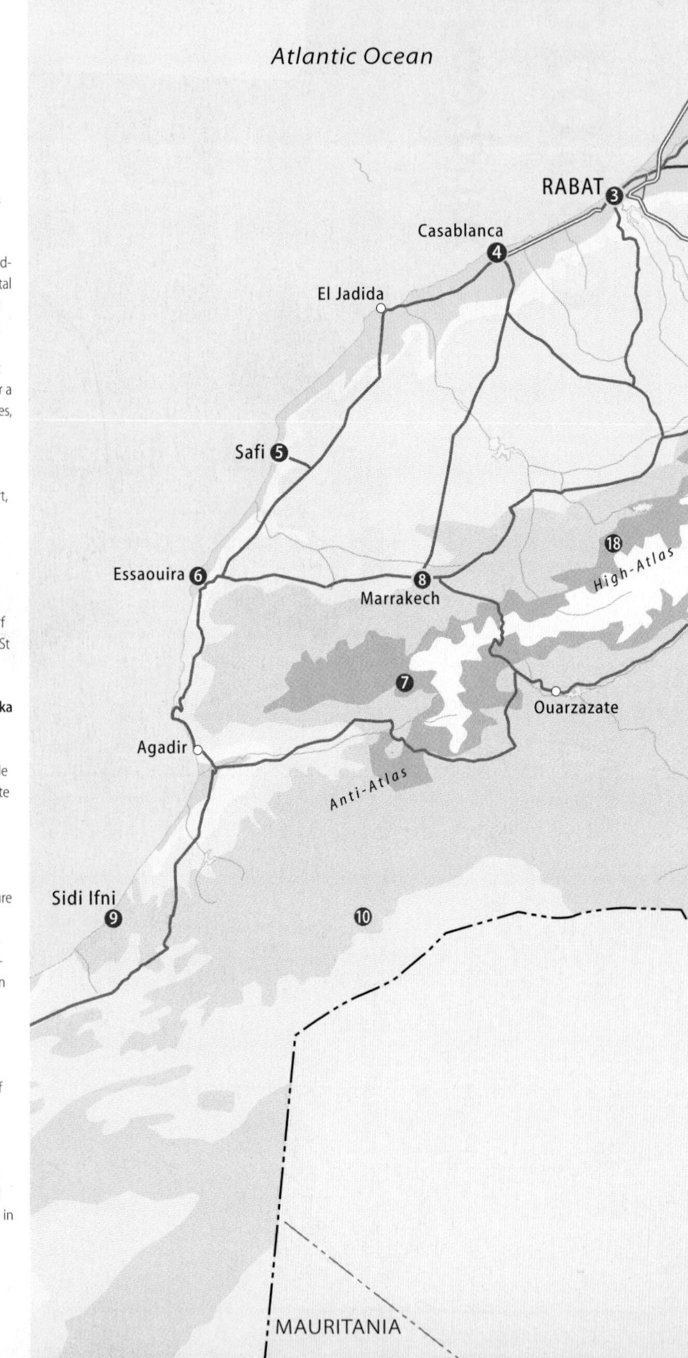

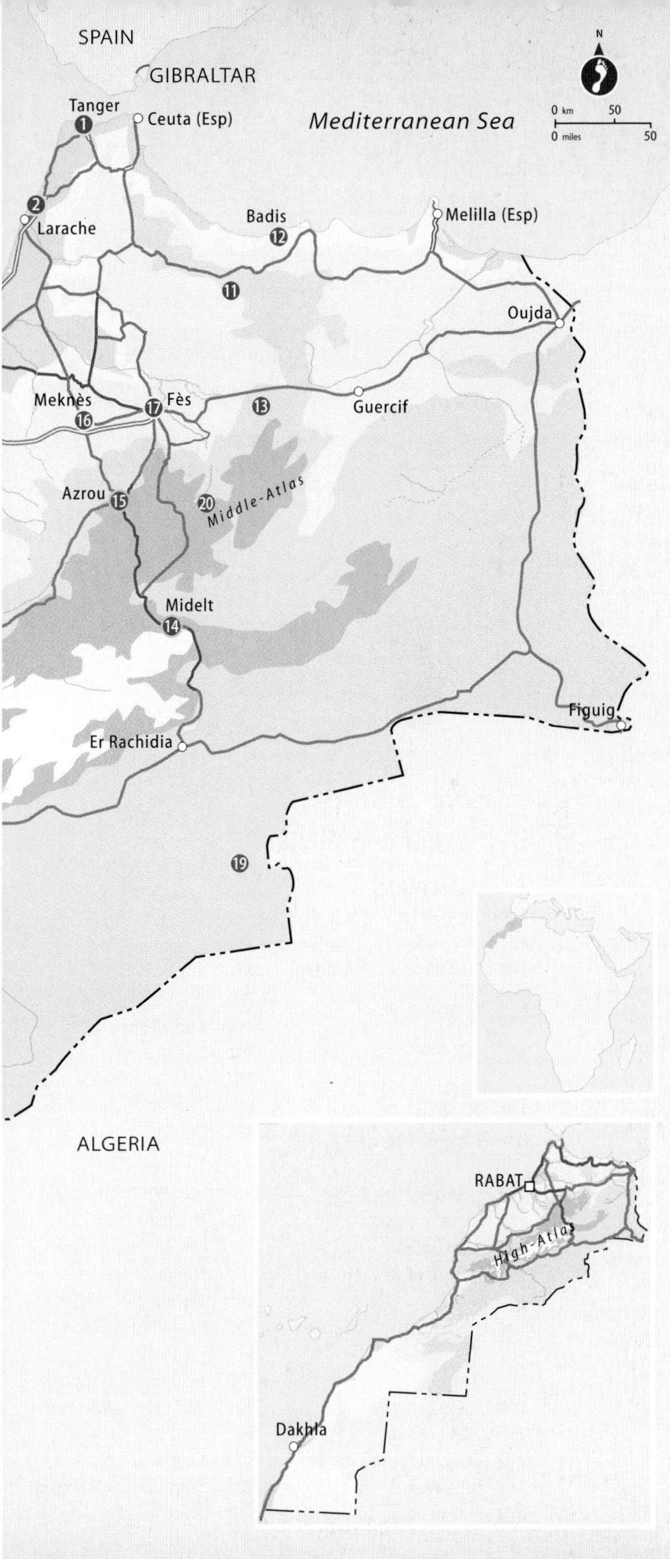

11 Jbel Tidghine
The Rif's highest mountain. Mountain forests

12 Badis
Near Al Hoceïma, isolated Mediterranean beach and site of Fès's long lost port

13 The Gouffre de Friouato
Jbel Tazzeka National Park, near Taza. 500 slippery stairs and a squeeze to view the stalactites

14 Midelt
Eerie abandoned mines in the Moulouya Gorge, Ahouli

15 Azrou and the cedar woods
Land of Barbary apes and hobbits

16 Imperial Meknès
Kilometres of crumbling pisé ramparts, a manageable médina

17 Labyrinthine Fès
Morocco's Athens, centuries of spirituality within the walls

18 Vallée des Aït Bougmez
Dinosaur footsteps in remote High Atlas of Azilal

19 The Tafilalet
The canyons of the Ziz, classic dunes at Merzouga

20 Skoura and the Dadès route
Earth-built fortresses in the palm groves

Contents

Introducing

9 Introducing Morocco

Essentials

18 **Planning your trip**
18 Where to go
19 When to go
19 Tours and tour operators
24 Finding out more
25 Language
26 Disabled travellers
26 Gay and lesbian travellers
26 Student travellers
26 Travelling with children
27 Women travellers
28 Working in the country
28 **Before you travel**
28 Getting in
29 What to take
30 **Money**
32 **Getting there**
37 **Touching down**
37 Airport information
38 Seaport information
39 Tourist information
40 Local customs and laws
40 Tipping
41 Security and terrorism
42 Safety
42 **Where to stay**
46 **Getting around**
53 **Keeping in touch**
53 Communications
54 Media
55 **Food and drink**
55 Moroccan cuisine
58 Cafés and restaurants
59 Drinks
59 **Shopping**
61 **Entertainment and nightlife**
62 **Holidays and festivals**
64 **Sport and activities**
70 **Health**
70 Before you go
71 Further information
73 On the road

Guide

Rabat and around

78 **Rabat**
99 **Salé**
104 Easy excursions from Rabat and Salé
105 Kénitra
105 Mehdiya
107 Ancient Thamusida
109 Moulay Bousselham
110 Ancient Banasa
112 South of Rabat

Casablanca and the central Atlantic coast

116 **Casablanca**
134 Mohammedia (ex-Fedala)
138 Azemmour
140 **El Jadida (ex-Mazagan)**
146 Oualidia
148 **Safi**
157 **Essaouira**

Tanger and the Northwest

172 **Tanger**
182 West of Tanger
183 East of Tanger
192 **South of Tanger**
192 Asilah
194 El Utad, the stone circle at Mzoura
195 Larache
199 **Ceuta**
205 **Tetouan**
210 Around Tetouan
211 **Chaouen**
215 The Northern Rif
217 **Al Hoceima**
221 Ouezzane and the Southern Rif

Imperial cities and the Middle Atlas

226 **Meknès**
238 **Moulay Idriss and Volubilis**
239 Moulay Idriss
239 Volubilis
242 **The Middle Atlas**
242 Azrou
244 Aïn Leuh, waterfalls and Aguelmane Azigza
245 Ifrane, Mischliffen and an excursion to the lakes
246 Khénifra, El Ksiba and Kasbah Tadla
248 **Fès**
254 Fès el Jedid
256 Fès el Bali
272 **Around Fès**
272 Moulay Yacoub
272 Sidi Harazem and Bhalil
273 Sefrou
275 **Taza**
278 Jbel Tazzeka National Park
281 **East of Taza**
281 Guercif
282 From Guercif to Midelt
283 Taourirt
284 Debdou

Northeastern Morocco

288 Eastwards from Al Hoceïma to Nador
288 **Nador**
293 **Melilla**
300 **Eastwards towards Algeria**
300 Berkane
301 Beni Snassen Mountains
302 **Saïdia**
304 **Oujda**
309 **South towards Figuig**
310 Figuig

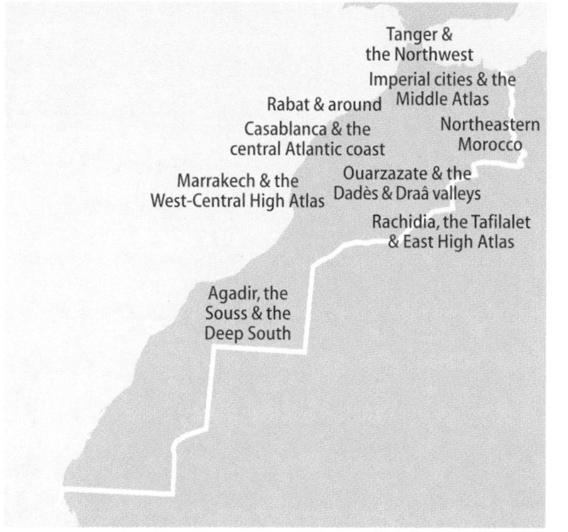

Marrakech and the West-Central High Atlas

316 **Marrakech**
322 Jemaâ el Fna
324 Koutoubia Mosque
325 North of Jemaâ el Fna
328 Kasbah quarter
358 **The Toubkal High Atlas**
358 Up the Amizmiz Road
360 Excursions up the Taroudant Road
362 Tin Mal
365 **Trekking in the Toubkal National Park**
365 Imlil
368 **The Ourika Valley**
370 Oukaïmeden
371 **The Tizi-n-Tichka route**
372 **Telouet**
373 Telouet to Ouarzazate via Aït Ben Haddou
374 **Azilal High Atlas**
374 Northeast of Marrakech: the Azilal High Atlas and Beni Mellal
374 To Azilal Demnate and Ouzoud
375 Azilal
376 Vallée des Aït Bougmez
377 The Massif du Mgoun
378 **Beni Mellal**
378 Northwest of Beni Mellal

Ouarzazate and the Dadès and Draâ valleys

384 **South of the High Atlas**
385 **Ouarzazate**
390 Aït Ben Haddou
391 **The Draâ Valley**
393 Zagora
395 South of Zagora
396 East from Zagora to Rissani
398 El Kalâa Mgouna
400 **The Dadès and Todgha Gorges**
400 Boumalne du Dadès
402 Tineghir
405 East from Tineghir to Er Rachidia

Rachidia, the Tafilalet and East High Atlas

410 **Er Rachidia**
413 South towards the Tafilalet
414 **Erfoud**
416 Rissani
418 Around Rissani
420 **The East High Atlas**
420 **Midelt**
421 Around Midelt
422 Imilchil
424 Trekking from Imilchil to Anergui and Zaouiat Ahansal

Agadir, the Souss and the Deep South

428 **Agadir**
437 Inezgane
438 **North of Agadir**
438 Taghazoute
438 Immouzer des Ida Outanane
440 **South of Agadir**
442 **Taroudant**
445 Taroudant to Ouarzazate, via Taliouine and Tazenakht
447 **Trekking in the Jbel Siroua**
447 Taroudant to Tata via Igherm
449 Tata to Bou Izakarn via Akka, Amtoudi and Ifrane de L'Anti-Atlas
452 **Tiznit**
455 **Tafraroute and the Ameln Valley**
458 Goulimine (Guelmin)
460 Sidi Ifni
463 Tan Tan
464 Tarfaya
465 **Laâyoune**
467 South into the Sahara
469 Boujdour and Dakhla

Background

472 **History**
482 **Modern Morocco**
492 **Culture**
499 **Architecture**
507 **Language**
509 **Music**
510 **Entertainment**
511 **Sport**
512 **Land and environment**
518 **Books**

Footnotes

522 Language in Morocco
532 Glossary
537 Indexes
548 Map symbols
549 Colour maps

Inside front cover

Overview
Price Guide

Inside back cover

Author

A foot in the door

South of the High Atlas *(previous page) Ochre evening light on the walls of a settlement in the Dadès region.*
Marrakech market *(right) The markets of Morocco are renowned for freshly ground spices. Each stall will have its specialities.*
Gate of the Victorious One *(below) Bab Mansour, entrance to the imperial palace complex in Meknès.*

Chechaouen blues *(above) Dreaming of a desert elsewhere in a northern Moroccan town.*
Honeycomb of colour *(right) Up to their waste in slimy liquids, the tanners of Fès hard at work.*

Introducing Morocco

For centuries, Morocco has enticed travelers. For some, it means souks, streets striped with sunlight filtered through lattice roofing, spice odours, the glow of carpets in a cavernous emporium, caftans, lipstick-red leather, the shine of copper. This is of course the land where Delacroix and Matisse discovered colour. For others, Morocco is the tawny smell of brasero-cooked tajine, frothy tea glasses stuffed with infusing leaves, honey sticky gazelle horns. Morocco is both remote and familiar. Its arid wastes and kasbahs star in films, its cities can be secretive, seething, contrasted: austere Fès and Rick's Casablanca, maverick Tanger and Goytisolo's Marrakech.

Northernmost state in Africa, on the western edge of the Muslim world, Morocco is also the closest Arab land to Europe. But the Arabness has taken the imprint of the region's original inhabitants, the mountain dwelling Imazighen. This unusual mix of the Arab and the Amazigh, with French and Spanish tints added during 20th-century colonization, distinguishes the Moroccans from the peoples of the Middle East. The country's history divides into the obscure pre-Islamic past and the centuries of often brilliant Islamic civilization following the Arab-Muslim conquest in the seventh century AD. From the 16th to the 19th century, the sultans were busy keeping expanding Europe at bay. A difficult coastline and high mountains enabled Morocco's peoples to maintain their independence into the early 20th century. And it is probably in the fierceness of the landscapes that Morocco is at its most spectacular. A couple of hours' flight from Europe are dune deserts and oasis gorges, arid mountains and cedar forests, cliffs falling sheer to the surf and ocean citadels. It may be a travel writer's cliché, but with the shores of Morocco, exotica begins.

Highlights

Morocco's relative isolation and late colonization meant that traditional ways of life continued undisturbed in many ways into the second half of the 20th century. Today the cities of Fès and Meknes, Marrakech and Tanger, among the greatest historic towns of the Mediterranean region, are the highlights of any journey.

Fès the spiritual

To start with the oldest, most secretive city: high-walled Fès, religious heart of Morocco and capital of a medieval empire. Narrow lanes where transport is by mule snake downwards to a labyrinthine centre. Here stands the Qaraouiyine Mosque, surrounded by crumbling religious colleges and thronging souks, niche-like shops where tailors painstakingly stitch caftans, eateries where calf trotters steam, alleys pungent with the smell of cedar wood shavings. But it is at night fall, gazing out over the terrace roofs of Fès, with the prayer call rising from the mosques and swifts whistling by, that you best sense the spirit of Fès.

Tranquil Meknès

Less visited is near neighbour Meknès, a médina onto which warring, restless sultan Moulay Ismail grafted a palace complex of Versailles-like scale in the 17th century. Kilometres of ramparts and gates, granaries, stabling and a vast reflecting pool have survived. Nearby, out in the olive groves, stand the scattered columns and arches of Roman Volubilis, perfect setting for a sword-and-sandal epic. From Meknès, you can head south across a region of cedar forests to Midelt, jumping-off point for an excursion up into the eastern High Atlas or to the abandoned mines of Ahouli.

Marrakech the joyful

Eating and a spot of shopping must be a highlight of any trip to Morocco. Marrakech, most frivolous of Morocco's cities, is the place for this. (Natives of Marrakech are nicknamed *bahja*, fun-timers.) Garden courtyard dining is of the essence with Andalucían lute music to aid digestion. (For post-prandial recreation, the city has a handful of nightspots from the brash to the extra-louche.) In the souks, everything is possible: monsieur requires fifty copper lanterns set with moonstones and one of those Boujaad rugs? No problem, we ship next week sir. The Marrakech region also has the most interesting range of accommodation. Old city homes are now guesthouses, most *mauresque* in character. While the uber-rich take their mini-breaks in the villas in the palm groves, there are plenty of backpacker places in Jemaâ el Fna. Further afield, in dusty villages, converted kasbahs stand sentinel to welcome the visitor. And in Atlas villages, kipping under the stars on your trek guide's roof is part of the experience.

Tanger the interloper

Least visited – except by migrants returning home in summer – is Morocco's Mediterranean north. Tanger in the far northwest, closest African metropolis to Europe, backdrop to many a literary life, is the most underrated of the major cities. Its international status is long gone, but its interloper air survives. Nearby are Mediterranean beaches, empty for most of the year, and hilltop Chaouen, a popular stop on the neo-hippy traveller trail. Cedar-clothed Jbel Tidghine, the Rif region's highest peak, is cool even in summer.

Perfect landscapes

Travelling between the great cities, the visitor discovers a land of spectacular landscapes. Snowcapped in winter, burnt ochre in summer, the High Atlas is the main range, with Toubkal one of Africa's highest peaks. On remoter plateaux, the visitor may find prehistoric rock carvings – and isolated valleys, home to Amazigh villages and their green terraced fields and walnut groves. South of the Atlas are the canyons and oases of kasbah-land, places for trekking, biking and birdwatching. And down in the southeastern corner of the country is desert fit for a Hollywood epic, the great dunes of Merzouga.

Wedding festival *(left) The moussem or annual late summer festival at Imilchil, essential to the Amazigh sense of identity.*

Real and imagined bargains *(below) A souk inside Marrakech's médina, where you can wander for hours through sunstreaked alleys.*

Casablanca style *(above) Street with boulevards of buildings reflecting Art Deco, Neo-Moorish and modern-movement influences.*

Marrakech, Jemaâ el Fna *(left) Powdery slilou served with ginger-flavoured tea is said to be an aphrodisiac.*

Biggest barbecue in the world *(next page) When night falls on Jemaâ el Fna, out come the barbecue coals and hissing gas lamps.*

42
30

***Ritual purity** (right) An essential part of daily life, the washing of feet, arms and face before prayer.*

***Camel train** (below) Not Rajasthan but Zagora. Beturbanned Berber leads his intrepid caravan across the shifting sands.*

***Window dressing** (above) A walk through the médina will reveal a surprise or two.*

***Horseshoe arches** (right) The restored mosque at Tin Mal, pride of the Almohad dynasty, in a remote High Atlas valley.*

***Yves Klein blue** (next page) A surprising splash of blue in the Red City. Surrounded by bamboo groves, the Villa Majorelle is a top attraction in suburban Marrakech.*

Kingdom in a time of change

21st-century Morocco

Morocco – or so the tourist literature would have it – is 'a feast for the senses', a land straight from the Arabian Nights. Though the landscapes are always spectacular, the reality of daily life is often more prosaic. Outside the main centres, a grinding poverty is all too often apparent. If cities like Marrakech are to continue as playgrounds for the uber-rich, then Moroccan governments will have a big task ahead of them to calm a growing swell of discontent. Remember, the wealth gap between Spain and Morocco is the biggest in the world between two neighbouring countries, bar the USA and Mexico. Literacy is pitifully low – around 56% of the population, and a quarter of the population lives below the poverty line. Thus educational reform is coming to the fore, along with ecological issues and bringing the country's industry up to international norms. The tourist business is concerned, with five new integrated beach resorts projected. Here niche-market travel is promising: wilderness walking and surfing, music festivals and heritage travel are all promising sectors. More broadly, Morocco has some good trump cards in its hand: relative political stability, a big internal market (30 million people), a highly educated elite, and a large and dynamic emigrant community.

Progress & tradition

Of the Arab states, Morocco is the hardest to classify. In Casablanca, the big smoke and one-time capital of a colonial dream, 'French California', the pace is hard. Gilded enclaves criss-crossed with palm-tree lined avenues sit alongside acres of tin-roofed shacks where the only thing to sprout is the satellite dish. In remote rural areas, life still beats to the rhythm of the seasons and the Muslim year. Walking in the Atlas, you'll come across scenes straight from Flemish old-master paintings: women stumbling down hillsides with bundles of firewood, donkeys trotting across the fields, taking children to the spring. But chances are that there will be a cybercafé in the nearest village, now sprawling dustily outwards. The new flats on spindly concrete legs will have been financed by migrants' earnings. The modernity versus tradition theme is a complex one: back in the cities, a francophone elite defends tradition avidly – too keenly, some would say, acting in the past like a colonial class on its own turf. Businessmen with palm pilots may well have a strong spiritual dimension to their lives, belonging to traditional religious brotherhoods. The great Muslim holidays are observed. Ramadhan is a time for family gatherings – and a general slow-down in the workplace, a true challenge to globalization.

An enduring welcome?

Above all, the general niceness of people will strike the visitor from north Atlantic lands. In the cities, at *paseo* time, the human tides are impressive. One rarely feels unsafe, however. Moroccans like to talk – and this is not always motivated by a need to extract extra tourist dirhams. They are always interested in others and their lives often show tremendous generosity with time and hospitality – even if the means available are limited. You will be made welcome in mountain homes, small restaurants and little cafés in a way impossible in more frenetic, 'up-to-date' lands. Morocco leaves few indifferent, and with its tremendous cultural and natural heritage, may leave you wanting to make another visit. The question is what sort of country will you find in five, ten years' time. Will Casablanca acquire a Barcelona sheen or descend into Lagos-like chaos? Will this be Portugal or Iran, a peaceful passage to democracy or a growing dour religious presence in government? One can only hope that shares in the national cake will be given out more fairly to all Moroccans than was the case in the 20th century.

Essentials

18 Planning your trip
18 Where to go
19 When to go
19 Tours and tour operators
24 Finding out more
25 Language
26 Disabled travellers
26 Gay and lesbian travellers
26 Student travellers
26 Travelling with children
27 Women travellers
28 Working in the country

28 Before you travel
28 Getting in
29 What to take

30 Money

32 Getting there
32 Air
34 Road
35 Sea
36 Train

37 Touching down
37 Airport information
38 Seaport information
39 Tourist information
40 Local customs and laws
40 Tipping
41 Security and terrorism
42 Safety

42 Where to stay

46 Getting around
46 Air
47 Road
52 Train

53 Keeping in touch
53 Communications
54 Media

55 Food and drink
55 Moroccan cuisine
58 Cafés and restaurants
59 Drinks

59 Shopping

61 Entertainment and nightlife

62 Holidays and festivals

64 Sport and activities

70 Health
70 Before you go
71 Further information
73 On the road

Planning your trip

Where to go

Morocco is a large country, with big distances between the major cities. To make the most of your stay, some careful planning is no bad thing. The question is, what can you reasonably expect to see, without overtiring yourself, within the time period you have for your trip? The following suggestions are based on circuits of a week, a fortnight and three weeks. Rather than try to take in a maximum of towns and areas, it's best to get to know a couple of places really well. There follow some suggestions for a city-based approach as well.

A week's holiday

All in all, given the distances, it is best to be selective - or have more than a week's break

If you have a week, you should try either to discover Marrakech and around really thoroughly or cover the main imperial cities. Using public transport, you can take in Rabat, Fès or Meknès, Marrakech and Casablanca. Most of the travelling would be done by train, but you would have a long bus ride from Fès to Marrakech. It would be pushing it to fit in Tanger as well.

As far as discovering Marrakech, you need three nights to do it justice. You could also have a day trip into the High Atlas. Three options here: either up to the Ourika valley to Oukaïmeden, to Imlil, Ouirgane and Tin Mal or up to the Tizi-n-Tichka pass and Telouet. Or you could reduce the time in Marrakech and do a little walking in the Atlas, either from Setti Fatma or Imlil. Finally, you could go to Essaouira on the coast for a couple of nights to contrast the rush of the Red City with the Atlantic coast.

For those with an interest in things architectural, in a week you could cover Fès and Meknès very thoroughly, visit the cedar forests in the Middle Atlas and then go back down to Rabat or Casablanca for a night or two before leaving. If you have come in for a business meeting at, say Casablanca, you can easily visit Rabat to the north or El Jadida and Azemmour to the south as a side trip.

Many tourists fly into Agadir which makes a good base for a driving holiday in southwest Morocco. In a week you could cover Taroudant (dubbed 'the little Marrakech'), the prehistoric rock carvings of the Akka area, Amtoudi, Sidi Ifni and the Anti-Atlas around Tafraoute. There would be plenty of time for the beach, too.

Two-week holiday

With two weeks, you could do a circuit by public transport, taking in the major cities, and then a week either trekking in the mountains or taking in some of the places on the southern side of the Atlas – the Draâ and Dadès valleys, or maybe Taroudant and Tafraoute, close to Agadir. You could combine a circuit including Rabat, El Jadida, Essaouira and Marrakech with walking in the High Atlas, for example. You could do the northwest along with Rabat, Fès and Meknès very thoroughly, with time to visit some more out of the way places like Moulay Yacoub (small spa town near Fès), and Larache and Asilah (old Atlantic port towns near Tanger). If in Marrakech, you might pick up an organized tour to take you right across to the Atlas to kasbah land, Er Rachidia and the dunes of Merzouga.

Three-week holiday

A three-week trip will enable you to get to know parts of Morocco really thoroughly: take a one or two week organized walking tour up in the High or Anti-Atlas (the latter in winter). For the hardy, the highlight of a three-week trip might be five or more days walking in the middle of the trip in the Vallée des Aït Bougmez, south of Azilal in the east-central High Atlas.This could be combined with time out at one of the coastal resorts (Essaouira, maybe Agadir), or travel by public transport along the Dadès Valley/Ziz Valley as far as Merzouga. And you would still have time to do some urban sightseeing.

On your fourth or fifth visit

Having visited Morocco a few times you will most likely have seen the 'must see' sights. You'll now be able to discover the delights of the Plateau des cèdres, south of Azrou, the springs of Oum Er Rabia, or the winding routes up into the Atlas beyond Beni Mellal. If you like the more obscure towns, then you can go and look at Youssoufia, difficult and much maligned Safi, Boujaâd and Kasbah Tadla. For those with a lot of time, then you might want to head for remote Figuig on the far eastern frontier, Debdou, odd Mediterranean resorts like El Hoceima or Saïdia, the remote beaches of Badis and El Jebha or the former mining town of Jerrada. Whatever, there will always be obscure places to discover. Happily, the roads are constantly being improved, and parts of the country once accessible only to 4WD are now open to the intrepid saloon car driver.

When to go

See also Climate, page 514, and Holidays and Festivals, page 62

Morocco is a good destination all year round, although January and February can be a bit cold and miserable in the North. Tanger and Fès under heavy rain are not too much fun. However, after a wet winter, the spring is delightful in the North and central regions. Routes from Tanger are busy in summer with returning migrant workers from Europe in overloaded cars and are best avoided as is Tanger itself with day-trippers from Spain. Urban sightseeing is fine all year round, although in Marrakech and Fès the heat can be oppressive during the day from July to late September. If you are going to do the southern routes such as the Dadès and Draâ Valleys, late February and March are magnificent. The blossom will be out, the days will be bright, and you won't suffer too much on public transport or driving.

For those coming to Morocco for an active sort of holiday, golf is pleasant from autumn to spring. For mountain walking, spring, summer and autumn are fine in the High Atlas. The Jbel Saghro, south of the High Atlas, is a winter walking destination. Windsurfers, based at, say Essaouira, will find winds stronger in summer, but the swell bigger in winter.

Morocco is known as 'a cold country with a hot sun'. Some of the coastal towns can be cold and damp in winter. Desert and pre-desert areas are obviously dry and hot, but from December to February are extremely cold at night. On the other hand, mountain areas can get quite hot during the summer days. Occasional but heavy showers occur turning the dry riverbeds into dangerous flash floods and snow blocks the passes of the High Atlas in winter.

Note also that some of the major cities, and in particular Casablanca, have high pollution levels due mainly to diesel vehicles. This, combined with the damp Atlantic air, can make life highly unpleasant for anyone with asthma.

For those with an interest in music, there are now a number of annual music festivals in the spring with which you could try to coincide. In late May/early June, Fès is host to the *Festival des musiques sacrées*. Essaouira has *Les Alizées*, a short season of European classical music in April, and the festival of Gnaoua music, including Afro-Jazz, in June. The Tanger Jazz Festival is also about this time. July weekends see the *Festival des arts populaires* in Marrakech. In September, Marrakech film festival is now an established event. The more traditional Moroccoan festivals or *moussems*, originally organized to commemorate a local saint, are important for locals, and can be part-agricultural fair, part-traditional gathering. In recent years, many have been cancelled by the authorities for health and security reasons.

Tours and tour operators

In the UK

Expensive *Abercrombie and Kent*, T020-7730 9600, www.abercrombiekent.com *Cadogan Travel*, T01703-332551, www.cadongantravel.com Main resort destinations. *CV Travel*, T020-7591 2810. Top of the range villa rental. ***Morocco Made to Measure (CLM)***, 4a William Street, Knightsbridge, London, SW3 1JJ, T020-7235 0123, F7235 3851. Made-to-measure itineraries, horse riding, trekking, birdwatching, cultural tours, golf, tennis. A reliable firm that knows its Morocco. **Mid-range** *British Airways*, T01293-723100. Moroccan city breaks. *Hayes and Jarvis*, T020-8748 5050. Tours of Morocco's main cities. **Budget** *Moroccan Travel Bureau*, 304, Old Brompton Road, London, SW5 9JF, T020-7373 4411. Reasonably priced flights and accommodation in main cities.

In Germany *Atlas Activ Tours*, Liebenhofen 42, D 88287 Grünkrant, T00-49-751-769340, www.atlas-activ-tours.de

Essentials

In Morocco

When ringing from the UK, prefix 00 212 and remove the initial 0 from the nine-digit number. In Morocco all numbers have nine digits which includes the regional code

Agadir *Complete Tours* (general manager Lesley Sanchez), 1 imm. Beau Souss, R du Camping, T048-823403, lessan@futurnet.net.ma **Casablanca** *Atlas Voyages*, 150 Av des FAR (travel agency) T022-314798, F316902. Central management at 44 Av des FAR atlasdg@ mbox.azure.net A major chain of travel agencies, link in with ABF Congrès, one of the main conference and incentive travel organiszers. About as reliable as they get. **Marrakech** *Atlas Sahara Trek*, 6 bis R Houdhoud, Quartier Majorelle, T044-313901, www.atlas-sahara-trek.com Highly recommended agency with 20 years experience of organiszing treks in Morocco. Casablanca-born director Bernard Fabry knows the south-eastern desert really well. Company also has a beautiful hostel, *Dar Itrane*, in the central High Atlas. *Complete Tours*, résidence Badr, 2nd floor, 220, Blvd Mohammed V, Guéliz, T061-708036 (Tim Buxton). Arranges all sorts of excursions around Marrakech and Essaouira. Works with a number of well-reputed British tour operators. Their Berber Trails 4WD excursion is a firm favourite with visitors. *High Country*, 31 Bab Amadil, Amizmiz, T044-454847, highcountry@cybernet.net.ma Agency based in Amizmiz in the foothills of the High Atlas. Organizes rock climbing, off-roading, mountaineering, kayaking on the Lalla Takerkoust dam lake. Founded 1997, works with UK, US and Italian groups. *Pampa Voyages*, 203 Blvd Mohammed V, Guéliz. T044431052, www.pampamaroc.com A big range of tours inclusing 4WD safaris.

Special interest travel

There are a number of companies which specialize in holidays in Morocco. Some of the trekking companies have many years of experience

UK and Ireland *Africa Explored*, Rose Cottage, Summerleaze, Magor, Newport, UK NP6 3DE. Overland camping expeditions and safaris which include a three-week comprehensive circular journey from Tanger called Morocco Encountered, visiting the main cities and main sites, and a shorter two-week Morocco Encountered with a flight back from Marrakech. Their 22-week Trans African expedition begins in Morocco and goes on through Mauritania to Nairobi. *Atlas Mountain Information Service (AMIS)*, 26 Kircaldy Road, Burntisland, Fife, KY3 9HQ T01592-873546. Small agency run by Hamish Brown, who organizes treks and climbing trips. *The Best of Morocco*, Seend Park, Seend, Wiltshire SN12 0NZ, UK, T01380-828533, www.morocco-travel.com Offer unlimited flexibility using quality hotels. *The British Museum Traveller*, 46 Bloomsbury St, London WC1B 3QQ, www.britishmuseumtraveller.co.uk Part of the British Museum. Advertises a nine-day accompanied tour of the Royal Cities of Morocco. Not cheap. *Exodus*

sightseeing.

exodus.co.uk

The Different Holiday

Leaders in small group Walking & Trekking, Discovery & Adventure, Biking Adventures, European Destinations, Overland Journeys, Snow and Multi Activity Holidays Worldwide.

Tel 020 8772 3822 for brochure.
e-mail: sales@exodus.co.uk

Exodus Travels Ltd ATOL

www.exodus.co.uk

Since 1982

"The ultimate look at the land and culture" — Vogue
"The tours emphasize authenticity" — Travel & Leisure

Specializing in

Custom-Designed Travel Arrangements for
Independent Travelers
Special-Interest Groups
Museum & University Study Tours to

Morocco

Feel like an "insider" with private arrangements, exclusive activities, unique sites. From Pasha-style luxury in deluxe lodgings to trekking and Land Rover explorations with warm hospitality in tribal hamlets.

Also

Mali ◊ Tunisia ◊ India

Cross Cultural Adventures

PO Box 3285, Arlington, VA 22203
(703) 237-0100 • FAX (703) 237-2558 • piotrk@erols.com

Travels, T020-8772 3822, sales@exodus.co.uk, www.exodus.co.uk Well-established worldwide operator. ***Explore Worldwide***, 1 Frederick Street, Aldershot, Hants GU11 1LQ, T0125-319448, www.exploreworldwide.com Offers small exploratory accompanied travels. On offer are eight days in the Jbel Siroua including Taroudant; 15 days trekking in the High Atlas attempting an ascent of Mount Toubkal; 15 days in the sparsely populated Jbel Saghro; 15 days exploring the mountains, desert and coasts in winter; 15 days visiting the Imperial Cities of Marrakech, Rabat, Fès and Meknès then moving on into the great sand sea. This group attempts to make the impact of tourism positive – by taking small groups, dealing with local suppliers for transport and food and controlling litter and waste disposal. ***Guerba***, Guerba Adventure & Discovery Holidays, Wessex House, 40 Station Rd, Westbury, Wiltshire, BA13 3JN, T01373-858956 (brochures), T826611 (reservation), www.guerba.com Tours and treks. ***Imaginative Traveller***, 14 Barley Mow Passage, Chiswick, London, W1 4PH, T020-8742 8612, www.imaginative-traveller.com Has well trained, motivated ground-staff who have worked in lots of countries. As you would expect, an imaginative choice of hotels. Main clients are experienced travellers with professional jobs who do not have the time to set up holidays for themselves. Lots of free time built into schedules. ***Insight Travel***, Insight International Bldg, 26 Paradise Road, Richmond, Surrey, TW9 1SE, T020-8332 29000, www.insight-travel.com. Trips combine Morocco with Spain and Portugal. ***Inspirations Morocco***, Inspirations East Ltd, Victoria House, Victoria Road, Horley, Surrey, RH6 7AD, T0129-3822244, F3821732. Very reliable, offer special interest section birdwatching, trekking, sport, but their advertised tailor-made travels can only be made up from the areas/hotels they use. ***Jasmin Tours***, High St, Cookham, Maidenhead, Berks SL6, 9SQ, T0162-8531121, F8529444. Escorted tours to Casablanca, Rabat, Fès, Zagora, and Marrakech. Advertised as cultural tours. ***I-escape.com*** (dir Laila Ram),

"In-depth Explorations
for the Sophisticated Traveler"

Custom Designed
Private Tours
Morocco · Spain · Turkey · South Africa

• Private custom-designed itineries
• Charming accommodations
• Luxurious private transport
• Excellent guides

Recommended by Travel & Leisure, Departures
and National Geographic Traveller

Heritage Tours

121 West 27th Street, Suite 1201, New York City, N.Y.
1 800 378 4555
www.heritagetoursONLINE.com

Essentials

42 Orlando Rd, London SW4 0LF. T0207-6524625, F6524632, laila@escape.com Personalized holidays to a range of destinations, including Morocco. ***Morocco Bound Ltd***, Triumph House, 189 Regent St, London W1R 7WE, T0207-7345307, F2879127. Guided tours, Land Rover tours, horse riding, short breaks. They can organize individual journeys using the hotels in their brochure. ***Nature Trek***, Chautara, Bighton, Hampshire, SO24 9RB, T01962-733051. Offer natural history and birdwatching tours in South Morocco. Use good accommodation. ***Prospect Music and Art Tours***, 454-458 Chiswick High Rd, London W4 5TT, T020-8995 2163. Accompanied tours with experts in art and art history, archaeology and architecture. ***Rambler Holidays***, Box 43, Welwyn Garden City, Herts, AL8 6PQ, T020-7733 1133. ***Sahara Trek***, T1800-9598820, wwwsahara trek.com US company offering weekly inclusive adventure and sightseeing tours. Package to custom designed. Desert trekking, Imperial cities, golf, whitewater rafting, beach resorts, skiing. ***Specialist – Golf International***, 36 Mill Lane, London NW6 1NR, T020-8452 4263, F8208 3894. They have agents in Rabat and Mohammadia. ***Sunbird Tours***, PO Box 76, Sandy, Bedfordshire, SG19 1DF, T01767-682969, www.sunbirdtours.co.uk Company catering to both the keen birdwatcher happy to be out from dawn to dusk and also those wishing to combine birds with other interests. ***Trafalgar Travel***, 5 Bressenden Place, Victoria, London, SW1E 5DF, T020-7828 8143. ***Travel Bag Adventures***, 15 Turk St, Alton, Hampshire, GU34 1AG, T01420-541007. Trekking holidays around Taroudant or in the Tafilalet, southeastern Morocco.

North America *Cross Cultural Adventures*, PO Box 3285, Arlington, VA 22203, T1-703-237-0100, piotrk@erols.com Custom crafted adventures for independent travellers and special-interest groups, from private Atlas treks to soft adventures by Mercedes cars. ***Heritage Tours***, 121 West 27th Street, Suite 1001, New York City, T1-800-378 4555, www.heritagetoursONLINE.com Custom designed in-depth itineraries. Specialize in cultural and historic tours, sahara encampments, crafts and architecture.

Europe and Israel *Alpinschule* of Innsbruck In der Stille 1, A-6161 Natters, Innsbruck, Austria. Organize walking tours based on Taroudant. The walks are not too strenuous and participants are taken to and from.

Finding out more

Moroccan tourist boards

Moroccan National Tourist Board (ONMT) Check www.exportmorocco.com/tourism. ONMT also has offices overseas. **Australia**, 11 West St, Sydney, NSW 2060, T9576711. **Belgium**, 66 R du Marché-aux-Herbes, Brussels 1040, T027361100. **Canada**, 2 Carlton St, Suite 1803, Toronto, Ontario M5B 1K2, T4165982208. **France**, 161 R Saint-Honoré, Place du Théâtre-Français, 75001 Paris, T42604724. **Germany**, 59 Graf Adolf Strasse, 4000 Dusseldorf, T49211370551/2. **Sweden**, Sturegaten 16, Stockholm 11436, T66099. **Switzerland**, Schifflande, 5, 8001 Zurich, T2527752. **UK**, 205 Regent St, London, T020-7437 0073. **USA**, 20 East 46th St, Suite 1201, New York NY 10017, T2125572520.

Morocco on the web

Many more can obviously found by typing 'Morocco tourism' or 'Maroc tourisme' in your favourite search engine

Background

www.biladi.net Semi-official site for Moroccans resident abroad.
www.emarrakech.info News of the Red City.
www.eudel.com Delegation of the European Union's site.
www.lexicorient.com/morocco Information on cities with photographs.
www.menic.utexas.edu/menic/countries/morocco Academic site with useful links.
www.north-africa.com Weekly analysis on economics, politics and business. Subscriber service.
www.usembassy-morocco.org.ma As the name suggests, the US embassy site for the country. Provides useful links.

Crafts and culture

www.alif-fes.com For those wanting to study Arabic and Amazigh languages.
www.cafmaroc.co.ma Mountain activities with the Casablanca chapter of the Club alpi
www.kelma.org French-based site with news and views from the gay community i the Maghreb, Belgium and France.
www.maghrebnet.net.ma/artisanat Lots of information on Moroccan crafts.
www.maroque.co.uk For design inspiration.

Festivals

www.festival-gnaoua.co.ma Details on the annual Gnaoua music festival in Essaouira.
www.morocco-fezfestival.com Information on the annual festival of sacred music held in Fès.
www.tanjazz.free.fr Mellow notes in early summer Tanger.

Places to stay

www.marrakech-medina.com For a look at some luscious houses for rent.
www.riadomaroc.com Personable accommodation across Morocco, including private houses and rural gites.

Transport

www.ferrimaroc.com Information if you want to get the ferry to Morocco.
www.royalairmaroc.com For those wanting to fly to Morocco.
www.oncf.com.ma All about Moroccan rail services.
www.comanav.co.ma Ferries to Morocco.
www.ctm.co.ma Leading Moroccan bus company.

Tourism

www.tourism-in-morocco.com Hotels, restaurants and crafts. Site developed in collaboration with the Moroccan National Tourist Board.

Spanish enclaves

www.conoceceuta.es.vg Introducing the Spanish enclave city of Ceuta.
www.turiceuta.com Tourism in Ceuta.

Language

Arabic is the official language of Morocco, but nearly all Moroccans with a secondary education have enough French to communicate with, and a smattering of English. In the North, Spanish maintains a presence thanks to TV and radio. Outside education, however, Moroccan Arabic in the cities and Amazigh in the mountains are the languages of everyday life, and attempts to use a few words and phrases, no matter how stumblingly, will be appreciated. Those with some Arabic learned elsewhere often find the Moroccan Arabic difficult. It is characterised by a clipped quality (the vowels just seem to disappear), and the words taken from classical Arabic are often very different from those used in the Middle East. In addition, there is the influence of the Berber languages and a mixture of French and Spanish terms, often heavily 'Moroccanised'. In many situations French is more or less understood. However you will come across plenty of people who have had little opportunity to go to school and whose French may be limited to a very small number of phrases.

See Footnotes, page 522, for lists of useful words and phrases

If you wish to learn Arabic, ALIF (Arabic Language Institute in Fes, T055-624850, F9331608, see www.alif-fes.com), an offshoot of the American Language Centre, has a very good name. They organize a range of long and short courses in both classical and Moroccan Arabic. Courses in Amazigh languages can be set up, too.

Disabled travellers

Morocco really cannot be said to be well adapted to the needs of the disabled traveller. However don't let this deter you. Some travel companies are beginning to specialize in exciting holidays, tailor-made for individuals depending on their level of disability. For those with access to the internet, a general site is provided by **Global Access - Disabled Travel Network Site** at www.geocities.com/Paris/1502 It contains useful information and includes a number of reviews and tips from members of the public. You might want to read *Nothing Ventured* edited by **Alison Walsh** (Harper Collins), which gives personal accounts of worldwide journeys by disabled travellers, plus advice and listings.

Gay and lesbian travellers

If there is no real public perception of what a lesbian might be in Morocco, foreign gays have long been a feature of life in towns like Marrakech and Tanger. The latter is long past its heyday of the 1950s and 1960s, while Marrakech continues to attract wealthy A-gays. However, according to the penal code, 'shameless or unnatural acts' between persons of the same sex can lead to short prison sentences or fines though this has never seemed to put anyone off. Note also that the body language is very different in Morocco. Physical closeness between men in the street does not indicate gay relationships. For the corruption of minors, the penalties are extremely severe.

Thanks to satellite television, there is an awareness among Moroccan gays that there is a certain 'international gay culture'. There is also an awareness of AIDS (le Sida in French), with an organization called the **ALCS,** Association de lutte contre le Sida, founded by Prof Hakima Himmich, doing sterling service with its information campaigns and info-lines. Much still remains to be done, however.

In Marrakech, gay travellers (or rather their friends) have run into problems with the brigade touristique, set up to ensure that visitors – of whatever persuasion - go unhassled. It should be stressed that given the poverty, there are a number of Moroccan men who are quite ready to have sex with visiting men for money. Marrakech is thus far from being a Mediterranean party island, rainbow-flag type destination. You'll find lots of good decoration ideas, however.

Student travellers

Morocco is a fairly good place for the budget traveller, as food and accommodation costs are very reasonable. Public transport is also very cheap, for the distances covered, but often slow for getting to out of the way places. Note that there are few student discounts of the sort available in Europe. The youth hostels have been upgraded, and most are now well run. Moroccan Railways (ONCF) are included on the European under-26 Inter-Rail pass, which also gets you half-price tickets on the ferries from Algeciras to Tanger. (Note that Inter-Rail is not valid on coaches run by *Supratours*, the ONCF sister company). Youth rail tickets are also available to Morocco, valid for six months along a pre-arranged route.

Travelling with children

Moroccans love children. This trait of the culture is particularly understandable when you realize how difficult life is for many families and how many children die in childbirth or infancy in the rural areas, due quite simply to a lack of basic health education in the Amazigh languages and Moroccan Arabic.

If you hire a car via an international agency, specifying the sort of child-seats you require, do not be surprised if your requirements get lost somewhere along the way. Most local car hire agencies will be unlikely to have kiddie-seats.

Children from the lands of supermarkets and industrial agriculture will find Morocco fascinating. Daily life is lived in the open, all sorts of activities which take place behind closed doors can be seen. There are workshops spilling out into the street and butchers with carcasses hanging outside, markets with mule parks, people ploughing with camels.

Kids from formal European cities will probably enjoy all the excitement of Moroccan urban life – and the vast landscapes of the South. If doing a lot of driving, make sure you have things for the car to entertain them. You could provide them with a contrast by trying to stay in hotels in Marrakech and Agadir with pools. When you book, however, check whether there is a shallow kids' pool and whether it is heated in winter (very often they are not). Though the sun is bright, the water will be damn cold.

On the health and safety front, make sure your kids are up to date with all their vaccinations. Tap water in major cities is safe to drink. In rural areas, give them sugary bottled drinks or mineral water. And on busy streets and squares, keep a tight hold, as the traffic is often very hectic. If staying in a riad with a plunge pool, check if it is fenced off in some way.

Women travellers

Young women travelling with a male friend report few difficulties – and couples with small children will find that the little ones attract a great deal of kindly attention. However, a woman going out on her own from the hotel without male escort will soon notice the difference. For women travelling alone, the hassle and stares can be extremely tiring after a while. So what do you do? In towns, dress fairly smartly, look confident, busy, and as though you know where you're going. (Depending on your age, this may make hustlers think twice – is this person with an official delegation, do they have a Moroccan husband?) Observe what smart Moroccan women are wearing, how they walk in public. Women from fairly traditional families will be wearing headscarves, others may be wearing expensive dark sunglasses.

Obviously you will want to strike up some acquaintances – and some women students waiting (say) for a grands taxi or in your train compartment will probably be delighted to have a chance to chat with an English speaker – as long as you don't look too outlandish by their modest standards of dress. Remember, a lot of importance is given to looking smart and respectable in Morocco. Many Moroccans lack the means to do this, and the unkempt European is really a bit of an extraterrestrial to them, the object of all sorts of prejudices, and not worthy of much respect.

And the hassling males? One way to deal with them is to develop a schoolmarmish manner. Modestly dressed, you are interested in Roman ruins, architecture, birds, women's issues (but probably not local politics), you are a serious person. This may put your hassler off – or lead to some intelligent conversation. (You'll probably get the 'convert-to-Islam' pitch at some point). And if you do decide you want someone to show you around, then agree on the fee beforehand (official guides get 100dh). This can save you time and prove entertaining too, if the person is genuine.

Role-playing can be tedious, however. In fact, in many places, despite appearances, the visitor has the upperhand. Since 1995, the plain clothes Brigade touristique has been in action in a number of the main holiday destinations. For a local observed giving a tourist a hard time, this can mean big problems, namely 1,000dh fine and/or a month in prison. Apart from Casablanca, Moroccan cities are really quite small provincial places where faces get known quickly. This is true even of Marrakech. The problem is then what happens if you are with a genuine Moroccan friend? You will have to convince the plainclothes policeman that you know the person you are with well and that there is no problem.

Working in the country

Morocco has a major un- and under-employment problem. University educated young adults find it hard to get work, especially those with degrees in subjects like Islamic studies and literature. At the same time, industry and business are desperately short of qualified technicians and IT-literate staff. Low salary levels mean that the qualified are tempted to emigrate – and many do, fuelling a brain-drain which has reached worrying levels. In cities, adults with a low level of skills find it hard to get work, basically as many simple jobs in small companies are done by badly paid, exploited adolescents. For the foreigner, this means that there are few opportunities for work, although international companies setting up in Morocco do employ foreign managerial staff, generally recruited abroad. Basically, the only opening if you want to spend time in Morocco is through teaching English, which is badly paid even with organizations like the British Council or the American Language Centres. It is your employer who will help you deal with the formalities of getting a *carte de séjour* (residence permit) in Morocco. For you to be able to work, your employer has to be able to satisfy the relevant authorities in Rabat that you are doing a job in an area which Morocco has a skills shortage. Anyone tempted to take up residence with the idea of doing a spot of Protestant conversion work should think twice. The authorities take a very dim view of potential missionaries.

Retired people (and others) from Europe can obtain residence relatively easily, providing they can prove that they have a regular source of income and that regular transfers of funds are being made into their Moroccan bank account. Towns where the police are used to processing the official paperwork for this sort of foreign resident include Agadir, Essaouira, Marrakech, Rabat and Tanger.

Before you travel

Getting in

Passports

Always carry photocopies of key pages of your passport with you

All visitors need a passport to gain entry into Morocco. Report the loss of your passport immediately to police giving the number, date and place of issue. The last hotel at which you stayed will have this information on the registration form. Getting fresh documents will probably entail a trip to Rabat and/or Casablanca. Tip: send your passport details to a personal email address for easy retrieval.

Visas

From the point of entry travellers can stay in Morocco for 3 months

No visas are required for full passport holders of the UK, USA, Canada, Australia, New Zealand/Aotearoa, Canada, Ireland and most EU countries. Benelux passport holders require visas at the present time. On the aeroplane or boat, or at the border, travellers will be required to fill in a form with standard personal and passport details, an exercise to be repeated in almost all hotels and guesthouses throughout the country.

Visa extensions These require a visit to the **Immigration** or **Bureau des Etrangers** department at the police station in a larger town, as well as considerable patience. An easier option is to leave Morocco for a few days, preferably to Spain or the Canary Islands, or to one of the two Spanish enclaves, either Ceuta, close to Tanger or Melilla, rather more remote in northeastern Morocco. People coming into Morocco from either of these Spanish enclaves for a second or third time have on occasion run into problems with the Moroccan customs. With numerous foreigners resident in Agadir and Marrakech, it may be easiest to arrange visa extensions in these cities. Approval of the extension has to come from Rabat and may take a few days.

Moroccan embassies and consulates

Australia *11 West St, North Sydney, T02-99576717.*
Canada *38 Range Rd, Ottawa, KIN 8J4, Ontario, T613-2367391.*
Denmark *Oregards Allé19, 2900 Hellerup, Copenhagen, T624511.*
Egypt *10 rue Salah el-Din, Zamalek, Cairo, T02-3409677.*
France *5 rue le Tasse, Paris 75016, T1-45206935.*
Germany *Goten Strasse 7-9, 5300 Bonn, T228-355044.*
Netherlands *Oranje Nassaulaan 1-1075, Amsterdam, T736215.*
New Zealand *See Australia.*
Norway *Parkveien 41, Oslo, T22556111.*
Spain *Serrano 179, Madrid, T1-4580950.*
Sweden *Kungsholmstorg 16, Stockholm, T8-544383.*
Switzerland *22 Chemin François-Lehmann, Grand Saconnex, Geneva, T22-981535.*
Tunisia *39 rue du 1 Juin, Tunis, T1-783801.*
UK *49 Queens Gate Gardens, London, SW7 5NE, T020-7581 5001.*
USA *1601 21st St NW, Washington DC 20009, T202-4627979.*

For foreign embassies and consulates in Morocco see individual town and city directories

Essentials

Customs

Visitors may take in, free of duty, 400 g of tobacco, 200 cigarettes or 50 cigars and such personal items as a camera, binoculars, a portable radio, computer or typewriter. You may also take your pet to Morocco. It will need a health certificate no more than 10 days old and an anti rabies certificate less than six months old. Foreign currency may be imported freely.

Prohibited items **Narcotics**: There are severe penalties for possession of or trade in narcotic drugs: three months to five years imprisonment and/or fines up to 240,000dh. You do not want to be involved in a Moroccan remake of *Midnight Express*. Morocco is under pressure from the European Union to reduce kif cultivation, and anyone caught exporting happy baccy will be turned into an example for others. **Wildlife**: Be aware that wild animal pelts and some other items openly on sale in Morocco cannot be legally imported into the EU. This also includes products made of animal pelts. Live wild animals may not be exported from Morocco and their import into EU is in most cases illegal.

Vaccinations

See Health, page 71, for further details

None required unless travelling from a country where yellow fever and/or cholera frequently occurs. You should be up to date with polio, tetanus, and typhoid protection. If you are going to be travelling in rural areas where hygiene is often a bit rough and ready, then having a hepatitis B shot is a good thing. You could also have a cholera shot, although there is no agreement among medics on how effective this is. If you are going to be travelling in remote parts of the Saharan provinces, then a course of malaria tablets is recommended.

What to take

Always take more money and fewer clothes than you think you'll need

Travellers usually tend to take to much. Be ruthless! A travel-pack will survive the holds of rural buses and sitting on the roof-rack of a share taxi. If you acquire a carpet, there is plenty of cheap luggage on sale. If you are going to go trekking without the benefit of mule transport, then you'll need a good rucksack.

If you need more clothes, most basic items are cheap should you need more. Outside summer you will need woollens or a fleece for evenings. It is advisable for women in particular to cover up in the country. Pack light trousers or skirts. In the towns Moroccans like to dress well if they have the money. Many don't, so smart appearance is appreciated. In many areas, especially in the northern cities, a lot of grinding poverty is apparent.

If you are aiming to travel into the Atlas take a pair of decent walking shoes or boots as getting to some of the rock art sites requires some scrambling. If planning to bivouac out in the desert, you will need a warm sleeping bag. The Saharan night-time cold is penetrating, so bring some warm clothing and items to wear in layers.

Checklists The following checklist might help you plan your packing: Air cushions for hard seating; earplugs; eye mask; insect repellant/cream, mosquito coils; neck pillow; international driving licence; photocopies of essential documents; plastic bags; short wave radio; spare passport photographs; sun hat; sun protection cream; handiwipes (wet-ones); Swiss army knife; torch; small umbrella; wet wipes; zip-lock bags. If you're going for **budget accommodation** you may also need: a cotton sheet sleeping bag or sheet; padlocks for luggage; student card; toilet paper; towel; universal bath plug.

See Health, page 71, for further advice on what to take

Health kit Anti-acid tablets; anti-diarrhoea tablets; anti-malaria tablets (chloroquin); antiseptic cream; condoms; contraceptives; mini first aid kit with disposable syringes; sachets of rehydration salts; tampons; travel sickness pills; water sterilization tablets if heading for rural areas.

Money

Currency

Currency is labelled in Arabic and French. Most transactions are in cash. There is a fixed exchange rate for changing notes and no commission ought to be charged for this

In July 2003, US $1 = 9.25dh, UK £1 = 14.97 dh, €1 = 10.63dh

The major unit of currency in Morocco is the **dirham** (dh). In 1 dirham there are 100 **centimes**. There are coins for 1 centime (very rare), 5, 10, 20 and 50 centimes, and for 1, 2 (new 2003), 5 and 10 dirhams, as well as notes for 10, 20, 50, 100 and 200 dirhams. The coins can be a little confusing. There are two sorts of 5 dirham coin: the older and larger cupro-nickel ('silver coloured' version), being phased out, and the new bi-metal version, brass colour on the inside. The bi-metal 10 dirham coin (brass colour on the outside), is replacing the rather scruffy red and pink 10 dirham notes. There is a brownish 20 dirham note, easily confused with the 100 dirham note. The 50 dirham note is green, the 100 dirhams brown and sand colour, and the 200 dirham note is in shades of blue and turquoise.

You can *sometimes* buy Moroccan dirhams at *bureaux de change* at the London airports. Dirhams may not be taken out of Morocco. If you have excess dirhams, you can exchange them back into French francs at a bank on production of exchange receipts. However, as European cash and Visa cards function in Moroccan ATMs (*guichets automatiques*), in major towns it is possible to withdraw more or less exactly the amount one needs on a daily basis. However at weekends and during big public holidays, airport and city-centre ATMs can be temperamental, so have cash and travellers' cheques to exchange. The most reliable ATMs are those of the ***Wafa Bank*** (green and yellow livery) and the *BMCI*.

Moroccans among themselves count in older currency units. To the complete confusion of travellers, many Moroccans refer to **francs**, which equal 1 centime, and **reals**, though both these units only exist in speech. Even more confusingly, the value of a real varies from region to region. A dirham equals 20 reals in most regions. However, around Tanger and in most of the North, 1 dirham equals 2 reals. *Alf franc* (1,000 francs) is 10 dirhams. Unless you are good at calculations, it's obviously easiest to stick to dirhams.

Credit cards

Morocco has a problem with card fraud

Credit cards are widely accepted at banks, top hotels, restaurants and big tourist shops. For restaurants, check first before splashing out. *American Express* are represented by *Voyages Schwartz* in Morocco, with limited services. Remember to keep all credit card receipts – and before you sign, check where the decimal marker (a comma in Morocco, as in Europe, rather than a dot), has been placed, and that there isn't a zero too many. You don't want to be paying thousands rather than hundreds of dirhams. To reduce problems with card fraud, common sense is to use your debit/credit card for payments of

Sample prices for basics, July 2003

For comparison, 1dh = 06.5p, 10dh = 65p, 10dh = 1 euro, 10dh = US$1 approx.

Cafés and restaurants

Good meal with wine in a medium-range restaurant, 200dh to 250dh
Kefta sandwich with chips, 15dh to 20dh
Mini bastilla from a pâtisserie, 20dh
Coffee and croissant in a good café, say 10dh with tip
Bottle of red wine 70dh (very good bottle, 150dh)

Food and drink

Litre of milk, 8dh
Litre bottle of Sidi Ali mineral water, 5dh
Litre of Coca Cola, 8dh90
Mid-range bottle of red wine, 40dh
Bottle of Flag beer, 5dh
4 natural yoghourts, 7dh60
Large round loaf of bread, 1dh10
Small tin of tuna, 7dh30
Kilo of tomatoes, 4dh,
Kilo of onions, 3dh
Kilo of oranges, 5dh
Kilo of mandarins, 7dh
Kilo of beef, 55dh
Kilo of mutton, 60dh

*(**NB** Meat prices higher in years when rain is good as more grazing for bigger flocks to be kept)*

Transport

A day's car hire, unlimited kilometrage, Fiat Punto, say 400dh to 500dh
Fill up (petrol) for the tank of a small car, say 400dh
First class rail-ticket, Casablanca Voyageurs to Marrakech, 110dh
Second class rail-ticket, Rabat to Casablanca Port, 27dh
CTM bus ticket, Marrakech to Fès, 65dh
Mercedes share taxi, Ouazarzate to Marrakech, 100dh
Marrakech, short daytime taxi ride Guéliz to Médina, say 10dh to 12dh
Marrakech, short ride on city bus, 3dh

Miscellaneous

Cheap mobile phone, 500dh
Small bottle of Cadum shampoo, 7.5dh
Small tube of toothpaste, 5dh
Men's haircut, 25dh to 35dh
Postcard, 3dh to 5dh
Stamp for letter to Europe, up to 20 g, 6.50dh

large items like carpets and hotel bills. If a payment is not legitimate, it is a lot less painful if the transaction is on the credit card rather than drawn from your current account.

Travellers' cheques

Although somewhat time consuming to change, travellers' cheques are probably the safest way to carry money (though a small commission will be charged for changing them). They are usable in Morocco, although the traveller may be sent from bank to bank before the appropriate one is found. Take travellers' cheques from a well known bank or company, preferably in euros. Some hotels and shops will exchange travellers' cheques. At the time of writing, the ***Banque Populaire*** and the ***Crédit agricole*** did not charge commission on cashing travellers' cheques.

Banking hours

Banking hours are 0830-1130 and 1500-1630. In the summer and during the month of fasting Ramadan, they are 0830-1400. Cities with returning summer migrant workers will have banks with longer hours in summer. Banks' bureaux de change in the major cities often open for longer hours (0800-2000). In theory rates of exchange are the same but commission differs. Main banks include the ***BMCE***, ***Crédit du Maroc***, ***Wafabank***, and ***Banque Populaire*** all widespread. The ***BMCE*** and the ***Crédit du Maroc*** seem to have the best change facilities, while the ***Banque Populaire*** is often the only bank in southern towns. Banking in Morocco can be a slow, tortuous process. The easiest way to get money is thus to use your Visa or cash card at a cash dispenser – always provided that this is in service.

Cost of travelling As a budget traveller, it is possible to get by in Morocco for £20-30/US$30-40 a day. Your costs can be reduced by having yoghurt and bread and cheese for lunch and staying in an 80dh a night hotel (there is even cheaper in small towns). Accommodation, food and transport are all cheap, and there is a lot to see and do for free, however this budget does not allow much room for unexpected costs like the frequent small tips expected for minor services. If you start buying imported goods, notably cosmetics and toiletries, foods and electrical goods, things can get expensive. Allowing £40/US$55 is more realistic.

In top quality hotels, restaurants, nightclubs and bars, prices are similar to Europe. Rabat, Casablanca and Agadir are the most expensive places while manufactured goods in remote rural areas tend to cost more. Around the 200dh mark, you can get a much better feed in a restaurant than you can in western Europe. Shopaholics will be more than satisfied with the gifty goodies on sale (prices negotiable). Prices for food and drink are non-negotiable, of course.

Cost of living Although prices for many basics can seem very low indeed to those used to prices in European capitals, the cost of living is high for most Moroccans. At one end of the scale, in the mountainous rural areas, there is Morocco's fourth world, still on the margins of the cash economy. In these regions, families produce much of their own food, and are badly hit in drought years when there is nothing to sell in the *souk* to generate cash to buy oil, extra flour and sugar. This precariousness means much 'hidden' malnutrition. Illiterate parents are uninformed about balanced diet and the long term impact of vitamin deficiencies.

Conditions are improving for the city shanty-town dwellers. Here families will be getting by on 2,000dh a month, sometimes much less. The urban middle classes, those with salaried jobs in the public and private sectors, are doing fairly well. A primary school teacher may be on 3,000dh a month, a private company employee at the start of their career will make around 3,000dh a month, too. This category has access to loans and is seeing a general improvement in living standards. Morocco's top-flight IT technicians, doctors, and business people have a plush lifestyle with villas and servants available to few Europeans. And finally, a very small group of plutocrats has long been doing very, very well, thank you.

To put the contrasts in perspective, there are parents for whom the best option is to place their pre-adolescent girls as maids with city families in exchange for 300dh a month. (You read that figure correctly). The Amazigh-speaking boy who serves you in the corner shop may be given 50dh a week, plus lodging (of a sort) and lodging. His horizons will be limited to the shop, there will be a trip back to the home village once a year. He may never learn to read, his language is despised at official level. At the other, distant end of the scale, there are couples who can easily spend 40,000dh a semester to purchase an English-language higher education for one of their offspring at the private Al Akhawayn University in Ifrane.

Getting there

Air

Major European airlines run frequent scheduled to Morocco's main airports at Casablanca-Mohamed V, Marrakech and Agadir, with most flights operating from France and Spain. National carrier ***Royal Air Maroc***, familiarly referred to as 'la RAM', is reliable (www.royalairmaroc.com). Prices are similar to Air France and British Airways. Most frequent flights run to Casablanca. Second rank airports include Casablanca-Anfa (private flights), Rabat/Salé, Tanger, Oujda, Fès, Al Hoceima, Ouarzazate and Laâyoune. Internal flights onward flights often man long waits at Casablanca-Mohamed V. A rail shuttle links this airport with Casablanca and Rabat.

Discount flight agents

In the UK and Ireland: ***STA Travel****, 86 Old Brompton Rd, London, SW7 3LH, T0207 361 6100 , www.statravel.co.uk They have other branches in London, as well as in Brighton, Bristol, Cambridge, Leeds, Manchester, Newcastle-upon-Tyne and Oxford and on many University campuses. Specialists in low-cost student/youth flights and tours, also good for student IDs and insurance.* ***Trailfinders****, 194 Kensington High Street, London, W8 7RG, T020-7938 3939, www.trailfinders.co.uk They also have other branches in London, as well as in Birmingham, Bristol, Cambridge, Glasgow, Manchester, Newcastle, Dublin and Belfast.*

In North America: ***Air Brokers International****, 323 Geary St, Suite 411, San Francisco, CA94102, T01-800-883 3273, www.airbrokers.com Consolidator and specialist on RTW and Circle Pacific tickets.* ***Council Travel****, there are retail outlets throughout the country but in New York you will find this company at 205 E 42nd St, New York, NY 10017, 254 Greene St, NY 10003 and 895 Amsterdam Av, NY 10025. Otherwise call T1-800-2COUNCIL, or check out www.counciltravel.com A student/budget agency with branches in many other US cities.* ***Discount Airfares Worldwide On-Line****, www.etn.nl/discount.htm A hub of consolidator and discount agent links.* ***STA Travel****, 5900 Wiltshire Blvd, Suite 2110, Los Angeles, CA 90036, 1-800-781-4040, www.sta-travel.com Also branches in New York, San Francisco, Boston, Miami, Chicago, Seattle and Washington DC.* ***Travel CUTS****, 187 College St, Toronto, ON M5T 1P7, T1-800-954-2666, www.travelcuts.com Specialist in student discount fares, IDs and other travel services. Branches in other Canadian cities as well as California, USA.* ***Travelocity****, www.travelocity.com Online consolidator.*

In Australia and New Zealand: ***Flight Centre****, with offices throughout Australia and other countries. In Australia call T133 133 or log on to www.flightcentre.com.au*

STA Travel*, T1300-360960, www.statravel.com.au; 702 Harris St, Ultimo, Sydney, and 256 Flinders St, Melbourne. In NZ: 10 High St, Auckland, T09-366 6673. Also in major towns and university campuses.* ***Travel.com.au****, 76 Clarence St, Sydney NSW Australia, T02 9249 5232, outside Sydney: T1300 130 482, www.travel.com.au*

NB *Using the web for booking flights, hotels and other services directly is becoming an increasingly popular way of making holiday reservations. You can make some good deals this way. Be aware, though, that cutting out the travel agents is denying yourself the experience that they can give, not just in terms of the best flights to suit your itinerary, but also advice on documents, insurance and other matters before you set out, safety, routes, lodging and times of year to travel. A reputable agent will also be bonded to give you*

From the UK & Ireland

Charter flights Charter flights run by package holiday companies fly mainly to Agadir. Sometimes they are a cheap alternative to scheduled flights. The disadvantage of such flights is that Agadir is 6 hrs bus travel from the nearest major tourist town, Marrakech. To protect the *RAM*, Casablanca airport currently receives no charter flights, although the situation is changing. New charter services may be run by ***Corsair*** from France.

Scheduled flights Cheapest fares from the UK to Morocco are normally with ***KLM*** and ***Royal Air Maroc***, 205 Regent Street, London W1, T0207-4394361. The latter fly from Heathrow, Terminal 2. London-Casablanca flights are almost daily, Marrakech, Tanger and Agadir less frequently served, with one or two flights a week, according to season and demand. Check www.royalairmaroc.com The RAM also flies out of Main western European airports.Services out of Paris to Morocco are more frequent to a wider range of Moroccan destinations, check also www.airfrance.com. *British Airways*, www.ba.com, has direct flights from London to Agadir, Casablanca, Marrakech and Tanger.

Royal Air Maroc offices abroad: Amsterdam, T020-6530007, F020-5158956; London, T020-74398854, T020-74394361, F020-72870127; Montréal, T514-2851619, 514-2851689 or 2851937, resa on T514-2851435, F514-2851338, New York, T212-7506071, F212-9807924. In Morocco, T090000800.

Fly-boat It is possible to get a flight to Gibraltar, Almería or Málaga, and then continue by boat to Ceuta or Tanger in north-west Morocco, or Melilla or Nador further east. *British Airways* flies to Málaga and Gibraltar.

From North America The *RAM* flies between Casablanca, Montreal and New York. (Flight time New York to Casablanca, 6hrs 40 mins).

From Africa & the Middle East The *RAM* runs regular services between Casablanca and**Algiers**, **Tunis**, **Tripoli** and **Cairo**. From the **Canary Isles** (Las Palmas) there are direct flights to Agadir and Laayoune. There are two flights a week between Casablanca and **Nouakchott**. Sub-Saharan Africa is served from Casablanca with flights to **Abidjan**, **Bamako**, **Conakry**, **Dakar** and **Libreville**. Middle Eastern *RAM* destinations include **Abu Dhabi**, **Jeddah** and **Riyadh**.

Road

Bus From London Victoria Coach Station there is **Eurolines/Iberbus** to Algeciras, taking 2 days, T020-7730 0202, www.eurolines.fr. An adult return is between £200-240. You then take the Algeciras-Tanger ferry. **Eurolines** main UK office is on T01582-404511.There are regular coach services to Morocco from Paris and other French cities.

Morocco's main coach company, the *CTM* has a website (www.ctm.co.ma) which mentions international services but doesn't seem to give prices and schedules. *CTM* services run between Tanger/Casablana and Alicante, Barcelona, Bolgna, Bordeaux, Brussels, Dijon, Frankfurt, Granada, Lille, Lyon, Madrid, Marseille, Paris, Rimini and Toulouse.

Car *See below for car ferries*

Import of private cars Foreigners are allowed temporary import of a private vehicle for up to six months in total (be it one or several visits) per calendar year. **Documents** required are car registration documents and a Green card from your insurance company, valid in Morocco which will be inspected at the border along with International Driving Licence (or national licences). The car will be entered in the drivers' passport, and checked on leaving the country, to ensure that it has not been sold without full taxes being paid. It should be noted that some car hire companies do not allow customers to take cars into Morocco from Europe. The minimum age of driving is 21. Car entry is not possible from Mauritania. From Algeria, in more peaceful times, the crossing points are Oujda and Figuig.

On arrival complete customs form D 16 bis called 'Declaration d'importation temporaire' and specify the intended duration of stay. Visitors arriving at the border without valid recognized insurance cover may take out a short-term policy available at any frontier post. A customs carnet is required for a trailer caravan but not for motor caravans. If using a vehicle or caravan of which you are not the owner carry with you a letter of authorization signed by the owner. Customs officials may require a detailed inventory in duplicate of all valuable items but routine items such as camping equipment need not be listed.

Sea

Shortest ferry crossings from Europe to Morocco are between Tarifa, Algeciras and Gibralter to Tanger and Ceuta. Longer crossings run from Almeria and Sète, France to Melilla and Nador. Ceuta and Melilla are Spanish enclaves so you actually cross a land border in Africa. This can be slow. Algeciras to Tanger is the most convenient crossing, Tanger being the northernmost point on the Moroccan rail network and (almost) the starting point of the autoroute down to Casa-Rabat. Algeciras to Ceuta is fast but the advantage is lost at the Fnideq land border crossing into Morocco.

Ferries

In the summer months, those with cars will find ferries booked solid months in advance as Moroccans working in Europe return home to visit family

When you leave Spain for Morocco, your passport is checked by the Spanish authorities before boarding. Moroccan border formalities are undertaken on ship: you fill in a disembarkation form and have your passport stamped at a guichet, generally as you get on board. Leaving Morocco, you fill in an embarkation form and departure card, which are stamped by the port police before getting on the boat. (Various characters will offer to sell you the police *fiches* but they can be found free when you check in.) When you travel from Spain to Spanish enclaves Ceuta and Melilla, this does not apply

Formalities on Spain to Morocco ferries

Websites providing details of ferry services (boats and hydrofoils) include www.transmeditteranea.es (click on South Straits zone) and www.frs.es for Ferrys rapidos del sur. Contact also ***Southern Ferries***, 179 Piccadilly, London W1V 9DB, T020-7491 4968, F7491 3502.

From Algeciras to Tanger

This ferry service is booked solid for cars in summer and around Muslim feast days

The main ferry route between Spain and Morocco is the Algeciras/Tanger passenger and car service, operated jointly by ***Trasmediterranea*** and ***Isleña de Navegación***. Algeciras has regular bus services from Gibraltar and Málaga, both towns having cheap flights from UK. Algeciras has a train service from Madrid, and tickets can be bought from London to Algeciras or Tanger. The ferry terminal, near the town centre, has a ticket office and money changing facilities. There are similar facilities in the Tanger terminal. The ferry takes two to three hours, and there are normally between six and 10 services a day, either way, with some seasonal variation. Be a bit early for your ferry, allowing at least an hour to clear the police and customs, particularly in Tanger. Be cautious about scheduling onward journeys on the same day, in view of the delays. Check the Moroccan railways (*ONCF*) website for latest train times.

One-way passenger fares are around 230dh, children from four to 12 years old are half price and under four year olds are free, cars from 320dh, motorbikes 215dh and bicycles are free. It is cheaper to buy a return in Tanger than two singles, if applicable. Tickets can be bought at either terminal or at numerous agents in both towns. The ferries have adequate facilities for the short crossing, including bars, restaurants, lounges, as well as a *bureau de change*. Food and drinks are on the expensive side and can be paid for in dirhams or euros.

In the summer there is an Algeciras to Tanger **hydrofoil service** running on most days, taking one hour. See www.frs.es

From Algeciras to Ceuta

The Algeciras to Ceuta connection is cheaper and quicker than Algeciras to Tanger, but should you need to overnight, accommodation in Ceuta is more expensive than in Morocco. (Ferries for Ceuta are run by the same companies from the same terminal in Algeciras. The crossing takes 1½ hours, slightly fewer services on Sunday. Passenger fares one way are from 210dh, children from two to 12 years old are half price and under two year olds are free, cars from 340dh, motorbikes are 195dh and bicycles are free. It is possible to buy tickets at either terminal or from numerous agents. There is also a faster (30 minutes) but more expensive and slightly less frequent **hydrofoil** (360dh), between Algeciras and Ceuta. Contact T956-509139 or ***Stirling Travel***, Gibraltar 71787.

From Gibraltar to Tanger

Direct services from Gibraltar run daily and take 2½ hours. Passenger fares start at about 300dh, return 420dh. Tickets can be purchased in Tanger from ***Med Travel***, Avenue Mohammed V, T935872/3, and in Gibraltar from ***Exchange Travel***, 241 Main Street, T76151/2, F76153 and ***Tour Africa***, 2a Main Street, Gibraltar, T77666, F76754. Day-tour travellers take precedence over booked return tickets, so be warned.

There are now high-speed **hydrofoil** services, crossing time 1½ hours from Gibraltar to Tanger. See www.frs.es

From Almería (and Málaga) to Melilla and Nador

In your own vehicle, to get to the Almería port, leave autovía E15 at exit 438. This is an 8 hour crossing, run almost every day by ***Transmediterranea***. The service is much used by migrant workers originating from the eastern Rif. Almería to Melilla leaves at around 2330, Melilla to Almería departs around 1430. One way passenger fare starts around 250dh, double cabins are 700dh, cars from 800dh. The Almería to Nador service is broadly similar, there being almost daily sailings in winter, up to 18 sailings a week in summer. A further service does the Málaga to Melilla run, generally leaving in the early afternoon and taking 7½ hours. At Málaga contact ***Transmediterranea***, Estacion maritima, Local E-1, T2224391. At Almería contact ***Transmediterranea***, 19 Parque Nicolas Salmeron, 236155.

From Sète to Nador or Tanger

Comanav, the Companie Morocaine de Navigation, run car and passenger ferry services from Sète in the South of France to Nador, (adjacent to Melilla) and to Tanger. For full details check out their website, www.comanav.co.ma

Return passenger fares from Sète to Tanger range from 2800dh to 4200dh depending on the time of year (June to September is the most expensive time to travel), car fares range from 3700dh to 5800dh. These are relatively luxurious services, running daily between Tanger (leaving 1800) and Sète (leaving 1900) a journey of 36 hours. Return passenger fares from Sète to Nador range from 2080dh to 4500dh again depending on the time of year, car fares begin at 3300dh. The service runs every four days at the height of the season (June to September).

Reservations via ***Comanav*** are at 7 Boulevard de la Résistance, Casablanca, T022-303012, F307838; 43 Av Abou El Alaâ El Maâri, Tanger, T039-932649, F306138; and Immeuble Lazaar Beni Enzar, BP 89, Nador, T056-608538, F608667. In France they are from ***SNCM Ferryterranee***, 4 Quai d'Alger, BP 81, 34202 Sète Cedex, T0677479305 and ***Compagnie Charles Leborgne***, 6 Quai François Maillol, 34 202 Sète Cedex, T067745055, F067743304. A Paris agent is ***SNCM*** at 12 Rue Godot de Mauroy, 75009, T33-1-91563666. Bookings also through ***Continental Shipping and Travel***, London, T0207-4914968.

Cruises

Major cruise line companies include Moroccan ports on their itineraries. Popular stopping places include Casablanca and Tanger. You will be allowed off the ship with a *laissez-passer*. Leaving the cushioned comfort of their ship, cruise passengers can be confused by the hurly-burly of these ports. Touts, pickpockets and miscellaneous hustlers are out there in the crowd, well aware that easy prey – and profits from selling your handicam – is at hand.

Train

Trains from London go via France and Spain and cross to Tanger. Rail entry from Europe is only through Tanger. Euro-Rail is valid in Morocco

Train travel to Morocco is a relatively cheap option for those under 26, and a convenient way to tie in a visit to Morocco with a short stay in Europe. (*ONCF* Moroccan rail services can be checked on www.oncf.com.ma) For those under 26 an **InterRail** ticket bought in any participating European country includes the *ONCF*, and a reduction on the Algeciras-Tanger ferry. Travelling through Spain often entails extra cost, as there are supplements to be paid on a number of trains. Trains on the Madrid to Algeciras see a lot of inter-railers during the summer

Essentials

Touching down

Business hours *The working week for businesses is Monday to Friday, with half day working Saturday. On Fridays, the lunch break tends to be longer, as the main weekly prayers with sermon are on that day. Any official business takes considerably longer in Ramadan.*

Banks: *0830-1130 and 1430-1600 in winter, afternoons 1500-1700 in summer, 0930-1400 during Ramadan.*

Post offices*: 0830-1230 and 1430-1830, shorter hours in Ramadan.*

Shops: *Generally from 0900-1200 and from 1500-1900, although this varies in the big towns.*

Museums: *Most close on a Tuesday. Hours generally 0900-1200 and 1500-1700, although this can vary considerably.*

Emergency services *Police: T19. Fire brigade: T15. Larger towns will have an SOS Médecins (private doctor on call service), and almost all towns of any size have a pharmacy on duty at night, the* pharmacie de garde. *Any large hotel should be able to give you the telephone/address of these. For most ailments, a* médecin généraliste *(general practitioner) will be sufficient.*

Directory enquiries *Dial T120 (business numbers) or T121 (personal numbers). For the operator dial T10, for information dial T16, for international calls when there is no direct line, dial T12.*

IDD code *T212. Dialling out of Morocco, first 00, and wait for the tone before dialling the country code. All Moroccan numbers have 9 digits beginning 0.*

Official time *Morocco follows GMT all year round, 1 hour behind the UK and 2 hours behind Spain in the summer.*

Weights and measures *Morocco uses the metric system.*

For more on student rail travel, see ***British Rail International***, London Victoria Railway Station, T020-7834 2345 (enquiries), T020-7828 0892 (tickets), only sell tickets to Algeciras, about £220 return. ***Eurotrain***, T020-7730 3402, and ***Campus Travel***, their agents for people under 26, T020-7828 4111, sell tickets from London Victoria to Tanger, including both ferry crossings, priced at around £265 return, and enable the traveller to stop off at any point on the fixed route for any length of time within the two month validity of the ticket. (If your route is to Morocco, then BIJ ticket validity is six months.) If Morocco is your main destination, then you might do better to get a cheap flight.

Touching down

The vast majority of tourists arrive in Morocco by air at Casablanca, Marrakech or Agadir. Another way to Morocco is by ferry, as detailed above, arriving at Tanger, Ceuta or Nador. Information on onward travel from point of arrival is given here by destination.

Airport information

Aéroport Casablanca Mohammed V

Casablanca's main airport is at Nouasseur, 30 km southeast of Casablanca, T022-339100. Formalities on arrival are brief. Your hand-luggage will go through a detector after passport control, though not your main luggage.The airport terminal has cafés, postboxes, *bureaux de change* and agencies for car hire companies. There are also ATMs on the main concourse, just after you pass customs. There is no hotel at this airport. Following 14 May 2003 Casablanca bomb attacks, the airport was put off-limits to all but travellers with tickets. Those meeting travellers wait outside.

Onward travel is by shuttle train or taxi. The station is under the main airport concourse, and the *Bidhaoui* blue regional express train runs services on the hour to Casablanca Voyageurs, the main station for inter-city trains. From here, you can take another train for the short ride to Casa-Port station, close to the hotels and the *CTM* bus terminal. (It is quicker to do this run in a red taxi, say 15dh maximum). The *CTM* now operates a bus service from the airport to the Casablanca terminus (40 mins), behind the Tour Habous building just off Av des FAR in the downtown area. Just outside the main door of the airport is the taxi rank. A grand taxi is 200dh to Casablanca city centre, 400dh to Rabat, non-negotiable. Expensive but good if you're in a hurry as there is only one train an hour.

When it comes to leaving Casablanca, check train times and your departure time carefully. At one of the stations, they can give you a small ticket-sized printout with train times. Mercedes taxis for the airport may be found at the *CTM* bus station or close to the Place des Nations Unies, on Avenue Moulay Hassan I.

Casablanca also has a second, smaller airport at Anfa, mainly for private traffic.

Aéroport Agadir Al Massira Agadir is the main destination in Morocco for large numbers of package tourists. This airport is a modern construction 28 km inland from the city, T048-839002, with connections by bus and Mercedes taxis. Banks and car hire companies are open during office hours, closed on Sundays. The No 22 bus runs to Inezgane (3dh), a transport hub near Agadir, with buses and Mercedes taxis to Marrakech, Taroudant and Agadir. Otherwise there are big Mercedes share taxis, 150dh standard fare for up to six people, into Agadir (arrange to share costs in terminal building). Grand taxi drivers may accept foreign currency – make sure you have the rough equivalent of the dirham charge in notes. However you can now *sometimes* buy Moroccan dirhams at London airports.

Aéroport Marrakech Menara Marrakech's airport is just 6 km outside the city. The *BMCE* and the *Banque Populaire* have bureaux de change, closed outside office hours. For the optimistic, there is the No 11 bus to Jemaâ El Fna, at the heart of the médina and near the budget hotels. Otherwise, the quickest way into Marrakech is by petit or grand taxi. A grand taxi should not set you back more than 50dh (60dh at night), for the run from airport to Guéliz, the modern town, which also has reasonably priced hotels. Euros may be acceptable to taxi drivers.

Aéroport Tanger Boukhalef Situated 15 km from Tanger, the Aéroport Boukhalef (T039-935720) has a couple of banks with bureaux de change but at the time of writing no ATM. Travel into Tanger either by bus or grand taxi. The taxi should cost 70dh for up to six people. Make arrangements with other travellers inside the terminal regarding taxi payment. There is a bus for the town centre.

Other airports There are also some international flights to **Aéroport Les Angads**, 15 km from Oujda, **Aéroport Charif Al Idrissi**, Al Hoceima; **Aéroport Fès Saïss**, Fès; **Aéroport Hassan I**, Laayoune; **Aéroport Taourirt**, Ouarzazate; and **Aéroport Rabat-Salé**, 10 km from Rabat. All these airports are well connected by buses or grand taxis.

Airport tax There are no airport taxes.

Seaport information

Arrival by ferry in Morocco will probably be by one of the following ports: Tanger or Nador, or one of the Spanish enclaves, Ceuta (near Tanger) or Melilla.

Arrival in Tanger

At the port, in the street, avoid all men who offer to take you to meet a real 'Berber' family in Asilah

Arriving by ferry in Tanger, generally from Algeciras, can be a pain in the neck. Getting off the boat and going through customs can take ages, and various hustlers and others are on hand to misinform fresh-faced backpackers and other innocents abroad as they emerge from the ferry terminal. For a woman travelling alone, arrival by ferry in Tanger can be extremely intimidating. Unless you are going to visit the town, you want to get to public transport as quickly as possible.

Happily, passport formalities have been accomplished on board. Once off the boat, there are various portacabins with exchange facilities. Cashpoints are only available at banks in the city centre.

Onward transport options from Tanger are train (*ONCF*) or bus. The Tanger-Ville station is now well and truly closed, trains now run from the Tanger-Moughougha station (also spelt Morora), out beyond the old bull ring and the city limits, say 10 km away. You will have to take a sky-blue petit taxi (20dh), or a Mercedes share taxi. In practice, the petits taxis work out as share taxis too. Generally, there are four train departures a day from Tanger-Moughougha to Casa-Voyageurs. The night departure, generally around 2230, goes through to Marrakech, arrival 0800 and has couchettes.

Inter-city ***CTM*** buses for main northern Moroccan towns run from outside the port gates. If there is no departure to suit you, take a petit taxi (15dh) to the main bus station (*gare routière*), which is some 2 km away. There are six passenger Mercedes taxis here for Tetouan (20dh), Chaouen and other destinations.

Arrival in Ceuta

Spanish time in use, one or two hours different from Moroccan time. Remember to adjust your watch as you leave the enclave

The Algeciras to Ceuta ferries are faster than the Tanger ones, which makes Ceuta a popular port. Once off the ferry, you take a bus to the border from Plaza de la Constitucion, in the town centre. Spanish customs is generally quick, the Moroccan customs can be slow for those with their own car. From Fnideq on the Moroccan side of the frontier, Mercedes taxis to Tetouan cost 20dh, to Chaouen 60dh a head. Moroccan banks have exchange facilities near the frontier. For information on Ceuta, see www.conoceceuta.es.vg

Arrival in Nador

The main ferry from Sète in France comes into Nador. Buses and Mercedes taxis leave from a terminal at the end of the Avenue des FAR, close to the waterfront (buses for Melilla from here). There is another bus terminal (***CTM*** and others) in the town centre, close to the Municipality.

Arrival in Melilla

Spanish time, and both euros and dirhams, in use

The Spanish-Moroccan border is best reached by bus from the central Plaza de España, 10-minutes' walk from the ferry terminus (20-minutes ride). The border can be crossed in five minutes on a good day. At peak times of year (Easter Week, end of August), the process can be much slower. You need to fill out a Moroccan entry card before getting to the passport window. Various lads will try to sell you these, otherwise ask for one at the window and return to your place in the queue (or huddle of people) at the window. Once over on the Moroccan side at Beni Enzar, there are Mercedes taxis and a bus to Nador.

Tourist information

Tourist boards

See individual towns for specific details

Main towns have an Office de Tourisme and a Syndicat d'Initiative (Information Office). There will be the usual glossy pamphlets and sometimes an enthusiastic employee.

Unofficial (& official) guides

See Getting around, page 53, for recommended maps

In the big tourist cities, unemployed lads will try to cadge some cash by offering guide services (local term: *faux guide*). They will offer to take you through the souks and show you the Berber market – 'open only today'. There have been cases of big and subtle rip-offs, ie the American student accepting hospitality for a couple of days and then feeling obliged to buy decorative items at a vastly inflated price from new friend's cousin in difficulty. The worst places for such hassle are Tanger, Fès and Marrakech. Sometimes, however, 5dh to a kid to guide you out of the souks is money well spent – and allows aforesaid kid to go to the town pool. If you are not on a budget, 100dh to a student to take you to the key sights will make the student's day – and yours too if the person is bright and uninvasive (agree on fee beforehand).

Official guides, supplied by big hotels, tend to be portly, officious gentlemen in djellabas who will deliver their blurb at high volume. They will have done the medina monuments a hundred times before and are rarely well informed. They will hasten you to carpet shops and gift emporia where they make commission.

Local customs and laws

Clothing & conduct In coastal resorts, you can wear shorts and expose arms and shoulders. However, when wandering round médinas and going to city centres, both men and women should cover shoulders. Sandals are fine but shorts should be baggy not skimpy. Expect lots of remarks and attention if you go wandering round in the souks in your brief running shorts. Have some smart but cool tops with you for summer travelling. Inland, winter is cold. Night temperatures in the desert and at altitude are low all the year – a fleece is handy, even as a pillow.

Eating Moroccan families may eat from a communal dish, often with spoons, sometimes with the hands. If invited to a home, you may well be something of a guest of honour. Depending on your hosts, it's a good idea to take some fruit or patisseries along. If spoons or cutlery are not provided, you eat using bread, using your right hand, not the left hand since it is ritually unclean (see below, loos). If the dishes with the food are placed at floor level, keep your feet tucked under your body away from the food. In a poorer home, there will only be a small amount of meat, so wait until a share is offered. Basically, good manners are the same anywhere. Let common sense guide you.

Loos
Budget travellers will see a lot of Turkish loos

The yeti-foot Turkish loo is widespread in Morocco. (Big hotels have standard sit-down ones). While loos in restaurants in main tourist towns like Marrakech have been much improved, they can be pretty primitive in out-of-the-way places. Moroccans do not use toilet paper (*papier hygiénique*), but wash with the left hand after performing. You'll see a plastic bottle next to the tap in the loo to help you with this. Procedures for washing are specified in Islam, and bodily cleanliness is very important to Muslims, there being two levels of ablutions: if you have had sex, the 'big ablutions' are necessary. Surprisingly perhaps, as it is source of life, sperm is considered impure.

If you are taken short in a medina, most mosques will have adjoining latrines or *midha*. The words *toilette* and *cabina* will be understood, otherwise ask for the *mirhadh*. The Musée de Marrakech had good clean loos as does the Fondouk Najjarine in Fes. Mini packs of tissue paper are available from street vendors everywhere for a couple of dirhams.

Tipping
Can be a bit of a 'hidden cost' during your stay in Morocco

Tipping is expected in restaurants and cafés, by guides, porters and car park attendants, and others who render small services. Make sure you have small change at the ready for this. Tipping taxi drivers is optional. Do not tip for journeys when the meter has not been used, because the negotiated price will be generous anyway. For handling baggage in hotels, tip around 3dh, on buses 3dh-5dh, and 5dh on trains and in airports.

Religion Sunni Islam is the religion of Morocco. The Gregorian calendar is used for all everyday matters, however. The Islamic or Hijra year, being a lunar year, is 10 or 11 days shorter. The Hijra calendar goes back to the seventh century AD, and year one corresponds to the Prophet Mohammed's emigration or *hijra* from Mecca to Médina in 622 AD. Friday is the Muslim holy day, when major sermons are given in mosques across the Islamic world. As a visitor, Islam won't effect you in the way it does on a visit to say, Saudi Arabia. In Ramadan, however, the 11th hijra month, and a time of fasting during daylight hours, the pace of public life slows down considerably.

How big is your footprint?

The point of a holiday is, of course, to have a good time, but if it's relatively guilt-free as well, that's even better. Perfect ecotourism would ensure a good living for local inhabitants while not detracting from their traditional lifestyles, encroaching on their customs or spoiling their environment. Perfect ecotourism probably doesn't exist, but everyone can play their part. Here are a few points worth bearing in mind:

- *Think about where your money goes, and be fair and realistic about how cheaply you travel. Try and put money into local people's hands; drink local beer or fruit juice rather than imported brands and stay in locally-owned accommodation wherever possible*
- *Haggle with humour and not aggressively. Remember that you are likely to be much wealthier than the person you're buying from*
- *Think about what happens to your rubbish. Take biodegradable products and a water bottle filter. Be sensitive to limited resources like water, fuel and electricity*
- *Help preserve local wildlife and habitats by respecting rules and regulations, such as sticking to footpaths, not standing on coral and not buying products made from endangered plants or animals*
- *Don't treat people as part of the landscape, they may not want their picture taken. Ask first and respect their wishes*
- *Learn the local language and be mindful of local customs and norms. It can enhance your travel experience and you'll earn respect and be more readily welcomed by local people*
- *And finally, use your guidebook as a starting point, not the only source of information. Talk to local people, then discover your own adventure*

Essentials

Prohibitions

Holy places Mosques in Morocco, except the Hassan II Mosque in Casablanca and the restored Almohad mosque at Tin Mal in the High Atlas, are off limits. Other Muslim religious buildings in use which you may visit are the very fine Medersa Bou Inania in Fès, the Tomb of Moulay Ismaïl in Meknès, and the Mausoleum of Mohammed V in Rabat. The remainder are strictly off the tourist track. People who are clearly non-Muslim will be turned away by door keepers from places where they are not wanted. Those who try to slip past the guardians should be sure they can talk their way out of trouble.

Narcotics *Kif* or marijuana represents a good source of income for small farmers in the Rif. However, the European Union has put pressure on Morocco to stop production. There is no serious attempt, however, to stop those Moroccans who so wish from having a gentle smoke. (*Kif* is also consumed in the form of ma'joun cakes, local variant of hash brownies, which have been known to lead to much merriment at otherwise staid occasions). However, as a tourist, under no circumstances do you want to be caught by the police in the possession of drugs of any kind. Expect no sympathy whatsoever if caught trying to export cannabis resin or other substances. You have been warned.

Security and terrorism

On the night of 14 May 2003, Casablanca was shaken by co-ordinated kamikaze bomb attacks targeting a Jewish social club and a major hotel. Over 40 Moroccans were murdered. Salafiya-Jihadiya fundamentalist groups organized these murders and the national security forces reacted with a wave of arrests. Summer 2003 saw the men responsible, including some of the suicide-bombers who survived, on trial. Some were condemned to the death penalty, which is not likely to be applied, however. The speedy trials were widely criticized as being more a vengeful reaction to the attacks rather than an attempt to apply justice.

Morocco has seen little urban terrorism and violence in recent years. (There were clashes between demonstrators and heavily armed police during urban riots in March 1965 and during the bread riots of 1984.) The influence of purist strains of Islam grew among the urban poor in the 1990s, in part due to the authorities' inability to provide any tangible improvement in standards of living. The gross double standards practiced by the USA with respect to the Israel/Palestine issue, which angers Muslim communities everywhere, angers Moroccans, too. In a sense, it is surprising that the attacks did not come earlier – except that Moroccans have always looked with surprise and disdain at the mess created in neighbouring Algeria by the violence of fundamentalists and the ruling military.

No prediction can be made of how the situation will evolve in Morocco. In July 2003, Hmidou Laanigri, head of the DST (Direction de la surveillance du territoire) was appointed head of the DGSN (Direction générale de la sécurité nationale, the urban police), thereby bringing two major wings of the Moroccan security apparatus together. New policy is expected to follow a line similar to that taken for over a decade now in Tunisia: tight monitoring of all fundamentalist activity, nil tolerance of anything which might lead to violence. The visitor will note fairly tight security. As anything Jewish is a sitting target, there are police outside synagogues. Only bona fide travellers can enter airport buildings. If driving, slow right down for checkpoints as you approach major cities.

Safety

For safety matters with regard to women travelling alone, see page 27

Morocco is basically a very safe country, although there is occasional violent street crime in Casablanca and (very rarely) Marrakech. Travelling on public transport, you need to watch your pockets. Do not carry all your money, cashcards, and travellers' cheques in the same place. A money belt and one of those small waterproof boxes (for credit cards or travellers' cheques), you wear round your neck are a very good idea. Never have more money than you can afford to lose in the pockets of your jeans. Thieves operate best in crowds getting on and off trains and at bus and taxi stations where they can quickly disappear into an anonymous mass of people.

One point is that you do need to be aware of the various skilled con-artists in operation in certain places. Hasslers of various kinds are active at the gates of Tanger port, and to a lesser extent in Tetouan. There are all sorts of ruses used by hasslers to extract a little money from tourists: 'the sick relative story', 'the grand taxi fare to Rabat to start university story', 'the supplement for the onward reservation to Chaouen 'story'. You need to be polite and confident, distant and sceptical – even a little bored by the whole thing. Some of the ruses, however, are pretty good, ie at Marrakech airport, 'would you like to make a contribution to the taxi drivers' football team fund?' Learn the values of the banknotes quickly (the yellow-brown 100dhs and the blue 200dhs are the big ones, a red 10dh is no great loss). Keep your wits about you. Remember, you are especially vulnerable stumbling off that overnight bus.

Should you be robbed, reporting it to the police will take time – but may alert them to the fact that there are thieves operating in a given place.

Where to stay

As anywhere, it's a good idea to take a look at a room before you take it

Morocco has a good range of accommodation to suit all budgets. There are well-appointed business hotels in the main cities, luxurious places for the discerning visitor – and clean basic hotels to suit those with limited funds. Independent travellers appreciate the growing number of *maisons d'hôte* or guesthouses (aka *riads*, see box, page 45 and listings, Marrakech), some very swish indeed, while in the mountain areas walkers and climbers will find rooms available in local people's homes. Modern

Hotel classifications

This table explains the hotel classification system used in this book. Prices are based on double rooms, singles are marginally cheaper.
LL (1500dh and over) *and*
L (1000-1500dh) *Indicates an international luxury class hotel as found in Casablanca or Rabat, or one of the famous luxury hotels of Morocco. Extremely good management means that everything works to the highest standard.*
A (800-990dh) *Indicates a hotel with top class facilities and services.*
B (360-790dh) *Indicates a four-star hotel with all basic facilities, including air-conditioning and probably a pool.*
C (260-350dh) *Denotes a three-star hotel run to a good standard. This will be a clean hotel, with all basic facilities. Service may be a bit lacking on occasion, however.*
D (180-250dh *A one- or two-star hotel, the best you may find in a small town. There may be a restaurant attached. Hot showers almost always available.*
E (120-170dh) *A one-star hotel, probably situated in an older area of a town. Will probably provide breakfast, but no restaurant. Shared WC and showers on corridor. Sometimes shower en suite. Hot water unavailable more often than not.*
F (60-110dh)

self-catering accommodation is also available in Agadir and the North, at Marinasmir and Kabila, close to Tetouan. This range of accommodation, growing constantly, is one of the main strengths of the Moroccan tourist industry.

So what should you expect of hotels in Morocco? Firstly, though there is an official star rating system, few hotels boast their membership of the one-, two- or even three-star categories. There does not appear to be very tight central control on how prices reflect facilities on offer. There are considerable variations in standards, and surprises are possible. Note too that breakfast is generally not included in the room price – except in *maisons d'hôte*.

Cheap

At the budget end of the market are simple hotels, often close to bus or train stations, where you will pay 30-60dh single, up to 90dh double for a small, simple room. There may be a washbasin, sometimes a bidet. Loos and showers (5-8dh), will be shared. The worst of this sort of accommodation will be little better than a concrete cell, stifling in summer. The best is often quite pleasant outside summer, with helpful staff and lots of clean, bright tiling. Rooms often open on to a central courtyard, limiting privacy and meaning you have to leave your room closed when out. Outside the big tourist cities, such hotels have almost exclusively Moroccan customers. Although such hotels are generally clean, it may be best to bring a sheet with you if you're planning to use them a lot. Water, especially in the southern desert towns, can be a problem. Generally, there will be a public bath (*hammam*) close by for you to take a shower after a long bus journey.

Mid-range

More expensive (say 90-120dh for a single) are one-star type hotels, generally in the new part of town (*ville nouvelle* neighbourhoods). Showers may be en suite, breakfast (coffee, bread and jam, a croissant, orange juice) should be available, possibly at the café on the groundfloor, for around 20dh. Next up are the two and three star-ish places, prices ranging from 120-350dh a single. In this category again, most of the hotels are in the *ville nouvelle* areas. Rooms will have high ceilings and en suite shower and loo. Light sleepers need to watch out for noisy, street-facing rooms. Some of these hotels are being revamped, not always very effectively. Still in this price bracket, you have a number of establishments with a personal, family-run feel, including the *Shehrazade* in Marrakech and certain southern hotels which despite aiming at tour groups are rather pleasant.

Expensive Top hotels are run by international groups such as ***Accor*** and ***Le Méridien***. Upmarket hotels in Morocco can either be vast and brash, revamped and nouveau riche, or solid but tasteful and even discrete with a touch of old-fashioned elegance. The main cities also have large business hotels, including a ***Hilton*** in Rabat and a long-established ***Hyatt Regency*** in Casablanca.

Hotel industry weaknesses For years, many of the large tourist hotels in places like Marrakech and Agadir were run as family businesses with little professional management. In the worst establishments, staff are poorly paid and generally on short term contracts (at the end of which they are sacked and recruited again after a month). Hotel owners are also tempted to use *stagiaires* (trainees on placement from hotel management school) as free labour in summer. Staff motivation in many of Morocco's hotels is thus poor, even in pricey establishments. It is thus a nice gesture to leave any unwanted shampoo, toothpaste etc for the *femme de chambre*. She will be working long hours on a very small salary, maybe only 1,500dh a month.

Riads & guesthouses

For more on riads check www.riadsomaroc.com, www.marrakech-medina.com, www.marrakech-riads.net or www.essaouira medina.com

The big phenomenon of the late 1990s in the Moroccan tourist industry was the development of the *maison d'hôte*. Wealthy Europeans bought old property in the médinas, the old towns, of Marrakech and Essaouira as second homes. Rather than leave the property closed for much of the year, the solution was to rent it out. A number of agencies specialising in the rental of *riads* (as these properties are generally called, after their garden courtyards or *riads*) were set up. Some *riads* are occupied for most of the year by their owners and so are more like guesthouses. If thinking of staying in a *riad*, you could make your first approach via a reliable agency like ***Riads au Maroc***, I Rue Mahjoub Rmiza, Marrakech, T044-431900, www.riadomaroc.com Certain UK travel companies now have *riads* in their brochures. Basically, they satisfy a growing demand for spacious accommodation with a personal touch. The service in a *riad* should be far better than in a four-star hotel. Generally, *riad* charges cover accommodation and breakfast. Meals can be laid on at extra charge, and as they are prepared to order for a small number of people, will be of excellent quality. In a place like Marrakech, hygiene in a *riad* should also be far better than in one of the city's jaded four-star establishments. There is now guesthouse accommodation to suit medium to large holiday budgets. In coming years, expect new riads to open in Fès and Casablanca.

When reserving *riad* accommodation, you need to be clear on how you will be met (finding such houses in complicated médina streets is generally impossible for taxi drivers). Also check whether your accommodation is ground floor (damper in winter) or top floor (hot in summer) and the nature of the heating. Moroccan nights can be very chilly in winter. Another consideration, if you have small children, is the presence of small pools without fencing.

Holiday rentals in highly individual restored homes in the medinas and mountains of Morocco

- Riads: historic city houses with garden courtyards and roof terraces in Marrakech, Essaouira and Fes
- Kasbahs in the Deep South
- Upscale desert bivouacs
- Rentals by room or whole property • Short and long stay
- Personalised service • Advice on excursions
- Prices range from 35 euros to 600 euros for a double room per night; breakfast included

Riads au Maroc

1, rue Mahjoub Rmiza 40 000 Marrakech Ménara Guéliz
Tél: (+212) 44 43 19 00 fax: (+212) 44 43 17 86
Email: riadomaroc@iam.net.ma Website http://www.riadomaroc.com

Best in town

The big development in Moroccan tourism in the last few years has been the growth of pleasant, owner-run guesthouse type accommodation. With no apologies for subjectivity, the following is a list of some of the more personable riads, guesthouses that make you want to stop and spend time in quiet corners of Morocco.

Tanger

***Dar Nour** 20 Rue Gourna, Kasbah, T062-112724, pgb.tanger@caramail.com Small new upmarket guesthouse in the Kasbah of Tanger, 400dh per night, suite 1000dh per night.*

Essaouira

***The Tea House** 74 Derb Laalouj, La Skala (in the heart of old Essaouira), T044-783543, www.aescalon.demon.co.uk /teahouse/ Offers 2 self-catering flats full of character.*

***House of the Caïd**, T061-708036 (mob). Recently restored, an upmarket guesthouse on the Bab Marrakech side of town.*

Marrakech

Particularly recommended in the highly expensive bracket are:

***Dar Caïs** T044-440141, Riad Enija, rahba el Qdima, 9 Derb Mesfioui, T044-440926 and **Dar el Qadi derb Debbachi**, T044-378655, riyadelcadi@iam.net.ma*

More reasonably priced are:

***Dar Mouassine** 148 Derb Snane, T/F044-445287.*

***Riad 72**, 72 Arset Awzel, Bab Doukkala, www.riad72.com Minimalist elegance with an African touch.*

***Riad Noor** 31 Derb el Kebir, Ben Salah neighbourhood, T044-386095, F386931, elisabeth.dianda@noorcharana.com*

***Riad Zina** 38 Derb Assabane, Riad Laârous, T044-385242, beate.prinz.tr.zi@gofornet.com A small, faintly hippyish place.*

Fès

***Riad al Bartal** 21 Rue Sournas, Ziat, Fès, T/F055-637053, riadlaroche@caramail.com Not cheap but worth it.*

***Ryad Mabrouka**, Derb el Miter, Talaa Kbira, T055-636345, www.riadmabrouka.com*

Dadès Valley

***Hotel Tomboctou** T044-834604, htomboctou@caramail.com Best at Tineghir and quite reasonably priced.*

***Kasbah Aït Ben Moro** T044-852116, black.condor@caramail.com At Skoura 40 km west of Ouarzazate. Splendid if expensive.*

***Kasbah Itren** T066-161147 (mob). A new venture, on the road to the Vallée des Roses, Kelaâ des Mgouna. Tiny and very reasonable.*

Youth hostels (Auberges de jeunesse)

There are 11 hostels in all affiliated to the **IYHA**, located in the cities (Casablanca, Rabat, Fès, Meknès and Marrakech, Oujda and Laâyoune) as well as Azrou (Middle Atlas) and Asni (High Atlas). The HQ is in Meknès, on Av Oqba ibn Nafi. Overnight charge 20-40dh, use of kitchen 2dh, maximum stay of three nights and priority to the under-30s. Summer opening hours are 0800-1300, 1830-2400, winter 0800-1000, 1200-15000, 1800-2230. For information try the **Moroccan Youth Hostel Federation**, Parc de la Ligue arabe, Casablanca, T022-220551, F226777. It is better to go for cheap hotels, more conveniently located and with better loos and showwers. The Casablanca hostel was improved in 2002, the Fès hostel has had good reviews but is in the *Ville nouvelle*, as is the Marrakech hostel. Both are convenient for the train station, but a long way from sights and old-town atmosphere.

Mountain accommodation

Walking in the Atlas, you will notice many children and adults have plastic shoes. Gifts of used kids' shoes are always welcome

In the mountains, you can easily bivouac out in summer or, in the high mountains, kip in a stone *azib* (shepherd's shelter). There are three main options for paying accommodation: floor space in someone's home, a *gîte* of some kind, or a refuge run by the **CAF** (Club Alpin Français, see www.cafmaroc.co.ma). The refuges are shelters with basic dormitory and kitchen facilities. Rates depend on category and season but about 15-50dh per night per person is usual. The **CAF** can be contacted via BP 6178, Casablanca, T022-270090, also BP 4437 Rabat, T037-734442. In France, the **CAF** is at 24 Av Laumière, 75019 Paris.

In remote villages, there are *gîtes d'étape*, simple dormitory accommodation, marked with the colourful *GTAM* (*Grande traversée de l'Atlas marocain*) logo. The warden generally lives in the house next door. Prices here are set by the **ONMT** (tourist board), and the *gîte* will be clean if spartan. The board also publishes an annual guide listing people authorized to provide *gîte* type accommodation.

In mountain villages where there is no *gîte*, you will usually find space in people's homes, provided you have a sleeping bag. Many houses have large living rooms with room for people to bed down on thin foam mattresses. It is the custom to leave a small sum in payment for this sort of service. On the whole, you will be made very welcome.

Camping There are campsites all over Morocco – the **ONMT** quotes 87 sites in well-chosen locations. Few sites, however, still respect basic international standards. Security is a problem close to large towns, even if the site is surrounded by a wall with broken glass on top. Never leave anything valuable in your tent. As campsites are really not much cheaper than basic hotels, and as even simple things like clean toilets and running water can be problematic, cheap hotel accommodation is preferable. There are some notable exceptions however. In Tinghir, on the route up to the Todgha Gorge, there are some campsites popular with the campervan brigade (*Chez Bernard – Camping du soleil*, and at Ksiba, the hills near Beni Mellal, there is a simple and pleasant new site. Near Meknès, on the Moulay Idriss road, the main city campsite is good. Other sites with a good name include *Camping Firdaous* at Marrakech, the *Camping International* on the Sefrou road outside Fes and *Chez Christian* at Ounara north-east of Essaouira.

Many Moroccan campsites lack shade. The ground tends to be hard and stony, requiring tough tent pegs. When choosing your tent pitch bear in mind factors like proximity to where people dump their rubbish (the bins may not be in a closed-off space). You may not get much sleep if other campers have decided to spend the night with a sing-a-long to the rhythm of the *darbouka* drum.

Getting around

When planning a trip in Morocco, remember that the distances are great, and that long trips on buses can be tiring. Bus journeys can be excruciatingly slow, even over say 200 km journeys between fairly important towns (emember these vehicles are used mainly by people who travel a lot by mule and donkey cart, too). To make maximum use of your time, if you don't mind dozing on a bus, then take night buses to cover the longer distances. If you have sufficient funds, then there is always the option of taking internal flights – although these may not always fit in with your schedule. Public transport is very reasonably priced. Car hire, however, is expensive: although you may be able to get a small car for 1800-2500dh a week, you still have petrol or diesel costs on top of this. The advantage, of course, is the flexibility in getting to obscure places where the public transport is slow or rare. And you can take photo-stops whenever you want.

Air

Companies offering private plane rental include Airstar, Marrakech T/F044-435502. Helicopter transfers by Hélisud Maroc, Marrakech T044-438438, heli-sud@iam.net.ma

Royal Air Maroc (Ram), see www.royailairmaroc.com, operates domestic flights, most unfortunately routed via Casablanca and therefore requiring waits in that airport. Cities served include Tanger, Marrakech, Agadir, Ouarzazate, Laâyoune, and Dakhla. If you are on business, a Marrakech to Fès via Casablanca may be preferable to an eight hour bus journey. (There are limited direct flights between **Marrakech** and **Fès**.) Unfortunately, promising domestic flights seem to disappear, ie the Casablanca to Essaouira service, but check. There are flights to and from Laâyoune on most days. A flight from Oujda to Casblanca (one a week) cuts out a 10-hour train journey. Though **Rachidia**

No rules of the road

Driving in Morocco is hazardous. Grands taxis, buses and lorries thunder along, forcing oncoming lesser vehicles on to the hard shoulder, if it exists. Sometimes there is a tyre-splitting gap between tarmac and dusty edge. Pedestrians wander out into the road and cyclists stray into the fast lane. On poor roads, will see Moroccan drivers holding a palm up to their windscreens. This is to reduce the risk of shattering due to stones shooting up from the wheels of oncoming cars.

People also seem to overtake in the most suicidal of places. Does the single continuous line have no meaning? In fact, driving in Morocco, you find yourself wondering how such a generally polite people manages to produce such appalling drivers. The answer lies in the fact that you can basically buy yourself a driving licence. The accident figures are appalling: 25.6 deaths per 1,000 accidents per annum in Morocco, as against 2.6 deaths per 1,000 accidents in France. The Gendarmerie royale is having a crackdown, however, especially on speed limits, and 400dh fines may be levied on the spot.

Do not rush, go with the flow and take your time. Apart from Casablanca, Morocco's cities are not large, and you will soon be out on the calmer country roads. Here you will share the roads with numerous animal-drawn carts and pack animals. This makes for slow driving but can also be hazardous at night. Most roads lack cats-eyes and most agricultural vehicles and mule carts drive without lights.

has an airport, demand is currently insufficient for regular flights. **Zagora** has a military airport which might one day come on line for tourist flights.

RAM head office is on T022-912000, F912397. All major towns have ***RAM*** agencies, generally on the main boulevard, as follows: Agadir, Av Général Kettani, T048-840793, F839296; Al Hoceima, Aéroport Charif al Idrisi, T039-982063; Casablanca, 44 Av des FAR, T022-311122, F442409; Essaouira, Aéroport Mogador, T044-476709, F476705; Fès, 54 Av Hassan II, T055-620456; Laâyoune, Pl Dcheira, T048-894071; Marrakech, 197 Av Mohammed V, T044-446444, F446002; Meknès, 7 Av Mohammed V, T055-520963/64, F523606; Nador, 45 Blvd Mohammed V, T056-606337, F605539; Ouarzazate, 1 Blvd Mohammed V, T044-885080, F886893; Oujda, Blvd Mohammed V, T056-683909; Rabat, Av Mohammed V, T037-709766, F708076; Tanger, 1 Pl de France, T039-935501; Tétouan, 5 Av Mohammed V, T039-961260, F961577.

Sample RAM prices: single Casablanca to Marrakech 800dh, return 1100dh. Single Casablanca to Nador 1140dh, 1350dh return

A small private airline company, ***Regional Airlines***, launched in 1998, runs flights with twin-prop planes between Casablanca, Agadir and Laâyoune, as well as Málaga, Las Palmas and Lisbon. Reservations on T022-53880, F538050. Their downtown Casablanca office is on Av des FAR, near the *Hotel Royal Mansour*, almost opposite the *Hotel Excelsior*.

Road

Bicycles & motorcyles

Theft from bikes is a problem

Mountain bikes, mopeds and sometimes small motorcycles can be hired in tourist towns. There is no shortage of mechanics to fix bikes and mopeds. Trains, buses and even grands taxis will take bikes for a small fee. An increasingly popular option is the cycle tour holiday. Some European companies now run such holidays, with bikes being carried on vans on the longer stretches. Off-road biking is popular near Tafraoute in the Anti-Atlas and the Gorges du Dadès.

If you go touring with a bike or motorcycle, beware of the sun. Wear gloves, cover those bits of exposed skin between helmet and T-shirt. For motorcyclists, helmets are complusory, believe it or not, and gendarmes will be happy to remind you so.

Riding a motorbike in Morocco is even more testing than driving a car. Watch out for stray pedestrians, note that vehicle drivers will not necessarily show you much respect. Where flocks of animals are straying across the road, try not to drive between a single animal and the rest of the flock, as it may well try to charge back to join the rest. Use your horn. If you are going to go off road, wear boots, make sure your tyres are in tiptop condition.

Theft from bicycle paniers is a problem. Anything loosely attached to your bike will disappear when you are being besieged by a horde of small kids in an isolated village.

Bus Domestic bus services are plentiful. Price variations are small while the quality of service varies enormously. Broadly speaking, if the train, a ***Supratours*** bus or grands taxi run to your destination, don't bother with the small bus companies. For early morning services it's worth getting your ticket in advance, also at peak times when many Moroccan are travelling, like the end of Ramadhan and around Aïd el Kebir (two months after the end of Ramadhan). You will find that there is a man who helps stow luggage on roof or in hold, so have a couple of dirham coins handy for him.

Interailers note: the pass is not valid with Supratours

Supratours and ***CTM*** In southern Morocco, the safest and most comfortable service is with ***Supratours***, an offshoot of the ***ONCF*** (see above). Next best is the *CTM*, *Compagnie de transport marocain* (white buses with blue and red stripes). VOften (but not always) their services run from stations away from the main *gare routière* (inter-city bus station). This is the case in Casablanca, Fès and Marrakech, for example. For Tanger, the *CTM* station is just outside the port zone gates. For information (*renseignements*) on *CTM* services try T022-458881. Both ***Supratours*** and ***CTM*** buses **usually** run on time. As an example of prices, a single Marrakech to Essaouira costs 50dh with ***Supratours***. The ***CTM***'s quadrilingual website, www.ctm.co.ma, may be updated to give schedules in the near future.

Local bus companies Other private bus companies are generally much slower, apart from a few *rapide* services with videos and the like – try ***Trans-Ghazala***. There are regional companies, like the ***SATAS***, which serves much of the south, and all sorts of minor companies with names like ***Pullman du Sud***. While such buses get to parts that the ***CTM*** cannot reach, they are often slow. Bus terminals have a range of ticket windows (*guichets*), displaying destinations and times of departure. Several companies may serve the same destination, and as you head into the bus station, you may be approached by touts who will urge you to prefer one company to another. The main Casablanca bus station functions on this basis, to the extent that the ticket windows are practically out of business.

Safety Vehicles used by many private bus companies do not conform to high safety standards. Winter 2000 saw a spate of horrible bus accidents in Morocco. The deaths and serious injuries meant they were given high media coverage. The reasons for this is that drivers are severely underpaid. To make up for their low wages, they leave half-full, aiming to pick up extra passengers (whom they won't have to declare to their employers) en route. This makes for a slow, stop/go service. On routes worked by several companies, drivers race each other to be first to pick up passengers in the next settlement. Given the poor condition of the vehicles and the often narrow roads, accidents are inevitable.

Although inter-city buses can be very slow, (and you may even see the road surface under your feet), for many of the people who use them speed is not an issue. Pack mules link mountain villages to the rest of the world, while on the coastal plains, mule and donkey drawn buggies provide transport to the weekly *souk*.

City buses Most towns have city buses which provide great opportunities for local pickpockets when crowded. Casablanca buses are terrible, so have 20dh notes ready for short red-taxi runs. The orange ***Alsa*** buses in Marrakech are fine. Note that there is no longer any bus service from Rabat or Casablanca to the Aéroport Mohammed V, Casablanca.

As distances are great having a car makes a huge difference in the amount you can cover. All the main hire car companies are represented (***Europcar***, ***Hertz***, ***Sixt-car***), and there are numerous small companies which vary hugely in reliability. Arriving at Casa-Mohammed V Airport, you will find hire-car companies on the main concourse to your left as you come out through the frosted-glass doors. The smallest car available is generally a Fiat Uno, more rarely a Renault 4. A large number of agencies now have Fiat Palios in their fleets. The Peugeot 205 is felt to be a more reliable small car, with slightly higher clearance and better road holding. A good deal would give you an Uno for 500dh a day, unlimited mileage, although certain Marrakech agencies (***Imzitours***, T044-433934/36, imzi_tours@usa.net for example) can be considerably cheaper. 4WDs available in Morocco include the Suzuki Gemini (2 persons) and the Vitara (4 persons), at around 800dh per day; long-base Mitsubishi Pajeros (6 persons) are hired at 900-1,000dh per day. Toyotas are said to be the best desert 4WDs. Landrovers are very uncomfortable for long cross-country runs on road, especially in summer without air conditioning.

Car hire

See individual city and town directories for details of companies.

There is huge demand for hire-cars during the Christmas and Easter breaks

Remember that you are responsible for damage if you take a car unsuited to the *piste* into areas suitable only for 4WDss. Regarding insurance, the best agencies will provide all risk insurance. As a matter of self preservation, do not agree to take a hire car other than in the daylight. Check such for tyre condition (this includes spare tyre), presence of jack and warning triangle, working lights and safety belts. When hiring an all-terrain vehicle, try to ascertain that the agency you are hiring from has a reliable, well-maintained fleet. Make sure that the vehicle will go into four-wheel drive easily and, as for ordinary cars, check the spare tyre. Look at the tyres closely – there should be no cuts on the sides.

In general, you will need dirhams to pay, as only the larger agencies take credit cards. They will take an imprint of your credit card as a guarantee.

Car insurance In terms of car insurance and damage to vehicle, there are several possibilities. A good agency will have agreements with garages across Morocco for repairs. The garage will talk to the agency about the nature of the repairs, and the matter will be handled. If the damage is your fault, that is because you have taken the car onto rough tracks in breach of contract, you will be responsible for covering the cost of repairs. In the case of accidents, you have to get a *constat de police* (a police report), which is a document drawn up by the police stating whose fault the accident is. Depending on the type of insurance, the client pays a percentage of the cost of repairs. You can have a *sans franchise* (rental contract) which means that you will have nothing to pay, or with a franchise set at a certain level, that is a 50% franchise means that you pay 50% more than rental cost, so that in a case of an accident, you pay only 50% cost of repairs.

Always try to have the mobile phone number of an agency representative in case of emergency

A good agency will have you sign a *fiche technique* (a technical details form) after you have viewed the car before hire, in daylight, and checked that everything, including tyres, spare tyre, jack, lights, windscreen, etc are in good order. It is important to check these things as there have been cases of unscrupulous hire-car agencies sending clients out with sub-standard vehicles which have broken down. Clients, in the lurch in remote towns, have then paid for repairs, which the agency has then refused to pay for.

Petrol and other costs You may have to pay for the petrol already in the tank of your hire car. Usually, the car will be almost empty, and you fill up yourself. In July 2003, diesel in Morocco was 5.82dh per litre, petrol (*essence*) was at 9.11dh. Hire cars in Morocco generally run on petrol (*super*) rather than diesel. Lead-free petrol is *sans plomb*. In 2003, a fill-up ((*le plein*) for a Fiat Uno or a Clio cost around 350dh. In such a car, 200dh does the four-hour trip on winding mountain roads from Marrakech to Ouarzazate. A fill-up with diesel for a Pajero 4WD costs 500dh, and on this the vehicle will do the 800 km trip Marrakech to Zagora and back.

Most cars do not as yet use unleaded petrol

In remote areas, remember to fill up whenever possible, preferably at one of the larger petrol stations (***Shell***, ***Mobil***, ***CMH***, in most cities, ***Ziz*** in the South). There have been cases of petrol being watered down, with unfortunate results, in certain places. New looking service stations are best, in towns.

Should you need tyre repairs, prices vary. Expect to pay upwards of 50dh as a foreigner in a hurry in a small town, rather less if you have time to wait in some rural outpost.

Basically always drive more slowly than you would in Europe

Risky roads There are a number of dangerous stretches of road which you may have to deal with in your hire car. Much concentration is needed on the four-hour drive on the winding, mountainous P31, Marrakech to Ouarzazate, via the Tizi-n-Tichka. Fog and icy surfaces are possible in winter. There are roads which seem excellent, you drive fast, and then meet sudden dips and turns, such as Ouarzazate to Skoura, Agdz to Nekob. The P7, Casablanca to Marrakech, is dangerous on Friday evenings as holidaymakers hasten towards the Red City, competing with lorry traffic (watch out for the final stretch through the Jebilet after Sidi Bou Othman). Drivers are also tempted to go far faster than necessary on the straight stretches of the P24 between Marrakech and Kelaâ des Sraghna. Care must be taken on the Rabat to Fès autoroute (which in fact is not much better than a European dual carriageway), especially as there are few crash barriers. In the Middle and High Atlas barriers are put down on routes to Azrou, Ifrane, Midelt and over the Tizi-n-Tichka and Tizi-n-Test when snow blocks roads. Basically always drive more slowly than you would in Europe.

Highway code The Moroccan highway code follows the international model. Speeds are limited to 120 kph on the autoroute, 100 kph on main roads, 60 kph on approaches to urban areas and 40 kph in urban areas. Speed restriction signs do not always follow a logical sequence. There are two types of police to be met on the roads: the blue-uniformed urban police and the grey-uniformed gendarmes in rural areas. The latter are generally stationed outside large villages, at busy junctions, or under shady eucalyptus trees near bends with no-overtaking marks.

The wearing of seat belts is compulsory outside the cities, and the gendarmes will be watching to see you're wearing them. (Many Moroccans who know the checkpoint locations well seem to think that seat-belts are worn just for the gendarmes.) It is traditional to slow down for the gendarmes, although as a foreigner driving a hire car you will generally be waved through. They will not, on the whole, ask for 'coffee money' from you. Note however that the police are empowered to levy on the spot fines for contravention of traffic regulations. Fines are now quite severe in response to the high number of fatal accidents due to careless driving.

Other highway code tips. Red and white curb markings mean no parking. Warning triangles are not compulsory – but highly useful. In the case of an accident, report to nearest gendarmerie or police post to obtain a written report, otherwise the insurance will be invalid.

Remember that 4WD vehicles, designed for rough tracks, do not perform as well as standard saloon cars on normal roads

Off-road driving In addition to well over 10,000 km of surfaced road, Morocco has several thousand kilometres of unsurfaced tracks, generally referred to as *pistes*. Some of these can be negotiated with care by an ordinary car with high clearance. Most cannot however, and 4WD vehicles are increasingly popular to explore the remote corners of Morocco. In south-central Morocco, a breathtaking but tough route is the 'Gorge to Gorge' piste from Msemrir at the top of the Gorges du Dadès round to Tamtattouchte at the top of the Gorges du Todgha. Another option in the High Atlas is the Telouet – Kasbah Anemiter – Aït Ben Haddou route, not however to be attempted after rain. There is a tyre-destroying piste from Nekob to Boumalne du Dadès across the Jbel Saghro (several spares necessary). For those with a yen for desert driving, it is now possible to drive down from Merzouga to Taouz, near the Algerian frontier, then westwards along the Oued Ziz to the intersection with the Oued Gheris, then north to join the Rissani to Nekob road (S3454) near Mecissi.

4WD adepts should plan their trips carefully, noting that bad weather can impede travel. Snow blocks mountain tracks in winter, rain and melt-water can make them impassable. Ask locals about conditions. In many areas, pistes are being upgraded – or are no longer well maintained, as they have been made superfluous thanks to the presence of a new tarmac road. However, not all road improvement works are of very high quality. A hard winter can leave mountain tarmac partly destroyed, or wash large quantities of rubble and clay on to the road surface.

If you are driving into remote areas, always travel with two vehicles. In the hostile desert environment, if things go wrong, there is nobody to get you out if you are by yourselves. If you are unused to off-road vehicles, employ the services of a driver (around 300dh a day). He will know the routes well and be able to chat to locals and other drivers about the state of the tracks. If you don't have a driver and get a bit lost, you can always pick up a local hitchhiker who will show you the way. Outside the main tourist towns, he is unlikely to be a 'fake' guide. When out in wild country, never take an unknown *piste* if a storm is on its way or as night is falling. Check before you leave the names of villages on the way and remember that some tracks lead to abandoned mining operations rather than helpful hamlets. Do not go full tilt into a ford without checking the depth of the water first by wading in. You do not want to be stranded in a *oued* in full flood. Remember that progress will be slow, and that after wet weather you may have to dig/pull vehicles out. Distances tend to be measured in hours rather than in kilometres.

Car parking In towns, parking is fairly easy. Parking meters rarely function and instead a sort of watchman, identified by blue overalls and a metal badge will pop up. Give him some spare change, say 5dh, when you return to your undamaged vehicle. At night, it is essential to leave your vehicle in a place where there is a night watchman (*le gardien de nuit*). In practice, all good hotels and streets with restaurants will have such a figure who will keep an eye out for eventual marauders.

Hitchhiking

Definitely unadvisable for women travelling on their own

It is possible to hitchhike in Morocco. There are lorries which go to and from Europe, and drivers can sometimes be persuaded to take a passenger. In remote areas, vans and lorries may pick up passengers for a bargained price. However, don't count on hitching, as vehicles out in the sticks are generally packed with locals. Landrover taxis (jeeps) and Mercedes Transit are not run for hitchers – they are public transport with a price.

Taxi

Taxi drivers' foreign language skills are highly variable

Long distance **grands taxis**, generally Mercedes 200 saloon cars, run over fixed routes between cities, or within urban areas between centre and outlying suburbs. There is a fixed price for each route and passengers pay for a place, six in a Mercedes, nine in a Peugeot 504 estate car. Taxis wait until they are full. You may however, feel rich enough to pay for two places in order to be comfortable at the front (and be able to wear a safety belt). In a Peugeot estate, the best places are undoubtedly at the front, or, if you are quite small, right at the back. The middle place in the middle row is probably the worst.

Between towns, grands taxis are quicker than trains or buses, and normally only a little more expensive. Each town has a grand taxi rank, generally, although not always, next to the main bus station. The drivers cry out the name of their destination, and as you near the taxi station, you may be approached by touts eager to help you find a taxi. The standard of driving sometimes leaves a little to be desired.

In mountain areas, the same system applies, although the vehicles are Mercedes transit vans (where there is tarmac) or landrovers, which have two people next to the driver and ten in the back.

Petits taxis are used within towns, and are generally Fiat Unos and Palios. They are colour-coded by town (blue for Rabat, red for Casa, khaki for Marrakech, tasteful pistachio green in Mohammedia). Officially they are metered, with an initial minimum fare, followed by increments of time and distance. There is a 50% surcharge after 2100. A petit taxi may take up to three passengers. In Marrakech, Rabat and Casablanca, drivers use the meters, in Tanger they try to charge what they like. In some cities (notably Rabat and Casablanca, where taxis are in short supply) drivers allow themselves to pick up other passengers en route if they are going the same way, thus earning a double fee for part of the route. No doubt this practice does not feature in the petit taxi driver's code of practice. In any case, taxi drivers welcome a tip – many of them are not driving their own vehicles, and make little more than 100dh a day. In terms of price, a short run between old and new town in Marrakech will set you back 10dh. Casa Port station to Casa Voyageurs is about 10dh too.

Train

ONCF timetables are available at all main stations and can be accessed on www.oncf.co.ma

The *ONCF* (*Office national des chemins de fer*) runs an efficient though slowish service between major cities. There are 1,900 km of railway line, the central node being at railway town Sidi Kacem, some 46 km north of Meknès. Coming into Casablanca airport, the traveller can take the blue *Bidhaoui* shuttle train to Casa-Voyageurs station on the **main north-south line**. This line runs from Tanger to Marrakech with significant stations being Kénitra, Sidi Kacem, Salé, Rabat, Casa-Voyageurs, Settat, and Benguerir. The *ONCF*'s **main west-east route** does Casa-Voyageurs to Oujda, main stations on this route being Rabat, Sidi Kacem, Meknès and Fès. A second fast *navette* (shuttle) serves commuters in the Casblanca-Rabat region, doing Casa-Port to Kénitra. This service **does not** run via Casa-Voyageurs. A two-tier Casablanca to Fès shuttle train is planned for the near future.

Prices & journey times Prices are reasonable. A first-class single ticket, Marrakech to Casa-Voyageurs, is 105dh, services between Casablanca and Rabat, depending on station and class, around the 35dh mark. Casa-Voyageurs to Tanger is 160dh first class. In terms of time, Casablanca to Marrakech generally takes 3 hours, Casablanca to Rabat just under 1 hour, Rabat to Fès nearly 4 hours. Fès to Oujda is another 5½ hours, while Rabat to Tanger is 4¾ hours.

Branch lines Railway enthusiasts may like the moderately obscure branch lines, mainly developed to serve the needs of the phosphate industry. There is a line from from **Benguerir to Safi** via phosphate town Youssoufia (ex-Louis Gentil) with a daily passenger service. Another branch line takes trains from **Casablanca to Khouribga** and Oued Zem, up on the Plateau des Phosphates. On Morocco's eastern flank, there is a weekly freight train from **Oujda to Bouarfa**, which unfortunately no longer takes passengers.

Most of the network is single track, apart from on the section Casablanca to Kénitra. Works are underway to double the line between Sidi Kacem and Meknès, and have started on the slow Meknès to Fès section. There are occasional delays on the Settat to Marrakech line as the tracks are being upgraded.

Train-bus link *Supratours* run buses to connect with trains from a number of stations. Routes covered include Tnine Sidi el Yamami, just south of Asilah, to Tetoutan; Taourirt to Nador and Khouribga to Beni Mellal. From just outside Marrakech station, ***Supratours*** has connecting buses to Ouarzazate, Essaouira, Agadir, Laâyoune and Dakhla. Sample prices in 2003 as follows: Marrakech to Agadir 75dh, Agadir to Laâyoune 200dh, Marrakech to Ouarzazate 65dh. Bus station numbers: Agadir T048-841207; Casa-Voyageurs T022-404299; Essaouira T044-475317; Laâyoune T048-894891; Marrakech T044-435525; Nador T056-607262; Ouarzazate T044-887912.

Train classes On the trains, first-class compartments are spacious and generally quieter than second class. Second-class rail fares are generally slightly more expensive than the *CTM* buses. You gain, however, in time saved, reliability and safety. Trains normally have a snacks trolley, a sandwich costing 12dh, a small coffee 5dh.

Maps

Of the road maps, the best is still probably the Michelin map, sheet 959, at scale 1:4,000,000, with insets at 1:1,000,000 and 1:1,600,000. You may find other maps in local bookshops.

If you are going to be hiking in the Atlas Mountains, and do not intend to engage the services of a guide, then you will want maps. These can be obtained from the Division du Cadastre et de la Cartographie, west of the town centre several kilometres down Avenue Hassan II, (T037-705311, F705191), open Monday-Thursday 0830-1100 and 0230-0530. Coming from the médina, take a petit taxi, look out for a large modern complex on your right near a big Renault garage on your left. Go straight into the complex and the map office is on the ground floor in a building towards the back. Arrive early. Most city and some mountain maps are immediately available – if you have an hour or so to spend. Be patient. Other orders take two working days to process. At the last count, the 1:100,000 scale maps cost 80dh. In Marrakech, maps can be obtained from reception at the *Hotel Ali* next to the Jardin Foucauld, Jemaâ el Fna, at the vastly inflated price of 140dh (you might get 10dh knocked off). The **Toubkal** 1:100,000 scale map is generally available, other sheets useful for the High Atlas of Azilal (Skoura, Tinghir, etc) are subject to availability. In London, *Stanfords*, generally has a pack of four maps for the Toubkal region (including Amizmiz, Oukaïmeden-Toubkal, Tizi-n-Test and Taliouine). If you are thinking of hiking the **Telouet to Ait Ben Haddou** route, get the 1:100,000 feuille NH-29-XXIII-2. For the **Tineghir to Gorges du Dades** routes, get 1:100,000 feuille NH-30-XIX-3.

More remote areas are covered, too. Although not strong on mountain relief, the 1:100,000 scale colour map, ref. STR HTA99, Maroc Haut Atlas, Carte des randonnées de **Zaouiat Ahançal**, also produced by the Division de la Cartographie, is handy as it shows a number of good circuits. For the whole **Azilal/Imilchil region**, a very useful map is the 1:250,000 scale Khénifra map, sheet, NI-30-13 which covers the whole region from **Khénifra** in the top northwest corner right across to **Midelt** and **Rich** in the east.

An excellent source of maps is ***Stanfords***: 12-14 Long Acre, London, WC2E 9LP, T 020-7836 1321, F 020-7836 0189, www.stanfords.co.uk. Also 29 Corn St, Bristol, BS1 and 39 Spring Gardens, Manchester, M2. Recommended.

Keeping in touch

Communications

Internet

See individual city and town directories

Internet cafés can by found in city centres and even quite out of the way places. Generally, you can get on line for as little as 30dh for half an hour. Areas of cheap hotels attracting budget travellers will have several cybercafés.The better private guesthouses have internet connections.

The world s finest map and travel book shops

Stanfords Flagship Store
12-14 Long Acre
Covent Garden
London WC2E 9LP
T: 020 7836 1321
www.stanfords.co.uk

Stanfords in Manchester
39 Spring Gardens
Manchester
M2 2BG
T: 0161 831 0250

Stanfords in Bristol
29 Corn Street
Bristol
BS1 1HT
T: 0117 929 9966

Inspiring exploration and discovery for 150 years

Essentials

Post
Letters to or from Europe can take up to a week

Posting letters is relatively easy, with the ***PTT centrale*** of each town selling the appropriate stamps. Postage costs to Europe are 6dh for a letter and 6.5dh for a postcard. Post offices are open 0800-1200 and 1500-1800 Monday-Friday in the winter, 0800-1500 in the summer. It is best to post the letter in the box inside or just outside this building as these are emptied most frequently. For those without a contact address to receive letters, instruct that they should be addressed clearly, with the surname underlined, to: Poste Restante, PTT Centrale, name of town, Morocco. Each ***PTT Centrale*** will have a post restante section, where letters are kept for a number of weeks. There is a small charge on collection ***American Express*** post restante is handled by *Voyages Schwartz*.

Telephone
Calling Morocco from abroad the code is 212

Phone shops or *téléboutiques*, clearly marked in distinctive blue and white livery are everywhere. (Lots of Moroccans have mobile phones, which they use to beep each other.) Téléboutiques stay open late in summer, are always supervised, with change available and (generally) telephone directories (*annuaires téléphoniques*). The machines are sometimes old French coin phones, and international calls are no problem. For internal calls put in several 1dh coins and dial the region code (even if you are in the region), followed by the number (a total of **nine** digits beginning 0). For overseas calls, put in at least three 5dh coins, dial 00 and wait for a musical sequence before proceeding. Most call boxes only accept the 'silver all over' coins, although this is changing. Calls can also be made from the *cabines téléphoniques* at the ***PTT Centrale***. Give the number to the telephonist who dials it and then calls out a cabin number where the call is waiting. NB It is significantly more expensive to phone from a hotel. Faxes can be sent and received from téléboutiques.

Media

The Press

Moroccan newspapers are produced in Arabic, French and Spanish. The main political parties all have their newspapers. From the mid-1990s, the general tone of the press became increasingly critical, dealing with issues once taboo. Of the daily newspapers, ***Le Matin du Sahara*** and ***Maroc Soir*** give the official line. The party press includes ***L'Opinion***, ***Libération*** and ***Al Bayane***. These newspapers are cheap and give an insight into Morocco and its politics. Coverage of overseas news is limited, but sheds interesting light on attitudes to major international issues. For the business visitor, the daily ***L'Economiste*** is essential reading for some insight into the general economic climate. For a weekly general review of the press, see www.ambafrance.ma.org

More interesting, and generally better written, are the weekly newspapers, which include ***Maroc-Hebdo***, and ***La Vie économique***. The best discussion of contemporary issues is provided by ***Le Journal***, which also provides major economic and business coverage. Morocco's best newsmagazine is ***Tel Quel***, see www.telquel-online.com ***Téléplus*** has some cultural events coverage. Aimed at a sophisticated urban audience, the glossy monthlies ***La Citadine*** and ***FDM*** (***Femmes du Maroc***), have articles on issues concerning Moroccan women alongside the fashion features.

The main foreign newspapers are available in town centre news kiosks, generally on the evening of publication. As these are expensive for most Moroccans, some kiosks run a 'rent-a –magazine' service for loyal customers. Occasionally an issue of a foreign news publication with a very critical article on Morocco will fail to be distributed.

Television & radio

Radio Télévision Marocaine, the **RTM**, is the state service, predominantly in Arabic and French. The news is given in Arabic, French and Spanish, with early afternoon summaries in the three main Berber languages. All agree that the **RTM** provides humdrum fare – hence the huge popularity of satellite television and the second channel **2M**, pronounce 'deux-em', which started life as a pay station, broadcasting North American and European feature films and some local current affairs programmes. **2M**'s news broadcasts are generally more lively than those on the **RTM**.

Most popular radio stations are **RTM-Inter** and theTanger-based commercial radio station **Médi 1** gives news and music in Arabic and French and is also available on the web. Northern areas can pick up broadcasts from Spain, Portugal, and Gibraltar.

Food and drink

Moroccan cuisine

See Footnotes, pages 536, for a glossary of food terms

The finest of the Moroccan arts is undoubtedly its cuisine. There are the basics: harira and bessera soups, kebabs, couscous, tagine and the famous pastilla, pigeon, egg and almonds in layers of filo pastry. And there are other dishes, less well known, gazelle's horns, coiling *m'hencha* and other fabulous pâtisseries. The Moroccans consider their traditional cooking to be on a par with Indian, Chinese and French cuisine – though the finest dishes are probably to be found in private homes. Today, however, upmarket restaurants, notably in Marrakech, give the visitor an idea of what fine Moroccan food can be. Moroccan cuisine is beginning to get the international respect it deserves, with new restaurants opening in European capitals. However, the spices and vegetables, meat and fish, fresh from the markets of Morocco, undoubtedly give the edge to cooks in old médina houses.

The climate and soils of Morocco means that magnificent vegetables can be produced all year round, thanks to assiduous irrigation. Although there is industrial chicken production, in many smaller restaurants, the chicken you eat is as likely to have been reared by a small-holder. Beef and of course lamb come straight from the local farms.

In addition to the basic products, Moroccan cooking gets its characteristic flavours from a range of spices and minor ingredients. Saffron (*zaâfrane*), though expensive, is widely used, and no Moroccan kitchen is without its saffron-substitute, the famous yellow *colorant*. Turmeric (*kurkum*) is also much in evidence. Other widely used condiments include a mixed all spice, referred to as *ra's el hanout* ('head of the shop'), cumin (*kamoun*), black pepper, oregano and rosemary (*yazir*). Prominent greens in use include broad-leaved parsley (*ma'dnous*), coriander (*kuzbur*) and, in some variations of couscous, a sort of celery called *klefs*. Preserved lemons (modestly called *bouserra*, 'navels', despite their breast-like shape) can be found in fish and chicken tajines. Bay leaves (*warqa Sidna Moussa*, 'the leaf of our lord Moses') are also commonly employed. Almonds, much used in patisserie, are used in tajines too, while powdered cinnamon (Arabic *karfa*, *cannelle* in French) provides the finishing touch for bastilla. In pâtisserie, orange-flower water and rose water (*ma ouarda*) are essential to achieve a refined taste.

Eating times vary widely in Morocco. Marrakech gets up early – and goes to bed early, too, so people tend to sit down to dine around about 0800. Casa-Rabat have a more reasonable rhythm, while Tanger takes a Spanish line, rising late, taking a siesta, and eating late. Across the country, the big meal of the week is Friday lunch, a time for people to gather in their families. The main meal of the day tends to be lunch, although this varies according to work and lifestyle. As anywhere, eating out in plush eateries is a popular upper-income occupation. Locals will tend to favour restaurants with French or southern European cuisine, while Moroccan 'palace' restaurants are patronised almost exclusively by tourists.

Starters

Harira is a basic Moroccan soup, ingredients vary but include chick peas, lentils, veg and a little meat. Often eaten accompanied with hard-boiled eggs. *Bissara* is a pea soup, a cheap and filling winter breakfast. *Briouat* are tiny envelopes of filo pastry, something akin to the Indian samosa, with a variety of savoury fillings. Also come with an almond filling for dessert.

Eating out

It is not easy to divide restaurants into price code categories, given the wide range of dishes which may be on offer at any one place.
Expensive *Above 250dh a head.*
Mid-range *Covers restaurants from 75-245dh a head.*
Cheap *Anything below 75dh. If you fill up with sandwiches and have perhaps one* mechoui *(barbecued meat) meal a day, you can easily manage on under 75dh a day. A lot of Moroccans do.*

Prices in cafés are fixed by the government according to level of service

Snacks Cheaper restaurants serve *kebabs* (aka brochettes), with tiny pieces of beef, lamb and fat. Also popular is *kefta*, mince-meat brochettes, served in sandwiches with chips, mustard and *harissa* (red-pepper spicey sauce). Tiny bowls of finely chopped tomato and onion are another popular accompaniment. On Jamaâ el Fna in Marrakech, strong stomachs may want to snack on the local **babouche** (snails).

Main dishes *Seksou* (couscous) is the great North African speciality. Granules of semolina are steamed over a pot filled with a rich meat and vegetable stew. Unlike Tunisian couscous, which tends to be flavoured with a tomato sauce, Moroccan couscous is pale yellow. In some families, couscous is the big Friday lunch, an approximate equivalent of old-fashioned English Sunday lunch.

Tagines are stews, the basic Moroccan dish. It is actually the term for the two-part terracotta dish (base and conical lid) in which meat or fish are cooked with a variety of vegetables, essentially, carrots, potato, onion and turnip. *Tajine* is everywhere in Morocco. Simmered in front of you on a brasero at a roadside café, is always good and safe to eat. Out trekking and in the South, it is the staple of life. For *tajines*, there are four main sauce preparations: *m'qalli*, a yellow sauce created using olive oil, ginger and saffron; *m'hammer*, a red sauce which includes butter, paprika (*felfla hlwa*) and cumin; *qudra*, another yellow sauce, slightly lighter than m'qalli, made using butter, onions, pepper and saffron, and finally *m'chermel*, a red made using ingredients from the other sauces. Variations on these base sauces are obtained using a range of ingredients, including parsley and coriander, garlic and lemon juice, *boussera* (preserved lemons), eggs, sugar, honey and cinammon (*karfa*).

In the better restaurants, look out for *djaj bil-hamid* (chicken with preserved lemons and olives), sweet and sour *tajine barkouk* (lamb with plums), *djaj qudra* (chicken with almonds and caramelised onion) and *tajine maqfoul*. Another pleasant little dish is *tajine kefta*, basically fried minced meat balls cooked with eggs and chopped parsley. In eateries next to food markets, delicacies such as *ra's embekhar* (steamed sheep's head) and *kourayn* (animal feet) are a popular feed.

A dish rarely prepared in restaurants is *djaj souiri*, aka *djaj mqeddem*, the only *plat gratiné* in Moroccan cuisine. Here, at the very last minute, a sauce of beaten eggs and chopped parsley is added to the chicken, already slow-cooked in olives, diced preserved lemon, olive oil, and various spices.

All over Morocco, lamb is much appreciated, and connaisseurs reckon they can tell what the sheep has been eating (rosemary, mountain pasture, straw, or mixed rubbish at the vast Mediouna tip near Casablanca). Lamb is cheaper in drought years when farmers have to reduce their flocks, expensive when the grazing is good, and is often best eaten at roadside restaurants where the lorry drivers pull in for a feed.

Desserts A limited selection of desserts are served in Moroccan restaurants. In the palace restaurants, there will be a choice between *orange à la cannelle* (slices of orange with cinammon) or some sort of marzipan pâtisserie like *cornes de gazelle* or *ghrayeb*, rather like round short-cake. *El jaouhar*, also onomatopoeically known as *tchak-tchouka*, is served as a pile of crunchy, fried filo pastry discs topped with a sweet custardy sauce

Top tables

Morocco's eating experiences are many, and a selection of the best addresses is hard to make. The following totally subjective choice mixes Moroccan with European cooking. While focused at the top of the price scale, it does include a couple of cheap (though memorable) addresses too. Prices given here are for the full whack.

Casablanca

A Ma Bretagne *Sidi Abderrahmane, about 4 km on from the Corniche, T022-362112. Seafood, ocean view, good choice of wines. One of the best restaurants in Morocco. Expensive.*

La Taverne du Dauphin *115 Blvd Houphouet Boigny, near Casa-Port station, T022-221200. Crowded, jolly restaurant, 200dh maximum a head.*

Le Cabestan *On the coast at Phare El Hank, T022-391190, closed Sunday and Ramadhan, for fish and lobster. Much appreciated by locals.*

Al Mounia *95 Rue du Prince Moulay Abdallah, T022-222669. A must for Moroccan cuisine.*

Marrakech

Dar Marjana *15 Derb Sidi Ali Tayir, Bab Doukkala, T044-385110, owner Chaouki Dkaier. From 500dh to 700dh, drinks included. Palatial surroundings.*

Ksar Es Saoussan, *3 Derb el Messaoudiyine, Rue des Ksour, owner Jean-Laurent Graulhet. T044-440632. More intimate than the* Marjana, *menus 300-500dh.*

Le Tobsil *22 Derb Abadallah Ben Hessayin, Leksour. Another excellent place for Moroccan food. 600dh, aperitifs and wine inclusive.*

Rabat

Dinarjat *6 Rue Belganoui, in the médina, close to the Kasbah des Oudaïas, T037-704239. Quality Moroccan cuisine.*

Essaouira

Auberge Tangaro *T044-784784. Some 5km out of Essaouira on the way to Agadir (can be reached by petit taxi). You have to stay at this small hotel to enjoy their cuisine.*

Riyad Bleu Mogador *23 Rue Bouchentouf, Essaouira-Médina. T044-784128. European and Moroccan cooking. A very good feed for 280dh. Cooking excellent as long as la patronne is there, on form and in control.*

Tanger

Saveurs de Poisson *escalier Waller. Leaving* Hotel el Minzah, *turn right and go down the steep flight of steps leading to a market area and Rue Salah Eddine el Ayoubi; the restaurant is on your right a few steps down. No menu, fish depending on the day's catch. Magnificent fish soup served from a terracotta pot, wooden forks and spoons, fruit and honey, herbal tea. Recommended and reasonable too.*

with almonds. Also on offer you may find *m'hencha*, coils of almond paste wrapped in filo pastry, served crisp from the oven and sprinkled with icing sugar and cinammon, and *bechkito*, little crackly biscuits.

Most large towns will have a couple of large pâtisseries, providing French pastries and the petits fours essential for proper entertaining. See *Pâtisserie Hilton*, Rue de Yougoslavie, Marrakech. Here you will find *slilou* (aka *masfouf*), a richly flavoured nutty powder served in tiny saucers to accompany tea. You won't find *maâjoun*, the Moroccan equivalent of hash brownies, made to liven up dull guests at wedding parties. On the more disastrous effects of *maâjoun*, see the 1952 Paul Bowles' thriller, *Let It Come Down*.

In local *laiteries*, try a glass of yoghurt. Oranges (*limoun*) and mandarins (*tchina*) are cheap, as are prickly pears, sold off barrows. In winter in the mountains, look out for kids selling tiny red arbutus berries (*sasnou*) carefully packaged in little wicker cones. Fresh hazelnuts are charmingly known as *tigerguist*.

Regional specialities

Bastilla is a sweet and sour dish, made from layers of fine filo pastry, pigeon, eggs and pounded almonds. A hint of saffron, cinnamon and icing sugar provide the finishing touch. The best bastilla is said to come from Fès.

The speciality of Marrakech is *tanjia*, a tall ceramic pot in which lamb or kid is baked in butter, spices and olives for hours, normally in the embers of the fire at the local *hammam*. This is a dish made by men before they go to work or sometimes when they have something to celebrate. In each *houma* in Marrakech, there will be one or two guys in a gang of friends who are famed for their ability to knock up a good *tanjia*.

On the south central Atlantic coast, the argan tree, a survival of the tropical forest that once grew all over the region, produces an oil highly valued for salads and cooking. Better still is *amlou*, a very runny Nutella, to be found in specialized shops in Essaouira and Agadir.

Dishes for Ramadan At sunset the fast is broken with a rich and savoury *harira* (see above), *beghrira* (little honeycombed pancakes served with melted butter and honey) and *shebbakia* (lace-work pastry basted in oil and covered in honey). Distinctive too are the sticky pastry whorls with sesame seeds on top.

Cafés and restaurants

Cafés offer croissants, petit-pain and cake (Madeleine), occasionally soup and basic snacks. Restaurants basically divide into four types: snack eateries, in the médina and *ville nouvelle*, generally cheap and basic. Some are modelled on international themed fast-food restaurants (*Taki Chicken* in Rabat). Then you have the *laiteries*, which sell yoghurt, fruit juices and will make up sandwiches with processed cheese, salad and *kacher* (processed meat). Full blown restaurants are generally found only in larger towns, and some are very good indeed – '*vaut le détour*' as the French guides say. There are long-established restaurants with interesting atmosphere, too (*Brasserie La Presse* or *La Corrida* in Casablanca or *Au Sanglier Qui Fume* in Ouirgane). And finally, in cities like Fès and Meknès, Marrakech and Rabat, you have the great palaces of Moroccan cuisine, restaurants set in old, often beautifully restored private homes. These can set you back 500dh or even more. Some of these restaurants allow you to eat à la carte (*El Fassia* in Marrakech, *La Zitouna* in Meknes), rather than giving you the full banquet menu (and late night indigestion).

Eating out cheaply If you're on a very tight budget, try the ubiquitous food stalls and open air restaurants serving various types of soup, normally the standard broth (*harira*), snacks and grilled meat. The best place for the adventurous open air eater is the Jemaâ el Fna square in Marrakech. Another good place is the fish market in the centre of Essaouira. Obviously there is a greater risk of food poisoning at street eateries, so go for food that is cooked as you wait, or that is on the boil. Avoid fried fish in the médina of Casablanca. A well known (and safe) cheap Casablanca fish restaurant is the ***Snack Amine***, Rue Colbert, off Av Mohammed V.

Vegetarian food Vegetarians will find that Moroccan food (unlike Indian cooking, for example) is not terribly interesting for them. They should be aware that 'vegetarian cuisine' in many cases means taking the meat of the top of the couscous or tajine. The concept is really quite alien to most Moroccans, as receiving someone well for dinner means serving them a *tajine* with good chunk of meat. There are some excellent salads, however. Be prepared to eat lots of processed cheese and omelettes.

Food markets Each city will have a colourful central market, generally dating back to the early years of this century, stuffed with high quality fresh produce. Try the one of Avenue Mohammed V at Casablanca (which has some good basket work stalls), the markets on the avenue Hassan II in Rabat (to your left off the Avenue Mohammed V as you enter the médina) and the Guéliz market in Marrakech, again, on the Avenue Mohammed V, on your left after the intersection with rue de la Liberté as you head for the town centre. Visiting food markets like this gives you an idea about everyday life – and is the time to stock up for a picnic or a hike.

Drinks

Tea

All over Morocco the main drink apart from water is mint tea (*thé à la menthe/attay*) a cheap, refreshing drink which is made with green tea, fresh mint and masses of white sugar. The latter two ingredients predominate in the taste. If you want a reduced sugar tea, ask for *attay msous* or *bila sukar/sans sucre*). In cafés, tea is served in mini-metal tea pots. In homes it is poured from high above the glass to generate a froth (*attay bi-rizatou*, 'tea with a turban') to use the local expression. Generally, tradition has it that you drink three glasses. To avoid burning your fingers, hold the glass with thumb under the base and index finger on rim. In some homes, various other herbs are added to make a more interesting brew, including *flayou* (peppermint), *louiza* (verbena) and even *sheeba* (absinthe). If you want a herb tea, ask for a *verveine* or *louiza*, which may be with either hot water or hot milk (*bil-halib*).

Coffee

Coffee is commonly drunk black and strong (*kahwa kahla/un exprès*). For a weak milky coffee, ask for a *café au lait/kahwa halib*. A stronger milky coffee is a *café cassé/kahwa mherza*.

Other soft drinks

All the usual soft drinks are available in Morocco. If you want still mineral water (*eau plate*) ask for Sidi Harazem, Sidi Ali or Ciel. The main brands of fizzy mineral water (*eau pétillante*), are Oulmès and Bonacqua, a new water produced by Coca Cola. You may want either *une grande bouteille* or *une petite bouteille*.

The better cafés and local laiteries (milk-product shops) do milkshakes, combinations of avocado, banana, apple and orange, made to measure. Ask for a *jus d'avocat* or a *jus de banane*, for example.

Wines & spirits

For a Muslim country, Morocco is fairly relaxed about alcohol. One hopes this situation won't change should the Islamists take some of the local councils in the coming municipal elections. In the top hotels, imported spirits are available, although at a price. The main locally made lager beers are ***Flag***, ***Flag Spécial***, ***Stork***, ***Castel*** and ***Heineken***. In the spring, look out for the extremely pleasant ***Bière de Mars***, made only in March with Fès spring water - the best beer in Morocco?.

Morocco produces wine, the main growing areas are Guerrouane and Meknès. Reds tend to prevail. ***Celliers de Meknès*** (CdM) and ***Sincomar*** are the main producers. At the top of the scale (off-licence prices in brackets), you have ***Médaillon*** (90dh) and ***Beau Vallon*** (CdM, 90dh, anything up to 185dh in a restaurant). A ***CdM Merlot*** will set you back 45dh. Another reliable red is ***Domaine de Sahari***, Aït Yazem. A pleasant claret, best drunk chilled in summer (30dh). The whites include ***Coquillages*** and ***Sémillant***, probably the best (40dh). At the very bottom of the scale is rough and ready ***Rabbi Jacob***, or, cheaper and still cheerful, ***Chaud Soleil***. The local fig fire-water is ***Mahia la Gazelle***.

If you want to buy alcohol outside a restaurant, every major town will have a few licensed sales points, ie just behind the *Hotel Balima* in Rabat, in the main food market in Guéliz in Morocco. Often they are very well stocked with local and imported wines. The ***Marjane*** hypermarket chain, now represented in all major cities, also has an off-licence section. ***Asouak Essalam,*** the main competitor, does not stock alcohol, however. In Ramadhan, alcohol is on sale to non-Muslim foreigners only and many of the off-licences shut down for the month. At Marjane, towards the end of Ramadhan, you may well be asked by locals to buy a few bottles for their end of fasting booze-up.

Shopping

Morocco has all manner of things to buy: carpets, lamps, jewellery, slippers, pottery. The list is endless. Marrakech, capital of retail therapy, produces craft items by the tonne. Prices are very reasonable compared with what you might be paying for the same thing in an arty-crafty shop in a European capital. Many of the main tourist towns now have fixed price shops, although some of these can be negotiated despite the label. Most of the historic towns have special government-run craft centres, referred to as an *ensemble artisanal*. These places can give you a good guide to the range of products available, although they tend to be a tad expensive. The best bargains, and the more authentic experience, are to be had in the *souqs*, the areas of traditional shops found in most historic cities. Village weekly markets tend to be interesting as an opportunity to see rural life, not for leisure shopping.

Bargaining Bargaining is expected in a lot of shops, and can prove a tedious business, on occasion ending with tantrums thrown by the vendo. To avoid hassle, don't express interest unless you are actually interested. Be polite – but not apologetic. Think – do you really need that blue and white ceramic bowl? that little wooden box? The answer is generally no. There are more interesting things to do than arguing over a 25dh price difference. If the item really pleases you, think whether you can afford it, and how much it would cost you back at home. Then go for a price which suits your pocket. Voices should on no account be raised. Remember, the salesman is on home ground, can shout louder, be ruder and unless you're the *souk* hound from hell, knows his clientele and profit margins very well. In any case, whether you buy or not, he's probably going to do well, as the goods are bought in cheap thanks to the young workforce in some dank workshop elsewhere in the médina.

Different nationalities react in different ways to playing at bargaining. The Moroccans and the French know each other well, the Germans play it serious, the Italians can give any *souk* vendor as good as they get, and with plenty of humour to boot. Above all, bargaining for souvenirs is not a life-and-death business, and should be treated as such.

Commissions In Fès and Marrakech, tourist guides – and in particular the officious official ones – tend to make a good living from commissions. An agency guide will be paid around 300dh for showing a group round Marrakech for half-a-day, around 700dh for a day trip up into the mountains. If offered the choice, they will always take the first option. Why? Because a large carpet shop will automatically pay 1,000dh to a guide for taking a group through, there will be commission paid to the guide on any sales, often of the order of 20% – which means the price you are paying for your carpet is automatically inflated. So if possible, go to a carpet shop unaccompanied – or with someone you like whom you don't mind getting commission. In Marrakech, a number of the palace restaurants also operate on a similar basis, paying commission to hotel reception staff making the reservation or to taxi drivers bringing clients.

In 2003, following the Casablanca May bombings, a lot of the tourist bazaars found themselves in trouble. They'd paid large sums to travel agencies to ensure a good through flow of charabanc tourists, only to find that none were coming.

What to buy Some of the main craft items to look out for in Morocco:

Babouches Babouches is the tourist name for the traditional slippers referred to by Moroccans as *belgha*. These come in a range of shapes and qualities. You can get a cheap pair for as little as 80dh. A good solid pair of yellow men's *belgha* can set you back 120-160dh, fashionably embroidered pair of women's slippers, with this season's motif, can cost even more. Best places to buy: médinas of Rabat, Fès or Marrakech.

Basketwork Splendid baskets in a range of shapes and sizes available from Casablanca *marché central* (off Avenue Mohammed V), and in the médina of Marrakech.

Clothing Obviously there are the usual souvenir T-shirts. However, if you have the right sort of physique, you may want to invest in an item of traditional clothing. A *djellabah* (for men), or a caftan of some kind can be handy for sloping off down to the pool. High quality traditional clothing is beautifully made by specialized tailors who can be seen at work in some of the médinas. Men wear hooded tunics over the work clothes on Fridays when they go to the mosque to pray. Regarding women's traditional dress, note that there are top caftan stylists, an annual caftan fashion show, and that there are regular changes of style. The caftan is still required dress for women at court receptions.

Carpets and weavings Morocco has some fine carpets, the best to be found in specialized shops in the médina of Marrakech. Other carpet buying destinations include places like Chichaoua, Taroudant and the souk at Khémisset which, although not the most picturesque of places has far lower prices than in Rabat.

The age of a carpet is not linked to how faded it is. Also, vegetable dyes do not make a carpet necessarily older – chemical dyes were sometimes cheaper in the past than natural dyes. Good buys include saddle-bags and decorative strips from tents, sold as *couloirs* (corridors) by carpet merchants. Main basic carpet types include the humble flat-weave *klim*, often cotton, the *akhnif*, a thicker flat-weave rug, and the *glaoua*, which combines deep-pile and flat-weave techniques.

Ceramics Safi and Fès ceramics are found all over the country. Ceramics are also produced at Oulja craft centre near Salé. Fès ceramics include large bowls, inkwells and dishes. Go for the more authentic, rougher, blue and white or yellow, green and cream pottery.

Leatherwork Morocco has long had a reputation for leatherwork, and *maroquinerie* is French for high quality leather goods. Top European names manufacture here, creating a skilled labourforce. Look out for top of the range leather goods in Guéliz, Marrakech. You might even want a gilt embossed leather *dossier* to take home for your desk.

Metal items Here you should look out for the lanterns which are available in a variety of metals, from shiny brass to rustic (and slightly rusty), iron. For tin lanterns, try ***Place des Ferblantiers*** near the Badi' Palace, Marrakech. There is also much wrought iron work of all shapes and sizes on sale.

Wooden items Look out for mirror frames and small boxes covered in painted arabesques or ***zouak***. See Rue des Consuls, Rabat, at the Kasbah des Oudaïas end for a good choice or near the Medersa Ben Youssef, Marrakech. For a small present, look out for something in fragrant **thuya wood** from the Essaouira region. The smell has been described as a mixture of cedar and pencil sharpenings. You'll also see thuya inlaid with mother of pearl or yellow citrus wood marquetry. There is so much thuya work produced now, that it's a wonder that there are any thuya trees left.

Entertainment and nightlife

As society is in many ways still highly gender-segregated, Western style night life is not really a major feature of life in Morocco. People tend to be very family orientated, which means that engagement parties and weddings, generally held in summer, are the big social events of the year. The annual month of fasting, Ramadhan, generates a social life all of its own. The BIG occasion is ***Aid el Kebir***, the 'Festival of the Sheep', which comes round once a year, two months after the end of Ramadan. Extended families gather in their home-towns or villages to sacrifice a sheep of some description or a calf in commemoration of how Allah sent down a lamb to Ibrahim so he wouldn't have to sacrifice his son.

Despite all this family-centred activity, in the main tourist centres, the visitor will find enough 'nightlife' to amuse them for a short stay.

Cinemas & theatre Casablanca in particular has some very fine cinemas dating from the 1930s and 1940s. The problem is the programming, which tends to be over-advertised Hollywood blockbusters, dubbed into French. The Dawliz cinema complexes (Casa-Corniche, Salé and Tanger) have slightly more imaginative programmes. More popular than these, however, are Hindi and karate films, generally subtitled in Arabic and French. Film buffs in the country for any length of time will want to look out for special film events at the *instituts français* in the main cities. These also programme theatre and, more rarely, contemporary dance. Moroccan films, with a few exceptions, tend to have very short runs. Consult the local press.

Nightlife Best for nightlife are Casablanca, Marrakech and Tanger. All these have a range of bars and nightclubs ranging from the plush to the rough. The average nightclub (if there is such a thing), will have a socially mixed clientele. There will be students and ordinary funsters, business men out for a night, even sex-workers of various kinds. Do not be surprised if the stylish person you meet expects a financial contribution. On the music front, there will be western club music, depending on the DJ's contacts. Main floor-fillers will be Egyptian pop, raï, and even some Latino. Not too surprisingly, Moroccans have a liking for reggae.

Good clubs in Casa: ***La Notte*** and ***Le Village***; in Rabat: the inevitable ***Amnesia***; in Marrakech: ***New Feeling*** (posh), ***Paradise*** (a bit stuffy), ***Le Diamant noir*** (not too rough), ***Star House*** (once very dodgy, new management), ***Shehrezade*** (often closed due to various scandals) and in Tanger: ***Olivia Valère*** (kind of posh), ***La Pasarela*** and ***Coco-Beach*** (dancey), ***Morocco Palace*** (much local colour); in Fès, the ***Phébus***, chic night club of the Jnan Palace.

Holidays and festivals

Religious holidays Religious holidays are scheduled according to the Hijna calendar, a lunar based calendar. Given the clear night skies of Arabia, it is easily comprehensible that the Muslims should have adopted a year based upon the cycles of the moon. The lunar year is shorter than the solar year, so the Muslim year moves forward by 11 days every Christian year. Thus in 10 years' time, Ramadhan, currently in the winter, will be at the height of summer. The start of Ramadhan can vary by a day, depending on the *ru'ya*, whether the crescent moon has been observed or not.

The main religious holidays are as follows:
1 Muharram First day of the Muslim year
Mouloud Celebration of the Prophet Mohammed's birthday
Ramadan A month of fasting and sexual abstinence during daylight hours
Aïd es Seghir (the Lesser Aïd) Two-day holiday ending the month of Ramadan
Aïd el Kebir (the Great Aïd) One-day holiday which comes 70 days after Aïd es Seghir. Commemorates how God rewarded Ibrahim's faith by sending down a lamb for him to sacrifice instead of his son. When possible, every family sacrifices a sheep on this occasion.

During ***Ramadhan***, the whole country switches to a different rhythm. Public offices go on to half-time, and the general pace slows down during the daytime. No Moroccan would be caught eating in public during the day, and the vast majority of cafés and restaurants, except those frequented by resident Europeans and tourists, are closed. At night, the ambiance is almost palpable. There is a sense of collective effort, shared with millions of other Muslims worldwide. People who never go out all year are out visiting friends and family, strolling the streets in Ramadhan. Shops stay open late, especially during the second half of the month. Ramadan is an interesting time to visit Morocco as a tourist, but probably to be avoided if possible if you need to do business.

Public holidays

New Year's Day 1 January.
Fête du Travail 1 May: Labour Day.
Fête de la Jeunesse 9 July.
Fête du Trône 30 July: Commemorates the present king Mohamed VI's accession.
Anniversaire de la Révolution 20 August.
Marche Verte/El Massira el Khadhra 6 November: Commemorates a march by Moroccan civilians to retake the Spanish held Saharan territories of Rio de Oro and Saguiet El Hamra.
Independence Day 18 November: Commemorates independence and Mohammed V's return from exile.

Festivals

Morocco also has a number of regional and local festivals, often focusing around a local saint or harvest time of a particular product, and are fairly recent in origin. The *moussems* or traditional local festivals have on occasion been banned in local years, the authorities giving as a reason the health risks created by gatherings of large numbers of people in places with only rudimentary sanitary facilities. The decision has been regretted, however, as the *moussems* are such an important part of Moroccan rural life. The main Moroccan festivals come in three categories: firstly, the more religious festivals, the timing of which relates to the lunar Islamic year, secondly the annual semi-commercial regional or town festivals with relatively fixed dates and thirdly, the new generation of arts and film festivals.

Movable festivals

The Mouloud in 2004 will be in May

Two festivals which may be worth getting to are held annually at Meknès and Salé, the day before the **Mouloud**, or the Prophet Mohammed's birthday:
Festival de Sidi Ben Aïssa, aka *Moussem du Cheikh El Kamel* In Meknès, this is one of Morocco's largest festivals, with adepts of the Aïssaoua brotherhood turning up to venerate their founder.
Moussem de Sidi Abdallah Ben Hassoun Held in Salé in honour of the patron saint of Salé and of travellers. Includes a large procession with wax lanterns held aloft on poles and local people dressed up in pirate costumes.

Regional or town festivals

February *Festival of the almond blossom* Tafraoute, near Agadir.
April *Honey festival* Immouzer des Ida Outanane.
May *Rose festival* El Kelaâ des Mgouna, Dadès Valley; *Moussem de Sid Ahmed Ben Mansour* Moulay Bousselham, north of Kenitra;
June *Cherry festival* Sefrou; *Festival of Folk Art and Music* Marrakech; *Moussem de Moulay Abdeslam ben M'chich* Larache; and *Moussem de Sidi Mohammed Ma El Ainin* Tan Tan.
July *Festival of Sea Produce* El Hoceima.
August *Moussem of Moulay Abdallah El Jadida; Festival des pommes Immouzer du Kandar; Moussem of Moulay Idris Zerhoun Moulay Idriss; Moussem of Setti Fatma Setti Fatma, Ourika Valley near Marrakech; Moussem of Sidi Ahmed ou Moussa Tiznit.*
September *Marriage Festival* Imilchil in the last week of September/first week of October); *Horse festival* Tissa near Fès; and *Moussem of Moulay Idris al Azhar* Fès.
October *Date festival* Erfoud.

Arts festivals

February *Salon du livre* Casablanca. Morocco's biggest annual bookfair. Prix du Grand Atlas, literary events.
April *Les Alizées* Essaouira. Small classical music festival.
May *Festival des Musiques Sacrées* Fès – generally late May running into June. Attracts a strange mixture of the spiritual, the hippy and the wealthy. Accompanied by popular music festival open to all. See www.morocco-fezfestival.com *Festival Gnaoua* Essaouira. One of Morocco's most successful music festivals, www.festival-gnaoua.co.ma.

May/June *Tanjazz* Tanger jazz festival, mixture of free and paying concerts, www.tanjazz.free.fr.
June/July *Festival estival de Rabat* The capital comes alive with concerts held in various venues.
July *Festival des arts et des traditions populaires* Marrakech, every July weekend, traditional song and dance from across Morocco. Try www.emarrakech.info to find out more. Once moribund, new management 2003.
Festival Rawafid des créateurs marocains de l'étranger Casablanca. Late July. Focusing on work by Moroccan creative artists abroad. Music and film.
August *Arts Festival* Asilah. Paintings of the medina, festival now in its 25th year.
September *Festival international du film méditerranéen* Tetouan. Long established but slightly erratic small film festival.
October *Festival cinématographique de Marrakech* end September /early October.

Sport and activities

Morocco's resort hotels will have swimming pools and tennis courts. The Atlantic coast resort of Agadir has all the usual beachy things to do, camel and horse rides, and beach buggies too. Elsewhere on the Atlantic coast – and especially at Essaouira – you will meet members of the **surfing** and **windsurfing** fraternity. Morocco is also known as a **golf** destination, and this, along with **mountain trekking**, is an area of tourism which is expanding rapidly. **Horse riding** is popular too. Moroccans themselves are keen on football and proud of their country's success in running and Marrakech regularly hosts cross-country events. Down in the desert, the annual Marathon des Sables, a gruelling cross-desert trek in which contestants must carry all their own food, grabs plenty of media space.

Ballooning There is a small Marrakech-based company, ***Ciel d'Afrique***, T044-303135, F303136, www.aumaroc.com/cieldafrique, which can organize hot-air balloon flights most anywhere in the country – at a price. The basic excursion involves leaving Marrakech very early for a flight over the Jebilet, the hills north of Marrakech. 4WD vehicle necessary to get to take-off point.

Camel trekking This activity saw a real growth in popularity in the 1990s with beasts being brought up from Mali to satisfy the growing demand. In the area covered by the present guide, treks through magnificent scenery along the Atlantic coast around **Essaouira** are the main option. For completeness sake, information is provided here on camel trekking in the desert, **Merzouga** (the Erg Chebbi) and **Zagora** being the two main camel trek bases. Apart from the quick camel ride into the dunes (especially popular at Merzouga), there are two options: the *méharée* and the *randonnée chamelière*. The **méharée** actually involves you riding the camel, the **randonnée chamelière** (camel hike) means you walk alongside the camels, used essentially as pack animals. Obviously, in the former option, you can cover a lot more territory. You will ride for about 4 to 5 hours a day, the only difficulty is getting used to the movement of the camel. Average daily cost is about 300dh/person. A good organizer will lay on everything apart from sleeping bags, although blankets are generally available. Best times of year for the south are October to April (NB sandstorms a possibility between November and February). A good 6-night camel hike out of Zagora would enable you to see a mix of dunes and plains, palm groves and villages, taking you from Zagora down to the dunes of Chigaga, with an average of 5 hours walking a day (4 hours in morning, 1 hour afternoon). For more on camel trekking in the south, contact ***Hotel Zagour***, BP 17, 45900 Zagora, T044-847451, F846178. In the Essaouira area, try ***Auberge de la Plage – club équestre***, T044-476600, 473383, aubplage@iam.net.ma

Hamman experience

A ritual purification of the body is essential before Muslims can perform prayers, and in the days before bathrooms, the 'major ablutions' were generally done at the hammam *(bath). Segregation of the sexes is of course the rule at the* hammam. *Some establishments are only open for women, others only for men, while others have a shift system (mornings and evenings for the men, all afternoon for women). In the old days, the* hammam, *along with the local zaouia or saint's shrine, was an important place for women to gather and socialize, and even pick out a potential wife for a son.*

Very often there are separate hammams *for men and women next to each other on the ground floor of an apartment building. A passage leads into a large changing room come post-bath area, equipped with masonry benches for lounging on and (sometimes) small wooden lockers. Here you undress under a towel.* Hammam *gear today is football or beach shorts for men and knickers for women. If you're going to have a massage /scrub down, you take a token at the cash desk where shampoo can also be bought.*

Next step is to proceed to the hot room: five to 10 minutes with your feet in a bucket of hot water will have you sweating nicely and you can then move back to the raised area where the masseurs are at work. After the expert removal of large quantities of dead skin, you go into one of the small cabins or mathara *to finish washing. (Before doing this catch the person bringing in dry towels so that they can bring yours to you when you're in the* mathara*). For women, in addition to a scrub and a wash there may be the pleasures of epilation with sokar, an interesting mix of caramelized sugar and lemon. Men can undergo a taksira, which although it involves much pulling and stretching of the limbs, ultimately leaves you feeling pretty good. And remember, allow plenty of time to cool down, reclining in the changing area.*

Diving

Morocco is not known as a destination for *la plongée* (diving). The construction of new ports on both the Mediterranean and Atlantic coasts has brought in a number of professional divers, and people dive for red coral at considerable depths off Al Hoceïma and Asilah. There is a well run **Club de plongée de Casablanca**, based at the Complexe sportif Mohamed V, Maârif. Members are mainly locals and the club runs diving courses and is approved by the **FFESSM**, the *Fédération française d'études* et de sport sous-mains. Contact: Dr Youssef Didi, T022-981941, 061-332972 (mob), or Mr Saïd Berrada, T022-992245, F992293.

Flying & parachuting

Moroccan Federation of Light Aviation and Aerial Sports can be contacted at Complex Sportif Prince Moulay Abdellah, Rabat, T037-708347, F706958. In the Casablanca area, flying courses are run by two private clubs, the ***Aéroclub Priv'air***, Aéroport de Casa Anfa, Hangar 775, T022-914188 and ***Aéroclub Tit Melil***, T022-332490. Planes are available for rental. Flying classes are around 720dh/hour, an annual club subscripton of 1500dh is required. There are **Royal Aero Clubs** at Marrakech, T044-447764 and Beni Mellal, T023-482095, where the ***RAM*** flying club is based. Try here for **gliding** (Centre royal de vol à voile). The ***Parachute Air Club de Marrakech*** organizes winter and spring courses in parachuting at Beni Mellal. Contact parachute.air.club@wanadoo.co.ma

Golf

Moroccan golf has a long history, first popularized by the sultans in the early 1900s (the first real course was in Tanger). Golf was the late King Hassan II's favourite sport, too. Major competitions such as the Trophée Hassan II attract international attention and much *RTM* television coverage. There are currently 15 courses designed by masters of the art and plans for more – presumably using recycled water, given the country's water problems. All courses are open to the public though evidence of handicap is

Essentials

required. Check locally for regulations, green fees and opening hours. The **Royal Moroccan Golf Federation** is at the *Royal Dar es-Salam Golf Cours*e in Rabat, T037-755960, F751026. In the UK, ***Best of Morocco*** (T00-44-1380-828533) produces a specialized golf holiday brochure.

A 10-day break in Morocco could keep keen golfers busy and the rest of the family amused, too. Golf and culture days could alternate. There are three areas with three or more courses of 18 holes: **Marrakech** and **Agadir** (courses close together), and the **central Atlantic coast** where hour or longer drives separate the courses at Rabat, Mohamedia, Casablanca, Settat and El Jadida. At Marrakech and Agadir, the best season is November to February. In March-April and October early starts will be necessary. On the Atlantic coast, the season is a little longer. Although buggies are not the norm on most Moroccan courses, caddies can be hired.

The locations of Moroccan courses are memorable. There are oceanside courses at Mohamedia, El Jadida and Agadir, while at the *Marrakech Royal Golf*, par 72, built in the 1920s by the Pasha of Marrakech, the course is planted with magnificent trees and in winter the mountains backdrop of the High Atlas is snowcapped. Marrakech also has country's most recent course, the *Golf d'Amelkis*, par 72, located close to the toney *Amanjena* complex. Up in the northwest, the Tanger course, designed by Henry Cotton and inaugurated in 1917, has many of its original features. There are views through mature trees to the sea and the city. On the Mediterranean coast, the Cabo Negro course has numerous water features.

Nine hole, more anecdotal courses can be found at Ouarzazate, near the waters of the Barrage Mansour Eddahabi – currently suffering from drought – and at Fès. There is an unusual course within the walls of the Meknès palace compound. A break in Morocco combining a decent amount of golf and plenty of entertainment for the rest of the family would probably combine Marrakech with either Agadir or El Jadida. It is likely that more courses will be developed in coming years, particularly in the vicinity of Agadir.

Hunting & fishing

Morocco has long been a destination for French and Italian hunters. In the Marrakech region, there are wild boar in the countryside around Asni and Amizmiz, partridge and quail in the Ourika valley. All foreigners wishing to hunt in Morocco must produce a valid hunting permit and permit to carry firearms from country of origin, and three photographs. A permit to hunt will be given which lasts 30 days and cannot be extended. It is compulsory to take out an insurance from a Moroccan company.

Keen fishers may find trout in the remote fast flowing but remote rivers of the High Atlas of Azilal. Licences for freshwater fishing can be obtained from the Ministry of Water and Forests, 11 Rue du Devoir, Rabat (also offices in most large towns) on a daily or annual basis for fishing in the rivers. A special licence must be obtained for fishing in the reservoirs and other artificial lakes. Fishing is not permitted anywhere between sunset and sunrise. Information regarding restrictions will be provided with the permit. In recent years, drought has had an effect on fish populations in both storage barrages and natural lakes, including notably the Barrage Lalla Takerkoust, Marrakech, the Barrage Bin el Ouidane near Beni Mellal and the great reservoir east of Ouarzazate

Motorbikes

Morocco has great stretches of desert roads to keep motorbikers amused. For off-road biking in the High Atlas, try ***Rand'Atlas***, near the Barrage Lalla Takerkoust, Marrakech, T044-484929.

Mountain biking (VTT)

Bikes (and mopeds) can be hired in Marrakech to potter round the city – but beware the hectic traffic. Areas popular with mountain bikers include Tafraoute in the Anti-Atlas and the region between the Dadès gorges and Toundoute, north of Skoura. There are some good tracks here. Clay washed onto the tracks by rain dries out to form a good surface for bikes.

Quad-biking

This is another of the expensive sports currently taking off in Morocco as tourism expands. Roar around on chunky tyred quad bikes especially designed to destroy the peace of the palm groves. Available in Marrakech and Ouazarzate. Try the ***Hotel Palma-Riva***, T044-305854, T061-153250 (mob) in Marrakech and in Ouazarzate ***Kart Aventure*** Av Moulay Rachid, between the hotels *Berbère Palace* and *Kenzi Belère*, T044-886374, F886216, half-day rental around 1,200dh, full day 1,700dh.

Riding

The horse is the object of a veritable cult in Morocco. Fantasias, spectacular ceremonies where large numbers of traditionally dressed horsemen charge down a parade ground to discharge their muskets a few metres away from tentfuls of banqueting guests, are an occasion to see Moroccan riding skills. The late King Hassan II assembled one of the world's finest collections of rare black thoroughbred Arab horses. Many towns have riding clubs, the television covers national show-jumping events, and the wealthy are keen to have their offspring learn to ride.

The following can provide riding: ***Ranch du Tijania*** at 8 km from Meknès, at Aït Berzouine on the El Hajeb road, T061-778528 (mob) or T067-820373 (mob). ***La Roseraie***at Ouirgane, on the Taroudant road, T044-439128, F439130, E roseraie@cybernet.net.ma The well-managed stables at ***Palmeraie Golf Palace***, Marrakech, also ***Club Boulahrir***, Km 8, Route de Meknès, T044-329451, F329454. In the Essaouira region, try ***Cavaliers d'Essaouira***, 14 km inland from Essaouira on the Marrakech road, next to restaurant *Dar Lamine*, T065-074889 (mob), and at Sidi Kaouki, ***Auberge de la Plage – club équestre***, T044-476600, F473383, aubplage@iam.net.ma (also do camel treks). Based in Ouazarzate, ***North Africa Horse*** (contact Joël Proust), T/F044-449464, T044-886689, F886690) can set up 6-day treks. They are often busy with film work, however.

Skiing

The Marrakech region has one ski resort often mentioned in the tourist literature: **Oukaïmeden**, an hour's drive up in the High Atlas south of the Red City. The up-and-coming winter sports would seem to be ski-climbing and ski-trekking. In all honesty, however, irregular and decreasing snowfall over the last decade or so has got the better of Morocco's reputation as a ski destination. Whereas 25 years ago, the ski season in Oukaïmeden lasted several months, today falls of snow rarely exceed 20 cm and tend to melt very quickly in the bright sun, only to refreeze leaving a brittle surface. Essentially, one cannot count on good snow for an Alpine-style skiing holiday. Skiers in Morocco tend to be locals who as soon as snow is announced on the news, rush down from Casa-Rabat for a weekend at one of the resorts. Hopefully, climatic change has not put paid to what could be a major supplementary attraction.

Best source of info on mountain sports is the **Club alpin francais**, see www.cafmaroc.co.ma. Try also the **Royal Moroccan Federation of Skiing and Mountaineering**, Parc de la Ligue Arabe, BP 15899, Casablanca, T022-203798, F474979. Another source of information might be Mountain Information Centre of the Ministry of Tourism, 1 Rue Oujda, Rabat, T073-701280. The best book is Claude Cominelli's 1984 *Ski dans le Haut Atlas de Marrakech* (Andorra: Cominelli ed), available from the Librairie Chatr on Av Mohamed V in Marrakech.

For the record, **Oukaïmeden** (2,600m) in the High Atlas, 74 km south from Marrakech, is Morocco's premier ski resort. There is a good range of accommodation from 3-star hotel to mountain lodges, and numerous chalets owned by wealthy locals. The ***Hotel Kenzi Louka*** (T044-319080/86, F319088) and the refuge managed by the **Club alpin français** (T044-319036, F319020) should be able to advise on skiing conditions. The summit above the plateau is Jbel Oukaïmeden (3,270m). There is a télésiège, and pistes ranging from black to green. The ski station infrastructure is managed by the **ONEP**, the Moroccan national water board, and is to undergo a major refit in the near future.

Skiing in the **High Atlas of Azilal** remains the preserve of the hardy and initiated for the moment. An enterprising soul has yet to open ski hire in the Aït Bougmez. Older mountain guides to this region suggest wilderness ski-touring possibilities. The **Jbel Azourki** (3,050 m), between Tabant and Zaouiat Ahansal, is held by many to be one the best mountains for off-piste skiing. The track to the bottom of this mountain, running south from Aït Mhamed (the old main track for Tabant, before the road was opened on the Oued Lakhdar/Agouti route coming in from the west), is not easy in winter. Ski trekkers could also use the Aït Bougmez as a base for short excursions to nearby mountains. More difficult of access in winter conditions, the **Irghil Mgoun** also provides ski trek opportunities. Basically, these are late season options, as with heavy snow you could be cut off in an isolated village for quite some time. The problem with late season skiing is that the snow surface can be 'corrugated' by wind erosion and melting. In recent years, as in the Toubkal High Atlas, snow cover has declined according to some locals with long memories. Take local advice or go through an agency if you want to ski-trek this region. You will almost certainly have to bring all your equipment with you. There is simple gîte type accommodation in Tabant.

Further east, in the **High Atlas of Imilchil**, the Jbel Ayyachi (3,747m) has some good ski descents. Here again, this is terrain for the committed wilderness-ski fraternity. The ***Auberge Tinmay***, T055-583434, timnay@ iam.net.ma, at Aït Ayach near Midelt may be able to provide information.

Swimming

A few large towns (Marrakech, Meknès) have municipal pools but these can be crowded and a grubby at the end of the summer season. They also tend to be all-male affairs. In the summer the pools of the luxury hotels are very tempting, and non-residents can on occasion use these pools for a fee. Note that very few hotels have heated pools (check on this when you book a winter break), and what actually constitutes the definition of 'heated' can vary. Beware of strong currents on the Atlantic beaches. On many of them, bathing is prohibited outside the summer season when a coastguard is present.

Surfing & wave sports

Surfing and windsurfing are popular in Morocco with both locals and visitors. Foreign surfers first arrived in the 1960s, and the sport caught on in a small way. Today, the weekends see lots of enthusiasts out surfing. On chill, bright winter afternoons, even the rather polluted waters of the Bouregreg Estuary up in capital city Rabat have their share of keen amateurs. In 2000, Dar Bouazza south of Casablanca hosted a stage of the European Bodyboard Tour. Fly surf has arrived, too. **Essaouira**, 'Wind City, Afrika' is the capital, but there are surf spots all along the Atlantic coastline. North of Rabat, surfing is possible at **Moulay Bouselham**, **Mehdiya Plage** (famed for its powerful waves, not for beginners) and **Plage des Nations**. Between Rabat and Casablanca, **Rabat estuary**, **Oued Cherrat** and **Bouznika Plage** are all popular. Things get more serious south of Casablanca in the El Jadida area, **Dar Bouazza** (difficult, lots of sea-urchins) and **Jack Beach** (used for competitions) being popular. South of El Jadida, **Oualidia** is ideal for beginners. Essaouira has surfing and windsurfing facilities. The surfers are around in the winter months, while from April to October the alizé winds bring the windsurfers in. A few kilometres south, **Sidi Kaouki** is popular with windsurfers due to persistently strong winds. Still further south, **Taghzaoute**, north of Agadir is popular with the winter surf set. **Mirhleft** and **Sidi Ifni** are popular destinations, too.

For further information on surfing, try the following: ***Océan Vagabond***, Blvd Mohamed V, Essaouira, right on the bay, T061-728340 (Bruno), T061-883013 (Catherine), bruno_erbani@yahoo.fr, oceanvagabond@hotmail.com Have good, recent equipment for rent and provide tuitition. Also see the UCPA, also nearby on the bay, although they may have to move soon, T044-472972, F473417. South of Essaouira, at Imessouane, try the ***Auberge Kahina***, T048-826032 (unreliable line), where Valérie and Hichem will do their best to provide wave-sport info and accommodation. Close to Tiznit, south of Agadir, ***Aftas Trip***, T048-866156, www.aftastrip.co.ma, can organize surfing instruction and a range of other outdoor pursuits.

Tennis

Morocco has an international tournament in Agadir. The big cities have tennis clubs and all the larger hotels will have a few courts. The country also now has a handful of male tennis stars playing to international standards.

Trekking

There are considerable opportunities for hiking in Morocco. The most popular area is the Toubkal National Park in the High Atlas. However, as roads improve and inveterate trekkers return for further holidays, new areas are becoming popular. Starting in the west, to the south of the High Atlas, the **Jbel Siroua**, east of Taroudant, is a plateau with pleasant spring walking. The **Toubkal High Atlas** is best from late April to October, with various loops up into the mountains staying in Amazigh villages possible. You will probably want to climb North Africa's highest peak, **Jbel Toubkal** (4,167m). The only problem is that the mountain has become almost too popular. South of Azilal, the beautiful **Vallée des Aït Bougmez** is becoming popular. For weekend trekkers, there are gentle walks along the flat valley bottom. The Aït Bougmez also makes a good departure point for tougher treks, including the **north-south crossing of the west-central High Atlas** to Bou Thraghar, near Boumalne and El Kelaâ des M'gouna. On this route, you have the chance to climb the region's second highest peak, Irhil M'goun (4,071m).

The **Middle Atlas** is much less well known to walkers. Certain parts are quite a Hobbit land, especially between Azrou and the source of the Oum er Rabi river, where there is beautiful walking in the **cedar forests**. Despite its proximity to the rich farmlands of Meknès and the Saïs Plain, this is an extremely poor region which would benefit from increased ecologically friendly tourism.

For walking in Morocco, you can either book through a specialist trekking operator in your home country or hope to find a guide available when you arrive. In popular trekking areas such as Toubkal, guides are available in trailhead settlements. For walking the best period is April to October, but in the high summer keep to the high valleys which are cooler and where water can be obtained. Note too that the views are not as good in the High Atlas at the height of summer because of the haze. Tents or bivouacking is fine in summer but indoor accommodation is necessary in autumn in refuges, shepherds' huts or locals' homes. The use of mules/donkeys to carry the heavy packs is common. Specialist maps and guides are useful and can be obtained via the *Hotel Ali* in Marrakech. Note that classified guest rooms in rural areas now have the GTAM (Grande traversée des Atlas marocains) label of approval. Places where trekking guides can be arranged include the ***Hotel Ali*** (T044-444979) in Marrakech (High Atlas), at the ***Auberge Tinmay*** (T/F055-583434) near Midelt (Middle Atlas and Jbel Ayyachi), and the ***Auberge Souktana***, (T048-534075), Taliouine, near Taroudant (Jbel Siroua).

If you are setting up a trek yourself, note that a good mule can carry up to 100 kg, i.e., the rucksacks of three trekkers. A mule with muleteer comes at around 120dh/day, a good guide should be paid 250dh/day, a cook around 150dh. When buying food for the trek with your guide, you will have to buy enough for the muleteers, too. Generally, trekkers will consume about 100dh worth of food and soft drinks a day. If you do not do a loop, you will generally have to pay for the 'mule-days' it takes to get the pack animals back to their home village.

Trekkers soon discover the beauties of the Atlas – and the secrets of ensuring that the walking is as comfortable as possible, ways of dealing with dehydration and fatigue. As on any hill trek, a steady, regular pace should be maintained. At higher levels, ensure you pause if a dizzy feeling sets in. A good trip leader will ensure you make an early start, to enjoy walking in the cool morning. Vehicle pistes look alluring to walk on but are in fact hard on the feet. Keep to the softer edges or go for footpaths when possible. Gorges are not the easiest places to walk in, so your local guide should know of the higher routes, if there is one which is safe. Pay particular attention if your route involves some scree running. You don't want to leave the mountains on a mule because of a sprained ankle. If you are not used to walking at altitude, try to avoid high routes in the early stages of your trip. In villages which see a lot of tourists, the kids will be on the look out, ever ready to scrounge a dirham or a bonbon. They can, however, be useful in showing you the way through to the footpath on the other side of the settlement. Always be nice to them (but make sure your rucksack pockets are well zipped up if you pause). And after all, they never have holidays at the seaside. A smile and a wave never hurt.

Avoid ghiardia: always put your steritabs in your water bottle when you fill up from a stream

There are few books on trek routes in English. For the central High Atlas, there is a seriously detailed work, André Fougerolles' 1982 *Le Haut Atlas central, guide alpin* (Casablanca: CAF). Walking and scrambling tours in the M'goun are described with small maps in the handy *Randonnées pedestres dans le Massif du M'goun* (Casablanca: Belvisi, 1989). Both books are generally available at the Librairie Chatr, Av Mohamed V, Marrakech. On the web, consult www.cafmaroc.co.ma

Spectator sports

The major cities have arenas with basketball, handball, athletics and football all popular. Check the local press for details. Football (*koura*) is seriously popular, with kick-arounds in the most remote locations, and an excellent standard of play on beaches and in town pitches. If you're watching a beach football game, and are a bit of a player, you may well be asked to join in.

Health

Written by Dr Charlie Easmon; see Acknowledgements, page 543, for his biography

The health care in the region is varied: there are some decent private and government clinics/hospitals. There are French or English speaking doctors in the major cities who have particular experience in dealing with locally occurring diseases. Any pharmacy or large hotel will be able to give you the name of a good *médecin généraliste* (GP). Major cities also have a private ***SOS Médecins*** service on night duty (will generally do hotel visits, cost 300-500dh). The **SAMU** is the emergency service. As with all medical care, first impressions count. If a facility is grubby and staff wear grey coats instead of white ones, then be wary of the general standard of medicine and hygiene. Its worth contacting your embassy or consulate on arrival and asking where the recommended (ie those used by diplomats) clinics are. Providing embassies with information of your whereabouts can be also useful if a friend/relative gets ill at home and there is a desperate search for you around the globe. You can also ask them about locally recommended medical do's and don'ts. If you do get ill, and you have the opportunity, you should also ask your medical insurer whether they are satisfied that the medical centre or hospital that you have been referred to is of a suitable standard.

However, before discussing the disease-related health risks involved in travel within Morocco remember to try to avoid road accidents. You can reduce the likelihood of accidents by not drinking and driving, wearing a seatbelt in cars and a helmet on motorbikes, but you should be aware that others on the road may think that they are in the remake of *Death Race 2000*.

Before you go

Ideally, you should see your GP or travel clinic at least 6 weeks before your departure for general advice on travel risks, malaria and vaccinations. Make sure you have travel insurance, get a dental check (especially if you are going to be away for more than a month), know your own blood group and if you suffer a long-term condition such as diabetes or epilepsy make sure someone knows or that you have a Medic Alert bracelet/necklace with this information on it.

Vaccinations for your Morocco trip

Polio Obligatory if nil in last 10 years
Tetanus Obligatory if nil in last 10 years (but after 5 doses you have had enough for life)
Typhoid Obligatory if nil in last 3 years
Yellow Fever Not required unless you are coming directly from an infected country in Africa or South America
Rabies Not normally required but the disease does exist in Morocco and careful consideration of your itinerary and activities is required
Hepatitis A Recommended as the disease can be caught easily from food/water

Malaria in Morocco

Malaria does not occur in tourist areas and for the few areas that it does exist medicines to protect against malaria are not needed. Evening and nighttime insect precautions are recommended in risk areas. The very slight risk (exclusively *P. vivax*) is in limited areas from May to October in Khouribga Province in rural areas. In the territory of Western Sahara, risk (exclusively *P. falciparum*) exists along the border with Mauritania. The cities of Tangier, Rabat, Casablanca, Marrakech, and Fez do not have risk.

What to take

For longer trips involving jungle treks taking a clean needle pack, clean dental pack and water filtration devices are common-sense measures

NB It is risky to buy medicinal tablets abroad because the doses may differ and there may be a trade in false drugs

Mosquito repellents Remember that DEET (Di-ethyltoluamide) is the gold standard. Apply the repellent every 4-6 hours but more often if you are sweating heavily. If a non-DEET product is used check who tested it. Validated products (tested at the London School of Hygiene and Tropical Medicine) include Mosiguard, Non-DEET Jungle formula and non-DEET Autan. If you want to use citronella remember that it must be applied very frequently (ie hourly) to be effective. If you are a popular target for insect bites or develop lumps quite soon after being bitten, carry an Aspivenin kit. This syringe suction device is available from many chemists and draws out some of the allergic materials and provides quick relief.

Sun Block The Australians have a great campaign, which has reduced skin cancer. It is called Slip, Slap, Slop. Slip on a shirt, Slap on a hat, Slop on sun screen.

Pain killers Paracetomol or a suitable painkiller can have multiple uses for symptoms but remember that more than eight paractemol a day can lead to liver failure.

Ciproxin (Ciprofloaxcin) A useful antibiotic for some forms of travellers diarrhoea (see below).

Immodium A great standby for those diarrhoeas that occur at awkward times (ie before a long coach/train journey or on a trek). It helps stop the flow of diarrhoea and in my view is of more benefit than harm. (It was believed that letting the bacteria or viruses flow out had to be more beneficial. However, with Immodium they still come out, just in a more solid form.)

Pepto-Bismol Used a lot by Americans for diarrhoea. It certainly relieves symptoms but like Immodium it is not a cure for underlying disease. Be aware that it turns the stool black as well as making it more solid.

MedicAlert These simple bracelets, or an equivalent, should be carried or worn by anyone with a significant medical condition.

Further Information

Websites

Foreign and Commonwealth Office (FCO) (UK), www.fco.gov.uk This is a key travel advice site, with useful information on the country, people, climate and lists the UK embassies/consulates. The site also promotes the concept of 'Know Before You Go', and encourages travel insurance and appropriate travel health advice. It has links to the Department of Health travel advice site, see below.

Essentials

Department of Health Travel Advice (UK), www.doh.gov.uk/traveladvice This excellent site is also available as a free booklet, the T6, from Post Offices. It lists the vaccine advice requirements for each country.

Medic Alert (UK), www.medicalalert.co.uk This is the website of the foundation that produces bracelets and necklaces for those with existing medical problems. Once you have ordered your bracelet/necklace you write your key medical details on paper inside it, so that if you collapse, a medical person can identify you as someone with epilepsy or allergy to peanuts etc.

Blood Care Foundation (UK), www.bloodcare.org.uk The Blood Care Foundation is a Kent-based charity "dedicated to the provision of screened blood and resuscitation fluids in countries where these are not readily available." They will dispatch certified non-infected blood of the right type to your hospital/clinic. The blood is flown in from various centres around the world.

Public Health Laboratory Service (UK), www.phls.org.uk This site has up-to-date malaria advice guidelines for travel around the world. It gives specific advice about the right drugs for each location. It also has useful information for those who are pregnant, suffering from epilepsy or planning to travel with children.

Centers for Disease Control and Prevention (USA), www.cdc.gov This site from the US Government gives excellent advice on travel health, has useful disease maps and details of disease outbreaks.

World Health Organisation, www.who.int The WHO site has links to the WHO Blue Book (it was Yellow up to last year) on travel advice. This lists the diseases in different regions of the world. It describes vaccination schedules and makes clear which countries have Yellow Fever Vaccination certificate requirements and malarial risk.

Tropical Medicine Bureau (Ireland), www.tmb.ie This Irish based site has a good collection of general travel health information and disease risks.

Fit for Travel (UK), www.fitfortravel.scot.nhs.uk This site from Scotland provides a quick A-Z of vaccine and travel health advice requirements for each country.

British Travel Health Association (UK), www.btha.org This is the official website of an organization of travel health professionals.

NetDoctor (UK), www.Netdoctor.co.uk This general health advice site has a useful section on travel and has an "ask the expert", interactive chat forum.

Travel Screening Services (UK), www.travelscreening.co.uk This is the author's website. A private clinic dedicated to integrated travel health. The clinic gives vaccine, travel health advice, email and SMS text vaccine reminders and screens returned travellers for tropical diseases.

Books *The Travellers Good Health Guide* by **Dr Ted Lankester** by ISBN 0-85969-827-0. *Expedition Medicine* (The Royal Geographic Society) Editors **David Warrell and Sarah Anderson** ISBN 1 86197 040-4. *International Travel and Health World Health Organisation Geneva* ISBN 92 4 158026 7. *The World's Most Dangerous Places* by **Robert Young Pelton**, Coskun Aral and Wink Dulles ISBN 1-566952-140-9.

Leaflets *The Travellers Guide to Health* (T6) can be obtained by calling the Health Literature Line on T0800 555 777. Advice for travellers on avoiding the risks of HIV and AIDS (Travel Safe) available from **Department of Health**, PO Box 777, London SE1 6XH. The Blood Care Foundation order form PO Box 7, Sevenoaks, Kent TN13 2SZ T44-(0)1732-742427.

On the road

Diarrhoea & intestinal upset

This is almost inevitable. One study showed that up to 70% of all travellers may suffer during their trip

Symptoms Diarrhoea can refer either to loose stools or an increased frequency; both of these can be a nuisance. It should be short lasting but persistence beyond two weeks, with blood or pain, require specialist medical attention. **Cures** Ciproxin (Ciprofloaxcin) is a useful antibiotic for bacterial traveller's diarrhoea. It can be obtained by private prescription in the UK which is expensive, or bought over the counter in Moroccan pharmacies. You need to take one 500 mg tablet when the diarrhoea starts and if you do not feel better in 24 hours, the diarrhoea is likely to have a non-bacterial cause and may be viral (in which case there is little you can do apart from keep yourself rehydrated and wait for it to settle on its own). The key treatment with all diarrhoeas is rehydration. Try to keep hydrated by taking the right mixture of salt and water. This is available as Oral Rehydration Salts (ORS) in ready-made sachets or can be made up by adding a teaspoon of sugar and a half teaspoon of salt to a litre of clean water. Drink at least one large cup of this drink for each loose stool. You can also use flat carbonated drinks as an alternative. Immodium and Pepto- Bismol provide symptomatic relief. **Prevention** The standard advice is to be careful with water and ice for drinking. Ask yourself where the water came from. If you have any doubts then boil it or filter and treat it. There are many filter/treatment devices now available on the market. Food can also transmit disease. Be wary of salads (what were they washed in, who handled them), re-heated foods or food that has been left out in the sun having been cooked earlier in the day. There is a simple adage that says wash it, peel it, boil it or forget it. Also be wary of unpasteurized dairy products, these can transmit a range of diseases from brucellosis (fevers and constipation), to listeria (meningitis) and tuberculosis of the gut (obstruction, constipation, fevers and weight loss).

Leishmaniasis

Cutaneous and visceral, transmitted by sandflies. Occurs in some areas. Insect precautions are recommended.

Schistosomiasis

Occurs throughout the country. Highest risk is on slopes of Atlas Mountains and on coastal strip. Avoid freshwater exposure.

Sun protection

Follow the Australians with their Slip, Slap, Slop campaign

Symptoms White Britons are notorious for becoming red in hot countries because they like to stay out longer than everyone else and do not use adequate sun protection. This can lead to sunburn, which is painful and followed by flaking of skin. Aloe vera gel is a good pain reliever for sunburn. Long-term sun damage leads to a loss of elasticity of skin and the development of pre-cancerous lesions. Many years later a mild or a very malignant form of cancer may develop. The milder basal cell carcinoma, if detected early, can be treated by cutting it out or freezing it. The much nastier malignant melanoma may have already spread to bone and brain at the time that it is first noticed. **Prevention** Sun screen. SPF stands for Sun Protection Factor. It is measured by determining how long a given person takes to 'burn' with and without the sunscreen product on. So, if it takes 10 times longer to burn with the sunscreen product applied, then that product has an SPF of 10. If it only takes twice as long then the SPF is 2. The higher the SPF the greater the protection. However, do not just use higher factors just to stay out in the sun longer. 'Flash frying' (desperate bursts of excessive exposure), as it is called, is known to increase the risks of skin cancer.

Hepatitis

Symptoms Hepatitis means inflammation of the liver. Viral causes of the disease can be acquired anywhere in Morocco. The most obvious symptom is a yellowing of your skin or the whites of your eyes. However, prior to this all that you may notice is itching and tiredness. **Cures** Early on, depending on the type of hepatitis, a vaccine or immunoglobulin may reduce the duration of the illness. **Prevention** Pre-travel hepatitis A vaccine is the best bet. Hepatitis B (for which there is a vaccine) is spread through blood and unprotected sexual intercourse, both of these can be avoided. Unfortunately there is no vaccine for hepatitis C or the increasing alphabetical list of other Hepatitis viruses.

Sexual Health

Sex is part of travel and many see it as adding spice to a good trip but spices can be uncomfortable. Think about the sexual souvenirs any potential new partner may have picked up or live with. The range of visible and invisible diseases is awesome. Unprotected sex can spread HIV, Hepatitis B and C, Gonorrhea (green discharge), chlamydia (nothing to see but may cause painful urination and later female infertility), painful recurrent herpes, syphilis and warts, just to name a few. You can cut down the risk by using condoms, a femidom or avoiding sex altogether. If you do stray, consider getting a sexual health check on your return home, since these diseases are not the sort of gift people thank you for.

Rabat and around

78 Rabat
78 Ins and outs
79 History
82 Sights
91 Essentials

99 Salé
100 Sights
103 Essentials
104 Easy excursions from Rabat and Salé
105 Kénitra
105 Mehdiya
107 Ancient Thamusida
109 Moulay Bousselham
110 Ancient Banasa
112 South of Rabat

Introducing Rabat and around

Rabat makes a good first destination in Morocco. It is a city for walking in, with plenty of historic sites, including a citadel overlooking the ocean and a mediaeval fortified royal town. Declared capital of Morocco under the French protectorate, Rabat has a wealth of Art Deco and Neo-Moorish architecture in the *ville nouvelle*, which along with the souks, can all be easily visited in a day. Across the River Bou Regreg is Rabat's twin town, **Salé**. The old walled city, once a pirate capital, is today something of a backwater.

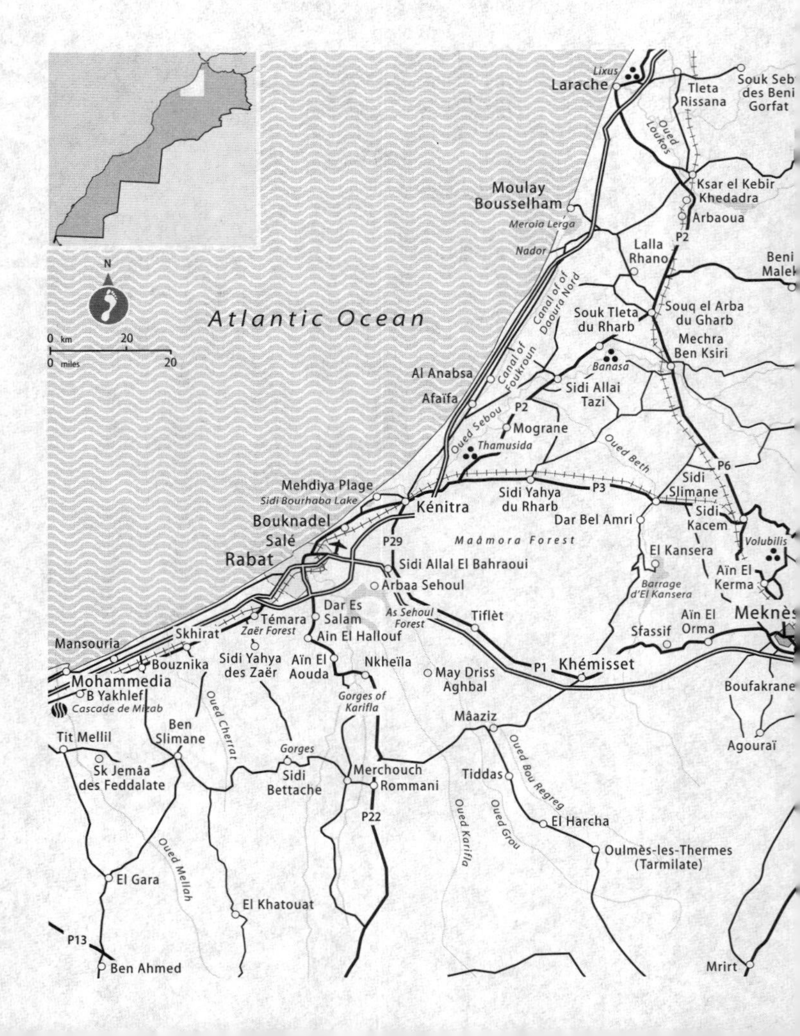

Salé El Jadida, or New Salé, is one of Morocco's largest new towns, however. Within easy day-trip distance from Rabat are **Moulay Bousselham** and its lagoon (an essential stop for birdwatchers), the historic fortress of **Mehdiya** and the lagoon of Sidi Bourhaba (another ornithologists' delight), and the ancient Roman sites of **Thamusida** (just north of Kénitra) and **Banasa**. South of Rabat are the resorts at **Temara** and **Skhirat** for those in desperate need of a beach. **Casablanca** is also an easy day trip from Rabat.

Things to do in Rabat

- Wander in the historic neighbourhoods of **Rabat**, taking in the **Kasbah des Oudaïas**, the **Médina** and the **Ville Nouvelle**. In the Médina, the Rue des Consuls is good for buying crafts and carpets.
- Get the feel of an ordinary small Moroccan town at Salé, across the Bouregreg from Rabat. Visit the historic *medersa* or college.
- Take a summer day trip north, visiting **Musée Belghazi** (a display of Morocco's material heritage), the **fortress at Mehdiya**, near Kénitra, and relax at **Plage des Nations**.
- Have a long archaeological day, driving up to the two Roman **archaeological sites** north of Rabat, **Thamusida** and **Banasa**. Have a picnic near the **stone circle of M'zoura**.
- Take a long day trip from Rabat (50 minutes by train) to see the **sights of Casablanca** (a small médina, the Grande Mosquée Hassan II, Quartier des Habous, the Villa des Arts in Maârif, architecture from the 1920s to the 1950s). Hop from site to site by red petit taxi.

Rabat الرباط

Phone code: 037
Colour map 1, grid B1
Population: 1,200,000

Behind its work-a-day façade, Rabat is a city which bears traces of numerous civilizations. It had Roman beginnings, as Colonia Sala Junonia, a prosperous settlement. Sala gave way to Berber Chellah, and then came the Almohads, who made Rabat el Fath, the Fortress of Victory, an imperial capital. (The unfinished Tour Hassan minaret dates from this time.) In the 17th century, Rabat was rebuilt by Andalucían refugees, for a short and vivid period becoming capital of a pirate republic. Under the first Alaouite ruler, Moulay Rachid, Rabat returned to central authority. The present ville nouvelle *dates from the early 20th century when Rabat was declared capital of Morocco, and the land between the sultan's palace and the médina was developed as a pleasant city of wide avenues and gardens. Rabat today is Morocco's second city and the country's political nerve centre.*

Ins and outs

Getting there

See Transport, page 97, for further details

Rabat is easily reached by public transport. There is a shuttle train service from Casablanca, and trains from Tanger, Fès and Meknès and Marrakech, as well as grands taxis. Rabat has a small airport (T037-808090/89), with some internal flights as well as some from France. Most international flights come into Casablanca Mohammed V Airport (for information on *RAM* flights, T09000800. Rabat is reached from this airport either by shuttle train (change at Casa-Voyageurs or Casa-Port stations), information on T037-736060. A grand taxi from Mohammed V airport will set you back 400dh. The coach service to and from Casablanca Mohammed V airport which used to leave from outside the *Hotel Terminus* has been discontinued. When coming into Rabat by bus, the principal bus terminal, for both *CTM* and private line buses, is located at Pl Zerktouni, 3 km out from the centre. For the city centre, catch a No 30 bus to Av Hassan II, or take a petit taxi for about 20dh.

Getting around

The main sites of Rabat are close enough to each other to do on foot. If time is limited, you may want to get one of the blue petits taxis between monuments, say from Chellah to the Kasbah des Oudaïas. This should cost no more than 10dh.

Tourist information

National Tourist Office, corner of Av al Abtal and R Oued Fès, T037-775171. **Office du Tourisme**, 22 Av d'Alger, T037-730562. **Syndicat d'Initiative**, Av Patrice Lumumba, T037-723272, not very useful.

History

Capital since 1913 Rabat has a long history

"They call Rabat the Pearl of Morocco" wrote Reginald Rankin in 1908. "It stands high on the steep southern bank of the Bouragrag where the green river lashes the blue sea, above cactus-grown ochre rocks, a long rambling line of white and yellow, everywhere dominated by the huge grey Tour Hassan." The name 'Rabat', a shortened and corrupted form of 'Ribat al-Fath', literally 'monastery of conquest', indicates an initial role as a religious retreat and strong point. From the citadel, the Kasbah des Oudaïas, the visitor can gaze out over the Atlantic as pirates and renegades must have done in the past. To the north, just across the Bou Regreg Estuary is Rabat's historic rival, Salé. The extensive city walls laid out by the third Almohad Sultan Abu Yusuf Yacoub al Mansour now enclose, with the river and the sea on the remaining sides, the kasbah, the old médina, and the core of the *ville nouvelle*, the old and new directly alongside each other. In this Rabat differs from Fès, Marrakech and Meknès, where the 20th-century new town was built some distance from the médina.

Early origins

The first settlement of this area was probably outside the present city walls, on the site of the later Merinid mausoleum of **Chellah**. There may have been Phoenician and Carthaginian settlement, but it is with the Roman **Sala Colonia** that Rabat's proven urban history began. Awarded municipal privileges, Sala Colonia was the most southwesterly town of the Roman Empire for two centuries, a trading post on the Oued Bou Regreg (which has since changed course), and a defensive settlement, located close to the line of frontier outposts, which ran ran through the suburbs to the south of the present city.

Sala Colonia came under Amazigh rule from the 8th to the 10th century. However, the heretic Kharajite beliefs of the Imazighen represented a challenge to the orthodoxy of the inland Muslims. In the 10th century the Zenata tribe built a fortified monastery, or *ribat*, on the site of the current **Kasbah des Oudaïas**. This functioned as a base from which to challenge the heretics on both sides of the river, and their supporters, the powerful Berghouata tribe. Sala Colonia was thus eventually abandoned.

Rabat under the Almohads

The *ribat* was used by the Almoravid Dynasty, but it was the Almohad Sultan Abd al-Mumin who redeveloped the settlement in 1150, transforming it into a permanent fortress town with palaces, the main mosque which still stands, reservoirs, and houses for followers, and using it as an assembly point for the large Almohad army. However, it was his grandson, Yacoub al Mansour, who from 1184 carried out the most ambitious programme of development, with his dream of Rabat as one of the great imperial capitals. He ordered an enormous city to be built, surrounded by walls. These walls were probably completed by 1197, and ran along two sides of the city, broken by four gates, most notably the **Bab er Rouah**. A grid of streets, residential quarters, a covered market, public baths, hotels, workshops and fountains were built, along with a new gateway to the médina. A bridge to Salé, and its **Grand Mosque**, were also constructed.

Yet the most impressive monument from this period, the **Hassan Mosque**, was never completed. Projected as the largest mosque in western Islam, little more than pillars remain. The vast minaret never reached its full height and remains a stubby tower. On Yacoub al Mansour's death in 1199 works were abandoned and Rabat then fell into decline. Parts of the city were destroyed in fighting between the Almohads and Merinids, to the point that Leo Africanus, visiting in 1500, found few inhabited neighbourhoods and very few shops. As Rabat declined under the Merinids, Salé prospered. The dynasty's most noteworthy contribution to Rabat was the funeral quarter on the **Chellah** site, with its impressive mausoleums, but even that eventually fell into neglect. It is impossible to know today to what extent the area within the Almohad walls – basically the core of the *ville nouvelle* – was actually built up.

Piracy & Andalucíans Rabat's fortunes revived in the 17th century. As maritime technology advanced and the Atlantic Ocean became important to international trade, corsairing, or piracy, boomed. For a time Rabat was the centre, with 'the Sallee Rovers' of historical repute more likely to have been based here than in present-day Salé. Robinson Crusoe was a fictional captive of 'a Turkish rover of Sallee'.

Rabat also benefited from the flow of Muslims leaving Spain during the Inquisition. First rejected by Salé, the Hornacheros settled in the Rabat kasbah in 1609, and the other Andalucíans in the Rabat médina in 1610. The médina they settled in was considerably smaller than the city Yacoub al Mansour had envisaged, as indicated by the 17th-century rampart, which, when built, demarcated the extent of the settlement, and now runs between the médina and the *ville nouvelle*. The area beyond this rampart was used for farming, and most of it remained undeveloped until the French arrived. In the Médina, the Andalucían influence is visible, notably in the street plan and the feel of the buildings.

Fierce rivalry existed between the Hornachero and the Andalucían communities, both setting up autonomous city-states. The period 1610 to 1666 was marked by intermittent strife between the three towns of the Bou Regreg estuary (Rabat, Salé and the Kasbah des Oudaïas). By 1627 the three were united under the control of the Hornacheros as the Republic of the Bou Regreg, a control against which the Andalucíans frequently rebelled, most notably in 1636. The Republic lost its independence in 1638. In 1641 the three cities were again united, and in 1666 when Moulay Rachid captured the estuary they came under the authority of the Alaouite Sultanate.

The principal background to these conflicts was the struggle for control over the profits from piracy, essentially a parasite form of trade. Rabat was especially popular with corsairs, many of whom had Mediterranean origins, because, unlike several other ports, it had not been occupied by Europeans.

Alaouite Rabat Under the Alaouites, Rabat changed considerably. Trade and piracy were taken over as official functions, the profits going to the sultanate. The port declined, replaced by Mogador (Essaouira) in the 18th century. Moulay Rachid took over the Kasbah, expelling its residents and built the **Qishla** fortification to overlook and control the médina. However, Sultan Moulay Ismaïl, most closely associated with Meknès, ignored Rabat, and broke the power of the corsairs.

In the late 1760s, Mohammed Ibn Abdallah had a palace built in Rabat, and since then the Alaouite sultans have maintained a palace there, making the city one of their capitals. Increased trade with Europe in the 19th century temporarily revitalized Rabat's role as a port, but it was gradually supplanted, perhaps because of the shallow mouth of the Bou Regreg and the poor harbour facilities, but also because newer towns and cities, notably Casablanca, were more easily controlled by Europeans. In 1832 the rebellious Oudaïa tribe were settled in the abandoned Kasbah, giving it its current name. The Kasbah continued to be administered separately from the médina until the 20th century.

Modern Rabat, experiment in urban planning

In 1912, after complex diplomatic and military manoeuvrings, Morocco was split into two protectorates, with a large French central region and small Spanish zones in the North and the Sahara. The Moroccan sultanate had had no fixed capital, the power centre being where the sultan happened to be. For the new French protectorate, a capital was necessary, and Rabat was chosen in 1913. The first Resident-General, Lyautey, with his architect Henri Prost, planned and built the majority of the new capital, the *ville nouvelle*, both within and outside Yacoub al Mansour's walls, leaving the médina much as they found it, although the main thoroughfares were paved.

Efficiency and beauty were Lyautey's watchwords as he supervised the creation of the new Rabat. The European neighbourhoods were initally laid out in an area between the médina, to the northwest, and the *mechouar* or sultan's palace complex, to the southeast. Prost created a system of parks and gardens. The tree-lined street between médina and the *ville nouvelle*, today's Boulevard Hassan II, became a meeting place for Muslim and foreign communities, with municipal markets, bus and taxi stations and cafés.

More revealing of the early Protectorate's attitude is what the planners did regarding heritage. The two main avenues of the new Rabat – Boulevard Dar El Makhzen, today's Avenue Mohammed V, and the Avenue de Casablanca, today's Avenue de la Victoire – lead to Moroccan monumental buildings, the former leading up to the Sunna Mosque, the latter to Bab Er Rouah, perhaps the city's finest Almohad gate. It would have been possible, given the freedom to act which Lyautey had, to build the Residency General at a focal point on a new avenue, somewhat like Lutyen's House of the Viceroy in New Delhi. Rather the new administrative buildings were built in a special area, close to the palace. With its luxuriant gardens, the Ministères neighbourhood recalls Anglo-American garden cities. The buildings, despite their importance to French rule, had simple whitewashed walls and green-tiled roofs and were linked by pergola walkways. They were kept unmonumental in scale (even the entrance to the Residency General had no obvious feature), hidden in vegetation. French policy was thus to use architectural devices to emphasize local culture, while keeping the seats of power hidden in a mini garden suburb. Buildings of the 1990s, such as the new Ministry of Foreign Affairs, clash radically with the original principal. It remains to be seen how the Résidence, until recently used as offices by the Ministry of Defence, will be refurbished as a Museum of Civilisations. Hopefully little of the gardens will be lost under concrete.

In short, in colonial Rabat, monumental buildings were only rarely used as a symbol of power. Today's Parliament Building, on the Avenue Mohammed V, is the exception, starting life as the Palais de Justice. Strongly symmetrical, with a massive colonnade, the building was probably designed to symbolize the equity and reason of French justice. Today, it is the centre of Moroccan political life.

After independence, Rabat continued to expand, its population swelled by the large number of civil servants required for the newly independent kingdom. Rabat's economy today is primarily based on its role as Morocco's capital, with massive numbers on the government payroll. The city has attracted large numbers of migrants from the countryside, and the formal housing market has been unable to keep up with the demand for accommodation, leading to the development of new self-built neighbourhoods like Douar Eddoum and Takaddoum. Rabat in many ways is a city of extremes, with streets of fine villas not far from crowded and largely insanitary slums, or *bidonvilles*. South towards Casablanca, the new planned residential area of Hay Ryad is larger than the whole colonial city centre, while at Madinat El Irfane ('City of Knowledge'), Rabat has the country's largest concentration of faculties and university institutes. Neither Almohad sultans nor Lyautey could have imagined that a city could grow so fast in just a couple of decades. This growth has not been without its negative consequences, however. The once fine gardens and tree-lined avenues have become distinctly scruffy and the pavements are often broken. Municipal management is clearly not keeping up with the pace of change. Morocco's capital, with its historic médina and one of the finest examples of 20th-century city planning, certainly merits proper upkeep. After all, Rabat is a sort of showcase for modern Morocco.

Sights

Route through the city

A day would be sufficient time for the energetic to explore Rabat, while two days would be perfect

The following route takes in most of the main sites. You would be advised, however, to take a petit taxi for one of the longer hops, either from the Kasbah to the Hassan Tower, or from the Chellah down to the far side of the médina. The three main sites of Rabat, namely the **Kasbah des Oudaias**, the **médina** and the **Chellah**, have to be explored on foot. If you started at the kasbah, you could next head for the **Hassan Tower** and the **Mohammed V Mausoleum** along Tarik al Marsa road with its thundering lorries and buses. From the Tour Hassan, you could then continue to skirt the city along Boulevard Bou Regreg,

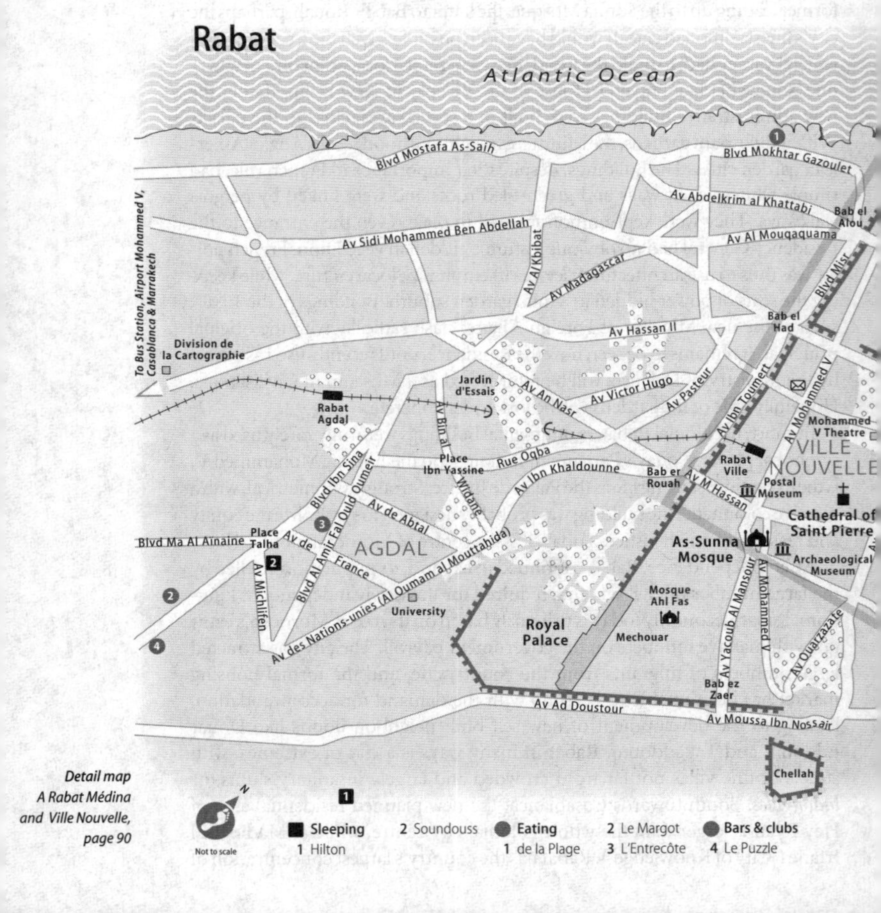

Detail map A Rabat Médina and Ville Nouvelle, page 90

Avenue Tariq Ibn Ziad and Avenue Moussa Ibn Nossair to the fortified **Chellah,** clearly visible down on your left from the road. After the Chellah, you would head into the *ville nouvelle* by **Bab ez Zaer** to the **Sunna Mosque**. Turn along Avenue Moulay Hassan and through **Bab er Rouah** to view it from the outside. Pass down Avenue Ibn Toumert, past **Bab el Had** to **Bab el Alou**, and right into the médina. Turn right down Boulevard Mohammed V and carry on through the médina to Avenue Hassan II. Those with transport must park here and explore the médina and the *ville nouvelle* on foot. Boulevard Mohammed V is the only drivable road in the médina, Avenue Mohammed V in the *ville nouvelle* is one way from Avenue Hassan II to the post office.

Walls & gates

Rabat has three sets of walls: the Almohad wall around the kasbah, the 5 km of Almoravid wall around much of the city centre dating from the 12th century, and the wall now separating the médina and the *ville nouvelle* built by the Andalucíans in the early seventh century. The walls are mainly built of *pisé* or *pisé*-cement and, though considerably repaired, strengthened and adapted, they are much as they were originally. There are four gates still standing in the Almoravid wall: **Bab el Alou, Bab el Had, Bab er Rouah** and **Bab ez Zaer. Bab er Rouah** is the most important and impressive of these, but **Bab el Had** is worth seeing. Located at the intersection of Avenue Hassan II and Avenue Ibn Toumert, the substantially remodelled **Bab el Had** has a blind arch and is flanked by two five-sided stone towers. Currently you pass through two chambers, at different levels. A number of scribes have their 'offices' in this gate, drafting correspondence and other documents for the illiterate.

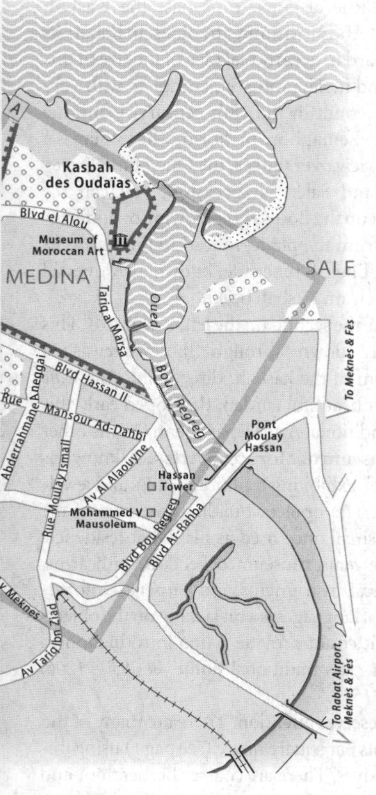

Bab er Rouah, also known as the 'Gate of the Winds', at Place An-Nasr, can best be approached along Avenue An-Nasr from outside the walled city, when its scale and beauty is most obvious. The gate is now used as an art gallery, and is only open when exhibitions are being held. The arch of the gate is framed by a rectangular band of Kufic inscription. Between the arch and the frame there is a floral motif, with the scallop symbol on either side. The arch itself, with an entrance restored by the Alaouites with small stones, is made up of three different patterns, of great simplicity, producing the overall effect of a sunburst confined within a rectangle. The entrance passage inside follows a complex double elbow. This, combined with the two flanking bastions outside, indicate that the gate was defensive as well as ceremonial.

Kasbah des Oudaïas

The Kasbah des Oudaïas, originally a fortified *ribat*, later settled by Andalucíans, is both beautiful and peaceful, and well worth a visit. It can be reached along Rue de Consuls through the médina, Boulevard el Alou along the western side of the médina, or by Tarik al Marsa which runs along the Oued Bou Regreg. There are a number of entrances to the kasbah, but the best is by the imposing **Bab al-Kasbah** gateway at the top of the hill. At this point avoid the unofficial guides as the kasbah is in fact small and easily explored without assistance. (In fact, to avoid them altogether, you could get up to the kasbah up the steps from the esplanade which runs along the beach below the cemetery.)

Bab al-Kasbah was located close to the **Souk el-Ghezel**, the main medieval market, whilst the original palace was just inside. The gateway was built by Yacoub al Mansour in about 1195, inserting it into the earlier kasbah wall built by Abd al-Mumin, and it did not have the same defensive role as the **Bab er Rouah**. The gate has a pointed horseshoe arch surrounded by a cusped, blind arch. Around this there is a wide band of geometric carving, the common *darj w ktaf*. The two corner areas between this band and the rectangular frame are composed of floral decoration, with, as in the **Bab er Rouah**, a scallop or palmette in each. Above this are more palmettes, a band of Koranic lettering, and on top a wide band of geometric motifs. The entrance to the kasbah is via stairs and through two rooms, a third room being closed to the public. The inside of the gate is also decorated, though more simply.

Inside the gate, the main street, Rue al-Jama, runs past the **Kasbah Mosque**, dating from 1150, the time of Abd al-Mumin, the oldest in Rabat. As is the case of most city mosques, it is hard to get any real idea of the size of this building, as homes are built all around it. The minaret, complete with very decorative arches, was substantially rebuilt in the 18th century. Continue along Rue al-Jama and you come to the semaphore platform, where there is a carpet factory. This gives an excellent view over the sea, the Oued Bou Regreg with its natural sand-bar defence, and Salé. On occasion, you can see windsurfers, surfers and, looking back up the Bou Regreg, rowing boats ferrying people over to Salé. Steps down from the platform lead to the *Caravelle Restaurant*, in a small fort built by an English renegade, known as Ahmed el Ingliz, and the popular, but none too clean, Kasbah beach.

Coming back from the platform take the second on the left, Rue Bazzo. This narrow and cobbled street winds down through the whitewashed Andalucían-style houses to the bottom of the kasbah, directly into the *Café Maure*, alongside which is a small but beautiful garden, developed early this century by Prosper Ricard and the Traditional Arts Department. On the other side of the garden is a section of the **Museum of Moroccan Arts**, also known as the Musée des Oudaïas, Souk el Ghezel, exhibiting traditional dress and jewellery from many regions of Morocco. The opulent buildings are part of the 17th-century palace, which Moulay Ismaïl once used as his Rabat residence. The central building now houses the main museum collection, with arms, instruments, jewellery, pottery, musical instruments and carpets. Unfortunately, information in a suitable array of languages is a bit lacking on the objects in this museum. If better managed, it could provide a fine introduction to Moroccan crafts and life in an upper class traditional home. ■ *0830- 1200, 1500-1830, except Tue. 10dh. T037-731512.*

If it is open, the carpet collection deserves attention. There are many of the carpets, defined by the number of knots per square metre (see page) using traditional motifs and natural fibres and dyes. There are coarser Berber floor and seat coverings, brighter and distinctive. It is a good place to visit before you purchase elsewhere. The rows of illuminated Korans are an unusual display.

The reconstruction of the interior of a typical Moroccan house is also worth examination – again if open. This is the spacious setting for low divans covered in silk covers with gold embroidery, large fine weave carpets, piles of brocade and silk cushions in brilliant hues, intimate alcoves and a huge central salon. There are reception rooms around a central courtyard. In particular seek out the palace baths, the *hammam*. The garden here is very pleasant, again in the Andalucían style. The flower beds are intended to be quite formal but the plants grow beyond the confines of the borders on to the paths.

Médina

Most of the buildings in the médina date from the arrival of the Andalucían Muslims in the 7th century

The Andalucían character of the buildings and decoration sets the médina apart from those such as Marrakech. Whilst Rabat médina is smaller and more limited in the range of markets, shops and buildings than Fès, Marrakech and Meknès, and less distinct in its way of life, its accessibility, size and the simplicity of its grid-like street pattern make it a good first experience of Moroccan médinas. Physically close to the *ville nouvelle*, the médina is very different in the design of buildings and open space, and the nature of commerce and socialization. It is an interesting and safe place to wander, with little risk of getting lost or hassled. Boulevard Mohammed V is one of the major arteries of the médina. As you enter the médina from the *ville nouvelle*, the second right, **Rue Souika**, and its continuation **Souk es Sebbat**, are the main shopping streets, with an unusually wide range of shops and a number of traditional cafés for such a small area. Souk es Sebbat, originally where the shoes were made, is easily recognized by its roof of woven straw and reeds. A great deal of leather work is on sale here, in particular worked leather for bags and the soft leather *babouches*. The mosque of Moulay Slimane at the junction of Rue Souika and Rue Sidi Fatah was constructed in 1812. The **Grand Mosque**, on Rue Souika, is a much restored Merinid building, the minaret of which is decorated with polychrome glazed earthenware tiles. Just opposite the **Grand Mosque**, on a side turning, is the interesting stone façade of a fountain, now a bookshop, but dating from the reign of the 14th-century Merinid Sultan Abu Faris Abd al-Aziz.

Souk es Sebbat leads down to the river, past the *mellah* on the right. The *mellah* is the former Jewish area, still the poorest area of the médina, with small cramped houses and shops, and narrow streets. It was built in 1808 by Moulay Slimane. Originally there were 17 synagogues, those remaining have become dwellings or storehouses. Today it is a triangular area of largely unsalubrious housing, bounded by Rue Ouqasson (the continuation of Rue des Consuls), the médina wall, and the river. As in many Islamic cities, Jews were kept in one area, for both protection and control, and so that they would be easily accessible to the authorities to carry out tasks Muslims could not perform. There are few Jews left in the *mellah*, most having emigrated to Israel. There is, however, a moderately interesting *joutia*, or flea market – and some very striking poverty.

Turning left off **Souk es Sebbat** one can follow the Rue des Consuls to the kasbah. This road was where many European consuls and important merchants lived until 1912. Rue des Consuls is now lined with expensive shops selling silk embroidery, souvenirs, traditional Moroccan items in copper and leather and carpets. Recently the street was enhanced with a range of roof features, one of which, with iron pillars and plexiglass vaults. There is a carpet market on the street on Tuesday and Thursday mornings. Turn right at the end of Rue des Consuls and you are in Tarik al Marsa (literally, Avenue of the Port). Here you may make a death-defying dash across the street to visit the kasbah and its traditional arts museum (see above). Also on the kasbah side of the street, to your right as you look at the kasbah, is the **Centre Artisanal**. All craft products sold here have fixed prices.

Hassan Tower & Mohammed V Mausoleum

The Almohad **Hassan Tower** dominates the skyline of Rabat, and even unfinished it is an impressive building, testimony to Yacoub al Mansour's unfulfilled vision of his imperial capital. It overlooks the Oued Bou Regreg and Salé, and can be reached most easily by Boulevard Bou Regreg, or by turning right at the end of Avenue Hassan II.

The building of the mosque was abandoned on Yacoub al Mansour's death in 1199, leaving most of the minaret, but just part of the columns and walls. All the portable parts, tiles, bricks and the roofing material, have been taken for use in other buildings. The remains of the mosque were excavated and reconstructed by the French and Moroccans. The mosque would have followed a T-shape, with the main green-tiled roof section between the minaret and the modern mausoleum. The *mihrab* (prayer niche) would have been in the south *qibla* wall, where the mausoleum is, and therefore was not properly orientated towards Mecca. It is also unusual to find the minaret opposite the *qibla* wall.

The incomplete minaret of the Hassan Mosque stands at 45 m. When completed, it would have been 64 m, four times as high as it was wide, with the lantern making it 80 m, five times as high. This is in keeping with the classic North African minaret style, as with the **Koutoubia** in Marrakech (see page 317). It is decorated with geometric designs, there being no inscription or floral decoration, but their scale and clarity of execution makes them clearly discernible from a distance. Each of the faces has a different composition, interweaving designs, arches and windows. The common Moroccan motif of *darj w ktaf*, resembling a tulip or a truncated *fleur de lys*, and formed by intersecting arcs with superimposed rectangles, is present, notably on the north and south upper registers.

Adjacent to the Hassan Tower is the **Mohammed V Mausoleum**, dedicated to the first king of independent Morocco and father of the current king. The building dates from 1971. The mausoleum is constructed on the site where Mohammed V, returning from his exile in 1955, gathered thousands of his people to thank God for giving independence to Morocco. The tomb chamber, but not the mausoleum's mosque, is open to non-Muslims, and features traditional Moroccan decorative motifs and techniques common in religious architecture, including a painted ceiling, the carved marble tomb, and the *zellige* tiles (mosaic) on the walls. Note the guards in their splendid uniforms. ■ *0800-1830 daily. Free.*

Merinid Mausoleum at Chellah

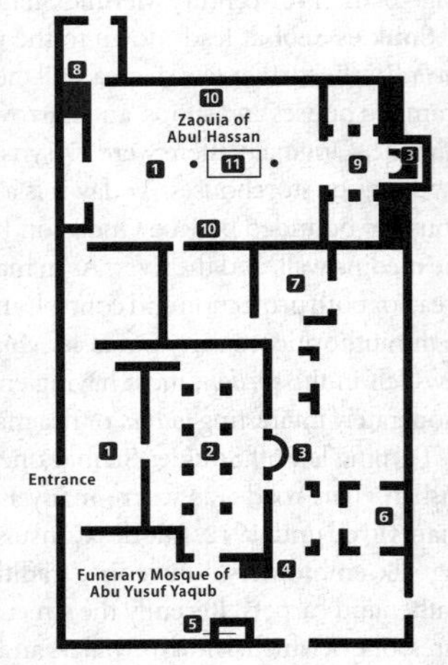

1 Courtyard
2 Sanctuary
3 Mihrab
4 Ruined Minaret
5 Pool - spring fed
6 Tomb of Abul Hassan
7 Tomb of Shams al-Dawha
8 Minaret (with storks)
9 Prayer Hall
10 Students' cells
11 Pool & two fountains

Chellah

The Chellah is reached by going past the main **As-Sunna Mosque** in the *ville nouvelle*, and carrying on south down avenue Yacoub al Mansour and through the **Bab ez Zaer**. There are five sides to the Chellah, all different lengths, and 20 towers. This walled Merinid necropolis was built between 1310 and 1334, approximately on the site of the Roman town of **Sala Colonia**. The second Merinid Sultan, Abu Yusuf Yacoub, built a mosque and Abul Hassan, the Black Sultan, then built the enclosure wall and the gate. The Roman ruins at the lower level of the Chellah enclosure have been excavated, and include a forum, baths, shops and a temple. These are not open to the public. ■ *10dh, residents 5dh.*

The gate is smaller and less impressive than the Almohad **Bab er Rouah**. It is decorated with carving, and coloured marble and tiles, with an octagonal tower on either side above which is a square platform. The entrance is on the elbow pattern and you turn right through three chambers, before walking out into a wild and lush garden. To get to the mausoleum take the wide path to the bottom, where it stands on the right, the Roman ruins on the left. On the far right are the tombs of local saints, surrounding a pool.

The door into the **Merinid mausoleum**, facing the Roman ruins, opens into the mosque of Abu Yusuf Yacoub, which consists of a small courtyard, followed by a three-aisled sanctuary. The arched doorway on the left has the remains of floral and geometric *zellige* in five colours. Entering the sanctuary, the *mihrab* is straight ahead. A door to the right leads to an area including the remains of the mosque's minaret, and a pool. From this one enters the area of tombs, including those of Abul Hassan and his wife Shams al-Dawha. The remaining area of the mausoleum is taken up with the *zaouia*, or mosque-monastery, of Abul Hassan. This includes a minaret, and a ruined funerary chapel, with very intricate carving, notably on the exterior of the south wall. The main part of the *zaouia* is a rectangular courtyard with a small mosque at one end, and surrounded by small cells. It had a pool surrounded by a columned arcade, the bases of the columns still discernible. The *mihrab* has some intricate stucco carving. The tiles on the upper portion of the minaret are perhaps recent, but the effect would have been a bright tiled structure.

Ville Nouvelle

The *ville nouvelle* contains some fine examples of French colonial architecture, which in Morocco incorporated an element of local design tradition, particularly the main post office (PTT Centrale) and the *Bank al-Maghrib*, both on Avenue Mohammed V. This main boulevard is wide and particularly impressive in the evening, when it is crowded with people out for a stroll. Off to the left, down a street opposite the railway station, is the **Catholic Cathedral of Saint Pierre**. Below the station is the Parliament building or Majlis an-Nuwwab. The lawns on the stretch of the central promenade between the entrance and the Balima are a favourite with demonstrators. A symptom of the Moroccan labour market, the protesters are likely to be unemployed graduates. Just past the *Hotel Terminus* is a small postal museum exhibiting stamps. The 18th-century but much restored **As-Sunna Mosque** dominates the view up Avenue Mohammed V.

Archaeological Museum

If you take the Rue Moulay Abdelaziz, opposite the Sunna Mosque, and turn right on the Rue Brihi, you will come to the Archaeological Museum, 23 Rue el Brihi. This was built in 1932 and enlarged a few years later. It has housed the National Museum collections since 1986. This museum houses the best archaeological collections in the country and is worth a good 30 minutes' visit. The section covering pre-history has human remains from 4000 BC. There are pieces of pottery, jewellery and metalwork from Mauritanian forbears, as well as some carved stones. Particularly fine is the Bronze Age Nkhila stela with its concentric curves and humanoid figure. ■ *0830-1200, 1430-1800, closed Tue. 10dh, residents 5dh. T037-722231.*

The museum is best known, however, for its Roman pieces, displayed in the Salle des Bronzes. (Usually kept locked, the caretaker will race off to open up when you buy your ticket.) The Hellenistic bronzes, restored a few years ago with UNESCO assistance, are superb and include an exquisite head of Juba II (ruled 25 BC to AD 23) and a most realistic dog from Volubilis, Morocco's most spectacular Roman site, near Meknès. Also from Volubilis is a portrait of Roman politician Cato the Younger (defeated by Julius Caesar in 46 BC at Utica, and who committed suicide by falling on his sword) and an *ephèbe* – a naked Graecian youth with ivy crown, victor in some games or just off to a party? The position of the left hand, however, suggests that he is a *doryphorous*, a spear carrier. There is a fine athletic horserider, probably based on a Greek original by Polyclitus. (Ultimately, it is interesting to see how the extent of the Roman Empire meant that Greek representations of male beauty were spread far and wide.) And there is a multitude of little dark greeny-grey statuettes. Again from Volubilis is a bronze armrest bracket in the form of a fierce-looking mule. The largest mosaics from Volubilis are still there.

All around the Salle des Bronzes also are a series of vitrines packed with archaeological finds. Unfortunately, the vast majority of the explanations are in French only, but you will be able to pick out candelabra, metal fittings from harnesses and furniture, a damascened trophy and a cuirass with lion and elephant heads. There are some small pieces of marble statuary, including some heads and a snoozing – or hungover – Silenus, with a jug from which water, or maybe wine would have trickled. And there is some jewellery, brooches, odd bronze feet, minute acrobats, a gold feather and a tiny bracelet with crescent moon.

Among the most interesting things are the pieces which tell something of life in the Roman garrison towns of Mauritania Tingitana. There is a display of builders' tools, including plumblines, compass and triangle from Banasa. And there is a bronze military diploma from Ceuta (Roman *Ad Septem*), conferring citizenship on a soldier who had completed his service in the legion.

Back in the main part of the museum, upstairs, are some more finds, again with explanations in French only. Regarding early Islamic times, there are photos and items from Belyounech, northern Morocco, a holiday area for neighbouring Ceuta (Sebta in Arabic) where the springs supplying the city were situated. A number of *munya*, as the tower houses were called, have been excavated. And there are details of sugar manufacture in the Chichaoua.

Given the size of Morocco, and the long period of ancient settlement, it is surprising in a way that the museum is so small. Doubtless funds are lacking to display all the finds. Perhaps UNESCO could be persuaded to come up with some finance for an extension/revamping of the displays. The collections are impressive, but need at the very least good explanations in a range of languages.

Natural Science Museum

The Natural Science Museum is part of the Ministry of Energy and Mining. Here there is a reconstruction of a sauropod dinosaur. The skeleton of this creature, which is almost 15 m in length, was discovered in 1979 in the Azilal region of the High Atlas.

Postal Museum

The Postal Museum was opened in 1970. It belongs to the PTT which has brought together this small and interesting collection of instruments once used by their service. The items range from a post van to an envelope and between are telegraph machines, belinographs which reproduced photographs over long distances and the Baudot telegraph with printer. Among the postage stamps is Morocco's first official stamp from May 1912 but the collections of more recent stamps will catch the eye. Philately is a good export earner.

At the top

In public buildings, offices and shops all over Morocco you will see portraits of the country's Royals, members of the ruling Alaouite dynasty which has been on the throne since the mid-17th century. Sometimes there is a triptych: a photograph of the late King Hassan II (ruled 1961-99) flanked by the two princes, the then crown prince Sidi Mohammed and his younger brother, Moulay Rachid. On the death of Hassan II in July 1999, the crown prince came to the throne as Mohammed VI. Increasingly, his portrait as a sober-suited young technocrat is replacing that of the late king on public display. (Trendy clothes shops may have the king in ski-gear complete with woolly gnaoua *cap.) In Hassan II's reign, shop-owners picked portraits appropriate to place: in a sports shop, there would be a picture of the king playing golf or in hunting gear while a crémerie would have the picture of the king alongside a Berber milkmaid; beauty salons favoured a picture of the king and one of his daughters fully made-up for her wedding day.*

Hassan II had five children. Elegant Lalla Myriem, the eldest daughter, now in her late thirties, was married to the son of former prime minister Abdellatif Filali. She won much admiration for her courage in getting a divorce, apparently against her father's will. She is much involved in charity work, as are the younger sisters, Lalla Esma and Lalla Hasna. Before the King married in 2002, the princesses accompanied their brother on official visits abroad. (Their mother never appeared in public life, and in court protocol, as in the Gulf states, there was never any reference to 'the queen'.)

Hassan II also had a brother, the popular prince Moulay Abdallah who died young. By his Lebanese wife he had several children. The eldest, Moulay Hicham, has had an international career and was involved in the UN peacekeeping mission in Kosovo. When his cousin came to the throne, it was thought that his expertise would be brought in to help the new monarch.

For the moment, Morocco's royal family are a popular lot. The king, a jet-ski adept, is seen as being wa'er, an almost untranslatable slang term meaning something like trendy or cool. Mohamed VI's popularity was further increased after his marriage to a university-educated woman of an ordinary Fassi family, now HRH Princess Selma. The couple's first child, Prince Hassan, was birn in May 2003. The other princesses are building themselves public profiles based on constant expression of their concern for the deprived. Some huge Iranian-style upheaval notwithstanding, they seem set to carry on chairing committees and visiting hospitals. Hopefully, government reform will provide the wherewithal for Morocco's people to pull themselves out of the poverty endemic to so many parts of the country.

Palace complex

To the right of the As-Sunna Mosque is the palace complex, where the sovereign spends part of the year. It is not possible to go beyond this point up the central avenue of the complex. Construction of the Royal Palace began in 1864. It is surrounded by a wall cut by three gates. Inside the complex is an open space known as the *mechouar*. Here stands the **Ahl Fas Mosque** where the King leads prayers each Friday when he is in the capital.

Lalla Soukaïna Mosque

A few kilometres south of the city centre, if you happen to be in the vicinity of Hay Ryad, the new Lalla Soukaïna Mosque (completed 1989) might be worth a look. The gardens are pleasant with scented shrubs and herbs. Non-Muslims are not permitted to enter the mosque, but the custodian will light up the centre so one can see through the glass doors to the yellow and green ceramic basins.

Rabat Médina & Ville Nouvelle

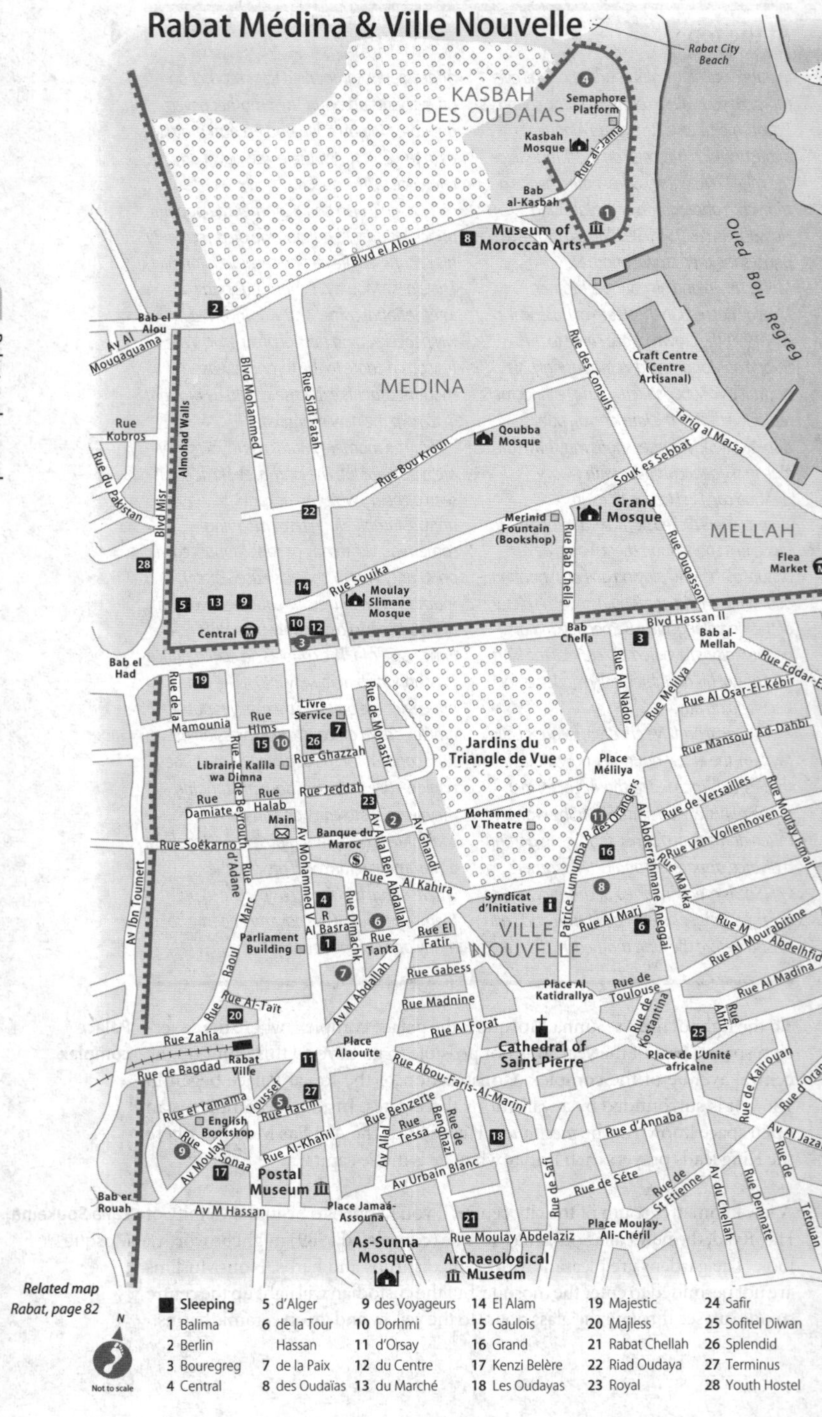

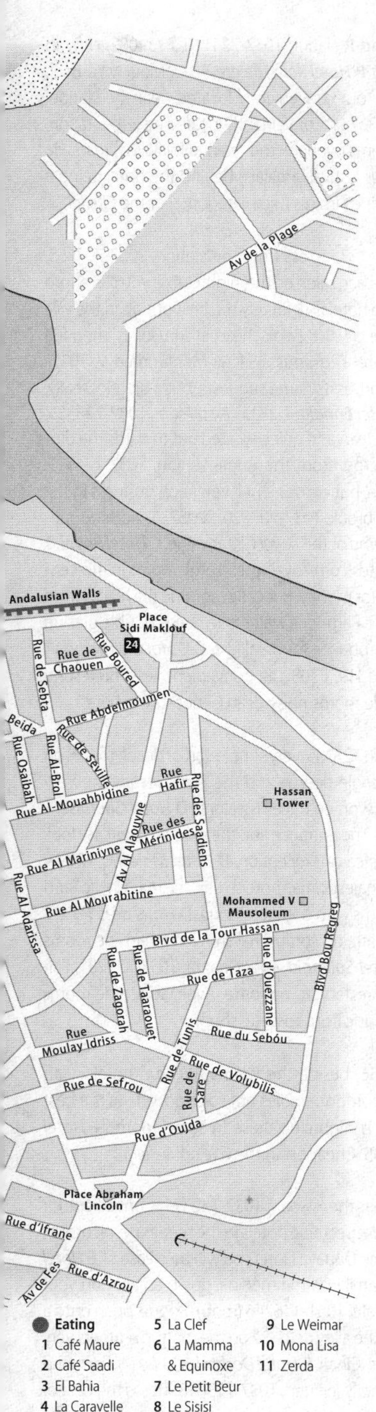

Essentials

Sleeping

Price codes: see inside front cover

In summer hotels can fill up early, especially in the mid-price range. There are plenty of reasonably priced hotels in Rabat. The cheapest hotels in the médina, for which prices can be very flexible, are best avoided (with a few exceptions). The centre of the *ville nouvelle* provides a wide range of good hotels.

Ville nouvelle

■ *on map, page 80*

L *Hotel Hilton*, Aviation Souissi, T037-675656, F671492. 220 rooms, 28 suites, luxurious, set in an extensive park on the road out past the Chellah, rather far from the city centre, but offers everything, including a business centre, mini golf course, art gallery, pool and *hammam*. **L** *Hotel de la Tour Hassan - Méridien*, 26 Av de Chellah, T037-704202, F725408, thassan@mtds.com 158 rooms, convenient location, a sprawling sort of hotel with pool fitted into a city centre site, excellent restaurants, conference room, bar. **L** *Hotel Safir*, Pl Sidi Makhlouf, T037-731091, F725408. Convenient, at end of Av Hassan II overlooking the river and Salé, built around a courtyard in an approximation of a Moroccan palace, pool, most other facilities and services. **L** *Hotel Sofitel Diwan*, Pl de l'Unité africaine, T037-262727, F262624. A recent (2001) respectable addition, handily located for embassies, banks and ministries in downtown Rabat. Simple, tasteful decor. Minor downside: immediate location on a busy junction. **L** *Hotel Soundouss*, 10 Pl Talha, Agdal. T037-675959, F675868. Recent hotel, handy if you are doing business in Hayy Riad or Agdal. Otherwise little to recommend it. **A** *Rabat Chellah*, 2 R d'Ifni, T037-701051/59, F706354. Right in centre of town and a few metres from the Archaeological Museum and the Sunna Mosque. All rooms with bath. Restaurant, bar and café. Downside: noise from corridors carries into rooms. Often used by groups so reserve in advance.

B ***Hotel Bouregreg***, corner Av Hassan II and R Nador, T037-724110, F734002. New in 1998, 70 rooms, well located for the médina. **B** ***Hotel Kenzi Belere***, 33 Av Moulay Youssef, T/F037-709801. A bit grim on the outside but conveniently located near the station. **B** ***Hotel Majless***, 6 R Zahla, T037-733726, F733731. Conveniently located near the station, but expensive for what it is. Street-side rooms overlook the main railway line, rear-side rooms are noisy during the annual summer festival, a palace behind the hotel being a main venue. Prefer the *Balima* or the *Bouregreg* in this price category – or the *Chellah*.

C ***Hotel Balima***, 173 Av Mohammed V, BP 173, across from the station, T037-707755, F707450. Popular café-bar, restaurant, snack bar, salon de thé, nightclub. If you can afford it, the faded grandeur of Rabat's former top hotel is definitely the best option in the *ville nouvelle*. Upper rooms have views over the city. NB Book ahead in Jun/Jul as often full with musicians etc over for festival. **C** ***Hotel Terminus***, 384 Av Mohammed V. T037-700616, F701926. Handy for the main station, as its name suggests, but a bit grim really. Prefer the *Balima* or the *Hotel d'Orsay*. **C** ***Hotel Ennakhil***, 23 bis Av d'Alger, T037-723355, F734268, 2 persons 450dh with breakfast. Clean and quiet, located out towards the diplomatic quarter. **C** ***Hotel Moussafir Ibis***, across from the Agdal station, T037-774919, F774903. Rather a long way from the centre, but convenient if you're on business in the Agdal area. **C** ***Hotel Les Oudayas***, 4 R de Tobrouk, T037-707820, F708235. Nothing special, but quite handy for the station. The *Balima* or the *Royal* better value. **C** ***Hotel Royal***, 1 R Amman, T037-721171, F725491, www.mtds.com/royalhotel Large rooms in this central, rather old-fashioned hotel. Good value for money. But early morning prayer call from mosque wakes you up in park-facing rooms. Partitions wafer thin, needs double glazing to cut out traffic noise. Nice café opposite entrance for breakfast. **C-D** ***Hotel d'Orsay***, 11 Av Moulay Youssef, near station, T037-701319, F708208. Convenient, less interesting than *Balima*. Range of room sizes. Streetside rooms noisy. Jean Genet stayed here.

D ***Grand Hotel***, 19 R Patrice Lumumba, T037-727285, very simple sort of decor, rooms on upper floors quieter. Near the Parc du Triangle de Vue and the *Zerda* restaurant. Very handy for médina – not recommended for women travelling alone. **D** ***Hotel Gauloise***, 1 R Hims, off Av Mohammed V, T037-723022. The entrance and the wooden staircase look promising, but the 59 rooms are tatty. Unpleasant reception. **D** ***Hotel Majestic***, 121 Av Hassan II, T037-722997, F709379, www.majestic.ma, hotel@majestic.ma Cheap and highly recommended. Refitted in 1998, rooms with double-glazing. **D** ***Hotel de la Paix***, 2 R Ghazza, T037-732031. Some rooms no bath, no communal shower. Streetside rooms very noisy – could do with a refit. **D-E** ***Hotel Splendid***, 24 R Ghazza, T037-723283. Fair rooms, pleasant planted courtyard. Handy restaurant opposite. Avoid streetside rooms as noisy due to traffic and overamplified music from cassette shop.

E ***Hotel Central***, 2 R Al Basra, T037-767356, beside the *Balima*. Wellrun hotel, clean double rooms, some with shower, wc on corridor, singles not so good, one of the best cheap options. NB Check whether there is nightclub noise in some rooms. **F** ***Hotel Berlin***, 261 Av Mohammed V, T037-703435. Cheapest in the *ville nouvelle*.

Médina
■ *on map, page 53*

D ***Hotel des Oudaïas***, 132 Blvd el Alou, near the kasbah, T037-732371. Convenient for sightseeing, and well fitted, one of the few respectable hotels in the médina. A bit grotty. Notice at reception says, "In the saloon of the Oudaya Hotel you will be pleased." **E** ***Hotel du Centre***, after you have crossed Av Hassan II into the médina, down an alley on your right, just before *Banque Populaire* and its café, T061-146246 (mob). Rooms open onto a long corridor, go for 14-23 which overlook the alley or 21-22 on the rooftop – others very hot in summer. Reservations not too reliable. Clean. **E** ***Hotel Dorhmi***, 313 Av Mohammed V, just inside the médina on your right, handily located, T037-723898. This is the best of the médina hotels, rooms and reception all on 1st floor up a flight of stairs. Rooms are clean, all face onto a central gallery. Showers extra. Reservations don't always work out. Selection of hotels down Souk Semara, alley on left after *Banque Populaire*, including **F** ***Hotel des Voyageurs***, T037-723720, just behind the market, 7 rooms, each with washbasin, clean, basic, next door to the **F** ***Hotel du Marché***, 22 rooms on 2 floors, doesn't encourage European clients, and **F** ***Hotel d'Alger***. **F** ***Hotel Maghreb al Jedid***, T037-732207, **F** ***Hotel El Alam*** (best of these 3), and **F** ***Hotel Marrakech***, T037-727703 – all 3 on R Sebbahi, right off Av Mohammed V, again very cheap. **F** ***Hotel La Kasbah***, R Sidi Mohammed Ghazi, off Av Mohammed V in the médina, T037-768537. ***Hotel National***, R Ben Rezouk, T037-737671. Rock-bottom prices.

Maisons d'hôte

If not exactly catching up with Marrakech and Fès, Rabat now has a few pleasant guesthouses in the upper price bracket. **L** ***Villa Mandarine***, 19 R Oulad Bousaa, Souissi, T037-752077, F632309, www.villamandarine.com In the upmarket Souissi neighbourhood, close to the Royal Golf Dar Es Salam. More of a small hotel than guesthouse (31 rooms, 5 suites). French and Moroccan food. Gardens and small pool. B&B (suite) 2,500-2,800dh. Half-board on request. Meals 280dh. Credit cards.

A ***Dar al Batoul***, 7 Derb Jirari, Médina, T037-727250, albatoul@iam.net.ma, www.riadbatoul.com Traditional patio house used as guesthouse, 8 rooms, 1 suite. Downstairs rooms used for small seminars. Evening meals available. **A** ***Riad Oudaya***, 46 R Sidi Fateh, Médina, T037-702392, Reservations via France on T/F0033-546413217. Riad is easily located just off the R Sidi Fatah, a parallel to the Av Mohamed V through the médina. Bused for small sem&B 1,300dh (rooms),1,600dh (suites); 2 rooms and 2 suites, meals available, fish a speciality.

Camping

Camping is an inconvenient option in Rabat, the 2 nearest sites being in Temara (see page 102). Sadly, the old site on the beach over the river at Salé is being built on by a local magnate. There are plenty of cheap médina hotels, however, which are probably better value and more secure.

Youth hostel

43 R Misr (Egypte), at Bab el Had, the intersection of Blvd Hassan II and R Misr. Very well located for sights, almost opposite Bab el Had, T037-725769. 60 beds, bed/breakfast 35dh for IYHA members, kitchen, basic and friendly, shower/loos a bit dodgy but improving. Train 1,200 m and bus 150 m.

Eating

● *on maps, pages 82 and 90*

Price codes: see inside front cover

Most higher quality restaurants are located within the *ville nouvelle*. A range of fairly cheap restaurants is to be found throughout the city, but the budget options – small Moroccan canteens and café-restaurants – are located in the médina, along Av Mohammed V, R Souika, R Sidi Fatah and adjacent streets. This is also a good area to wander. There are plenty of *crémeries* doing juices, pâtisseries, snacks and sandwiches to order.

Expensive

Dinarjate, at 6 R Belganoui, in the médina, close to the Kasbah des Oudaïas. T037-704239, 722342. Upscale, traditional Moroccan with Andalucían music. No alcohol – could make more of an effort but is the only 'traditional' restaurant in the old town. Reserve. If in own car, park up on Blvd Bab el Alou. ***L'Entrecôte***, 74 Av Amir Fal Ould Oumeir, Agdal, T037-671108. French cooking. Business clientele, occasional tour groups. Reliable. ***Le Goëland***, 9 R Moulay Ali Chérif, in the diplomatic quarter, T768885. Discrete dining in large room opening onto covered patio, credit cards. ***Le Margot***, 20 Av Ibn Sina, T037-672602. Expensive, excellent reports. Try to reserve. ***Kanoun Grill***, in *Hotel Chellah*, 2 R d'Ifni, T037-701051. Reservations recommended, a big menu of Moroccan food. ***Restaurant de la Plage***, close to the Plage des Oudaïas, Rabat, T037-733148, F738024. Reservations recommended in summer. Around 300dh per head, plus wine. Fish and sea food.

Mid-range Two areas with a good selection of restaurants: immediately behind the *Hotel Balima* and in the neighbourhood uphill on your right, roughly behind the hotels *Orsay* and *Terminus*. ***La Caravelle***, up in the Oudaïas, overlooking the ocean, T037-738844. Splendid location, food fine. Nice for a beer and fish overlooking the Atlantic. Allow 200dh per head for a good feed. Busy at weekends. ***La Clef***, R Hatim, T037-701972, close to the station, off Av Moulay Youssef. Popular upstairs restaurant. Loyal clientele, licensed. ***La Mamma***, 1 R Tanta (ex-Paul Tirard), T037-707329, behind the *Hotel Balima*. Italian food. More cheaply, try the ***Equinoxe*** next door. ***Le Petit Beur***, Dar Tajine, 8 R Damas, T037-731322, again behind the *Hotel Balima*. Traditional decor. Rather formal, dark interior at lunchtimes. Better as an evening place. Under same management as the upmarket *Dinarjate* in the médina. Excellent Moroccan cooking, good *pastilla* at 55dh. ***Café Restaurant Saadi***, 81 bis Av Allal Ben Abdallah, T037-769903. Good Moroccan meals, licensed. ***Le Weimar***, restaurant of the Goethe Institut, 7 R Sanaâ, T037-732650.A good little place for pizzas, salads and chocolate cake, handily located in the neighbourhood behind the *Hotel Terminus* and main PTT. ***Zerda*** (literally 'the banquet'), 7 R Patrice Lumumba, T037-730912. Jewish Moroccan cooking, live music. Recommended for a jolly night out. At the lower end of this price bracket, try ***Le Sisisi***,19 R Moulay Rachid, T037-724378, open from early to 2300, popular with a young crowd (close to the *Grand Hotel*).

Cheap ***Café Anoual***, Av Moulay Abdallah. Good *tagines*, salads and juices, European food also. ***Mona Lisa***, passage Derby, 258 Av Mohammed V. Reasonable *tagines*, Moroccan food, salads. ***Restaurant El Bahia***, Av Hassan II, in the wall near junction with Av Mohammed V. Moroccan food in a courtyard, good value, erratic service. Lots of cheap eateries doing set lunches, *harira* and *brochettes* in the evening near the *Hotel Dorhmi* and the Central Market off Av Hassan II.

Cafés, pâtisseries & cafés-glaciers There are many good cafés, pâtisseries and glaceries on or near Av Mohammed V, including: ***Au Délice – Pâtisserie suisse***, 285 Av Mohammed V, up from the *Balima*, opposite the Parliament. Looks as though it hasn't changed since the late 1950s. Good cake and croissants. ***Café Les Ambassadeurs*** is for reading the papers. Note large portrait of the late king. ***Pâtisserie Gerber***, 258 Av Mohammed V, lovely Moroccan sweet cakes. ***La Comédie***, 269 Av Mohammed V. ***Salon de Thé Lina***, 45 Av Allal Ben Abdallah, near the French consulate. Very French (a smoke-free café with excellent pâtisseries). ***Le Petit Poucet***, on Av Mohammed V. ***Café Maure***, in the Kasbah des Oudaïas, has mint tea and pastries, good views, waiters in traditional dress, a pleasant place to while away the time. Try also stand-up juice bars in the médina. ***La Génoise***, Blvd Oued Akrech, opposite Dar Es Salam school, French cakes at reasonable price.

Bars and clubs

Rabat has little of the nightlife one might expect in a capital city, particularly late at night. The rich kids tend to go over to Casablanca to the clubs on the Corniche, or in the summer season to seasonal places at one of the beach resorts between Rabat and Casablanca or even up to Tanger.

Bars ***Piccadilly Piano Bar***, in *Hotel Hyatt Regency*. Popular for those who can afford it, nightly jazz band on patio by pool. ***Hassan Bar***, in *Hotel de la Tour Hassan*, 22 Av de Chellah. Similarly expensive, with dated charm. ***Hotel Balima***, 173 Av Mohammed V. One of the most popular places to drink a beer or coffee, particularly during the evening promenade. Bit of a gay rendezvous.

Clubs ***Amnesia***, 18 R Monastir, T037-701860, entrance 100dh. City centre club frequented by more affluent Moroccans and Europeans. Doesn't really get going until 0200. ***Hotel***

Balima on Av Mohammed V has a small nightclub (access on street at back of hotel).. *Day and Night*, Av du Chellah, 35dh, again not salubrious. *Fifth avenue*, Av Bin el Ouidane, Agdal, 60dh, music. Bar next door with pool tables. Take a petit taxi to get there – get out at the lively Pl Ibn Yassine. *La Kasbah*, large red house on the right on the coast road out of Rabat, Fri night busy, T037-749116. *Le Puzzle*, 79 Av Ibn Sina, T037-670030, F674144. Chic bar, live music, Agdal quarter – take a petit taxi from city centre. *Le Yucatan*, expensive little bar with a Mexican theme, 7 R Oskofia, T037-720557 (before the flower market on Pl Pietri, when coming from Av Mohammed V). A recent addition to the political capital's night life is *La Pachanga*, a piano bar with jazz in basement, 2 doors up from *Café Hawaii* opposite the main station.

Entertainment

Keep an eye on the newspapers, including *Le Journal*, *La Vie économique*, *L'Economiste* or *Le Matin du Sahara* for cultural events and reviews.

Art galleries

The following all hold occasional exhibitions of varying quality. **Galerie Marsam**, 6 R Oskofiah. **Galerie Moulay Ismaïl**, 11 Av Bin El Ouidane. **Galerie Bab Rouah**, Av de la Victoire. Set in an old city gate, turn right just before Sunna Mosque at top of Av Mohammed V. Also check out the main gate to the Kasbah des Oudaïas where occasional exhibitions are held.

Cinema

The 4 biggest cinemas are easily found, 3 in Av Mohammed V, and 1 at the junction of Av Allal Ben Abdallah and R al Mansour ad-Dahbi which has perhaps the best range of films. Most films are dubbed in French. You could also go to the Dawliz multi-screen complex over the River Bou Regreg, just outside Salé.

Cultural centres

France, Germany and Spain all maintain cultural centres which programme events. **Alliance Franco-Marocaine**, R Benzerte, with instruction in Arabic and French. **British Council**, 36 R de Tanger, T037-760836. **Goethe Institut**, 7 R Sanaa, near the station, T037-706544, F708266. **Institut Français** , 2 R Yanboua, T037-701138. **Instituto Cervantes**, 5 R Madnine, T268121, adrabat@cervantes.org.ma Events are often held at the Theatre Mohamed V – see below.

Theatre & music

Theatre Mohammed V, R Al Kahira (du Caire) puts on a range of plays and concerts.

Festivals

Annual summer ***Arts festival***, with a mix of musical styles, held in **Jun/early Jul**. Book accommodation in advance.

Shopping

Bookshops

American Language Centre, 4 R de Tanger, has a small bookstall, with some books on Morocco in English, including books on crafts and birdlife. ***Le Bouquiniste de Chellah***, 34 Av du Chellah, opposite the Lycée Hassan II, T061-592135 (mob). Owner Abadallah el Ghouari will be able to help you find that elusive title; small stock of antiquarian books on Morocco. ***English Bookshop***, 7 R El Yamama (close to the station). Small, but stocked with a good range of academic titles and some fiction in English. A booklover's bookshop. ***Librairie Kalila Wa Dimna***, 344 Av Mohammed V, T037-723106. Probably the best bookshop in Rabat, run by the people who own the *Carrefour du Livre* bookshop in Maârif, Casablanca. ***Librairie Populaire***, 4 R Ghazza (was 18 Juin), T037-738867. ***Livre Service***, 40-46 Av Allal Ben Abdallah, T037-724495. Good postcards, wide selection of books in French – could be the place to buy one of those Moroccan art photography books. ***Librairie du 6 Novembre***, Av Fall Ould Oumeir.

Maps For hiking maps go to the **Division de la Cartographie**, now a 20dh taxi ride out of the centre at Km 4, Av Hassan II, T037-295548, 295117, which sells official maps (*cartes d'état major*). Most areas of the country, apart from those close to the Algerian border, are available, also some quite recent city maps. Allow a good 2 hrs for the whole operation, including travel time from the city centre.

Markets Local markets are on Thu at Salé, Av du 11 Janvier, Fri at Bouznika, Sat at Temara, Sun at Bouknadel and Skhirat. In Rabat médina the vegetable market is best on Sun, and carpets in R des Consuls on Tue and Thu morning. Agdal Market, off Av des Dadès, to the west of the university is noted for its fruit and vegetables. It is, however, a long way to travel. The Municipal Market, clearly marked off Av Hassan II after the gate into the *mellah*, also has good fruit and vegetables and a selection of fresh aromatic herbs. In the *ville nouvelle* there is an underground vegetable and fruit market at Pl Moulay al Hassan, with excellent flower sellers above ground outside. Supermarkets for easy shopping, ***Makro*** (with items in large quantities) and ***Marjane***, both on the road to the airport. Note that there is a huge new *Marjane* out in the plush Souissi residential area. Both *Marjane* supermarkets stock alcohol, as does a small shop behind the Balima, on your right as you go downhill.

Moroccan craftwork Use the ***Centre Artisanal (Coopartim)*** in Tarik al Marsa to get an idea of the range, then bargain in the small boutiques in the médina, on or just off Av Mohammed V, R Souika, ***Souk es Sebbat*** and R des Consuls. There are many larger shops, in the *ville nouvelle*, on Av Mohammed V, or in the malls just off, where the high prices may be negotiable.

Newspapers & magazines There are places on Av Mohammed V stocking a full range of English language, French and international press. The best is perhaps inside the main railway station.

Sports clothing & equipment ***Delta***, Av Al Amir Moulay Abdallah, supplies for golf too. ***Filo***, 105 Av Hassan II. ***Suchart***, 4 R Mamounia for riding equipment.

Sport and activities

Clubs Rabat has little public provision for sport. Locals who want to play tennis or swim in a pool tend to join one of the following clubs. ***Club des Cheminots***, Agdal, T037-770048. ***Club El Wifak***, Route de Zaërs, T037-754539. ***Olympique Marocain***, 2 R Ibn Khaldoun, T037-771872, 7 courts. ***Riad Club***, R Abdelaziz Boutaleb, Agdal, T037-722776, 6 courts. ***Stade Marocain***, Av Haroun Rachid, T037-771903, 7 courts.

Golf ***Royal Golf Dar Es Salam***, 12 km from Rabat on R de Zaërs, T037-755864, F757671, www.royalgolfdaresalam.com.ma The most famous course in Morocco, with 45 holes, fees approximately 500dh per day. For information, check also **Moroccan Royal Federation of Golf**, 2 R Moulay Slimane, T037-755960.

Horse riding & polo ***Royal Polo Equestrian Club***, at *Royal Golf Dar Es Salam*, R de Zaërs, T037-754692. ***Club Equestre Al Foursane***, at Aïn el Aouda, some 27 km south of Rabat, closed Sun. ***Club Equestre Yquem***, T037-749197, on the coast road 20 km south of Rabat, just across Oued Yquem, offers riding on the sands.

Jogging There are tracks through the eucalyptus woods behind the *Hotel Hilton*, courses of 800 m, 1,500 m and 3,000 m.

Swimming

Nothing in the way of swimming pools for the occasional visitor – although you could try the *Hotel Hilton*. The main beach in Rabat is the one below the kasbah, which is popular but none too clean. Lots of surfies here in the winter. Look out for the jet-ski set, too. The beach at Salé is similar, and both have dangerous currents from the river. You really need to go further afield, to the Plage des Nations (see page 104, Temara or Skhirat (see page 112).

Tennis

Hotel Hilton, Aviation Souissi.

Walking & climbing

Information from ***Club Alpin Français Rabat***, T037-673364, activ@cafmaroc.co.ma

Watersports

Yacht Club de Rabat, Quai de la Tour Hassan, T037-720254. ***Fath Union Sport***, Port de Rabat, T037-733679. ***Olympique Marocain***, Quai Léon Petit, T037-725123. Information from Yachting Federation, Av Ibn Yassine Bellevue, Agdal, BP332, T037-771782.

Tour operators

Afric Voyages, 28 bis Av Allal Ben Abdallah, T037-709646. ***First International Tours***, 32 Av Ben Khattab, T037-775060. ***Gharb Voyages***, 289 Av Mohammed V, T037-767311. ***La Royale***, Immeuble Montfavet, Pl Mohammed V, T037-707031. ***North Africa Tours***, Residence El Minzah, R Kadira, T037-769747, F762298. ***Rainbow Travel***, 1 R Derna, Pl Piétri, T037-762563. ***Safir Voyages***, *Hotel Safir*, Pl Sidi Makhlouf, T037-731093. ***TAK Voyages***, 1 bis Av Ibn Sina, Agdal, T037-771684. ***Wagons-Lit Tourisme***, 1 Av Amir Moulay Abdallah, T037-709625. ***Welcome Voyages***, 29 Av d'Alger, T037-702871, F702873.

Transport

Local

Road **Bus**: buses run all over the city, many originating from Av Hassan II, near **Bab el Had**, or just past Parc du Triangle de Vue. Nos 6 and 12 go to **Salé**, 17 to **Temara**, 1, 2 and 4 for the **Chellah**, get off at **Bab des Zaër**. The main bus terminal for all buses, T037-795124, is at Pl Zerktouni, 3 km from the centre, to the west of the city in the direction of Casablanca. Catch a petit taxi there, or a No 30 bus from Av Hassan II. ***CTM*** and other companies. Buses to **Casablanca**, 10 a day (1½ hrs), **Tanger**, 2 a day (5 hrs), **Meknès** 3 a day (4 hrs), **Fès** 6 a day (5½ hrs).

Petit taxi: in Rabat they are blue and some of the best in Morocco, nearly always metered, and often shared. They can be picked up anywhere, most easily at the stand on Av Hassan II, close to the junction with Av Mohammed V. Alternatively, T037-720518. Sample fare from Av Mohammed V to Hassan Tower, 8dh. A Rabat petit taxi cannot take you to Salé, which has its own taxis – take a grand taxi instead.

Grands taxis: shared between 6 passengers, these run from the stand on Av Hassan II, just past the Parc du Triangle de Vue, for local locations such as **Temara**, **Skhirat**, **Salé** and **Bouknadel**, and from the bus station for long-distance locations.

Long distance

Air Buses to Airport Mohammed V used to run from in front of *Hotel Terminus*, Av Mohammed V. The service may be resumed, journey time 90 mins. To get to the Mohammed V airport by train, take the train from Rabat to Casa-Port or Casa-Voyageurs, where you will need to change. There are 11 daily between 0512 and 1900. For Rabat-Salé airport, T037-727393, follow the P1 Salé-Meknès road. Daily direct flights to **Paris** and **Casablanca**, 1 a week to **Tetouan** (Fri).

Airline offices: *Royal Air Maroc*, 2 agencies in downtown Rabat. ***Agence A*** is almost opposite the train station on Av Mohammed V, T037-709766, F708076, central

Rabat, key phone numbers

Rabat-Salé Airport T037-808090/89
RAM (Royal Air Maroc) Call Centre T090-000800
ONCF (trains) Rabat and region T037-736060
CTM (bus) T037-795124
Gare routière Bettana T037-795124
Budget car T037-705789
Hertz T037-769257
Avis T037-767959

reservations on T037- 709710. ***Agence B***, 9 R Abou Faris al Marini, T037-709700, up the hill opposite the station. ***Air France*** is further down, after the *Hotel Balima*, T037-707728. There is no ***British Airways*** office in Rabat, contact their main office in Casablanca on T02- 229464 (reservations) or T02-339524 (flight information). ***Iberia***, 104 Av Mohammed V.

Rail Rabat Ville station, T037-767353, Av Mohammed V, departures – **Casablanca**: Regular services between 0437 and 2337. **Marrakech**: 8 daily between 0437 and 2337. **El Jadida**: 1957, **Oued Zem**: 0815, 1527, 1930. **Meknès and Fès**: 9 daily between 0752 and 2349. **Taza and Oujda**: 1047, 1522, 2141, 2349. **Tanger**: 0748, 1327, 1656 and 0155. **Rabat Agdal** station, T037-772385, R Abderrahman El Ghafiki, departures – **Casablanca, Marrakech, El Jadida** and **Oued Zem**: as above, 4-6 mins later, Meknès, Fès, Oujda and Tanger: as above 6-8 mins earlier.

Road Car hire: ***Avis***, 7 R Abou Faris el Marini, T037-767503, also at Rabat-Salé Airport. ***Budget***, Rabat-Ville Railway Station, T037-767689. ***Citer***, *Residence el Minzah*, R el Kahira, T037-722731. ***Hertz***, 467 Av Mohammed V, T037-709227, also at Rabat-Salé Airport. ***Holiday Car***, 1 bis Av Ibn Sina, T037-771684. ***Inter Rent-Europcar***, 25 bis R Patrice Lumumba. ***La Royale***, Immeuble Montfavet, Pl Mohammed V, T037-763031. ***Sixt***, *Hotel Hilton*, Rabat, T675656.

Directory

Banks ***BMCI*** ATM just as you turn left out of Rabat main rail station, on the corner. Further ATMs at ***Wafa Bank***, where Av Mohammed V meets Av Hassan II. ***ABM***, 19 Av Allal Ben Abdallah, T037-724907. ***Banque Marocaine de Commerce Exterieur (BMCE)***, 241 Av Mohammed V, T037-721798. The best for change (cash, TCs and Visa/Mastercard) for which it has a separate door (open 0800-2000 weekdays, 1000-1200 and 1600-2000 weekends). ***BMAO***, Av Allal Ben Abdallah, T037-769980. ***Crédit du Maroc***, Av Allal Ben Abdallah, T037-721961 (ATM). ***Wafa Bank***, Av Mohammed V, T037-721181/82 (ATM).

Communications **Internet**: ***ACDIM***, 44 R Abou Derr, Agdal, T673600, 671998. ***Cyberinfo***, 68 Av Fal Ould Oumeir, Agdal, Rabat, T683712. ***Cyberplanete***, 23 Av d'Alger, appt 1, Tour Hassan (10-mins walk from main station). ***Glacier-Web***, 1 bis R Maârif, Aviation, T652980. Try also upstairs at the ***Librairie Livre Service***, on Av Allal Ben Abdallah, almost opposite *Crédit du Maroc*. **Central Post Office**: ***PTT Centrale***, Av Mohammed V, 0800-1200, 1400-1830. R al Mansour ad-Dahbi, just off Av Mohammed V, opposite the post office has a permanent facility for telephoning and collecting letters. Check with staff that previous call is cleared before using cabin. Otherwise there are plenty of téléboutiques around the city centre.

Embassies & consulates **Algeria**, 46-48 R Tarik Ibn Ziad, T037-765474. **Austria**, 2 R Tiddas, T037-764003. **Belgium**, 6 Av de Marrakech, T037-76474. **Canada**, 13 bis R Jaafar Assadik, Agdal, T037-672880. **Denmark**, 4 R de Khemisset, T037-767986. **Egypt**, 31 Av d'Alger, T037-731833. **France**, 3 R Sahnoun, T037-777822. **Germany**, 7 R Madnine, T037-765474. **Israel**, Av Beni Znassen, T037-657680/1. **Italy**, 2 R Idriss El Azhar, T037-766598. **Japan**, 70 Av Al Ouman al Mouttahida, T037-674163. **Mauritania**, 6 R Thami Lamdour, off Av John Kennedy, T037-770912, 756817. **Netherlands**, 40 R de Tunis, T037-733512/3. **Portugal**, 5 R Thami

Lamdouar, T037-756446. **Saudi Arabia**, 43 Pl de l'Unité Africaine, T037-730171. **Senegal**, R Cadi Ben Hammadi Senhadji, T037-754171. **Spain**, 3 R Madnine, T037-768988. **Sudan**, 9 R de Tedders, T037-761368. **Sweden**, 159 Av John Kennedy, T037-759313. **Switzerland**, Sq Berkane, T037-706974. **Tunisia**, 6 Av de Fès, T037-730576. **UAE**, 11 Blvd Al Alaouiyine, T037-730976. **UK** (also used by **Australia**, **Ireland** and **New Zealand**), 17 Blvd de la Tour, Hassan, T037-731403. USA, 2 Av de Marrakech, T037-762265.

Libraries & research centres

Centre Jacques Berque (CESHS) - Centre d'études en sciences humaines et sociales, 35 Av Tarak Ibn Ziad, T037-769691/92, F769685, cjb@iam.net.ma, www.ambafrance-ma.org/cjb Well-run small French research centre providing a focus for academics working on contemporary Morocco. **British Council**, 36 R Tanger, BP427, T037-700836. Free entry, reference books, novels, some books on Morocco, magazines and newspapers, TV news, small café. **Centre national de documentation**, Av Ma El Ainain. Open to academic researchers. **La Source**, 26 Av Chellah, Mon-Fri 1430-1830, research library on all things Moroccan. **Centre for Cross-Cultural Learning**, Av Bab el Alou, derb el Jirari, 11 impasse el Hassani, Médina, T202365/66, F202367, www.cccl-ma.com Despite the grand title, this small centre has a good name for putting together educational courses.

Medical services

Ambulance: T15. **Chemists**: ***Pharmacie du Chellah***, Pl de Melilla, T037-724723, and another on R Moulay Slimane. ***Pharmacie de la Préfecture***, Av Moulay Slimane opposite town hall. If not open, look in any chemist's door for details or T037-726150 for the name of the night chemist. **Hospital: Hôpital Avicenne**, Av Ibn Sina, T037-773194/774411. **SOS Médecins**: Rabat and Salé, T037-202020. Emergency private medical service.

Useful addresses

Archaeological Institute (Institute National des Sciences de l'Archéologie et du Patrimonie), Bab Zaër, Av President Kennedy, PO Box 503, Souissi, Rabat. **Garages** *Concorde*, 6 Av Allal Ben Abdallah. *Garage Citroen* (SIMA), at the junction of R de Congo and R de Senegal. **UNICEF** in Agdal at junction of R Oum-Errabi and R Oued Baht. **Emergency numbers** **Fire**, T15. **Police**, R Soekarno, behind the *PTT Centrale*, T19.

Salé سلا

Phone code: 037
Colour map 1, grid B1

Historic Salé, on the north bank of the Bou Regreg Estuary, was once a rival to Rabat in the days of piracy and Andalucían Muslims fleeing the expanding power of Catholic Spain. Today it takes second place to Rabat, although its population, close on 600,000, seems set to grow with the creation of Salé El Jedida new town. The médina of Salé has a fine medersa *and a striking early Merinid gate, the Bab Mrisa. For those with enough time, Salé is worth a visit.*

Ins & outs

See Transport, page 102, for further details

Salé is most easily reached from Rabat by grand taxi (from the grand taxi rank just past the Parc du Triangle de Vue, on Av Hassan II). Travellers coming in from the north may want to get off at Salé railway station. In practice, however, given the small size of the médina at Salé, and the limited accommodation, most people prefer to make it a half-day trip from Rabat, perhaps combining it with a look at the craft centre at Oulja.

Background

Salé, Sala or Sla in Arabic, derives from the Roman *Sala Colonia*. Salé was founded in the 11th century, and its Great Mosque dates from 1163-1184. The town was embellished and fortified by the Merinids in the 13th century, becoming an important commercial centre. Great rivalry, even armed conflict, has existed between Rabat and Salé, although they were united in the

Republic of the Bou Regreg. Up until the 17th century Salé had enjoyed long periods as the more important of the two cities, being known for religious learning and piety. In the 20th century Rabat outstripped Salé, the latter gradually turning into a dormitory settlement for the former. New businesses and light industries, however, are gradually springing up on the road north out of Salé. While Rabat is known as the city of gardens, Salé is perhaps the city of sanctuaries. The 14th-century Medersa Abul El Hassan is well worth visiting.

Sights

As elsewhere, early 20th-century French planners at Salé preserved the historic city walls and left a wide space between the médina and land for new building. The visitor arriving by grand taxi will get out by the gardens adjacent to the Bab Mrisa gate, one of the most unusual city gates in Morocco.

Bab Mrisa Bab Mrisa, or 'Gate of the Little Harbour', was originally the sea gate of the médina, as there was once a channel running to it from the River Bou Regreg. The gate is wide, and its 11-m high horseshoe arch would have allowed the sailing boats of the day to pass within the walls for repairs. Since medieval times, the access canal has silted up. Although Bab Mrisa was built by the Merinid Sultan Abu Yusuf in the 1260s, in style it is closer to the Almohad gates – the triangular space between the arch and the frame is covered with floral decoration centred on the palmette, with the use of the *darj w ktaf* motif down the sides. Originally it had a porch. Alongside the tower there are two tall defensive towers. It may be possible to get access to the top of the gate. A

caretaker may be found by a small door on the left, inside the gate, which gives access to a small garden leading to a round tower. From this tower walk back along the top of the rampart to the gate. There is another similar sea gate, the next gate around the wall to the left.

Abul Hassan Medersa

This *medersa*, or religious school, is the most important building to visit in Salé, being the only *medersa* in the region. It was built by the Merinid Sultan Abul Hassan, the Black Sultan, and was completed in 1342. To reach it follow the city walls around to the left from Bab Mrisa to a small square at **Bab Bou Hajar**, alongside a park. Just beyond this there is an area where cars should be parked. Take the small lane off to the far right at the end of this area. Take the first left, then the first right. Some 200 m later, just after the lane passes under a house, turn left. ■ *0800-1200, 1430-1800.*

The particularly large **Grand Mosque** in front was built by the Almohad Sultan Abu Yusuf Yacoub in the late 12th century, although the minaret and door are both modern. Just beyond the mosque is the tomb of Salé's patron saint, Sidi Abdallah Ben Hassoun. The *medersa* is to the left of the mosque.

Before you pass through the beautiful Merinid doorway, note the intricate decorations below a green-tiled roof resting on cedar lintels. The *medersa* is quite small, with a courtyard surrounded by a gallery, its columns decorated with *zellige* mosaic tiling. The walls above the columns are decorated with geometric and floral motifs, while the ceilings of the ground floor have panelled wood in geometric patterns. Both the wood carving of the prayer hall ceiling and the stucco have been restored, but much of the decoration is original, and in good condition. To reach the upper floors, return to the entrance and climb the stairs. These are the students' cells, which seem tiny and ill-lit, but give an insight into the nature of *medersa* life. From the roof is a view of Salé, and beyond it, Rabat.

Abul Hassan Medersa

From Medersa du Maroc, Charles Terrasse, 1927

1 Vestibule
2 Columns decorated with tilework
3 Marble pool
4 Heart shaped corner column
5 Prayer hall
6 Mihrab
7 Stairs up to students' cells & roof

The médina

Salé médina is small and easy to explore. Walking in any direction you are likely to arrive at the souks, the **Grand Mosque** and **Abul Hassan Medersa**, or the city walls. The **Mausoleum of Sidi Ben Ashir at-Tabib** is located close to the western wall of the cemetery that lies between the médina and the sea. This 14th-century Muslim saint was famous for curing people, and the sick still visit his tomb for its curative powers. This is a very striking building, quite tall, brilliant white in contrast to the blue sky and the background of ochre of the city walls. Adjacent, in the walls, cannon still point defensively out to sea.

Foundouk al Askour

The Foundouk al Askour is worth seeing for its portal. From **Bab Bou Hajar** follow Rue Bab al-Khabbaz, and take the fourth lane on the left past

Medersa – place of education for Islam

"Learning is a city, one of whose gates is memory, the other is comprehension" – an Arab saying.

The medersa *in North Africa is a college of higher education in which Islamic teachings lead the syllabus. The institution originated in Persia and developed in the Islamic West in the 13th century. The construction of places of advanced learning was a response by orthodox Sunni Islam to the growth of Shi'ite colleges, but they soon became important centres in their own right as bastions of orthodox Islamic beliefs. Subjects other than theology were taught at the* medersa, *but only in a limited form and in ways that made them adjuncts to Sunni teachings and acceptable to a very conservative religious hierarchy. Unfortunately, therefore, the* medersa *became associated with a rather uninspired and traditional academic routine in which enquiry and new concepts were often excluded. Knowledge and its transmission sadly fell into the hands of the least academic members of the theological establishment. The poor standards of science, politics, arts and ethics associated with the Arab world in the period since the 13th century is put down to the lack of innovation and experiment in the* medersa, *a situation which has only very recently begun to break down in Sunni Islam. It can, however, be argued that formal Islam needed firm basic teachings in the face of rapidly expanding popular Islam and its extravagant Sufi beliefs.*

The shortcomings of the medresa *in creative teaching terms was in part compensated for by the development of the buildings themselves. They were mainly modelled on the Medersa Bou Inania at Fès (page), founded under Sultan Abu Inan (1348-1358), itself based on designs from Syria. The main courtyard* sahn *is surrounded by cloisters/galleries separated from the* sahn *by ornate screens of wood. The mosque is to the east and the long* qibla *wall has a deeply set* mihrab *(see plan,). The Merinids founded seven* medersas *in Fès during the 14th century.*

Entry is restricted for non-Muslims, though at the Medersa of Bou Inania at Fès (page) visitors are allowed into the mosaic paved courtyard even if not to the mosque, and when the repairs are completed the roof terrace of the Atterin Medersa (see page 261) will once again allow views of Fès. Meknès has its own Bou

the park, which is obstructed by three concrete posts. This leads to a textile souk. After 120 m the souk passes under an arch. On the right is the *foundouk*. It was originally built in about 1350 as a *medersa* by Abu Inan, son of Abul Hassan. It was later a merchants' hostel. The door is surrounded by a partially restored *zellige* mosaic of the *darj w ktaf* pattern. Above this is a panel of *zellige* with the traditional eight-pointed star motif, and above that a row of nine niches carved into a plaster panel. Inside there is a courtyard with two storeys of arcades.

Souks In this area there are some interesting souks, which are perhaps more traditional than those of Rabat, and worth exploring. The textile market is **Souk el-Merzouk**, while **Souk el-Ghezel** is the wool market. There are stonemasons and carpenters in Rue Kechachine, and blacksmiths and brassworkers in Rue Haddadine. The Souk el-Merzouk is noted for its jewellery and embroidery. The médina of Salé is also noted for a procession of multicoloured candles, or thick poles bearing various representations, which occurs every year on the afternoon before the Prophet's birthday, Mouloud an-Nabi. This proceeds through the town, culminating at the **Tomb of Sidi Abdallah Ben Hassoun**. He is the patron saint of Salé and this is the most venerable of the sanctuaries in the city. It is also the most picturesque, with a most

Inania Medersa (see page 232) and the Medinid Abul Hassan Medersa in Salé should be noted too.

"Let your eyelids enjoy my splendid beauty – you will find a marvellous virtue to chase away cares and sadness", reads one of the many carved inscriptions in the 16th-century Ben Youssef Medersa in Marrakech (see page 327), which is the largest medersa *in North Africa and considered one of the finest. Originally a Merinid foundation but remodelled in the 16th century, it has an arcaded courtyard with intricate mosaic work, lace-like carved stucco weathered to a faint rose coloured patina and finely worked cedar beams.*

Nicolas Clinard, a French humanist, left an account of his time studying in Fès in the 16th century. Writing about the religious scholars he says: "The faqirs do not show off their wealth even if they are rich, and they do not consider it dishonourable to walk in the streets unaccompanied by servants, just like our Parisian doctors with a breviary under the arm and mud on their shoes".

Clinard also tells us about the teaching methods in use: on learning the Koran, he writes that the young students "impress into their memory a book they do not understand". The basis of the different subjects – Arabic language, the Koran, law, astronomy and mathematics – were treatises written in verse or rhymed prose, which facilitated the task of committing them to memory. Ibn Malik's Alfia *(treatise in a thousand verses) was the essential grammar book. The emphasis on memorizing texts in a society without masses of printed material bore fruit later on in the educational process. Debate was enriched as all could readily refer to a common body of material, and literary discussions were common. With his basic studies completed, the student might return to his home town – or continue the quest for learning in a* medersa *elsewhere. However, the student seeking material wealth would go for legal studies: detailed knowledge of the law according to the Malekite rite was a precondition for a successful public career.*

Moroccan medersa*, were, until quite recently, used for student accommodation and even for teaching, but the traditional life has now disappeared and the* medersa*, remain as intriguing monuments to an educational past where religious belief and education were tightly linked.*

curious dome and an exterior gallery decorated with polychrome tiles. The seafaring past of the city is particularly visible in this event, with the men in pirate costumes.

Essentials

Sleeping & eating

Very few travellers stay in Salé, as there are few hotels, and the city is easily accessible from Rabat. It's also rather a sleepy sort of place, with little streetlife of an evening. **B** ***Hotel Le Dawliz***, T037-883277, F883279, handy for those travelling in own vehicle as located near Bou Regreg river on Rabat road. Pool, cinema complex nearby. **E** ***Hotel des Saadiens***, T037-783645, by the bus station. ***Camping de la Plage***, T037-782368. By the river and the sea, with toilets, showers, pool, shop, laundry, electricity for caravans, petrol 300 m just 100 m from beach and on a plot of nearly 4 ha. There are a number of small and cheap café-restaurants just inside both main gates, and along R Kechachin.

Shopping

The artisans of Salé are as talented as their neighbours and quality goods are available in the médina. Look at the pottery (some is very distinctive), tooled leatherware, iron-ware (though this is difficult to transport home), carpets (perhaps not the best place to buy these), fine embroidery, drapery and, for the beach, rush matting.

Pottery Easily accessible by petit taxi from Salé (say 10dh) is the *Complexe artisanal d'Oulja*, some 3 km from the town. There is a central exhibition space with café and small restaurant. A series of craft potters, basket makers and blacksmiths are based in purpose-built workshops with adjoining exhibition space. Although many of the items on sale (apart from the pottery) are a little bulky and heavy to take home by plane, the Oulja centre does give a good idea of the range of products available. The high quality basket work is particularly good value. The *zellige* work table tops are also very reasonable in price – but extremely heavy. To get back to Rabat from Oulja, there are buses running from the nearby crossroads.

Transport

Rabat petit taxis are not allowed to cross the river

To get to Salé take a **bus** No 6 or 12 from Av Hassan II in Rabat, a **grand taxi** from the stop on the same street, or walk down to the quay below the kasbah and take a rowing **boat** across the river, from where you can walk up to **Bab Bou Hajar**. Once in Salé it should be possible to explore most of the centre on foot, if not, the city has its own **petit taxis**. If you have your own transport, go along Tarik al Marsa, Av Hassan II or Blvd du Bou Regreg and cross the bridge below the **Hassan Tower**. It is possible to walk this route in 30 mins.

Easy excursions from Rabat and Salé

Mamora Forest To the northeast of Rabat, the Marmora Forest is a peaceful area of cork and eucalyptus trees, and a possibility for a picnic. Around half the cork oaks of Morocco are found here. The eucalyptus is also harvested for commercial purposes and there are plantations of pine and acacia. More unusual is the Mamora wild pear, a tall tree, growing up to 15 m, which has white flowers in spring. There are *dayats* (shallow lakes) in the region and in wetter years these attract the white stork. The spotted flycatcher is a summer visitor, as is the magnificent blue roller. The turtle dove, visiting from the South, is declining in numbers as human hunting continues. Indeed, the whole area is under human pressure, as the neighbouring settlements expand and people use the forest as a source of charcoal and a place for grazing their livestock. Bissected in part by the main north-south autoroute, the forest can also be accessed off the Meknès road. Turn off left at Sidi Allal Bahroui. Return via the P2 and P29.

Jardins Exotiques About 15 km north of Rabat, at **Bouknadel** on the P2, and the No 28 bus route, these 4 ha of garden were the work of French horticulturalist and Moroccophile, M François, in the 1950s. Originally, there were over 1,500 species and varieties of plants from all over the world, laid out in a network of pools, bridges and summerhouses. There was a Japanese garden with bamboo bridges and flat-stone paths, a section of Brazilian rainforest, and an area of plants from Polynesia. Unfortunately, the Moroccan pavilion is in ruins, the Middle Atlas apes look miserable in their minute cages, and the general tendency is towards Barbary jungle. Children with a taste for adventure could have a whale of a time exploring, however, with appropriate supervision. There are some fine palm trees and flowering datura. Things horticultural apart, the Jardins Exotiques seem to function as a minor Garden of Eden where local couples discourse in the shade, safely out of the way of prying family. ■ *0900-1830. 5dh, children 3dh.*

Plage des Nations The Plage des Nations at Sidi Bouknadel, about 25 km northeast of Rabat, is very popular with the affluent, and more a family beach than those of Rabat-Salé, but the currents can be dangerous. Take bus No 28 from Salé, and walk 1 km from the turning, or in summer share a grand taxi from Salé. The C *Hotel Firdaous*, T037-780407, has a bar, restaurant, pool, open to all comers for a small charge.

Dar Beghazi

The Dar Beghazi is another sight close to Rabat accessible for those with their own vehicle. Situated opposite the turn-off to the Plage des Nations, on the P2 road northward from Salé, this home has been turned into a private museum to house the Beghazi family's collection of carpets, weapons and jewellery. Access is expensive, but there is a lot to see, including a rather splendid coach. ■ *Mon-Sat. 40dh for main rooms, 100dh for whole collection. T037-822178.*

Bou Regreg Dam

Cross the Oued Bou Regreg to Salé and take the P1 eastward towards Fès and Meknès. After 18 km turn southwards on the S204 to Arbaa Sehoul for 7 km. You eventually come to the access to the lake and some popular picnic areas.

Kénitra

Phone code: 037
Colour map 1, grid B2

Kénitra is an industrial and military centre of importance within Morocco. It was a small military fort until 1913 when the French built a new town, as well as an artificial harbour used as a military port and to export citrus fruit and other products from the rich agricultural areas of the surrounding Gharb region. The port was developed to replace Larache, in the Spanish zone, and Tanger, in the International Zone. In 1933, Kénitra was renamed **Port Lyautey** by the French, after the first Resident-General of the Moroccan Protectorate. US troops landed here in November 1942 as part of Operation Torch, and experienced heavy casualties under fire from the port at Mehdiya. In 1947 the US returned to establish an important naval base, which they used until 1977. After independence, Port Lyautey was renamed Kénitra and it remains important as a military centre and port. It lies on the P2 from Rabat to Tanger. For the first-time visitor to Morocco, the attraction of Kénitra (beyond some early 20th-century architecture) could be as a base for excursions to the nearby Roman site of Thamusida and Mehdiya, with its fine kasbah, on the coast.

Sleeping & eating

B *Hotel Safir*, Pl Administrative, T037-371921. Good but unexciting, part of an established chain, with restaurant, bar, and pool. Avoid rooms overlooking service station. **C** *Hotel Mamora*, Av Hassan II, T037-371775, F371446. Good restaurant, bar and pool. Clean. **D** *Hotel La Rotonde*, 60 Av Mohammed Diouri, T037-371401. Extremely noisy. Not for single women. Restaurant and bar. **E** *Hotel de la Poste*, Av Mohammed Diouri, perhaps the best of the cheap hotels. Showers in most rooms. Try also **F** *Hotel de France*, Av Mohammed V, where there are other cheap hotels. There is no shortage of restaurants on Av Hassan II and Av Mohammed V. *Hotel Mamora* and *Hotel La Rotonde* are recommended as places to eat and drink. There is even a *McDonalds* right in the town centre on the ground floor of the *Hotel Europe*.

Transport

Road: the *CTM* **bus** station is on Blvd Mohammed V. Bus No 9 for **Mehdiya**, share taxis easier. **Train**: from the railway station, south of town centre, T363736, trains leave regularly to **Asilah**, **Tanger**, **Meknès**, **Fès**, **Oujda** and **Marrakech**, and there are almost hourly services to **Rabat** and **Casablanca** between 0400 and 2309.

Directory

Airline offices *Royal Air Maroc*, 435 Blvd Mohammed V, T037-376234, F371184. **Banks** *BMCE*, corner of Av Hassan II and Blvd Mohammed V, has ATM. **Communications** **Post office**: Blvd Mohammed V.

Mehdiya

Phone code: 037
Colour map 1, grid B2

Mehdiya (also spelt Mehdia and Mahdia) Plage is Kénitra's one-horse beach resort, noted for windsurfing but more interesting to visit for its kasbah (some way from the town's seafront) and the nearby nature reserve around Lac de Sidi Bourhaba. Mehdiya is 11 km from Kénitra, with plentiful grands taxis and there is a bus service up the P2 from Rabat to Kénitra. Bus 9 from Kénitra has its terminus just opposite the kasbah entrance.

If you are driving up from Rabat, turn left off the P2 for Mehdiya Plage as you head north at a complicated junction (police presence) with the *Café Bustan* and petrol. The road winds over heathland to drop down to Mehdiya Plage, (lots of new villas). For the kasbah, head through the town. You'll note a crumbling flight of steps up to the kasbah on your right (east). Parking may be awkward. Otherwise, follow the road round and up the hillside (estuary on your left), turn right (new housing area on your right), eucalyptus wood on your left. The entrance gate to the kasbah soon comes into view.

History Historians think that a Carthaginian trading post was established here in the sixth century BC. Around the 10th century, the site was occupied by the Berbers. Naval shipyards were established here by the Almohads. By the 16th century, a small and active commercial port visited by European merchants, Al Mamora, had grown up close to the site of present day Mehdiya. The Portuguese, then expanding along the African coast after taking Ceuta in the 15th century, became interested in the area, and thus it was that King Manuel of Portugal sent out an expeditionary force which took the little town in June 1515, renaming it São João da Mamora. The Portuguese were quickly defeated, however, and the little port became a lair for pirate adventurers. By the early 17th century, along with Salé and Algiers, it was one of the leading pirate ports in North Africa, and a source of irritation to the European trading nations. Like Salé (Sila in Arabic), home of a band of renegades known as the Sallee Rovers, it functioned as a sort of autonomous republic. For a while Mamora was ruled by the English adventurer Henry Mainwaring, who later continued his career in the Royal Navy before becoming a member of the English parliament (1620-23). And it was also at Mamora that another adventurer, Saint Mandrier, was captured by Moroccan forces; this enterprising Frenchman was later to become technical adviser to the sultan on fortifications and cannon foundries.

The pirate republics of Morocco harmed European trade with the Indies. In 1614, Spanish forces took Mamora, and on a hillside overlooking the river a new fortress was constructed, named San Miguel de Ultramar, the basis of most of the kasbah still surviving today. In May 1681, this fortress in turn fell to the advancing armies of the Alaouite Sultan Moulay Ismaïl. The victory marked the end of the Spanish presidios: Larache and Tangiers were subsequently evacuated.

The newly taken fort was renamed El Mehdiya, 'the citadel delivered'. (Henceforth the name Mamora was to be used for the vast cork oak forests to the northeast of Salé.) Moulay Ismaïl installed a garrison, strengthened the walls and began work on a new port at the mouth of the River Sebou, ultimately abandoned in the late 18th century.

Under the French, the fortress was occupied by the military, and it was the scene of clashes between US and French forces during the American Expeditionary Force landings of November 1942.

Sights Uninhabited apart from a few cows, the **Kasbah of Mehdiya** is definitely worth a visit on a second or third trip to Morocco. If you have your own transport, it is very easy to get to. There is no entrance fee, although there may be a man sitting at the gate who should be given a small tip. Within the walls, the small mosque with its whitewashed minaret is still used by local people. The smaller of the two entrance gates, **Bab el Aïn**, is of Spanish origin, while the other gate, the grander **Bab Jedid** (New Gate), flanked by two massive rectangular towers, was erected by Moulay Ismaïl. From the roof terraces there is a magnificent panorama of the river and ocean to the northwest, and over to the **Sidi Bourhaba** lagoon, a protected area, to the south. The northwest bastion, or **Borj Bab el Aïn**, is well preserved with seven cannons still in place. Below, next to the estuary, is a labyrinth of extensive storerooms, well protected by a sea wall.

The most important building, however, is the governor's house, the **Dar el Makhzen**, which with its great mosaic patio must have been an extremely fine residence in its day with extensive outbuildings – close to the main entrance are the remains of a hammam and a merchants' hostel or *foundouk*. A flight of brick steps leads up to dusty weedgrown terraces. Today, however, the bustle of traders and soldiers in the fortress overlooking the Sebou belongs very much to the past: goats graze on the weeds growing out of the paving, fig trees sprout from the walls, and there is no foreign army to menace the great bastions and moats. Despite the neglect, the cobbling and some other features indicate that this kasbah was restored and used under the French. Birdwatchers will find finches flitting between the crab-apple and tamarisk bushes.

The southern section of the **Lac de Sidi Bourhaba** and adjacent marshes are the focus of the nature reserve, popular for birdwatching, and in the summer, for picnicking. The *koubba* has a festival in August. Approaching from Mehdiya the road (S212) runs along the lagoon.

The northern section of the lake is a pleasant area for picnicking, either by the water's edge which tends to be marshy or better in the surrounding woodlands. Overwintering waterbirds are the main interest (literally thousands of ducks) and/or an April visit for spring migrants. African marsh owls are frequently reported. There is a keeper's residence on the east side.

Sleeping & eating

D ***Hotel Atlantique***, T037-388116. 21 rooms, nothing particularly special, but has a popular nightclub. Much frequented by holidaymakers and locals in season. **F** ***Auberge de la Forêt*** and ***Camping Mehdia***. Open in the summer with pool, restaurant and shop, site of 15 ha, distance to beach 100 m, bar, snacks, showers, laundry, first aid, electricity for caravans, petrol at 20 km, situated north of the town adjacent to Oued Sebou. There are cafés near the beach. Try the ***Restaurant-Café Dauphine*** for fish.

Ancient Thamusida

Colour map 1, grid B2

Though not really a priority visit, the remains of the ancient Roman town of Thamusida can make an interesting excursion from Kénitra feasible if you have your own car or a lot of time. Ideally, you would have a car and try to cover Thamusida along with Mehdiya, the Roman site at Banasa and the stone circle at Mzoura in a long day trip.

Ins & outs

Getting there The remains are located in open agricultural land near **Sidi Ali Ben Ahmed** on the left bank of the Oued Sebou 18 km from the *oued* mouth, just off the P2 some 10 km north of Kénitra. At the major roundabout north of Kénitra, take the turn-off signposted Tanger 222 km, Tetouan 249 km. After passing under a railway bridge, follow through northwards. The turn-off left is easily missed: look out for a pink café, some 25 m before a small *Total* petrol station and a mosque. Turn left at the café, and a sandy track will take you past small houses and market gardens to a sort of crossroads (go straight on, not left for another small mosque). Crossing the fields, eventually you approach the riverbank where the track follows round to the left. Markers to look out for are the distinctive white dome or *koubba* of Sidi Ali Ben Ahmed, a stand of trees and, on the river, the boatmen. In the far distance, the hill of the Mehdiya kasbah is just visible. Note that access in wet weather is problematic in a small hire car. If coming down the P2 from the north, you should look out for the roadside houses of the village of Ouled Slama. On the right of the road, you should see the cream-painted administrative building of the Commune rurale Ouled Slama. The *Total* garage and pink café are about 100 m further on.

Thamusida was built in an excellent position, protected from flooding (being on a flattish hillock about 12 m above sea level) but accessible from the sea by good-size boats making use of the tidal flow. The site of Roman Thamusida had been settled on and off since prehistoric times. Its first recorded mention is by Ptolemy. The Roman garrison was established here under the Flavians and monuments have been found dating from that period. So far discovered are the remains of a temple with three shrines beside the *oued*, the baths and some dwellings; one named the House of the Stone Floor. This Maison du Dallage to the east of the complex has the traditional open central courtyard with the *triclinium* (dining room) at the eastern end. The baths, close to the *oued*, have been altered and extended a number of times, finally covering an area of around 3,000 sq m – the ground plan showing a division into separate sections for men and women. Some evidence also points to the existence of fish-salting works for the production of *garum*, an iron works and shops.

The large camp to the southwest of the site was constructed by order of Marcus Aurelius. It measures 166 m by 139 m and is considered to have been large enough to house a substantial military presence. The walls of the fort had four gates, one more or less central in each wall, and 14 towers which project inwards. In the centre is the praetorium, a rectangular porticoed courtyard 45 m by 30 m with rooms on three sides. In the southwest side one of the

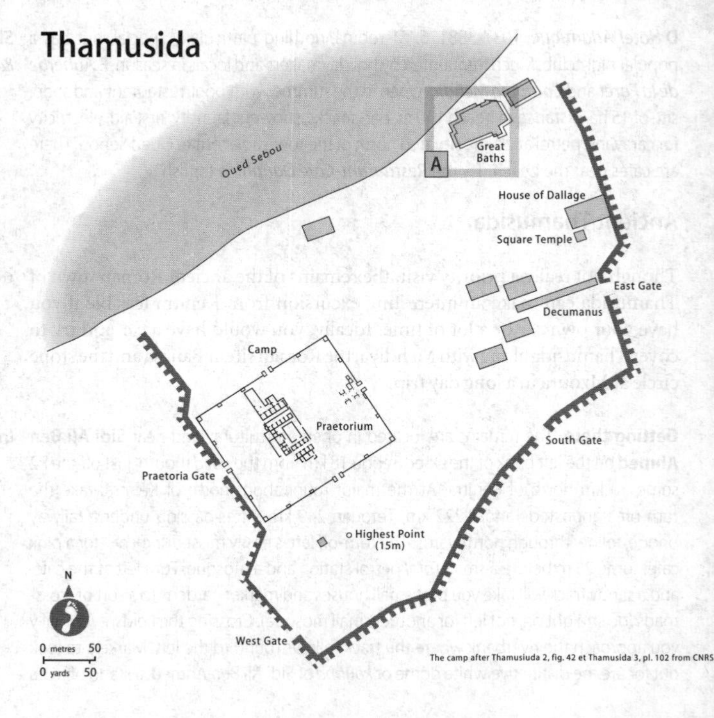

The camp after Thamusiuda 2, fig. 42 et Thamusida 3, pl. 102 from CNRS

rooms, built on a podium and reached by four steps, is larger. On the northwest side of the praetorium, projecting into the main courtyard, are the remains of a hall constructed in the time of Septimus Severus.

A wall with a number of entrance gates encloses the town on the three land sides, the fourth side being protected by the *oued*. At intervals along the wall are semicircular towers which project outwards.

Excavations began in the early 1930s. On the basis of the finds, the settlement can be assumed to have been prosperous and quite active well into the third century AD. However, it is thought that the whole area was abandoned quite suddenly between 274 and 280 AD. Excavation continues sporadically and Thamusida remains a sleepy place, the croaking of frogs and drone of irrigation pumps occasionally disturbed by flights out of the Kénitra airbase.

Souk el Arba du Gharb

Souk el Arba du Gharb (Rharb), the 'Wednesday souk in the West', is an important market town. It is the focal point for the rich agricultural region of the Gharb which extends as far north as Larache, and as far south as Kénitra. Once important for cereal production, the region later became a centre for citrus and vegetable production. It is from Souk el Arba du Gharb that you will turn westwards for Moulay Bousselham on the coast. If you wish to stay there is **E** *Hotel Gharb*, Route de Rabat-Tanger, T037-902203, with a restaurant and bar; also a number of basic hotels and restaurants, but little else. ■ *Getting there: there are regular trains to Tanger, Meknès, Fès, Oujda, Rabat, Casablanca and to Marrakech, as well as regular buses and grands taxis to Ouezzane and Moulay Bousselham.*

Moulay Bousselham

Phone code: 037
Colour map 1, grid A2

The small beach resort of Moulay Bousselham is a relaxed summery place, increasingly popular with Fassis and others who have built second homes there. There is a fine stretch of coast, with rough swimming conditions. Moulay Bousselham is best known for its lagoon, however, **Merdja Zerga** ('the blue lagoon'), an important wintering site for migrating birds. Moulay Bousselham also had regional renown for its *moussem*, or festival, although this has not been held in recent years.

Ins & outs

Although easily reached from Souk el Arba du Gharb, only 44 km along the S216, Moulay Bousselham is bypassed by most tourists. The village is located just off the northern autoroute, midway between Rabat and Tanger. It is 130 km from Rabat, an easy 1 hr 20 mins drive. A grand taxi from nearby Souk el Arba du Gharb takes 25 mins. Buses from Souk el Arba can take much longer, depending on the number of stops.

Background

Moulay Bousselham, 'the man of the cape', is named after a 10th-century saint and mystic, who supposedly came from Egypt and converted the Atlantic Ocean to Islam. He is commemorated in a nearby *koubba*. The memory of Moulay Bousselham was commemorated in a *moussem*, in July. The beach is spectacular but dangerous for swimming, although not bad for fishing. You will probably want to stay in Moulay Bousselham for the birdlife, however. If you have a car, you could take in the nearish Roman sites of Banasa, near Souk Tlata du Gharb, and Thamusida, near Kénitra, on the way south to Rabat.

The lagoon & birdlife

The lagoon, Merdja Zerga, is one of Morocco's largest lagoons, covering over 30 sq km. This and the surrounding wetlands are a designated reserve offering protection for migrating and overwintering waterbirds.

By car it is possible to approach the reserve from the south. Proceed from Souk El Arba du Gharb and after 34 km turn left on the 2301. After crossing the Nador Channel (Canal de Daoura) turn sharp right and park in the village, Daoura Oulad Mesbah. Access to the reserve from Moulay Bousselham is across the Oued Drade which flows to the south of the village. Arrange a lift or hire a rowing boat. Bargain firmly. Arrange for a return trip with the fisherman who ferries you across. The track down the west side of the lagoon goes through Daoura Roissia and to the minor coast road, but provides ample opportunity for peaceful observation. It is estimated that half of the ducks and small waders wintering in Morocco north of latitude 30°N are found here. It will be impossible to miss the greater flamingos and spoonbills and the familiar wigeon, mallard, shoveler, shelduck and teal. Sighting a slender-billed curlew is less likely.

Sleeping **C** *Villa Nora*, T037-432017. Guesthouse run by Alan Gabriel and his sister Jean Oliver who can provide you with information on the region's birdlife. **D** *Hotel Le Lagon*, T037-902603. With restaurant, bar, nightclub and pool. Attractive location overlooking the lagoon. Definitely past its prime – serves mainly as the local drinking hole in a rather dry area. May be revamped in near future. **D** *La Maison des Oiseaux*, down on your left as you approach the village, a very pleasant auberge-type place with garden run by Franco-Moroccan couple, Gentiane and Karim. Accommodation to suit families and school groups (bring own sleeping bags). Excursions onto the lagoon (200dh per day) to see the birds. Reservations with Gentiane Edmundson in Rabat, T037-673903, ring before 0900 or on weekday evenings. Highly recommended.

Camping *Camping Moulay Bousselham*, a rather basic sort of place, with many mosquitoes in summer. Site of 15 ha, with bar, snacks, restaurant, grocery shop, pool, showers, laundry, electricity for caravans, petrol at 100 m. Eat at ***L'Ocean*** or ***La Jeunesse***, or at one of the restaurants down by the lagoon, where the fishermen's rowing boats are pulled up on the beach.

Ancient Banasa

Colour map 1, grid B2

If you need to prioritize, Banasa is the most important (in terms of visible ruins) of the ancient sites reached from the Rabat-Tanger P2 road. Like Thamusida, it is located south of the Oued Sebou, probably bridged here in ancient times. Unlike Thamusida, access is by metalled road. Banasa is awkward to get to without own transport.

Ins & outs **Getting there** Travelling north from Rabat on the P2, you need to turn right at a minor junction south of Souk Tlata du Gharb ('Tuesday Souk in the Gharb'): look out for some abandoned farm buildings just before the turn and an avenue of eucalyptus trees on the main road. Big road signs near the turn (showing Rabat 100 km and Tagner 173 km) are parallel to the P2 and so are not easily visible. After the turn, follow the narrow road to the bridge, follow over. Here the road is being widened and follows the river to your left. At a T-junction, go left and after about 2 km you will find a rusty sign telling you to turn off left for Banasa. The track runs across the fields and the site is easily located by a mosque and the domed shrine of Sidi Ali Boujnoun.

Excavation at Banasa was not easy as remains were buried beneath many layers of alluvium deposited by the flooding *oued*. The earliest settlement recorded here was third century BC, but the main colony was founded at the end of the first century BC by Caesar Augustus. Remains include traces of houses (some indicating wealthy owners), five baths and shops. A wealth of pottery, mosaics and inscriptions has also been discovered. Banasa pottery was of a distinctive style. The alignment of the streets on a northeast-southwest grid can be seen, with a forum marking the centre of the town. Unfortunately, most of the better building material was removed and 'recycled'. The discovery here of a number of bronze inscriptions, legal texts, military diplomas and decrees of patronage, some of which are now visible in the Rabat Archaeological Museum, make this an important site.

A few mosaics were found on the site. They include an ornamental design with the head of the ocean in the centre from one of the excavated baths; one containing fighting cocks and a bag of money; and a number with marine scenes. In one of the baths, traces of painted stucco and a very faint mural in a niche can just about be distinguished

Arbaoua

Arbaoua is signed to the west of the P2, and with its shade trees is a popular stopping place for Moroccan families making the journey back from Europe by car. NB mosquitoes can be a nuisance. The old frontier post between the Spanish and French zones of protectoral Morocco is at Kedhadhra, marked by a fine reinforced concrete building and lots of stalls selling pottery and wicker furniture. North of here the first major town is Ksar el Kebir.

Sleeping **E** *Hotel Route de France*, T039-902668. Bath, mid-range meals. A lunch stop. There is a 4-ha campsite with showers, laundry, electricity for caravans.

Ksar el Kebir (formerly Alcazarquivir)

Kasar el Kebir means the 'Great Fortress' and probably stands on site of the Roman colony *Oppidum Novum*, 'new town'. Off the main P2 road, it is only a must if you have an interest in neo-Moorish Spanish colonial architecture.

The exact location of the Roman town is uncertain. Two funerary inscriptions were found here, one in Greek and one in Latin. In its favour, Ksar el Kebir is close to other ancient settlements, and if the Romans had wanted a strongpoint to guard a crossing of the Oued Loukkos, where better than here? An 11th-century settlement here was expanded and fortified by Yacoub al Mansour in the late 12th century.

But Ksar el Kebir's chief claim to fame is that it lies near the site of a great battle. Nearby, in 1578, the famous Battle of the Three Kings was fought, where King Sebastian of Portugal, Saâdian Sultan Abd al-Malek, and a claimant to the throne, former Sultan El Mutawakkil, all died. The flower of Portuguese chivalry was wiped out, leading to the end of Portugal as an independent nation for some 100 years. Moulay Ismaïl destroyed much of the town in the 17th century.

The Spanish occupied Ksar el Kebir in 1911, rebuilding it and calling it Alcazarquivir, and developing it as a military centre. There are a number of Spanish buildings in various stages of decay. Particularly fine is the Alhambra-style decoration of the former officers' mess, now housing local Ministry of Education offices. The women who work there may allow you to have a look in. In the same area, there is a flag factory with weavers using handlooms to make red cloth for flags for official buildings. The regional market is held on Sunday outside the station. There is also a much transformed **Grand Mosque** (an Almohad foundation) near to a Merinid *medersa*.

Sleeping **E** *Hotel Ksar Alyamama*, 8 Av Hassan II, T039-907960. Fine if you need to stop over. **F** *Café-Hotel Andaluz*, as basic as they come really.

Transport There are 6 trains a day from **Tanger**, 4 a day from **Fès, Meknès** and **Oujda**, 4 a day from **Rabat** and **Casablanca**, and 2 a day up from **Marrakech**.

South of Rabat

Zaër Forest
Colour map 1, grid B1

The region to the south of Rabat, inland from the bustle of the coast roads, is known as the Zaër Forest, with valleys, the Karifla Gorges and rolling hills clothed with cork oak, juniper and acacia. It is basically impossible to explore this area without a car. A possible circuit leaves Rabat on the P22, follows the side of the *oued* and passes through the small village of **Aïn el Aouda** at Km 28. Turn right after a further 11 km towards **Merchouch**, almost immediately crossing the Oued Karifla. At Merchouch turn west along the S106 and across the **Karifla gorges**, to the ancient rest site of **Sidi Bettache** on the old road from Rabat to Marrakech. Enjoy a steep descent and ascent on this winding route. Take time to admire the views. The S208 leads north to **Sidi Yahia des Zaër** and on to **Temara**. There are numerous small tracks into the forest and down to the streams.

One of the best times to do this tour is the spring: if the winter has been rainy, the *dayats* will have water, and there will be abundant wild flowers. There are numerous larks, warblers and shrikes in the open fields. The road between Sidi Bettache and Sidi Yahia des Zaër is reported to offer the best chance of sighting a double-spurred francolin. The valleys too have their bird populations, in particular the magnificent bee-eaters with their cliffside nests.

A second route into this area leaves from **Ben Slimane**, a market town on the edge of the Zaër forest. There are some interesting tracks through this area, suitable for cars. The route recommended in the forest leaves Ben Slimane on the S106 going east. Ignore the turn right to El Gara and after 15 km take the next right into the forest. After 16 km turn left to **Bir el Kelb** and **El Khatouat**. This is a climb up the side of Jbel Khatouat (830 m). At El Khatouat turn west. Subsequently, either the first turn right after 12 km or the second turn right after a further 10 km will take you back to Ben Slimane. The first is slower but more scenic.

Temara
14 km from Rabat, off the P36

The town and the ruins of a kasbah, built by Moulay Ismaïl, can be reached on Bus 17 from Avenue Hassan II in Rabat. The beach is 4 km to the west. It is a popular destination as the beach is long, sandy and clean.

Temara Zoo, the former royal menagerie, has a small collection of animals and birds. Crowded at weekends. ■ *1000 to sunset*.

Sleeping C *Hotel St Germain en Laye*, T037-744230. An upmarket option. **C** *Hotel La Felouque*, T037-744388, F744065. 23 rooms, restaurant, bar, tennis. Crowded at weekends. **C** *Hotel Panorama des Sables*, T037-744289. Terrace overlooking the beach.

Campsites *Camping de Temara*, the first from Rabat on the coastal road. *Camping la Palmeraie*, T037-749251. A 3-ha site, 100 m to beach, bar, snacks, restaurant, groceries, showers, laundry, petrol 600 m, electricity for caravans. *Camping Gambusias*, 100 m from beach, bar/restaurant, showers. *Camping Rose-Marie* at Ech Chiahna, south of Temara Plage, 100 m from beach, restaurant, showers, laundry, electricity for caravans.

Skhirat

Skhirat has little of interest except a Sunday souk. The palace near the beach was the scene of a bloody but unsuccessful coup attempt in July 1971. Skhirat beach is upmarket, as are the restaurants and hotels nearby. Skhirat is 31 km from Rabat and is clearly signposted off the P36, P1 and RP36. There are infrequent trains from Rabat-Ville each day (check station for times), taking 17 minutes.

Sleeping and eating C *La Kasbah*, Rose-Marie Plage (north of Skhirat), T037-749133, F749116. 42 rooms, pool, tennis, restaurant, bar, parking. **C** *La Potinière*, T037-742204, an auberge-type place, with French management, open Jul-Aug only.

Casablanca and the central Atlantic coast

116 **Casablanca**
116 Ins and outs
117 Background
121 Sights

127 **Essentials**
127 Sleeping
129 Eating
130 Bars and clubs
131 Entertainment
131 Shopping
131 Sport and activities
132 Tour operators
132 Transport
133 Directory

134 Mohammedia (ex-Fedala)

136 Routes from Casablanca

138 Azemmour

140 **El Jadida (ex-Mazagan)**
140 Ins and outs
140 Background
142 Sights
143 Excursions
144 Essentials

146 Oualidia

148 **Safi**
148 Ins and outs
149 Background
150 Sights
154 Essentials
156 Routes from Safi

157 **Essaouira**
157 Ins and outs
158 Background
158 Sights
161 Essentials

Introducing Casablanca and the central Atlantic coast

Sprawling, dynamic **Casablanca** may well be your first contact with Morocco. A city of more than four million people, it is

Morocco's economic capital. Although lacking the exotic charms of the imperial cities and the far south, as a modern metropolis with a Franco-Arab feel it has a certain appeal. The city's Neo-Moorish and Art Deco architecture will appeal to architecture buffs in particular. North of Casablanca, **Mohammedia** is a pleasant side trip along the coast, while southwards lie the old Portuguese coastal bastions of **El Jadida** and **Azemmour**, an easy day trip away, as is the Kasbah of **Boulaouane**. More distant are gentle **Oualidia** (its lagoons a must for birdwatchers) and a rougher, working town, phosphate-processing and pottery-producing **Safi**. And where Atlantic Morocco meets the South, as yet untouched by mass tourism, is remote **Essaouira**, with its ramparts overlooking the Atlantic and a vast, windswept beach.

Things to do on the central Atlantic coast

- Take an architectural walk around **Casablanca's** central neighbourhoods. Look out for gems of neo-Moorish, art deco and functionalist building in the central neighbourhoods, gawp at the gigantesque Mosquée Hassan II, Africa's biggest, right on the ocean-front.
- Explore the great Portuguese citadel of **El Jadida**, then visit the shrine of Moulay Bouchaïeb in nearby **Azemmour**.
- Visit the crumbling 17th-century kasbah at **Boulaouane**.
- Out of season, eat oysters and swim at **Oualidia**.
- Explore the potters' quarter at **Safi**.
- Spend a peaceful few days at **Essaouira**. Enjoy surf-sports, riding, walking on the beach, contemplating works by the local school of art naïf, eating at the fish market, hanging out as one of the neo-Beat generation.

Casablanca الدار البيضاء

Phone code: 022
Colour map 2, grid A4

In the 1930s, only two French achievements are said to have surprised the Americans: the First World War ('la Grande Guerre') and Casablanca. A boom town, nicknamed 'the African Marseilles', 'Casa' for short, it was a city where you could drive around at 130 kph and where the streets were filled with luxurious cars. The city grew from a small trading port at the end of the 19th century into one of Africa's biggest cities. With a centre planned by Henri Prost in the early 20th century, Casablanca, with its wide avenues, elegant buildings and huge port, was held to be the finest achievement of French colonial urbanism. It has remained the economic capital of independent Morocco, the centre for trade and industry, finance and the stock exchange.

Ins and outs

Getting there

See Transport, page 132, for further details

Should you be arriving late in the evening, bear in mind that it may be difficult to find a reasonably priced restaurant open in the city centre

You may well fly into Casablanca. In which case, from the airport, you will either take a grand taxi (200dh, set rate) to the city centre (where most of the hotels are) or the shuttle train (25dh) to either Casa-Port station (the terminus, again close to the central area where the hotels are) or to Casa-Voyageurs, where there are connections onward for all the other main cities. Casa-Port station is also 10-mins' walk from the main *CTM* bus station, just off Av des FAR behind the *Hotel Sheraton*. From there a coach departs for destinations across the country. Note that there are car hire agencies, ATMs (not always working) and banks at the airport – but no hotel. Arriving by train at Casa-Voyageurs station, you will find that the taxi drivers do not want to take individual clients. Rather, they want to take several people going the same way, thereby maximising their income. From Casa-Voyageurs to the city centre should not cost more than 15-20dh, depending on the traffic.

Getting around

Casablanca is a big place. The central area, with most of the interesting architecture, between the médina/Casa-Port station and the Parc de la Ligue Arabe, is just about small enough to do on foot. Other sites which you may want to visit – the Corniche with its restaurants and beach clubs at Aïn Diab, the Hassan II Mosque or the Quartier des Habous, a sort of garden city for Muslim notables – are short trips from the centre in one of Casablanca's red taxis (10-20dh for the trip). Have change ready. There are numerous public and private bus lines, but if you're on a short trip, maximize time by taking taxis.

24 hours in the city

The day starts with a stroll around the **central neighbourhood** near the market on the Avenue Mohammed V and the Rue du Prince Moulay Abdallah. Next, take a petit taxi over to the **Quartier des Habous**, a perfectly planned 1920s neighbourhood built for the notables of Fes to get them to settle in Casablanca. Plenty of souvenir places here – and have a look at the the Tribunal du Pacha, too. Take another petit taxi over to the **Grande Mosquée Hassan II**, right on the Atlantic shore, the westernmost mosque of the Islamic lands. (Visiting times are fairly regular, generally 1030, 1130 in the mornings). Next stop is the Restaurant du Port de peche, actually inside the port compound, for a long lunch. Follow this with a quick siesta. Then back to touring the city, taking a petit taxi out to Maârif to visit the **Villa des Arts**, (contemporary Moroccan art and exhibitions). Finally, in the early evening, those who like the crowds might want to explore the **médina** or the area round the **Parc de la Ligue arabe**. Evening activities could include a trip to a **hammam**, perhaps the Bain Zaiani, or one of the hammams near Boulevard Zerktouni and the Mosquée el Badr. Casablanca has plenty of good restaurants: try Taverne du Dauphin in the town centre or the expensive A ma Bretagne out beyond Ain Diab. Casa nightlife centres on the Corniche, where there are bars and clubs to suite most tastes: La Notte (jeunesse dorée), the Villa Fandango (for the discrete and well-heeled), Le Village (quite trendy, a bit gay). There are plenty of low-life cabaret bars in the centre near the Avenue Mohamed V, too. Finally, in the small hours, you could head over to the abattoirs for barbecue and unfocused conversation with the other night-owls.

Tourist information

Office du Tourisme, 55 R Omar Slaoui, T022-271177, F225929. **Syndicat d'Initiative**, 98 Av Mohammed V, T022-221524. The latter is perhaps the more helpful of the two.

Background

Bold Phoenician pilots founded a trading post close to the present site of Casablanca during the seventh century BC. The discovery of a Roman galley indicates use if not settlement of the area in the first century BC. The silver coins found on this vessel are on show at the Banque National du Maroc in Rabat. In the seventh century AD the Berber tribe, the Barghawata, held this area. It was conquered by the Almohads in 1188, and developed by Sultan Abd el-Moumen as a port. In the 14th century the Portuguese established a settlement here on the site of the village of Anfa, but when it became a pirates' base in 1468, they destroyed it, repeating this act in 1515. The Portuguese re-established themselves in the late 16th century, and stayed until 1755, when an earthquake destroyed the settlement. The town was resurrected in the mid-18th century for strategic reasons, under Sultan Mohammed Ben Abdallah. There are various stories about how the town acquired its name ('the white house', El Dar el Baydha in Arabic). One version says that it was named after the Caïd's house, a large white building visible from a distance. Mohammed Ben Abdallah built walls, military installations and a customs house. There was neither palace nor monuments, and no urban bourgeoisie at first.

French colonization

In the 19th century, European traders settled at Casablanca, and at the beginning of the 20th century the French obtained permission from Sultan Abd al-Aziz to construct an artificial harbour. This was the beginning of Casablanca's rapid expansion. The French occupied Casablanca in 1907 (and the rest of Morocco in 1912). Adventurers of all kinds were attracted to the city, which had a Wild West feel to it. This first wave of French immigration greatly displeased the aristocratic French resident-general, Lyautey, who wrote that "The citizens were Frenchmen who had built, beside the Moroccan city, a town to their own liking, but of the same disorderly, speculative and soulless nature as the American boom towns."

The town grew quickly: in 1907, the population was 20,000, including 5,000 Jews and 1,000 Europeans; in 1912, the population was 59,000, of which there were 20,000 Europeans and 9,000 Jews. Morocco's first factory was founded in 1908 in Casablanca, the first labour union was founded in 1910, and the first modern banks came with the Protectorate. Land speculation was rampant, with both Muslims and Europeans involved.

Lyautey was highly suspicious of the European inhabitants of this boom town on the coast of 'traditional' Morocco. (When he decided that Rabat should be the capital in 1913, there were street protests in Casa.) However, it became imperative to do something for the city: in 1913, an observer described it as "an ocean of hovels, a sort of unstructured suburb to an as yet unbuilt metropolis".

Planning the new city

In 1915 the French resident-general, Lyautey, and his chief architect, Henri Prost, began work on planning the new city centre, creating a grid of wide

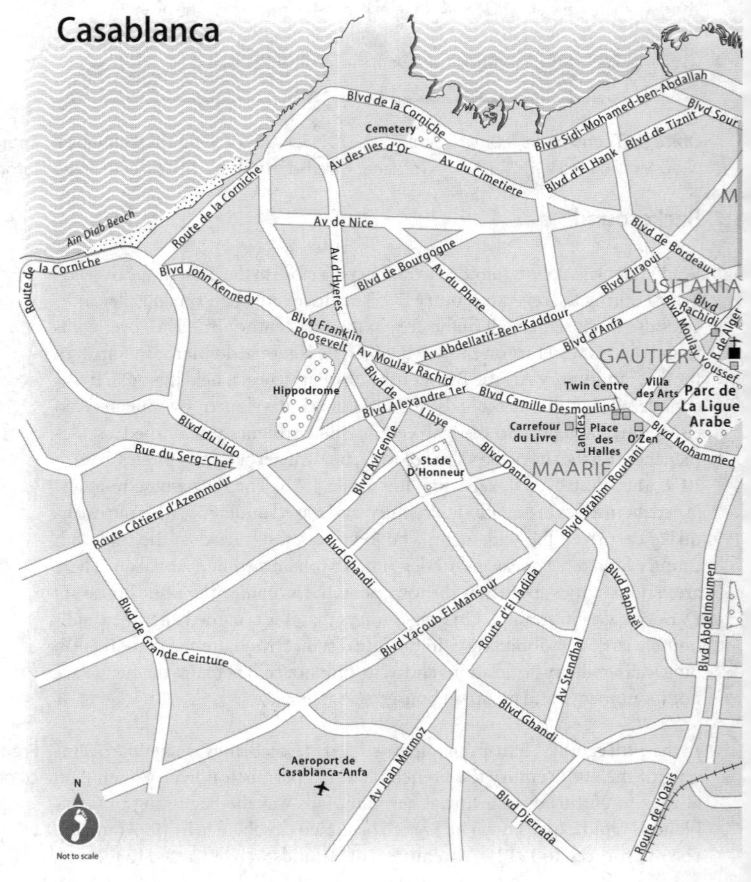

Detail maps
A Casablanca centre, page 124
B Casablanca Médina, page 123

boulevards, lined with fine stucco office and apartment buildings. Key state buildings (as in Rabat) were styled with detailing derived from Moroccan traditional architecture, a style known as *Arabiasance.*

One of the first acts of the new city administration was to create a 4 km ring boulevard, considered far too wide at the time. But the city was to grow far more rapidly than anyone predicted.

Prost certainly had no easy task, given the settler interests at stake. His plan covered an area of 1,000 ha. With a proposed density of 150 people per hectare, the city was designed for 150,000 people – which led to accusations of megalomania. Industrial areas were situated north and east of the centre, on rocky ground, while residential areas, on more fertile soil, were to the west and southwest. Between the two, Prost laid out a centre focusing on two large public squares, the Place de France, centre for commercial activity, and the Place Lyautey, site of the main administrative buildings. The walls of the médina were in part demolished. The Avenue du 4ème Zouaves, today's Avenue Houphouêt Boigny, led down to the railway station and the port. A fan-shaped system of roads and ring boulevards structured the new city – and it is a tribute to Prost's planning that the traffic runs as smoothly as it does today.

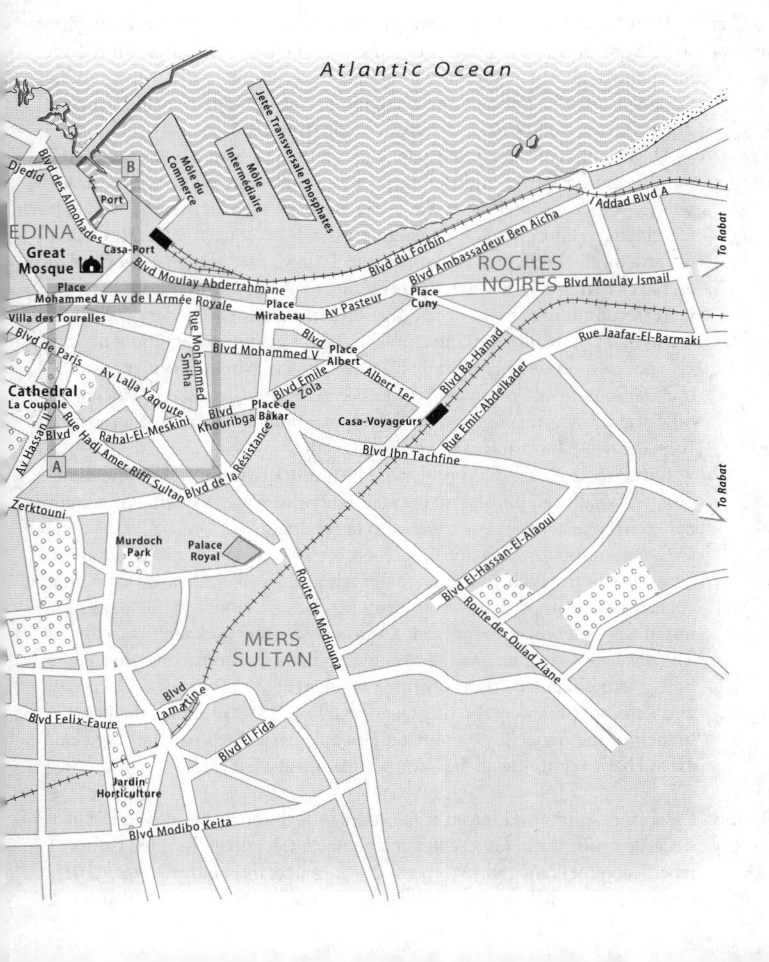

Unfortunately, the new metropolis was to lack the green spaces characteristic of Rabat and Marrakech. A sports ground was left behind the Parc Lyautey (today's Parc de la Ligue Arabe), and there is the Parc Murdoch up beside the Royal Palace. But after Prost's departure in 1923, settler pressure swallowed up green space, and also led to the abolition of height restrictions.

In terms of physical planning, colonial Casablanca was a relatively successful city – even though Prost's zoning was not always respected, and the suburbs subsequently sprawled far beyond the core, with vast planned projects and unplanned *bidonvilles* (the original *bidonville* or tin can city was in Casablanca). The Second World War saw Casablanca with a population of 700,000. Between 1921 and 1951 the number of inhabitants grew by 85 – due to an exodus from the Moroccan countryside and arrivals fleeing the wars of Europe. With rising unrest in the expanding slums, it was essential to improve housing conditions. Planner Ecochard and the Atbat-Afrique team developed the concept of culturally adapted housing for the masses, i.e. inward looking, multi-storey patio houses for the poor Muslim communities. However, as André Adam, chronicler of Casablanca's development, put it, "in her hanging patio, today's woman is like a bird in a cage".

After the war In 1950, Casablanca was an exciting place to be, drawing in capital fleeing the socialist government in France, and where the focus of debates was Moroccan independence. A new building boom produced some modest skyscrapers. Casablanca-based trade unions were important in the nationalist struggle, notably in the riots of 1952 and insurrection from 1953-55.

The city has continued to expand, and in the 1980s and 1990s acquired a number of new architectural landmarks: new préfecture buildings, the headquarters of TV channel 2M at Aïn Sebaâ, the dark, angular mass of the Office Chérifien des Phosphates, the gigantic Hassan II Mosque, right on the Atlantic, and on the Boulevard Zerktouni, the Twin Center, designed by Catalan architect Richard Bofill, dwarfing the Maârif neighbourhood. Despite the increased amount of building speculation at the expense of older property, it seems that Casablanca's architectural heritage is gaining recognition: the city is to have a museum, financed by the ONA, in a villa in the Gautier area, the once famous *Hotel Transatlantique* has been restored, and there is increased official awareness that the city's architecture is potentially a draw for tourists. (Can the neo-Moorish *Hotel Lincoln* be saved?)

But Casablanca also has problems. The mix of ocean-humid air and diesel pollution makes an unpleasant cocktail. There are huge disparities of wealth between the wealthy villa quarters of Anfa Supérieur and Aïn Diab and extensive areas of substandard housing. There are still numerous *bidonville* areas. Some, like Beni Msick, have seen major rehousing projects, others form little enclaves of tin-roofed poverty – around the lighthouse at El Hank, for instance, or on odd strips of land next to railway lines and derelict factories. The distances are often great, and although there are numerous private bus lines, there is neither a tramway nor a regional light rail network. Electricity and water supplies were recently taken on by a private company, the *Lydec*, a branch of the *Société Lyonnaise des Eaux*. Time will tell whether they can extend basic services to all the city's population at a fair price.

Upstart city Casablanca, grimy and frayed at the edges though it may be, also has a glitzy side. Alongside the imperial cities, it is an upstart. Its streets bear the names of rebel heroes, of French and Moroccan cities – and of trees and artists. If Rabat is a home-loving civil servant, and Fès an austere imam, then Casablanca is a golden boy, often stressed-out but always on the move. Casablanca has a go-getting air which builds glamorous careers for some – and leaves many in the gutter. The old Lusitanian port, destination for camel and mule trains coming up from plains and mountains far inland, is a very long way away. Casablanca is a place where an anonymity impossible in the traditional city can be found, where identities can sometimes break free of the old constraints. Although not the most attractive or hospitable of places to visitors, it is definitely the place where Morocco's future is made. Casablanca, stylish child of French colonial capitalism, has grown up. The vast city, made a household name by a Hollywood film, watches the world on satellite TV. Morocco watchers observe its potentially turbulent suburbs and listen to the gossip in its villas and cafés to follow how things in the wider country are going. Unlike Cairo and San Francisco, Lisbon and Istanbul, it has yet to find a novelist to describe its multiple lives. However, the names of its neighbourhoods – Mers Sultan and Plateau, Oasis, Le Polo and Californie, Roches Noires, Aïn Diab (Spring of the Wolf) and Sidi Beliout (Lord of the Lion) are certainly evocative enough.

And, finally, before moving onto the sights of the Great White City, it is probably worth noting that no part of the Warner Bros 1942 production *Casablanca* was filmed in Morocco.

Sights

With drought frequently hitting small farmers, Casablanca is a place of dreams for the rural poor, for whom the city was a magnet right from the beginning. And it also attracted the great families of the imperial cities as they settled into modern business. Casablanca, where the towering Twin Center sits a few minutes' walk away from slum housing, is a place where extreme poverty and wealth coexist. It has a *Bonfire of the Vanities* air to it – and feels like the place where contemporary Morocco's history, as well as money, is being made. But beware, Casablanca is a tough place, polluted and sometimes tense. Visitors in need of a restful holiday should head straight away for Essaouira or Oualidia.

You may want to devote a day or two to Casablanca, however, if you're on a two-week trip. With half a day, you could see something of the city centre and the Hassan II Mosque or the Quartier des Habous. With a full day, you could take in all of these easily, taking a look round Maârif in the late afternoon, and a stroll along the Corniche in the evening. Day trips to El Jadida, Azemmour (south) and Mohammedia (north) are very easy from Casablanca – which is also easily visited by train as a day trip from Rabat.

When visiting Casablanca, you may note changes in street names. The older French names in the central area are still in use. On new plaques, the French *rue* is written in Latin letters as *zanka*, while *avenue* is *chari*.

The médina – & a few saints

The **médina**, site of the old city, is a ramshackle quarter, dating primarily from the 19th century (the fortifications are 18th century). In 1907, the médina covered some 60 ha. There were three main sections: a bourgeois area with consuls, merchants, government officials and Europeans; a *mellah* or Jewish neighbourhood – atypically not walled off; and the *tnaker*, housing rural migrants. (The term *tnaker* refers to a compound with a cactus hedge.) For much of the early 20th century, the médina was dominated by its Jewish population. Still densely populated, the médina can easily be explored in a couple of hours, entering from Place Mohammed V. The **Great Mosque** was built by Sultan Sidi Mohammed Ibn Abdallah at the end of the 18th century to celebrate the recapture of Anfa from the Portuguese. The médina is a good place to shop, especially for clothes, but high quality handicrafts are in short supply.

The *koubba* of **Sidi Bou Smara** stands in the southwest corner of the médina near an old banyan tree. It is said that in the 10th century Sidi Bou Smara ('man of the nails') was passing through the town and asked for water to perform his ritual washing before praying. Insults and stones were thrown at him instead. Undaunted, he struck the ground with his staff and there issued from that place a spring which continued to flow. It seems that the inhabitants' earlier inclination to send him away changed to a reluctance to let him go, so he settled in the corner of the médina and planted a banyan tree which grew quickly and to an immense size. Here he lived. The tree is now studded with nails driven in by supplicants for the saint's assistance.

The *koubba* of **Sidi Beliout** (off-limits to non-Muslims) is the small complex of whitewashed buildings to your left on the Avenue Houphouêt Boigny (ex-Avenue du 4ème Zouaves) as you walk towards the city from Casa-Port station. It used to be in the médina, until the demolitions created the boulevard linking station and city. Sidi Beliout is said to have blinded himself and gone to live with the wild animals, finding them preferable to the human race. The animals cared for him and a lion carried him to this resting place after his death. He is appealed to by those needing consolation. Near his shrine is a fountain. Those who drink the water may well return to Casablanca. Sidi Beliout is now the name of the central district close to the shrine.

The remains of **Sidi Allal el Kairouani** and his daughter Lalla Beida are in a shrine on Rue Tnaker to the north of the médina. He was the patron of fishermen and she was known as the White Princess due to the attractive pale colour of her skin. One story goes that Dar el Baydha (House of the White Princess) was the name given to the town in 1770 when it was rebuilt, and only later took the Spanish translation Casa Blanca. The story recounts how Sidi Kairouani, travelling from Tunisia to Senegal, was shipwrecked off the coast here, but rescued by the locals. He sent for his motherless daughter who was not so fortunate. Her ship sank too but she drowned. Her body was carried to her grieving father who buried her facing the sea and left a place beside her for himself.

City centre architecture

For Resident-General Lyautey, Casablanca was to be the commercial nerve centre of the French Protectorate. (Perhaps, in some way, he hoped to avoid 'contaminating' the old imperial cities with modern influences.) The decision was taken to build a vast new port – at a site which many critics saw as totally impracticable. The technical difficulties were overcome, and in 1921, the new port complex, with its kilometre long Delure Jetty, was inaugurated, confirming Casablanca's status.

The city centre is increasingly known today for its architecture. The early period of the Protectorate, the Lyautey years, were characterized by a variant of the Neo-Moorish style, already used in neighbouring Algeria and Tunisia (see the sadly derelict **Hotel Lincoln** opposite the Central Market on Avenue Mohammed V). Lyautey wanted Morocco's official buildings to be simple and sobre in style, and some of the results can be seen in the central administrative square, the place Mohammed V.

Art Deco

Later, in the interwar period, a local variant of art deco took root, using geometric motifs in low relief and wrought ironwork, and occasionally incorporating plaques of Moroccan *zellige* mosaic decoration. Set-back terraces on the top storeys and horizontal detailing gave the larger buildings a sculptural quality. The art deco aesthetic, strengthened by the success of the 1925 Paris Exhibition of Decorative Arts and Modern Industries, can be traced in buildings as diverse as the **Hotel de Ville** – by Marius Boyer, undoubtedly the leading architect of the city – and Paul Tournon's **Cathédrale du Sacré Coeur**, set to be transformed into performance space. **NB** Just across from the cathedral, you'll find the **Villa des Tourelles** now housing an art and heritage foundation.

Laboratory of urban planning

One of the first cities to be planned with aerial photography and formal zoning regulations, Casablanca was also one of the first places to see the use of revolutionary construction techniques like concrete formwork. In the early 1930s, streamlining and speed stripes were all the fashion – hence the horizontal window bands of many buildings – and the first mini-skyscrapers appeared, marking a break with the six-storey apartment buildings. Plot size and land prices (and the enterprising spirit of 'French California') allowed the construction of buildings difficult to envisage in the crowded cities of France. And of course there were numerous adaptations to local conditions: terraces and belvederes, granito floorings for the daily washing of floors, and separate servants' quarters. 1951 saw the completion of Morandi's Immeuble Liberté –

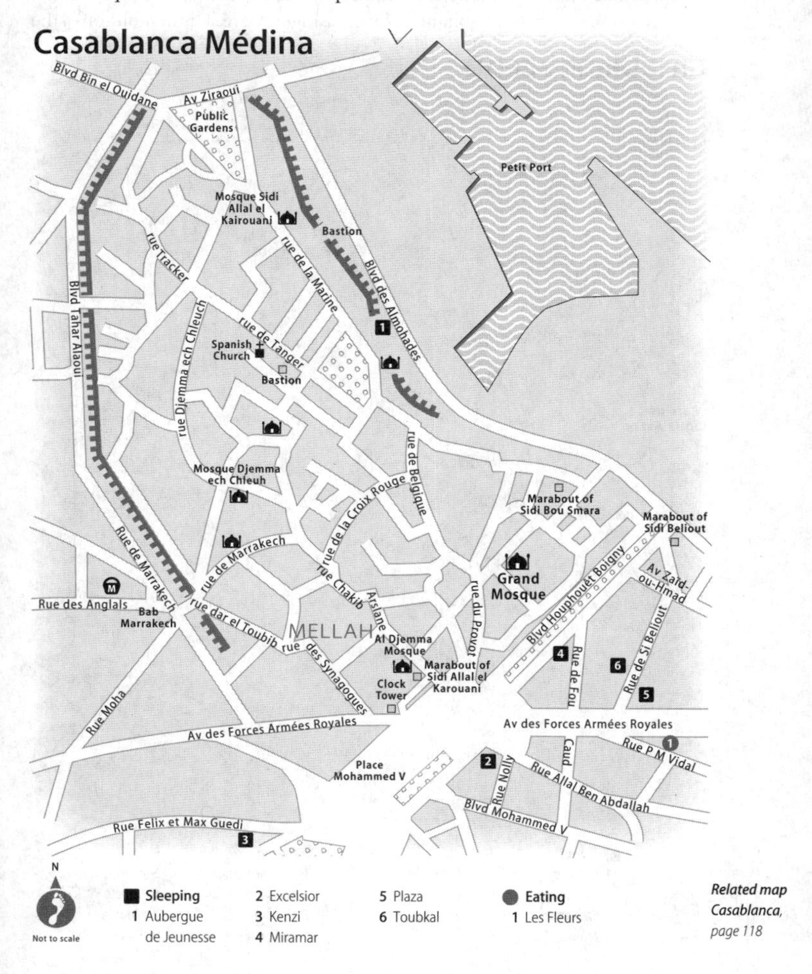

Related map Casablanca, page 118

17-storeys high, in the finest ocean liner style. (If you have time, take a look at the **Villa Souissi**, near the Espace Anfa, a private 1950s home unfortunately transformed into a bakery/pâtisserie.

With the arrival of the Allies in 1942, and the new US base at Nouasseur, American influence grew. American cinema, and its capital Hollywood (with a similar climate to Casablanca), inspired the city's wealthy families. The new villas of the *zones de plaisance* like Anfa and Le Polo were luxurious and functional according to the tenets of the modern movement. The bourgeoisie, enriched by the war and the influx of capital from France, showed their taste and status in Scandinavian-style homes. In a few decades, their city had acquired the most up-to-date facilities for work and leisure: office buildings and the great Auto-Hall, modern abattoirs and the International Fair. Cinemas had a key place: the Rialto (1930) and the Vox (by Boyer, 1930, now demolished).

Conserving Casablanca Casablanca was always more than just another colonial city – due to Protectorate policy and the populations which moved there. Casablanca somehow epitomized Jazz Age modernity, and today the city has a great architectural heritage of which its inhabitants are increasingly aware. The demolition of the

Boyer-designed Villa El Mokri in 1995 aroused widespread criticism and media interest. A new association, Casa Mémoire, is now working for the preservation of the city's unique heritage of buildings.

Quartier des Habous

Resident-General Lyautey's respect for things Moroccan reached an apogee at the Quartier des Habous. (Close to Mers Sultan train station, but better take a petit taxi and ask for Derb el-Habous; alternatively, take a city bus (number 4 or 40) from the bus station at the junction of Boulevard de Paris and Avenue des Forces Armées Royales.) Only too aware of the housing problems facing the Muslim population, Lyautey's planner Henri Prost proposed a new traditional town. The aim was to provide medium-cost housing for Muslims. Top families from Fès, wary of settling in 'impure' areas inhabited by Europeans, were to be attracted to a stylish mini-médina, close to the Sultan's new palace but a fair distance from the new city centre. The land was put forward by the Habous, a sort of religious property institution. (In Islam, land or other property can be held in mortmain to benefit descendants, a foundation of some kind.) A Jewish merchant added a plot, but as the Habous could not accept gifts from the Jews, he gave the land to Sultan Moulay Youssef, who turned it over for development.

The task of designing the mini-médina was given to architect Albert Laprade, a great observer of traditional architectures in Europe. Too busy designing the residency in Rabat, he handed the project to Cadet and Brion, who produced a whole neo-traditional area with all the necessary modern infrastructure. There were all the facilities familiar to former residents of an old city: a market, public ovens, *hammams*, Koran schools, and mosques – situated on public squares, rather like churches in a French village. The Pasha's Courtrooms (**Mahkamat el Pacha**), completed in the 1950s and rather Lutyens in style, make a final focal point, close to the palace. Wealthy Fassis moved to the area, keen to be close to the heart of things while living in a traditional environment.

Today, Derb el-Habous is often a whistle-stop on tours for official visitors. There are a number of shops selling *belgha* (leather slippers), Moroccan clothing and copperwork. Close to the Pasha's Courtrooms are a number of good bookshops, stocking mainly Arabic titles.

Bousbir

Another interwar building project was the Bousbir neighbourhood – rather less noble, but still with vernacular architectural motifs inspired by the médinas of Rabat and Salé. Bousbir (so-named after Prosper, the engineer responsible for building it) was Casablanca's red-light district. Its function as a centre for prostitution ended in 1954, but the Neo-Moorish trappings remain. Fairly close to Derb el-Habous but a long way off the tourist circuit, visitors to Bousbir may find themselves unwelcome in a poor residential neighbourhood with a past that most would prefer to forget.

One final architectural note. Those interested in church architecture may want to visit **Notre Dame de Lourdes**, close to the Nouvelle médina, at the junction of Avenue du 2 Mars and the Rond-Point de l'Europe. Built in the 1950s, the church is famous for its stained-glass windows by Gabriel Loire.

Hassan II mosque

The Hassan II Mosque took five years of intensive labour by over 30,000 workers and craftsmen. It stands at the most western point in the Muslim world. Works were undertaken by French contractors Bouygues, also responsible for the huge Basilica of Yamasoukrou on the Côte d'Ivoire. The minaret, some 200 m high, was inspired by the minaret of the Koutoubia Mosque in Marrakech, and is Casablanca's chief landmark. Sometimes a laser beam, visible over 35 km

Sidi Abderrahman, the flautist

The story of Sidi Abderrahman – like that of so many saints – has been smudged over like an old manuscript. Sidi Abderrahman was a pious man or wali salih, *who took refuge on an islet off the Atlantic coast, to better contemplate the Almighty. But he was unable to pray. To serve the Lord, he played sweet music on a reed flute. Another wali, Sidi Bouchaïb Arradad, hearing of the piety of Sidi Abderrahman, came to see him, and said that he should lay down his flute and that he would explain to him the intricacies of prayer. The two remained together for seven days, and on the eighth day, Sidi Bouchaïb spread his carpet on the sea and went away. Deep in prayer, Sidi Abderrahman didn't see him leave. When he realized that his guide had left, he called him back, then threw himself into the sea to try to catch up. The waves drew back and an island appeared. Sidi Bouchaïb, seeing this miracle, cried out, "Oh Sidi Abderrahman, forget what I taught you and play your flute. Your baraka is greater than mine." And so Sidi Abderrahman stayed on his island to worship God until he passed away.*

Of course there are many other legends explaining the past of Sidi Abderrahman. His tiny island retains a mystic fascination; it is a place where women may go to seek the saint's blessing, a cure for sterility, bad health and other maledictions. They come from all over Morocco, travel across to the island on makeshift 'boats', consult soothsayers in tiny damp rooms, visit the shrine, maybe organize a lila *– a night-time ritual of dance and trance – and return home relieved of their cares.*

away, indicating the direction of Mecca, probes the night sky. The mosque is huge: in terms of covered area it is the largest in the world, and has space for 80,000 worshippers, as well as buildings for a library and a museum. There are upper prayer areas on a mezzanine floor with space for 5,000 female worshippers. The mosque is often toted as a building contributing to the renaissance of Moroccan craftskills, with hundreds of square metres covered in traditional decorative detailing, including ceramic mosaic, carved plasterwork and painted wood. The 50 chandeliers were imported.

The mosque is built on a rocky site, right next to the ocean, the water practically washing the bay windows of the prayer hall (which has a mobile roof allowing it to be opened to the sky). Visitors will pass through the main prayer hall, the ablutions room (ritual ablutions are compulsory before prayer) and the two public baths, beautifully decorated but still closed. As one approaches the wide esplanade leading to the mosque, the buildings on either side were planned to house a *medersa*, a library and a museum of Islamic art. The necessary funding has yet to be found. The costly operation was paid for by public subscription. Unusually for a mosque in the city, the Hassan II Mosque is managed by the Agence urbaine de Casablanca, and a small part of maintenance costs is covered by visitors. A report in early 2003 suggested that even larger sums would have to be found in the near future, as the mosque was facing severe structural problems. On a more positive note, the esplanade is popular with locals from the crowded housing areas nearby. ■ *Open to non-Muslim visitors by guided tour only. 0900, 1000, 1100 and 1400. 100dh.*

Aïn Diab & the Corniche This ocean promenade is easily reached by petit taxi or by local bus (number 9) from the junction of Boulevard de Paris and Avenue des Forces Armées Royales. The Corniche is most definitely a place to stroll and be seen. (If on a business trip, you might find yourself in one of the Corniche hotels.) Along the ocean front, beach clubs with open-air pools have been built on the rocks, their names – Miami Plage, Tahiti, Tonga – practically enough to give you a suntan, as thriller writer Tito Topin put it. At the 'city' end of the Corniche, there is a *McDonalds* and the Dawliz cinema complex. After the beach clubs and hotels, out on the coast road, you will come to the shrine of **Sidi Abderrahman**, built on a rocky islet.

Excursions

Cascades de Mizab are about 24 km along the old road P1 towards Rabat. They are a popular visit for the people of Casablanca, a place to picnic and relax. There is a minor excursion to **El Gara** and **Ben Ahmed** through a rich farming area, with cereals and citrus orchards, which also supplies market garden produce for Casablanca.

Essentials

Sleeping

■ *on maps, pages 123 and 124*
For ease of reference, hotels are listed here under city centre and Corniche

Casablanca does not seem to have quite enough hotels, and mid-range hotels are often booked up early in the day. This is especially true when there is a major national event on in the city, and the authorities make block reservations. The lower range hotels are often more expensive than elsewhere in Morocco. Cheap hotels in the médina are of the flop-house variety on the whole – avoid. Another consideration is noise: Casablanca is a city where the traffic starts moving early, and hotels which may have been fine in their heyday in the 1950s will have street-facing rooms which are very noisy in summer. If you have an early departure, go for a hotel near Casa-Port railway station. (There are only 2 hotels near Casa-Voyageurs.) Another option (but a 20-min taxi ride from the centre, depending on the traffic) are the hotels on the Corniche at Aïn Diab.

Since Driss Benhima's appointment as governor of Casablanca in 2002, existing hotels have improved and more are on the way. New 4-star addresses will be the *Marhaba* on Av des FAR and another hotel on Av Houphouet Boigny near Casa-Port station. A personable upmarket guesthouse was in the planning stages in the Médina in 2003.

City centre

L ***Hotel Hyatt Regency***, Pl Mohammed IV, T022-221234, F220180. Plush business hotel, one of the centrepieces of the town, 300 rooms, 5 restaurants, bar, nightclub, health club, art gallery, squash courts and pool. **L** ***Hotel Royal Mansour Méridien***, 27 Av des FAR, T022-313011/2, www.lemeridien.com/morocco/casablanca 170 rooms ranging from standard to royal club suites, 2 restaurants, coffee bar, bar, health club and small pool. **L** ***Hotel Sheraton***, 100 Av des FAR, T022-317878, F315136. 306 spotless and well-equipped rooms, helpful reception, 5 restaurants, 3 bars, high quality business centre, special meeting room, health club, *hammam* and nightclub. **A** ***Hotel Safir***, 160 Av des FAR, T022-311212, F316555. Recently renovated, 310 pleasantly decorated and well-equipped rooms, 4 restaurants, 2 bars, nightclub, sauna and heated pool.

B ***Les Almohades***, Av Hassan I, T022-220505. Accor group business hotel, takes tour groups, 140 rooms. **B** ***Hotel Al Mounia***, 24 bis Blvd de Paris, T022-220727, F223314. Pleasant, nicely decorated central hotel. Recommended. One of the better ones in this price bracket. **B** ***Hotel Idou Anfa***, 85 Blvd d'Anfa, T022-224004, F220029. 20 mins from airport, pool, conference room, restaurants. **B** ***Hotel Kenzi Basma***, 30 Av Moulay Hassan I, T022-223323, info@kenzi-hotels.com Modern, comfortable. **B** ***Hotel Toubkal***, 9 R Sidi Beliout. Not terribly exciting, but very handily located for downtown area and Casa-Port station, a/c, quiet, kind of gloomy, double-glazed rooms.

C ***Hotel Majestic***, 55 Blvd Lalla Yacout, T022-310951, T/F446285. Satisfactory hotel close to the R Moulay Abdallah. Well renovated, immaculate bathrooms, TV. Street-side rooms noisy. Good value. **C** ***Hotel de Paris***, on the pedestrian R Prince Moulay Abdallah, address 2 R Ex-Cherif Amziane, ex-R Branly, T022-273871, F298069. Popular, best to book. Rooms small but with satellite TV. Overpriced.

D ***Hotel Aviatic,*** 197 Blvd Brahim Roudani, T022-257855. Spartan, clean hotel on busy avenue, handy for the Maârif neighbourhood. Street-side rooms extremely noisy. **D** ***Hotel du Centre***, 1 R Sidi Beliout, T022-312448. Fair prices, clean and convenient. **D** ***Hotel Excelsior***, 2 R Nolly, T022-220048. 54 rooms, 32 with bath, central, with a more illustrious past. Street-side rooms have traffic noise, inward-facing rooms have noise from a/c plant at bank next door. Currently (2003) undergoing renovation. **D** ***Hotel de Lausanne***, 24 R Tata, ex-R Poincaré, T022-268083. Popular central hotel which has seen better days (broken windows do not seem to get repaired). Some rooms with terraces. Plenty of hot water, and handy for some good breakfast cafés, including *La Loge*, just down the street. **D** ***Hotel de Noailles*** 22 Blvd du 11 Janvier just off Blvd Lalla Yacout, T022-310951. Centrally located. Top-floor rooms have terraces. Must have been very swish in its day. Recently refurbished; very clean. Now has a bar. Recommended. **D** ***Hotel Plaza***, 18 Blvd Houphouêt Boigny, T022-297698. 27 spacious rooms, very satisfactory; rooms at back may be noisy because of public hall used for weddings next door. 2 persons 273dh, triple 356dh, 4 bed 440dh, breakfast expensive at 30dh. Very handy for Casa-Port station. Refit due in 2003 – the original charm is to be restored.

E ***Hotel Colbert***, 38 R Chaouia, T022-314241. Staircase entrance opposite the flower sellers outside the Central Market. Some rooms with showers. Very handy for the *Snack Amine* fish restaurant. **E** ***Hotel de Foucauld***, 52 R Araibi Jilali, T022-222666. Useful central location. **E** ***Hotel Guynemer***, 2 R Périgord, T022-275764. A friendly, good and clean hotel in a quiet but central location. **E** ***Hotel Rialto***, 9 R Claude, T022-275122. Fine. **E** ***Hotel Touring***, 87 R Allal Ben Abdallah, T022-310216. Large rooms, fills up early as handy for *CTM* and Casa Port.

F ***Hotel Bon Rêve***, R Allal Ben Abdallah, T022-311439. **F** ***Hotel Les Négociants***, R Allal Ben Abdallah. Good and cheap.

Corniche

A ***Hotel Riad Salam***, at start of Blvd de la Corniche, T022-391313, F391345, www.1stmaroc.com/salam/salam.html 189 rooms and 8 suites, a/c, restaurants, bar, nightclub, tennis, pool, sun terraces, conference room and shops, parking, all major credit cards, thalassotherapy centre 'Le Lido'. 2 sorts of accommodation: bungalow rooms around pool (damp in winter) and more recent quieter rooms in 3-storey blocks; best place by the beach, handy for the clubs. Expensive for what's on offer. In something of a decline. **B** ***Hotel Bellerive***, on the Corniche, T022-391409, F393493. All facilities, most rooms refurbished, ocean view, pool in small garden, some rooms noisy at night because of disco. **B** ***Hotel Suisse***, Blvd de la Corniche, T022-360202, F367758. Slightly cheaper than the *Bellerive*, not on ocean side of Corniche road. 200 rooms, all services including small gym, sauna, nightclub, and pool. Sometimes used by business travellers.

Camping

Camping de l'Oasis, Av Mermoz (the continuation of Blvd Roudani), T022-253367. This is the nearest, in the direction of El Jadida, take bus 31 from Av des FAR. Noisy, poorly maintained site with shade, 10 km from beach, petrol and shop close by, electricity for caravans. ***Camping International Tamaris***, about 16 km out of Casablanca on the coast road to Azemmour, T022-330060. Only 100 m from the beach (crowded in summer), 9-ha site, 10dh per person per night, snack restaurant, grocery shop, showers (cold?), laundry, first-aid post and electricity for caravans, noisy.

Youth hostel

6 Pl Amiral Philibert, T022-220551, a square in the médina off Blvd des Almohades, near the harbour. 80 beds, meals available, overnight dormitory fee 45dh including breakfast, or small double rooms at 120dh. Bus and train nearby, renovated, airy and well maintained. Some noise from nearby mosque.

Eating

● *on maps, pages 123 and 124*

Casablanca has a good range of restaurants, including cheap fried fish places, eateries which have survived from more cosmopolitan times and rather sleek lounge-bars with minimalist pretensions. You can eat good Moroccan food, too, and there are a number of popular Italian restaurants in the more prosperous neighbourhoods. Arriving late in central Casa it will be problematic finding anything to eat.

Expensive

La Cambuse, at Aïn Diab, T023-367105. Noted for fish dishes. ***A Ma Bretagne***, Sidi Abderrahman, Blvd de la Corniche beyond Aïn Diab, T022-362112, www.amabretagne.com Excellent fish and good wine cellar, sea view, one of the best in Casablanca, pricey but recommended. (Chef André Halbert is a maître cuisinier de France.) ***La Mer***, Blvd de la Corniche, near the El Hank lighthouse, T022-363315. Good reputation for seafood. ***Restaurant Wong Kung***, *Hotel Hyatt Regency*, T022-221234. Said to be the best Chinese restaurant in Morocco, including excellent seafood dishes.

Mid-range: general

Restaurant de l'Etoile Maroccaine, 107 R Allah Ben Abdallah, adjacent to market. No alcohol. ***La Corrida***, 59 R Guy Lussac, T022-278155. Good Spanish food, faded decor tells of the days when Casablanca had a bullring. Take a look at their *livre d'or* for an idea of past glories. Closed Sun and Sep. ***La Marignan***, 63 R Mohammed Smiha. Excellent Japanese food. ***Al Mounia***, 95 R du Prince Moulay Abdallah, T022-222669. Probably the best Moroccan restaurant in Casa. Very good value. ***Las Delicias***, 18 Av Mohammed V. Good Spanish restaurant. ***Le Petit Poucet***, 8 Av Mohammed V. Licensed French restaurant. ***Brasserie La Presse***, Blvd Roudani, Maârif, take a taxi as long way from centre. Popular with both eaters and drinkers – need not cost too much. Unfortunately, lost some charm in recent refurbishment. ***Restaurant Ryad Zitoun***, 31 Blvd Rachidi, T022-223927, F365021, closed Sat and Sun lunch. Moroccan food, restaurant popular with business people. Nice terrace in summer. Top end of mid-range bracket. Advertises a lot. ***Restaurant Saigon***, 40 R Colbert, T022-286007. Good Asian food. ***Tri Camelli***, 5 R des Rosiers/Mutanabbi, T022-491565. Highly popular Italian restaurant in the Gautier district. ***Toscana***, 7 R Yaala el Ifrani, Quartier Racine, T022-369592. Another popular Italian restaurant, open all day Sun. ***Restaurant Vertigo***, 110 R Colbert, aka R Chaouia, opposite the *Hotel Transatlantique*, T022-294639. A trendy little place, posher than the nearby cheap fish snack restaurants on Av Lalla Yacout.

Mid-range: seafood

Le Cabestan, 90 Blvd de la Corniche, T022-391190. Closed Sun. A la carte. At the upper end of this price bracket. Take a taxi from the centre. ***Restaurant du Port de Pêche***, T022-318561, close to the médina in the fishing port compound. (Leaving Casa-Port station on your right, go straight ahead and then turn left for port area.) Excellent fish dishes in smart but simple atmosphere. Service on the slow side, try to reserve. A good lunchtime spot. ***Ostréa***, T022-318561, just inside port compound on right. Again, very pleasant for lunch – try to get a table by the window upstairs so you can look down on the bustle of the port below. Can work out pricey. Sister restaurant in Oualidia.***Taverne du Dauphin***, Blvd Houphouët Boigny, T022-221200. One of Casablanca's best known restaurants, good for seafood. Try the Oualidia oysters. Highly rec, closed Sun.

Cheap

La Grotte, 18 R Mohamed Fakir, just off Av des FAR behind the *Café-Restaurant des Fleurs*, T022-268082. Tiny, easily recognizable by its nomad decor and waiters in blue chèches (turbans). ***Snack Amine***, on the R Chaouia, opposite the flower sellers at the Central Market. Speciality, big plates of seafood in batter. Highly recommended. A cheap area for eating is around R Colbert and R Allal Ben Abdallah, try ***Café-Restaurant Anwal***, 116 R Allal Ben Abdallah, T022-319630. Standard Moroccan fare. ***Café Intissar***, R Allal Ben Abdallah. Reliable. Another cheap area is in the médina, with the ***Restaurant Widad*** a good choice. However, the fish restaurants in the médina are perhaps best avoided as there have been cases of food poisoning. If waiting for a train at Casa-Voyageurs, there is a cheap though rather forlorn snack restaurant over the road from the station on the left side of the square.

Cafés & pâtisseries Casablanca has a number of cafés-glaciers. If you are wandering up the Av Hassan II, try *Oliveri* for ice cream. In the central area, good cafés for breakfast include ***La Loge*** on R Tata (ex-R Poincaré) – highly recommended – ***La Choppe***, at the most strategic corner at the start of pedestrian street R Prince Moulay Abdallah, and ***La Princière***, on R Idriss Lahrizi. ***Café de France***, on Pl Mohammed V, has a slightly rakish air to it in the small hours when nightclubbers come into town from the Corniche. Also on Pl Mohammed V, ***Café de l'Excelsior*** does breakfast and is handy for a kiosk with foreign papers. For good Moroccan pâtisserie, the best place is said to be the ***Pâtisserie Bennis***, a little difficult to find at 2 R Fkih El Gabbas in the Derb el-Habous (ask a local).

Bars and clubs

Bars Various bars in the town centre can tend towards the rowdy. Try ***Le Petit Poucet***, 86 Blvd Mohammed V, where they will proudly show some old photos of the city centre and explain how aviator St-Exupéry would drink here when he stayed at the *Hotel Excelsior*. More upmarket, with big-screen sports coverage some nights, is ***La Bodega***, just behind the Marché central at 129 R Allal Ben Abdallah. Terribly chic and decorated in a Lusitano-Indian style is ***La Villa Fandango*** on the Corniche (expensive), T022-798508. Heading up the Corniche with ocean on right, turn left down the street just before the *Restaurant Croc-Magnon*.

Lounge bars The new trend in 2003. Try ***O-Zen***, 21 R Zaid Bnou Rifaâ, Maârif, T022-252563, F252538. As you face the Twin Centre, go left on Blvd Zerktouni and take the 2nd street right before Fiat. Minimalist decor, elegant wining and dining. Small portions, attentive service. Closed Sat midday. Very popular at weekends. On the same street is ***Palladium***, 29 R Ziad Bnou Rifaâ, T022-989748. Also worth a look, though more beach-side than lounge, is ***Le Petit Rocher*** at El Hank, on the Corniche, near the lighthouse, T022-395748. Fine terrace, ocean view. Beers at 30dh, trendy mixed crowd. Recommended in summer.

Clubs Most of the nightclubs are situated on the Corniche at Aïn Diab. The mix of punters is often interesting: media people, expatriate kids and *créatifs*, yuppies letting go and young women who might (or might not) be sex workers, trendsters and Saudis on the razzle, hustlers and a handful of gays. Popular places include: ***Le Balcon***, 33 Blvd de la Corniche. Also along the same strip are ***Le Village*** (fairly gay) run by the redoubtable Omariya, and ***La Notte***, haunt of Casa's rich kids. Up-and-coming is ***Manhattan***, R de la Mer noire, T022-798630, closed Sun. Still in fashion is ***La Réserve***, T022-367110, perhaps the most chic of the lot. Also functions as an upscale restaurant. In the town centre, try ***Le Sintra***, in street parallel to Blvd des FAR and near Central Market. 1950s Strasbourg bar decor, Moroccan music downstairs, sometimes a flautist upstairs. Some heavy drinking till late, no fights. In the small hours, revellers may take a taxi over to the abattoirs for barbecue sandwiches. Though the new city abattoirs have opened, this remains a haunt for revellers at the end of the night.

Entertainment

Cultural centres

The local press often advertises and reviews events at the **Complexe culturel Sidi Beliout**, at 28 R Léon l'Africain, T022-303760, located just behind the *CTM* bus station. As in other major Moroccan cities, the **Institut français** (121 Blvd Zerktouni, T022-779870, F779871, culture@institut-francais-casa.org, ambafrance.ma.org) is active, showing films and hosting visiting theatre and dance groups. The IF also has a small cafeteria.

Shopping

Books & newspapers

The city's best bookshop, ***Le Carrefour du Livre***, is in the Maârif neighbourhood (sometimes considered Casablanca's equivalent of St Germain-des-Prés), a short taxi ride away. Literary buffs should check as both established and up-and-coming Moroccan writers have their book launches here. If you are looking for photography and art books on Morocco, or contemporary novels, try the large bookshop on R Tata (ex-R Poincaré), almost opposite the *Hotel Lausanne*. They also have good postcards. There are stalls, some selling European newspapers, on Pl Mohammed V and along Av Mohammed V.

Clothes

Try the boutiques on central pedestrian street R Moulay Abdallah, or for something a little more upmarket, shops in the Maârif neighbourhood or the Twin Center (*Célio* for men, *Mango* just opposite). Try ***Alpha 55***, at 55 Av de Mers Sultan in city centre, department store with a good range of items.

Food

There is a fine covered market on Av Mohammed V which stocks all the usual fresh produce. If in need of some cheap presents, there are a number of stalls selling beautifully made basketry of various kinds. There are also a couple of souvenir stalls with fossils and miscellaneous pottery. At the Twin Center, there is Morocco's first urban hypermarket, ***Marjane***, where you can find a big range of imported items. There is also a suburban branch of the chain in L'Oasis.

Handicrafts

The best fixed-price shop, and a friendly place just to look, is the government-run ***Coopartim*** in the Grande Arcade Complexe Commerciale, just off Pl des Nations Unies, T022-229444. There are plenty of smaller shops in the médina, close to Bab Marrakech, and along Blvd Houphouêt Boigny. There is also a large shop stocking everything from carpets to metal lamps in the Centre 2000, just next to Casa-Port station. Handicrafts, and in particular traditional Moroccan clothing, can be found in the Quartier des Habous.

Sport and activities

Football

Casablanca's football clubs are the Raja (green and white strip) and the WAC (Widad Athletic Club – red and white). Both have grounds in the Beauséjour neighbourhood. Matches generate a lot of enthusiasm and should not be attended by the faint-hearted: the Casablancan crowd is fierce though not given to hooligan-style violence.

Golf

Royal Golf d'Anfa, 10 mins from the centre of the city, 9 holes, T023-365355, F393374. A prestigious course with a luxurious clubhouse and a restaurant. See also *El Jadida* course (page) and *Mohammedia* course (page 136), both 18 holes, par 72. There is also a 9-hole course at Ben Slimane about 50 km northeast of Casablanca.

Hammams

The men's *hammam* at R Imam el-Ghazali in the Quartier des Habous is modelled on a traditional médina bath house. Closed for works in late 2002. Closer to the city centre, try ***Les Bains Zaiani***, reputedly the only 'bain oriental' in Casablanca, at 59 R Abou Rakrak, ex-R Verdun, T022-319695, F314495. (Coming from R du 11 Janvier, turn right along Blvd

Rahal El-Meskin, and left up R Abou Rakrak shortly after the *Cinéma Liberté*.) Open 0700-2200. Choose your masseur from the photo at the desk. More expensive at weekends. There are 2 clean and popular *hammams* (men and women) in the Bourgogne neighbourhood, off Blvd Zerktouni, a short taxi ride from the city centre (ask for the Clinique Badr): ***Hammam Beidaoua***, 3 R du Chevreuil/R Abou Kacem Kattabari, T022-271063, is open daily 0600-2200; ***Hammam Idéal***, 9 R Ramée/R Annaba, has similar opening hours. Both are busy Thu evenings and at weekends. A visit here might give you some insight into daily life in an ordinary residential part of Casablanca.

Hiking *Club Alpin Français*, 50 Blvd Moulay Abderrahman (ex-Blvd de la Grande Ceinture), T022-270090/990141, www.cafmaroc.co.ma Postal address BP 6178, Casablanca 2000. Premises near the Lycée Lyautey. Organizes outdoor activities. Might be worth joining if you are going to be resident in Morocco. Otherwise, might put you in touch with outdoor enthusiasts interested in climbing, canyoning and the like.

Horse riding *L'Etrier*, Quartier des Stades, Route d'El Jadida. ***Club Equestre Bayard***, R Schuman. *CAFC*, Quartier des Stades, Route d'El Jadida, T022-259779.

Swimming The Grande Mosquée has taken the place of what was once Africa's largest open-air swimming pool. However, you could try taking out a day-ticket at one of the private beach clubs at Aïn Diab. On the other side of the city, at Aïn Sebaâ, there is the ***Piscine Océanique***. Otherwise, near Maârif is the ***Stade d'honneur***, with 2 pools, one of which requires a monthly subscription card.

Tennis *Cercle Athlétique de Casablanca*, Av Jean Mermoz, T022-254342. 18 courts. ***Cercle Municipal de Casablanca***, Parc de la Ligue Arabe, T022-279621. 6 courts. ***Union Sportive Maroccaine/Tennis Club de Casablanca***, Parc de la Ligue Arabe, T022-275429. 8 courts.

Tour operators

Comanav Voyages, 43 Av des FAR, T022-312050. For ferry reservations. Try small travel agents left of *CTM*. ***Discover Morocco***, 62 R de Foucauld, T022-273519. ***Gibmar Travel***, 8 R Nolly. ***Menara Tours***, 19 R Chenier (close to Pl du 16 Novembre and *Hotel Hyatt Regency*), T022-225232, F225199. ***Olive Branch Tours***, 35 R de Foucauld, T022-220354, F260976. Reliable agency who can set up trips almost anywhere in Morocco. ***Sun Tours and Travel***, 75 R Driss Lahrizi, T022-220196. ***Wagons-Lit Tourisme***, 60 R de Foucauld, T022-223051.

Transport

Local **Road Car hire** All the main car hire agencies are represented at the airport. After baggage reclaim, go left when you come through the frosted-glass doors into the main concourse. ***Avis***, 19 Av des FAR, T022-312424, T339072 (airport). ***Euro Rent***, 3 R Assaâd Ibnou Zarara, T022-254033. ***Hertz***, 25 R de Foucauld, T022-312223, T339181 (airport). ***Inter-Rent Europcar***, Tour des Habous, Av des FAR, T313737. ***Leasing Cars***, 110 Blvd Zerktouni, T022-225331, a cheap option.

Long distance

Most major world cities are connected to Morocco through Casablanca. *See Touching down, page 37, for further details*

Air Departures for foreign and internal destinations from Mohammed V Airport, T339100, south of the city at Nouasseur, connected by trains from Casablanca Voyageurs and Casablanca Port and by grands taxis from the bus station near the *Hotel Hyatt Regency* (200dh by day, 300dh at night). There are no bus services to and from this airport. Flights to/from Casablanca to **Agadir** (at least 2 daily), **Al Hoceima** (2 weekly), **Dakhla** (weekly), **Fès** (daily), **Laayoune** (daily), **Marrakech** (2 daily), **Ouarzazate** (4 weekly), **Oujda** (daily), **Rabat** (daily), **Tanger** (daily), **Tan-Tan** (weekly) and **Tetouan** (weekly).

Airline offices: *Air Afrique*, Tour des Habous, Av des FAR, T022-312866. *Air France*, 15 Av des FAR, reservations on T022-293030. *British Airways*, 7th Flr, Centre Allal Ben Abdallah, R Allal Ben Abdallah, Angle Faker Mohammed, T022-229464, F229711, T022-539524 (airport). *Iberia*, 17 Av des FAR, T279600, T022-339260 (airport). *KLM*, 6 Blvd Mohammed El Hansali, T022-223232. *Lufthansa*, Tour des Habous, Av des FAR, T022-312371. *Royal Air Maroc*, T022-912000 (airport); 44 Av des FAR, T022-311122; 90 Av Mers Sultan, T022-228712; 44 Pl Mohammed V, T022-223270; reservations, T022-314141. *Sabena*, 41 Av des FAR, T022-313991. *Swissair*, Tour des Habous, Av des FAR, T022-313280. *Tunis Air*, main office, 10 Av des FAR, T022-273914.

Road Bus: the *CTM* terminal is at 23 R Léon l'Africain, off R Colbert and Av des FAR, behind the *Hotel Sheraton*, T458800, try also T228061-7. Daily services to **Essaouira** (5 hrs), **El Jadida**, **Agadir**, **Tiznit**, **Beni Mellal**, **Marrakech**, **Fès**, **Tanger** and **Rabat**. Private line buses leave from the new terminal, the **Gare routière des Ouled Ziane**, a hefty hike from the city centre (best to get a petit taxi from the centre, say 10dh). There are many touts in operation here, to the point that the ticket windows don't always seem to function. All major Moroccan cities are served daily. **Taxi**: **grands taxis** to **Mohammedia** and **Rabat** from the first street left as you leave Casa-Port rail terminal. For **El Jadida**, take a **petit taxi** to the Blvd Laouina. Plenty of departures.

Sea Ferries: *COMANAV*, 7 Blvd de la Résistance, T022-303012. *COMARINE*, 65 Av des FAR, T022-311941.

Train From **Casablanca Port**, T022-223011, to **Rabat** almost hourly between 0645 and 2035. 3 or 4 departures a day for **Meknès**, **Fès**, **Taza** and **Oujda**. The mainline **Tanger** to **Marrakech** service runs through Casablanca-Voyageurs. Trains every hour (the Bidhaoui Service) to **Mohammed V Airport**, starting at **Aïn Sebaâ**, calling at **Casa-Voyageurs** (departure on the hour), **Mers Sultan**, and **Oasis**. Service to **El Jadida** has been resumed. Full details on www.oncf.ma, generally reliable, or on T022-220520, 223011.

Directory

Banks

Handy central ATMs include the *Wafa Bank*, Av Hassan II just after the *Ramsès* restaurant, and *BMCI*, corner of Av Mohamed V and Pl des Nations-unies, just across from the *Café de Paris*. There are further banks with ATMs, including *Crédit du Maroc*, further down Av Mohamed V towards the Marché central.

Communications

Internet: there are a couple of handy internet cafés close to the *Café La Loge* near the intersection of R Tata and Blvd de Paris. *Euronet* is across from *La Loge*, a second cyber is just round the corner, past the *Café La Comédie*, on Blvd de Paris, on your left. Try also the ground-floor arcade of the Centre Allal Ben Abdallah, between the Marché central and the *CTM*, on R Allal Ben Abdallah, a street parallel to the Av des FAR. Also try *Cyberclub* at Groupe Open SA, Résidence Adriana, 63 Blvd Moulay Youssef, T022-293450. At corner of R Normandie/R Salaheddine Al Afghani, T022-390039. Open 7 days a week, 70 computers. **Post**: main *PTT* is on Pl Mohamed V, for collecting poste restante and sending parcels. **Telephone**: plenty of téléboutiques in central area for phoning home – try the one next to the *Café Ramsès*.

Embassies & consulates

Algeria, 159 Blvd Moulay Idriss I, T022-804175. **Austria**, 45 Av Hassan II, T022-226904. **Belgium**, 13 Blvd Rachidi, T022-222904. **Denmark**, 30 R Sidi Beliout, T022-316656. **France**, R Prince Moulay Abdallah, T022-225355. **Germany**, 42 Av des FAR, T022-314872. **Greece**, 48 Blvd Rachidi, T022-277142. **Italy**, 21 Av Hassan Souktani, T022-277558. **Japan**, 22 R Charam Achaykh, T022-253264. **Netherlands**, 26 R

Nationale, T022-221820. **Norway**, 44 R Mohammed Smiha, T022-305961. **Portugal**, 104 Blvd de Paris, T022-220214. **Russia**, 31 R Soumaya, T022-255708. **Spain**, 29 R d'Alger, T022-220752. **Sweden**, 88 Blvd Lalla Yacout, T022-319003. **UK**, 43 Blvd d'Anfa, T022-221653. **USA**, 8 Blvd Moulay Youssef, T022-224550.

Medical services **Emergency**: T15 is the emergency number. Or dial **SAMU**, emergency service, T022-252525; or **SOS Médecins**, T022-444444; or **Moroccan Red Cross**, T022-252521. **Hospital**: T022-271459. **Chemists**: There is a Pharmacie de Nuit (chemist's open at night) on Pl Mohammed V, T022-229491, and another on Blvd d'Anfa where it intersects with Pl Oued le Makhazine. Otherwise, any pharmacy closed at night will have a list of the closest pharmacies de garde (night chemists) up on its door. **Doctors**: Any major hotel should be able to put you in touch with a doctor. For a first visit, ask for the SAMU, T022-444444 or a *médecin généraliste* (a GP).

Useful addresses **Chamber of Commerce:** *Chambre Britannique*, 185 Blvd Zerktouni, T022-256920. **Fire service**: R Poggi, T15. **Police**: Blvd Brahim Rodani, T19. **Traffic police**: T177. **Garage Services:** *Renault-Maroc*, Pl Bandoeng. Fiat at Afric-Auto (T022-279285), 147 R Mustapha El Maoui. Peugeot at Siara (T022-301762), at 193 Av des FAR. **Motoring club**: *Touring Club de Maroc*, 3 Av des FAR (0900-1200 and 1500-1830, Mon-Fri). **Transport**: Casa-Port station T022-243818, Casa-Voyageurs station T022-271837, *Royal Air Maroc* central reservations T022-314141, F442409, *RAM* office on Blvd des FAR T022-311122. ***CTM*** bus station T022-448130.

Mohammedia (ex-Fedala) . المحمدية

Phone code: 023
Colour map 2, grid A4

Mohammedia, known as Fedala until 1960, when it was renamed after the present king's father, Mohammed V, is a curious, sleepy sort of town. It is home to the Samir Refinery, and is the second biggest port in the country. There is a small walled médina – and a neighbourhood of fine, wide avenues lined with palm trees, and a park with a modern church – all somehow on a scale unsuited to such a quiet place. It is as though grandiose plans for city development in the 1920s never actually quite got off the ground. Beachside Mohammedia, with its promenade and cafés, comes alive in summer. A likeable little town, it could be the place to spend a last night at the end of a trip, perhaps if you have a late flight the following day out of Casablanca.

Ins & outs
See Transport, page 136, for further details

Getting there Mohammedia is easily reached by the shuttle train running between Casablanca (10 mins) and Rabat (25 mins). Another option is to take a grand taxi from Blvd Moulay Abderrahman in Casablanca (turn first left just before the Centre 2000 as you leave Casa-Port station). **Getting around** The town is easily explored on foot, although there are plenty of lime-green petits taxis, if you need to get back to the station quickly. From in front of the Kasbah gate, take the Av des FAR as far as the R de Fès. A left turn will take you to the R Farhat Hached, where the nicer restaurants are located. It's only about 1½ km from the station to the main park area. **Tourist information** Tourist office at 14 R Al Jahid, T023-324299.

Background Just to the north of modern Casablanca, the future Mohammedia was a thriving port in the 14th and 15th centuries. Its trade with Europe expanded in the 17th and 18th centuries, notably with the export of horses, and the kasbah was built in 1773 to support this activity. A decline in trade left Mohammedia subordinate to adjacent Rabat. Specializing in the handling of petroleum gave it a new lease of life and the oil refinery, opened in 1961, raised its status to one of Morocco's major ports. Industrial activities are centred around a rock salt factory. Its 3 km of sandy beaches make it a popular recreational area for the people of Casablanca, both for weekend breaks and as a summer holiday haunt.

On a sombre note, Mohammedia was severely hit by flooding in autumn 2002. Torrential rains caused a dam above the town to burst, with terrible results for poor housing areas and the refinery.

Sights

The distinctive mosque, **Jama' Radouane**, was opened in 1991. There are three doors, in arched apertures, approached by shallow steps across a gleaming white marble courtyard. More impressive is the wide open park which some planner must have intended as the focus for a rather grand coastal resort.

Note that Mohammedia gets packed in summer and that the beach, nicely located near the oil refinery terminals, is none to clean. If you want a beach destination near Casa-Rabat, prefer Plage des Nations to the north of Rabat or Dar Bouazza, the closest surf destination to Casa, south from the city.

Sleeping

Accommodation in Mohammedia is going through some changes at the moment, no doubt due to the privatization of the hotel industry. Closed at the time of writing were the 2 biggest establishments, the *Hotel Samir* and the *Hotel Miramar*, both of which are no doubt too potentially profitable to leave closed for very long.

B ***Hotel Sabah***, 42 Av des FAR, T023-321451. A recent hotel, mainly aimed at business travellers. Ugly furniture, 1st floor rooms noisy because of nightclub. Expensive for what it is. **C** ***Hotel Hager*** R Farhat Hached, T023-32592, F32592. Probably the best address in Mohammedia. Small, clean rooms, ocean view from some top-floor rooms. **D** ***Hotel La Falaise***, R Farhat Hached, T023-324828. Close to the beach. Some of the 10 rooms have showers en suite. Generally used by oil industry people. Reservations necessary, as popular and books up quickly. **E** ***Hotel Ennasser*** Av Abderrhamane Sarghini (as you stand in front of the kasbah entrance, on the left a few doors down the avenue). Most of the 11 rooms have no outside windows. For those wishing to go self-catering, try ***Complexe Skoura***, northeast of the town on the beach next to *Camping Les Mimosas*, T023-311993, F311995. Large holiday flats sleeping up to 8, minimum let a fortnight.

Camping ***Camping International Loran***, T023-322957. Pool, restaurant and shop, site of 4 ha, beach 100 m, bar, snacks, showers, laundry, first aid, electricity for caravans, petrol at 500 m. ***Camping Mimosa***, site of ½ ha, 3 km outside town, beach 100 m, grocery, showers, laundry, electricity for caravans, petrol 5 km. Clean site with shade. ***Camping Oubaha***, at Mansouria, 10 km north up the coast, site of 3 ha, only 100 m to beach, groceries, showers, laundry, first aid, electricity for caravans, petrol at 600 m. ***Camping Océan Bleu***, located on the coastal track 2 km from Les Mimosas, and ***Camping Saïd***, a small site 2 km from Mohammedia on the Rabat side of town, also have good reputations.

Eating

Most of the more expensive restaurants are on or around the R Farhat Hached end of town, close to the sea. Cheaper, still-acceptable places with terraces can be found at the roundabout opposite the kasbah gate (poor kids may show up, however, hoping to grab a share of your lunch or a couple of dirhams). **Expensive** ***Restaurant du Port***, 1 R du Port, T023-322466. Terrace, good food and service. ***Restaurant Sans Pareil***, R Farhat Hached, near *Hotel La Falaise*, T023-322855. A little snobbish, Casa bourgeoisie packs the terrace for Sun meals. Good seafood. ***Auberge des Grands Zenata***, T023-352102, midway between Casablanca and Mohammedia, seafood specialities, pricey. **Mid-range** ***La Frégate***, R Oued Zem, near *Hotel La Falaise*, T023-324447. Good for fish, try the paella. ***Restaurant des Sports***, R Farhat Hached, near *Hotel La Falaise*. Gets the Almodovar prize for tacky decor. Good seafood. ***Restaurant du Parc***, R de Fès, near the park and a wide avenue of araucarias.

Sport & activities

Golf Despite high winds, the 18-hole course is one of the best in Morocco, 5,917 m, par 72, 220dh per round, closed Tue, T023-322052. There is also a 9-hole course at Ben Slimane 30 km east of Mohammedia, 3,100 m, par 36, 200dh per round, open daily, T023-328793.. **Horse riding** *Club Equestre*, Blvd Moulay Youssef. **Sailing** *Yacht Club de Mohammedia*, Port de Mohammedia, T023-322331. Regattas Oct-May, well-equipped clubhouse.**Tennis** *Tennis Club de Mohammedia*, 9 courts, T023-322037. **Watersports** *Ibn Batouta Base Nautique de Mohammedia*. Water skiing popular here.

Tours & tour operators

Fedala Voyages, 35 Av des FAR, T023-327390.

Transport

Road Bus/taxi: frequent bus and grand taxi services into **Casablanca**. **Train** To **Rabat** between 0707 and 0107, to **Casablanca Port** between 0547 and 2306, and to **Casablanca Voyageurs** between 0526 and 0033, as well as to all other major destinations.

Directory

Airline offices *Royal Air Maroc*, junction of Av des FAR and R du Rif, T023-324841. **Banks** *BMCE*, on R Rachidi, a continuation of the wide Av Mohammed V, parallel to the Av des FAR, not far from *Hotel Sabah*. *BMCI*, on the roundabout at entrance to kasbah.

Routes from Casablanca

To Beni Mellal via Boujad & Kasbah Tadla

See Northwest of Beni Mellal, page 378, for further details

If you wish to reach the central High Atlas quickly from Casablanca, the **Beni Mellal** route is no bad option. From downtown Casablanca, follow signs for Oasis, Aéroport Mohammed Vand **Berrechid**, the centre of an important cereal producing area, with a ruined kasbah and an annual *moussem*. Next take the P13 past Ben Ahmed (ruined kasbah) off the highway to the south and on to **Khouribga**. This is not one of the most beautiful spots on earth, being the centre for phosphate extraction – these are said to be the world's richest phosphate deposits and some 65% of Morocco's annual phosphate production originates here. Film buffs note that Khouribga has an annual cinema festival with an emphasis on African and Arab films. **Oued Zem**, 33 km further east (once a military post and now an important market town), is reached after crossing the mining area (see page 379). Some 22 km further on, **Boujad**, definitely worth a quick stop, is known as a pilgrimage centre. Birthplace of the painter Ahmed Cherkaoui and once famed for its rugs (see page 379), it is an old town, founded perhaps in the 11th century with many shrines and a *moussem* in the autumn. After Boujad, the P13 continues south-southeast to **Kasbah Tadla** (also worth a quick stop), to intersect with the Marrakech to Azrou/Fès P24 road. Here you go right (south) for **Beni Mellal**.

To Marrakech

For the moment, Marrakech is practically a four-hour drive from Casablanca. Lorry traffic can be heavy, making overtaking perilous on certain stretches, and you will certainly need to pause at some point. Traffic south can be heavy on Friday evenings with Casa-Ribatis heading to Marrakech for their weekend. By late 2003, the dual carriageway as far as Settat should be completed. A full blown autoroute for Marrakech is on the drawing board.

Direct route Head south out of Casablanca on the dual carriageway through Oasis to **Berrechid** (or take the more restful minor road through Bouskoura) and on to **Settat**, a prosperous, well-planned town in the rich Chaouia plain. There are industries associated with agriculture (cereals, cattle and sheep), textiles and chemicals. Settat, hometown of Driss Basri, all-powerful interior minister in the 1980s and 1990s, pulled in major infrastructure investment. The town has higher education facilities and a golf course. South of Settat, you cross the Oum er Rbia, Morocco's major river, just after Mechra Benâbou. At **Skour Rehamna**, you are rather more than halfway to Marrakech. Here the lorries pull over at the barbecue road restaurants. Between Skhour and Benguerir there are some tricky places for overtaking. **Benguerir** is home to a major airbase, said to be important to the Americans as it is one of the few military aerodromes capable of handling space shuttles and the like. At Benguerir, a branch railway line runs west to Youssoufia (see below) and Safi. Next major settlement (and train stop) on the P9 is **Sidi Bou Othmane** (future site of the Marrakech international airport?). Next you cross the Jbilet, the low hills north of Marrakech, and soon the palm trees of the Red City are in sight.

Via Boulaouane and Youssoufia For those with plenty of time, there are other options to the easy P7 route, allowing you to take in the kasbah at Boulaouane (pronounced Boulawan) and the former mining town of Youssoufia. At Settat, head west-southwest on the S105 for Sidi Bennour. Your first stop is **Boulaouane** nicely located near the Oued Oum er Rbia in vine-growing country, home of the widely consumed *gris de Boulaouane*. Here, at a most strategic position above a meander of the *oued*, stand the remains of the kasbah built in 1710 by Moulay Ismaïl. (Best view, from the S105 where it crosses the Oum er Rbia.) One story runs that it was put up for his favourite concubine. A more likely reason is that it was a good idea to have a strongpoint on Morocco's only permanently flowing river, just out of day-trip distance for the marauding Portuguese ensconced in El Jadida. In its day, with crenellated ramparts flanked by seven bastions, the kasbah must have been very impressive. The ruins consist of a well, a tall square tower with arched gateway and part of the minaret. Some underground chambers have been located. After Boulaouane, continue on the S124 to Sidi Bennour. Here you go south on the P9 for Marrakech.

About 48 km south of Sidi Bennour, the S125 takes you 26 km west to **Youssoufia** (ex-Louis Gentil), a French-founded phosphate town renamed for Sultan Moulay Youssef after independence. It was once also known as Kachkat. If you like obscure early 20th-century mining settlements, this is the place for you. Up on the hill, the fine villas of the mining engineers would not look out of place in Normandy (give a palm tree and a stork or two). If you get lost, ask for Diour Ennasara. The phosphate industry is apparently running down at the moment, although trains to Safi, another polluted, industrial town, still run. Today, the town is hard-drinking and said to be a centre of mild, Tablighi, back-to-Islamic-roots type fundamentalism. The effect of phosphates in the water can be clearly seen in the locals' blackened teeth (or is it due to too much sweet tea?). Should you be thinking of staying, Tuesday is souk day in Youssoufia, with people travelling in from across the Abda region by horse and mule-drawn buggy. The only accommodation is at the **F** *Hotel Atlas*, T044-688050. As you come into town from south, go right opposite the *Total* station. The hotel is on your right after *hammam*, chemists and just before the *Wafa Bank*.

After Youssoufia, return to the P9 which will take you across the austerely beautiful Plateau des Ganntour and down into the Haouz plain and Marrakech. Another option is to continue south for 21 km on the S125 to **Chemaïa**, another mushrooming rural town. From here it is 78 km southeast to Marrakech on the P12/P9 (or 68 km west to Safi).

To Azemmour & El Jadida

There are two options for travelling southwest towards Azemmour and El Jadida. The inland P8, also the principal bus route, is quicker than but the more scenic coastal S130. This route leaves Casablanca via the busy Boulevard de la Corniche (hotels, beach terrace clubs, shops and bars) and follows the coast towards the **Marabout of Sidi Abderraman**. There is ample roadside parking here if you decide to take a closer look at the shrine. After turning left at the renowned restaurant *A Ma Bretagne* (see page 129), the road swings inland and, although the sea is often tantalizingly out of sight for much of the drive to Azemmour, there are glimpses of wide, empty (out of season) beaches. Approaching Azemmour, the vegetation becomes more lush, with eucalyptus lining the road. For camping, try **Tamaris Plage** at Km 16 (see page 128), *Camping Hawaii International*, T022-330070, at Km 25 and **Plage Sidi Rahad** at Km 29 (45 km from Azemmour).

Azemmour

Phone code: 023
Colour map 2, grid A3
Population: about 25,000
80 km SW of Casablanca

Perhaps the least visited of the old Portuguese coastal bastions, Azemmour has a backwater air. It is a town with a dual identity. There are the obvious attractions – the walk along the old ramparts, the stroll through the narrow streets of the médina, the view of the Oum er Rbia River – and then there is the walk up to the Zaouia of Moulay Bouchaïb. Here you can see the whole gammut of stalls and actitivites which are so much a part of a pilgrimage centre: herbalists, apothecaries and fortune tellers, henna-tattoo ladies and candle sellers. And for a summer bathe, about 1 km from the town is Haouzia beach.

Ins & outs
Reports of tourists being hassled

Getting there Azemmour is an easy excursion from El Jadida, with plenty of grands taxis doing the 20-min trip. There are now 5 trains a day from Casablanca and Rabat. The station, however, is a good 30-min walk from the town. If you arrive by car, park near the ramparts, where there will be some sort of 'warden'. **Getting around** All the sights are in easy walking distance. A child may show you up to the ramparts, while the beach is about 30 mins' walk away. The busy R Moulay Bouchaïb takes you up to the zaouia of the same name.

Background

There was a trading post here called Azama in the Carthaginian period, but earlier marble columns dating back to Punic times and Roman coins have also been found in the area. In the 15th century Azemmour was an important trading port on the routes between Portugal and West Africa, trading horses, carpets, *jallabah* and *haiks* with Guinea and cereals with Portugal. The Portuguese occupied Azemmour in 1513 as a base from which to attack Marrakech, but under opposition from the Saâdians had to withdraw in 1541. The town assumed regional importance under the Saâdians, but soon lost ground to the growth of its near neighbour, El Jadida. Azemmour is known for embroidery. The town is sometimes referred to as Moulay Bou Chaib, after its patron saint, who has a *zaouia* above the town. This town on the Oued Oum er Rbia was once noted for the widespread shad fishing throughout the cooler part of the year. The fish were caught as they went upstream to spawn. Water control barrages have drastically reduced the numbers.

Sights

Azemmour is still partly surrounded by imposing ochre ramparts with several attractively carved bastions often decorated with cannon. It is located at the mouth of the Oued Oum er Rbia. From the hill above the bridge on the east side of the river there is a most striking view of the médina with its white, square-fronted, flat-roofed houses stretching along the top of the steep bank opposite. The beach is also one of the best, but the town attracts few visitors.

The walls of the old médina can be explored by the rampart walk, also with excellent views of the town. The steps are at the northeast end of the walls. Via **Bab es-souq** enter the médina, with its clear Portuguese architectural influences and impressive wooden doors generally round-arched with carved keystones, and visit the *kissaria*, or covered market, and the **Sanctuary of Moulay Abdallah Ben Ahmed**. The doors of this house have a particular style, reminiscent of the Portuguese. A passageway to the left leads to the **kasbah**, which also had a role as a *mellah*, or Jewish quarter. In the kasbah, visit the **Dar el Baroud** building, the house of the powder, built within the ramparts between the médina and the kasbah. It is dominated by a tower from which there are views back over the rooftops towards the *oued*. The 16th-century kasbah gate is a strikingly simple semicircular arch. Climb its tower for a view of the town.

Sleeping
■ *on map*

Only 2 options here as the gentrifying guesthouse brigade has yet to arrive. **F** ***Hotel de la Poste***, next to the *PTT*, opposite the city walls. T023-357702. Clean and basic. **F** ***Hotel de la Victoire***, 308 Av Mohammed V, T023-347157. Cold showers, but friendly and handy if you need to stay over. Don't be tempted to **camp** in an isolated spot at Haouzia, the beach near Azemmour. There have been cases of violent theft.

Eating
● *on map*

Close to the médina the choice of cafés and restaurants includes ***Café l'Etoile de l'Atlantique***, a colourful place with a good terrace, and ***Café El Manzeh***, Av Mohammed V, close to Pl du Souk. You might also try ***Restaurant d'Azemmour***, for fresh fish, or ***Café Belle Vue***, a good vantage point for a view of the town. Outside the town is the popular, fine sandy beach of Haouzia, a ½-hr walk away, with the usual cafés, including ***Restaurant La Perle***, T023-347905, signposted from Pl du Souk (good in summer, a bit sad out of season).

El Jadida (ex-Mazagan) الجديدة

Phone code: 023
Colour map 2, grid A3
Population: 120,000

Popular in summer with Casablancans, El Jadida hibernates out of season. With its avenues and araucaria trees, it has a faint elegance reminiscent of some forgotten Mediterranean resort, the sort of place where you might film a Moroccan remake of Death in Venice. *El Jadida is best known, however, for its massive-walled citadel, the Cité Portugaise, its bastions and lookouts harking back to a time of armies equipped with pikestaffs and blunderbusses, of days when caravels were sailing for the Indies and Brazil.*

Ins and outs

Getting there

See Transport, page 145, for further details. In summer, try to get your bus tickets to major destinations a day ahead

El Jadida is easily accessible by public transport. There are plenty of buses to Casablanca (2 hrs), Marrakech (4 hrs, depending on service), and Essaouira (a punishing 7-hr ride). The town is a rather slow 1¾ hr drive from Casablanca, taking the coast road. There are grands taxis. The train service to Casa/Rabat has been reinstated, with 5 daily services. The bus station is south of the centre, along Av Mohammed V. From here it is a 5-10-min walk to Pl Mohammed V, the focus of the town. The train station lies 3 km south of El Jadida off to the west of the P8 (the Marrakech road) and, unfortunately, is not well signposted from the centre of town. Info on trains, T023-352824 or T022-220525.

Getting around

El Jadida is sufficiently small to do all the main sites on foot, and the cheap and reasonably priced hotels are all in the centre. You will want to do the Cité Portugaise, and stroll in the squares nearby. For beaches, the better ones are a short taxi ride away, past the Sidi Ouafi lighthouse (Phare de Sidi Ouafi), a beach popular with Moroccan families camping. The more distant Sidi Bouzid beach is also popular – and has more facilities (take bus No 2 or a grand taxi). If you have your own transport, the coastal village of Moulay Abdallah, with its zaouia complex, is 11 km southwards.

Tourist information

Délégation du Tourisme, Immeuble Chambre du Commerce, Av Ibn Khaldoun, T023-332724. **Syndicat d'Initiative**, Av Rafii opposite site of the Municipal Theatre, daily 0830-1200, 1430-1830. Limited range of information available but helpful staff are happy to provide details of hotel accommodation and tourist brochures of a general nature.

Background

El Jadida is short for 'El Médina El Jadida', the 'New Town'. Over its long history, however, the town has had at least four other names – El Breija, 'Little Fort', Mazagão for the Portuguese, El Mahdouma (The Destroyed) in the 18th century, and Mazagan under the French.

The area was probably occupied by the Phoenicians, and may well have been the trading post referred to as Rubisis by the ancient authors. Apparently a safe mooring and a strong defensive position, the site was occupied by the Almohads who built a *ribat*, or fortress, later abandoned. In the 16th century, the Iberian powers were building their empires in the Indies and the Americas. With trade growing, Portugal was wealthy enough to establish strongpoints along the African coast, and the fortress town they founded and named Mazagão in 1515 was to become one of their most important bases, and one of the longest lived, holding out after the fall of their other enclaves in northwest Africa.

Sultan Mohammed Ben Abdallah retook the town in 1769. But the town had been mined by the defeated Portuguese, who, according to legend, left someone behind to light the fuses; in the explosion, large numbers of celebrating

Moroccan soldiers were killed. The old fortress town thus acquired a sinister reputation – and the nickname El Mahdouma, 'The Demolished'. On the wild Atlantic coast, the massive defences left by the Portuguese were far too valuable to be left abandoned for long. Reconstruction works were launched in 1815 by Sultan Sidi Abd al-Rahman. In 1844, after the Moroccan forces had been defeated by the French at Isly – and the sultan's authority duly weakened – the Doukkala tribes looted the town. However, European merchants were to settle and the town began to expand beyond the walls of the original Portuguese city. There was also an influx of Jews from neighbouring Azemmour in the 19th century, and the town was further developed by the French as the chief town of the Doukkala region, also handling much of the trade with Marrakech. Under the French Protectorate, the usual new avenues, gardens, along with administrative and residential neighbourhoods, were carefully laid out.

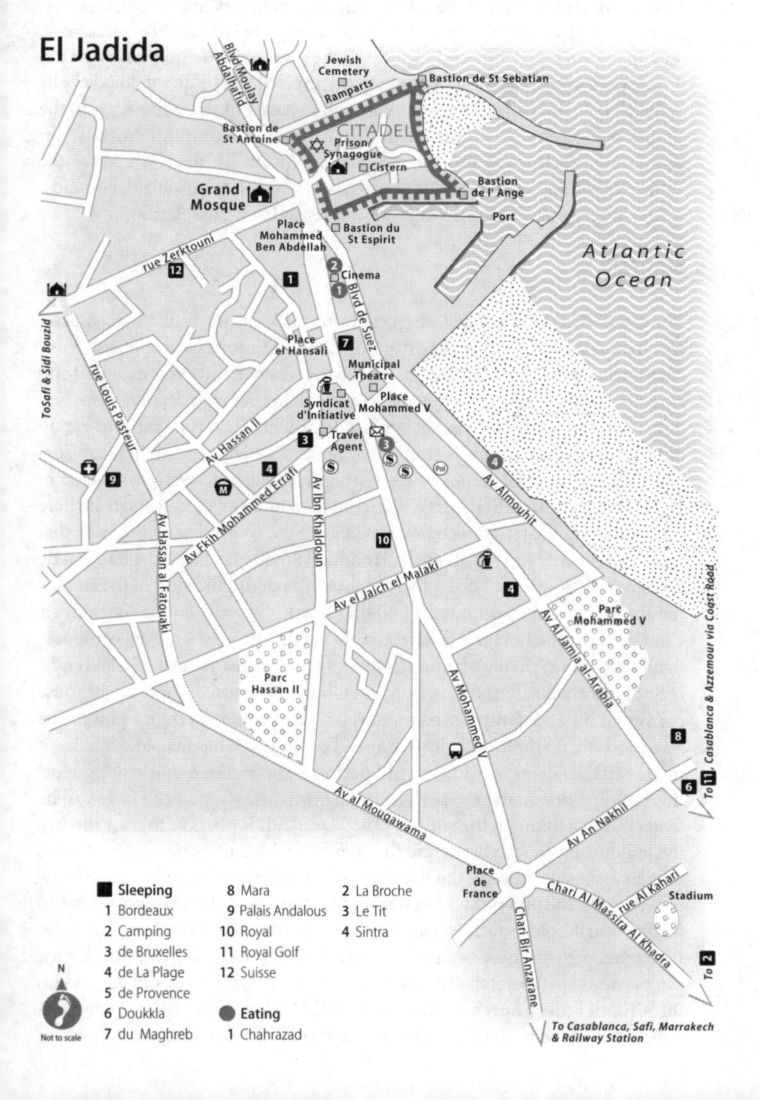

Today, El Jadida is a sleepy sort of small town, home to provincial administration, a university and a busy port, much involved in sardine fishing. Without the development of ports at Safi and of course, Casablanca, it would no doubt have been much bigger. There are, however, deep-water port facilities just to the south of the town, at Jorf Lasfar ('Yellow Cliff'), developed in the 1980s for processing and shipping phosphate rock from the Gantour and Ouled Abdoun regions to the south. Artificial fertilizers are manufactured and exported. There is also a major petrochemical complex. The main 'curiosity' is the old Portuguese cistern dating from the 16th century.

Often referred to as 'Deauville of Morocco' in the 1930s, El Jadida had rather lost its reputation as a tourist destination in the 1980s, not least due to the pollution of coastal waters and the mucky state of the beach. Poor rural migrants from the Doukkala plain settled on the city edge. The summer influx of mainly Moroccan tourists is short (mid-July to mid-September), after which hibernation sets in. However, things look set to change as El Jadida is too pleasant to remain undeveloped forever. In late 2000, the scandalous demolition of the old municipal theatre raised lots of protest, and revealed that the town does have its defenders. On a positive note, the Portuguese have put some money into the citadel, the golf course is attractive, and the Moroccan authorities' emphasis on promoting beach resort tourism may have spin-offs for the town. Once the autoroute is completed, El Jadida (and the beaches to the south at Sidi Bou Zid), will be in very easy driving distance for weekends from Casablanca.

Sights

Citadel

The Citadel was built by the Portuguese from 1513, and its distinctive character was maintained after their departure in 1769 by European and Jewish merchants who settled here from 1815. The quarter is small and easily explored and contains some attractive Portuguese and Jewish houses with decorated, arched doorways and wrought-iron balconies. Check whether it is possible to get up onto the ramparts. Access is from the right of the main gates. These are surmounted by the escutcheons of the Portuguese kings and were completed in 1541. The **Bastion du St Esprit** is located at the southwest corner and from here the walk along the ramparts follows a canal on the south side, which is all that remains of the old moat that once surrounded the citadel. From the **Bastion de l'Ange** at the southeast corner there is a superb panoramic view of the citadel, the fishing harbour and beach. Looking north the walls are broken on the coastal side by the **Porte de la Mer**, the old sea gate from where the Portuguese finally left in 1769; many of the other interesting features of the old walled city – including a chapel, hospital, prison and Governor's palace – and a lighthouse converted into the **Grand Mosque** can be seen from this vantage point. The minaret, built on the foundations of an old watchtower, has five sides making it unique in the Islamic world. The **old prison** was converted into a synagogue; this building dominates the skyline to the north and the Star of David can be seen clearly high up on the white-fronted facade. It is possible to gain entry to the building if you are able to find the guardian with the key but there is little of note to see inside. Beyond the Porte de la Mer, the ramparts walk can be completed via the **Bastion de St Sébastian** and the **Bastion de St Antoine**. From this final section the old Jewish cemetery can be seen to the north outside the city walls. If you choose to make use of the services of a guide for this tour, make sure that the price is negotiated beforehand. Located between the entry gates and the Bastion du St Esprit is the **Church of Our Lady of the Assumption**, a Portuguese construction restored by the French in 1921, and later converted into a mosque.

The **Cistern**, a most distinctive feature of the citadel, below street level on Rue Mohammed Ahehami Bahbai, dates from the 16th century and was probably originally designed to store munitions. It served as a fencing school before being used after completion of the town walls in 1541 as a tank to store water for times of shortage. When full, the Cistern reportedly held 4 million litres of water. The symmetrical construction has a vaulted roof supported by 25 circular and rectangular pillars, with just one central window in the ceiling, 3.5 m in diameter, producing a single shaft of light. Covering the flagstones is a shallow sheet of water, producing a shimmering reflection of the vaulted ceiling in the half-light. In the entrance hall to the Cistern there is a small display of 17th-century muskets and other Portuguese weaponry originally found on the ramparts. ■ *0830-1200, 1430-1800. 10dh.*

Orson Welles filmed scenes of his epic Othello in the Cistern. It was also used in the 1980s' neo-Orientalist pic, Harem, starring Nastasja Kinski and in a recent Moroccan TV ad for coffee!

Outside the citadel, the other main focus of interest is the area between Place Mohammed V and Place Mohammed Ben Abdallah and the immediately adjacent streets. The main shops, banks and restaurants are here, together with cinemas and the Municipal Theatre, and the pedestrianized Place El Hansali provides a pleasant alternative to the corniche for a relaxing drink on a café terrace.

Excursions

Beaches & Moulay Abdallah (Tit)

The beaches south of El Jadida on the S121 are reached by bus No 2 and grands taxis. First is **Sidi Ouafi**, then the more developed (and polluted) **Sidi Bouzid**, with a bar, café-restaurants and a campsite. Here at Sidi Bouzid the gulls congregate in their hundreds between November and February each year. **Moulay Abdallah (Tit)** is a fishing village with an attached site of religious importance, lying 10 km from El Jadida. Tit, meaning 'the source', was founded by Ismaïl Amghar, an ascetic from Arabia, who settled here in the 11th century. The minaret of Ismaïl Amghar dates from the Almoravid period, and is almost intact. The place was renamed Moulay Abdallah after a son of Ismaïl Amghar who founded a *zaouia* and another mosque here and built the fortifications. The shrine attracts many pilgrims to its annual *moussem* in August. This is one of the major festivals of the Moroccan calendar with up to 200,000 visitors. Thousands of horsemen take part in the parades and displays, magnificent in their skill and their costumes. In recent years, the *moussem* has been called off, the authorities being concerned about health and security problems generated by large numbers assembling in informal campsites.

Kasbah of Boulaouane

See also Casablanca to Marrakech via Boulaouane and Youssoufia, page 137

Travelling south on the P8 turn off left after 20 km onto the S105. This route crosses a flat, fertile arable landscape of fields divided by low stone walls before reaching the treelined entry to **Had Ouled Frej**, an untidy settlement with the saving grace of having a petrol station in an emergency. **Boulaouane** is another 19 km from here and areas of low bushy vines planted in the reddish-brown soil become increasingly frequent. The best view is obtained by turning left to the bridge over the Oued Oum er Rbia, but access to the kasbah itself is only by turning right on the S124 towards Sidi Bennour and then left and left again.

Gorges de Méhéoula

Also known as the Gorges des Orangers. Take the road south out of Azemmour, turning right just before the Oued Oum er Rbia, and left at the first junction to keep alongside the *oued*. About 9 km from here, there is a signed turning left (north), giving the best view of this gorge.

Essentials

Sleeping

■ on map, page 141

Hotels are often heavily booked in the summer, so ring ahead, particularly if arriving late at night

The **Délégation du Tourisme** on Av Ibn Khaldoun (T023-344788) may be able to help if you are stuck. Moroccan families often rent villas or flats for the summer. This could be an option to investigate if you like El Jadida enough to stay for a week. There is 1 really good hotel, and some nice surprises among the cheap addresses.

L ***Sofitel Royal Golf Hotel***, Km 7 Route Casablanca, BP 542, T023-354141. Next to the *Royal Golf Club*, complex of whitewashed buildings with beautiful gardens, 220 rooms, 2 restaurants, pool, sauna, 2 tennis courts, nightclub, hairdresser and shop, conference room, parking, room price includes breakfast, dinner menu 200dh. Secluded location only 100 m from the 1st hole of the golf course and close to beach, all facilities. Can provide information on horse riding. **C** ***Hotel Doukkala***, Av de la Ligue Arabe, T023-343737, F340501. Situated some distance south of the Cité Portugaise, a modern but unexciting hotel with 81 rooms, restaurant, bar, tennis court, pool, parking. Ideally located for those requiring a beach holiday. Ask for one of the revamped rooms, some have nice balconies. Canteen smell in public areas, too expensive for what's on offer, but prices open to negotiation out of season. **D** ***Hotel Palais Andalous***, Blvd Docteur de Lanoë, T023-343745. 31 rooms, parking. In Protectorate days, this hotel was the residence of Pacha Hammou. With its fine courtyard, it should be a fantastic hotel. The rooms smell damp, the 'suite' looks as though it was mis-decorated from a 1970s junk shop, the restaurant is sinister, general atmosphere glacial. Hotel situated a little way out of town off Av Hassan II close to the *Hôpital Mohammed V*. **D** ***Hotel de Provence***, 42 Av Fkih Errafi, T023-342347, F352115. 16 rooms. A popular choice but not good value. Windows don't close, bathrooms tiny, no towels nor soap. Nice manager.

E ***Hotel de Bruxelles***, 40 Av Ibn Khaldoun, T023-342072. 14 rooms, balconies with wrought iron, old tiles, all a bit 1930s. Parking, some rooms with bath, convenient central location, Kamel on reception very pleasant. Best value in this bracket, even though it doesn't look much. **E** ***Hotel Royal***, 108 Av Mohammed V, T023-341100, T342839. 38 rooms, TV room, gardens, terrace, comfortable establishment with restaurant, well situated for the bus station which is only a short walk up Av Mohammed V. Street-side rooms noisy. **E** ***Hotel Suisse***, 145 R Zerktouni, T023-342816. 21 rooms, most without shower, restaurant, parking, reasonable value. **F** ***Hotel Bordeaux***, 47 R Moulay Ahmed Tahiri, T023-342356. Old but clean, hot showers available. Difficult to find, despite all the signs. **F** ***Hotel de la Plage***, Av Al Jamia al Arabia, T023-342648. Cheap and reliable. **F** ***Hotel du Maghreb (et de France)***, R Lescoul, just off Pl Mohammed V, T023-342181. Feels like a mansion furnished with broken camping furniture. Marble staircase and peeling formica. Convenient, good low-budget option – could be magnificent. Views from roof terrace. **F** ***Hotel du Port***, on Blvd Suez (near *Snack Ramsès*), the ocean-side street leading to the Cité Portugaise. Masochists only.

If you are thinking of swimming at the main beach at Sidi Bouzid, note that water and sand are polluted as the resort has no sewage facilities

Sidi Bouzid and down the coast **B** ***Hotel Hacienda***, Centre Balnéaire de Sidi Bouzid, T023-348311. 12 rooms, restaurant, bar, pool, tennis, kiosk, conference room, parking. **B-C** ***Hotel Le Relais***, 26 km south of El Jadida on Safi road, T023-345498. Best rooms have balconies with ocean view. Good menu at 120dh, alcohol served, popular at weekends. **D** ***Hotel-Restaurant La Brise***, 37 km from El Jadida on Safi coast road, T023-346917. Half-board compulsory, meals around 100dh, mainly fish, small pool (pay for access).

Camping *Camping International*, Av des Nations Unies, T023-342755. At entrance to El Jadida, coming from Casablanca. Restaurant, shop and pool, site of 4 ha, only 500 m from beach, showers, laundry, electricity for caravans. Also has chalet accommodation for 260dh/night. ***Camping Sidi Bou Zid***, by beach, bus No 2, 5 km out of town.

Eating
• *on map, page 141*

Expensive ***Restaurant Le Tit***, 2 Av Al Jamia al Arabia, T023-343908. Open 1200-1500 and 1900-2300, closed Mon, expensive (for El Jadida) but good quality, main courses range from 45-90dh, Visa and Mastercard, convenient central location. 'Tit' means spring or source in Amazigh.

Mid-range ***Restaurant La Provence***, 42 Av Fkih Errafi, T023-342347. European and seafood dishes 50-60dh, fixed price menu 74dh, a/c, credit cards. Not really worth bothering with – go for ***Le Tit*** instead. ***Restaurant Ali Baba***, Av Al Jamia al Arabia, on the coastal route to Casablanca, 5-min walk from *Hotel Doukkala*, T023-341622. Upstairs restaurant with excellent views of the sea and the Cité Portugaise, 3-course menu 85dh, plenty of choice from à la carte dishes, open lunchtimes and 1930-2230. Recommended but you will need a car or petit taxi from the centre of town; also café and pizzeria downstairs. ***Chez Chiquito***, fish by the port.

Cheap ***Restaurant La Broche***, Pl El Hansali. Small restaurant on 2 floors on a busy square, popular with locals, offering keenly priced choice of dishes and quick, friendly service, dinner menu mainly fish 35-80dh but you will also find couscous, chicken and other meat courses for 25-40dh, also open lunchtimes. Probably the best of the cheaper restaurants. ***Restaurant Le Caporal***, 40 Blvd de Suez. Open midday till late. Good value. ***Restaurant Chahrazade***, Pl El Hansali. Broadly similar to *La Broche*, from which it is separated by the *Cinéma Le Paris*. Very good value, 20dh *tajine*, 5dh small salad. ***Restaurant La Portugaise***, just inside the citadel when you come from the new town. Small, good value restaurant. ***Restaurant Ramsès***, Blvd de Suez, simple snack restaurant next to the ***Hotel du Port***, not far from Cité Portugaise.

Cafés *Café Sintra*, Av Almouhit. Has a good open-air terrace with sea views; look for other cafés along this stretch of the seafront (warden controlled street parking available here) and also in and around Pl el Hansali.

Bars

Not much choice for drinkers in El Jadida. Try ***Hotel le Palais Andalous***, Blvd Docteur de Lanoë, T023-343745. Also try ***Hotel de la Plage*** (for an ordinary sort of bar) at 3 Av Al Jamia al Arabia.

Entertainment

Cinemas There are 2 in Pl el Hansali, **Cinéma du Rif** and **Cinéma Le Paris**. The theatre has been demolished.

Shopping

The main traditional shops and stalls are around R Zerktouni. El Jadida also has a reputation for craftwork in brass, on sale in Pl Mohammed ben Abdallah and Pl Moulay Youssef at its junction with R Zerktouni close to the entrance to the Citadel. North of the ramparts near the Bastion de St Antoine there is an open-air market, providing cheap clothes and household goods to locals. A souk is held near the lighthouse on Wed. To find this, take the coastal route to Sidi Bouzid via R Zerktouni.

Sport & activities

Golf *Royal Golf Club*, T023-352251. 6,274 m, 18 holes, par 72, fees 300dh weekday, 350dh weekend, club hire 75dh. **Riding** *Real Club Equestre S/C de Tribunal Regional*, best contacted via the *Sofitel Royal Golf Hotel*. **Tennis** *Tennis Club Jedidi*, Parc Hassan II, T023-342775. 5 courts. Also at the *Sofitel*.

Transport
Bus times change regularly

Road The bus station is in Av Mohammed V, approximately 1 km south of Pl Mohammed V. The *CTM* service from **Marrakech** has been discontinued, leaving only badly maintained buses on this run. (The 200 km to Marrakech can take around 3½ hrs.) For **Safi**, first bus at 0400 followed by a further 7 buses with the last at 1830. For **Casablanca/Rabat**, 9 buses at hourly or 2-hourly intervals, 0620-1730. For **Agadir**, 7 buses,

0700-1800. For **Oualidia**, 1 bus for most of the year, 2 in summer. For **Taroudant**, change at Agadir. Other destinations include **Settat** (0500, 0700, 0800 and 1130) and **Sidi Bennour** (1030, 1330 and 1730). **Train** The old 0810 to Casablanca no longer runs.

Directory **Banks** *BMCE Bank*, on Av Fkih Errafi. *BMCI Bank*, on Av Al Jamia al Arabia. *Crédit de Maroc*, *Bank al-Maghrib* and *WAFA* banks on and around Pl Mohammed V. **Communications** Post: *PTT Centrale*, Pl Mohammed V. **Medical services** Chemists: night pharmacies available at *Sidi Daoui*, 14 Blvd Moulay Abdelhafid, T023-353448, and *Pharmacy Ennour*, 77 Av Jamal Eddine el Afghani, T023-351240.

Oualidia

Phone code: 023
Colour map 2, grid A3

Almost midway between El Jadida and Safi, Oualidia is a restful, unspoiled sort of place. Named for the Saâdian Sultan El Oulalid, who built a kasbah there in the 1630s, the town is best known today for its oysters and its restaurants. There is a small fishing port, a lagoon, safe swimming – and ample amusement for twitchers, as the inlets and beaches are much appreciated by migrating birds in autumn and spring. Busy in summer, it's very tranquil for the rest of the year.

Ins & outs Oualidia is 78 km south of El Jadida – say 45 mins by car – and 66 km north of Safi. There is 1 slow bus a day (2 in summer) from El Jadida, taking well over an hour, and 3 from Safi, taking around 1½ hrs.

Sights The village of Oualidia forms a crescent shape around a peaceful lagoon, entered by the sea through two breaches in a natural breakwater. Above the beach, the skyline on the wooded hillside is dominated by the **kasbah** built in 1634 by a Saâdian sultan to defend the pleasant and potentially useful harbour (a track to right off the S121 opposite the turning to Tnine Gharbia leads up to the building).

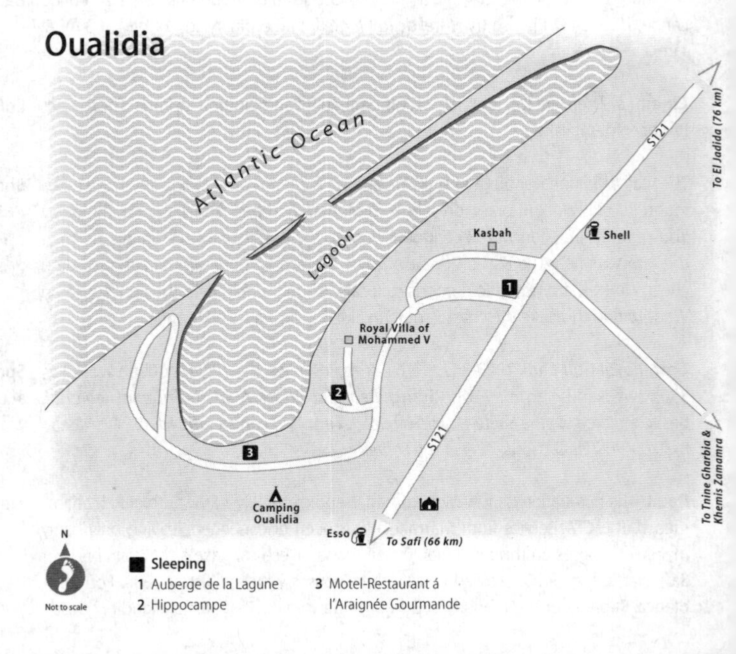

Birds in paradise

After the industrial port of Jorf Lasfar, south of El Jadida, the coast starts to become of interest to birdwatchers. At times, the road runs close to the seashore past a series of small, deserted sandy beaches, little bays and inlets dotted with fishing boats. At Sidi Moussa, there are dunes, which further south give way to salt marsh and a long chain of lagoons. This part of the Moroccan Atlantic coast is thus popular with birdwatchers during the spring and autumn migrations, particularly between Sidi Moussa and Oualidia and at Cap Beddouza. The range of habitats, including rocky coast, lagoons and salt flats to dunes and scrub, makes for a variety of species. In addition, given its latitude, the area is important for over-wintering. All year there are flamingoes, cattle and little egrets, white storks and grey herons and even the tiny Sardinian warbler. Migrants include the collared pratincole and little tern,gulls and waders. The slender-billed curlew has also occasionally been spotted. Access is possible by bus, if you ask to be dropped off at a suitable place, but travel by car is far easier.

Below it is the now disused **royal villa** built by Mohammed V as a summer palace. The town has a market (Saturday) for local agricultural produce. The lagoon and beach provide an ideal sheltered location for sailing, surfing, windsurfing and fishing. From late June to September, Oualidia is very busy, being referred to in some circles as 'le St Tropez de Marrakech'. The beach gets very crowded and the water is none too clean. Off-season, you have the beautiful surroundings almost to yourself. The oyster beds came into production in the late 1950s, and annual production is of the order of 200 tonnes, mainly for local consumption. Early fruit and vegetables, and in particular tomatoes, are produced here under plastic for local and European consumption.

For a change of beach, you could head for **Lalla Fatna**, just 2 km outside the main village, signposted. For those with a car, a possible side-excursion is to the **Kasbah Gharbia** about 20 km to the southeast on the S1336. The kasbah is a huge enclosure, with a large white building in the centre, no doubt the home of a local notable in Protectorate times. The locals will be pleased to have a visit, and will no doubt show you round.

Sleeping & eating

Oualidia can get very crowded in high summer. Hotel reservations essential

If a holiday home on the Moroccan Atlantic attracts you, contact www.oualidia.net and take a look at *Les Jardins de la Lagune* or contact their Casablanca office on T022-982332. **B** *Hotel Hippocampe*, T023-366108, F366461. 20 rooms, small, very relaxed, good restaurant, bar, tennis and immaculate pool, beautiful setting above lagoon. **C** *Hotel Auberge de la Lagune*, currently closed due to internal management problems. **D** *Motel-Restaurant à l'Araigneé Gourmande*, T023-366447, F366144. 15 rooms all with balconies, 6 with ocean view, good restaurant particularly for fish, street parking, welcoming staff, slight damp smell, dining room a bit gloomy but terrace views of the lagoon, royal villa, recommended. Cheap menu 70dh, 200dh menu with lobster. **D** *Hotel Restaurant l'Initiale*, T023-366246. Opened 2000, 6 spacious rooms near ocean, 1 with ocean view, very clean, charming. Good Italian menu at 90dh, expensive menu at 180dh. **D** *Restaurant Ostréa II*, on your right as you come into Oualidia from the Casablanca direction. Oysters and white wine, nice lagoon view. (*Restaurant Ostréa I* is in Casablanca).

For **cheap** eats, *Les Roches* has a good 80dh menu, nice service and air of the 1960s, while *Tomato Beach* with its little terrace does seafood, including a plate of fried fish for 40dh and a splendid *tajine de poisson*. WC none too clean. *Le Thalassa*, opened in 1999, has a restaurant and a few rooms. Nice terrace for dining, menu at 50dh.

El Jadida – Oualidia road **C** *Le Relais*,T023-345498, at Sidi Abed. Restaurant all year round (except Ramadhan), accommodation in summer. A handy coffee stop if you're on a long drive. **D** *Villa La Brise*, T023-346917. With bar and good cooking.

Camping *Camping Municipal* and *Camping International de Oualidia*, T023-366160. Site of 30 ha, bar, snacks, restaurant, grocery shop, hot and cold showers, laundry, petrol at 1 km, electricity for caravans in summer only 10dh per night, other charges per night: caravan 30dh, tent 30dh, car 2dh, person 3dh.

Southwards to Safi

Travelling south from Oualidia, the S121 is elevated with the land falling away to the east towards a cultivated plain; to the west there are beautiful views of craggy coastlines, broad reaches of deserted beach and the Atlantic Ocean beyond. Despite the isolated nature of much of this route, you are unlikely to travel far before passing optimistic traders offering bead necklaces and other trinkets for sale. The landscape becomes more barren approaching the rocky headland and green-topped lighthouse at **Cap Beddouza** (ex-Cap Cantin), a dominating, fortress-style building. This remote promontory is believed to be where a shrine to the sea god Poseidon was built in the fifth century BC by the Carthaginian navigator Hanno. The final 30 km of the route into Safi has some splendid cliff scenery as the road follows the sweep of the bay towards **Cap Safi** and then beyond to **Sidi Bouzid** (see page 154). Make sure that you stop here to enjoy the extensive views of Safi, notably the commercial port and fishing harbour, the Portuguese fortress, médina and the new town on the hill above the old town.

Safi آسفي

Phone code: 044
Colour map 2, grid A2
Population: about 400,000

Safi is the largest of the five historic Atlantic coastal towns, with fortifications and other sights going back to a Lusitanian past, a good deal of industry and much poverty. Despite its médina and renown as a centre for fine, traditional pottery, it is probably for enthusiasts only. For those in search of architectural oddities, the médina contains a fragment of a cathedral in the Manueline Gothic style, all that the Portuguese had the time to build during their brief occupation in the 16th century. Unlike El Jadida to the north, Safi was an enclave where they stayed a mere 33 years.

Ins and outs

Getting there

See Transport, page 155, for further details

Safi is easily accessible by bus from Casablanca (4¾ hrs), Essaouira (4 hrs) and El Jadida (2½ hrs). There is 1 daily train from Casablanca which goes via Benguerir on the Casablanca to Marrakech line. If driving, Safi is on the S121 coastal road from El Jadida and the P12 from Marrakech. Approaching on the main P8 from Casablanca and El Jadida to Essaouira and Marrakech, turn along the P12 from Tleta de Sidi Bouguedra.

Getting around

The train station is south of the town centre – take a taxi to the médina. The bus station is southeast of the town centre, say 1½ km from the médina. Turn out of the bus station onto Av du Président Kennedy, past the *Hotel Abda*, at the first main junction, Pl Idriss, bear right (north) and follow the road north for the Pl de l'Indépendence and the médina. Parallel to this street, further west, the R du Caïd Sidi Abderrahman, subsequently becoming R de R'bat, will also take you there. All the major sites in the old town are within walking distance of each other. Beaches are a different matter. South of the town, the coast is highly polluted by the chemical industry. Local buses (Nos 10 and 15) run up to Lalla Fatna, a sheltered beach 15 km north of the town.

Tourist information

Tourist offices Ave de la Liberté, Ville Nouvelle. Open Mon-Fri 0900-1200, 1500-1830. The office is in a portacabin in a side street opposite the *Hotel Assif*. Although you will receive a friendly welcome only generalized tourist literature about Morocco seems to be available, so expect little by way of specific maps and information about Safi itself.

Background

Safi is a port and an important industrial centre. Its harbour has been important since pre-Roman times and it was one of the first areas of Morocco to receive Islam. Later it was the site of a ribat held by ascetic Muslim warriors.

The Almohads surrounded the city with ramparts and built the **Zaouia of Sheikh Mohammed Saleh**. During their rule, Safi had an active intellectual and religious life. The first written mention of the town goes back to 11th-century geographer, El Bakri, who wrote that ".. the ships sail up along the coast from the Oued Souss to Marsa Amegdoul (today's Essaouira).. and then to Marsa Kouz (the mouth of the River Tensift), which is the port of Aghmat, and thence to Marsa Asafi". El Idrissi, writing in the mid-12th century, said that ships could load at Safi "when the Ocean of Shadows was calm".

The Portuguese had had a trading centre at Safi since 1481 and took control of the town in 1508, building a citadel, repairing the kasbah and building the distinctive **Dar el Bahr** (Castle of the Sea) in 1523, to defend the northern entrance of the port and to be the official residence of the governor. Some of the cannon, cast in Spain and the Netherlands, remain today, 'protecting' the town. The Portuguese left in 1541. Under the Saâdians in the later 16th century, Safi developed a role as the port for the sugar produced at Chichaoua and for Souss copper, a strategic raw material much in demand in the foundries of Europe. The Saâdians also built the **Grand Mosque** in the médina.

Detail map
A Safi centre, page 153

In the 17th century, European countries had a significant trading presence in Safi, and Moulay Ismaïl was instrumental in developing the city in the early 18th century. Under Sidi Mohammed Ben Abdallah, trade intensified, with France, England, the Dutch Republic and Denmark all having agents. An indication of the effects of contact with Europe is given by a Dr Lempriere, an English visitor in 1789: "During the time I spent in the town, I lodged in a Jewish house where I saw two Arabs who had been to London, and who spoke a few words of English. They thought to please me greatly when they proffered a chair and a small table. Since I had left Tangiers, I had only seen this furniture, now completely indispensable to us, at the French consul's house in Rabat".

However, developments were cruel to Safi. Its position as the chief diplomatic port for the capital, Marrakech, was removed when Essaouira was rebuilt in the late 18th century. Between 1791 and 1883, no less than 18 natural catastrophes of various kinds hit the town. Nevertheless, not all was doom and gloom: in the mid-19th century, potters from Fès came to settle, bringing with them their craft skills. The Jewish community developed – it says much for the open-mindedness of Safi that there was never any walled-off *mellah* area – and a mixed Franco-Hispano-Portuguese commercial and fishing community gradually took root.

Safi was the base of a large sardine fishing fleet, which continues to this day, and, for many years, Safi was the biggest world sardine port. Large schools of sardines are present as a result of the currents of cold water bathing the coasts south of El Jadida in the summer, and more than 30,000 tonnes of fish now pass through the port annually – hence an important processing and canning industry, providing much employment for women.

Under the French, Safi was developed as a port for exporting phosphate rock, connecting it by rail to the mines around Youssoufia. In 1964 a new processing complex for Maroc-Chimie to the south of the town came on line, allowing the export of phosphate fertilizers, as well as unprocessed phosphates, and established Safi as one of Morocco's largest ports.

The development of Safi has been rapid, with the population rising from 40,000 in 1960 to 400,000 today. The once bustling multinational sardine port has become a provincial city where a combination of factors have produced rather negative results. Chemical products poured into the sea have had a bad effect on the fish population. There are no useable town beaches, and scant respect has been paid to the town planning regulations. There is a huge sub-standard housing problem, especially in the médina. A few years ago, a large number of the urban poor of Agadir and Marrakech were apparently relocated to Safi, creating a certain climate of insecurity – no doubt much exaggerated. A Safi lobby has yet to get together to 'do something', and many former Safiots who grew up there in the 1950s and 1960s prefer not to go back. This is all rather unfortunate, given the fact that the town does have an interesting history and sights. Although it will never be a major destination, it would be a pity if Safi's tourist potential was totally neglected.

Sights

The médina

The médina, with its ramparts and large towers, slopes westwards towards the sea and can be entered by the main gate, **Bab Chaaba**. The main thoroughfare which runs from Place de l'Indépendence to Bab Chaaba is Rue du Socco, around which are located the main souks. It is a busy, bustling area, with shops and street stalls selling all manner of food, jewellery, cheap toys and plastic goods. Close to the northern wall of the médina near Bab Chaaba is the pottery souk, a colourful alleyway and courtyard crammed with pots and plates displaying a wide variety of local designs. This leads on up some steps to an open courtyard with attractive archways housing some further pottery stalls. Just off the Rue du Socco is the **Grand Mosque** with a notable minaret, and behind it a ruined Gothic church built by the Portuguese, and originally intended as part of a larger cathedral. There is also an interesting old *medresa*. On the east flank of the médina is the **Kechla**, which houses the **National Ceramics Museum**, a large kasbah built by the Saâdians, clearly identifiable with its towers and green-tiled roofs. It offers some outstanding views over the médina and the potters' quarter at Bab Chaaba. The entrance opens out into the main courtyard, gardens and a terrace. Displays of ceramics here are divided into three sections: contemporary, local and ancient and, amongst these, are some very fine pieces of 20th-century Safi pottery. The visit might even inspire you to visit the local potters, where a cruder form of pottery is available and the construction can be observed. ■ *0830-1200, 1400-1800. 10dh. T044-463895.* On the right of its entrance is a large round tower built by the Portuguese, and within the **Kechla** is the **Bahia Palace**, an 18th-century governor's residence flanked by gardens.

Dar el Bahar

Just outside the médina ramparts, overlooking the sea, is the Dar el Bahar fort and prison built by the Portuguese in 1523. Used by them as the governor's residence, it was restored in the 1960s. Entry is under an archway, inscribed 'Château de Mer', opposite the *Hotel Majestic*. Just to the left of the pay kiosk is a *hammam* and to the right is the prison tower. You can see the dungeon area and climb the spiral staircase of the tower (narrow and dark in places) for views of the médina, Kechla and port from the top. Back at the foot of the tower, access to the ramparts on the seaward side of the fortress is via a ramp. Here can be seen an impressive array of Dutch and Spanish cannon pointing out to sea; castings on two of these show 'Rotterdam 1619' and two others are marked 'Hague 1621'. From the top of the southwest bastion there is a further opportunity to enjoy a fine panorama, including the coast southwards towards Essaouira. ■ *0830-1200, 1430-1800. 10dh.*

Town centre

Modern Safi has two main squares, the Place de l'Indépendence and Place Mohammed V. Located just to the south of the junction of Avenue Moulay Youssef and Boulevard du Front de Mer, Place de l'Indépendence is a busy street with a central, treelined reservation, flanked by shops, banks, cafés and restaurants. Street markets are also to be found here and in the Rue de R'bat to the south. Dar el Bahar sits at the northwest corner of the square. In contrast, on the hill high above the old town, Place Mohammed V is a large, modern paved area somewhat lacking in character, a focal point for the seven streets converging on it. The town hall is the main building here and the principal post office, the tourist office and the more expensive hotels are close by.

The Potters Quarters

These quarters at **Bab Chaaba** are well worth a visit: you can see all the stages of the pottery process happen in and around tiny workshops. From the port side of the old town, you can cut straight through to the potters' area which centres on the marabout Sidi Abderrahman, Moula El Bibane, 'Protector of the city gates' and patron of the potters; the whole area was given official listing as being of historic importance in 1920. Safi once produced pottery with an international reputation (and also continues to make the green tiles found on many major buildings throughout Morocco). The recent development of the potteries is an interesting story, shedding light on French policy towards traditional crafts in Morocco.

Lamali and the invention of art pottery in Safi

First French resident-general in Morocco, Hubert Lyautey had a great interest in all things Moroccan, and in particular in its traditional heritage. A special Service des Beaux-Arts was set up in Rabat to study traditional crafts. A ceramics unit was established and the director, on a visit to Paris to discuss plans, was introduced to one Boujemaâ Lamali, a master potter from Kabylia (Algeria). The result of this chance meeting was the birth of art-pottery in Safi.

Born in 1890, Lamali had wanted to be a potter from childhood. He studied under master-ceramicist Soupierau at the Fine Arts School in Algiers, and subsequently in Paris. After the First World War, he was sent to Fès to train apprentice potters to give new life to the local pottery industry – but preferred to settle in Safi, where things were less hidebound. From 1918 to 1935 he ran the Safi pilot workshop. Although there was some resistance from local potters at first, the tiny unit attracted some keen students, some of whom were later to become master potters. Under the influence of Lamali, the purest old shapes were revived, experiments were made with iridescent colours and turquoise-blue backgrounds, and new decorative motifs were introduced, including the khidous design, with its lozenges evoking weavings from the High Atlas. Safi firing techniques were applied to Rif-type pottery, traditionally hand-modelled with matt black decoration. Safi pottery was to win international fame at the universal exhibitions in the interwar period, leading to major orders from clients in Paris and elsewhere.

Today a number of potters continue the Lamali tradition, and pieces by Ben Brahim El Fakhkhari, Ahmed Serghini and the Laghriss family are much sought after by collectors. Although much contemporary Safi pottery is not to tastes used to Habitat minimalism, the visitor will find Safi production right across Morocco, such was the success of Boujemaâ Lamali in creating a recognizable style.

The simplest pottery produced in the Safi area comes from Lamaâchate, on the north coast road, where amphorae are made. This manufacture is no doubt very ancient: Safi always had water shortages, and there were many springs at Lamaâchate. In the 12th century, the Andalucíans brought by Youssef Ben Tachfine the Almoravid may have contributed to the development of pottery: glazed green water jars for the haji, the pilgrimage to Mecca, are said to have been made there. At the end of the 18th century, the *amine* or leader of the Potters' Corporation had a Fassi potter brought to Safi. In the 19th century, talented ceramic artists came from Fès to settle, and for many years, only blue pottery with Fassi motifs was produced. Blue was the cheapest colour, readily available as it arrived by sea, unlike the other colourants (iron oxide, chrome and manganese), which came from the remote Tafilalet and Fès. After the First World War, Safi pottery was hit by the mass availability of cheap enamelled metal dishes. Local hand-modelled pottery was hard hit.

However, thanks to the energetic Boujemaâ Lamali, a master potter of Algerian origin (see box above), the Safi pottery industry was to take a radical new direction in the 1920s and 1930s. In many ways a product of the Lyautey system, Lamali's reinvention of Safi pottery, in terms of both shapes and decoration, was to have a long-lasting impact.

See Footprint Handbook to Marrakech & the High Atlas for more detail on the pottery of Safi

Today, the techniques in the 140 or so workshops have changed little since the beginning of the 20th century. Equipment is simple: potter's wheel, basin, reed, pot-shard and a few planks to leave pots drying in the shade are quite sufficient. The clay comes in large chunks which need to be broken up and softened in water. On the second day of preparation, the clay is left in the sun before being kneaded with the feet in big round pats on a bed of ashes. After a secondary kneading with the hands and the removal of stones, it is ready for transformation. In dark workshops, well out of the bright daylight, the potters can be seen hard at work at their foot-operated wheels.

The kilns, essentially fired by *rtem* or brushwood, are designed to avoid huge leaps in temperature. On day one, the temperature does not rise above 200°C, and big pots stay three or four days at this temperature. (Clay, a highly malleable substance, only really begins to change texture significantly at 600°C, and solidifies at 900°C.) During firing, a pot loses 15-20% of its volume, and imperfections due to poor technique during throwing become apparent. After the kiln has cooled fully, pots can be removed.

Painting and glazing were areas in which numerous experiments were conducted under Lamali. Before painting, the pot has to be dipped in a mixture of white clay and water, to cover the original clay colour. Traditionally, the glaze – a liquid composed of tin, lead and silicate – was applied before coloured designs. Pots must be extremely clean before glaze is applied. Generally five colours are used: white, blue, green, yellow and brown. (Lamali revived the old colours of Safi pottery, which had disappeared with the ease of producing Fassi blue and white designs.) The motifs are painted in outline by the *maâlem*, and the apprentice does the colouring in. Different chemical substances produce the colours: cobalt blue is the most highly valued, green is produced by copper oxide, while a lead oxide is used to produce the deep green roof tiles. Manganese is the base for the browns, deep purple brown being referred to as *zbibi*, from *zbib* (raisin).

Safi centre

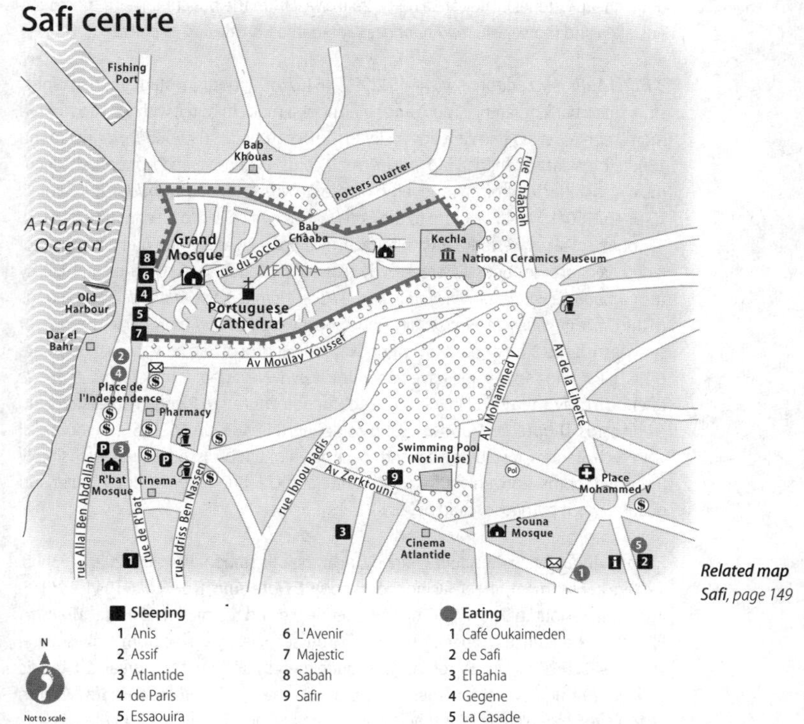

Related map
Safi, page 149

The pot-painters, often women, are highly skilled workers. The pots are carefully piled in the kilns before re-firing. A small tripod or *chouka* is used to separate the bigger pieces so that air can circulate in the kiln. The three marks left after this second firing are painted in afterwards. The motifs have names like honeycomb, scorpion and *jnaweh boufertoto* (butterfly wing), olive kernel and bull's eye. However, many of the designs today are somewhat garish. Note that the best place to buy is not always the stalls below potters' hill. You could also try the pottery *souk* in the médina, off Rue du Socco.

Profits for the workshop owners are potentially very good. The clay brought in from quarries some 5 km outside Safi costs a mere 200dh the lorry load. Skilled potters operate on a piecework basis, making between 500dh to 600dh a month. The guys who do the carrying, clay-kneading and kiln-stoking obviously make less. If you had time, you could even design and order your own dinner service.

Beaches The best local beach is **Sidi Bouzid**, just north of the town and on the No 15 bus route, with cafés and the very good *Le Refuge* seafood restaurant. Further afield is the **Lalla Fatma** beach, just past Cap Safi. If they can, locals go further afield to **Plage Souiriya**, some 30 km to the south.

Essentials

Sleeping

■ on map, page 153

In Safi the budget traveller can find hotels at a fraction of the price of those in Essaouira. The cheap hotels are all concentrated in the southwestern side of the médina, opposite the port, just below the long, sloping Pl de l'Indépendence (where there are some good cheap eateries). They are a hefty, 2-km walk from the bus station. For those with nostalgia and more cash, the *Atlantide* is an Agatha Christie sort of place.

B ***Hotel Safir***, Av Zerktouni, T044-464299, F464573. 90 rooms, restaurant, bar, nightclub, snack bar, conference room and small pool, a modern hotel, with well appointed rooms, some having fine views over city to the ocean. Suites 690/960dh, dinner menu 160dh, breakfast 50dh, parking, major credit cards, expensive and not entirely decorous – a reflection of the poverty of the town. **C** ***Hotel Atlantide***, R Chaouki, T044-462160/1, F464595. Close to the *Hotel Safir*, to which it is to be entirely preferred. 47 rooms, pleasant restaurant with terrace, nice pool. An old-style hotel with an air of faded elegance not entirely wrecked by recent renovation work. Opened in 1920 by the *Compagnie Paquet de Navigation* as the *Hotel Marhaba*, the *Atlantide* now belongs to the *Office Chérifien des Phosphates*, and is mostly used by company personnel (lots of seminars). It has a quiet position overlooking the centre of Safi new town. Rooms are plain but comfortable, some have panoramic views. Next door is the *Cinema Atlantide* offering a daily afternoon film performance for hotel guests, parking in quiet street, no credit cards. **D** ***Hotel les Mimosas***, R Ibn Zeidoun, T044-463208, F625955. 34 rooms, all with bath, 2 suites, restaurant, bar and snack bar, nightclub/discotheque, clean, simply furnished rooms. Convenient for town centre and Pl Mohammed V. Not as quiet and decorous as it perhaps should be.

E ***Hotel Abda***, Av du Président Kennedy, near the bus station, T044-610202, F463868. 1990s establishment, street-facing rooms noisy. **E** ***Hotel Anis***, R de R'bat, T044-463078. 36 rooms, restaurant, close to Pl de l'Indépendence and the médina. **F** ***Hotel Majestic***, Pl de l'Indépendence (corner of Av Moulay Youssef), clearly visible from main square, T044-464011. 20 rooms, TV room, basic, quite friendly and clean, no breakfast, public parking 20 m. Round the corner and up a side street, try **F** ***Hotel/Café de l'Avenir***, T044-462657, kind of gloomy, tiny restaurant at back, hot shower shared, cold showers in rooms with WC. Further up the street, on right, is **F** ***Hotel de Paris***, T044-462149. Old house built round a courtyard, spartan, clean accommodation, big, airy rooms. If stuck try **F** ***Hotel Sabah*** in same street.

Camping ***Camping de Sidi Bouzid***, 3 km north of Safi at Sidi Bouzid, T044-462871. Site of 6 ha, bar/snacks, grocery shop, pool, showers, laundry, petrol 2 km, electricity for caravans. ***Camping Balnéaire***, at Kédima 32 km south, site of 2 ha, beach 3 km, showers, laundry, electricity for caravans, petrol at 18 km.

Eating

• *on map, page 153*

Expensive The restaurant in the ***Hotel Atlantide*** has a pleasant terrace. Also good is the ***Restaurant La Trattoria***, aka ***Chez Yvette***, a large Italian restaurant on R Aouinate, on an uphill road leading south of the médina, T044-620959. A good feed for 200dh, salad and fish main course for 150dh, pizza, lasagne, osso bucco and occasionally tiramisu. A good address. **Mid-range/cheap** Centrally located and easily identified by bright displays of vegetables and plastic flowers are ***Restaurant de Safi***, 3 R de la Marine, T044-610472, and ***Restaurant Gegene***, 8 R de la Marine, T044-463369. Specializing in fish and Italian dishes; both are just off the Pl de l'Indépendence near the *Wafa Bank*. Cheaper places are to be found around the médina. Although out of Safi to the north (a petit taxi or car needed), also try ***Restaurant Le Refuge***, Route de Sidi Bouzid, T044-464354. Has a good reputation for French cuisine, particularly fish dishes (closed Mon) and ***Restaurant La Corniche***, also on Route de Sidi Bouzid, T044-463584. Moroccan food and shellfish. Often, restaurants in Safi do not display menus outside so check inside to be sure of prices and range of food on offer.

Cafés Try ***Café-Restaurant El Bahia*** at the southern end of the Pl de l'Indépendence for a pause. In the area around Pl Mohammed V, ***Café Oukaimeden*** on Av Zerktouni has a pleasant street terrace. Other possibilities include ***Café al-Marjan***, also on Av Zerktouni, and ***Café La Cascade***, next door to *Hotel Assif* on Av de la Liberté.

Shopping

Best bargain in Safi is **pottery** (see above). In the médina, numerous stalls sell cheap shoes and clothes.

Sport & activities

The beach at Sidi Bouzid is known for **surfing**. There is **horse riding** at *Club Equestre*, Route de Sidi Ouassel. There are signs to a **swimming pool** from Pl Mohammed V along Av Moulay Idriss. However, the pool site on Av Mohammed V next to the public gardens is neglected and unused at present.

Transport

Local Bus: No 7 takes you from main bus station into town centre, 2dh. **Car hire**: *Europcar*, Pl Ibnou Sina, T044-462935.

Long distance Train The railway station is to the south of the town, on R du Caïd Sidi Abderrahman, the continuation of R de R'bat, T044-464993. There is 1 train daily at 0815 to **Benguerir**, journey time approximately 1 hr, which connects with services to **Casablanca**, **Rabat**, **Kénitra**, **Meknès**, **Fèz**, **Marrakech**, **Asilah** and **Tangier**. The daily arrival at Safi from all these destinations is at 1846.

Road The bus terminal is on Av Président Kennedy to the south of the town. *CTM* runs services to **Casablanca**, **Marrakech**, **El Jadida**, **Essaouira** and **Agadir**. Try to reserve ticket day before. Other operators include ***Chekkouri*** with frequent daily services to **Marrakech** and **Agadir**; (0100-2330) and 9 to **Casablanca** (0200-2300); they also have departures for **Taroudant** and **Rabat**.

Directory **Banks** *BMCE*, Pl Ibnou Sina, and *BMCE*, *BMCI* and *Banque du Maroc*, Pl de l'Indépendence. *Bank Populaire*, Av de la Liberté, close to Pl Mohammed V. **Communications** Post: *PTT*, Pl de l'Indépendence and **Post Office:** Av Abdallah, at junction of Av Zerktouni.

Routes from Safi

Safi to El Jadida An option for travelling inland to El Jadida uses the P12 Marrakech exit from the town. Once into open countryside beyond the roadside snack and butchers' stalls on the outskirts of Safi, the first 26 km stretch to **Bouguedra** runs through an area of fertile farming land. At Bouguedra, which has a few shops, cafés, a *Crédit Agricole* bank and a brick factory but otherwise little else of interest for the traveller, turn north on the P8 towards Casablanca. After a further 18 km through more arable country with views of distant hills to the right, you reach **Jemâa-Sahi** a sizeable town with the usual facilities, including cafés and tyre repair. Less attractive, 33 km further north, is the bustling town of **Khémis des Zémamra**, a busy place cluttered with sugar-beet lorries. A detour can be taken here to **Sidi Bennour** (31 km) by turning right on the S123, an undulating route across a productive farming landscape criss-crossed with irrigation ducts, past grazing camels and local people splashing and washing in roadside pools. The western side of Sidi Bennour is a busy, somewhat scruffy area full of roadside market stalls, but once the junction with the P9 is reached, the character of the town changes to one of pleasant apartments, shops and pavement cafés. There are petrol stations and banks here. Turn north on the P9, past factories manufacturing pipes and processing sugar beet, for another 21 km to **Sidi Smail**, another large town at the junction of the P8 and P9 where there is a good choice of facilities. The landscape for the remainder of the journey is mainly agricultural but given added variety by roadside traders selling pottery, live pigeons and eggs. On the outskirts of El Jadida, the train station is down a turning to the left immediately after driving under the railway line; the route passes through a residential area before it reaches the large roundabout at Place de France.

Safi to Agadir– via Chichaoua & the High Atlas This route is an alternative to the more direct option using the P8 via **Talmest** and **Ounara** and, later in the journey, provides a good opportunity to enjoy some of the fine scenery of the western High Atlas mountains. Leave Safi on the P12; beyond Sidi Bouguedra the road climbs steadily into the hills for the first part of the 42 km to **Chemaia** and then levels out to give views of high plains in all directions. Petrol is available outside Sidi Tiji. In Chemaia, turn south on the S511 for **Chichaoua** (63 km). This is a very isolated section (no petrol), travelling across wide plains with flat-topped hills in the far distance, crossing the Oued Tensift after 35 km. Reaching the busy junction with the P10 road to Marrakech offers the chance to refuel and stop at one of the shops or cafés here. Chichaoua is noted for the distinctive animal designs of its good quality, brightly coloured carpets. Travelling south on the P40 the impressive High Atlas range soon comes into sight on the way to **Imi-n-Tanoute**; a detour off the main road into this busy but unattractive town provides the chance to visit shops and banks but little else. Leaving Imi-n-Tanoute the route winds upwards through the pass of **Tizi Maachou** (1,700 m) through some beautiful mountain scenery. Beyond the summit there are fine views of the higher peaks to the east before you reach the reservoir and **Barrage Abdelmoumen**; on the way you will pass many local traders offering bottles of argan oil for sale. A rapid descent to the viewpoint at

Ameskroud then follows; it is worth stopping here to enjoy the extensive views southeast over the plain towards **Taroudant** before completing the remainder of the journey to Agadir.

Safi to Essaouira – on the coast road

After the beach resort of Sidi Rosia is **Jorf el Yhoudi** – also known as the Jew's Cliff. On the coast at **Souira Kédima**, 32 km south of Safi, is a rebuilt/restored Portuguese *ribat*, more or less open to the public, dating from the early 16th century. Across the Oued Tensift, the ford having been replaced by a new road and bridge, and beyond Dar Caiid Hadji is the more recent **Kasbah Hamidouch**, built in the 18th century by Sultan Moulay Ismaïl to control this region. At one time the river surrounded the building as a moat. It is a splendid building, with crumbling turrets and crenellations in abundance. This coastal area gets busy in summer. There's a good campsite here, *Camping Balnéaire* – see Camping, page 155, for further details.

The road continues through **Akermoud** with Jbel Hadid (Iron Mountain) to the east. In this region are a number of white shrines. That of Moulay Bouzerktoun set among the sand dunes is most striking.

Essaouira الصويرة

Phone code: 044
Colour map 2, grid B2

Essaouira, 'little picture', is one of those stage set places: you half expect to see plumed cavalry coming round the corner, or a camera crew filming some diva up on the ramparts. It is a beautifully designed 18th-century military port, and somehow hasn't been too much changed since. The walls are white, the windows and shutters are often cracked and faded blue, while arches and columns are sandy camel-brown. Three crescent moons on a city gate provide a touch of the heraldic, while the surfers and the much exhibited local naïve school of artists hint at Essaouira's hippy days, a couple of decades ago. Tall feathery araucaria trees and palms along the ramparts add a Mediterranean touch. The new airport has reduced Essaouira's isolation (the town is over six hours by road from Casa). Large numbers of foreigners have bought picturesque property and there are two successful music festivals.

Ins and outs

Getting there

See Transport, page 167, for further details

Essaouira is easily accessible by bus from Agadir (3½ hrs), Marrakech (3-4½ hrs), Casablanca (6 or 9 hrs, depending on route) and from Safi and El Jadida. Both *CTM* and private lines arrive at the bus station about 1 km from the town – a 20-min walk with luggage or a 7dh petit taxi ride (10dh at night). Grands taxis also run to the bus station, although arrivals will be dropped off next to Bab Doukkala. Drivers may want to use the car park (24-hr warden) close to the harbour next to Pl Prince Moulay El Hassan. Depending on the season, *RAM* runs flights from Rabat, making it a possible long-weekend destination for the capital's wealthy.

Getting around

One of the most appealing aspects of Essaouira is that all the principal tourist sites can be comfortably reached on foot; cars can be left in the parking area to the south of Pl Moulay Hassan. There are some good walks along the windswept beach to Borj El Beroud. The walk to Cap Sim is an all-day excursion.

Tourist information

Tourist office Av du Caire, open Mon-Fri 0830-1200. Rather basic office, don't expect too much useful information. In fact, they tend to send you to hotels that will pay them commission.

Background

Gnaoua Music Festival held at the end of June (www.festival-gnaoua.co.ma). Classical music lovers are catered for by Les Alizés, a small festival held in April

Essaouira is a quiet sort of place with a long history. There was a small Phoenician settlement at Essaouira, previously called Magdoura or Mogador, a corruption of the Berber word *Amegdul*, meaning 'well-protected'. The Romans were interested in the purple dye produced from the abundant shellfish on the rocky coast, which they used to colour the robes of the rich (see box). Mogador was occupied in the 15th century by the Portuguese who built the fortifications around the harbour. The town was one of their three most important bases, but was abandoned in 1541, from which time it went into decline. Mogador was also visited by Sir Francis Drake, Christmas 1577. In 1765, the Alaouite Sultan Sidi Mohammed Ibn Abdallah transformed Mogador into an open city, enticing overseas businessmen in with trade concessions, and it soon became a major commercial port, with a large foreign and Jewish population establishing the town as a major trading centre. The sultan employed the French architect Théodore Cornut to design the city and its fortifications. In his design, Cornut chose a rectangular layout for the main streets, resulting in a very uniform style, and constructed ramparts in the Vauban style. The fortifications were not always that effective, however. From time to time, the tribesmen of the region would raid the town, carrying off booty and the merchants' wives – who it is said, were not always that happy to return. Perhaps life in the *bled* was more pleasant than listening to the wind in the damp counting houses of Mogador.

Orson Welles stayed here for some time, filming part of *Othello* at the **Skala du Port**. At Independence the town's official name became Essaouira, the local Arabiac name meaning 'little picture' – perhaps because Essaouira is 'as pretty as a picture'? In the 1960s Essaouira had a brief reputation as a 'happening place', which attracted hippies and rockstars, including Jimi Hendrix. Essaouira now seems to be emerging from several decades of decline, for on top of fishing, fish processing, a small market and handicraft industries, the town is attracting greater numbers of tourists, notably surfers – who refer to it as Wind City, Afrika. Upmarket and activity tourism may yet bring some wealth to the inhabitants of this most relaxed town, without spoiling its gentle atmosphere. Essaouira has some useful friends in influential places, including André Azoulay, one of HM the King's special advisers, and there is an artistic lobby, too, including gallery owner Frederick Damgaard and Edmond Amran-Mellah, the writer. Hopefully the charm will not fade under the impact of oversized hotel developments and day trippers from Marrakech. The town's annual music festivals – *Les Alizés* for classical music in the spring and the Gnaoua Festival in the summer – have become hugely popular.

Sights

Essaouira does not have a lot in the way of formal sites (another reason perhaps for its failure to attract mainstream tourist investment), and it is more of a gently atmospheric sort of place than anything else.

Médina Enclosed by walls with five main gates, the médina is the major attraction. Entering from **Bab Doukkala** the main thoroughfare is Rue Mohammed Zerktouni, which leads into Avenue de l'Istiqlal, where there is the **Grand Mosque**, and just off, on Darb Laalouj, the **Ensemble Artisanal** and the **Museum of Sidi Mohammed Ibn Abdallah**, which houses the Museum of Traditional Art and Heritage of Essaouira and which has an interesting collection of weapons, as well as handicrafts such as woodwork and carpets. This house, once the home of a pasha, has an interesting ethnographic collection, including examples of stringed instruments beautifully decorated with marquetry and documents on Berber music. ■ *0830-1200 and 1430-1800, except Fri 0830-1130 and 1500-1830, closed Tue. 10dh. T044-472300.*

Avenue de l'Istiqlal leads into Avenue Okba Ibn Nafi, on which is located the small **Galerie des Arts Frederic Damgaard**. At the end of the street a gate on the right leads into Place Moulay Hassan, the heart of the town's social life. The town's souks are mainly located around the junction between Rue Mohammed Zerktouni and Rue Mohammed El Gorry, although there is an area of woodworkers inside the **Skala** walls to the north of Place Moulay Hassan, where some fine pieces can be picked up with some good-natured

Essaouira

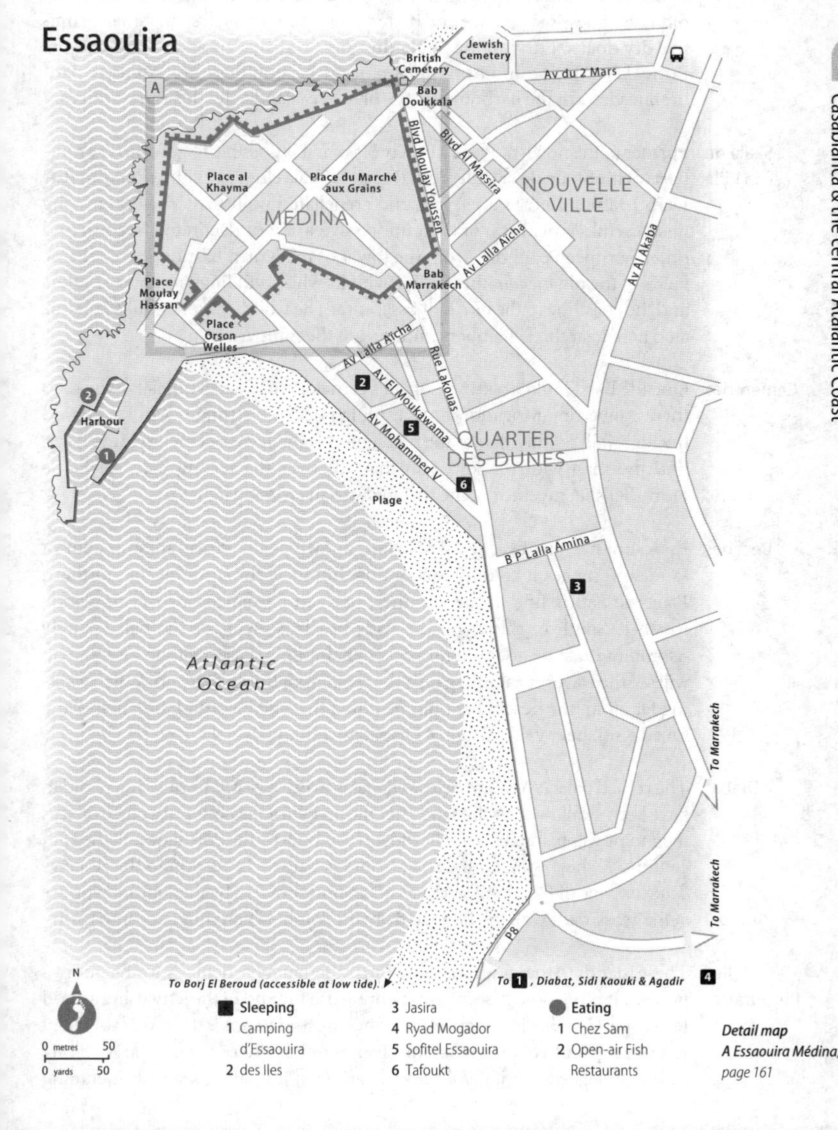

Detail map A Essaouira Médina, page 161

bargaining. At the northeast end of Rue Zerktouni, close to Bab Doukkala, is the much decayed **mellah**, or old Jewish quarter. Although the Jewish community no longer remains, it made a substantial contribution to the commercial and cultural development of the town.

The Harbour & Skala Off Place Moulay Hassan is the small harbour, busy with its fishing fleet. Tourists tend to lunch at one of the open-air restaurant stalls serving grilled fish. The sea gate (**Porte de la Marine**) which serves to link the harbour with the médina was built in 1769, it is said by an Englishman converted to Islam, during the reign of Sidi Mohammed Ibn Abdallah. The gateway is built of stone in the classical style and the year of its construction (1184 of the Hegira) is inscribed on the pediment. It is connected to the ramparts on the **Skala**, an old Portuguese sea defence and battery, by a bridge which spans small primitive dry docks. Entry to the **Skala du Port** (10dh) is via a kiosk close to the Porte de la Marine and from the top of the bastion there are extensive panoramic views of the harbour and the offshore islands, the **Iles Purpuraires**.

Skala de la Ville Further to the north of Place Moulay Hassan it is possible to get onto the ramparts of the **Skala de la Ville** from Rue de la Skala close to its junction with Rue Darb Laalouj. Entry here is free and crenellated walls protect a 200 m long raised artillery platform and an impressive array of decorated Spanish and other European cannon. From the tower of the North Bastion there are fine views of the old *mellah*, the médina with its white buildings and blue shutters and the coastline to the north of Essaouira. The woodworkers' souks are situated here in arched chambers underneath the ramparts.

Cemeteries Outside Bab Doukkala is the Consul's cemetery for British officials, who died there converting Mogador into a trading post with strong UK links. Behind the high wall on the road to the bus station is the Jewish cemetery. If you can find the man with the key, you may discover the resting place of Leslie Hore-Belisha, inventor of the first pedestrian crossing light.

Beaches Essaouira has fine beaches. The wind, known as the *alizée*, stirs up a lot of sand, and makes it cold for swimming, but ideal for surfing. The northern Plage de Safi is fine in the summer, but can be dangerous during windy weather. South of the town, the wide beach is great for football – surely Essaouira must be a school for soccer champions. Past the Oued Ksob, you will see the waves breaking against the remains of Borj El Baroud. When walking far along the beach it should be noted that the incoming tide makes the Oued Ksob below the village of Diabat into an impassable river.

Diabat The ruined palace/pavilion below Diabat is worth a visit. The building is said to have been swallowed by the sand after the people of the Sous put a curse on it as their trade was being ruined. The old fort was built by the Portuguese in the 18th century. A short walk up the road from Diabat will bring you to the *Auberge Tangaro*, one of Essaouira's better known hotels; 500 m further on, and you are at the crossroads with the P8 road from the south, which runs back into town.

Iles Purpuraires These islands to the southwest are a bird sanctuary, particularly for Eleonora's falcons. It is possible to see these falcons from the end of the jetty using a good telescope. One particular area frequented by the falcons is the mouth of Oued Ksob to the south of the town. This river mouth is also noted for a large colony of yellow-legged herring gulls and a variety of migrating seabirds including black, little, sandwich, whiskered and white-winged terns. The *oued* can be reached from a track off the P8 south of the town but access to the sea is not easy. The scrubland in the same vicinity provides sufficient sightings to satisfy any birdwatcher. It is possible to visit the main island, the Ile de Mogador, and the ruins of a prison, by contacting the Tourist Information Office on Place Moulay Hassan. They will direct the visitor to the Province office off Avenue Mohammed V where a permit can be obtained for 50dh, and will arrange a boat for transport for the 15-minute trip, for a negotiable price. The creation of a regular daily ferry service to the islands is hopefully only a rumour: nothing should be allowed to disturb the rare Eleonora's falcons when they are nesting – after all they are rare and have flown all the way from Madagascar.

Essentials

Sleeping

■ *on map, page 159 and below*

Parking can be tricky, especially during the festivals. If you leave your car under a street lamp, it may get covered in guano

Accommodation in Essaouira divides into 4 areas: the southwest side of town/Quartier des Dunes with a couple of big hotels and some guesthouses; the médina with upmarket guesthouses and damp cheap hotels; near the train station; and finally the country guesthouses south in Diabat, Ghazoua and Cap Sim. Médina guesthouses are listed separately. For cheap hotels in Essaouira it is important to get a well ventilated room with windows, and preferably a view of the ocean. There are now a good number of restored old properties operated as guesthouses. The typical Essaouira house rose up 2 storeys around a courtyard with rooms opening onto balconies on all 4 sides. If the courtyard is small, the result is often a bit gloomy to modern western taste. High-ceilinged rooms and decoration schemes compensate.

The amount of accommodation is expanding. It is important to ring ahead for the small *hotels de charme*, especially during the annual Gnaoua Festival. If you are looking for self-catering accommodation, you could try ***Jack's Kiosk***, at 1, Pl Prince Moulay El Hassan, T044-475538, F476901, or, more upmarket, ***Essaouira Médina***, T/F044-472396, www.essaouiramedina.com If you are interested in buying property, contact the latter as they have a good name. See Directory for further advice.

Quartier des Dunes/ Agadir road

A *Sofitel Essaouira*, Av Mohammed V, T044-479000, F479037, www.sofitel.com. Recently built by the *Groupe Accor*. Right opposite the beach. Very comfortable establishment indeed, just what the town needed. Nice bar (which could be anywhere, however), good restaurant. Recommended. **A** ***Hotel Ryad Mogador***, out of town on the Agadir road, T044-783555, www.net-tensift.com/mogador Package hotel built round a central pool, quiet, clean and ultimately boring. Rooms cramped, no alcohol allowed. Plus point: tennis courts. **B** ***Hotel des Iles***, Av Mohammed V, T044-472329, F472472. 70 rooms of which 46 are bungalow-style around a central swimming pool, others in the older part of the hotel built in 1948. On the grim side – but then you're likely to be out most of the day. Seafood and international restaurants (views of harbour and beach), bar, nightclub and secure parking, tourist menu 180dh (3 course), breakfast 55dh, convenient for beach. All major credit cards. **B** ***Hotel Tafoukt***, 98 Av Mohammed V, BP 38, T044-784504/05, F784416. Reasonable hotel just across the road from the beach but an appreciable walk (about 1 km) from the centre of town, 40 rooms, tea room, bar and restaurant; ask for a room with sea view. **C** ***Hotel Jasira***, 18 R Moulay Ali Cherif, Quartier des Dunes, T044-784403, aljasira@iam.net.ma 30 rooms and 4 small suites, pool, restaurant, but no booze.

Médina

Hotels A-B *Hotel Palazzo Desdemona*, Av Okba Ibn Nafi, T044-472227, F785735 (same management as *Auberge Tangaro*, see below). From 500dh for simplest room on terrace to 950dh for a suite. Fireplaces in some rooms, plenty of hot water, but had a couple of bad reviews from readers in 2002 (some rooms with no outside windows). No food available apart from breakfast. **A-B** ***Hotel Villa Maroc***, 10 R Abdallah Ben Yassin, T044-476147, villamaroc@casanet.net.ma Converted merchant's house, beautifully decorated around a central court festooned with plants and greenery, roof terrace with superb views, 17 rooms, apartment sleeping 4 available for 1,200dh, restaurant for guests only, dinner 150dh, public parking (approximately 200 m) near Pl Orson Welles, all major credit cards. A personable establishment but a victim of its own success. Hot water for showers (gas-fired water heaters) a problem if several people showering at same time.

B *Maison du Sud*, 29 R Sidi Ben Abdellah, T044-474141, maisondusud@iam.net.ma, www.essaouiraweb.com/maisondusud 14 rooms, including split-level suites, 2 terrace rooms. Supper available on request. A good recent address, worth a try. **B** ***Hotel Riad al Madina***, 9 R Attarine, T/F044-475727, www.riadalmadina.com A former hippy hotel which has been over-expanded to 30 rooms. Though the decorator's hand is much in evidence, rooms are very pokey. Too little privacy at this price as almost all suites and rooms open onto a central courtyard.

C *Hotel Emeraude*, 228 R Chebanate, near the little gate of Bab Marrakech, T044-473494, www.essaouirahotel.com Small, attractive Franco-Moroccan-run hotel on the dry side of the médina. One of the nicest small hotels in town. **C** ***Hotel Le Grand Large***, 2 R Oum er Rabi, T044-472866, www.essaouiranet.com/legrandlarge Tastefully restored place on main street. Very clean, rooms on small side. Pizzeria on ground floor – noise rises to upper landings. Good for a couple of nights. **C** ***Riad Lalla***, 12 R de l'Iraq, T044-476744. 7 rooms, nice reception.

D ***Hotel Beau Rivage***, Pl Moulay Hassan, T/F044-475925. 18 rooms, central, rooms available with and without showers, some with balconies overlooking main square (noisy), others with sea view, TVs in room may prove to be more decorative than functional, clean, basic and with friendly, helpful management, roof terrace, no restaurant but breakfast available from café outside hotel. **D** ***Hotel Dar el Qdima***, 4 R Malek Ben Rahal, T044-473858, F474154. Just off main drag (Av de l'Istiqlal), on your right as you come from port area, on same alley as *Azurette* the herbalist. Old building restored, very pretty decor, if you like beige *tadelakt* you will love this place. Rooms around central court. Weak point: the hot water. Very, very good value. **D** ***Hotel Kasbah***, 4 R Tetouan, close to Pl Moulay El Hassan, T044-475605. A large old house with craftwork for sale in the courtyard. Some rooms with views over the town. **D** ***Hotel Le Poisson Volant***, 34 R Labbana, T044-472150, F472152. 8 rooms. A bit damp, but otherwise fine. Windsurfer clientele. **D** ***Hotel Shahrazad***, 1 R Youssef el Fassi, T044-476336. Small hotel, some rooms with bathroom. Acceptable.

E ***Hotel Cap Sim***, 11 R Ibn Rochd, T044-785834. Clean and cheap, just round the corner from Pl Moulay Hassan. **E** ***Hotel Majestic***, 40 Darb Laalouj, T044-474909. Nothing very majestic about this place. 18 rooms, cheap and charmless, youths hanging around outside. Nice views from terrace. For the record, this was the first French courthouse building in town, opened 1914. **E** ***Hotel Mechouar***, Av Okba Ibn Nafi, T044-784828. 25 rooms, uninviting appearance, not the best value option in this price range, no breakfast, restaurant reported as open in the season. **E** ***Hotel des Remparts***, 18 R Ibn Rochd, T044-475110. 27 rooms on 3 floors around a courtyard, a popular place with friendly staff and a spectacular view from the roof terrace. However, a bit run down, rooms reported as dark and damp, no restaurant for evening meals, public parking in a restricted area. **E** ***Hotel Sahara***, Av Okba Ibn Nafi, T044-475292. 70 rooms, in the médina next door to the *Hotel Mechouar*, comfortable and central, range of rooms, some quite pleasant, cheaper rooms on inner courtyard are darker, less well ventilated and noisy, terrace, no restaurant, public parking near Pl Orson Welles 200 m. **E** ***Hotel Smara***, 26 R Skala, T044-475655. 17 rooms, just inside the ramparts in the woodworkers' souk north from Pl Moulay Hassan, clean and friendly, most rooms have washbasins, showers cost extra, WCs shared, make sure room has ocean view, others can be damp and dark, no restaurant, breakfast available. Roof terrace with a view as good as anywhere in Essaouira, very restricted parking in street, probably best cheap option. **E** ***Hotel Souiri***, 37 R Attarine, T/F044-475339. 20 rooms, central, clean. **F** ***Hotel du Tourisme***, R Mohammed Ben Messaoud, at the southeast corner of the médina. Some rooms damp, not recommended.

Guesthouses This type of accommodation took off in a big way in Essaouira in the late 1990s, and by the time this goes to press, new addresses are sure to have appeared. The following is a small selection of the better ones. Most guesthouses can do evening meals, prices around 100-150dh – enquire. In some cases, the whole establishment can be rented for a few days for a house party. **Recommended agency**: *Essaouira Médina*, 8 R Ibn Rochd, Essaouira, just off Pl Moulay Hassan, T/F044-472396, www.essaouiramedina.com (manager Abd el Fatah Mazouz). Traditional **A-C** houses and flats to rent and buy. Very reliable, honest agency (welcome in a place full of sharks).

Médina
Check whether the guesthouse accepts credit cards – many in Essaouira do not

A ***Dar Loulema***, 2 R Souss, T/F044-475346, T061-247661 (mob), www.darloulema.com Centrally situated next to the the *Café Taros*. 6 rooms with a/c, 1 with bath. **B** ***Casa del Mar***, 35 R d'Oujda, T044-475091, T068-943839 (mob), www.lacasadelmar.com Attractive, simple house restored by owners of Spanish origin. 4 rooms with shower. Highly recommended. **B** ***Dar Adul***, 63 R Touahen, T044-473910, T061-245241 (mob), michelgandin@iam.net.ma. 5 rooms with shower or bath. Popular. Best room on 1st floor has a fireplace. **B** ***Dar Al Bahar*** ('the House of the Sea'), 1 R Touahen, T044-476831, daralbahar@yahoo.fr 9 rooms with shower in a restored house set in the north walls. Views over médina and ocean from terrace. Simple, clean, recommended. **B** ***Riad Gyvo***, 3 R Mohamed Ben Messaoud, T044-475102, T061-686156 (mob), www.riadgyvo.com 3 studios (ground floor ones on dark side), 2 small flats with cooking facilities, roof terrace. Impeccably kept. Mini-weights room. **B** ***The Tea House***, 74 Derb Laalouj, La Skala. Despite its English name, this small guest-house is very much 'traditional Essaouira'. 2 self-catering 5-room flats are available for rent, beautifully decorated, each accommodating 4 people. Each flat has kitchen, large bathroom, living/dining room with open fire (a definite draw) and 2 bedrooms. Break-fast included, along with firewood. Recommended, reservations on T044-783543 teahouse@iam.net.ma (owner-manager Alison McDonald). **B** ***House of Caïd***, R Chebanate, close to Bab Marrakech (ie good location on the dry side of the médina), T061-708036 (mob), houseofcaid@joymail.com, also via www.riadchelita.com **B** ***Villa Quiéta***, 86 Blvd Mohammed V, T044-785004, F785006. Located at end of promenade, 15 mins from médina. Suites very nice, some rooms have a hint of British seaside resort. A former family house transformed into a guesthouse. Modern, a bit lacking in charm, but still one of the nicest places in Essaouira. **B** ***Riyad el Zahia***, 4 R Mohammed Douiri, a side street left off Darb Laalouj as you head towards the ramparts, T061-347131 (mob). 6 rooms, 2 suites, beautifully decorated. **C** ***Les Chandeliers***, 14 Darb Laalouj, opposite the museum, T044-476450. Via *Restaurant Les Chandeliers*, you can rent a good value guest suite or a simple room in a historic building at the heart of old Essaouira. **E** ***Chez Brahim***, 41 R el Mourabitine, near Bab Marrakech, T044-472599. A very good budget option. Prices tend to be negotiable, around 80dh for a single, breakfast 15dh. Clean establishment, rooms around a courtyard, pleasant terrace for breakfast. One of Brahim's scouts meets likely guests at the Supratours bus stop or the gare routière. Room for surfboards on ground floor. No sign, you get the house keys to let yourself in.

Near the bus station

There is a sprinkling of small, reasonably priced hotels here, ideal if you are allergic to the ocean damp or have an early departure. **D** ***Hotel Palais d'Essaouira***, 5 Av du 2 Mars, right opposite the gare routière, T044-472887, F472387. 29 rooms, some triples, opening onto central covered courtyard, no damp, very clean. Noisy at night if TV on in central area? Much Moroccan decoration, ground-floor restaurant. **D** ***Hotel el Andalous***, T044-472951. As you leave bus station, cross over main road towards pharmacy. The hotel is 3 storeys, café on ground floor, on this avenue on right. Preferable to *Palais d'Essaouira* if you need quiet. No damp, clean, much Moroccan decor. **E** ***Hotel Marjane***, T044-476691, sign-posted just round corner from the *Andalous*. 10 rooms, good cheap address, better than *Argana*. **E-F** ***Hotel Argana***, just outside the ramparts at Bab Doukkala, T044-475975. Ade-quate travellers' hotel. Turkish loos. Go for newer 2nd-floor rooms some of which have view of ocean and Christian and Jewish cemeteries. Smell of urine on 1st floor.

South of Essaouira

Diabat The one-time favourite hippy destination of Diabat, about 5 km from Essaouira, is easily reached by petit and grand taxi, say 40dh. **B** ***Auberge Tangaro***, T044-784784, F785735. Same management as *Hotel Palazzo Desdemona* (T472227) in town. 13 rooms, 5 suites, half-board compulsory, 2 persons 800dh. A pleasant farm-type place. No electricity, good food, hot water a bit dodgy sometimes. Recep-tion not what it should be. Suite No 6 has good ocean view. Camping possible.

Ghazoua **B** ***Villa Argana***, about 11 km from Essaouira on the Sidi Kaouki road, look out for a turn left, T044-474365, T061-618532, agrgw@excite 3 eccentrically pleasing rooms with a cave-like feel. On the expensive side, around 600dh for 2. No electricity as yet. English-owned. **C** ***Baoussala***, El Ghazoua, T/F474345, T066-308746 (mob), www.baoussala.com Small guesthouse, 5 en suite rooms, peaceful location 10 km from Essaouira and 10 km from Sidi Kaouki, purpose built by owners Dominique and Bruno Maté in extensive grounds. Whole house can be rented.

Agadir road and Sidi Kaouki Leaving Essaouira, there is the stratospherically priced **LL** *Dar Mimosas*, on Agadir road about 3 km south of Essaouira, T044-475934, T061-109180 (mob), www.skara-bee.com/~moa/darmimosas/gb.swf Prefer the Teima and Tafaya suites in the main villa with ocean view. **B** *La Maison du Chameau*, off the Agadir road some 13 km from Essaouira, take the left turn for Marrakech, T044-785077, F476901, maisonduchameau@yahoo.fr Traditional whitewashed farm buildings converted into guest accommodation. **B-C** *Hotel Villa Soleil* , Plage de Sidi Kaouki, about 20 km south of Essaouira, T044-474763, T070-233097 (mob), www.hotelvillasoleil.com 9 simple rooms and 1 suite, a good basic address. Belgian owned. **C** *Dar Kenavo*, 13 km out of Essaouira on Agadir road, take the left turn for Marrakech, T061-207069 (mob), F044-476867. Out in argan country, a small house with rooms around a pleasant patio. A quiet corner to see something of Moroccan rural life. **C-D** *Auberge de la Plage*, Sidi Kaouki, T044-476600, F473383. Italo-German management, 11 rooms, shared showers and loos. No electricity (yet). Also do horse riding and camel excursions. **D** *Résidence Le Kaouki*, T044-783206, or via the *Villa Maroc* in town. 10 rooms. Ideal for windsurfers – near the beach. **D** *Auberge de l'Etoile de la Mer*, T044-472537. Tiny 3- room guesthouse close to the mausoleum of Sidi Kaouki.

The turn-off for Sidi Kaouki is some 15 km south of Essaouira on the Agadir road

Camping *Camping d'Essaouira*, 2 km out of Essaouira on the Agadir road, well protected, clean loos.

Eating

● *on map, pages 159 & 161*

Expensive *Chez Georges*, probably the best food in Essaouira, near the Skala. Couscous on terrace under tents, small dining room in house. Doesn't advertise. ***Chez Sam***, T044-473513, in the harbour with fine views of the port, a fish and seafood restaurant and bar, with good food and drink and a distinctive atmosphere, particularly good lobster, although pricey, seafood platters, *Amex* and *Diners Club* credit cards. ***Les Chandeliers***, 14 Darb Laalouj, just opposite the museum, T/F044-476450. Pleasant surroundings for candlelit supper, excellent *magret de canard*, fish in a variety of sauces. Southwestern French dishes, as owners Patrick and Martine Dupeyrat from that part of the world. Also pizzas. Recommended. Also have guest rooms over restaurant (see Sleeping, above). ***Riyad Bleu Mogador***, 23 R Benchtouf, T044-784128, F784583, down a side street off R Mohammed el Qorry, on your right as you head into the médina leaving Bab Marrakech behind you. European and local cooking. Highly recommended if the chef is on good form.

Mid-range *Chalet de la Plage*, 1 Av Mohammed V, T044-472972, F473419. Good fish dishes but also a wide-ranging menu, also open for lunch. If the wind isn't too severe, try for a table on attractive terrace directly overlooking the beach. ***Le Coquillage***, inside the port, T044-476655. Sometimes overrun with charabanc parties at lunchtime. ***Dar Baba***, 2 R de Marrakech, T044-476809. Top end of this category. Italian food, alcohol, credit cards accepted, recommended. ***Pizzeria L'As Dos***, 34 R Lattarine, on left just after first arch on Av de l'Istiqlal as you come from port direction, T044-473553. Candlelit but no booze. ***Pizzeria Le Grand Large***, 2 R Oum er Rabi, perfectly adequate pizzeria in the heart of the médina. ***Restaurant El Khaima***, in a small square off Darb Laalouj, opposite the museum. A good licensed restaurant with Moroccan specialities and a separate lobster menu. ***Restaurant Bab Lachouar***, southwest end of Pl Moulay Hassan. ***Restaurant La Licorne***, 26 R de la Skala, turn left at the ramparts end of Darb Laalouj, T044-473626, lalicorne_restau@yahoo.fr Traditional Moroccan food. ***Café-Restaurant Taros***, 2 R de la Skala, up street on your left as you face Pl Moulay Hassan with port behind you, T044-476407, F476408. Good food, open late, closed Sun, lots of books and magazines in café area, Breton management. Recommended. *Taros* is the local name for the ocean wind.

Cheap By far the best cheap eating option is to sample the freshly caught fish grilled at open-air restaurants between Pl Moulay Hassan and the port; accompanied by a tomato salad this makes a meal at a reasonable, negotiated price. The standard of hygiene has improved. Make sure you are absolutely clear on the price when you order. Another cheap option is the little fish barbecue place in *souk el Hout*, the fish market in the town centre (the one on the left as you come from the port area down Av de l'Istiqlal). ***Laâyoune***, 4 bis R Hajjali, close to Pl Moulay Hassan, T044-474643. Cheap and cheerful, young crowd some evenings. ***Les Alizés***, 26 R de la Skala, ground floor of *Hotel Smara*. Alcohol. A good little address. Cheap eateries off to the left of R Mohammed Zerktouni as you head for Bab Doukkala. Other good cheap options include ***Café-Restaurant Essalam*** on Pl Moulay Hassan offering good value local dishes such as couscous, open daily 1200-2300; and ***Mustafa's***, on Av Mohammed Ben Abdallah, a street that has a number of other cheap places.

Cafés The best places for breakfast are on Pl Moulay Hassan, particularly ***Café L'Opéra*** and ***Chez Driss***, a good place to have breakfast, or watch the evening social life pass by. Breakfast here will be better value than in a cheap hotel, and no one seems to mind if you bring your own cakes. There are several beachside cafés, too.

Bars Essaouira is not really the place for wild nightlife, although it livens up nicely during the annual **Gnaoua music festival**. Try *Chez Sam*, in the harbour; or ***Hotel des Iles*** and ***Hotel Tafoukt***, both on Av Mohammed V. The best upmarket bar is in the ***Sofitel***. For buying booze, the main off-licence is near the *Cinéma Rif*. Turn right out of Bab Doukkala, the off-licence is on your left, before the cinema, identifiable by small black and white tiles and beer posters.

Shopping

In its own quiet way, Essaouira offers some rather good opportunities for spending surplus cash

The main tourist shops are roughly between Pl Moulay Hassan and Darb Laalouj. Objects made in fragrant, honey-brown thuya wood are everywhere, from small boxes inlaid with lemon-wood to chunky, rounded sculptures. More expensively, you can pick up **paintings** by the local school of naïve and pointillist artists. Traditionally, the town's women wore all-enveloping **cotton/wool mix wraps**, in cream or brown, just the thing to keep out the ocean mists. Islamic fashions change, and happily, the weavers have found a new market providing fabrics for *maisons d'hôte* and their denizens. New colours and stripes have been added, and you can get a nice bedspread for 300dh. A visit to Essaouira is also a good opportunity to stock up on **argan oil** and **amlou**, a runny peanut-butter type product. In Essaouira, you can also find plenty of flowing shirts and pantaloons in greys, creams and beiges. However, the ultimate nouveau-hippy item must be the delicate, totally impractical **raffia-work sandals**, available direct from the cobbler in the odd dank workshop.

Chez Kabir, Raphia Mogador, on the central Souk des Grains (the market square on your right off Av de l'Istiqlal as you come from the port), is the ultimate supplier of *babouches* and raffia sandals, which in fact are made from doum-palm fibre. The best are the pointy-toed Aladdin ones. Can be ordered to suit your feet in colours ranging from natural cream to electric green and purple. Argan products can be picked up in quite a few places. Try ***Co-operative Amal***, Village de l'Arganier, Tamanar, T044-788141. Get to understand the production process by visiting this women's cooperative in the Essaouira region. Sample prices: 20 g bottle of amlou, 40dh, Arganati oil, 25cl for 80dh. Try also ***Essaouira Médina***, 8 R Ibn Rochd, Essaouira. This property rental agency also sells argan products.

Sport & activities

Cycling Bikes, including mountain bikes, can be seen for hire in the old town and from the *Hotel Shahrazad*, close to the tourist office. **Hammams** Several in the neighbourhood between Bab Doukkala and the bus station, easily identifiable by chimneys producing black smoke. Try also the more expensive 'European *hammam*', the ***Mounia Hammam Café***, complete with ambient music, plants. **Riding** ***Cavaliers d'Essaouira***, 14 km inland from Essaouira on the Marrakech road, next to restaurant *Dar Lamine*, T065-074889 (mob). New stables, riding by the hour and short treks in beautiful rolling countryside, all argan and olive groves and thuya plantations. Try also ***Auberge de la Plage***, at Sidi Kaouki, 27 km south of Essaouira, take bus No 5, T044-476600, F473383, aubplage@aim.net.ma Budding cameleers can take lessons at ***La Maison du Chameau***, off the Marrakech road, T044-785077, F476901, maisonduchameau@yahoo.fr Accommodation too, see Sleeping above. **Surfing** Winter is the surfing season in Essaouira. From Apr to Oct, the wind is up and the windsurfers are out in force. If you don't have your own gear, you can rent. However, the problem with surf gear is that it gets such intensive use that it ages quickly. Check carefully when you rent. There are a couple of surf places, of which the best is probably ***L'Océan Vagabond*** right on the main beach, T061-728340 (mob), bruno-erbani@yahoo.fr Try also ***Palais d'Océan***. Gear is about a year old but in good condition, 60dh/hr for wave-riding gear, 180dh/hr for windsurfer. They also do snacks and drinks. Surf scene tends to focus here. ***UCPA***, a well-managed surf centre close to ***L'Océan Vagabond***, T044-472972, F473417, was scheduled for removal as it got in the way of visitors to the new *Sofitel*. In town, ***No Work Team***, 7 bis R Houmane el Ftouaki, T044-475272, F476901, just off R Mohammed Ben Abdallah, almost opposite *Maison du Sud*, does clothing and gear.

Transport

Air Check whether ***RAM*** is still running flights from Casablanca to the tiny new Aéroport de Mogador, reservations and information on T044-476709, F476705. Demand seems to be insufficient for services to be maintained.

Road Bus *CTM* and private line bus services operate from the terminal north of Bab Doukkala, with connections to Casablanca, Safi, Marrakech and Agadir. There are lots of touts competing for custom – go inside terminus and look at ticket windows where departure times are clearly posted. The best onward service is with ***Supratours*** (Essaouira office, T044-475317) service to **Marrakech**, to connect with onward trains to **Casablanca-Rabat**, depart at 0620 (48dh single), from the big square outside Bab Marrakech. Buy your ticket at the kiosk on the square the day before, as this is a popular bus. ***CTM*** has departures for **Safi** at 1115 and 1500, **El Jadida** 1115, **Casablanca** 1115 and 2400, **Agadir** 1230 and 2030, **Tiznit** 1230. ***Pullman du Sud*** does a midnight departure for Casa, *guichet* 9 has frequent departures for Marrakech. **Taxi** Grands taxis operate from a parking lot beside the bus terminal. (You may have to wait a while for the vehicle to fill up if you are going to Marrakech.) There are frequent departures for **Diabat**, **Ghazoua**, **Smimou** and other places in the region, also for **Marrakech** and **Agadir**. Petits taxis are numerous, 5dh for a short ride in town. There are numerous *calèches* to be caught from the cab rank outside Bab Doukkala.

Buses from Essaouira can get very full in summer and during the Gnaoua Festival in Jun. Check your departure times the day before you travel and try to reserve

Directory

Banks Branches of ***Bank Commercial du Maroc***, ***Bank Populaire*** and ***Crédit du Maroc*** (you can change money here Sat morning in addition to normal banking hours) are in and around Pl Moulay Hassan. Foreign residents say that ***Wafa Bank***, Av de l'Istiqlal, (ATM, bureau de change) is the most practical when dealing with abroad. **Communications Internet**: places clearly signed almost opposite *Hotel Agadir* on Av de l'Istiqlal and on R Mohammed el Qorry. Best is probably ***Essaouira Informatique***, 127 R Mohammed el Qorry, T044-473678, esinfo@iam.net.ma **Post**: *PTT* is on Av Lalla Aicha, back from the seafront and Av Mohammed V. Stamps also available from telephone booths opposite *Restaurant Chalet de la Plage*. **Medical services** Dentist: Dr Elacham, 1 Blvd de Fès, T044-474727. Also Dr Sayegh, on Pl de l'Horloge, T044-475569.

Doctor: try Dr Mohammed Tadrart, opposite the post office, T044-475954. Also Dr Haddad, Av de l'Istiqlal, close to the *Wafa Bank*, T044-476910. **Hospital**: Outside the old town on Av El Mouqawama (the one behind the *Sofitel*). Emergencies on T044-474627. **Pharmacies**: in médina there are pharmacies on Av de l'Istiqlal and on Pl de l'Horloge. Several pharmacies on Av Al Massira near Bab Doukkala. **Useful numbers** Police: main commissariat on T044-784880.

Essaouira to Safi via the coast

For the journey northwards to Safi the main route travels east on the P10 to Ounara and then northwards on the P8 through the market village of Talmest to Sebt-des-Gzoula. Here there is the option to branch off northwest on the P120 or continue north to Tleta-de-Sidi-Bouguedra (126 km from Essaouira) and then west on the P12. If you are travelling by car, following the coastal route is a much more attractive alternative; make sure, though, that you have sufficient petrol for the 125 km drive as there are no service stations once you leave the main road. Leave Essaouira on the P10 to Marrakech and after about 6 km turn left on a new road signposted to Safi. For about 15-20 km this fast stretch of well-metalled road travels through open scrub landscape before descending at Km 244 towards the sea near **Cap Hadid** to give superb views of Atlantic waves breaking onto a long, windswept beach. For much of the next 35 km there is plenty of opportunity to enjoy the wild, unspoiled beauty of the coastline and the mountains of the Chiadma region to the east. The highest peak in this range is Jbel Hadid (Iron Mountain), 725 m. At Km 221 there is a rough track to the left to Plage Bhibhab and, on an otherwise isolated route, *Café Voyageur* is passed just before Km 206. Before reaching the new bridge across the Oued Tensift at Khemis-Oulad-el-Hadj, look for the ruins of **Kasbah Hamidouch**, an 18th-century fortress built by hyperactive builder Sultan Moulay Ismaïl. The road narrows and deteriorates as it follows the river estuary northwards but improves again at Souira Kédima (see page 157) where the rather dreary looking *Café Echabab* is close to the beach. For the next 15 km the route becomes more elevated with some fine clifftop scenery before the left turn at the *Café-Restaurant Essaouira*, 17 km from Safi. Much of the remaining journey is through a large industrial complex; on reaching the ring road, head for the centre of town as signposting is certainly not Safi's strong point.

Essaouira to Agadir

The road southwards runs some distance in from the coast. Although Essaouira has extended there are remnants of the argan tree forest that once covered this area now cut through by the P8 to Agadir. At Km 161 a track goes west to Sidi Kaouki on the coast. After a further 19 km another track leads west to more marabouts. At Smimou a road leads east by the side of Jbel Amardma to Souk el Tnine and Sebt des Ait Daoud, an interesting detour. The road then descends the side of Jbel Amsittene with many bends to cross the two parts of the Oued Iguezoulen, then climbs up the other side. Tamanar is built round a large kasbah. A winding road of 21 km leads down to the resort, shrine and viewpoint at Point Imessouane. A steep ascent leads up to Tamri, Cap Ghir (also spelt Rhir) offers good views, Paradise Plage is not as pleasant as its name suggests, Taghazout is a fishing village, and then you come to sprawling Agadir (see chapter on Agadir and the Souss).

Tanger and the northwest

172 Tanger
172 Ins and outs
173 Background

178 Sights

182 Excursions
182 West of Tanger
183 East of Tanger

184 Essentials
184 Sleeping
187 Eating
188 Cafés and pâtisseries
189 Bars and clubs
189 Entertainment
189 Festivals
189 Shopping
190 Sport and activities
190 Tour operators
190 Transport
191 Directory

192 South of Tanger
192 Asilah
194 El Utad, the stone circle at Mzoura
195 Larache

199 Ceuta
199 Ins and outs
201 Sights
203 Essentials
204 Tanger to Tetouan

205 Tetouan
205 Ins and outs
206 Sights
208 Essentials
210 Around Tetouan: the beach resorts

211 Chaouen
211 Ins and outs
211 Background
212 Sights
213 Essentials

215 The Northern Rif

217 Al Hoceima
217 Ins and outs
217 Background
218 Sights
219 Excursions
220 Essentials

221 Ouezzane and the Southern Rif

Introducing Tanger and the northwest

Tanger is a city at the crossroads of Africa and Europe, the Mediterranean Sea and the Atlantic Ocean. In recent memory it was both a wheeler-dealer enclave outside Moroccan jurisdiction and a resort where international rich met an artistic demi-monde. Although it has rather lost its glamorous patina, Tanger is still a bustling city, shabby on the edges but full of character.

A short drive from Tanger is **Ceuta**, would-be Hong Kong of the Mediterranean and still a Spanish enclave. Inland from Tanger, historic towns such as **Chaouen**, **Ouezzane** and **Tetouan** reflect links with Andalucía, long lost to the Moors. South of Ceuta is a string of small resorts: **Restinga-Smir**, **Cabo Negro**, and **Martil**, along with many small fishing villages. Much further east, **Al Hoceima**, today a quiet Mediterranean resort, is a recent implant, a creation of the Spanish Protectorate of the first half of the 20th century. The Rif, inland, is a land of wild and beautiful mountains with a history of strong independence.

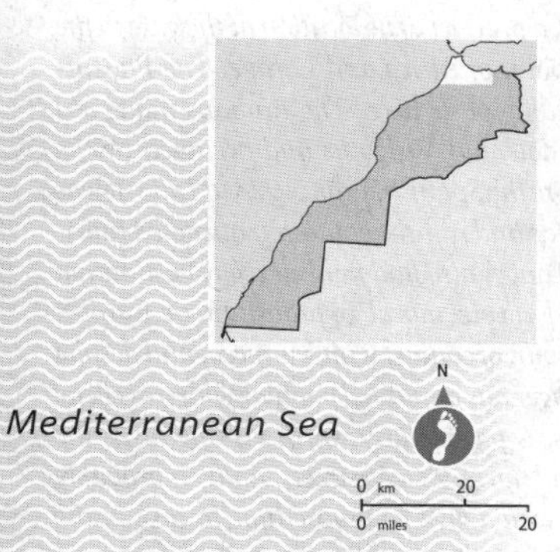

Things to do in the Northwest

- Explore **Tanger**, cityscape with literary and artistic ruins. Try to coincide with the ***Tanjazz festival***, now held in May/June (see www.tanjazz.com).
- Visit **Larache** (Spanish colonial architecture, Atlantic beach) and the sketchy but memorably sited remains of ancient **Lixus**.
- Visit the small but perfect médina of **Tetouan**.
- Near Issaguène, climb **Jbel Tidghine**, highest mountain in the Rif range.
- From Al Hoceïma, head west for the remote Mediterranean villages of **Torres del Kelaâ** and **Badis**.

Tanger طنجة

Phone code: 039
Colour map 1, grid A3

Tanja in Arabic, often referred to as Tangiers in English

Tanger has a highly individual character, a product of its location at the gate to the Mediterranean Sea and at the meeting point of Africa and Europe. The Phoenicians and Carthaginians established trading posts here. The Romans made it a capital city. It was invaded by the Vandals and Visigoths and occupied by the Arabs. The Portuguese took the town before the Spanish. From 1923 to 1956, it was an international city, and its tax-free status and raffish reputation attracted European and American writers and artists. Tanger also had fame as a gay destination in the days when such things attracted severe moral opprobrium in Europe. Arriving by sea, it may well be your first point of contact with Morocco, and despite a certain reputation as a hassly place, Tanger has remained popular with travellers. The kasbah, former residence of sultans, is particularly worth visiting, as is the médina, a dense maze of houses, shops and narrow, steep streets. A day is probably enough to see the main sights; two days would give you more time to take in the atmosphere and make a side trip to the Caves of Hercules on the Atlantic coast.

Ins and outs

Getting there

See Transport, page 190, for further details

Tanger's Boukhalef Airport, T039-935129, is 15 km southwest of the city on the P2 road to Rabat. Entry formalities can be slow. Catch bus 17 or 70 from the terminal to the Grand Socco (Pl du 19 Avril 1947), or take a grand taxi (70dh by day, 105dh after 2100 in winter and 2200 in summer, rates displayed on wall by customs).

The **train** no longer stops at Tanger Ville and Port. Rather, the terminal is at Tanger Moghougha, a 15dh petit taxi ride from the town centre, 20dh for the port, more at night. Have change ready. Taxi drivers will want to fill up their vehicles so you may have to wait. *CTM* buses arrive at the terminal in Av des FAR, adjacent to the port gates, and the former Tanger Ville railway station. Private lines arrive at the terminal at the end of R de Fès.

There are plenty of **buses** to Tanger, from Casablanca, Fès, Meknès and Rabat, as well as from local places like Asilah, Larache and Tetouan. The bus station is a short (12dh) petit taxi ride from the city centre hotels.

Driving into the city in the summer from the south, expect slow traffic north of Asilah after the motorway ends. The P2 from Rabat brings the driver into Tanger along R de Fès. The S704 from Ceuta feeds into Av Mohammed V, as does the P38 from Tetouan.

To get to Tanger by **sea**, there are car/passenger ferry services from Algeciras, Spain and Gibraltar. Within the port compound, there is a rank for both kinds of taxi. Negotiation over prices will be probably be necessary but hard.

Getting around

Tanger is actually quite a small place. However, the bus station (*mahattat el kirane*) is a good way out, so you will need to get a petit taxi (12dh), which ought to be metered, or a beige grand taxi. A trip within the city by petit taxi is 5dh. These taxis can be flagged down even when they have other passengers. If it is going in your direction, it will take you. A grand taxi ride will cost 10dh for a trip within the city. Note that prices go up by 50% after 2000. There are handy Boughaz minibuses and grands taxis from the Grand Socco for getting out to the bus station and the Atlantic coast sights.

There are 3 main hotel areas: off the Petit Socco, near the port entrance (ask to be dropped near *Hotel Marco Polo*, for example), and around the Blvd Pasteur.

Tourist information

Tourist offices **Office du Tourisme**, 29 Blvd Pasteur, T039-938239, F948050, open Mon-Sat 0800-1400. **Syndicat d'Initiative**, 11 R Khalid Ibn El Oualid, T039-935486.

Background

Perhaps the oldest city in Morocco, Tanger was active as early as 1600 BC. There was a Phoenician settlement here. Roman mythology ascribes its founding to the Greek giant Antaeus, son of Poseidon, god of the Earth, and Gaia, goddess of the earth. Antaeus challenged Hercules, but the hero killed the giant and had a child by his widow, Tingis. Hercules pulled apart Spain and Africa to give this son, Sophax, a city protected by the sea. Then, out of filial piety, King Sophax named his city Tingis.

Tanger, known to Phoenicians, Romans, Vandals and Byzantines, has always been important due to its location on the Straits of Gibraltar. At one point, Rome made it capital of the empire's North African provinces, its people receiving Roman citizenship in AD 38. It controlled the city until AD 429. Later, the Vandals and Byzantines struggled to control the region. The Muslim Arabs took the city in AD 706. It was to remain a point of conflict between the major Arab and Berber dynasties, before achieving commercial importance in the Mediterranean during the 1300s.

Tanger was first conquered by the Portuguese in 1437, and subsequently reoccupied in 1471, became Spanish in 1578 and Portuguese again in 1640. They built fine houses, Dominican and Franciscan chapels and a cathedral. The city was part of the dowry brought by the Portuguese Catherine of Braganza when she married Charles II of England in 1661. The English succeeded in alienating the Portuguese population, forcing both religious orders and Jews out of the city, before finally departing themselved in 1684, destroying the kasbah as they left. Sultan Moulay Ismaïl rebuilt the town after the English left.

In the 19th century Tanger became a popular base for European merchants and housed a large European colony. It was also the focus of political

competition between expansionist European powers. In 1923 the city became a tax-free International Zone controlled by a 30-member international committee. From then until the early 1960s was Tanger's heyday as a hedonistic, decadent freeport, playground of an international demi-monde, thus reinforcing the truth of earlier descriptions of the city. St Francis had seen it as a centre of sin, while in the 17th century Samuel Pepys had described it as a latter-day Sodom.

Celebrity visitors, wealthy & often talented

The streets of Tanger are full of artistic and literary memory. Among the illustrious visitors were 17th-century diarist Samuel Pepys, Camille Saint-Saëns (who drew on Issaoua trance music for his *Danse macabre*), film stars Marlene Dietrich and Errol Flynn, Oscar Wilde, author-translator Paul Bowles, Ian Fleming, Richard Hughes (*High Wind in Jamaica*), James Leo Herlihy (*Midnight Cowboy*). Woolworth-heiress Barbara Hutton had a house here, as did the heiress to the Knoll furniture fortune, the crumbling York Castle, up in the kasbah. Winston Churchill, Ronnie Kray, and the photographer Cecil Beaton all passed through. Painters who discovered light and the Orient in Tanger include Eugène Delacroix in 1832, Henri Matisse (1912), Kees Van Dongen and more recently Francis Bacon. The city's reputation as a haven of freedom for the likes of Tennessee Williams and Truman Capote, William Burroughs, Allen Ginsberg and Jack Kerouac, Brion Gysin and Joe Orton in the 1950s and 1960s continues to draw visitors. Today backpackers relive something of those heady days by visiting the *Tanger Inn*, Rue Magellan, a surviving fragment of Burroughs' *Interzone*.

Though many of the city's literary sites were lost in the demolition-rebuilding of the 1990s, the romantic-minded can still find something of Tanger's artistic soul. There are plenty of decaying apartment buildings, restaurants and low-life bars. The *Grand-Hôtel Villa de France* still survives, home to Gertrude Stein and Matisse, as does the Teatro Cervantes. Down near the port, next to the *Hôtel Cecil* (a favourite with Roland Barthes), is the *Immeuble Renschaussen*, where Burroughs and Gysin did artistic cut-ups in one of the lofts. Up at the kasbah, the Palais Menebhi was home to Gysin's 1001 Nights bar. Further west on the Montagne at the Villa Mimosa, Bowles finished *Let it come down*, yet another tale of an American adrift in the mysterious East. Still west of the city, the Plage Merkala was the setting for numerous tales by M'rabet, Charhadi and other members of Bowles' coterie. And the *Salon de thé Porte*, though heavily revamped, still carries a hint of a literary yesteryear.

The end of cosmopolitan Tanger

Tanger as a centre of easy money and loose morals was not to last, and the freeport was reunited with Morocco in October 1956. Tax-free status was maintained until 1960. Since Independence, Tanger has declined in international economic importance. Tourism was soon overshadowed by the enormous development of the industry elsewhere in the Mediterranean and today functions essentially for the Moroccan market. In the summer, up to two million migrant workers and their families pass through the port, and Tanger is their first contact with their homeland. In the 1980s, the green cliff tops of La Montagne, west of the city, came to be favoured by Gulf amirs as the place for a holiday home. Vast palaces in the Neo-Kuwaiti style appeared like UFOs in the pine and eucalyptus woods.

1990s Tanger

Tanger has always been through highs and lows, and the 1990s were in many ways the trough of a low period. A building boom, in part financed by the profits of the kif trade, meant masses of new building as profits were recycled in. Many historic buildings were torn down, replaced by blocks of

With William Burroughs in Interzone

William Burroughs got interested in visiting Tanger after reading a couple of Paul Bowles Tangerine novels. In 1953, just after the publication of Junkie, *he left New York for anywhere – and wound up in Tanger. Disappointment was quick to set in, the city's literary coterie was hostile and Burroughs wrote in a 1954 letter to Alan Ginsberg: "There is an end-of-the-world feeling in Tangiers, with its glut of nylon shirts, Swiss watches, Scotch and sex and opiates sold across the counter. Something sinister in complete laissez-faire. And the new police chief up there on the hill accumulating dossiers. I suspect him of unspeakable fetishistic practices with his files." Paul Bowles proved hostile and manipulative, too. A moment of vengeance came, however, when the the city's senior writer was set upon by enraged baboons in the countryside and forced to flee for his life. Wrote Burroughs: "They got vicious purple-assed baboons in the mountains a few miles out of town ... I intend to organise baboon sticks from motorcycles. A sport geared to modern times."*

The exotic splendours of Tanger left Burroughs unmoved. As he put it in a letter to Ginsberg: "Don't ever fall of this inscrutable oriental shit like Bowles puts down." No adoration of the mysterious East here. Burroughs' life in the city gradually decayed into a drugged-up blur. He was dubbed the Invisible Man, *rarely emerging from his hotel in the Petit Socco, dividing his time between writing, 'delicious afternoon sleeps in a darkened room' and the half-light of the* Bar Mar Chica. *The denizens included fellow addicts and his lover Kiki. A cure at the Hôpital Benchimol produced meagre results, "the philosophic serenity conveyed by an empty scrotum" was not enough to break the opium habit. Eventually, Burroughs left for England for further treatment. He returned to take up residence at the Villa Mouniria and in 1957 finished the manuscript which was to become* The Naked Lunch. *The International Zone of Tanger features here as* Interzone, *(first title of the book), a place of shady deals and narcotic visions. Over time, Burroughs' idea of the city changed, and he came to find it had 'a wild beauty'.*

For more on Tangerine atmosphere in the 1950s, look out for the Bowles' novels Let it come down *(1952) and* The Sheltering Sky *(1949), both republished in paperback.* The Letters of William S Burroughs *(London: Viking Press, 1983) give a frank view of the writer's tribulations in Tanger.*

concrete-brutalist ugliness. And then came the late king's 'clean up public life' campaign. Corruption scandals and court cases hit the city, various local figures disappeared behind bars or overseas, all to the good many would say. But the big change came with Mohammed VI's accession to the throne in July 1999. The new king made the Northwest the first region he visited outside the capital. Tanger was ecstatic. The long-ignored Palais Marshan was dusted down, there seemed to be some hope for a region too long forgotten by the powers that be.

The second half of the 1990s also saw groups of local notables, business people and intellectuals try and 'do something' to improve things in Tanger. A feisty local press with newspapers like *Les nouvelles du Nord* and *D3* (pronounced Dé-trois, like Detroit) kept things moving along, associations were set up to do something for street kids, to support the unemployed and illiterate, to save the kasbah and the Teatro Cervantes. The death of local literary figure Paul Bowles put the city back in the international press while a certain intellectual design set, tired of crowded (and increasingly polluted) Marrakech rediscovered the virtues of Tanger. Yves St Laurent bought a place, as did Alberto Pinto, designer responsible for the Mamounia's 1999

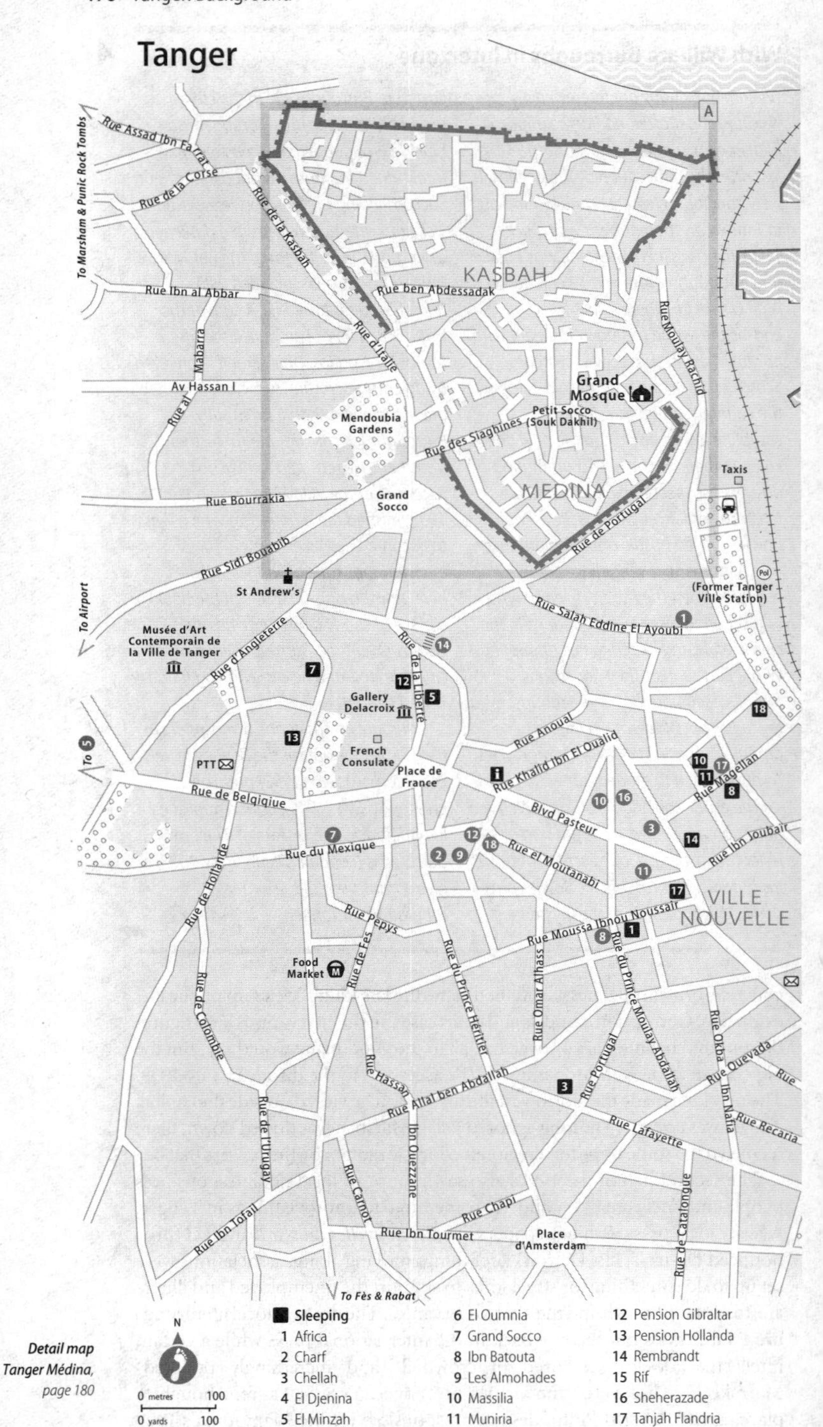

Detail map Tanger Médina, page 180

Sleeping
1 Africa
2 Charf
3 Chellah
4 El Djenina
5 El Minzah
6 El Oumnia
7 Grand Socco
8 Ibn Batouta
9 Les Almohades
10 Massilia
11 Muniria
12 Pension Gibraltar
13 Pension Hollanda
14 Rembrandt
15 Rif
16 Sheherazade
17 Tanjah Flandria

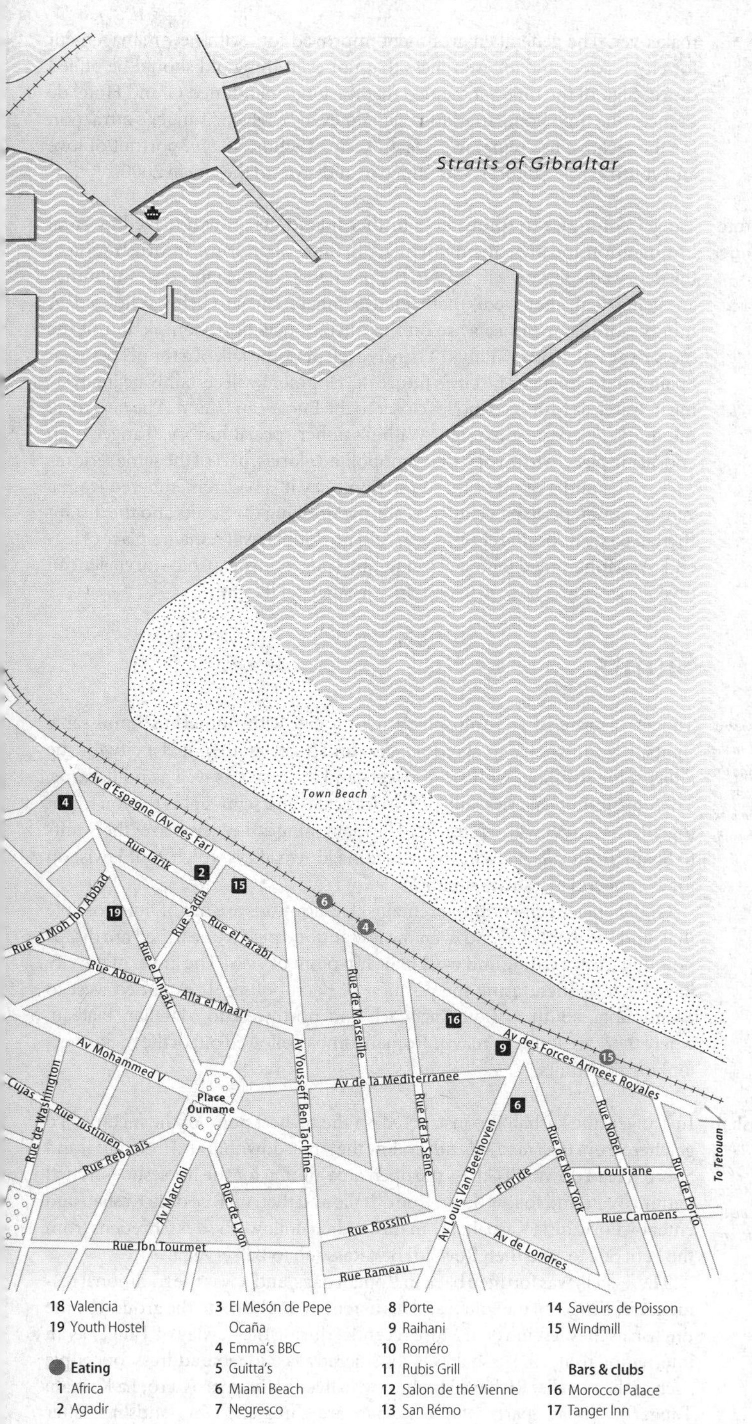
Straits of Gibraltar
Town Beach
Av d'Espagne (Av des Far)
Rue Tarik
Rue Sadia
Rue el Farabi
Rue el Moh Ibn Abbad
Rue el Antaki
Rue Abou
Alla el Maari
Av Mohammed V
Place Oumame
Av Yousseff Ben Tachfine
Rue de Marseille
Av de la Mediterranee
Rue de la Seine
Av des Forces Armees Royales
Rue Nobel
Rue de New York
Rue de Porto
To Tetouan
Louisiane
Floride
Rue Camoens
Av Louis Van Beethoven
Av de Londres
Rue Rossini
Rue Rameau
Rue de Lyon
Av Marconi
Rue Ibn Tourmet
Rue Rebalais
Rue Justinien
Cujas
Rue de Washington
18 Valencia
19 Youth Hostel
Eating
1 Africa
2 Agadir
3 El Mesón de Pepe Ocaña
4 Emma's BBC
5 Guitta's
6 Miami Beach
7 Negresco
8 Porte
9 Raihani
10 Roméro
11 Rubis Grill
12 Salon de thé Vienne
13 San Rémo
14 Saveurs de Poisson
15 Windmill
Bars & clubs
16 Morocco Palace
17 Tanger Inn

makeover. The general environment improved too, with new management for city services and an awareness that not everything old should be pulled down. Sign of the times, it seemed that the long abandoned Grand Hotel de France, one time home to Matisse, might even be saved. Tanger's attraction for the creative has remained intact: André Téchiné's *Loin*, portrait of love and youth across cultures, was filmed in and around the city in 2000.

The future of Tanger

Tanger continues to sprawl ever further inland, its growth fuelled by rural in-migration and high unemployment. In times of pressure, the frustration of the deprived spills over in riots in the poor areas on the city edge. But things are better than they were, the *bidonville* inhabitants are being rehoused. A number of major projects are on the cards: a new port, completion of the motorway link to Casa-Rabat. There is even periodic talk of a tunnel between Spain and Morocco. The city's future development will certainly be interesting to watch as Morocco moves closer to the European Union. The new royal interest is a very positive sign. With its rather special history, Tanger is an endearing place, a town of past cosmopolitan glories, part of the same series as Alexandria and Tripoli of the West. Some say it is best remembered from a vantage point, perhaps a cliff-top café, overlooking the Straits and the distant Iberian coast across the choppy sea. And no doubt it will remain a place of legend. As Mohammed Choukri put it, "In Tanger, any capable storyteller can invent a story and be sure to convince listeners of its truth."

Sights

Best view of Tanger: from the café terrace and the McDonald's (sorry) in the Dawliz Complex, R du Hollande

Tanger is more of an atmosphere than a city with numerous unmissable sights. If you manage to avoid hasslers and hustlers, then it is a city for the *flâneur*, for strolling, with steep streets and stairways as well as boulevards. There are minor galleries, out-of-the-way cafés and semi-sights for you to put together a wander with a purpose. The main thing is the views: over the Straits to Spain, from *ville nouvelle* to the médina, down alleys which could twist on for ever or end in a sticky situation.

Of the ancient city nothing remains. Descriptions are full of 'it is possible that' and 'probably be' and even the few antique pieces unearthed are disappointing from a dating and workmanship point of view. The limits of the city have been defined, using the position of necropolises. It extended west to Mendoubia, south to Bou Kachkach and northwest to Marshan Plateau, where there are Punic or maybe Roman tombs hollowed out of the rock, overlooking the Straits.

Kasbah

Kasbah means 'strongpoint', and in north African cities means the citadel area

In Tanger, the kasbah is constructed on the highest point of the médina. To get there from the *Hotel Minzah*, follow the street downhill and into the Grand Socco. Head downhill across the open area aiming for the horseshoe-arched entrance gate and follow down Rue d'Italie and then up Rue de la Kasbah and enter by Porte de la Kasbah. From the médina, follow Rue des Chrétiens from the Petit Socco, and then Rue Sidi Ben Rassouli to Bab el Assa.

The kasbah was fortified back in Roman days, and it was the traditional residence in Tanger of the sultan and his harem. It was burnt to the ground by the English as they left in 1684. More recently, during the heyday of Tanger as an international city, the kasbah was considered a fashionable address for people such as the novelist Richard Hughes (who lived at 'Numéro Zero, La Kasbah, Tanger'). Today, parts of the kasbah are threatened by landslips: after particularly heavy rains, the locals hold their breath and wait to see whether a section of the cliffs will slither down towards the sea. Especially at risk is York Castle, 17th-century home of English governor, the Duke of York.

Musée de la Kasbah

The Musée de la Kasbah is in the former palace of the kasbah, the **Dar al-Makhzen**, and includes Moroccan arts and antiquities. The palace was built by the Sultan Moulay Ismaïl in the 18th century, and was used as the Sultan's palace up until 1912, when Sultan Moulay Hafid, exiled to Tanger, lived there. The palace is itself worth seeing, with an impressive central courtyard. ■ *0930-1300, 1500-1800, closed Tue. T039-932097.*

Museum of Moroccan Arts

Note the painted wooden ceilings, sculpted plasterwork and exquisite mosaics

The Museum of Moroccan Arts is housed in the prince's apartments. This is truly a magnificent setting for the displays. The museum has a wide range of carved and painted woods, carpets and textiles. Items of note are the firearms from the North enhanced with delicate marquetry; pottery decorated with flowers and feathers also from the North; unique carpets from Rabat. The Fès room is certainly outstanding; firstly for the room itself with its intricate wall and ceiling carvings, and secondly for the ancient ceramics from Fès and Meknès, centuries old dishes embellished with brilliant colours ranging from golden to the renowned Fès blue. In the Fès room, too, are dazzling silks, and illuminated manuscripts of the finest calligraphy, all superbly bound.

Museum of Antiquities

The former kitchens of the palace is now the Museum of Antiquities. On display are bronzes and mosaics from the Roman sites. A major item is the famous mosaic known as 'The Voyage of Venus' found at Lixus. This quite spectacular mosaic shows Venus in a vessel propelled by oars with nymphs (in and out of the water). The colours and the countenances of the major figures are still remarkably clear. Many of the artefacts relate to the history of Tanger and the surrounding region. In Room 3, which is devoted to ancient funeral rites, is a life-size replica of a Carthaginian tomb and a number of lead sarcophagi.

The garden of the palace is worth exploring, a beautiful mature Andalucían arrangement, with fragrant plants. The ancient necropolis incorporated into the garden is a very good reproduction. As you leave the palace stop at *Le Detroit* for a drink and pastries, and an impressive view of the city and sea.

Other sights in the kasbah

To the left of the palace is the **Museum of Ethnography and Archaeology**. In front of the palace is the Place de la Kasbah, where criminals were once punished or executed. Note the **Grand Mosque** adjacent to the port. In the sea wall a gate leads out onto a belvedere with excellent views of the seascape. On the other side of the Place de la Kasbah, just outside the kasbah gate on Rue Sidi Hassani, is the **Musée International d'Art Contemporain**. Also nearby is **Villa Sidi Hosni**, former residence of Barbara Hutton, the American heiress who was famous for her parties, amongst other things (read all about it in Iain Finlayson's '*Tangier, City of the Dream*').

Below the kasbah, the médina

Lying below the kasbah, and running from the Grand Socco (Place de 19 Avril, 1947) down to the port, the **médina** is focused on the Petit Socco, and is full of narrow, twisting streets and old houses, many of which are now shops, hotels or restaurants catering for tourists. It is a quarter which has captured the imagination of numerous European and American writers, with the stories of Paul Bowles amongst the most evocative. It is easy to get lost here, so it might be advisable for the visitor with limited time to take an official guide. Unaccompanied, unofficial guides will hawk for business continuously.

The Grand Socco is where the médina begins, Tanger's answer to Jemaâ el Fna in Marrakech. Nowadays it is a bit of a car park, although stalls and cheap cafés and restaurants seem to do a good trade. Note the tiled minaret of the **Sidi Bou Abid Mosque** (1917) on the corner of the Grand Socco and Rue Sidi Bou Abid. On Thursday and Sunday Rifi Berber women sell all sorts of wares in Rue de la Plage (Rue Salah Eddine El Ayoubi). Along Rue d'Angleterre they also sell woven blankets. On the Rue Bourrakia side of the Grand Socco, the arch with Arabic on it leads into the **Mendoubia Gardens**, a quiet and impressive foresty place in the heart of Tanger, unfortunately usually closed. These gardens were formerly part of the residence of the Mendoub and contain 30 bronze cannon, the remains of old French and British warships. The **Mendoubia Palace** is the former residence of the sultan's representatives on the International Commission.

Rue Siaghine, the old silversmiths' street, running from the Grand Socco to the Petit Socco, is still an important commercial area of the médina, and the easiest route by which to enter the main area of the médina. To the right of Rue Siaghine, is the *mellah*, the Jewish quarter.

One also passes the **Spanish Cathedral**, now boarded up. Rue es Siaghin leads down into the Petit Socco, the heart (or belly?) of the médina. This market square was once bigger, but now seems strangely cramped. It is surrounded by a number of famous but primitive *pensiones*, and the *Café Central*, formerly a café-bar attracting the likes of William Burroughs, Allen Ginsberg and Jack Kerouac. Today, with no alcohol sold in the médina, it is just a fairly ordinary café with a terrace from which to watch life pass by.

Tanger Médina

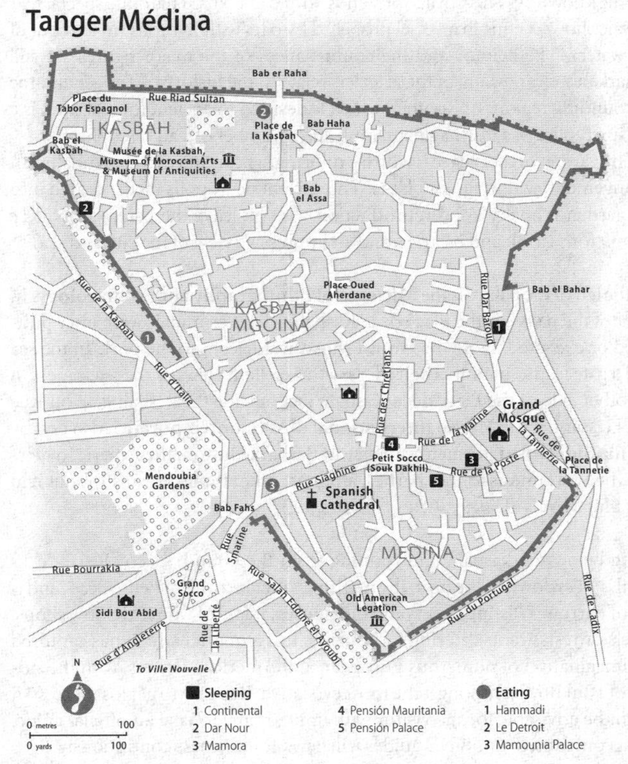

Related map
Tanger, *page 176*

Below the Petit Socco, the **Grand Mosque** lies in between Rue de la Marine and Rue des Postes. This is built on the site of a Portuguese cathedral, although that had been predated by a mosque and, probably, a Roman temple. Opposite is a 14th-century *medersa*. Also on Rue des Postes (Rue Mokhtar Ahardan) is the *Pensión Palace*, where Bertolucci filmed scenes for *The Sheltering Sky*, based on the Paul Bowles novel.

The **Old American Legation**, 8 zankat Amerika, is the oldest American diplomatic property, given to the US by the Moroccan sultan in 1821 and used as a Consulate until 1961. It has the distinction of being the only historical monument to have remained in US possession since the birth of the American Nation. It is now a museum and study centre. On display is a letter from George Washington to Moulay Abdallah and a collection of mirrors, also a good collection of prints including works by Lecouteux and Ben Ali Rbati, an early Moroccan naïve painter. ■ *0930-1200, 1600-1830. T039-935904.*

Ville nouvelle

Tanger's *ville nouvelle* is a veritable catalogue of late 19th/early 20th-century architectural styles. Place de France (Place de Faro) has a good view of the bay, with the famous *Café de France* alongside, where wartime agents met and made deals. Next to it is the Terrasse des Paresseux, where would-be emigrants can see across the Straits to Spain and shoeshine boys and Polaroid-snappers harass the tourists (just opposite is a famous Madini ersatz perfume store). Boulevard Pasteur (becoming Avenue Mohammed V further down) is the main shopping and business street of the new town. Find time to explore the area behind the Boulevard Pasteur. Here the streets once had names like Rue Delacroix, Rue Jeanne d'Arc and Rue Tolstoï. Look out for the 1940s cinemas, have tea at *Pâtisserie Porte*, drop in at the Librairie des Colonnes back on the main boulevard. Then wander médina-wards again down Rue de la Liberté (the one with the *Hotel Minzah*) perhaps stopping off at the **Galerie Delacroix** if there is an exhibition.

Near the Grand Socco

At 50 Rue d'Angleterre, is the Anglican **Church of St Andrew's** consecrated in 1905. The churchyard gate is discrete, in a low whitewashed wall, just left of some birdsellers' stalls, at the top side of the Grand Socco. Inside, the church hides in luxuriant vegetation. The key is kept by the friendly and helpful groundsman, Mustapha, who will unlock the church and give you a guided tour. Architecture and internal decoration are modelled on Moorish Granada. Note the Arabic inscriptions of the Lord's Prayer and Gloria at the altar end. Memorials and graves, both inside and outside, feature a number of important former residents of Morocco, including 19th-century British consul Sir John Drummond Hay, early 20th-century *Times* correspondent Walter Harris, Caïd Sir Harry McLean, Scottish adviser to Sultan Moulay Abd al-Aziz, and Emily Keane, 19th-century wife of the Sherif of Ouezzane. Turn right out of the churchyard gate, follow the wall uphill and you will come to the former British Consulate, now the **Musée d'Art Contemporain de la Ville de Tanger**, at 52 Rue d'Angleterre. Here there is a small but fine selection of late 20th-century Moroccan painters. There are a couple of wacky pictures by wild woman Chaïbia Tallal, plus early works by the likes of Farid Belkahia, founder of the Casablanca Ecole des beaux arts, Saâd Hassani and others. ■ *10dh. T039-938436.*

In the Marshan neighbourhood

Until recently, the **Forbes Museum of Military Miniatures** was the main attraction in this early-20th-century neighbourhood of villas up on the Marshan Plateau west of the Kasbah. (The others are the *Café Hafa* and the Punic necropolis.) Housed in the former Palais Mendoub on Rue

Shakespeare, overlooking the sea near the stadium, the museum consisted of military dioramas assembled by US magazine magnate Malcolm Forbes. In late 2000, the palace was purchased by the Moroccan state to be used for important guests. Further along the Rue Shakespeare, large neo-classical villas bear witness to past prosperity and taste in Tanger.

The *Café Hafa*, the clifftop café, lies down a narrow street near the former museum. Crowded at weekends with local youth, it is the place for a sticky, Polo-mint tasting tea, flavoured in season with orange-blossom. The **Punic rock tombs**, little more than large coffin-sized shapes hollowed out of the soft rock, are nearby, signposted by large boards indicating that the local authorities are going to landscape the site. The closest clifftop viewing place near the poorer parts of the city, it is popular with local women and kids on weekend afternoons.

Beaches Back in the centre, the **town beach** and the clubs alongside it were previously an expatriate zone where anything was permissible and a good time easily available. In its heyday, this beach was said to be the third most beautiful in the world, after Rio de Janeiro and Miami. Jack Kerouac and Joe Orton were among the habitués, the latter meeting a sticky end after one particularly lively stay in Tanger. Roland Barthes enjoyed *Las Tres Caravelas*, which then gave way to the *Miami*. More recently, Mario Testino photographed the local wildlife. The clubs offer a range of drinking, eating and dancing opportunities. Nostalgics might try *Emma's BBC* or *The Windmill*. *La Pasarela* and the *Coco Beach* are the clubs of the moment, packed at weekends with people up from Casa.

During the day, the locals are out playing football on the beach, which gets particularly crowded in July and August. There is even talk of a beach football league. Out of season parts of the beach are none too clean – watch out for used needles, avoid after dark. The pollution problem has been partly resolved, too.

For the moment, families with frazzled parents, small children and the means to rent a car would be advised to go for more relaxing, less crowded and cleaner beaches east along the coast – possibly on the stretch south of Ceuta. Nearer Tanger, there is bathing at **Playa Blanca** and **Sidi Kankouch**, also further on near **Ksar Es Seghir** and **Plage Dahlia** (11 km after Ksar Es Seghir). Beaches west of Tanger such as **Plage Merkala** can be dangerous, with unsuspected depths, partly caused by building contractors being authorized to excavate beach sand. The advantage of the Atlantic beaches is that in summer there is sun until the early evening. Here, too, beware currents and heavy breakers.

Birdwatching Tanger is a splendid place for watching the birds which migrate across the Strait of Gibraltar, the easiest crossing place between Europe and Africa. Literally hundreds of species make use of the thermals to cross northwards in spring and southwards in autumn, the flocks of huge storks and vultures being the most impressive sight. Head east for **Jbel Moussa**, Gibraltar's African twin for such ornithological sights.

Excursions

West of Tanger

Atlantic beaches The excursion west is a rewarding experience, with a dramatic drive en route. The coast of Southern Spain can be easily seen on a clear day. From the coast road to the north of the town, a special viewpoint is provided. The options are to negotiate a round-trip price with a grand taxi driver in Rue d'Angleterre, take a

Boughaz minibus from the port gates, or in your own transport, follow Rue Sidi Bou Abid and Rue Sidi Amar on to the S701. This goes up into the Montagne, an exclusive suburb of royal palaces and villas, past discrete gates with plaques bearing names like Siddartha. In places, the road and woods would not be out of place in Devon, plus a few palm trees. You may see pines sculpted by the Chergui wind. After dense eucalyptus woods, the landscape opens up, with views of the ocean and fine stands of parasol pine. **Drive carefully**. Weekenders in fast Mercedes can be reckless and the narrow road is due for resurfacing.

Some 11 km from Tanger, the extreme northwestern corner of Africa is reached. Coming from Tanger, bear right for the **Cap Spartel** lighthouse with its *Café-Bar Sol*. Going left, you have rocky coastline followed by the wild Atlantic or **Robinson Beach**. This is a dramatic place, and swimmers should exercise caution (there are drownings every year and very little the coastguard can do). In spring, there are plenty of wild flowers, while in summer, tiny temporary cafés with cane awnings spring up among the rocks above the crashing surf, a place to savour grilled sardines, sweet tea and maybe a quiet smoke.

If you wish to overnight on this coast, the options include the **L** *Hotel-Club Le Mirage*, near the caverns, T039-333332, F333492, excellent service, the discretely rich rent holiday chalets for the whole season. Also nearby are the **C** *Hotel Les Grottes d'Hercules*, T039-938765; and the **E** *Hotel Robinson* as well as *Camp Robinson* and the *Robinson Café-Restaurant*.

Caves of Hercules

The Caves of Hercules are natural formations which have been extended by quarries for millstones up to the 1920s. Later prostitutes worked here, and Tanger's rich and famous held parties. From a window shaped like Africa which overlooks the sea there is an impressive view. ■ *1000 to sunset, nominal charge.*

Ancient Cotta

After the Caves of Hercules take a rough farm track off the road to the Ancient Cotta. This is a small site, less impressive than Volubilis, centred around a factory for *garum*, or anchovy paste. Also note remains of the temple.

East of Tanger

Cap Malabata

From Tanger, 10 km east along the S704 road around Cap Malabata, tourist developments, including the *Hotel/Casino Mövenpick* complex, numerous cafés as well as some excellent beaches used by the people from Tanger. Cap Malabata is where the Atlantic and the Mediterranean meet and it is said the waters (with a little imagination) can be seen as two different colours. Despite this the views are magnificent. The Victorian pile on the hill is the **Château Malabata**, a Gothic folly inhabited by a family.

Ksar es Seghir

Ksar es Seghir is a small seaside town 37 km east of Tanger, dominated by the ruined Portuguese castle. The town was named Ksar Masmuda under the Almohads, and Ksar al Majaz under the Merinids, who added walls and gates in 1287. The Portuguese took the town in 1458. The floor of the hammam and mosque should be noted, as well as the intact sea gate arch. The **F** *Café-Restaurant Hotel Kassar al Majaz Tarik Ibn Ziad* is basic. There are other cafés and restaurants, including the recommended *Restaurant Caribou, Café Dakhla* to the west of the town, *Café Dahlia* to the east and *Café Lachiri* on the bridge (seafood). There are possibilities for camping, and a splendid beach. Onwards, between Ksar es Seghir and Ceuta, there is a string of beautiful and deserted beaches. Bus 15 from Grand Socco, Tanger, serves this route. The road is busy on a Sunday and very busy in summer. Out of season many places are closed.

Bird migration

Without doubt this is the best place in North Africa to watch the migrations to and from Europe. Over 250 different species have been counted crossing this narrow strip of water, and while the main movements are from March to May and August to October, early and late movers ensure that there are always some birds to observe. The stretch of coast from Cap Spartel in the west to Punta Ceres in the east and the advantage of height gained by Jbel Kebir and Jbel Moussa provide ample viewing spots. The massive migration of large raptors is very impressive. Flocks of white stork can be spotted too. Smaller birds take this route including warblers and wheatears, swallows, larks and finches. The routes are determined by the direction and strength of the wind.

Gibraltar/ Algeciras

Excursions take only 1¼ hours. Day trips cost 60dh to Gibraltar, 250dh to Algeciras. See Transport, page 191, for further details.

Essentials

Sleeping

■ *on maps, pages 176 & 180*
Price codes: see inside front cover
Tanger has hotels to suit all budgets

For the budget traveller, easiest to find and deal with are the hotels near the **seafront**, best of which are the *Hotel Excelsior*, and, more expensively, the *Muniria* and the *Hotel Nabil*. Women travelling alone should avoid **Petit Socco** hotels if possible – you don't want to be caught up in nocturnal brawls as you return from a restaurant. However, there are reasonably priced establishments in the **upper médina** and off **Blvd Pasteur**, aka **El Bolibar**, handy for banks, bars, boîtes de nuit and pâtisseries the morning after. Best in the upper-mid-range is the *Continental*, followed by the *Intercontinental*. East of the city, Tanger also has a number of large **beach hotels**, including a *Club Méditerranée*. These hotels tend to get the smell of raw sewage when the wind's blowing the wrong way. For toney people, there is the indispensable *El Minzah* and, out west at **Cap Spartel**, the discrete and calm *Mirage*, Tanger's equivalent of the Mamounia. Note that in the lower price brackets, many of the hotels near the seafront and on the Petit Socco can be pretty damp. Some are frequented by potential *harragas*, Moroccans and Nigerians hoping to get across the Straits to Spain. In Jul and Aug, prices tend to rise by 20-30% and some hotels make breakfast compulsory at extra charge.

One of Tanger's most famous institutions, the *Grand Hotel de France*, used by Matisse during his time in Morocco, is currently closed. The owner seems to have abandoned his intentions to demolish it and put up a shopping mall, so there is every hope for a pleasant new institution. The *Hotel Rif*, a large 1970s hotel on the seafront, also remains firmly closed. The guesthouse phenomenon has now reached Tanger, too. Perched up in the kasbah, there is the personable *Dar Nour*. On a grander scale, the *Palais Ben Abbou* can be rented via www.riadmaroc.com

Seafront & on the slope

Av des Forces Armées Royales is abbreviated to Av des FAR

B ***Hotel Rif***, 152 Av des FAR (ex-Av d'Espagne), T039-937870. Closed at time of writing but too good a hotel to be left derelict for long. Has sea views and nice pool. **C** ***Africa Hotel***, 17 R Moussa Ben Noussair, T039-935511. 86 rooms, comfortable and lively, bar, pool, restaurant, nightclub. **C** ***Hotel El Djenina***, 8 R El Antaki (R Grotius), just off Av d'Espagne, T039-942244, elejenina_hotel@caramail.com 21 well renovated, airy rooms, helpful reception. A good option. **D** ***Hotel Charf***, 25 R Dante, behind the *Rif*. T039-943340. Compulsory 35dh breakfast in summer. **D** ***Hotel Marco Polo***, Av d'Espagne, T039-931877. Small comfortable hotel, 9 rooms, German run, much used by lorry drivers. Nice reception, best hotel near port. **D** ***Hotel-Résidence Karim***, 6 R Cook, below the *Muniria*, T039-937790. 7 apartments of various sizes, studio 1000dh per week low season, apartment sleeping 4 2000dh per week high season. Prices vary according to season and client. Some rooms have bad damp. **E *Hotel Massilia***, behind the *Rembrandt*, now closed. Another part of Tangier's mythical past disappears. Expect demolition and a new building on the site blocking the sea view from the back rooms of the *Rembrandt*. **E *Hotel Muniria***, R Magellan, T039-933537. Only 8 rooms, hot water not always available in mornings. Nice views from terrace. Taxi drivers will often tell you that it is closed. To find, locate *Hotel Rembrandt*, go down hill towards *Hotel Massilia*, turn left at this hotel. After 40 m, turn right. *Muniria* and *Ibn Batouta* are down the slope. *Tanger Inn* (bar next door) is popular too, former clients including William Burroughs, Kerouac and Ginsberg. So if you're intent on making a Beat Generation pilgrimage... **E *Hotel Ibn Batouta***, 8 R Magellan, with restaurant. Opposite the *Muniria*. Has been expanded, suites 600dh per 2 persons, new rooms 200dh, but avoid pokey, damp single rooms at 100dh. Nice management, some rooms with good views. An address which should have charm. Cleaning ladies patrol the corridors. **E *Valencia***, 72 Av d'Espagne, junction with R de la Plage (zankat Salah Eddine el Ayoubi), T039-930770. 45 rooms, clean but basic, no restaurant. **F *Hotel Cécil***, 112 Av d'Espagne, T039-375331. Cold showers, occasional hot water. Finest marble staircase in Tanger, vast rooms with double doors, abandoned dining room. Original decoration early 20th-century classical, Moroccan and 1970s touches. Michel Foucault stayed here. Not too suitable for women.

On Rue de la Plage

There are also cheap and basic pensiones on R de la Plage, where prices do not seem to be fixed. Many do not have showers, including **F *Royal*, *Madrid*, *Le Detroit*, *Playa*** and ***Atou***, the last being particularly cheap, while *Le Detroit* is about the best.

Grand & Petit Soccos

The Petit Socco is the heart of the médina. Its pensiones are on the grubby side but do have a history. Watch your pockets in this area

If you have just arrived in Morocco by ferry, you may find the route to the Petit Socco (aka Pl Souk Dakhil) a little confusing, although it is in fact simple – from the seafront Av d'Espagne, aka Av des FAR, go straight up either R de Portugal or R de la Plage to the entrance to the médina, and then down R es Siaghin to the Petit Socco. **D *Hotel Mamora***, 19 R des Postes, aka R Mokhtar-Ahardan, T039-934105. Only really decent hotel in the centre of the médina. Immaculately clean but faintly downcast. Downside: noisy street-side rooms. Rooms looking towards port have call to prayer from Great Mosque. Great views from abandoned roof terrace restaurant. If pushed, probably best to go for this rather than risk a very downmarket place. **F *Hotel Grand Socco***, R Imam Layti, behind the Grand Socco. Cheap, dirty and noisy. **F *Pensión Mauritania***, T039-934671. In full decline too, as is the *Pension Olid*. The *Pension Lutétia* tends to be used by women sex workers. Probably best of the lot, on R des Postes, is the **F *Pensión Palace***, 2 R Mokhtar-Ahardan, T039-936128. A rambling sort of place with new bits round the back. Some rooms cramped and airless, others high-ceilinged and spacious. Reception used to backpackers off the ferry.

Upper médina

A *Palais Ben Abbou*, see www.riadmaroc.com 5 double rooms, courtyard, available for rent in its entirety in Jul-Aug, for shorter periods at other times. **C *Hotel Continental***, 36 R Dar Baroud, T039-931024. Not on the seafront but in the médina with view of the port, a good mid-range option, owned and managed by 2 brothers. Go for the refurbished rooms (nice restyling by local decorator Itaf Ben Jelloun). Service catastrophic – never mind, there is lots of charm and a sea view. Used by Bertolucci in the filming of the Paul Bowles novelette, *The Sheltering Sky*. Some clients rent a room all year round. **C *Dar Nour***, R Gourna, La Kasbah, reservations T062-112724 (mob), also pgb.tanger@caramail.com. Twin rooms 400dh, large suite 1000dh, 1 small room 150dh. 4 new suites added in 2002. Views over the Parc de la Mendoubia to the cathedral and new mosque. Big breakfasts. An excellent address. After acquisition of house next door, is to add 3 new suites. May lose the intimate touch. Khadija can cook excellent meals to order.

Near Parc Brooks A *Hotel Intercontinental*, Parc Brooks, T039-936053, inter@wanadoo.net.ma One of the best addresses in the city, even if a bit lacking in charm. And only 15 mins' walk from the Blvd Pasteur. Spacious rooms with a/c.

Off Blvd Pasteur L *Hotel El Minzah*, 85 R de la Liberté (zankat el Houria), T039-935885, F934546. 100 rooms with bath, pricey but central, dates from the 1930s, beautiful gardens set around an Andalucían courtyard, convenient for exploring the médina, 2 restaurants, wine bar, coffee bar, tea room, mini-golf, tennis, pool. **B** ***Hotel Rembrandt***, Av Mohammed V, T039-937870/2. Conveniently located at centre of *ville nouvelle*, best town centre hotel after *El Minzah*, restaurant and popular bar. **B** ***Tanjah Flandria Hotel***, 6 Av Mohammed V, T039-931231, F934347. Centre of the new town, top of the slope on the Av Mohammed V, 5 mins downhill to town beach, all rooms a/c, bath, phone and radio, 170 rooms, comfortable, 2 restaurants, piano bar, art gallery, pool, garage. *Crédit du Maroc* ATM and bureau de change in same building. **B-C** ***Hotel Chellah***, 47-49 R Allal Ben Abdallah, T039-943389. Has a beach club feel despite being mid-way between the Bolibar and the beach, 180 rooms (standard and superior), 10 suites, good value, disco, tea room, parking with warden. Nice pool. **D-F** ***Pension Hollanda***, 139 R de Hollande (up the hill on Av de Belgique from Pl de France, turn right, is near the *Dawliz* multiplex), T039-937838. A badly converted villa with 2 categories of room: pleasant . . . and terrible, roof-terrace accommodation. A bit noisy, safe parking. Reservations essential in summer, used by Moroccans on the drive home. **D** ***Hotel de Paris***, 42 Blvd Pasteur, T039-931877. Clean, central hotel, which should be ideal, given its location. But street-facing rooms are horribly noisy in the small hours. A real pity. **D** ***Pension Villa Caruso***, 60 R du Prince Héritier, T039-936361. 15 rooms in converted house, shared showers on ground floor. **E** ***Pension Gibraltar***, 62, R de la Liberté, opposite *Hotel Minzah*. The building is a prime example of the lost splendours of Tanger, the rooms are terrible. OK for a night.

Beachside, east of city Over the oued east of the city, **L** ***Hotel Mövenpick Malabata***, T039-329300, F941909, is the city's best run and most expensive beach hotel. Also has one of Africa's biggest casinos, plus conference facilities. **A-B** ***Hotel Les Almohades***, 43 Av des FAR, T039-940755, F946317.138 rooms, near the beach, most with sea views, well appointed, restaurants, bar, nightclub, small pool overlooked by neighbouring blocks of flats. Of little interest. **B** ***Hotel Ahlen***, Km 5 Route de Rabat, T039-350001/2, F350003/5. Low line hotel, all on 2 floors, 2 bars plus poolside bar, 350 beds. All rooms have bath, heating, phone and private balcony; mini-suites have a/c, TV, minibar; suites have spacious living room. 3 restaurants and a snack/grill, Olympic pool plus children's pool, water polo, table tennis, tennis, horse riding, disco, 2 shops, free parking. Airport and port are 5 km, free shuttle bus to beach club. **B** ***Hotel Tarik***, Route de Malabata, T039-940363, F940944. On the beach, 154 rooms with bath and balcony, tennis, disco. Badly managed, mice. **B-C** ***Apart-Hotel Alia***, 13 bis Route de Malabata, T039-321782. Self-catering apartments of a good standard. **B** ***Hotel Sheherazade***, Av des FAR, T039-940500. Close to the sea, 146 rooms, pool, private beach, bar and terrace, tennis, fishing, horse riding, separate a/c and central heating, quite pleasant, disco. **B** ***Solazur***, 43 Av des FAR. A 10-storey concrete monster of a place on the seafront. 360 rooms with bath, telephone and radio, 2 restaurants, disco. Cavernous reception, mucky pool, returning migrant worker clientele. Rooms high up have good sea view. **B-C** ***El Oumnia***, seaward end of Av Beethoven, not far from *Hotel Les Almohades*, T039-940367, F940366. A fine example of a 1970s hotel, small pool, rooms period pieces with much ageing formica. A bit run down and due for a refit in 2003 (they say). "Water guaranteed even trough out drought" advises the leaflet.

Youth hostel 8 R El Antaki, T039-946127, at right angles to Av d'Espagne, 60 beds, overnight fee 30dh, advanced booking essential, bus 100 m. Good reports given on this hostel, near the *Hotel Djenina*, clean and well run.

★

Five good restaurants in Tanger

- Cheap and cheerful: *Agadir*, Avenue du Prince Héritier, just off the Bolibar, cheap, food and service pleasant.
- Tapas and live-music: *Rubis Grill*, off the Bolibar, up the side street behind the *Hotel Tanja Flandria*, T039-931443. Animated sort of place, can get quite loud.
- Family and relaxed: *Casa d'Italia*, in the Palais des institutions italiennes, T039-936348. Impeccable service, lots of room for kids to run around, safe parking.
- Un peu chic: *San Remo*, off the Bolibar, T039-938451. Resolutely Italian, said to be one of the best tables in Tanger.
- Local authenticity: *Hotel Minzah*, restaurant marocain. T039-935885. Probably the best formal Moroccan restaurant in the city. Expensive.

Camping

Camp sites are not much cheaper than a budget hotel and rather far from the city. Camper vans should be secure enough

Camping Miramonte, 3 km west from city centre, not far from Marshan district, very handy for Plage Merkala, T039-937138. Well-kept site up on a hillside with lots of shade, bar/snacks, small pool, showers, laundry, petrol at 400 m. Deutsche leitung. ***Camping-Caravaning Tingis***, 6 km east of town on Route de Malabata, T039-940191. A once well-equipped site of 6 ha which could be good. Beach 800 m, not recommended. ***Camping Achakar, Les Grottes d'Hercule***, at Cap Spartel, near the Caves of Hercules, 12 km west of town, T039-333840. Probably the best bet.

Eating

● *on maps, pages 176 and 180*

Price codes: see inside front cover

Even if there is a *McDonalds* in Tanger, its yellow-arched sign glowing balefully above the Dawliz multiplex, not all is lost. Though not all restaurants have that William Burroughs touch (an "extraordinary Arab restaurant that looked like a remodelled bus station"), there are plenty with ambiance, from cheap eateries with alcohol like the *Agadir* to the upscale *Minzah* and the *Marquis de l'Orient*.

Expensive

Le Marquis de l'Orient,18 R el Bouhtouri, T039-941132. Not widely known. Roccoco decor a little on the sinister side, impeccable service. ***Le Citoyen de Tanger***, the former *Nautilus*, 9 R Khalid ibn Oualid, T039-931159. Modern decor with lots of silverware, German owner, French chef. ***El Erz***, *Hotel El Minzah*, 85 R de la Liberté, T039-935885. Reservations recommended, popular restaurant with a wide range of European dishes, often with music. ***El Korsan***, *Hotel El Minzah*, 85 R de la Liberté, T039-935885. Reservations recommended, Moroccan food amid traditional decor and music; Argentinian oriental dancer. ***Le Mirage***, out at Cap Spartel, T039-333331. Site magnificent, international cuisine with a loyal following. The chef trained *Chez Toni*.

Mid-range: European

La Casa d'Italia, Palais des Institutions Italiennes (ex-Palais Moulay Hafid), T039-936348. Excellent Italian nosh, licensed, very pleasant outside eating in summer. Recommended. ***Las Conchas***, 30 R Ahmed Chaouki (ex-Murillo), T039-931643. French cuisine, good service, reservations necessary. ***Hotel Continental***, 36 Dar Baroud, T039-931024. Has a restaurant with middling food and service. ***Guitta's***, Pl du Koweït, second major junction as you come from the town (20-min walk up the R de Belgique from the *Café de France*, across the street from the Mohammed V Mosque), T039-937333. Once the city's chic garden restaurant, now described by one local as 'a glorious ruin'. So if you're feeling nostalgic... Could soon fall prey to property developers. ***London's Pub***, 15 R Mansour Dahabi, T039-942094. Smooth sort of place. International food. Fine for just a drink, too. Closed lunchtimes. ***Restaurant El Mabrouk***, R Ahmed Chaouki, off Pl de France. Very reasonably priced set menus with good Moroccan food. ***Restaurant le Detroit***, Av du Prince Moulay Abdallah. Spanish food, cheaper than nearby *Romero's*. ***Mesón de Pepe Ocaña***, on the street behind the *Hotel Rembrandt*. Easily missed. A good address for a drink and tapas. Recommended. ***Negresco***, 14 R du Mexique, close to the *Café de France*. Part of the Tanger tradition. Hearty bar, simple food on the restaurant side. ***San Rémo***, 15 R Ahmed Chaouki, T039-938451. Closed Mon. Though the Italian owner has died, fresh pasta is still on the menu. A good address, though on the expensive side. Go for the *poisson au sel*. ***Roméro***, 12 Av du Prince Moulay Abdallah, T039-932277. Paella, fish and seafood. ***Rubis Grill***, 3 R Ibn Rochd, T039-931443. Handy city centre place with tapas and the like.

Mid-range: Moroccan No really good choices here – best to splash out and go for the *Qorsan* (Arabic for pirate) in the *Hotel El Minzah* if you are not going to get to Marrakech. ***Dar Tajine***, 29 R du Commerce, T039-947709. Moroccan meals, some tour parties, middling quality. ***Restaurant Hammadi***, 2 R de la Kasbah, opposite junction with Paseo del Docteur Cenarro, next to the *Banque populaire* at the bottom of the Kasbah hill, T039-934514. Moroccan meals in the usual surroundings. Acceptable. ***Restaurant Mamounia Palace***, 6 R Semmarine, Petit Socco, T039-935099. Set menus of Moroccan food with 'authentic' decor and music. Nothing special. ***Restaurant Marhaba Palace***, R de la Kasbah, on your left before you turn right for the kasbah gate, T039-937643. Poor food, tour parties – but great decor. ***Raihani***, 10 R Ahmed Chaouki (ex-Murillo), T039-934866. Last choice for Moroccan palace restaurant type food. ***Saveurs de poisson***, just after the *Hotel El Minzah*, on your right at the top of a flight of steps as you go downhill. No menu. Splendid fish soup, seafood dishes, a famous herbal tea. Welcome variable, make sure you know what you're paying. Recommended.

Mid-range: on seafront ***Emma's BBC***, Av d'Espagne, famous and cheap beachside bar-restaurant, open summer only. ***L'Marsa***, right on the seafront, on your right as you leave the port gates. Nice café-restaurant terrace overlooking busy street. Good value. ***Miami Beach***, Av des FAR, T039-943401. Beachside bar-restaurant, 1000-1800; gayish bar and disco at night. ***Windmill***, Av des FAR, T039-940907. Oldest beachside restaurant patronized by writer Joe Orton – fish, Moroccan and Spanish food. ***Valencia***, Av Youssef ibn Tachfine, just behind the *Hotel Miramar*. Paella and seafood, a good address even if the food is a bit on the oily side.

Cheap ***Restaurant Africa***, 83 R de la Plage (R Salah Eddine El Ayoubi), T039-935436. ***Agadir***, a tiny fragment of the 1950s near the Blvd Pasteur at 21 R du Prince Héritier. The cheapest civilized licensed place, it does fish and some excellent Moroccan dishes. ***Dallas***, a clean, well-managed fish restaurant in R du Mexique. ***Restaurant Hassi Baida*** and ***Restaurant Cleopatre*** are in the same road and similar; the Grand Socco has several cheap open-air places to eat, if your stomach flora has adapted to Morocco; in the médina, there are a number of cheap, basic restaurants, such as ***Mauritania*** and ***Assalam*** in R de la Marine, and a similar selection on R du Commerce.

Cafés and pâtisseries

In the *ville nouvelle*, the ***Café de France***, 1 Pl de France, has a history as a meeting place for artists and intellectuals. Mixed clientele of local notables, tourists and *passeurs* looking out for potential emigrants to hustle across the Straits. Try also ***Salon de thé Vienne***, corner of R du Mexique and R Moutanabi. Large and showy. ***Porte***, R el Moutanabi (R Sanlucar). Reopened in 1999, a shadow of its former elegant self, the nostalgics say. Hercule Poirot would have taken tea here. In and around the old town, there are a number of places to sip mint tea. ***Café Central***, in the Petit Socco, also a former artistic rendezvous, now just a place to watch the crowd. As you leave the palace in the kasbah, stop at the ***Salon de Thé/Restaurant le Detroit***, T039-938080, which is pricey for food, but good for tea, coffee, pastries and a panoramic view of the Straits. Created by writer/musician Brion Gysin, now a stop for charabanc parties.

Bars and clubs

Tanger has bars and discos to suit all tastes, from smooth wine bar to late night dive, from Arabesque cabaret to souk à putes

Casa-Ribatis head up to Tanger for a good time as an alternative to overcrowded Marrakech. ***Coco Beach*** may be reopened by the time this goes to press. ***Patio Wine Bar***, *Hotel El Minzah*, 85 R de la Liberté, T039-935885. A wine bar in which to explore the wines of Morocco and overseas, a little pricey and rather uneven in service and quality. ***The Pub***, 4 R Sorolla, T039-934789. Food, beer and other drinks in a pub atmosphere. ***Caïd's Bar***, *Hotel El Minzah*, 85 R de la Liberté, T039-935885. Moroccan decoration and expensive drinks in an atmospheric bar. ***Tanger Inn***, 1 R Magellan, T039-935337. Small bar popular with those reliving the Beat experience. The first stage on a long Tangerine night out. ***Le Monocle***, R du Prince Héritier. Minute bar just off Blvd Pasteur. The last, drunken stage, the lower reaches of nocturnal Tanger. Potentially dangerous. ***Morocco Palace***, 11 Av du Prince Moulay Abdallah, T039-938614. An Oriental-disco mix with floorshow including performance by a singing dwarf. A Fellini film set. ***Number One***, 1 Av Mohammed V, T039-931817. Popular with gays, it is said. ***Olivia Valère***, *Hotel Ahlen*, out on the Rabat road, 5 km from Tanger. Local middle-class kids and friends up for the weekend. ***Pasarela***, Av des FAR, T039-945246. Club of the moment along with *Coco Beach*. Can you fit *Pasarela* and *Morocco Palace* into the same soirée? ***Régine***, on rond-point du Roxy. Serious local money goes dancing here. ***Scotts***, R Moutanabi (R Sanlucar). Formerly a gay address. Paintings of Rif boys in Highland gear by local decorator Stuart Church. ***Hotel Shéhérezade, Les Grottes***, Av des FAR. Popular club in seafront hotel. ***Solazur***, nightclub in the hotel of the same name on Av des FAR. Slightly gay, cheap and cheerful.

Entertainment

Art galleries *Galerie Delacroix*, R de la Liberté. ***Tanjah Flandria Art Gallery***, R Ibn Rochd, behind the *Hotel Flandria*, T039-933000. **Cinemas** *Ciné Alcazar*, junction of R de l'Italie and R Ibn Al Abbar (Paseo del Doctor Cenarro). May reopen as gallery space. ***Cinema Rif***, Grand Socco, specializes in Hindi and karate films for médina lads and countryfolk in town for the market. Preferably look around Blvd Pasteur, try the ***Cinema Goya***, near Blvd Pasteur. **Cultural and language centres** **Institut français**, R de la Liberté, easily identified by the Galerie Delacroix sign. Good temporary exhibitions.

Festivals

The annual ***Jazz festival***, www.tanjazz.com, seems set to have a slot in **late May/early June**. There are street parades and free concerts on the Grand Socco, paying concerts in the Mendoubia gardens.

Shopping

Food

There is a food market between R d'Angleterre and R Sidi Bou Abid. The stalls along R d'Angleterre are not very impressive. There are numerous fruit sellers along R de la Plage and its side streets. Just off, on R El Oualili, is another food market.

Handicrafts & antiques

Tanger is not the best place to buy handicrafts, for although shops have a large selection, production tends to be in Marrakech

The pressure to buy in Tanger can be intense, with bazaarists and hawkers used to gullible day trippers from Spain. The cheapest shops and stalls, with the most flexible prices, will be found in the médina. Shops in the *ville nouvelle* may claim fixed prices but in most cases this is just another ploy. ***Coopartim, Ensemble Artisanal***, R de Belgique, T039-931589, is a good place to start, a government controlled fixed-price craft centre with a number of workshops. There is a particularly good bookbinder with a small stock of antiquarian books, and an enthusiastic octogenarian slipper seller, with albums of addresses and letters from his clients all over the world. In the médina, try

Marrakech la Rouge, 50 R es Siaghin. For crafts and antiques see ***Galerie Tindouf***, 64 R de la Liberté, T039-931525. For kitting out your villa on the Montagne with Indian antiques, try ***Adolfo de Velasco***, down on Av Mohammed V on the opposite side to the Post Office. Also has a branch in the *Hotel Mamounia* in Marrakech.

Newspapers & books Foreign newspapers can be bought from shops in R de la Liberté or outside the post office in Av Mohammed V. For books in French, Spanish and a few in other languages, go to ***Librairie des Colonnes***, 54 Blvd Pasteur, T039-936955.

Sport and activities

Flying *Royal Flying Club*, Boukhalef Airport, T039-934371. **Golf** *Royal Club de Golf*, Boubana, T039-944484, F945450. 18 holes, 5,545 m, par 70, 200dh per round. **Riding** *Country L'Etrier*, Boubana. **Tennis** *M'Sallah Garden Tennis Courts*, R de Belgique, T039-935203 and ***Municipale***, Av de la Paix, T039-943324.

Tour operators

Holiday Service, 84 Av Mohammed V, T039-933362. ***Wagons-Lit Tourisme***, R de la Liberté. *Limadet Ferry*, Av du Prince Moulay Abdallah, T039-932649. *Comanav Ferries*, 43 R Abou Alaâ el Maâri, T039-932649. ***Transtour Ferries***, 4 R el Jabha al Outania, T039-934004.

Transport

Local **Road** **Bus**: Av Jami' al Duwal al Arabia, T039-946682. Tanger is fairly small and thus it is unlikely that you will want to use local buses. If you do they can be picked up in the Grand Socco or in Av des FAR outside the port gates. Boughaz minibuses, from just outside the port gate, may be useful to get to the private bus station, or on excursions from Tanger westwards. **Bicycle and motorcycle hire**: *Mesbahi*, 7 R Ibn Tachfine, just off Av des FAR, T039-940974. Renting bicycles, 50cc and 125cc motorbikes, deposit required for 3 days or more. **Car hire**: *Avis*, 54 Blvd Pasteur, T039-938960, and at the airport. ***Budget***, 7 Av du Prince Moulay Abdallah, T039-937994, and at the airport. ***Europcar***, 87 Av Mohammed V, T039-938271. ***Hertz***, 36 Av Mohammed V, T039-933322, and at the airport. *Leasing Cars*, 24 R Henri Regnault, and at the airport, a little cheaper. **Grands taxis**: can be picked up from the Grand Socco or in front of Tanger Ville railway station, to destinations within or outside of the city. You will need to set a fare with the driver. **Petit taxis**: turquoise with yellow stripe, may be cheaper, although that will depend on your skill as the meters are not always operated. For a taxi T039-935517.

Long distance **Air** Tanger's Boukhalef airport is 15 km from the city along the P2, T039-935129, 934717. Catch bus 17 or 70 from Grand Socco or a grand taxi. Arrive 1-2 hrs early. There are direct flights to **Agadir**, **Al Hoceima** and **Casablanca** and direct international flights to European cities including **Amsterdam**, **Barcelona**, **Brussels**, **Frankfurt**, **London**, **Madrid** and **Paris**. **Airline offices**: *Air France*, 20 Blvd Pasteur. *British Airways*, 83 R de la Liberté, T039-935877. ***Iberia***, 35 Blvd Pasteur, T039-936177. *Royal Air Maroc*, Pl de France, T039-935501/2.

Road **Bus**: information, T039-932415. *CTM* buses depart from the ticket office near the entrance to the port in Av des FAR. Departure times (subject to change) include: **Kenitra, Rabat and Casablanca**: 1100, 2230, 2330, 2400. **Souk El Arba du Gharb, Ksar el Kebir, Larache, Asilah**: 1100, 1630, 1800, 2230, 2330, 2400. **Sidi Kacem, Meknès, Fès**: 1800. **Agadir, Tiznit**: 1630. **Paris**: 0500. Private buses, running from the terminal at the end of R de Fès, go to most destinations and are generally cheaper. **Tetouan**: every 15 mins (1 hr).

Asilah: 0915, 0945, 1100 (30 mins). **Larache**: every hour (1½ hrs). **Meknès**: 0700, 1000, 1300, 1600 (5 hrs). **Fès**: 1000, 1600 (6 hrs). **Chaouen**: 0545, 0800, 1045, 1300, 1330, 1815 (2½ hrs). **Ceuta**: 0730, 0945, 1245 (2 hrs). **Ouezzane**: 0900, 1400 (4 hrs). To get to the terminal take a petit taxi or a Boughaz minibus. **Taxi**: to many destinations take a shared grand taxi from the bus terminal at the end of R de Fès. To **Tetouan** and **Ceuta** this is a quick, practical and not too expensive option. For excursions from Tanger to the Caves of Hercules or Cap Malabata negotiate for a grand taxi in R de Hollande.

Sea Ferry tickets to **Algeciras** can be bought at the ***Limadet Agents*** in Av du Prince Moulay Abdallah, just off Blvd Pasteur, T039-932649, at travel agents in Blvd Pasteur, or at the ferry terminal. ***Trasmediterranea*** and ***Limadet*** jointly operate this car and passenger service 3 or 4 times a day in the summer and 2 in the winter. Passengers from 196dh, cars from 8,500dh. Check in at least 1 hr early, to allow time to collect an embarkation card, complete a departure card, and have your passport stamped. For tickets for the *Bland's Line* ferry to **Gibraltar** go to ***Med Travel***, 22 Av Mohammed V, T039-935872, or to the port. Departures Mon 0930, Wed, Thu and Fri 1430, Mon and Fri 1830 and Sun 1630. Single 250dh, return 360dh, day trip 400dh, motorcycles and bicycles 200dh, vehicles up to 6 m 600dh. Journey takes 1 hr on hydrofoil and 2-2½ hrs on traditional ferry. Holding a return ticket for a specific sailing is no guarantee you will be allowed on the boat – *Bland's* excursion customers come first. Tickets to **Sete** can be bought from ***Voyages Comanav***, 43 R Abou el Alaâ el Maâri, T039-932649, F932320. There is a ferry every 3-4 days. Passenger tickets from 2,720dh. Car and 2 passengers from 3,740dh.

At the port avoid all touts selling embarkation cards which are free from the officials

Train There are no longer any city rail stations in Tanger. The former port station on Av des FAR is firmly closed. Trains now arrive/depart from the suburban Moughougha station, a 15dh taxi ride out in the new suburbs. Departure times change, in general there are 3- 4 a day, including a 2230 overnight train with couchettes for **Marrakech**. Departures include **Rabat**, **Casablanca** and **Marrakech**. **Meknès**, **Fès** and **Oujda** can be reached by making a connection at Sidi Kacem. All trains stop at **Asilah**.

Train times can be checked on T039-952555

Directory

Banks

All the usual banks with ATMs are on Blvd Pasteur/Av Mohammed V. The ***Crédit du Maroc***, on the ground floor of the *Tanja Flandria Hotel*, has a bureau de change, as does the ***BMCI***, down the street opposite the Terrasse des paresseux, next to the *Café de France*. The ***Wafa Bank*** (ATM) is further down the slope, on your left just before the *PTT*. Banks are open 0830-1130 and 1430-1630. **American Express**: c/o ***Voyages Schwartz***, 54 Blvd Pasteur, T039-933459, open Mon-Fri 0900-1230, 1500-1900, Sat 0900-1230.

Communications

Internet: *Cybercafé Momnet*, 53 Av Moulay Abdallah, T039-324248. **Post**: *PTT*, 33 Av Mohammed V, T039-935657, Mon-Fri 0830-1200, 1430-1800, Sat 0830-1200. **Telephone**: International phone (24 hrs) far right of post office. Also telephone from the *PTT* at the junction of R El Msala and R de Belgique. There are also the usual téléboutiques, and *Cybercafé Momnet* above.

Embassies & consulates

Belgium, 124 Av Mohammed Ben Abdallah, T039-931218. **Denmark**, 3 R Ibn Rochd, T039-938183. **France**, Pl de France, T039-932039. **Germany**, 47 Av Hassan II, T039-938700. **Italy**, 35 R Assad Ibn Fourat, T039-931064. **Netherlands**, 47 Av Hassan II, T039-931245. **Norway**, 3 R Henri Regnault, T039-931245. **Portugal**, 9 Pl des Nations, T039-931708. **Spain**, R Sidi Bou Abid, T039-937000, 935625. **Sweden**, 31 Av Prince Héritier, T039-938730. **Switzerland**, R Henri Regnault, T039-934721. **UK**, 9 R d'Amerique du Sud, T039-935895. **USA**, 29 R El Achouak, T039-935904.

Library *Tanger Book Club*, Old American Legation, 8 R d'Amerique, the médina, T039-935317. Open Tue-Sat 0900-1200.

Medical services **Ambulance**: T15. **Chemists**: *Pharmacie de Fès*, 22 R de Fès, T039-932619. 24 hrs a day. *Pharmacie Pasteur*, Pl de France, T039-932422. **Dentist**: Dr Ibrahim Filali, 53 Av du Prince Moulay Abdallah, T039-931268. Speaks English. **Doctor**: Dr Joseph Hirt, 8 R Sorolla, T039-935729, speaks English, and will pay calls to hotels. 24-hr medical visits, T039-333300, 331111, 339797. **Hospital**: Emergencies: T039-930856, also try T039-934242. *Hospital civil Mohammed V*, Val fleuri, Ancienne Route de Rabat, T039-938056. *Hôpital Español*, T039-931018. **Private clinics**: *Clinique Sidi Amar*, 52 R Sidi Amar, Souk Bakr, Tanger, T039-331400, F330459. *Clinique Tingis*, R Aboubakr Arrazi, T946992.

Useful addresses **Fire**: T15. **Garage**: Tanjah Auto, 2 Av de Rabat. **Police**: (general) R Ibn Toumert, T19; (traffic) T177.

South of Tanger

Asilah

Phone code: 039
Colour map 1, grid A2
40 km S of Tanger

Also referred to as Arzila

Asilah, south of Tanger, is a striking fishing port and coastal town of white and blue houses, surrounded by ramparts and lying alongside an extensive beach. It is the northernmost of the former Portuguese outposts (the others include Azemmour, El Jadida and Safi). Today a small place with a Mediterranean feel, Asilah might provide a pleasant introduction to Morocco, in spite of the extent to which tourism dominates. You could try turning up in August to coincide with the annual influx of toney people for the *International Festival of Asilah*, which should include some jazz and Moroccan music, and exhibitions by contemporary Moroccan artists.

Ins & outs
See Transport, page 194, for further details

Asilah lies off the main P2 Tanger to Rabat road. It is accessible both by road (buses and grands taxis take 60 mins from Tanger) and by rail (50 mins from Tanger). The rail station is some 2 km north of the town, and there aren't very many taxis in Asilah. Buses and taxis stop at the Pl Mohammed V, close to the old town. There are buses from Larache, too, taking about 1 hr.

Background Modern Asilah stands on the site of the Phoenician town of *Silis*, or perhaps *Zilis*. The area was subsequently settled by Romans in Anthony's reign and the Byzantines. In 966, the town was rebuilt by El Hakim II, ruler of Cordoba. It was the last stronghold of the Idrissid dynasty. The Portuguese occupied Asilah from 1471, and built the town's fortifications, and in 1578 King Sebastian landed there on his way to defeat at what was to become known as the Battle of the Three Kings. This defeat led to the Spanish absorption of Portugal, and thus of Asilah, but the Portuguese influence on the town is still quite discernible.

The Moroccans recovered Asilah in 1691, under Moulay Ismaïl. In 1826 Austria bombarded Asilah, then a base of piracy, as did the Spanish in 1860. In the late 19th and early 20th century Ahmed al-Rasouli, the bandit chief who terrorized much of northwestern Morocco, was based in the town, as described by his one-time hostage and later friend, Walter Harris, in *Morocco That Was*. Al-Rasouli built his palace in the médina, and from it exercised power over much of the region, being for a time its governor. The Spanish took Asilah in 1911, as part of their Protectorate of northern Morocco.

In more recent years, Asilah has become home to an international summer arts festival founded by local politico Mohammed Ben Aïssa who eventually rose to become Morocco's foreign minister in the late 1990s. Today, the old neighbourhoods are almost too squeaky clean. The local people have been largely bought out – not always very fairly, it is rumoured. Weekend retreats for wealthy Casablancans have replaced family homes. Though the result is pretty and whitewashed, the authenticity, to use a much overworked term, has largely gone. For a macho version of Asilah, try Larache further down the coast. Still, Asilah has some pretty good fish restaurants.

Sights

The **médina** is the main interest of Asilah, a quarter of predominately white and blue buildings, reflecting in their design the influence of the Iberian powers. Note the modern murals on some of the houses in the médina, painted by artists during the festival. The ramparts were built by the Portuguese in the 15th century, and are set with a number of important gates, including **Bab el Kasbah**, **Bab el Bahar** ('the sea gate'), **Bab el Homar**, a structure topped with the eroded Portuguese coat of arms, as well as **Bab el Jbel** ('the mountain gate') and **Bab Ihoumer**. At points it is possible to climb the fortifications for views of the town and along the coast. Within the médina, **Le Palais de la Culture** is a cultural centre converted from the former residence of the brigand Ahmed al-Rasouli, built in 1909 right beside the sea. It is difficult to gain access except during the festival, but it is possible to visualize those who incurred al-Rasouli's wrath being made to walk the plank from the palace windows over the cliff front.

The **souk** has a Thursday market attracting farmers from the surrounding area. In addition to the sale of the usual fruit, spices and vegetables, handicrafts distinctive of the Rif region are also on display.

The **International Festival of Asilah** is a cultural festival which has taken place in Asilah since 1978 and involves performers from all over the world. Events throughout the town each August attract many spectators. The festival has its ups and downs, some years good, others not so.

The **beach** is often windy, frequented by bathers, men touting camel rides, and fishermen, but at times can be quite perfect. The beach stretches beyond the building works to the north of the town, and to the south.

Sleeping

For private houes to rent, try the Spanish site www.elbaraka.net

C *Hotel Al Khaima*, Km 2 Route de Tanger, outside town towards Tanger, BP 101, T039-917317, F917566. 113 rooms with bath, some with telephones, restaurant, disco, bar, pool, tennis. Best out of season, too noisy in summer. **C** *Hotel Zelis*, 10 Av Mansour Eddahabi, T039-417069, F417098. A good, clean recent hotel, just behind the *Hotel Oued el Makhazin*. Prices higher in summer. Small pool, Moroccan restaurant.

D *Hotel Oued El Makhazine*, Av Melilla, T039-417090, F417500. 36 rooms with showers, breakfast extra, 100 m outside médina, opposite a bit of open ground, OK restaurant, bar and café, tiny pool and telephone, safe parking. **D** *Hotel Mansur*, 49 Av Mohammed V, T039-917390. 8 rooms with bath, reliable. **D** *Hotel Patio de la Luna*, 12 Pl Zelaka, T039-416074, F416540. Charming new small hotel, Spanish owned, highly recommended. Go for the terrace rooms. Reservations essential in summer. **D** *Hotel Sahara*, 9 R Tarfaya, T039-917185. 24 rooms, clean, hot shower, avoid rooms with tiny windows.

E *Hotel Asilah*, 79 Av Hassan II, T039-917286. 11 rooms, entrance round the side, 1st-floor rooms have showers, 2nd floor give onto terrace with view. Closed out of season. **E** *Hotel l'Oasis*, 8 Pl des Nations Unies, T039-917186. 12 rooms, an old palace with restaurant and bar. **F** *Hotel Marhaba*, 9 R Zelaka, T039-917144, near the médina. Adequate and cheap, rooms poorly soundproofed but with colourful decor, nice roof terrace. Room with bath extra. Terrace with views over the médina.

Camping There are numerous camping sites just north of the town along the road to Asilah. ***Camping As Sada***, on the Tanger road, some 300 m out of town, T039-917317. Overlooks the ocean, also has some chalet-type accommodation. Wash-block inadequate. ***Camping Echrigui***, 500 m from the town and 1 km from station, T039-917182. Has chalet-type accommodation too (no water). Wash-blocks inadequately maintained. Not quite as good as *Camping As Sada*. ***Camping International***, site of 1 ha, 50 m to beach, showers, laundry, petrol 300 m, electricity for caravans. ***Camping Atlas***, 100 m to beach, snacks, showers, laundry, grocery, first aid, electricity for caravans.

Eating In some of the more expensive restaurants, you will be shown a great dish of fresh fish to choose from. Your chosen fish is then weighed, and you are charged by the 100 g. If this is the case, make sure you know how much you will be charged. In the cheaper restaurants, go for grilled rather than fried fish, as the oil is sometimes used far more than it should be. **Mid-range** *La Alcazaba*, 2 Pl Zellaca outside the ramparts, T039-917012. Has a good reputation for fish. ***Casa Garcia***, on the seafront, is also recommended for similar food, as is the ***El Espignon***, a few mins walk further up the front. **Cheap** *El Oceano*, aka *Chez Pepe*, on Pl Zelaka, just outside the médina walls, T039-917395. Has declined slightly, make sure you know how much your fish will cost. For cheaper eating, try the small restaurants like the ***Rabie*** and the ***Miramar*** near the old ramparts, alongside the main square.

Transport **Road** **Bus**: the station is on Av de la Liberté, T039-987354. There are regular bus links with **Tanger**, **Ouezzane**, **Tetouan**, **Meknès**, **Rabat** and **Casablanca**. **Taxi**: grands taxis, particularly convenient for Tanger, leave from Pl Mohammed V. **Train** Asilah railway station, T039-987320, is just outside the town alongside the P2 to Tanger and can be reached by local bus or by either petit or grand taxi from Pl Mohammed V. There are 6 trains daily to **Tanger**, 4 daily to **Meknès**, **Fès** and **Oujda** and 2 daily to **Rabat** and **Casablanca**.

Directory **Banks** *Banque populaire*, Pl Mohammed V. For the moment, there is no ATM in town. **Communications** *PTT*, Pl des Nations Unies. **Medical services** Chemist: *Pharmacie Loukili*, Av de la Liberté, T039-917278. **Hospital**: Av du 2 Mars, T039-917318. **Useful addresses** Police: Av de la Liberté, T19 or T039-917089.

El Utad, the stone circle at Mzoura

Colour map 1, grid A2

For prehistory buffs, the stone circle at Mzoura makes a good excursion from Rabat or Tanger for those with plenty of time in northwest Morocco and a car. Though there are numerous prehistoric rock art sites in the High Atlas and Djebel Beni, the **barrow at Mzoura** is the only one of its kind in the country – and actually quite accessible. This is not a highly spectacular outing, but if twinned, say, with visits to Thamusida and Banasa, it makes a good day out from Rabat, or linked with visits to Asilah and Lixus, a good long day from Tanger. The best time to visit Mzoura is in late summer when the vegetation has died back. After a rainy winter, the countryside will be at its best.

Ins & outs

When driving on sandy tracks, it helps to wiggle your steering wheel a little when the sand is thick

Getting there On the GP2 north of Larache – a winding, busy road likely to get less crowded when the final Larache to Tanger section of the north-south autoroute is opened – there is a major roundabout near **Sidi Tnine el Yamani** where you should branch off for Tetouan (P37). Just under 4 km from the roundabout, turn left at the *Somepi* garage and head up the recently widened road for Sidi Yamani. After about 3 km, in the village, you reach a Y-junction, where you need to take the left-hand fork. (A seedy character will come running out from a café at the approach of any hire car. No need to stop – if you do, he will present himself as the official guide to the site.) About

6½ km after the village, after passing a large abandoned Spanish building on your left, amongst other things, you should turn off right onto a sandy track – one of numerous sandy tracks running across the rolling landscape of open fields, stands of eucalyptus and occasional corrugated-iron roofed homesteads. The one you want comes after a minor cutting, with the road running slightly downhill. (If in doubt, ask a local for *el utad*, the funerary monument.) Once you turn off, the track doubles back sharply, the good but sandy track taking you the 2½ km to the hamlet where the circle is located. When you get to the hamlet, keep left; the track to the circle runs between the bramble hedges of the farmsteads, eventually veering round to the left.

The first trace of prehistoric occupation you meet are three great stones (*menhirs* in French), lying on the ground. Look out for the scooped-out 'bowls' in one of the stones, referred to as 'cup and circle' by English archaeologists and testimony to some obscure cult after the stones had fallen. Further on, to your right, the stones of the circle once ringed a high barrow, heavily excavated by the Spanish. Most stones are only 1.5 m high, and within them lies a sort of stone walkway – possibly the original base of the barrow. The most spectacular feature is a stone standing 4.5 m high. You can also locate a sort of lintel in the circle, once the entrance to the barrow. Burial sites like this were in use over very long periods of time and the site was no doubt operational in several different ways. Curiously, perhaps, it is in heathland like this that similar barrows in southern England and Brittany are located.

As there is no information available at the site, you can let your imagination work overtime. This excursion is a good one for birdwatchers, giving them a focus point in a landscape unspoiled by industrial agriculture. It also gives you a glimpse into the living conditions in the countryside. Though there is new building, for most families, life in the countryside is extremely rudimentary in material terms.

Larache العرائش

Phone code: 039
Colour map 1, grid A2

Bigger than Asilah, and rather less bijou, Larache is a relaxed, faded seaside town, with a good beach and not too many tourists, a halfway house between Spanish and Moroccan urban life. It is a sleepy sort of place, with views over the ocean and the Loukkos Estuary, plus the evocatively named Château de la Cigogne, the Fortress of the Stork – a minor bit of 16th-century building. It was at Larache that Jean Genet was to find a haven, writing his last novel here.

Background

Larache (El-Arayis in Arabic) is named for the vine arbours of the Beni Arous, a local tribe. The area has one of the longest histories of human occupation in Morocco, going back to Phoenician, Carthaginian and Roman times at the settlement of nearby Lixus. Larache was occupied by the Spanish during 1610-89 and as part of their Protectorate, from 1911. At that time, the harbour was added and the new town was developed. Larache became the principal port of the Spanish northern zone. Today, the town draws its livelihood from the agro-food industry and fishing, although it has lost its status as a major port. Revenues from migrant workers and the building industry are important, too. Tourism may become the major activity as a large resort complex is planned on the Atlantic beach north of the river.

Sights

Larache is a small place, easily visited in a day. However, Roman history enthusiasts might want to stay the night, giving themeselves plenty of time to see the somewhat unspectacular **ruins of ancient Lixus**, at its best in the late afternoon light.

On the very edge of the old town of Larache is a large piece of Renaissance military engineering, with the usual pointy bastions, dating from the 16th century. The isolated structure, now housing the local museum of antiquities, is the **Château de la Cigogne** (also called Castillo de las Cigueñas or Al Fath). The museum contains a small amount of material from Lixus. ■ *Wed-Sun 0900-1200, 1500-1730. T039-912091.*

The Avenue Mohammed V is the main street of the new town. At the eastern end, heading for the central plaza, there are the fortifications and then the post office on the right and the **Iglesia de Nuestra Señora del Pilar** on the left. The circular Place de la Libération, with a fountain, is the heart of the town; the entrance to the médina, an arched gate, **Bab el Khemis** is on the north side.

Exploring further, on the clifftop overlooking ocean and estuary, the 16th-century **Kebibat Fortress** was used by the Spanish as a hospital. Shamefully, it has been left to fall into ruin. The **Spanish Consulate** occupies a fine art deco building, and you will also easily locate the Neo-Moorish style **Central Market**, recognizable by its towers.

The médina is a poor quarter of steep and narrow streets and high walls. Just inside is the Spanish-built market square. There are a number of souks in the médina, notably **Socco de la Alcaiceria**, the cloth market, moderately

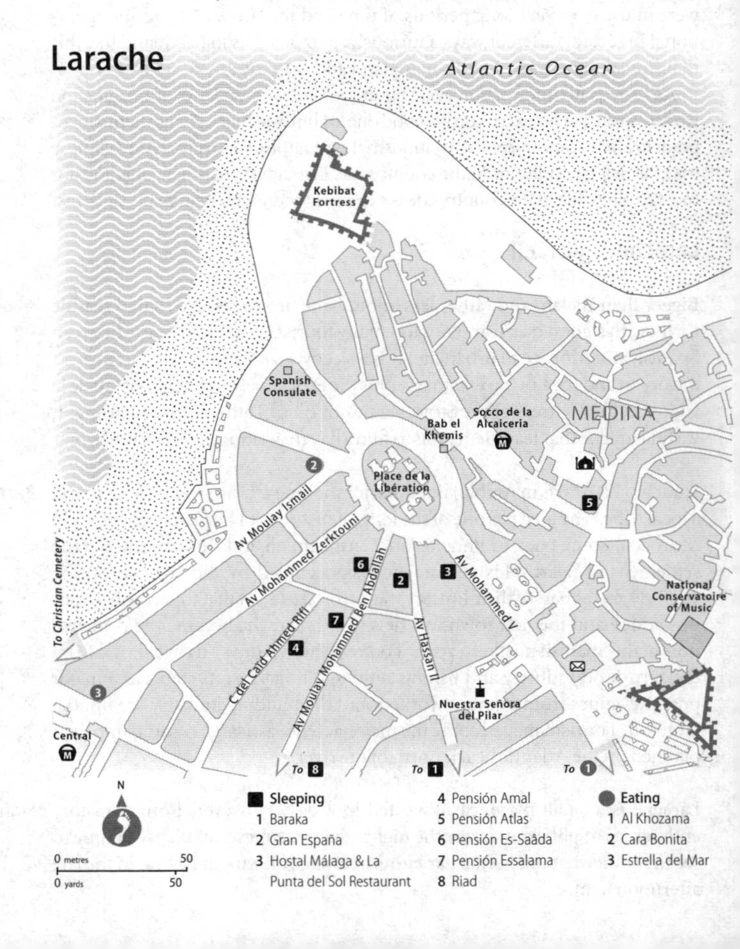

picturesque. In fact, the médina is best viewed from below or the north side of the estuary. You can wind your way back to the east side of town to visit the archaeological museum. The repainted Neo-Moorish building is the **National Conservatoire of Music**, built by the Spanish in 1915, near to Château de la Cigogne (see above).

The main beach is an extensive strip of fine (though littered, in season) beach, with a number of cafés nearby. ■ *Getting there: See Ancient Lixus below.*

For the literary minded, one final port of call in Larache is the **tomb of writer Jean Genet** (1910-86) out in the old Christian cemetery near the lighthouse and prison. The cemetery has been cleaned up, part of the works currently being financed by the regional government of Andalusía. The cemetery has a caretaker, and should you wish to pay tribute to the author of *Querelle de Brest* and *Les Bonnes*, there is a thick visitors' book for you to sign. With the views over the ocean, Genet could hardly have chosen a better final resting place. Larache could be the place to have a read of Genet's poems (*Le condamné à mort*, Gallimard, pocket edition,1999).

Excursion to Ancient Lixus

See plan, page 198

The second most important Roman site in Morocco after Volubilis, located on a spectaular site on right bank of the Oued Loukkos about 4 km from the sea, Ancient Lixus is a must visit on a second trip to Morocco. Tchemich Hill, on which the town is located 50 m above sea level, was obviously an excellent location for defensive reasons and the views from here are beautiful, especially in the early evening, when the sun is going down over the meanders of the estuary. For some ancient writers Lixus was the location of the Garden of Hesperides, where Hercules harvested golden apples to gain his place on Mount Olympus. (Today's city shield shows an orange tree.) The first traces of settlement date from the 7th-6th century BC and in pre-Roman inscriptions the future Lixus is referred to as Semes. The oldest evidence of building goes back to the fourth century BC. There was a seventh-century Phoenician and later a Carthaginian settlement here. Rome annexed the town in 40 BC. Coins with Latin and Neo-Punic inscriptions suggest the inhabitants had a dual culture, as was the case in so much of Roman North Africa. The town became a colony under the Emperor Claudius I, when salt, olives and fish were the main exports. Eventually reaching an area of 62 ha, Lixus prospered until the late third century AD, in part because of its strategic position on the road from Tingis (Tanger) to Sala Colonia (Rabat). It remained active and was occupied until the fifth century AD and in Arabic historiography, re-emerges as Tohemmis. This remained a Muslim settlement until Larache was founded in the 14th century. Recent archaeological finds in the region will shed further light on the town's history. ■ *The site is just over the Oued Loukkos, on a hillside to the west of the GP2. For those without own car, you may have to walk or take a petit taxi (say 40dh). Best option is to get the bus No 2 (3dh) which runs from the port to the beach, Plage Rimmel. The site is open during daylight hours (it says), but there is no ticket booth. The east side of the site next to the GP2 is fenced in by green railings. Best parking is probably under the eucalyptus trees after the turn off for the beach. Note that there is often a Gendarmerie royale presence at the junction. A small site map on a metal plaque can be found next to the locked entrance gate.*

The easiest way up into the site is via the track near the gate, generally closed, at the north end of the garum (fish salting) basins behind the railings on the GP2 (just nip around the railings). Head uphill to find the **amphitheatre**, excavated in 1964 and probably the best ruin on account of its quality stonework. Spectators would have been able to enjoy a play and superb views of the flood plain beyond at the same time. And just beyond the theatre is a small bath complex. There are some **mosaics** still in situ in the hall area, although the central mosaic of Neptune has been removed. In the circular caldarium are traces of painted plaster. Clear evidence of demolition/rebuild can be seen from the column drums inserted into a wall.

After the amphitheatre, either follow the track uphill to discover the remains of **apsed temple** (crumbling half-tower) or cut across left (west) and scramble up to visit the **acropolis** area. Look out for the impressive vaulted cisterns. It is possible to make out an oratory (?), a small open space with a stubby column in the middle and twin semicircular niches. The layout of the colonnaded forum can also be seen. Dominating the highest point of the site is a rectangular, vaulted chamber some 4 m high, probably a cistern for feeding the nearby bath complex. Water supply must have been quite an issue at Lixus. Was there an aqueduct or were all cisterns fed by rainwater running off the roof terraces? Heathland butterflies and the occasional raptor are added bonuses to visiting Lixus – the salt flats should provide some good sightings, too. And on no account wear shorts here in summer. The scrubby vegetation is very prickly indeed.

Remember that the Atlantic undertow is very powerful

Beyond Lixus the road leads onto the beach, where there is a car park and camping areas. In summer, there are lifeguards and organized beach activities for the local children. All may change here if the plans for a new *zone touristique* at Khémis Sahel to the north go through.

Sleeping

■ on map, page 196

Reserve in summer when the town is busy. For the budget traveller, there are many basic hotels

In the cheap category, the *Hotel Avenida* and the *Hostal Málaga*, in a side street just off Pl de la Libération, are good value. **C *Hotel Riad***, R (or calle or zankat) Moulay Mohammed Ben Abdallah, signed from Av Mohamed V, T039-912626, F912629. Converted former residence of the Duchess of Guise, 24 rooms, gardens, restaurant but no bar, small pool, half-board sometimes required. Recently refurbished, the place has some vaguely stylish wrought-iron furniture. In summer, a good night's sleep is impossible because of karaoké in the garden. Other downside: slightly smelly corridors. A good bet out of season? **D *Hotel Essalam***, 9 Av Hassan II, T039-916822. Clean and bright, nice reception, all new, big roof

Lixus

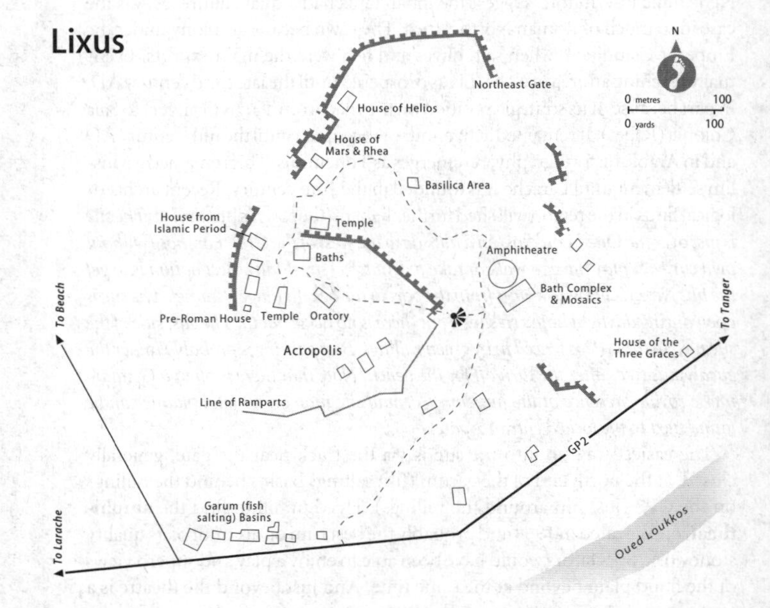

terrace. Perhaps the best cheap option. **D** *Gran Hotel España*, 2 Av Hassan II/Pl de la Libération, T039-913195, F915628. Once a grand place in an outpost of Spanish provincial life. 45 rooms, TV, super clean, communicating parents/kids rooms, view over *Café central*. Neon lighting. Some street-facing rooms noisy. **E** *Hotel Avenida*, R de Salé, T039-501920. Fairly spacious rooms. **E** *Hostal Málaga*, R de Salé, T039-911868. 25 rooms. Small rooms without bath, no view, bigger rooms balcony and bathroom. Recently refurbished. Nice reception. **F** *Hotel Cervantes*, 3 R Tarik ibn Ziad, close to Pl de la Libération, T039-910874, ali621@caramail.com Sea view, bright, spacious rooms, bathrooms none too clean, nice reception. Has some character. There are a number of other *pensiones*, most just off Av Moulay Mohammed Ben Abdallah. **F** *Pensión Es-Saada*, T039-913641. Very mucky, run down, avoid. **F** *Pensión Amal*, T039-912788; 10 R Abdallah Ben Yassine. The closest to bus and grand taxi stations. 14 rooms, clean, quiet, nice reception. Better than the other cheapies. **F** *Pensión Essalama*, T039-910192. 20 rooms, not too clean. Old and kind of ugly. **F** *Pensión Palmera*, no phone, on same street as *Hotel Riad*. 15 rooms. Quiet, a bit damp, needs a paint. **F** *Pensión Atlas*, T039-912014, in the médina close to R du Petit Souk. The best of the médina pensiones – the others are fairly terrible. **F** *Hotel Baraka*, 70 Av Hassan II, T039-913127. 24 rooms, clean, quiet, new building with a little lounge area on each floor.

Eating

■ *on map, page 196*

For a meal with alcohol, try the Estrella del Mar or the Casa de España

Expensive *Restaurant Al Khozama*, 114 Av Mohammed V, T039-914454. No alcohol, nice service, credit cards. ***Restaurant Estrella del Mar***, 68 C Mohammed Zerktouni, on the street opposite Bab al Khamis, T039-912243. Town's best address. Views of ocean, fish, paella, tea room on 2nd floor. **Mid-range** *Cara Bonita*, 1 Pl de la Libération. Serves seafood, nice service. **Cheap** *La Punta del Sol*, R de Salé, next to the *Pensión Málaga*, open midday to late. ***Restaurant Eskala***, just inside the médina as you enter from Pl de la Libération. ***Restaurant Larache***, R Hassan II, for its seafood.

Transport

The town is easily reached by the P2 from Tanger or Rabat. The bus station is just off Av Hassan II. There are **buses** from **Asilah** (1 hr), **Ksar el Kebir**, **Rabat** (3½ hrs) and **Meknès** (5½ hrs). There are **grands taxis** from **Rabat** and **Souk El Arba**.

Directory

Banks All major banks, some with ATMs, can be found on Av Mohamed V or Pl de la Libération. **Communications** Internet: try *Cyber Marnet* on R Motamid Ibn Abbad, opposite the entrance to the *Hotel Riad*, signed, T039-916884.

Ceuta سبتة.

Phone code: 0034956
Colour map 1, grid A3

Ceuta is an odd sort of place, an enclave of provincial Spain, an African equivalent of Great Britain's Gibraltar. However, unlike Gibraltar, Ceuta has not established itself as a minor tourist attraction. Ceuta gives the impression that it would like to be a Mediterranean Hong Kong: it has the right sort of location, between two continents, developed Europe and upcoming Africa. But the Gibraltar-Spain frontier was opened in 1985, and in many ways Ceuta has been sidelined into becoming a sort of passenger transit port. In 1995, Ceuta, like Melilla, became an 'autonomous town', with a special status within Spain. The Ceuta-Fnideq frontier may well be your first point of contact with Morocco.

Ins and outs

Getting there

See Transport, page 204, for further details

There are frequent ferries from Algeciras to Ceuta, and the journey is rather quicker than Algeciras to Tanger. (The advantage of Tanger is that you are at the start of the Moroccan rail network.) It's best to arrive early in Ceuta, so you have plenty of time to clear the frontier and move on to Tetouan or Tanger, if there's time.

Coming from Morocco, the Fnideq-Ceuta frontier is reached most easily from Tetouan by grand taxi. The taxis leave Tetouan from opposite the main bus station, expect to pay around 25dh a place. There are also occasional buses from Tetouan to Fnideq. Note that on the Moroccan side of the frontier, formalities can be slow.

Driving up to Ceuta from Tetouan you can take the direct route or go via Martil, passing a string of resort villages, including, from south to north, Martil, Cabo Negro (M'diq), Kabila and Smir Restinga, before reaching Bab Sebta. The drive will take around 45 mins.

Getting around Unless you intend to stay the night to explore Ceuta, you will need to get from port to Moroccan border at Fnideq, 3 km away. There is a bus from Ceuta city centre, leaving from Plaza de la Constitución. To get there, turn left as you leave the ferry terminal, and follow round along Paseo de las Palmeras (a 15-min walk, maximum). You can spend both pesetas and dirhams in Ceuta in restaurants and shops. Like mainland Spain, the enclave has a long afternoon siesta with shops closed 1300-1600. Sun is very much a day of rest.

Tourist information **Patronata Municipal de Turismo**, at the exit to the ferry port. See also www.turiceuta.com, the tourism office's website.

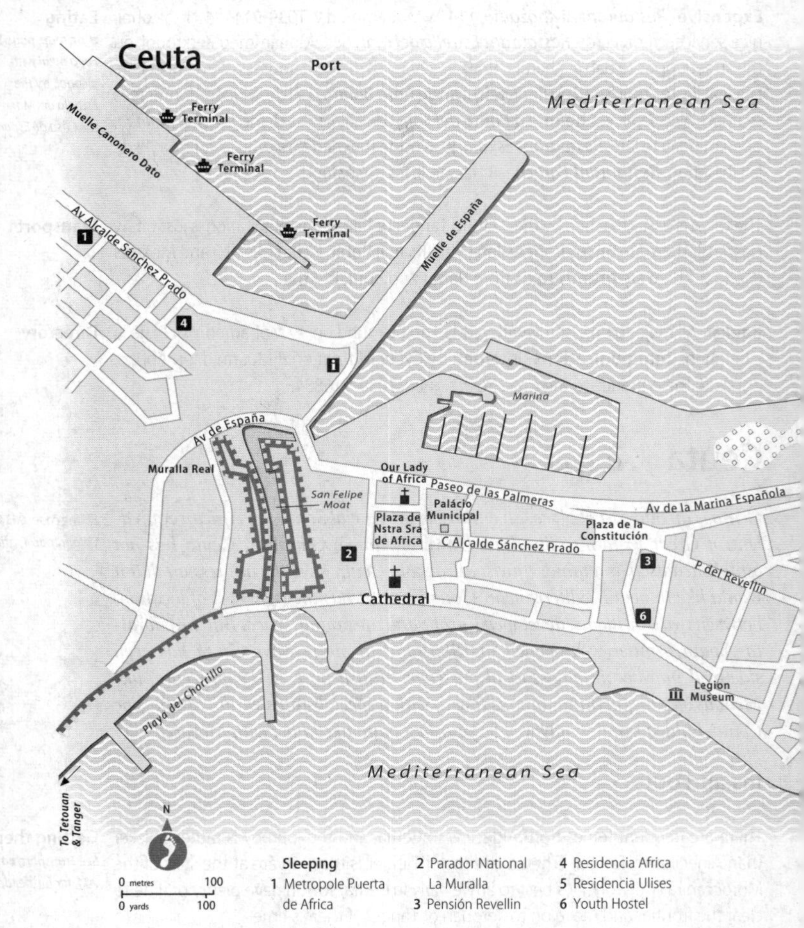

Background

Ceuta is Sebta in Arabic

Ceuta is a Spanish enclave on the Moroccan coast, which since 1995 has had the status of 'autonomous town', putting it somewhere between the Spanish autonomous regions and the municipalities. Ceuta has an excellent strategic position on the Strait of Gibraltar and was occupied by the Carthaginians, Greeks and Romans. After being taken in the Arab conquest, the site was captured by the Portuguese in 1415 but on the union of Spain and Portugal was transferred to Spain in 1581, under whose control it has remained ever since as little more than a military prison. Its later fame arose from its importance as a supplying fortress for Spanish forces during a series of 19th-century sieges of the northern *presidios*. Fighting near Ceuta in 1859 nearly led to the total loss of the enclave. In 1860 a Spanish military force invaded Morocco from Ceuta in what was described as 'a wretched affair' which led to the fall of Tetouan. In the 20th century Spain once again became embroiled in a bloody war in northern Morocco in which it badly lost important battles at Anoual in 1921 and in the Chaouen-Tetouan campaign in late 1924. Ceuta ultimately survived this episode thanks largely to Abdelkarim's internal political difficulties and the improved Spanish generalship under Franco. And it was from Ceuta that the future *caudillo* launched his forces to impose his form of law and order on mainland Spain in 1936.

Sights

Ceuta is basically a small, heavily urbanized peninsula, the Punta Almina, on the Strait of Gibraltar. It occupies a mere 19 sq km with an unexciting coastline. **Monte Hacho** is the highest point (204 m), though the adjacent **Sierra Cimera** which forms the boundary with Morocco rises to 350 m.

Ceuta harbour lies tucked into a bay on the north of the peninsula with the town largely packed onto a narrow isthmus lying between Monte Hacho in the east and hills adjacent to the frontier with Morocco in the west. The town itself is Spanish in character with a heavy military presence – the armed forces occupy most of the larger and older buildings including the fortress areas. The shopping streets such as Paseo del Revellin and Calle Real concentrate heavily on duty-free luxury goods such as electrical items, electronic equipment, perfumes and fashion boutiques, rather like Gibraltar. The town is saved from banality by areas such as those in the old town around the base of Monte Hacho, and in Paseo Revellin together with individual buildings such as the cathedral and **Casa de los Dragones**. Recent investments in facilities such as the new Mediterranean theme gardens near the Paseo Espanola covering some 55,000 sq m and the splendid Paseo de las Palmeras pedestrian shopping precinct have added to the charm of the enclave.

Much more than Melilla, Ceuta is, however, a transit port between Spain and Morocco and lacks the air of peace and good taste of its twin enclave. Good restaurants are fewer and, other than the duty-free lines, shopping as a whole is less varied.

Plaza de Africa

A visit to Ceuta probably starts on Plaza de Africa, home to two large Catholic places of worship, the Cathedral and the Church of Our Lady of Africa

The **Cathedral Museum** is situated in the side wall of the cathedral itself off Plaza de Africa and has ecclesiastical items in its collection including the highly decorated montage of the *Virgen Capitana*. The **Cathedral** is located in the south of Plaza de Africa and stands on the site of a pre-Muslim church and a mosque from the Arab period. The present building dates principally from the 17th century, though there were large-scale renovations in 1949-58. ■ *Afternoons only*. The **Church of Our Lady of Africa** is also on Plaza de Africa. The main building dates from the 15th century with many later additions, the largest in the 18th century, and is on the site of a former mosque. Its importance was as a great Christian monument in Islamic North Africa. The **Palacio Municipal** (town hall) is a modern building dating from 1926 of interesting design and containing some fine panelling and frescoes by Bertucci. The *Peñon Municipal* (municipal banner) is kept in the town hall. The centre of the Plaza de Africa is taken up with a large monument to those Spaniards who fell in the country's African wars (1859-60). Note the bronze reliefs of battle scenes by Susillo. The **Church of San Francisco** stands in Plaza de los Reyes, which reputedly contains the bones of the Portuguese King Sebastian.

Municipal Museum

The Municipal Museum on Paseo del Revellin is well laid out and attractive. Rooms I and II have some fine Punic and Roman amphorae (earthenware jars) and display the activities of Ceuta and the sea including the salt-making pans on the ancient site of what is now the Parador and the Plaza de Africa. Room III has items relating to underwater archaeology with some well-preserved and decorated amphorae and pots, a corn-grinding wheel and a lead depth sounder. Other rooms (IV and, downstairs, V) display medieval crafts of Hispanic-Islamic origins. Rooms VII and VIII are given over to scenes and artefacts of the Spanish-Moroccan war (1859-60) with a wide selection of written sources on the war although exclusively a Spanish view of events.

Legion Museum

More military materials are on show at the Legion Museum on Paseo Colon, which celebrates the founding and activities of the Spanish special forces Legion force. There is a variety of armaments, uniforms and military memorabilia on show. ■ *Mon-Fri 1000-1400, Sat 1000-1400 and 1600-1800, closed Sun.*

City walls

The city walls form an impressive ring around the city. These Portuguese-built fortifications of forts, towers and curtain walls are at their best adjacent to the San Felipe moat and the Muralla Real. The exterior fortifications are also impressive – **Fort (Museum) Desnarigado** and **Fortaleza del Hacho**, though the latter, still occupied by the military, is closed to the public. Fortaleza del Hacho is of ancient foundation, probably Byzantine in origin but strengthened in the Arab period under the Ommayyad dynasty. It was reconstructed by the Portuguese and redeveloped by the Spanish in the 18th and 19th centuries. In the west of the town above the Ramparts Pedro La Mata are the **Merinid Walls**, a 14th-century construction on earlier buildings. The ramparts here are spectacular and well worth a visit. Of the original 2 km of walls, there now remains only a 500-m section, interesting nevertheless, including the old Fès Gate. Adjacent to Plaza de la Paz on Paseo Marina are the ruins of the **Arab baths**, heavily reconstructed but accessible and a useful reminder of the high urban forms of the Arab period.

To the east of the town is a tree-covered hill, a pleasant place for a stroll. At the far eastern edge is an old Portuguese fort. Stop off at the **Ermitada de San Antonio**, a convent rebuilt in the 1960s. From the walls is a good view of the town.

Beaches

Either avoid the rubbish on the town beaches, or head out west to the more pleasant beach at Benzu.

Essentials

Sleeping

■ on map, page 200

If you are thinking of staying in Ceuta and will arrive late in the day, make sure that you reserve your hotel room in advance. Accommodation can be tight

L ***Parador National Hotel la Muralla***, Pl Virgen de Africa 15, opposite the Cathedral, T514940, F514947. 106 rooms, pool, bar, nightclub. **A** ***Hotel Metropole Puerta de Africa***, Av Alcalde Sánchez Prado, T517191. **A** ***Hotel Residencia Ulises***, 5 C Camoens, T514540. 124 rooms, with pool. **B** ***Hotel Residencia Africa***, Juan Ignacio Quero Rivero, Muelle Cañonero Dato, T509470. 3-star hotel well situated almost opposite the *Shell* station near the ferry terminal. **C** ***Hostal Residencia Skol***, Antonio López López, Av Reyes Católicos 6, T504161. The main area to try for cheaper hotels is Paseo del Revellin, C Cameons and C Real. In C Real, try **C** ***Pensión Real***, T511449. 11 rooms. **C** ***Pensión La Perla***, T515828. 7 rooms. **C** ***Atlante***, 1 Paseo de las Palmeras, T513548. Also very good in C Real is **D** ***La Rociera***, T513559. At the foot of Paseo del Revellin, opposite the *Banco Popular Español*, is the **D** ***Pensión Revellín***, T516762, 16 rooms; and **D** ***Bohemia***, C Cameons, clean, recommended.

Youth hostel (Pousada de Juventud) 27 Pl Viejo, T515148. Only open in Jul and Aug. Often crowded but the cheapest place in summer.

Eating

■ on map, page 200

Expensive *La Torre*, 15 Pl de Africa, T514949. Recommended, but a dear do. ***Casa Silva***, C Real 87, T513715. Expensive array of Spanish fish and seafood dishes, as well as good wine. ***El Sombrero de Copa***, Padilla 4, T518284. Seafood specialists. ***Casa Fernando***, at the Benitez Beach, T514082. Good for seafood. ***Vincentina***, Alférez Bayton 3, T514015. ***Delfin Verde***, Muelle Cañonero Dato, T516332. ***La Terraza***, Plaza Gilbert 4, T514029. **Cheap** Sample some of the tapas in a number of the bars. Small cafés with tables outside on Paseo de las Palmeras, ***Café Tempo*** and ***Café Levant*** with a better view of the harbour (and the traffic).

Bars & clubs

Bars *Royal Automovil*, Beatriz de Silva 12, T512722. **Nightclubs** *Bogoteca*, C Real. *Coconut*, Carretara del Jaral. *San Antonio*, Monte Hacho.

Festivals

Fiesta de Nuestra Patrona, La Virgen de Africa, 5 Aug. *Carnival* in Feb.

Shopping

There are numerous shops selling duty-free goods. The savings are not enormous but shop around for bargains, especially spirits. Fuel is cheaper here than in Morocco. For travellers heading on to Morocco, stock up on Spanish cheese and wine from the local supermarkets. Excellent fresh fish and shellfish.

Sport & activities

Horse riding Martine Catena, T56-511048. **Watersports** Marina has capacity for 300 vessels, weather information, security and dry-dock facilities, T513753. Subaquatics, T513753. Windsurfing, enquire at larger hotels.

Tour operators Most of the agencies are on Muelle Cañonero Dato. Try *Viajes Dato*, T507457. *Viajes Dimasur*, T503428. *Viajes Flandría*, C de la Independencia 1, T508960. *Viajes Multimares*, T509107. *Viajes Punta Europa*, T509226. *Viajes Tourafrica*, T509302. Also *Independencia*, 1 edif Inmaculada, T512074, F514559.

Transport **Local Car hire**: *Africa Car*, SL through *Flandria Travel Agents*, Independencia 1, edif Inmaculada. **Helicopter**: *Transportes Aereos del Sur* advertise helicopter flights from Ceuta to Jerez and Málaga. Details, T504974. **Taxis**: in Ceuta, T505406.

Road From Ceuta follow the signposts to Morocco. The frontier post is on the south side of the peninsula, a little way out. Petrol is cheaper in Ceuta than Morocco. For those without transport, pick up a Spanish taxi or take bus 7 from Pl de la Constitución. There are some long-distance Spanish buses, from the bus station on the south coast road in Ceuta, to **Casablanca**, **Al Hoceima** and **Nador**. **Tetouan** is a better option for finding bus services. From Morocco, drive through Fnideq to the frontier. There are bus and grand taxi services between Fnideq and Tetouan, and between Fnideq and Tanger. Between the frontier and Fnideq there is a grand taxi, currently costing 4dh. **The Frontier**: passports have to be checked and stamped by Moroccan officials both ways, and there are often lengthy queues. Travellers with their own transport have to have their vehicles registered and their papers, including insurance, registration and licence, checked. This can take some time. Cash can be exchanged on the Moroccan side of the frontier at the *Banque populaire* booth.

Sea The **Algeciras-Ceuta ferries** are cheaper and quicker than those between Algeciras and Tanger, with passengers from 130dh and cars from 645dh, taking 80 mins. There are normally 6 services a day Mon-Sat, 5 each Sun generally with refreshments available. Tickets can be bought from *Trasmediterranea* in Muello Cañonero Dato, T509496, F509530; from *Isleña de Navegación*, in the port building, T509139; or from the numerous travel agents around the town centre. The port is in the centre of the town and the main destinations are clearly signposted. The **hydrofoil** service to Algeciras should be booked in advance at 6 Muelle Cañonero Dato, T516041. These frequent (6 or 7 daily) Rapido services by catamaran or hydrofoil carry foot passengers only, take 30-45 mins depending on sea conditions and cost 3,000 ptas single.

Directory **Banks** *Banco de España, Pl de España.* ***Banco Popular Español**, 1 Paseo del Revellin.* **Communications** Pl de España, T509275. **Useful addresses** **Fire:** T513333. **Police** (municipal): T092. **Police** (national): T091. **Red Cross:** T514548.

Tanger to Tetouan

Tetouan is about 70 mins from Tanger, as a fast grand taxi runs, through beautiful hilly country. Note that there are police checkpoints at all major junctions, so keep your speed down. Watch out too for hairbrained overtaking on the seemingly fast, winding sections of the road. On the last stretch into Tetouan, the road becomes triple lane as it goes up and over a high ridge. The middle lane is for overtaking, for Tetouan-bound traffic on the northwest side, for Tanger-bound traffic on the southeast side. You run into Tetouan through its sprawling suburbs, past a turn-off right onto the main route for Chaouen and Fès.

Tetouan

Tetouan has a striking location, between the Rif and the Mediterranean Sea. The city has a certain dramatic beauty with the white buildings of the médina contrasting with the backdrop of the Rif Mountains. Some impressive colonial architecture is found in the Spanish town dating from the 1920s and 1930s. The city is an interesting place to explore, albeit with more noise and hassle than Chaouen to the south. There are a number of resorts - some rather fashionable, others with a more downbeat appeal - between Ceuta and Tetouan and also further round the coast which can be visited en route, or as an excursion from Tetouan. For the tourist, Tetouan's main sites can be covered in a rather rushed half day; a full day would give you time to explore the city pretty thoroughly.

Phone code: 039
Colour map 1, grid A3

Ins and outs

Getting there

See Transport, page 209, for further details

Tetouan is easily visited as a day trip from Tanger, if you don't want to stop over. There are buses in from Chaouen, Fès, Meknès, Ouezzane and of course Tanger, operated by both the *CTM* and private companies. There is also a bus from Casablanca (7 hrs). Chaouen to Tetouan takes around 1 hr, Tanger to Tetouan 1½ hrs. There is also a daily bus from El Hoceima (5 hrs). Coming from Ceuta, it's best to get a grand taxi from the frontier.

Getting around

Taxis from Tanger and Tetouan arrive in the new town, close to the bus station, about 10 mins' walk from the médina. (From the bus station, to get to the médina, head up R Sidi Mandri and turn third right down Av Mohammed V, which will bring you to Pl Hassan II.) In summer, if you want to go to Martil or Cabo Negro, buses go from Av Massira, near the old train station, instead of from the main bus station. To get there, take Av Hassan II, to the right of the main bus station, which meets Av Massira after the Ensemble Artisanal on the right.

Tourist information

Office du Tourisme (ONMT), 30 R Mohammed V, T039-961915, F961914. Syndicate d'Initiative, Blvd Hassan II, Residence Nakhil, T039-966544.Tourists to Tetouan must be careful as seedy characters are out in force. Travelling by bus, you are at your most vulnerable arriving at the main bus station, where there are various con artists with a keen eye for tired backpackers stumbling off a late bus from Fès. Pay attention to your belongings and avoid having any dealings with *faux guides*. The tourist office and the larger hotels should be able to arrange for official guides, but the city is really small enough for you to manage on your own.

Background

Tetouan was founded in the third century BC as **Tamuda**, but was destroyed by the Romans in AD 42. The Merinid ruler Sultan Abou Thabit built a kasbah at Tetouan in 1307. Sacked by Henry III of Castille in 1399 to disperse the corsairs based there, Tetouan was neglected until it was taken over by Muslims expelled from Granada in 1484. They were to bring with them the distinctive forms and traditions of Andalucían Islamic architecture, still observable in the médinas of Granada and Cordoba. Many of the Andalucíans worked as corsairs continuing the tradition. A Jewish community was established here in the 17th century which gave the impetus to open up trade with Europe. Trade with the West continued to boom in the 18th century during the reign of Moulay Ismaïl. In 1913 Tetouan was chosen as the capital of the Spanish Protectorate over northern Morocco. The Spanish created the new town, which has remained an important regional centre in independent Morocco.

Sights

Ville nouvelle A good point to start is **Place Hassan II**, the focal point of the city and former market, and the best place to stroll or sit in a café terrace in the evening. It is dominated by the gleaming **Royal Palace**, lots of white walls and green-tiled roofs, a 17th-century building completely transformed under Hassan II. Here, in the centre of the square among the palm trees, is a smart green and white column surmounted by a flag. Looking onto the square is the Pasha Mosque with its distinctive green door and green-and-brown-tiled minaret. Bab er Rouah has also had a facelift. The other major centre in the *ville nouvelle* is **Place Moulay el Mehdi**, along Boulevard Mohammed V from Place Hassan II, dominated by an impressive golden-yellow **cathedral**.

Médina **Bab er Rouah**, in the corner of Place Hassan II, leads into the médina where Andalucían influence is still apparent in the whitewashed walls and delicate

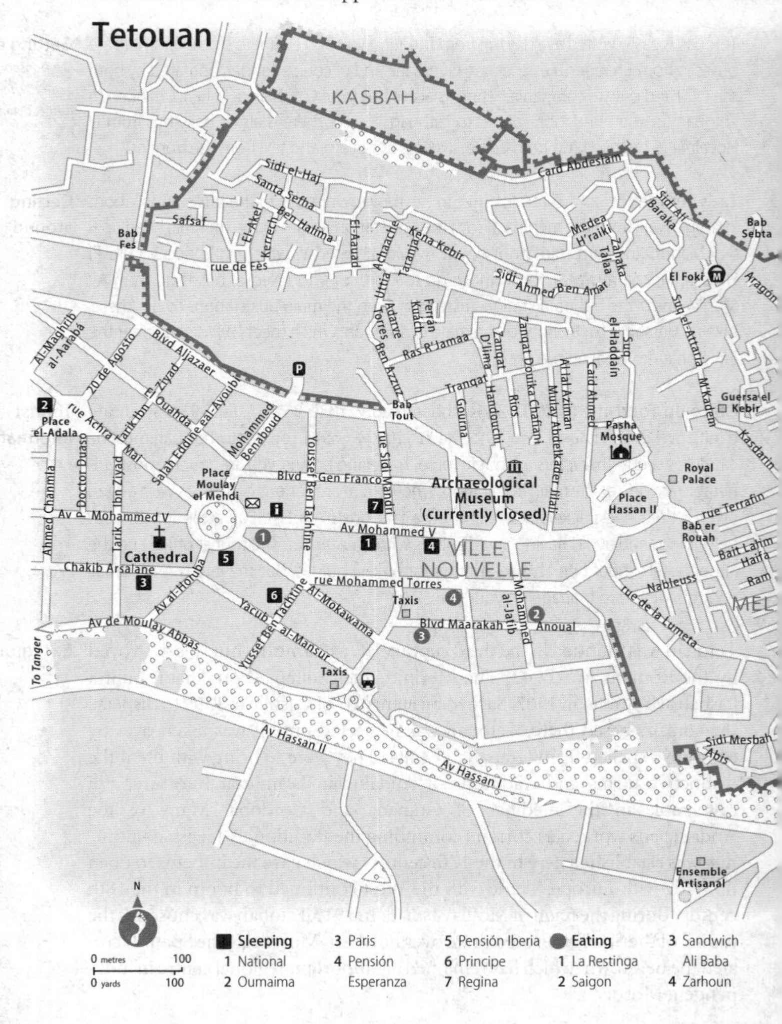

wrought-iron decorations on the balconies. The médina of Tetouan is a confusing maze of streets and souks, well worth exploring, although perhaps with the assistance of an official guide. In the souks look out for artefacts with Tetouan's favoured red coloration. Rue Terrafin is a good route through the médina, leading into Rue Torres and Rue Sidi el Yousti, and out at Bab el Okla. North of Rue Sidi el Yousti is an area with some of the larger and more impressive houses.

Souks

Souk el Hout, with pottery, meat and fish is to the left of Rue Terrafin behind the palace. Here there is a delightful leafy square, pleasant surroundings for admiring the wares. Behind the souk is a small 15th-century fortress, the **Alcazaba**, now taken over by a cooperative. Take the left hand of the two north-bound lanes from the Souk el Hout and on the right is **Guersa el Kebir**, a textile souk, selling in particular the type of striped, woven blanket worn by Rifi women. The colours are particularly striking, the red, white and blue striped fabrics on sale by women dressed in the same colours. **El Foki** market can be found by following your nose – the smell of the traditional, flat, round loaves is impossible to miss. Look out for the **L'Usaa Square**, with its white houses around a mosaic fountain and a rose garden.

Further on from this souk, leading up to **Bab Sebta**, are a number of specialist craft souks and shops. Running between Bab Sebta and **Bab Fès** is Rue de Fès, a more general commercial area, although with a number of souks around. From Bab Sebta the road out of the city passes through a large cemetery. Above the médina is the crumbling kasbah (closed to visitors), and nearby a vantage point providing stunning views over the city.

Jewish quarter

On Place Hassan II, the first alleyway south of Bab er Rouah leads onto the main street of the *mellah*, the 19th-century Jewish quarter, where there are a number of abandoned synagogues. The original Jewish population has all but disappeared. The earliest *mellah* was near the Grand Mosque.

Archaeological Museum

Built in 1943, this museum contains a small archaeological collection from the prehistoric and pre-Islamic sites of the northern region of Morocco, plus some pieces from the once-Spanish Saharan provinces and a large library. Of most interest, however, are the Roman statues and mosaics found at ancient **Lixus** near Larache. The most notable mosaic portrays the Three Graces of Roman mythology. Other rooms display prehistoric tools, bronzes and pottery. Of note here is the Sumerian ex-voto statuette found close to Asilah. Most of the small figures date from the first century AD. Note particularly the Roman coins and mosaics. ■ *Currently closed, presumably due for renovation. Blvd Aljazaer, near Pl Hassan II. T039-967103.*

Musée d'Art Marocain/ Musée Ethnographique Housed in Bab el Okla and renovated in 2002, this small museum is definitely worth a visit, perhaps at the end of your meander through Tetouan. There are samples of local textiles and dress, weapons and musical instruments, plus a small Andalucían garden at the back. There is also a display of traditional tiles. Note that the technique for making tiles in vogue at Tetouan was different from the more mainstream Moroccan or Fassi *zellige* technique. The latter is a mosaic technique involving the assembling of thousands of tiny coloured ceramic pieces. The artisans of Tetouan produced tiles imitating the *zellige* mosaics using the *cuerda seca* ('dry cord') technique, by which the different coloured glazes were separated by a pattern of geometric lines. ■ *Mon-Fri 0830-1200 and 1430-1730, Sat 0830-1200. T039-970505.*

Ecole de Métiers Outside the médina, across the road from Bab el Okla, there is the Ecole de Métiers (craft school), built by the Spanish. Here are craftsmen and students at work on *zellige* tiles, leatherwork, carpentry and pottery. The school, generally closed for holidays in August, may be visitable.

Tamuda The remains of ancient Tamuda are really only for enthusiasts. The site, unsigned, lies to the south of the P38 road running west out of Tetouan. It was founded in the third-second centuries BC. Later, during the Roman period, in the third century AD, the original settlement disappeared under a Roman camp. So far only remains of dwellings have been excavated, no public buildings or religious buildings. Finds from Tamuda are in the Archaeological Museum in Tetouan.

Essentials

Sleeping
■ *on map, page 206*

The budget hotels or *pensiones*, in and near the médina and Pl Hassan II, are often primitive and unhygienic. Make sure you are very clear about the price you will be paying. Note that demand can outstrip supply in the summer months. If on a budget, perhaps best to go for something slightly more expensive than usual, for security, in Tetouan.

B ***Hotel Chams***, Av Abdelkhalak Torres, T039-990901, F990907. A few kilometres east towards Martil, 68 rooms, 12 suites, all with bath, TV, pool, restaurant. Comfortable rooms. Safe car park, conference facilities. **B** ***Hotel Malaga***, west of the town. **B** ***Hotel Safir Tetouan***, Av Kennedy, T039-970144. 5 km from town centre. Good reputation, 100 rooms with bath and phone, frequented by package tours, garden, pool, tennis, restaurant, nightclub (2300-0300). **D** ***Hotel Oumaima***, R Achra Mai, T039-963473. Central, convenient and respectable. **D** ***Paris Hotel***, 11 R Chakib Arsalane, T039-966750. 40 rooms, nothing special, parking. **E** ***Hotel National***, 8 R Mohammed Torres, T039-963290. Recommended and not too expensive, with a café. **E** ***Hotel Principe***, 20 Av de la Résistance, T039-962795. 61 rooms, large and generally clean. Not all rooms have hot water. **E** ***Hotel Regina***, 8 R Sidi Mandri, T039-962113. Cheaper hotel in the *ville nouvelle*, all 58 rooms with bath, occasional tepid water. **E** ***Hotel Trebol***, 3 Av Yacoub El Mansour, T039-962093. Handily located behind the bus station, thus a little on the noisy side. Clean, showers in all rooms. **F** ***Pensión Iberia***, above the *BMCE*, Pl Moulay el Mehdi. Small and cheap with hot water. **F** ***Pensión Esperanza***, Av Mohammed V.

Camping There are a number of camping sites a short distance from Tetouan along the coast, the nearest by the river and beach at Martil. ***Camping Tetouan***, site of 6 ha, beach only 200 m, bar/snacks, restaurant, shop, showers, laundry, electricity for caravans, petrol at 200 m. ***Camping Municipal***, at Martil Beach. Security might be a problem. ***Camping Ch'bar***, at Cabo Negro. ***Camping Fraja***, at Restinga Smir. Rather austere.

Eating

• on map, page 206
Tetouan does not have any exceptional restaurants. The city is known for its sweets

Expensive *Hotel Safir Tetouan*, Av Kennedy, T039-967044. Well recommended and reliable. **Mid-range** *La Restinga*, 21 R Mohammed V. Good well-priced Moroccan food with good *tagines*. ***Restaurant Marrakech de Tetouan***, in the médina. Has good Moroccan food and music, busy at lunchtime. ***Restaurant Saigon***, R Mourakah Annual. Moroccan and Spanish food. ***Zarhoun***, 7 Av Mohammed Torres, near the bus station. Moroccan decor and music, and set Moroccan meals, bar. **Cheap** *Café-Restaurant* ***Moderne***, 1 Pasaje Achaach, near the bus station. Cheap Moroccan food. ***Sandwich Ali Baba***, R Mourakah Anual, a popular place for cheap local food. Also try the places around R Luneta and Bab er Rouah.

Shopping

Ensemble Artisanal, the government fixed-price shop, is on Av Hassan I. Also the souks.

Sports & activities

Al Menara Complex, Torreta el Mers, provides swimming, tennis and basketball. **Golf**: *Cabo Negro Royal Golf Club*, Cabo Negro, T039-978303, F978305, 200dh per round, open daily. **Horse riding**: *La Ferma*, Cabo Negro, T039-978075. **Hunting**: *Sochanord*, Mdiq, T039-974415. **Tennis**: *Kabila Tennis*, Tetouan-Ceuta Rd, T039-977051. **Yachting Club**: Mdiq port, T039-977694.

Tour operators

Akersan Voyages, Av FAR, T039-963034. ***Hispamaroc***, Av Mohammad, T039-963812. ***Maroc Consult***, R Achra Mai, T039-965832.

Transport

Local Much of Tetouan can be reached on foot. A petit-taxi is a cheap alternative.

Long distance **Air** Aéroport de Sania R'Mel, 5 km, T039-971233. There were no civil flights for either domestic or foreign services to Tetouan in 2002-03. ***Royal Air Maroc***, 5 Av Mohammed V, T039-961260.

Road **Bus**: the bus station, at the corner of Av Hassan I and R Sidi Mandri, T039-966263, has both *CTM* and private line services to most major destinations. Services to **Fnideq** (for Ceuta, 30 mins), **Chaouen** (1 hr), **Tanger** (1 hr), **Meknès** (8 hrs) and **Fès** (6 hrs). *ONCF* also operates a coach service to link up with the rail network at Tnine Sidi Lyamani. Through tickets can be bought from the office at Pl el Adala, where the coach also departs from each day. Buses to **Martil, Cabo Negro** and **Mdiq** leave from near the old railway station on Av Massira, those for **Oued Laou** from the main bus station. **Taxi**: much of Tetouan is quite manageable on foot, but a cheap and reasonable alternative is a petit taxi. Grands taxis to **Tanger**, **Fnideq** (for Ceuta), **Chaouen**, the beaches and other places, leave from Blvd Maarakah Annoual or nearby. **Car hire**: *Amin Car*, Av Mohammed V, T039-964407. ***Zeite***, Yacoub el Mansour.

Directory

Banks *Banque Marocaine*, Pl Moulay el Mehdi. *BMCE*, 11 Av Mohammed Ibn Aboud (Mon-Fri 0800-2000, Sat-Sun 0900-1300, 1500-2000). *BMCI*, 18 R Sidi el Mandri, T039-963090. **Communications** Post office: Pl Moulay el Mehdi, T039-966798. **Embassies and consulates** Spanish Consulate, Av Al Massira al Khadra, T039-963590. **Medical services** Chemist: 24-hr, R al Wahda, T039-966777. **Useful addresses** Police: Blvd General Franco, T19.

Around Tetouan: the beach resorts

Restinga Smir From Fnideq to Tetouan, the P28 passes through a flat strip of beaches and marshes, and a number of tourist developments. Restinga Smir, 22 km from Tetouan, has a long beach and a correspondingly long line of holiday complexes, hotels, bars, restaurants, bungalows and camping areas. Until recently it was still a small fishing village frequented only by a small number of local visitors. Now it enjoys an international reputation. There is, however, sufficient space on the vast beaches for the activities on offer which include horse riding, mini-golf, tennis, underwater fishing and windsurfing. There's also the small marina/pleasure port of **Marina Smir**.

Sleeping and eating Includes a *Club Mediterranée*. **D** ***Hotel Carabo***, T039-977070. 24 rooms, bar, restaurant, pool, tennis and disco. Recommended restaurant ***Nuevo Le Chariot*** has a sea view and fine seafood. There are many good campsites to choose from including ***Al Fraia*** campsite and ***Camping Andalus***.

Mdiq After Restinga Smir the road passes through **Kabila**, another beach and marina, to Mdiq, a small fishing port with some traditional boat construction. Mdiq shares the same coastline and the same clientele as Cabo Negro (see below) and there is a certain feeling of competition. Mdiq is a well-established resort offering a range of modern hotels and restaurants (mainly fish of course), nightclubs, swimming pools and the usual selection of watersports on the beach. This is certainly a popular family resort which is spreading to the north. The town centre has banks, a post office and telephones and a number of shops selling handicrafts unlikely to tempt a discerning buyer.

Sleeping and eating Accommodation ranges from **A** ***Hotel Golden Beach***, T039-975077, F975096, 86 rooms, on beachside opposite bus station; **A** ***Kabila Hotel***, T039-975013, 96 rooms, to **E** ***Hotel Playa***, T039-975166, and a campsite. Eating options include the ***Restaurant du Port*** and ***Restaurant Al Khayma*** in centre of town.

Cabo Negro After Mdiq turn for Cabo Negro (also known as Taifor or Ras Tarf) which is 3½ km off the P28. Here the beach is more rugged with the low hills which overlook the sea dotted with small houses. This is a slightly less commercialized region though the number of discos and nightclubs is growing. Riding is very popular here with horses for hire by the hour and day. The roads through the town follow the contours and rise at various levels up the hill. At the coast there is a small pleasure marina by the jetty. The *Royal Golf Club of Cabo Negro*, currently only a nine hole (par 36) course, is popular with Casa-Ribatis on holiday.

Sleeping and eating There is another large *Club Mediterranée* adjacent to the golf course. **D** ***Hotel Petit Merou***, T039-978115/6. 23 rooms, restaurant, bar, disco. ***Restaurant La Ferma***, T039-968075, with French cuisine is only 1 km from main road.

Martil Martil, Tetouan's former port, and a pirate base, stands at the mouth of the Oued Martil. It is now another popular resort, with over 10 km of sandy beach. Once it was the particular resort of the people from Tetouan who established holiday homes here on the coast but now Martil welcomes visitors from far afield. Buses from Tetouan to Martil, Cabo Negro and Mdiq leave from Avenue Massira, near the old railway station.

Sleeping and eating **A** *Karia Kabila*, 14 Route de Ceuta, T039-975013. Right on the beach, 90 double rooms and 10 suites with bath, telephone, some with TV, restaurant, disco, 2 pools. **E** Hotel Nuzha, R Miramar. ***Camping Martil***, by the river, or ***Camping Oued La Malah***, signed further out of town. ***Municipal Camping*** at Martil Beach, T039-979435, site of 3 ha, beach, showers, laundry, electricity for caravans, petrol at 600 m; ***Ch'bar***, Martil Rd, Cabo Negro. ***Hotel/Café Addiyafa***, on right towards Tetouan. Recommended.

Oued Laou & the coastal road south of Tetouan

Oued Laou is 44 km southeast of Tetouan, along the spectacular coastal road, the S608. It is a relaxed fishing village with an excellent beach but only basic facilities. Stay at **F** *Hotel-Café Oued Laou*; **F** *Hotel-Restaurant Laayoune*; or *Camping Laayoune*. Eat at the hotels or foodstalls. An option from Oued Laou is to drive inland or to Chaouen.

The road continues along the coast through the villages of **Targa**, **Steha**, **Bou Hamed**, and **Dar M'Ter**. Possibly a more convenient place to stop is the fishing village, **El Jebha** (souk Tuesday). Stay at the **F** *Grand Hotel* or the **F** *Petit Hotel*, neither very good. It is served by buses from Tetouan and Chaouen. A tortuous mountain road, the 8500, takes the intrepid traveller to meet the P39 west of Issaguen (Ketama).

Chaouen شفشاون

Phone code: 039
Colour map 1, grid A3
60 km S from Tetouan

Chaouen, also called Chefchaouen, and even spelt Xaouen (the Spanish version), is a fine if sprawling Andalucían town in the Rif, set above the Oued Laou valley and just below the twin peaks of the Jbel ech-Chaouen, the 'Horned Mountain'. The town can be easily explored in a day, but with a room in the right hotel, you might want to stay longer to relax and explore the surrounding countryside. Note that the selling of kif is big business here, the main production regions being to the east. Suitably persistent refusal should rid travellers of unwanted attentions.

Ins and outs

Getting there

See Transport, page 215, for further details

By bus and grand taxi, Chaouen is within easy travelling distance of Tetouan (1 hr) and Ouezzane (1¼ hrs). The journeys from Meknès (5 hrs) and Fès (7 hrs) will require early morning starts. Driving your own car, you might take the P28 which runs close to Chaouen from Ouezzane to the south to Tetouan. Note that as Chaouen is midway between central Moroccan towns and Tanger/Tetouan, buses often arrive full.

Getting around

Chaouen has a new bus station, a ½ hr walk out of the town centre. Coming in by grand taxi, you arrive close to the old town on Av Allal Ben Abdallah. Everything is accessible on foot. Up a flight of steps, and on your right, on the Av Hassan II, there are some reasonable hotels (the *Marrakech*, the *Salam* and the *Madrid*) close to Bab El Hammar.

Tourist information

Syndicat d'Initiative, Pl Mohammed V, open mornings.

Background

Set in the Djeballa region, Chaouen was founded in 1471 by Sherif Moulay Ali Ben Rachid, a follower of Moulay Abd es-Salam Ben Mchich, the patron saint of the area, in order to halt the southwards expansion of the Spanish and Portuguese. The city's population was later supplemented by Muslims and Jews expelled from Spain, particularly from Granada, and for a time the rulers of Chaouen controlled much of northern Morocco. The town also grew in importance as a pilgrimage centre.

From 1576 Chaouen was in conflict with, and isolated from, the surrounding area, with the gates locked each night. Prior to 1920 only three Christians had braved its forbidding walls: the Vicomte de Foucauld disguised as a rabbi in 1883; Walter Harris, *The Times* correspondent and author of *Morocco That Was*, in 1889; and the American William Summers, poisoned in Chaouen in 1892. In 1920 Chaouen was taken over by the Spanish as part of their protectorate. Until that time the few Europeans who ever visited the town found Jews still speaking 15th-century Andalucían Spanish. The Spanish were thrown out from 1924 to 1926, by Abd el Karim's Rif resistance movement. They then returned to stay until Independence in 1956.

Modern Chaouen has extended across the hillsides, and the old town is now ringed by a suburb of the usual three-storey family apartment buildings. Though it is now well established on tourist itineraries, both mainstream and backpacker, Chaouen manages to retain a village feel. Here you may have your first sighting of the distinctive garments of the women of the Rif, the red and white striped *fouta* or overskirt and the large conical straw hat with woollen bobbles. And you will certainly come across a lot of other visitors, here to relax away from the Imperial cities.

Sights

There are few major sites. The centre is Place Mohammed V, with its small Andalucían garden. Avenue Hassan II leads to Bab el Aïn and the médina. The market is down some steps from Avenue Hassan II, on Avenue Al Khattabi. Normally a food market, there is a local souk on Monday and Thursday.

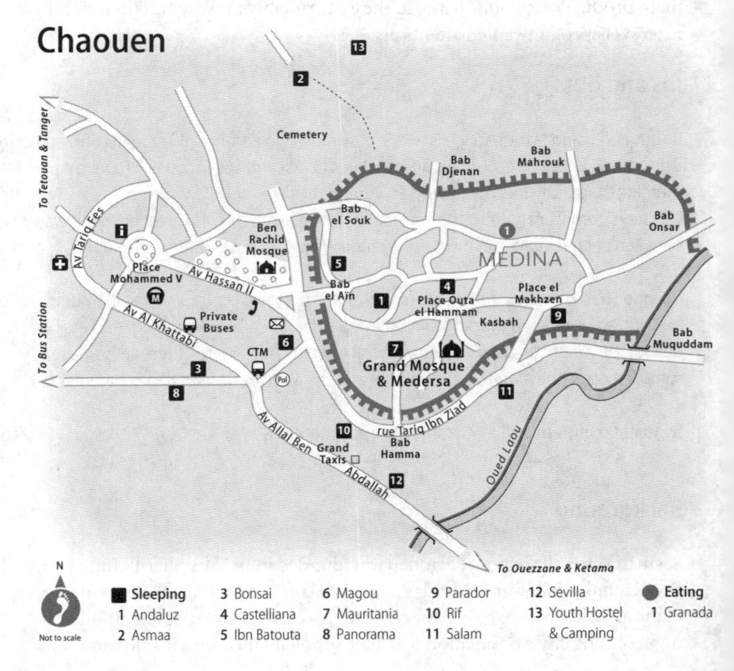

Médina

The médina of Chaouen is rewarding to explore, sufficiently small not to get lost, but with intricate Andalucían architecture, arches, arcades and porches, white- or blue-washed houses with ochre-tiled roofs and clean, quiet cobbled streets. In the maze of these narrow streets you run into water points, small open squares with shops and the solid ramparts of the kasbah. By car, park in Place el Makhzen and explore the rest on foot. Approaching the médina on foot, enter by Bab el Aïn. From Bab el Aïn a small road leads through to **Place Outa el Hammam**. This is the main square, lively at night, and surrounded by a number of stalls and café-restaurants, popular with kif smokers.

The square is dominated by the 15th-century **kasbah**, now the **Musée de Chefchaouen** (including the Centre d'Etudes et de Recherches Andalouses), by Pasha Ahmed Errifi. As a prison it housed the Rifi leader Abd al-Karim from 1926. The museum has an exhibition of local costumes, some with very delicate embroidery, tools, musical instruments, pottery, weapons and a collection of decorated wooden caskets. These illustrate the customs and popular art of the region in particular and northern Morocco in a more general way. It is an interesting building, worth climbing to the top for a good view of the town from the roof, and exploring the dungeons and prison cells below. There is a quiet garden constructed in the Andalucían style in which to relax. ■ *1000-1200 and 1400-1900, 0900-1700 in Ramadan. T039-986761.*

Note the beautiful **Grand Mosque**, with its octagonal minaret, beside the kasbah, dating from the 15th century, but restored in the 17th and 18th. Next door is a 16th-century *medersa*, unfortunately closed. Opposite the *Restaurant Kasbah*, at No 34, is an old caravanserai. Further on, **Place el Makhzen**, the second square, has stalls along the top side, the *Ensemble Artisanal* at the end. Chaouen has a large number of artisans employed in metalwork, leatherwork, pottery and woodwork, amongst other crafts, and is particularly known for weaving the striped Rifi blankets, as seen on country women.

Chaouen has many sanctuaries for pilgrims and each year thousands of visitors are attracted to pay homage to the memory of Sidi Ben Alil, Sidi Abdallah Habti and Sidi el Hadj Cherif.

Hillwalking

Chaouen is a good base for hillwalking, with some spectacular scenery and plentiful animal and birdlife. Expect suspicious questioning, however, from the military involved in cracking down on kif cultivation in the area, and be prepared for a long and strenuous day. Taking a guide is well worth considering, and could set you back around 100dh, maybe less. In particular look out for the natural spring called **Ras el Maa** just 3 km out of town in the direction of Jbel Tisouka. The manager of the *Casa Hassan* (see below) may be able to advise on mountain walking. You are withing striking distance of the **Parc naturel de Talassemtane**, still basically undiscovered by tourists. **El Malha, Beni Ahmed** and other isolated villages in this park are reached by landrover taxi from **Bab Taza**, 25 km to the southeast of Chaouen on the P39 road to Issaguen (Ketama).

Essentials

Sleeping

■ *on map, page 212*

Chaouen is a popular place for budget travellers as it has a good supply of clean cheap hotels (in addition to other more narcotic attractions). However, note that it gets pretty cold here in winter. Light sleepers will be awakened by the heavily amplified call to prayer from the numerous mosques.

B *Hotel Parador*, Pl el Makhzen, T039-986324, F987033, next to kasbah and médina. Lovely views, 37 small rooms with bath, telephone and a/c, no TV, safe parking, bar, restaurant, pool, the best in Chaouen, good location, try to reserve. Expensive for level of service. **C** ***Hotel Asmaa***, T039-986002, F987158. 94 rooms, placed insensitively on a hill above the town, but with an excellent view of the médina and the valley beyond, pool, bar, 2 tea rooms, restaurant. A group tour sort of place. Could be much better. **C** ***Hotel Panorama***, 33 R Moulay Abderrahman Cherif, T039-986615, F987498. New hotel, quiet as out of town, convenient for bus station, lives up to its name as has good views from the roof.

D ***Bab El Aïn***, 77 R Lalla-Horra, T039-986935. Not much charm, but a cut above the other pensions. Probably the cheapest with showers. **D** ***Casa Hassan***, 22 R Targhi, T039-986153, F988196. Recommended. Small hotel up a side street giving onto Pl Outa el Hamamm. Not easy to find. Pretty decor, but rather resting on its laurels, some visitors say. Showers on corridor. **D** ***Hostal Gernika***, 49 R Onssar, at the eastern end of the old town, not far from Pl el Makhzen, T039-987434. Highly recommended. **D** ***Hotel Madrid***, Av Hassan II, T039-987496, F987498. Good hotel, clean, plenty of hot water, friendly management. **D** ***Hotel Magou***, 23 R Moulay Idriss, outside Bab el Aïn, T039-986257. 32 rooms with bath, clean and recommended, currently closed. **D** ***Hotel Rif***, 29 R Tarik Ibn Ziad, T039-986207. Friendly hotel, bar and restaurant, good view from higher (but noisy) rooms. **E** ***Hotel Bonsai***, 12 R Sidi Srif, T039-986980. Small hotel, 12 very basic rooms, quieter, being out of town, convenient for the walk to the bus station. Nice patio with orange trees. **E** ***Hotel Ibiza***, R Sidi Mandri, on the entry to the town from Tetouan, T039-986323. Another small place. **E** ***Hotel Salam***, 38 R Tarik Ibn Ziad, T039-986239, just below the médina. Clean rooms with hot water, breakfast. **E** ***Residencia Estrella***, 2 Av Sidi Abd el Hamid, T039-986526. Roof terrace.

The cheap hotels and pensiones in Chaouen are often very good, basic but clean and reasonably priced

F ***Andaluz***, a few mins walk from Pl Outa el Hammam, follow signs. Clean and friendly with hot water. **F** ***Pensión Castilliana***, signposted just off the main square. **F** ***Auberge Granada***, up R Targhi from Pl Outa el Hammam. **F** ***Hotel Ketama***, R Allal Ben Abdallah, not far from *PTT*, T039-986094. Very basic but popular with pipe-of-peace people. Roof terrace. **F** ***Pensión Mauritania***, 20 Kadi Alami, T039-986184, below the square. Friendly place with music and café. **F** ***Pensión Ibn Batouta***, just off the road between Bab el Aïn and Pl Outa el Hammam. Clean and quiet. **F** ***Pensión Znika***, 10 R Znika, T039-986624. Small establishment (9 rooms) near the kasbah on a street going up to the left.

Youth hostel and camping Located next to each other, 2 km from centre near the *Hotel Asmaa*. Follow the signs from the road in from Tetouan, or walk (diplomatically) through the cemetery above the médina. ***Youth hostel***, T039-986031. 30 beds, meals available, kitchen, overnight fee 20dh. Poorly maintained, go for a cheap hotel instead. ***Camping Municipal***, T039-986979. Small café, shop, simple toilets and showers, tents amongst the trees, good view of the valley.

Eating
• *on map, page 212*

Expensive *Hotel Asmaa* and the ***Hotel Parador***, the latter with an extensive French-Moroccan menu. Both are good for a drink and a view. **Mid-range** Not too many choices, but look out for ***El Baraka, chez Didi*** down the narrow streets near Pl Outa el Hammam. On the expensive side for what's on offer. For a modestly priced licensed restaurant go to ***Restaurant-Bar Oum Rabi***, on R Tarik Ibn Ziad, not far from Av Hassan II. Lunch only, does fish and fried squid, alcohol. **Cheap** There are several cafés and restaurants on the main square, Pl Outa el Hammam, such as ***Restaurant Azhar***, R Moulay Idris. Friendly restaurant near the *Hotel Magou*. ***Estrella Verde***, Pl Mohammed V. Has a pleasant terrace and very reasonable prices. ***Restaurant Kasbah***. Also try ***Restaurant Tissemlal***, 22 R Targhi. Excellent Moroccan food. ***Restaurant Zouar***, R Moulay Ali Ben Rachid, near the main square. Wide range of cheap Spanish dishes including fish. ***Restaurant La Plaza Grande Kazba***, R Targhi. Cheap Moroccan food near the main Pl Outa el Hammam. ***Pâtisserie Magou***, Av Hassan II. Good for bread and cakes.

Transport
Try to reserve your bus seat in advance when you want to move on

Road Bus: the bus station is out of town. Buses are often through services and can thus be full. There are several buses a day for **Ouezzane**, 2 daily for **Meknès** (5 hrs), 1 daily for **Fès** (7 hrs), several a day for **Tetouan**, 2 daily for **Al Hoceima** (8 hrs), 2 weekly for **El Jebha** (7 hrs). **Grands taxis**: leave from the bus station on Av Allal Ben Abdallah to most of the above destinations.

Directory

Banks *Banque populaire*, Av Hassan II. *BMCE*, Av Hassan II, also *Crédit agricole* on Pl Outa el Hammam Communications **Post office:** PTT, Av Hassan II. Medical services **Chemist:** Beside the Hotel Magou.

The Northern Rif

Colour map 1, grid A3

The P39, the 'route of the crests' from Chaouen to Al Hoceima, is one of Morocco's most dramatic journeys, a route through a succession of small villages with stunning views over the remote valleys and towards the snow-capped Rif Mountains. Care must be taken on this narrow, hill-top road which may be closed by snow in winter. Traditionally this was an area of unrest against central authorities, notably in the Rif rebellion of Abd el Krim against the Spanish from 1921 to 1926, whilst more recently bandits are said to have preyed on travellers. Today the situation has improved, and the main dilemma is how to replace one of the major sources of income for local families, cannabis cultivation. (The term *kif* refers to the dried and chopped leaves and flowers, not the resin.) Government development programmes and pressure from the EU have had little impact, simply because the cannabis plant, especially if irrigated, grows very well on the region's hillsides. If you stop over in the area, you may be invited to see the process of turning the leaves into a ball of uncut, smokeable material, the understanding being that you will buy. Do not even think of smuggling cannabis out of the country. There are links between the police and vendors, who may try to blackmail you. The European consuls in Tanger have plenty of would-be smugglers to visit in the local prisons already. In any case, the varieties of cannabis now grown in the Netherlands give far better results.

Chaouen to Issaguen, aka Ketama

Leaving Chaouen, there is a major *Somepi* petrol station after you turn off onto the road for Issaguen (Ketama). The first stretch is quite fast and drivers are tempted to do some risky overtaking. The first place worth stopping at is **Cherafat** (try the salon de thé with the butcher's at the front on your right, go for mechoui and salad). The road winds up into the hills, and there are spectacular views to the south. Next 'major' stop is **Bab Berrad** where there is the cheap and very scruffy *Hotel Rif*, a pharmacy, and an old Spanish post office in the Andalucían vernacular style. After Bab Berrad, the forest begins, and there are views northwards towards the distant Mediterranean. A road to **El Jebha** on the coast is signed left, 55 km. If you want to do this route by grand taxi, you may find that you have to do it in two hops, Chaouen to Bab Berrad and Bab Berrad to Issaguen. Drivers may want to travel at night, the reason being that the headlights signal oncoming traffic immediately. The occasional visitor should do this route during daylight.

Issaguen (Ketama)

On the tourist maps the town marked as Ketama on the main east-west road linking Al Hoceima to the Tanger-Tetouan region is in fact called Issaguen, although there is nothing to tell you that in the way of roadsigns (the blue-and-yellow *CIH* petrol station at the junction, after a run through cedar forests, is the main indication). In fact, Ketama is a smaller place with a weekly Tuesday souk a few kilometres away on the S302 south to Fès.

Issaguen has long had a sulphurous reputation for being Morocco's capital of cannabis, a reputation not entirely undeserved. Although much money is made from kif, it doesn't really seem to have found its way into this particular town, although there is, as everywhere in Morocco, some new building. Issaguen could perhaps have been an important centre for summer hillwalking, being at the heart of a region where the mountains are covered in cedar trees. Spanish hunters used to visit in season looking for wild boar and fowl. Pleasant in winter, the town can sometimes be snowbound in winter. The main point of interest in the area is to climb the nearby **Jbel Tidghine**, the highest mountain in the Rif at 2,448 m.

If you settle for a couple of minutes in a café in Issaguen, someone is certain to approach you with an offer of cannabis. But the Gendarmerie royale are watching, so avoid making any purchases. Close to the main road, the once-splendid *Hotel Tidghine*, the old Maroc Touriste hotel, a splendid chalet-type place, has long died a death. There is an acceptable option in the form of **F** *Café-Hotel Saada*, T039-813061, on the main drag and easily identified by its shaded terrace, about 100 m on from the *Hotel Tidghine*.

Excursion up Jbel Tidghine (Tidiquin)

Remember to bring a water bottle – there is a spring where you can refill it

For Jbel Tidghine, you need to head for the village of **Azila**, the closest village, about 5 km from Issaguen. If driving, take the road south out of Issaguen and turn left at the new, low angular building. Alternatively take a local taxi (clapped-out car, 5dh a seat) from outside the *Hotel Saada*. The houses of Azila are scattered around a valley below Jbel Tidghine. If driving, follow the road through to the open 'football field' where the odd taxi parks up, or before this, turn off right by some trees on a dirt track to come out just above the mosque. Hopefully, a local kid will volunteer to show you the way across the valley. You will dip down through the village, over a rough plank bridge past small cannabis plantations under the walnut trees. Then passing some quite large, recent concrete houses, and more cannabis plantations, you reach the bracken and first cedars of Tidghine's lower slopes. For the climb, there are two options: either wind slowly up the old forestry department piste, or cut straight up, a bit of a vertical take-off exercise, to intersect with the forestry track further up – a good option if with a local. It is said that strong 4WDs can get to within 30 minutes of the summit. Climbing time should be about 2¼ hours, the descent 1¾ hours.

The forest is truly beautiful (butterflies in late summer) but under threat from locals in need of more sources of income than livestock and the barely profitable cannabis cultivation. To bring the great trees down, the practice is to light the needles under the trees in summer. The resinous trunks burn easily, weakening the whole tree, which is then easy to fell in winter when the forestry wardens are less likely to make tours of inspection.

The last stretch up the mountain is shaley scree, quite easy to deal with but slow. At the top, the views are magnificent. There are two, stone-built, corrugated-iron roofed huts where you could kip the night if you have a warm sleeping bag.

Route de l'Unité

The S302 runs southwards from Issaguen (Ketama) to Taounate, Aïn Aicha and Fès with views of deep valleys and forested slopes. This road, the Route de l'Unité, was built just after Independence by voluntary labour battalions, to link the Spanish Protectorate of the north with the former French areas. The whole region is untouched by tourism, despite its cedar woods and mountainous terrain, which in a sense is a pity. Settlements are scattered, and although not always prosperous, always pretty clean. In similar villages in the High Atlas the poverty is often more grinding, while the Rif, despite having been ignored in government development projects for decades, does seem to have managed a minimum of prosperity.

Issaguen (Katama) to Al Hoceima via Targuist

East of Issaguen, along the winding P39, the Rif becomes increasingly barren. If driving, allow about 2 hours to cover the 115 km between Issaguen and Al Hoceima. After 12 km, the 8500 branches off to the left, a 61-km drive to the small resort of **El Jebha** (see page 211). After a further 30 km, the 8501 branches left to Beni Boufrah and **Torres de Alcalá**, a coastal village from which you can explore further to **Kalah Iris** and **Badis** (see Al Hoceima Excursions, page 219). The first major town on the P39, **Targuist**, 65 km west of Al Hoceima, sits down in the valley and can be avoided. Claim to fame? This is the place where Abd al-Karim finally surrendered. It also gave the title to a Paul Bowles short story, 'The Wind in Targuist'. There is basic accommodation at the **F** *Hotel Chaab* or **F** *Hotel Café-Restaurant El Mostakbel* by the square where the buses stop. There are regular buses and grands taxis to Al Hoceima. After Targuist, the road, shaded in part by lines of eucalyptus, descends to the red-soil lands around **Ajdir** (Fès signed 263 km, Tanger 323 km).

NB If driving in this region in summer, note that car accidents are frequent. Returning migrant workers out to impress in powerful cars fail to appreciate the dangers of the winding roads.

Al Hoceima

Phone code: 039
Colour map 1, grid A4

Al Hoceima has one of the most beautiful natural sites on the Moroccan Mediterranean coast. Although the town, a Spanish creation of the 1920s and 1950s, has no great monuments, there is compensation in the form of nearby beaches. Despite these coastal attractions and greenery of the surrounding hills, the difficulty of getting to Al Hoceima by road reduces the flow of casual visitors. There is an airport, however, bringing in a few package tourists. In summer there are huge numbers of migrant workers and their families back from Europe, while the winter is very, very quiet. East of the town is a fertile plain enclosed on three sides by hills. And off the Plage de Sfiha, also to the east of Al Hoceima, is an intriguing group of islands, the Peñon de Alhucemas, Spanish territory since 1673, and once disputed by the French and English for their strategic position.

Ins and outs

Getting there

See Transport, page 220, for further details

Al Hoceima is possibly the most isolated resort town in Morocco. You can fly there from Casablanca (in summer), or, given the distances, take an early morning bus from Chaouen, Fès, Nador, Tanger, or Taza. There are also grands taxis, especially from Nador (3 hrs) and more rarely from Taza and Fès.

Getting around

Al Hoceima is not a big place. However, you might want to take a beige-and-blue petit taxi out to one of the beaches. The beaches at Torres de Alcalá and Kalah Iris, some 60 km away to the west, can also easily be reached by public transport. Note too that Issaguen (Ketama) and its mountain, Jbel Tidghine, is a feasible day trip by grand taxi from Al Hoceima.

Tourist information

Délégation Regionale du Tourisme, Immeuble Cabalo, R Tarik Ibn Ziad off Pl de la Marche Verte, T039-982830, 0830-1200 and 1400-1800, small but friendly.

Background

The islands off the coast of today's Al Hoceima first attracted the attention of the European nations in the 16th century. When the Saâdian dynasty weakened in the mid-17th century, the French envisaged setting up a trading post. The

Fréjus brothers from Marseille were authorized by the French crown to begin trading from the Albouzeme Islands, as they were called. Negotiations with the new Alaouite sultan, Moulay Rachid, proved unfruitful, however, and the project was abandoned. Further French projects for the islets were ruined by the War of the Spanish Succession and England's growing control of the seas.

The character of the town centre of modern Al Hoceima (ex-Alhucemas) is distinctly Spanish, reflecting the Protectorate years. Established by the Spanish in 1926 as Villa Sanjurjo, it was built as a garrison to control the Beni Ouriaghel tribe, of which Abd al-Karim was the chief, immediately after the Rif rebellion. (For those interested in colonial place names, the town was originally named Villa Sanjurjo, after one General Sanjurjo who led Spanish troops ashore here. The old part of town is still sometimes referred to by this name.) To the east of Al Hoceima is the long and less busy beach of the Alhucemas bay, while offshore is the Peñon de Alhucemas, a remarkable idiosyncrasy of history. This small island is owned and occupied by Spain and apparently used as a prison. It is completely dependent on Melilla for supplies and even water, and has no contact with the Moroccan mainland, off which it sits like a ship at anchor.

Today Al Hoceima has a population of some 60,000. Off season, it has an isolated feel: Tanger lies 300 km away to the west, Melilla is 170 km to the east, Oujda some 250 km away. The image in the holiday brochures is of a villageish sort of place with low, whitewashed houses atop a cliff, surrounding a few colonial buildings. In fact, modern Al Hoceima has streets and streets of three- and four-storey blocks, sprawling across the hillsides. This is where migrant workers put their savings. So Al Hoceima is turning into a big town, without any industry or major official functions. Nador and Al Hoceima are the key towns for the Ta'rifit speaking region, and Arabic-speaking outsiders are not all that much appreciated here. (Newsagents sell badges and stickers with the image of Abd el Karim, hero of the Rif War against the Spanish.) Some cultural resistance aside, Al Hoceima is very sleepy outside the summer season when the migrants from the Netherlands and Belgium pour in.

Sights

Buses and taxis pull into the neighbourhood of the **Place du Rif**. You should thread your way over to the Avenue Mohammed V (banks and cafés) which leads down to the wide paved expanse of **Place de la Marche Verte**. (The well maintained colonial building at the bottom is the Spanish school.) The cafés on your right as you head down are worth a pause with their views over the horseshoe bay. At the *Hotel Mohamed V*, the road curves down to the main beach. The **port**, extended in 2002-03, is worth a look if you have time, and there are a handful of restaurants. A gentle stroll round the town will reveal various other remnants of Spanish times.

Just before the *Hotel Mohamed V*, a steep flight of steps leads down to the *Hotel Quemado* complex and the **beach**. This gets pretty crowded in summer, although the sand is cleaned and raked every morning. There are pedalos and rowing boats for hire, and, unfortunately, jet skis. There is a rock to swim out to, and lots of enthusiastic playing of beach tennis.

Beaches east of town

Cala Bonita beach is just within the urban area (campsite, café-restaurant, and crowds in summer, also sewage smells from the creek around the cliff). Further east are Isri, Sfiha, Souani, and Tayda. The beach at **Isri** has gravelly sand and, being below a brick factory, receives a certain amount of rubble. The left turn-off for Isri beach, coming from town, is 50 m after the Centre de visite technique, a large white building. The gravelly beach also has the rock (no heritage-trail labels) where Abd el Karim el Khattabi made a famous speech in 1926, urging his resistance fighters to give up their arms and accept a form of autonomous government under Spanish rule. The tribes rejected this proposal and subsequently took a pounding from the Spanish airforce, a nasty precedent repeated by the Italians in Libya and many times by the USA in Indochina and elsewhere. Note that city taxis do not run this far out.

The beach at **Souani** ('the orchards') is rather better. The turn-off left is signed. There is a 2-km drive down to the car park next to the beach. Take care on the looping road, and don't get distracted by the superb views over to the Spanish-held island of Peñon de Alhucemas (Nkor or Ma'ziza). The sand is dark and fine, and there are few seasonal beach cafés, showers (pink building) and the *Restaurant Yasmine*. In summer, for a modicum of quiet, you will need to walk along the beach towards the forest and **Tayda**, where there is an exclusive *Club Med*. To get to Souani, without own transport, take a grand taxi, 7dh a place, and get out at **Sfiha**. Then walk along the beach to Souani.

Excursions

There are some good day trips to the tiny fishing communities west of Al Hoceima, namely Torres de Alcalá, Kalah Iris, and rather remote Badis. Torres de Alcalá, is the middle of the three, Kalah Iris lying west of it, Badis to the east. Without own transport, easiest approach is to take a grand taxi from Al Hoceima to Beni Boufrah, via Imzouren. **Beni Boufrah** is a small rural community about 7 km from Torres. Here you change for a local share taxi. (There is also occasional transport from Beni Boufrah to Targuist.)

Torres de Alcalá has a pebbly beach and seasonal café. Just behind the beach is a campsite among the eucalyptus trees (practically no facilities). Up on the hill are the remains of a fortress, which gives the village its name, 'the towers of the citadel', Alcalá being a Spanish word derived from the Arabic for citadel.

More interesting than Torres is **Badis**, a tiny fishing settlement about 90 minutes' walk along a good piste to the east. The track starts just behind the two-storey houses of Torres village. You could drive (and there is another, more direct, piste off the Imzouren to Beni Boufrah road), but note that in summer Badis is off-limits to all outside vehicles as there is a royal campsite here. Princess Lalla Amina, Hassan II's sister, takes her annual holidays on the beach at Badis, which is unofficially off-limits to all but locals. The track runs along the clifftop and makes a good walk. You have to scramble down the last 100 m or so to reach the beach. Behind the beach, a wide valley runs inland. There is no accommodation. You can buy a few basic things at the tiny shop in the settlement about 300 m from the sea, behind the royal camping area. In summer, one of the royal security guards will probably come and have a chat. Activities in Badis? Swimming, perhaps a long scramble up to what is said to be a ruined windmill high above the beach, and a look at the tiny shrine to Abou Yacoub al Badis, born around 1260, hidden in the trees. As the Mediterranean port for Fès, Badis was once an important settlement. It was destroyed by earthquake in 1564. The Spanish-held Peñon de Velez de la Gomera, generally described in the press as an islet but in fact attached to the beach at Badis by a pebbly spit, may have some fortifications which go back to Merinid times.

Finally, **Kalah Iris**, 60 km west of Al Hoceima and 9 km from Beni Boufrah, has an attractive beach. Italian funding is helping to construct a new port. Sometimes fishermen can be persuaded to run trips out to see the impressive cliffs.

Essentials

Sleeping

Difficult to get a quiet night's sleep in Al Hoceima in summer. There are practically no street names shown

Al Hoceima has a fair range of hotels, all with fair drawbacks. The *Hotel Karim* was closed in 2002, as was the *Hotel National*. The Hotel Marrakech is very noisy and best avoided. A new beach hotel, west of the town at Tala Youssef, may open in 2003.

B-C ***Hotel Mohamed V***, T039-923314. Just off Pl de la Marche verte, above the beach, twin to the *Quemado* down below. Could be superb, but badly run. **C** ***Hotel Khozama***, T039-985669, F985696. Linking rooms for families, nice café. Probably the best choice. Same owner as the *Hotel Etoile du Rif*. **C** ***Hotel Quemado***, T039-822233, F983314. Down on the beach. Big, plain rooms, bungalows on the hillside behind the hotel, restaurant, bar, run-down tennis courts. Fights and noise when nightclub shuts. Open Jun-Sep.

D ***Hotel Afrique***, R el Alaouiyine, T039-983065, close to Pl du Rif, clean, not too noisy. **D** ***Hotel Maghreb El Jadid***, Av Mohammed V, T039-982504. 40 good-sized rooms, a good option in the town centre. The problem? Traffic noise. Also has an annex on passage Saoussen Yaacoubi, T039-982511. 11 clean rooms with clean bathrooms, WC on corridor. **E** ***Hotel Etoile du Rif***, 40 Pl du Rif (Sahat Rif), T039-840847. A stylish pink and white Spanish building dominating the main square, once the town's casino, friendly, clean, best rooms overlook the square, cold showers, restaurant, café. Handy for bus station, recommended. **F** ***Hotel de Station***, Pl du Rif. Basic, cold showers, convenient for buses. **F** ***Rif Hotel***, R Sultan Moulay Youssef. Basic, close to Pl du Rif, handy for buses. Other options near the main square include the **F** ***Hotel Hanae***, 17 R Imzouren, with noisy restaurant on ground floor, and the **F** ***Hotel Oriente***, 18 rooms.

Camping sites *El Jamil*, also referred to as *Camping Cala Bonita*, T039-982009. East of the town, crowded in summer as close to the beach. Awful wash-blocks. ***Club Méditerranée***, T039-982222, is 10 km from Al Hoceima. Main activities are watersports and riding. Best booked through Club Med in your home country, but you could perhaps ring up.

Eating

Expect plenty of fish on all menus

There are few top eating options in Al Hoceima but try ***Hotel Maghreb El Jadid***, Av Mohammed V, T982504. A mixed French, Spanish and Moroccan menu. At the port there are several good fish restaurants including ***Restaurant Scorpio Sahara***, ***Restaurant Chez Mimoune***, and the rougher, licensed ***Bar-Restaurant des Poissons***, most do not speak French, try broken Spanish. Other economic options in town are ***Restaurant Mabrouk*** or ***Restaurant Al Hoceima*** in R Imzouren just off Pl du Rif, both serving tagines. Try also the shwarma place on Av Abd el Karmi Khattabi. In summer, the snack restaurant in the park opposite the post office stays open late.

Cafés

There are some nice cafés with sea views

Try any of the cafés off Pl de la Marche verte overlooking the Playa Quemado. Try also the ***Café Miramar***, or near Pl du Rif, also with seaview. ***Café Alfain/2000***, Av Mohamed V, opposite *Hotel Maghreb al Jadid*, is another good bet.

Tour operators

Chafarinas Tours, 109 Blvd Mohamed V, T039-841323, F841325, chafarinas.tours@caramail.com Works mainly with Moroccans from Europe.

Transport

Local The town is small enough to explore on foot but for the port or beaches hail one of the blue and beige petit taxis.

Long distance Air The airport, Aéroport Côte du Rif, T039-982005, is at Charif al Idrissi, 17 km southeast from Al Hoceima on the Nador road, with flights to **Amsterdam** (2 a week) and **Brussels** (1 a week), and **Casablanca** (2 a week) in season. ***Royal Air Maroc***, T039-982063.

Road Bus: all buses leave from Pl du Rif, which has ticket booths for the different companies. Most buses leave early in the morning. ***CTM*** (T039-982273) has services to **Nador** (0530, 1230, 7 hrs), **Tetouan** (3 per day, 1330, sometimes late as this is a through service from Nador, 2130 and 2230), all via **Targuist**, and **Fès**, 0630, 2000. There are many private bus companies. ***Nejme Chamal*** (Etoile du Nord) and ***Trans-Ghazala*** are recommended. **Grands taxis**: for **Nador** and **Taza** leave from Pl du Rif. For destinations west of Al Hoceima, they leave from C al Raya al Maghrebiya, off top of Av Mohamed V, between *Mobil* and *Total* garages and opposite the *BMCI*.

Directory

Banks All the usual banks, with ATMs, on or around Av Mohamed V. **Books and newspapers** *Librairie Jamouni*, on an unnamed street off Av Mohamed V, near the *Hotel Maghreb al Jadid*. There is a goodish bookshop on Av Tariq Ibn Ziad, near Pl de la Marche verte. **Communications Internet**: ***Cyberclub***, Av Mohamed V, above the *Méditel* shop near the turn-off for *Hotel Khozama*. Also ***Internet Bades***, Av Tarik Ibn Ziad, next to *BCM*, on left as you come from Pl de la Marche verte. **Medical services** **Hôpital Mohammed V**, Av Hassan II. Pharmacies on Av Mohamed V.

Ouezzane and the Southern Rif

Phone code: 039
Colour map 1, grid B3

Ouezzane is now a good sized town, rumoured to be the centre of cannabis-resin trading since the clean-up in Tanger in the late 1990s. For visitors, there is little to see. Nevertheless, it may just merit a little exploration, especially if you want to look at Rif building traditions. You might have to spend some time here if you are on a long drive travelling between northwestern Morocco and south-eastern Morocco, going via Fès and Meknès.

Ins & outs

Getting there Ouezzane lies 60 km (1¼ hrs) from Chaouen down the P28 road (look out for the Pont de Loukkos, which used to mark the border between the two Protectorates). There are grands taxis from Chaouen and Souk El Arba, as well as buses from Fès (5 hrs), Meknès (4 hrs) and Chaouen. **Getting around** The bus and taxi terminals are close to Pl de l'Indépendence, with budget hotels located close by. Note that travelling on from Ouezzane can be awkward by bus, as a lot of buses are through services, which arrive full.

Background

Ouezzane, perched on the north-facing slopes of Jbel Ben Hellal, has a dramatic hillside location. A short track from the town (only 3 km) leads up to the peak (609 m) and gives a splendid view across towards the Rif. Just 9 km north of the town is Azjem, burial place of an important Rabbi, Amram Ben Djouane, who came from Andalucía in the 18th century. Here again are impressive views of the

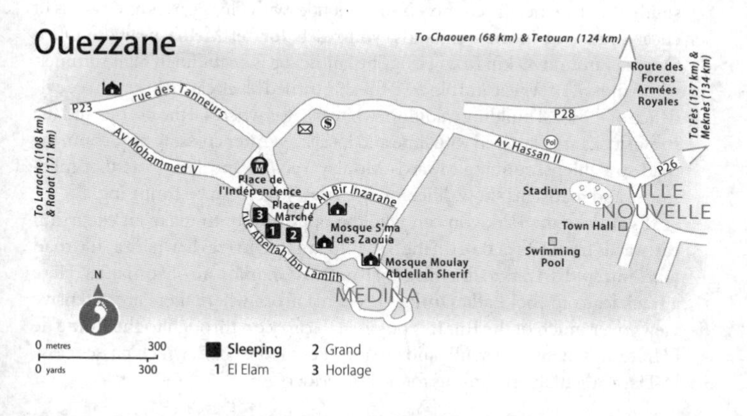

rugged Rif Mountains and the verdant valleys between. Azjem would be well worth visiting en route from Chaouen to Meknès or Fès.

Ouezzane, today an important regional centre with a population of 41,000, was founded in 1727 by Moulay Abdallah Cherif founder of the Tabiya Islamic order. This brotherhood achieved great national prominence from the 18th century, when the zaouia they had founded in Ouezzane became the focus of extensive pilgrimage activity. Ouezzane had close links with the sultan's court, which was often dependent on the zaouia and its followers for support.

Perhaps somewhat ironically, in view of the veneration Muslims accorded the Cherifs, a mid-19th cherif of Ouezzane married an Englishwoman, Emily Keane, in 1877 in an Anglican service – they had met at the house of the American consul where Keane was governess, although she later separated from him to live out her dotage in Tanger, where she is now buried in the Anglican Church. The zaouia's importance was destroyed by the sherif's growing connection with the French.

Ouezzane has importance today in the production of olive oil and, because of its Thursday souk, is a draw for local farmers and tradesmen.

Sights Ouezzane's **médina** has some of the most interesting architecture in the Rif, with the picturesque tiled-roof houses along winding cobbled streets. The focus of the town is the 18th-century **zaouia**, on Rue de la Zaouia, a distinctive green-tiled building with an octagonal minaret. Non-Muslims should not approach too close. Nearby are old lodgings for the pilgrims and the decaying cherifian palace.

Place de l'Indépendence, the centre of the médina, is busiest during the town souk on Thursday. To get to the **craft souks**, centred around Place Bir Inzarane, follow Rue Abdallah Ibn Lamlih up from Place de l'Indépendence. Ouezzane is known for woollen carpets woven in the weavers' souk at the top of the town. The blacksmiths' souk is along Rue Haddadine. There is a *Centre Artisanal* on Place de l'Indépendence, and another on Avenue Hassan II. ■ *0800-1900.*

Sleeping & eating Ouezzane is very limited for hotels, and is perhaps best visited in passing or as an excursion from Chaouen. Budget hotels include **F** *Marhaba*, **F** *Horloge*, and **F** *El Elam*, on Pl de l'Indépendence, or the more basic **F** *Grand Hotel* on Av Mohammed V, although none of these is an attractive option. Eat at the basic café-restaurants on Pl de l'Indépendence. If you are driving, *Café Africa*, 10 km north of the town, is a good place to stop for a drink.

South & east of Ouezzane to Fès From Ouezzane, there are two routes possible to Fès and Meknès, the P28 which runs south to intersect with the P3 east to Fès (134 km), and the slower P26. (A daily bus from Ouezzane to Fès follows this route.) Taking the P28, south of Ouezzane, the country is more gentle, with olive groves and stands of eucalyptus. Out in the cornlands, you reach **Jorf el Melha** near the Oued Ouerha (around 89 km from Fès). The landscape is beautiful in high summer, with a mosaic of wheat and blocks of freshly turned black earth. You will see evidence of the local building tradition, white villages where all the houses and the straw stacks are plastered with lime and local clay. After crossing the Sebou, the road straightens, running towards Moulay Yacoub and Fès. Note that milestones and roadsigns show different distances, which can be confusing.

If you take the P26, you can take the opportunity to make an excursion eastwards from **Fès el Bali** on the S304, 17 km to **Ourtzarh**, where a side road takes intrepid drivers to the village of **Rhafsai** (Ghafsai), an olive market. Here a track leads to **Jbel Lalla Outka** (1,595 m), from where there are extensive views over much of the Rif. It is possible to carry on through to the Route de l'Unité and then head south and west for Fès on the S302, which passes close to **Tissa**, a settlement famous for its horseriders.

Imperial cities and the Middle Atlas

226 **Meknès**
226 Ins and outs
227 Background
230 Sights
234 Excursions

235 **Essentials**
235 Sleeping
236 Eating
237 Entertainment
237 Shopping
237 Sport and activities
237 Transport
238 Directory

238 **Moulay Idriss and Volubilis**
239 Moulay Idriss
239 Volubilis

242 **The Middle Atlas**
242 Azrou
244 Aïn Leuh, waterfalls and Aguelmane Azigza
245 Ifrane, Mischliffen and an excursion to the lakes
246 Khénifra, El Ksiba and Kasbah Tadla

248 **Fès**
248 Ins and outs
249 Background

254 **Sights**
254 Fès el Jedid
256 Fès el Bali: Adoua el Quaraouiyine
262 Fès el Bali: Adoua el Andalus
263 The palaces of Fès
264 Fès vantage of points

264 **Essentials**
264 Sleeping
268 Eating
270 Sport and activites
270 Shopping
270 Tour operators
270 Transport
271 Directory

272 **Around Fés**
272 Moulay Yacoub
272 Sidi Harazem and Bhalil
273 Sefrou

275 **Taza**
276 Ins and outs
276 Background
276 Sights
277 Essentials

278 **Around Taza**
278 Jbel Tazzeka National Park

281 **East of Taza**
281 Guercif
282 From Guercif to Midelt
283 Taourirt
284 Debdou

Introducing the Imperial cities and the Middle Atlas

The area of central Morocco around the Jbel Zerhoun and the Saïss Plain was important even in ancient times, a strategic, fertile region on the trade routes leading from eastern North Africa to the Atlantic coast. Power has often been concentrated in this region - witness the ancient Roman city of **Volubilis**, and the imperial cities of **Fès** and **Meknès**.
Volubilis is one of the finest Roman sites in North Africa, and its ruins still manage to evoke life in a prosperous frontier town in the second and third centuries AD. Nearby, **Moulay Idriss**, the father of the Moroccan state, is honoured in the pilgrimage town of the same name, a memorable settlement, with houses cascading down hills on either side of a large mosque.

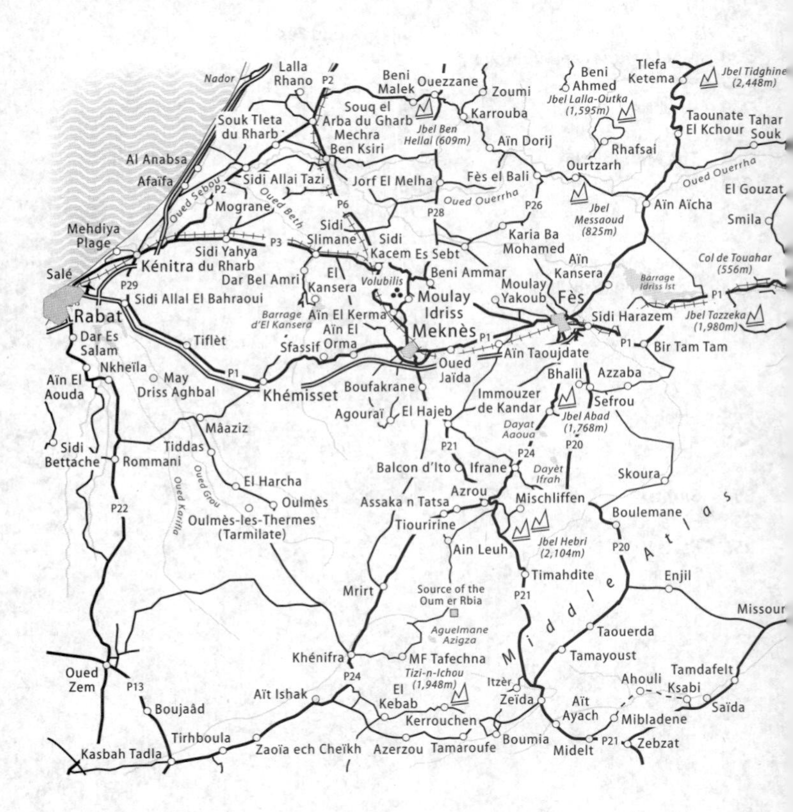

Moulay Idriss founded Fès which went on to become an imperial capital, the undisputed intellectual and spiritual centre of the country. Today, the city has stunning examples of late mediaeval architecture, as well as souks, each with its own speciality, still largely functioning as of old. Meknès, lying to the west of Fès , is a quieter city with a pleasant médina and the ruins of Sultan Moulay Ismaïl's vast capital - a must if you haven't the time and energy to face the pressure of Fès. To the east of Fès, towards Algeria, **Taza** and **Oujda** are regional centres which have held vital strategic roles. To the south of Fès and Meknès lie the **Middle Atlas** mountains. **Azrou** and **Ifrane** are the two main towns, giving access to a Hobbit-ish region of cedar forests, hills and limestone plateaux.

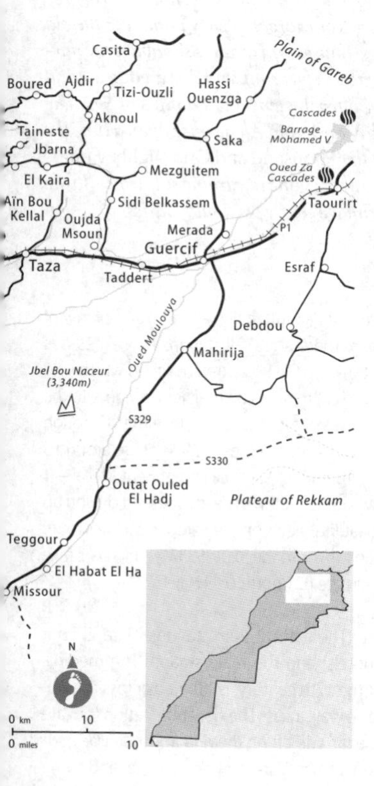

Things to do in the Fès – Meknès – Taza region

- Explore **Fès el Bali**, the oldest part of the medina of Fès, visiting historic medersas and abandoned palaces.
- Have a **Fassi's day out** and take a day trip to the springs at **Moulay Yacoub**, near Fès.
- Drive up to the hobbity landscapes of the **Plateau des Cèdres**, south of Azrou and Aïn Leuh
- After a morning exploring the **médina of Meknès**, spend the afternoon at **Volubilis**, Morocco's largest ancient Roman site.
- Scramble and slither underground at the **Gouffre de Friouato**. Located in the Jbel Tazzeka, south of Taza, this is probably the most important cave system the country.

Meknès مكناس

Phone code: 055
Colour map 1, grid B3

Meknès never set out to be an 'imperial city'. Chance would have it that as the inhabitants of Fès and Marrakech showed little enthusiasm for 17th-century ruler and builder Moulay Ismaïl, he was to turn Meknès, strategically situated at the heart of Morocco, into his capital, embarking on a massive building programme. Meknès was known as well as a city of minarets – gentle green or grey in colour, the tall, angular, linear minarets of Morocco. They dominate the old town, which with its cream colour-washed houses and terraces sits above the narrow valley of the Oued Boufekrane. There are pleasant souks, a medersa - *and above all, an easy pace, almost relaxing after the tension and press of Fès. The most famous monument is the great Bab Mansour El Aleuj, once upon a time the great gate to a palace complex worthy of the* Thousand and One Nights. *Little is left except for vast pisé walls. Meknès also offers some rewarding side trips – to the Roman site of Volubilis, and to the pilgrimage centre of Moulay Idriss.*

Ins and outs

Getting there
See Transport, page 237, for further details

Meknès has direct rail links from Casablanca and Rabat (8 daily) and Fès, and plenty of buses and grands taxis to other destinations. There are 2 rail stations in Meknès, see below. If coming by car from Rabat, you will travel on the P1, a stretch of road which sees some pretty dangerous driving as people try to cut minutes off their journey time to the capital. The autoroute linking Rabat and Fès to Meknès is not much safer either, although it has relieved congestion on the P1. Sample bus journey times to Meknès are around 5 hrs from Rabat, 7 hrs from Tanger and 9 hrs from Marrakech, calling at Beni-Mellal – 1 daily bus only. The landscape on this journey is rather dull in the early stages. If driving up from Marrakech, however, you have some beautiful views on the Azrou to Meknès route (the P21), with the Belvédère d'Ito, or you can turn onto the S209/S3331, which will take you from Mrirt through fine landscapes to join the P21 north of El Hajeb.

Getting around

Meknès is a fairly spread out sort of place. There are 2 train stations, Gare El Emir Abdelkader (closest to the *ville nouvelle* hotels) and the main station. The médina, along with the ruined palace complexes of the 17th century, is situated across the valley of the Oued Boufekrane, a good kilometre walk away. The new bus station (private buses), however, is at Beb El Khemis, on the far side of the médina from the *ville nouvelle*. The old *CTM* bus station is on Av Mohammed V in the *ville nouvelle*, and some grands taxis leave from nearby on ave des FAR.

The 'golden age' of Moulay Ismaïl

Moulay Ismaïl became sultan in 1672 as head of the Alaouite Dynasty. His reign is associated with a period of great stability and city building, especially at Meknès, which was his chosen capital. Old sites were cleared so that a new kasbah, stores and gardens could be constructed at Meknès. The military zone of the town was extended to accommodate an army numbering more than 150,000 men. His empire was extensive and no less than 76 garrisons were set up to defend the sultan's interests. He enforced a strong central rule on the country, overwhelming the regional tribal leaders. He was also notably successful against the Europeans, pushing the British out of Tanger in 1674 and the Portuguese from Asilah in 1691.

Moulay Ismaïl is remembered for his authoritarian rule. He permitted no opposition, putting down any possible source of political challenge ruthlessly. Indeed he is known as much for his cruelty as his tremendous effort at building roads, dams and cities. He also failed to train and introduce a successor to take over after his 53 years of absolute rule. His death was followed by a struggle for the succession during which the country declined into anarchy. For those who wish to see the architectural achievements of Moulay Ismaïl, go no further than the imperial city in Meknès, where the gates and palaces give a sample of the grand status of the Sultan Ismaïl.

When visiting Meknès in summer, it can get hot, and the distances between the different parts of the 17th-century palace city are considerable. You may need a full day, most of a morning for the palace complex. In half a day, you could do the médina very nicely.

Tourist information

Office du Tourisme (ONMT), 27 Pl Batha-l'Istiqlal, T521286. Very helpful.

Background

Coming up to Meknès by road from Rabat, you get a good idea of why Moulay Ismaïl chose the town as his capital. The P1 passes through the Mamora Forest and a belt of fertile, relatively prosperous countryside. The only major town en route is Khemisset (with a reputation for the fine *brochettes* in the small restaurants along the main street).

Meknès is a striking town, a fact accentuated by the distant views of the Jbel Zerhoun, rising over 1,000 m to the north. The wooded foothills and orchards of olives, apples and pears below provide a green background to the city for much of the year. Meknès is one of the great historic cities of Morocco, pre-eminent during the reign of 17th-century Sultan Moulay Ismaïl when its vast, and now mostly ruined, imperial city was built. This is memorable more for the impressive size and feeling of space than for the architecture. Another distinct part of Meknès is the historic médina which includes the intricately decorated **Medersa Bou Inania**, vibrant souks, the **Dar Jamaï** palace museum and numerous mosques. The cream-washed walls and daily life of the residential areas just behind rue Dar Smen still carry a 'Morocco that was' feel. (But how could things be otherwise when neighbourhoods have names like Koubbat es Souk, 'Dome of the Souk' and Kaâ el Ouarda, 'Bottom of the rose'.) To the east of the médina, on the opposite bank of the Oued Boufekrane, there stands the early 20th-century *ville nouvelle*. Carefully laid out by planner Henri Prost, the new town commands impressive (and as yet unspoiled) views over both médina and the imperial city. It has a relaxed atmosphere, a calm place to drink a coffee or tea and watch the evening *promenade*.

Early origins Meknès was originally a kasbah from the eighth century, used by the Kharajite Berbers against the Arabs. The town itself was founded by the Zenata Amazigh tribe called Meknassa in the 10th century and then destroyed by the Almoravids in 1069. A later kasbah was destroyed by the Almohad Sultan Abd El Moumen in order to build a new grid-patterned médina, some features of which still remain. This city was ruined during the conflict between the Almohads and the Merinids, but was partially rebuilt and repopulated in 1276 under Sultan Moulay Youssef. A fine *medersa* was built under the Merinids as they sought to expand Sunni orthodoxy to reduce the influence of Soufi leaders.

The reign of Moulay Ismaïl The reign of the Alaouite sultan, Moulay Ismaïl (1672-1727), saw Meknès raised to the status of imperial capital. Even before his succession to the imperial throne, Moulay Ismaïl developed the city. Meknès was chosen as his capital rather than the rebellious and self-important rivals of Fès and Marrakech. Moulay Ismaïl is renowned for his ruthless violence, but many of the stories recounted by the

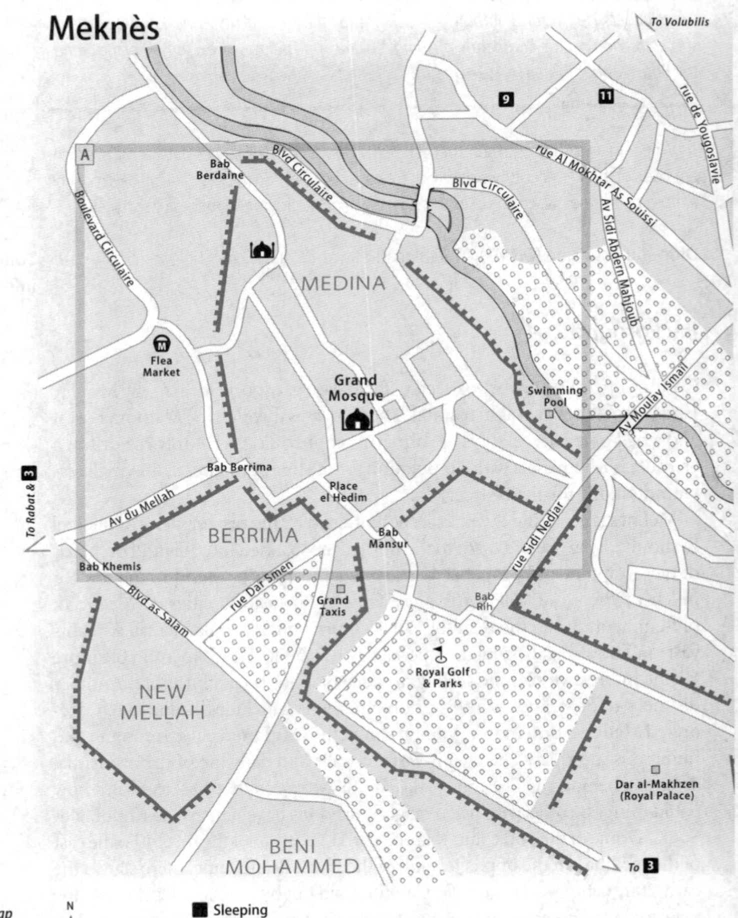

Detail map A Meknès Medina, page 231

Sleeping

1 Akouas
2 Bab Mansour
3 Camping
3 de Nice
4 Excelsior
5 Majestic
6 Rif
7 Touring
8 Transatlantique

guides may be apocryphal. What is certain is that he made an impression on European visitors to the court. Meknès was described as a Moroccan Versailles. Indeed, some suggest that the sultan was trying to rival Louis XIV, then involved in building his palace complex outside Paris. Having conquered Morocco, Moulay Ismaïl left his mark all over the country. Kasbahs were built by his troops as they pacified the tribes, cities acquired mosques and public buildings.

Moulay Ismaïl's vision of Meknès was vast, and although much of the pisé and rubble walls are in ruins, those still standing are testimony to its original scale. The city was built by a massive army of slaves, both Muslim and Christian, and the sultan was in particular famed for his barbaric treatment of these people, supposedly having them buried in the walls. He built several palaces to accommodate his wives, concubines, children and court, as well as quarters for his army the Abid Bukhari, an élite praetorian guard of black slaves, the chief instrument of his power. The city contained within it all that was necessary for such a large military machine, with store houses, stables, armouries, gardens and reservoirs.

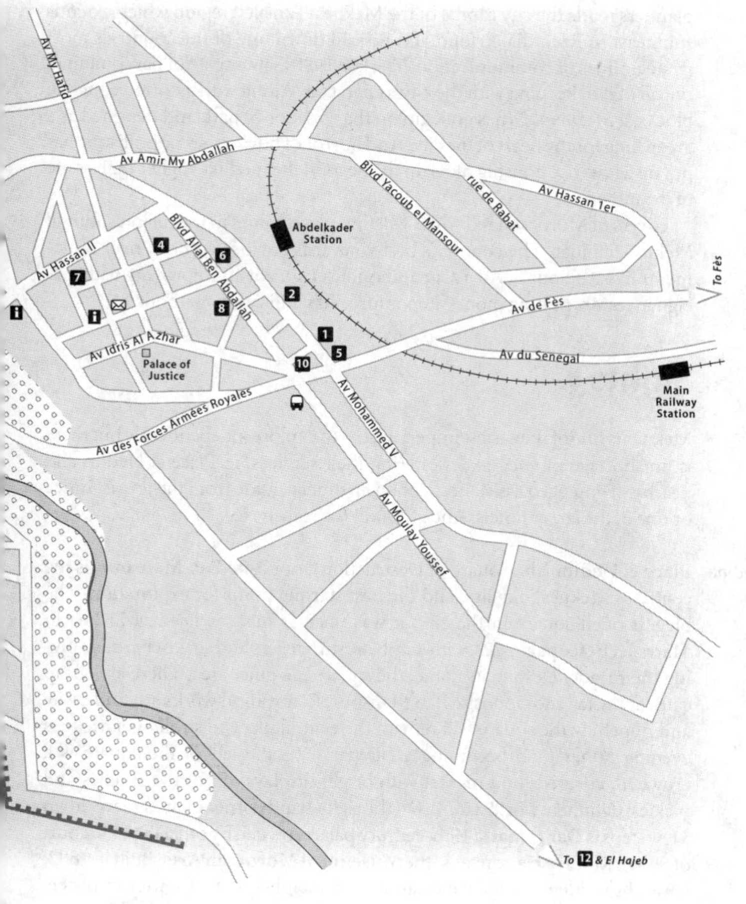

9 Volubilis
10 Youth Hostel
12 Zaki

After Moulay Ismaïl

After Moulay Ismaïl's death, Meknès gradually declined. His huge court and army could not be held together without his immense ego, and his successors Moulay Abdallah and Sidi Mohammed returned the emphasis to Fès and Marrakech. Furthermore, the earthquake of 1755 destroyed many of Moulay Ismaïl's creations. The French revitalized Meknès, appreciating its strategic position in the corridor linking eastern Morocco and Algeria with the coastal belt around Rabat and Casablanca. They built their *ville nouvelle* apart from the médina and the imperial city, on the east bank of the Oued Boufekrane, as part of their policy of separate development of Moroccan and European quarters. During the Protectorate, Meknès became the most important garrison town in Morocco, and continued as an important military town after independence.

Meknès today

Although Meknès is perhaps overshadowed by its near neighbour Fès, it is today the fifth largest city in Morocco with both tourism and industrial activities, and the centre of a highly productive agricultural region. After a period of relative stagnation, Meknès is re-emerging as an important town. National planners made the city capital of the Meknès-Tafilalelt region which extends southeast to Rachidia, Erfoud and Rissani down one of the country's most strategic lines of communication. The late 1990s saw a spate of new building, not all of it in keeping with the city's character. Along with assorted concrete blocks, a *McDonald*'s has gone up on the corridor of parkland designed as a green lung for the heart of the city. And horror of horrors, some philistine has put up a low-rise housing block in the heart of the médina, higher than some of the minarets.

Lovers of Moroccan red wines will find place names in the region south of Meknès familiar. The country's best vineyards are located here, near settlements like Aït Souala, Aït Yazm and Agouraï. Quality is improving with foreign investors putting money into improved vinification methods.

Sights

Meknès is one of the easiest imperial cities to explore independently but there is no shortage of *faux guides* offering their services, in Place el Hedim and nearby. If you need assistance, obtain an official guide from the tourist office or one of the larger hotels. About 100dh is a realistic fee.

Médina

Place el Hedim (the Square of Destruction), opposite **Bab Mansour**, is the centre of Meknès' old city, and the best starting point for exploration. The biggest open square in the city, it was once as busy as Djemaa El Fna in Marrakech (see page 322), with acrobats, storytellers and snake charmers plying their trade. Despite its name, the square is a quiet area. There are cheap cafés at the far end opposite Bab Mansour. Renovation works are underway and hopefully the square will remain the central place to stroll on a Meknès evening rather than becoming a car park. To the left of the square is a crowded, covered food market with bright displays of fresh vegetables and pickles; definitely worth a look. On the right-hand corner of the square down a few steps is **Dar Jamaï**, a 19th-century palace, owned by officials at the court of Sultan Moulay Hassan, now the **Museum of Moroccan Arts**. Built in 1882, it was the residence of the Jamaï family, two members of which were ministers to Moulay Hassan. It was used as a military hospital after 1912 and only in 1920 used to display Moroccan Art. Exploring the house gives one an insight into the lifestyle of the 19th-century Muslim élite. On display are wrought iron, carved wood, weaving, leather and metal work, and various antique household items. Look out for richly painted wooden chests and panels. Upstairs is a furnished reception room. The garden planted with cypress and fruit trees is a pleasant halt in the heat of the day. NB Closed for renovation work in early 2003. ■ *0900-1200, 1500-1800. 10dh. T055-530863.*

Souks

The médina of Meknès has seven traditional souks, which whilst not quite of the order of those in Marrakech or Fès, are worth exploring. Immediately to the left of the **Dar Jamaï** a small entrance leads to the souks. The alley bends around to the right behind Dar Jamaï past some undistinguished clothes shops. Just before a carpet shop turn left. The passage, now covered, widens slightly, and continues past a range of shops selling modern goods, a bank, and various minor side turnings. At the junction, on the left, is **Souk Nejjarine** (see below). **Souk Sebbat** is the right-hand turning including sellers of *baboushes*, modern clothes and kaftans, several tourist and handicraft shops, a *fondouk* on the right, and another on the left before the **Bou Inania Médersa**. A turning on the right opposite the *medersa* leads directly onto Rue Dar Smen, a good alternative route to remember.

Grand Mosque

Although non-Muslims are not permitted to enter the Grand Mosque, it is possible to view the green-tiled roof and the minaret from the neighbouring Médersa Bou Inania. The Grand Mosque, situated in the heart of the médina, is a 12th-century Almoravid foundation with 14th-century alterations. It is one of the oldest in Meknès and also the largest.

Meknès Médina

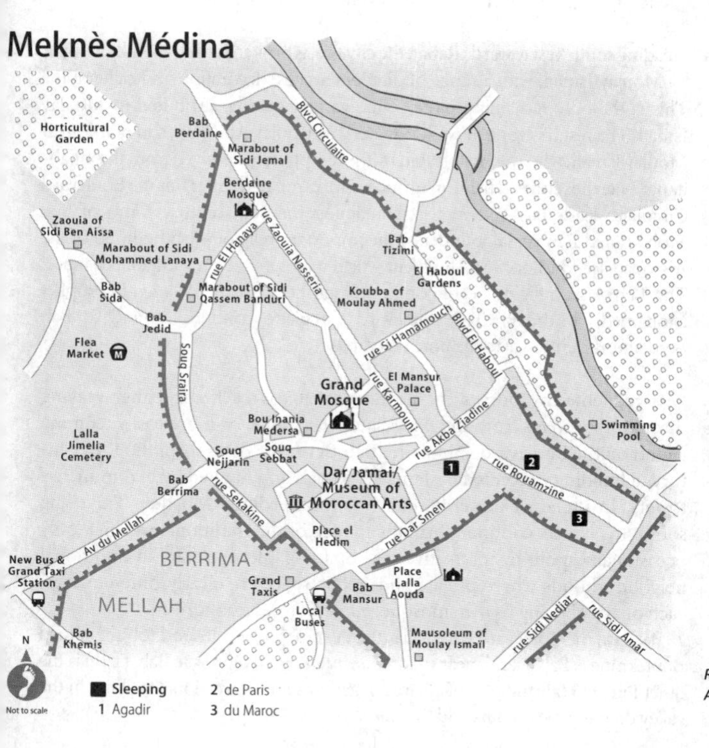

Related map
A Meknès, page 228

Medersa Bou Inania

Climb up onto the roof for a view of the médina, including the roofs of the Great Mosque, the minaret of the Nejjarine and other mosques

Founded circa 1345 by Merinid Sultan Abou El Hassan as a college dispensing religious and legal instruction, the Medersa Bou Inania is a must visit, best approached from Souk Sebbat. The door to the *medersa*, part of a cedar screen, is just under a dome (notable for its ribbed design) at an intersection in the *souk*. Altogether, the college had 40 cells for its students, on both floors, around an oblong courtyard including a pool, with arcades surrounded by a screened passageway. As with many of the *medersas*, there is eye-catching *zellige* tiling and carved wood lintels. Take a look at the green-and-yellow-tiled prayer hall. The doorway is ornamented with *zellige* tiling, as well as the customary and perhaps a little over-the-top stalactite-style plasterwork. ■ *0900-1200, 1500-1800.*

Souks

Souk Nejjarine includes sellers of textiles, and carpenters, another entrance to the carpet *souk*, and a *fondouk* hardly changed since it was built. This route passes the Almoravid **Nejjarine Mosque**. At the end one can turn left towards the *mellah* or Place el Hedim or right into the dusty and noisy **Souk Sraira**, just inside the city walls, used by carpenters and metalworkers. At the very end, on the left, is the 12th-century Almohad **Bab Jedid** gate, around which are some interesting stalls selling musical instruments. **Souk Cherchira**, initially occupied by tentmakers, runs parallel to Souk Sraira but outside the city walls.

Mellah

To the west of Place El Hedim, through a street popular with hawkers of household goods, turn left into Avenue de Mellah. On the left is the *mellah*, a quarter built by Moulay Ismaïl in 1682 for his large Jewish community, walled off from the Muslim médina. The **Bab Berrima Mosque** dates from the 18th century when the *mellah* was becoming increasingly Muslim. Few members of Meknès' once important Jewish community remain today.

Bab El Khemis

Heading southwest towards Rabat, the city wall is broken by Bab El Khemis, built by Moulay Ismaïl, with a range of different arches, decoration and calligraphy. This is the only remaining piece of the garden quarter attributed to Moulay Ismaïl. The rest has gone. It was destroyed by Moulay Abdallah, son of the great Moulay Ismaïl, who was not pleased by the reception he received from the inhabitants when he returned from an unsuccessful campaign. After this the Boulevard Circulaire leads past a cemetery containing the 18th-century tomb of Sidi Mohammed Ben Aissa, founder of the important religious brotherhood of the Aissoua, closed to non-Muslims but worth a look from a respectable distance. The Ben Aissa religious ceremonies are still held on the *Mouloud* (Prophet Mohamed's birthday). The Boulevard Circulaire continues round to Bab Berdaine, the entrance to the north médina.

Northern médina

Less frequented by tourists, the northern médina is reached by either weaving through the streets from the *medersa* or the souks, or more easily, coming round on the Boulevard Circulaire. **Bab Berdaine** dates from the 17th century, a building decorated by Jamaa el Rouah and flanked by two immense towers. Inside, on Place el Berdaine, is the **Berdaine Mosque**. Travelling south, the streets continue through an area of the traditional médina, only occasionally spoilt by insensitive new building. Here you are in traditional neighbourhoods where private and public space are clearly differentiated, each quarter having its own mosque, *hammam* and public oven.

Back on the Boulevard Circulaire, the next major gate around towards Oued Boufekrane is Bab Tizmi, near to *Restaurant Zitouna*. Opposite Bab Tizmi is the quiet **Parc el Haboul**, part of an area of gardens and recreational facilities in the valley dividing the médina and the *ville nouvelle*.

Bab Mansour

Claimed by some to be the finest gateway in North Africa

Meknès is dominated by the monumental gate at the top of the hill in the médina, opposite Place el Hedim. It dates from the reign of Sultan Moulay Ismaïl, and was completed by his son Moulay Mohammed Ben Abdallah in 1732, and marks the entrance to the huge grounds of his imperial city. The gate is named after one of the sultan's Christian slaves, Mansour the Infidel. The huge size is more of a testimony to its sultan than a reflection of defensive strength. The gate is clearly more about imperial splendour than anything else. The decorated flanking towers do not even have firing posts. The *outrepassé* arch is surrounded by a blind arch, including the usual lozenge network motif and *zellige* tiling. Between the arch and framing band is a black-tiled area with floral patterns. The overall effect of the main gate is exuberant and powerful. The gate has come to be a symbol of Meknès. During the Année du Maroc in France (1998), a canvas painted reproduction of the gate went up in the heart of Paris on Place de la Concorde.

Imperial city

The Imperial city of **Moulay Ismaïl** is a massive area of crumbling walls and ruins, well worth taking a day to explore at leisure. Immediately through Bab Mansour from Place el Hedim there is Place Lalla Aouda, once the public meeting point during the period of Moulay Ismaïl and now a relaxing and pleasant area to rest. In the far corner is the **Lalla Aouda Mosque**, the story being that it was built by Princess Aouda as penance for eating a peach during the Ramadan fast.

Directly opposite Bab Mansour, in the right-hand corner of the square, a space in the walls leads through to a second square, the Mechouar. To the right note the domed **Koubat al Khayyatine** situated in a small park behind a fence; a plain building with pleasing simple decor. In the 18th century this was used to receive ambassadors, and later to make uniforms. ■ *Tickets 10dh, on the left of the entrance to the building*. Koubat el Khayyatine translates as 'the tailors' dome'. Inside is a (temporary?) display of photos of old Meknès. Outside, right of the entrance, a flight of stairs leads down to dank and vaulted underground chambers, said by guides to be the prison of the Christian slaves, although why one should want to keep a workforce down here is anyone's guess.

In the wall opposite the small park the right-hand gate leads to a golf course. This was originally to have been a lake, but was converted into its present usage by the present king. Behind the golf course is a later palace of Moulay Ismaïl, the **Royal Palace** or **Dar al Makhzen**, still in use and now heavily restored, closed to visitors.

Mausoleum of Moulay Ismaïl

Unusually for religious buildings in Morocco, the mausoleum is open to non-Muslims, and there is an entrance fee (sometimes). Access is via the monumental entrance in the cream wall opposite an arcade of craft shops (stock-up on film here). The mausoleum contains the tombs of Moulay Ismaïl, his wife and Moulay Ahmed. Non-Muslim visitors can enter as far as an annex to the mosque section and admire from there the plaster stucco, *zellige* tiling and distinctive and exuberant colouring. The guardian normally allows visitors to take photos of the interior of the mosque from the annex.

Dar El Kebira

Just past the mausoleum is an entrance to **Dar el Kebira** ('the big house'), Moulay Ismaïl's late 17th-century palace. The palace is in ruins, but the nature of the original structure of the building can be discerned. Since the 18th century, houses have been built into the walls of the palace. Back out on the road pass under the passage of the **Bab ar Rih** ('Gate of the Winds'), a long, arched structure. Follow the walled road, running between the Dar el Kebira and the Dar al Makhzen and turn right at the end. Carry straight ahead through another arch and after around 200 m you reach another chunky *pisé* wall, the **Heri es Souani** building.

Heri es-Souani
Have a post-visit drink at the café in the nearby campsite

Close to the city campsite and a hefty 35-minute walk from the médina, Heri es Souani, also called **Dar el Ma** ('the Water Palace'), is a large, impressive structure dating from the reign of Moulay Ismaïl, used variously as granary, warehouse and water point, to provide for the court, army and followers in either the normal run of events or in case of conflict or drought. It is a good indication of the scale of Moulay Ismaïl's imperial ambitions. From the roof there would be a good view if one were allowed up. The nearby Agdal basin is now used for storing water for irrigation purposes. Once it was presumably a vital reserve in case of siege. Popular at weekends and summer evenings with strollers, the location is a little stark on a hot summer afternoon. ■ *0830-1200, 1430-1830.*

Outlying crumbling sights

For completeness sake, you may want to take in the **Heri al Mansour**, yet another large and crumbling ruin. Starting at Heri es Souani, turn right through the narrow arch, follow the road straight for 100 m, then go left onto the main road. On your left, you will see the **Dar al-Baida**, or White Palace, built by Sultan Mohammed Ben Abdallah in the 1790s, now a military academy closed to visitors. Here you turn right and eventually reach the low **Rouah Mosque** also built by Mohammed Ben Abdallah in 1790, using columns from the Badia Palace in Marrakech. (There is a small *medersa* used as a Koranic school.) Go left here along an avenue of low-rise apartment buildings and you will come to the the massive structure of the **Heri al Mansour**, also known as the **Rouah**, on your right. Struggle under the barbed wire barring the ground-floor entrance and scramble up onto the weed-grown first floor. There is nothing to tell you who inhabited this palatial structure or when it was abandoned. Beyond the walls, fields and new housing areas stretch into the distance.

Excursions

See also page 238 for Moulay Idriss and Volubilis

Agouraï, about 20 km south of Meknès, is in the foothills of the Zaiane Mountains. Many of the people have names more akin to Europe than to the Middle Atlas. As explanation, Moulay Ismaïl is said to have given this area to his Christian prisoners for services rendered. This is an important vine growing region producing some reasonable wines.

On the P21 south of Meknès, **El Hajeb** is a small town at the top of the scarp slope overlooking the Saïss Plain. In earlier times, it must have been pretty picturesque. There are the remains of a small kasbah and one or two minor bits of early 20th-century architecture.

Another minor excursion from Meknès, if you have lots of time, might be to the springs at **Jerri**, off the Rabat road, a grand taxi ride from the centre.

West of Meknès

Khémisset, halfway between Rabat and Meknès, is in the heart of the Zemmour region, a busy town in a region of olive groves and grain lands. From here you can travel north on the S205 to the **Barrage d'El Kansera** or southwest on the S106 to the popular inland resort of *Dayat er Roumi*, camping site of 1 ha, swimming in lake (depends on water level), electricity for caravans. If you need to stop over, there is the **C** *Hotel Diouri*, T055-552645, on the Meknès side of the town.

The P1 continues west to **Tiflèt**, an important local market town where Oulmès bottled water is produced. Here the spring comes from the banks of the Oued Aguennour at the bottom of a deep canyon. Access to the spring, a drop of 700 m, is by jeep along a road with hairpin bends and a precipitous drop. The area is wooded with ancient cork oaks. The bottling takes place some 7 km from the site. In recent years, the canyon bed has had little more than a trickle of water, making this a side trip for enthusiasts of deepest Morocco. The **C** *Hotel Les Thermes*, Oulmès Tarmilate, T037-552293, closed July-August, is a place to stay with rooms near the spring.

Essentials

Sleeping

Meknès is short on hotels in all categories. Mid-range hotels can get filled with tour groups. At peak times, especially spring holidays, try to book in advance or arrive early.

■ *on maps, pages 228 & 231*

Ville nouvelle
There are some very reasonably priced central hotels here

Some of the older hotels near the top end of Av Mohammed V and the Av des FAR, tend to be noisy as there are a number of bars here. **B** ***Hotel Transatlantique***, R el Meriniyine, T055-525051, F520057, transat@iam.net.ma, transatmeknes.com Central, 120 a/c rooms, 2 restaurants, bar, tennis, 2 good pools, credit cards. A fading, stylish 1930s hotel. Rooms in the old wing (*l'aile ancienne*) have balconies with view over gardens or the old town. The 60 rooms of the new wing, built in the 1960s, have been modernized. Largest rooms are Nos 14, 62 and 64. **C** ***Hotel Rif***, R d'Accra, *ville nouvelle*, T055-522591, F524428. 120 rooms, a/c, seriously tacky reception area, lively nightclub (2130-0300), 2 restaurants, good bar, pool, safe parking. Rooms over restaurant exit are noisy. Used by groups as most comfortable hotel near to old town. **C** ***Hotel Zaki***, Blvd Al Massira, on city outskirts, T055-520990. Modern, 230 a/c rooms, 2 restaurants, 2 bars, nightclub and pool. **D** ***Akouas Hotel***, 27 R Emir Abdelkader, T055-515967, F515994. New, 52 rooms, 2 restaurants, bar, nightclub (2200-0100). **D** ***Hotel Bab Mansour***, 38 R Emir Abdelkader, T055-525239, F510741. 76 rooms and 2 suites, new, all with carpets and TV, restaurant, bar, nightclub. **D** ***Hotel de Nice***, 10 R d'Accra, T055-520318. Restaurant, bar, central, safe parking, good rooms. **D** ***Hotel Palace***, 10 R de Ghana, T055-511260. Just opposite the side entrance to main post office. Has very clean, basic rooms, also rooms with bathrooms. No breakfast, noisy bar which does not however impinge on your sleep, safe parking for 10dh or park in street with warden. Recommended. **D** ***Hotel Volubilis***, 45 Av des FAR, T055-520102. Bar, nightclub, quite old, conveniently located. **E** ***Hotel Excelsior***, 57 Av des FAR, T055-521900. 42 rooms. **E** ***Hotel Majestic***, 19 Av Mohammed V, T055-522033, F527427. 42 clean rooms, excellent value, friendly staff. Recommended. The buts? Rooms on street are on noisy side, inner rooms are quieter but smaller. **E** ***Hotel Touring***, 34 Av Allal Ben Abdallah, T055-522351. Cheap, respectable, large rooms, café.

Médina

There are now 2 guesthouses in the Dar Lakbira area. **A-B** ***Le Riad***, 79 Ksar Chaacha, T055-530542, F531320, riad@iam.net.ma Run by a former tour guide, 6 suites each decorated to a theme (Sherazade, Ali Baba, Berber, etc). The building is in fact modern. Though heavily decorated, the rooms have no views and the courtyard is used as a restaurant. Overpriced. Same management is opening a further guesthouse, *Riad Didi*, in the same neighbourhood. The cheap médina hotels are located on the R Rouamzine, which runs up from Bab Bou Ameir, the entrance point for the old town as you come from the *ville nouvelle*. The first major left at the top is the busy R Dar Smen, also with cheap hotels, which takes you along to Bab Mansour (on the right) and the Pl el Hédim. **F** ***Hotel Agadir***, 2 R Dar Smen (on the small square), T055-530141. 18 tiny, basic rooms in a bizarre, distinctively decorated rabbit warren. **F** ***Hotel du Maroc***, 7 Derb Ben Brahim, off R Rouamzine, T055-530075. The best cheap hotel, 28 rooms, quiet, clean and efficient, cold showers. **F** ***Hotel Nouveau***, 65 R Dar Smen (on the small square), T055-533139. Handily located opposite the *Banque Populaire*. **F** ***Hotel de Paris***, 58 R Rouamzine, above *La Comtesse de Paris salon de thé*. 11 good rooms but no showers. Arrive early as soon fills up.

Out of the city **C-D** *Ranch du Tijania*, 8 km out of Meknès at Aït Berzouine, down a road right off the El Hajeb road, T067-820373 (mob), T061-359245 (mob). Accommodation and riding.

Camping *Camping Agdal*, 2 km out of Meknès centre, opposite the Heri es Souani, T055-551828. Take buses 2 or 3, or better, a petit taxi. The 4-ha site with shop, café, laundry, electricity for caravans, and hot showers, clean and well organized, petrol only 2 km. Some rooms soon available, alcohol – a bit noisy near the café area, piped music. Lots of shade. *Camping Belle-Vue*, on the road to Moulay Idriss some 15 km north, T068-490899. Site of 3 ha, 60dh 2 people with car and tent, small shop, showers, laundry, electricity for caravans, petrol 100 m. Loo blocks could do with some maintenance.

Youth hostel Av Okba Ibn Nafii, near the municipal stadium and *Hotel Transatlantique*, 1000-1200, 1600-1700, T055-524698. This is the **YHA headquarters** in Morocco and is one of the best and most friendly hostels with dormitories around a garden. Well maintained, 60 beds, 25-35dh per night, kitchen, meals available, bus 25 m, train 1,200 m.

Eating

Ville nouvelle **Expensive** *Restaurant Belle Vue*, in *Hotel Transatlantique*, R El Marinyen, T055-525051. Extensive international menu, good wines, excellent views over Meknès médina from its hilltop location. ***La Hacienda***, Route de Fès outside Meknès, T055-521092. French and international food in a farm atmosphere, nightclub below. Recommended. ***Palais Terrab***, 18 Av Zerktouni, T055-521456. Two fairly heavy menus served in Moroccan decor. Much used by groups.

Mid-range *Restaurant Bar Brasserie Metropole*, 12 Av Hassan II, on the corner near the Central (food) Market, T055-522576. Brochettes and chicken, licensed. ***Bar Restaurant La Coupole***, Av Hassan II, down the street from the *Hotel Palace*, T055-522483. French/Moroccan menu, plush interior, reasonable food, over-elaborate service, licensed, upmarket bar next door. ***Café Restaurant Gambrinus***, Av Omar Ibn el Ass, opposite the market, off Av Hassan II, T055-520258. French, Spanish and Moroccan cuisine, kindly service, just lacks alcohol. Interesting wall murals – a bit of a survival. ***Le Dauphin***, 5 Av Mohammed V, T055-523423. Licensed Moroccan restaurant, seafood. ***Pizzeria Le Four***, 1 R Atlas, T055-520857. Reasonable international cuisine and truly terrible pizzas, alcohol. Interesting mix of tour groups, local businessmen entertaining their women friends, independent travellers, and local students.

Cheap Try ***Rôtisserie Karam***, 2 Av Ghana. Good chicken, brochettes and salads. ***Novelty***, Av de Paris, T055-522156. Moroccan food, licensed. On Av Mohammed V, uphill from the *Hotel Majestic*, opposite the *BCM*, are a couple of cheap and cheerful roast chicken eateries, the ***Coq Magique*** and the ***Restaurant Sana***. Up on the Av des FAR, under the *Hotel Excelsior*, are more barbecue-type places. Same area also has lots of bar-eateries indicated by Flag Spécial signs.

Médina

Meknès has a small but growing range of Moroccan restaurants catering mainly to tour groups

Expensive *Restaurant Zitouna*, 44 Jamaa Zitouna, T055-532083. In the style of a Moroccan palace in a médina side street near Bab Tizmi, Moroccan menu, no alcohol. **Mid-range** *Restaurant Collier de la Colombe*, 67 R Driba, T055-525041, F556599. Housed in a fine 19th-century city residence, a short walk off Pl Lalla Aouda in the médina. Moroccan food for tour groups during the day. Interior is all very peach, good views over to the *ville nouvelle*. Fine. ***Le Riad***, 79 Ksar Cha'acha, Dar Lakbira, T055-530542, riad@iam.net.ma. Cheapest menu at 120dh. Small médina house transformed into restaurant. Dining either on patio or inside. No booze. Can get very crowded with tour groups. **Cheap** For a bowl of pessara soup or a brochette, there are a couple of places on the left, under the arcades on Pl el Hédim, as you stand with Bab Mansour behind you. Otherwise, there are places on R Dar Smen, including ***Restaurant Economique***, perhaps the best. Will do omelettes for vegetarians.

Cafés

Meknès produces the best mint in Morocco, so go for mint tea here. Try one of the noisy cafés on R Dar Smen. The picturesque roof-terrace café, ***Sari as-Souani***, at the great reflecting pool has been closed for years 'for security reasons', which is a real shame. In the *ville nouvelle* try ***Crémerie-Pâtisserie Miami***, Av Mohammed V.

Bars & clubs

Hotel Transatlantique, R el Marinyen. An excellent place for a relaxing drink, not least because of the view over the médina. Also try the ***Hotel de Nice***, 10 R d'Accra; ***La Caravelle***, 6 R de Marseille; ***Bar Continental*** and ***La Coupole***, both in Av Hassan II. Nothing very exciting here in the ways of nightclubs – after all, this is a rather conservative, small Moroccan city. Nice local girls do not go out clubbing. The rumbustious bars are at the top of Av Mohammed V. Try ***Bahia***, *Hotel Rif*, R d'Accra (2130-0300). ***Le Diamant bleu*** (they're always called the diamant something or other) in ***Hotel Akouas***, 27 R Emir Abdelkader (2200-0100) and ***Hotel Bab Mansour***, 38 R Emir Abdelkader. Loud local music bands and lots of smoke. Also ***Cabaret Oriental***, *Grand-Hotel Volubilis*, 45 Av des Forces Armées Royales. You could also try ***Hotel Zaki*** (see Sleeping), out of town centre.

Entertainment

Cultural centres *Institut français*, zankat Farhat Hachad, Av Hassan II, T055-524071. Organizes lectures and films, hosts occasional concerts and plays. Closed mid-Jul to early Sep. A bright note in Meknès' rather sleepy cultural life.

Shopping

A Meknès speciality is iron work decorated with beaten silver thread, or *metal damasquiné*. For this and other specialities try the médina.

Sport and activities

Golf *Royal Golf Club*, El Mhancha, T055-530753. 9 holes, 2,707 m, par 36, fee per round 200dh, closed Mon. **Hammam** *Hammam des Jardins*, aka ***Hammam Maha***, very handy for the *ville nouvelle*. Heading towards the médina on Av Hassan II, take a right between *BCM* and *Agora salon de thé*. After 25 m, drop left down some steps, then go right. Hammam, separate entrances for men and women, overlooks a semi-abandoned small park. Try also ***Hammam Sidi Omar Bou Aouada***, turn right as you face Dar Jamaï museum on Pl Hedim, baths on your right about 25 m further on, unmarked. **Riding** *L'Etrier* (Haras Régional), on the El Hajeb road, 8 km from Meknès at Aït Berzouine. A piece of the countryside in the urban sprawl. ***Ranch du Tijania***, T067-820373 (mob) or T061-359245 (mob). Riding ring and hacking. Horse lovers may want to call in at the Meknès stud farm or *haras*, open 0900-1100 and 1500-1700, on the Azrou road. **Swimming** 2 pools in Meknès, in the Oued Boufekrane Valley: ***Lahboul Park***, rond-point Bou Amer, BP 45, T055-520415; there is another more expensive pool further on up the valley. **Tennis** *Club de Meknès*, Parc Lahboul, rond-point Bou Amer, BP 45, T055-520415.

Transport

Local

Bus: buses No 5, 7 and 9 run between the *ville nouvelle* and the médina. **Car hire**: *Stop Car*, 3 R Essaouira, T055-525061. ***Zeit***, 4 R Antsirebe, T055-525918. **Taxi**: use the light blue petits taxis to speed up the hop between *ville nouvelle* and médina.

Long distance **Bus** *CTM* buses to **Rabat**, **Casablanca** and **Fès** (7 a day), **Tanger**, **Ifrane, Azrou**, **Ouezzane** and **Er Rachidia** (daily) leave from 47 Av Mohammed V, T055-522583/4. Private line services go from the terminal below Bab Mansour.

Taxi Grands taxis, which are a particularly good option to both **Fès** and **Azrou**, leave from the car park below Pl el Hédim, opposite the private line buses. Ask the drivers hanging around for the destination. Grands taxis for **Moulay Idriss** (and then a short walk to **Volubilis**) leave from near the *Shell* station on your right as Av Hassan II descends. Negotiations over prices can be long and painful, with various people hanging around to act as intermediaries and take their cut. See also the taxi rank near the Palais de la Foire.

Train The main station is some way from the centre, T055-520017/520689. Regular departures for **Rabat** and **Casablanca**, for **Tanger** with a change at Sidi Kacem, and eastwards for **Fès**, **Taza** and **Oujda**. **NB** If you are going to stay in *ville nouvelle*, get off at the Meknès Amir Abdelkader station, the first of the 2 Meknès stations as you come from Casa/Rabat. This station is just below Av Mohammed V, and closer to the centre of the *ville nouvelle* than the other main station.

Directory

Airline offices *Royal Air Maroc*, 7 Av Mohammed V, T055-520963/523606. Closest airport is at Fès. **Banks** *Banque du Maroc*, 33 Av Mohammed V. *BMAO*, 15 Pl 2 Septembre. *BMCE*, 98 Av des Forces Armées Royales, T055-520352. Bureau de change open daily 1000-1400, 1600-2000. ***Credit du Maroc***, 33 Av Mohammed V. *SGMB*, Pl Al Wahda Al Ifriquia, T055-527896. ***Wafa Bank***, 11 Av Mohammed V, T055-521151. As usual, the most useful. **Communications** *PTT Centrale*, Pl Administrative, 0800-1400, T0800-2100. Also the *PTT* on R Dar Smen, in the médina. Medical services **Chemists**: ***Pharmacie d'Urgence***, Pl Administrative, T055-523375, 0830-2030. ***Depot de Nuit: Medicaments d'Urgence***, *Hotel de Ville*, Pl Administrative, 2030-0830. **Hospitals:** ***Hôpital Mohammed V***, T055-521134. ***Hôpital Moulay Ismaïl***, Av des FAR, T055-522805. Probably the best of the bunch is ***Polyclinique Cornette-de-St-Cyr***, at 22, Esplanade du Docteur Giguet, T055-520262. **Useful addresses** **Emergency**: Ambulance, T15. Fire, T15. Police, T19.

Moulay Idriss and Volubilis

Phone code: 055
Colour map 1, grid B3

The shrine town of Moulay Idriss and the Roman ruins at Volubilis are an easy day trip from Meknès, although there is a hotel at Volubilis for those who want to stay over and get a really early start, a good idea in summer when the heat can be oppressive. Volubilis, set in open fields, is a delight in spring, with wild flowers abounding. The ruins cover over 40 ha, there is a noble forum and a triumphal arch to Caracalla. The ruins have poetic names – the House of Orpheus and the House of the Nymphs, the House of the Athlete and the House of the Ephèbe. There are ancient oil presses, too. The vanished splendour of Volubilis is echoed by legendary evocations of early Islam at Moulay Idriss nearby. This most venerable pilgrimage centre, set between steep hillsides, was founded in the eighth century by one Idriss Ibn Abdallah, great-grandson of Ali and Fatima, the Prophet Mohammed's daughter. Today he is referred to as Idriss El Akbar, 'the Great'. His son, Idriss II, is buried and venerated in Fès.

Ins & outs The shrine town of Moulay Idriss is 30 km north of Meknès, Volubilis a little further north. For Moulay Idriss, take a grand taxi from R de Yougoslavie, or from the square below Pl el Hédim (a 10dh ride). There are also regular buses from below Bab Mansour. The last bus back is at 1900. Volubilis is a clearly signposted 5-km drive from Moulay

Idriss, a pleasant walk on a nice day, or a short taxi ride. Alternatively, for Volubilis bargain in Meknès for a grand taxi all the way (split cost with others, say 50dh the trip), or take a bus for Ouezzane and get dropped off near the site. If travelling by car, leave Meknès by R de Yougoslavie in the *ville nouvelle*, and follow the P6 as far as Aïn el Kerma, and from there the P28 to Moulay Idriss.

Moulay Idriss

Coming round the last bend from Meknès, Moulay Idriss is a dramatic sight, houses and mosques piled up around two rock outcrops, with the *zaouia*, or sanctuary, in between. The centre of the Jbel Zerhoun region, Moulay Idriss is a pilgrimage centre, including as it does the tomb of its namesake, Idriss Ben Abdallah Ben Hassan Ben Ali, the great-great-grandson of the prophet Mohammed. The town is a Mecca in Morocco for those unable to do the ultimate pilgrimage. Moulay Idriss came to Morocco from Arabia, after defeat at the Battle of Fakh in 786. In 788 he was accepted as *Imam* by the Amazigh Aurora tribe at Volubilis, and continued the rest of his life in Morocco, before he was poisoned in 791, to win over the loyalty of the tribes to the Idrissid Dynasty he established, and to spread the faith of Islam. This town and Fès were two of his major legacies.

However, the town of Moulay Idriss was mainly developed in the 18th century by Sultan Moulay Ismaïl, in part using materials lifted from nearby Volubilis, which the sultan plundered without restraint. Moulay Idriss was closed to non-Muslims until 1912, and even today is primarily a Muslim sanctuary, best visited during the day as an excursion, and although not unfriendly, certainly a place to be treated with cautious respect. A religious festival, or *moussem*, is held here in August, when the town is transformed by an influx of pilgrims and a sea of tents.

Buses and taxis stop in the main square where there are some basic restaurants and cafés. Above it is the **Zaouia of Moulay Idriss**, as well as shops for various souvenir items associated with pilgrimage: rosaries, scarves, candles, and a delicious array of nougats, candies and nuts. The sanctuary itself, with its green-tiled roofs, a succession of prayer halls, ablution areas and tombs, is closed to non-Muslims.

Looking up from the square, the médina clings to the two hills, on the left is Khiba, while Tasga is on the right. Steep paths climb through the residential areas. After the climb there is a rewarding view over the sanctuary, showing the courtyards and roofs, and the adjacent royal guesthouse. The road through the town, keeping right, leads to a Roman bath just above the stream. Further on, beyond the road, there is a ruined 18th-century palace with a good view of the town.

Sleeping & eating

Only 1 (expensive) option for sleeping in this area, **B** ***Volubilis Inn***, T055-544405/08, F544369. 52 rooms, 4 suites, 2 restaurants, pool, terrace, excellent views, just to the north of the archaeological site of Volubilis. Decor cheap and tacky, but the location saves the day. Owner also has a riad in Fès. For **camping**, try ***Zerhoune Belle Vue***, en route to Meknès. Also, opposite the turning to Volubilis, the proprietor of the café allows people to camp.

Volubilis

By far the most impressive Roman site in Morocco

Although nowhere near as splendid as the Roman cities further east in North Africa, Volubilis merits a visit. While much has been removed to adorn other cities over the centuries, or taken to museums such as the one in Rabat, the structure of the town, and the design of the buildings are clearly discernible from the ruins. Some floor mosaics are still intact. Situated below the Jbel

Zerhoun and 5 km from Moulay Idriss along the P28, the site is signed from the road, has free parking, a café and ticket office but little else. It can be viewed in a day trip. In summer start early to avoid the heat. On the way in, note the collection of mosaics and sculptures, an 'open-air museum'. ■ *0800 to sunset. 20dh.*

Background

Cinema buffs will recognize that the site was used in the filming of Martin Scorsese's The Last Temptation of Christ

Archaeological evidence points to the possibility of a Neolithic settlement at Volubilis, whilst tablets found show there was a third-century BC Phoenician settlement. In AD 24 it was the Western capital of the Roman kingdom of Mauretania, and from AD 45 to 285 the capital of the Roman province of Mauretania Tingitana. Under the Romans the immediate region prospered from producing olive oil. However, as Volubilis was at the southeastern extremity of the province, connected to Rome through the Atlantic ports, its weak position necessitated extensive city walls.

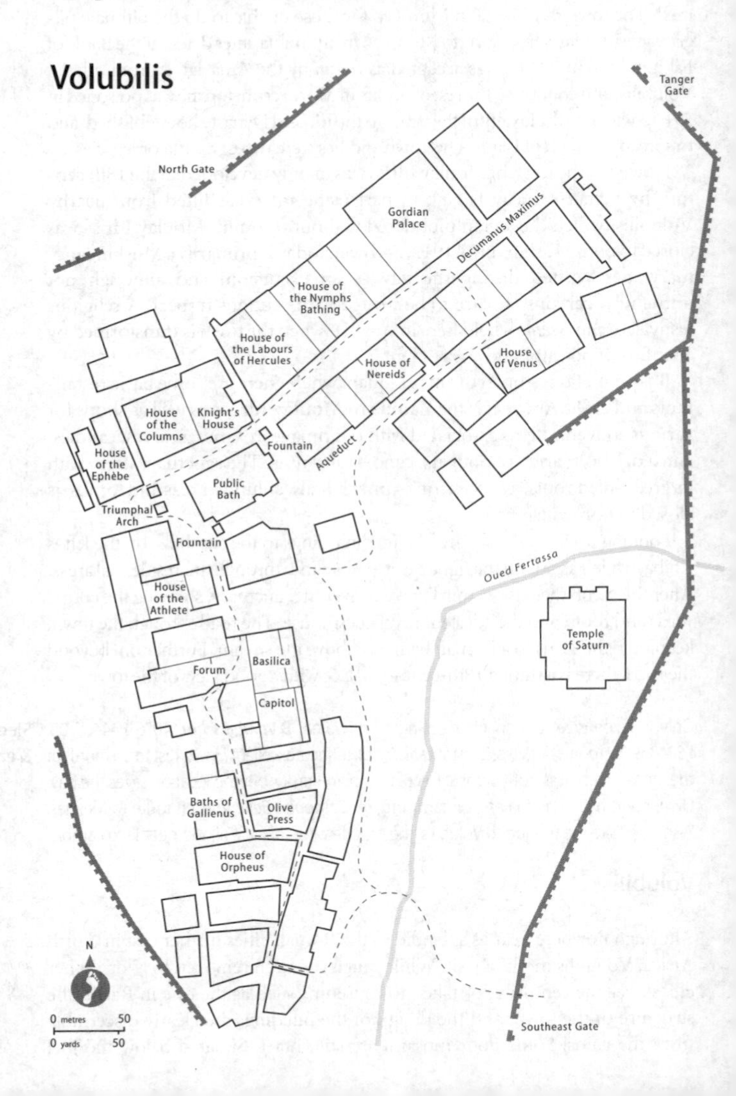

Under the Emperor Diocletian, Rome withdrew to the coastal areas, leaving Volubilis at the mercy of neighbouring tribes.The city survived and its Christian and Jewish population survived with diminished importance, becoming the Christian enclave of Oualila during the eighth century. Though proclaimed sultan in Volubilis, Moulay Idriss preferred Fès. By the 11th century, Volubilis was totally deserted. It suffered again when Moulay Ismaïl ransacked the ruins to build Meknès, and further in the earthquake of 1755. French excavations and reconstruction began in 1915. The metal tracks on the site date from this period.

The site

From the ticket office the entrance to the city is by the southeastern gate. A path, with sculptures and tombstones alongside it, leads down to a bridge across the Oued Fetassa. Up on the other side the first important remains in an area of small houses and industrial units is of an **olive press** complex. The mill stones, for crushing the olives, and the tanks for collecting and separating the oil, can be seen. Olive presses can be found through much of the city, as olive oil production was an essential element in its economy, as it is in the area today, where many of the same techniques are still used.

House of Orpheus

Right of the olive press is the House of Orpheus, a large mansion. In this building, as in most, some areas will be clearly roped off, and it is advisable to respect this, to avoid the whistle and wrath of the otherwise very friendly guardian. The first entrance gives access to a room with an intricate dolphin mosaic, to a kitchen with a niche for religious figures, and to a paved bathroom and boiler room. Note the complex heating system. The second entrance leads to an open court with a mosaic of the goddess Amphitrite, with living rooms around, including a dining room with an Orpheus mosaic, showing the hero playing his harp.

Some public buildings

Roman imperial settlements, even the most provincial, had impressive arrays of public buildings to cement a general feeling of Romanity. This was architecture as identity, and Volubilis was no exception. Heading further down into the site, and then to the right, lie the **Baths of Gallienus**, public baths which are the distant ancestor of the Moroccan *hammam*. Beyond this, the large public square in front of the Basilica is the **Forum**. In this area are a number of monuments to leading Roman figures. The **Basilica** is one of the most impressive ruins, with a number of columns intact. This third-century building was the court house for the city.

Beside the Basilica is the **Capitol**, also with columns. In the court in front there is an altar, and steps leading up to the temple. This temple is dedicated to Juno, Minerva and Jupiter Optimus Maximus. This building had great state importance, being the place where the council would assemble on great occasions.

House of the Athlete

Adjacent to the Forum is the **House of the Athlete**, named after the mosaic of an athlete winning a cup. The **Triumphal Arch** dominates the skyline, as well as the **Decumanus Maximus**, the roadway leading to the Tanger Gate. This was built in AD 217 to honour Emperor Caracalla and his mother Julia Domna. Originally finished with fountains, and medallions, the arch was heavily reconstructed by French archaeologists. Although not of the same finesse as the honorary arches surviving in the Roman cities of Tunisia and Libya, it is nevertheless impressive.The **Decumanus Maximus**, the main street, had a colonnade with small shops, in front of a series of large houses, some containing interesting mosaics.

Starting on the left, from just beside the **Triumphal Arch**, the **House of the Ephèbe** was built around a courtyard with a pool. The house is named after the bronze statue of a beautiful boy or *ephebos* found in the ruins. Adjacent is the **House of Columns** and then the **Knight's House** which has an interesting mosaic of Bacchus, good-time god of wine. In a more serious taste, the **House of the Labours of Hercules** has a mosaic with individual pictures of Hercules' life, and another of Jupiter. Further up, the **House of the Nymphs Bathing** has a mosaic showing nymphs undressing. The largest house on this side, the **Gordian Palace**, is fronted by columns, but the remains are quite plain. This may have been the governor's residence from the time of Gordian III, with both domestic quarters and offices.

On the right hand side of Decumanus Maximus from the Triumphal Arch there is a large public bath and fountains, fed by an aqueduct. Three houses up is the **House of Nereids** with a pool mosaic. Behind this and one up is the **House of Venus**, which has one of the best array of mosaics. The central courtyard pool has a mosaic of chariots. There are also mosaics of Bacchus, on the left, and Hylos and two nymphs, on the right. Nearby is a mosaic of Diana and the horned Actaeon. From the House of Venus cross back over the Oued Fetassa to the remains of the **Temple of Saturn**, a Phoenician temple before the Romans took it over. From here, follow the path back to the entrance, perhaps for refreshments in the café after the labours in Volubilis.

The Middle Atlas

Based in Fès or Meknès, there are a number of interesting towns to visit in the Middle Atlas, possible stopovers to break a journey south to Marrakech, places to escape the summer heat in the imperial cities and do some walking in hills and cedar forests. If you already know more major sites and towns in Morocco well, you may want to do a full circuit to take in some of the Middle Atlas towns. In a week you could comfortably combine visiting Fès and Meknès (plus Volubilis and Moulay Idriss) with a circuit southwards which might include overnights in Azrou, and then Ifrane or possibly Sefrou or Immouzer du Kandar. A loop southwest of Azrou would take you down to Khénifra and back up via the Aguelmane Azigza and the source of the Oum er Rbia, Morocco's largest river which flows into the Atlantic at Azzemour.

Azrou

Phone code: 055
Colour map 1, grid B2
70 km S of Meknès

Azrou is a small Amazigh market town and hill resort at the heart of the Middle Atlas. The word 'azrou' means rock in Tamazight, and at the middle of the town next to the large new mosque is the rock which gives the settlement its name. The town has a relaxed air and good hiking in the wooded vicinity. The ruined kasbah was built by Moulay Ismaïl.

Ins & outs

There are plenty of buses from Meknès and Fès to Azrou, which is situated at a crossroads of routes leading up from Marrakech (via Beni Mellal and Khénifra) and Er Rachidia (via Midelt). Coming from Marrakech, you will have to change at Beni Mellal if you don't get a direct bus. All buses, except those of *CTM*, arrive at the bus station opposite the Grand Mosque. The grand taxi station is close by, near the roundabout. Grands taxis for Khénifra are close to the rock. Azrou is a one-horse sort of place, so no difficulties getting around.

Background

One of Azrou's claims to fame is that under the French Protectorate, it was chosen to be home to the **Collège berbère**, a training school for Moroccan Berbers which was founded on the premise that Arabs and Imazighen were fundamentally different – and should be educated and ruled as such. The divide and rule policy backfired – it was in the interests of neither Arabs nor Imazighen for a colonial regime to continue to control Morocco, and both were Muslims; in any case, loyalty to Islam and the Alaouite throne proved to be stronger than ethnic ties, a fact which somehow escaped French colonial ethnographers. After Independence, the Collège berbère became the Lycée Tarik ibn Zayid, symbolically named for the Arab conqueror of Andalucía. In the late 1990s, Amazigh cultural movements began demanding more official recognition of their cultural identity. How Morocco handles its large Amazigh minorities will be interesting to watch in coming years.

Sights

Azrou's traditional character, once created by the green-tiled roofs of the arcades round the market square, has taken a beating. Although Azrou has a few good hotels and is ideally located as a base for exploring the cedar forests, it has yet to find its place in the tourist market. It seems to function as a sort of suburb to its more upmarket neighbour Ifrane.

The heart of Azrou, Place Mohammed V, is to the right on leaving the bus stop. There is a covered **market** near Place Mohammed V, while the *Ensemble Artisanal* (0830-1200, 1430-1800) is situated off Avenue Mohammed V, with a fixed-price shop and a number of craftsmen working on the premises – look out for the Middle Atlas carpets. A large Amazigh **souk** is held just above the town on Tuesday, with vegetables, textiles and some interesting Middle Atlas carpets, as well as traditional entertainment from musicians and others. The town also has a small pool for summer use.

Excursions

If you have time, you should definitely seek out the region's largest and most famous cedar, the **Cèdre de Gouraud**, still named for some half-forgotten French military commander. This is signposted off the Azrou to Ifrane road, down a track left off the Azrou to Midelt road. Barbary apes will be anxiously waiting among the trees to share the contents of your picnic.

Of more specialized interest is the abandoned Benedictine monastery at **Tioumliline** (turn right a few hundred metres up the hill after the *Ifriquia* petrol station above Azrou on the Midelt road). The monastery, founded in 1920, was finally relinquished in 1963, becoming a vocational training centre, abandoned along with the dispensary in the 1980s. Low stone buildings, a cloister planted with cypress, lilac, and a Judas tree survive on this beautiful site, as does the church building and the graves of five fathers. The location is beautiful; birdwatchers may find things of interest in the mixed deciduous/cedar woodlands here. The monastery was important as a meeting place for Moroccan intellectuals in the heady days after independence, providing a refuge to abstract painter Gharbaoui, amongst others.

Sleeping

A *Hotel Amros*, 3 km out of town on the road towards Meknès, T055-563663, F563681. 66 rooms, 8 suites, restaurant, nightclub, pool (empty out of season), tennis courts (out of use), reservations don't quite work. **B** *Hotel Panorama*, T055-562010, F561804, panorama@extra.net.ma 39 rooms, good restaurant and bar, view, as the name suggests. Definitely better than the *Amros*. **B** *Villa des Oliviers*, T061-216624 (mob), T061-067788 (mob), francoise-reda-fathmi@hotmail.com, or villa_les_oliviers@hotmail.com Large Provençal-style villa in the countryside outside Azrou on the P24 Khénifra road.12 km out of Azrou, turn left and keep left on the track. 2 large guest rooms, more planned. French and Moroccan food, pool, safe parking. **E *Hotel Azrou***, Route de Khénifra opposite the *Crédit agricole*, about 600 m down from central mosque, T055-562116, F566473. Spotless, 9 rooms, breakfast 23dh, restaurant with menu 85dh and noisy bar. **E *Hotel des Cèdres***, Pl Mohammed V, T055-562326. A clean establishment with hot water, heavy old-fashioned sheets, communal showers and a fair restaurant. Local *faux guides* will come and say hello as you're having your breakfast (23dh) on the terrace. **F *Hotel Salam (Chez Jamal)***, T055-562562, hot shower 8dh, hot water in rooms. Opposite the *BMCE*, entrance on the Pl Saouika off Pl Mohammed V. Nice management, kind of tacky decor. Roof terrace. **F *Hotel Beau Séjour***. 45 Pl Saouika. OK. Cold showers.

Youth hostel T055-563733, Route de Midelt, Azrou, BP147, to get to it follow the signs from Pl Mohammed V, and turn left off the road to Midelt. Clean and friendly, 40 beds, kitchen, overnight fee 20dh, about 1 km from town centre.

Eating The best meals are in the restaurant of ***Hotel Panorama***; at the ***Café Restaurant Relais Forestier*** next to the *Hotel des Cèdres*; or possibly the restaurant of ***Hotel des Cèdres***, both on Pl Mohammed V. Lots of cheaper places along the road to Marrakech and around the bus station, also near big new mosque.

Transport **Road** ***CTM* buses** depart from near Pl Mohammed V, early departures for **Casablanca**, **Midelt**, and **Meknès**. There are further *CTM* and private line services from Azrou to **Rissani, Er Rachidia, Marrakech, Khénifra** and **Fès**, and numerous **grands taxis** to **Khénifra, Ifrane, Immouzer du Kandar, Meknès** and **Fès**.

Directory **Banks** The *Banque Populaire* and the *BMCE* (cashpoint) are on Pl Mohammed V.

Aïn Leuh, waterfalls and Aguelmane Azigza

Colour map 1, grid C3

If you have a car – and are interested in birdlife – then there are some beautiful routes to cover south of Azrou. One loop would take you up to Aïn Leuh, past Lac Ouiouane and across the Plateau des cèdres to the source of the Oum er Rbia (Morocco's major river) and the Aguelmane Azigza to Khénifra (a possible overnight?), or back up from Khénifra on the main P24 to Azrou via Mrirt (large Thursday souk). The landscapes are truly beautiful. This would, however, take time without own transport.

At 19 km south of Azrou, a turning off the P24 leads to **Aïn Leuh**, an Amazigh village with a Wednesday **souk** important to the semi-nomadic Beni M'Guild tribe, a ruined **kasbah** from the reign of Moulay Ismaïl, and nearby **cascades**. You then follow a narrow road through cedar forest and across a plateau, past **Lac Ouiouane** and its 1930s chalets to the source of the River Oum er Rbia, 20 km away. In places, the cedar forest has been cut back to form a thick green crown on the tops of the hills. The villages here are desperately poor, there is little vehicle traffic and children will come racing out at the first sign of a passing vehicle. Many of the houses are little more than stone shelters with crude plank roofs, now partly rendered more watertight with plastic. Drive slowly as the road is narrow. Eventually, you drop down to the **source of Oum er Rbia**, clearly visible with its water works from above. There is a car park (lots of men wanting to warden your car) and steps leading to a series of concrete platforms built on the rocks where the river waters come boiling out from between the boulders. (Some of the springs are said to be sweet, others salty.) After the platforms, you can clamber on to where the water comes crashing into a small, but not actually very deep pool (no diving). After the source, you can head west on a narrow and in places much deteriorated metalled road through beautiful landscape to join the main P24 south of Mrirt. The other option is to head on south to **Aguelmane Azigza**, a crater lake surrounded by forest, ideal for swimming. The tree-lined spot has its devoted followers amongst Moroccan campers and is a fine location for some birdwatching. There also used to be accommodation in a café. The road continues to rejoin the P24 at **Khénifra**.

Ifrane, Mischliffen and an excursion to the lakes

Phone code: 055
Colour map 1, grid C3
17 km N of Azrou, 63 km S of Fès

Ifrane is a mountain resort founded by the French in 1929 which today has numerous large villas and chalets, as well as a royal palace and hunting lodge. When this is occupied by the king, the town becomes busy with staff and politicians. From the town there are good walks in the cedar forests, and a drivable excursion round the *dayats* (crater lakes). There is some skiing at the nearby resort of **Mischliffen**. Ifrane still manages to have something of a colonial hillstation feel to it – despite the arrival of a large new campus university housed in chalet-type buildings and vast new social housing developments on the Azrou side of town. There is a small airport maintained for private and royal flights.

The **University Al-Akhawayn** at Ifrane is an elite private institution modelled superficially on a North American campus university. The institution in fact functions rather like a French university with classes in English. The clientèle is the offspring of the Moroccan bourgeoisie. (Those who can afford the high fees, but need to improve their English, use it as a launch pad before going on to further studies abroad.) Unsure of the status of the new institution, well-qualified staff have proved difficult to lure away from the main universities in Rabat and Casablanca, while students, internet or no internet, find that the attractions of isolated Ifrane pall after a while. In any case, there are plenty of private higher education institutes with links with European and North American universities in the main cities.

Sleeping

Ifrane does not have a huge range of good accommodation. What there is may be block-booked by athletics teams in training, so try to reserve in advance

A ***Hotel Mischliffen***, BP 18, T055-566607, F566623. Big 1970s hotel with 107 rooms, restaurant, bar, and pool (full in summer), 2 conference rooms. The decaying luxury choice, no doubt built to house royal retinue. **C** ***Grand Hotel***, Av de la Marche Verte, currently closed for refurbishment, hopefully original character will not be destroyed. **C** ***Hotel Perce Neige***, R des Asphodelles, T055-566210, F567116. A friendly place, 22 rooms, 5 suites, good restaurant and bar. Decor a bit stuck in the late 1970s. Best upmarket choice. *Restaurant Atlas* has menu for 120dh, eat à la carte for 200dh. **D** ***Hotel Le Chamonix***, T055-566028, 64 bright clean rooms, a bit overpriced. Restaurant with alcohol, better choice than the *Tilleuls*. Ski hire from bar. **D** ***Hotel des Tilleuls***. T055-566658, F566079, 39 rooms. Has lost all charm since its refurbishment/extension. Best avoided, bar on ground floor.

Camping *Camping International*, signposted from the town centre, T055-566156. Very busy in the summer but open all year, 6-ha site, laundry facilities, petrol only 2 km.

Eating

Ifrane is not exactly a gastronomic destination. Wander round and you'll find somewhere to eat

The ***Restaurant Atlas*** in the *Hotel Perce Neige* is the good **expensive** bet where you can try Middle Atlas trout. Otherwise, lots of **mid-range** places. ***Restaurant La Paix***, T055-566675, grilled meat, no alcohol. ***Café-Restaurant de la Rose***, 7 R des Erables, next to the *Mobil* station, T055-566215, menu 70dh, no alcohol, try their *truite en papillottes*. You can also ask for obliging local mountain guide Izem here who knows some good routes in the local outback. ***Au Rendez-Vous des Skieurs***, on the main street. Try also pâtisserie ***Cookie-Craque***, Av des Tilleuls, next to *Hotel des Tilleuls*.

Sport & activities

Skiing at Mischliffen Near Ifrane, season Jan-Mar, good but short slopes, sometimes with patchy snow cover. Hire equipment from the *Chamonix* restaurant in Ifrane and take a taxi to the resort. This is a small area with cafés and ski lifts but little else. Ski equipment (120dh for everything) and sledges (40dh) can be rented at the *Chamonix*. During the summer the area is popular with walkers.

Directory

There is a **Syndicat d'Initiative** information centre and a municipal swimming pool in the town, and regular buses from Ifrane to both Azrou and Fès. The café ***Le Croustilant***, opposite the *Mobil* station, has internet access. For wines and beer, there is a *débit d'alcohol* next to *Le Croustillant*. For films and photography equipment, there is a shop next to the ***Hotel Le Chamonix***.

Aaoua, Afourgan & Ifrah Dayats

North of Ifrane, leave the P24 to the east for a tour of the *dayats*, lakes formed by solution of the limestone. There are five lying between the P24 and the P20: Aaoua, Afourgan and Ifrah. Dayat Aaoua, 12 km from Ifrane, could be a scenic place to picnic if the lake is full, which is not the case in drought years, making the area disappointing for birdwatchers. The **D** *Auberge Chalet du Lac*, Route de Fès, T055-603197 is an atmospheric hotel with restaurant (trout, snails, lamb) and bar, adjacent to lake, ring to confirm it is open (manager Mme Régine Beccari). The circular route also takes in Dayats Ifrah and Hachlaf before returning to Ifrane.

In good circumstances the *dayats* are home to coots, herons and egrets, look out for the black-winged stilt, and numerous reed warblers. The surrounding woodland, made up mainly of holm-oak and cedar, is alive with small birds, tits, chaffinches and short-toed treecreeper, and not-so-small birds like the jay and greater spotted woodpecker and raptors including black and red kite, Egyptian vulture and booted eagle. In the woodland near Ifrane the Barbary apes can be seen and where the woodland gives way to more open plateau look out for the jackals.

Immouzer du Kandar

Phone code: 055
80 km S of Fès

A small hill resort, beautiful in spring with the apple blossom, Immouzer is also a lively place during the **Fête des Pommes** in July. Market day is Monday in the ruined kasbah. Immouzer is a popular excursion from Fès, from where there are regular buses and grands taxis. **Aïn Erreggada** is clearly signed to the west of the road, the approach from the centre of town near the taxis being the easier. Just north of Immouzer du Kandar are the popular picnic/camping springs, **Aïn Seban** and **Aïn Chifa**, clearly signed to the west of the road. In drought conditions they are less attractive.

Sleeping Not too much choice at Immouzer du Kandar, as you might expect; a place to stay if Ifrane and Azrou are full up. **C** *Hotel Royal*, Av Mohammed V, T/F055-663080. 40 rooms, TV lounge, restaurant and bar, nothing special. **C** *Hotel Chahrazed*, T055-663670, F663445. Basic, central, a bit boring but comfortable.

Eating Mid-range *La Chaumière*, near the southern exit of the town. Moderately priced European food. **Cheap** *Hotel des Truites*. Popular, pleasant atmosphere.

Khénifra, El Ksiba and Kasbah Tadla

Khénifra & surrounds

Colour map 1, grid C2
96 km SW of Ifrane

Khénifra, capital of the Zaïane region, is a relaxed (if rather dull) Middle Atlas town with a population of around 100,000 whose men are famed for their horsemanship. It has large Wednesday and Sunday souks, the place perhaps to pick up an Amazigh rug. The town was developed by Moulay Ismaïl in the late 17th century, due to its strategic location at the heart of the Middle Atlas. In the late 19th century, Sultan Hassan I named local strongman Moha ou Hammou ez Zaïani as caïd. The French had considerable difficulty in bringing Khénifra under their control, and suffered a major setback there in 1914, at the hands of Moha ou Hammou. The town only came under the Protectorate's control in 1921 when he was killed in a battle with French forces. A few kilometres south of the town on the P24 is a monument to this resistance hero.

Khénifra still has a somewhat military feel to it. There is a main avenue with the usual buildings on stilt-legged arcades (cybercafés here). At the north end of town near the horse-monument roundabout are a large number of steep-roofed French buildings, often topped with storks' nests, while over the river is the kasbah area with an old bridge and one or two historic buildings drowned in a mass of new constructions. A possible place for a coffee stop might be the *Café des Cascades*, on a low rise between town centre and horse roundabout. There is a **tourist office** at Immeuble Lefraoui, Hay Hamou-Hassan.

A popular excursion from Khénifra is to the tree-lined lake of **Aguelmane Azigza**, 24 km along the 3485. The road continues to the source of the Oued Oum er Rbia and Aïn Leuh, and then back onto the P24 just southwest of Azrou (see page 244 for further details).

Sleeping and eating **B** *Hotel Hamou Azzayani Salam*, in the new town, the top place to stay, T055-586020. 60 a/c rooms, restaurant, bar and pool. Poorly maintained. **C** *Hotel Najah*, on the P24, T055-588331. Modern place, hot water, comfortable rooms. Café and restaurant attached. **E** *Hotel-Restaurant de France*, Quartier Forces Armées Royales, T055-586114. Good size rooms and a decent restaurant. **E** *Hotel Mlilia*, T055-384609, close to the bus station. Acceptable. Has reasonable restaurant.

Khénifra to Kasbah Tadla via El Ksiba

Continuing south on the P24 the next major settlements are Zaouiat ech Cheikh and Kasbah Tadla. The road winds through beautiful farming country, all red earth and green in the springtime. Agriculture here is not heavily mechanized, people with pack animals move through the open fields as in an early Flemish landscape. Some 17 km south of Khénifra the P33 turns off east across the Middle/High Atlas divide for Zeïda (see below). A few kilometres further on, the town of **Aït Ishak** can be seen to the west. Roughly halfway between Meknès and Marrakech is the **C** *Hotel Trans-Atlas*, T055-399030, restaurant and bar, clean rooms round a pool. **Zaoaï ech Cheikh** (a lorry driver's stopping point and said, like El Hajeb, to have something of a reputation for women sex workers), has lots of tagine restaurants. Just 22 km before Kasbah Tadla, the P24 passes the turn off for **El Ksiba**, a small agricultural town in the Atlas foothills which might be a pleasant place to stay. The town has expanded hugely in recent years, but the small belvedere up by the twin mosques has a lot of charm with locals playing pétanque in the early evening. Accommodation includes the decaying former hunting lodge, the **E** *Auberge Henri IV*, T023-415002, with shower. Prefer however the nearby new campsite *Auberge Les Artistes*, on the Aghbala road out of El Ksiba, T/F023-415490 (postal address Sarif El Ksiba, BP10, Province de Beni Mellal). The 2½-ha site has beautiful views. Facilities include small restaurant, simple rooms and hot showers. Owners can advise on walking in the region. El Ksiba also has a *Crédit agricole*.

The approach to Kasbah Tadla is a fast stretch of road across open cornlands. (A suitable point for a break on the long slog up between Marrakech and Meknès, Kasbah Tadla is dealt with – along with Boujaâd and Oued Zem – in the chapter on Marrakech, see page 379.)

Khénifra to Zeïda via El Kebab & Kerrouchen

An attractive west-east route takes you across from the P24 to Zeïda, a former mining town on the P21 Azrou to Midelt/Rachidia road. Prefer the 3409 to the wider P33. Follow signs up to the hillside town of **El Kebab**. Although the new building is unattractive, the views west are beautiful. The chunky lines of the table mountain behind Khénifra are clearly visible on the horizon. Down a narrow alley above the main street you will find a metal door set with a cross, the hermitage-house of *le Père*. For more than 30 years Father Albert Peyriguère (died 1959) lived here, providing basic medical treatment for the poor – and winning many friends in the region for his pro-independence stance. His successor, Père Michel Lafon, continued his work. After El Kebab, the narrow 3409 follows the contour lines to the village of **Kerrouchen**, a village high above the valley. After rains, watch out for mud slides on the road. Villages of clay-red flat-roofed houses sit in olive groves above terraced fields. There is a steep climb up to the **Tizi-n-Ichou** (1,948 m). Here you reach the southern reaches of the cedar forests. Then the road descends to join the P33. Off right is the large rural town of Boumia. Some 18 km after the turn-off for Boumia, the approach to **Zeïda** (1,453 m) is across open plain with views of the Cirque de Jaffar in the eastern High Atlas away to the south.

Fès

Phone code: 05
Colour map 1, grid B3

Fès (also spelt Fez in English) is a fascinating city - perhaps as near to the Middle Ages as you can get in a couple of hours by air from Europe. It is not an easy city to get to know, but probably repays time and effort. With three main sections, the city has numerous historic buildings, centred around the Qaraouiyine Mosque and some memorable souks. Fès is also a base from which to explore nearby regions, Bhalil and Sefrou to the south and the spa towns of Sidi Harazem and Moulay Yacoub, as well as sites further afield, the Middle Atlas resorts of Azrou and Ifrane. Also nearby is the other central Moroccan imperial city of Meknès, with Volubilis and Moulay Idriss close by.

Ins and outs

Getting there

See Transport, page 270, for further details

Fès is accessible by train, bus and grand taxi. There are direct train services from Rabat and Casablanca, all via Meknès, taking respectively around 4 hrs and 5 hrs. Coming by train from Tanger (nearly 6 hrs), you will change at Sidi Kacem or Sidi Slimane. There are plenty of bus services to main cities, with some useful late-night services for points south; Marrakech and Er Rachidia are around 9 hrs away, for example, Tanger 6 hrs. There are 2 bus stations: the main one is outside the city walls near Bab Mahrouk, while the *CTM* station is on Av Mohammed V in the *ville nouvelle*. If you come in from Taza and all points east, you will probably arrive at yet another bus terminus, at Bab Ftouh.

Fès also has a small airport, with flights all year round to Casablanca. There are fewer scheduled flights to Marrakech. Check with *RAM* for details of flights to Europe. The Aéroport de Fès-Saïss, 15 km south of town, is a grand taxi ride out of town.

Getting around

Distances in Fès are greater than they may seem at first

Fès is a spread out sort of place, so look forward to some considerable hikes from one place to another, or petit taxi rides. If you are based in a *ville nouvelle* hotel – probably the best bet – you can get a taxi from the Pl Mohammed V or the main PTT on the Av Hassan II. Getting around the historic neighbourhoods of Fès, which divide into Fès El Bali (the Old) and Fès El Jedid (the New), is another matter. You will be dealing with a complex network of lanes and alleys. Especially if your time is limited, it may be better to engage an official guide – rather than get lost and have (possibly unpleasant) dealings with an unofficial guide. From the Information Office on Pl de la Résistance in the *ville nouvelle* to Bab Boujeloud, effectively the beginning of Old Fès, is a 3-km trot. The train station is a similar distance from Fès El Bali, the *CTM* terminus roughly 4 km.

Tourist information

Office du Tourisme, Pl de la Résistance, T055-623460, F623146. Syndicat d'Initiative, Av Mohammed V, T055-625301.

Background

Spiritual capital

"The best of cities," wrote Abou Zar El Fassi, "has five characteristics: a river with running water, arable land, forests close by, well-built ramparts; and a powerful authority to ensure every success to its people and protect them." Fès, which has enjoyed some or all of these features over its long history, also has a highly strategic location. The city is situated in the Oued Sebou basin, astride the traditional trade route from the Sahara to the Mediterranean, as well as on the path from Algeria and the Islamic heartland beyond into Morocco. For centuries the dominant axis within Morocco was between Fès and Marrakech, two cities linked by their immense power as well as by their rivalry. Even today, while the coastal belt centred on Rabat and Casablanca dominates the country in demographic, political and economic terms, Fès continues to fascinate, for it has another characteristic, perhaps its dominant feature, which Abou Zar failed to mention: Fès is a religious sort of place, and is felt to be the spiritual capital of Morocco.

The influence of a saintly person, the *baraka* or blessing of a protector, was also felt to be essential for a Moroccan city in times gone by. Fès, founded by Idriss II, El Azhar, 'the Splendid', has a patron, too. The life of the city once gravitated around the cathedral-mosque where Moulay Idriss and his descendants are buried. In recent memory, the end of each summer saw great celebrations for the *moussem of Moulay Idriss*. The craftsmen's corporations would take part in great processions to the shrine of the city's founder, a sacrificial bull, horns and head decorated with henna, the heart of every procession. Some early European writers saw the city as a great Mont-St-Michel, a prayer-saturated place with its mosques, *zaouïas* and oratories.

The people of Fès were deeply religious. Dr Edmond Secret, writing in the 1930s, said that "the majority do their five daily prayers. Draped in modesty in the enveloping folds of their cloaks, the bourgeois, prayer carpets under their arms, recall monks in their dignity." This air of religiosity still clings to the city, especially in the month of Ramadhan, the month of fasting during daylight hours. Of the nights of this month, the most spiritual is the 27th, so beautiful that the angels ask God for permission to descend from Heaven to pass the night on Earth. And on every night of the year, in the hours which precede the dawn, a time hard for those who are sick and in pain, a company of muezzins maintains a vigil in the minaret of the Andalucían Mosque, praying for those asleep and those awake. This prayer is called *mu'anisi el murdha*, 'the companions of the sick'.

Intellectual heritage

The city's religious life was for long closely tied to education. "If learning was born in Médina, maintained in Mecca and milled in Egypt, then it was sieved in Fès," went the adage. In the early Middle Ages, it was a centre of cultural exchange. One Gerbert d'Aurillac, later to become Pope Sylvester II, from 999 to 1003, studied in Fès in his youth, and brought Arabic numerals back to Europe. Famous names to have studied or taught in Fès include Maimonides, the Jewish philosopher and doctor, Ibn' Arabi (died 1240) the mystic, Ibn Khaldoun (died 1282), and the mathematician, Ibn El Banna (died 1321).

Thus Fès for long supplied the intellectual élite of the country, along with many of its leading merchants, and the Fassis (the people of Fès) are to be found in most towns and cities. The Fassis are rightly proud of their city and history; their self-confidence, verging at times on self-satisfaction, is a distinctive trait, making them rather different from most other Moroccans. Therefore, Fès does not have the immediate friendliness of the villages, the mountains or the desert. It is, however, a city well worth spending time in - and like it or not, will not leave you indifferent. Author Driss Chraïbi, for one, in his 1954 breakthrough novel *Le Passé Simple*, certainly did not mince his words: "I do not like this city. It is my past and I don't like my past. I have grown up, I have pruned myself back. Fès has quite simply shrivelled up. However, I know that as I go deeper into the city it seizes me and makes me entity, quantum, brick among bricks, lizard, dust - without me needing to be aware of it. Is it not the city of the Lords?"

The three cities of Fès

The city is composed of three distinct parts. On either side of the Oued Fès, a tributary of the Oued Sebou, lies Fès El Bali, the oldest part of the city, a médina divided by the river into Adwa al Andalusiyin (the Andalucían quarter on the east bank) and Adwa al Qaraouiyine (the Qaraouiyine quarter on the west bank). On a plateau just to the west lies Fès El Jedid, containing the royal palace and the *mellah* or former Jewish quarter. This is the most recent part of the historic city, founded under the Merinids in the late Middle Ages. To the southwest, on another raised area, lies the *ville nouvelle*, the modern city built by the French which has taken over many of the political, administrative and commercial functions of old Fès.

Settlers from Andalucía & Kairouan

The first settlement here was the village Medinat Fès founded in 789/90 by Moulay Idriss, the sultan and saint commemorated in the shrine town bearing his name near Meknès. (The word *Fès* in Arabic means axe - a possible reference to tools used in its construction?) However the town proper was founded by his son Idriss II as Al-Aliya in 808/9. Muslim families, refugees from Cordoba and surrounding areas of Andalucía soon took up residence in the Adwa al Andalusiyin quarter. Later 300 families from Kairouan (in contemporary Tunisia), then one of the largest Muslim towns in North Africa, settled on the opposite bank, forming Adwa al Qaraouiyine. The **Qaraouiyine Mosque**, perhaps the foremost religious centre of Morocco, is the centre of a university founded in 859, one of the most prestigious in the Arab World. The influence of the university grew a few centuries later under the Merinids with the construction of colleges or *medersas*. On the right bank of the Oued Boukhrareb, the **Jamaâ Madlous** or Andalusian Mosque was also founded in the ninth century and remains the main mosque of Adoua el Andalus.

Almoravids & Almohads

The two parts of Fès El Bali were united by the Almoravids in the 11th century, and became an important city to anyone ruling North West Africa. Fès became one of the major cities of Islam. In the 12th century the Qaraouiyine mosque was enlarged to its present form; one of the largest in North Africa, it can take up to 22,000 worshippers. The Almohads strengthened the fortifications of the great city. Under both dynasties Fès was in competition with the southern capital of Marrakech.

The growth of Fès under the Merinids

Fès reached its peak in the Merinid period, when the dynasty built the new capital of Fès El Jedid reflecting its power, containing the green-roofed Dar al Makhzen still occupied by the monarch, the **Grand Mosque** with its distinctive polychrome minaret dating from 1279, and the *mellah*, to which the Jews of Fès El Bali were moved in 1438. The Merinid sultans Abu Said Uthman and Abu Inan left a particularly notable legacy of public buildings, including the **Medersa Bou Inania**, several mosques and the **Merinid Tombs**. The **Zaouïa of Moulay Idriss**, housing the tomb of Idriss II, was rebuilt in 1437. In the 15th century Fès consolidated its position as a major centre for craft industries and trade.

Saâdian & Alaouite Fès

Under the Saâdians (15th to 16th centuries) Fès declined, with a degree of antagonism between the authorities and the people. The Saâdians did however refortify the city, adding the **Borj Sud** and **Borj Nord** fortresses on the hills to the south and north of the city.

Under the Alaouites, Fès lost ground to the expanding coastal towns, far better located to benefit from trade with Europe. The occupation of Algeria also meant Fès was out of phase with the huge changes taking place to the east. In 1889 the French writer Pierre Loti described it as a dead city. However, the dynasty had added a number of new *medersa* and mosques, and reconstructed other important buildings. The French entered Fès in 1911, but proved unable to gain full control of the city and its hinterland. Plans to make it the Protectorate's capital were thus abandoned. In any case, Rabat on the coast was better located with respect to fertile farmlands and ports. Although the ***ville nouvelle***, also often referred to as **Dar Dbibagh** was founded in 1916, it dates principally from the late 1920s. French policy was to leave the historic quarters intact, preserved in their traditional form. Since the early 1990s, the city has exploded beyond its former limits, with huge new areas of low rise housing on the hills behind the Borj Sud at Sahrij Gnaoua and to the north at Dhar Khemis and Bab Siffer.

Fès: three cities

Detail maps
A Fès El Bali, page 258
B Fès el Jedid, page 255
C Fès Ville Nouvelle, page 265

The Fassia

'Fassi', an inhabitant of Fès, in contemporary Moroccan parlance, is synonymous with taste and refined urban living, of knowing how to do things in 'the right way'. Born in Casablanca or Rabat, your Fassi origins will still be important. And even born in Fès, you may not really be a Fassi, a person having that lineage which goes back generations into the soul of the city. Travellers visiting Fès were in agreement that there was a definite Fassi mindset, imbued with el-qa'ida, *tradition – and very different from the outlook of the Marrakchis, for example, whose city , set on the plain, was wide open to influences from mountain and desert.*

Could it be that there is an actual physical 'Fassi type', linked to the Fassi personality, wondered Roger Le Tourneau in his learnèd work, Daily Life in Fès in 1900, adding that "centuries of urban living, frequent marriages between different ethnic groups, climate, food, identical habits have over the years shaped a veritable Fassi type: pale-skinned, even under a summer tan, muscles only slightly developed, slow heavy gait, sensitive nerves, a crabbed body, fine and noble features, a penetrating gaze." However, Le Tourneau also felt that the Fassi personality was shaped by the fact that to co-exist, a mixed bag of races had to make a great effort to create a common moral code, a way of life: "The Arab contributed nobility, the Andalucían refinement, the Kairouanais dexterity, the Jew shrewdness, the Berber tenacity; to this alloy of aptitudes was added a social rule, qa'ida *(rule, model), a keen taste for study and matters of the spirit, a natural penchant for religious life, a penetrating and caustic turn of mind."*

In the late 19th century, the Fassis considered their city in all respects superior to the rest of Morocco: it was the centre of civilization in a rural world. Few of these condescending Fassis had travelled – apart from merchants and pilgrims to the Middle East – to be able to think otherwise. The technical superiority of Europe was attributed to some maleficent force.

But the world was changing. While earlier generations of Fassis had been suspicious of central power, resisting predatory rulers, under reforming Hassan I the picture changed. Certain families had already settled in Casablanca, the up-and-coming port, becoming active in finance or diplomacy. Later, in the 1920s, members of the great Fassi families settled in Casablanca close to the sultan's new palace in the purpose built Derb el Habous. Casablanca's dynamic bourgeoisie was taking shape: privileged, tied to each other by a web of marriages, bound together by the same education, some Fassi notables worked for independence, too. They were to be important in business and finance after Independence. To their ancient lineage, they added French university educations, becoming aristocrates du diplôme *as well. Today, the label of a Fassi family name can still be a help in getting ahead, even though most of the most go-ahead families have long since left the city of the Idrissids, leaving the great homes occupied by poor relations or rural migrants. More importantly, perhaps, the adjective Fassi continues to denote the epitome of everything traditional and refined.*

Saving Fès During the 20th century Fès was largely overshadowed by the growth of Rabat and Casablanca, even though many Fassi notables did well out of the Protectorate – witness the palaces and splendid houses of the Ziat, Douh and Batha areas of the médina. The city declined in the post-independence period as the élite moved to the cities of the Atlantic coast, leaving their fine courtyard homes to the poorer members of the family or rural immigrants. The money for the upkeep of large, ageing buildings has gone elsewhere, and today much of the médina faces critical problems, not the least of which is the pollution of the Oued Fès and the Oued Sebou, along with the disintegration of the historic, but much decayed, drinking water network.

Building in Fès

In old Fès, building a new house was a long and often protracted process for the future happy home owner. There were no architects or contractors as such, only different craft corporations, with whom the future home owner would have to deal directly, even going to recruit the labourers in person. A master builder and a master carpenter would do most of the work, but only the owner would supervise the whole process. A whole series of small enterprises were concerned, each specialized in a different domain: roofing, rendering and painting, laying brick floors or doing the wall mosaics, carving and painting wooden and plaster surfaces. The craft corporations had very close loyalties, often cemented by regional origins. The builders, for example, were almost all from the Figuig region. Everything was done by hand – absolutely no machine tools were involved.

Certain craftsmen, notably those using decorative techniques, were famed far beyond Fès. The ceramic mosaic workers, the stucco and wood carvers and the painters had Morocco-wide reputations. Almost all belonged to ancient local families, and their geometric designs gave homes their particular Fassi feel. The detailed patterning of mosaics and stucco work, like fine embroidery, comes as something of a surprise to visitors used to more sobre interiors. The skill of the craftsmen in producing endlessly repeated motifs and arabesques is consumate. (The zelligeurs, composing intricate mosaics out of coloured ceramic fragments placed face down on the ground, are particularly amazing.) However, the repetition of a limited repertoire of forms can become a little tiring on the eye. The craftsmen are certainly skilled – but not always terribly creative. On the whole, technique tends to prevail over innovation.

Today the crumbling houses of Old Fès are home to a poor population. Official figures give 35% of old city's population as being under the poverty line, the figure rising to more than 40% in some areas. The ADER (Agence pour la dédensification et la réhabilitation de Fès) was set up to improve living conditions, to date with only limited success. With houses regularly disintegrating after the winter rains, the ADER's main aim is to ensure that people are moved out of the most dangerous housing – so reducing the potential for street protests. In 1981, the city was added to the UNESCO-sponsored World Heritage List. In the 1990s, the ADER began restoration works on a small number of gates and monuments. A special traditional building crafts training centre was established.

Projects & initiatives

The scale of the problems of Fès is enormous, however. In 1985, UNESCO estimated that $585 million were needed to save the old city – frightening figures. In 1992, the UNDP put the cost of creating a pilot conservation district at $70 million. The ADER and local government proved to have insufficient technical know-how to put together a project to justify the loan of this sum. Finally, in 1995, the World Bank came up with $14 million for infrastructure improvement – and works are finally underway. So more than twenty years after being listed, the Médina continues to decay, with demolitions leading to gaps in the once dense urban fabric. There has been much controversy over the building of two roads into the centre, one leading to Talaâ Kebira, and the other over the existing course of Oued Fès. Although some restoration projects seem to go on for ever – the Medersa Bou Inania, for example, private and foreign finance has been used to restore a number of buildings at the heart of Fès el Bali, including the Foundouq Najjarine (Fondation Lamrani) and Dar Adil (Italian foreign ministry). To really save Fès, official bodies like the Municipality, the ADER, the Urban Planning Agency and the Ministry of

Culture will have to work more closely together. In particular, some sort of housing improvement loan policy will have to be created to persuade the often absent owners to invest in their historic property. On a positive note, Fès now has some upmarket private guesthouses, and plans for quite a number of others are said to be on the drawing-boards.

Sights

Writing in the 1930s, the Tharaud brothers, chroniclers of the Morocco that was disappearing, wrote that "in Fès there is only one age and one style, that of yesterday. It is the site of a miracle, of the suppression of the passage of time." Which is fine if you are a visitor, but not always much fun if you happen to have to live there. Largely abandoned by its once deep-rooted, urban élite, it has fallen prey to ineffective government and poverty. Nor are its sights are easily discovered. Although several days are really necessary to take in the city's atmosphere, circuits of Morocco tend to give you just one day.

Essentially, there are **three main areas** to visit: **Fès el Bali**, which really merits at least a day, **Fès el Jedid**, a good half-day, and the **ville nouvelle**, where you are fairly likely to stay, given the lack of mid-priced accommodation in the old neighbourhoods. You'll also need to have energy to get up to the Borj Nord/Merinid tombs for views across Fès el Bali at sundown. While Fès el Jedid is fairly flat, Fès el Bali has long sloping streets. In the winter it can rain heavily, turning Talaâ Sghira and Talaâ Kbira into minor torrents. Many of the main sites are decayed – the Boujeloud Gardens, for instance, and maintenance works to the monuments of Fès seem to last for ever: the Bou Inania Medersa, the Batha Museum were both undergoing restoration in early 1993 – and had been for several years. The Medersa Essahrij is in parlous condition. It might be worth getting hold of a local guide and try to get access to one of the semi-abandoned palaces (Dar Ababou, Dar el Mokri, Dar el Glaoui) in the Ziat neighbourhood. For Dar el Glaoui, ring Abdelkhalek Boukhars on T067-366828 (mob).

Fès is spectacular, but not as immediately attractive as Marrakech. Unlike the capital of the South, a crossroads for caravans and peoples, Fès is more secretive, its old ways hidden behind the cliff-like walls of its alleyways. Although it may not be a city for everyone, few will leave this once imperial capital unmoved.

Fès el Jedid

Allow a short half-day stroll, taken perhaps in the late afternoon before heading for the Borj Nord at sunset

The one-time Merinid capital, containing Royal Palace and the old Jewish neighbourhood or *mellah*, is now a pleasant old quarter between the hustle and bustle of Fès El Bali and the *ville nouvelle*. The chief points of interest here, apart from the atmosphere of a busy, 'real' neighbourhood, are the small **Synagogue Aben-Danan** in the *mellah* and the square at **Bab Dekakene**, often used during the Festival des musiques du monde for concerts.

A promenade in the *mellah* and Fès el Jedid is probably best started at the Place des Alaouites, close to the Royal Palace, instantly recogniszable by its spectacular doors giving onto a vast esplanade, used essentially on ceremonial occasions – or, in the early 1990s, during urban riots. (If you want to stay in this area, the small and cheap *Hotel Glacier* overlooks the square). Over on the right, at the edge of a small garden terrace, is the elegant **Bab Lamar**. Between this and the Rue Bou Kssissat, opt for the small gate which takes you into Rue des Mérinides in the *mellah*, a term derived from the Arabic *milh*, salt, the story going that in harsher times the Jews were the 'salters' of the criminals' heads displayed for public delectation on the gates of Morocco's cities. This sounds a bit too much like a tale dreamed up by some unpleasant French colonial to be true. In fact, the term would seem to derive from the Oued Melah, literally 'salty river' which once ran close to this part of Fès, but which, like so many of the watercourses in the region, has disappeared.

Off Rue des Mérinides, the streets once had names which reflected the area's Jewish past. Take the fourth street on the right, Rue de Temara, which will take you to the **Synagogue Aben-Danan**. (There used to be two other synagogues, the Em Habbanim and the Mansour). In fact, until the 13th century, the Jews lived in Fès el Bali in the Bab Guissa area, still referred to as Fondouq el Yahoudi. In the main hall of the synagogue, there is a collection of objects which will give some idea of the material context of Fassi Jewish life. After the synagogue-museum, past a small square, head across to the Nouaïl area. Next to the Jewish cemetery, a new museum of Jewish life is scheduled to open soon. (If you go right here, the street leads down to a door which will take you down to the American animal hospital or **Fondouk el Amerikan**. From the Nouaïl area try to cut through to the continuation of Rue des Mérinides, Rue Sekkakine and the imposing **Bab Semmarine** which leads you to Fès el Jedid proper. (If you double back on Rue des Mérinides, you'll find **Bab Magana**, the 'clock gate', whose scruffy timepiece stopped a while ago.) All along the street are the elegant facades of the houses built by prosperous Jewish families in the early 20th century.

Bab Semmarine, a chunky structure characterized by a double horseshoe arch and lozenge motifs, takes you through into the wide main street of Fès el Jedid, often referred to as Avenue Moulay Slimane. This divides the *madina al bayda*, the white city founded by the Merinids in 1276, in two and takes you through to Bab Dekakene. On the right, **Jamaâ el Hamra** 'the red mosque' is the first of the two mosques, so called because it was founded by a red woman

Fès El Jedid

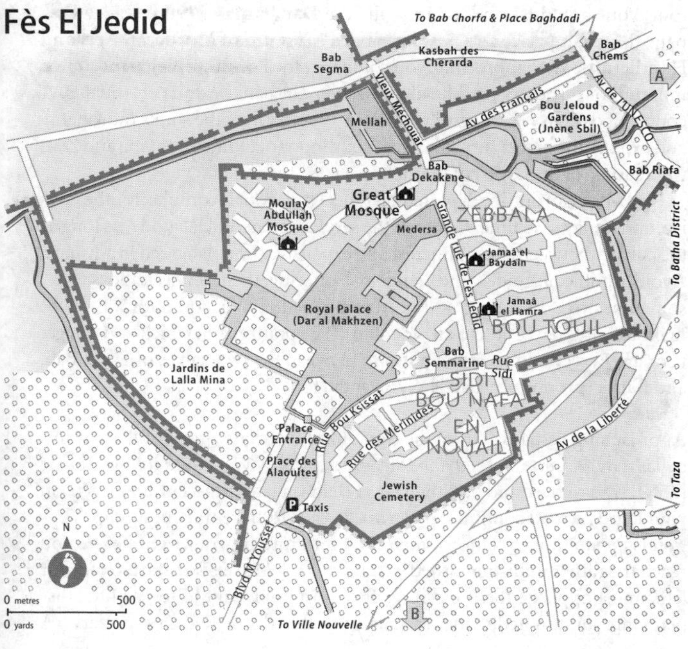

Related maps
Fès: three cities, page 251
A Fès El Bali, page 258
B Fès Ville Nouvelle, page 265

from the Tafilalelt. The second mosque on your right is the **Jamaâ el Bayda**. Continue straight ahead and at the end of the avenue you can cut through an arched gate in the walls to your right which will take you past the dry course of the Oued Chrachar to a decrepit waterwheel and a small café-restaurant. Double back, cut through left, and you are at **Bab Dekakene**. Here you want to go through to the right to the walled square referred to as the **Vieux Mechouar**. On the left are the Italianate entrance gates to the **Makina**, originally built in the 19th century to house an arms factory. It now handles various functions including rug factory and youth club. Going straight ahead, you come to **Bab Sba'**, which takes you through onto the main road running along the north side of the city, linking the *ville nouvelle* to Fès el Bali. You might take a look at the unusual twin octagonal towers of **Bab Segma**, flanking the ring road. The fortified structure to the north is the **Kasbah des Cherarda**, built 1670 by Sultan Moulay Rachid and today housing a branch of the university and a hospital.

For those with plenty of time, the trail through Fès Jedid could be extended to include a dawdle through Moulay Abdallah neighbourhood, north of the palace. (A couple of mosques for non-Muslims to look at from the exterior here.) Those with plenty of energy can head through the Boujeloud gardens and along Avenue des Français to **Bab Boujeloud**, the western end of Fès el Bali.

Fès el Bali: Adoua el Quaraouiyine

With its long narrow sloping streets, Fès el Bali requires a lot of walking. Start early, especially in hot weather

On the left bank of the Oued Boukhrareb, the Adoua el Quaraouiyine is a rewarding place to visit, as long as you don't expect too many well structured heritage sites. If time is very short, then the minimum **half-day circuit** will allow you down the main street, Talaâ Kbira, to the central souks and main religious monuments, the **Moulay Idriss Zaouïa** and the **Qaraouiyine Mosque**, closed to non-Muslim visitors. Either at the start or the end of the tour, you should take a look in at the the **Dar Batha**, a 19th-century Hispano-Moorish palace and now home to a **Museum of Moroccan Arts and Handicrafts**. With more time, you could visit the **Fondouk Nejjarine**, now a museum of carpentry, and head up to the right bank, Adoua el Andalus. A couple of days in Fès will give you time to get to know the souks thoroughly and explore the higher, upscale neighbourhoods of Douh, Zerbtana and Ziat, where some of the largest of the city's palaces are located.

Fès El Bali can only be explored on foot. The layout is complex for the novice, and it may save time to engage the services of an official guide, as long as the balance between sites of interest and expensive shops is agreed in advance. Avoid unofficial guides and 'students' offering their services. So saying, sometimes you do get lost and need someone to guide you out (5dh might make a child's day, 10dh to an older kid). The points from which you can get taxis are **Errecif**, down at the bottom, between the two halves of Fès el Bali, and **Batha** (pronounce 'bat-Ha'), up at the top.

Boujeloud Gardens & the Batha Museum

Approaching Fès El Bali from the **Boujeloud Gardens** (Jnène Sbil or Jardins de la Marche Verte) – ■ *0900-1800 except Mon* – you could follow Rue de l'UNESCO right round past the **Dar el Beida**, a late 19th-century palace, on your left. The road continues past a line of early 20th century buildings (*Pension Campini*, police station), then the Préfecture on your right before you reach the rather undistinguished entrance to the **Musée Dar Batha**, on your left almost opposite the Préfecture. The most important features of the displays are undoubtedly the carpets and the distinctive Fès pottery. A

10th-century technique enabled the use of cobalt to produce the famous 'Fès blue'. On Talaâ Kbira there are a couple of shops stocking this traditional pottery. In the museum. Look out too for the *minbar* or preacher's chair from the Medersa Bou Inania. ■ *0900-1130 and 1500-1800 except Tue. T055-634116.*

Bab Boujeloud & around

If you're staying in a cheap hotel, it's likely that you'll be at **Bab Boujeloud**. The neighbourhood takes its name from the striking gate which marks the main western entrance to Fès El Bali. With blue zlij on the outside, green zlig on the inside, Bab Boujeloud makes a fittingly stylish access point to the city – and was revamped under the French in 1913. Just to the right of the gate as you arrive from the Place Boujeloud, there is a small gate in the wall, generally kept closed, which leads into the recently restored brick **water collector**. Though this may not sound very exciting, it was a rather good piece of late mediaeval hydraulic engineering, channelling the waters of the Oued Fès into underground pipes which supplied the distributors of each neighbourhood. The whole system was still in operation in the late 19th century. The two minarets visible from the gate are those of the 14th-century **Medersa Bou Inania Medersa** and the simpler ninth-century **Sidi Lazzaz Mosque**.

Still on the subject of gates, on your left as you arrive at Bab Boujeloud, the impressive gate flanked by twin octagonal towers is **Bab Chorfa**, leading into **Kasbah Nouar**, or Kasbah Filala, so named as it was once occupied by people from the Tafilalet who arrived with the early Alaouite rulers. Behind you as you face Bab Boujeloud, the **Place Baghdadi** was being redeveloped in early 2003, probably with the idea that it would become a Fassi version of Marrakech's Jmaâ el Fna. Inside Bab Boujeloud there are plenty of cheap restaurants. Following down and round to the right are some good cafés for people watching, just before you get to the *Cinema Boujeloud*.

There are two routes onto the main thoroughfares of Fès El Bali. Talaâ Seghira leads to the right. Talaâ Kebira leads to the left, directly past the Sidi Lazzaz Mosque, and the next major building, the **Bou Inania Medersa**, one of the most important sites in Fès.

Bou Inania Medersa

One of Fès' main monuments, the 14th-century **Medersa Bou Inania**, is located handily close to Bab Boujeloud, with the main entrance being between some lock-up shops near the top of Talaâ Kbira. Built by the Merinid Sultan Abu Inan between 1350-55, it was used to accommodate students until the 1960s. Restoration works and the site manager permitting, you enter through a highly decorated vestibule roofed by a stalactite dome. The building centres on a large, stone-flagged courtyard, at the far end of which a sort of dry moat, where once flowed water derived from the Oued Fès, separates the prayer hall from the square courtyard. The mosque area has a highly decorated minaret, indicating that it was far more important than most *medersas*, which normally do not have minarets or even pulpits for the Friday prayer. Indeed, the *medersa* has the status of a Friday mosque, and for a time rivalled the Qaraouiyine Mosque.

The courtyard is decorated with ceramic mosaic, badly damaged by the building works, Koranic inscriptions, and some fine carved woodwork. Around the courtyard on ground and first floors are the students' cell-like rooms, some with decorated ceilings. Try to gain access to the roof for a good photo of the minaret.

There used to be a complex 14th-century **clepsydra** (water clock) built in the wall opposite the *medersa*. Complete with chimes, it is said to have been used to allow the Medersa Bou Inania, visible from both the Qaraouiyine Mosque and the Mosque of Fès el Jedid, to signal the correct time for prayer.

Down Talaâ Kbira to the Qaraouiyine, the souks & medersas

The narrow **Talaâ Kebira**, the principal street in Adoua el Qaraouiyine, descends steeply towards the spiritual and commercial heart of the city, a tangle of streets and alleys around the shrine or zaouïa of **Moulay Idriss** and the **Qaraouiyine Mosque**. Beware of the heavily laden mules carrying goods across the city, guided by muleteers crying out 'Balak!' to warn pedestrians. Such are the distractions of the shops and crowd as you head downwards that you will be hard pressed to look out for interesting architectural features. Never mind, pick up on these on a second visit and enjoy the experience of the main thoroughfare of a mediaeval city. Once you get to the bottom of Talaâ Kebira, the main religious monuments are off limits, of course. It may be

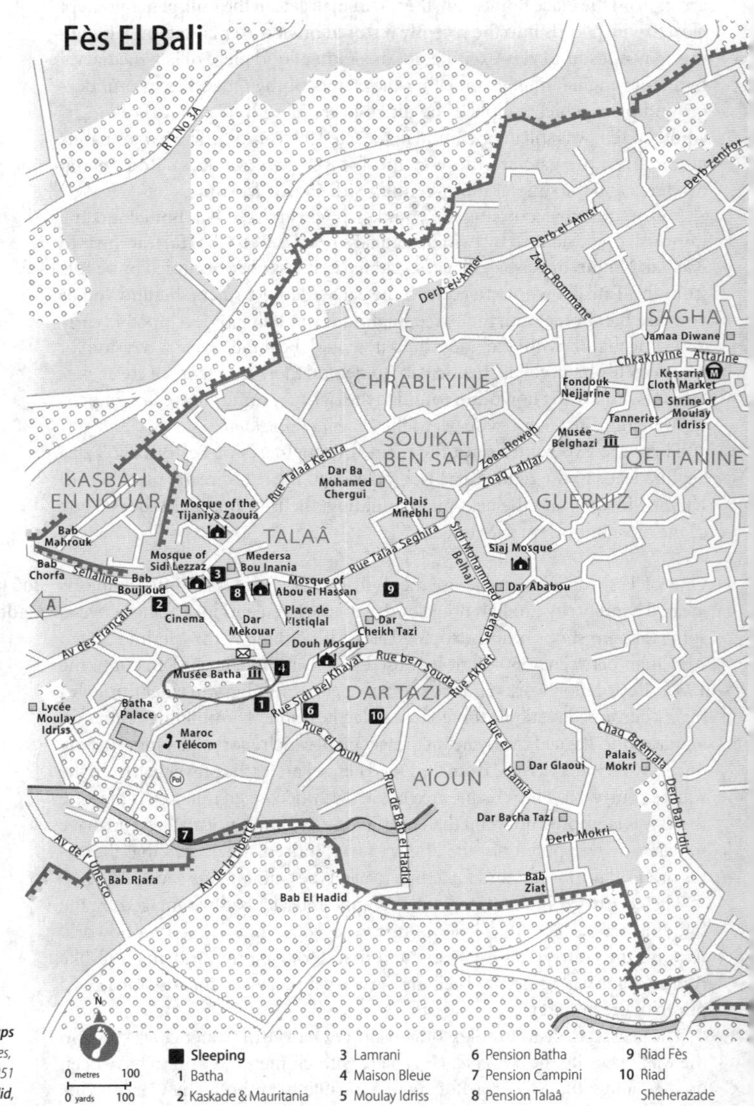

Related maps
Fès: three cities, page 251
A Fès El Jedid, page 255

possible, depending on restoration works, to get into one of the medersas which ring the Qaraouiyine Mosque. Try to see the **Medersa el Attarine** and don't miss the restored **Foundouk Nejjarine**, the Carpenters' Fondouk, the main accessible historic building in the central part of Fès el Bali. The other don't-miss sight is the main tannery or **Dar Debbagh**, located quite close to the well-signed **Musée Belghazi**.

As Talaâ Kebira descends, it goes through frequent identity changes, taking on the name of the different crafts which are (or were) practised along different sections of the street. First it becomes **Rue Cherabliyine** (slippermakers) where each afternoon except Friday people hawk secondhand shoes and

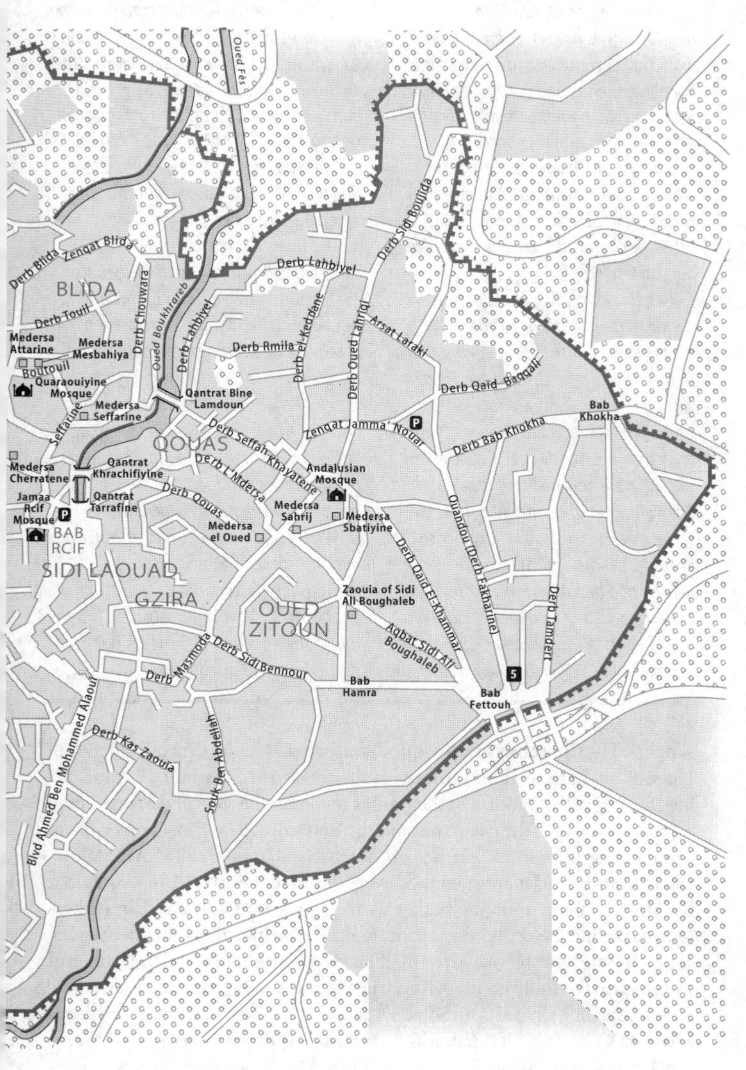

Saintly Sultan Abou Inane

A number of ancient colleges in the medinas of Morocco – among them medersas *in Meknès, Salé and Fès – bear the name Bou Inania, after their royal founder. Sultan Abou Inane's most important building works were in this latter city: he constructed the Jama'a Zhar, a fine mosque close to his palace, and the Koubba of the Karaouiyine Library. Today's non-Muslim visitor can see the Medersa Bou Inania in Fès, considered to be one of the finest in existence. Tradition has it that when the sultan was presented with the final accounts, he tore up the paperwork, declaring that "Beauty is not expensive, whatever the sum may be. A thing which pleases man cannot be paid too dear." What the contractors said is not recorded by popular tradition.*

Born in Fès in 1329, Abou Inane Faris de-throned his father aged barely 20, when he had himself proclaimed sultan at Tlemcen in June 1348. By all accounts he was an imposing figure. Wrote Ibn El Ahmar, chronicler of the Merinids: "He was taller than everybody else. His body was slim, his nose long and well-made. He had hairy arms. His voice was deep, but he spoke quickly in a staccato manner, so that it was sometimes difficult to understand him. He had beautiful, finely shaped eyes, full eyebrows, and an agreeable face of great beauty. A magnificent beard covered his chest, which divided into two when the wind blew ... My eyes have never seen in his army a soldier with a fuller beard, a finer and more pleasing figure." Abou Inane was also by all accounts a skilled horseman, and had a good knowledge of law, arithmetic and Arabic. Ibn El Ahmar also mentions that he left behind 325 children.

On being proclaimed sultan, Abou Inane took the throne name of El Moutawakkil, 'he who places trust in God'. Although a strong ruler, he was also a pious man (he knew the Koran by heart), and this was reflected in a number of ways. He instituted a tradition of having a blue flag hoisted to the top of the minarets on Friday to indicate prayer time, and had oil-lamps placed on the minarets to show prayer times at night.

Like many a mediaeval ruler, however, Abou Inane had an unfortunate end. In 1358, returning to Fès from Tunis, he fell sick. Arriving in his capital on the eve of Aïd El Kebir, he had sufficient strength to lead the great prayers on the musalla *outside the city. He was too ill, however, to receive homage from the notables of the realm. The vizier, Hassan El Foudoudi, had been plotting in the wings: he had the sick sultan smothered in his bedclothes.*

Where Abou Inane is buried, however, remains something of a mystery. Perhaps it was too risky to allow such a good ruler to have a mausoleum, which might then become a focus for public gatherings and discontent?

slippers. The **Cherabliyine Mosque** dates from 1342, the reign of Sultan Abul Hassan, and has a small and attractive minaret tiled in green and white including the *darj w ktaf* motif. On the right is the *Palais des Merinides*, one of the more impressive of the palace restaurants, and worth a look inside even if you cannot afford the food. Further on, Rue Cherabliyin is called **Aïn Allou**, where leather articles are auctioned every day except Friday. After Aïn Allou, the street is named for the basket weavers (Msamriyine) and bag makers (Chakakyrine), before becoming the **Souk el Attarine**, the former perfumers' souk, the most prestigious in the médina. Between Attarine and the Zaouïa of Moulay Idriss is the lively main **Kissaria**, the place to buy traditional clothing.

Before getting tangled up in Souk el Attarine, you should take a right and then a left down some steps off Chrabliyine to get to the square in front of the 18th-century **Fondouk Nejjarine**, an impressive building now home to displays of traditional craft tools. ■ *10dh*. Restoration was financed by a foundation created by former Moroccan prime minister Karim Lamrani. NB Very clean loos on ground floor. Apart from taking a look at the traditional woodwork for which Fès was famous, the fondouk is definitely worth a visit for its roof terrace. Back on the square, the **Nejjarine Fountain**, also carefully restored, is reputed for the fever-curing properties of its waters. On the far side of the square from the fondouk is **Hammam Laraïs**, the wedding baths, once much used by grooms and brides before a pre-marriage trip to the Zaouïa of Moulay Idriss. At Nejjarine, you are close to the tanneries or **Dar Debbagh**. To get there, go right at the far end of the Nejjarine Square and follow the street round.

Surrounded by narrow streets, the 18th century **Zaouïa of Moulay Idriss**, last resting place of the 9th-century ruler Idriss II, is off-limits to non-Muslim visitors – although parts of the interior can be seen by tactful glances through the large unscreened doorways. Shops around the *zaouïa* sell candles and other artefacts for pilgrims, the distinctive chewy sweets which are taken home as souvenirs of a pilgrimage, and silverware. Each entrance to the precinct is crossed by a wooden bar, ensuring no pack animals go wandering into the sacred area. On your way round, note a circular porthole through which offerings can be discretely passed.

The Qaraouiyine Mosque (see below) is also surrounded by narrow streets on all sides. In the immediate vicinity of the mosque are four medersas: going clockwise, the **Medersa Attarine** (the most important, visitable, see below), the **Medersa Mishbahiya** (partly ruined), the **Medersa Seffarine** (the Coppersmiths' Medersa, recently restored) and the **Medersa Cherratène** (more modern, three storeys). All of these medersas were in use by students well within living memory.

Dating from 1323, the **Medersa Attarine** was built by Merinid Sultan Abu Said. It used to accommodate students from the northwest of Morocco, studying at the nearby Qaraouiyine University. The courtyard is one of the most elaborately decorated in Morocco, with the usual carved stucco and cedar wood, and *zellige* tiling. The courtyard has a solid, white marble fountain bowl. In the dark prayer hall, a chandelier bears the name of the *medersa*'s founder and the date. As with most *medersas*, the second floor has a succession of students' cells. From the roof (if accessible) there is a good view of the minaret and courtyard of the Qaraouiyine Mosque. ■ *0900-1200, 1400-1800.*

Qaraouiyine Mosque

Inaccessible to non-Muslims. From the narrow streets, take diplomatic glances through unscreened entrances where possible, but no photographs

At the end of Souk El Attarine, the Quaraouiyine Mosque, the focal point of Fès El Bali, is probably the most important religious building in Morocco. With space for some 20,000 worshippers it is one of the biggest mosques in North Africa. Original funding to build this mosque was provided in 857 by a wealthy immigrant family from Kairouan (in present day Tunisia), hence the name. The building was enlarged in 956 and again – most importantly – under the Almoravids between 1135 and 1144. The Almohads added a large ablution hall, whilst under the Merinids the courtyard and minaret were rebuilt. The twin pavilions in the courtyard are 17th-century Saâdian additions. While the minaret goes back to 956, the 'Trumpeters' Tower or **Borj an-Naffara**, is later and used during Ramadan to signal time to begin fasting again. Built under Sultan Abou Inan in the second half of the 14th century, the tower originally functioned as an observatory. There are said to be plans to convert the tower into a museum dedicated to astrolables and astrology – an important science in the Muslim world given the religion's use of a lunar calendar and the need to calculate the precise direction of Mecca for prayer.

For those who like figures, the Qaraouiyine has 14 doors, 275 pillars and 3 areas for ablutions. Features include elaborate Almohad carving and a venerable wooden pulpit. Some of the chandeliers were made from church bells.

Women have a separate worship area, on a sort of mezzanine floor, behind the men. The Qaraouiyine was a major centre of mediaeval learning, with professors in law, theology, algebra, mathematics, philosophy, and astronomy. Students would gather around their teacher who would have his particular pillar

A minor sight on the Derb Bou Touil, the street running along the eastern side of the mosque, is the 14th-century three-storey **Fondouk Titouani**, originally built to accommodate merchants from Tetouan, and today used by artisans and a carpet shop. Both this and the nearby *Palais de Fès* restaurant have good views of the Qaraouiyine's courtyard.

Place Seffarine

On the southeast side of the Qaraouiyine, the triangular **Place Seffarine** (Brassworkers' Square) is marked by a tree visible in views over Fès el Bali from the north or south Borj. On the right is the **Qaraouiyine Library** founded in 1349, still operational and home to an ancient collection of books (closed to non-Muslims). Of passing interest, behind the tree on Hyadriyine are two of the oldest hammams in Fès. The **Medersa Seffarine**, built in 1271, was the first in the city and much simpler in style than the other, later medersas. It continues to be used by students.

If you head left of the tree on Seffarine, you can follow through to one of the bridges over the Oued Boukhrareb, either Qantarat Kharchifiyine or after Sebbaghine, Qantarat Terrafine. Here you come out onto Rcif, where there are buses and taxis.

Chouara tanneries

There is another set of tanneries north of the Place Seffarine. As you face the Medersa Seffarine, go straight ahead into Derb Mechattine. This alleyway leads to the Chouara tanneries. Although this is a smelly place, it is a memorable experience for the courageous. (See page 332 for a full account of the traditional tanning process.)

Fès El Bali: Adoua el Andalus

If time is short, the Adoua el Andalus, the south bank of Fès el Bali, is probably best left for your second visit to Morocco. However, with the Medersa Bou Inania still closed for works, your best chance of seeing a medersa is the **Medersa Essahrij**, next to the **Jamaâ Madlous**. You can approach the neighbourhood from the southeast, taking a petit taxi to **Bab Fettouh**, or by climbing up out of **Bab Rcif**, losing yourself in the maze of streets of the Qouas neighbourhood. (The simplest route, if there is such a thing, is to cross the river at **Qantrat Bine Lamdoun** bridge and follow Derb Seffah and Derb Khayetène upwards. If you're sense of direction is none too good, the simplest option is to head for Bab Fettouh. Once inside the gate, take Aqbat Sidi Ali Boughaleb, which leads directly down to the **Medersa Essahrij**, or Derb Qaid el Khammar, which will lead you down to the small 'square' in front of **Jamaâ Madlous.**

With its green and white minaret, **Jamaâ Madlous** is a distinctive building dating from the same period as the great Qaraouiyine Mosque. The minaret dates from the 10th century, and the mosque was enlarged in the 13th century, with an architect from Toledo designing the grand main doorway, particularly impressive if you approach the mosque coming up the steps from below. If interested in a relic of the city's commercial life, take a look in at the **Fondouk el Madlous**, a few steps down from the mosque entrance on the left. Restored under Moulay Hassan I in the 19th century, this fondouk is still used for accommodation and storage.

As you face the main door of the mosque, go right along Derb Yasmina to reach the entrance of the nearby **Medersa Essahrij** ('School of the Reflecting Pool'), built 1321-23 to house students studying at the mosque. There has been no major restoration campaign. Cats snooze atop the weathered wood screens topped with scallop designs and the square *bassin* generally has bright green slime. The white marble basin, after which the *medersa* was named, has been removed from the courtyard. The large prayer hall contained the library against the *qibla* wall at either side of the *mihrab*, the niche indicating the direction of Mecca and therefore prayer. Try to get up onto the roof for the view. In between the mosque and the medersa is the **Medersa Sebbayine**, now closed. It is named *sebbayine* after the seven ways of reciting the Koran. After visiting the Medersa Essahrij, you could carry along the same street, past the unmarked **Medersa el Oued** on your right. A few metres further on, a sharp right will take you onto Derb Gzira. Just after the turn is a house which bears the strange name of **Dar Gdam Nbi**, the 'house of the Prophet's foot', so called because a sandal which supposedly once belonged to the Prophet Mohamed was conserved there. Once a year, just before the Prophet's birthday or Mouloud, the Tahiri family would open their home to allow the faithful to approach the semi-sacred item of footwear. Unfortunately, the owners have sold up and the property has been divided. Continue therefore on Derb Gzira which winds down to **Er Recif** where you could find a bus (No 18) to take you back up to Place de la Résistance in the *ville nouvelle*. There will be red taxis here as well.

The palaces of Fès

The Fassis were famed for their building mania, and the city is famed for its palaces, few of which are open to the public. Hidden in the narrow streets of the **Douh**, **Zerbatana** and particularly **Ziat** neighbourhoods, just east of the Batha, are some truly huge 19th and early 20th century palaces. The heirs having long since migrated to more promising elsewheres, the high-ceilinged rooms are semi-squatted by poor relatives or rural migrants. You will probably need to find a local to guide you in. As you are going into someone's home, a tip of around 20dh per visitor is probably reasonable for the disturbance. If your time is limited, try to see **Dar el Glaoui** and **Dar el Mokri**, both down in Ziat.

The Riad Fès guesthouse, T055-741012, may be able to put you in touch with a suitable guide. Try also the multilingual Abdellatif Riffi Mbarki, T068-220112 (mob)

Most often visited, as it is right on Talaâ Kebira, is the **Palais Mnebhi**, which now functions rather efficiently as a restaurant for groups. Its former owner, a minister of war under Sultan Moulay Abd el Aziz, probably didn't have the serving of Moroccan cuisine in industrial quantities in mind when he built the vast courtyard. Maréchal Lyautey, first résident-général, resided here. Garden buffs should try to get a peek at the garden patio of **Dar Ba Mohamed Chergui**, located on Derb Horra, linking Talaâ Kebira to Talaâ Seghira. The overgrown raised flowerbeds are laid out according to the *mtemmen*, figure-of-eight motif traditional in *zellige* (ceramic-mosaic). On Rue Sidi Mohamed el Haj, a right off Talaâ Seghira as you descend, is **Dar Ababou** which has a garden courtyard overlooked by balconies. Currently inhabited by members of an extended family, it is no doubt earmarked for restoration – if ever the heirs can be identified and their part-shares bought up.

Dar el Glaoui is the most easily visited of the big palaces. Abd el Khalek Boukhars who lives there can be contacted via *Riad el Bartal* (see Sleeping, page 268), T055-637053. Three tennis courts, if not four, would have easily fitted into the main courtyard. From the roof terraces there are views across the city. When the Glaoui family fell from favour after independence, the palace was abandoned. No less splendid is **Dar el Mokri**, named for the grand vizir El

Mokri who held office for the whole of the French period. There are additions in the taste of the 1930s and a sadly run-down garden. Off the big courtyard, the rooms are partly converted to workshops, partly squatted. There is an off-chance that if you are passing down Derb Chaq Bedenjala on your way to Bab Jedid a lad will spot you and ask if you want to take a look at the palace.

Close to the Batha (*batha* is Arabic for open area) are a number of easily located patrician residences. Right on the square, **Dar Mekouar** , once a cradle of the nationalist movement, is easily located a few metres to the left of the *Maison Bleue* guesthouse (see plaque on wall). Next to the café to the right of the *Maison Bleue*, a narrow street, Derb Salaj, runs directly into Fès el Bali. Follow along and you will find, down a blind alley, the house used by the local Institut français for occasional concerts. Further along, the *Riad Fès* guesthouse (very chic) is signed, and you will find **Dar Cheikh Tazi**, now headquarters of the Association Fès-Saïss, an organization working to promote the region. Once the home of Sultan Moulay Abd el Aziz's finance minister, it was taken over by the French protectoral authorities. The whole Douh area was important under French rule, being home to consulates and the like.

Fès vantage points

Fès El Bali from the outside

Three excellent vantage points enable you to view Fès El Bali from the outside, permitting one to piece together the places explored or plan visits

The **Borj nord**, built by the Saâdian Sultan Ahmad al Mansour in 1582, is a small but still interesting example of 16th-century fortress architecture. There are good view of parts of Fès El Bali from the roof. Inside, the Arms Museum, T055-645241 (closed Tuesday), has displays of weapons and military paraphernalia from all periods, including European cannon. The collections have been built up mainly as a result of royal donations and include a number of rare pieces. Many of these killing tools have a certain splendour as crafted items. Look out for the largest weapon of all, a 5 m long cannon weighing 12 tonnes used during the Battle of the Three Kings. From the Borj nord, you can head along the hillside to the 14th-century **Merinid Tombs**. The tombs are ruins, and much of the ornamentation described by earlier visitors has not survived. A word of caution – this is not a safe place to go alone at night. In the late afternoon, the garden promenade behind the Borj nord and tombs is busy with locals out for a stroll. The views over Fès el Bali are splendid. Nearby is *Hotel Les Merinides*, also with an excellent view.

From the 13th-century **Borj sud**, occupied by the military, you can look north over Fès. The nearby **son et lumière** auditorium bathes Fès el Bali in white light. Unfortunately there are no lasers to pick out the parts of the city being described in the commentary. Until the late 1990s, this southern military outpost of the city stood in isolation. The low-rise flats of the sprawling Sahrij Gnaoua neighbourhood have marched up the hills, threatening to engulf it.

Essentials

Sleeping

■ *on maps*

There are hotels in Fès to suit all budgets, including some very luxurious ones from which you can make forays down into the tangled lanes of the médina, and some very shady places indeed at the bottom end of the scale. The improvements in the budget hotels which have taken place in Marrakech have yet to reach Fès. If your budget is not too tight, go for a slightly better hotel in the **ville nouvelle**. (Good medium priced hotels include, in descending order of price, the *Splendid*, *Grand*, *Olympic* and *Amor*.) However, the best way to get a real feel of old Fès is by staying in the médina – which probably means a cheap hotel (choose carefully) in the **Boujeloud district**, today the main way into Fès El Bali. Well placed for sights like the Dar Batha Museum and the Bou Inania Medersa. You could try the **Bab Ftouh area** (a few hotels), handy for grands taxis to Sidi Harazem.

Ville nouvelle
■ *on map below*

L *Hotel Jnan Palace*, Av Ahmed Chaouki, behind the craft centre off Av Allal Ben Abdallah, T055-652230, F651917. Beautiful grounds, pool. **A** *Hotel Menzeh Zelagh*, 10 R Mohammed Diouri, T055-625531, menzeh.zalagh@fesnet.net.ma close to Pl de la Résistance in an odd residential neighbourhood. Gardens, pool open to outsiders for a

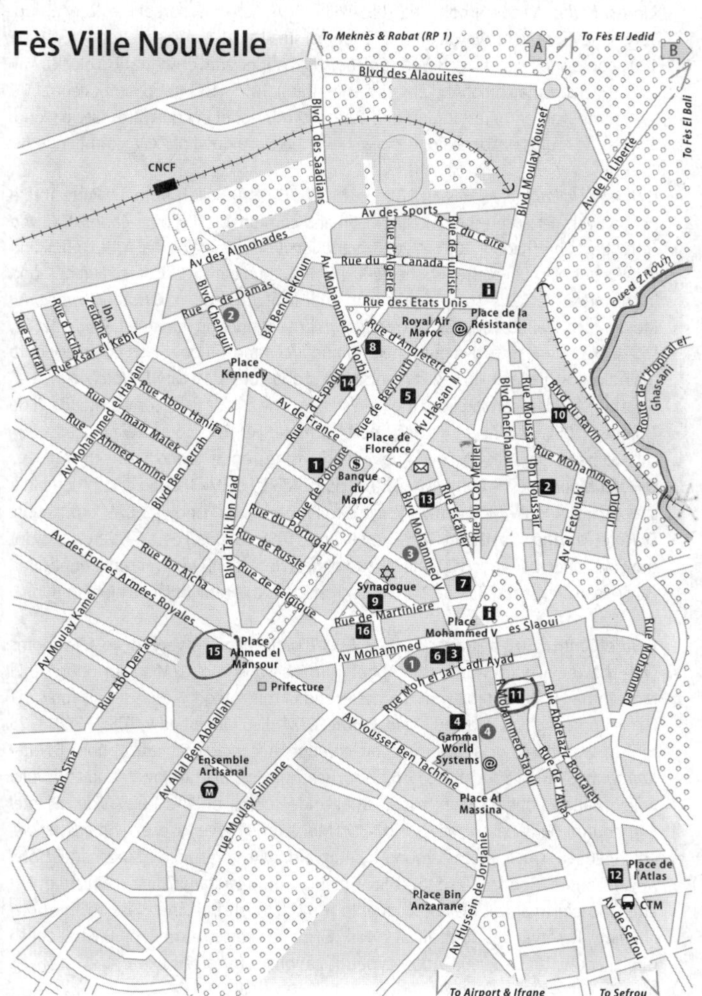

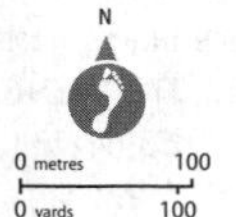

Sleeping
1 Amor
2 Auberge de Jeunesse
3 Central
4 CTM
5 de la Paix
6 du Maghreb
7 Grand
8 Kairouan
9 Lamdaghri
10 Menzah Zelagh
11 Mounia
12 Nouzha
13 Olympic
14 Royal
15 Sheraton
16 Splendid

Eating
1 Al Khozama
2 La Cheminée
3 La Médaille
4 Marrakech

Related maps
Fès: three cities, page 251
A Fès El Jedid, page 255
B Fès El Bali, page 258

small fee, tennis courts. Go for upper rooms with fine views over to the médina. Avoid restaurant. **A** ***Hotel Sheraton***, Av des FAR, T055-625002, F620486. 280 rooms, modern, comfortable, extensive gardens, 2 restaurants, coffee shop, bar, tennis and pool, used by tour groups, grab your buffet meal before it goes cold. **B** ***Hotel Sofia***, 3 R de Pakistan, just off Av Hassan II, in heart of city, T055-624265-67, F626478, 120 a/c rooms (doubles at 640dh, breakfast included) and 4 suites, 2 restaurants, 2 bars, nightclub, pool, safe parking. A good address. **B** ***Hotel Volubilis***, Av Allal ben Abdallah (the continuation of Av Hassan II, moving away from the *ville nouvelle*), T055-654484, F621125. Restaurant, bar, good hotel with pleasant garden and pool. Used by tour operators. **B** ***Hotel Moussafir Ibis***, Av des Almohades, T055-651902/07, F651909, part of the *Accor* group. Very handy for the railway station. 122 rooms, small pool, conference room for up to 180 people, secure parking. **B** ***Hotel Splendid***, 9 R Abdelkarim el Khattabi (a block away from the pedestrian bit of Abd el Karim el Khattabi), T055-622148, F654892, central. 70 a/c rooms with bath, restaurant, bar, TV room, mini-pool in courtyard, safe parking. Street-side rooms on lower floors noisy. Nevertheless, a good place, recommended.

C ***Hotel de la Paix***, 44 Av Hassan II, T055-625072, F626880. Stylish, from the Protectorate period, with bar and restaurant, a/c, clean and comfortable. Recommended. **C** ***Grand Hotel***, Blvd Chefchaouni, T055-932026, grandhotelfes@menara.co.ma A 1930s building in centre of *ville nouvelle*, refurbished 2001. Stylish. Loud bar at back of restaurant. Good in this price bracket – some rooms with a/c. Helpful reception. **C** ***Hotel Olympic***, Av Mohammed V, almost opposite the *Wafa Bank* but entrance on side street. T055-932682, F932665. Central, recently refurbished, TV and a/c in most rooms. Plus point: opposite main alcohol sales point in Fès, Ets Ben Saïd, and good breakfast café. **D** ***Hotel Amor***, 31 R d'Arabie séoudite, coming from the train station, take a left as you come onto the Pl de Florence, T055-622724. 35 rooms, most with shower, no groups. Clean beds. Bar, café-pâtisserie in street below. Avoid street-facing rooms. Good value for money.  **D** ***Hotel Mounia***, 60 R Cuny (R Asilah), T055-624838, F650773. Good cheap hotel in a street parallel to Av Mohammed V, close to Pl Al Massira. Handy for *CTM* bus station. **D** ***Hotel Nouzha***, 7 R Hassan Dkhissi, off Pl Atlas, T055-640002, F640084. Very handy for the *CTM* station but a good 20-min hike from the train station. Cybercafé on ground floor. Fairly clean, efficient staff, café, bar. A good option in this category for a night or two.

E ***Hotel Central***, 50 R du Nador, T055-622333. Big, clean rooms, very cheap. 50% rooms with shower, all with washbasin. About 10-mins' walk from *CTM* station, close to Pl Mohammed V. Acceptable – at the cheap end of this category, especially if you can't face summer heat of Bab Boujeloud. **E** ***Hotel CTM***, Blvd Mohamed V, T055-622811. 25 rooms, washbasin or shower, wc on corridor. Acceptable cheap option. **E** ***Hotel Kairouan***, 84 R du Soudan, T055-623590. Reasonable, near railway station and *Hotel Royal*. Handy pâtisserie next door. Street-side rooms on the noisy side. **E** ***Hotel Lamdaghri***, 10 R Abass el Massadi, off Blvd Mohammed V, very close to *Hotel Splendid*, T055-620310, small, rooms around a courtyard, with a restaurant and bar. **E** ***Hotel Royal***, 36 R du Soudan, T055-624656. Coming from the station, first main street left after the big Imam al Malik mosque. In a modern-ish building close to the *Hotel Kairouan*. Reservations don't always work. **E** ***Hotel Savoy***, in a street off Blvd Abdallah Chefchaouni, T055-620608. Above a petrol station. Hot showers extra.

In the *ville nouvelle* there are a number of cheap options too. **F** ***Hotel du Maghreb***, 25 Av Mohammed es Slaoui, close to Pl Mohammed V. T055-625999. Reception on 1st floor. A couple of blocks from the *CTM* bus station. **F** ***Hotel Régina***, 21 R du 16 Novembre, T055-622427. Acceptable. **F** ***Hotel Rex***, 32 Pl de l'Atlas, T055-642133. Rather a long way from the town centre, but good value. Go straight down Av Mohammed V and turn left onto Av Youssef ibn Tachfine, which leads into Pl de l'Atlas.

Médina

■ *on map, page 258*

L ***Hotel Le Méridien Mérinides***, Borj nord, T055-646218, F645225. 80 rooms, 11 suites. Superb views over the médina. Pool, restaurant, bar, nightclub, modern, conference room. One of Fès' premier addresses. Recommended. **L** ***Hotel Palais Jamaï***, Bab el Guissa, T055-634331/3, F635096. A former palace with superb views of the médina and a beautiful garden, 100 rooms, 20 suites, 2 restaurants, bar, *hammam*, sauna, tennis, pool heated in winter, reservations advisable, service slow, breakfast disappointing. **D** ***Hotel Batha***, R de l'Unesco, T055-634860, F741078. Popular, reasonably priced hotel, comfortable, a/c, handy for sites. Small pool, miserable reception, breakfast pathetic – go for café over the road.

Budget accommodation in the Médina fills up very quickly in spring and summer

At the budget end of the scale, the following are in the **Bab Boujeloud** area of the médina, a 10-min walk from the Borj Nord bus station. The best, but not cheapest, option is the recently opened (2002) **E** ***Pension Campini***, in a converted family house about 150 m up the street from the Batha Museum, T055-637342. Prices seem to be a bit flexible (higher in summer). Some rooms sleep 3 or 4. Popular with student groups. Outside Bab Jeloud, down a side street on your right as you approach the gate, is the sad, run-down **F** ***Hotel du Jardin Publique***, T055-633086, near the Boujeloud Mosque. Just inside the gate, on your right, are **F** ***Hotel Mauritania***, clean, 9 simple rooms, efficient management, and **F** ***Hotel Kaskade***, 26 R Serragine (on the corner after the *Hotel Mauritania*), T055-638442. Not a bad option. One hot shower, loos just about clean. Courtyard rooms quieter. **F** ***Hotel Erraha***, Pl Boujeloud, T055-633226. Adequate but kind of smelly. Head down past the restaurants onto Talaâ Sghira and there are 2 further cheap options, just after the cinema. On your left is **F** ***Hotel Lamrani***, T055-634411, 16 impeccably clean rooms, some with up to 4 beds, shower on ground floor only (cold free, hot 10dh). Manager a little eccentric. On your right is the **F** ***Pension Talaâ***, T055-633359, just 6 rooms without washbasin. Roof terrace rooms would be boiling in summer. Very austere. Small plus point? View of Bou Inania Medersa.

At **Bab Ftouh** on the southern side of Fès el Bali are a couple of cheap hotels. The advantage of being here might be that there are fewer *faux guides* to hassle you as you leave your accommodation. The **F** ***Hotel Moulay Idriss***, on R Saïd Khammer. Clean and simple.

Another option is to stay in **Fès Jdid** where there are a couple of hotels on or close to Pl des Alaouites, the busy square in front of the *Palais Royal*. Try the spartan **F** ***Hotel du Commerce***, T055-622231. Hot showers and loo on corridor. Breakfast at café downstairs. Street-facing rooms noisy.

Riads

Reservations are essential and someone will be sent to meet you

Private guesthouses in restored historic properties began to open in Fès in the late 1990s. If the rate of restoration/conversion continues as in 2002-03, there should be some 20 guesthouses open by 2004, according to one local builder. For the moment, accommodation of this type is on the hugely expensive side as demand far exceeds

Fez Medina

Small Palaces, Royal Suites, & Traditional Houses in the 12th Century Souks of Fes, Morocco

The Fes Medina Project is the only organization making historic properties available for rent in the intact medieval medina of Fes. Authentically restored with traditional materials, properties range from an antique royal suite to the expansive inner world of the traditional Riyad. The Fes Medina Project, www.fesmedina.com 215-833-1896, reservations@fesmedina.com

supply. Most of the luxurious riads are in the **Batha** neighbourhood, with parking 5-10 mins' walk away. ***Invisible World Fez***, T215-833189, www.fesmedina.com, is an agency that offers luxury accommodation, from palaces to riads, in the médina.

LL *Riad Fès*, 5 Derb Ben Slimane, T055-741012, F741143, www.riadfes.com Owner Chakir Sefrioui takes huge pride in the complex operation which transformed this vast, early 20th-century house into an upscale guesthouse with 17 rooms. Diplomats and the like stay here. **L** *Dar el Ghalia*, 13/15 Ross Rhi, T055-636393. Another restored property, partly 18th century, belonging to the Lebbar family, more intimate than *Riad Fès*, 1,500dh per suite, 3,000dh per grande suite, dinner 500dh. Contact owner-manager Omar Lebbar. Same management as the hotel at Volubilis. In the Batha *quartier*, the best upscale choice is **L** *Riad Sheherazade*, 22 Arsat Bennis Douh, T055-741642, T061-189860 (mob), www.sheheraz.fr.st Small pool, superb views from the roof terrace. Cedar-wood ceilings perfume the large rooms. Downside? Possibly a slight lack of privacy if the riad is very full.

In the **Ziat** neighbourhood, not far from the historic Dar el Glaoui, is **A** *Riad el Bartal*, 21 R Sournas, Fès El Bali, T/F055-637053. Various types of rooms, from 550-1,250dh per 2 persons with breakfast. Moroccan decor with French touches, owners Mireille and Christian Laroched. Highly recommended if you get one of the big rooms. **A** *Maison Bleue*, 2 Pl de l'Istiqlal, Batha, T/F055-741843, www.maisonbleue.com Also functions as restaurant, hence some rooms enjoy piped music from the courtyard restaurant. Overpriced. Acceptable if top hotels full. The same company also has a 7-room separate guesthouse, **A** *Maison Bleue – Le Riad*, 33 Derb el Miter, Talaâ Kbira, T055-741873, T061-196851 (mob), www.maisonbleue.com Not recommended. High prices, 2,800dh a night for a suite! The carpet merchants' approach to the guesthouse. Some rooms low ceilings, cluttered. Courtyard with unfenced pool. Off the main drag, Talaâ Kebira, is **A** *Riad Mabrouka*, 25 Derb el Miter, T055-636345, www.ryadmabrouka.com Prices from 800dh small room low season to 1,900dh suite high season. Usual big rooms. Plus point: views over médina from terrace. Unsuitable for those with small children. Unfenced pool and central fountain. Highly recommended. Owners have a real appreciation of the city. In the **Batha** neighbourhood, a good choice is **A-B** *Riad Louna*, 21 Derb Serraj, a street linking Talaâ Sghira with the Batha, T/F055-741985, riadlouna.com Pleasant garden courtyard. Reserve well in advance in May/Jun and at year's end. The whole riad, sleeping up to 12 people, can be rented for 4200dh per night.

Youth hostel 18 R Abdesslam Serghini in the *ville nouvelle*, T055-624085. 60 beds, kitchen, bus 150 m, train 1,200 m, overnight fee 25dh, cheap option for those with a YHA card. Will rent space out on the roof if all the dormitories are full. Has some 2 persons rooms, clean bathrooms. Open only 0800-0900, 1200-1500, 1800-2200. According to a reader, one of the best Yhs in Morocco.

Camping *Camping du Diamant vert*, near Aïn Chkeff, right off the P24, expensive but site with shop and snack restaurant, can be reached by bus No 19 from Fès from outside the PTT. Shade trees but poorly maintained wash-blocks. If staying here, you can use the next door aqua-fun complex (out of use out of season). Packed in summer. ***Camping international***, on the Sefrou road, some 3 km from Fès, reached by bus No 38 from Pl Atlas. T055-731439, F731554. Well maintained but expensive site with pool and shops. Bars with alcohol make this a lively, even noisy site.

Eating

Fès is far from having the same selection of European restaurants as Marrakech. Nevertheless, there are a few reasonable options.

Ville Nouvelle
• *on map, page 265*

Expensive *Restaurant el Hambra*, 47 Route d'Immouzer, T055-641687, menu at 350dh. Out in the suburbs, the restaurant is housed in a series of villas. Collection of traditional musical instruments on display, good service. ***La Cheminée*** 6 Av Lalla Asma (ex-Blvd Chenguit), T055-624902. Under the arcades on your right as you head towards the station, about 250 m away. Alcohol, Franco-Moroccan cooking. ***La Médaille*** 25 R Laarbi Kaghat, T055-620183, near the central market, off Blvd Mohammed V to your right as you come from Pl de Florence. **Mid-range** *Restaurant Mounia*, 11 Blvd Mohammed Slaoui, R Houceine El Khaddar, T055-626661. Moroccan and European food but unlicensed. ***Restaurant du Centre***, 106 Av Mohammed V, T055-622823. Good Moroccan food. There are also reasonable licensed restaurants in the *ville nouvelle*: ***Oued de la Bière***, Av Mohammed V, T055-625324. Moroccan and French cuisine, good *tagine de kefta*, clean and relaxed. ***Restaurant Pizzeria Chez Vittorio***, 21 R Brahim Roudani/R Nador, T055-624730. Good Italian food, wine, no credit cards. **Cheap** Try ***Sicilia***, 4 Av Chefchaouni, T055-625265, pizzas and sandwiches, recommended. ***Al Khozama***, 23 Av Mohammed es Slaoui, almost opposite the *Hotel Jeanne d'Arc*, good simple food. ***Le Nautilus***, 44 Av Hassan II, small restaurant, often full with tour groups, part of the *Hotel de la Paix*, service a bit slow. ***Restaurant Chamonix***, 5 R Mokhtar Soussi, off Av Mohammed V, T055-626638. Moroccan, European and pizzas. Also try ***Croque Burger***, 26 Av Mohammed es Slaoui, T055-654029. Takeaway, delivery and eat-in burgers and pizzas. ***Fès Mondi Sportif***, near intersection of Av des FAR and Av Hassan II. ***Marrakech***, opposite *Hotel Nouzha* off Pl Atlas. Absolutely fine. ***Marhaba***, 23 Av Mohammed V. Good *tagines* and salads. ***Chawarma Sandwich***, 42 R Normandie. Reasonable and clean.

Médina
• *on map, page 258*
Many of the medina restaurants are not licensed

Many of the 'traditional Moroccan' restaurants in converted médina premises are open for lunch only and much used by tour groups. When you ring to make an individual reservation, these restaurants will offer to send someone to take you to the restaurant. The other option is to go for the Moroccan restaurant in one of the 2 big hotels. The most sumptuous food, according to one local, is to be had in the *Dar el Ghalia* (see Sleeping, riads, above).

Expensive *Al Fassia*, in the *Hotel Palais Jamaï*, Bab El Guissa, T055-634331. Reservations advisable, one of the best Moroccan restaurants with a vast array of dishes including quail *tagine*, plus traditional music. Extra charge when there is floorshow with Oriental dancers. ***La Koubba du Ciel***, in *Hotel Les Merinides*, Borj Nord for the best view of Fès El Bali. More convenient for sightseeing is ***Restaurant Dar Saada***, 21 Souk El Attarine, T055-637370, F637371, alcohol served. ***Le Palais de Fès***, R Makhfia, near the *Cinéma el Amal*, via Bab Errsif, T055-761590, F649856. Lunch menu at 350dh, evenings will set you back about the same. ***Palais Mnebhi***, 15 Souk Ben Safi, Talaa Sghira, T055-633893. Cavernous covered courtyard. Only if you can't get into any of the others. ***Dar Tajine***, 15 Ross Rhi, 055-T634167. Fixed Moroccan menus in 19th-century palace, try the *pastilla*. ***Restaurant Palais des Merinides***, 99 Zkak Roah, T055-634028. Serves lunch and dinner, splendid setting, around 110dh per course. **Mid-range** *Restaurant Zohra* 3 Derb Aïn Nass Blida, near the Medersa el Attarine, T055-637699. Menu at 80dh. A good option. ***Restaurant Zineb***, 3 Derb el Kateb Zkak Romane, T055-741966, F055-741967. A new place near Pl Nejjarine, menu 80dh, à la carte around 120dh, no groups, owner Rachid Lamrani. **Cheap** There is no shortage of cheap restaurants in Fès El Bali, particularly near Bab Boujeloud; one of the more upscale is ***La Kasbah***, 18 Bab Boujeloud, T055-741533. Cheap menu including excellent *brochettes*. Make sure you know what you are paying when you order, otherwise prices tend to be a bit arbitrary.

Cafés

In the *ville nouvelle*, try ***L'Elysée***, 4 R de Paris or ***Café Les Ambassadeurs*** on Pl de Florence.

Bars & clubs A drink in the *Hotel Palais Jamaï* is a good break in the médina, the *Hotel des Merinides* has a good view of the city. In the *ville nouvelle* try ***Es Saada***, on Av Slaoui, or ***Bar du Centre***, Av Mohammed V. The *Hotel Menzah Zalagh* has the local chic nightspot, the ***Disco Galileo***.

Sport and activities

Golf ***Royal Golf Club***, Route d'Ifrane, T055-763849. 9 holes, 3,168 m, par 37. Fees per round 400dh, hire of clubs 100dh, closed Mon. **Swimming** In the large hotels, mainly *Hotel Menzah Zalagh*, R Mohammed Diouri, or at the municipal pool, Av des Sports. **Tennis** ***Sporting Club Fassi***, Clos de la Renaissance, 10 R Moulay Slimane, T055-641512, 5 courts. ***Tennis Club Fassi***, Av Mohammed El Kori, T055-624272, 7 courts.

Shopping

Fès El Jedid is a quieter but slightly more pricey area to shop in

Moroccan goods Fès has for long been one of the great trading centres of Morocco. The souks, *kissaria* and boutiques offer a splendid selection for visitors. Many of the boutiques in the hotels, the *ville nouvelle* and near the important tourist attractions will try to charge inflated prices. As elsewhere, the large carpet shops have very experienced salesmen who work with guides to whom they pay a commission for sales completed. Best buy in Fès? The blue and white painted, quite rustic pottery, once typical of the city. For smaller gift items, slippers and traditional clothing wander in the Kessaria (clothes market) area between the Zaouia of Moulay Idriss and the Qaraouiyine Mosque. For a good selection of crafts in the *ville nouvelle*, try ***Coopartim Centre Artisanal***, Blvd Allal Ben Abdallah, T055-625654 (0900-1400, 1600-1900).

Tour operators

Azur Voyage, 3 Blvd Lalla Meryem, T055-625115. ***Fès Voyages***, 9 R de Turquie, T055-621776. ***Number One***, 41 Av Slaoui, T055-621234. ***Tak Voyages***, 41 Av Mohammed V, T055-624550, F652736. ***Wagons-Lits Tourisme***, *Immeuble Grand Hotel*, T055-654464.

Transport

Local **Bus** These can be a convenient option in Fès, a ticket costs 2dh. No 1 runs from Pl des Alaouites to Dar Batha, No 3 from Pl des Alaouites to Pl de la Résistance, No 9 from Pl de la Résistance to Dar Batha, No 10 from Bab Guissa to Pl des Alaouites, No 18 from Pl de la Résistance to Bab Ftouh and No 20 from Pl de Florence to *Hotel les Merinides*.

Car hire ***Avis***, 50 Blvd Chefchaouni, T055-626746. ***Budget***, adjacent *Palais Jamaï Hotel*, T055-620919. ***Europcar-Inter-Rent***, 41 Av Hassan II, T055-626545. ***Hertz***, Kissariat de la Foire No 1, Blvd Lalla Meryem, T055-622812; airport T055-651823. ***Holiday Car***, 41 Av Mohammed V, T055-624550, F652736. ***SAFLOC***, *Hotel Sheraton*, T055-931201. ***Zeit***, 35 Av Mohammed Slaoui, T055-625510.

Grands taxis Leave from Pl Baghdadi, except for Sefrou and Azrou which leave from R de Normandie.

Taxi Red, cheap and a quick way to get around Fès, they can be found around much of the city, and generally have meters. Sample fares, Bab Boujeloud to Pl Mohammed V, 10dh; Pl Mohammed V to *Hotel Les Merinides*, 15dh. Parking can be a problem approaching the médina, so it is perhaps better not to use one's own car.

Long distance

Air Aéroport de Fès-Saiss is 15 km to the south of the city, off the P24, T055-624712. There are flights to **Casablanca** with connections to internal and international destinations, 1 a week to **Er Rachidia**, as well as direct flights to **Marseille** and **Paris**. To get to the airport take Bus 16 from the train station. **Airline offices** The *RAM* office, T055-625516/7, reservations T055-620456/7, is centrally located at 54 Av Hassan II in the *ville nouvelle*.

Road Fès lies at a crossroads in Morocco, and is an excellent base from which to plan and carry out the next stage of travels.

On the routes into the city, men on motorbikes often drive alongside motorists to tout for unofficial guide work: best to ignore them

Bus *CTM* buses depart from the station on Av Mohammed V, T055-622041, for **Beni Mellal**, **Marrakech** (early morning departure, 8 hrs), **Tetouan**, **Tanger** (in the small hours), **Taza** , **Oujda**, **Nador**. For **Casablanca**, 8 departures a day, 0700-1900, for **Rabat**, 7 a day, and for **Meknès,** 8 a day, 0700-1900. Most other private line buses leave from the new terminal off the Route du Tour de Fès, below the Borj Nord and not far from Bab Boujeloud. Buses for the **Middle Atlas** leave from the Laghzaoui terminal, R Ksar el Kebir.

Train The railway station is at the end of Blvd Chenguit, in the *ville nouvelle*, T055-622501. To get to the town (*ville nouvelle*), head down this road and slightly to the left into Av de la Liberté. This joins Av Hassan II, the main street of the new town, at Pl de Florence. If you arrive by train, check your potential departure time at the station. Trains run east to **Taza** and **Oujda** and west to **Meknès**, **Tanger**, **Rabat** and **Casablanca**.

Directory

Banks

Lots of banks in *ville nouvelle* on Pl Florence and Av Mohamed V. Most reliable ATM is the ***Wafa Bank***, Av Mohammed V, T055-622591. Other banks with ATMs in the big Immeuble Mamda, Pl de Florence. ATMs in Fès el Bali difficult to locate but many shopkeepers will change euros.

Communications

Internet: internet cafés can be found on Av Hassan II in the *ville nouvelle* and near the intersection of R Douh and the Batha in Fès el Bali. **Post/telephone**: the *PTT Centrale* is at the junction of Av Hassan II and Av Mohammed V, phone section open 0800-2100. In the médina, main PO is on Pl Batha. **Books and newspapers**: try the *English Bookshop* of Fès, 68 Av Hassan II, near Pl de la Résistance. Newspapers from the stalls in Av Mohammed V.

Cultural & language centres

Institut français, 33 R el-Bahrein, T055-623921, library and films. ***Alif*** (Arabic Language in Fès), in the *ville nouvelle* at 2 R Ahmed Hiba (close to the *Hotel Zalagh*), T055-624850, www.alif-fes.com Has a good reputation for organizing courses in Arabic, both literary and spoken Moroccan. They can cater for specific language needs, and at any one time have around 30 or more students, from various backgrounds.

Medical services

Chemists: there is an all-night chemist at the Municipalité de Fès, blvd Moulay Youssef, T623380 (2000-0800). During the day try ***Bahja***, Av Mohammed V, T622441 or ***Bab Ftouh*** at Bab Ftouh, T649135. **Hospital**: ***Hôpital Ghassani***, Quartier Dhar Mehraz, T622776.

Useful addresses

Emergency: Fire, T15. Police, Av Mohammed V, T19.**Garages**: try ***Mécanique Générale***, 22 Av Cameroun. Fiat repairs at ***Auto Maroc***, Av Mohammed V, T055-623435.

Around Fès

Moulay Yacoub

Phone code: 055
Colour map 1, grid B3
20 km NW of Fès

Moulay Yacoub is a short journey through rolling countryside and some interesting capital-intensive irrigated farming. Taxis from Bab Boujeloud stop near the car park above the village. The ride from Fès to Moulay Yacoub takes about 45 minutes. Steep flights of steps lead down into the village to the *hammams*. There are plenty of small shops, cafés and a number of cheap lodging houses, some with rudimentary self-catering facilities. This is a pilgrimage sort of place, every bit a country spa-town.

Moulay Yacoub is most definitely a destination for local tourists, and a visit to the *hammam* can be quite an experience. There are baths for both men and women. The buildings date from the 1930s, and could do with some maintenance, but at the price, you can't complain. The men's *hammam* has a pool of extremely hot sulphurous water – a bucket of Moulay Yacoub water poured on your head is guaranteed to boil your brains. There are few foreigners; beware the masseur, who may well delight in making an exhibition of you with a poolside pummel and stretching designed for Olympic athletes. Merely bathing in the hot spring water will leave you exhausted – and hopefully rejuvenated. There is also a luxury spa down in the valley.

Sleeping & eating
At quiet times, there will be plenty of rooms in private homes on offer

C ***Hotel Moulay Yacoub***, also called the ***Fès Motel***, stands above the village, T055-694035, F694012. 60 rooms with TV, bath and terrace, 60 bungalows, restaurant with magnificent views, bar, tennis, pool. A new treelined road leads down to the medical treatment centre using thermal springs, with neat gardens, café and practice golf.
E ***Hotel Lamrani***, T055-694021. Perhaps the best of the cheap accommodation.

Sidi Harazem and Bhalil

Sidi Harazem
Colour map 1, grid B3

In restaurants all over Morocco, Sidi Ali and Sidi Harazem are the most widely available mineral waters, along with sparkling Oulmès. The saintly Sidi Harazem is said to have died in Fès in 1164. He taught in that city, at the Qaraouiyin Mosque, and it is said his classes and lectures were so interesting that even the djinn, the 'other ones', attended.

The village of Sidi Harazem, with its spring and spa centre, is an easy day excursion from Fès, being only 4 km along the P1 from the capital of the Idrissids, with buses from the *CTM* bus station and Bab Boujeloud, and other buses and grands taxis from Bab Ftouh. The area around the thermal baths is still very popular for swimming and picnics. That said, the once impressive watercourses, pools and spas have been disappointingly neglected. There is too much concrete and trinket sellers can be a little tedious. There is a 17th-century *koubba*, dating from the time of the village's establishment as a resort under Sultan Moulay Rachid. If you want to stay there is the **C** *Hotel Sidi Harazem*, T055-690057, F690072, with 62 air-conditioned rooms, health facilities, restaurant and bar. Pricey for what it is.

Bhalil

En route to Sefrou, 5 km before the town off the P20, is Bhalil. This small hill village may have had a Christian population before the coming of Islam. Behind the picturesque village are several troglodyte dwellings, with people still inhabiting the caves. The road takes you round the town, giving excellent views on all sides, and two good clean cafés on the outskirts when approaching from the east.

Bump in the baths

Early in the 19th century, Fès was visited by the Spaniard Domingo Badia y Leblich, travelling in the Cherifian lands under the pseudonym Ali Bey El Abbassi. He noted the importance of the public baths or hammams *of Fès ... "The baths are open to the public all day. The men go in the morning, the women in the afternoon. I generally used to go in the evening, taking the whole bathhouse for myself so that there would be no outsiders ... The first time I went there, I noted that there were buckets of water placed symmetrically in the corner of each room and each cubicle. I asked what they were for. 'Do not touch them, sir,' the personnel of the* hammam *replied in haste. 'Why?' 'These are buckets for the people down below.' 'Who are they?' 'The demons who come to wash during the night'."*

A few centuries earlier, Leo Africanus described the traditions of the hammams *of Fès ... "The companions and the owners of the steam-baths hold festivities once a year, celebrating in the following way. First of all they invite all their friends, and go through the city to fife, tambourine and trumpets, then they take a hyacinth bulb, placing it in a fine copper container which they cover with a white cloth. Then they go back through the city, accompanied by music, to the door of the* hammam*. There they put the bulb in a basket which they hang over the door, saying, 'This will bring seed to the hammam, because of it there will be many visitors'".*

Traditions related to the hammam seem to have died away today. However, even in the 1920s and 1930s, superstitions were very much alive. Dr Edmond Secret, a French doctor working in Fès, noted how those who went to the hammam very early, washing alone, were considered courageous: genies were held to live in damp corners and in the water pipes.

Sefrou

Phone code: 055
Colour map 1, grid B3

Sefrou is 32 km south of Fès along the P20. It is not the sort of place you would visit if travelling south, as the P24/P21, via Ifrane and Azrou, is a better route from Fès to Er Rachidia and the South. However, Sefrou is certainly worth visiting as a side trip from Fès or even for an overnight stay, as it is one of the most appealing towns in Morocco, a poor but relatively unspoilt historic walled town lying in a beautiful wooded valley, with a calm and genuinely friendly atmosphere.

Ins & outs

Getting there Buses and taxis arrive and leave from Pl Moulay Hassan, by Bab Taksebt and Bab M'kam, where the road from Fès meets the old town. Buses from Fès leave from Bab Boujeloud and many go on to Er Rachidia. Grands taxis from Fès leave from Bab Ftouh.

Background

Although now bypassed by new roads, Sefrou once lay astride the major caravan routes from Fès and the North, to the South and the Sahara beyond. It does however remain an important marketplace for the surrounding agricultural region. Like Debdou and Demnate, Sefrou was one of those small inland Moroccan towns which had a distinctive character due to a large Jewish population which predated the Islamic conquest. Although many Berbers and Jews were converted to Islam by Moulay Idriss, Sefrou's Jewish element was reinforced with the migration of Jews from Tafilalet and Algeria in the 13th century. After the Second World War, large numbers of Jews emigrated to Morocco's large cities, Europe and Israel. The 1967 Arab-Israeli War was the final blow. Sefrou has fascinated American academics, with anthropologists Geertz, Rosen and Rabinow carrying out research here. Recently Sefrou was created capital of a new province, receiving new and badly needed investment. A town declining into shabby anonymity, it may yet rescue something of its heritage and find a place on the tourist map.

Sights The market place below and east of Avenue Mohammed V is a relaxed place to wander, best during the Thursday **souk**. The town, which is known for olive and cherry production, has a large **Fête des Cerises** in June, and other smaller *fêtes* during the year. There is a *moussem*, or religious gathering, for Sidi Lahcen Lyoussi.

Entering from the north the road curves down to the Oued Aggaï, past the *Centre Artisanal* (0800-1200 and 1400-1900, except Sunday) into the busy Place Moulay Hassan. From here Bab M'kam is the main entrance to the médina which lies north of the river and Bab Taksebt the main entrance, over the bridge, into the *mellah*. Both are small, maze-like quarters, but it is difficult to get seriously lost. The *mellah* can also be entered from the covered market-place through Bab M'Rabja. Beside a mosque built into the wall, bend right and down the main street, beside small restaurants, butchers, shops and craftsmen, and then left to reach one of several small bridges over the Oued Aggaï. Alternatively, take one of the small side turnings to discover the cramped design of the *mellah*, now mainly occupied by poor rural migrants, with houses often built over the narrow streets.

In the médina, the **Grand Mosque**, restored in the 19th century, lies beside the river, and the souks just upstream. Past the souks is the **Zaouïa of Sidi Lahcen ben Ahmed**. In the médina there is a clearly discernible difference in the design of the quarter, reflecting the strict regulations and conditions under which Jews in the *mellah* lived. Sefrou is quite remarkable, however, in that the *mellah* is as large as the médina.

Avenue Moulay Hassan crosses the Oued Aggaï, where there is a *Syndicat d'Initiative*, T055-660380, past the Jardin publique, which has a swimming pool and continues as Avenue Mohammed V, the main street of the unexciting new town, with the post office, and a few shops and simple café-restaurants including the *rôtisseries*, for grilled chicken.Turn into Rue Ziad by the post office, past *Hotel Sidi Lahcen Lyoussi* and continue uphill on the black top road. Camping is signed to the left but continue up to the *koubba* of Sidi Bou Ali, white walls and distinctive green-tiled roof. There is a café, a few stalls and a magnificent view. Another small excursion beginning south of the river leads west to a rather small waterfall (*les cascades*).

Sleeping & eating **B** *Hotel Sidi Lahcen Lyoussi*, off Av Moulay Hassan, T055-660497. Dated but comfortable place with 24 rooms, a restaurant, bar and pool. **F** *Hotel La Frenie*, Route de Fès, T055-660030. A small but generally OK place. **Camping** Follow R Ziad, by the post office on Av Mohammed V, to a campsite, *Camping de Sefrou*, T055-673340. 2 km from the town, in site of 4 ha, bar/snack, grocery, showers, laundry, petrol at 2 km, and on a fork off that road, the **F** *Hotel-Café Bouserghine*, by the green-roofed Koubba of Sidi Bouserghine, Sefrou's patron saint.

Valley of Ouergha The triangle formed by the S302, S304 and the P26 makes an interesting tour. Aïn Kansera stands off the road to the right before the track to the Idriss I Dam is reached. This large lake on the Oued Inaouena is some 20 km in length and stores water for Fès. It is a popular picnic site. At Tissa there is an important annual gathering of horses and their riders. Aïn Aicha is an important regional market in the Oued Ouergha. Take time to visit picturesque Rafsai, 10 km beyond Ourtzarh. Jbel Messaoud (825 m) can be reached from Ourtzarh and affords fine views over the valley and the Rif.

Return to Fès travelling south on the P26. Where Tnine stands on the east of the road, Moulay Bouchta stands on the west, a venue for the annual horse and rider *moussem*.

Fès to Taza

Fès to Taza by the P1 road is 113 km, with a driving time of 1 hour 50 minutes, provided there aren't too many lorries. Getting out of the eastern suburbs of Fès can be slow, especially on a Sunday when there is a market. The first stage of the journey takes you along a fertile river valley with poplar trees, stands of cane and market gardens. A winding but quite fast section of road then takes you up to a plateau, with views over to the waters of the Barrage Idriss Ier set against rolling hills. Then a long, straight, eucalyptus-lined road takes you past the turn-off for Tissa to the north and up to the **Col de Touahar** (556 m), some 98 km from Fès. **NB** Watch your speed, the stubby grey jeeps of the Gendarmerie royale are lurking behind the trees. The turn-off for the Tazzeka circuit, eastern approach, is before the col. Look out for signs to **Bab Zahra**, 12 km, 86 km from Fès. There is a big green sign for the **Jbel Tazzeka** national park behind the Bab Zahra sign and the road takes you left before doubling back under the railway bridge to rise to a 4 km wild and russet-rock gorge with suggestive caves in the cliffs. (The full route is described below, page 278, departing from Taza.)

After the Bab Zahra turn-off, there will be lots of olive oil for sale along the road. At the first major junction in Taza (petrol on your right, rail-station signposted left), you can turn right and wind up into Taza – Ville Nouvelle.

Taza

There was a time when Taza was quite a happening place, given its strategic location controlling the easiest route from the Moroccan heartland of Fès and Meknès to the eastern plains. The town, a rather quiet place today, is divided into three quite separate parts: the area around the railway and bus station; the ville nouvelle *around Place de l'Indépendence; and the quiet médina on the hill (whose main historic buildings are closed to non-Muslims). Nevertheless, the médina, with its narrow streets , is an interesting place to stroll. After the hurly-burly of Fès, low-key Taza makes a good base from which to explore up into the Jbel Tazzeka.*

Phone code: 055
Colour map 1, grid B4
Population: nearly 80,000

Taza Médina

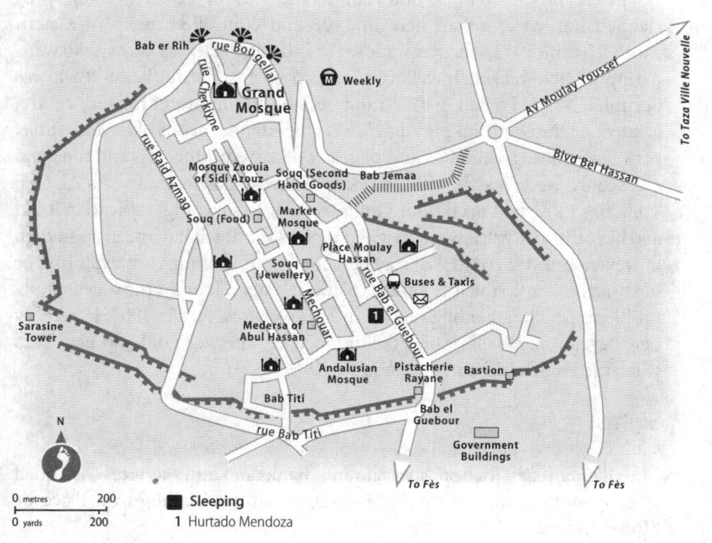

Ins and outs

Getting there

See Transport, page 278, for further details

Taza is easily accessible by public transport from Fès, 120 km to the west. Coming from eastern Morocco, you will necessarily pass through Taourirt and Guercif, a major meeting of the roads some 40 km from Taza. There are trains daily from Oujda, taking around 4 hrs, and from Meknès, say 3½ hrs and Fès, 2 hrs. There are occasional grands taxis from El Hoceima, north of Taza on the Mediterranean coast. From both El Hoceima and Nador, also on the Mediterranean, there are buses to Taza, via Aknoul, taking around 4 hrs.

Getting around

Arriving by train, bus or grand taxi, you will come into the north of the *ville nouvelle*. The médina is a fair 3-km trek away, and as there is only 1 hotel there you will probably stay in the *ville nouvelle*. (Go straight down Av de la Gare, there are 3 hotels on Pl de l'Indépendence at the end.) There is a regular bus service from Pl de l'Indépendence to Pl Moulay Hassan in the médina. A light blue petit taxi will cost you around 3dh from station to Pl de l'Indépendence, say 6dh from station to médina.

Background

Though of considerable regional importance in the past due to its strategic location on routes across northern Morocco, Taza today is a modest market town. The site was first settled in Neolithic times. Later it was developed by Meknassa Amazigh groups, eventually becoming an important but finally unsuccessful fortification against the advance of the Fatimids from the east. The Almohads under Sultan Abd el Moumen captured the city in 1141-42, making it their second capital, and using it to attack the Almoravids. The Almohads built a mosque and expanded the fortifications.

Taza was the first city taken by the Merinids, who extended the Almohad city considerably. Its important defensive role continued under the Merinids and the Saâdians, and was again pivotal in the rise to power of the Alaouites, who further extended and fortified the city, later using it as a strong point in their defence against the threat from French-occupied Algeria to the east.

The eccentric pretender, Bou Hamra, 'the man on the she-donkey', proclaimed himself as sultan here in 1902 and controlled much of eastern Morocco until 1912, when he was caught and killed. He was known as a wandering miracle-maker, travelling Morocco on his faithful beast. Taza was occupied by the French in 1914, and became an important military centre, located on the route linking Algeria with the Atlantic plains of *le Maroc utile*, between remote mountains and plateaux of eastern Morocco and the great cities to the west. Today, with the decline in cross-border trade with Algeria, Taza, like its distant neighbour Oujda, sees far less passing traffic than it did and has a distinctly sleepy feel to it. A couple of the hotels have been upgraded, however, and you could well stay here for a couple of nights if exploring or birdwatching up in the Jbel Tazzeka National Park. Happily, the water supply problems which rather blighted life in Taza were resolved in 2002. Hopefully new development will respect the distance kept between old and new Taza when the French laid out the *ville nouvelle*.

Sights

The *ville nouvelle* – for hotels, restaurants, banks and other services – is a quiet place centred around early and mid-20th century buildings on Place de l'Indépendence.

Médina

The older buildings are in the small attractive médina perched on the hill 3 km away from the railway station and 2 km from the centre of the new town. From the bottom of the hill there is an interesting short cut to the kasbah via a flight of steps which provide remarkable views. Beyond this point, further along the main road on the right, are the **Kifane el Ghomari** caves, inhabited in Neolithic times.

The transport hub of the old town is Place Moulay Hassan, just outside the main entrance to the souk, where the post office, bank, cafés, téléboutique et cetera are to be found. The focus of the old quarter is the main street, with a number of names, but commonly called the Mechouar from end to end, which runs behind Place Moulay Hassan along the entire length of the médina from the Andalucían Mosque to the Grand Mosque at the opposite end of town by the Bab er Rih gate. Between the two mosques are the various souks. Hassle is practically non existent, as there is a few articles which might be thought to interest the tourist. The fact that there is no motor traffic in the médina makes it all the more pleasant. The best thing to do is just wander – the old neighbourhoods are quite small and sooner or later you will come out on the outside road ringing the town.

Turning left just past the main gate to the souk by the *Cinema Friouato* is the jewellery section of the souk. From here you can turn left along a very straight and narrow section of road towards the Andalucían Mosque, or right toward the Grand Mosque. Following the latter route, the food and spice souk is off to the left, behind the broader section of the *mechouar*. Further along, one can perhaps gain a glimpse of the Zaouia of Sidi Azouz and note its beautiful wall-basin by the door. It is difficult to gain a good view of the **Grand Mosque**. The mosque, including its existing minaret, was built by the Almohads in the second half of the 12th century, with further elaboration by the Merinids in the late 13th century, and the Alaouites in the 17th. In its classic proportions of 1:5, the minaret resembles that of the Koutoubia Mosque in Marrakech. Only Muslims can view the beautiful chandelier bearing 514 oil lamps which lights the mosque.

To the right of the Grand Mosque, down a steep flight of steps, you reach a section of the ramparts, with good views over the surrounding countryside, lower Taza, and the mountains beyond. Going left after the steps to start a rampart tour, the first section, with some steep drops, is referred to as Bab er Rih, 'the Gate of the Wind'. From here you have perhaps the best view of the Almohad minaret. Eventually, keeping to the outside of the town, you could look out for the the circular Sarasine Tower, also dating back to the Almohad times – and showing clear European influence.

Good views over old Taza from the road up into the Jbel Tazzeka

At the far end of the mechouar from Bab er Rih is the Andalucían Mosque with its 12th-century minaret. Just before, on the right, stands the 14th-century Medersa of Abu el Hassan, named after a Merinid sultan. This is closed, but the exterior shows a carved lintel in cedar wood, and a porch roof overhanging the road. At the end of the Mechouar, in a lane to the right of the mosque, Zankat Dar el Makhzen, there is the former house of Bou Hamra the pretender. The weekly market takes place outside the walls at this end of town, outside Bab Titi.

Essentials

Sleeping

There is at present no campsite

D ***Hotel Friouato Salam***, Av de la Gare, T055-672593. Top hotel in town, 58 rooms, bar, restaurant, tennis and pool (in summer), room heating in winter. Inconvenient location between the médina and the *ville nouvelle*, to get there turn left at the foot of the steps that climb the hill to the old town. Has seen better days and capacity outstrips demand but good for a drink in the large peaceful garden. **E** ***Grand Hotel du Dauphiné***, at the centre of the town on junction of Av de la Gare and Pl de l'Indépendence, T055-673567. 26 rooms, recently (2002) renovated and all the better for it, even though the 'period charm' and dust have gone. **E** ***Hotel de la Gare***, at the main crossroads near the station, T055-672448. The best cheap option in the new town, adequate standard of cleaning, friendly owners, café, téléboutique next door, best rooms are on the 1st floor, cold showers only. Very handy for early starts with grand taxi and bus stations close by as well as 'la gare'. **F** ***Hotel de la Poste***, Pl de l'Indépendence, by the *CTM* office above a café, T055-672589. Very austere, tiny rooms, at times very noisy. **F** ***Hurtado Mendoza*** (alias *Hotel du Garage de l'Etoile*), Moulay Hassan, T055-270179. Very cheap: 40dh single, 80dh double, shower now available. (They quote prices in riyals.) Located behind some arcades at the entrance to the médina, opposite the post office, only hotel in the old town. Basic, clean accommodation around a courtyard with an old walnut tree. Lots of pink paint and tiles. Nicest rooms are on the upper floors, which are better ventilated and have good views. The proprietor, Mr Mendoza, is Spanish and lives here with his Moroccan wife and children. **F** ***Hotel Guillaume Tell***, Pl de l'Indépendence. Spartan, clean but not a fun place.

Eating **Mid-range** *Hotel Salam Friouato*, T055-672593, has reasonable, unexciting meals. A better option is ***Grand Hotel du Dauphiné***, junction of Pl de l'Indépendence and Av de la Gare, T055-673567. Huge 1950s dining hall, good value if you don't mind a limited menu (sometimes only steak and chips), beer available. **Cheap** ***Café Restaurant Majestic***, Av Mohammed V, Moroccan food, and on same street ***Restaurant Azzam***. ***Snack Bar Youm Youm***, behind *Hotel de la Poste* on Blvd Moulay Youssef, serving *brochettes*. **Cafés** ***Pâtisserie des Festivités***, 1 Blvd Mohammed V, just off Pl de l'Indépendence, cosy salon at rear, good for breakfast and cakes. ***Café Andalous***, in the old town where terrace overlooks the animated Pl Moulay Hassan. A place to sit and observe the local scene. ***Café el Ghissani***, opposite *Café Andalous* by the main entrance to the souk. Popular café, again good for people-watching. ***Café des Jardins***, Av Ibn Khatib. Pleasant, situated in the municipal gardens on route to the old town, terrace with views, closed at night.

Shopping *Pistacherie Rayane*, 5 Av Moulay Hassan, by the entrance to the old town. Sells factory-fresh nuts, very much cheaper than elsewhere.

Transport **Road Bus**: *CTM* buses leave from their office on Pl de l'Indépendence for **Oujda** and **Fès/Meknès/Casablanca**. Other companies operate from near the railway station, turn right at the end of Av de la Gare. Regular services to **Oujda/Guercif/Taourirt**, (4 hrs), **Fès** every hour (2 hrs), **Nador** (4 hrs), **Al Hoceima** (4 hrs) and **Aknoul** (1 hr). Make sure you take a new looking bus by a reliable company for Al Hoceima and Nador. **Taxi**: grands taxis leave from the transport cafés by the bus station to **Oujda**, **Fès**, **Al Hoceima** and **Nador**, amongst other places.

Train At Taza the ONCF locomotives switch from electric to diesel, hence pace going eastwards is slow. There are at least 3 daily departures for **Oujda** (stopping at Guercif and Taourirt). **Casablanca** is 7 hrs away, **Tanger** a good 8 hrs away, if you are lucky with the *correspondance* at Sidi Kacem. **Fès** is 2 hrs by train, **Meknès** 3 hrs.

Directory **Banks** Banks with ATMs include the *BMCE*, near the *Hotel Dauphiné*, in the new town.

Around Taza

Jbel Tazzeka National Park

Colour map 1, grid B4

An area of fine mountain scenery, the Jbel Tazzeka National Park, south of Taza and the P1, can be visited with own transport on a long but rewarding day trip from Fès. The region's cork-oak forest and its undergrowth has plenty to keep ornithologists happy – look out for the rare black-shouldered kite. If you're feeling very fit and energetic, bring scruffy kit and good boots: scenery and kites apart, the main reason for doing this side trip up into the Tazzeka is to go intrepidly down into the **Gouffre de Friouato**, an immense series of hobbity caverns with scrambles, stalactites and mud aplenty.

From the plateau of old Taza, the S311 winds its way south and west, eventually linking up with the the P1 some 31 km further west. If you have parked up close to the walls of Taza, then head back as though you were returning to new Taza, leaving the Préfecture on your left, and go straight ahead at the next roundabout. The excursion up into the Jbel Tazzeka is primarily for those with their own transport, although you might bargain for a grand taxi to take you part of the way, from the rank by the railway station. In own car, with no stops, a careful driver will take 1¾ hours to reach the P1. (NB Take water in case engine overheats.) After a rainy winter, the **Cascades de Ras el Oued**, a few kilometres out of Taza and a popular picnic spot, might be worth a look. Next stop, some 14 km along the route, is the **Vallée des oiseaux**, which starts with a thick stand of cork oak. Nearby lies the **Dayat Chiker**, a seasonal lake. Next you will reach a fork in the road signed Maghraoua (left) and Bab Boudir (right). Go right, and 3 km further on, about 35 minutes from Taza, you will reach the turn-off right heading uphill to the Gouffre de Friouato.

Gouffre de Friouato

A descent into this magnificent cave system is not for the weak-kneed. Near the car park is a stone-built guichet building where smiling, bright-eyed Mustapha Lachhab presides over piles of biscuits, sweets, torches and batteries – everything an amateur caver could need. The officially authorized organizer of guides, he also has photocopied sheets with a cross section of the caverns. Access to the first flights of steps costs 3dh, 100dh gets you a guide to take a small group (up to four people), down the 230 m and 520 steps of the first section, through a narrow squeeze and scramble bit and into the Salle de Lixus, as the first main cave is rather grandly known, after the Roman site near

Jbel Tazzeka National Park

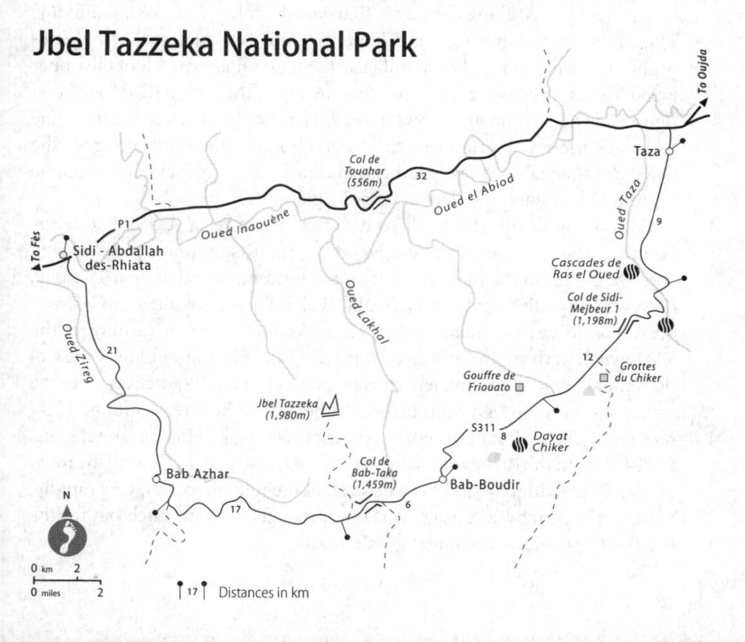

modern Larache. Here there are stalactites, including a sort of crystal platform looking for all the world like a Renaissance pulpit, a be-turbaned individual (use your imagination) and a *hallouf* (pig). From here the caves run on at least a further 2 km, an exploration best left to the enthusiastic and well equipped. Getting down and back from the Salle de Lixus will take you about an hour. The squeeze to this section is easier coming up, by the way. If you're a real speleologist, it would definitely be worth spending time in the region as there are further caverns elsewhere. Note that, having done the descent so many times, the local guides really do know how to pace a group. They now have quite a lot of ropes and other material left behind by cavers.

After the caves, the next major stopping point, 30 km from Taza, is an unlikely *station estivale* with red-roofed houses, more under construction and various seasonal eateries including the *Café Bouhadli*. Continue on to the Bab Taza pass from which a rough and challenging track goes north up to the **Jbel Tazzeka**, where there are incredible views of the surrounding mountains. After, or avoiding, the Jbel Tazzeka, the road continues through cork forest, past another signed picnic area, the **Vallée des cerfs** and then down and through the narrow gorge by the Oued Zireg and back to the P1. The map shows distances between major points and the quality of the roads. For excursions south to Immouzer du Kandar and the Dayats of Aaoua, Afourgan and Ifrah, see page 246.

From Taza to Casita

Lying north from Taza is a section of the Rif mountains that can be visited easily in one day. Although less dramatic and tamer than the mountains further west, it is a pleasant trip if you have your own transport, particularly on market days (see below) which make for more entertaining halts. If you are heading for Nador the S312 is more scenic than routes further east. The road branches off from the P1, 2 km to the east of Taza station, and after 20 km reaches the village of **Aïn Bou Kellal**, which has a large bustling market on Saturday. It is important to arrive early to enjoy the event at its best (and coolest).

The next village along the way is **Jbarna**, which has a market on Sunday. Thereafter the road begins to climb more steeply, and mature Aleppo pines begin to appear. Some 5 km past Jbarna the road joins a stretch of the upper Oued Msoun which is very pretty. Near the top of the pass, a road to the east signposted to Mesquitem follows the *oued* downstream back to the P1, while to the west a less well surfaced track leads to El Gouzat and south alongside the Oued el Hadar back to the P1. Either makes an interesting excursion but these are not short distances and would require planning.

Continuing north, the small administrative centre of **Aknoul** is disappointing. There are hardly any shops and no place to stay, only a petrol station and two banks on the main road. If you are passing through on a Tuesday, however, its worth stopping for the souk, which draws a colourful crowd from the surrounding mountains. Shortly after Aknoul there is the turning for the S304 which leads precariously westwards into the Rif heartland over the Col du Nador. There is a permanent *sureté* roadblock at this T-junction. Expect a courteous but thorough routine check. The next 18 km are scenic and high, reaching 1,300 m. But this is nothing to the towering Jbel Berkane on the east (1,774 m) and the Rif massif to the west, over 2,000 m. It is not until the town of Tizi-Ouzi (Monday souk) is reached that the road descends, very rapidly, towards the plains and Casita. This is a speedy 21 km but watch out for the *oued* bed just before reaching the main road.

Casita

This is little more than a junction town on the P39 with the usual new building. It is located just inside the former Spanish zone of influence. There are buses to Nador and Al Hoceima every hour, so there is little reason to stay unless you are heading back to Taza, in which case you may have to wait some time for public transport. A bus departs at 1500 back to Taza. If you're stuck here the only acceptable option is the basic *Hotel Andalous* opposite the Taza Road, above a simple café/restaurant.

Transport From Taza taxis to Aknoul/Casita/Al Hoceima depart from the rear of the long taxi queue behind the transport cafés near the station. Waiting for a taxi to fill up can take some time.

East of Taza

From Taza to Oujda Msoun

Some 20 km to the east of Taza along the P1 is the fortified farming village of Msoun. Built around 1700 in Moulay Ismael's reign to guard the approaches to the strategic Taza Gap, it is still inhabited by members of the semi-nomadic Houara tribe. The village has a shop, post office and even a teahouse. The compact, walled settlement stands isolated on a hillside, clearly visible from the main road where there is the convenient *Motel-Restaurant Casbah*, and a petrol station. It is possible to walk to the village from here, just 2 km.

Guercif

Phone code: 055
Colour map 1, grid B5

Guercif is an unremarkable modern agricultural town noted for its olives and shoe industry. In the 14th century, it became a stronghold of the Beni Ouattas Tribe, who later overran Taza and replaced Merinids to form the Ouattasid Dynasty. The main part of town, which lies to the south of the main road, is centred around Boulevard Mohammed V, its solid 19th-century mosque, and two adjacent squares: the central square, which functions as a commercial and transport hub, and the Place Zerkatouni with the public gardens and post office. The railway station is reached via a driveway from the opposite side of the main road. Market day is Sunday.

Sleeping

E ***Hotel Howary***, Av Moulay Youssef, T055-625062. A busy small hotel on the Oujda road near the railway station, rooms are very variable, and the plumbing is unreliable, you may have to ask for clean bed linen but staff are friendly and helpful. **E** ***Hotel/Restaurant des Voyageurs***, R Ibn Battuta, between the mosque and the main road. A faded piece of colonial France frozen in time, atmospheric, threadbare, large rooms, nonchalant staff, in spite of the name, no restaurant.

Eating

The best eateries are the group of transport cafés known as '***le complexe***' on the main road, the meat used for the *brochettes* is very fresh, direct from the in-house butcher. The *Place Centrale* has several snack places and grocery stores catering for travellers. **Cafés** *Café Nahda* is a small, friendly, efficient place on the corner of R Mohammed V and R Ibn Battuta near the mosque. The café opposite is also good.

Transport

Bus *CTM* connections to **Oujda**, **Fès** , **Midelt** and **Er Rachidia**. The *CTM* Offices are located between the central square and Pl Zerkatouni. Private lines: **Taourirt/Oujda** and **Taza/Fès**, **Nador**. **Er Rachidia** 2100 departs from '*le complexe*' on the main road. **Train** ONCF services to**Taourirt/Oujda** and **Taza/Fès/Casablanca**.

Directory **Banks** *Banque Populaire*, on market square. *BM* and *BMCE*, near *Shell* petrol station on Oujda road. **Medical services** Chemists: *Pharmacie centrale* on the market square.

From Guercif to Midelt

Colour map 1, grids B5 to C3

About 4 km east from Guercif towards Oujda is the turning for the S329, a long, straight narrow road that follows the middle reaches of the Oued Moulouya parallel to the Atlas mountains. It is a little used route, ideal for those wishing to head southwards as quickly as possible. Note that *Café/Snack Bar des Voyageurs* on the P1 is the last place for refreshments until Outat Ouled el Hadj, another 200 km. Petrol stations are also few and far between on this route, and there is only one hotel, at Missour (250 km). Initially barren and uncultivated, the landscape becomes attractive around the farming village of Mahirija, with the Debdou massif to the east. However, this green respite soon disappears entirely as the route enters the vast semi-desert territory of the Rekkam Plateau, Morocco's 'empty quarter'. From here until Outad Ouled el Hadj much of the road follows the path of a dismantled railway line used by the French in their arduous campaign to conquer the tribes of the middle and upper Moulouya (1913-23). Along the way are viaducts and the remains of former stations. The snowclad peaks of the Middle Atlas are a constant presence throughout the length of this route. This trans-Rekkam road is criss-crossed by *oueds*, generally with no water, that require slowing down to a snail's pace as the road surface at crossing-points is very bumpy. The first small town is **Outat Ouled el Hadj**, attractively situated with Jbel Bou Naceur (3,340 m) in the background, and the Oued Moulouya running through the centre, which is leafy and compact. There is a souk on Monday in the enclosure by the river. Unfortunately the attractions stop here. Transport connections are poor with one daily bus to Guercif/Nador in the morning and an afternoon bus to Missour, Midelt and Er Rachidia. Make sure you don't get stuck here, as there is no accommodation. A much better option is to proceed to the next town, Missour, which has a reasonable hotel.

Missour A tranquil rural town with many donkeys and unpaved roads, Missour comes alive for the weekly market. Though unaccustomed to foreigners, the people are helpful. There is a fair medium-priced hotel here. Most of the commercial activity in Missour is concentrated behind the central section of the main boulevard. If you are lucky enough to be here on a Wednesday, there is a large local souk situated on the hill by the water tower, past the new mosque. The lower part of the market is disappointing, but the top end of the main enclosure has the fruit and vegetable market, and a separate area beyond encloses the livestock market. The latter is the most interesting part. Both enclosures have tea tents (breakfast served). There is a view of the town and the mountains from the adjacent hill.

Sleeping **D** *Hotel Baroudi*, Blvd El Bassatine, T055-585651. Take the dirt track by the *Credit Agricole* bank and follow the signs to a veritable oasis of a hotel with a swimming pool and a large garden where a couple of mischievous semi-wild monkeys roam, good restaurant (menu around 75dh), nice staff, prices negotiable.

Transport All transport arrives and departs from the street 2 blocks from the main road, behind the *Banque Populaire*. Buses for **Guercif** and **Nador**, **Midelt/Er Rachidia** and **Fès**.

Directory **Banks** *Banque Populaire*, on the main road. **Medical services** Chemist: *Pharmacie Echifa*, opposite the new mosque. **Useful addresses** Petrol: At the south end of the main boulevard before the bridge.

On to Midelt

Past Missour, the road continues for about 30 km through a still bare but slightly more dramatic landscape that would make a good location for a Western movie. After Tamdafelt, the road runs along an attractive stretch of the Oued Moulouya, with pisé villages and richly cultivated riverbanks. Two fortified kasbahs built by Moulay Ismaïl around 1690 to guard the imperial route from Fès to Sijilmassa are still inhabited: Saida and Ksabi. The inhabitants of these kasbahs, originally forming an agglomeration of 10 *ksours*, are mostly descendants of Alaouite guardsmen from the Tafilalet. At over 1,000 m, the freshness of the air and quality of light in this remote region is exhilarating. After Ksabi the road swings away from the Oued Moulouya and crosses the high plain of Aftis until it joins the P21 15 km east of Midelt (see page 248).

Taourirt

Phone code: 055
Colour map 1, grid B5

Halfway between Taza and Oujda, Taourirt is an important local commercial centre with a large weekly market on Sunday. In the past the town functioned as the junction between two major trade routes: the east-west trans-Maghreb route and the route from Melilla to the Tafilalet. The centre of town is located around the junction of the P1 and the Debdou road (the ancient caravan route to the south which is packed with shops, garages, cafés and small workshops). The only tangible historical attraction in Taourirt is the remains of the **kasbah** on the hill 1 km to the northwest of the town centre. Unfortunately, the site has been despoiled by electricity pylons and is occupied by the army. But there is an excellent view.

Excursions

There are several excursions around Taourirt that make it worthwhile stopping for a day or two, if you have time. The mountain village of Debdou (see below) and surroundings; the Zaâ waterfalls and the Zaâ Gorges. For the cave dwellings you will need a guide.

Providing there is enough water in the *oued* (unlikely between August and December), **Zaâ Waterfalls** make an enjoyable picnic and bathing excursion. Camping is possible. To get there, turn right at the signpost 6 km along the Taza road. It is a further 9 km to the waterfalls. The track continues to Melga el Ouidane and the large lake known as Barrage Mohammed V. This looks better when it has a good quantity of water. There are a number of picnic spots along the route.

Zaâ Gorges are deep, very impressive and well worth the journey. As you leave Taourirt on the Oujda road, there is a turning off to the right for the Zaâ Gorges (about 12 km). You cannot drive through the narrow defile. Leave the car where the road ends and walk from there.

Sleeping

F *Hotel Mansour*, T056-694003, on the Debdou road just off main crossroads. Large rooms, adequately clean, good café below. Hot water available.

Transport

Road Bus: for **Oujda** (every ½ hr) and **Nador** (around 5 a day) depart from the *Agip* petrol station past the main crossroads. **Guercif/Taza/Fès** (virtually every ½ hr during the day and hourly at night) depart from near the *Shell* petrol station on the same road, as do the **grands taxis** that ply the P1. Grands taxis for **Debdou** leave from the rank on the Debdou road. **Train Oujda** 0530, 0800, 1800, 1930 (approximate times). **Taza/Fès/Casablanca** 0830, 1045, 2030, 2230 (approximate times).

Directory

Banks *BMCE*, *CMD* and *Wafabank* next to *Hotel Mansour*. **Medical services** **Chemists**: on the road out to Debdou: Al-Jabri; Al-Qods.

Debdou

Colour map 1, grid B5
50 km to the SW of Taourirt

Nestling in a verdant bowl formed by the surrounding massif, Debdou is an island of rural tranquillity. The fact that Debdou is on a road 'to nowhere' has helped to preserve its own identity. The surrounding area is very scenic and provides good opportunities for walking and exploration. There is an interesting **kasbah** halfway up the mountainside above the main village. There are no tourist facilities, and transport links are poor.

Until the 1960s over half the population of Debdou were Jewish, most of whom were the descendants of Jews from Taza who fled persecution and chaos of Bou Hamra's rule (1902-08). The 'main street' branches off the main road at the entrance to the village and zigzags for about 1 km, past store houses to a square at the top end of the village known as Aïn Sbilia. Overlooking the square is a balcony shaded by four huge plane trees. A small sluice gate allows water to flow into a channel bisecting the square below which has a café. It is all very restful, with the locals playing cards and backgammon and drinking mint tea.

High above the village is the still-inhabited **Kasbah of Caïd Ghomriche** built by the Merinids in the 13th century as a fortress and subsequently handed over to the Beni Ouattas, a related tribe, around 1350 when the Merinids ruled Morocco. Follow the signposted track (2 km) starting from the bottom end of the village. Note the colourful dwelling housing the *hammam* which is still heated by a wood stove. Along the way there are pretty views of the town on the right and the waterfalls high above on the left. Just before entering the kasbah there is a grassy ledge with good views over the valley, and the entrance to a cave. The settlement is a mixture of ancient ruins, small vegetable gardens and mud houses.

At the back of the village, past the walls, and a dry moat, is a field where jagged stones stick out of the ground – the sunken headstones of tombs. Take care not to trip over them. By crossing the field and turning left for 30-40 m and then sharp right, there is a pathway (1 km) linking up with the main road and the source of the Oued Debdou. The same location can be reached by the main road which swings to the left just before Debdou, and runs along the mountain crest, or Gaada de Debdou, for 5 or 6 km. There are fantastic views from here and good walking opportunities. Beyond this the road descends from the plateau down into the arid Rekkam plain where it becomes a rough track, eventually leading to Outad Ouled el Hadj (see page 282). Market day is Wednesday.

Eating There are no restaurants in Debdou. Apart from the café at Aïn Sbilia (see above), the only other café is at the entrance to the town, at the start of the track leading to the kasbah.

Transport **Road Bus**: **Taourirt**, an early morning and an early afternoon departure. **Taxis**: to **Taourirt** are unpredictable, but most frequent in the morning and early evening. If you don't want to get stuck here, try to leave before 1800.

El Aïoun Situated halfway between Taourirt and Oujda, and within easy reach of the Beni Snassen Mountains (see page 301), El Aioun was founded by Moulay Ismaïl in 1679. It has a small kasbah that was restored in 1876 by Sultan Moulay Hassan in response to the threat of French expansion from Algeria. To the south of the town is a cemetery where those who died fighting colonialism are buried. During the first half of the 20th century, El Aioun became a centre of the Sufi Brotherhood of Sheikh Bou Amama, whose *zaouia* is located here. The weekly souk is held on Tuesday and frequented by members of the local Ouled Sidi Sheikh tribe.

Oujda is described in the chapter Northeastern Morocco, along with the coastal resorts Saïdia, the port of Nador, and the Spanish enclave of Melilla.

Northeastern Morocco

288 Eastwards from Al Hoceïma to Nador

288 Nador
289 Ins and outs
290 Sights
290 Essentials
292 Capes and coastal wetlands

293 Melilla
293 Ins and outs
293 Background
294 Sights
297 Essentials

300 Eastwards towards Algeria
300 Berkane
301 Beni Snassen Mountains

302 Saïdia
303 Sights
303 Essentials

304 Oujda
304 Ins and outs
304 Background
305 Sights
305 Excursions
307 Essentials

309 South towards Figuig
310 Figuig

Introducing Notheastern Morocco

For centuries, the regions which today constitute northeastern Morocco – the hills and plains to the east of the Rif – were the domain of nomadic tribespeople. Once used as a transit route for invasions and for trade from the East and the Mediterranean, several dynasties arose, notably the Merinids and the Wattasids, using it as a base to harass and eventually conquer the key city of Fès.

From this turbulent past, northeastern Morocco has few historic sites. Unfortunately, it is also rather economically depressed. The closure of the border with Algeria has hit the regional capital **Oujda** hard, giving the town a sad air which it is hard not to escape. Nearby, however, the beach resort **Saïdia** does come alive in the summer with returning migrant workers.

Away from the coast, northeastern Morocco is noticeably drier than other parts of the country, as the Rif and Atlas Mountains block rain coming in from the Atlantic. For the visitor, some of the fine mountain scenery offers good hiking opportunities, notably the **Jbel Tazzeka**, just to the south of Taza, and the **Beni Snassen mountains** between Oujda and the sea. The 20 km stretch of coast between Ras Kebdana and **Saïdia** is largely unspoilt, while the peninsula of **Cap des Trois Fourches** is wild, rocky and windswept. The water temperature along the Mediterranean coast is fine for swimming from April to November. Much further south lie deserted expanses and remote **Figuig**, oasis town without tourists, close to the Algerian frontier in the far southeast.

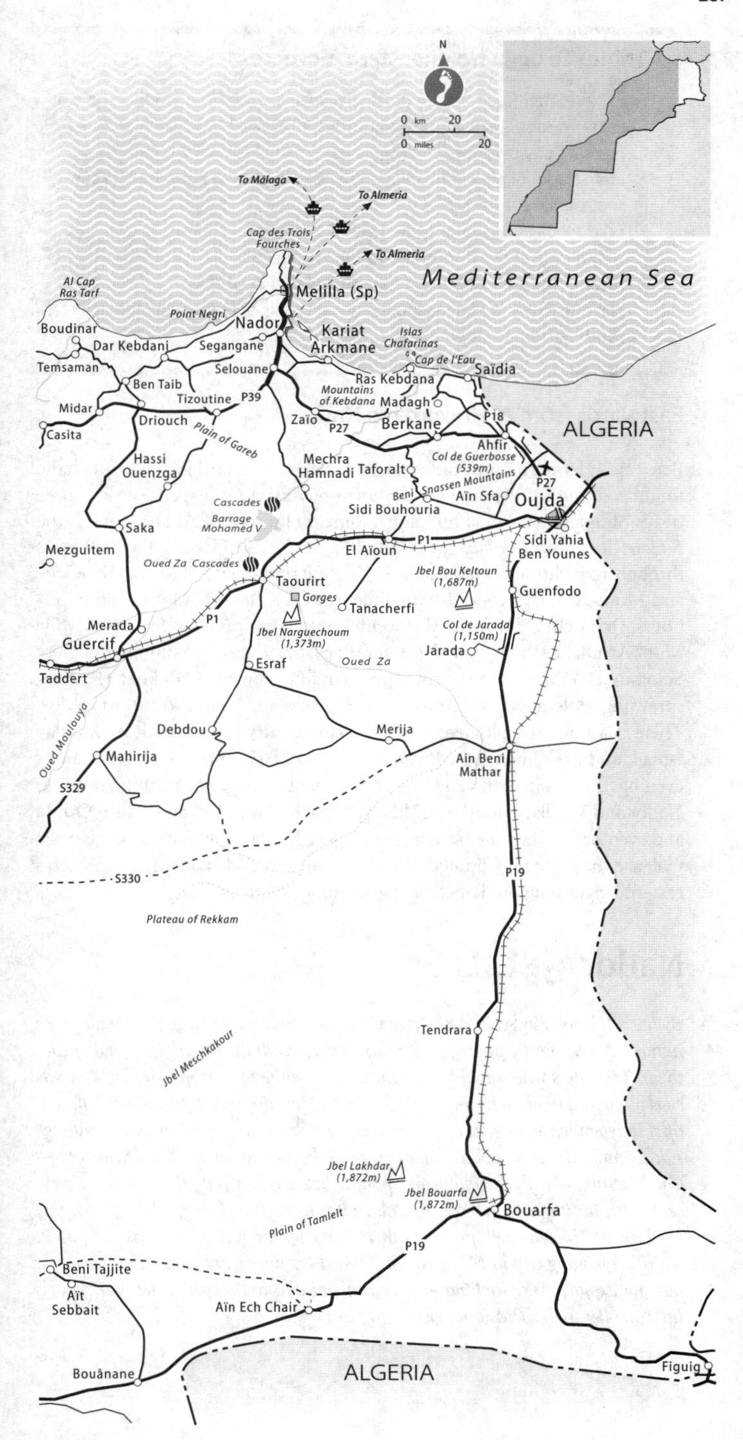
N
0 km 20
0 miles 20
To Málaga
To Almeria
To Almeria
Cap des Trois Fourches
Mediterranean Sea
Al Cap Ras Tarf
Melilla (Sp)
Point Negri
Nador
Boudinar
Kariat Arkmane
Islas Chafarinas
Dar Kebdani
Segangane
Cap de l'Eau
Temsaman
Selouane
Saïdia
Ben Taib
Ras Kebdana
Mountains of Kebdana
Midar
Tizoutine
P39
Madagh
Driouch
Zaïo
P18
Casita
Plain of Gareb
P27
Berkane
ALGERIA
Ahfir
Col de Guerbosse (539m)
Hassi Ouenzga
Mechra Hamnadi
Taforalt
P27
Beni Snassen Mountains
Aïn Sfa
Oujda
Cascades
Sidi Bouhouria
Barrage Mohamed V
Saka
P1
Sidi Yahia Ben Younes
El Aïoun
Mezguitem
Jbel Bou Keltoun (1,687m)
Oued Za Cascades
Taourirt
Gorges
Guenfodo
Tanacherfi
Merada
P1
Col de Jarada (1,150m)
Jbel Narguechoum (1,373m)
Guercif
Jarada
Taddert
Esraf
Oued Za
Debdou
Merija
Oued Moulouya
Mahirija
Ain Beni Mathar
S329
S330
P19
Plateau of Rekkam
Tendrara
Jbel Meschkakour
Jbel Lakhdar (1,872m)
Jbel Bouarfa (1,872m)
Bouarfa
Plain of Tamlelt
P19
Beni Tajjite
Aït Sebbait
Aïn Ech Chair
Bouânane
ALGERIA
Figuig

Things to do in Northeastern Morocco

- Explore **Melilla**, a touch of provincial Spain on Morocco's Mediterranean coast. To see: Renaissance fortifications, 1920s and 1930s architecture, a pleasant city beach.
- From Nador or Melilla, head up to the **Cap des Trois Fourches** for some spectacular coastal scenery.
- Take a look at **Oujda**, last town before the Algerian border. Take a steam-bath at the **Hammam du Jardin**, near Bab el Gharbi.
- Drive from Oujda or Nador to the **Gorges du Zegzel**.
- Travel across arid plateaux to the distant oasis of **Figuig**, on Morocco's far south-eastern frontier.

Eastwards from Al Hoceïma to Nador

Between Al Hoceïma and Nador the P39 winds northward inland through the foothills of the Rif. At the junction town of **Casita** (also spelt Kassita, some traces of Spanish colonial building), some 60 km out of Al Hoceïma, is the **F** *Hotel-Restaurant Andalous* (T056-364706). After Cassita, the P39 runs through agricultural plains and the expanding rural towns of Midar, Drouiche and Mont-Aroui. A good driving time from Kassita to Nador would be 1¾ hours. **Driouch**, 97 km from Al Hoceïma, has the basic **F** *Hotel Es-Salam*, while Mont Aroui, has the **E** *Hotel Hassan* (T056-362392). A few kilometres before **Selouane**, you pass Nador airport on the right. Selouane (315 km to Fès) is a sprawling settlement 144 km from Al Hoceïma and just 12 km from Nador. There is a fine example here of a late 17th-century kasbah built by Moulay Ismaïl, and the rather good *Restaurant Brabo* (T056-609033, closed Sunday evenings). From here the P39 turns into a dual carriageway running north to Nador and Melilla, while the P27 leads off east to **Zaïo**, **Berkane**, **Ahfir**, **Oujda** and eventually, when the border is open, to **Algeria**. Levels of fundamentalist violence there are now limited to isolated pockets, indicating that Morocco's eastern neighbour could open up considerably to tourists.

Nador ناظور

Phone code: 056
Colour map 1, grid A5

By the salt lagoon of Sebkha Bou Areq, the provincial capital and port Nador (the name is Arabic for lighthouse) is a relaxed place with the atmosphere of a border town. Travellers will probably pass through en route to or from Melilla. With its steel plant and modern harbour, Nador was a flagship for Moroccan development after independence, when the new town was developed on a gridiron pattern alongside a small Rif village. Today, it is a centre for the agri-food business, fish farming – and contraband with neighbouring Spanish-held Melilla, only 10 km away. Funds sent back by migrant workers are also vital to its well-being, More politically, Nadoris are increasingly proud of their Amazigh origins. (Nador is the largest Ta'rifit-speaking city in Morocco). Birdwatchers may want to use the town as a base for exploring the wetlands and coastal habitats to the east. Otherwise there is little on offer to the occasional visitor to Morocco.

Ins and outs

Getting there

See Transport, page 291, for further details

Nador is easily reached by bus from Al Hoceïma (3½ hrs), Melilla, Oujda (2½ hrs), and Taza. *ONCF*, the national railway company, have a bus from Taourirt which meets the train between Meknès/Fès and Oujda. There is also a daily bus from Casablanca (12 hrs) and from Tetouan (9½ hrs). Nador, if you come from France, might be your first meeting with Morocco if you take the ferry from Sète. There is also an international airport.

Getting around

The grid pattern of the town makes orientation straightforward. Streetnames are notable by their almost total absence, although a plan was announced for new trilingual signs in the Amazigh, Arabic and Latin scripts in early 2003.

Buses and grands taxis arrive at a large and fairly confusing terminal at the lagoon end of Av des FAR. *CTM* and *SATAS* buses have a city centre terminus near the *Hotel Ryad* and the Municipality. The *ONCF* buses from Taourirt arrive on Av Sidi Mohammed.

One principal street, Blvd Youssef Ben Tachfine (at right angles to the lagoon), cuts right through the centre from the roundabout on the Melilla road to the *Hotel Rif* on the waterfront. The administrative quarter, post office, and the modern Grand Mosque with its unusually tall and slender minaret are all located on this road. If you come in by public transport, turn right out of the bus/grand taxi terminus and walk into the centre along the Av Hassan II. You pass the main concrete contraband goods market on your right and meet Blvd Ben Tachfine. A couple of the better eateries are near here. Go left, uphill for banks with ATMs. Further on, Av Hassan II is crossed by the palm tree and café-lined Blvd Mohammed V connecting the promenade by the lagoon with the town hall. This is the nicest part of town.

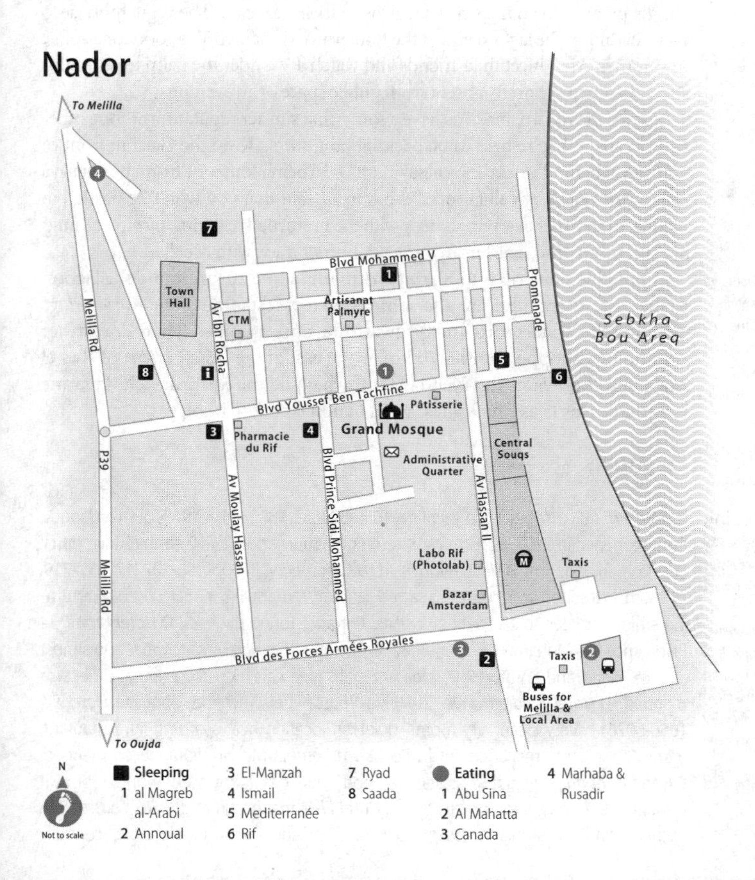

Tourist information

Tourist office, 3rd Flr, 88 Blvd Ibn Rochd, T056-606518. Ask to speak to Mr Addouche who is as helpful as possible, given his resources.

Sights

Nador is a recent town, its people almost all of Rif Amazigh origin. As in El Hoceïma to the west, the people feel very strongly about their *Amazighité*, and in fact you will hear far more Ta'rifit (the main Amazigh language of northern Morocco) spoken than Arabic. The region has sent huge contingents of migrants to Belgium, the Netherlands and Germany, and the money they send back is crucial to the region's economy – as is the contraband trade with the nearby Spanish enclave of **Melilla**, a good day trip from Nador (see page 293 for further details). There is a good selection of hotels, busy in summer.

Nador's attractions are limited, it has to be said. The original centre was developed on a gridiron pattern by the Spanish in the 1920s and 1930s. After independence, the town mushroomed in size, the population reaching 100,000 in the late 1980s. When relations collapsed with Algeria, large numbers of Moroccans resident in that country settled in Nador. With the MRE (Marocains résidents à l'étranger) spending their money on homes for family left behind, Nador has become a magnet for the rural poor seeking work. In summer, the people-watching can be quite interesting, as the *fakansiya*, the MRE back for their *vacances*, parade up and down the small corniche in their new cars. The vaguely art deco pier building at the lagoon end of the Boulevard Mohamed V is good for a coffee in summer. Men meet their friends and watch TV under the palm trees on this street. Women are pretty absent from public space of an evening.

Just for the record, Nadoris have a somewhat sinister reputation among other Moroccans – they're held to be backstabbing sorts. 'Keep the Galai in front of you, never behind' goes the local saying, a Galai being someone from the Guelaya clan of the region. In all fairness, it has to be said that you won't be hassled in Nador. In summer everyone is busy with their returned relations, in winter things are fairly comatose, apart from the cross-border trade with Melilla.

See Capes and coastal wetlands, page 292, for further details

A possible side-trip is to **Kariat Arkmane**, some 20 km round the lagoon to the east, where there are also some good fish restaurants, the *Kariat Plage* camping site, watersports and birdwatching opportunities. There are further ornithological opportunities 70 km to the east at the beach resort of **Ras el Ma'a**, also known as Ras Kebdana, off which lie the Spanish-held Ja'farine Islands, aka las Islas Chafarinas, and a national park to boot.

Essentials

Sleeping

■ *on map, page 289*
Prices: see inside front cover

Best hotels fill up quickly in summer, as migrant workers return with their families. Try to reserve ahead

B ***Hotel Rif***, 1 Blvd Youssef Ben Tachfine, T056-603635, F333384. A 1970s gem on lagoon front reopened in 2002, 62 a/c rooms, restaurant, murky pool and 2 earth tennis courts. Best upmarket option. **B** ***Hotel Ryad***, Blvd Mohammed V, BP60, T056-607717, F607719. 41 rooms, 18 suites, lavish decor to say the least, restaurant, 2 bars, café, used by returning emigrants keen to display their wealth. Entrance round the back. **D** ***Hotel Ismail***, 34 Blvd Prince Sidi Mohammed, T056-606280. Cheaper than *Hotel Mediterranée* and almost as nice, clean and comfortable, pleasant staff, nice café but no restaurant. Recommended. **D** ***Hotel Mediterranée***, 2-4 Blvd Youssef Ben Tachfine, opposite *Hotel Rif*, T056-602611. Very clean, airy rooms, quiet-ish location near seafront, lift, restaurant, menu 80dh. Same management as *Pension Tuhami* in Melilla. Highly recommended. **E** ***Hotel Annoual***, overlooks bus station, good value, check hot water works, rooms at front are very noisy, large ornate café. **E** ***Hotel El-Manzah***, corner of Blvd Youssef Ben Tachfine and Av Moulay Hassan, T056-332578. Adequately comfortable, centrally located, with a receptionist who speaks English and a guarded parking space, private bathrooms. **F** ***Hotel al-Maghreb al-Arabi***, on street of the same name just off Blvd Mohammed V in the best part of town. Very cheap, very simple, but clean. **F** ***Hotel al Mahatta,*** 38 Av Abbas Mohammed Akkad, T056-602777. Large and cheap hotel with restaurant, to the left off Av des FAR with sea and bus station behind you. **F** ***Hotel Saâda***, 26 R Ibn Rochd, T056-602881. Central location roughly behind the town hall. A rambling hotel, fairly clean. 1px 40dh, large multi-bed rooms, showers on corridor.

Camping *Kariat Plage* at Kariat Arkmane, east end of salt lagoon. 2 ha, 20 m to beach, bar, snacks, restaurant, grocery shop, showers, laundry, electricity for caravans, petrol at 400 m.

Eating

• *on map, page 289*

Expensive *Hotel Rif*, T056-606535, and ***Hotel Ryad***, T056-607715. Both have international and Moroccan cuisine. **Mid-range** Slightly less expensive, with good fish dishes, is ***Restaurant Romero***, corner of Av Hassan II and Av Yacoub El Mansour. ***Marhaba***, 2 R Ibn Rochd near *Hotel Ryad.* Large establishment with a fast service aimed at Spanish day trippers, wide choice. ***Rusadir***, next to *Marhaba* but slightly more upmarket, speciality is fish. The *Hotel Méditerranée* has an acceptable, clean restaurant. **Cheap** *Abu Sina*, R Abu Sina, just off Blvd Youssef Ben Tachfine on right as you head towards Blvd Mohamed V. Busy small restaurant open at lunchtime, wide selection including fish soup, grilled prawns and paella. Plenty of cheap eateries close to bus station, including ***Canada***, Blvd des FAR.

Cafés & pâtisseries

Try Blvd Mohammed V for cafés and ice cream. The mirador building jutting out into the lagoon at the end of this avenue is the nicest place for a coffee and cake.

Entertainment

In summer there are occasional displays of regional crafts just off the Corniche. Despite the Spanish influence, Nador is practically a dry town, so head for nearby Melilla for café terraces with cold beer.

Shopping

The clothes and electrical goods on offer in the main market of Av Hassan II are definitely aimed at the local market. Prices are broadly similar to Europe. **Photography** *Labo Rif*, 210 Av Hassan II, near bus station.

Transport

Apart from Melilla, Nador is a fair distance from other major towns: 175 km from Oujda, 120 km from Al Hoceïma on an often tortuous though beautiful road, 275 km from Taza, 400 km from Fès

Air Flights to Nadar Airport have been irregular. Choose *Iberia* connections from Spain to nearby Melilla. **Airline offices**: *Royal Air Maroc*, 24 Blvd Mohammed V, T056-606478.

Road There are 3 main **departure points** for public road transport: the busy, grotty main station, shared with grands taxis, at the junction of Av des FAR and Hassan II; *CTM* and the better private line departures from Av Ibn Rochd near the Municipalité; and grands taxis for Melilla from behind the town hall. **NB** The *CTM* departure for Al Hoceïma leaves from the Av des FAR terminus.

Bus: *CTM* buses run to **Tanger** (1900, 180dh for the 700 km, via Fès, Meknès, Larache and Asilah), **Al Hoceïma, Oujda** and **Fès, Meknès, Rabat and Casablanca**. For Melilla, take a private line bus to **Beni Enzar** (frequent departures). If you want a seat be sure to board the bus at the terminal as it fills up rapidly along the way (journey time 30 mins). Other private line destinations include **Er Rachidia** (8 hrs via Missour/Midelt), **Figuig** (9 hrs via Oujda), **Kariat Arkmane, Ras el Ma'a/Ras Kebdana, Taza, Fès and Meknès** (several departures, including early morning), **Casablanca, Guercif, Oujda** (numerous during day), **Chaouen, Tetouan and Tanger**, (take early morning bus to see mountainous route), **Targuist** (0415, 1115, 1700), **Al Hoceïma, Rabat ,Taourirt,** and **Berkane**. Note that the *ONCF* runs to **Taourirt** to connect with the trains to **Fès, Meknès, Rabat** and **Casablanca**.

Taxi: grands taxis from beside the bus station, with numerous destinations including **Ahfir** (over 1 hr) and from there to **Saïdia**, to the border with **Melilla** (4dh), to **Al Hoceïma** (50dh), **Meknès** and **Fès**. Taxis for Beni Enzar (border) and other points north depart from the main road near *Hotel Ryad*.

Sea There is a ***Comanav*** car and passenger ferry service from **Nador** to **Sète** in France, every 4 days Jun-Sep, tickets and information from ***Comanav Passages***, Immeuble Lazaar Beni Enzar, BP 89, T056-608538, or from the same company in Casablanca, 43 Blvd des FAR, T022-310015/6. The new ferry service between **Nador** and **Almería** operated by ***Ferrimaroc***, www.ferrimaroc.com, is a nightly service (except Sun) departing from Nador at 2330, arriving in **Almería** 8 hrs later. Cost is 240dh minimum fare 1-way for foot passenger. Cabins from 475dh (2 people).

Directory

Banks There is no shortage of banks to process money sent home by migrant workers. Try ***Wafa Bank***, on your right on Blvd Ben Tachfine as you head uphill, not far from *Hotel El Menzah*. Other ATMs are on or near this street. **Medical services** Chemists: ***Pharmacie du Rif***, corner of Blvd Ben Tachfine and Av Moulay Hassan. ***Pharmacie Ibn Sina***, top end of Blvd Ben Tachfine under the arches.

Capes and coastal wetlands

Kariat Arkmane
20 km E of Nador

At the extremity of the lagoon, Kariat Arkmane (souk Wednesday) is a small settlement divided into three separate parts some distance away from each other. The main village, on the lagoon, is a bustling, rough and ready sort of place. There is a morning fish market behind the square. Beyond the modern residential area, situated about 1 km inland along the road, you will find the turning to Kariat Plage, which is itself a further 2 km further on, across a stretch of marshlands. Although the swimming is safe and clean here, the beach is litter-strewn and very crowded in high summer.

Sleeping and eating There are no hotels, but family-sized apartments are available in the large block at the beach next to *Restaurante Arena de Oro* for 350dh per day in the high season, less in the low season. Ask around for other cheaper possibilities. The well known *Arena de Oro* specializes in fish. For simpler fare, there are a couple of places by the beach.

Transport Buses for **Nador** leave hourly in the morning and at 1600. For **Ras Kebdana/Ras el Ma'a**, at 1130 and 1400. All depart from the main village where there are also frequent **grands taxis**.

Directory Banks *Crédit du Maroc*, in main village by taxi rank. **Medical services** Chemist: *Pharmacie Centrale*, next to bank.

Ras Kebdana (Ras el Ma'a)

From Kariat Arkmane to Ras Kebdana is about 40 km and the 8101 winds inland across attractive rolling farmlands and seasonal riverbeds eroded into the soft, red sandstone. On the right stand the jagged and wild Kebdana mountains and on the left the sea appears from time to time. It can be reached on foot by following one of the many dry *oued* beds for 2 or 3 km although there is no beach, only low, muddy cliffs. The village of Ras Kebdana is entirely devoted to fishing, and is dwarfed by its large modern harbour, beyond which there is a wonderful unspoilt beach stretching for 6 km to the estuary of the Oued Molouya, and beyond that to the resort of **Saïdia**. The view from the headland over the coast and the Spanish-held Ja'farine Islands is spectacular. From the breakwater at the far end of the harbour a flight of steps leads up to the lighthouse where a bored sentry may stop you out of curiosity. Take care walking along the crumbling cliff edge. It is possible to walk back along the crest of the headland to the road and down another flight of steps to the back of the village. The headland itself has been spoilt by military installations.

Sleeping and eating **Camping** on the large space behind the beach, no facilities as yet. ***Café restaurant du Port***, T055-605972, is a large mid-range restaurant situated in the middle of the port area, clean and friendly. Huge portions of very fresh fish and prawns.

Transport

Buses to **Nador**, 0830, 1500; **Berkane**, 1230, 1530. **Grands taxis** run from time to time to **Kariat Arkmane** and **Berkane**.

Cap des Trois Fourches

The scenery along the way to the cape is very beautiful, but there are strong currents around the peninsula and swimming can be dangerous

Jutting some 30 km into the Mediterranean, north of Nador, the Cap des Trois Fourches peninsula is rocky, wild and windswept. To get out to the peninsula you will need your own transport – or get a taxi from Beni Ensar or Farkhana as far as they will go, and then walk. For the adventurous there are a couple of tiny beaches close to the lighthouse, accessible by a 14 km long rough hilly track from the village of Taourirt north of the border post of Farkhana. Past Taourirt, there is a turning on the left to another tiny beach at Cala Tramontana 4 km away. There are few settlements, just a couple of impoverished hamlets.

Melilla مليلية

Phone code: 0034-95
Colour map 1, grid A5

Melilla time is 1 -2 hours different to Moroccan time

Melilla is the main town of a small Spanish enclave on the eastern stretch of Morocco's Mediterranean coast. It stands on the promontory, facing eastwards, just 16 km south of Cap des Trois Fourches and 12 km north of Nador. A sleepy sort of place, the enclave is worth a day's visit for the fortifications of Medina Sidonia and the pastel and stucco buildings of the early 20th century town. There is a relaxed, clean beach, a small archaeological museum, streets like those of any provincial Spanish city. The Cap des Trois Fourches, north of Melilla is a beautiful natural site, however.

Ins and outs

Getting there

See Transport, page 299, for further details

You may well come into Melilla by ferry from Málaga or Almería, or by plane from Málaga. Flights and boats tend to be full up in the height of summer and Easter week (Semana Santa). Otherwise, you can reach Melilla – or rather the border at Beni Enzar – by grand taxi or bus from Nador. Border formalities can be very slow. Stumbling into Melilla half-asleep off a night-boat, you are particularly vulnerable to pickpockets. Have your wallet and passport well stowed away under your clothing.

Getting around

From the border post, the town centre is a good 40 mins' walk on foot, so take one of the buses which run regularly from 0700 to 2200 (taking 20 mins) to Plaza de España. The town centre is easily covered on foot.

Tourist information

Oficina de Turismo, C Fortuny 21, in the conference centre behind the bull ring, T2675444, F2679616, dsi@camelilla.es, open 0830-1500, closed Sat-Sun.

Background

Melilla started life as Phoenician Rusadir. The Greeks and Romans were here too. The Spanish captured the town from the Berbers in 1497. Occupied by the usual dynasties in the Middle Ages, Melilla was taken by the Merinids in 1272, and along with Badis, was to become one of the ports for Fès and Taza, involved in trade with Genoa, Pisa, Marseille, Catalonia and Aragon.

The ancient citadel area is today called Medina Sidonia, after the Duke of Medina Sidonia, who was urged by Ferdinand of Aragon and Isabel of Castille to take the town. In 1497, Melilla fell to Don Pedro Estepiñan with a contingent of 700 men and a fleet later to participate in Columbus' second voyage to the Americas. Under the Spanish, the old fortified town on its huge rocky outcrop rising out of the sea was rebuilt, the first fortifications being completed in 1515, final touches being made in 1739.

From the late 15th century on, the history of Melilla was one of sieges and clashes. In 1774, Sidi Mohammed Ben Abdallah led 40,000 troops to take the town – but to no avail. In 1909, Spain appropriated large territories around the old fortress core, which then had barely 9,000 inhabitants. In the early 1920s, however, Abdelkarim El Khattibi's Rif forces, fighting for an independent state, nearly put an end to this expansion of Spanish Melilla.

Spain had become interested in the town for economic reasons. A local potentate sold to a Spanish mining company one of the largest open-cast iron ore mines of the time, at Bou Ifrour. Spain built a railway line between the mine and Melilla, and the town's development was rapid. By 1925, the population was 25,000 – more than many Andalucían cities – and reached a high of 90,000 in 1950. However, when the rest of the Spanish Protectorate was returned to Morocco in 1956, Mellila, along with Ceuta, remained as a somewhat sleepy symbol of Spanish pride on the coast.

Since the late 1960s, the bright entrepreneurs of Melilla have built themselves fortunes via the contraband trade with Morocco, based on a clientele in an area which stretches far beyond the immediate Rif region. Today the Spanish Christian population is around 30,000, and there are some 6,000 Spanish Foreign Legion soldiers. The Muslim population numbers around 30,000, many of whom once lived in the slum Cañada de la Muerte neighbourhood. They received Spanish papers in 1987, and Muslim areas like the Cañada and María Cristina have been much improved. Morocco continues to demand the return of the city, but the city's mixed Rif and Spanish population plies its trade in foodstuffs, household goods and clothes regardless. Although lots of Nadori residents have the right to come into Melilla on a daily basis for work, the border has been tightened up considerably, as Spain fears mass influxes of Algerians and sub-Saharan Africans claiming refugee status.

Sights

Melilla has enough to keep you busy for a long half-day

Approaching from the frontier post to the south, Avenida General Astilleros takes you through an undistinguished suburb (barracks and army housing to the left). The main beach area is behind the buildings to your right. After the concrete bridge over the Río de Oro (River of Gold!), a large modern mirror-glass construction, put up to celebrate the 500th anniversary of the discovery of the Americas, hoves into view, rather marring the vision of the old town, **Medina Sidonia**, just behind. The **modern city**, an example of late 19th and early 20th century planning, starts with the round Plaza de España from which the twin main shopping streets, Ejército Español and Juan Carlos Rey, run. Plaza de España was something of an architectural showcase in its day, still home to the *Banco de España*, the town hall building and the ferry office (also banks with ATMs).

Abd El-Karim – rebel of the Rif

Abd al-Karim (Al-Khattabi) was born in the Rif Mountains of Morocco in 1882. He led a long resistance movement against both Spanish and French occupations of his homeland. He was educated in Spanish as well as Islamic schools. His objective became the establishment of an independent Rif republic in northern Morocco. He was particularly eager that the Rif should become a state on an Islamic but modern model with a flag and full freedom of action in foreign policy. His difficulties arose on two sides. First, his colonial opponents were well equipped and organized. He mainly faced the Spanish, whose army he defeated at Anoual in 1921 and again in the Chaouen-Tetouan campaign in late 1924. Secondly, he faced the difficulty that the Rif was fragmented into tribal factions, whose allegiance to the concept of a Rif republic was never sure. Constant political in-fighting between the tribes of the Rif and of adjacent areas of northern Morocco gave Abd el-Karim perpetual problems as he tried to keep his armies provisioned and united. He showed great skills as a diplomat and politician, successfully maintaining tribal loyalty.

His military successes against the Spanish and his encroachments, as local tribes joined him, deep into French controlled Morocco, almost reaching Fès in 1924 and 1925, brought the European powers to a joint agreement against him. In 1926 the Spanish army, better organized under General Franco, was heavily reinforced along the Mediterranean coast. The French moved in from the south and by autumn the Rif was surrounded on all sides. By January the area was short of food and there were defections by tribes not directly affiliated to the Rif. In April 1926 a peace conference was convened to no avail as a result of Abd al-Karim's failure to return European prisoners. In May the French and Spanish moved into the Rif and, other than a short resistance in Azilaf in the extreme north, collapse came quickly and on 27 May he surrendered to the French commander. He went into exile, first to Réunion, and eventually died in Cairo in 1963.

Abd al-Karim was the forerunner of North African political leaders with ideas of statehood and independence. His resistance to colonization was organized and sustained. He had ideas of sovereignity, justice and political structures that most countries of North Africa still have not achieved.

Nueva Melilla, aka El Ensanche

Twentieth century Melilla is interesting in a cosy Spanish provincial sort of way. The town was laid out by one Don Enrique Nieto, the money for its expansion coming from the export of iron ore mined in the hinterland. (The Edificio Quinto Centenario sits on what was the old ore loading quay or *cargadero*.) Take a look at the neo-Moorish or *historicista* style mosque. Architecture buffs have your cameras ready for there are a few gems along the streets named after Spanish generals and cultural heroes. Buildings in the *estílo ondulante* draw inspiration from natural forms; for the *estílo geométrico* see the Edificio de la Asamblea on the Plaza de España. If you have lots of time, walk up to the *Parador de Melilla*, for good views of the city. Below it, the Parque Lobera is pleasantly shady and has slides and an aviary which might please small children.

Medina Sidonia

If short of time, head directly for Medina Sidonia, a fine example of elaborate 16th-century fortifications, now a sleepy sort of place, where palm trees wave over stone facades decked with mustard-coloured classical detailing. At Melilla, the Spanish picked one of the best defensive locations on the north Moroccan coast to construct an elaborate fortified settlement, divided into two parts by a moat and gates. The entrance to the main, earliest section, (parking nearby) is below the walls at the end of Avenida General Macías. On foot, you head up a ramp and come out onto a small square with the Chapel of Santiago over to your left. You can then wander through the narrow streets in search of views across the Mediterranean, the **Museo Amazigh**, the Church of the Immaculate Conception and the small but well planned **Municipal Museum**. The ground floor of the museum is set aside for visiting exhibits. More interesting, on the first floor, the archaeological section has Carthaginian coins, amphorae, an exquisite Etruscan oinochoé and a pair of dove-shaped gold earrings beside the skull whose ears they once adorned. Look out for the model of a Punic burial with amphorae. The top floor has some good displays on the development of Melilla. There is access to a small walkway with views across the town. Through gaps in a defensive wall cannons stand ready to bombard the Parador! ■ *Daily 1000-1400, 1700-2130, closed Sun afternoon and Mon. T952-699158.* Next to the museum, dedicated by the people of Melilla in 1970, stands a statue of a be-armoured Don Pedro de Estepiñan, waving his sword at 'the mainland'.

The highest point of Medina Sidonia is occupied by a bastion, the **Baluarte de la Concepción**, a mixture of medieval and 18th-century building on the site of the first walled area. The nearby **Cuevas del Conventico** played a key role in the siege of 1774. In the same area, the 17th-century **Iglesia de la Puríssima Concepción** has some period carving, and the statue of Nuestra

Senora de la Victoria, the patroness of Melilla, who is celebrated on 17 September. NB Church may be locked. When you get back to the bottom of the city, try the *Cafetería Miramar* for a snack or lunch.

A great deal of Medina Sidonia is still occuped by the military – and a prison, in the case of the San Fernando barracks. There is obviously a lot more to the town's history than meets the eye in the museum and church. (For more information, try the Asociación de estudios melillenses on road down from Callejón del Moro in Medina Sidonia.) Now that the EU has funded a good deal of restoration work, it will be interesting to see if more cultural tourism develops – or whether the city's odd geopolitical position (and other factors) maintain its backwater status. Certainly, large sums will have to be invested in the sub-standard housing, much of it occupied by families of Moroccan origin, which sprawls up the hillsides above the modern town.

Beaches

Close to the city, the beaches of Melilla are well equipped with ice-cream kiosks, stands renting loungers, and showers. Playa San Lorenzo is nearest to the town and least attractive. Playa de los Carabos is fine, Playa de la Hípica is the furthest away, only walkable for the very, very energetic.

Essentials

Sleeping

■ *on map*

In the smaller hotels you may be able to pay in dirhams as well as euros

The city has a range of good accommodation. Reasonably priced hotels fill up early, so phone ahead. The *Parador* is to be preferred to expensive hotels in Nador. Best of reasonable hotels is the *Tuhami*. A number of medium-priced hotels have closed. **NB** Melilla is part of Spain, so if phoning from Morocco, dial 0034 (for Spain), then 95 (Melilla) before the 7-figure local number.

A *Parador de Melilla*, Av de Cándido Lobera, T2684940, www.parador.es, 40 rooms, 76 beds, telephone, TV, parking, lift, facilities for disabled, credit cards, exchange, a/c, heating, restaurant, coffee shop/bar, small pool. **A** ***Rusadir***, 5 Pablo Vallescá, T2681240, F2670527. Smart hotel, 35 rooms, telephone, credit cards, a/c, lift, TV. Expensive, no pool. **B** ***Anfora***, 16 Pablo Vallescá, T2683340, F2683344. Big hotel opposite the *Rusadir*, near main roundabout. 145 rooms, garage, lift, a/c, telephone, TV. **B** ***Avenida***, 24 Av Juan Carlos I Rey. 8 rooms, currently closed, but may possibly get renovated. **B** ***Nacional***, 10 Jose Antonio Primo de Rivera, T2684540. 30 rooms, credit cards, exchange, telephone, bar/café. Central. **B** ***Parque***, 15 General Marina, T2682143. 28 rooms, telephone, overlooking central park. **C** ***Mirasol***, 31 General Astilleros, nr the frontier, T2674686. 13 rooms, bar/café.

Colonial confetti: the Spanish enclaves in Morocco

Just as the Arabs had swept into the Iberian peninsula during their great period of expansion (711-1212 AD), the Spanish Reconquista (1212-1492) had a momentum that, along with the growing wealth of the Spanish Empire, led it into a crusade into Africa. In 1492 the King of Castille permitted the Duke of Medina Sidonia to claim West Africa by force of arms. Imperial ambitions were mixed with religious expansionism and Spanish military expeditions seized a variety of cities and towns along the North African coast – Algiers, Asilah, Bougie, Larache and Tripoli. However Spanish attention moved rapidly away from Africa to the New World of the Americas and ultimately the Pacific Ocean. Only five minor holdings or presidos *remained in North Africa –* **Ceuta, Melilla, Peñon de Velez de la Gomera (Badis), Peñon de Alhucemas (al-Nakur)** *and the* **Islas Chafarinas***, the latter three being no more than groups of islets. Politically and culturally, these presidios became largely detached from Morocco and survive as little fragments of provincial Spain in Africa.*

The effective integration of the five presidios *into metropolitan Spain has not prevented the contemporary Moroccan state from reviving claims to sovereignty, using the same arguments for change that Spain itself deploys into its claim to Gibraltar from the British, including historic rights. The people of the Moroccan Rif have their own tribal and traditional claims to the enclaves, bred by 400 years of episodic warfare against the Spanish fortresses.*

That the Moroccan claims on the presidios *has been muted is explicable by the fact that the Government of Morocco has more important political objectives in Western Europe. A close relationship with the EU is vital if Morocco is to continue to achieve rapid economic growth and construction of a permanent crossing of the Strait of Gibraltar would certainly be impossible if a major dispute were to exist with Spain. There is some gratification for Morocco in the changing demography of Ceuta in particular, where the element of Arab-Berber ethnic stock is growing quite rapidly while the number of those of Spanish extraction permanently resident in the enclave is static or falling.*

Meanwhile, Spain is happy to hold on to its presidios, *since Ceuta is still a major national port and the five possessions as a whole give Spain a very strong strategic influence over the world's third most busy strait.*

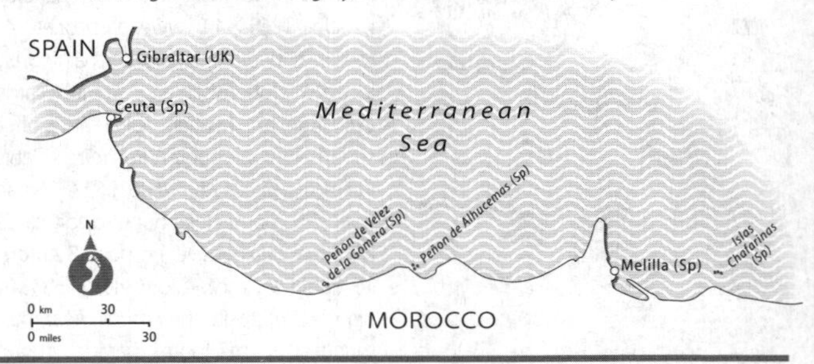

C-D *Cazaza*, 6 Jose Antonio Primo de Rivera, T2684648. 8 rooms, next to *Hotel Nacional*. **C-D** *Hostal Tuhami, C.B.*, 13 General Margallo, T2686045, F2686174, hostaltuhami@hotmail.com Clean and highly recommended. Same management as the *Hotel Méditerranée* in Nador. **D** *Hostal Residencia Rioja*, 10 Ejercito Español, T2682709. Good value cheap hotel. Has had some odd reports and is not recommended for women travelling alone. **D** *Pension El Porto*, T2681270. Facing the port, as its name suggests. Perhaps the cheapest hotel in Melilla but not at all advisable for women alone.

Camping Camp site is closed. Avoid camping in own car – reports of break-ins.

Eating

• on map, page 296

Expensive *Zayka*, 32 Montemar, T2681037. The most expensive, the food is excellent. **Mid-range** For Spanish food at mainland prices try ***Los Salazones***, 15 C de Alcaudete, and for a good fish selection ***Granada***, 30 Montemar, T2673026, and ***Victoria***, 9 General Pareja, T2677946. There is a pleasant eatery below the walls of Medina Sidonia, at the end of Av Grl Macías. **Cheap** *Casa Martin*, 11 General Polavieja. ***El Mesón***, 9 Av de Castelar. In summer, try cheap eateries along the beachfront.

Bars & cafés

Plenty of small bars, including ***Bodega Madrid***, 10 Castelar, cafeterías like ***La Palma***, 20 Av Juan Carlos I Rey. For ice cream try ***La Ibense***, Plaza Héroes de España.

Entertainment

Bull ring C Querol, T2699213. **Theatres** *Auditorium Carvajal*, Parque Lobera. *Grand Teatro National*, 8 Candido Lobera.

Shopping

Main shopping streets are Av Juan Carlos I Rey including Plaza de los Héroes de España (crowded with shoppers and socializing groups in the evening), Ejército Español and C O'Donnell. Duty free shops offer a limited range of electrical goods. Moroccan craft goods can be found at fairly high, fixed prices so wait till you get to Morocco for the real thing. Check prices at one of the bazaar shops near *Hotel Anfora*. Best book shop by far is ***Rafael Boix Sola***, 23 Av Juan Carlos I Rey, T2681983. Books in Spanish on local history. Surf and windsurf equipment at ***Ultrafun***, 36 C General Polavieja.

Sport & acrtvities

Watersports *Municipal Swimming Pool*, Av de la Juventud, covered pool. *Marina, Club Maritimo*, C Muelle, T2683659. Annual watersports week in the second half of Aug.

Tour operators

Renfe, 113 C O'Donnell, T2683551, for rail/sea travel. See also Transport below. Independent travel agents include ***Andalucía Travel***, 13 Av de la Democracia, T2670730, F2676598, and ***Viajes Melvia***, Pasaje Av, T2688526.

Transport

Taxis to/from the airport take 10 mins

Air Good air services from Melilla to Spanish mainland including **Madrid, Málaga** and **Almería**. *Panair* runs BAe146 jets and *Trasmediterranea* flies propeller-driven aircraft in a 30-min 8 flight per weekday (6 flights Sun) return service Málaga-Melilla. Flight frequencies can vary on a quarterly basis – check in Melilla with the appropriate agency: ***Panair***, 2 C Musico Granados, T2674211, ***Trasmediterranea***, 1 General Marina/Plaza España, T2681918 or ***Iberia***, 2 C Cándido Lobera, T2670386 (at airport, T2673123/2673800).

Hire cars cannot normally be taken from Melilla into Morocco

Road **Bus**: cheap bus services within Melilla, most services calling at Plaza de España. **Taxi**: comparatively cheap, pay on the meter. For services ring T2683623 or 2683621. **Car hire**: available at the airport and from agencies in the town such as ***Rent-a-car La Mezquita*** who have agencies in Oujda and Nador, too, ring T061-363396 (mob) or T056-349389 for the Beni Ansar border office. For travel to the **border** take the regular bus from Plaza de España (every 15-30 mins, 0700-2200).

If crossing the border from Morocco to catch the ferry, allow for the fact that Spanish time is 2 hrs ahead of Moroccan time Apr-Sep and 1 hr ahead Oct-Mar

Sea *Trasmediterranea* runs a regular ferry service to **Málaga** and **Almería** from the terminal just off the old town. The crossing takes 7½ hrs from **Málaga** and 6½ hrs from **Almería**. Frequency of service varies with season, reserve ahead for summer months. Cheaper rates apply to ordinary deck/public cabin tickets but the margin against the air fare for a half hour flight is close. Info and tickets at ***Trasmediterranea***, 1 General Marina/Plaza España, T2681918 in Melilla; Estación Maritima, El Puerto, T0034-95-2224391 in Málaga; Parque Nicolàs Salmeron 19, T0034-95-0236155 in Almería. The UK agent is ***Southern Ferries***, T020-7491 4968.

Directory

Banks *Banco de España*, Plaza de España. *Banco Español de Crédito*, 10 Av Juan Carlos I Rey. *Banco Hispano Americano*, 5 Plaza Menéndez Pelayo. Money changers operate outside the *Trasmediterranea* office on Plaza de España. **Communications Internet**: internet cafés on Av Juan Carlos Rey and at the intersection of Candido Lobera and Ejército Español. **Post office**: on Pablo Vallescá. **Embassies and consulates** France, Muelle Ribera, T2681511. **Medical services** Hospitals: *Hospital Comarcal*, Remonta, T2670000. *Red Cross Hospital*, Av Duquesa Victoria, T2684743. **Useful addresses** Ambulance: T2674400. **Fire service**: T080. **Guardia Civil**: T2671300/2671400. **Police**: (Local) T092 (emergencies), also T2674000, (National) T091. **Red Cross Ambulance**: T2672222.

Eastwards towards Algeria

From just south of Nador, at **Selouane** (Saturday souk), the P27 branches off the P39 and goes east across the barren foothills of the **Kebdana mountains** towards the Algerian border. At Zaïo, a left turn onto the 8100 takes you east and north to Cap de l'Eau (Ras el Ma) (51 km). About 10 km after Zaio the P27 crosses the Oued Moulouya, once the easternmost limit of the former Spanish protectorate, into the plain of Triffa or Saïdia. To the south the isolation of the Beni Snassen Mountains comes into view.

During the period of French administration (1911-56), this tiny corner of northeastern Morocco was transformed into one of the richest agricultural areas in the country, thanks to the construction of the Triffa Canal diverting water from the Oued Molouya. European settlers came in to run farms on the same model as that prevailing in neighbouring Algeria.

One of the most enduring legacies of this period is the Beni Snassen vineyards, which produce a good wine of the same name. Since the departure of the settlers in the 1950s and 60s, the area has remained industrious and relatively wealthy although there are still wide gaps in income. In recent decades, Moroccan expatriates have returned from France, Belgium and the Netherlands to build houses for their families and invest in farming and small businesses.

For the visitor, there are two easily reached attractions: the beach at **Saïdia** (launched in 2001, there are five main beach tourism projects in Morocco, the most advanced at Taghazoute; Saïdia is one of these projects) and the unspoilt **Beni Snassen Mountains** south of Berkane.

Berkane

Phone code: 055
Colour map 1, grid B6

Berkane is a bustling modern agricultural centre with little of historical or cultural interest. It is, however, a convenient base for excursions to the nearby mountains and there is a comfortable hotel with a good restaurant. A sharp contrast exists between the leafy, well-to-do end of town close to the administrative and military buildings on the Oujda Road, and the busy crowded dusty streets which characterize the rest. Most facilities can be found on the main Boulevard Mohammed V, which is also the Nador to Oujda main road. At the western end of this road, before the bridge over the *oued*, is a large open space with the main mosque, several cafés and a large weekly market each Tuesday. The town is also a main centre for the Boutchitchiya soufi brotherhood.

Sleeping **C** *Hotel Zaki*, 27 Route Principale d'Oujda, opposite the municipality building, T055-613743. Stylish little hotel with excellent restaurant. **E** *Hotel Ennajah*, Blvd Moulay Youssef, T055-612914. Simple hotel with clean rooms, street noise can be bothersome in early morning, no hot water, there is a café/restaurant below. **E** *Hotel Mounir*, just off Blvd Mohammed V on R Cheraa, T055-611867. A popular, efficiently run hotel, which doubles as a rooming house, with a friendly and helpful owner, self catering possible.

Eating

Mid-range *Restaurant des Orangers*, in *Hotel Zaki*, T055-613743. Excellent little restaurant whose kitchen is run by Haji Sakhraji, who featured on a BBC food programme in the 1980s, menu 95dh. For a snack try ***Sandwich Venisia***, 144 R Sultan Moulay Mohammed. A cheerful drink and snack with the locals can be sampled in the tiny wine cellar at 21 Blvd Mohammed V opposite the post office, probably the best evening entertainment available.

Tour operators

Oriental Voyages, 94 Blvd Mohammed V, friendly and helpful.

Transport

Road Bus: the *CTM* offices are located midway along Blvd Mohammed V next to the *Café des Jardins*. There is a bus to **Oujda** at 1030 and one to **Fes/Casablanca** at 1900 from here. Most other bus services depart from Blvd Moulay Youssef opposite *Café des Jardins*. From here there are hourly departures for **Ahfir** and **Oujda**. Buses for **Nador** stop to pick up every hour on the hour (roughly) by the Grand Mosque. There is normally only 1 bus for **Saïdia** at 1400 departing from the same place as the taxis (see below). **Taxi**: grands taxis for **Nador**, **Taforalt**, **El Aioun** and **Taourirt** leave from the parking space under the tall trees by the Grand Mosque. For **Saïdia**, the taxis leave from the Saïdia road at the opposite end of town (bear left at the roundabout with the emblem in the middle). All other grands taxis depart from the main bus stop in Blvd Moulay Youssef.

Directory

Banks *BMCE*, opposite *Shell* petrol station. ***Crédit du Maroc***, 44 Blvd Mohammed V. **Communications** On Blvd Mohammed V. **Medical services** Chemist: ***Pharmacie de la Mosquée***, Pl de la Grand Mosquée.

Beni Snassen Mountains

Colour map 1, grid B6

The whole area is riddled with underground caves, most of which remain unexplored

In geological terms, the Beni Snassen mountains are a continuation of the Rif. The hillsides are covered with Mediterranean vegetation – almond and orange, lavender and oleander, olive, juniper and pine – and the rockscapes are dramatic. Well tended orchards cling to the lower slopes. In the Zegzel Gorge, terraced cultivation is necessary, ordering the scenery with changing bands and blocks. Certain caves here have fine formations of redeposited calcium and other shapes formed by water erosion of the limestone. In the Plombo caves there are rare prehistoric cave drawings. The highlights are the **Gorges du Zegzel** and the **Grotte du Chameau**, where it is possible to camp. A warm

Northeastern Morocco

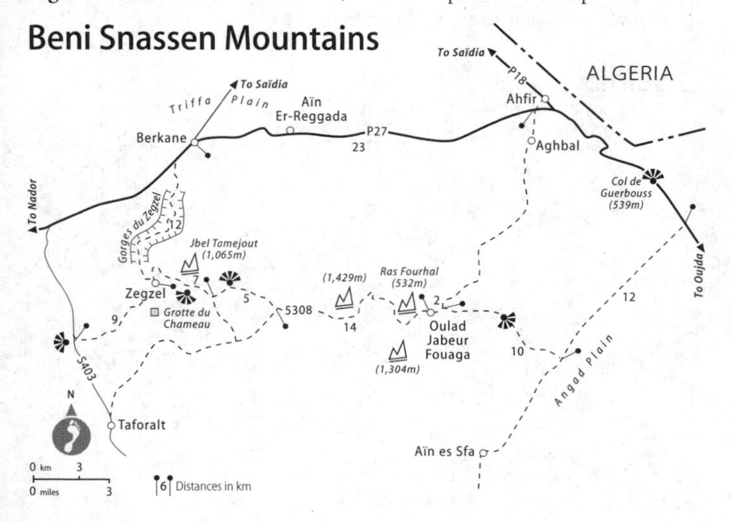

stream flows out of the main entrance of the cave and joins the nearby Oued Zegzel. Inside the cave there are stalactites and an extensive warren of unlit passageways. (Unfortunately at the time of writing these were closed to visitors, as works to ensure visitor safety were planned.) Both sites are easily accessible from Berkane, even on foot, in a couple of hours if one is feeling energetic.

Ins & outs

Lifts are easy to come by in this area, but you should always offer to pay

There are several ways to get into the Beni Snassen Mountains. If you are pressed for time, and don't have your own transport, the best way is from Berkane via a circular route that takes in the gorges and the caves. This can be done easily in 2-4 hrs, either by taxi or by using a combination of taxis, walking and lifts. Taxis from Berkane don't normally pass via the gorges, so you may have to charter one. Make sure the price you agree on is for a return trip including stop-offs. A cheaper option is to do the circuit anti-clockwise by taking a shared taxi heading for Taforalt (20 km) along the S403 and getting off at the pass shortly before the village. From here there is a signposted road winding 9 km to the caves along a very attractive valley of fruit trees and tiny hamlets. From the Grotte du Chameau you can return to Berkane, a further 10 km downhill, via the Zegzel Gorges. Eastwards, a rough but very scenic corniche road (the 5308) branches off from the Zegzel defile, and runs along the crest of the range for 30-40 km, down to the Angad Plain and on to Oujda. Distances and the most rewarding viewpoints are marked on the map on page ???. Back on the P27, the next town after Berkane is Ahfir, a quiet border town. From here there are 2 options, northwards to the resort of Saïdia, or south to Oujda by the panoramic 539 m Col de Guerbouss.

Saïdia

Phone code: 055
Colour map 1, grid A6

Saïdia is a pleasant resort popular with Moroccans, not yet overly developed, and hence perhaps lacking in some comforts. It has an old 17th-century fortress from the time of Moulay Ismaïl and a more recent 19th-century construction. It is packed in the summer, with no shortage of places to eat, but limited and expensive hotels, some of which are closed in winter, when the place is fairly deserted.

Ins & outs

See Transport, page 303, for further details

Saïdia is easily reached from Oujda, with plenty of buses and grands taxis running between the 2 towns. The road to Saïdia runs parallel to the Algerian border, at one point through a narrow gorge when all that separates the traveller from Algeria is the narrow Oued Kiss (no translingual pun intended here).

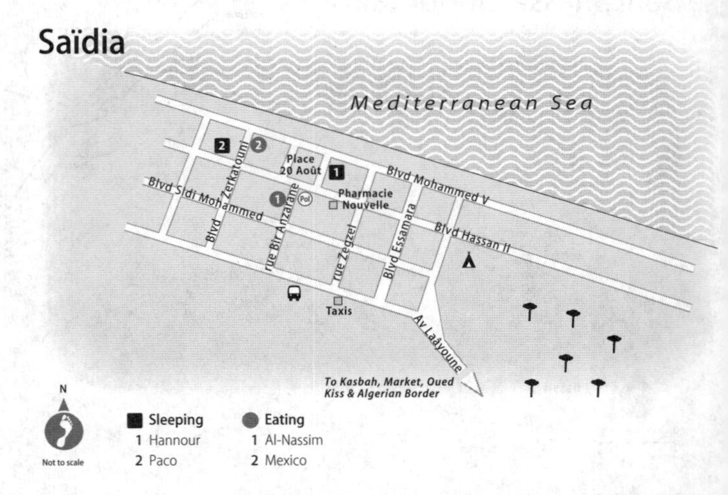

Sights

The Saïdia region has orchards, vineyards and market gardening. Saïdia itself is located on the coastal plain of Triffa, with forested mountains not far to the south. There is an attractive sandy beach which stretches for 12 km, and views of the Spanish Islas Chafarinas (Ja'farine Islands) and east to Algeria. Saïdia is easily explored, with a grid of brightly coloured houses, restaurants and hotels parallel to the beach.

The 20 km between the Algerian border and the estuary of the Oued Moulouya was the only section of the Moroccan Mediterranean coast to have been occupied by France for any length of time

In the low season, Saïdia feels like an empty film set, waiting for the big show, which in a sense it is; the **Saïdia Music Festival**, in August, marks the high point of the year, when virtually the entire population of Oujda and Berkane seems to migrate here to escape the heat. Unfortunately, the beach cleaning services cannot always keep up with the invasion.

The tiny, square 19th-century **kasbah**, with its intact walls and humble dwellings, was all that existed here prior to the 1930s. It was built by Hassan I to guard against the French, then occupying Algeria. The adjacent market enclosure, which holds a souk on Sunday, backs onto the Oued Kiss which marks the border with Algeria.

From the kasbah, it is a short walk to the beach through a eucalyptus forest. A new tourist complex is planned here to include hotels, restaurants, golf courses and a marina.

Essentials

Sleeping

■ *on map*

For Jul and Aug, try to reserve

C *Hotel Hannour*, Pl 20 Août, T055-625115. Centrally located, the smartest hotel in Saïdia, with a good restaurant and a bar, open Jun-Oct. **D** *Hotel Paco*, Blvd Hassan II, T055-625110. Comfortable, friendly, family hotel close to the beach, 15 rooms , restaurant, open Jun-Oct. **E** *Hotel El-Kalaa*, R Layoune, T055-625123. Open all year round. Also **E** *Sherif*, which is also open all year, some distance from the beach. Apartments can be rented cheaply Sep-May if you bargain. The owner of the *Al-Nassim* restaurant may be able to help.

In season, the campsites get packed and services do not always keep up with the demand

Camping *Camping Caravaning Al Mansour*, R de Moulouya. Site of 6 ha. *Camping Centre Autonome*, at Saïdia Plage. Site of 8 ha, beach only 200 m, bar/snack, grocery shop, pool, showers, laundry, petrol at 500 m, electricity for caravans. *Camping Essi*, site of 2½ ha, beach 200 m, groceries, showers, laundry, electricity for caravans, petrol 500 m.

Eating

● *on map*

Mid-range *Café/Restaurant Al-Nassim*, R Bir Anzarane, T055-625008. Open all year, breezy panoramic salon, very fresh fish. Recommended. **Cheap** *Café/Restaurant Mexico*, Blvd Zerkatouni. In the centre, facing the beach, friendly proprietor who speaks English, very good value, open all year. Several standard restaurants on R Sidi Mohammed, open all year, including *Café Restaurant Plus*. Try *Café Bleu*, R Laayoune, relaxed and friendly atmosphere.

Transport

Road Bus: depart from R Laâyoune to **Ahfir/Oujda**, services more frequent in summer. **Taxi**: grands taxis leave from R Laâyoune or from the treelined road behind and parallel to R Sidi Mohammed, to **Ahfir** (20 mins), and on to **Oujda**, **Berkane** and **Nador**. Grands taxis also depart from R Laâyoune or from the taxi rank by the kasbah.

Directory

Banks Nearest are in Ahfir, 20 km away. In high summer, a mobile branch service operates in Pl du 20 Août. **Medical services** *Pharmacie Nouvelle*, Blvd Hassan II.

Oujda وجدة

Phone code: 055
Colour map 1, grid B6
Population: about 500,000

Founded in the late 10th century, capital of the Zenata tribe for nearly a century, Oujda then largely disappears from the history books until the 19th century, when it was twice occupied by the French. In the 20th century, Oujda was developed by the French as the capital of Maroc Oriental. The city has a distinctive feel to it, more relaxed than the Rif towns to the west, and has a university and some light industry. Until the border with Algeria was closed, Oujda, first stop in Morocco for tourists from Algeria and Tunisia, used to have a flourishing hotel trade. However, given the appalling security situation in Algeria, the border has been shut since the mid-1990s and shows no signs of being reopened. Although Oujda has few sights, it might make a convenient stop before moving on to Spanish Melilla, or planning to journey southwards to Figuig, in the Sahara. The place makes a welcome break from the hassle of other Moroccan cities, as people see few Westerners

Ins and outs

Getting there

See Transport, page 308, for further details. *You can fly to Oujda from Casablanca, Paris, Amsterdam and Brussels*

Oujda is a long haul over the P1 from Casablanca (nearly 12 hrs), Fès (6½ hrs) and Taza. Figuig is a hard 7-hr drive across bare expanses of eastern Morocco. The P27 leads into Oujda from Melilla and Nador (2½ hrs) and Ahfir. There are grands taxis from Taza and Saïdia, and buses from Casablanca, Fès, Taza and Figuig. Oujda is at the eastern end of Morocco's rail network, the station not far from the town centre. Arriving by air, the Aéroport Oujda – Les Angads, T055-682084 – is 15 km north, a grand taxi ride away.

Getting around

After exploring Oujda, you may want to take a town bus from Bab el Ouahab out to the oasis of Sidi Yahia, 6 km away

Oujda is easily covered on foot. From most destinations, if you arrive by bus or grand taxi, you have a fair 15-min walk (or a cheap petit taxi ride) from the Oued Nachef terminal to get to the hotels on Blvd Zerktouni, which runs down to the city centre from the train station. Some *CTM* buses, however, arrive in the centre, on Pl du 16-Août, behind the central clock tower and mosque. Grands taxis from Nador, Berkane and Ahfir terminate near Pl du Maroc in the town centre. Pl du 16-Août is just a short walk away down the R de Marrakech.

Tourist information

Délégation Régionale du Tourisme, Pl du 16-Août, BP 424, T055-684329 (open 0800-1200 and 1430-1830), unhelpful.

Background

Although Roman ruins have been found at Marnia, in 944 Zenata Berbers founded Oujda, located on the main route from Rabat and Meknès to Algeria. Traditionally, the town was fought over by the rulers of Fès, in Morocco, and Tlemcen, in Algeria. Captured by Sultan Youssef Ben Tachfine in 1206, it was a major centre for the Almohads who added to the fortifications. The Merinid ruler Abou Youssef rebuilt the city in 1297, constructing new walls and a kasbah, a mosque and a palace. Later the Ottoman Regency of Algiers gained control of the city, but Moulay Ismaïl regained it in 1687, subsequently doing much to develop the city. Though acknowledged as part of Morocco by international treaties, the city was occupied by French forces in 1844 after the decisive Battle of Isly, fought 8 km west of the city, and again in 1859. In 1903 Oujda was the centre of the uprising led by Bou Hamra, and was again taken by French forces from Algeria in 1907.

Oujda is now the most significant city in northeastern Morocco. Occupied by the French several decades before the rest of Morocco, modern education was available earlier than elsewhere in the country. Thus Oujda's inhabitants consider themselves rather more sophisticated than many of their co-nationals. Indeed, a large number of Oujdis were active in the national independence movement. The contact with neighbouring Algeria also gives Oujda a slightly less provincial feel than one might expect. This is particularly apparent when coming from the Rif. Sadly, after the border with Algeria was closed in 1995, the sharp fall in the number of visitors crossing from Algeria hit the local economy badly, affecting Oujdans' morale. (Signs of economic hardship are evident, although not overwhelming.) Until the late 1980s, many locals relied on regional tourism and cross-border business for revenue. Revenues from migrant workers do something to compensate, however, and in the last couple of years, the king has visited the city several times, with a number of regional development initiatives promised.

Sights

Ville nouvelle

In its heyday in the mid-20th century, Oujda must have been a prosperous sort of place. The town centres on a 1930s municipal clock tower on Place du 16-Août and the central section of Boulevard Mohammed V, home to the best cafés and setting for the evening promenade. Close to the 1970s *Hotel Oujda*, is the **French Cathedral with its bell-tower topped by a stork's nest.**

Médina

Oujda's médina has interesting souks used by ordinary Moroccans

Oujda's heavily rebuilt **small médina** is surrounded by the *ville nouvelle*. There are no notable buildings accessible to the visitor and in 2002 even the tiny ethnographic museum, located in the slightly tatty **Lalla Meryem** gardens, was closed. No one seemed to know when it would be back in action. Still on this southeastern side of the médina, a short section of *pisé* Merinid ramparts tries to compensate for the lack of formal sights. Continuing along the line of the walls, you come to the most animated part of the old town, the area around the **Bab Sidi Abd el Ouahab** at the end of Avenue du Marché, where you will find the fish, meat and vegetable markets.

Just outside the Bab Sidi Abd el Ouahab is a large area where street entertainers used to perform for the evening crowds. Sadly, the square has now been designated as a parking lot. Some of the former atmosphere can be enjoyed on the far side of Place Bab Sidi Abd el Ouahab, where there is also a **junk market**. Inside the gate is a super fresh produce market, suitably confusing in layout. Nearby, there is an extensive *kissaria*, with all sorts of cloth and clothing on sale. Past the vegetable stalls, try to locate Place Al-Attarine, with the *koubba* of Sidi Abd el-Ouahab, as well as the heavily restored 13th-century **Merinid Grand Mosque** (one of the city's finest buildings) and medressa, built by Sultan Abu Yaqub. Still in this area, ask for the **Hammam du Jardin**, a public bath built in the early 20th century which will give you a good introduction to the arts of the Moroccan bath.

Excursions

There are a handful of things to do from Oujda, the most obvious being a trip to the shrine of Sidi Yahia (see below). On the way, the **Lalla Aïcha Park** is popular with locals. In summer, the **beach** at Saïdia is a huge draw. If in Oujda for any length of time, the gorges of the **Beni Snassen Mountains** to the northwest are in easy day-trip distance. (NB Lots of day trippers from Spanish Melilla at weekends.) Another side-trip option, some 25km south of Oujda, is the plateau-like **Djebel Mahceur** on the Touissite road. Taking the Berkane/Nador road, **Ras el Ma** and its long beach is another option for a day out.

Sidi Yahia Ben Younes

On summer evenings, the **Shrine of Sidi Yahia Ben Younes**, located in the oasis of the same name, is popular for Oujdans seeking a spot of fresh air and room to let their kids run around. Set in a pleasant if slightly scruffy park area of tamarisk and eucalyptus trees, the shrine is thought by some to be the tomb of St John the Baptist. It has been revered by Jews, Christians and Muslims alike. A series of small stalls selling pilgrims' needs, sandwiches and drinks precedes the shrine. If travelling by yourself, you might be invited into the shrine, to sit in the cool on the carpets and contemplate the green-silk covered tomb. There are two annual *moussems* (religious festivals) in honour of Sidi Yahia, in August and September. To get there, take a town bus from Bab Sidi Abd el Ouahab, service every 10 minutes, ride takes 20 minutes, or a petit-taxi to here from the city centre (12dh).

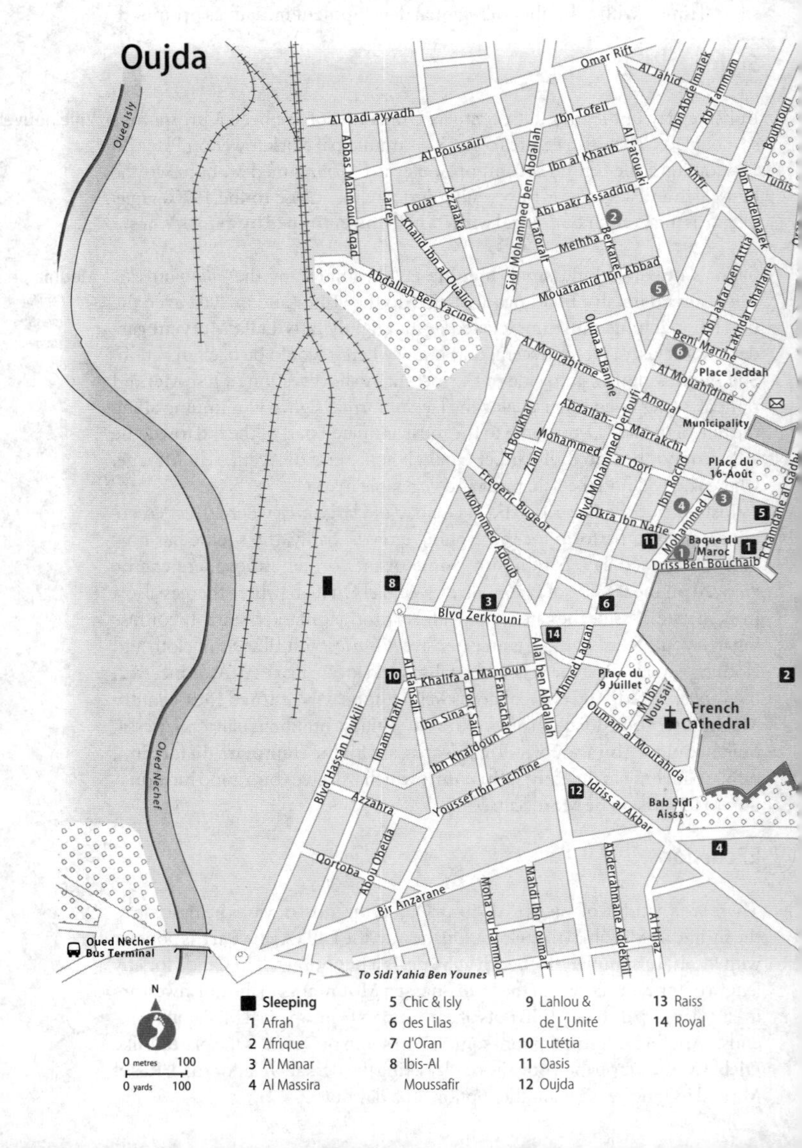

Essentials

Sleeping

■ on map

Since the closure of the Algerian border in 1995, times have been hard for hotels in Oujda. For the time being, this often means no hot water, darkened corridors, poor plumbing as hotels struggle to economize. This state of affairs is particularly noticeable in some of the more expensive hotels, where, apart from the *Hotel Al Moussafir*, you can bargain prices down.

Essentially an area with large hotels built in the 1950s to early 80s, often very empty

Ville nouvelle B *Ibis – Al Moussafir*, corner of Blvd Abdallah Chefchaouan and Pl de la Gâre, T055-688202. Perhaps the best hotel in town, 74 good rooms with a/c, TV, shower, telephone, bureau de change, pool, packed in summer, restaurant (menu 120dh), parking. **C** *Hotel Al Manar*, 50 Blvd Zerktouni, near the station, T055-688855, F681670. Well-managed establishment, better value than the *Moussafir*. Reserve in summer, a/c. **C** *Al Massira*, Blvd Maghreb al-Arabi, T055-710797, el.massira@wanadoo.net.ma Pool (murky water), noisy band on summer nights, pleasant in its day. **C-D** *Hotel Oujda*, the big 1970s block on Blvd Mohamed V near the church, T055-685063, F685064. Another hotel for those nostalgic for the 1970s. TV, a/c, small clean pool.

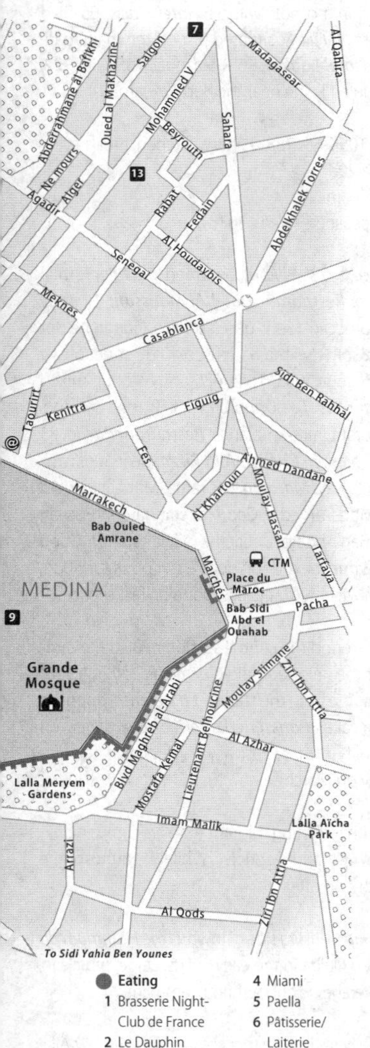

D *Hotel de la Concorde*, 57 Av Mohammed V, T055-682328, close to Pl du 16-Août 1953. 36 room, clean, simple, but centrally-located hotel with restaurant and bar. 2px 200dh. *Hotel des Lilas*, R Jamal Eddine el-Afghani, T055-680840. Clean, 36 slightly cramped rooms, central location, (coming up from rail station, take the last left before you reach Blvd Mohamed V), reliable hot water, underground garage, cafés nearby. **D** *Hotel d'Oran*, Blvd Mohammed V, Route d'Alger, T055-701001. Tastefully decorated, comfortable and friendly family-run hotel, very clean, efficient, reliable hot water, heating, all rooms with bath, TV, restaurant. **D** *Hotel Raiss*, Blvd Mohammed V, Route d'Alger, T055-703058. Newly built, elegant, all rooms with bath, comfortable and very clean, enthusiastic staff, lift, café, TV, garage.

E *Hotel Royal*, 13 Blvd Zerkatouni, on your right heading away from the station, T055-682284. 60 good rooms, has seen better days, worth bargaining hard, no hot water at time of writing, insist on towels, soap, etc. Street-side rooms noisy. **F** *Hotel Lutétia* 44 Blvd Hassan Loukili, T055-683365. Worn and deserted, go right on first main avenue as you leave the station.

All rooms with w/b, shower, wc on corridor. **F** ***Hotel Victoria*** Blvd Mohamed V, near station, opposite *BMCI*, T055-685020. Multi-bedded rooms, no hot water. Good cheap choice.

The central area near the clock tower, off Av Mohamed V and the Pl du 16-Août 1953

Médina **E** *Hotel Tlemcen*, 26 R Ramdane el Gadhi, down a side street just off Pl du 16-Août 1953, T055-700384. Basic, clean hotel. Best of the cheapies. **E** ***Hotel Afrah***, 15 R de Tafna, T055-682328. Central position, clean and good value. Near *CTM* and cheap eateries, ask for a *bit dakhlani* (inward facing room). **F** ***Hotel Afrique*** or ***Ifriqiya***, 2 impasse Achakfane Barrani, T055-682095. Good choice in the médina, located just off R Mazouzi (jewellery souk), clean but very simple, no showers. **F** ***Hotel Chic***, 2 R Ramdane El Gadhi just off Pl 16-Août, small and simple, rooms rather dark, no private bathrooms or hot water, good value for the budget traveller. **F** ***Hotel Isly***, 24 R Ramdane El Gadhi, off Pl 16-Août, T055-683928. Old fashioned French-style establishment, clean and pleasant but rather spartan, no hot water. **F** ***Hotel Oasis***, 65 Blvd Mohammed V, T055-683214. Very similar to *Hotel Isly*, situated just off the main road. Other basic hotels in the médina include ***Hotel Lahlou***, 96 R Mazouzi, T055-682122, and ***Hotel de l'Unité***, down the narrow R Ouled Rzine near the Bab Ahl Jamal.

Youth hostel 11 Blvd Allal ben Abdallah, T055-680788. 45 beds, kitchen, meals available, bus 100 m, train 500 m, overnight fee 20dh.

Camping The nearest is at Saïdia on the coast (see page 303).

Eating
● *on map*

Expensive *Brasserie Night-Club de France*, 87/89 Blvd Mohammed V. Rather formal establishment serving international cuisine. ***Restaurant Hotel Al Moussafir***, Pl de la Gare, T055-688202. International and Moroccan food, good service, adequate set menu at 120dh. **Mid-range** *Comme chez soi*, R Sijilmassa, left up a side street off Av Mohammed V as one nears the Pl du 16-Août 1953, T055-686079. Alcohol, mixed Moroccan and European menu. ***Restaurant Le Dauphin***, 38 R de Berkane, T055-686145. Smart but homely fish restaurant, nice ambiance. ***Restaurant Paella***, 83 Blvd Derfoufi. Cheaper alternative to the *Dauphin*. **Cheap** *Allo Pizza*, near *Sandwich Sindibad*. Best choice for pizza eat-in or takeaway. ***Marajan***, 9 R Tafna. Moroccan food, speciality is tagine, 30dh. ***Miami***, 67 Blvd Mohammed V. Good for standard Moroccan cuisine. ***Restaurant National***, 17 Blvd Allal Ben Abdallah, near the railway station. Good cheap tajines and brochettes. ***Pizzeria Diwane***, next door, does a big pizza for 50dh. ***Sandwich Sindibad***, 95 Blvd Derfoufi. Sandwiches, fruit juices, popular, fast service.

Cafés & pâtisseries

The best cafés in Oujda are located in and around the central section of Blvd Mohammed V. The smartest is ***Le Royal***, handy for the neighbouring *Cinéma de Paris*, on your right down Blvd Allal Ben Abdallah as you come from the station. ***La Défense***, opposite the Wilaya building, is also pretty smart. For cakes, ***Pâtisserie/Laiterie Sheherazade***, on R Ben Attia, off Pl Jeddah. The local speciality *karane*, basically chick peas eaten in a sandwich, can be found on stalls on the Av du Marché.

Shopping

The central souks are packed in summer with returning migrant workers' families buying clothes and electric goods to kit out newly married couples. While the atmosphere is interesting, there is little 'typical' craftwork on offer.

Sport & activities

Hammam Over on the Bab Sidi Aissa and *Hotel Massira* side of town, is the ***Hammam du Jardin***, built shortly after the French occupied Oujda in the early 1900s. Large and clean, architecturally more interesting than your average neighbourhood hammam.

Transport

Local **Car hire**: demand for hire cars is heavy in the summer season. ***Avis***, 110 Av Allal ben Abdallah, T055-683993, and at the airport. ***Budget Cars***, on left just as you leave the rail station, T055-681011. ***Hertz***, 2 Immeuble El Baraka, Blvd Mohammed V, T055-683802, and at the airport. ***Mezquita Rent-a-Car***, Blvd Zerktouni, immeuble Essaâda, T055-703452, T061-363396 (mob). **Taxi**: petit-taxis are red. Watch out for unofficial red vehicles without signs. Taxi from Av Mohammed V to Oued Nachaf bus station, 5dh.

Long distance Air *Aéroport Oujda-Les Angads* is 15 km from the city, off the P27, T055-683261. Take a grand taxi into town. To get there take a grand taxi from Pl du Maroc. There are flights to **Casablanca** (6 a week), **Amsterdam**, **Brussels**, **Dusseldorf**, **Frankfurt**, **Marseille** and **Paris**. Flights more frequent in summer season. ***Royal Air Maroc*** has an office at the *Hotel Oujda*, Av Mohammed V, T055-683963-4, as does ***Air France***.

Road Bus: 2 bus departure points, the Oued Nachaf bus station and the centrally located *CTM* office. Check whether *CTM* still has departures from the Oued Nachaf for Fès and Nador. The ***CTM*** office, 12 R Sidi Brahim, is easily located behind the central clock tower and mosque, just off Pl du 16-Août, T055-682047. Services to **Fès**, **Nador** and **Casablanca** (evening). The Oued Nachaf bus station, T055-682262, is a short (4dh) taxi ride from centre. On foot, the centre is 20 mins away. Leave bus station and head for busy roundabout with *Petrom* station. Turn left, keeping *Petrom* on right and a long treelined avenue brings you to the rail station roundabout. Oued Nachaf gare routière has private line services to **Casablanca** (Express Tassaout), **Fès**, **Meknès**, **Taza**, **Midelt**, **Figuig** (get the early morning service to avoid the heat, 50dh, guichet 6), **Bouarfa**, **Nador** (lots of services), **Al Hoceïma**, **Berkane**, **Saïdia**, and **Ahfir**. **Taxi**: grands taxis to **Berkane**, **Ahfir** (40 mins) and the **border** leave from just off Pl du Maroc. For **Saïdia** change at Berkane or, preferably, Ahfir. To **Taza**, **Figuig** and **Bouarfa** leave from the bus station. There are regular grands taxis for **Nador**.

Train The train station is on Pl de l'Unité africaine, T055-683133. Check departures when you arrive. The line runs west via Taza, Fès and Meknès to meet the main north-south, Tanger to Marrakech line at Sidi Kacem, north of Kénitra/Rabat. Journey times are long, you may have to change at Sidi Kacem. Expect to do Oujda to **Tanger** in 12 hrs, Oujda to **Marrakech** in not much less. The goods train for Bouarfa no longer has passenger wagons. In summer, there are 4 trains a day on the Oujda-Casa Voyageurs run.

Directory

Banks Most banks are on Blvd Mohammed V where both the ***Wafabank*** and ***Crédit de Maroc*** have ATM machines. Closest ATM to rail station is the *BCM*, almost opposite *Hotel Manar*. Outside normal banking hours, the main branch of the ***BMCE*** is open on Sat. Otherwise, there is the *Hotel Al Moussafir* bureau de change. **Communications Internet**: on Blvd Allal Ben Abdallah, ***Internet Essalam*** and bookshop almost opposite *Pizzeria Diwane*. Try also ***Alfanet Cyberclub*** next to *Banque du Maroc* and *Relax Chez Miss Poulet* (sic) eatery. On the southeast side of the old town, there is an internet club (blue and yellow facade) almost opposite the entrance to the kissaria on Blvd du Maghreb arabe. **Post**: *PTT*, Av Mohammed V/Pl du Jeddah. **Embassies and consulates Algeria**, 11 Blvd de Taza, T055-683740-1. **France**, 16 R Imam Lechaf, T055-682705. **Medical services Chemist**: all night on R de Marrakech, T055-683490. As you arrive by train, there is a handy pharmacy almost in front of the station on your right. Also try pharmacy opposite *Café Royal*. **Useful addresses Fire**: T15. **Police**: T19.

South towards Figuig

Colour map 1, grids B6 & C6

The journey south by road is long, monotonous, and very hot and is to be avoided if possible in summer. Only the initial part of the road, climbing up towards the Col de Guerbouss and the mining district of Jerada is green and varied. The rest of the route crosses the eastern edge of the vast Rekkam Plateau, which extends across into the high plateaux of Algeria. A low carpet of esparto grass and wormwood stretches to the horizon. Travel by bus is punctuated by frequent stops to pick up and set down shepherds who miraculously survive in this scorched, windswept emptiness. The only towns along the route are Guenfouda, Ain Beni Mathar, Tendrara, and Bouarfa, none of which holds much interest other than their remoteness and an opportunity to stretch the legs and buy basic provisions.

Bouarfa The administrative and garrison town of Bouarfa serves as transport hub for the southeastern corner of Morocco. A stop here is unavoidable for those travelling to/from Er Rachidia. The town is well provided with shops and services. The Saturday market is held in the large enclosure off to the right below the bus station. It is a major event, attracting shepherds and traders from the whole southeastern region.

Sleeping F *Hotel des Hauts Plateaux*, (no phone) situated above the bus station by the mosque, panoramic location at the foot of the Jbel Bouarfa. **F** *Hotel Tamalt*, T055-798799, on the high street below the bus station, above a café. Clean, well-ventilated rooms with attractive tiling.

Transport Road Buses from Oujda to Figuig pass through Bouarfa. 2 buses a day to Er Rachidia. **Train** The weekly train from Bouarfa to **Oujda** leaves at 0920 on Sun and arrives there at 1701. The return journey is the following Sat at 2200 getting into Bouarfa on the Sun at 0635.

Directory Banks The only bank with an exchange facility is the ***Banque Populaire***, some distance from the centre. To get there, turn left at the foot of the high street and then right at the next junction. **Medical services** 2 pharmacies on the main street.

Figuig

Phone code: 056
Colour map 3, grid B6

The route from Bouarfa to Figuig (100 km) is mesmerizing in its isolation and quality of light, particularly along the final stretch, where the valley narrows. Although the first 60 km or so out of Bouarfa are difficult, the road is being improved, with the last 40 km now widened. Figuig itself, tucked away in a remote southeastern corner of Morocco, right next to the Algerian border, is 400 km south of Oujda. The four-wheel drive hordes have no reason to make the trek this far east, so you can enjoy the oasis and desert environment. The charms of Figuig are not instantly apparent in the new administrative centre. However, some exploration away from the centre of town should make your trip worthwhile.

Ins & outs There are buses to Figuig from Oujda and Er Rachidia, running via Bouarfa. Although relations between Morocco and Algeria were improving in early 2003, the border seemed set to remain closed for at least another year. If driving, there will be a close check on your papers by the Gendarmerie royale a few km before Figuig.

Background Figuig's frontier location has given it a strategic significance, and it has often been fought over by the Moroccan sultanate and the powers to the east. Most recently in 1963 and 1975, there were clashes between the armies of Morocco and Algeria. The border has been closed for some years now, resulting in even fewer visitors to this least-frequented of the southern oases and not much of a livelihood for its inhabitants, apart from small-scale farming and the date harvest.

Figuig comprises seven distinct villages situated on two levels: the upper level consists of Ksour El Oudaghir, which straddles the main road where most shops and facilities are located, and the adjacent villages of El Maiz, El Abid, Ouled Slimane, and El Hammam Foukani; the lower plain, or 'Baghdad' as it is known here, supports a large area of palmgroves connected by a network of alleyways, with Zenaga, the largest of the *ksour*, in the middle. The two levels are separated from each other by an escarpment, the Jorf.

Sights

Friday souk

Until recently, each of the *ksour* of Figuig was independent, and their history was one of continuous feuding with each other, mainly over the issue of water. Centuries of management and protection of this precious resource have moulded the appearance of each *ksar*, with their watchtowers, high walls, and winding irrigation channels. Reached by turning between the hotels *Sahara* and *Meliasse*, **Ksar Oudaghir** has springs and an interesting round stone minaret which it may be possible to climb. See if a local will take you to one of the *ksar*'s underground *hammams*. Of all the *ksour*, perhaps **Ksar Zenaga** has the most to offer, being the largest, most distinctive and also furthest from the administrative centre. Zenaga has a pleasant square with a café and a mosque from where several alleys radiate into the palmery. A platform with excellent views over the lower half of Figuig can be reached by turning right at the bottom of the main street, through the small market enclosure (Friday souk), and following a narrow path across fields. On the horizon is a gap between two mountains which marks the Moroccan/Algerian frontier. A good panorama of the Figuig ensemble can be obtained in the evening (for the best light) from the rocky pass situated on the road that encircles Figuig to the west. **Ksar el Maiz** with its vaulted streets and arcaded square is close to the main road and easily accessible. **Ksar el Hammam Foukani** ('Ksar of the Upper Hammam') is so called because of its underground *hammam*, fed by hot springs and reached by a slippery flight of steps. Another possible trip (fine views) is to the **Oued Zousfana Valley** and the **Taghla Pass** 4 km to the southeast of the administrative centre. To avoid any unnecessary arousing of border guards' suspicions, it is advisable to notify the police station if visiting the Zousfana Valley and surrounding hills.

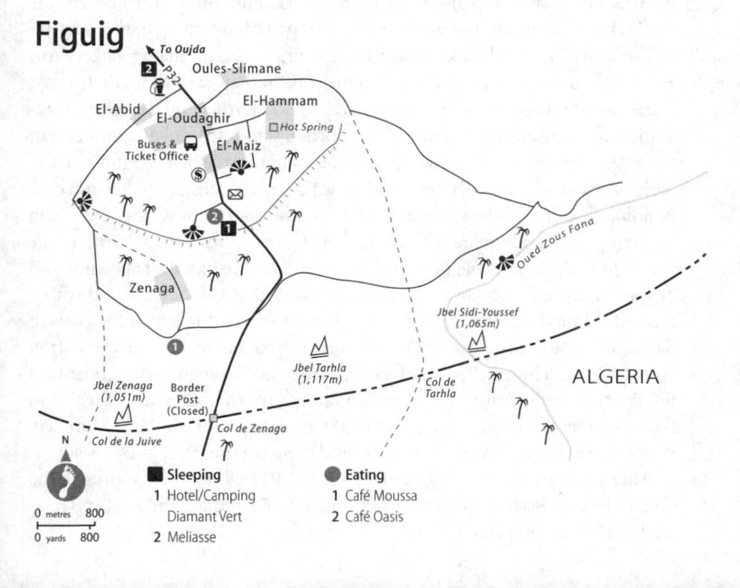

Sleeping
■ *on map, page 311*

At the time of writing there were only a couple of functioning hotels in Figuig. Best bet is the **E** ***Hotel Figuig***, T056-899309. Only 6 rooms so try to reserve. Also some cheaper dormitory-type accommodation. Less agreeable is the basic **F** ***Hotel Meliasse***, T056-899062, next to the petrol station at the entrance to the town. No comforts, very cold on winter nights. Enquire at the petrol station – it may be possible to **camp** in the grounds of the attractive ***Hotel/Camping Diamant Vert***, which may reopen in the near future.

Eating
● *on map, page 311*

Figuig is hardly a gastronomic destination, although dew-fed mushrooms are picked by the local shepherds and sometimes sold in the market. There are no real restaurants, but the following 2 places do simple meals (eg omelette, tajine). **Cheap** *Café Oasis*, situated in the municipal gardens at the end of the main street, Av Hassan II. *Café Moussa*, down in Zenaga new town (take second turning signposted for Zenaga after Hotel/Camping), garden at rear with a stage, where concerts are sometimes held.

Sport & activities

If spending some time in Figuig, you might try a spot of **hot sand therapy**, as delivered by Abderrahmane Sassi, T056-899493 in Ksar el Hammam el Foukani. The idea is that you are partly buried in holes in the sand. The treatment is said to be very effective against rheumatism. From early Jun to mid-Sep only.

Transport

Road Buses leave from Av Hassan II, in front of the *Hotel Sahara*, which operates as the ticket office. There are 4 buses a day to **Oujda** 0500, 0645, 0815, 1400 (check all times, later service is irregular, enquire from ticket office). At one time there was a daily morning service to **Er Rachidia**, although for this destination you will probably have to take a bus for Oujda and change at Bouarfa. In summer, get the early bus to avoid the afternoon heat.

Directory

Banks *Banque Populaire*, on the main street. **Medical services** Chemist: on the main street or in Zenaga. **Hospital**: near the barracks. There is usually at least a nurse present. The doctor lives next door.

From Bouarfa to Er Rachidia

Now a large sized town, Er Rachidia (good selection of hotels, plus petrol and garages) is described in detail on page ???

With the border closed, there is little choice but to retrace one's steps from Figuig to Bouarfa and from there on to Er Rachidia (or Oujda if you are travelling around Morocco anticlockwise). The hauntingly dramatic landscape along the P32 more than compensates for the lack of facilities along the route. For the first 70 km or so the road runs close to the Algerian border along the broad plain of Tamalt with little to break the horizon. The first stop is the dusty village of **Aïn Ech Chair**, 1 km off to the left, with a tiny café and grocery shop, that comes alive briefly for the twice-daily bus service. Some 12 km beyond the village, inaccessible from the Moroccan side of the border, stands the isolated monument to General Leclerc. The next settlement is **Bouanane**, the first significant palm oasis, situated on the *oued* river of the same name. The village's reddish-brown buildings, gardens and leafy streets make for a pleasant halfway stop; there is an attractive porticoed square with a café away from the main road. North of the town along the bed of the *oued* is the picturesque **Kasbah of Takoumit** and beyond it a rough network of mountain tracks that can be explored with a four-wheel drive vehicle. About 35 km further on, on the left, is the oasis of **Sahli**, with its low profile desert architecture seeming to merge into the barren surroundings. The inhabitants of Sahli are regarded as chérifs, descendants of the Prophet Mohammed. **Boudnib** is a rather forlorn military town which in colonial times operated as the French military quarters for southern Morocco. Buses stop in the central garden square and there is a single very basic hotel.

After more desert, the P32 finally joins the P21 close to the source of the Oued Meski. It is a further 18 km from here to Er Rachidia along a flat and relatively fertile stretch of the Ziz Valley.

Marrakech and the West-Central High Atlas

316 Marrakech
316 Ins and outs
317 Background

320 Sights
320 Main areas of interest
322 Jemaâ el Fna
324 Koutoubia Mosque
325 North of Jemaâ el Fna: souks and monuments
328 Kasbah quarter
330 Down Riad Zitoun el Jedid: craft museums and palaces
331 Tanneries near Bab Debbagh
333 Ramparts and gates
334 Gardens

335 Essentials
335 Sleeping: hotels
342 Sleeping: riads
346 Eating
350 Cafés
350 Bars and clubs
351 Entertainment
351 Shopping
354 Sport and activities
355 Tour operators
355 Transport
357 Directory

358 The Toubkal High Atlas
358 Up the Amizmiz Road
360 Excursions up the Taroudant Road
362 Tin Mal

365 Trekking in the Toubkal National Park
365 Ins and outs
365 Imlil
366 Climbing Toubkal

368 The Ourika Valley
370 Oukaïmeden

371 The Tizi-n-Tichka route

372 Telouet
372 Ins and outs
372 Background
373 Telouet to Ouarzazate via Aït Ben Haddou

374 Azilal High Atlas
374 Northeast of Marrakech: the Azilal High Atlas and Beni Mellal
374 To Azilal Demnate and Ouzoud
375 Azilal

376 Vallée des Aït Bougmez
377 The Massif du Mgoun

378 Beni Mellal

378 Northwest of Beni Mellal

Introducing Marrakech and the West-Central High Atlas

Marrakech has attracted European visitors since at least the 1920s. The mythical Red City, so called because of the terracotta wash used on its buildings, lies within reach of cool high Atlas valleys and arid plains. Marrakech is one of the great historic cities of North Africa. Focus points are the 12th-century **Koutoubia Mosque** and the **Jemaâ el Fna** 'square', famed for its entertainments and open-air restaurants. Around them stretches the médina, a place of narrow streets, flat-roofed houses and minarets. The souks are thronged with handicrafts of every shape and size, from silken caftans and pottery drums to carved wooden chests and the orange-woollen expanses of Chichaoua carpets.

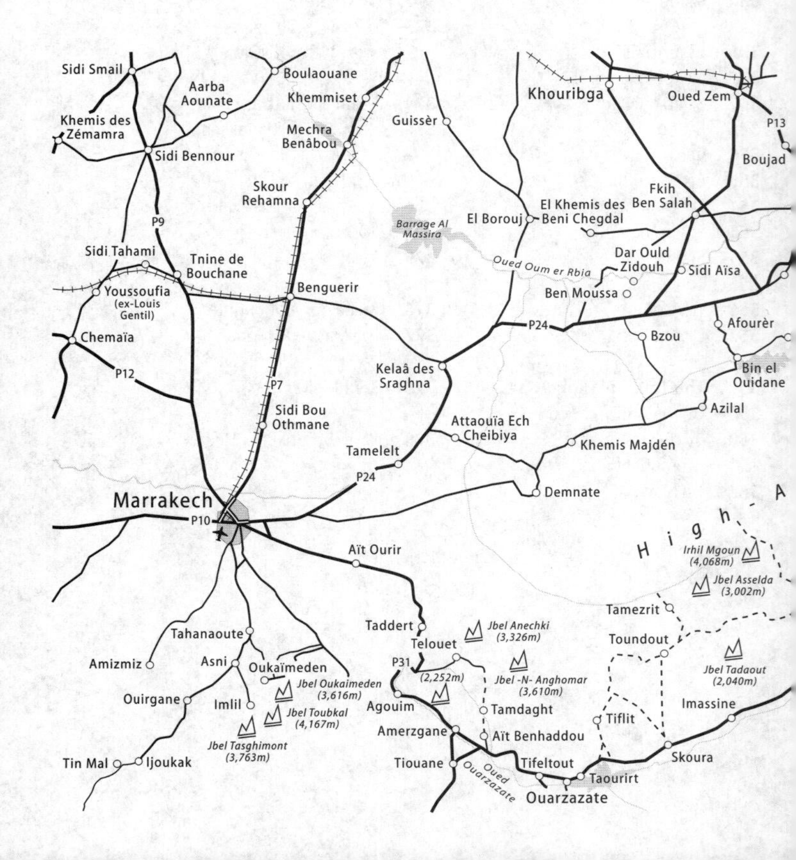

For the outdoor minded, there is plenty to do in day-trip distance: the **Ourika Valley** and the **Toubkal National Park**, centring on Jbel Toubkal, North Africa's highest peak. Also within easy distance of Marrakech are sites like the Cascades d'Ozoud. South of **Azilal**, committed walkers can head for the **Vallée des Aït Bougmez**, an excellent base for gentle walking and tough trekking into the fastness of the Irhil Mgoun, second highest summit of the Atlas range. Heading south of Marrakech, you can visit the Glaoui citadel of **Telouet** and cross the range at the **Tizi-n-Tichka** pass before descending to Ouarzazate. Even more spectacular is the **Tizi-n-Test**, which takes you over the Atlas to Taroudant and the Souss plain.

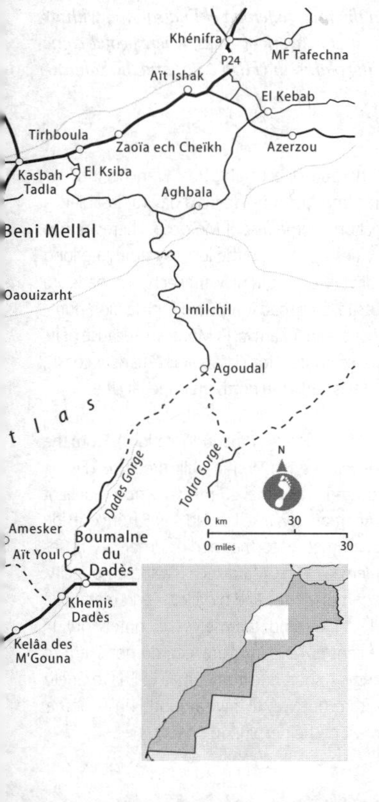

Things to do in Marrakech

- Get to **Jemaâ el Fna**, aka 'la Place', in late afternoon. Watch the musicians and snake charmers, tumblers and tourists, have a feed at one of the smokey barbecue stalls, or even a bowl of steamed snails.
- Visit the great **palaces** (the vast ruined Badi', the Dar Si Saïd for its museum). Textile and carpet buffs must not miss the **Maison Tiskiouine**.
- Do a spot of **souking** for that essential Berber dagger, silk embroidered velvet slippers, lipstick-red tooled leather desk set, cedar-wood harem door feature (for shipping).
- Find your way through from chic **Mouassine** via the **Medersa Ben Youssef** to **Bab Debbagh**, home of that smelliest of attractions, the **tanneries**. (Getting lost in the medina is such a pleasure.)
- Fast all day to be ready for Marrakchi gastronomics in a discrete **riad restaurant**.
- Take a day trip up to the **Atlas mountains** and the ruined fortress of Telouet.

Marrakech مراكش

Phone code: 044
Colour map 2, grid B4

Marrakech has a memorable beauty, with its palm-lined streets and red earth walls, surrounding a huge médina of flat-roofed, red houses. The High Atlas mountains, snow-capped until April, form a dramatic backdrop to the city, and a venue for numerous excursions. Above all, Marrakech is worth visiting to experience the vibrant mass of people milling around in the unique Jemaâ el Fna square, with its grillstalls, traders and entertainers and the vast network of souks, where people come to buy and sell from all over the surrounding plains, the High Atlas and the Sahara.

Ins and outs

Getting there

See Transport, page 355, for further details

Marrakech is accessible by air, road and rail. There are direct flights from French and some other European cities to Marrakech-Menara airport, and 5-7 trains a day to Casablanca (journey time 3½ hrs), with onward connections to the rest of Morocco. There are bus and grand taxi connections with all major cities – although the journey times are long (around 8 hrs to Fès, for example). For car drivers, once out of Marrakech, the roads are rarely crowded. However, the Marrakech-Casablanca road is reputed for the high number of accidents. Marrakech makes an excellent point of arrival in Morocco because of its centrality, situated at the meeting point of routes for Essaouira (Atlantic coast), Ouarzazate (key to the gorges south of the Atlas), and the northern imperial cities.

Getting around

The airport is a short taxi ride from the city (50dh during the day, 60dh at night). From the railway station to Guéliz, the heart of the *ville nouvelle*, is a 15-min walk; the Jemaâ El-Fna area, where most of the budget hotels are located, is a further 20-min walk from Guéliz. It is best to get a taxi into the city (say 10dh). Alternatively, take bus No 3 or 8 from outside the station along Av Hassan II and Av Mohammed V, to the médina. Inter-city buses arrive at Bab Doukkala, a 15-min walk from Jemaâ El-Fna. Marrakech is a spread-out city, built on a plain – hence the large number of mobylettes and bicycles – and rental of a 2-wheeler is an option. Upmarket travellers may find themselves in hotels out in Semlalia, which run shuttle services to the centre. Taxis in Marrakech do not seem to bother with meters: remember to have change. A short ride from Jemaâ El-Fna to Guéliz should not be more than 10dh. The most picturesque way to drive around is in a *calèche*, a horse-drawn carriage. The energetic do most of their exploring on foot.

Hassle

The 'hassle' which deterred some visitors in the past is reduced a little thanks to the unseen but ever-vigilant *Brigade touristique*. The predominant atmosphere is relaxed, best appreciated from a café terrace beside Jemaâ el Fna! If you are robbed or hassled, the Brigade touristique is situated on the Mamounia side of the Koutoubia, near the *CMH* petrol station (blue and yellow livery), in a small building on a public square with a few trees. Believe it or not, if you are spending some time in the city, you may have to visit them to do the paperwork authorizing a Moroccan friend to accompany you so they don't have hassle with the Brigade. This seems to apply only if the Moroccan is not of a recognizably educated background.

Tourist information

Office du Tourisme, Pl Abd el-Moumen Ben Ali, T044-448889. **Syndicat d'Initiative**, 176 Av Mohammed V, T044-432097/434797. Rather sleepy.

Background

The city

In some early European maps Marrakech appears as 'Morocco city', although 'Maraksh' is the Arabic name. The origins of the name are obscure: some see it as a corruption of 'aghmat-urika', the name of an early town (see Aghmat, page 368). The city is surrounded by extensive palm groves, into which areas of villas and hotels are gradually spreading. Yet there are also sandy, arid areas near, and even within, the city which give it a semi-Saharan character. And then there are the mountains. Arriving from Fès or Meknes one runs alongside the bald arid Jebilet 'the little mountains', or cross them at Sidi Bou Othmane as one runs in from Casa-Rabat. (Perhaps the most beautiful approach to Marrakech is on the P9, from Casa and Sidi Bennour, which crosses the Plateau des Gantours and the end of the Jebilet.) However, from most points in Marrakech, cloud and heat haze allowing, it is the High Atlas, the Adrar (literally 'the mountains'), in Tachelhit, which dominate. At times the optical illusion is such that the snow-covered mountain wall appears to rise from just behind the city.

Marrakech covers a large area, with distinct zones separated by less populated areas. For the visitor this will entail long walks between the main points of interest in the médina, Guéliz (the *ville nouvelle*), and the two olive groves of the Agdal and the Menara, or more probably reliance on taxis, *calèches,* buses or your own transport. The long, wide treelined boulevards of the *ville nouvelle*, a number of which are focused on the beautiful Koutoubia Mosque, give the city an impressive feeling of spaciousness, which contrasts with the equally impressive density of the médina.

Marrakech is Morocco's fourth largest city. The official population in 1993 was 550,000, although today the figure is probably nearer the 800,000 mark. Its people are a mix of Arab and Amazigh; many are recent migrants from surrounding rural regions and further south. For centuries important as a regional market place, Marrakech now has a booming service economy. There is still a wide range of handicraft production and small-scale industry, particularly in the médina. Out in the western suburbs are new factories. Increasingly, tourism is seen as the mainstay of the city's economy. Marrakech is one of the major tourist attractions of Morocco and many of the city's large unemployed or under-employed labour force supplement their incomes by casual work with tourists, their unwanted attentions having in the past given the city a bad name.

Almoravid origins & role

Marrakech was first founded properly in 1062 by one Youssef Ibn Tachfine, the Almoravid leader, as a base from which to control the High Atlas mountains. A kasbah, Dar al-Hajar, was built close to the site of the Koutoubia

24 hours in the city

Marrakech has so many visitors these days that the main historic sites are at visitor saturation level. Before the rush, start your day with lots of walking in the southern part of the old town to take in the museums, maybe the **Dar Si Said**, the **Palais Bahia** (19th- century), and the **Palais Badi** (a vast 16th-century ruin). The **Saadian Tombs** are a must do, but get very, very crowded. Next, whizz over to the small but perfectly planted **Jardin Majorelle** in a petit taxi. From here you could get another petit taxi over to **Gueliz** for a spot of light shopping (area around Rue de la Liberte) and then on to lunch at a restaurant like *La Bagatelle* or *La rotisserie* du *Café de la Paix*, on Rue de Yougoslavie (both with outside terraces, latter two the best). After a quick siesta at your hotel, you can soldier back to the **médina** for more monuments (area north of Jamaa el Fna, Ben Youssef Medersa, Musee de Marrakech) and even some **shopping**. Sundown will see you on **Jamaâ el Fna**, having your photo taken with gnaouas/snake charmers/acrobats and retiring for a mint tea and patisserie at the *Café Argana* or perhaps the *Café CTM* (more locals than tourists). Marrakech sits down to **dinner** relatively early. Choose one of the more discrete restaurants in the Mouassine/Bab Leksour area of the old town (*Ksar Saoussan*, *Le Tobsil*, possibly *Dar Moha*). Or go for brochettes at one of the eateries on the **great square** (the largest open-air barbecue in the world?). The scene here will entertain you for hours.

Mosque. Under Youssef Ben Tachfine, Marrakech became the region's first major urban settlement. Within the walls were mosques, palaces and extensive orchards and market gardens, made possible by an elaborate water transfer and irrigation system. The population was probably a mixture of *haratine* or blacks from the Oued Draâ, Imazighen from the Sous Valley and the nearby Atlas, and Jews of Amazigh stock. The city attracted leading medieval thinkers from outside Marrakech.

Marrakech was taken by the Almohads in 1147, who almost totally destroyed and then rebuilt the city, making it the capital of their extensive empire. Under the Almohad Sultan Abd el-Moumen, the Koutoubia Mosque was built on the site of Almoravid buildings, with the minaret added by Ya'qub al Mansur. Under the latter Marrakech gained palaces, gardens and irrigation works, and again became a centre for musicians, writers and academics, but on his death it declined and fell into disarray.

Merinid neglect & Saâdian revival

Whilst the Merinids added several *medersa* to Marrakech, Fès received much of their attention, and was preferred as the capital, although from 1374 to 1386 Marrakech was the centre of a separate principality. Marrakech was revitalized by the Saâdians from 1524 with the rebuilding of the Ben Youssef Mosque, and the construction by Ahmed al Mansour Ad-Dahbi of the El Badi Palace and the Saâdian Tombs. Marrakech also became an important trading post, due to its location between the Sahara and the Atlantic.

Alaouite Marrakech

The Alaouites took control of Marrakech in 1668. In the early 18th century the city suffered from Moulay Ismaïl's love of Meknès, with many of the major buildings, notably the El Badi Palace, stripped to glorify the new capital. The destructive effects of this period were compounded by the civil strife following his death. However, under Alaouite Sultan Moulay Hassan I, from 1873, and his son, the city's prestige was re-established. A number of fine palaces still visitable date from this time.

Early 20th century: Glaoui rule

From 1898 until independence, Marrakech was the nerve-centre of southern Morocco, ruled practically as a personal fiefdom by the Glaoui family from the central High Atlas. The French took control of Marrakech and its region in 1912, crushing an insurrection by a claimant to the Sultanate. Their policy in the vast and rugged southern territories was to govern through local rulers, rather as the British worked with the rajahs of India. With French support, Pacha T'hami el Glaoui extended his control over all areas of the South. His autonomy from central authority was considerable, his cruelty notorious. And of course, there were great advantages in this system, in the form of profits from the new French-developed mines. In the 1930s, Marrakech saw the development of a fine *ville nouvelle*, Guéliz, all wide avenues of jacarandas and simple, elegant bungalow houses. Acquiring a railway line terminus, Marrakech reaffirmed its status as capital of the South. And it was at this time, when travel for pleasure was still the preserve of the privileged of Europe, that Marrakech began to acquire its reputation as a retreat for the wealthy.

Capital of the South

In recent decades Marrakech has grown enormously, its population swelled by civil servants and armed forces personnel. Migrants are attracted by the city's reputation as 'city of the poor', where even the least qualified can find work of some kind. (For many rural people, the urban struggle is hard, and as the Tachelhit pun puts it, Marrakech is *ma-ra-kish*, 'the place where they'll eat you if they can'.) North of the médina, new neighbourhoods like Daoudiate and Issil have grown up next to the Université Cadi Ayyad and the mining school. South of the médina, Sidi Youssef Ben Ali, referred to in Marrakchi slang as SYBA, is an extension of the old town with a reputation for rebellion. West of Guéliz, north of the Essaouira road, are the vast new housing areas of Massira, part low-rise social housing, part villa developments. The most upmarket area is on the Circuit de la Palmeraie, however. Little by little, the original farmers are being bought out, and desirable homes with lawns and pools behind by high walls are taking over from vegetable plots under the palm trees. East of the médina is the vast Amelkis development, a gated community complete with golf course and the discrete Amenjana 'resort'. Here the money and privilege are accommodated in an area equal to one third of the crowded médina. It is a tribute to Morocco that enormous wealth and intense deprivation can sit so close to each other without street crime of the Latin American kind being a problem.

Future of Marrakech

The late 1990s saw Marrakech in an upbeat mood. The Brigade touristique set up in the mid-1990s had managed to reduce the hassling of tourists. All forms of tourist activity were on the up, with hotels reporting record booking levels. According to one report, there were over 80 private guesthouses in the médina, many owned and run by Europeans. The problem was how to deal with the influx. Certain monuments had reached saturation point: the exquisite Saâdian tombs were home to a permanent people jam. On the drawing boards was a major new tourism zone of over 1,000 ha, the *Oliveraie de Marrakech*, to be located on land southwest of the old city. The Avenue de France is to be extended for a few more kilometres. The plan's opponents worry whether this will be the final blow for what remains of the city's rural character, destroying working olive groves and the open approach to the southern side of the city. On a positive note, the airport is to be moved further out, probably to Sidi Bou Othmane on the future Casablanca to Marrakech autoroute. There remains the problem of transport in the central areas. At peak times, the area around Jemaâ el Fna is a seething mass of vehicles and mopeds, bicyles, carriages, buses and humanity. One rumour has it that the square is to be dug up to create an immense underground car park.

The 'Venice (or Lausanne) of Morocco'?

Nevertheless, Marrakech continues to draw the visitors in. Thanks to public relations campaigns like the 1998 *Année du Maroc* in France, the city maintains its hold on the Western imagination. The setting is undeniably exotic, eccentricities are tolerated, and (rather less honourably) domestic help is cheap. Features in international decoration magazines fuel the demand for property; major monuments are being restored. Occasional resident Yves St Laurent even dubbed Marrakech 'the Venice of Morocco' – which might seem an appropriate description on a February day with torrential rain on Jemaâ el Fna. The city authorities are engaged in a major *embellissement* campaign, consisting mainly in installing wrought-ironwork, rosebeds and pergolas around the médina. Locals murmur darkly that the unstated objective of all these prettifications is to turn Marrakech into the Lausanne of Morocco. The effect is more that of a magnificent wild feline transformed into a lapdog with ribbons in its tail. Still, the Red City remains the closest Orient one can find within a few of hours flight of the grey north European winter, and provided the city authorities can keep vehicle pollution in check, it looks set to maintain its popularity.

Sights

Main areas of interest

Marrakech is clearly divided into the large historic city, the médina, and the *ville nouvelle*, Guéliz. The focal point of the médina, and indeed of the whole city, is the **Jemaâ el Fna**, an open place full of street entertainers and food sellers, adjacent to which are the most important souks. Handily for the tourist, it is located between the two main areas of historic sights. **North of Jemaâ el Fna** are the souks and the Sidi Ben Youssef Mosque, the city's main mosque after the Koutoubia. On a walk in this neighbourhood, you can visit the Almoravid Koubba, the Ben Youssef Medersa, and the Museum of Marrakech. **South of Jemaâ el Fna**, down Riad Zitoun el Qadim, you have an area of palaces, the Saâdian Tombs and a tiny ethnographic museum, the Maison Tiskiwine. If you are staying in a riad, you may well be in the **Bab Doukkala** or **Leksour/Mouassine** neighbourhoods, the former on the Guéliz side of the médina. The latter is very central, just north of Jemaâ el Fna, and is fast becoming the 'chic enclave', home to bijou gallery places like the Ministero del Gusto (sic) and the Dar Chérifa *café littéraire*. Bab Doukkala is handier for the bus station. For visitors with more time, the cheap goods market at **Bab el Khemis** is busy on a Sunday morning. Another point of interest are the tanners at **Bab Debbagh**.

Another popular feature of a visit to Marrakech is a tour of the gardens. This will include the **Jardin Majorelle**, quite close to Bab Doukkala, the **Menara**, a large square pool set in a vast olive grove south of Guéliz, and the **Agdal**, another pleasant olive grove close to the Sidi Youssef Ben Ali neighbourhood. To the east and north of Marrakech, across the Oued Issil, is the **Palmeraie**, increasingly built up but with a narrow road for intrepid bike riders. Close to the médina, the gardens between Koutoubia and Mamounia have been totally replanted with roses. Even once scruffy **Arset Moulay Slimane**, opposite the Municipality on your way to **Jemaâ el Fna**, is being given the treatment.

Most visitors will spend some time in **Guéliz**, the suburb laid out by the French in the 1920s. Despite all the new apartment buildings and traffic, it has a pleasant enough atmosphere with its cafés, upmarket boutiques and food market. The main thoroughfare is **Avenue Mohammed V** and the evening promenade here is popular.

The **Festival national des arts populaires** brings together music and dance troops from all over Morocco and some international acts. Under new management in 2003, festival activities were programmed for every weekend in July. The **Festival cinématographique** is held annually in the early autumn.

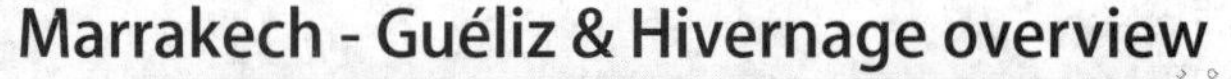

Marrakech - Guéliz & Hivernage overview

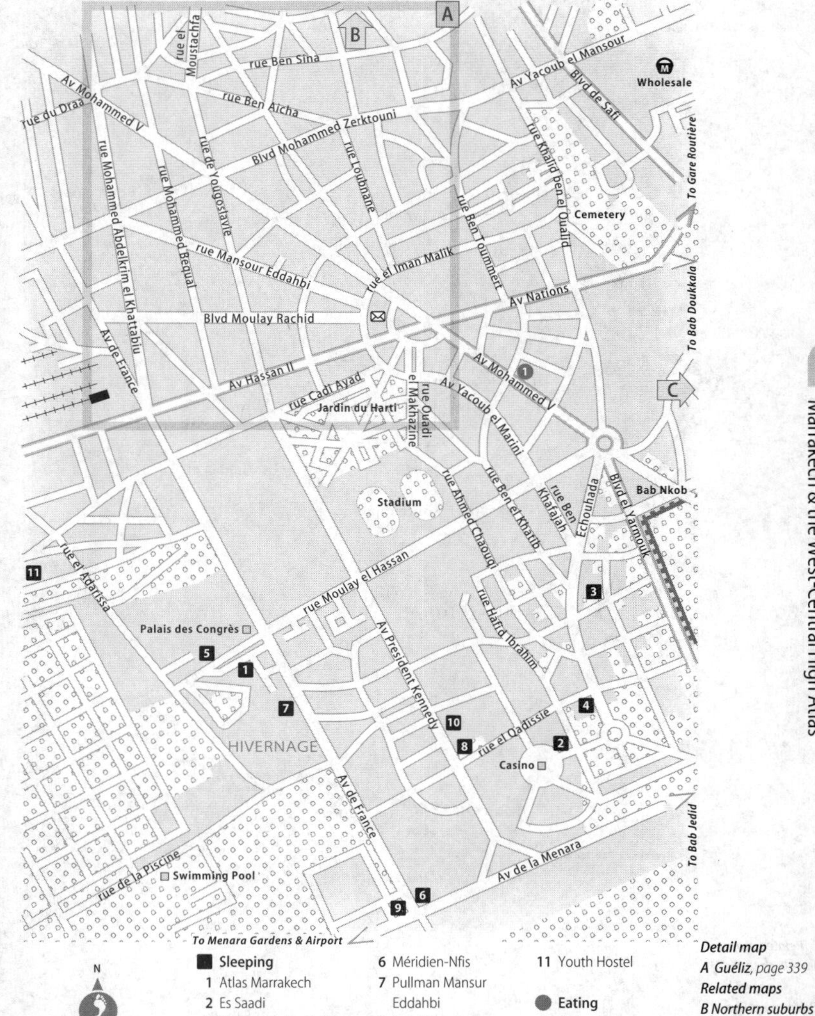

N

0 metres 300
0 yards 300

Sleeping
1 Atlas Marrakech
2 Es Saadi
3 Grand Hotel Imilchil
4 Imperial Borj
5 Mansour Ed Dahbi
6 Méridien-Nfis
7 Pullman Mansur Eddahbi
8 Safir Marrakech
9 Sheraton
10 Siaha Safir
11 Youth Hostel

Eating
1 Al Fassia

Detail map
A Guéliz, page 339
Related maps
B Northern suburbs & Palmerie, page 341
C Marrakech Médina, page 322

Jemaâ el Fna

Popular photo point: the terrace-roof of the Hotel CTM

The Jemaâ el Fna, unique in Morocco, is both the greatest pull for tourists and still a genuine social area for the Marrakchi people and those flooding in from the surrounding regions. 'La Place' is full of people hawking their goods or

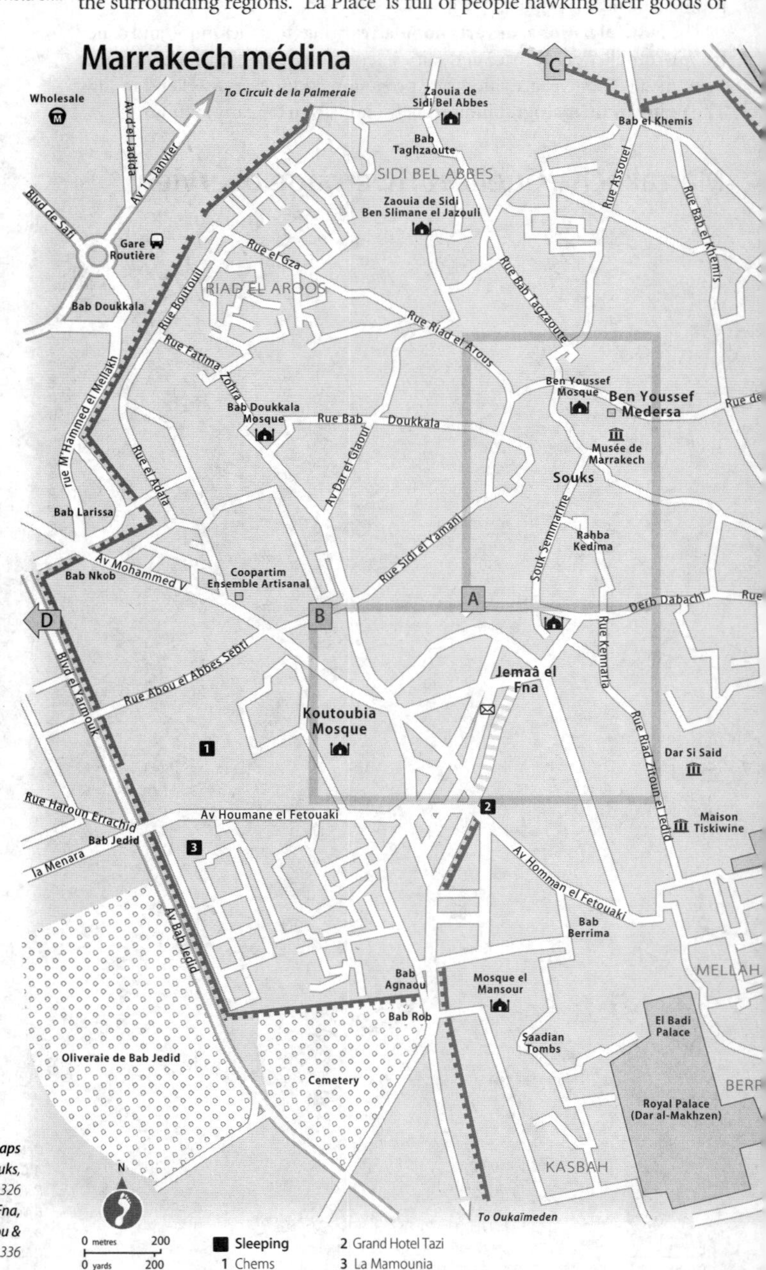

Related maps
A Marrakech souks, page 326
B Jemmâ el Fna, Bab Agnaou & around, page 336

talents and others watching, walking, talking and arguing. It is particularly memorable during Ramadan when the day's fast ends. Whatever the time of day or year, Jemaâ el Fna is somewhere that the visitor will return to again and again, responding to the magnetic pull that affects locals as much as tourists, to mingle with the crowd or watch from the terrace of the *Café de France* or *Café-Restaurant Argana*.

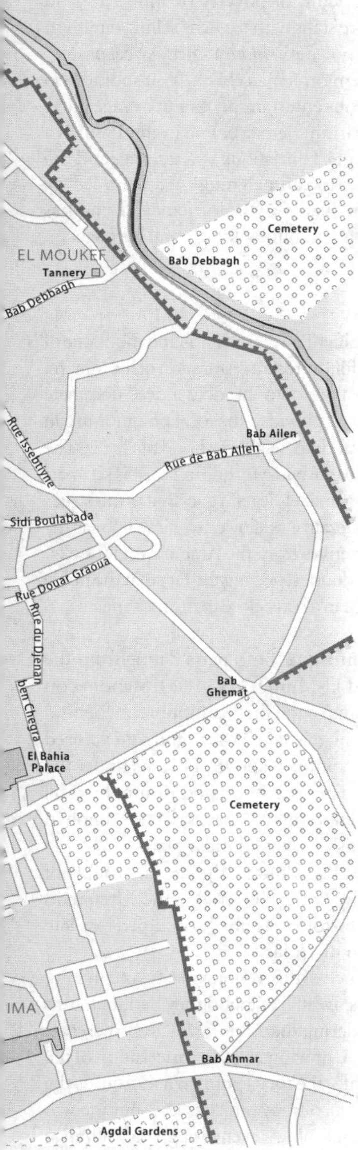

Background

Jemaâ el Fna means 'assembly of the dead', and may refer to the traditional display of the heads of criminals, executed here until the 19th century. In 1956, the government attempted to close down the square by converting it into a corn market and car park, but soon reverted it to its traditional role. In the late 1980s, the bus station was moved out to Bab Doukkala. In 1994, the square was fully tarmacked for the GATT meeting. The food stands were reorganized, and the orange juice sellers issued with smart red fezzes and white gloves. Today, Jemaâ el Fna, despite the pressures of tourism and poverty, retains its attraction.

At 'La Place'

Watch your wallet on Jemaâ el Fna. Lots of small change required for entertainers

During the day you can explore the stalls and collections of goods: fruit, herbs and spices, clothes, shoes, alarm clocks and radios, handicrafts too; there are snake charmers and monkey tamers, watersellers and wildly grinning gnaoua musicians with giant metal castanets, all too ready to pose for photographs. Sheltering from the sun under their umbrellas, the fortune tellers and public scribes await their clients. In the evening, the crowd changes again, a mix of students and people pausing on the way home from work, smart tourists strolling to exclusive patio restaurants in the médina – and backpackers ready for hot tagine or harira soup at one of the foodstalls. You may see Ouled el-Moussa tumblers or a storyteller enthralling the crowd. Sometimes there are boxers, usually groups of musicians: after much effort to extract a few dirhams from the crowd, an acoustic band will get some Berbers dancing, while around a hissing gas lamp a group will perform a song by Jil Jilala, an activist group popular in the 1970s.

More recent attractions include the *nakkachat*, women with syringes full of henna, ready to pipe a design onto your hands. 'Hook the ring over the coke bottle' is popular, while a lad with a dumb bell improvised from two old mill-stones will let you do some exercises for a dirham or two. You may find an astrologist-soothsayer tracing out his diagram of the future on the tarmac with a scrubby piece of chalk. A modern variation on the traditional *halka* or storyteller's circle touches harsh social reality: local people listen to a true tale told with dignity by the relatives of a victim of poverty or injustice. And should you need an aphrodisiac, there are stalls with tea urns selling cinamon and ginseng tea and little dishes of black, powdery *slilou*, a spicey sweet paste.

Pickpockets are occasionally a problem on Jemaâ el Fna. You should also have plenty of change handy for the various entertainments and orange juice. The hassling of tourists which marred visiting Jemaâ el Fna in the 1980s is a thing of the past: the plain clothes Brigade Touristique is watching, and the penalties are severe. And finally, thanks to campaigning by a team led by Spanish writer and Marrakech resident Juan Goytisolo, Jemaâ el Fna has received UNESCO recognition for its place in humankind's oral heritage.

Koutoubia Mosque

As this is a place of prayer, and in every way the most important mosque in the city, dress decently if you are going to approach the site to view it at length. Behind the mosque are gardens, and some nice photo opportunities

The Koutoubia is to Marrakech what the Eiffel Tower is to Paris and the Statue of Liberty is to New York (or so the publicity for the recent restoration of the minaret would have it). The 65-m high **minaret** of the Koutoubia does indeed dominate the whole of Marrakech. Visible from afar, it provided the focal point for urban planner Henri Prost when he laid out the modern neighbourhood of Guéliz. The Koutoubia is clearly visible as, unlike the Qarawiyin Mosque in Fès, it is set apart from the dense building of the old town. An unlikely legend goes that as this structure overlooked the harem, only a blind muezzin was allowed to climb it to call the faithful to prayer. The name Koutoubia derives from the Arabic *kutub* (books) and means the 'Booksellers' Mosque', no doubt reflecting the fact that the noble trade of selling manuscripts was conducted in a souk close to the mosque.

Background

Unusually, the Koutoubia is a **double mosque**, both parts dating from the reign of the second Almohad ruler, Abd El-Mumin (1130-63). Standing on the esplanade facing the minaret, the ruins of the first Koutoubia are behind railings to your right (first excavated in the late 1940s, and re-explored recently). The bases of the prayer hall's columns, and the cisterns under the courtyard, are clearly visible. The ground plan of the second Koutoubia, still standing, is the same as that of the ruined one (17 naves). The Almohad mosque at Tin Mal, visitable for non-Muslims, has a similar plan.

So why, back in the 12th century, did the Almohads go to the trouble of building not one but two mosques? Why bother destroying the Almoravid mosque? The site of the mosque is itself historic, originally occupied by a late 11th-century kasbah, the Almoravid **Dar al-Hajar**.

The successful Almohads destroyed much of the Almoravid city, and in 1147 built a large mosque, close to the fortress. In all likelihood they had to do this because, puritan as they were and considering the Almoravids to be heretics, they could not pray in a tainted building. Unfortunately, the orientation of the new Almohad mosque was not quite right – the focus point in a mosque is the direction of Mecca, indicated by the *mihrab*, or prayer niche. The solution was to build a second mosque – the present Koutoubia – even though the faithful at prayer can correct this directional problem themselves, under the direction of the imam, once the right direction has been worked out.

Thus two mosques existed for some time side by side, the first probably functioning as a sort of annexe. Given Almohad religious fervour, the congregations were no doubt large. Today, the bricked-up spaces on the northwest wall of the Koutoubia Mosque indicate the doors which connected them. However, the complex was excessive in size and the older structure fell into disrepair and eventual ruin. The excavations of 1948 also revealed a *maqsura*, or screen, in front of the *mihrab*, which could be wound up through the floor to protect the Sultan, and a *minbar*, or pulpit, which was moved into position on wooden rollers. The two cisterns in the centre may have been from a previous Almoravid structure. On the eastern flank of this mosque was an arcade of which a niche and the remains of one arch remain.

Existing Koutoubia Mosque

The existing Koutoubia Mosque was built by Abd el-Mumin in 1162, soon after the building of the first mosque. The **minaret** is 12.5 m wide and 67.5 m to the tip of the cupola on the lantern, and is the mosque's principal feature, rightly ranked along with later Almohad structures, the Hassan Tower in Rabat (see page 86) and the Giralda in Sevilla. The minaret, a great feat of engineering in its day, was to influence subsequent buildings in Morocco.

The minaret is composed of six rooms, one on top of the other. The cupola on top of the minaret is a symmetrical, square structure topped by a ribbed dome and three golden orbs. These are alleged to have been made from the melted down jewellery of Yaqoub al Mansour's wife, in penance for having eaten three grapes during Ramadan. The cupola has two windows on each side, above which is a stone panel in the *darj w ktaf*, 'step-and-shoulder' motif. (For a close-up view of the top of the mosque and this design feature, consult your 100dh banknote.) The main tower has a band of coloured tiles at the top.

The Koutoubia, a vast structure for 12th century North Africa, had to be a mosque equal to the ambitions of the western caliphate. It is held to be the high point of Almohad building, a cathedral-mosque of classic simplicity. It is here that the innovations of Hispano-Moorish art – stalactite cupolas, painted wooden ceilings – reach perfection. There are perspectives of horseshoe arches, no doubt an aid to contemplation. (Although the prayer hall is off- limits to the non-Muslim visitor, an idea of what it is like can be gained at the Tin Mal mosque in the High Atlas.) The unique *minbar* (preacher's chair), set against this apparent simplicity, is all decoration and variety – and very much in keeping with the elaborate taste of Ummayad Spain. (The *minbar*, also recently restored, can be viewed at the Badi Palace.) Both prayer hall and chair were to be a source of inspiration for later generations of builders and decorators.

Ultimately, the Koutoubia is striking because it is the work of one ruler, Abd el Moumine. Comparable buildings in western Islam – the Great Mosque of Cordoba and the Alhambra – were built over a couple of centuries. If you want to climb a mini-Koutoubia try the semi-ruined Almohad minaret at Akka.

North of Jemaâ el Fna: souks and monuments

Souks

An unofficial guide can be more trouble and expense than he is worth – and don't believe the 'Berber market, only open today' line

Many of the souks of Marrakech retain their original function and a morning's souking is one of the pleasures of the city. Before leaping into impulse purchases, get an idea of prices in Guéliz – perhaps in the stalls in the market there. The main souks lie to the north of Jemaâ el Fna. The entrance to them is to the left of the mosque. Follow this round to the left and then turn right in the main thoroughfare, **Souk Semmarine**. Alternatively, enter through the small tourist pottery market, further round to the left on Jemaâ el Fna. Souk Semmarine is a busy place, originally the textiles market, and although there are a number of large, expensive tourist shops, there are still some cloth sellers. To the left is a covered *kissaria* selling clothes. The first turning on the right leads past **Souk Larzal**, a wool market, and **Souk Btana**, a sheepskin market, to **Rahba Kedima**, the old corn market, now selling a range of goods including traditional cures and cosmetics, spices, vegetables and cheap jewellery, and with some good carpet shops. Walk back onto the main souk via a short alley with wood-carved goods. Here the souk forks into **Souk el Attarine** (perfumers' souk) on the left and **Souk el Kebir** on the right.

Clean toilets just north of souks in Museé de Marrakech café

To the right of Souk el Kebir is the **Criée Berbère**, where carpets and *jallabahs* are sold. This was where slaves, mainly from across the Sahara, were auctioned until 1912. Further on is the **Souk des Bijoutiers**, with jewellery. To the left (west) of Souk el Kebir is a network of small alleys, the *kissarias*, selling Western goods. Beyond the *kissarias* is the **Souk Cherratine**, with leather goods, somewhere to bargain for camel or cowhide bags, purses and belts.

Continuing back on the other side of the *kissarias* is the **Souk des Babouches**, a far better place to buy slippers than in the tourist shops. This feeds into Souk el Attarine, the spice and perfume souk, which itself leads back into Souk Semmarine. West of the Souk el Attarine is the carpenters' **Souk Chouari**. From here walk on to a Saâdian fountain and the 16th-century **Mouassine Mosque**. South of Souk Chouari is the **Souk des Teinturiers**, or dyers' market, where wool recently dyed is festooned over the walkways. Nearby are the blacksmiths' and coppersmiths' souks.

Islamic monuments

Once you have threaded your way up Souk Semmarine, onto Souk el Kebir and past Souk Cherratine, you are in the neighbourhood of some of the city's most important Islamic monuments, the **Almoravid Koubba** and **Medersa Ben Youssef**. With the **Museum of Marrakech** and the **Fondation Belarj**, there is also much evidence of private money creating new heritage sites.

Koubba el Baroudiyine

Now protected by neo-Versailles wrought-iron railings, the 11th-century **Almoravid Koubba** (Koubba el Baroudiyine) is the only complete Almoravid building surviving. It dates from the reign of Ali bin Youssef (1107-43), and perhaps formed part of the toilet and ablutions facilities of the mosque that at the time existed nearby. At first glance it is a simple building, with a dome surmounting a square stone and brick structure. However, the dome has a design of interlocking arches, plus a star and chevron motif on top. The arches leading into the *koubba* are different on each side. Climb down the stairs to view the ceiling of the dome, noting the range of Almoravid motifs, including the

Related maps Marrakech Médina, page 322 A Jemmâ el Fna, Bab Agnaou & around, page 336

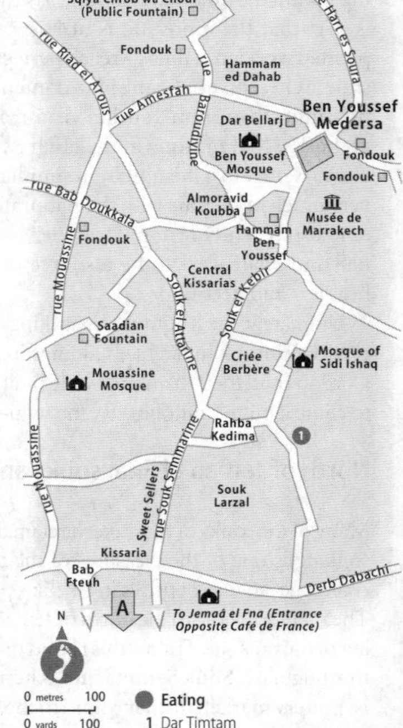

palmette, pine cone and acanthus. Around the corniche is a dedicatory inscription in cursive script. Set into the floor is a small, almost square, basin.

Musée de Marrakech

Clean loos in the café of the Musée de Marrakech

The entrance to the Musée de Marrakech is clearly in evidence just off the open area in front of the Almoravid Koubba. The museum is housed in Dar M'nebhi, the early 20th-century palace of a former Moroccan minister of war. ■ *0900-1800, closed Mon. 20dh. T044-390911.* After the entrance courtyard (good café and clean loos, on left, bookshop on right), a narrow corridor takes you into the exhibition areas proper. The simple whitewashed walls of the domestic wing shelter temporary exhibitions of contemporary art. Off the main courtyard, now entirely paved and protected by a plexi-glass roof and a brass chandelier as big as a small UFO, are displays of Koran manuscripts, coins, ceramics and textiles. Note the Portuguese influence in the elaborate wooden façades to the rooms on the left. A small passageway to the left of the main reception room takes you through to the restored hammam, now home to a small collection of early engravings on Morocco.

Medersa Ben Youssef

Standing with the Almoravid Koubba behind you, the minaret of the large 12th-century **Ben Youssef Mosque**, rebuilt in the 19th century, is clearly visible. Turning right out of the Museé de Marrakech, follow the street round and you will come to the entrance to the city's most important Islamic monument, the 16th-century Medersa Ben Youssef. One of the few Islamic buildings open to the general public, it is currently being restored by the Fondation Ben Jelloun. Founded in 1564-65 by the Saâdian Sultan Moulay Abdellah, on the site of a previous Merinid *medersa*, it functioned as a boarding school for students of the religious sciences and law. The *medersa* is centred around a square courtyard containing a rectangular pool, and with arcades on two sides. Each student had a separate cell with a sleeping loft and a window looking onto the courtyard. Note the much worn but still fine cedar wood of the upper façades around the courtyard. You will see fine *zellij* tiling on the arcade floor, walls and pillars. Inscriptions are in Kufic and cursive lettering, interwoven with floral patterns.

At the far end is the **prayer hall** covered with an eight-sided wooden dome. Beneath the dome plaster open-work windows illuminate the tilework. In the *qibla* wall is a five-sided *mihrab*. Note the stalactite ceiling of the *mihrab*, and the carved stucco walls with pine cone motif. (Why did they go for pine cones?) The inscription here, dedicated to the Sultan, has been translated as: "I was constructed as a place of learning and prayer by the Prince of the Faithful, the descendant of the seal of the prophets, Abdellah, the most glorious of all Caliphs. Pray for him, all who enter here, so that his greatest hopes may be realized." Note also the massive Carrara marble columns.

Ben Youssef Medersa

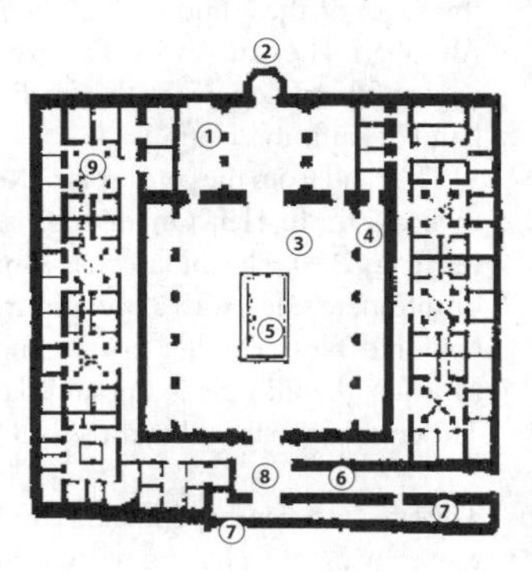

1 Marble pillars
2 5-sided mihrab
3 Open courtyard paved with marble
4 Marble pillars with wooden lintels to support two galleries
5 Marble pool
6 Entry
7 Stairway to students' cells
8 Vestibule
9 Individual students' cells around courtyard

On the way out of the *medersa*, the toilets on the right of the vestibule have an elaborate stalactite design on the ceiling. ■ *0900-1200 and 1430-1800, closed Fri.*

Dar Bellarj

Turning right out of the *medersa*, then left under a covered street, you will come to the entrance of Dar Bellarj, 'the House of Storks', on your left. The building, restored recently by a couple of Swiss artists, dates from the 1930s. Prior to this there was a *fondouk* on the site which housed the only hospital for birds in North Africa. Here there dwelt a wise man who had the gift of curing wounded storks. Today, the building, austerely but simply refurbished, is used primarily as gallery space. It is definitely worth calling in. Events have included an exhibition on the earthen architectures of the Draâ Valley. If director Susan Biederman is on hand she may have time to explain the house and its restoration.

North of the Ben Youssef Medersa

North of the Medersa Ben Youssef, you can wander through recent residential neighbourhoods, built on the site of former orchards and market gardens. You begin to realize the contrast with Fès. Whereas Morocco's spiritual capital has steep and narrow streets, accessible only by pedestrians and mules, flat Marrakech is teeming with bicycles and mopeds, mini-taxis and handcarts. Eventually, your wandering might take you to the open square of **Bab Taghzaoute** and on to **Zaouia of Sidi Bel Abbes**, one of the seven saints of Marrakech. Born in Ceuta in 1130 (some authorities say 1145), he championed the cause of the blind in Marrakech and was patronized by Sultan Yaqoub al Mansour. The shrine, recently restored, is strictly closed to non-Muslims. Nearby is the **Zaouia of Sidi Ben Slimane el Jazouli**, a 14th-century sufi.

Kasbah quarter

Bab Agnaou, meaning the gate of the blacks, marks the entrance to the kasbah quarter. To get to it, follow Rue Bab Agnaou from Jemaâ el Fna, or enter the médina at Bab Rob. The kasbah quarter dates from the late 12th century and the reign of the Almohad Sultan Ya'qub al Mansour. Bab Agnaou is also Almohad. The gateway itself is surrounded by a series of arches within a rectangle of floral designs, with a shell or palmette in each corner and an outer band of Kufic inscription.

The road from the gate leads to Rue de la Kasbah, turn right along here and then take the first left. On this road is the much restored **Kasbah Mosque**, dating from 1190. The minaret has Almohad *darj w ktaf* and *shabka* (net) motifs on alternate sides, with a background of green tiles, above which is a band of coloured tiles. Though not as impressive as the tower of the Koutoubia Mosque, the minaret is a notable landmark en route to the Saâdian Tombs. The entrance to these lies directly to the right of the mosque.

Saâdian Tombs

Try to visit early in the day as the place gets horrendously crowded with tour groups

The late 16th-century Saâdian Tombs were discovered thanks to aerial photography in 1917, having been been sealed off by Moulay Ismaïl in the 17th century in a vain attempt to condemn the Saâdian rulers to oblivion. A series of chambers around a small garden, decorated with carved cedar and plaster, is the final, and ultimately rather moving, resting place of the Saâdian family. The *mihrab* of the first main burial chamber is particularly impressive. Here lies the prince Moulay Yazid. The second room contains the tomb of Ahmed al Mansour. The second and older mausoleum was built for the tombs of Ahmed al Mansour's mother, Lalla Messaouda, and Mohammed esh Sheikh, founder of the Saâdians. In the garden and courtyard are the tombs of numerous other princelings and followers. ■ *0800-1200 and 1400-1800.*

El Badi Palace

El Badi Palace was built by the Saâdian Sultan Ahmed al Mansur ed-Dahbi (the Golden) between 1578 and 1593, following his accession after his victory over the Portuguese at the Battle of the Three Kings, at Ksar el Kebir in northern Morocco. To get there return to the Bab Agnaou and head right inside ramparts, and then take the second right. Road leads more or less directly to Place des Ferblantiers, a square with a number of workshops where they make lanterns and other items in tin. Pass through Bab Berima, the gate on the southern side. The entrance to the palace is on the right, between high pisé walls. ■ *0900-1200 and 1430-1730.*

The 16th-century palace marks the height of Saâdian power, the centrepiece of an imperial capital. It was a lavish display of the best craftsmanship of the period, using the most expensive materials, including gold, marble and onyx. Today only the great walls have survived as a reminder of one of the periodic royal re-foundations of Marrakech. The palace was largely destroyed in the 17th century by Moulay Ismaïl, who stripped it of its decorations and fittings and carried them off to Meknès. No austere royal fortress, the Badi was probably a palace for audiences – and it was at one of these great court ceremonies that the building's fate was predicted: "Among the crowds taking part at the banquet was a visionary who, at the time, enjoyed a certain reputation for his saintliness. 'What do you think of this palace?' asked the sultan El-Mansour in jest. 'When it is demolished, it will make a big pile of earth', replied the visionary. El-Mansour was lost for words at this answer. He felt a sinister omen". El-Ifrani, a historian writing in the early 18th century, noted the inauspicious numerical meaning of the palace's name. The value of its letters is 117 – exactly the number of lunar years the palace remained intact (from 1002 AH to 1119 AH, that is 1594-1708).

The name El-Badi ties in with the palace's once elaborate decoration. In Arabic, *'ilm el-badi* is one of the main varieties of classical Arabic rhetoric, the art of stylistic ornament – and the palace was certainly one of the most decorated in its day. Above one of the main gates, the following inscription was placed in flowing Arabic calligraphy: "This gate is as beautiful as the eloquent beginning of a fine poem, and the palace is as the continuation of this poem. Thus it was named *badi*, using hyperbole, assonance and pleonasm."

In its day, the Badi Palace was the physical symbol of the golden sultan's glory. El-Mansour had conquered the Soudan (Arabic for 'blacks'), bringing them under Islamic rule. Deeply influenced by Ottoman court traditions, he no doubt hoped to establish the imposing ceremonial of the Istanbul court in Morocco. The palace drew in wealth and skilled craftsmen from all over. The colonnades were of marble, apparently bought, or rather exchanged, with Italian merchants, for their equivalent weight in sugar. El-Mansour had sugar-cane presses built. Perhaps there is an allegory here, the power of the prince transforming crystalline sugar into powder white marble and stucco. Sugary sweets were distributed to the sultan's guests – at a time when well refined sugar was a rarity.

The ill omens which had so frightened El-Mansour were realized: not only was the palace destroyed, but all its fine building materials were dispersed. The glory of the palace was dismantled, and in the words of one contemporary observer, "there was not a single city in Morocco which did not receive some debris of El Badi." The vaulting ambition and power of the great Moulay Isma'il in turn had to find an expression in stone – or rather adobe – walls, but at Meknès, not Marrakech. Perhaps there was a political logic to all this building activity. Moulay Ismaïl is said to have declared: "If I have a sack full of rats, I must move the sack constantly to prevent them from escaping." The moral of the tale? 'Keep your subjects busy.'

El-Atlal – lamenting the past

Sometime in the 16th century, Leo Africanus visited the ruined Almohad palace (on which El-Badi palace was later to be built) of Marrakech: "Despite the slight remains of the past which have survived in this town," he wrote, "they still bear witness to the pomp and grandeur which reigned at the time of Yaqoub El-Mansour. Today only the palace of the royal family and the palace of the archers are inhabited. In the latter are housed the porters and muleteers of the present sovereign. All the rest is home to rock doves, crows, owls and birds of this sort." The palaces of old Morocco – like the kasbahs of the southern regions – were built of pisé, a sort of earth, lime and gravel mix. With heavy rains and wind, they were eroded away, and needed constant repair and rebuilding. When a dynasty disappeared, its capital would often disappear with it, sometimes for good. Across the Arab world, there are abandoned royal capitals – legendary Samarra in Iraq, the ruined cities of Islamic Andalucía, Raqqada near Kairouan in Tunisia, Chellah outside Rabat, and Tin Mal in the High Atlas, of which only the mosque has survived.

In poetic descriptions of such remains, Arab and other writers would draw their moral conclusions about the ruins, meditating on the rise and fall of dynasties, and the hubris of domineering builder-rulers. Contemplating remains of the past, reliving better days goes right back to the earliest days of recorded Arabic poetry in the sixth century AD. Nomad poets wrote of the emotions aroused as they looked at the charred remains of a campfire, the only trace of the encampment of the departed loved one. El-Atlal (The Remains), sung by 20th-century Egyptian diva Um Kalthoum, opens with just such a lament. If there is one Arab song you should try to discover while you are in Morocco, it is El-Atlal, perhaps the most famous piece of 20th-century Arab music.

On July weekends, El Badi comes alive for the annual **festival of traditional dance and music**. Most of the year, however, it is a quiet sort of place, the high thick walls protecting the vast courtyard from the noise of the surrounding streets. The courtyard is divided by water channels connecting a number of pools. The largest of these even has an island. The ruins on either side of the courtyard were probably summer houses, the one at the far end being called the **Koubba el Khamsiniya** after the 50 pillars in its construction. The complex contains a small museum which includes the movable *minbar*, a sort of pulpit, from the Koutoubia Mosque. The scattered ruins of the palace, with odd fragments of decoration amidst the debris, include also stables and dungeons.

Other sights To the south of the El Badi Palace is the **Dar el Makhzen**, the modern-day Royal Palace, one of the late King Hassan II's favourite residences. The present king has had a new palace constructed, close to the Mamounia.

Nearby, the **Musée Dar al Funoun ash Shaâbia** has audio-visual displays on various themes of Moroccan arts including dance, theatre and the marriage ceremony, each lasting 20-45 minutes. ■ *154 Derb Sahrige, R Arset Moussa, Riad Zitoune Kedim, T044-426632.*

Down Riad Zitoun el Jedid: craft museums and palaces

If you are keen on traditional craftwork, you could follow a visit to the Badi' Palace with a look at a couple of museums devoted to Moroccan artisanat at the south end of Riad Zitoun el Jedid. Starting on Jemaâ el Fna, to get to the museums follow Rue des Banques from just past *Café de France*. At the first junction, follow through to the right onto Riad Zitoun el Jedid. (If you go left, you intersect with Derb Debbachi which if you go right will take you right through to Bab Aylen on the far eastern side of the medina). Eventually, on Riad Zitoun el Jedid, you'll see signs indicating the **Dar Si Said** off to the left and the smaller **Maison Tiskiwine**.

Museum of Moroccan Arts & Crafts

Built by Si Said, Visir under Moulay El Hassan and half-brother of Ba Ahmed Ben Moussa, the Dar Si Said is a small, late-19th century palace housing the Museum of Moroccan Arts and Crafts. The collection includes pottery, jewellery, leatherwork and Chichaoua carpets. It is particularly strong on Amazigh artefacts such as curved daggers, copperware, and jewellery. On the first floor is a salon with Hispano-Moorish decoration and cedarwood furniture, while around the garden courtyard you'll find old window and door frames. Look out for a primitive four-seater wooden ferris wheel of the type still found in *moussems* (country fairs) in Morocco. Those interested in traditional Moroccan artefacts will want to continue to the neighbouring Maison Tiskiwine. ■ *0900-1200, 1600-2100 summer, 1430-1800 winter, closed Tue. T044-442464.*

Maison Tiskiwine

Don't miss the beautiful Saharan leatherwork

Between the Dar Si Said and the Bahia Palace a few streets further south is the Maison Tiskiwine ('the House of the Horns'), home to a fine collection of items related to Moroccan rural culture and society. This small museum was put together by the Dutch art historian Bert Flint. There is an exhibition of craftsmen's materials and techniques from regions as far apart as the Rif, High Atlas and the Sahara, including jewellery and costumes, musical instruments, carpets and furniture. The building itself, around a courtyard, is an authentic and well-maintained example of traditional domestic architecture. Flint was also instrumental in setting up another collection of traditional Moroccan craftwork for the city council in Agadir. ■ *T044-443335. 8 R de la Bahia.*

Bahia Palace

Further to the south is the Bahia Palace (Bahia means 'brilliant'). It was built in the last years of the 19th century by the Vizir Ba Ahmed Ben Moussa, or Bou Ahmed, a former slave who exercised power under sultans Moulay Hassan and Abd el-Aziz. Generally packed with tour groups, the palace is a maze of patios planted with fruit trees, passageways and empty chambers with painted ceilings. The story goes that Bou Ahmed was so hated that, on his death in 1900, his palace was looted and his possessions stolen by slaves, servants and members of his *harem*. Subsequently, the building was occupied by the French authorities. As you gaze at a marble-paved courtyard, the guides will tell you that each wife and concubine had a room looking onto the patio. ■ *0800-1200 and 1430-1800.*

The Jewish quarter

See Fès el Jedid, page 254, for the etymology of the term mellah

South of the Bahia and east of the El Badi Palace, the *mellah* or Jewish neighbourhood was created in 1558. The Jewish community has all but vanished, and there is little to tell you of its former role in the life of Marrakech. There were several synagogues, and under the control of the *rabbis*, the area had considerable autonomy. It is worth asking around to be let into one of the synagogues. There is a small one down an alley as you face the restaurant *Dar Douiria*, on your right as you leave Place des Ferblantiers behind.

Tanneries near Bab Debbagh

You can get a view of the area from the leather shop terrace next to Bab Debbagh

The tanneries near Bab Debbagh ('Tanners' Gate') are one of the most interesting (if smelly) sites in Marrakech. Wandering towards the tanners' area, you will in all likelihood be approached by some lad who will offer to show you the tanneries (20dh is a very reasonable tip). Through a small metal door, you will be shown an area of foul-smelling pits, where men tread and rinse skins in nauseous liquid. In small lean-to buildings, you will find other artisans scraping and stretching the skins. Located close to the seasonal Oued Issil, the tanners were on the edge of the city with plenty of water and space to expand away from residential areas.

Founding myths The tanners are said to have been the first to settle in Marrakech at its foundation and a gate is named after them, the only one to be named for a craft corporation. 'Bab Debbagh, bab deheb' – 'Tanners' Gate, gold gate' – the old adage goes, in reference to the tanners' prosperity. One legend runs that seven virgins are buried in the foundations of the gate (sisters of the seven protector saints of Marrakech) and women who desire a child should offer them candles and henna. Another legend runs that Bab Debbagh is inhabited by Malik Gharub, a genie who dared to lead a revolt against Sidna Suleyman, the Black King, only to be condemned to tan a cowhide and cut out *belgha* soles for eternity as punishment.

The tannery was considered a dangerous place – as it was the entrance to the domain of the Other Ones, and a beneficial one, since skins were a symbol of preservation and fertility. Bab Debbagh was the eastern gate into the city, and there was a symbolism based on the sun rising in the east and skin being reborn as leather. The tanners, because they spend their days in pits working the skins, were said to be in contact with the unseen world of the dead; they were also seen as masters of fertility, being strong men, capable of giving a second life to dry, dead skin.

Cycles & processes The tanneries used to be regulated by an annual cycle, with work more intensive in summer, when the skins can be cleaned in the fermenting water more quickly and dried on the walls and riverbanks. In the winter, the tanners of country origin would return to their fields to plough and sow.

In the old days, the complex process of tanning would start with soaking the skins in a sort of swamp – or *iferd* – in the middle of the tannery, filled with a fermenting mixture of pigeon guano and tannery waste. Fermenting would last three days in summer, six in winter. Then the skins would be squeezed out and put to dry. Hair would be scraped off. Then the skins would go into a pit of lime and argan-kernel ash. This would remove any remaining flesh or hair, and prepare the skin to receive the tanning products. The lime bath lasts 15-20 days in summer, up to 30 in winter. Then the skins are washed energetically, trodden to remove any lime, and any extra bits are cut off. Next the skins spend 24 hours in a *qasriya*, a round pit of more pigeon dung and fresh water. At this stage the skin becomes thinner and stretches. (This is a stage to be undertaken with care, because a djinn lives in the pit, and skins can be ruined if left too long.) There follows soaking in wheat fibre and salt, for 24 hours, to remove any traces of lime and guano.

Then begins the actual tanning process. The word *debbagh* actually means tannin. Traditional tanneries used only plants – roots, barks and certain seeds and fruits. In Marrakech, acacia and oak bark are used, along with *takkut*, the ground-up fruit of the tamarisk. A water and tannin mix is prepared in a pit, and the skins get three soakings.

After this, the skins have to be prepared to receive the dye. They are scraped with pottery shards, beaten and coated with oil, alum and water. Then they are dyed by hand, with the dye traditionally being poured out of a bull's horn, and left to dry in the sun (traditionally on the banks of the nearby Oued Issil – where a large social housing development has replaced the local bidonville).

Note that the characteristic yellow of leather for belgha slippers was derived from pomegranates. Finally, the skins are worked to make them smoother and more supple, stretched between two ropes and worked on smooth pottery surfaces. Skins were sold at auction.

Symbolism of tanning

The process of tanning skins is strongly symbolic – the tanners say that the skin eats, drinks, sleeps and 'is born of the water'. When the skin is treated with lime, it is said to be thirsty; when it is treated with pigeon dung, it is said to receive *nafs*, a spirit. The *merkel* (treading) stage prepares the skin to live again, while the *takkut* of the tanning mixture is also used by women to dye their hair. At this point, the skin receives *ruh* (breath). Leather is thus born from the world of the dead and the *ighariyin*, the people of the grotto, and is fertilized in the swampy pool, the domain of the dead – who are also said to have the power to bring rain.

In Marrakech, you will probably be told that there are two tanneries: one Arab, the other Berber. In all likelihood, the workforce is ethnically mixed today. Certainly there are specialities, with one set of tanners working mainly on the more difficult cow and camel skins, and the others on goat and sheep skins. For the record, the tanners were known to be great nocturnal hunters, doing a trade in hedgehog skins for magic. They were also known as big *kif* smokers: working in such difficult conditions with the foul odours and the presence of spirits would have been difficult without a daily pipe of *kif*.

The interesting thing is to see a pre-industrial process, still alive and functioning not far from the heart of the médina – even though the traditional dyes have been replaced with chemical products. If walking precariously between pools of nauseous skins and liquid is too much, you could always take a carriage around the city walls to one of Marrakech's gardens.

Ramparts and gates

The extensive ramparts of Marrakech (20 gates and 200 towers stretching for 16 km) are predominantly Almoravid, excepting those around the Agdal Gardens, although extensively restored since. The reconstruction is a continual process as the *pisé*-cement walls, made of the distinctive earth of the Haouz plains, gradually crumble. The ramparts and gates are one of the distinctive sights of Morocco. A ride in a horse-drawn *calèche* will allow you to see part of the ramparts. In places, there has been much beautification going on of late, with fancy wrought-iron railings and rose gardens taking the place of the dust on the Hivernage side of town.

Bab Rob, near the buses and grands taxis on the southwest side of the médina, is Almohad, and is named after the grape juice which could only be brought through this gate. **Bab Dabbagh** (the Tanners' gate, see above), on the east side, is an intricate defensive gate with a twisted entrance route and wooden gates, which could shut off the various parts of the building for security. **Bab el Khemis**, on the northeast side, opens into the Souk el Khemis (Thursday market) and an important area of mechanics and craftsmen. Check out the junk-market here on a Sunday morning. There is a small saint's tomb inside the gate building. **Bab Doukkala**, on the northwest side by the bus station, is a large gate with a horseshoe arch and two towers. The médina side has a horseshoe arch and a cusped, blind arch, with a variation on the *darj w ktaf* (step and shoulder) motif along the top. There are occasional exhibitions in the guardroom inside the gate. The esplanade has been badly neglected, the orange trees have died off… but then few wealthy visitors to

Five good inexpensive hotels in Marrakech

- *Hotel Jnane Mogador*, 116 Riad Zitoun Kedime, Derb Sidi Bouloukat, T044-426323, jnanemogador@hotmail.com 17 rooms in neo-traditional style, roof terrace, 1px 250dh, 2px 300dh.
- *Hotel Le Toulousain*, Rue Tarik ibn Ziad, Guéliz, T044-430033, F431446. Very popular, 2px 170dh. Upstairs rooms hot in summer
- *Hotel Sherezade*, Riad Zitoun el Jedid, Médina, T044-429305. Cheapest simplest double at 180dh, more expensive rooms too. Charming.
- *Hotel Central Palace*, off Rue Bab Agnaou, Médina, T044-440235, F442884. A good cheapie, easy to find, in area of lots of cheap hotels, 2px 100dh. (*Hotel Amal* in this area gets good reviews.)
- *Hotel Mimosa*, Rue des Banques, Médina, behind *Café Hotel de France*, T044-426385. 3px 80dh. Very good value.

Marrakech see this gate. At night, this is the place to locate a black-market booze merchant. A road is being opened up running across the palm grove north of Bab Doukkala, to complete the circuit of the ramparts.

Gardens

Agdal Gardens

The Agdal Gardens, stretching south of the médina, were established in the 12th century under Abd el-Moumen, and were expanded and reorganized by the Saâdians. The vast expanse, over 400 ha, includes several pools, and extensive areas of olive, orange and pomegranate trees. They are in the main closed when the king is in residence, but can generally be visited at other times. Of the pavilions, the **Dar al-Baida** was used by Sultan Moulay Hassan to house his *harem*. The largest pool, **Sahraj el Hana**, receives its coachloads of tourists, but at other times is a pleasant place to relax, although not to swim.

Menara Gardens

From the médina and the Agdal Gardens, Avenue de la Menara leads past the Oliveraie de Bab Jedid, earmarked for hotel development, to the Menara Gardens, essentially an olive grove centring on a rectangular pool. A short moped hop from central Marrakech, the area is much appreciated by locals for picnics. The presence of such a large expanse of water generates a pleasant microclimate. The green-tiled pavilion alongside the pool was built in 1866. With the Atlas Mountains as backdrop, it features heavily on postcards.

Jardin Majorelle

The garden now belongs to Yves St Laurent, who has a house close by

The Jardin Majorelle, also called the **Bou Saf-Saf Garden**, is off Avenue Ya'qub al Mansour. This is a small tropical garden laid out in the inter-war period by a French artist, Louis Majorelle, scion of a family of cabinet-makers from Nancy who made their money with innovative art nouveau furniture. Majorelle portrayed the landscapes and people of the Atlas in large, strongly coloured paintings, some of which were used for early tourism posters. Strong colours and forms are much in evidence in the garden: the buildings are vivid cobalt blue, the cactuses sculptural. Bulbuls sing in the bamboo thickets and flit between the Washingtonia palms. A green-roofed garden pavilion houses a small Musée d'Art Islamique with a fine and easily digestible collection of objects. Sensitive souls tempted to try Majorelle Garden blue in decorating schemes back home in northern climes should beware – the result depends on bright sunlight filtered by lush vegetation. ■ *0800-1200 and 1400-1700 in the winter, 0800-1200 and 1500-1900 in the summer.*

The Palmeraie

Marrakech is surrounded by extensive palm groves. In the original Prost development plan of the 1920s, no building was to be higher than a palm tree – and it is illegal to cut down a palm tree – hence palms have been left growing in the middle of pavements. In recent years the Palmeraie has suffered as the urbanized area round Marrakech has expanded, and certain areas have been divided up for upmarket holiday development. Nevertheless, it is a good place for a drive or a *calèche* tour. Take the Route de la Palmeraie, off the P24 to Fès, to explore it.

Essentials

Sleeping: hotels

■ on maps
Price codes: see inside front cover

If planning to visit Marrakech at peak times (winter holidays, spring) it is a good idea to reserve rooms, as demand far outstrips supply of accommodation

The **upmarket hotels** are located in 3 areas: in the **Hivernage** garden city area and along the neighbouring **Av de France**; in a development on the Casablanca road in the **Semlalia** neighbourhood; and in the **Palmeraie** east of the city. Hivernage is close to **Guéliz**, and a short taxi ride into Jemaâ el Fna in the old town. Upmarket **guest-house**-type accommodation is located in the **médina** (favoured locations: Bab Doukkala and Bab Leksour/Mouassine) and the **Palmeraie**. **Medium price hotels** tend to be located in **Guéliz**, with quite a few along Av Mohammed V and Av Zerktouni. Hotels *Toulousain*, *Moutamed* and *Oasis* are all OK, a step up from médina traveller hotels. More expensively, there is some good city-tour type accommodation here, see hotels *El Kebir, Nassim, Oudaya, du Pacha, Tachfine* and *Tafoukt*.

In terms of **cheap accommodation**, the vast majority of small hotels are 5-10-mins' walk from Jemaâ el Fna, in the alleys off pedestrian street **Bab Agnaou** (hotels *Central Palace, Ichbilia, Amal* and *Arset el Bilk*), off **Riad Zitoun el Kedim** (hotels *Essaouira* and *Sherazade* for example), and the **Kennaria** neighbourhood behind the *Café-Hotel de France*. (Coming by rail and *CTM* buses, you will need to take a petit taxi, say 10dh to Jemaâ el Fna/Arset el Bilk. If your rucksack isn't too heavy, it is just about walkable from the Bab Doukkala bus and taxi station.) To get to Jemaâ el Fna, you also have the No 1 bus down Av Mohammed V from near the tourist information service on rond-point Abd el Moumen.

Médina

■ on maps, pages 322 & 336
See also Riads, page 342

LL *La Mamounia*, Av Bab Jedid, T044-444409, F444660. Now part of the *Leading Hotels of the World* network. A Marrakech institution, one of the first hotels in the city, built just within the walls a couple of mins' walk from the Koutoubia. Originally owned and run by Moroccan railways, it was patronized by the rich and famous back at its beginnings in the 1930s. The major 1980s refit was undertaken by royal decorator André Paccard and was in its turn revamped in the late 1990s by Alberto Pinto. Although the art deco-Arabesque mix is a little overwhelming in places, there is much perfection. Prices start at around 2,000dh for a double in low season (excluding petit déjeuner, for which add 190dh). 171 luxurious rooms, 49 normal suites, 8 themed suites, 3 villas, outstanding service, 5 restaurants, 5 bars, casino, conference room, business centre, boutiques, fitness and beauty centre, *hammam*, pool, tennis, 5 ha of gardens. All in all, kind of nouveau riche. **L** ***La Maison Arabe***, 1, Derb Assehbe, Bab Doukkala, T044-391233, F443715. A restaurant now converted into very swish accommodation, run by the Prince Ruspoli and Pierre Cluzel. Private house atmosphere – which may soon be destroyed by the addition of a further floor. 10 rooms, including 6 suites with private terraces covering 2 courtyards. Price includes breakfast and afternoon tea. Evening meal by arrangement. New in 2002, close to the Koutoubia, is **A-B** ***Jardins de la Koutoubia***, 26 R de la Koutoubia, T044-388800, hotel.jardinskoutoubia@iam.net.ma. A *faux riad* on the site of one of Marrakech's finest palaces, the sadly demolished Dar Louarzazi. Well situated for the nights.

Good selection of cheap hotels in streets like Sidi Bouloukat off the pedestrian Rue Bab Agnaou, off Jemaâ el Fna. Also very handy for ATMs, internet cafés and other services

R Bab Agnaou (aka Le Prince) and around Bab Agnaou is the pedestrian street leading into Jemaâ el Fna, R Bani Marine runs parallel to it, R Moulay Ismaïl is the one which runs along the Jardin de Foucault, aka Arset el Bilk. Coming from Jemaâ el Fna, R Bani Marine is best identified as 'the street through the arch to the right of the post office'. **C *Hotel Chems***, Av Houmane El Fetouaki (listed here for convenience), BP 594, T044-444813. Small, restaurant, bar and nightclub. **C-D *Hotel Gallia***, 30 R de la Recette, T044-445913. Clean, conveniently located. Head down R Bab Agnaou from Jemaâ el Fna, the *Gallia* is at the end of a narrow street on the left. A 1930s building with beautifully planted courtyard. Had a rather sulphurous reputation but is now very smart. Popular, so reserve well in advance. Some very good rooms, plenty of hot water. **D *Hotel de Foucauld***, Av el Mouahidine, T044-445499. 33 rooms, a good hotel with restaurant and bar, same management as the *Tazi*. Easily located just opposite the well-planted Sq de Foucauld, aka Arset el Bilk. Used by trekking groups. **D *Grand Hotel Tazi***, R Bab Agnaou, T044-442787, F442152, at the far end of pedestrian R Bab Agnaou from Jemaâ el Fna. Memorable rooms with extravagantly painted ceilings and furniture, one of the few bars close to the médina, reasonably priced Moroccan restaurant. Though convenient for the sights and services, expensive for what it is. Reception unpleasant. **E *Hotel Afriquia*** 45, Derb Sidi Bouloukat, T044-442403. Close to *Hotel Central Palace*. Patio and roof terrace, washbasins in rooms. **E *Hotel Ali***, R Moulay Ismail, T044-444979, F440522. Especially recommended for those intending to go climbing/trekking in the Jbel Toubkal region as the guides are here. Friendly but has had mixed reports on cleanliness, good cheapish Moroccan food, has 2 entrances, main one facing Jardin Foucault, the back on the R Bani Marine, as does the neighbouring **E *Hotel Arset el Bilk***, R Moulay Ismaïl, rooms en suite with shower, wall fan, hygiene acceptable. **E *Hotel Central Palace***, T044-440235, F442884. Well signed in an alley off R Bab Agnaou, on your left as you come from Jemaâ el Fna. 40 rooms, annex to house overflow, one of the best cheapies. **E *Hotel Ed Dakhla*** 43, Derb Sidi Bouloukat, T044-442359. Keep going down alley after *Hotel Afriquia*. Prefer the *Afriquia* or the *Central Palace*. **E *Hotel La Gazelle***, 13 R Beni Marine, T044-441112, F445537. Showers on corridors, well managed, small terrace. **E *Hotel Ichbilia***, on street linking R Beni Marine and R Bab Agnaou (turn left off the latter just before *Cinéma*

Jemaâ el Fna, Bab Agnaou & around

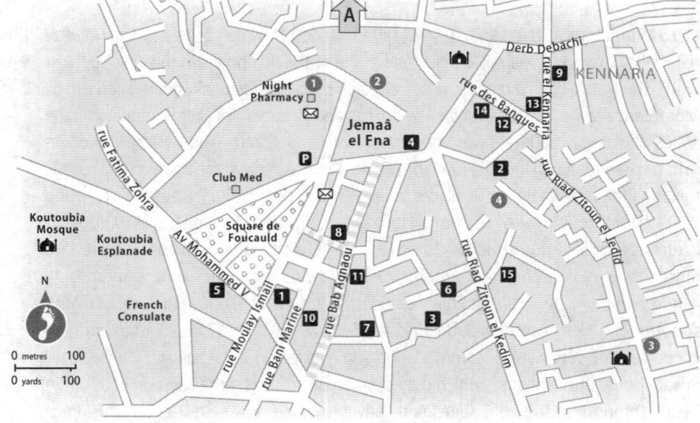

Related maps
A Marrakech Médina, page 322
B Marrakech souks, page 326

Sleeping
1 Ali
2 Badr
3 Chella
4 CTM
5 de Foucauld
6 Essaouira & Médina
7 Gallia
8 Ichbilia
9 Kennaria
10 La Gazelle
11 Mabrouka
12 Mimosa
13 Mounir
14 Résidence de la Place & Café-Hotel de France
15 Sherazade

Eating
1 Al Baraka
2 Café Restaurant Argana
3 Palais Gharnatta
4 Riad Temsna

Mabrouka), T044-390486. Street-facing rooms noisy. Fine for a night. Cybercafé in basement of building. **F *Hotel Azhar***, down the alley to the left of the *Hotel CTM*, with lots of other sleeperies, T044-445955. Clean and cheap. **F *Hotel el Atlas***, a friendly, efficient place on R de la Recette. **F *Hotel Mabrouka***, on R Bab Agnaou, just opposite *Cinéma Mabrouka*. 10 cell-like rooms off 2 tiny courtyards, acceptable, good location if not much else. **F *Hotel Nouazah***, on 1st left off R Bab Agnaouent.

Arset el Maâch Coming up R Bab Agnaou, from 'La Place' go left at the top, just before the *Hotel Tazi* for this area. **D *Hotel Fantasia***, 184 Arset El Maâch, T044-426545. Opened in 2002, this is the Marrakech hotel closest to an Oriental house of the three little pigs. The tiling truly hurts the eyes. That said, the 35 en suite rooms are clean and comfortable, the roof terraces extensive. The secret? Rush across through the courtyard to your room. Nearby is the **E *Hotel Minaret***, 10 R du Dispensaire Arset Moha, T044-443139, F443773. En suite rooms, ground floor rooms dark.

Kasbah L *Les Jardins de la Médina*, 21 Derb Chtouka, T044-381851, www.lesjardinsdelamedina.com Opened in 2001, an unusual small (36 rooms) hotel in a refurbished and extended palace. All rooms a/c, small heated pool, good restaurants, hammam, safe underground parking. Lacks the individuality of a true guesthouse.

Riad Zitoun el Kedime and around C *Hotel Belleville*, 194 Riad Zitoun el Kedime, just after *Hotel de France*, T044-426481, T061-193218 (mob). 9 en suite rooms, impeccable beds, lots of wrought iron, roof terrace with tent. **C *Hotel Jnane Mogador***, 116 Riad Zitoun Kedime, T044-426323, www.jnanemogador.com New in 2002, 17 rooms with shower/wc, extensive roof terrace, neo-traditional decor, pleasant. **C *Hotel Sherazade***, 3 Derb Djama (3rd narrow street on your left as you come up Riad Zitoun el Kedim from Jemaâ el Fna, big awning over door), T/F044-429305, sharazade@iam.net.ma, also reservations via Herr Khan in Germany on T0621-771633. Germano-Moroccan management. Spotlessly clean. Varied accommodation around large, pleasantly decorated courtyards. Rooftop terraces. Can organize excursions and car hire. **E *Hotel Chella***, T044-442977, heading down Riad Zitoun el Kedim from Jemaâ el Fna, take 3rd narrow side street on your right. Small, clean establishment, showers extra. **E *Hotel Essaouira***, 3 Derb Sidi Bouloukat, down an alley left off Riad Zitoun el Kedim as you come from Jemaâ el Fna (just before the left turn for the *Hotel Sherazade*). T044-443805. Fine for a couple of nights. **E *Hotel Médina***, 1 Derb Sidi Bouloukat, T044-442997. Similar but smaller to *Hotel Essaouira*. **E *Hotel CTM***, on the Jemaâ el Fna, T044-442325. Good and clean rooms, some with a view of the square (noisy), often full. Note that *CTM* buses now go from Av Zerktouni near the big cinema in Guéliz. **E *Hotel de France***, 197 Riad Zitoun el Kedim. Another cheapie, with be-rucksacked figure striding out on sign.

Kennaria and around There is a small selection of cheap hotels in the side streets behind the *Café de France*, on Riad Zitoun el Jedid, aka Kennaria. To get into this area, take R des Banques, the road that runs straight ahead of you as you face the *Café de France*; this intersects with R el Kennaria, which then turns into R Riad Zitoun el Jedid. **E *Hotel-Résidence de la Place***, right on Jemaâ el Fna, next to *Café-Hotel de France*, T061-776169 (mob). 16 rooms, No 25 the best (?). Best classified as *un hôtel de passe*. How they got planning permission for this is anyone's guess. Good views of the square from the café-restaurant. **E-F *Hotel Kennaria***, 10 R el Kennaria,T044-390228. 23 rooms off a courtyard, clean but spartan. **F *Hotel Badr***, R des Banques, down a long alley. Quiet during the day. Cold showers. **F *Hotel Mimosa***, R des Banques, T044-426385. Built 1997, 16 rooms with washbasin and cupboard. Shower free, terrace. Tiles everywhere. **F *Hotel Mounir***, R el Kennaria, T044-444356. 13 rooms, hot showers. Slightly better than *Hotel Kennaria*, rooms less cell-like and look outwards onto street.

Hivernage
■ *on map, page 321*

L ***Sheraton Marrakech***, Av de la Menara (at south end of Av de France), T044-448998, F437843. 291 comfortable a/c rooms and suites, Moroccan and international restaurants, pizzeria, heated pool, tennis, shops, salon, very friendly atmosphere. Has a well-established American Jewish clientele. **A** ***Hotel el Andalous***, Av President Kennedy/Jnan el Harti, T044-448226. 200 double rooms each with 2 queen-size beds, bath, a/c, balcony, telephone and radio, authentic Andalucían style, 2 restaurants (Moroccan and international), pool, tennis, sauna, fitness centre. Service poor for this category. **A** ***Hotel Es Saâdi***, Av Kadissia, T044-448811. Luxurious hotel built in 1950s style and set in large and pleasant gardens (best feature), with a fair restaurant, bar, nightclub, tennis and pool. Popular with older clients of upmarket tour companies, but generally felt to be in need of a refit. Service poor. **A** ***Imperial Borj***, 5 Av Echouhada, T044-447322. 187 rooms, modern, conference centre, restaurant, bar and popular nightclub. Houses overspill from the palace when the court is in residence. Popular for small conferences. Almost opposite chic piano bar and restaurant *Le Comptoir*. **A** ***Hotel Kempinski - Mansour Eddahbi***, Av de France, T044-448222. 450 rooms, restaurant, pool, tennis. Vast hotel next to Marrakech's (and indeed Morocco's) largest conference centre. OK if you're in Morocco for a conference, too impersonal for real holidays. Recently refitted. **A** ***Hotel Safir Marrakech***, Av President Kennedy, T044-447400, F448730. 280 rooms. Facilities include disco, 2 tennis courts, bar, restaurant, shops, *hammam* and a pool surrounded with palm trees. **A** ***Hotel Sofitel Marrakech***, R Haroun Errachid, T044-425600, F437131, sofitel.com Opened 2002, 260 rooms, 62 suites, all with internet connection. Good sized pool, 5 conference spaces. Set to become the city's premier conference address. **C** ***Grand Hotel Imilchil***, Av Echouhada, T044-447653, F446153. 96 rooms with a/c, quiet street, pool, restaurant and bar. Used by tour groups. Location good for both Guéliz and the médina. **C** ***Hotel Menara***, Av des Remparts, T044-436478, F447386. Typical Moroccan-style hotel, situated halfway between the médina and the European Centre, views over the ramparts to the High Atlas, 100 rooms with bath, balcony, a/c, central heating, telephone, Moroccan and French cooking, bar, TV room, garden, pool, tennis, free parking. A bit run down. **C** ***Hotel Siaha Safir***, Av President Kennedy, T044-448952, F448730. 243 rooms, pool and hammam.

Guéliz
■ *on map, page 339*

Quite a good mix of accommodation here, city hotels with pocket-size swimming pools plus 1 or 2 cheapies. Without wishing to cast aspersions, avoid the *Hotel Boustane*.

B ***Hotel Agdal***, 1 Blvd Zerktouni, Guéliz, T044-433670. Ugly block of a hotel with 129 rooms and 4 apartments, all with a/c, balcony, telephone, radio, bath. Pool heated in winter, bar, restaurant, breakfast room with panoramic view. Very handy for the train station, *CTM* bus offices and services near rond-point Abd el Moumen in Guéliz. Used by tour groups. **B-C** ***Hotel Kenza***, Av Yacoub el Mansour, T044-448380, F435386. Expensive for what it is. Small pool. Marrakech low-life to be found in the hotel's nightclub, the *Shehrazade*, provided it hasn't been raided by the police recently.

C ***Hotel du Pacha***, 33 R de la Liberté (left turn off Av Mohammed V, just before the market, as you head médina-wards), T044-431327, F431326. Just about creeps into the **C** category. Small hotel which could be loads better. Some rooms with a/c, lousy breakfast. **C** ***Hotel el Harti***, 30 R Cadi Ayad, T044-448000, F449329. A recent hotel close to the Jnene el Harti stadium, on a street parallel to the Av Hassan II. Used by young male Marrakchis and their women friends? Pretty close to the train station. **C** ***Hotel Myriem***, 154 R Mohammed el Beqal. Rooms have a/c, TV, direct telephone and radio, 2 restaurants, pool and safe parking. **C** ***Hotel Ibis Moussafir***, Av Hassan II, right next to the train station, T044-435929, F435936. Improved by recent works. **C** ***Hotel Koutoubia***, 51 Blvd Mansour Eddahbi. At present closed, this small hotel was one of the best in Guéliz. Site no doubt earmarked for redevelopment. **C** ***Hotel Nassim***, 115 Blvd Mohammed V,

T044-446401, htlnassim@cybernet.net.ma Centrally located city hotel, practically next to tourist office on rond-point Abd el Moumen. All rooms with a/c, TV and bath. Tour groups and people on business only. **C *Hotel Oudaya***, 147 R Mohammed El Baqal, T044-448512, F435400. As you face the *Cinéma Colisée*, go left and take 1st right. City hotel, typical of those built in the 1990s. Used by *Panorama* and other tour operators. 15 suites, 77 rooms, small unheated pool, restaurant and bar. Very clean. Pool-side rooms quietest. Fine for a couple of nights. **C *Hotel Résidence le Grand Sud***, 25 Blvd Mansour Eddahbi T044-449762, www.cybernet.net.ma/grandsud 1990s block with small self-catering flats close to Guéliz centre. Small unheated pool. Fine for a short stay. **C *Hotel Tachfine***, Blvd Zerktouni/R Mohammed el Beqal, next to the *Cinéma Le Colisée*, T044-447188, tachfine@iam.net.ma 50 rooms with small balcony, TV, a/c. Adequate city hotel, have breakfast at nearby café.

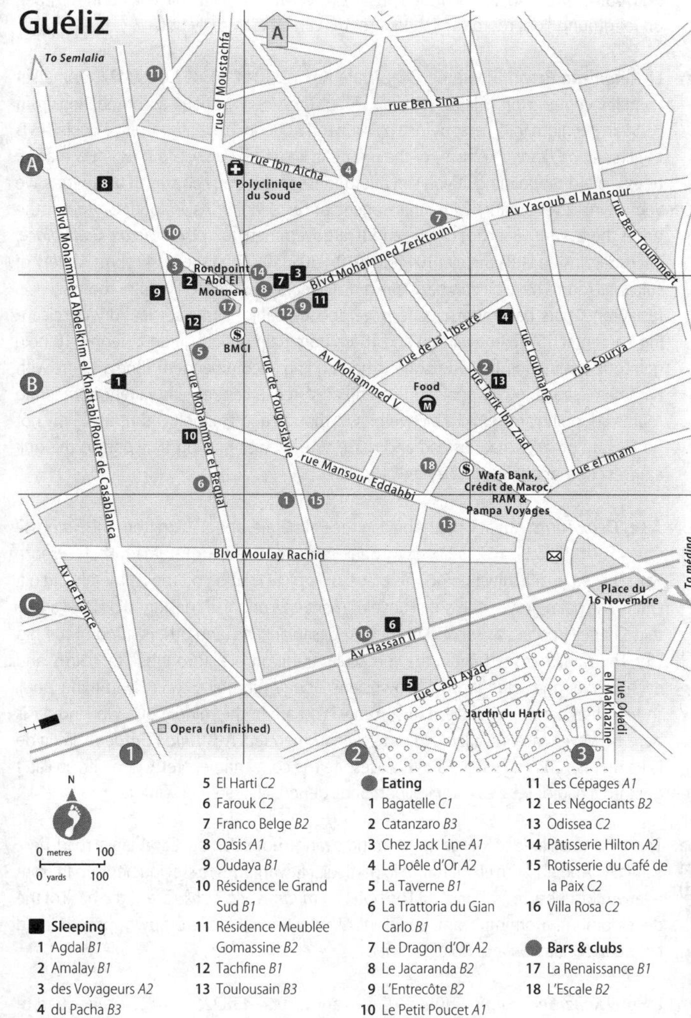

Related maps
***A Marrakech - Guéliz & Hivernage overview**, page 321*
***B Northern suburbs & Palmeraie**, page 341*

E ***Hotel des Voyageurs***, 40 Blvd Mohammed Zerktouni, T044-447218. Almost opposite *Café Les Négociants*. Reasonable and central but *Oasis* is better choice. **E** ***Hotel Farouk***, 66 Av Hassan II, near the main post office, T044-431989, F433609. A long established Marrakech address, same management as *Hotel Ali*. Acceptable. **E** ***Hotel Franco Belge***, 62 Blvd Mohammed Zerktouni, just down from *Restaurant Le Jacaranda* on rond-point Abd el Moumen, T044-448472. Entrance, almost exactly opposite *Somepi* petrol station and *Europcar*, is easily missed. Old-style traveller's hotel which has seen better days. Pleasant courtyard planted with orange trees, old furniture. Quiet – if your people in next room are quiet. Clean, but could do with a bit of attention. Rooms cold in winter. **E** ***Hotel Oasis***, 50 Av Mohammed V (same side as *Hotel el Moutamid*), T044-447179. Good but noisy, with restaurant and bar, clean, large rooms, some with shower. **E** ***Hotel Toulousain***, 44 R Tarik Ibn Ziad, Guéliz, T044-430033. Handily located behind the Guéliz food market, this is the best cheap option in the *ville nouvelle*. Rooms open onto courtyards – so not too much privacy. Nevertheless, a reliable choice. In summer, go for ground floor rooms as 1st floor rooms can be extremely hot.

Palmeraie (east & north of city)

■ *on map, page 341*

LL ***Amanjena Resort***, Route de Ouazarzate Km 12, T044-403353, F403477. Upmarket complex centring on a large reflecting pool (*bassin*). Luxurious accomodation from 6,950dh per night for 2 persons for a pavilion to 18,000dh for a *maison* with a pool. This is the first *Aman Resort* in Africa. For the moment, it's all a bit new. Grounds – few mature trees – are disappointing. If you can afford these prices, you can stay in a riad (or have your own). 2 restaurants with stratospheric prices, 1 doing Asian food. On top of the prices there is a 10% service charge and 10% government tax. **LL** ***Palmeraie Golf Palace***, in Les Jardins de la Palmeraie, T044-301010, F305050. 77 ha site, 314 rooms, variety of suites, all rooms have balcony, a/c, direct dial telephone, satellite TV. 24-hr room service, restaurants, bars, baby sitter, crèche, travel agency, bank, hairdresser, laundry/dry cleaning, car rental, 15 km from airport and 10 km from train station, gardens, tennis, 18-hole golf course, mini-golf, bowling, squash, horse riding (recommended), fitness centre with hammam, sauna, etc, 5 pools (2 heated), conference centre with variety of meeting rooms, shopping arcade. All a bit overblown, though good for golf enthusiasts. Why not go for an upmarket riad instead and make sure they can lay on transport to the golf courses? Pool accessible for day fee of 200dh.

A ***Les Deux Tours***, out at Douar Abiad in the Palmeraie, about 1 km from the *Hotel Issil Club*, T044-329525, F329523, www.deux-tours.com Pick-up at Marrakech airport. Taxis will have difficulty finding this place, off a piste leading off the Palmeraie Circuit. Out in the palm groves, this small development was originally designed by local architect Charles Boccara as second homes for Casablancans (and others) tired of the big city. The small houses, built in the vernacular tradition, are surrounded by palms, and each has its own plunge pool. Downside? Dodgy plumbing. Nice swimming pool, though flies can be a problem in summer. You are in the middle of a working oasis here, however. Meals available to order. Recommended. **A-B** ***Tikida Garden***, Circuit de la Palmeraie, T044-329595, F329599. Despite the corny name, pretty good if you can't get into a riad or *Les Deux Tours*. Good pool, generally heated in winter.

Semlalia (Casablanca road)

■ *on map, page 341*

There is a small area of 5 large upper-middle range hotels on the Casablanca road, here called Av Abd el Karim el Khattabi. No particular advantages to staying here, apart from relative closeness to *McDonald's*! The hotels *Semiramis* and *Tichka* are at the back of the development. Coming from *McDonald's* direction, turn left down private road between *Sahara Inn* and *Hotel Tafilalet*.

L ***Hotel Kenzi Semiramis***, Route de Casablanca, T044-438226, F447127. Once part of the *Méridien* chain. Nice (but small) grounds with lawns and mature palm trees.

Tennis, pool with paddling area for kids, conference rooms for anything up to 300 people. Free gold shuttle bus to Amelkis course (green fees 450dh). Vastly overpriced for what's on offer. Service good 'if they know you'. At this price, a more convenient hotel could be found in Hivernage or the médina. **A *Hotel Tichka***, Route de Casablanca, T044-448710, F448691. 138 rooms, beautifully decorated, restaurant, international and Moroccan menus, bar, nightclub, tennis, heated pool in which you can just about do lengths, shop, conference rooms for 20 and 150 people. Credit cards. Used by companies for incentive trips. Likes to call itself 'the little Mamounia'. **B *Hotel Amine***, Route de Casablanca, T044-436376, F438143. A/c and heating, TV. Small pool in garden area which has constant noise from nearby busy road. West-facing rooms have view of back of *Total* petrol station and poor neighbourhood built in a quarry over the road. Handy for *Société générale bank* and *Le Diamant vert café-glacier* next door. Tour groups only. **B *Hotel Tafilalet***, Route de Casablanca, T044-449818, F447532. The first hotel in this area, dating from the early 1970s. Consists of 2 kasbah-like blocks. Rooms small but pleasant. Grounds too small, pool with terrace restaurant. Now belongs to the *CIH*, the national hotel and housing development

Northern suburbs & Palmeraie

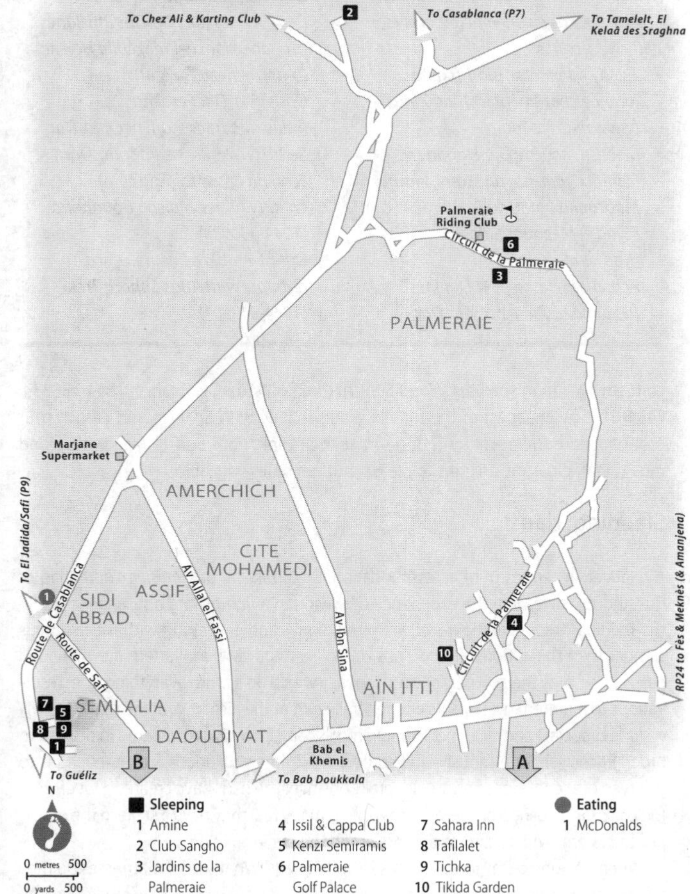

Sleeping
1 Amine
2 Club Sangho
3 Jardins de la Palmeraie
4 Issil & Cappa Club
5 Kenzi Semiramis
6 Palmeraie Golf Palace
7 Sahara Inn
8 Tafilalet
9 Tichka
10 Tikida Garden

Eating
1 McDonalds

Related maps
A Marrakech Médina, *page 322*
B Guéliz, *page 339*

Choosing a riad

The rumour goes that Marrakech now has more than 80 old houses refurbished to provide holiday accommodation, mostly in the medina. In addition to these, there are what might be termed 'guest villas', out in the Palmeraie. A night in a quality riad does not come cheap, however. Prices are by the room, at anything between 1,000dh and 2,500dh the night, although it is possible to find simpler accommodation around the 600dh/night mark. As riads have quite often been renovated in very personal ways by their owners, you need to make sure that you'll be staying somewhere which suits your temperament. After all, your tired eyes don't need to deal with canary yellow tadelakt and over-wrought iron furniture. The following is an attempt to classify some of the better riads:

- *Trendy minimalist:* ***Riad Tchina*** *(bruno.richez@noos.fr),* ***Riad Zina*** *(www.riadzina.ma)*
- *Moorish modern:* ***Dar Hanane*** *(contact@dar-hanane.com),* ***Riad Mabrouka*** *(info@riad-mabrouka.com),* ***Riyad el Mezouar*** *(info@riyad-el-mezouar.com)*
- *At home in the médina:* ***Dar Inès*** *(riadomaroc@iam.net.ma),* ***Dar Mouassine*** *(T044-445287, T061-341784),* ***Dar Taliwint*** *(taliwint@dartaliwint.com),* ***Riad el Az*** *(riadelaz@yahoo.fr),* ***Riad Noor Charana*** *(elisabeth.dianda@noorcharana.com),* ***Riad 72*** *(riad72@wanadoo.net.ma),* ***Dar Soukaïna*** *(www.riadmania.com)*
- *Comfortably elegant with antiques:* ***Dar el Assad*** *(T044-427065, T061-130820),* ***Riad Kaïss*** *(riad@riadkaiss.com),* ***Riad Malika*** *(jean.luc@iam.net.ma)*
- *Marrakchi grandee:* ***Riad Charaï*** *(maisons-traditions@iam.net.ma),* ***Riad Madani*** *(T044-431900),* ***Riad el Ouarda*** *(elouarda@yahoo.fr)*
- *Déco-Arabesque villa:* ***Dar Rhizlane*** *(rhizlane@iam.net.ma),* ***Villa Hélène*** *(bruno.richezz@noos.fr)*
- *Oasis villa:* ***Dar Feracha*** *(atlassaharatrek@iam.net.ma),* ***Dar Sedra*** *(www.dar-sedra.com),* ***Dar Temsna*** *(info@tamsna.com)*
- *Country basics:* ***Maison Boughdira*** *(T044-330999)*
- *Out-of-Arabia camping: upscale bivouacs with* ***Atlas Sahara Trek*** *(T044-313901)*

company. Nothing special. **C** ***Hotel Sahara Inn***, Route de Casablanca, T044-438334, F434610. The cheapest of the bunch, works mainly with Spanish and French tour groups. Bedrooms recently redone in salmon-pink. Pool and terrace with piped music. Staff pleasant, anxious to please, but not really very able.

Sleeping: riads

The riad experience A relatively recent form of accommodation in Marrakech, the *maison d'hôte* (riad or guesthouse) gives you the experience of staying in a fine private house, generally in the médina. The prices, however, are often high – and in keeping with the luxurious standards of these houses. The riads, often restored and converted, are managed either directly by their owners or via an agency which deals with everything from reservations to maintenance. Clients are generally met at the airport, and the rental fee will include breakfast and cleaning. Evening meals can generally be prepared in the riad to order. Prices vary enormously, and some are extremely luxurious. Client reactions to this type of accommodation are generally positive. The riads have created a lot of work for locals (and pushed property prices up), so many feel they have a stake in the guest-house system. With regard to tipping, err on the generous side.

When booking a stay in a riad, check these details. What sort of mattresses do they have (foam mattresses are very hot in the summer)? How is the shower water heated (electric water heating will provide plenty of hot water, a gas *chauffe-eau* providing water for several rooms is inadequate if more than 1 person is having a shower)? What is included in terms of catering, if anything? Note that cooler, darker ground floor rooms are preferable in summer, 1st floor rooms in winter. Note too that in winter it can rain heavily in Marrakech, turning streets in the old town to muddy tracks.

Riad rental agencies

Before you book your riad accommodation, it may pay to shop around and see what is offered by the 3 main riad rental agencies (all **C** and above). *Marrakech-Médina SARL* is the longest established. Though having a smaller list of properties, *Riads au Maroc* is very efficiently run while *Marrakech-Riads* has a handful of exquisite riads restored primarily for rental.

Agency Marrakech-Médina SARL, 79 Derb El Qadi, Azbest. Offices at 2 Derb Tizogarine, near Dar El-Pacha, Bab Doukkala, médina, T044-429133, F391071, rak.medina@cybernet.net.ma From Paris, reservations on T00-33-143259877. A range of self-catering accommodation from this Belgo-Canadian partnership. A very personalized service. Houses are rated by palm trees. For example, a 2 palm tree home starts at €60 a night, plus daily service charge of €10 a head for a riad sleeping 5 people in the low season. Airport transfer charges €15 a head. The agency has much larger and more luxurious riads on offer as well. They also act as agents for self-catering holiday accommodation in Essaouira, Telouet and Oualidia.

Ryads au Maroc, 1 R Mahjoub Rmiza, Guéliz, T044-431900 (manager Serge Meadow), www.riadomaroc.com Located in a small modern block just off Av Mohammed V. Heading towards the médina, just before Bab Nkob, go left and then left again; office is on your left. Functions as a centralized reservation service for both rooms in riads and whole riads. Highly personalized service. A choice range of homes for rent, including the elegant *Villa Hélène* in Guéliz (with pool) and the faintly minimalist*Dar Tchina*. Properties rated by lanterns (1 to 5). Rooms are available as in a hotel for short periods. Cheapest room is 300dh. An average property, 3 lanterns, eg *Dar Nimbus*, sleeping 8, costs 2,400dh a night. Most spectacular property? ***Riad al Kadi***, Derb Debbachi. Great attention paid to bathrooms and mattresses. Meals can be cooked in-house to order, average cost 100dh a head.

Marrakech Riads, 8 Derb Charfa Lekbir, Mouassine, T044-385858, T061-163630 (mob), www.marrakech-riads.net Small agency managed by Abdellatif Ait Ben Abdallah. Properties include the simple *Dar Sara* and the beautiful *Dar Zellije* (Sidi Ben Slimane), double rooms 1,200-1,500dh per night. The agency's headquarters, the beautiful Dar Cherifa, a 17th-century house converted with gallery space on the ground floor, are worth a visit in their own right.

Magesor SARL, Villa Le Grillon, R Oumou el Banine, Marrakech – Guéliz (managers Florence and Jean Marie Milicent), T063-040104, F436997. Small agency with 2 properties for rent in Marrakech: a villa in Guéliz with large suites at 600dh per day for 2 people and a riad in the Bab el Khemis neighbourhood, close to the new Museum of Marrakech, which can sleep up to 12 people for 7,200dh per day. Prices include maid service, breakfast and all taxes.

Riads for rent directly from owners (Médina)

Always double check your riad reservation at peak times of year (end of year holidays, Easter, May/June)

L *Riad Charaï*, 54 Diour Jdad, Zaouïa, T044-437211, www.maisons-traditions.co.ma Manager Mme Nazik Salmouni. The former residence of the Pacha of Marrakech's secretary. Sleeps up to 12, fair-sized pool (4 m x 9 m), huge garden patio. **L** *Riad el Ouarda*, 5 Derb Taht es Sour, Zaouia el Abbasia, T044-385714, www.riadelouarda.com Located in the northern side of the médina, beautifully decorated. 2 suites and 4 rooms. Prices are steep: suite for 2 persons is 1,850dh, 1,700dh for 1 person; rooms clock in at 1,300 for 1 person, 1,400 for 2. Breakfast included. **L** *Riad Enija*, 9 Derb Mesfioui, Rahba Lakdima, T044-440926, F442700. A truly jungliferous courtyard and absolutely fabulous artistic beds ('remarkable fabrics, darling'). You too can slip under the gloss of a decor magazine. Best visited with one's personal photographer. Not all rooms have en suite bath and shower. Blue room is coolest, the Suite Harem has roof terrace. **L** ***Riad Mabrouka***, 56 Derb el Battia, Riad Zitoun el Jedid, T044-377579, www.riad-mabrouka.com 3 rooms and 2 suites. Simple decoration. Owner Catherine Neri is a cookery enthusiast. **L** ***Villa des Orangers***, 6 R Sidi Mimoun, T044-384638, www.villadesorangers.com Close to both Hivernage and médina. Near the new royal palace and the Kasbah area. Chic. Agreeable although more of a discrete hotel than a guesthouse. Closed mid-July/mid-Aug. **L** ***Les Yeux bleus***, near the *Maison arabe* at 7 Derb el Ferrane, Bab Doukkala, T044-378161, T061-422682 (mob), owner Mme J Despin. Luxurious and tasteful.

A ***Dar Hanane***, 9 Derb Lella-Azouna, T044-377737, T063-839292 (mob), F044-377074, near El Moukef and Medersa Ben Youssef. 1 suite and 4 rooms. Superb terrace view, thematic weeks (painting, golf). **A** ***Dar Moha***, 81 R Dar el Bacha, T044-386400, F386998. Very accessible for both médina and Guéliz in Rmila neighbourhood. 3 double rooms at 1,700dh (with breakfast), 1 single room at 1,300dh. Fine decoration, but downstairs functions as a restaurant (with piped music), so this is not as private and exquisite as it should be for the price. Tiny pool is in the restaurant courtyard downstairs at the back. **A** ***Riad Malika***, 29 Derb Arset Aouzal, Bab Doukkala, T044-385451, www.riadmalika.com. Features many nice old chairs and art deco bits and a patio thick with vegetation. **A** ***Riyad El Mezouar***, 28 Derb el Hammam, Issebtine, T/F044-380949, www.riyad-el-mezouar.com Near the Medersa Ben Youssef, 2 rooms and 3 suites. Simple elegant decor in a restored 18th-century house. **A** ***Riad Noga***, 78 Derb Jedid, Douar Graoua, T044-443386, F441941. TV and internet access from most rooms. Not the most traditional of riads, but very comfortable.

A-B ***Dar al Assad***, 29 Derb El Hajra, Derb Debbachi, T/F044-427065, T061-130820 (mob). 4 smallish but beautifully decorated rooms with full bath or shower. Beautifully furnished. **A-B** ***Dar el Cadi***, 59 Derb el Cadi, Azbezt, Derb Debbachi. (Mail to BP101 Marrakech-Médina.) Definitely one of the best riads in the médina. 4 patios, plunge pool, cool and simple decoration. Living room. Highly recommended. Advance reservations essential, T044-378655, F378478, riyadelcadi@iam.net.ma **A-B** ***Dar Mouassine***, 148 Derb Snane, Mouassine, T/F044-445287, T061-341784 (mob). Contemporary styling, all rather sleek, 3 suites and 2 rooms. Good video library, lots of books, too. Recommended. **A-B** ***Riad Cais***, T044-440141. In the Riad Zitoun el Kedim area, close to the Badi Palace, a 10-min walk from Jemaâ el Fna. (Owner-manager, architect Christian Ferré, lives on premises.) Named after Cais, the Romeo of early Arabic poetry (Leila was his Juliet). One of the finest riads, beautifully decorated, full of nooks and crannies. Open fires everywhere in winter. Garden patio with tall, mature trees. Lots of staff to look after you. Difficult to fault in fact. (Used by UK agency *Simply Travel*.)

B ***Riad el Arset***, 10 bis Derb Chemaâ, near Dar Glaoua, Arset Loughzail, T044-387567. Fine colonnades and a beautiful suite in the summer house. **B** ***Riad el Az***, 152 Derb Sidi M'barek, Sidi Mimoune, T065-070900, riadelaz@yahoo.fr Small, highly personal riad. 3 en suite rooms and 'studio'. Recommended. **B** ***Riad Catalina***, 21 Derb Abdallah Ben Hssaine, Bab Leksour, T044-426701, F426702. More of a small hotel than a riad, despite the courtyard. Accommodation for up to 35 people – might suit a group holiday. Fully a/c, satellite TV, diminutive roof-terrace swimming pool accessible to all. Clean, located in a part of the médina close to Av Mohammed V and Guéliz, but is to a traditional home what Paris Disneyland is to Chambord. **B** ***Dar el Borj***, hidden away at 63 Derb Moulay Abd el Kader, Derb Debbachi, just 10 mins' walk from Jemaâ el Fna, T/F044-391223, T061-675942 (mob), www.riyads.com Manager: Rachid Bouabid. One of the most reasonably priced riads. Good central location and good value in low season with it. Roof terraces and a small, pleasantly planted courtyard. Week's rent for 8 people: low season 13,000dh, high season 21,500dh. **B** ***Dar el Farah***, Arset

Bouachrine, Riad Zitoun el Jedid, T044-441019, F427522. Close to Jemaâ el Fna. Can sleep up to 12 people. Weekly rent for full house party in high season, breakfast included, about 25,000dh. Pleasant terrace and plunge-pool in main patio. French owned and managed. **B** ***Dar el Hana***, T/F044-429977, very small riad which would suit a (well-heeled) family. Sitting room with fireplace. 7 rooms. **B** ***La Maison Alexandre-Bonnel***, 4 Derb Sania, Bab Leksour, near therestaurant *Ksar Es Saoussan*, T/F044-429833. (3 rooms available). Personable small house in a central neighbourhood. Owners Christophe and Valérie Crouzet live on the premises and know the region really well. Can set up excursions, advise on restaurants, etc. An excellent address. **B** ***Riad Noor Charana***, 31 Derb el Kebir, Ben Salah neighbourhood, T044-386094, www.noorcharana.com. Pleasant, small French-run riad, 6 rooms and roof terrace. Highly recommended. **B** ***Dar Taliwint***, 26 R de la Bahia, T044-377805, T068-048799 (mob), www.dartaliwint.com Opened 2003, 4 a/c en suite rooms on 1st floor in Riad Zitoun el Jedid neighbourhood. Highly recommended. **B** ***Riad Nisrine***, Mouassine, T061-341357 (mob), also via France T00 33 148780273. Beautiful garden courtyard, fine roof terrace. **B** ***Riad Zina***, 38 Derb Assabane, Riad Laârous, T044-385242, F061-249197. Well-managed small riad, 3 rooms only, with an agreeable laid-back, post-minimalist feel. Recommended. **B-C** ***Dar Zerqa***, 30 Derb Kaâ Akhij, Sidi Ben Slimane, T061-340463 (mob). Attractive small riad. 1st floor with 2 double rooms, living room downstairs with couches. Would suit a family. Located between Sidi Bel Abbès and Dar el Bacha. Some reports of double bookings, however.

Guesthouses in Guéliz & Hivernage

AL ***Dar Rhizlane***, Av Jnane el Harti, T044-421303, www.dar-rhizlane.com 19 a/c rooms and suites, starting at 2,300dh per room. Princely. Pool. **A-B** ***Villa Occitane***, 3 R Nador, T/F044-448319. In a quiet corner of l'Hivernage. 6 rooms. Prices include breakfast and laundry. 1 person 500dh, a little extra for half-board. Has an Oscar Wilde touch.

Guesthouse accommodation directly from owners (Palmeraie)

There is now a small selection of upmarket accommodation out in the Palmeraie and in the rural areas close to the city. At the rate building works are going, there will be plenty more in the near future. Some of the newer offerings are truly Arabian-Disney-Nightmare, however (not listed here).

L ***Dar Temsna***, and the new ***Jnane Temsna*** For reservations contact owner Meryanne Loum-Martin (speaks perfect English), T044-329423, 329884, T061-242717 (mob), www.tamsna.com. Same management as the beautiful *Ryad Tamsna* eatery boutique in the médina. Well away from the bustle of downtown Marrakech, the twin villas (10 suites) of Dar Temsna make an ideal base for the upscale visitor. Close to the Palmeraie golf course. Highly personalized service. ***Jnane Temsna*** has organic food, massages, tennis courts and pools. One of the best addresses in Marrakech – at a price. Highly recommended. **L** ***Dar Sedra***, Douar Abiad, near Les Deux Tours, reservations on French T00 33 146570087, www.dar-sedra.com House for rent at €2,300 per night (5 rooms). Whole property sleeps up to 14. **L** ***Kasbah des Roses***, Km 9 Route de Ouazarzate, T044-329305, F329303, kasbahdesroses@iam.net.ma 1 room and 3 suites in private pink concrete farmhouse on a 35-ha flower farm east of the city. Small pool. Owners will tell you all about growing roses. Overpriced. **A** ***Dar Faracha***, T044-313901, F313905, www.atlas-sahara-trek.com Out on the edge of the palm groves, pleasant low villa with arcaded veranda, pool and garden, sleeps 6-8. Recommended.

Self-catering flats Simple catering accommodation in the form of sparsely equipped holiday flats is also available in Marrakech. Such *résidences*, generally blocks of flats of a few storeys, are located in Guéliz and the newer residential area Daoudiyet. Many flats are run with hotel-type facilities. This sort of accommodation (modern, clean, but a bit lacking in charm) tends to be favoured by Moroccan families down

Five special restaurants in Marrakech

- *Ksar Essaoussan*, Leksour, Médina, T044-440632. Chic and elegant Moroccan cuisine, though seating a bit cramped.
- *Les Jardins de la Médina*, 21 Derb Chtouka, Kasbah, T044-381851. Dining in a Marrakchi garden.
- *Dar Moha*, Dar el Bacha, Médina, T044-386400. Where well healed locals might go to enjoy Moroccan food.
- *Bagatelle*, Rue de Yougoslavie, Guéliz. Pleasant dining in gardened courtyard. French food. Very reasonably priced. T044-430274.
- *Le Tobsil*, Leksour, Médina. T044-444052, 441523, 444535. Most elegant Moroccan nosh.

from Casablanca for the weekend. If you have the money, try to go for a riad instead. **B *Résidence el Bahja***, corner of R Ibn Aicha and R Mohammed el Beqal, T044-448119, F346063. 13 spacious self-catering flats, but not within easy walking distance of the médina. Moroccan meals to order. Street-facing rooms noisy. **B *Résidence Zahia***, Route de Casablanca, T044-437815, F430028. 44 self-catering flats and studios able to sleep 4 people. Avoid street-facing accommodation. Pool. **C *Résidence meublée Gomassine***, 71 Blvd Mohammed Zerktouni, Guéliz, T044-433086, F433012. Facing the *Café Les Négociants*, go left, this apart-hotel is about 70 m down the street on your right. New in 1999. Very clean. Prices: 300dh 1 person, 400dh 2 persons, 460dh 3 persons, 700dh 5 persons. Larger flats have living rooms. Fully equipped kitchens and a/c. Large café with good cakes on ground floor.

Youth hostel R el Jahed, Quartier Industriel, off Av de France, T044-447713. 80 beds, kitchen, meals available, bus 200 m, train 700 m, overnight fee 30dh, hot showers, IYHF cards only. Open 1200-1400 and 1800-2200 in winter, 0600-2400 in summer. Difficult to find (barely signed), a long way from the sights – and there is plenty of cheap accommodation in the médina for a few extra dirhams.

Camping *Camping Municipal*, off Av de France, 5 mins south of the railway station, with shop, showers and café, site of 2 ha, bar, laundry, first aid, electricity for caravans, petrol at 800 m, quiet, clean and pleasant. For those with own transport, 13 km out of the city on the Casablanca road, the *Camping Firdaous*, T044-313167, is a possible clean option.

Eating

Guéliz
● *on maps*
There is a good selection of places to eat in Guéliz

The older bar restaurant places tend to be located on the main Av Mohammed V. There is a small selection of restaurants, including *Pizzeria Niagara*, at the end of the avenue farthest from the médina. More interesting (and slightly more expensive) are the European-style places, located in the side avenues, such as *L'Entrecote*, *Odissea* and the *Trattoria di Gian Carlo*. Guéliz also has some smart cafés (notably *Les Négociants* on rond-point Abd el Moumen). For a panoramic drink, take the lift up to the mirador of *Bar La Renaissance*, also on aforesaid rond-point.

Expensive *Al Fassia*, 232 Av Mohammed V, T044-434060. Excellent Moroccan restaurant which allows you to dine à la carte and avoid the surfeit of Moroccan food you automatically get in the 500dh a head palace restaurants. Reservations recommended. Easy to find on Av Mohammed V, about halfway between rond-point Abd el Moumen and Jemaâ el Fna. Recommended. ***Le Dragon d'Or***, 10 bis Blvd Mohammed Zerktouni, T044-433341. Chinese food. ***Le Jacaranda***, 32 Blvd Mohammed Zerktouni (opposite

Café Les Négociants), T044-447215. Long-standing restaurant with good reputation. Elaborate French food, strong on fish and creamy sauces, closed Tue and Wed lunchtime, bar. Eating à la carte, expect to pay 250dh. The menus are much cheaper. Terrace very noisy, sit upstairs inside for quiet. ***La Trattoria di Gian Carlo***, 179 R Mohammed el Bequal, T044-432641, www.latrattoriamarrakech.com To locate, find *La Taverne* (opposite *Cinéma Le Colisée* near rond-point Abd el Moumen), which is on corner of Blvd Zerktouni and R Mohammed el Bequal. *La Trattoria* is 2 blocks down, next to *Café L'Amandine*. Gian Carlo has gone but standards are being maintained. The city's best Italian restaurant? Excellent selection of wines, superb desserts. ***Villa Rosa***, 64 Av Hassan II, T044-430832. Small Italian restaurant specializing in pasta and fish. Full meal 200-300dh. A good address, easily located by taxi drivers. Best to eat out on patio, if possible.

Lots of places in the medium-price bracket, many of which are very good

Mid-range *Restaurant Bagatelle*, 101 R Yougoslavie, T044-430274. Good French food served in the restaurant and vine shaded courtyard, open 1200-1400 and 1900-2300, closed Wed. Very pleasant lunch stop in summer. Try the *salade fermier*. Light lunch for around 100dh, the full wack for 200dh. Recommended. ***Rotisserie du Café de la Paix***, 68 R Yougoslavie, T044-433118. Reasonable grilled food all year round; with garden in the summer. ***Catanzaro***, R Tarak ibn Ziad, behind the market in Guéliz, next to the *Hotel Toulousain*, T044-433731. Excellent Italian food. Full meal for around 150dh, though you can spend far less. A very popular lunchtime address. Reservations essential in evening. ***La Concha Basque***, R Loubnène, not far from the Guéliz food market, T044-4436471. ***Chez Jack'line***, 63 Av Mohammed V, T044-447547. Atmospheric, in a 1950s bistro sort of way. Meat beautifully cooked. French and Italian cuisine. Ideal for a European meal when you've just spent 2 weeks up in the mountains eating tagine. There is a resident parrot, too. The lion cub has long gone, sadly, as has the monkey. ***La Poêle d'Or***, R Allal ben Ahmed, on a square behind the *Hotel Boustane*. (To get there, starting with *Les Négociants* on your right, take 1st left on R Tarik ibn Ziad, after *Hotel Boustane*.) A reliable little address. Franco-Moroccan cooking, small shaded outside dining areas. Nice lunch for 160dh. Recommended. ***La Taverne***, 23 Blvd Mohammed Zerktouni (opposite *Cinéma Le Colisée*), T044-446126. Fixed standard menus and a bar. Lighting on the bright side, fine for a beer and cheap eat out. ***L'Entrecote***, 55 Blvd Zerktouni, T044-49428. Manager Abdel Ghani Khatir, T061-245042 (mob). To locate: Start at rond-point Abd el Moumen, facing *Les Négociants*. Go left. *L'Entrecote* is on your right, about 20 m from roundabout, in the ABN Amro building, at back of small mall. Recommended. Meat particularly good. Menu 120dh, lunchtime quick menu 70dh, 150dh for a good feed. ***Le Jardin des Arts***, 6/7 R Sakia el Hamra, T044-446634, F446649. Near *Hotel Amine* and *Café le Diamant Vert*. In Semlalia rather than Guéliz but included here for convenience. A newish (Apr 2001) French restaurant that fills the gap in the Semlalia hotel zone. Overpriced. ***Odissea***, 83 bis Blvd Mansour Eddahbi, T044-431545, F449921. To get there, coming from the médina on Av Mohammed V, locate the main *RAM* agency and *Wafa Bank*. Go left, and left again. *Odissea* is a few metres down on your right. The decor of this Italian-run restaurant is molto Versace, with impeccable waistcoated waiters and giant paintings of leopards. Excellent pizzas: pizza and wine for 2 will work out at about 200dh. Highly recommended. ***Pizzeria Niagara***, Route de Targa (take a taxi), T044-449775. Good pizzas. Covered terrace. Gets crowded in the evenings with chic locals, so reservations essential. Recommended.

Cheap Top of the cheap range in the *ville nouvelle* is ***Brasserie du Regent***, 34 Av Mohammed V, T044-448749; also try ***Badr***, R de la Liberté, Guéliz. ***Le Petit Poucet***, Av Mohammed V, T044-448238. Bar and restaurant with basic but good French dishes. ***Tiffany***, under the arcade on Av Mohammed V, near the post office. Basic meals and breakfasts, good service, stays open during the day in Ramadan; or ***Café Agdal***, 86 Av Mohammed V, T044-448707, good for chicken, no alcohol. Highly recommended is the ***Bar L'Escale***, almost opposite the main market in Guéliz. Coming from the médina, go left at the *Wafa Bank* and it is a few doors along on your right. The eating area is at the back. Go for charcoal-grilled *coquelet* and chips with your Flag beer. Not really for unaccompanied women.

L'Hivernage
Although a quiet district of villas and large hotels, there are now a few restaurants

Although not exactly in L'Hivernage, the famous *Hotel Mamounia*'s restaurants are nearby in easy walking distance of the area's hotels.

Expensive *Le Comptoir*, Av Echouhada (almost opposite the *Hotel Imperial Borj*), T044-437702, F447747. A toney establishment with much muted lighting and elegant waitresses in caftans. The place for a pre-dinner drink perhaps. They also have a little boutiquey place at the back. Dinner will set you back around 400dh. Trendissimo. ***Restaurant La Calèche***, in the *Hotel Mamounia*, Av Bab Jedid, T044-448991. French food with a view over the hotel's famous gardens. ***Restaurant Marocain de l'Hotel Mamounia***, also in the *Hotel Mamounia*, Av Bab Jedid, T044-448991. Reservations recommended, lavishly decorated restaurant introducing élite Moroccan cuisine. Expensive for what it is.

Mid-range *L'Amandier*, corner of R de Paris and Av Echouhada, T044-446093. Quite near hotels *Impérial Borj* and *Saâdi* and *Polyclinique Koutoubia*. French cuisine. ***Safran et Cannelle***, 40 Av Hassan II, T044-435969, F434274. Trendy, popular place close to Jnene el Harti on a busy main avenue. Apart from restaurant on ground floor, there is a noisy bar in the basement and the karaoke bar *L'Hacienda* on 1st floor. Not for those in search of a quiet night out. Lots of beer for 20dh a go.

Médina
These listings are generally in the expensive category

The upmarket Moroccan restaurants in restored houses with garden courtyards are part of the Marrakech experience. Reservations are essential. Generally, they are indicated by a discrete wall plaque – taxi drivers know where they are, or someone from the restaurant will come to accompany you. You make your reservation, and they will give you a place to tell the taxi driver to drop you off. There you will be met by the restaurant doorman, generally togged up in traditional gear. Most of the traditional restaurants are located in one of 3 districts: **Riad Zitoun and la Kasbah**; **Bab Leksour** (*Ksar Saoussen*, *Stylia*, *Tobsil*); or **Dar el Bacha and Bab Doukkala** (*Dar Moha* and the *Marjana*). Note that the médina restaurants vary greatly in size and style. The profits to be made by catering for large groups means that not all can offer intimate courtyard dining. Indeed, behind discrete doors in alleyways are some big restaurant operations – for example, the *Stylia* in Leksour or the vast *Dar Haj Idder* off Derb Debbachi. Here you will be eating in the company of jolly coach parties from Agadir or *IBM* employees on their convention spree. Latest addition? The elegant *Foundouk* near the Médersa Ben Youssef.

Close to the Koutoubia *Dar el Baroud*, 275 Av Mohammed V, T044-426009, F311443. A good address for refined Moroccan food and not excessively expensive at 400dh per head. Easily located down an alley opposite the Koutoubia, on your left as you come from Guéliz. ***Restaurant Relais Al Baraka***, Jemaâ el Fna, near the police station, T044-442341. Moroccan meals around a courtyard with fountain, convenient after sightseeing, reservations recommended.

Riad Zitoun and Kasbah *Dar Douiriya*, 14 Derb Jedid Hay Essalem, off Av Houman el Fetouaki (and very close to the Pl des Ferblantiers and the Badi' Palace), T044-403030, F403055. 4-course dining at around 380dh a head in slightly gaudy surroundings with the usual trimmings (live music, belly dancer doing her brief bit). Ideal for an a/c lunch stop after doing the palace museums. Main plus points: easy accessibility by taxi, nice service. A good if unexciting introduction to Moroccan food. Can seat up to 120 but has intimate corners. ***Dar Mima*** (not to be confused with *Dar Mimoun*). Near the Dar Si Saïd at 9 Derb Zaouïat el Kadiria, T044-385252. Around 250dh a head. Alcohol. A la carte, evenings only. Portions can be on the small side. Recommended. ***Ryad Temsna***, Riad Zitoun Jedid, 23 zanka Daïka,T044-385272, F385271, in the Kennaria district, down an alley on the right after the old cinema (see map or call, they'll send someone to meet you at the *Café de France* on Jemaâ el Fna). Beautifully restored riad open for lunch, about 200dh. Lebano-Moroccan cuisine. A fine eating experience. Highly recommended. Occasional exhibitions of painting, too. No booze.

Bab Leksour area *Ksar es Saoussan*, T044-440632, F426075. Dinner only, seats up to 40. Three fixed price menus, 300dh, 400dh and 500dh. Prices include an aperitif and half bottle of wine. An early 17th-century house with a new function as a restaurant, located next to one of the oldest houses in Marrakech, the ruined Dar el Messaoudiyine. Red-robed porter will meet guests at the entrance to R Leksour. Small – even a bit cramped – by médina restaurant standards but highly recommended. Food excellent. Manager, Jean-Laurent Graulhet. ***Le Pavillon***, 47 Derb Zaouia, T044-387040. Near *La Maison arabe*, opposite the mosque at Bab Doukkala, at the end of an alley. One of the first of this kind, originally restored by a French decorator, now under new management. Dinner only, closed Tue. Good wines, around 350dh per head. Recommended. ***Restaurant Stylia***, 36 R Ksour, T044-443587. One of the largest traditional palace restaurants, reservations required, with all the usual Moroccan traditional dishes. Unfortunately, hasn't been able to maintain the original quality. Service is poor. Works mainly with groups (can cater for up to 700 people, they say), as the restaurant consists of several interlinked houses. Easy access – torch-bearers will show you the way. Around 400dh per head. For information, *stylia* means 'bucket-makers'. ***Le Tobsil***, 22 Derb Abdallah ben Houssein, Ksour district, T044-444052, 441523, 444535, F443515. A safe bet. Elegant Moroccan cuisine. Reservations absolutely essential as there are not very many tables. 550dh a head, wine and spirits included. *Tobsil* means plate. Highly recommended.

Bab Doukkala and Dar el Bacha *Dar Marjana*, 15 Derb Sidi Ali Tair, T044-385110, F385152. Down an alley almost opposite the entrance to Dar el Bacha, currently the royal residence when the king is in Marrakech. Lunch for groups, dinner for all-comers. Choice of 3 5-course menus: 600dh (tagine and couscous), 650dh includes *tlaâ* (succulent shoulder or lamb), 700dh includes *mechoui* (barbecued lamb). Prices include aperitifs and alcohol. Recommended. If the manager has had too much to drink, women guests may get a little hassle. ***Dar Moha***, 81 R Dar el Bacha, reservations on T044-386400, F386998. One of the better médina restaurants, digestible Moroccan nouvelle cuisine. Easily located by a taxi as on the busy R Dar el Bacha. On foot, if heading towards Jemaâ el Fna, turn back left at 20 mins to the hour just opposite the Koutoubia minaret. Follow busy R Rmila for some 200 m. It curves round to right, becoming R Dar el Bacha. The smooth, clean façade of Dar Moha is on your left after 100 m. Originally restored by Pierre Balmain, the house now functions partly as an exclusive guesthouse (upstairs). In summer, try to get a table in small patio out back.

Arset Ihiri/Riad Laârous *Dar Fès*, 8 R Boussouni, Riad Laârous (car park Arset Ihiri), T044-382340. Not as chic as some of the old city restaurants, but pleasant nonetheless. Comfy blue velvet sofas in a garden patio. ***El Yacout***, 79, Derb Sidi Ahmed Soussi, T044-382929, F382538. Closed Mon, dinner only. Reservations essential. 600dh a head. The full Moroccan culinary experience. Atmospheric, but has been enlarged and in the process totally lost the intimate touch. (*Une usine à bouffe*, as the French say.) Caters for large groups – popular with the American market.

Close to Jemaâ el Fna Mid-range and cheap ***Restaurant de Foucauld***, in the *Hotel Foucauld*, Av el Mouahidine. Good couscous and tagines near the Jemaâ el Fna. ***Restaurant Tazi***, in the *Grand Hotel Tazi*, R Bab Agnaou. Similar restaurant run by the same management, the cheapest licensed establishment in the médina. Buffet dinner in ***Hotel Ali***, R Moulay Ismail, good choice and very reasonably priced. ***Café-Restaurant Argana***, Jemaâ el Fna. Food with a view, popular with locals and tourists. Gets very busy at sundown. Café on ground floor is a strategic meeting place, as no one can miss the large red Argana sign atop the restaurant. ***Restaurant Etoile de Marrakech***, R Bab Agnaou. Good value set meals with view of Jemaâ el Fna from the roof.

Near Rahba el Kadima ***Dar Timtam***, 44 R Rahba el Kadima, T044-391446. Near the square of the same name. Turn right off the square on the far side from the *Wafa Bank*. A funny sort of place, trying hard. Patio roofed over. Currently does light meals for about 150dh, excluding drinks. No booze. Handy as a tea-stop if you are in the central souks? Included in this section for convenience, located near the Medersa Ben Youssef, is ***Le Foundouk***, 55 Souk Hal Fassi, Kaât Ben Hadid, T044-378190, F378176. One of the most elegant addresses in Marrakech, Franco-Moroccan nouvelle cuisine, at the top of the mid-range bracket, the full wack for 250dh a head, but you can eat for less. Drawback? Alcohol licence pending.

In the médina the most popular option is to eat at the open-air restaurants on the Jemaâ el Fna

On 'La Place' Piles of salads and steaming tagines are set up under hissing gas lamps. Each stall has a different variety of cooked food. Although conditions are pretty sanitary, in summer it is best to go for the food cooked to order while waiting. The salads always look pretty fresh, however. Another possibility is ***Chez Chekrouni***, on Jemaâ el Fna, left of the *Café de France* in the Derb Debbachi direction, the one with the counter seating overlooking the square (packed at lunchtimes). Also almost opposite the *Café de France* is a new place for reasonably priced pasta, pizzas and salads, ***Les Terrasses de l'Alhambra***. Neo-Marrakchi deco but no tajines. Popular.

There are more cheap restaurants, often packed with locals, along Bani Marine (the one which runs behind the *Cinéma Mabrouka*, parallel and between R Moulay Ismail and pedestrian R Bab Agnaou), such as ***Casse-Croûte des Amis***. Also, behind the souvenir stalls opposite the nut sellers, there is a covered area of cheap restaurants.

Cafés

On Jemaâ el Fna try ***Café-Restaurant Argana***, with a good view from the top terrace. Good lemon tartlettes. Another good meeting place is the ***Café de France***, with several levels and an excellent panorama over the square and the médina beyond. In Guéliz, the rond-point Abd el Moumen has lots of popular cafés on each side, including the ***Café Les Négociants*** and ***Café La Renaissance***; ***Boule de Neige***, on R de Yougoslavie, just off this roundabout, is a trendy place for pricey but excellent drinks, ice-cream and breakfasts; next door is ***Pâtisserie Hilton***, with a full range of Moroccan sweets and cakes. For late-night coffees or ice-creams (most places close by 2130), try ***Café-Glacerie Siroua***. ***Café Zohor***, R de la Liberté, gets crowded in the early evening (try also the neighbouring ***Pâtisserie Zohor***). ***Café Firdaous***, Av Mohammed V, also has a local clientele. ***Café Caruso***, corner of R Ibn Malek and Av de France. For a coffee after work.

Bars and clubs

The trendiest address in town, perhaps too trendy for its own good, is ***Le Comptoir Paris-Marrakech***, on Av ech Chouhada, opposite the *Hotel Impérial Borj*. More conservatively, there is the ***Piano Bar***, at the *Hotel Mamounia*, Av Bab Jedid, 1800-0100, drinks not cheap. More cheaply, for a beer with a view, you have ***La Renaissance***, Av

Mohammed V. Go up the lift to the rooftop bar for the best view of the Guéliz. (You pay for your 1st drink at the counter downstairs.) For a beer, chicken and chips, go for ***L'Escale***, just off Av Mohammed V, after the *Wafa Bank*. ***Le Petit Poucet***, 56 Av Mohammed V, has fairly cheap drinks. Reaching further downmarket, the ***Ambassadeurs***, 6 Av Mohammed V, must have been a good address years ago. More trendily, opened in 2002, the ***Le Montecristo***, 20 R Ibn Aïcha, Guéliz, could fill the gap between pleasant pizzerias and low-life bars. Dance and drink the night away. Finally, the latest glitzy offering is in the sub-Buddha bar mode: ***Al'anbar***, T044-380763. The premises are cavernous, the music deafening, the décor over the top and beyond. Same management as *Chez Ali*, the gaudy fantasia people. You have been warned.

Nightclubs

Disco Paradise, at the *Hotel Pullman Mansur Eddahbi*, Av de France, T044-448222. Admission 80dh, 2200-0700, a large disco with the latest equipment. ***Cotton Club***, at the *Hotel Tropicana*, Semlalia, T044-433913. Admission 60dh, 2100-0500. Also try ***L'Atlas***, ***Le Flash*** and ***Le Diamant Noir*** at the *Hotel Marrakech*, both on Av Mohammed V.

Entertainment

Casinos

Grand Casino de la Mamounia, at the *Mamounia Hotel*, Av Bab Jedid, T044-444570. Open from 2000 or 2100. ***Hotel Es Saadi***, Av Kadissia, T044-448811.

Cinemas

The major cinemas showing films in French are the ***Colisée***, Blvd Mohammed Zerktouni, and the ***Regent***, Av Mohammed V. Try also the ***Centre Culturel Français***, Route de Targa, Guéliz, T044-447063.

Cultural & language centres

Institut français, Route de la Targa, Guéliz, daily 0830-1200 and 1430-1830 except Mon. With a recommended café, open-air theatre and pleasant garden, shows films, holds exhibitions and other cultural events. Library has small stock of books in French on Morocco-related subjects.

Folklore & fantasia

The ***Cappa Club*** at the *Hotel Issil*, the ***Hotel le Marrakech***, Av Mohammed V, and the ***Club Mediterranée*** all have large folklore displays but can be difficult to get into. The best bet is the ***Restaurant Riad***. For fantasia, drive or take a taxi to: ***Chez Ali*** in the Palmerie, after the Tensift bridge, T044-448187; ***El Borj***, after the Tensift bridge, T044-446376; ***Zagora***, Route de Casablanca, T044-445237; and ***Ancien Casino de Marrakech***, Av el Kadissia, T044-448811. Food and extravagant displays from 2100, admission 100dh. ***Restaurant Chaouia***, near the airport, T044-442915. Displays of horsemanship, swordplay, dance and music.

Shopping

Handicrafts

Marrakech is something of a shoppers' paradise. Since the early 1990s, craft production has taken off in a big way, with a range of new products, notably in metal and ceramic, being added to classic leather and wood items. The influence of the international decorator set can clearly be felt. Close to the Dar El Pacha, in the Bab Doukkala neighbourhood, are plenty of antique dealers, and in Guéliz, the keen shopper will find chic boutiques with clothing, fine leather and other items. Prices in Guéliz are fixed, and more expensive than the médina. A feel for prices can also be gained by visiting the workshops in the large craft training centre (the *Coopartim Ensemble Artisanale*), on your left as you go from Guéliz to the médina. Here again prices are non-negotiable, and slightly more expensive than in the old city. However, in a very short time you can see people at work at practially all the main crafts, including embroidery, ceramic mosaic and basketry, felt hats, wood painting and slipper making. In the médina, there is so much on offer that you begin to feel a little dazed – craftwork overdose, or something like the *syndrome de Stendahl*, the result of seeing too many souks rather than too many Italian churches and paintings.

In the médina, prices are of course negotiable. Remember, you are buying non-essential articles for decoration – so it really doesn't matter if you have them or not. Keep a sense of humour (remember how absurd it all is when some salesman whom you met 5 mins ago reasons that "you are not my friend because you don't want to buy from me". Always be polite, and you may just come away with some bargains. The price you pay for that bijou plate or mirror is really only what a decorative item is worth to you.

Good items to buy in Marrakech include thuya wood boxes and trays, painted wood mirrors, ceramics and *belgha* (leather slippers). You can also find very nice wrought-ironwork mirror frames. Baskets, available from stalls in the Guéliz *marché* are also a good buy.

Guéliz There are quite a few souvenir shops and shops selling clothes and luggage on Av Mohammed V. There are number of little boutique-type places on R de la Liberté, which cuts across Av Mohammed V just after the main food market in Guéliz, on your left as you come up from the médina. Also have a quick trawl along R Mohammed Bequal (turn left just after the restaurant *La Taverne*, which itself is almost opposite the *Cinéma Colisée*).

R de la Liberté *Côté Sud*, 4 R de la Liberté (as you come from the médina on Av Mohammed V, turn left after *Place Vendôme* clothes shop; *Côté Sud* is about 30 m along on right). Boutique owned by craft specialist Sabine Hmami-Bastin. Good choice of embroidery, ceramics and small paintings and frames, also perfumes, candles and incense. Many articles made especially for the shop. ***Intensité Nomade***, corner Av Mohammed V/R de la Liberté. Tasteful clothes and leather goods for toney people. ***L'Orientaliste***, 15 R de la Liberté. Ceramics and perfumes, paintings and semi-antiques. ***Place Vendôme***, 141 Av Mohammed V, almost opposite the food market. High quality leather and *maroquinerie*. ***Yves Rocher***, R de la Liberté. For the lotions and potions you forgot in the rush to pack.

R Mohammed Bequal *Chic Caftan*, Immeuble 100, No 2, T044-435093. Almost opposite the *Galerie Bikenmeyer*. As the name suggests, a good choice of upmarket traditional women's gear. Beautiful babouches with a modern touch.

The médina It can be terribly confusing for shopping. Originally each souk specialized in a given item. This system has largely broken down, however, on the main tourist drag (Souk Semmarine and its continuation, Souk el Kebir) up to the area around the Ben Youssef Medersa. Basically, there are shops specializing in slippers, traditional gear, wood and ceramics, and a number of large antique shops.

You could make your way into the médina at the 'entrance' just opposite *Résidence de la Place*. You will wind round and eventually come through an arch into the wide, paved ***Souk Semmarine***. There are some big antique shops and carpet emporia here, some of them very expensive. At the end of Souk Semmarine, you come to another arch, the street rises slightly, and you are in Souk el Kebir (good choice of babouches and djellabas). ***Rahba Kedima***, off to the right, also has some interesting small shops. Further on, Souk el Kebir successively becomes Souk el Najjarine and, under a wooden lintel Souk Chkaïria. Leather goods can be bought here. Up ahead you will see the minaret of the Ben Youssef Medersa.

Near the Ben Youssef Medersa *Chaussures Ben Youssef*, Kaâte Bennahi, 6 Souk Ahl Fès, T044-377810. Small workshop, easily missed, behind the *medersa*. (Go straight on instead of turning left for Dar Belarj, the workshop is on your right.) The place to buy the best babouches, prices 200-280dh, materials used include old flat weaves and modern silks. Beautiful presents.

Leksour and Mouassine neighbourhoods *Au Minaret de Mouassine*, 56 Fhel Chidmi, Mouassine, T044-441357 T061-181194 (mob). Owner Hassan Errijaji is an English-speaking carpet dealer. Good place to buy. ***Beldi***, a maison de haute couture at 9-11 Souikat Leksour, T044-441076. Fine selection of traditionally tailored clothes, mainly for women. Waistcoats and flowing shirts for men. ***D'Altro 1***, 21 Fhal Chidmi, Mouassine, T044-444289, owner Abd el Moumen Mhaidi. Minimalist decorative thingies. Lamp bases in tadelakt, simple wood picture frames. A surprising little shop. ***Dar Bou Ziane***, 20-21 R Sidi el Yamani, Leksour, T044-443349, F443367. Asiatic, Syrian and Moroccan antiques on premises which used to be a flour mill. The place to buy your marble fountain or Damascene mother-of-pearl love seat. Everything for the ideal oriental home including wild wrought iron and ram-horn chandeliers by designer Med. But who knows how many kasbahs were pillaged to stock their antique door section. ***Trésorie du Sud***, R el Mouassine, T044-440439. Small jewellers.

Books

Despite the presence of the Université Cadi Ayyad, Marrakech is not the most intellectual of towns. Nevertheless, there are a few book shops where you can stock up on large coffee table books, maps and recent Moroccan fiction in French. Foreign newspapers can be bought from the stands along Av Mohammed V, and in the large hotels. **Guéliz** *Librairie d'Art ACR*, 55 Blvd Zerktouni, Guéliz (in the ABN Amro arcade, to find it, go left as you face the *Café des Négociants*). Expensive art books and a variety of other reading material, including guides and a few books in English. ***Librairie Chatr***, under the arcades at the top end of Av Mohammed V, near the *Shell* station and the intersection with R Abd el Krim el Khattabi. Best choice of books in the city from coffee table books to novels in English and Atlas Mountain guidebooks (in French). The ***Librairie Gilot***, almost opposite, is not quite as well stocked. **Médina** ***Librairie-Papeterie el Ghazzali***, 51 Bab Agnaou, next to *Café Lipton* just off Jemaâ el Fna. North African novels in French, some maps and guidebooks, also newspapers.

Food & wine

On the Casablanca road, the vast but rather appalling ***Hypermarché Marjane*** stocks just about everything (Europeans can buy alcohol here during Ramadan), as does the central food market in Guéliz. In this market, ***Hassan Oumlile*** (shop 19, sort of in the middle, to the right as one goes through the main entrance) has a good range of booze and will deliver wine to riads in the médina. Telephone your order on T044-433386 (shop opening hours 0800-1400, 1600-late, Fri and Sun 0800-1400). Another, a couple of doors left of the *Hotel Nessim* on Av Mohammed V, is the ***Entrepot alimentaire*** which has a good selection of imported wines and alcohols. Further up the Av Mohammed V, just after the restaurant ***Le Petit Poucet***, a good *épicerie* on the corner of R Mohammed Bequal sells wine and beer. The best known stock-everything shop in Guéliz is ***Achkid*** (which is Tachelhit for 'come along'), coming from the médina, turn left at the *Wafa Bank* on Av Mohammed V, shop is on your left about 30 m beyond the junction.

Country markets

A look in at a country market can be fitted in with an excursion out of Marrakech

Such markets serve local needs, although there are inevitably a number of persistent trinket pushers. Men from the mountain villages come down on mule, bicycle and pick-up truck to stock up on tea and sugar, candles and cigarettes, agricultural produce, maybe have a haircut or a tooth pulled. This is the place to sell a sheep, discuss emigration or a land sale. There may be some Islamists peddling cassettes of sermons, perfumes and religious texts. At such markets, just how different living standards in the countryside are really hits home. The markets are dusty, rough-and-ready sorts of places, people are paying with the tiny brass coins hardly seen in the city. You really feel that people are living from the land, how hard drought can hit them. Country market days as follows: **Ourika** (Mon), **Amizmiz** (Tue), **Tahanaoute** (Tue), **Ouirgane** (Thu), **Setti Fatma** (Thu), **Asni** (Sat) and **Chichaoua** (Sun).

Sport and activities

Ballooning Only an option from Oct to May when the balloon can ride on the thermals. Try T044-303135, prices around 2,000dh for 1 hr. You can't overfly Marrakech, but will get some good views of the surrounding area.

Football The *Kawkab* (KACM) football club of Marrakech, one of the best in Morocco, can be seen at the Stade al Harti, R Moulay El Hassan, Hivernage.

Go-Karting At ***Kart Hotel***, Sud Quad.

Golf ***Royal Golf Club***, 6 km south off the Ouarzazate road (P31), T044-444341. 18-hole course set in orchards, 6,200 m, par 72, fee per round 300dh, club hire 100dh, open daily. ***Palmeraie Golf Palace***, 18-hole, par 72, 6,214 m, fee 350dh, 15 km south of town.

Hammams Try one of those on Riad Zitoun el Kedim or ***Hammam Dar El Bacha***, R Fatima Zohra. This is a large hammam dating from the early 1930s. The vestibule has a huge dome, and inside are 3 parallel marble-floored rooms, the last with underfloor heating. The men's hammam on Souk el Bayadine, just off Derb Debbachi, is handy for the cheap hotels in Kennaria (but has a rather scurrilous reputation). The closest hammam to the Bab Agnaou hotels is the ***Bain Polo***, on the same street as the *Hotel Gallia*. In the Sidi Ben Youssef area are 2 hammams. The bigger one is almost opposite the entrance to the Musée de Marrakech. As this is a poor neighbourhood, so is the clientele. The much older ***Hammam ed Dahab*** is almost opposite the entrance to the Fondation Dar Belarj. Outside the médina, there are more salubrious hammams in the Quartier Majorelle and close to the wholesale market near Bab Doukkala. One of the best hammams, outside weekends, is ***Hammam ez Zohour***, located in Massira III, about 20 mins' drive out of the centre.

Riding At ***Club de l'Atlas*** (Haras Régional), Quartier de la Menara, T044-431301. Or there is ***Club royal équestre***, 4 km along the road to Asni, T044-448529. Most suitable for children are the stables at the ***Palmeraie Golf Palace*** or PGP as it is known to locals.

Skiing The best site is 76 km from Marrakech at Oukaïmeden (see below). Snow irregular.

Swimming At the municipal pool in the ***Moulay Abd es-Salam Garden***, R Abou el Abbes, near the Koutoubia Mosque. Refurbished 2002, open summer only, gets crowded. The water gets a little mucky at the end of the season. Not really for women. There are other municipal pools for SYBA, Daoudiate and the Menara, the best being the one in Daoudiate, a short taxi ride from the centre. The large hotels have pools, not always heated, however ***Sheraton***, ***Tichka*** and ***Méridien-Nfis*** are. The best pool in Marrakech is said to be at the ***Hotel-Club Sangho***, off the Casablanca road.

Tennis ***Royal Tennis Club de Marrakech***, 8 courts, central location at Jnane el Harti, R Oued el Makhazine, T044-431902. 30 tennis courts in hotels.

Trekking ***Atlas Sahara Trek***, 6 bis R Houdhoud, Quartier Majorelle, T044-313901, atlassaharatrek@iam.net.ma One of the best trekking agencies in Marrakech with 20 years' experience. Moroccan-born founder Bernard Fabry knows his deserts well. Did the logistics for the Eco-Challenge. Also runs upmarket accommodation in the Vallée des Aït Bougmez. ***Erg Tours***, 22 Av Mohammed V, T044-438471, F438426. Landrover hire. ***TTM-Trekking Tour Maroc***, 107 R Saad Ben Errabia, Issil, T044 308055, F434520. Offer ski trekking in Toubkal from 15 Jan-30 Apr, camel trekking by the Atlantic coast, mountain walking guides, meals and all camping equipment provided. ***Pampa Voyage (Maroc)***, 203 and 213 Blvd Mohammed V, Guéliz, T044-431052, F446455. Another agency with a good reputation. Small groups will find English-speaking ***Mohamed Nour***, T/F044-302189, very helpful for setting up treks.

Tour operators

See also Trekking, opposite

Menara Tours, 41 R Yougoslavie, T044-446654. Has English speaking staff, runs popular day trips, much used by English tour agencies. Also try ***Atlas Tours***, 40 Av al Mansour Eddahbi, T044-433858. ***Atlas Voyages***, 131 Av Mohammed V, T044-430333.***Sahara Tours***, 182 Av Abdelkrim El Khattabi, T044-430062. ***Wagons Lits Tourisme***, 122 Av Mohammed V, T044-431687. ***Royal Air Maroc***, 197 Av Mohammed V, T044-436205.

Transport

Local

Bus Enquiries, T044-433933. Can be caught from R Moulay Ismaïl, just off the Jemaâ el Fna, and elsewhere along Av Mohammed V and Av Hassan II. No 1 is the most useful, running from Jemaâ el Fna along Av Mohammed V, No 3 and 8 run from the railway station to the bus station, via Jemaâ el Fna, No 10 from Jemaâ el Fna to the bus station, No 11 from the Jemaâ el Fna to the Menara Gardens.

Bicycle/motorcycle hire *Hotel de Foucauld*, Av El Mouahidine, T044-445499. *Peugeot*, 225 Av Mohammed V, several cheaper places in Bani Marine, the road in between R Moulay Ismaïl and R Bab Agnaou.

Experienced throughout Morocco since 1977 in:

INCENTIVES	EXCURSIONS
SEMINARS	HOTEL BOOKINGS
CONGRESSES	CAR HIRE
GROUPS & FITS	AIRLINE TICKETING

Tailor-made programs for groups and individuals with cultural, educational, adventure and leisure interests.
Web: www.menara-tours.ma

Head Office:
41 rue Yougoslavie
40,000 Marrakech
Tel: 212-44-446654
Fax: 212-44-446107

Branch:
Imm. Iguenwane
Blvd. Mohammed V
80,000 Agadir
Tel: 212-48-842732
Fax: 212-48-821108

E-mail: tours@menara-tours.ma

Calèche Green-painted horse-drawn carriages can be hailed along Av Mohammed V, or from the stands at Jemaâ el Fna and Pl de la Liberté. There are fixed prices for tours around the ramparts, other routes are up for negotiation, but they are not normally prohibitively expensive, and this is a pleasant way to see the city.

Car hire 2,000dh for 3 days is a reasonable rate. You should be able to do better, getting something like a small Fiat for 500dh per day, unlimited kilometrage. Avoid the lesser known firms if possible. ***Avis***, 137 Av Mohammed V, T044-433727. ***Europcar Inter-Rent***, 63 Blvd Mohammed Zerktouni, T044-431228, and at the airport. ***Euro Rent***, 9 Av al Mansour Ad-Dahbi, T044-433184. ***Hertz***, 154 Av Mohammed V, T044-434680, airport T044-447230. ***La Royale***, 17 R Mauritanie, T044-447548. A good bet is ***Imzi Tours*** off R de Yougoslavie, take 1st right after *Patisserie Hilton*, T044-433934, F438295. Lesser known firms with more competitive rates are ***Concorde Cars***, 154 Av Mohammed V, T044-431114 (speak English), and ***SAFLOC***, 221 Av Mohammed V, T044-433388. Avoid ***Set Car*** at 213 Av Mohammed V. For 4WD vehicles, agencies with a good reputation include ***Imzitours***, T044-433934/36, imzi_tours@usa.net, ***Ballouty Trans***, T044-447377, F447315, and ***Lune Car***, T044-447743, F447354, lunecar@iam.net.ma

Taxi **Petit taxi**: the city's khaki coloured petits taxis are much in evidence. As you get in, check the driver switches the meter on. From the médina to Guéliz should cost 8-10dh during the day, 10-15dh during the late evening and night. A journey out to the *Marjane* supermarket from Guéliz will cost nearly 20dh. Few journeys should cost much more than this. Major ranks are to be found in Jemaâ el Fna, at the Gare Routiere by Bab Doukkala, and outside the *marché municipal*, Guéliz. **Grand taxi**: normally more expensive, can be found at the railway station and the major hotels. They also run over fixed routes, mainly to outlying suburbs, from Jemaâ el Fna and Bab Doukkala, most rides cost 3dh/1 person when there are 6 people squeezed in.

Long distance

Air Aéroport Marrakech Menara, T044-447862, is 6 km west of the city, by the Menara Gardens, and clearly signposted from the centre. There are flights to **Casablanca** (2 a day), as well as to **Brussels** (Fri), **Geneva** (Sun), daily to **Paris** and almost daily to **London** and to **Madrid**.

Airline offices: *RAM*, 197 Av Mohammed V, T044-436205/446444, information T044-447865, open 0830-1215, 1430-1900. The ever helpful ***Menara Tours***, 41 R de Yougoslavie next to the *Café Atlas*, is the representative for *British Airways*, T044-446654. ***Airstar***, 33 R Loubnane, Guéliz, T/F044-435502, provides an excursion and transfer service in southern Morocco. Try also ***Maint'aero*** (Vincent Duroc/Patrick Simon), T044-300658. Has a small Cesna, subcontracts with other agencies. Helicopter transfers by ***Hélisud Maroc***, 2 R Ibn Aicha, Guéliz, T044-438438, F420488.

Road **Bus**: Run from the gare routière at Bab Doukkala, T044-433933, which is easily reached by taxis and local buses. There is often a choice between a number of different companies with different prices and times. Long distance buses – when leaving Marrakech, as there is more than 1 bus company, make sure the number of the booth where the tickets are bought matches the bus stop number where you intend to catch the bus. Always be there in advance even if the bus does not leave on time. It is worth trying the bus driver with 10dh for a seat near the front. Most CTM departures are from the office near the *Cinéma Colisée* in Guéliz. Destinations include **Casablanca**, **Ouarzazate**, **El Rachidia**, **M'hamid**, **Beni Mellal**, **Agadir** and **Laâyoune**. There are also private line services to **Beni Mellal**, **El Kelaa des Sraghna**, **Rabat**, **El Jadida** (very slow), **Essaouira** (best service with *Supratours*), **Ouarzazate** and **Skoura**, **Agadir** (also very slow), **Safi**, **Taroudant** (2 a day), as well as to **Asni**, **Oualidia**, **Khouribga** and **Demnate**. It is wise to call at the station the previous day as some services, notably across the High Atlas to **Taroudant** and **Ouarzazate**, leave early in the morning. There are *CTM* services to **Paris** every day except Fri and Sun at 1700, cost 1,150dh. The private line alternative leaves at 1200. *CTM* services for **Agadir** and **Casablanca** can also be taken from Guéliz, in Blvd Mohammed Zerktouni, but places should be reserved a day in advance. Buses to the **Ourika Valley**, **Asni** and **Moulay Brahim** run from Bab Rob. **Grands taxis:** running over fixed routes, with fixed prices, leave from a variety of places around the city. For **Ourika**, **Asni** and **Ouirgane**, leave from Bab Rob. For most other destinations, including **Chichaoua**, **Essaouira** and **Agadir**, go to Bab Doukkala. For destinations east, check out Bab Doukkala or Bab el Khemis.

Train The railway station is in Guéliz, on Av Hassan II, T044-447768. Although there are very long-term plans for an extension of the line south to Agadir and Laâyoune, at present *ONCF* operates only bus services to the south, connecting with the arrival of the express trains. Express trains for **Casablanca** (3 hrs) and **Rabat** (4 hrs) leave at 0900, 1230, 1400 and 1900, and non-express services at 0700, 1705, 2050 and 0130. Timetable subject to modification during Ramadan and major public holidays.

Directory

Banks

The main concentrations of ATMs are on R Bab Agnaou, on Av Mohammed V next to the *RAM* agency and near the rond-point Abd el Moumen, Guéliz. As elsewhere in Morocco, ATMs can go unpredictably off-line. If stuck at weekends and public holidays, then the *BMCI*, almost opposite the *Cinéma Colisée* on Blvd Zerktouni, is open 0930-1130 and 1600-1900. Otherwise it opens 0900-1300 and 1500-1900. ***ABM***, 55 Blvd Zerktouni, T044-448912. ***Banque Al Maghrib***, Jemaâ el Fna, T044-442037. ***Banque Populaire***, 69 Av Mohammed V, T044-434851. ***BCM***, Blvd Zerktouni, T044-434805. ***BMCI***, Blvd Mohammed Zerktouni. ***Credit du Maroc***, Av Mohammed V, T044-434851. ***SGMB***, 59 R de Yougoslavie, T044-448702. ***Wafa Bank***, 213 Av Mohammed V, T044-433840. **American Express**: ***Voyages Schwartz***, Immeuble Moutaouakil, R Mauritania, T044-433321.

Communications

Internet **Internet cafés**: try those signed off the pedestrian R Bab Agnaou or in the building opposite the *Cinéma Colisée* in Guéliz. Also ***Cyberland***, 61 R de Yougoslavie, passage Ghandouri, No 46, T044-436977. Small and friendly, in centre of Guéliz. There is another close to the Jardin Majonelle. **Post** *Central PTT* for post is normally very busy. For telegrams, poste restante and payphones outside, head for the big post office on Pl du 16 Novembre, Guéliz, open till 1800. There is also a reasonable post/telephone office on the Jemaâ el Fna. There are now plenty of *télé-boutiques* scattered across the city – just keep your eyes open. Close to Jemaâ el Fna, there is one on Derb Debbachi (on your right, after the *Café-Hotel de France*).

Embassies & consulates

French Consulate, R Ibn Khaldoun, right next to the Koutoubiya Mosque, T044-444006. Open 0830-1145.

Medical services

Chemists: ***Pharmacie Centrale***, 166 Av Mohammed V, T044-430151. ***Pharmacie de Paris***, 120 Av Mohammed V. At the Jemaâ el Fna, end of R Bab Agnaou, there are a couple of pharmacies, also next to *Café de France*. The préfecture operates an all-night pharmacy, the ***Dépôt de nuit***, which looks like a ticket window on Pl Jamaâ el Fna (with the Koutoubia behind you, turn left after the stone wall of the Club Med compound). You may have to queue for some time. There is an all-night chemist, ***Pharmacie de Nuit***, at R Khalid Ben Oualid, T044-430415. **Dentists**: Dr Hamid Laraqui, 203 Av Mohammed V, T044-433216, and Dr E Gailleres, 112 Av Mohammed V, both speak English. **Doctor on call**: T044-404040 (ambulance service too), SAMU T044-433030. **Doctors**: Dr Ahmed Mansouri, R de Sebou, T044-430754, and Dr Perez, 169 Av

Mohammed V, T044-431030. Both speak English. **Private hospital**: ***Polyclinique du Sud***, 2 R de Yougoslavie, T044-447999, F432424, green number T08002525. ***Polyclinique Les Narcisses***, Camp el Ghoul, 112 Route de Targa (behind the Petit marché), T044-447575. Also try ***Clinique Ibn Tofail***, R Ibn Abd el Malik, Quartier des Hôpitaux, Guéliz, T044-438718, F438717, T061-181370 (mob) (Dr Driss Bouyousfi).

Useful addresses

Emergency services **Private ambulance service**: 10 R Fatima Zohra, T044-443724. **Fire**: R Khalid Ben Oualid, T16. **Police**: R Ibn Hanbal, T19. **Garages** ***Peugeot***: Toniel S A, R Tarik Ibn Ziad. ***Renault***: CRA, 55-61 Av Mohammed V, T044-432015. Others are ***Auto Hall***, R de Yougoslavie, and ***Garage Ourika***, 66 Av Mohammed V, T044-430155.

The Toubkal High Atlas

Phone code: 044
Colour map 2, grid B4

Note that much fuller details of all these areas can be found in the Footprint Handbook to Marrakech and the High Atlas

In easy day-trip distance of Marrakech, the High Atlas of Toubkal has long been a draw for tourists. In addition to the Toubkal National Park, named for Jbel Toubkal, the highest peak in North Africa, the region also has some excursions, including the much-visited Ourika and the ski resort of Oukaïmeden. Up the Nfis Valley, there are pleasant hotels at the mountain retreat of Ouirgane, and the striking, restored mosque of Tin Mal, on the spectacular road to the Tizi-n-Test pass. Heading south from Marrakech in the Ouarzazate direction – and still within day-trip distance – is another striking high pass, the Tizi-n-Tichka, and the village of Telouet with its brooding Glaoui fortress. You can travel on south across the Atlas by road, or, in a 4WD vehicle, take the rough mountain tracks from Telouet down to Tamdacht and the famed kasbah of Aït Ben Haddou, just north of Ouarzazate.

The Toubkal region began to become well known to trekkers back in the 1970s. The landscapes are spectacular and for walkers there are plenty of bivouac and accommodation opportunities. For the less energetic, many interesting parts of the region can be visited as part of an organized 4WD excursion from Marrakech. Particularly popular are trips up onto the Plateau du Kik and across from the Ourika to the The problem is that certain treks, including the ascent of Toubkal (referred to by one French climber as being a 'boulevard-type' hike), are almost too popular in the summer season. Nevertheless, there are plenty of alternative routes. If not hiking with a foreign-based tour company, you should be able to work out some sort of interesting route to suite your capabilities with an experienced local guide, contacted via *Hotel Ali* in Marrakech or in a trail-head village.

Up the Amizmiz Road

Take the main S501 road south out of Marrakech (straight over at the junction near the Hivernage). A few kilometres after the Club royal equestre, the road forks. You go left for Asni (S501), right for Amizmiz in the foothills of the Atlas. The road passes through a number of small settlements, including Tamesloht, and the Lalla Takerkoust Lake, where accommodation is available.

Tamesloht, 3 km to the west of the S507, is a typical rural settlement on the Haouz Plain. Agriculture has been much effected by the drought, and those with the means to run a water pump are needing to bring water up from even greater depths. On the main road you will pass shops selling the large terracotta food storage jars now popular for plants in the tasteful houses of Marrakech.

Oumnass is a poor settlement of packed-earth houses. A wealthy European has a discrete fortified retreat at the nearby village of Tagadirt. Here a

Five things to do in the west and central High Atlas.

- In winter, take a drive up to **Oukaïmeden** to see the snow and Morocco's premier ski resort in action.
- A couple of nights out in the mountains. Climb North Africa's highest mountain, **Jbel Toubkal**. With a week in hand, do a walking circuit in the area.
- Drive the Taroudant road for **Ouirgane** (lunch stop) and **Tin Mal** and its (heavily) restored Almohad mosque.
- Take a summer day trip from Marrakech to **Demnate** and the **Imi-n-Ifri** cavern, then on to the crashing **Cascades d'Ozoud** near **Azilal**.
- Head up to the **Vallée des Aït Bougmez** near Tabant for a spot of trekking.

British-Moroccan company has constructed a new kasbah-retreat hotel, *Le Caravan' Serai* (see Sleeping below). A few kilometres further on, the road reaches the small gorges of the Oued Nfis below the Barrage Cavagnac, now renamed **Barrage Lalla Takerkoust**. A turn-off left takes you on a road around the shores of the 7-km long lake. In recent years water levels have been extremely low. Restaurants and campsites, once right on the lake shores, now find themselves 100 m or more from the water. After this detour, going back down the lake shore road, you return to the main road which takes you on to Amizmiz, 21 km further on.

Around Marrakech

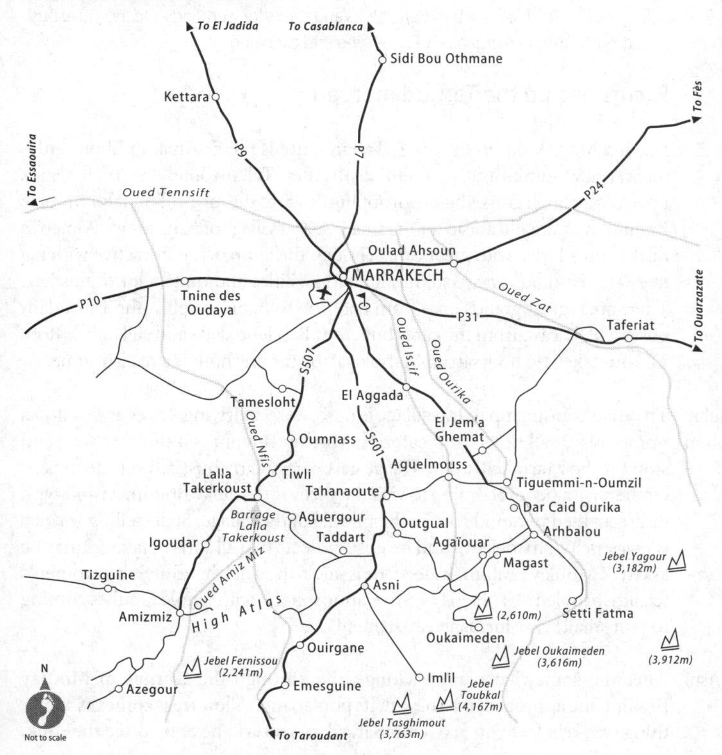

Amizmiz, 55 km southwest from Marrakech at the end of the S507, is a growing rural centre interesting as the starting point of some pleasant hikes and a Tuesday souk. There are regular buses (2½ hours), and much quicker grands taxis, to and from Bab Rob in Marrakech. The post office, bank and internet café are all situated in a new district on the main road as you arrive from Marrakech.

Turning off right just after the 'administrative zone', you can wind up into the foothills to the *maison forestière*. Parking in the shade, there is some gentle walking along a track above the Assif Anougal, with views down over the villages. From Amizmiz, there is also a metalled road eastwards to **Ouirgane**, via the Tizi-n-Ouzla (1,090 m), where you have a view of the Assif Amassine valley, with the Toubkal Massif as backdrop. There then follows a winding descent to the junction with the S501, where you can go right for Ouirgane (accommodation) or left for Asni and Marrakech.

In a wet year, clay hillside may crumble onto the upper sections of the Amizmiz to Ouirgane road

Sleeping Before you reach Amizmiz, there are several options if you want to make an overnight stop. At the expensive end of the market, at **Ouled Ben Rahmoun**, there is the **L** *Le Caravan' Serai*, T044-300302. On the same lines, with a larger pool, is **L** *Tigmi Tagadert*, T061-124422 (mob), www.tigmi.com A suite will knock you back 3,000dh. If sustainable tourism interests you, then there is an interesting initiative near **Tamesloht**, 100 m off the main road, the simple **B** *Ferme d'accueil*, T061-342837, look out for yellow signs, run on a sustainable basis by Myriem and Mustapha Nassef. They have 2 small guest chalets and will be operating their venture as an educational farm. At **Lalla Takerkoust**, on the lake shores, is the country style **C** *Relais du Lac*, T044-484924, which has accommodation for up to 20 people in small bungalows. This would be ideal for kids, combined with 3 nights in a riad in Marrakech. In the neighbouring restaurant area, the Relais also has 185 places in traditional tents and caters for weddings and incentive business groups. They can organize VTT, trekking and canoeing.

Excursions up the Taroudant road

Leaving Marrakech on the S501, **Tahanaoute** is the first main ribbon settlement (new administrative buildings). After Tahanaoute, the road winds upwards through gorges before dropping down to the turn-off right for Moulay Brahim. (Go straight ahead for the small market village of Asni, a few kilometres further on.) Drive with great care. Though the approach is attractive with tall trees and rustling cane, Asni has limited facilities and quite a lot of hustlers. There are regular grands taxis from Bab Rob to Asni, as well as the Taroudant buses which leave from the gare routière at Bab Doukkala and call at Bab Rob. The bus takes 1½ hours from Marrakech, by car one hour is a realistic time.

Moulay Brahim

The road winding up to the village is narrow, so if driving, take care. With its numerous small hotels and eateries, Moulay Brahim is a popular weekend stop for the Marrakchis. The village gets particularly busy from June to September, with people coming to visit the shrine of Moulay Brahim, visible with its green-tiled pyramid roof in the middle of the village. Stalls selling various scraggy pelts, chameleons and incense indicate that all sorts of favours may be asked of Moulay Brahim. Indeed, he is said to be a dab hand at fixing women's fertility problems. There is a festive atmosphere, with whole families coming to rent small semi-furnished apartments.

Asni

After the somewhat nerve-racking drive through the **Gorges of Moulay** Brahim, the approach to Asni with its poplar and willow trees comes as something of a relief. If you arrive on Saturday, you will be able to see the souk, (located in a big dusty enclosure on your left as you come from Marrakech) with its accompanying chaos of grands taxis, mules and minibuses. The village is in fact quite extensive, with houses scattered in clusters in the valley. Asni is a good place for a quick break en route to Ouirgane, Tin Mal or Taroudant, or on to the Toubkal National Park, if you can deal with the attentions of the trinket sellers. The Saturday market attracts locals from the surrounding valleys and a few tourist 4WDs. Walkers may want to set up a trek into the country around Asni. There are good routes along the **Plateau du Kik** to the west of Asni, north to Moulay Brahim and southwest to Ouirgane.

A popular 4WD excursion takes you from Marrakech to Asni, up to Moulay Brahim and thence up above the village onto the Plateau du Kik (see local map Amizmiz NH-29XXII-2). From here you may drop down to the villages around **Tiferouine** before heading some 8 km northwest across country to the settlement of **Lalla Takerkoust** and its reservoir lake. Tourist agency trips tend to picnic at encampments near the receding lake shore. The return north to Marrakech is on the S507 Tizi-n-Test road.

Sleeping The main option used to be the **D** ***Grand Hotel de Toubkal***, a converted kasbah, at the south end of the village. At the time of writing, the hotel was closed. If stuck, check out the small hotel opposite the entrance to the souk – although you will do best to carry on to Imlil. ***Youth hostel***, on Route d'Imlil at far end of village where the road goes out left to Imlil, T044-447713. Take sleeping bags, blankets can be hired, can be cold in winter, 40 beds, quite spartan but beautiful setting, kitchen, overnight fee 20dh, open all year, open to non-members.

Eating Limited choice available. In the centre of the village are a number of stalls and cafés cooking *harira* soup and tagines. This is the last major place to stock up on basic supplies for a visit to the Toubkal region.

Transport Buses/taxis to Imlil go from just south of the youth hostel.

Ouirgane

Ouirgane is another pleasant place to pause on the S501, about one hour's drive (61 km) from Marrakech. The settlement's houses are scattered on the the valley sides, out of reach of flash-flood prone Oued Nfiss. Ouirgane can be reached by bus from Marrakech (the Taroudant service), or by grand taxi from Asni. The four main hotels in Ouirgane have good food and offer the opportunity to explore the valley in easy rambles.

Sleeping and eating **L** ***Le Val de la Roseraie***, BP 769, Marrakech 40000, T044-439128, booksings@laroseraie.com Peaceful hotel set in extensive gardens, with 23 a/c rooms, 2 restaurants, bar, hammam, hydrotherapy centre, tennis, horse riding, outdoor pool and small indoor pool. The *Roseraie* has a well-established clientele, but is said to be on the expensive side for the level of services on offer. Food variable. **B** ***Auberge Au Sanglier Qui Fume***, T044-485707/8, F485709, address CP 42150, Ouirgane, Marrakech. Small country hotel run by a French couple, the Poucets, daughter and son-in-law of the Thévenins who founded the auberge back in 1945. It has 22 chalet-style rooms, a restaurant serving excellent French country food, a bar, tennis and a pool in the summer, and would make a nice stop-off for a family. Mountain bikes for rent, and the management will put you in touch with guides should you wish to do some walking. Horse riding by arrangement with the neighbouring *Roseraie*. **B** ***La Bergerie***, about 2 km before Ouirgane village as you come from Marrakech, turn off right for Marigha, signposted, French management, T044-485716, F485718, labergerie13@hotmail.com, www.passionmaroc.com, postal address BP 64

Marrakech. Set in 5 ha of grounds in a valley away from the village, 8 nice rooms in a farm-type atmosphere. Meal without wine about 150dh. Highly recommended. **B-C** *Chez Momo*, T044-4485704, F485727, reservations unreliable, otherwise recommended. Finally, cheap rooms in private homes opposite the *Auberge Au Sanglier* have been recommended. For reasonably priced eating, on the Tizi-n-Test side of Ouirgane, there is the ***Restaurant Le Mouflon***, T044-485722. Tagines as per usual, 60-75dh per head.

Tin Mal

Colour map 2, grid B3

Tin Mal is a small settlement high in the Atlas mountains, off the S501 from Marrakech to Taroudant. Once upon a time, it was the holy city of the Almohad Dynasty. For the non-Muslim visitor, it offers a rare opportunity to see the interior of a major mosque, with examples of 12th-century Almohad decor intact amidst the ruins.

Getting there & around

Tin Mal is 100 km from Marrakech (about 1¾ hrs drive, taking things easy), just past the village of Ijoukak. If you are not driving, you can take a Taroudant bus or a grand taxi as far as Ijoujak, where there are several basic cafés with rooms. Just after the village, on the right, is the Talat-n-Yacoub Kasbah, home of the Goundafi clan, who formerly ruled the area, and a ruined summer pavilion with a ribbed dome, and further along, on the left, another kasbah of the Goundafi family. Carry on walking, and across the river to the right can be seen the square structure of the Tin Mal Mosque, built 1153-54. Cross the river on the next bridge (often impassable by car), and walk up past Tin Mal village to the mosque.

Background

To appreciate Tin Mal, fast rewind back to the early 12th century. In 1122, one Ibn Toumert, after much roaming in search of wisdom, returned to Morocco. He created too much trouble in Marrakech with his criticisms of the effete Almoravids, and shortly after, when the mountain tribes had sworn to support him and fight the Almoravids in the name of the doctrines he had taught them, he was proclaimed Mahdi, the rightly guided one. In 1125 Ibn Toumert established his capital at Tin Mal, an anonymous sort of hamlet strategically situated in the heartlands of his tribal supporters. The rough and ready village was replaced with a walled town, soon to become spiritual centre of an empire, a sort of Muslim Lhasa. The first mosque was a simple affair. The building you see today, a low square structure, was the work of Ibn Toumert's successor, Abd el Mu'min – a student whom the future Mahdi had met in Bejaïa.

Looking across at the mosque from the Taroudant road, you need to imagine it surrounded by a walled town, with banners on the ramparts and smoke rising from the hearths. Tin Mal was the first *ribat*, as the austere Almohad fortresses were called – and subject to a puritan discipline. The Mahdi himself, the very infallible imam, was by all accounts a sober, chaste person, an enemy of luxurious living. All his efforts went into persuading his followers of the truths of Islam – as he conceived them. In fact, his task was not unlike that of the Prophet Mohammed at Medina back in the early days of Islam: how to build a unified community out of a heterogeneous set of tribespeople. There was a council of 50 elders to represent the tribes – who cannot have willingly given up their independence.

Tin Mal was subject to a pitiless discipline. Prayers were led by the Mahdi himself and all had to attend. Public whippings and the threat of execution kept those lacking in religious fervour in line. As well as prayer leader, the Mahdi was judge, hearing and trying cases himself according to Muslim law – which had barely begun to penetrate the mountain regions.

Warriors from the mountains

Visiting remote Tin Mal, you need to imagine your way back to early medieval times, when Islam was not as stable as it is today – and when the narrow rocky valleys of the Atlas Mountains must have been very remote indeed. One Ibn Toumert, a Masmouda Berber born around 1080 in the Anti-Atlas, was to found a religio-politico movement which was to overthrow dynasties and control the whole of North Africa. In 1106, Ibn Toumert set out for Cordoba – and later the Middle East, in search of learning. On his return to his native Atlas in 1117, he had very definite ideas about what a good Muslim should be. His basic principle was that the true Muslim could not be satisfied merely with carrying out the religious obligations of Islam – he would take it upon himself to ensure that others did so too.

The year 1121 found Ibn Toumert in Marrakech, the capital of the Almoravids, denouncing the use of musical instruments and other forms of pleasure ... He raised an uproar in the capital by declaring that it was unbefitting for the Emir, Ali Ben Youssef, to wear the litham *or veil of the men of the desert, and told him that the dyed mat on which he sat in the mosque was ritually unclean because of the droppings used in the dye. The Emir could not ignore these provocations, and summoned the troublesome Ibn Toumert to a debate with the religious leaders. Needless to say, Ibn Toumert got the better of them – and the court savants advised the Emir to put him to death. Unfortunately for the Almoravid dynasty, the Emir's great piety prevented him from doing this; he merely banished Ibn Toumert from Marrakesh, even though he had thrown the Emir's sister her horse when he saw her riding along unveiled.*

Ibn Toumert withdrew to the mountains to preach his doctrine of the unity of God – and the stage was set for a major rebellion, as our dour religious leader preached ardently to the Masmouda Berbers. In 1125 he settled at Tin Mal, and gradually built up a strong community whom he called el-muwahhidoun *'unitarians', hence the term Almohad, a Spanish corruption of the Arabic name. Tin Mal was an ideal HQ, for the enemy Almoravid forces were composed of cavalry which could not operate along the twisting, dangerous mule tracks of the Nfis valley.*

In 1130 Ibn Toumert died, but his work was carried on by his right-hand man Abd el Mu'min, aged just 36. It is said that Ibn Toumert's death was kept secret for three years, time enough for his successor to establish his authority. 1144 saw the final rout of the Almoravids near Tlemcen, and Marrakech fell in 1147. Abd el-Mu'min was to lead the Almohad movement for over 30 years, unifying North Africa under his rule. Perhaps the most impressive thing of all in this tale is the power of an austere set of ideas to give scattered tribes the drive to build an empire.

Tin Mal mosque

Standing in the quiet mosque, today mostly open to the sky, looking down the carefully restored perspectives of the arcades, it is difficult to imagine what a hive of religious enthusiasm this place must have been. And after Ibn Toumert's death, it was to remain so, as his simple tomb became the focal point for a mausoleum for the Almohad sovereigns.

The prototype for Tin Mal was the Great Mosque at Taza (near Fes), also built by Abd el Mumin. The Koutoubia at Marrakech (Almohad capital as of 1147) was in turn modelled on it. Completed in 1154, also under Abd el Mumin, the Tin Mal Mosque has a simple exterior. (Was there once an elaborate minaret?) The *mihrab* (prayer niche) is built into the minaret. To the left, as one stands before the *mihrab*, is the imam's entrance, to the right is a space for the minbar, the preacher's chair, which would have been pulled out for sermons. The decoration is simple: there are several cupolas with restored areas of stalactite plasterwork and there are examples of the *darj w ktaf* and palmette motifs, but little inscription. The technique used, basically plaster applied to brick, is a forerunner of later, larger Almohad decorative schemes.

Essentially, the Tin Mal Mosque marks the firm establishment of Ibn Toumert's doctrine under his successor, his long-standing follower and companion, Abd el Mumin, who was to lead the Almohad armies into Marrakech. But although the new empire acquired a fine capital well located on the plain, Tin Mal was to remain its spiritual heart – and a sort of reliable rear base. It was to Tin Mal that Abd el Mumin sent the treasures of Ibn Tachfin the Almoravid.

The tombs of Ibn Toumert, Abd el Mumin, Abu Ya'qub and Abu Youssef were at Tin Mal as well and the town became venerated as a pilgrimage centre, even after the Merinid destruction of 1275-76. The tombs inspired deep respect – and Ibn Toumert became a great saint – quite the reverse of what he would have wanted. The Almohad rulers, whenever they were to undertake a military expedition, would visit Tin Mal to seek success.

The end of the Almohads

Eventually, the Almohads were to collapse in internecine struggles. The final act came in the 1270s. The last Almohads took refuge in Tin Mal, led by the Vizir Ibn Attouch. However, the governor of Marrakech, El Mohalli (named by the rising Merinid sovereign), isolated the tiny Almohad group in their mountain retreat. In 1275 the Almohads made a last desperate attempt to retake Marrakech – without success. El Mohalli pursued them into their mountain fastness, and besieged and took the seemingly impenetrable town. The Vizir died in battle and the Almohad caliph and his followers were taken prisoner and executed. But the winners went even further. An adventurer, one Abu Ali (who after a failed revolt against the Almohads had taken refuge with the Merinids), decided to take his revenge. The great Almohad sovereigns, Abu Yaqoub and Abu Youssef, were pulled from their tombs and decapitated. The Merinid sultan is said to have been scandalized. The Almohads, one time conquerors of the whole of the Maghreb and much of Spain, were destroyed in their very capital, barely 150 years after they had swept away the Almoravids.

Restoration of the mosque

When Tin Mal was studied and surveyed by French art historians in the 1920s, the mosque was in an advanced state of decay. The tombs had long since disappeared, the rigour and puritanism of Almohad Islam belonged to the remote past. Strange cults has taken over in the abandoned sanctuary: the inhabitants of the region came to venerate the stone of Sidi Wegweg. The central authorities rejected the Caïd Goundafi's proposal to restore the mosque – fearing perhaps a revival of a long-vanished dynasty?

In the early 1990s, the state of the mosque came to the attention of a charitable foundation of the *ONA*, Morocco's largest conglomerate. Six million dirhams (circa £400,000) was put forward for restoration work. Only local materials were used, although a special lime for repairing the plasterwork came from Spain. Cedar from Azrou was used for the ceilings. No cement or concrete was used: the restoration is as ecological as can be. There remains, however, the question of the site museum. Will there eventually be a display of the unique square silver coins struck by the Almohads at Tin Mal? The spiritual heart of a medieval Muslim Empire has survived. The villagers, who for centuries had a decaying basilica-mosque at their disposal, now live next to what might one day become a major stop on the heritage tourism trail. Or alternately, the mosque may return fully fledged to religious use. As it is, it is used for Friday prayers.

Onward to Taroudant via the Tizi-n-Test

The S501 from Marrakech to Taroudant is one of the most spectacular routes in Morocco, winding its way up and then down through the High Atlas mountains, above the beautiful valleys and past isolated villages, eventually reaching the Tizi-n-Test pass, with its breathtaking views across the Sous valley to the Anti Atlas mountains. There are buses between the two cities, although check that they are *par Tizi-n-Test*. Driving has been possible since the road, a traditional trading route, was formally opened in 1928, following the work of French engineers. Some of its sections are a bit scary, but it is a highly recommended experience, particularly when tied in with visits to Asni, Ouirgane and Tin Mal. Signs on the exit to Marrakech will indicate if the pass is open. The S501 joins the P32 from Taroudant to Ouarzazate.

For a lunch stop on this route, there is the cheap *Restaurant La Belle Vue*, about 1 km after the pass on the Taroudant side. Cheap rooms available, have sleeping bag ready – it gets cold at 2,100 m altitude.

Trekking in the Toubkal National Park

Ins and outs

Getting there

Toubkal National Park is reached by a road/track, which leads off left after the centre of Asni and the *Grand Hotel de Toubkal*. For those without transport either hike or negotiate a grand taxi, easy to find especially on market day. It is possible to walk from Asni to Imlil, or to Tachedirt, which has a refuge run by the *Club Alpin Français*, information, T022-270090, F297292.

Getting around

Walking Options include the **Aremd circuit**, a refreshing hike through remote villages and past breathtaking views, and a hike to the **Lac d'Ifni**. Another is to walk to **Setti Fatma**, in the Ourika Valley. Much more challenging is to climb **Jbel Toubkal**, the highest mountain in North Africa at 4,167 m. It is necessary to break the walk at the ***Club Alpin Français Toubkal Refuge*** (ex-Refuge Neltner), a simple dormitory place with no meals at 3,106 m. In winter this is a difficult trek and full equipment is essential. A wise plan is to purchase specialist hiking books (such as Robin Collomb's *Atlas Mountains*) and maps (ie the 1:100,000 scale Oukaïmeden/Toubkal map, feuille/sheet NH-29-XXIII-1) for the region before arriving, possibly available at the *Hotel Ali* in Marrakech. More up to date, with extremely detailed indications for walking in the Toubkal region, is Richard Knight's *Trekking in the Moroccan Atlas* (Hindhead: Trailblazer, 2001). Mules and guides can be hired in Imlil, most easily in the *Refuge* or at *Ribat Tours*.

Imlil

Phone code: 044
Colour map 2, grid B4
Altitude 1,790 m
17 km S-SE from Asni

Imlil is the most important village of the Aït Mizane Valley. It is the start of the walks in this area. In the centre of the village is the car park/taxi area with the stone-built Club Alpin Français (CAF) hut at the corner of the road, guides hut and *Café du Soleil*. There are numerous small cafés and shops, a good baker and a travel agent. Mules are 'parked' to the south of the village, on the left, before the junction. There is a utilitarian concrete route indicator on the right, should you be unsure of your direction. When you arrive, you may be besieged by lots of underemployed blokes, keen to help you in some way or other.

Sleeping & eating

In Imlil, the top option is the **C** ***Kasbah de Toubkal***, T044-485611, F485636. Contact also UK office: *Discover Ltd*, Timbers, Godstone RH9 8AD, T01883-744392, F744913. The kasbah (which played the role of a Tibetan fortress in director Martin Scorsese's film

Kundun) has dormitory-type accommodation much used by student and British public school groups, and a couple of very nice rooms on the terrace. The building, once HQ of the local caïd, has been well restored and for a 20dh contribution to the local development fund, you can have mint tea and walnuts on the roof terrace. More reasonably, try **D** ***Atlas Gîte***, T/F022-485609, manager Jean-Pierre Fouilloux. 3 double rooms, 2 larger rooms. Will advise on setting up treks. A good little address. Cheaper options are **F** ***Café du Soleil***, a tiny and basic place; the **F** ***Etoile de Toubkal*** (8 rooms), T044-449767, F434396; the **F** ***Hotel-Café El Aïne***, as you arrive in the village from Asni on your right (best rooms upstairs), or the **F** ***Refuge du Club Alpin Français*** (no reservations), which provides clean but minimal facilities. 40 beds in dormitories, open all year round, more expensive if you aren't a CAF member. For information try T022-270090. The ***Café Aksoual***, opposite the CAF, also has some very cheap, rudimentary rooms.

The *Bureau des Guides*, in the centre of the village, can provide information on accommodation in local homes. The locals who are used to walkers are generally anxious to provide a floor or mattresses to sleep on. *Aït Idr Mohammed* in Targa Imoula, just through Imlil, has been recommended for accommodation and hire of mules and guides. Information is available through ***Ribat Tours***, the ***Hôtel-Café Soleil*** and at the CAF refuge.

Climbing Toubkal

Having a local Tachelhit-speaking guide is essential on treks

There are a number of routes up North Africa's highest peak. Imlil is often the departure point for groups heading for the mountain. The least technical route, which requires a little scrambling from the Neltner Refuge to the summit, is used by several thousand visitors each year. A good guide, mule back-up and the correct equipment are essential.

Best time to visit The best time for walking is after the main snows, at blossom time in the spring. Mules cannot negotiate passes until Mar/Apr. For some, summers are too hot, visibility in the heat haze is poor. Nov-Feb is too cold and there is too much snow for walking, although frozen ground is often more comfortable than walking on the ever-moving scree. Deep snows and ice present few problems to those with ropes, ice axes, crampons and experience. Without these – stay away in winter.

Tours Customized walking tours are organized by Hamish M Brown, ***AMIS***, 26 Kircaldy Rd, Burntisland, Fife KY3 9HQ, Scotland, who also provides maps, briefing sheets and sound advice. He has been walking in these mountains for over 30 years. Other recommended group walking tour operators are listed on pages 19 and 355.

Maps Walking in the Toubkal area requires the following 1:100,000 scale maps: Tizi-n-Test (NH-29-XVI-4), Toubkal (NH-29-XXIII-1) and Amizmiz (NH-29-XXII-2).

Imlil to Jbel Toubkal Imlil is the end of the surfaced road but it is possible to reach **Aremd** (also spelt Aroumd) by car up the rough track. Takes about 45 minutes to walk. *Café Lac d'Ifni* makes a good stop here. Sidi Chamharouchouch is reached in another 2½ hours, going steadily uphill. It is important to bear right after the *marabout* to find the initially very steep, but later steady slope up to the **Nelter Refuge** (3,207 m). Allow 4½ hours from Imlil. The *Neltner Refuge*, with dormitory space for 30 persons, US$5 per night, is often crowded. On the plus side, the warden sells bottled water, soft drinks, and can do food for small groups. Campers using level site below the hut can use the facilities.

Jbel Toubkal by the South Cwm

This is the usual approach for walkers, a long day's walking and scrambling if you want to do up and back. The route is clearer on the map than it is on the ground. First observe the route from the rear of the Neltner Refuge and the large boulders on the skyline. These are a point to aim for. Leave the refuge and go down to the river. Cross over and up the other side is the main path to the foot of the first of the many screes. Take the scree path up to the boulders which can be reached in just over an hour. From there is a choice, the long scree slope to the north of the summit or the shorter, steeper slope to the south of the summit ridge. Either way, allow 3½ hours.

The summit is not in itself attractive, especially if people are making calls from their mobile phones. (Who carried up the pieces of iron for the strange pointed structure on the top?) The stone shelters make fairly comfortable overnight camping for a good view of sunrise. Views are excellent – if there is no heat haze – to the Jbels Saghro and Siroua but as the summit here (4,167

Jbel Toubkal region

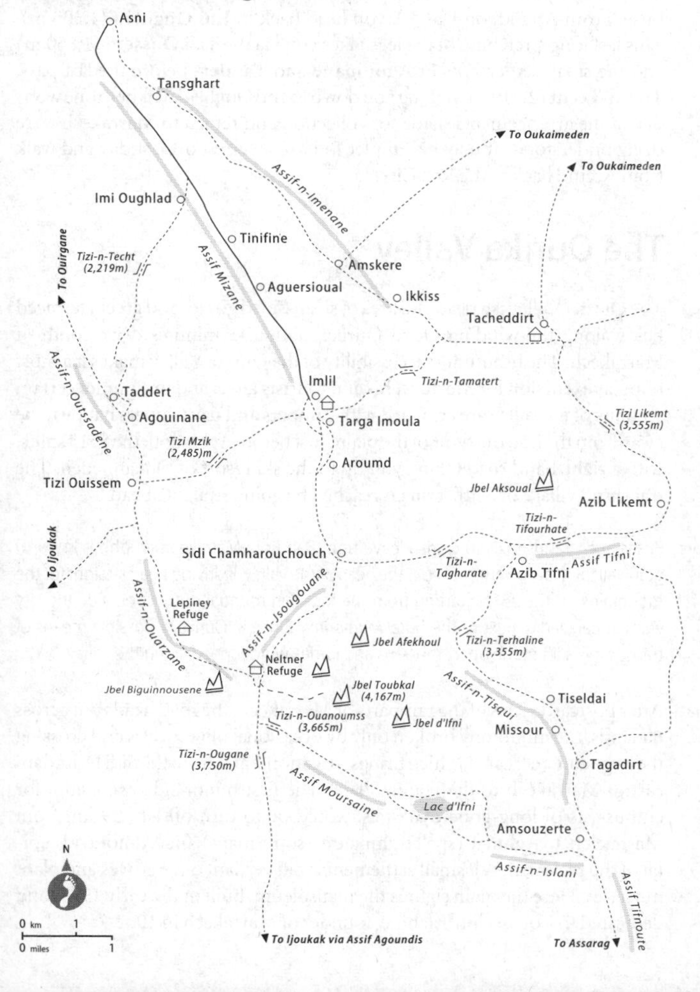

m) is a plateau other views are limited. Be prepared for low temperatures at this altitude and for the bitter winds that blow three out of four days in the spring and autumn. The descent is quicker, allow 2-2½ hours.

The Toubkal Circuit

This circuit starts and ends at Asni

In 10 days, a good walking circuit can give you a feel for life in the High Atlas and take in Jbel Toubkal too. The accompanying map shows the main overnights. Day 1 would take you from **Imi Oughlad** or **Aguersioual** to **Amskere**. On Day 2, the first full day getting used to the mountains, a 5-hour trek takes you to **Tacheddirt**. A long Day 3 runs via the **Tizi Likemt** (3,555 m) to **Azib Likemt**. From here, you have a long Day 4 over to **Amsouzerte** where there is a gite, a little difficult to find – ask (30dh a night) – and Landrover taxis back down to Marrakech. From Amsouzerte, on Day 5, you head for **Lac Ifni** (2,290 m). Day 6 takes you to the **Neltner Refuge** (3,106 m) via the **Tizi-n-Ouanoumss** (3,665 m), and a long Day 7 is the climb up **Jbel Toubkal** (see details above) and back down to the refuge. Day 8 takes you down to **Aroumd/Aremd** (1,920 m), via the shrine of **Sidi Chamharouch** (2,340 m) and its tiny collection of stalls. At the time of the pilgrimage this shrine is very busy. From Aremd, on Day 10, you head back to **Imi Oughlad** (1,300 m). This last long stretching of the legs takes you via the **Tizi Oussem** (1,850 m) and the small settlements of **Agouinane** and **Taddert** before the last pass, **Tizi-n-Techt** (2,219 m), taking you down to Imi Oughlad. It is here one wonders if the arrangements made for collection and return to Marrakech were really understood. It may be simpler to have a very short last day and walk from Aremd back to the Red City.

The Ourika Valley

Colour map 2, grid B4

The Ourika Valley is a beautiful area of steep-sided gorges and green, terraced fields along the winding Oued Ourika, about 45 minutes drive south of Marrakech. The beauty and accessibility of the Ourika Valley makes it a most popular excursion for Marrakechis and tourists alike, and in summer certain sections of the valley are crowded with campers and day trippers happy to be away from the hot, dusty air of the plain. Just before Aghbalou, the S513 splits, with a right-hand road taking you up to the ski resort of Oukaïmeden. The trail-head village of Setti Fatma is reached by going straight ahead.

Ins & outs

The valley has a problem with flash floods, which campers should bear in mind

Buses and grands taxis to Ourika leave from Bab Rob, Marrakech (20dh). It is worth going all the way to Setti Fatma, at the head of the valley. If driving head straight for the mountains on the S513, starting from the fountain roundabout just outside the city walls at Bab Jedid, next to the *Hotel Mamounia*. Once in Ourika, a possible means of transport is a lift in the open-top vans and lorries which speed along the valley.

To Aghmat

After postcard views of the ramparts of Marrakech, the road heads out across flatlands, the monotony broken only by occasional olive groves and crossing the large concrete canal, which brings irrigation water from the Sidi Driss dam east of Marrakech to the Haouz Plain. The first minor side excursion, for enthusiasts of long-gone dynasties, would be to turn off left, 29 km from Marrakech, to Aghmat (spelt Rghmate on some maps), first Almoravid capital of the region, now a small settlement set in verdant olive groves and plant nurseries. Here the main sight is the mausoleum, built in the early 1960s and dedicated to Youssef ibn Tachine, founder of Marrakech in 1062.

Dar Caïd Ourika

Despite the tourists, this is still a good opportunity to see rural Morocco

Some 35 km from Marrakech another left turn takes you down to the main market town at the foot of this part of the mountains, Dar Caïd Ourika, also referred to as Tnine Ourika, ie Monday souk on the Ourika. Thus on Mondays, the place is lively, local colour added to by giant tour buses and crowds of foreign visitors. Arriving on market day, look out for the mule and donkey park as you cross the bridge over the usually dry riverbed.

As you head up into the foothills, the road winds past a large pottery on your left. Indeed, the whole road is lined with shops selling terracotta ware – it's surprising there's very much of the foothills left, so much clay must have been mined. After the pottery, there is a sign for the *Camping Amassine*, a woody (peach trees) and apparently secure sight with room for camping cars. No restaurant. Drawback? Some traffic noise from the road above during the day.

After the right turn for Oukaïmeden, the next big village is **Aghbalou** (also Arhbalou). From here on, there are a number of pleasant hotels along the roadside.

Sleeping and eating **B** *Hotel Ourika*, before the turn and Aghbalou, T061-120999 (mob). A large 1970s establishment with 27 a/c rooms, restaurant, bar and pool. About 1 km after that turn, look out on your right for **C** ***Le Maquis***, T044-484531, just before the roadside settlement of Oulmès. With Franco-Moroccan management, *Le Maquis* has both proper guest rooms (1 person 260dh with breakfast) and 6-sleeper bunk rooms. Accommodation here is bright and cheerful, the restaurant slightly less so (basic menus 55-120dh). After Aghbalou, there is the **D** ***Hotel-Restaurant Amnougour***, which has fantastic views and a disappointing restaurant. (On this stretch, are ***Restaurant le Lion de l'Ourika*** and ***Restaurant Kasbah de l'Ourika***, patronized by coach parties.) Next along, at Km 50, try the **D** ***Auberge Ramuntcho***, T044-444521, F484522, T061-165182 (mob), with a large (too large?) restaurant (pleasant outside terrace), bar and pool, plus 14 nice-sized rooms. Set up by a Basque – hence the name, Ramuntcho being 'king of the mountains' in a Pierre Loti novel. Some 5 km from Aghbalou, 52 km from Marrakech, at **Oulmès** (not to be confused with Oulmès-les-Thermes, between Meknès and Rabat, where the fizzy water comes from), on your left as you arrive, is the chintzy, cosy **D** ***Dar Piano***, T044-484842, T061-342884 (mob), darpiano@wanadoo.net.ma 4 rooms plus a small flat sleeping 4 for 400dh. Closed Jun-Aug. The restaurant has a good menu at 150dh. In the village itself, the **E** ***Hotel Raha*** is probably the best of the cheapies.

Setti Fatma

The road ends at Setti Fatma, noted for its annual summer *moussem*, seven waterfalls and 100-year-old walnut trees. There is a small weekly market, a *Bureau des guides de montagne* and quite a choice of basic accommodation, as befits a popular summer tripper destination. Setti Fatma must once have been quite pretty. Today, the impression is of lots of new, breeze-block housing set with satellite dishes built among the older stone homes. The sound of the river saves the day, and Setti Fatma could be a good starting/end point for a trek.

Up to the Cascades The main part of Setti Fatma is further on, entailing a climb on the far side of the river to the road. At the main village, cross over to the boulders and grassy area where the youth of Marrakech picnic and relax. There are a number of café-restaurants along the bank, including **F** *Hotel Café Bouche de la Source*, which provides basic rooms and cheap tagines; alongside, and marginally better, is **F** *Auberge des Routards/Restaurant les 7 Cascades*; beyond is the *Restaurant des Cascades*. The seven cascades are a 30-minute scramble up from Setti Fatma, following the path up behind the first café, and there are plenty of young men and kids who will help you find the way. There is a café perched up where the path ends, beside the first waterfall.

Walking from Setti Fatma Setti Fatma makes a good base for exploring the **Jbel Yagour**, a plateau region famed for its numerous prehistoric rock carvings. About 10 km from Setti Fatma is Tachedirt, where there is a *Refuge du CAF*. If you don't have much time in Morocco, it is feasible to do three-day treks up onto the plateau. To set up a trek, contact the *Bureau des guides de montagne*, on your right before the hotels. They have leaflets laying out details of itineraries and prices. The staff, including English-speaking Hassan Aït Brahim, are the same people who ran the Asgaour trekking office. Contact trained guide Abderrahim Mandili on T044-426113.

Sleeping and eating **F** ***Hotel Tafoukt***, on your left as you approach Setti Fatma. 6 rooms and 2 small flats. Run by the friendly Slimane Bouhliha. Lunch 70dh. Views over the valley. Wonderful location. Like much of the new building in the valley, the hotel is an aesthetic disaster. *Tafoukt* means sun. **F** ***Hotel Asgaour***, on your right, several hundred metres after the *Tafoukt*. 20 basic, clean rooms. **F** ***Hotel Billa***, right at the top end of the village, on the right, after the crossing to the cascades, identifiable by green façade. 20 rooms, large *salon marocain* with river view. Probably the best of the cheapies. For reservations, contact Omar on T066-186607. Still among the cheapies, if stuck try **F** ***Hotel Café Atlas***, good rooms and **F** ***Hotel Zohour***.

Oukaïmeden

Phone code: 044
Colour map 2, grid B4

Oukaïmeden, 'the meeting place of the four winds', is Morocco's premier ski resort. It's some 2,600 m up in the Atlas and a two-hour drive from Marrakech, making it a fine day trip from the city. It is also possible to climb the Jbel Oukaïmeden in a day. In winter hotels and restaurants are open but in summer it is less busy and many places are closed.

Ins & outs Daily buses from Marrakech in the winter. Also reached via the S513 Ourika Valley road – but forking right 43 km out of Marrakech, instead of left for Setti Fatma. Another option is to walk the piste which leaves the road south of Oukaïmeden, and cross the hills to the S501 to south of Asni. See also routes below.

The resort & surrounding area The resort is open for skiing from December to March, with a high ski lift up the Jbel Oukaïmeden (3,273 m), though it's not always in service. The skiing is very variable and good skiable snow cannot be counted on. The hot African sun means that the snow melts, only to freeze again at night. Nevertheless, as soon as there is snow, people flock down from Casablanca with their gear. Instructors work in the resort, and there is a ski shop near *Hotel de l'Angour*.

In summer visitors can walk, climb and even parasail. Look out for the prehistoric carvings on the rocky outcrop below the dam wall. Takes about 20 minutes with the right guide. There are further carvings on the flat rocks among the new chalets.

Routes to Oukaïmeden In a 4WD, Oukaïmeden is accessible from the west by winding roads and tracks from Tahanaoute and Asni on the S501 Tizi-n-Test road. Although the villages and landscapes are beautiful, the villages are very poor, and small children are eager to cadge pens, notebooks and a few dirhams. When you pull away from a village, watch out that the bolder elements are not clinging onto the back of your vehicle for a thrilling (if dangerous) dare.

Sleeping & eating Oukaïmeden has a small but adequate supply of accommodation. In practice, the resort only gets crowded on snowy weekends, and many Moroccan visitors prefer to return to Marrakech to sleep. Out of season, rooms in mountain chalets can be found. Oukaïmeden has 1 or 2 local shops with expensive tinned goods for sale. In the restaurants, prices for tagines vary wildly according to the customer; 40dh is plenty to pay.

B ***Hotel Kenzi Louka***, T044-319080, F319088. Large, triangular-shaped hotel open all year round, comfortable rooms. Outside pool (generally heated), information and advice on skiing and trekking. **D** ***Hotel Imlil***, T044-319032, a comfortable place with restaurant and good bar. Tends to close in summer. Beautiful views from terrace. **D** ***Hotel de l'Angour*** (aka *Auberge Chez Juju*), T044-319005, information and reservations via Marrakech on T/F044-448378, open all year (except Ramadan). 8 rooms, reasonable restaurant with French cuisine, bar with cold beer, half-pension required (250dh), but fair prices for clean sheets and hot showers. **D** ***Hotel Panoramique***, open all year, 14 rooms and a 20-bed dormitory. **D** ***Le Chouka***, only open in winter, 8 rooms and a 30-bed dormitory, restaurant, modern and comfortable. **F** ***Refuge of the Club Alpin Francais***, T044-319036. Space for 100, but not bunks for all, often has spaces for non-members, restaurant with reduced prices for *CAF* members, very comfortable considering position, skiing equipment, mountain bikes etc can be hired here, open all the year, bar room, games room, showers (sometimes with hot water), very clean. **F** ***Chalet de la Jeunesse et des Sports***, just before the *CAF*, T044-319004. Sleeping bag required, no heating. ***Camping Oukaïmeden***, small site, open only to caravans, has electricity and petrol 1 km. Self-catering chalets available via Marrakech-based company, ***Magesor SARL***, Villa Le Grillon, R Oumou el Banine, Marrakech – Guéliz, T063-040104, F044-436997.

The Tizi-n-Tichka route

Phone code: 044
Colour map 2, grid B4

Of the two mountain routes over the High Atlas to the southern side of the mountains, the P31 from Marrakech to Ouarzazate, and its Tizi-n-Tichka pass, is a larger road and safer option than the route over the Tizi-n-Test to Taroudant. Completed in 1936 by the Foreign Legion, the P31 gives stunning views. It runs through the full range of Atlas environments, from the Haouz plains, through the verdant *dir* foothills of the Oued Zat, to the barren peaks of the Atlas and the arid regions around Ouarzazate. Drivers need maximum concentration on this route, especially in the twilight when as likely as not you will meet donkeys and flocks of sheep wandering across the road, guided by small children. Clapped out local buses break down, and there are some very hairy bits leading up to the pass after Taddert. Don't cut corners. A further hazard are the fossil sellers who hang out at viewpoints and café stops. Also note that in winter there can be heavy cloud, snow storms and icy rain, reducing visibility and making the road extremely slippery. In such conditions, the road is not much fun at night. If snow cuts the pass, the snow barriers will be down.

The total distance from Marrakech to Ouarzazate is nearly 200 km. You should pace yourself. Good places to stop include upper **Taddert** (very busy, 86 km from Marrakech), the **Tizi-n-Tichka** itself which is almost exactly halfway, or **Ighrem-n-Ouagdal**, about 118 km from Marrakech where there is an old agadir (granary) to visit. Driving carefully in good conditions, Marrakech to Taddert will take you two hours, while Taddert to Ouarzazate is about another two. You will need to stop for photographs of course, and may want to do side-trips to **Telouet** and/or **Aït Ben Haddou**.

Leaving Marrakech, the best way out is on the Fès road. Then after 7 km after a large service station you go right onto the Aït Ourir and Ouarzazate road which runs through a sparse eucalyptus plantation and past olive and fruit tree groves. After 15 km, you intersect with the road coming out from the Médina of

Marrakech. At 22 km from Marrakech, you reach a possible accommodation option, the **D** *Complexe touristique du Dadès* (main advantage a pool). At 36 km from Marrakech, you are on the **Aït Ourir** bypass. (A turn-off left takes you into this rather undistinguished town.) On the right on a bend is a possible stopping place, the small restaurant *Le Coq hardi* which also has some accommodation. Then the road climbs through the foothills with some splendid views of the green valley of the Oued Zat.

Before the pass is the roadside village of **Taddert**, which now sprawls in two fairly unsightly parts. Pause for tagine, biscuits and drinks in upper Taddert. A few kilometres after the Tizi-n-Tichka pass is a turning on the left leading to the **Kasbah Telouet** (see below). From the pass the road winds and sweeps down to Ouarzazate. At **Ighrem-n-Ouadgal** (1,970 m) there is a fine fortified granary to visit – and accommodation in the form of **D** *Maison I'Roccha*, T067-737002, postal address Douar Tisselday, BP7, Ighrem-n-Ouadgal 45250, with 5 simple rooms and Moroccan/Mediterranean cooking. At **Agouim**, 126 km from Marrakech, a piste comes in from the west. Next point of interest is **Amerzgane**, where there is a turn-off right (west) for Taroudant and the neighbouring ruins of Tasgedlt. At 167 km from Marrakech a track leads off east to Aït Ben Haddou. The next major junction is a right turn for Taliouine and Taroudant. Then, about 176 km from Marrakech, at a fairly built-up junction, there is a left turn onto the road for **Aït Ben Haddou** (see below). At 191 km from Marrakech a right turn onto the road for Zagora enables you to avoid Ouarzazate – and passes just by the spectacular Kasbah of Tiffoultoute. Otherwise you can carry straight on into Ouarzazate, past the film studios (left, Egyptian temple decor) and the bus station.

Telouet

Colour map 2, grid B4

An eagle's nest of a place, high in the mountains, Telouet is something of a legend. It has one of the most spectacular kasbahs in the Atlas. Today, it is on the tourist circuit, as the hordes of 4WD vehicles which can be met there testify. Within living memory, however, its name was synonymous with the repressive rule of the Glaoui brothers. Easily accessible, it is one of the great sites of mountain Morocco, and is a good starting point for a 4WD journey southwards to Aït Ben Haddou.

Ins and outs

A narrow road, rather in need of resurfacing and with some nasty tyre-splitting edges, takes you from the Tizi-n-Tichka road to Telouet (turn left 106 km from Marrakech, or turn right 85 km after coming up from Ouarzazate). For those without their own vehicle, the trip is problematic, though there may be grands taxis up from Ighrem-n-Ouagdal. Adventurous 4WD people may want to try to reach Telouet from the south by the piste which runs up from Aït Ben Haddou via Tamdaght, Tizgui-n-Barda and Animiter (see below for description of route in reverse).

Background

The history of Telouet and its kasbah is short but bloodthirsty. It is the story of how two brothers of the Glaoua tribe, sons of an Ethiopian slave woman, by force of arms and character, managed to achieve absolute dominance over much of southern Morocco in the early 20th century. As it is a story in which neither of the main players, French and Moroccan, appear in an exactly glorious light, the main episodes of the Glaoui Empire's history have tended to be left alone by serious contemporary historians. For the English-speaking reader, Gavin Maxwell's *Lords of the Atlas* (1965) gives a vivid portrait of the turbulent times in Marrakech and the mountains as first the Moroccan monarchy and then the French skirmished with the southern tribal leaders to achieve dominance. The denouement, which came shortly after Moroccan independence in 1956, was fatal to Glaoui power.

Visiting Telouet

Surprisingly perhaps, we have few eyewitness accounts of Telouet in its heyday. None of the former inhabitants have written on their home, perhaps the foreign writers and intellectuals of the 1930s were too preoccupied with Marrakech to make it up to the mountains. Gavin Maxwell left a short description of the fortress in winter, just after a great blizzard which left thousands of goats suffocated on the mountainsides. As the snow melted, ravens, crows and kites gorged themselves on the carcasses. At sundown, "the air was dark with them as with a swarm of locusts; they homed for Telouet in their thousands, … till the branches of the trees broke under them, till the battlements of the castle were foul with their excreta."

Abandoned before completion, the Kasbah of Telouet as we see it today is in fact mainly the result of 20th-century building schemes implemented by the last great Glaoui lord, T'hami. Generally, as visitors arrive, someone will emerge to show one around. Although not exactly in splendid condition, the great reception rooms with their cedar ceilings and crumbling stucco, perfect transposition of late 19th century Moroccan urban taste to the mountains, are worth a visit. Some will see in it 'the labyrinth at whose heart one might expect the minotaur' described by earlier visitors. Others will be amazed at how such a display of quasi-medieval power was created in the 20th century.

Sleeping

For the moment, there is little on offer in terms of accommodation in Telouet, apart from a couple of cheap and insalubrious hotels. A better option, especially if you are in a group, is to look out for the man who has a couple of old French-built houses for rent (2 bedrooms, 300dh per night, no hot water, but still fairly charming). The better of the 2 houses is above the souk, but much less accessible. Key is with the hammam keeper, immediately north of the souk.

Telouet to Ouarzazate via Aït Ben Haddou

For those with 4WD, Telouet is also the starting point for an 80-km excursion down to Ouarzazate. You need to ask for the road to Animiter, the first main village. Leaving Telouet, after a few kilometres, a turn-off to the left, near the foot of Jbel Amassine, takes you up to the source of the Glaoui family's wealth, a salt mine. **Animiter**, some 9 km east from Telouet, was famous in the early days of Moroccan tourism as its kasbah, painted by Jacques Majorelle, was featured on an early poster. Here the surfaced road runs out. It should be possible to camp near the Oued Mellah. The next village, **Timsal**, lies a few kilometres to the south. After Timsal, follow the track along the Adrar Taqqat, used when they put in the electricity lines. You reach **Tioughassine** and the track follows the Ounila Valley. At **Assaka**, note abandoned granaries located under the cliffs. The track then follows up onto a sort of plateau above the canyon. Next, the main track drops steeply down to the valley bottom; **Tizgui-n-Barda** is the next main village, about 29 km from Telouet. Continue along the Assif Ounila to reach **Tamdacht**, meeting point of the oueds Marghene and Ounila and the start of the metalled road. **Aït Ben Haddou** is reached 50 km from Telouet.

In fact, this route was used in earlier times by caravans coming up from the south to pick up salt from the Telouet mine. Today, it is increasingly popular as an off-road excursion. The main difficulties are that in wet weather parts of the track turn to red-clay mud, extremely trying if you get stuck. As for other off-road adventures, it is to be tackled by vehicles in pairs as if you get stuck, you will definitely need someone to dig you out of trouble.

Azilal High Atlas

Northeast of Marrakech: the Azilal High Atlas and Beni Mellal

Colour map 2, grid B4

The P24 Marrakech to Fès road runs northeast out of the Red City through flat countryside to **El Kelaâ des Sraghna**, and thence eastwards to **Beni Mellal**, a large town of growing regional importance for both the rich irrigated areas of the Tadla Plain and a section of High Atlas to the south. A key place in this mountainous hinterland is **Azilal**, which gives access to the high valley of the **Aït Bougmez**, an area increasingly popular with walkers. The landscapes are beautiful, accommodation is possible in village gîtes. Between Marrakech and Azilal, off the S508 road, other attractions include the grotto of **Imi-n-Ifri** near Demnate and the **Cascades d'Ouzoud**, Morocco's highest waterfall. North of Beni Mellal, still on the P24 heading for Meknès, the visitor passes through Kasbah Tadla. Here the P13 runs north and west via pilgrimage centre **Boujad**, and the phosphate towns of **Oued Zem** and **Khouribga**, the latter best known for its annual film festival.

Well watered like the High Atlas of Toubkal, the High Atlas south of Azilal has a very different character, due perhaps to the inaccessibility of its valleys, hidden away in the heart of the mountains. The people here are Tamazight speaking, and in many ways more limited contact with mainstream Morocco makes them more conservative. Formal education has had little impact in the high valleys. It was only in the late 1990s that roads began to replace some of the landrover tracks. Much of the region's charm comes from the architecture of the villages, as yet unspoiled by the concrete constructions which have disfigured so many of the villages in the High Atlas of Toubkal.

To Azilal via Demnate and Ouzoud

Colour map 2, grids B4 & B5

Journey time from Marrakech to Azilal on this route is around three hours (with a 20-minute coffee stop), not allowing for side trips to Demnate and the Cascades d'Ozoud. Take the P24 out of Marrakech heading for Fès. A few kilometres after Temelelt (watch your speed because of Gendarmerie checks here), take a right fork onto the S508 for **Ettouia**, a mushrooming town on the plain with a couple of good cafés. The landscape improves, with views of the High Atlas over to the south. About 50 km after Ettouia, the road rises, there are conifers and you are at the turn-off right for Demnate, some 10 km away.

Demnate About two hours' drive from Marrakech, Demnate is worth the 10-km detour off the S508. It was once a picturesque place – all whitewashed, if the old guidebooks are to be believed. It had an important Jewish community, now vanished. Unfortunately, Maréchal Lyautey's planners didn't do a good job on Demnate and the crumbling kasbah, once set in the middle of olive groves, is surrounded by unsightly new building. There is also a chunky old minaret.

After a quick look round, continue up the much improved road to **Imi-n-Ifri** ('the door to the cave'), a natural rock bridge formed by the partial collapse of a huge cavern. If you don't have transport, there are transit vans which do the short run up from Demnate. At Imi-n-Ifri, opposite the closed auberge of the same name, a path winds down to the stream bed. There is a small reservoir where local lads come to swim and camp. Concrete steps, partly gone, take you up to the grotto. Above your head, there are great sheets of calcareous rock, technically called dripstone. Mind you don't slip on the guano underfoot, created by cawing choughs (*alzoui* in Amazigh) circling overhead. You may also see the odd Barbary squirrel. All that is lacking are a few Barbary apes.

Back up at the top, there is a café with a lawn. The road forks. The left fork takes you onto the black-top road all the way to Iouarden, where there are fossilized dinosaur footprints. Taking the right fork, the tarmac runs as far as Aït Imlil.

Sleeping and eating F *Hotel Café d'Ouzoud*, on main Av Mohammed V, T062-239972 (mob) manager, T061-241099 (mob) owner. 24 small clean rooms. At Imi-n-Ifri, taking the right-hand fork past the café, there is a new ***gîte d'étape***, T044-456473, clearly signposted. Open only in summer.

Cascades d'Ouzoud

Locals can be over-insistent in their desire to show you the way down to the foot of the falls. You could give in, but agree on a fee beforehand

After visiting Demnate, return to the S508 which runs east to the signposted turn-off for the Cascades d'Ouzoud. The winding road has been much improved. For those without a hire car, a grand taxi from Azilal is an option if you get an early start. After the turn-off, the road heads north through beautiful landscapes where the dominant colours are red earth, dark green thuya and the paler grey green of the olive trees. Arriving in the village of Ouzoud, various local men will emerge waving sticks to help you park. For the cascades, head past the new riad, and a few metres of market garden land crossed by rivulets of fast flowing water lead you to the edge of the precipice (watch out for slippery clay). Look out for the traditional water-driven barley mills. There are various paths which will take you down to cafés on the rocks below the falls. All in all, this is a most picturesque spot, popular for camping in the summer. The word *ouzoud* comes from the Amazigh *izide*, meaning delicious, which is what bathing below the falls should be. (No diving, as the pool under the falls is very shallow.)

After visiting Ouzoud, return to the much improved S508 road and turn left. The main centre for the region, Azilal, is reached 21 km to the east.

Some good options for staying at the Cascades these days

Sleeping and eating C *Riad Cascades d'Ouzoud*, T023-459658. 6 tasteful rooms, nice roof terrace. Check to be sure they're open. Try their traditionally milled couscous *balboula*. Can set you up with a guide for 150dh. In the village, the **D** ***Hotel de France***, T023-459017. Cheap but lacks atmosphere. **D** ***Hotel les Cascades***, above the téléboutique, noisy (in summer), slightly boozy post-hippy atmosphere. **D** ***Hotel Dar es Salam***, T023-459657, next to the car park. Mucky and best avoided. Camping is possible at various small sites, generally very noisy in summer and lacking in hygiene. Try ***Camping Cascades d'Ouzoud*** in 4 ha of land, first aid, nearest petrol 32 km.

Azilal

Phone code: 023
Colour map 2, grid B5

Sprawling west from a small core of kasbah and French military buildings, terracotta red Azilal is less of a one-mule place than it used to be. In fact, it is turning into a major town with the usual stilt-legged buildings, a big gare routière, a Thursday souk and a tourist office (Avenue Hassan II, T023-488334).

Accommodation and eateries can be found on the main street

Sleeping and eating Best option is the **D** ***Hotel Assounfou*** ('relaxation' in Tachelhit), coming in from Marrakech look out for the blue balconies on your right on main street, T023-459220, F458442. 29 rooms, 2 suites, satellite TV, everything very pink, solar-heated water, which only partly explains why it is generally cold. Nice management. **F** ***Hotel Dadès***, just as you arrive from Marrakech, on your right, T023-458245. Basic, 3-bed concrete box room 50dh, hot showers 5dh. **F** ***Hotel Tanout***, T023-488281. 12 rooms, on your left next to the *Shell* station as you leave Azilal for Beni Mellal.

Transport Azilal is the transport hub for the regions of the High Atlas to the south, with a gare routière next to the main mosque. **Bus**: for **Marrakech** at 0600 and 1400, for **Casablanca** at 0700, and for **Beni Mellal** at 1400. **Grand taxi**: Landrovers (2 a day); Mercedes transit vans (2 a day) to **Tabant**; Landrovers for **Zaouiat Ahansal**, too, although for this destination it is probably best to get a Peugeot or Mercedes grand taxi to Ouaouizaght and then switch to the less comfortable Landrover.

Azilal to Tabant

From Azilal you have a slow, 2¾-hour drive south over the mountains into the **Aït Bougmez**. The tarmac now runs nearly the whole way to Tabant. At the first major intersection, about 20 km from Azilal, you go right, taking the new route over and round to **Agouti**, to the west of Tabant, rather than the older, rougher route via Aït Mohammed. Drivers need to have their wits about them, your vehicle should have excellent brakes – which you will no doubt begin to smell as they heat up after particularly long descents such as the one down to **Ighir** where the **Oued Lakhdar** comes in from the west. Some 7 km further on, the piste turns east for Tabant. You should not start on this road if it looks like snow – you might find yourself cut off for a few days. The piste was just about doable in a Fiat Uno – but remember, if you set out on rough tracks in an ordinary hire car with low clearance, the insurance will not cover any damage.

If you have already done the High Atlas of Toubkal south of Marrakech, the differences with the High Atlas of Azilal soon become apparent. Despite human pressure, there is more vegetation with conifer forests surviving at high altitude. If you go trekking, you will discover wide flat valleys, deep gorges and small rivers which can easily turn to flood after a rainstorm on the mountains. The highest mountain in the region is the long shoulder of the **Irghil Mgoun** (4,071 m).

Vallée des Aït Bougmez

Colour map 12 grid B5

The Aït Bougmez is one of the most beautiful valleys of the High Atlas, so far unspoiled by breeze-block building. Electricity arrived in early 2001, and the completion of the black-top road will bring further changes. Hopefully, improved transport will not destroy the region's vernacular architectural traditions. The stone and pisé built villages above the fields of the valley bottom are fine examples of housing, perfectly adapted to local environment and needs.

One of the most isolated regions of the High Atlas, the Aït Bougmez was until very recently cut off by snow for part of the winter. The villagers had to be highly self-reliant, a factor that explains the reluctance to abandon traditional crops such as barley, which can be cut for fodder and will sprout again to produce grain. Unlike Imlil in the Toubkal region, there is as yet no major switch to more profitable fruit trees. Though tourism in the form of small hiking groups is beginning to make a contribution to the local economy, life is still hard for most.

Tabant

Tabant, 1,850 m up in the Aït Bougmez, is the main administrative centre. There is even a new post office and a very handy téléboutique (no internet café as yet), also a number of basic shops. Down behind the téléboutique is a small café where the locals play bar billards and baby-foot. East of the village are the modern buildings of the *Centre de formation aux métiers de la montagne* (CFAMM), a vocational school which trains mountain guides.

Sleeping and eating *Gîte d'étape* is the best in the nearby village of Imelghas. Accommodation for up to 40, clean loos and showers. Owned and run by Abdellah Ben Saïd El Ouakhoumi, who can be contacted via the Tabant téléboutique on T023-459341, postal address Gîte d'étape Imelghas, Aït Bougmez, Tabant, 22480 Azilal. The upmarket option is a fine *gîte* owned by Marrakech-based *Atlas Sahara Trek*, contact T044-313901, F313995. Reservations via Marrakech office essential.

Options are limited in Tabant. In many villages in the valley there is simple sleeping-space in GTAM gîtes

Walking around the Aït Bougmez

The Aït Bougmez provides some excellent walking. The wide, flat-bottomed valley provides pleasant day walks out from Tabant for occasional walkers and those with young families. You could find a local to walk you up to the dinosaur footsteps near Rbat. Tabant (or Imelghas) to Agouti is a very easy walk, say 8 km, along the valley road. Look out for the granary of Sidi Moussa up on a mound-like hill. There is another, rather longer walk (say 9 km), from Tabant to Ifrane along the old main piste to Aït M'hamed.

The valley can also work as an excellent starting point for hiking tours, in particular into the Massif du Mgoun to the south. Setting up a longish circuit with a local guide generally requires you to give a couple of months' notice. The guide will need to have an idea of the group's walking experience and fitness levels. For setting up a trek, contact Saïd el Ouakhoumi at the Tabant téléboutique, T023-459341/42. A week-long trek with transfer to the valley from Marrakech airport will cost 3,500-4000dh, meals excluded. A hiker consumes around 100dh worth of food and drink a day.

Maps and books Any properly organized guide will obviously have the maps necessary for hiking in the region. If you want to buy 1:100,000 scale maps, try *Chez Ali* in Marrakech (expensive) or, if you have lots to time in Rabat, the Division de la cartographie. The eastern part of the Aït Bougmez is on the Zaouiat Ahansal sheet, ref NH-29-XXIV-4, as is most of the Ighil Mgoun. The western access to the Aït Bougmez, with most of the road from Azilal, Abachkou, administrative village of the Aït Bou Ouilli and Jebal Ghat, are shown on the NH-29-XXIV-3 Azilal sheet. Trekking south of the Ighil Mgoun, you will need the Qalaa't Mgouna NH-29-XXIV-2. The sheet west of this, the NH-29-XXIV-1, Skoura, shows Amezri and the Oued Tessaout. If you read French (and even if you don't there are some handy, small maps), in Marrakech you may be able to obtain a small publication called *Randonnées pédestres dans le Massif du Mgoun* ('Walking tours in the Mgoun Region').

The Massif du Mgoun

Colour map 2, grid B5

With its alluring, extraterrestrial sounding name, the Mgoun is Morocco's second highest mountain massif. Although not the most aesthetically pleasing of mountains (no soaring peaks), it has the largest area of land above 3,000 m in the whole country. The best time to climb the mountain is probably summer or early autumn, for snow remains late into the year in these highlands. The easiest route to the summit is from the south side of the mountain, which means starting form **El Kelaâ des Mgouna** in the Dadès Valley (see page 398). The alternative is to head south from the Aït Bougmez to approach the massif from the east. Taking this option, you will probably head south from Tabant over the Tizi-n-Aït Imi (2,905 m) to Tighremt-n-Aït Ahmed, and thence west to the foot of the mountain along the course of the Assif Oulliliymt on a second day's trek. The ascent to the highest point (4,068 m) is not actually difficult. Note that the summit is in some way sacred. In a survival of some obscure pre-Islamic tradition, the mountain's help (protection) may be asked, even today.

A popular hiking option is to trek from the Aït Bougmez south to **Bou Thrarar** and **Kelaât Mgouna**. This is a six-day trip, with possible bivouacs at **Tarzout**, **Aguerzka** and **Bou Thrarar**. It will be up to your guide to break up the route as they see fit. Apart from the high pass on the first day, there are no huge climbs, and you will be walking for between six and seven hours a day.

Beni Mellal

Phone code: 023
Colour map 2, grid B5
Population: about 140,000
200 km NE of Marrakech

This is one of the major centres of central Morocco, with an important souk on Tuesday. Like a number of other towns in the region, it has grown thanks to remittances from migrant workers in Italy. Main monuments include the **Kasbah Bel Kush**, built in the 17th century by Moulay Ismaïl, but heavily restored in the 19th century. The main thing to do in Beni Mellal is to walk up to the small, quiet gardens below the ruined **Kasbah de Ras el Aïn**, perched precariously on the cliffside. There is a nice café in the gardens. A tourist office is located on the first floor of Immeuble Chichaoui, Avenue Hassan II, T023-483981. Coming from Marrakech, if you wish to avoid Beni Mellal go left for the bypass just before two petrol stations (*Somepi* on left, *Shell* on right).

Sleeping

There are 1 or 2 good options in Beni Mellal

C ***Al Bassatine***, Route de Fkih Ben Salah, T044-482227. 61 a/c rooms, pool, restaurant, TV, direct telephone, parking, conference facilities. **C** ***Hotel Chems***, Route de Marrakech, BP 68, T023-483460. 77 rooms, restaurant, bar, nightclub, tennis, pool, nice grounds. Could do with some renovation, has a 1970s air, far out from the centre. Has a certain run-down charm (some would say). **C** ***Hotel Ouzoud***, Route de Marrakech, T023-483752/3. Restaurant, bar, tennis, pool. In the new town, try **D-E** ***Hotel Gharnata***, Av Mohammed V, easily located near *Petrom* station and *PTT*, T023-483482. Must have been excellent in the 1950s, badly refurbished, 14 noisy rooms. **D** ***Hotel El Amria***, Av des FAR, T023-483531. Simple. **D** ***Hotel de l'Aïn-Asserdoun***, Av des FAR, T023-483493. Modern place with restaurant. Of the cheapish hotels near the gare routière, best is probably **D** ***Hotel Kamel***, T023-486941. Street-facing rooms noisy. In the older part of town, several good cheap options, the best **E** ***Hotel Tasmmet***, T023-421313, not that easy to find, but if you get onto the street which runs parallel to the main street behind the *CTM* offices you eventually see it down a side street to your left as you head towards the kasbah. On the small square in the old town (reached by heading up the souk street which leads uphill to the right of the big ceremonial gates and square), 2 simple options with rooms around courtyards: **F** ***Hotel Marhaba***, T023-483991, 11 rooms, 27 beds, sleep on roof terrace for 25dh, and **F** ***Hotel El Fath***, no phone, opposite the *Marhaba*, no shower, damp in some rooms.

Eating

The best place used to be the ***Auberge du Vieux Moulin***, Av Mohammed V. Try the restaurant of the ***Hotel de Paris***, T023-282245, a little way out of the town centre on Kasbah Tadla road. Serves alcohol. More decorously, try the ***Salon de Thé Azouhour***, 241 Av Mohammed V. There are the usual *laiteries* and cafés along the main street.

Transport

Road *CTM* **buses** leave from the terminal in the town centre. Connections with **Marrakech** and 3 a day for **Fès**. From the bus station it is a 10-min walk up Av des FAR to the centre. **Casablanca** service irregular. **Grand taxis** up to **Ouaouizaght** and to **Azilal**, whence you can pick up tougher transport to the **Aït Bougmez** and **Zaouiat Ahansal.**

Northwest of Beni Mellal

If you are on a circular tour with a hire car, possibly flying out from Casablanca, there are some minor places of interest as you head back coastwards from the mountains. Casablanca-bound from Beni Mellal and the High Atlas of Azilal, you take the P24 Casablanca road north from Beni Mellal to **Kasbah Tadla**, and then the P13 northwest to **Boujad** and **Oued Zem**. Here the P22 runs north to Rabat via **Rommani** and Aïn el Aouda. The P13 continues to the phosphate town of Khouribga across the Plateau des Phosphates, to intersect with the main P7 Marrakech to Casablanca road at **Berrechid**. Kasbah Tadla and Boujad are must visits for those doing their advanced Moroccan studies diploma.

Heading north out of Beni Mellal, a fast stretch of the P24 takes you through well-irrigated orchards and olive groves out into open grainlands. To your right are views of the northwestern side of the High Atlas. At a major junction (curious concrete monument to your left), Kasbah Tadla comes into view. Head straight on for the town, its ramparts visible above the Oum er Rbia, or go right past the closed *Hotel Bellevue* to continue on the P24 for Khénifra.

Kasbah Tadla

Kasbah Tadla doesn't really have enough attractions to warrant a stopover. Souk day is Monday

Kasbah Tadla was founded in 1687 by the Alaouite Sultan Moulay Ismaïl, no doubt because it is ideally located more or less halfway between Marrakech and Meknès and Fès, the imperial cities of the Saïss Plain. The crumbling terracotta ramparts sit above the shrivelled course of the river. The view is little changed since the town's foundation, although a new social-housing project on the flood plain is changing that. On the 'plateau' behind the kasbah is a rather derelict *jardin public*, splendid in a quiet sort of way when the purple jacarandas are in flower. Within the **kasbah** there is a lot of self-built housing, put up by soldiers and their families, and two mosques, one with the distinctive Almohad lozenge design on the minaret. The other has a Sahelian feel with poles protruding from the minaret. Some lad might offer to show you into the courtyard building behind the mosque which was the sultan's residence. Today, it is inhabited by poor residents, so be discrete when you are taking photos. If 17th-century engineering is your thing, get some shots of the 10-arched bridge over the Oum er Rbia.

The best view of the kasbah is from the austere monument to four resistance heroes on a low rise on the south side of the town. Four parallel concrete blades rise skywards, but there is no inscription to recall who the heroes were and local youths sitting in the shade of the monument don't seem to know either.

Sleeping and eating Unfortunately, the *Hotel Bellevue*, just outside the town off the P24 from Fès to Beni Mellal, is now derelict and there do not seem to be any plans to re-open. There are 3 very basic hotels in the centre. **F *Hotel des Alliés***, Av Mohammed V, T023-418587. Perhaps the best though lacking in hot water. Founded in 1921, it still has many of its original characteristics, albeit in desperate need of attention. **F *Hotel El Atlas***, R el Majati Obad, T023-418046. **F *Hotel Oum er Rbia***, 26 Blvd Mohammed Zerktouni, no shower. There are a few basic restaurants in the town centre. Try ***Restaurant Salem*** on the main drag. **Campsite** *Auberge des Artistes*, at El Ksiba, just 30 km east of Kasbah Tadla, T023-03415490. Well-run site in 2 ha of grounds, showers, electricity for caravans, clean wash blocks. See page 423 for further details of the route from El Ksiba to Imilchil.

Transport *CTM* **buses** for Fès, Marrakech and Beni Mellal run via Kasbah Tadla. Private line buses from *Agence SLAC* for **Beni Mellal** at 1300, **Boujad** and **Oued Zem** at 1700, and **Rabat** at 0430, 0730 and 1300. These can all be caught from the bus station on the Boujad side of town, ie the far side to the old kasbah.

Boujad

Just a 25-minute drive from Kasbah Tadla, Boujad is something of a surprise. In recent memory, it was an important town, essentially a pilgrimage centre for the semi-nomadic inhabitants of the Tadla plain. It gets plenty of coverage in guidebooks of the 1930s. The historic médina has an almost Mediterranean character with its arcaded square, whitewashed walls, shrines and paved streets and white houses. The main *zaouia* is a 16th-century foundation. Much of the town was destroyed in 1785. The key buildings are the **Zaouia of Sidi Othman** and the **Mosque of Sidi Mohammed Bu'abid ech Cherki**, the town's founder.

Sleeping, eating and transport There is 1 hotel on the main square, Pl du Marché, the **F** *Café-Hotel Essalyn*, and several cheap restaurants nearby. People on pilgrimages rent rooms in private houses near the shrines. Regular **buses** and **grands taxis** leave for **Kasbah Tadla** and **Oued Zem** from the main square.

Khouribga

Khouribga (35 km west from Oued Zem, just south of the P12) is an important working town due to its central role in the phosphates industry. For the tourist, it is singularly lacking in any charm or appeal.

Sleeping, eating and transport There is 1 luxury hotel, the **A** *Hotel Safir*, T022-492013, F493013. With restaurant, bar, tennis and pool. The best cheap hotel is the clean **F** *Hotel de Paris*, 18 Av Mohammed V, T022-492716. The only other is **F** *Hotel des Hotes*, 1 R Moulay Ismaïl, T022-493030, a basic and unfriendly place. Around the market, just off the main street, are a number of basic restaurants. There are **trains** to **Casablanca**, with connections to **Marrakech**.

Kasbah Tadla to Khénifra

Leaving Kasbah Tadla in the Azrou/Fès direction, the P24 runs across fast, open corn lands. After about 22 km is the turn-off right to **El Ksiba**, the starting point for the north-south route to Imilchil. Next stop is **Zaouiat ech Cheikh**, best known for its roadside tagine restaurants. The road takes an increasingly winding route along the contours, so keep your speed down and watch out for wild-card grands taxis. **Aït Ishak** is signposted off to the left, and then you reach the junction with the P33, which will take you east to **Zeïda** and the P21 Azrou to Midelt road. Distances between main towns as follows: Khénifra to Zeïda 110 km, Kasbah Tadla to Zeïda 159 km, journey time to Midelt 2¼ hours. If you need a break, the roadside **C** *Hotel Transatlas* – T055-399030, 25 rooms, air-conditioning, bar, small pool, noisy in evenings – is acceptable. There is nothing much better until you reach Azrou.

After this junction, Khénifra is about 35 km further on. After 12 km, you reach the turn-off for **El Kebab** and an alternative (and attractive) route across to Zeïda via **Kerrouchen** (26 km to El Kebab, 59 km from Khénifra).

Khénifra

Khénifra is another of the Middle Atlas towns that stood up to the French military in a big way, before becoming an important town in the colonial enterprise. Like Marrakech, it is a *ville rouge*. The locals have a tradition of horsemanship. Various kasbahs are signposted. There is an old bridge over the rubbish-strewn bed of the Oum er Rbia. If you need a break from driving, have a drink at the *Café des Cascades*, on a rather minor precipice to your right as you head north out of town.

Sleeping Not much choice. **A** *Hotel Salam Zayyani*, T055-586020. Restaurant, pool, poorly maintained. **C** *Hotel Najah*, 187 Blvd Zerktouni, the main street, T055-588331, F587874. Simple clean rooms. The best cheap hotel has rather gone down, **F** *Hotel Restaurant de France V*, quartier des FAR, on the west side of the town, T055-586114. Restaurant overpriced. There are several new places on the main drag.

Ouarzazate & the Dadès and Draâ valleys

384 South of the High Atlas: Ouarzazate and the Dadès and the Draâ Valleys

385 Ouarzazate
385 Ins and outs
386 Sights
386 Excursions
387 Essentials
390 Aït Ben Haddou

391 The Draâ Valley
393 Zagora
395 South of Zagora
396 East from Zagora to Rissani

397 The gorges of the Dadès and Todgha
398 El Kalâa Mgouna

400 The Dadès and Todgha Gorges
400 Boumalne du Dadès
401 Gorges du Dadès
402 Tineghir
404 Gorges du Todgha
405 East from Tineghir to Er Rachidia

Introducing Ouarzazate & the Dadès and Draâ valleys

South of the High Atlas, place names like Ouarzazate and Tifeltoute, Zagora and Tamegroute, Boumalne and Tamtatouchte speak of palm groves and the distant blue of desert horizons. In the great valleys of the region, palm groves and startling earth-built fortresses stand out against arid hills. Travelling over the High Atlas from Marrakech, the first major town is **Ouazarzate**, legionnaire base turned tourist town and centre of the Moroccan film industry. Within a short drive, you have the star of several films, the **Kasbah of Aït Ben Haddou**. Still close to Ouarzazate, but more discrete, are the **Kasbah of Tifeltoute** and the **oasis of Fint**.

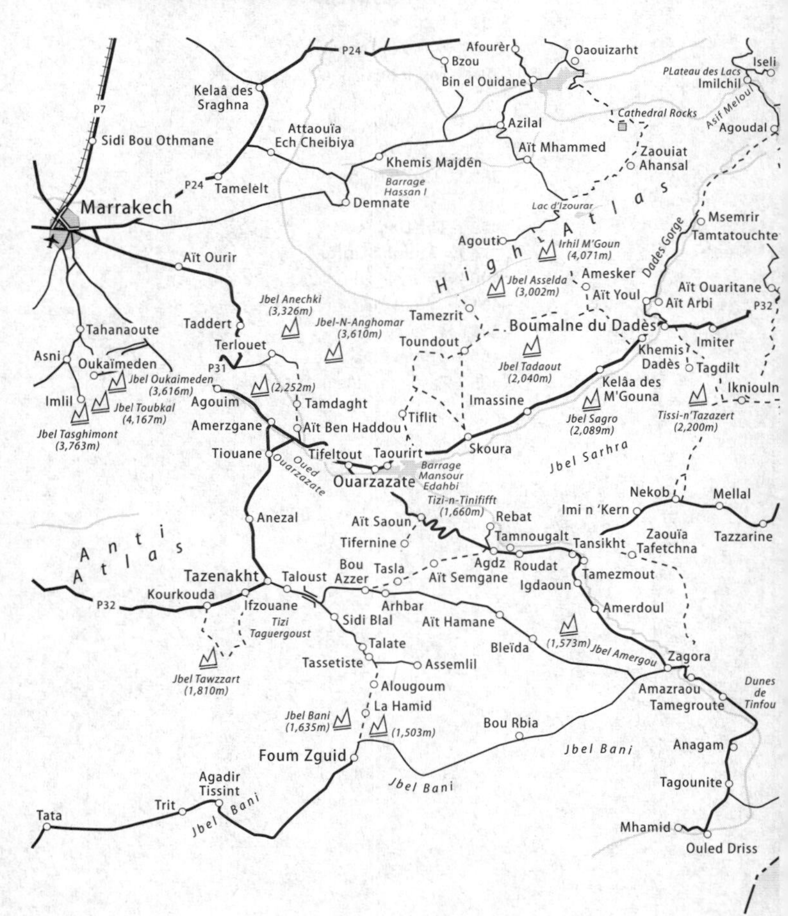

Within a day's drive of Ouarzazate, the contrasts in the landscapes are impressive. There are two classic routes, south to the Sahara and east along the southern flank of the High Atlas. The southern route begins with a spectacular switchback drive to **Agdz**, then down to **Zagora**, **Tamegroute**, former centre of Islamic learning, and **M'hamid**, gateway to the Sahara.

East of Ouarzazate, the Dadès Valley route takes you through **Skoura** (still more kasbahs) and **El Kelaâ des Mgouna** (rose-ville) to **Boumalne**, base for travelling up into the **Gorges du Dadès**. Here you can overnight, before heading on to **Tineghir**, access point for the **Todgha Gorges**. Both Boumalne and Tineghir make excellent starting points for treks up into the Atlas, either by 4WD or on foot. East of Tineghir, the road rises to Goulmima and on to Rachidia, base for exploring the Tafilalet and the Ziz Valley.

Things to do out of Ouarzazate and Zagora

- Take a look at the kasbahs at **Tifeltoute** and **Aït Ben Haddou**, a short half-day trip out of Ouarzazate. Stay in a **kasbah hotel** at Skoura or Tineghir (*Timboctou* reasonable).
- Discover the secrets of the rose-essence industry at **Kelaâ des Mgouna** – or just enjoy the mountainous landscapes north of the town.
- Visit the spectacular **Gorges du Todgha**. The adventurous with 4WD can attempt the gorge-to-gorge route, looping back down the **Gorges du Dadès**.
- Drive down the Draâ valley to Zagora and take a **camel trek** into the desert to see the **dunes near Tamegroute or M'hamid**.
- Explore the region round Nkob for **prehistoric rock carvings**. Stay in the kasbah hotel there.

South of the High Atlas: Ouarzazate and the Dadès and Draâ valleys

The great valleys south of the High Atlas have some of the finest scenery in Morocco, with some magnificent drives for those with their own transport, ranging from arid mountains to gentle oases, a volcanic massif and some splendid canyons. Almost all travellers will pass through **Ouarzazate**, where the Tizi-n-Tichka route over the mountains from Marrakech meets the main east-west Rachidia to Agadir axis running parallel to the south side of the High Atlas. Although Ouarzazate is served by charter flights from France, most visitors will come in by road.

While Ouarzazate has some very smart hotels, all the smaller settlements like **Agdz** and **Zagora**, **Boumalne** and **Tineghir** have plenty of acceptable, though not always luxurious, accommodation. Those on a budget will be well served in hotel terms, too, though small concrete-built hotels can be stifling in summer. There are now some very nice restored kasbah hotels, notably at **Skoura** and **Nkob** (highly recommended) and a small number of personable guesthouses (**Ouarzazate** and **El Kelaâ**). On the minus side, the public transport is a little slow and the distances great. Those driving should take great care. The main roads are narrow, wind up and over high passes and can get very busy with vehicles driven too fast by experienced local drivers.

Possible routes

Local tour companies often sell Ouarzazate as a long day trip from Marrakech. This is only really worthwhile if the journey includes **Telouet** (see page 372). It would be better to make an overnight stop in Ouarzazate, after a leisurely drive over the **Tizi-n-Tichka** taking in the kasbahs at Telouet and **Aït Ben Haddou**. The following day, you would explore sights east from Ouazarzate (**Skoura**, **Kelaâ des Mgouna**) before making the long drive back. Alternatively, Ouarzazate or any of the **Dadès** towns and **Tineghir** can be used as overnights on a big round the Atlas tour, other possible overnights being **Er Rachidia**, **Midelt**, **Beni Mellal** or **Azilal**. Another option, if you are more of a day walker, is to take it easy and spend a couple of nights in (say) **Skoura**, **Boumalne** and **Tineghir** in order to explore palm groves and gorges. There is some good mountain biking from Skoura and Boumalne.

Ouarzazate

The very name Ouarzazate evokes a desert fort. The reality of Ouarzazate is a little more prosaic. The once isolated French military outpost now has an international airport and a core of luxury hotels alongside its kasbah. Though the garrison remains, the needs of the regional administration and migrant worker remittances have created a large town. Ouarzazate should thus be seen as a base for exploring valleys and oases south of the High Atlas, as a transit point for mountain and desert. The region is at its best in early spring when blossom is on the almond trees and snow still covers the summits of the Atlas.

Phone code: 044
Colour map 2, grid C5

Ins and outs

Getting there

See Transport, page 390, for further details

Taourirt Airport is 2 km northeast of Ouarzazate. From there get a petit taxi to your hotel. Ouarzazate is well served by buses and grands taxis. By bus, the run from Taroudant takes 5 hrs, from Agadir 7½ hrs, from Marrakech hopefully under 5 hrs. In winter, the Tizi-n-Tichka col can be closed with snow. By grand taxi, Zagora to Ouarzazate takes 3 hrs, rather longer by bus. The *CTM* bus terminal is on a square on the main street, Av Mohammed V, private line buses arrive at the out of town bus station on the Marrakech exit to the town, and grands taxis on Pl Mouahidine.

Getting around the town

Hotels are located in the town centre or over the causeway in Hayy Tabount. It is a hefty walk from the out of town bus station to both of these – best take a petit taxi. Main reference points in the town centre are Av Mohamed V and, running parallel, R du Marché. As you come down Av Mohamed V from the bus station, there are quite a few services on or near the large Pl du 3 Mars, a large, rather impersonal square on your left.

Getting to sights in the region

Ouarzazate is a small place, more of a base than anything else. Getting to the spectacular kasbah at Aït Ben Haddou is awkward without your own car. You could club together with other tourists and hire a grand taxi, or you could get a bus going up the P31 Marrakech road, and get off at the turn-off for the kasbah – and walk the rest. A few kilometres out of Ouarzazate, on the bypass, is the well preserved kasbah of Tiffeltoute, easily reached by grand taxi. Another place you may want to get to from Ouarzazate is the oasis of Skoura, east along the Boumalne du Dadès P32 road, easily accessible by local bus.

Tourist information

Tourist office Av Mohammed V, opposite *CTM* bus terminal, T044-882485 (Mon-Fri 0900-1200, 1430-1830). **Syndicat d'Initiative et du Tourisme**, Kasbah de Taourirt.

Background

Some good kasbahs can be visited in the region

Strategically placed at the confluence of three rivers, Ouarzazate has had a military presence since the Almohad period. In the late 19th century, the kasbah came under control of the Glaoui family, who used it as a power base to develop their control of the South. In 1926, the first airfield was built, and in 1928 a regular French military garrison was installed. Ouarzazate was henceforth the main administrative town for the region, the nerve centre for the Lyautey method of expanding French influence into tribal areas. A few buildings from this period straggle along the main street. Around and above them are the large hotels, built mainly in the 1980s. Today, Ouarzazate is a solid (if sleepy) little town (market days Sunday and Tuesday). Neat low-rise housing developments painted magenta brown with white trim are going up, and there is a new bus station.

The immediate vicinity of Ouarzazate is often used as a film location. Since *Lawrence of Arabia* was filmed at Aït Benhaddou, the region, close to mountains and desert, has been a popular director's choice. The Atlas Studios never seem to be out of work. (Look out for the mock Egyptian statues signalling the studios off the road north of the town.) Ouarzazate also has a small handicrafts fair in May and the *moussem* of Sidi Daoud in September.

Sights

Though Ouarzazate has a large modern mosque, the first stone of which was laid by King Mohammed V in 1958, the historic highlight of Ouarzazate is the **Kasbah Taourirt**, located east of the town 'centre' along Avenue Mohammed V. Constructed largely in the 19th century, the building had its heyday in the 1930s and would have housed the Glaoui chief's extended family, servants and followers, as well as a community of tradesmen, artisans and cultivators. Today the kasbah is one of Ouarzazate's poorest areas. The part adjacent to the road, probably quarters for the Glaoui family, has been maintained and can be visited. ■ *Mon-Fri 0830-1200 and 1500-1800, Sat 0830-1200.*

Opposite the kasbah in the *Ensemble Artisanal* there are handicrafts. ■ *Mon-Fri 0800-1200 and 1300-1800, Sat 0830-1200. T044-883449.* In the town centre there is also a *Coopérative Artisanale des Tissages de Tapis*, another fixed-price shop. *Atlas Studios*, where film work is done , is open to public view (0800-2000), and is 3 km from the centre, along the road to Marrakech.

Excursions

Mansour Edahbi Dam
The best time to do this trip is spring or autumn

To the east of Ouarzazate, the Mansour Edhabi Dam on the Oued Draâ has created a lake over 20 km long. Birdwatchers come here to see the wintering and migrating wildfowl. Visitors include spoonbills and flamingos, when there is sufficient water in the dam. In recent years, water levels have fallen spectacularly, the lakeside golf course is a ghost of its former self, and the villas built as pricey lakeside retreats are now a fair way from the water. Tracks from the P32 lead down towards the northern shore. One is signed into a gated reserve. You should be able to enter if you show your binoculars and say you

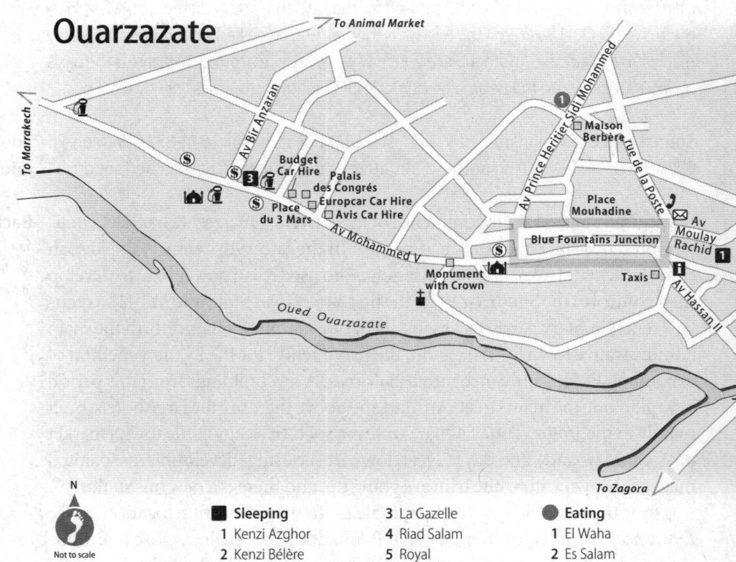

are a birder. Another access point is via the golf club. The southern shore is more difficult to reach and access to the dam itself is prohibited.

Kasbah of Tifeltoute

A visit to the Kasbah of Aït Ben Haddou (see page 390) could be combined with a visit to the Kasbah of Tifeltoute. Take the road from Ouarzazate west across the causeway and turn right (north). After about 7 km you will come to the village of **Tifeltoute** with its splendid kasbah built for the Glaoui family in the early 20th century. It stands alongside the Oued Igissi. Still owned by the family, it is now used as a simple hotel, with adequate food and magnificent views, T044-882813. You can visit for a small fee and climb up to the roof terrace for views of the countryside and a stork's nest on one of the turrets. After visiting the kasbah, continue to the main junction with the P31, whence you go right and 5 km south back to Ouarzazate or left in the Marrakech direction to visit Aït Ben Haddou.

Oasis of Fint

For those with 4WDs or hardy cars, the oasis of **Fint** is a possible destination, a few kilometres out in the desert west of Ouarzazate, aross the Tabount causeway.

Essentials

Sleeping

■ *on map*
Price codes: see inside front cover

Travelling by public transport, you come into the *gare routière* on the Marrakech side of town. After a hot bus journey, you may want to take a petit taxi to run you into town, a couple of kilometres away. (*CTM* buses come into Av Mohammed V.) Hotels are basically in 3 areas: around Av Mohamed V/R du Marché; further east in the Quartier Erraha (big neo-kasbah hotels); and over the causeway in Hayy Tabount.

As Ouarzazate is basically a one-mule sort of place, a lot of streets have yet to get name plaques

LL-L *Hotel Berbère Palace*, T044-883105, www.ouarzazate.com/leberberepalace 232 good rooms off garden patios, pool, bar, tennis, restaurants Moroccan, Italian, international, piano bar, even a hammam, prices start at 1,400dh 1 person, rising to the vizierial suite at 3,000dh a night. Clientele includes tourists, business people, film producers and even the odd star. Downside? Smooth but impersonal. **A** *Hotel Bélère*, 22 Av Moulay Rachid, T044-882803, F883145. 270 rooms and 11 suites, a/c, pool, tennis, restaurants (poor

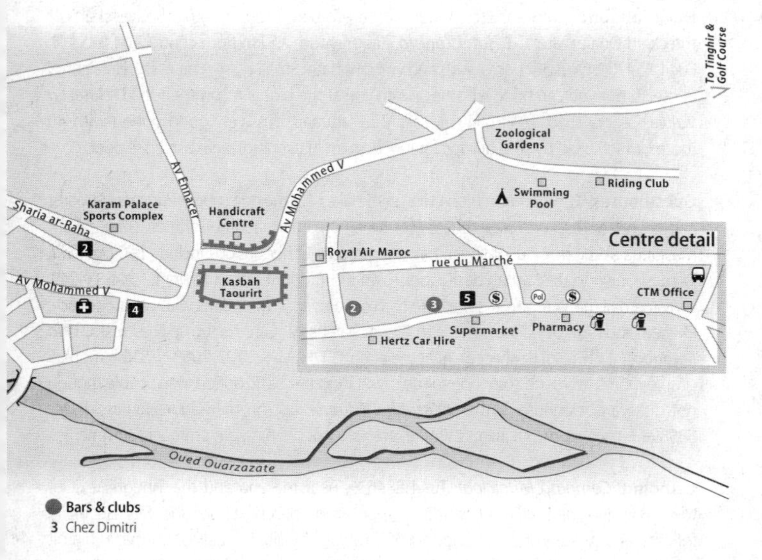

Ouarzazate & the Dadès and Draâ valleys

service), nightclub, cool, spacious, views over palm groves, excellent facilities, helpful manager, 2nd best hotel in town. Downside? Tour groups, a little frayed at the edges. **A** ***Hotel Riad Salam***, Av Mohammed V, T044-883335, F882766. 2 converted kasbahs, luxuriously equipped, 14 suites, 63 rooms, with TV, restaurant, bar, spectacular pool, sauna, massage, horse riding and tennis, shops, conference facilities, a bit overpriced.

B ***Hotel Oscar Salam***, on northern outskirts, at Tassoumaate, Route de Marrakech, right next to the *Atlas Corporation Studios*, T044-882212, www.atlastudios.com 64 rooms, a/c, lush pool – Egyptian gods watch over you. Downside? A bit tatty, poor service. **B** ***Hotel Sol Karam Palace***, T044-882225, F882642, Av Moulay Rachid, near the *Bélère*. Nice grounds and pool, next to *Sporting Club* (tennis courts). **C** ***Hotel Kenzi Azghor***, Blvd Prince Moulay Rachid, T044-886501/05. 150 rooms, restaurant, bar, pleasant pool, used mainly by tour operator *FRAM* so often full.

D ***Hotel la Gazelle***, Av Mohammed V, T044-882151. A good option with 30 rooms, bar-restaurant, small pool, a little out of town on the Marrakech road. **D** ***Résidence Ouarda***, Av Mohammed V near Palais des Congrès, T061-871499 (mob). Slightly mucky, decaying, last resort. **E** ***Hotel Amlal***, easily located on side street behind *Wafa Bank* and *RAM* office, signed, next to *Nekob Car Hire*, T044-884030, F884600. Clean rooms with showers, some rooms with 4 beds. Recommended. **E-F** ***Hotel Royal***, 24 Av Mohammed V, T044-882258, near the *BMCE*. Friendly place with clean rooms with shower, also some basic rooms. Well located, fair prices, 1st floor rooms slightly better but hot in summer. A better option than *Hotel Salam*. **E** ***Hotel Salam***, over the road from *Hotel Royal*, T044-882512. 3 floors, 55 rooms, many poorly ventilated, around long courtyard, rather like being in a large pink cake, fairly clean, requires payment in advance – an option if all else fails. **F** ***Hotel Atlas***, 13 R du Marché, T044-882307, behind the main street. Cheap and more or less clean. **F** ***Essaâda***, R de la Poste, T044-883231. Only has cheapness to recommend it. **F** ***Hotel Habib***, in low-rise building diagonally across waste ground from grand taxi station, T044-882024. Clean. **F** ***Hotel Safsaf***, on left after Palais des Congrès as you come from Marrakech, T044-884121. Austere metal bedstead type hotel. Good value, used by tour-group drivers.

Hayy Tabount There are a few hotels over the Tabount causeway on the west bank of the Oued Ouarzazate. **C-E** ***Hotel Zaghro***, Zagora road, 2.5 km from centre, T044-85413, F044-854709. Over 50 rooms, with and without bath. Small pool. A bit noisy. No alcohol at meals, but you can bring a bottle, as can you at the highly recommended **D** ***Hotel La Vallée***, Zagora road, T044-854034, zaid172@caramail.com Very good option with 40 rooms, much used by tour groups for lunch, quiet in evening, pleasant small pool.

Guesthouses The ultimate chic? A villa on the lake near the golf course. Princess Margaret and Leonardo Di Caprio stayed here (not together). Information on the off-chance from Mustapha at the golf club if you're passing through. Other options include **B-C** ***Dar Daïf***, Talmasla, next to the Kasbah des Cigognes on the Tabount side of town, T/F044-854949, www.dardaif.ma 4 rooms, 7 suites, a/c bath or shower. Some rooms with private terrace. Owned and run by Zineb and Jean-Pierre Datcharry. Can set up excursions. **C** ***Villa Kerdabo***, 22 Blvd Sidi Bennaceur, near the airport., T/F044-887727, T068-675164 (mob). 5 simple rooms, will send someone to meet you. Another basic option, personable though not quite a guesthouse, is the **D** ***Kasbah Tifeltoute***, out on the Zagora bypass, T044-885899. Only 6 rooms, clean and simple, possibility of sleeping out on roof in summer.

Camping *Camping Municipal*, T044-884636, near the zoo and the Tineghir exit of town. Running water, café and restaurant, pool at complex next door, showers, electricity for caravans, grocery shop and petrol 800 m away, the site is small, only 1 ha, and a bit expensive, clean pitches. Can be noisy when there is a show on at the complex.

Eating

• on map, page 386

Expensive Asterix fans see ***Obélix***, Av Moulay Rachid, T044-882829, menu at around 160dh, created after *Astérix et Cléopatre* was filmed here. Decor featuring pharaonic statues, frescoes, etc. Tour groups are taken to the ***Complexe de Ouarzazate***, next to the campsite on the Skoura exit from town, T044-883110. Set menus 130-290dh, lots of traditional decoration and tents.

Mid-range There are a growing number of eateries doing more than just multiple tajines and couscous. Oldest address is ***Chez Dmitri***, on Av Mohammed V, in the town centre. Once the focus of Ouarzazate (as the bar of the Foreign Legion), the restaurant serves excellent European/Italian food, with a good lasagne. Downside? Lives on its fame, service poor. Further out from the centre is the restaurant of the ***Hotel la Gazelle***, Av Mohammed V, T044-882151. For French and Moroccan food try ***Le Relais de Saint-Exupéry***, aka ***Le Petit Prince***, 13 Av de Moulay-Abdallah, Quardier El Qods, T044-887779, in the Skoura direction, leaving Ouarzazate on your left just before the *Total* station. More varied cuisine than elsewhere, recommended. Management used to run the *Hotel Rosa Damaskina* at Kelaâ des Mgouna. In centre, try in particular ***La Kasbah***, opposite the Kasbah Taourirt, T044-882033, menu 100dh, no alcohol, nice service, eat outside on terrace. Also ***La Datte d'Or***, on Av Moulay Rachid, T044-887117, ladattedor@caramail.com, a recent establishment with a 100dh menu. Decor is Alpine-Berber chalet, service attentive and efficient. Recommended.

Cheap The cheapest places are along R du Marché and nearby streets. ***Restaurant Salam***, Av du Prince Heritier Sidi Mohammed, on corner with *Hotel Atlas* (and nothing to do with Hotel Salam), is a cheap touristy option for Moroccan food. ***Restaurant Chez Hellal***, 6 R du Marché, is a good choice, just to left of entrance to market (terrace good for people watching). If passing through Ouarzazate, have lunch at the roast chicken restaurant almost opposite *Chez Dimitri*. Make sure you know what you're paying when you order. For breakfasts, try the ***Café du Sud***, on Av Mohammed V towards the Kasbah Taourirt.

Bars

Ouarzazate is not the best place for lads' night out. In memory of the Foreign Legion, have a quiet drink at ***Chez Dmitri***, Av Mohammed V. More lively is the nightclub of the ***Hotel Kenzi Bélère***, popular with locals as well as tourists. Raï, techno, etc.

Shopping

Films, batteries for cameras, sun cream, writing paper and stamps can be obtained on Av Mohammed V. Almost opposite *Chez Dimitri* there is a supermarket which even sells alcohol (last place before Tineghir as you head east). On the same side of the street as the supermarket, look out for Abdallah Medkouri's shop sellling various local souvenirs and in particular pieces of *hizam*, a sort of carpet belt once worn by women in the region.

Sport & activities

Biking *Rent-a-Bike*, Av Moulay Rachid near the big hotels, T044-887117, 140dh a day. Can provide guide and helmet. An excellent way to get to know the region. **Golf** *Ouarzazate Royal Golf Club*, 9 holes, par 36, T044-882653, F883344. Open daily, a rather parched sort of course. **Go-Karting** ***Kart aventure***, Av Moulay Rachid, between hotels ***Berbère Palace*** and ***Kenzi Belère***, T044-886374, F886216, full day's excursion in off-road go-kart 1,700dh. Try also: ***Quad Aventure***, in Hayy Tamassint, near *Atlas Studios*, T044-884021, www.quadaventure.com, about 1,000dh/day. Also rent mountain bikes. **Riding** *North Africa Horse*, 5 Résidence Bab Sahara, Pl Al Mouahidine. Provide beasts for films, sometimes do day rides and treks. **Swimming** At major hotels and in particular the Complexe de Ouarzazate, next to the campsite. The *Hotel Bélère* pool can be used by non-residents for 50dh. Try also pool of the *Hotel Karam*. **Tennis** At the ***Sporting Club*** on Av Moulay Rachid, next to the *Hotel Karam*. 6 floodlit tennis courts, ball boys, fine view.

Tour operators

Amzrou Transport Touristique, 4 Av Mohamed V, T044-882323, amzrou@iam.net.ma Rental of 4WD vehicles with driver, treks and circuits for small groups. ***Daya Travels***, also rent bikes. T044-887707/T062-498287 (mob), www.dayatravels.com ***Ksour Voyages***, Pl du 3 Mars, T044-882840, turn left before the Palais des Congrès as you come from Marrakech. ***Palmiers Voyages***, Pl de la Poste, T044-882617. ***Top Voyages***, *Hotel Karam*, T044-883645, for excursions in the region.

Trek operators

Trekking agencies *Désert et Montagne Maroc*, contact via *Dar Daïf* guesthouse, or on T044-885146, F886352, desert@iam.net.ma Sets up mule and camel treks. ***Iriqui Excursions***, Pl du 3 Mars, T044-885799, www.iriqui.com In-depth knowledge of the region.

Mountain guides *Fatima Aoujil, Bureau des guides*, Hayy el Ouarda 1581, T061-148225 (mob), ayomofat@iam.net.ma Fully qualified mountain guide who can advise on and set up treks. ***Lahcen Ahansal***, 2 Av Mohamed V, T044-847942. Lahcen is 4-times champion of the Marathon des Sables, Morocco's desert challenge. He and his brother, a trained mountain guide, run treks.

Transport

Local **Car hire**: *Budget*, Av Mohammed V, near *Résidence Ouarda*, T044-882892. ***Hertz***, Blvd Mohammed V, T044-882048. ***Inter-Rent***, Pl du 3 Mars, T044-882035. Other agencies around Pl du 3 Mars. For petrol, there is *Shell* in the centre and service stations at the main exits to the town. Lead-free petrol available – check *Afriquia* in Marrakech direction.

Long distance **Air** Flights from Taourirt airport, northeast of the city, T044-882348, to **Casablanca** and possibly **Marrakech** and **Agadir**. International flights to **Europe** (mainly France) both charters and regular. For internal flights, airport formalities are confusing. **Airline offices**: *RAM* Av Mohammed V, T044-885080/885102/882348

Road **Bus**: to **Marrakech** across the High Atlas by the Tizi-n-Tichka pass. Several services a day to **Zagora**, east to **Boumalne**, **Tineghir**, **Er Rachidia**, and west to **Taroudant** and **Inezgane**. *CTM* buses, T044-882427, leave from the offices on Av Mohammed V, next to the *PTT*, private line buses including ***SATAS*** from the gare routière outside town. For distant destinations, get your ticket the day before.

Grand taxi: 2 departure points: from Pl Al Mouahidine, destinations include **Hayy Tabount**, **Skoura**, **Boumalne** and **Zagora**; for further afield, head for the gare routière.

Directory

Banks ATMs near the *RAM* on Av Mohammed V. *BMCE*, Av Mohammed V, has a bureau de change open Sun. Otherwise try the large hotels to change money. **Communications** **Internet**: try ***Internet Info-Ouar*** on the alley between the hotels *Atlas* and *Amlal*, also ***Cyber-Café Ouarzazate*** on Av Mohammed V, between supermarket and *Amzrou Transporte*. **Post**: *PTT*, Av Mohammed V. **Medical services** **Chemist**: *Pharmacie de nuit*, Av Mohammed V, T044-882708, also on Av Al-Mouahidine. **Useful addresses** **Fire**: T150. **Police**: Av Mohammed V, T190.

Aït Ben Haddou

Phone code: 044
Colour map 2, grid B4

Up on a dramatic hillside, the Kasbah of Aït Ben Haddou, 30 km from Ouarzazate, is one of the largest complexes of traditional packed-earth buildings in Morocco, hence its place on the Unesco-sponsored World Heritage List. The place's fame has spread far and wide and in season coach after coach drives up, pauses for a photograph to be taken and then leaves.

The turn-off for Aït Ben Haddou is clearly signed from the P32, 22 km from Ouarzazate. A large *marabout* with ridged cupola and crenellated edges on the tower is a prominent landmark to make sure you don't miss your way. The route follows the valley, with the *oued* on the right. The first village is Tissergate.

After a further 10 km the much-filmed kasbah comes into view on the right, set up above the bright green of the irrigated fields. The kasbah towers offer views across the area and the old village also includes a large *agadir*, or store house.

Aït Ben Haddou no doubt grew because of its strategic location on the south side of the Atlas, near the convergence of the Draâ and Dadès Valley routes. The village is a must for tourists, both because of its unique architecture and its role in the film industry, with *Lawrence of Arabia* and *Jewel of the Nile* filmed here, as well as *Jesus of Nazareth*, for which part of the settlement was actually rebuilt. Despite all the visitors, the area is not really spoilt.

Sleeping & eating

As you drive up to Aït Ben Haddou on the metalled road, the hotels and restaurants are on your right, in the following order: *Auberge Bin el Ouidane*, *Auberge La Kasbah*, *Restaurant Saghro*, *Auberge Baraka* and *Auberge Etoile filante*, the latter being 400 m further on the left. At peak times of year, try to reserve accommodation in advance. **C-D** ***Auberge Bin el Ouidane***, T044-890312, F893737. 8 en suite rooms with view, 9 without view, all painted sandy brown. **C-D** ***Auberge la Kasbah***, T044-890302/08, F883787. 40 rooms, small, nice decor, 10 with shared bathrooms, 3 price categories, nice management, does car, mule and bike hire, pool, courtyard rooms hot in summer. Best choice here. **E** ***Auberge-Restaurant Al Baraka***, T044-890305, F886273. Small place with a restaurant, ugly plastic tent out front and 5 fairly clean rooms, primitive washing arrangements, standards here are low, direct access to unprotected roof terrace extremely dangerous for children. **E** ***Auberge Etoile filante***, T044-890322, F886113. 9 rooms, set menu 70dh, nice welcome. A good cheap address.

To Tamdaght

The road continues to the ford at Tamdaght, with accommodation at the gîte d'étape **E** *La Kasbah* adjacent to the Oued Mellah (contact Abd el Aziz Taoufik, T044-890371). This is a splendid site. A bridge has been constructed, and with a 4WD you could carry on the 40 km or so remaining up to Tourhat along the Asif Ounila and then west to Telouet (see page 372). The route is not to be risked when there is lots of melt water or after late summer thunderstorms. Even the best off-road vehicle can become bogged down in the wet clay.

The Draâ Valley

Phone code: 044
Colour map 2, grids C5 & C6

The road from Ouarzazate to Zagora is spectacular, first winding its way across the Jbel Anaouar mountains, and then down along the Draâ valley, a strip of intense cultivation, a band of vivid colour weaving through the desert. Here and there are red-earth coloured kasbahs and villages of flat-roofed houses, there rooftops edged with crenellations. Once, the Draâ was one of the longest rivers in North West Africa. Today, the cultivated areas give way to the desert near M'hamid, south of Zagora. In this region, the classic sights are the village of Tamegroute, once famed as a centre of Islamic learning, and the dunes of Erg Lehoudi and Chigaga.

Ins & outs

Getting there The P31 is a good road, much improved by recent works. Regular buses and grands taxis connect Ouarzazate, Agdz and Zagora. A car allows you to make photo-stops at will, and visit the smaller, less spoilt oases and villages. (Tamnougalte has a particularly good kasbah.) The most difficult section of this route is between Ouarzazate and Agdz, with a winding climb up to the Tizi-n-Tinifitt.

Getting around Once in Zagora, you can visit the oasis on foot. Tamegroute is 20 km from Zagora, and you might be able to get a grand taxi or a lift of some kind if you don't have your own transport. There are buses from Zagora to Tamegroute. (The once much visited dune site of Tinfou is a further 10 km on from Tamegroute.) There is a slow local bus between M'hamid and Zagora, which means that M'hamid, only 88 km further south, is not a day-trip option without your own car. The dunes of Chigaga require 4WD.

Background

The Draâ Valley region south of Ouarzazate was not always so arid – as is attested by the rock carvings of animals which have been discovered in the lower Draâ. The Draâ was known to the ancient writers: for Pliny, it was the *flumen Darat*, for Ptolomey, the *Darados*, and Polybius mentions it as a river full of crocodiles. After Zagora, near M'hamid, the Draâ disappears in the sandy Debaïa plain. The river only very rarely runs its full course to the Atlantic coast near Tan Tan, some 750 km away (the last time was in 1989). In years of sufficient rainfall, there is good grazing for the nomads in the Debaïa, and even some cultivation.

Agdz

Agdz has numerous overpriced carpet and pottery shops. Pestering can be a problem

Travelling south from Ouarzazate, Agdz, with its Thursday souk, is the first major settlement of the Draâ Valley, about an hour's drive from Ouarzazate. The buses, often full, pass through here, but there are grands taxis for moving on. There are no banks here.

Sleeping and eating C *Maison d'hôte Tansiffte*, T044-341056, fermeagdz@hotmail.com As you head out of Agdz for Tazenakht, the guest-farm is about 2 km from the *Total* station. 5 rooms, shared washing facilities. Meals. **D** ***Hotel Kissane*** (named for the neighbouring Jbel Kissane), Av Mohammed V, northern end of town, T044-843044, F843258. 29 rooms, an upmarket option said to be in decline. Restaurant heavily used by tour groups, always a bad sign. **F** ***Hotel-Café-Restaurant du Draâ***, T044-843024. 17 rooms, breakfast, a friendly place, price includes hot shower (evenings only). **F** ***Hotel des Palmiers***, on main square near petrol pump (access on side street), T044-843127.15 small rooms, some badly ventilated, clean loos. ***Camping Kasbah de la Palmeraie***, T044-843640, some 5 km out of the village centre, also rents rooms, simple restaurant. Wash block could be a lot cleaner, early morning call to prayer from mosque nearby. The palm groves nearby can be a pleasant place to wander, however. Through both the campsite and the *Hotel des Palmiers*, it may be possible to arrange excursions, and **mountain bikes** can be rented from *Horizon Sud* on the main square, T044-843065.

At Tamnouglat D *Au Jardin de Tamnougalt*, T/F044-843614, freenet.de/jardin-tamnougalt Guesthouse 6 km south of Agdz at the kasbah village of Tamnouglat, well signed after the little road on the left opposite the kasbah ruins. All rooms with shower, camping possible.

From Agdz to Zagora

If off-roading in this area, go with at least 2 vehicles

Heading south of Agdz, you are entering real kasbah land, a region which with the Ziz Valley is one of the most beautiful oasis valleys in Morocco. With a 4WD, there are a couple of opportunities for some off-road driving here. Try to take in the **Kasbah de Tamnougalt**, some 6 km south of Agdz, on the north bank of the Draâ. Some 30 km east of Agdz, you come to **Tansikht** and the intersection with the 6956, a metalled road running east to Nekob, where it becomes the 3454. This route eventually takes you right across to Rissani in the Tafilalet.

There are two rough track options to take you down to Zagora from near Tansikht. Option one, to be undertaken with a minimum of two vehicles, involves turning east onto the 6956 (which becomes the 3454 after Nkob). After about 15 km, there is a track leading right (south-southeast) towards a col. It then takes you across rocky plain to the small settlement of **Zaouia Tafetchna**, and then more or less south to Zagora. (A left-hand fork after

Zaouia takes you east to Tazzarine.) For option two, you follow a track on the eastern bank of the Draâ. Cross the bridge at Tansikht onto the 6956 for Nekob, and the track is a couple of kilometres further on to the right. The off-road drive to Zagora will take around six hours.

Zagora

Phone code: 044
Colour map 2, grid C6

Zagora is the main town at the southern end of the Draâ valley, the best place to overnight before heading off into the desert. In the 1990s, the town woke up to tourism. The arrival of 4WD vehicles and the improvement of the P31 road has allowed an influx of visitors. In the space of a decade, the desert settlement has been transformed out of all recognition. Zagora in fact goes back to the 13th century, when it was founded by an Arab tribe.

Ins & outs

Hassle The fact cannot be ignored – the people of Zagora see visitors as having a great deal more money than they do and, given the poverty levels, many locals want to make something out of the tourist trade. To avoid potential hassle, try to use official guides and make travel arrangements into the desert through your hotel or recommended agencies.

Sights

Alhough there are few architectural traces of the town's life before tourism, the paths through the date palm groves to the various *ksour* can help you imagine a time when the world was much, much slower. Of these promenades, one of the more pleasant, despite the potential pestering, is around the **Amazrou date palm oasis** across the river. There is also some accommodation here. Amazrou features a kasbah once famed for its silverwork. Above Zagora and within walking distance are two hills, from where there is an excellent view over the valley and towards the desert. Nearby are the ruins of an 11th-century Almoravid fortress.

During the *mouloud*, there is a major religious festival held in Zagora, the *Moussem of Moulay Abdelkader Jilala*. The town's market days are on Wednesday and Sunday. The souk is an important place for the exchange of produce and livestock for the surrounding region.

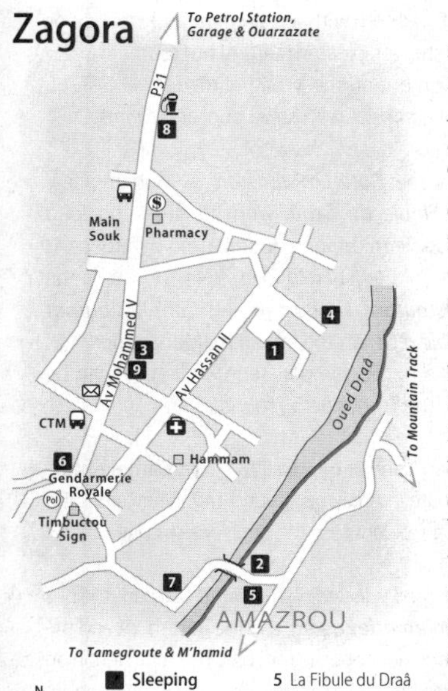

Sleeping

For a small town, Zagora has a reasonable selection of hotels

B ***Hotel Reda Zagora***, Route d'Amazrou, near the Oued Draâ at the southern side of town in the palm groves, T044-847079, F847012. 155 rooms, restaurant, bar, tennis, 2 pools. Posh, 800dh 2 persons, rates negotiable out of season. Overpriced. **B** ***Hotel Riad Salam***, Av Mohammed V, T044-847418, F847551. At entrance to the town, 60 double rooms and 4 suites, with shower and telephone, OK-ish restaurant, pool and private parking. Elegant. **B** ***Hotel Ksar Tinzouline***, northern end of town between Av Hassan II and Oued Draâ, T044-847252, tinsouli@iam.net.ma 90 rooms, beautiful gardens, restaurant, bar, excellent pool. Fraying a little at the edges.

Run by *Fibule du Draâ* management. **D** ***Hotel La Palmeraie***, Av Mohammed V, near road junction to south of town and bus station, T044-847008. Friendly, 60 rooms, a few with a/c, restaurant, small pool, beer available, compulsory half-board Apr and Dec at 170dh 1 person. A popular choice. **E** ***Hotel Vallée du Draâ***, Av Mohammed V, T044-847210. Basic but adequate, with restaurant, street-side terrace, very central, some rooms with showers. Recommended. **F** ***Hotel-Café-Restaurant des Amis***, Av Mohammed V, roughly halfway between the bus stations. Friendly, clean and with a reasonable restaurant, hot water evenings only, the cheapest option but rooms very hot in summer.

In Amazrou **D** ***Hotel-Restaurant Kasbah Asmaa***, 2 km from centre, just over the bridge to Amazrou on eastern side of and adjacent to Oued Draâ, T044-847599, F847527. Restaurant, pool, garden. Best to reserve in high season. Popular hotel now living on its reputation (badly maintained bathrooms etc). Glitzy Touareg approach to desert Morocco. **D** ***Hotel La Fibule du Draâ***, about 200 m on from the *Kasbah Asmaa* on right before irrigation channel, T044-847318, F847271. 26 rooms, pool and restaurant-bar, used by tour groups. 270dh 1 person without breakfast, simple rooms 100dh, also sleep out possible. Mountain bikes available for rent. Good reputation. **D** ***Hotel Sirocco***, go left over bridge as you come from Zagora, hotel is 150 m on left, T044-846125, F846126. A nice new address in Amezrou in the usual bogus kasbah style, nice pool, alcohol, desert trips organized. Recommended. **D** ***Hotel-Restaurant Zagour***, Route de M'hamid, BP 17, Zagora, T/F044-847451. Concrete block-type hotel 600 m after the bridge. 18 double rooms, all a/c, restaurant, minute pool. Prefer the *Sirocco*. **D** ***Villa Zagora***, guesthouse in the palm groves near Jbel Zagora. French run, reservations via Paris on T00 33 146337084, minimum 3 nights stay.

Camping ***Camping d'Amazrou***, 1 km to the south in M'hamid direction, T044-847419. Basic and friendly, 100 m on from the *Hotel La Fibule du Draâ*. Wash block needs to be cleaner. ***Camping la Montagne***, 3 km to south, site of 1 ha, friendly, plenty of shade and water, on the spartan side, petrol 1 km. ***Camping Sindibad***, T044-847553, near the *Grand-Hotel Tinsouline*, in a small palmery with a restaurant and small pool. Rooms available 50dh, with toilet and hot shower, pleasant setting but rooms are very damp. ***Camping Auberge Tomboctou***, 6 km out on the M'hamid road, T044-847165 and (via Casablanca) T022-356653. Recent campsite with small pool and rooms.

Eating

As in many southern towns, cheap eateries need to be treated with caution. If worried, stick to food cooked before you and processed products

Hotel Tinzouline, T044-847252, and the cheaper ***Hotel La Palmeraie***, Av Mohammed V (alcohol available). In Amezrou, try ***La Fibule du Draâ***, with its large and loud Arabo-kitsch decor (serves alcohol). A possible mid-range option, used by groups, is the ***Restaurant La Baraka***, after the *Fibule* on the M'hamid road, T044-847722. In the town, basic food can be had at the ***Restaurant Timbuctou*** and ***Café-Restaurant Essaada***; or ***Restaurant l'Afrique***. The ***Sable d'Or***, on the left on Av Mohammed V as you go towards the Tombouctou sign, is a good little pâtisserie, while beer can be bought at the ***Hotel La Palmeraie***, also on the Tombouctou roundabout.

Sport & activities

Bicycling Bicycles can be hired in Av Hassan II and at the *Hotel La Fibule*. **Camel excursions** Try ***La Fibule du Draâ***, 2 km to the south in Amazrou, around 140dh for camel and meals. **Swimming** *Hotel Tinsouline* lets non-residents use the pool for a small fee.

Directory

Anything of any importance is on Av Mohammed V, including the grand-taxi park, the bus station, post office, the ***Banque Populaire***, ***Pharmacie Zagora***, and the best shops and the souk. For medical care, there are 2 doctors' surgeries opposite the souk. The *Total* station on the Ouarzazate road can do minor vehicle repairs, while there is a larger garage opposite the police station, on your left as you come from the Ouarzazate direction. ***Cyber Club***, 87 Av Mohammed V, T066-943855, supplies internet access, while newspapers are available at the Librairie Najah, also on the main avenue, just down from the gare routière.

South of Zagora

Tamegroute
20 km SE from Zagora

Tamegroute lies on the left bank of the Oued Draâ and is visited mainly because of the *zaouia*, founded in the 17th century, headquarters of the influential Naciri Islamic brotherhood, which had great importance in the Draâ region until recently, and is visited by scholars from the Islamic world. The outer sanctuary and library are open to public view (closed 1200-1500), the latter containing a number of impressively old *korans* and 12th-century antelope hide manuscripts. The village is interesting to explore, a close-knit area of old housing typical of the region, with potters at work producing the characteristic green and brown pottery, and a souk, main day Saturday. There is a daily bus and grands taxis to Tamegroute.

Some 8 km south of Tamegroute, the **Tinfou dunes**, once popular with tourists, are a thing of the past due to a violent storm.

Sleeping and eating Tamegroute D *Jnane Dar*, opposite the library, T044-848622. 6 rooms and nomad tents, garden area, has had some good reports. There are a couple of places to stay at the **Tinfou Dunes**, the family run **E** *Auberge du Repos des Sables*, T044-848566, now in a period of decline, and the pricier **C-D** *Porte au Sahara*, 1 km from the road, contact via *Sahara Express*, BP 28 Zagora, T044-848562, F847002. 10 well-furnished rooms or roof space with mattresses. Restaurant with alcohol.

Tagounite

Driving south from Tinfou, the road takes you up over the Jbel Bani and down into oasis country again and the village of Tagounite, at the junction with the other road coming southwards from Zagora. Some 5 km before you reach Tagounite, a sign on the left indicates the **D** *Kasbah Aït Isfoul*, which has rooms and camping space, T044-848302, also via local téléboutique on F044-848127. Further on, outside the village of **Ouled Driss**, around 6 km before M'hamid, another sleeping option is the *Carrefour des caravanes*, T/F044-848665, with accommodation in small rooms or under nomad tents. Wash block could be cleaner, can lay on treks into desert.

M'Hamid

M'Hamid can be reached by bus or by a negotiated grand taxi from Zagora. Note that there are two routes, one via Amazrou, Tamegroute and Tinfou, described immediately above, the other being a 90-km drive south along a reasonable road through the desert. M'Hamid has basic facilities, cafés and accommodation, a Monday souk, and dunes nearby. If visiting on a Monday, there may be some 'blue men of the desert', as per traditional tourist literature. In reality, great camel caravans led across the desert wastes by indigo-swathed warriors are a mirage from the last century. Nevertheless, M'Hamid is a good place from which to arrange short camel rides and stays overnight in the desert, possible destinations being the sands of the **Erg Lehoudi**, some 8 km north of M'hamid, and the dunes of **Chigaga**, 55 km out towards the Algerian frontier, a 90-minute drive by 4WD. Try to get there for sunrise or sunset. Go with a trek operator.

Sleeping F *Hotel Iriqui*, T044-848023 or (via Ouarzazate) T044-885799, F884991. Basic, clean rooms, can organize treks out to Chigaga dunes. **F** *Hotel Sahara*, 10 rooms, separate showers. Very rudimentary, none too clean. Camel trips can be arranged.

Camping *Auberge al Khaima*, T062-132170 (mob), in the palm groves, over the bridge, rough and ready a few simple rooms available. More sophisticated is *Camping Hamada du Draâ*, T062-132134 (mob), clean, a couple of showers and loos. Contacts with official guides.

East from Zagora to Rissani

Colour map 3, grids B2 & B3

Leaving Zagora, there are two main options if you want to avoid going northwards back over your tracks. The first route, the rough track running northeast from Zagora to Tazzarine, a settlement on the main metalled west to east route to Rissani in the Tafilalet, is for 4WD only and needs careful planning. Ask at Zagora hotels for details of the vans and lorries covering this route.

Nekob & Tazzarine

In a hire car, there is a better route to Rissani which, although it means retracing steps 60 km up the Ouarzazate road as far as Tansikht, takes you across some wonderful arid scenery on metalled road all the way east to Rissani (essentially the 3454, although some maps label the middle section as the 3458). Although the route can easily be driven in a half-day, there is now an excellent overnight halt at **Nekob** (42 km from junction) where the restored citadel has been given new life as the *Kasbah Baha Baha* (see Sleeping below), with a tiny ethnographic museum, lots of information on the region, including prehistoric rock art. After Nekob, **Mellal** is the next settlement before **Tazzarine** (conveniently located 75 km from junction), a small settlement with *Ziz* petrol (no unleaded) and basic shops, where the direct north-south track from Zagora joins the road. Tazzarine is a good base for searching out the *gravures rupestres* (prehistoric rock carvings) at Tiouririne or Aït Ouazik – see Sleeping below for details about guides.

After Tazzarine, you pass through **Tiguerna** (128 km from the junction), the airstrip where anti-locust spray planes are parked, before reaching the more major oasis settlement of **Alnif** – petrol, mechanics, small stores and two hotels (see below). Over the remaining 90 km to Rissani, you pass through small villages such as **Achbarou**, with shops and a café, and (30 km after Alnif) **Mecissi**, which makes a good starting point for off-road journeys into the desert areas of the Oued Mharch and Oued Gheris. **NB** Such expeditions are best set up with expert local help. Finally, 55 km beyond Mecissi, after crossing a dry riverbed, you reach the junction (petrol) with the P21 Erfoud-Rissani road. Turn right (south) for the last 3 km into Rissani (see page 416 for further details).

Sleeping & eating

Nekob D *Kasbah Baha Baha*, T044-839078, F446724. Cool, quiet rooms. Interesting displays of traditional artefacts, a small pool, and discrete staff in local gear. Highly recommended.

Tazzarine D *Hotel Bougafer*, next to *Agip*, T044-839169, F838086. Restaurant, 45 clean, basic rooms, showers a bit mucky, be very clear about prices (do they show any in restaurant yet?). **Camping** *Camping Amasttou*, signed as you arrive from Nekob, T044-838078, F446724. 50dh 2 people with tent, also basic rooms available. *Camping Bougafer*, on left, just after oued as you arrive from the west, T044-838084, F838086. Very basic, belongs to hotel of same name, has contacts with local guides.

Alnif F *Hotel Restaurant Bougafer*, T055-783809, F884289. 10 basic, fairly clean rooms, well-meaning staff, and opposite the similar **F** *Gazelle du Sud*, T055-783813. Very cheap, 5 basic none too clean rooms. Meals provided at both places.

Transport

In practical terms, a **grand taxi** from Zagora to **Rissani** via Tazzarine is around 100dh per person, or 600dh for the whole taxi. A 4WD with driver from Zagora to **Rissani** is 900dh and takes 6 passengers.

Tracks from the 3454 to the Dadès road

Always check you have a good spare tyre before setting out on piste into rough country

With a solid 4WD, there are a couple of routes from the 3454 across wild country to the P32 Rachidia to Ouarzazate road. Heading east out of Nekob, you will find a sign showing right for Tazzarine, left for **Iknioun**, a settlement lying some 65 km to the north in the Jbel Saghro. It is best to travel this route with a local as the tracks are confusing. Some of the better ones lead up to mines, in fact. After crossing the **Tizi-n-Tazazert-n-Mansour** (2,200 m), you will have the option of going north on a rather better piste to **Boumalne** (about 42 km), or right to Iknioun and then **Tineghir**, via the **Tizi-n-Tikkit**, a rougher but more beautiful route.

The easiest route up from the 3454 to the P32 heads north from **Alnif**, however. Although it is best tackled in a 4WD, it can just about be done in a hire care with high clearance. After the **Tizi-n-Boujou**, the track takes you onto the P32 some 20 km east of Tineghir, 35 km west of Tinejdad.

West from Zagora to Foum Zguid

Colour map 2, grids C6 & C5

This route was off-limits for years due to the risk of Polisario rebel incursions from neighbouring Algeria. It is another difficult journey best attempted in a 4WD with accompanying vehicles. Much of the road (the 6953) is a very poor surface and 124 km in these conditions are not to be undertaken lightly. The thrill of the open spaces, the wide horizons and the faint prospect of sandstorms makes this a memorable journey. Basically, the road runs east-west following the line of the **Jbel Bani** to the south. From **Foum Zguid**, further rough tracks take you southwest and west towards **Tata** in the Anti-Atlas.

The gorges of the Dadès and Todgha

Colour map 2, grids B5 & B6

The 'Road of the Thousand Kasbahs', as it is termed in the tourist blurbs, takes you from Ouarzazate up to Tineghir, via Skoura, El Kelaâ des Mgouna and Boumalne du Dadès, through arid plains and oases where the backdrop is one of harsh mountain landscapes, where semi-nomadic Berbers pasture their flocks. The modern world has arrived, however: tourist buses and four-wheel drives bring their flocks to the growing villages at the start of the spectacular gorges, and the new buildings replacing the crumbling kasbahs use concrete breeze blocks rather than pisé. Nevertheless, there is plenty of interest and walking opportunities along this route. Oases near to Ouarzazate like Skoura and El Kalaâ can be covered as day excursions, or you could do stop-overs while heading east to Er Rachidia. Those with 4WDs can try the bumpy mountain tracks leading into the Massif du Mgoun, from Skoura round to El Keleâ via Toundoute and Bou Thraghar, or the rugged gorge-to-gorge route from Boumalne to Tineghir, via Msemrir and Tamtatouchte.

As you set out travelling east of Ouarzazate on the P32, the land is flat and barren plain. To the north, outlying hills of the High Atlas become increasingly visible. To the right signs indicate the presence of **El Mansour Eddahbi Barrage** whose waters, in a good year, are just about visible south of the road. The golf course is a landmark: 'traditional style' villas can just about be glimpsed.

The large oasis fed by the Oued Idelssan has irrigated gardens with palms, olives and cereals. The Oued Hajag crosses the road on the western side of Skoura. The small settlement here has a white square mosque with white cupola.

Skoura oasis

Colour map 2, grid B5

You can now bypass the old oasis settlement of Skoura (souk Monday and Thursday) on the main road. Nevertheless, the palm groves have much of interest. Before the actual village, to the left of the road, is **Kasbah Amerhidl**, the largest of Skoura's kasbahs. The village also includes two kasbahs formerly occupied by the El Glaoui family, **Dar Toundout** and **Dar Lahsoune**.

The older part of the town is to the north, providing all the usual services. There is petrol (*Ziz*), and small shops in arcades on both sides of the road include bakers and pharmacy. If you stop, groups of children and youths will want to take you to the kasbahs. *Café Atlas* is clean and fairly welcoming and the *Café du Sud* is not too bad either. Since the construction of the bypass to the west, new buildings have filled in the space among the palm trees. To get the most out of a wander round Skoura, you might as well take a local as a guide (50dh is a generous tip for a couple of hours for a student guide).

Sleeping **LL** *Dar Ahlam*, T/F044-852239, www.lamaisondesreves.com One of the most exclusive addresses in Morocco. Prices start at around 3,800dh per day per person with everything thrown in. **C** ***Kasbah Aït Ben Moro***, 3 km before Skoura proper, T/F044-852116, receptionist Aziz Sabir T067-194760 (mob). A beautifully refurbished building a few metres off the main bypass. With so many concrete kasbahs around, it is splendid to find such a well restored building. Rooms are dark, as kasbah rooms had to be, decor is austere and elegant. From the roof terrace, views over the palm groves to the Kasbah d'Amerdihil. 24 rooms, meals 120dh. Can organize horse riding, 350dh per day. Highly recommended. The alternative, some 200 m from the Kasbah d'Amerdihil, is **E** ***Chez Slimani***, a simple gîte-type place. **F** ***Hotel Nakhil***, a primitive establishment for emergency use.

Imassine At Imassine, just east where the road crosses the Oued Dadès, there are two small places for a drink, the *Café des Amis* and the *Café Salem*. New houses in **Aït Ridi** indicate money from abroad. This is the beginning of the rose-growing area. All the fields have hedges of roses, but there are no flowers to be seen because as soon as the bud opens the petals are picked.

El Kalaâ des Mgouna

Phone code: 044
Colour map 3, grid B1

Another ribbon-development sort of place, El Kalaâ des Mgouna, 1¼ hours' drive from Ouarzazate, is the capital of the Moroccan rose-essence industry and centre of the M'Gouna tribe. (The name means 'Citadel of the M'Gouna' and is also spelt Qalat Mgouna.) The former French administrative centre has become a sprawling town with banks, police, small shops for provisions, petrol and a Wednesday souk. The **rose festival** is held in late May/early June with dances and processions under a shower of rose petals. The children at the roadside will try to sell bunches of roses and garlands of rose petals, and there are plenty of shops selling rose water, *crème à la rose*, rose-scented soap and dried roses.

Background How is it then that El Kalaâ came to be a centre for this industry? A picturesque local legend runs that pilgrims travelling back from Mecca brought with them 'the Mother of All Flowers', the Damascus rose. It may be, however, that sometime in the 20th century, French perfumers realized that conditions in this out of the way part of southern Morocco would be ideal for the large-scale cultvation of the bushy *Rosa centifolia*. Today, there are hundreds of kilometres of rose bush hedges, co-existing with other crops, and two factories, distilling rose essence. (The one in a kasbah-like building can be visited.) To produce a litre of good quality rose oil requires around five tonnes of petals, you will be told. The locals feel, however, that the price paid by the factories is too low, and prefer to sell dried rose petals on local markets. Pounded up, the petals can be used mixed with henna or other preparations. Rumour has it that Bulgarian rose growers are providing stiff competition for El Kalaâ.

Sights

Based in El Kalaâ, the energetic may want to head northwards 15 km up the Mgoun Valley to the **Ksar de Bou Thrarar**, at the entrance of the Mgoun Gorges. Less adventurously, there is a dagger-making co-operative on the eastern outskirts of the town. For trekking options in the Massif Mgoun, see Azilal High Atlas section, Vallée des Aït Bougmez, on page 376.

Sleeping & eating

El Kalaâ does not have a vast range of accommodation – and you need to reserve if you are going to coincide with the rose festival (which, in all honesty, is more for locals than tourists). **C** ***Hotel Les Roses de Mgouna***, T/F044-836007. 102 rooms, above the town at 1,927 m, a pure relic of the 1970s, with accommodation built around courtyards planted with bamboo and fruit trees. Reasonable restaurant, bar, nice pool with views of the Mgoun Massif. A sleepy sort of place, apart from the bar that is much used by locals. Prices negotiable out of season. **C** ***Hotel Rosa Damaskina***, pont d'Alnou, 6 km before El Keläâ, to north of road, T044-836913, F836969. Restaurant *Le Képi blanc* (more memories of *la Légion*), beautiful views over river valley to poplar trees and ruined kasbah, small rose garden, tacky restaurant tent. An odd little place, fine for a night but long past its best. **D-E** ***Kasbah Itren***, a tiny new auberge run by a Spanish-Moroccan partnership, up on a cliff on the road up into the Massif du Mgoun. 5 simple rooms, views of Kasbah Mirna to south and Kasbah du Glaoui to north. Mountain guide Mohammed Taghada, T066-161147 (mob), can organize treks for 350dh 1 person night all in. **F** ***Hotel du Grand Atlas***, Av Mohammed V, T044-836838. 12 rooms, basic and friendly. Communal showers. The owners can help you set up trekking into the nearby Massif du Mgoun.

Shopping

Apart from the ubiquitous rose products (best buy: large pink heart-shaped rose-flavoured soap), you could try the ***Coopérative du poignard***, the Dagger Makers' Cooperative, on the right shortly after the centre. Making daggers is a craft tradition carried on from the now-departed Jewish communities in the region, and most of the artisans are concentrated in Azlague, south of the Cooperative. A good dagger, purely for ornamental use of course, may cost anything up to 400dh.

Sport & activities

Trekking El Keläâ is a good base town for trekking, call in at the **Bureau des guides de montagne**, 1 km before the town centre, on south side of road, clearly signed, T044-836311. As elsewhere, the daily rate for a guide is around 200dh. The *Hotel du Grand Atlas* has plenty of contacts with guides. Ambitious walkers in late spring and summer may want to try to climb Irhil Mgoun, at 4,068 m one of the highest peaks in the central High Atlas. A good 7-day circuit would take you up to Amesker and back via Aït Youl.

Directory

Banks *Wafa Bank* and *Banque populaire* right on main intersection. **Medical services** **Pharmacy**: on left (east) after *Banque populaire*, also on street leading to *Hotel Rose de Mgouna*. **Doctors**: Dr Brahim Charaf, T044-836118, home T850061.

El Keläâ to Boumalne du Dadès

After El Keläâ des Mgouna, the 20 km to Boumalne is heavily built up, in some places three blocks deep. As you leave El Keläâ heading east, watch out for a bad bend marked by red/white crash barriers on the right. Much of the building is financed by locals who have emigrated to Europe and are putting up something for their retirement. Behind the houses is a string of prosperous oasis gardens, with dilapidated kasbahs popping up at intervals.

Dadès and Todgha Gorges

Phone code: 044
Colour map 3, grid B2

Over the centuries, coming down from the High Atlas, the Oued Dadès and Oued Todgha have carved out narrow and spectacular gorges. These make attractive excursions from Boumalne (for the Dadès) and Tineghir (for the Todgha). Both gorges offer options for walking up into the mountains beyond. For the really rugged, it is possible to travel north up into the High Atlas to Imilchil and the Plateau des Lacs via remote Agoudal, and there is also a rough piste leading from Msemrir, on the Dadès round to Tamtatouchte, on the Todgha. However, most people choose just to walk in the lower gorges and enjoy the scenery from the pleasant vantage point of the restaurants located nearby. There are some fine opportunities for birdwatching.

Ins & outs

Getting there Both Boumalne (116 km from Ouarzazate), for exploring the Dadès Gorge, and Tineghir (170 km from Ouarzazate), for exploring the Todgha, are easily accessible by bus and grand taxi. Both places are situated on the P32 road linking Ouarzazate to Er Rachidia. There are grands taxis between Boumalne and Tineghir, taking about an hour. Tineghir is 5 hrs by bus from Ouarzazate. If in own car, note that when passing through ribbon settlements in this region in the evening you need to drive with care, watching out for small children, bicycles, mopeds and donkeys. There is quite a lot of 4WD tourist traffic, too, which tends to race along too fast. Alternatively, you might approach Tineghir and Boumalne from the east, coming in from Er Rachidia or Erfoud via Tinejdad. On public transport, both Er Rachidia and Erfoud lie about 3 hrs from Tineghir.

Boumalne du Dadès

Approaching from the west, there is usually a Gendarmerie royale checkpoint at the intersection before the bridge, so slow down

Boumalne is a small town (Wednesday market), with a reasonable selection of hotels. The town grew from a very basic settlement to its current size mainly in the second half of the 20th century. In the Muslim cemetery there is the domed shrine of one Sidi Daoud. He is commemorated in an annual festival, when bread is baked from flour left at the grave, and fed to husbands to ensure their fertility.

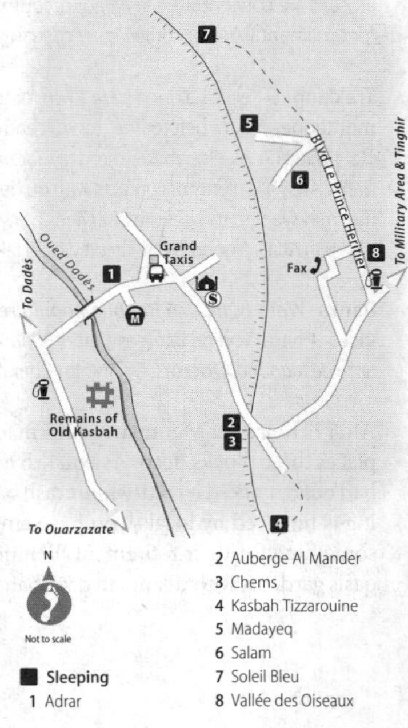

Excursions
See also Gorges du Dadès below

Visitors go to Boumalne for the landscape, harsh and rocky. From a high point above the town, a barracks and some hotels look out over the landscape. If you are a birdwatcher, you may well want to head off south to the **Vallée des Oiseaux** (the road from Boumalne to Iknioun). Otherwise, there are rewarding short walks up into the gorge. **Msemrir**, 60 km up the gorge, is a possible destination using local transport. Should you want to stay in the gorges, there is some basic accommodation at **Aït Oudinar**.

The track southeast which leaves the P32 road just east of Boumalne gives easy access into the desert environment. It rises steadily to **Tagdilt** and provides an experience of the desert, and possibilities for spotting desert birds and, less likely, desert fauna.

Sleeping

■ *on map*

Price codes: *see inside front cover*

C ***Kasbah Tizzarouine***, T044-830690, T061-34812 (mob), F044-830256. A largish hotel complex on the plateau overlooking Boumalne from the south (at top of slope, turn right just before large mural). Fine views over the Oued Dadès and the mountains to the north. Accommodation includes fairly traditional buildings with all modern comforts, tiny underground rooms (troglodyte), cool in summer and cosy in winter, or even nomad tents kept cool by the breeze. Establishment is now too big, with tent for entertainments and tour group lunches plus large conference rooms. A fairly well-run address if lacking the personal touch. Prefer the *Kasbah Tomboctou*, Tineghir, at this price, or the *Aït Ben Moro*, Skoura, slightly dearer. **C** ***Hotel Madayeq***, T/F044-830763. 100 rooms, comfortable, a/c, restaurant, bar and rooftop pool. Reception is very off-hand, once past them it is sunshine all the way. **D** ***Hotel-Restaurant Chems***, T044-830041, F831308. 10 double rooms, 5 single rooms, at the top of the slope heading for Rachidia, on the right on the bend. Well maintained, nice reception, restaurant.

E ***Auberge de Soleil Bleu***, to the right before the *Hotel Madayeq*, T044-830163. 12 rooms with bath, good restaurant, fine views, camping permitted, treks organized into High Atlas and Jbel Saghro by local guide Mustapha Najim. Popular with walkers and bird-watchers. **E** ***Hotel-Restaurant Salam***, T044-830762, near the *Hotel Madayeq*. 15 rooms, shared showers, heating, rooftop terrace and restaurant with local food. A friendly and helpful place which provides free transport to Aït Oudinar in the gorge, and organizes skiing, trekking, 4WD, mountain bikes, contact Daoud in Boumalne. Recommended. **E** ***Auberge Al Manader***, T044-830172, on the Rachidia road, near the *Hotel Chems*. 8 good clean rooms, 4 with bathroom, small restaurant, panoramic views as the name in Arabic suggests. **E** ***Hotel-Restaurant Vallée des Oiseaux***, T044-830764, on the Rachidia side of Boumalne, near the *Shell* station. 12 comfortable rooms and restaurant, can set up trips into the mountains, cheap rooms 70dh, with shower 110dh, open fire in winter. **F** ***Hotel Adrar***, opposite the souk, T044-830355. 27 rooms around a courtyard, with restaurant.

Eating

The best restaurant in town was once at the ***Hotel Madayeq***. Cheaper options include ***Hotel-Restaurant Salam*** and the ***Café Atlas***, in the centre, good for food or just a tea or coffee; just outside Boumalne, on the Er Rachidia road, ***Restaurant Chems*** is perhaps the best option with its pleasant terrace.

Gorges du Dadès

The 6901 leaves the P32 at Boumalne and follows the Oued Dadès through limestone cliffs, which form the striking Gorges du Dadès. The principal destination is the section of the gorges following Aït Oudinar, but the track continues up into the High Atlas, with public transport as far as Msemrir. There are very basic pistes into the mountains, and around into the Gorges du Todgha.

Just beyond Boumalne is **Aït Arbi**, where there are a series of striking *ksour* above the road. The road continues past areas of unusual rock formations, through **Tamnalt** and **Aït Oudinar**, where there is basic accommodation. The valley narrows after Aït Oudinar, creating the most striking area of the gorges, where the cliffs are in vivid shades of red. The road, now surfaced practically all the way, continues alongside the *oued* as far as **M'semrir**, just beyond which it branches. The right-hand branch turns into a difficult track, running east across the pass (2,800 m) and continuing to link with the 6902 through the Gorges du Todgha, and up into the High Atlas. The gorges and crags offer a good environment for golden and Bonelli's eagles and lammergeiers, and the scree slopes for blue rock thrushes.

Sleeping & eating

There are a number of small places to stay up in the Gorges du Dadès. However, standards of hygiene are variable, and the loos don't always seem to keep up with the influx of visitors. By the time of going to press, electricity should have arrived, which should lead to an improvement in food standards. When staying in simple places like these, make sure you know what you have to pay when you settle in. Note that Aït Oudinar makes a good starting point for a walking circuit.

Tamnalt 14 km from Boumalne, accommodation and food are available at the **E** ***Hotel-Restaurant Meguirne*** and further on at the ***Hotel-Restaurant Kasbah***, 13 rooms and insufficient loos. **Aït Oudinar** 25 km from Boumalne, **C** ***Auberge Chez Pierre***, T044-830267, a tasteful Belgian-run establishment with rooms and excellent food. Try also the **E** ***Auberge des Gorges du Dadès Aït Oudinar***, T044-831710, 25 rooms, restaurant, téléboutique. Variable reports on this. Facilities for campers and camper-vanners nearby. **Further on** **F** ***Auberge des Peupliers***, 27 km up in the valley, T044-831748, 4 rooms and camping, and the **E** ***Kasbah de la Vallée du Dadès***, about 27 km from Boumalne. Good reports. Most basic of all is the ***Auberge Tissadrine***, T044-831745, cheap and fairly clean. **Aït Hammou** Simple **F** ***Café-Hotel Taghea***, several rooms but no electricity. **Msemrir** Basic accommodation available at ***Café Agdal*** and ***Hotel Ouarda***.

Boumalne du Dadès to Tineghir

From Boumalne to Tineghir the P32 road runs across a flat plateau land, between the southern side of the High Atlas, to the north, and the eastern end of the arid Jbel Saghro, to the south, forming a clear line. This is mining country, also a land of resistance to French forces. A track leads south to the 2,200 m Tizi-n-Tazazert shortly after Boumalne, and to Iknioun and Jbel Bou Gafer. The mining centre of **Imiter** is signed. At **Timadriouine** a track leads south to mines (silver) which can be seen from the road, and northwards to Arg Sidi Ali ou Bourek. A number of ruined *ksour* stand in the valley at Imiter, some quite tall. There is sparse pasture land between. At 52 km from Boumalne, 166 km from Ouarzazate, **Tineghir** appears in the distance down a long straight stretch of road.

Tineghir

Phone code: 044
Colour map 3, grid B2

Once a tiny oasis settlement, Tineghir is a modern administrative centre, its population swelled by technicians and staff working for the local mining company. Tourism is taking on importance, and the town is an ideal stay on the road east to the Tafilalet, the **Gorges du Todgha** being the sight to see (see below). It also makes a good first night on a walking holiday.

Tineghir is an unexpectedly large place. There is the modern hub, now ribboning east and west along the P32. And then there are the older kasbah settlements, a few kilometres north from the town, overlooking irrigated plain as one climbs out of the

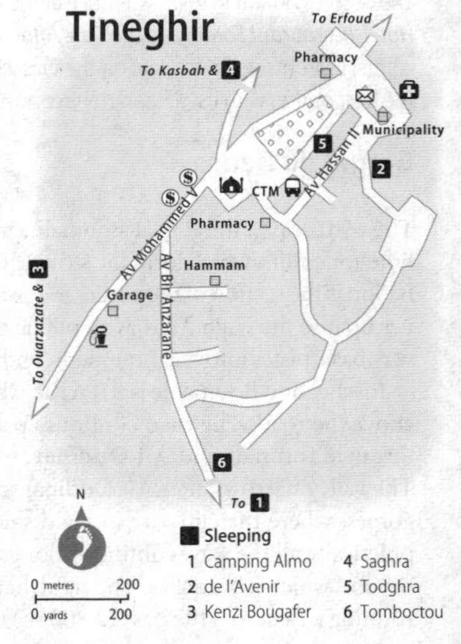

town towards the Gorge du Todgha. There is a stark contrast of magnificent barren mountains and verdant oases. For the rushed, there are views from the gorge road – otherwise you might explore on foot. Hire a guide for 40dh. You will find olive and fruit trees inter-cropped with cereals and vegetables, herds of sheep and goats out to pasture in the foothills. As elsewhere in the region, there is much new building along the roads, the old *ksour* partly abandoned to the side. The main population belong to the Aït Atta tribe. Try to visit the **Kasbah El Glaoui**. Although officially closed, it is normally possible to get in.

Sleeping

■ *on map*
Price codes:
see inside front cover

Nothing too complicated about Tineghir, which focuses on 2 squares, one with trees on the main road, and another a block back from the main street, sort of behind the post office. Town hotels are located around these 2 areas. The other option for accommodation is to head up into the gorges, taking a local grand taxi from the centre, or, with own transport, turn left before the low bridge on the eastern side of town (see below).

B ***Hotel Kenzi Bougafer***, Blvd Mohammed V, T044-833200/80, F833282. An early 1990s hotel 2 km west of town, comfortable, clean, good pool, alcohol, noisy. **C** ***Hotel Saghro***, T044-834181, F834352, on the Ouarzazate road, with the appearance of a *ksar*. 62 comfortable rooms, restaurant, bar and pool. **D** ***Hotel Todgha***, 32 Av Hassan II, T044-834249. 30 rooms, restaurant, overpriced .**D** ***Hotel Tombouctou***, Av Bir Anzane (take 1st major left coming into Tineghir from west), T044-834604, F833505. Nice cool rooms in restored kasbah, small pool, secure car parking available. Mountain bikes for rent, plus sketch maps of region. Best hotel. **E** ***Hotel l'Avenir***, on the 2nd square, T044-834599. On 1st floor above a pharmacy, 12 small rooms, very clean, good beds, roof terrace. Some rooms only open onto corridor, square below is noisy. Still the best cheap hotel. Bike hire. **F** ***Hotel El Fath***, Av Hassan II, T044-844806. Next to the *CTM* bureau. Hot showers. Café-restaurant. **F** ***Hotel Houda***, R Moulay Ismaïl. A recent hotel, on a side street off Av Hassan II. **F** ***Hotel Oasis***, Pl Principale. Cheap, clean, central, welcoming, upstairs restaurant with good food and views over town. **F** ***Hotel Essalam***, on a side street behind the Pl Principale. Basic, 1 person 25dh, hot foam mattresses. Acceptable if all else fails.

Camping *Camping Almo*, centre of town on south of road, very secure, pool, shop, only open in summer. ***Camping Ourti***, south of road at western end of town beyond *Hotel Bougafer*, very secure, restaurant, bungalows, pool but quite a walk from town. All sites have electricity for caravans. Perhaps the best of the bunch.

Eating

No exciting gastronomic choices here. ***Hotel Saghro*** has a fair though expensive restaurant. ***Hotel Todgha***, 32 Av Hassan II, and ***Hotel Oasis***, Pl Principale, are a little cheaper. ***La Gazelle d'Or***, in the town centre, is also good. ***La Kasbah***, Av Mohammed V, a friendly place with good food. A good café is ***Chez Habib***.

Shopping

There is a Tue souk, behind the *Hotel Todgha* and small shops on the main square (Pl Principale). For alcohol and stores try ***Chez Michelle***, T044-834668, a supermarket, on your right after ***Ziz*** petrol as you come in from west. Look out for green facade.

Transport

Buses and **grands taxis** to all locations, including **Ouarzazate**, **Boumalne** and **Er Rachidia**, leave from Pl Principale. Grands taxis and vans run from here to the Gorge. In some hotels, staff may organize trips to the Gorge for 60dh. For locals, a place in a share taxi up the Gorge costs 6dh, the whole taxi 36dh. Tineghir to **Boulmane**, 25dh by grand taxi, Tineghir to **Er Rachidia**, 45dh.

Directory

Banks *Banque du Maroc*, along with other banks, on the Av Mohammed V. **Communications** Post: *PTT*, on main square.

Gorges du Todgha

Colour map 3, grid B2

The Gorges du Todgha are more spectacular than the Gorges du Dadès, particularly in the evening when the rocks are coloured in bands of bright sunlight and dark shadow. There are campsites and places to stay near the narrowest part of the gorge, a highly recommended break from the activity of the major towns.

The 14 km route is very narrow, and you will have to slow down for kids playing near the road. Also watch out for the tyre-splitting road edge when you move over for a bus thundering towards you. (Tourist buses and 4WDs head up to the Gorge for lunch.)

Just north of Tineghir as the road climbs up is the village of **Aït Ouaritane**. There are many good views. The safest place to stop is generally picketed with camels, the most spectacular has the usual fossil and scarf sellers. Photocall for neat strips of crops in the oasis gardens and crumbling kasbah villages.

Some 9 km from Tineghir are campsites in an idyllic location in a palm grove. About 6 km further on is the most visited section of the gorge, where the high cliffs leave just enough space for the road and river. As you might imagine, rocks, palm groves and river make this a good environment for birds. There are a couple of hotels (*La Vallée* and *Etoile des gorges*) before the ford, and in the past there was a small toll to pay for taking one's car up beyond this point. Or someone would say that 'the gorges are closed', obliging you to park and pay them a car park fee. The ford should present no problems for ordinary cars, and you can carry on up to the next two hotels, *Les Roches* and *Yasmina*, which squat in the bogus kasbah style under a spectacularly overhanging bit of gorge.

Sleeping

There are plenty of options in the gorges, for all budgets, including campsites with facilities for campervans, and a number of hotels, some now quite substantial. In winter it gets pretty chilly at night, and in late summer the river can swell suddenly after thunderstorms in the mountains, so choose your camping place with care.

D ***Hotel Amazir***, on your right after *Camping Les poissons sacrés*, stone building, T044-895109, F895050. Opened 2001, 15 rooms (6 triple, 9 double), manager Omar Aït Chaoui very anxious to please. Recommended. **E** ***Hotel-Restaurant Auberge La Vallée***, T044-835580, on your left as you arrive. Small basic rooms, nice management. **E** ***Auberge Etoile des Gorges***, T044-835158. Another tiny, adequate hotel, 6 rooms, some with en suite hot shower. **D** ***Hotel Les Roches***, T044-834814, F833611, at the end of the road. Perfectly adequate, 30 rooms, 50dh to sleep out on terrace with mattress, lunchtime menu 90dh, tour group restaurant in plastic ceremonial tent. Why put such an ordinary building in such an extraordinary place? **D** ***Hotel Yasmina***, T044-895118, F833013. Amazingly kitsch shiny green bedspreads in new rooms, restaurant in tent for tour groups. Camping here by arrangement. Sleeping on roof (mattress provided) 20dh per person and includes a hot shower. For these 2 hotels, hot water is only provided when the generator is working to produce light – so have your shower in the evening. Take a torch.

Camping As you head up into the Gorges, the first accommodation is a campsite, 8 km from Tineghir, on your left. The better is ***Hotel-Camping du Soleil***, aka ***Chez Bernard***, T044-895111, open since Dec 2000, small pool, a bit lacking in shade, otherwise excellent, new loo block, washing machines, some rooms, 1 person 100dh without shower, 200dh with bath and loo, night under tent 25dh, restaurant 114 seats, meal around 100dh. Recommended, ably run by Bernard, formerly with the Légion, and Issa. The best option, although a fair way from the gorges. Can put you in contact with a local for mule rides in the region. Next door is the **E** ***Hotel Camping Azlag***, T044-896050, 5 nice rooms, small campsite out back with bamboo canopy, breakfast 15dh, meal 55dh. There are 3 camping sites on the right a bit further on along the road leading towards the gorges, all of which do rooms. First along is **E *Hotel-Camping Atlas***, just opposite téléboutique, T/F044-895046. 6 rooms, also camping 20dh, campervan 1 person 10dh, tent 15dh, car 15dh, hot shower included. Rooms are in small building overlooking site, meals to order 60dh, definitely the best of the 3, same management as *Hotel Amazir*. ***Camping du Lac***, T044-895005. Bar, restaurant, more expensive. Has rooms as well in building over the road. ***Camping des Poissons Sacrés ('Sacred Fish' campsite)***, T044-895139. 10 tent pitches, 5 rooms, faintly smelly, has a slightly dodgy feel to it. Management needs changing, basically. Have a look in to see the fish if you're nearby.

Tamtatouchte & around

The more adventurous will want to continue beyond the narrow confines of the Gorge du Todgha. The village of Tamtatouchte is a walk of about four hours considering the steady climb. The *Auberge Baddou*, the *Auberge Bougafer* and various other rudimentary establishments provide food and accommodation. A few lorries returning from the souk use this route and would provide a lift, which will prove to be a very slow, very dusty and very bumpy ride. With 4WD many of the smaller villages to the north can be reached. By far the greatest danger to walkers are the fleets of Fronteras and squads of motorbikes. With a good driver, connections can thus be made westward with the Dadès Gorge or northwards to Imilchil.

Gorge to Gorge route

Though rough, the 42 km west to **M'semrir** from **Tamtatouchte**, rising to 2,800 m, is popular with the 4WD brigade. It can be done in five hours, they say. This journey is best undertaken in a good 4WD vehicle with reliable local driver. Ensure that tyre pressure is higher than normal, as tracks are very stoney, and that you have a full tank. Find out about the condition of the piste before departure. This route is best undertaken between May and September. At other times of year, potential flash floods make it dangerous. It is probably best to do this route starting at the Todgha Gorge so you do the most difficult pass, the one after Tamtatouche, 2,639 m, first. At **M'semrir**, a popular base village for treks, there are a couple of simple places to stay, including the *Auberge el Ouarda* and the *Auberge Agdal*.

Excursions south from Tineghir

The village of **Aït Mohammed** is southeast of Tineghir and clearly visible from the main road. It stands on the minor road which goes along the *oued* to **El Hart-n'Igouramène**. A track due south leads into the Jbel Saghro, aiming for the village of Iknioun which nestles under the central heights.

The road from Tineghir keeps to the south of the imposing Jbel Tisdafine. At 10 km from town a track to the right goes to Alnif (63 km) and a connection with the desert road from Erfoud to Zagora. See Tracks from the 3454 to the Dadès road, page 397.

East from Tineghir to Er Rachidia

In terms of public transport, buses run from Tineghir to Er Rachidia, or from Tinejdad, en route, across to Erfoud. There are grands taxis from Tineghir to Tinejdad, Tinejdad to Goulmima, and Goulmima to Er Rachidia. Tineghir to Tinejdad takes about an hour on public transport. Er Rachidia is roughly two hours from Tinejdad, as is Erfoud.

Tinejdad

East from Tineghir, the first major stop is Tinejdad, where the road forks and you have the choice of heading northeast for Er Rachidia or more directly east for Erfoud, Rissani and Merzouga. Tinejdad is an Amazigh and Haratine town in a large oasis, with some significant kasbahs, notably the **Ksar Asrir**; and the **F** *Hotel-Restaurant Tizgui*, with basic accommodation and food. There are an amazing number of bicycles in Tinejdad, every child seems to own one so be particularly careful when driving through. The central square offers a post office, the town gardens, town hall, telephones, taxis and *Total* petrol. There is a weekly souk. *Café El Fath*, *Café Assagm* and *Café Ferkla* are possibilities for refreshment. *Café Oued Ed-Dahab* stands north of Tinejdad at the junction with the road to Erfoud. It is a good place to stop offering cold drinks and juice, but you may find the place overrun with people on 4WD tours or even convoys of campervans.

The P32 road from this Tinejdad junction goes due north, leaving the palms of the oasis gardens for dry farming cereals on the level plain and aiming for a gap in the scarp, a gorge cut by the Oued Gheris. This is an extension of the scarp through which the gorges of Dadès and Todgha are cut.

Goulmima
Market day Monday

Goulmima (not to be confused with Goulimine, aka Guelmime, south of Agadir) is one of a series of expanding small towns, mainly Amazigh in population, round the eastern side of the High Atlas. Rachidia, Rich and Midelt are others of similar ilk. There is a lot of new property on the outskirts, well served with water, electricity and telephones. The centre of Goulmima is similar to Tineghir, and there are a large number of *ksour* out in the palm groves. Much of the town is to the north of the road in the main oasis.

Approaching the centre, after passing through the usual mechanics and carpenters on the outskirts, the road becomes wider. There are ministry buildings on both sides, a hospital on the left, village gardens on the right desperately in need of some attention. Opposite the garden is a bus station and a walled area for grands taxis, which extends about 200 m into town. An *Agip* petrol station is on the left before the market square. Sleeping options include a guesthouse, **D** *Les Palmiers* (Franco-Moroccan management, recommended), T055-784004, with five clean rooms and space for small tents in garden. More basic is the **F** *Hotel Gheris*, T055-783167, with 10 reasonable rooms, restaurant with good food. In this area are situated the pharmacy, telephone boutique, and after 50 m *Petit restaurant* advertising sandwiches, with chairs under the trees, all on the right. In the arcade of shops you will find another café, telephone, shop for stamps and postcards, *Restaurant Badou* and beyond up on the left the covered souk. *Camping Tamaris*, on a site of 4 ha, showers, petrol station 100 m.

Heading east out of Goulmima, the road sweeps up and over the *oued* after the *Ziz* petrol station. A high bridge indicates potential floods. The road climbs up sharply between the gardens, through the scarp (good views looking back).

Alternative routes from Goulmima

There is a road north from Goulmima leading to the villages of the High Atlas, only suitable for 4WD. It is 'surfaced' for the 55 km to **Amellago**, from where it is possible to circle back to the Todgha Gorge and/or the Dadès Gorge. More handily, Amellago is on the recently surfaced Rich to Imilchil road, cutting right into the heart of the eastern High Atlas. There is a road southeast to **Gaouz** (4 km) and eventually to **Touroug** on the road to Erfoud.

The last 58 km to Er Rachidia are up on the plateau, where the Jbel Timetrout runs parallel to the road on the north side. The land offers scrappy pasture for large flocks of sheep and goats and in places dromedaries herded by the nomads. Changes in animal husbandry are under way. Shepherds sometimes ride motorbikes, while water is provided at evenly spaced drinking and penning areas. More spectacularly, livestock owners transport their flocks in lorries to find the best seasonal grazing.

Rachidia, the Tafilalet and East High Atlas

410 Background

410 Er Rachidia
411 Ins and outs
411 Sights
411 Excursions
412 Esssentials

413 South towards the Tafilalet

414 Erfoud
414 Ins and outs
415 Sights
415 Essentials

416 Rissani
418 Around Rissani

420 The East High Atlas
420 Midelt
421 Around Midelt
422 Imilchil
424 Trekking from Imilchil to Anergui and Zaouiat Ahansal

Introducing Rachidia, the Tafilalet and East High Atlas

The variety and scale of the landscapes is the attraction of east-central Morocco. South of Rachidia, you have palm-filled canyons, crumbling ksour at **Rissani** and the **high dunes of Merzouga**. North of Rachidia, the **Oued Ziz** runs through a fearsome defile to Rich, where a metalled road now takes you west to **Imilchil**. Centring on a crumbling kasbah topped with

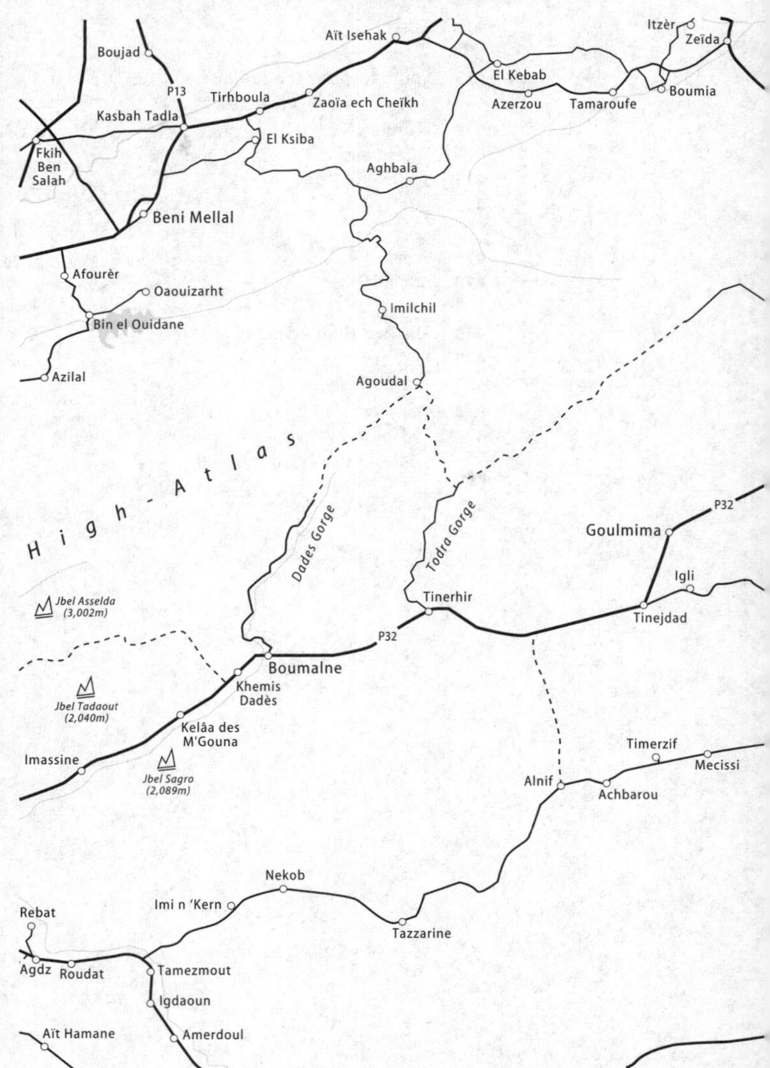

storks' nests, the village is a crossroads sort of place whence trekking expeditions set off into the **eastern High Atlas**. The region is particularly beautiful in late spring, when the greens of young barley and poplars coming into leaf contrasts with the creamy-brown nakedness of the cliff-sides above. In this region, long shoulder-mountains dominate, snowcapped into early summer. In the high pastures, semi-nomad lifestyles still subsist. Near to Imilchil are the calm twin lakes of **Isli** and **Tislit**. Moving westwards, tracks lead across the mountains to another major meeting of the ways, **Zaouiat Ahansal**.

North from Rich, over the Tizi-n-Tighemt, the rough and ready mining centre of **Midelt** is a good base for more excursions, to the abandoned mines of **Ahouli** in a defile of the Oued Moulouya, or off-road to the **Cirque de Jaffar**, a natural amphitheatre in the side of **Jbel Ayyachi**, paramount peak of the region.

Things to do at the eastern end of the High Atlas

- From Rachidia, take a day trip down to the Tafilalet. Overnight at the Erg Chebbi, the great **dunes of Merzouga**.
- With 4WD, explore the **Oued Gheris region**, remote desert south and west of Merzouga: Taouz, Hassi Ouzina and Hassi Remlia.
- North from Rachidia, take the spectacular road along the **Gorges du Ziz** to Midelt.
- Based in **Midelt**, explore the **abandoned mining settlement of Ahouli** on the upper Moulouya.
- Go **trekking from Imilchil** in the eastern High Atlas.

Background

Rachidia, east-central Morocco's largest town, is generally used by visitors as an overnight stop on a 'round the High Atlas' circuit. Coming from Ouarzazate, after a day visiting gorges and kasbahs, it makes a good place to pause before heading down to **Rissani** (more crumbling kasbahs) and the **dunes of Merzouga**. If you can't get accommodation at Merzouga or Erfoud, the dunes are visitable from Rachidia on a long day out.

Heading north from Rachidia, there is still more spectacular landscape: the **Gorges of the Ziz** and, after Rich, the hillscapes along the road to Midelt. Going west from Rich, you head up for **Imilchil**, in some ways 'capital' of the **Eastern High Atlas**, taken here as the region between Midelt in the east and Zaouiat Ahansal in the west. Only now beginning to feature on walking tours, the region is substantially different to the Toubkal High Atlas. Gone are the long deep winding valleys with their terraced fields. This is an area of shoulder mountains, bare plateaux and occasional deep canyons. High points include the **Jbel Ayyachi** and the deep gorges of the **Assif Melloul**, thick with vegetation.

Back on the P21, the former mining-town of **Midelt** is another useful base in the region. There are plenty of interesting day trips into the hill-country. On a Moroccan motor tour, Midelt is also handily located for an overnight stop about halfway between the Imperial Cities and the Tafilalet. Marrakech is also within a long half-day's drive of Midelt. For the moment, a difficult unmetalled section north of Imilchil on the Rich – Imilchil – El Ksiba route (bringing you out on the P24 east-west road) makes this route off-limits for small hire cars.

Er Rachidia

Phone code: 055
Colour map 3, grid B3

Er Rachidia, previously known as Ksar Es Souk, was renamed after the first Alaouite leader, 17th-century sultan Moulay Rachid, after independence. The Alaouites came from the Tafilalet region. The present town was established by the French, initially by the Foreign Legion, as a military and administrative centre, a role it retains today. The town has little of interest for the visitor, beyond a 19th-century ksar near the Erfoud exit. It has the usual concrete architecture. Behind the new brown and red buildings, the older mud-walled dwellings still exist. Er Rachidia, however, is a convenient stopping point at the meeting of routes to Ouarzazate, Erfoud (south), Midelt and Meknès (north) and distant Figuig (east), and so has reasonable facilities and a relaxed atmosphere, with lots of people out strolling in the evenings after the heat of the day. Main market days in Er Rachidia are Sunday, Tuesday and Thursday.

Ins and outs

Getting there
See Transport, page 412, for further details

You will probably head for Er Rachidia by road. (There were no regular flights to the Aéroport Er Rachidia, T055-572350, at time of writing. Should there be flights, a short taxi ride will take you into town.) There are several buses a day for Erfoud and Rissani (2 hrs), Midelt (3 hrs), Tineghir (3½hrs), Fès (9 hrs) and Meknès (8 hrs), and one each morning to Figuig (8 hrs). There are frequent grands taxis to Erfoud and Meski, Goulmima and Tinejdad, from the taxi rank opposite the bus station.

Getting around

The grid-iron street pattern, so typical of French garrison towns in the Sahara, makes orientation simple. The main road, Av Moulay Ali Cherif, leads down to the new bridge over the Oued Ziz, after which it becomes Av El Massira. The *gare routière* (T055-572024) is on the right in the town centre as you head east.

Tourist information

Av Moulay Ali Cherif, T055-572733 (open 0830-1200 and 1400-1800).

Sights

Er Rachidia is not exactly blessed with myriad sights. Architecture buffs may want to take a look at the historic **Ksar Targa**, about 5 km from the centre. Of passing interest are the **social housing developments** on either side of the Midelt road. Here the architects put new homes within neo-ksar type walls, painted a strong, Marrakech terracotta colour. As the largest town in the southeast, close to the Algerian frontier, the modern Moroccan state clearly needed to mark its presence by such projects. Er Rachidia is supplied with water by the Hassan al Dakhil dam on the Ziz and also has a large airport. The visitor will note quite a number of soldiers – there is a large garrison – and lots of shoeshiners, who will readily apply black polish to dusty walking boots. Otherwise, the hassle is fairly low key.

Excursions

For the **Source Bleue** (Blue Spring) at Meski, 21 km south of Er Rachidia on the Erfoud road, take a grand taxi, paying the same price as for Erfoud – the Source and campsite are a few hundred metres from the road. Moving on from Meski, you might be able to get a bus, or (easier) hitch a lift with other tourists.

North to the Gorges du Ziz

The P21 north to the Gorges of the Ziz is a superb route. For the first 20 km the road follows the Oued Ziz. Caves can be seen cut into the cliff, no doubt used to store crops. On your right is the western shore of the **Barrage de Hassan Addakhil**, completed in 1971. The dam supplies water to Er Rachidia and the region's oases. It also limits the potentially destructive flash flooding of the Oued Ziz. Migrating birds stop over on the lake, too. Travelling this route in the evening, the sun accentuates the landforms, highlighting bands of hard rock with screes between. And then you come to the Gorges of the Ziz, a spectacular ride in a narrow defile 2 km in length. At around 29 km from Er Rachidia, where a bridge crosses the river, there is the small settlement of **Ifri** where picnicking and camping are possible.

If you have lots of time, then continue on the P21 through the Legionaire's Tunnel, to the **hot springs of Moulay Ali Cherif**, 42 km north of Er Rachidia. Otherwise, backtracking to Er Rachidia on the P21, you could see if the road running left (east) to follow the dam wall is open (on some maps it is shown as off-limits). Follow through to the gardens of **Tirhiourine**. The surfaced road links with the P32 a few kilometres east of Er Rachidia, near the airport.

If you are travelling north on the P21 from Er Rachidia to complete a High Atlas circular tour, Midelt is the next major town with fairly decent accommodation, 156 km from Er Rachidia.

Essentials

Sleeping
■ *on map*
Price codes: see inside front cover

There is not a huge choice of hotels in Er Rachidia, especially at top of the range. **B** ***Hotel Kenzi-Rissani***, Av El Massira (de la Marche Verte), in the direction of Erfoud, T055-572184/86, F572585. Pleasant location on the town's outskirts, 60 rooms, restaurant, bar, disco, tennis and pool, open to non-residents for 50dh daily. Gets booked up by tour groups at peak times. **D** ***Hotel M'daghra***, R Allal Ben Abdallah, T055-574047, F790864. Popular, try to reserve. If coming from west, turn left at *Café Lipton* on main drag, hotel 100 m down on right. 29 rooms, a little noisy, very clean, nice reception (goldfish), the best bet, have breakfast in café nearby. **D** ***Hotel Oasis***, 4 R Sidi Abou Abdallah, T055-572519. A modern place with 46 small hot rooms, lovely wallpaper, restaurant and bar, if stuck only. **E** ***Hotel Meski***, Av Moulay Ali Cherif, T055-572065, near the intersection with the Midelt road. 25 rooms with uninteresting restaurant, café and small pool, streetside rooms noisy. **F** ***Hotel Ansar***, 34 R Ibn Batouta, T055-573919. Clean, 14 rooms, on street leading away from main street behind bus station. **F** ***Hotel Renaissance***, 19 R Moulay Youssef, T055-572633. 15 none too clean rooms, people are helpful, restaurant, has limited choice but OK food. Close to bus station. **F** ***Royal***, 8 R Mohammed Zerktouni, T055-573068. 21 rooms, 31 beds, ask when you get to Pl Hassan II. **F** ***Zitoune***, 25 Pl Hassan II, T055-572449. 10 beds in 7 rooms, very basic, no hot water.

Camping The campsite is closed, the nearest possibility being at Meski, 18 km southeast of Er Rachidia.

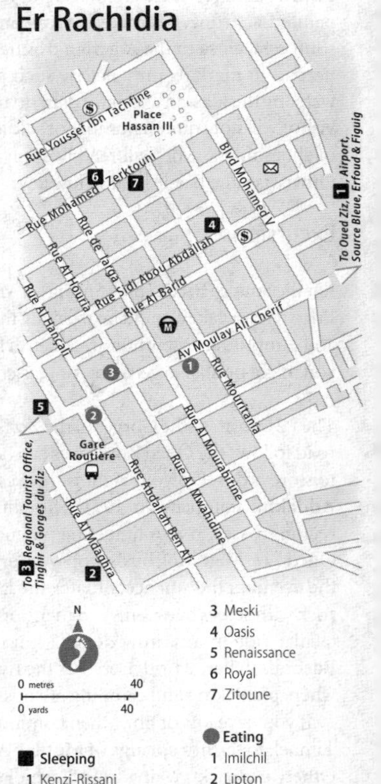

Eating
● *on map*

Hotel Oasis, 4 R Sidi Abou Abdallah, T055-572519. Serves Moroccan food and alcohol. ***Restaurant Lipton***, Av Moulay Ali Cherif. Good food throughout the day and night – and handy for the bus station. ***Restaurant Imilchil***, Av Moulay Ali Cherif, T055-572123. Moroccan standards served on a terraced establishment overlooking the main drag. The most economic place is ***Restaurant Sijilmassa***, Av Moulay Ali Cherif, with a simple but good menu. ***Hotel-Café la Renaissance***, 19 R Moulay Youssef, T055-572633, is reliable, with excellent couscous. There are other cheap places along Av Mohammed V. Try the ***Café Bousten***, next to the bridge on right at the eastern end of town.

Transport

Air From Er Rachidia, there used to be a weekly flight to Fès. At the moment, there is little traffic apart from the occasional private flight, usually emirs flying in with their falcons to hunt in the desert (Aéroport Er Rachidia, T055-572350). **Road Bus**: leave from the bus station off Av Mohammed V, T055-572760. For the long ride to **Figuig** early morning departure (0500, but check time).

Directory

Bank *Banque Populaire*, Av Mohammed V. *BMCE* on Pl Hassan II. **Car parts** Renault and other vehicle parts, also tyre repair, at place opposite the *Hotel Meski*. **Communications** Post: *PTT*, just off Av Mohammed V, near the *Banque Populaire*. **Medical services** Chemist: Blvd Moulay Ali Cherif, open all night. Pharmacy near *Café Lipton* and next to bridge in same building as *Café Bousten*. **Useful addresses** Police: T190. Fire: T150.

South towards the Tafilalet

Meski

Colour map 3, grid B3

Heading for the Tafilalet from Rachidia, you have 94 km to go before Rissani. Meski, lying to the west of the Erfoud road about 18 km east of Er Rachidia, is the first halt, famed for its Source Bleu. Developed by the Foreign Legion, Meski has a springwater pool surrounded by palms, and a popular camp site, the Camping de la Source Bleu, about 40dh for two with tent and car. Almost too lively in summer, the campsite is said to have improved considerably. Lots of fossil sellers nearby.

The **Ksar of Meski** is around 500 years old and the ruins make an attractive silhouette. Continuing south on the P21 towards Erfoud, you could easily miss one of the most spectacular views in Morocco. Keeping an eye out, you will eventually glimpse the huge **oasis-canyon of the Oued Ziz** to the right (west). There is a track, marked by a small cairn, which runs to the edge of the gorge. The view is magnificent – and there will be others there admiring the scenery.

Along the Ziz Canyon

After the viewpoints, the road soon drops down into the valley, some 20 km long, where a succession of ksour house the farming people who make their living from the area. Many of the settlements of the valley were destroyed in the flood of 1965. The southern stretches of the Ziz valley, a region known as the Tafilelt, are particularly fertile. 1930s writer Patrick Turnbull referred to the region's 'palm forests', a particularly apt term. Historically, the region was of considerable importance, due in part to its location on the trans-Saharan trade routes. The town of Sijilmassa was a major mediaeval centre whose rapid decline has not yet been fully explained. In the eighth and ninth centuries the region was a separate kingdom, and became known as a centre of religious unorthodoxy – of the Kharijite Berber heresy and later of Shi'ism. The ruling Alaouite Dynasty originated in Rissani. From 1916 to 1931 French control of the region was challenged and effectively thwarted by local forces.

Today the region, while it produces figs, olives and dates (not very special), is noted its tamarisk trees. Tamarisk fruit, appropriately dried, is used in the leather industry for its tannin, essential to the curing process.

If you have time, take a 4WD and a guide along the small roads by the river through the small settlements rather than speed along the P21. Here you will see a great contrast between the green fertile ribbon of palms and oasis gardens and the surrounding scorched landscape. In each loop of the river stands a ksar or fortressed village made of mud brick guarding the valley and providing protection for the village and also supervision for the trade in slaves and precious metals that used this route.

At 28 km from Rachidia, the road drops to the valley floor along a road descending down the cliff face. **Zouala** is the first settlement, and a sign indicates new guesthouse type accommodation there – *Chez Moha*, aka *Maison Zouala*, T055-578182, T061-602890 (mob). You could take time to explore the oasis here. Above are soaring crags, below are palms and the water, a fine dual environment for birds, the green contrasting with the rock faces. Further on, the large settlement, strung out along the road, is **Aoufouss**, about 45 km from Rachidia. There is *SOMEPI* petrol and a *CTM* stop. Red-washed concrete houses line the road, the old pisé dwellings are clearly visible further back. On the northern outskirts, look out for the circular threshing floors where there is sufficient level land. For a break, try the *Café Saada*, sit under trees on the opposite side of road. 28 km from Rachidia, the road rises out of the canyon floor onto an arid plain for the final approach to Erfoud.

At **Borj Yerdi**, 14 km north of Erfoud you will see a small geyser to the west of the road. Unfortunately, the water, red and iron-rich, is unsuitable for agrigulture. Experiments are underway to see if other benefits can be drawn. As per usual for a tourist halt, there are fossil sellers. The first small dunes come into view. Watch out for sand on the road, despite the tiny fences of palm fronds put up to control the ever shifting dunes.

North of Erfoud to the east of the road stands the ksar of **Ma'adid**. Here it is said the streets are so narrow and the arrangement so complicated that only locals can find their way in and, more importantly, out. Take a guide if you visit. There will be crowds of excitable small children, eager, as usual for bonbons and stylos. West of the P21 to Erfoud, look out for a spanking new development, the *Hotel-Complexe Kasbah Xalucca Ma'adid*.

Erfoud

Phone code: 055
Colour map 3, grid B3

Erfoud is another of these southern Moroccan garrison towns, founded by the French in the 1930s to administer their desert territories. The modern centre of the Tafilelt, it is not terribly exciting – but it does make an excellent base for exploring the valley and nearby desert areas. The small town of Rissani and its ksour and the dunes of Merzouga are close by. Lovers of dates may try to coincide with the annual date Fèstival held in October.

Ins and outs

Getting there Erfoud is easily accessible from the Dadès Valley further west. You can travel by bus from Tinghir to Tinejad, changing there for Erfoud (2hrs). Er Rachidia to Erfoud is 1½hrs. There is also a daily bus from Fès, 11hrs away.

Getting around Erfoud is a small place, easily explored on foot. You will probably however want to visit the ksour at Rissani, easily accessible by grand taxi. A number of ksour are a few kilometres out of the main settlement. The dunes are at Merzouga, about an hour from Erfoud, down a metalled road which then gives way to a few km of track. The dunes can be reached by 4WD excursion, with hotels like the *Salam* and the *Tafilalet* in Erfoud offering the trip. Otherwise, try to join up with some people with a car. There are grands taxis and minivans in the early morning between Merzouga and Rissani, leaving from the main square of Rissani near the *Ziz* petrol pump.

Sights

On the other side of the river from the town of Erfoud is the **Borj Est**, a military fort – no admittance, but get a taxi up to the top for the view – overlooking the village and palms, shadows of their former glory, the Tafilelt oasis and the desert. There is a souq on Sunday in the centre, and a Date Fèstival in October.

Marmar Marble Factory

Here they polish a black rock estimated to be about 650 million years old, embedded with fossilized shells known as goniatites (ammonites). Artistically enhanced fossils may not be everyone's thing, but they could make an interesting 'decorative feature', as they say. In fact, the stone isn't really marble as in a true marble the shells would have been metamorphosed to oblivion. The slabs, rather reminiscent of tomb stones, appear in all the hotels and bars in town. The main quarries are out of town on the road to Merzouga, near the *Hotel Salam*.

Essentials

Sleeping

■ *on map*

Price codes:

see inside front cover

Erfoud has a clutch of pricey hotels at the Rissani (southern) side of town, facing towards the distant Merzouga dunes. Coming from Rachidia, cheaper hotels and eateries in the town centre are reached by going left onto Av Mohamed V, at the crossroads with the post office. **B** ***Hotel Salam***, Route de Rissani, large hotel on left as you leave Erfoud for Rissani, T055-576665, F576426. Modern, well equipped in traditional style, 100 rooms, 45 de luxe suites, bar, exchange, a good restaurant, pool (not always!), shops, gardens, private parking, vehicle and driver hire including 4WDs with guides, used by tour groups, ask for Abdoul Oudai or ring him in Er Rachidia, T055-572486, to book in advance. Has had mixed reports. **B** ***Hotel Kenzi El Ati***, T055-577372, F577086. Large place on right after Tourism School on southern exit to Rissani. 110 rooms and 8 suites, breakfast 45dh, lunch and dinner 180dh. Better option than the *Salam*? **C** ***Hotel Kasbah Tizimi***, 2km out of town on the Tinghir road, T055-576179. 50 rooms around patio, pleasant pool, good restaurant. **D** ***Hotel Farah Zouar***, Av Moulay Ismail, on right as you leave Erfoud for Rissani, T/F 055-576230. 30 a/c rooms, restaurant serving European and Moroccan food, good views from roof terrace. Small rooms, dodgy hot water, suitable for slightly better-off independent

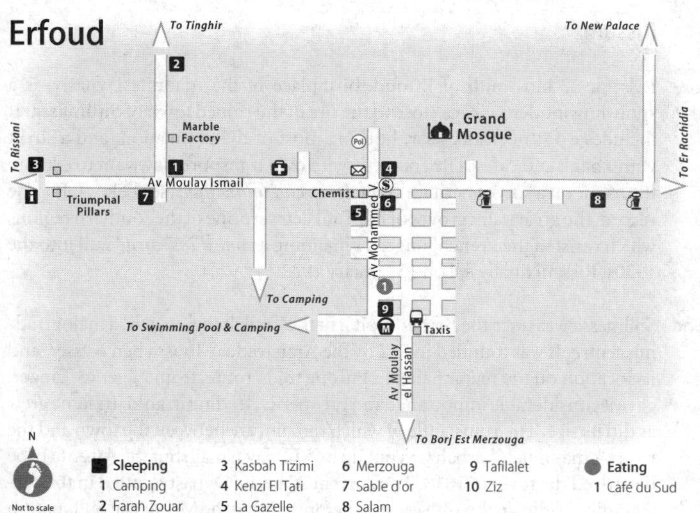

travellers. **D *Hotel Tafilelt***, Av Moulay Ismail, in town, on left as you arrive from Rachidia, T055-576535, F576036. 64 a/c rooms, bar, restaurant, pool and garden. Again, has had mixed reports – a bit run down, used by tour groups. **D *Hotel La Gazelle***, Av Mohammed V, T055-576028. 9 rooms, hot showers, good apart from noisy rooms at the front, reasonable restaurant. **D *Hotel Ziz***, 1 Av Mohammed V, T055-576154, F576811. 39 a/c rooms round courtyard, some with showers, good licensed restaurant, hire of 4WDs to see sunrise over dunes etc. **F *Hotel Sable d'Or***, 141 Av Mohammed V, T055-576348. Rooms with shower and loo, view of distant dunes from top floor. **F *Hotel Merzouga***, 114 Av Mohammed V. Basic, use own sheet, nice reception, will let you kip on roof terrace.

Camping, located close to Oued Ziz, with basic facilities, no shade, not recommended at all. OK for those with campervan. Avoid the chalet rooms.

Eating

● on map, page 415

You can eat in (relative) luxury at the *Kenzi El Ati* and the *Salam*. For those on a budget, there are places on Av Moulay Ismail and Av Mohamed V. **Mid-range** ***Restaurant Erg Chebbi***, Av Moulay Ismail, between the *Hotel Tafilalet* and the *Café des Dunes*, T055-577527, around 90dh a head, though you can eat for less. Also have hotel at dunes.**Cheap** As always in cheap restaurants in southern Morocco, check what you will be paying when you order. Cheap and fairly cheerful is ***Hotel-Restaurant de la Jeunesse***; try also the well-known ***Café-Restaurant des Dunes*** near the *Ziz* petrol station (standards have fallen of late). Also possible are the ***Restaurant-Café du Sud***, very handy for the bus station on Av Mohamed V; also on this street are the ***Restaurant Merzouga*** (prices shown) and ***Hotel-Bar Ziz***.

Transport

There are buses each day to **Er Rachidia** and on to **Meknès**. Transport onwards to **Rissani** is by bus, grand taxi, or by a hired 4WD.

Directory

The post office and branch of the ***Banque Populaire*** are located in the town centre on the central junction where main Av Moulay Ismail crosses Av Mohammed V. Nearby are the ***Crédit agricole***, a pharmacy and Dr Abdelkader Khouya, T055-576084. There is a *BMCE* ATM next to the *Total* garage on the east side of the main drag, just before the *Hotel Tafilalet*, as you go north. There is a men's hammam next to the *Hotel Sable d'Or*.

Rissani

Phone code: 055
Colour map 3, grid B3

Rissani, 22 km south of Erfoud, birthplace of the Alaouite Dynasty, is a sprawling modern village close to the site of the ruined town of **Sijilmassa**. It includes a 17th-century ksar, housing most of the population, and a street with a bank and cafés. The energetic with own transport may want to explore the ksour on a sort of heritage trail, the *circuit touristique* (see below). For the record, the great palm groves of the Tafilalet were one of the southern regions which resisted the French longest, remaining a *zone d'insécurité* well into the 1930s. Rissani finally fell on 15 January 1932.

Background

Sijilmassa was once the Berber capital of the Tafilelt region, and a major trading centre. It was founded in 757 by the Arab leader Moussa ben Nasser, and its location on the major Sahel to Europe trade route, from Niger to Tanger, gave it considerable importance and prosperity, trading in gold. Its fame grew as did its size. The ruins, little of which remain, are between the town and the river. A major new kasbah was put up by Moulay Ismail, but the Aït Atta tribe destroyed the town in 1818. The current Alaouite Dynasty settled in the surrounding region in the 13th century before gaining the Moroccan Sultanate in

Hassle and scams in Rissani

Rissani is an end of the line sort of place (the Alaouite dynasty used to exile potentially troublesome relatives down here). Most tourists getting out this far have one big objective in their minds: the dawn (or sunset) photograph of the great dunes of Merzouga. Though Rissani has some good sights too, the number of tourists staying in the town has fallen. Are they put off by the small number of hotels – or is it the hassle from the Rissanis? Arriving in a hire car, you will be assailed by kids eager to be its parking gardien. Then in the souk, authentically blue-robed figures may pursue you. Long-time Morocco visitors are in agreement: the hassle in Rissani is worse anywhere else – apart from the occasional incident in Fès. Whereas Marrakech's plain-clothes brigade touristique have worked wonders on the 'false guides' and other denizens of the souks, the local authorities in Rissani have shown no willingness to act.

The hassle here can take on a slightly nasty edge. And they don't give up that easily, either. So you've fended off the guy in the Touareg togs? There will be a swarm of kids around the corner. Coming from countries where one is generally ignored on an ordinary stroll round town, the constant demands for attention in desert outposts can be exhausting. Constant questions about one's nationality, job etc wear you down. With the desert heat and light (plus the Saharan runs), it's all a bit too full on. And even in a group, things can turn awkward. There was a report of an incident at Merzouga where some older members of a tour group got left behind in the dunes; local 'guides' caught up with them and refused to help them out unless a large sum of money was handed over immediately.

Other tactics used to get maximum financial gain are worked over several days. A classic case: young travellers meet calm, English-speaking local and spend lots of time with them, relaxing after hassle of journey. Local finds out all about travellers' lives, jobs and most importantly, spending power. On third day, visit to needy student friend with some nice articles to sell. Travellers buy goods with absolute confidence. Later, travellers find out that they have paid hugely over the odds – and feel pretty abused.

What to do then? First, understand that there is much poverty down in Rissani. Not perhaps on the scale of certain parts of the eastern High Atlas where there is child malnutrition too, but enough to make any potential source of a few dirhams worthy of attention. The kids are easiest to deal with of course. Try to be bemused, detached, don't lose your temper. If it's kids demanding pens and bon-bons, say donnez-moi un stylo first. You could even try to talk to them, learn a name or two. Remember, these children are in an education system based on rote learning in formal Arabic (not even in their first language, which will be Tachelhit or Moroccan Arabic). So any adult who actually tries to communicate will get a good response. They'll be here all summer, no weekends by the ocean in Essaouira. And after all, it's their ksar you're looking round.

the 17th century. The ruins are of historical interest only and the guides are ill informed – but can be entertaining. The tales of earthquake destruction are on the fanciful side.

To find out more about Rissani's past, you might call in at the **Centre d'études alaouites**, located in the large austere ksar on the main square (the former *Bureau des affaires indigènes*), just along from the *Hotel Sijilmassa*. There is a library and a museum, in practice a few small cases of pots from recent excavations and large panels with information in French about the region's history. There is a detailed 1 :100,000 scale map of the region, and some of the staff may helpfully speak English.

Sleeping & eating

There are few hotels in Rissani and at peak times of year, they tend to get booked up. It is probably better to stay in Erfoud, where there is much more choice, and make Rissani a day out. Another option would be to stay at one of the various dune hotels at Merzouga. **C** ***Hotel Kasbah Asmaa***, north of the town at road junction, 15km from Erfoud, T055-574083, F575494. Run by the Alaoui family. 34 rooms, lunch 110dh, can organize sorties to the dunes at Merzouga for small groups. **D** ***Hotel Tomboctou***, T055-575826, on the way to Merzouga. If all else fails. **E** ***Hotel-Café-Restaurant Sijilmassa***, Pl Massira El Khadra, T055-575042. Pass through the triumphal arch, the hotel is over on the left, near the mechanics. 10 high-ceilinged en suite rooms, modern and clean, some with 2 double beds. Perfectly adequate food, in cellar restaurant (ask to be served on terrace). **E** ***Hotel El Filalia***, T055-575103. Go right after you come through triumphal arch, hotel is 100m straight ahead. 18 good size spartan rooms, awful loos. On the main square, next to *CTM* office, *Banque commercial du Maroc* and *Ziz* petrol. Good view from roof terrace. Handy for hammam.

Not many eating options in Rissani. There are small places serving salad, tajine or roast chicken just next to the *Hotel El Filalia* at around 35dh a throw.

Shopping

Rissani has a lively market on Sun, Tues and Thur, and there are several handicraft shops. The region was once famous for its leather, although none of this tradition has survived. People with large 4WD vehicles may like to pick up a hefty chalky-white khabiya (water jar) or two, as still used in the region. Alternately, you could kit yourself up with full touristic 'blue man' gear, including gandoura 'air-conditioned' robe, slit down sides, baggy seroual, a chèche (3 m of cotton, sand-proof scarf).

Transport

Although there is a new gare routière, before the ceremonial arch as you come into town from the north, lots of buses still seem to come into the main square, as to the Mercedes minivans and grands taxis for Merzouga. There is a CTM bus (T055-575103), leaving for Rachidia and Meknès every evening, around 2000, plus occasional grands taxis across to places on the 3454 road across to the Zagora to Ouazarzate road.

Around Rissani

The Ksour circuit

see map opposite

To the southeast of Rissani is the **Zaouia of Moulay Ali Cherif**, the founder of the Alaouite Dynasty. This is a new building as the previous one was destroyed by flash flood. Non-Muslims may not enter and are prevented therefore from viewing the beautiful glazed tilework, the central courtyard with fountain and surrounded by palms. Moulay Ali Cherif was buried here in 1640. Sort of behind this is the **Ksar d'Akbar**, a ruined Alaouite palace from the 19th century quite unhappily derelict – but no doubt has some tales it could tell of the rejects of important families it accommodated and the vast treasures it stored. It is also said to be the palace of Moulay Abd el Rahmane, brother of reforming nineteenth century sultan Hassan I.

About 2 km to the south is the **Ksar Ouled Abd el Helim**, nicknamed the 'Alhambra of the Tafilalet'. It was built in 1900 by Moulay Rachid, elder brother of Moulay Hassan, as a governor's residence. Its decorated towers, monumental gateway and cloistered courtyards provide a little grandeur in the oasis.

Tinrheras is the most southerly *ksar* at 770 m above sea level. There is a splendid view from the walls, the *hammada* to the south and the panorama of the oasis to the north.

Off the road to Erfoud, in the vicinity of the *Hotel Kasbah Asmaa*, are some more minor sights, including **Ksar Jebril**, a large, still-populated village to the west, and **Al Mansouria**, another village to the east, about 300 m into the palm groves. Here there are yet more crumbling remains of vanished palaces, including a rather spectacular gate.

The whole feel of the Rissani oasis is rather Mesopotamian, with mud monuments crumbling away to fine dust. The region was once obviously very prosperous, as the palace buildings are architect designed, unlike the ksar villages. And in the light of the isolation of Rissani, separated from Erfoud by salt flats and nothingness, the palace remains become even more fascinating. Much eroded by the action of the wind, sun and occasional floods, the lost Alhambras of the Tafilalet must have been truly impressive for wandering nomads and caravans coming up from far distant Mali. It was clearly the Arabian Nights city of the Mediaeval imagination.

Great dunes of Merzouga

Some 61 km southwest from Erfoud, **Merzouga** has one attraction, the huge dunes 50 m high called **Erg Chebbi**, a vast pile of sand stretching into the Sahara. There is little else, beside the other tourists and a small village with a Saturday souk, but then the calm and wilderness is part of the appeal. A short walk across the dunes is a must once there. There are also camel excursions organized by the various auberges, and some good birdwatching in the adjacent Dayat Merzouga when it has water. Another (summer) option is to have a sand bath, said to be good for rhumatism The piste continues south to **Taouz**, and the 4WD brigade now travel along the once 'forbidden track' (shown as the *piste interdite* on the maps) west to **Remlia** and the confluence of the dry river valleys of the Gheris and Ziz. More simply, a grand taxi from Rissani to Merzouga will cost 40dh.

Sleeping It is possible to stay at Merzouga, although accommodation is often taken early in the day. Best to try to reserve in advance. Most of the accommodation is concentrated at the north-west tip of the dunes, with a couple of places in the village of Hassalbeid and some further south towards the seasonal lake. Note that there are numerous faux guides in the area who will do their best to convince you that certain auberges are closed, simply because the owners refuse to pay them a commission for hustling potential clients to the door. **A-B** *Auberge-Kasbah Derkaoua*, T/F055-577140, reservations via riadomaroc@iam.net.ma, near the dunes at Erg Chebbi, BP 64. Licensed restaurant, pool, riding on beautiful Arab horses. By far and away the best option. Magnificent food, apple tajine, French desserts and sorbet in the desert. Book in advance (closed Jan, Jun and Jul). Highly recommended. **D** *Ksar Saniya*, by the Grand Dune and the seasonal lake, close to the *Auberge Touareg*, T055-577414. run by Gérard and Françoise Tommaso, a friendly sort of place, attractive rooms, short camel rides, longer treks, 4WD rental. Owners have excellent knowledge of the region. Recommended.

The Tafilalet oases

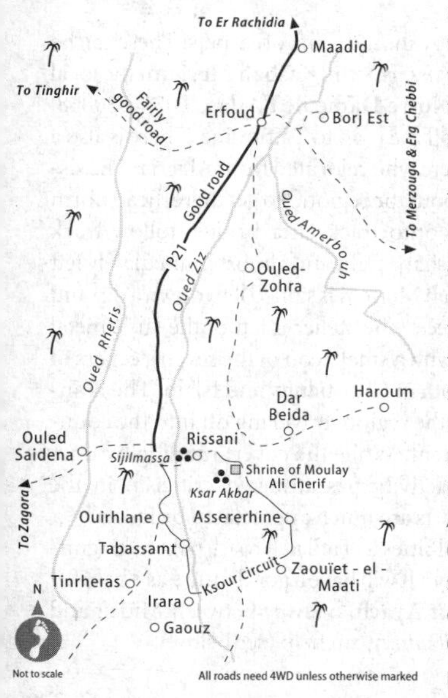

The other addresses are all very similar. **E-F** ***Hotel Merzouga***, a friendly place which is an annexe to the *Hotel Tafilalet*, T055-576322, rooms and nomad tent. Not the best, but showers are hot. Good food. **E** ***Auberge Les Dunes d'Or***, BP 3 Merzouga, T 061-350665 (mob), F044-887214 (Ouazarzate number). Good reputation, 14 simple rooms, also terrace to sleep out on, hot water, showers. **F** ***Café-Auberge l'Oasis***, T055-577321. 12 rms with shared showers and toilet, acceptable. **F** ***Kasbah des Dunes***, T/F055-577287 also in the village of Hassalbeid. Simple rooms, hot showers, night on terrace for 20dh; **F** ***Café Yasmina***, T055-576783, a fort-like building with simple clean rooms, or night under tent for 20dh. Recommended. **F** ***Auberge du Trésor***, on the way from Rissani to Merzouga, right out in the desert. 4 simple rooms, meals; **D** ***Camping La Khaima***, at the foot of the dunes, T055-577216. 20dh for a night under a nomad tent, meals possible, cold showers, clean loos.

The East High Atlas

Er Rachidia to Midelt via Rich

The P21 running north from Er Rachidia to Midelt, one of the finest routes in Morocco, is also useful for the visitor, enabling you to travel back up to Fès and Meknès, via Azrou. After the Gorges du Ziz, the landscape opens up, and the town of **Rich** is visible below the range to the west. To the east are some beautifully mysterious small mountains. Rich has two small, unclassified hotels, *Hotel Salama*, 14 rooms, T055-579343; *Hotel El Massira*, 7 rooms, T055-579340. Remember, however, that you are just an hour's drive from Midelt (75 km). Rich is the starting point for the only metalled road – for the moment – up to Imilchil (see page 422 for further details).

Midelt

Phone code: 055
Colour map 3, grid A3
Altitude: 1,525 m

High on the plateau lands between Middle and High Atlas, Midelt is a good stopover en route from Er Rachidia (138 km) to the Imperial Cities. Despite high unemployment, the town has a calm, friendly atmosphere.

Sights

Sunday souk
For other excursions see Around Midelt, page 421

Those in need of some shopping therapy should think of carpets. These can be bought at a weaving school (*atelier de tissage*), the **Kasbah Meriem**, the local name for the monastery/convent of **Notre Dame de l'Atlas**, T055-580858, run by Franciscan sisters in premises off the road to Tattiouine. There is also a tiny community of Trappist monks here who relocated from Algeria. The sisters may be a source of information about the region. To get there, head north out of Midelt centre, take left turn onto track after bridge, follow track towards kasbah village, where you go sharp right and almost immediately left up the hill. After about 1 km, the Kasbah Meriem is signed left, down a dip and up again, its presence indicated by trees. The atelier is left of the large metal gate. Inside, there is a simple church with a small icon of the seven sleepers of Ephesus, symbol of a myth present both in Christianity and Islam. The Franciscan sisters do lots of good work in the region, travelling off into the countryside with mules and a dispensary tent. While the covert funding by USA churches of Protestant missionary activity has attracted criticism in the Moroccan press, the Franciscans' efforts are much appreciated by locals.

Strategically located on the Imperial cities to Tafilalelt road, next to magnificent mountains, Midelt looks as though it will have a good future as a base for hikers. For more on this, head for **Aït Ayach**, halfway between Midelt and Zeïda on the P21, where the *Auberge Timnay* can help (see below).

Sleeping

Even remote Midelt is getting its share of tourists. Reservations are recommended in the spring

D *Hotel Ayachi*, R d'Agadir, a few minutes from the town centre, signposted behind the post office, T055-582161, F583307. Very 1930s, 30 big rooms with shower, quiet, big restaurant, nightclub, safe parking and garden. Try to reserve, as sometimes it's full with tour groups. The old mining company hotel and best address is **D *Hotel Kasbah Asmaa***, on right on southern exit, the neo-kasbah building, T055-583945, F580408. 20 en suite rooms, nomad tents, garden, fireplaces, can set up treks. **E *Hotel Bougafer***, Av Mohammed V, T055-583099. Up the hill round behind the bus station, best cheap option, en suite rooms and simple 3- and 4-bed rooms on top floor. Spotless, good food. Recommended. There are several more basic hotels, including: **E *Hotel Roi de la Bière***, T055-582625, near the southern exit. Only 1 shower and loo. **F *Hotel Atlas***, R Mohammed Amraoui, T055-582938. Small family-run hotel. Very clean. **F *Hotel Mimlal***, on left as you come into town from north, 1½ km walk from bus station, T055-582266. Food fine, cheap rooms and 'suite' at 150dh. **F *Hotel Toulouz***, in the centre, behind the *Shell* station near the main roundabout. 4 rooms, you don't get more basic than this. **Camping** You may be able to camp in the grounds of the *Hotel Ayachi*, but the *Timnay* (below) is really the best option.

Zeïda road **D-E *Auberge-Restaurant Timnay***, T055-583434, timnay@iam.net.ma 20 km from Midelt. This is an efficient set-up, with a range of accommodation, including simple rooms, camping, nomad tents and sites for campervans. There is a restaurant, shop and pool, also 4WD rental, with guide for exploring the region. For a 4WD, 4 people are necessary to cover costs. Possible circuits on offer include Zaouiat Sidi Hamza and the upper Taâraârt Valley (2 days, 415dh per person). A good day trip: Canyon de Tatrout.

Eating

Groups tend to use the restaurant of the ***Hotel Ayachi***, perfectly acceptable, alcohol. Otherwise cheap options include ***Restaurant de Fès***, 2 Av Mohammed V, which has very good couscous; ***Excelsior***, also in the town centre, on the corner as you go uphill from central roundabout, alcohol, seedy inside, nice service; ***Brasserie Chez Aziz***, by the Er Rachidia exit. Plenty of cafés for breakfast opposite the central *gare routière*.

Around Midelt

Colour map 3, grid A3

There are some excellent excursions from Midelt. Walkers will want to head for the mountains and the **Cirque de Jaffar**. For those with hire car, a good half-day adventure is to drive via **Mibladene** up to the abandoned mines at **Ahouli**. In the heart of the eastern High Atlas, **Imilchil** is now feasible as a long day trip on the metalled road via Rich. Note that, as elsewhere in this plateau region, the winters are very cold and the summers very hot, so the best time to visit is the spring. Here the spring is later, and May or even early June are recommended for walking.

Mines of Ahouli

This excursion north from Midelt goes along the S317 to **Mibladene** (10 km) and over the head of the Oued Moulouya to the abandoned mining settlement of **Ahouli**. The road is signed right a few metres north from the central, bus-station junction in Midelt. The first long straight section to Mibladene is badly potholed, then improves slightly after Mibladene, a former mining community, to the right of the road. You then wind into spectacular gorges. The road deteriorates after an Indiana Jones-style bridge, parts of it washed away by floods.

Ahouli must have been a hive of activity. Copper and lead were the main products. The gorge is beautiful, with poplar, oleander and even the odd weeping willow. Mine infrastructure and housing clings to the cliffs. The community even had its own rather splendid cinema (now sanded up) and swimming pool. The lower floors of the houses had heavy metal doors, to keep out eventual flood water. There is a caretaker here, and he or his son may show you round.

After Ahouli, you can drive up out of the gorges on a well-made track, turning left to more abandoned dwellings on the plateau. Turning left, and a couple of kilometres brings you to the small village and semi-abandoned ksar of **Ouled Taïr** next to the oued, reached by a wobbly footbridge.

NB When driving out to Mibladene, men will try to flag the car down. Most will be selling fossils or stones of some kind. With all three mines in the region (Mibladene, Ahouli and Zaïda) now closed, there is a lot of poverty and selling stones is about the only thing left to do for many.

Jbel Ayyachi

The first ascent of the mountain was made in July 1901 by the Marquis de Segonzac

Midelt it also the jumping-off place for treks up to Jbel Ayyachi which at 3,747 m is eastern Morocco's highest mountain, an impressive 45 km stretch of solid mountain, unbroken by any peaks. The heights can remain snow-covered into late June. In the right conditions, on a long summer's day, the climb can be done in a day. Better, however, to take two days and bivouac out on the mountain. To tackle the Jbel Ayyachi, head first for **Tattiouine**, 12 km from Midelt (grand taxi transport available). Here it should be possible to find mules and a guide. For a fit party, the climb and back should take around 12 hours. Make sure you have plenty of water. Even in summer, it can be very cold at the summit.

Impressive and seemingly impenetrable with its snow-capped heights, the Jbel Ayyachi functions as a water tower for southeastern Morocco, its melt water feeding both the Moulouya to the north and the Oued Ziz to the south. Jbel Ayyachi derives its name from the local Aït Ayyach tribe. Within living memory, caves in the cliffs were occupied by freedom fighters resisting the Makhzen and the incoming French. The last of such mountain strongpoints were only finally taken by the central authorities in 1932.

Cirque du Jaffar

One of Morocco's best known 4WD excursions takes intrepid off-roaders up to the Cirque de Jaffar (map NI-30-II-3), one of the natural arenas hollowed out on the north side of the Jbel Ayyachi. In fact, in a good off-road vehicle it is just about possible to travel over from Midelt, via the Oued Jaffar, to Imilchil, a distance of 160 km. The initial part through the Oued Jaffar gorges is the most scenic. The route is not to be attempted in winter, however, and certainly not risked in spring if there are April snows. Consult the Gendarmerie royale in Midelt or the people at *Auberge-Restaurant Timnay* on the Zeïda road (see page 421).

Imilchil

Rich to Imilchil

138 km, 3 hours

Although geographically closer to Beni Mellal than to Rich, Imilchil is dealt with here via the easiest access route, the newly completed road from Rich (halfway between Er Rachidia and Midelt on the P21). After crossing the wide Oudlalas plain to **Amouguer**, the road takes you up into the eastern High Atlas, through splendid landscapes with lots of geological convulsions clearly visible. Though good, the road is slow as it winds constantly, as befits a former mule track. There are straight bits where the temptation is to zip along, and then you meet sudden bends. Go carefully, especially when passing through villages. **Outerbate**, set among poplars and tiny fields, about 80 km from Imilchil, is the first major settlement, then you climb up towards the plateau regions.

Imilchil is famous for its annual *Moussem des fiançailles*, a sort of summer wedding festival which was an occasion for people from all over the region to get together. The *moussem* site is in fact at **Allamghou**, signed left off the route, some 20 km before Imilchil and near the meeting place with the mountain piste up from Tinghir. The local legend goes that two young people fell in love and wanted to marry. Their parents said no, and they cried so much that two lakes formed: Tislit for the girl, and Isli for the bridegroom. With such results, the parents could hardly continue to refuse and thus allowed their offspring to choose the partner of their choice. The *moussem* was a great occasion for locals to turn out in all their finery, and there were plenty of traditional dances and singing. In recent years, the occasion has suffered from the incursions of tourists – and drought. In all of Morocco's rural communities, weddings – expensive, once-in-a-lifetime occasions that they are – require a lot of available capital, always in short supply in drought years.

Nevertheless, in villages along the route to Imilchil, there is some new prosperity, lots of new building, for the most part using traditional packed-earth construction methods. In Imilchil itself, reinforced concrete has arrived, with unsightly new building ruining the area around the village's beautiful kasbah, sadly being allowed to crumble away by the owners.

The village

A good contact is Zayid the butcher (el jazzar), who speaks English and can put you in contact with guides and muleteers for a trek

The end of a slow drive up from Rich, the village of Imilchil does not exactly dazzle. There is a dusty, sloping main street, where you will find a couple of small cafés, the local dispensary and the entrance to the souk enclosure. The town's finest feature, the kasbah, is sadly sagging, its earthen walls deteriorating with every passing winter. Behind the kasbah, the *Hotel Izlane* can provide a little information on possible treks and may be able to put you in contact with suitable guides.

Sleeping Options are few but adequate, the best being the **E *Hotel Izlane***, clearly visible behind the Kasbah, T023-442806, run by mountain guide Khalla Boudrik. Large restaurant, 15 rooms, 39 beds, 3 showers, 4 loos. Has regional maps and can advise on treks. Try also **E *Café-Hotel Atlas***, T023-442828, 14 basic rooms, ably managed by the voluble Moha Ougourar. There is simple dormitory accommodation elsewhere in the village. Halfway between Imilchil and Lac Tislit, try the **E *Auberge-Kasbah Adrar***, BP 23, 52403 Imilchil, T/F023-442184. 1 person 100dh, 2 persons 200dh with breakfast, also 50dh with breakfast for night in nomad tent. Nothing very authentic but rooms are big and clean.

Towards Lac Tislit & Lac Isli

Just 5 km north of Imilchil lies Lac Tislit, an exquisite austere oval of blue ringed by reeds, set in an arid hollow of the mountains. Unfortunately, the natural splendour has been marred by a bogus kasbah, complete with plastic ceremonial tents and 4WD park. After Lac Tislit, the larger Lac Isli is an easy day's 4WD trip.

North from Imilchil by road

Until recently, the easiest access to Imilchil was from the east, on the metalled road from Rich. The shorter, but much slower northern route, from either El Ksiba (see previous chapter, Azilal High Atlas for accommodation options) and Aghbala, difficult to metal in parts, was for 4WD enthusiasts only. Total distance between El Ksiba and Imilchil is 110 km, taking about 5 hours if the piste in the Tassent Gorge is not in too bad condition (stress on the *if* here). Ask for latest track information in Imilchil.

Trekking from Imilchil to Anergui and Zaouiat Ahansal

For walking in the Anergui area, you will need the 1:100,000 scale sheets for Zaouiat Ahansal, Imilchil and Tinghir

One of the best treks in the Atlas takes you from the plateaux of the Imilchil region, via the Assif Melloul and the beautiful village of Anergui to the former pilgrimage centre of Zaouiat Ahansal. This route, part of the **Grande traversée de l'Atlas marocain**, takes you through remote regions where knowledge of French (and even Arabic) will be rudimentary to say the least. Take a local, preferably Tabant-trained, guide who will be aware of conditions in terms of snow (if travelling outside summer) and water levels in the Assif Melloul. At Zaouiat Ahansal, you link in with further routes south-west to the Aït Bougmez and north to the so-called Cathedral rocks of Tilouguite and Ouaouizaght. A number of European-based travel companies now do treks in this region. Accommodation will be in mountain gîtes, bivouacking out or in locals' homes.

Imilchil to Anergui

There are various trek routes from Imilchil to Anergui, a distance of roughly 57 km. The route you take will depend on weather conditions. Some routes require better than average physical condition. If the **Assif Melloul** is not in flood, your guide will take you along the riverside route, which will involve some wading and goes via the small settlements of **Oudeddi** and **Oulghazi**. After Oulghazi, you may head up out of the river valley and head for Anergui via the **Tizi-n-Echfart**. The other option is a more perilous route high above the river. Note that the river will be in full flood in spring, and that ice in shady areas can make high paths perilous for both people and mules.

With the green of its fruit and walnut trees, **Anergui** is one of the most beautiful sites in the eastern High Atlas. The village now has accommodation, the *Wihalane* ('the right place'), capacity 24. For information, contact Lahcen Fouzal on T023-442331 via *Studio La Nature* in Ouaouizaght or via José Garcia, 17 Rue de Sermaize, 90000 Belfort, France, T0033-384266049.

Anergui to Zaouiat Ahansal

The Assif Melloul continues west from Anergui to meet the Assif ou Ahansal near the so-called **Cathedral Rocks** near Tamga. A basic piste from Anergui to Zaouiat Ahansal can (just about) be done with 4WD, a distance of around 92 km. For walkers, this route is one of the finest in the High Atlas, taking you through the beautiful gorges of the Assif Melloul.

Zaouiat Ahansal

Once centre of the Ahansaliya brotherhood, the Zaouiat Ahansal (altitude 1,600 m) became important due to its location at a meeting of the ways between the eastern and central High Atlas. In terms of accommodation, there are a couple of gîtes. As in many poor, out of the way places with few visitors the children can be a bit trying.

Note that the easiest way to Zaouiat Ahansal is from **Azilal**, a distance of 83 km, much of it now metalled. There are fairly frequent 4WD taxis doing this run. About 17 km out of Azilal, a junction is reached where you either go right for the **Aït Bougmez** or left for **Aït Mhamed** (Saturday souk), 3 km further on. From here it's another 63 km to Zaouiat Ahansal. The tarmac runs out a few kilometres out of Aït Mhamed. The track continues east-southeast towards the **Tizi-n-Tsalli-n-Imenain** (2,763 m, 50 km from Azilal), in the shelter of the great **Jbel Azourki** (3,677 m). A further col, the **Tizi-n-Ilissi** (2,600 m), comes 16 km further on, below Jbel Arroudane (3,359 m). Then comes the drop down to Zaouiat Ahansal.

Agadir, the Souss and the Deep South

428 Agadir
428 Ins and outs
429 Background
431 Sights
432 Essentials

437 Inezgane

438 North of Agadir
438 Taghazoute
438 Immouzer des Ida Outanane
439 Agadir to Essaouria: unspoiled coastline

440 South of Agadir
440 Agadir to Tafraoute
441 Agadir to Tiznit

442 Taroudant
442 Ins and outs
442 Sights
443 Essentials
445 Taroudant to Ouarzazate, via Taliouine and Tazenakht

447 Trekking in the Jbel Siroua
447 Taroudant to Tata via Igherm
449 Tata to Bou Izakarn via Akka, Amtoudi and Ifrane de L'Anti-Atlas

452 Tiznit
453 Ins and outs
453 Background
454 Sights
454 Essentials

455 Tafraroute and the Ameln Valley
456 Sights
457 Essentials

458 Goulimine (Guelmin)
460 Sidi Ifni
463 Tan Tan
464 Tarfaya

465 Laâyoune
465 Ins and outs
465 Background
466 Sights
466 Essentials

467 South into the Sahara
469 Boujdour and Dakhla

Introducing Agadir, the Souss and the Deep South

South of the High Atlas, the landscapes are worthy of some yet-to-be-made Moroccan road movie. The scenery of the Anti-Atlas is pure orographics. Here you feel how the land rose and folded to become mountains. The **Saharan coast** has an austere magnificence, too.

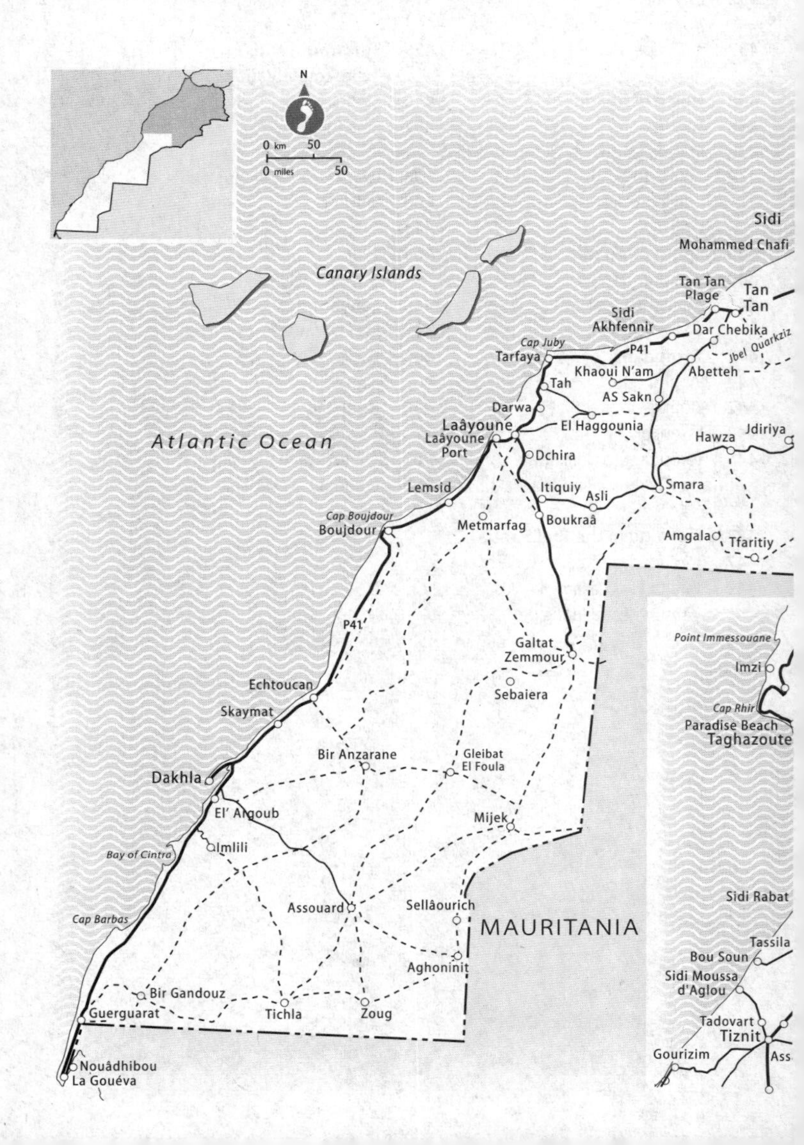

Though burgeoning ocean-side **Agadir**, Morocco's first package holiday resort, may be your first point of call you can soon escape to more remote interiors. Inland from Agadir, in the agricultural Souss Valley, lies walled **Taroudant**, 'Marrakech's elder brother'. From here you can travel up into the **Jbel Siroua** or down across wild, folded hills via **Igherm** to **Tata**, an ideal base from which to reach south to the prehistoric rock art sites at **Akka** and **Oum el Aleg** or east to **Tissint**. Moving west, there are fortified granaries at **Amtoudi** and in the great rock amphitheatre of **Tafraoute**. On the coast, the surf fraternity meets up in the one-time Spanish enclave of **Sidi Ifni**, sports fishing is on offer at remote **Dakhla**, last stop before the border with Mauritania. Though bumpy tracks are giving way to tarmac, Morocco's southern provinces are little visited by the general tourist. This may change: the new tourist zone at **Taghazoute** near Agadir is under way, another such development is planned for **Plage Blanche**, near the mouth of the Oued Draâ and **Goulimine**. Even **Laâyoune**, former Spanish-garrisoned Villa Cisneros, may get its share of tourists. For the moment, the great horizons and mountainscapes are the preserve of more determined visitors.

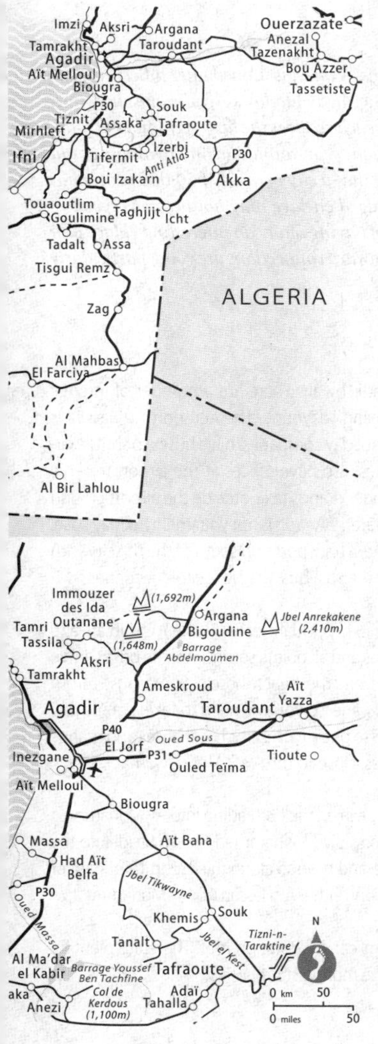

Things to do in the Agadir region

- In **Agadir**, take a look at Coco Paolozzi's neo-Berber fun **medina** – or head for the **Tafraoute** region for the real thing in spectacular hill country.
- Take the road across the **Jbel Bani** from Taroudant via Tiout and Igherm to the pre-Saharan oasis of **Tata**.
- With a guide, search the desert for **prehistoric rock carvings** at **Oum Aleg** and **Akka**.
- Explore the **fortified granaries** of **Amtoudi**, high above the oasis villages in the gorge.
- Surf, swim or just walk on the beach at **Sidi Ifni**, survival of an obscure Spanish colonial presence. Or try the **Playa de la Guezira**, a few kilometres to the north.

Agadir

Phone code: 048
Colour map 2, grid C2

Atlantic Agadir, at the mouth of the Souss Valley, is named after a Berber fortified granary. But simple rural life is an age ago in today's Agadir: the city which has grown up along the sweeping 9 km beach receives the largest number of tourists in all Morocco. The microclimate means year-round sun and swimming, and it is in part thanks to the travel industry that a city of nearly 850,000 people has grown up. Although tourism in a packaged enclave may not be to everybody's taste, the city does have the advantage of having many an interesting village and natural sight close by. In addition, the onward connections are good, particularly by bus from Agadir or nearby Inezgane.

Ins and outs

Getting there
See Transport, page 436, for further details

The vast majority of tourists arrive in Agadir by air. There are a number of internal flights, including arrivals from Casablanca and Laâyoune. The Aéroport Al-Massira is some 25 km inland from the city. Package-holiday companies have buses to shuttle clients to their hotels. The car hire companies also have offices at the airport (reserve beforehand). Otherwise there are 6-passenger grands taxis outside the airport (150dh to the town centre, you could arrange to share). If Agadir is not your main holiday base, then you could take a grand taxi to Inezgane, a transport hub south of the the city with connections to various destinations. There is also a bus, the No 22, for Inezgane.

There are buses for Agadir from Marrakech (5 hrs), Ouarzazate (7½ hrs), Casablanca (9 hrs), Essaouira (3½ hrs), the main local towns and all points south. Intercity buses arrive at the Gare Routière Talborjt, some way from the beach hotels. Some buses from southern destinations only go as far as Inezgane, so you will need to take a grand taxi (say 3dh a place) or a local bus (Nos 5 and 6) to get into the city. Local buses and grands taxis arrive in the city centre on the R de Fes, close to the Av El Mouqawama.

Arriving by road, from the north you will come in on the P8, leading into Av Mohammed V; from Marrakech and the P40, turn left along Blvd Mohammed Cheikh Saadi into the town centre. From the airport and Inezgane, and beyond along the P32 to Taroudant or the P30 to Tiznit and the South, one enters along either Av Hassan II or Av Mohammed V.

Getting around

Agadir is not a huge place, and most things can be done on foot. There are plentiful petits taxis, useful for getting to some of the more distant hotels.

Tourist information

Office du Tourisme, Immeuble A, Pl Prince Heritier Sidi Mohammed, T048-822894, open Mon-Fri 0800-1500 (Jun-Sep); 0800-1200 and 1430-1830 (Sep-Jun). **Syndicat d'Initiative**, Av Mohammed V, T048-840307.

Background

Although Agadir has the relaxed air of beach resort, it has perhaps little which is distinctively 'Moroccan', as the old settlement was almost totally destroyed in the earthquake of 1960, and has been rebuilt and developed to the standards of an international beach resort.

Agadir's rise & fall

Agadir first features in written history in the early 16th century, when a Portuguese noble built a fortress named Santa Cruz de Cap de Gué, somewhere close to the present city. The fort was sold on to the King of Portugal in 1513, and it became a further link in the chain of trading posts the Portuguese were establishing along the Atlantic coast of Africa. But not for long. The Imazighen of the Souss valley launched a *jihad* against the isolated fort, and the Saâdian Emir of the Souss, Mohammed Echeikh el Mehdi, captured it in 1541, heralding the Portuguese departure from most of their other Atlantic strongholds. His son, Moulay Abdallah el Ahalib, built the kasbah on the hill overlooking the city, the ruins of which still stand. As the Saâdians developed farming in the Souss valley, Agadir grew in importance, eventually becoming an important trading centre in the 17th and 18th centuries. Exports were sugar cane, olive oil, gold and spices, both from the immediate hinterland of the Souss valley, and further afield from the Sahara. However, Agadir declined during the reign of Sidi Mohammed Ben Abdallah, who preferred to develop Essaouira, to the north, and closed down Agadir's port. At the start of the 19th century, Agadir had all but disappeared.

In the early 20th century, Agadir hit the international headlines briefly. The European powers were running out of places to colonize, and Germany, under Kaiser Wilhelm II, was miffed at the growing influence of France and Spain in Morocco. (Germany had joined the scramble for Africa relatively late.) In 1911 an incident occurred in the Bay of Agadir: a German gunboat appeared 'to protect German interests', despite the 1906 Algeciras treaty. This crisis was settled by negotiations between the French and Germans, recognizing France's rights in Morocco, in exchange for territorial concessions in the Congo. The French occupied Agadir in 1913. They constructed the port in 1914, and enlarged it in 1930 and 1953.

On 29 February 1960, disaster struck: old Agadir was completely destroyed by a terrible earthquake. Newly independent Morocco faced the challenge of rebuilding the town. An entire new settlement was laid out south of the old centre, planned for development as a major tourist resort, with distinct functional zones separated by green swathes, and the large hotels carefully distanced from the local residential areas. The ruined kasbah was encased in concrete. Set in the wall are Mohammed V's words, commemorating the dead: "If destiny desired the destruction of Agadir, its reconstruction depends on our faith and our determination." More clearly visible, on an arid hillside, in giant Arabic letters, is the national motto 'Allah, Al-Watan, Al-Malik' - 'God, the Nation, the King'. With reconstruction, the city gained some chunky functional buildings, all brutalist concrete, by the likes of star 1960s Moroccan architects like Zevaco. The port (which escaped total destruction) was developed as the base for a large fishing fleet and as the centre of an industrial zone.

Agadir 1541: the Portuguese meet their match

The Portuguese-held port of Agadir fell to Saâdian leader Mohamed Cheikh in 1541. The fall of this crucial entrepot to the Saâdians, along with financial difficulties, was to lead to the collapse of the Portuguese colonial system in Morocco. Portuguese expansion in Morocco reached its height in the late 15th century, with Tangier occupied in 1471, Larache in 1473, and Azemmour in 1486. Trade was the motive, with horses and fine cloth from Morocco being traded for slaves and gold in the ports of West Africa.

Further south, the Sous Valley attracted interest, and in 1505 came the turn of Agadir: João Lopes de Sequeira occupied the tiny settlement and built the fortress of Santa Cruz. Trade developed with the tribes. But the Portuguese dominance made a new political unity possible among the scattered Muslim communities of Morocco. The Saâdians – with all the prestige that comes from being cherifs, descendants of the Prophet Mohamed – came forward to lead the fight against the Christians. One story runs, however, that the motive to unite actually came from the Portuguese. Having taken some Moroccan warriors captive, the Portuguese refused to hand them back unless the tribes put forward a single ruler with whom negotiations could be held. The story goes that a certain Sidi Baraket, a mystic respected in the region, conducted the talks. In about 1510, he influenced the tribes to recognize Mohamed el Kaim, head of the Saâdian house, to lead them against the infidel.

Simplifying heavily, Saâdian raiding was initially focused on Safi and Azemmour. (Exports of Sous Valley sugar via Portuguese protected European merchants in Agadir were too important financially to be interrupted.) Then in the early 1540s, Mohamed el Kaim's second son, Mohamed el Sheikh, began his bid to become ruler of all Morocco. Taking Agadir in 1541 was a good strategic move: the Portuguese evacuated Safi and Azemmour further up the coast, and the Saâdian leader gained the moral upper hand. The Wattasid sultan in Fès, Ahmed, had been pursuing a policy of peaceful co-existence with the Portuguese in northern Morocco. The influential religious leaders of Fès could hardly continue to support rulers who collaborated with the infidel. The Saâdian ruler was well on the way to unifying the country under a Cherifian (rather than purely tribal) dynasty, and Fès fell to the Saâdians in 1549.

Agadir today In the 1990s, tourism in Agadir suffered from the impact of the Gulf War and the huge growth in popularity of Marrakech. The attraction of the beach holiday product was not what it had been, as Europeans realized that long hours in the sun increase risks of skin cancer. Nor did Agadir develop a nightlife to compete with the Balearics or the Canaries. Rather, the town became a destination for a wealthy Gulf Arab clientele seeking a discrete playground. From the town's nightclubs, prostitution developed. Poor housing areas on the margins expanded, with rural people fleeing the drought-stricken countryside in the late 1990s. Thanks to this exodus, Agadir is now the largest Tachelhit-speaking city in Morocco, and its people, the Gadiris, are rightly proud of their Amazigh origins. There is a dynamic local bourgeoisie with business interests across Morocco. Today, tourism looks set to take off again: new hotels are going up and plans for a large *zone touristique* at Taghazoute (also spelt Tarhazoute), 19 km north of the city, are well advanced.

Sights

The beach is Agadir's main asset, clean and well provided with cafés, camel rides and watersports. The beaches in front of the hotels are patrolled by wardens who keep the trinket-sellers at a distance. On the more public beaches, controls are laxer and the sellers are both determined and thick skinned. Small children should not be left to paddle unattended because of the strong undertow – let them splash safely in the kiddie pool at the hotel. There is a summer-only municipal pool at the north end of the beach.

Beaches
Be aware that this is an Atlantic ocean beach, there is a strong undertow

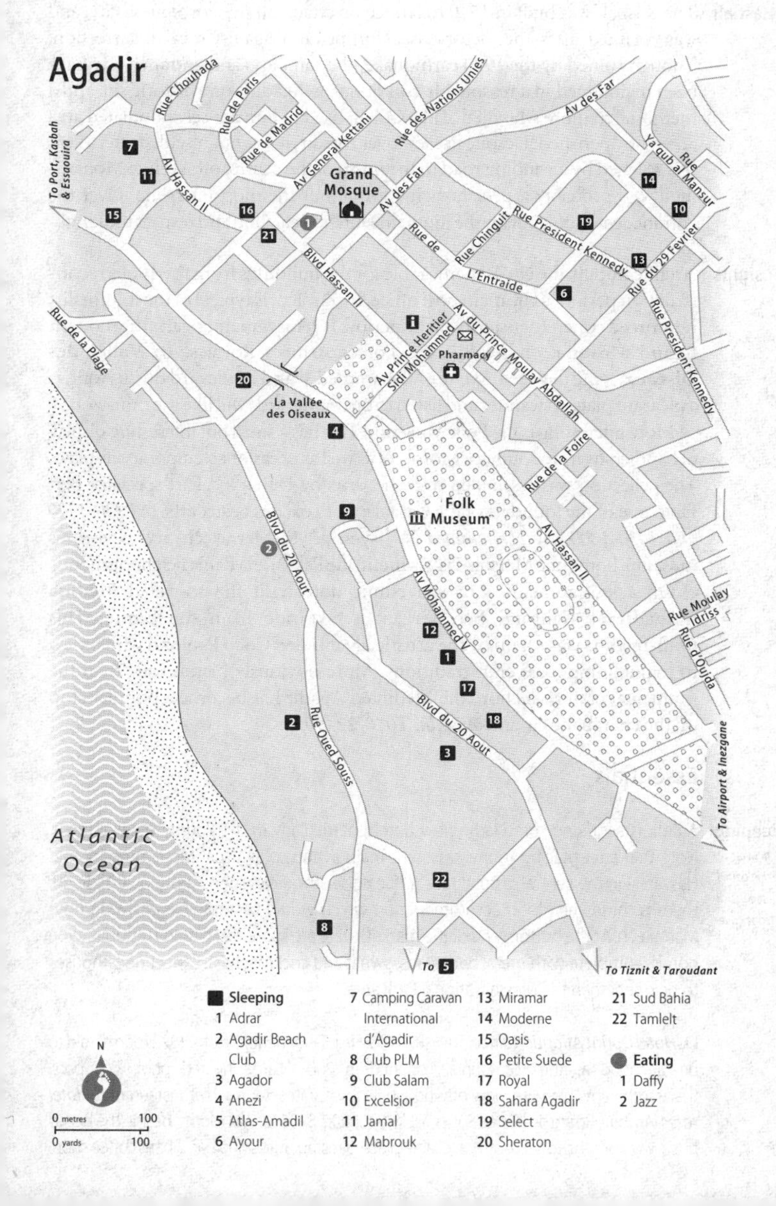

The northern end of the beach is quieter than the centre or southern end, where hotels continue to sprout. Sunbed hire, around 20-30dh per day, includes toilet/shower facilities where available. Most of the private sunbed hire units have snack bars and restaurants.

Port To get to the port take a petit-taxi for 6dh, or bus No 1, or walk along from the beach. The main reason for visiting is to eat at the small fish restaurants right of the port entrance.

Kasbah The Kasbah was built in 1540 to launch an attack on the Portuguese city, and was retained after the victory as a fortification against local insurrection. Though ruined by the 1960 earthquake, the ramparts and entrance way have been maintained in a reasonable condition, as Agadir's one historic site and a memorial to those who died. This Kasbah used to be a densely populated area and many perished. Despite its view over Agadir, it was not resettled after 1960. It is reached by a winding road to the north of the centre, off Avenue Mohammed V – probably a petit taxi ride for all but the most energetic. Over the entrance gate, look out for the motto in Dutch, 'Fear God and respect the king'.

Other sights Architecturally the city is memorable for the buildings from the 1960s reconstruction period. (The main post office, by Zevaco, is typical of the minimalist reinforced concrete austerity of the period.) Of marginal appeal is the modern **Grand Mosque**, on Avenue des Forces Armées Royales. **La Vallée des Oiseaux**, lying between Avenue Mohammed V and Boulevard du 20 Août, is a pleasant place to wander and listen to bird song; kids will like the mini-zoo.

More interesting is the **Folk Museum**. This has a small but interesting display of handicrafts from southern Morocco, as well as occasional temporary displays. The collection was assembled over the years by Dutch local art specialist Bert Flint, one of the founders of the Casablanca Ecole des beaux arts. ■ *0930-1300 and 1430-1800. Av Mohammed V*. If you get to Marrakech, try to visit his museum-home, the **Maison Tiskiwine**, in the Palais de la Bahia neighbourhood.

On a less authentic but still ethnic note, visit the so-called **Médina d'Agadir** at Aghroud Ben Sergao, a taxi ride from the centre. This mini-médina was set up by the artistically minded Coco Paolozzi with a view to maintaining local craft traditions. More obviously picturesque than the municipal craft collection, the Médina d'Agadir has become a popular stop on the charabanc circuit. ■ *20dh. T048-224909*.

Essentials

Sleeping
■ *on map*
Price codes: see inside front cover

Agadir is acquiring some large new hotels, particularly in the Founty development. Note that street-facing rooms on the 2 main avenues (as usual Mohammed V and Hassan II) in the central district have traffic noise. If you can spend around 200-250dh, there is some very good accommodation which would be more expensive in (say) Marrakech. At the bottom end of the market, there are some real banana republic-type hotels (complete with metal bedsteads, sweat and cockroaches). Expect guesthouses to be opening in the Massa National Park area.

LL *Hotel Dorint Atlantic Palace*, T048-824146. First 5-star de-luxe hotel (322 rooms, said to be 'as good as the Mamounia'), opened in 2000. Large heated pool, kids pool, thalassotherapy, bar with view of whole bay, royal suites, tennis, diet restaurant. **L** *Hotel Atlas-Amadil*, Route de l'Oued Souss, T048-840620, F823663. 322 rooms, beside the beach but away from the town centre, a reliable place, 3 restaurants, wine bar, 2 bars, coffee shop, nightclub, hairdresser, laundry, library, pool, tennis. Used by major tour operators. **L** ***Europa Hotel Safir***, Blvd du 20 Août, T048-821212, F823435. 221 rooms, Moroccan-style decor, 3 restaurants, 2 bars, business centre, art gallery, tennis, pool. **L** ***Hotel Madina Salam***, Blvd du 20 Août, facing the sea, about 100 m from beach, T048-845353, F845308. Traditional style decoration,165 rooms and 40 suites with a/c, direct telephone, TV, heated pool, sauna, conference facilities, 3 restaurants, bar by pool, 24-hr room service. **L** ***Hotel Sheraton***, Av Mohammed V, T048-843232, F844379. A *Sheraton* resort hotel and reports are that it is not up to the high standard of, say, the *Sheraton Marrakech*.

A ***Adrar***, Av Mohammed V, T048-840417. 174 rooms, another package tour hotel, but the food is excellent even if it is crowded round the pool, useful rear access to beach area. **A** ***Anezi***, Av Mohammed V, T048-840940. Good position, 254 rooms, terrace, gardens, pool, hammam, usual problems of road noise, but cheerful, helpful staff a compensation here. **A** ***Club PLM Dunes d'Or***, on beach, T048-840150. 450 rooms, price includes all activities, famous tennis courts which host professional events, sauna, hammam, gym, horse riding, volleyball and basketball, 2 pools, 5 restaurants, 6 bars, nightclub, constant activity, not the place for a rest. **A** ***Hotel Sahara Agadir***, Av Mohammed V, T048-840660, F840738. Popular and luxuriously equipped with 300 pleasant rooms, 4 restaurants, 2 bars, nightclub, hairdresser, sauna, hammam, tennis, horse riding and volleyball, children and adult pools. **A** ***Hotel Tamlelt-Agador***, Quartier des Dunes d'Or, T048-841525. 659 rooms. This complex links 2 hotels: the *Tamlelt* inspired by Moroccan médinas, the *Agador* by the kasbahs, large gardens, fountains, 4 restaurants, nightclub, hairdresser, several bars, 4 pools, not suitable for disabled people. **A** ***Transatlantique***, Av Mohammed V, T048-842083, F842076. 208 rooms with a/c, TV, some bargaining can be done here if the package tours have not taken all the places, friendly atmosphere despite the size, note our comment about traffic noise.

B ***Agadir Beach Club***, T048-840791, F825763. 374 rooms, luxurious rooms, 2 bars, nightclub, laundry, hairdresser, tennis, magnificent pool. **B** ***Hotel Aladin***, R de la Jeunesse, T048-843228, F846071. Comfortable, small pool, good breakfast. **B** ***Hotel Club Salam***, on Av Mohammed V, right in the centre of town and the best beaches, T048-840840, F841834. 50 bungalows and 150 double rooms, restaurant for international and Moroccan dishes, buffet bar at pool, has had some negative reviews. **B** ***Hotel Jamal***, junction of Av Hassan II and Av Général Kettani, T048-842346, F844367. 36 rooms (standard and de-luxe), good rooms with balcony, minibar etc. Restaurant with booze, bar, rooftop terrace, small pool, lounge, off-street parking, used by tour groups and near beach. **B** ***Hotel Oasis***, just off Av Mohammed V, T048-843313-6, F842260. Excellent view, 132 rooms, 2 restaurants, 2 bars, pool, sauna, *hammam*, nightclub, tennis and golf. **B** ***Hotel Talborjt***, R de l'Entraide, T048-841832. Pleasant garden setting.

C ***Hotel Aferni***, Av du Général Kettani, T048-840730. Small hotel with nice pool. **C** ***Hotel Atlantic***, Av Hassan II, T048-843661. Clean, comfortable and cool courtyard for outside meals. **C** ***Hotel Atlas***, Av Mohammed V, T048-843232, F844379. 156 rooms, bungalows amidst the gardens, a recommended and reasonably priced option, 2 restaurants, tennis, pool, nightclub. **C** ***Hotel Ibis Mousafir***, Route de Marrakech, about 1 km out of town centre, T048-232842-47, F232849. As is usually the case with the *Mousafir* hotels, it is noisy and the walls between the rooms are rather thin. **C** ***Hotel Karam***, R de la Foire, T048-844249. **C** ***Hotel des Palmiers***, Av Sidi Mohammed, T048-843719. Recommended at this price range.

D ***Aït La'ayoun***, R Yacoub El Mansour, T048-824375. Popular at this price range and can be fully booked, plenty of hot water, reports of unclean rooms, bus stop outside reduces chances of a good sleep. **D** ***Hotel Ayour***, 4 R de l'Entraide, T048-824976, F842474.

Modern, comfortable, satellite TV, entirely acceptable in this category. 20 clean, quiet rooms, 10 mins' walk from the beach. **D** ***Hotel Itrane***, 23 R de l'Entraide, T048-821407. **D** ***Hotel Mabrouk***, Blvd du 20 Août, T048-840606. 40 rooms, near town centre, reasonable place, pool and bar. **D** ***Hotel Miramar***, Av Mohammed V, T048-840770. Good, well-furnished rooms, separate bathroom and loo, some balconies with sea view. Pleasant, quiet place near the port, extremely good value. Restaurant has strong reputation (eat for around 300dh à la carte). **D** ***Hotel de Paris***, Av du Président Kennedy, T048-822694. 2 courtyards with huge rubber trees. Rooms have showers, no TV. No ventilation in bathrooms, musty rooms, depressingly little maintenance. **D** ***Hotel Royal***, Av Mohammed V, T048-840675. 73 rooms/bungalows amidst pleasant gardens, bar, restaurant and pool. **D** ***Hotel Petite Suede***, Av Hassan II, T048-840779. Friendly place with reasonably priced and comfortable rooms in town centre, very handy for the beach and on the quietest, greenest section of the Av Hassan II. A little bit run down. **D** ***Hotel Sindibad***, Pl Lahcen Tamri, T048-823477. Small and popular place on busy square with bar and adjoining restaurant. Good size rooms with phone, but a bit on the noisy side – go for the ones on side street. Handy for the *CTM*. **D** ***Hotel Sud Bahia***, R des Administrations publiques (sic), T048-840762, F846386. 246 rooms with a/c, bath and phone. Good restaurant, pool generally heated in winter (check), a short walk to the beach. Recommended. In this category – very good value. Near the *Hotel Ayour*.

E ***Hotel de la Baie***, corner R Allal Ben Abdallah/R du Président Kennedy, T048-823014. Truly terrible. A few sad plants in a courtyard, rooms as welcoming as a barracks, with grey blankets. Don't enter bathrooms barefoot. **E** ***Hotel El Bahia***, R El Mehdi ibn Toumert, T048-822724. Breakfast available, very friendly, recently renovated, with spotless, well-equipped rooms. Patio a bit noisy at night if several people talking. Outstanding decorative feature: the chunky wallpaper. **E** ***Hotel Excelsior***, R Ya'qub El Mansur, T048-821028. Near the bus station, but otherwise not brilliant and rather noisy, hot communal showers. **E** ***Hotel Moderne***, R El Mehdi ibn Toumert, T048-823373. Quite good and quiet. **E** ***Hotel Select***, behind *Restaurant Salam*, R Allal Ben Abdallah. **F** ***Diaf***, R Allal ben Abdallah, T048-825852. Adequate, hot water supply unreliable. **F** ***Hotel Tour Eiffel***, R Allal Ben Abdallah. Small and simple. **F** ***Hotel Amenou***, 1 R Ya'qub al Manour, T048-823026. Clean and welcoming. **F** ***Hotel Tifawt***, R Ya'qub al-Mansur, T048-824375. Basic. Cheaper accommodation can be found at: ***Anezi***, Av Mohammed V, T048-840940; ***Nejma***, Av des FAR, T048-841975; and ***Yasmine***, R de la Jeunesse, T048-842565.

Self-catering *Residence Sacha*, Pl de la Jeunesse, T048-825568, F841982. High season, around 500dh for a studio for 2, 300dh low season. Well located in downtown Agadir. Small pool, beach only 10-min walk away. Well managed. Credit cards.

Camping *Camping Caravaning International d'Agadir*, Blvd Mohammed V, T048-840981. Well equipped and reasonably priced place near the centre, with showers, site of 3 ha only 300 m from beach, pool, laundry, first aid, snack bar, restaurant, fair grocery shop, shade but no grass, electricity for caravans, petrol only 500 m away, very, very crowded in summer – security a problem. ***Camping Taghazoute***, Km 12, north of town on road to Essaouira, also full in summer.

Eating
● *on map*

Jazz, Blvd du 20 Août, T048-840208. Pasta, fish and pizza, meat dishes too. Good desserts. With wine etc, you're heading for 300dh a head. Very good. ***Miramar***, T048-840770, on Blvd Mohammed V, in the same premises as the hotel of the same name. Seafood and fish, Italian food. Highly recommended. ***Restaurant Daffy***, R des Oranges, set menus, good value. ***Via Veneto***, Av Hassan II, opposite the Vallée des Oiseaux, T048-841467. High quality European food and a very popular place, reservations advised, alcohol. ***Le Jardin d'Eau***, Blvd du 20 Août, T048-840195. Good French and

Moroccan dishes, particularly the lamb *mechoui*, reasonable prices, recommended. ***Darkhoum Restaurant Marocain***, Av du Général Kettani, T048-840622. Reservations advised, below the *Hotel Sud Bahia*, Moroccan decor, food and music. ***Restaurant du Port***, T048-843708. Seafood restaurant by the port with mixed reports. ***Pizzeria Annamunda***, Av du Prince Heritier Sidi Mohammed. Music and Italian food.

The restaurants by the port have cheap and excellent fresh fish, open 1230-2030, standards and reasonable prices maintained through hectic competition. Take a petit-taxi there for 5dh, or bus No 1. Also try the Nouveau Talborjt area with its tree-shaded Pl Tamri. ***Restaurant Sindibad***; ***Restaurant Mille et Une Nuits***, north end of R du 29-Février, which has good Moroccan main courses and salads; or ***Restaurant Coq d'Or***, all on Pl Lahcen Tamri; nearby, there are 2 good fish restaurants on R du 29 Février.

Cafés & pâtisseries

La Maison du pain, 19 Av Hassan II, close to the *Hotel Petite Suède*. Cakes, fruit juice and ice-cream. ***Oufella's***, R Allal Ben Abdallah, adjacent to the *Hotel Select* (undergoing renovation), is a *pâtisserie* with a good selection of cakes, sweets and drinks. ***Pâtisserie Tafarnout***, Av Hassan II, opposite the Chamber of Commerce. Breakfast on the terrace and cakes to take away.

Entertainment

Discos and clubs Plentiful in the large hotels, but they are of variable quality. Some are the preserve of local sex-workers and their clients. ***Tan Tan***, at the *Hotel Almohades*, Blvd 20 Août, T048-840233, T840096. ***Byblos***, at the *Club PLM Dunes d'Or*, on the beachfront, T048-820150, open 2130-0500, admission 60dh, popular and the drinks are reasonable.

Shopping

Handicrafts Agadir has no shortage of handicrafts for sale, notably from the traders displaying their wares along the paths and roads leading from the big hotels to the beach. A good display (inflexible prices) is to be found at the ***Centre Artisanal Cooperative***, in R du 29-Février.

General Best stock at the supermarket ***Uniprix***, Av Hassan II (open 0830-1230 and 1430-1930), also does alcohol. There are a number of good beer and wine shops on Av Mohammed V, right from Av du Général Kettani. European newspapers can be bought from stalls outside the major hotels and on Av Hassan II.

Sport & activities

Golf ***Royal Golf d'Agadir***, 12 km from Agadir, between Inezgane and Aït Melloul, T048-241278, F844380, snack bar and play area for children, weekends can be very busy. ***Golf Les Dunes***, more central, on Route d'Inezgane, T048-834690, F834649, 18 holes, 107 ha, best to book in advance, caddy compulsory. ***Golf du Soleil d'Agadir***, chemin Oued Souss, T048-843005, F841858, the most recent.

Horse riding ***Royal Club Equestre***, 7 km Route d'Inezgane. ***Ranch les Pyramides***, 8 km Route d'Inezgane. ***Ranch REHA***, 17 km north on the road to Essaouira, T048-847549. ***Club de l'Etrier***, 5 km Route d'Inezgane, expect to pay 250dh for 2 hrs, bring your own hard hat.

Surfing Try locations known as Banana 12 km north of Agadir, Mystery 23 km north and Killer 25 km north

Swimming Apart from the sea, there is a pool by the beachfront, off Av Mohammed V by the ***Syndicat d'Initiative***.

Tennis Clay courts at ***Royal Tennis Club d'Agadir***, Av Hassan II.

Tour operators *Sahara Tours*, Av Général Kettani, T048-840634, organize a range of excursions outside Agadir starting at 130dh, including visits to Taroudant, Marrakech, Tafraoute and Essaouira, usually includes at least 1 meal. Other agents in the same building also organize trips to Immouzer des Ida Outanane, Tata and Akka. ***Air France***, 287 Av Hassan II, T048-842546. ***Comanav Voyages***, 5 bis Av Mohammed V, T048-840669. ***Menara Tours***, 341 Av Hassan II, T048-821108. ***Royal Air Maroc***, Av du Général Kettani, T048-840145/840793.

Transport

Watch departure boards with care as tannoyed information is almost impossible to understand

Air Aéroport d'Agadir-Massira on Taroudant road, 28 km from city, T048-839122. Has bureaux de change, cashpoints and car rental. A blue grand taxi from the airport will cost 150dh by day, 200dh at night. Flights for **Casablanca**, occasionally scheduled for **Laâyoune**, also **Las Palmas**, and major European cities.

Road Bicycle/motorcycle hire There are several individuals hiring bicycles, mopeds and motorbikes from Blvd du 20 Août (prices high). Try ***Dynamic Loisirs***, T048-314655, F314654, out at Tamraght. They also do surf equipment.

Bus Services run to and from the gare routière on R Ya'qub al Mansur, new Talborjt area. *Supratours* buses can be found on Pl des Orangers, T048-841207, services connecting with the trains at **Marrakech**. *CTM* and private line services leave from the same place. There are private line services to **Marrakech** (5 a day), **Casablanca / Rabat** and **Taroudant** (4 a day), **Essaouira** and **Tiznit**, **Tata and Tan-Tan** and **Akka**; also **Tafraoute**. Bus companies: ***CTM***, T048-822077, ***SATAS***, T048-842470, and ***Pullman du Sud***, T048-846040. Local buses to the airport, **Inezgane** (5 and 6) and **Taghazoute** (12 and 14), leave from Pl Salam. From Blvd Mohammed Cheik Saadi, Nos 5 and 6 go to **Inezgane**, bus No 1 goes to the port. Taking bus to/from the airport is more difficult as a change in Inezgane is required.

Car hire *Afric Car*, Av Mohammed V, T048-840750. ***Agadir Voitures***, Immeuble Baraka, R de Paris, T22426. ***Avis***, Av Hassan II, T048-841755, and at the airport, T048-840345. ***Budget***, Av Mohammed V, T048-840762. ***Hertz***, Bungalow Marhaba, Av Mohammed V, T048-840939, and at the airport, T048-839071. ***Inter-Rent Europcar***, Av Mohammed V, T048-840367. ***Lotus Cars***, Av Mohammed V, T048-840588. ***Tiznit Cars***, Av Hassan II, T20998. ***Tourist Cars***, Av Mohammed V. ***Week-End Cars***, Av Mohammed V, T20567.

Taxis Agadir is a sprawling sort of city and therefore its plentiful **petit-taxis**, painted orange, can be useful, particularly to get to the kasbah or the port, insured for 3 passengers, metered, cannot go outside town limits, prices go up by 50dh after 2000 (*majoration*). **Grands taxis** are blue, insured for up to 6 passengers, operate within town limits and further afield. They leave for various destinations, particularly **Inezgane** and **Taroudant**, from Pl Salam.

Directory **Banks** Banks with ATMs, including *BMCE* and *BMCI*, are on Av du Général Kettani, on your right as you head towards Blvd Mohammed V and the ocean. Try also ***Wafa Bank*** in this area. ***American Express***, see *Crédit du Maroc*, Pl des Taxis. **Communications** **Post**: *PTT*, corner of Av Prince Heritier Sidi Mohammed and Av du Prince Moulay Abdallah. **Embassies and consulates** **Belgium**, Holidays Services, Av Hassan II, T048-824080. **Finland**, Good Year, Av Hassan II, T048-823821. **France**, Blvd Mohammed Saadi, T048-840826. **Italy**, R de Souvenir, T048-843093. **Spain**, R Ibn Batouta, T048-822126. **Sweden**, R de l'Entraide, T048-823048. **UK**, R des Administrations Publiques, T048-827741. **Medical services** **Ambulance**: T15. **Chemists**: *Pharmacie*, Municipalité d'Agadir, next to the post office, T048-820349, open all night. **Doctors**: Dr Martinez Espinoza Grich, Oumlil building, Av Hassan II, opposite *Royal Tennis Club*, T048-841750 or (home) T048-844808. Dr Hamid Grich, T048-426727, also in the Oumlil building. **Dentists**: Mme Berrada, Oumlil building, T048-844243. **Hospital**: ***Hôpital Hassan II***, Route de

Marrakech, T048-841477. Red Cross, T048-821472. Better to try one of the private clinics like ***Clinque Assoudil***, T048-843818, or the ***Polyclinque d'Agadir***, R Moulay Youssef, T048-824956. **Useful addresses** **Fire**: T150. **Police**: R du 18-Novembre, T190.

Inezgane

Phone code: 048
Colour map 2, grid C2
13 km S of Agadir

Busy Inezgane is now almost a part of Agadir The streets get choked with traffic, there are sheep on the road, goats grazing, women in bright garments carrying packages on their heads, and the usual plastic brooms and buckets, industrial items cheap and cheerful, for sale in the shops. Inezgane is above all a transport hub, which is why you will probably have to deal with it if you are travelling in the southwest, for which there are numerous coach, bus and grand taxi connections. It may also be handy as a stop-over, if you do not want to go into Agadir.

Ins & outs

Getting there Coming up from the south to Inezgane, there are 2 approaches. The one via Aït Melloul across the Oued Souss is to be avoided, and this can now be done by using the bypass.

Excursions

Inezgane provides access to the mouth of the **Oued Souss**, an important place for birdwatchers. There are no signposts, but you need to reach the north bank. The best visiting times are February to April and September to November, when many varieties of gulls and terns are in residence. The surrounding area has colourful residents which include the black-headed bush shrike, the great grey shrike, brown-throated sand martin and De Moussier's redstart.

Sleeping

Transport connections are likely to be the main reason for staying overnight in Inezgane. Unfortunately, the buses make most hotels extremely noisy. Cheap hotels are near the gare routière and around the Pl El Massira. The best hotel lies just outside Inezgane: the **C** ***Hotel Club Hacienda***, Route de l'Oued Souss, T048-830176. Bar, restaurant, nightclub, tennis, pool and horse riding. **D** ***Hotel-Restaurant les Pergolas***, T048-830841 (also rec) along the road to Agadir. 23 rooms, a bar and a restaurant serving French food. **D** ***Hotel Provencal***, nearby, T048-831208. 44 rooms, bar, restaurant and pool. **D** ***Hotel les Pyramides***, Route de l'Oued Souss, T048-834705. A quiet place with 20 rooms, a pool, restaurant, bar and horse riding. **D** ***Hotel Hagounia***, 9 Av Mokhtar Soussi, T048-830783. 48 rooms with shower and WC, located on the road just before the town centre. **F** ***Hotel El Merjane***, cheap and clean with communal facilities, the preferred choice on the main square.

Eating

There is no shortage of restaurants, but a good inexpensive one is the ***Café-Restaurant Bateau de Marrakech***, on the main square. Try ***Café/restaurant*** adjacent to *Hotel Hagounia* right in the centre for a view of the activity. There are plenty more adjacent. Also recommended is ***Saada*** on Blvd Moulay Abdallah opp. the stadium.

Transport

There are public transport services to Inezgane from **Casablanca** and **Essaouira**, **Marrakech** and **Taroudant** (1 hr), **Ouarzazate**, **Tiznit** and **Laâyoune**, amongst other places. In short, it is far better connected than Agadir, which you get to via grand taxi (2.5dh a seat) or local bus (Nos 5 and 6) from Inezgane. The airport bus is No 22. All long distance buses and grands taxis stop along the wide, busy main street lined by bus agents (including the ***CTM***), small shops and cheap restaurants. At the end of this is the main square, with the local bus stands. Off to the right of the square is a relaxed and mildly interesting covered market, with the main market day on Tue. Coming from Taroudant, you may have to change grands taxis at Ouled Teïma.

North of Agadir

The coast to the north offers the potential for rewarding excursions, and some limited opportunities for staying out of the city. Although this potential is gradually being realized by developers, the area remains idyllic and tranquil, with the ***Paradise Beach*** *and others stretching 30 km northwards from Agadir. Eastwards,* ***Paradise Valley*** *is a beautiful gorge and river basin, dotted with palm trees and waterfalls, leading up into the mountains and the village of* ***Immouzer des Ida Outanane****.*

Taghazoute

Phone code: 048
Colour map 2, grid C2
19 km N of Agadir

Once upon a time, the sleepy village of Taghazoute was a hippy sort of place. Today, it is waking up to the fact that it is close to Agadir, and could well eventually become a mainstream holiday town. Although new homes are currently being built, it remains a relaxing place and the beach is superb. To get there, catch bus 12 or 14 from place Salam in Agadir. Three kilometres to the south of Taghazoute is Tamraght, famous for its banana grove. From late autumn to spring, the Atlantic winds make this whole section of coast popular with surfers.

Sleeping & eating

C *Résidence Amouage*, Taghazoute, T/F048-200006. Basic self-catering accommodation, 350dh 2 persons. Out on the north (Essaouira) side of Taghazoute. **D** *Auberge du Littoral*, at Aourir, T048-314726, F314357. 20 good rooms, 4 small self-catering flats. **E** *Mamy Salerno Surf Dynamic Loisir*, Tamraght, T048-314655, F314654. Good rooms in a converted house. Used by surfers. Mountain bikes available for rent. French surf school sets up shop nearby from Oct to Mar. It is possible to rent cheap rooms in private houses, normally for a week minimum (**NB** no piped water). Be careful, however, as there have been cases of theft.

Camping The official campsite, opening onto a magnificent stretch of coast, is to the south. Partly shaded, café and basic facilities. Wash block just about kept clean. There are unofficial sites along the ocean front, where equally unofficial watchmen will make a small charge for keeping an eye out. Near the camp site is the restaurant, *Taoui-Fik*, try also *Paradise*, opposite the campsite. Other cheap eating options in the village. At Aourir, try *Al Baraka* next to the *Afriquia* petrol station.

Immouzer des Ida Outanane

Phone code: 048
Colour map 2, grid C2

Named after the local confederation of Berber tribes, Immouzer des Ida Outanane (Thursday market) is a pleasant, relaxing place for a short stay. Local claim to fame is honey (see festival in May. Immouzer's most famous sight, however, is its seasonal waterfalls, impressive in spring after a wet winter. This is an arid region, and generally the water is used, more prosaically, for irrigation.

Cascades

To reach the foot of the seasonal waterfalls, located below the village, turn left in the main square (signposted) and descend for 4 km past the *Café de Miel* and the *Restaurant Amelon*. This road, although a little rough in places, is driveable with care. Although they have been reduced in volume in recent years, the falls are popular for both sightseeing and bathing. The village is also a good place for birdwatching and walking. The *Hotel des Cascades* may advise. **NB** No petrol at Immouzer.

Sleeping

Camping is possible near the *Café de Miel* near the foot of the cascades, but the best option is the **C** ***Auberge des Cascades***, T048-826016 (or contact via Agadir agent T048-842671), a wonderful hotel with 27 rooms, terrace or balcony, with bath, excellent food in the restaurant, no TV, bar, tennis, pool lined with pomegranate and pear trees, and a delightful, tiered garden of fruit and olive trees located above the seasonal waterfalls, recently extended with 9 new spacious, rooms. Lunch possible on shaded terrace with wonderful views of the mountains, dinner menu 170dh, breakfast 48dh.

Transport

Immouzer is accessible by bus from Agadir, with a departure from close by the gare routière at 1400 (return bus to Agadir leaves at 0800). On market day (Thu), there are minibuses up from Agadir. For those with a car, drive north out of Agadir. At Km 12 north of Agadir at Aourir, just before Tamraght, a road turns off to the right and then forks right again in the village to Immouzer (50 km). This route, which is well metalled but narrow in places, winds steadily upwards through a green steep-sided valley. After approximately 15 km it descends into Paradise Valley, through a beautiful gorge. Stop on the way at *Café-Restaurant Tifrit*, a good restaurant 30 km from the main coast road, with simple rooms too (T048-826044). The spectacular scenery continues for the rest of the ascent through hillsides dotted with beehives, until at the end of this valley, 61 km from Agadir, at an altitude of 1,160 m, you come to the small market town of Immouzer des Ida Outanane.

Agadir to Essaouira: unspoiled coastline

The 173 km journey on the P8 follows the coast for about the first 70 km and thereafter runs some distance inland, often through hills covered with argan trees. On this route, you have three of Morocco's finest natural sites, the bird reserve at **Imzi**, one of the last refuges of the bald ibis, **Plage Tafadna**, and **Cap Sim**, possibly the windiest beach in Morocco.

Leaving Agadir, you have good views back over beach and port. After 12 km, however, beyond the turning to Immouzer at Aourire, the attractive beaches around Tamraght come into view, followed by those at Taghazoute at 19 km. Northwards from here, the road often stays close to the shoreline which alternates between outcrops of rock and deserted sandy bays, with some very picturesque views entering and leaving the small settlement of Aghrod. The lighthouse and viewpoint at **Cap Rhir** is reached after 40 km at a point where the most westerly point of the High Atlas falls over 360 m to the sea. There are opportunities for birdwatching around a lagoon, as the road swings inland along the wide estuary valley of Asif Aït Ameur past the banana plantations to the small settlement of **Tamri**. The piste turn-off for the reserve at **Imzi** comes some 8 km north of Tamri, marked by a sign *Ministère des eaux et des forêts, site protégé*. Imzi is unique in that there are large sand dunes atop the cliffs, formed by eroded matter being blown back onto the land. At km 89 there is a left turn off to the resort and shrine at Point Imessouane and the clifftop viewpoint of **Point d'Igui-n-Tama**. Look, too, for the **Gouffre d'Agadir Imoucha** at km 77, a ravine over 1 km long cutting into the plateau from the sea; you can find it by walking west across the fields. Soon, **Tamanar**, said to be the capital of the argan tree, is reached. There is a small hotel, *L'Etoile de Sud*, cafés, including *Café Argan*, shops, *tajine* stalls and petrol stations. From here the P8 soon descends to cross the two parts of the Oued Iguezoulen, passing a left turn to **Plage Tafadna**, sometimes marked on maps as **Cap Tafelney**, and then climbs through many bends around the side of Jbel Amsittene (905 m) to the village of Smimou (cafés and petrol). Here, a road leading east by the side of Jbel Amardma to Souk el Tnine and Sebt des Ait Daoud offers an interesting detour into the mountains of the Haha region. After a further 24 km, a turning to the left leads you 12 km to the **Marabout of Sidi Kaouki** on the coast. From here, **Cap Sim** can be reached. With its regular, strong swell, it is one of Morocco's best surf spots. To reach Essaouira, the best route is via the P8 and P10 roads; the alternative via Diabat starts promisingly enough, but then degenerates into a poor quality track.

Agadir to Marrakech

This is a very busy 268-km long road through some very striking country. Shortly after leaving Agadir, the road climbs to begin the long journey across the western extension of the High Atlas. This is the northernmost region in which the argan tree survives. Argan oil is sometimes offered for sale at the roadside (though it doesn't keep well). Here the argan trees and the browsing goats are common, but once north of the village of Argane these trees disappear to be replaced by juniper. The Tizi Maachou pass (1,700 m), while not as spectacular as those further east, has the advantage of being open to traffic all the year when the others are closed due to snowdrifts. Imi-n-Tanoute is an administrative centre (market Monday), where the 'short cut' to Marrakech runs northeastwards.

South of Agadir

Agadir to Tafraoute

Colour map 1, grid C2

The S509 runs for 170 km from Agadir to Tafraoute. Frequent louages and service buses No 8 and 13 cover this route. **El Kolea**, a dusty settlement is popular with Moroccans from Agadir. Water from the central fountain apparently has curative properties and is taken home by these visitors. Further on, **Biougra** is neat and clean with trees set into the tiled pavement along the central dual carriageway. Between the two settlements the busy road winds across an almost level plain, through a plasticulture region.

After Biougra, the land slowly rises. Workings in the huge limestone quarry on the left throw white clouds across the land. Beyond **Imi Mgourn** the first foothills are encountered and the road rises up with good views towards **Aït Baha**. The first of the fortified settlements are up here. Driving requires great concentration as large stretches of this narrow winding road are being repaired, or may need repair after damage by heavy rain.

Aït Baha, has the usual just adequate services, basic hotels, *souk* on Wed, 92 km still to go to Tafraoute, there is a road south to Tanalt. This makes an interesting detour of 100 km, the first 64 km being surfaced. There are three villages of note and an opportunity to strike northwards into the massif just before Aougounz. From Tanalt to Tioulit the scenery is very attractive, but the track is exceedingly rough so don't begin what your hire car cannot finish.

There are one or two small villages on the main route such as **Hadz Aït Mezzal**, and many abandoned villages high up the slope with the new settlements much lower now that conditions are safer. As the road swings over the cols there are good views and café stops at around 60 km from Tafraoute. If you miss these, the *Café Madou* in **Aguerdn'tzek**, right in the centre of village will do. The landscape grows increasingly spectacular, with the strata at an angle of 45°. After the **Tizi-n-Taraktine** pass (1,500m) you drop down to the junction with the 7038 turn off left for Igherm. Go right to sweep down into the **Ameln Valley**.

Agadir to Tiznit

Colour map 2, grid C2

Follow the signs from Agadir towards the airport, 20 minutes on a quiet day, then take the P30 south to Tiznit. This is a good straight and fast road through rich agricultural land. Tifnite to the west is a beach resort.

Sidi Rabat and **Massa** are signed on the right at 46 km from Agadir. Follow the 7128 west across the flat coastal plain. Soon you will be running through a large and busy agricultural settlement, busy with buses and service taxis. Stands of cane along the Oued Massa can be glimpsed over to the left. Take the right turn marked to Sidi Rbat, with a deep *oued* to the right hand. The road surface stops very suddenly, turning into sandy track over open farmland. Depending on your vehicle, you will have to cover the last few km to the Oued Massa Nature Reserve on foot.

Held back by large sandbanks, the waters of the Oued Mass have formed a lagoon. The vast reed beds, the massive fringing dunes to the southwest, sandbanks at the mouth of the river, the water course itself and the mud banks to the north provide are home to both birds and mammals. Visit between February and April, and between September and November when there are over-wintering birds.The estuary is home (temporary or permanent) to crane, avocet, spoonbill, great flamingo, osprey, and night, squacco and purple heron. One of the few surviving groups of the endangered bald ibis (*Geronticus eremita*) live here. (The other main site is north of Agadir at Tidzi). Although not an attractive creature, it did not deserve to be hunted almost to extinction. Several kinds of raptor are attracted by the populations of birds, including small groups of ospreys.

Detour to the Youssef Ben Tachfine Dam

Birdwatchers may also like to make a detour off the P30 Agadir to Tiznit to the Barrage Youssef Ben Tachfine, which retains the waters of the Oued Massa. The turn off left as you head to Tiznit is clearly signed and a surfaced road takes you up to the actual dam. A track running left just beyond the dam wall might give you some twitching opportunities. The detour then continues southwestwards to Tiznit through Souk el Arba des Ersmouka back to the P30. See page 452for further details about Tiznit.

Inland from Agadir to Taroudant

Buses No 11 and 20 from Inezgane cover this route

This is an interesting 73 km which improves after the urban sprawl of the Agadir region is left behind. The initial part is very built-up - but rural life is always present, and dromedaries may be seen grazing adjacent to the Agadir bypass. Traffic crawls through **Temsi** but clears at **El Jorf**, where the speed limit ends. In season the sweet smell of orange blossom is very strong and the road is lined with wild flowers. The first argan trees are to the east of El Jorf, with thin cereals underneath. The first major town is called **Ouled Teïma** situated at a busy crossroads. (If you are travelling by grand taxi to Taroudant, you may have to change here.) New tall buildings, mainly four-storey with lock-up shops beneath, line the main street. All is neat and tidy and there are the usual features of a small Moroccan town: market, various government offices, hospital and schools. Market day (Monday) attracts an interesting mixture of people. Right until mid-summer the High Atlas to the north have a covering of snow, a contrast to the dry plain. Beyond Ouled Teïma, the plain of the Oued Souss, one of Morocco's most productive regions, lies ahead.

Taroudant

Phone 'code': 048
Colour map 2, grid C3

Taroudant is famous for its red-brown crenellated walls. Nicknamed by locals 'the grandmother of Marrakech', it has some of the character of its more famous neighbour across the Tizi-n-Test pass, albeit on a far smaller and sleepier scale. The médina is enclosed by impressive rammed earth ramparts. Inside are two largish squares, higgledy-piggledy streets and some souks. Much of the older building has been replaced by new concrete stuff, however. Taroudant makes a good overnight stop on an exploration of Southern Morocco. Agadir and the coast are a short hop westwards. Much farther afield are the pre-Saharan oases of Tata and Akka (rock carvings close by). North is the western High Atlas, while eastwards are routes to Ouarzazate and the Draâ, Dadès and Ziz valleys.

Ins and outs

Getting there

See page 445 for further details

Taroudant is easily accessible from Agadir and its transport hub, Inezgane, by bus and grand taxi. There are further bus and grand taxi links across to Ouarzazate and north across the mountains to Marrakech. If you are planning to visit the oases of Tata and Akka, there are grands taxis, plus onward connections to Tiznit. Buses and taxis arrive at Bab Zorgane. There are no longer any buses coming into the central squares. Note that the buses can be very slow – the *CTM* from Marrakech on the easy Chaouia route has been known to take a ridiculous 6 hrs for what is only a 223 km trip.

Getting around

The town centres on Pl Assarag (aka Pl des Alaouites) and Pl Talmoklate (aka Pl Ennasr). The sights, such as they are (basically the ramparts and souk), can be done on foot. You might hire a bike from an outfit on Pl Assarag to explore a bit more. From Taroudant, possible day trips include the old village of Freija, some 10 km from town, and the oasis of Tioute, which has an old kasbah. Pale-brown petits taxis do runs in the local area, and there are a few horse-drawn calèches, too.

Background

Located at the heart of the fertile Souss valley, Taroudant was always an important regional centre, and even managed to achieve national prominence on a few occasions. Taken by the Almoravids in 1056, it achieved a certain level of independence under the Almohads. Temporary fame came in the 16th century with the rise of the Saâdians (they of the beautiful hidden necropolis in Marrakech). From 1510, the first Saâdian leader, Mohammed el Qa'im, was based in Taroudant as the Emir of the Souss. Even after the Saâdians had gained control of the rest of Morocco, Taroudant remained their capital for a while. Later, in the 17th century, Taroudant supported Moulay Ismaïl's nephew in his rebellion. When the great sultan took the town in 1687, he took his revenge by slaughtering the population and destroying much of the town. Decline set in, continuing into the 18th and 19th centuries. In the early years of the French protectorate, Taroudant harboured the rebel Sultan el Hiba and was consequently sacked by colonial forces. Today, the town is a regional market. Two luxury hotels attract visitors. Most tourists, however, are day-trippers from Agadir or people over-nighting on their way to other southern destinations. And finally, just for info, an inhabitant of Taroudant is called a Roudani.

Sights

Walls

The 16th and early 17th-century Saâdian pisé walls, nicely crenellated and set here and there with chunky square towers, are Taroudant's best sight. You could follow the wall's round the town, possibly in a *calèche* (horse-drawn carriage), generally available from outside the *Hotel Salam* for around 40dh per hour. There were originally only five gates (running clockwise from the bus station Bab Zorgane, Bab Targhount, Bab Oulad Bounouna, Bab el Khemis and Bab el Kasbah), and you can go up at least one of these for a look out over olive groves, orchards and much new building. En route you'll pass the Kasbah, the most densely populated and poorest part of town. This in fact was a fortress re-built by Moulay Ismaïl in the 17th century. Outside the walls, you might try to visit the tanneries, left from Bab el Khemis ('the Thursday gate'), where skins of a variety of animals are still cured using pretty traditional methods.

Souks

Although nowhere near as extensive as those of Marrakech, the souks of Taroudant are fairly good. They are perhaps an easier, calmer place to look around for souvenirs than Marrakech, where handicraft indigestion sometimes sets in. Thursday and Sunday are busy days, with people coming in from the surrounding villages. The souks lead off from Place Assarag, beside the bank. Notable specialities of the town include jewellery and mock ancient carvings in local limestone. Carpets can also be found. There are small stalls and a few bigger tourist shops. Off the far side of Place Talmoklate ('square of the Little Pot') is an area with shoplets selling spices, herbs, medicines and pottery.

The town

Apart from its walls, Taroudant is not the most picturesque of places by day. Originally, part of the area within the walls was devoted to orchards and market gardening. Much of this has now been built up, and the majority of the original low pisé buildings have long since been replaced by charmless concrete housing. In the evening, however, Taroudant takes on a more interesting air, and men stay up late socializing in the cafés in the centre. Essentially, this is a farming centre, and there is much poverty, evident from the number of shoe-shiners willing to clean your walking boots as you sit at one of the café terraces. However, tourism may yet bring some limited prosperity. There is apparently a scheme to redevelop one of the squares with fountains and the like. Deterred by the high prices of property in Marrakech, there is money around looking for riads to restore. Hopefully, the ramparts will not be disfigured by further restaurant-type developments.

Essentials

Sleeping

■ *on map, page 444*
Price codes: see inside front cover
All numbers begin with the code 048

Taroudant is lacking in good accommodation. If you can't pay the stratospheric prices of the Gazelle d'Or, you have the choice of the Palais Salam (should be better than it is), some unprepossessing mid-range places - or a spartan, noisy room in one of the very cheap central hotels (early morning call from nearby mosque). For budget-ish travellers, either the *Hotel Le Soleil* or the *Hotel Taroudant* will be fine for a night or two. For groups, there is also a self-catering type place, Jnène Remane.

LL *Hotel La Gazelle d'Or*, Route d'Amezgou, T048-852039/48, F852737. A truly toney place, some 2 km outside Taroudant. Originally built by a Belgian aristocrat. Generally closed in summer. 100 ha of beautiful grounds, pool, tennis, hammam, riding and croquet. Half-board around 4,000dh in one of the garden houses. Suites much more expensive. Said to be one of the best hotels in Morocco. **A** ***Palais Salam***, built into the ramparts around the Kasbah district, in a building which was the local pacha's palace, T048-852501, F852654. 2 pools, including one in the shape of a Moroccan horseshoe arch (bit tacky, really). Not in fact as classy as it likes to make out, witness the piped music at the poolside. The only place where you can get a beer (for the moment).

E *Hotel Saâdiens*, Av du 20 Août, Borj Oumansour, T048-852589, F852118. Well signed, even though in the middle of the old town. Small pool. All in all, not a very exciting deal. **E** *Café-Hotel-Restaurant Le Soleil*, close to Bab Targhount, just outside the walls in the Agadir direction, T048-551707. Pleasant place with a small garden and big rooms, old fashioned bathrooms (baths Egyptian sarcophagus model) and hot water. Quiet by day. At night tends to be rather noisy: clients arrive from late buses, water trickles in unseen pipes. At the last count, management seemed to consist of two 14-year-old kids who, considering they kip on the kitchen floor, were doing a very good job. **E** *Hotel-Restaurant Taroudant*, Pl Assarag, T048-852416. From 55dh for the simplest rooms to 160dh for the best twin with shower and loo. As usual, prefer inward facing rooms, although these are noisy when the bar is in action, if it ever re-opened since the last licence holder died. Staff very nice. A good address, if a little basic with its linoleum and air of the 1950s. Try for room 14. **E** *Hotel-Restaurant Tiout*, Av du Prince Héritier Sidi Mohammed, T048-850341, F854480. 37 rooms including 12 with tiny balcony. Re-opened in 1999 after 'major renovation work', ie much artistic paintwork to mask a basic concrete building as cheaply as possible. Ugly terrace ('solarium'). A false *bel hôtel*. **F-E** Creeping into the **E** category are a number of small hotels on Pl Assarag, including the hotels ***Les Arcades***, ***El Ouarda*** ('the Rose') ***de la Place*** and ***Roudani***. Very basic, tiny and none-too-clean rooms for 60-70dh. Best of the bunch? Possibly *El Ouarda*.

Self-catering *Jnène Remane* ('Garden of the Pomegranates'). Well-run small outfit with private flats and dormitory accommodation, located in the old town. Ecologically managed by a UK-based company, *Naturally Morocco Ltd*, T044-0709-2343879, www.naturallymorocco.com Locally-based staff are very knowledgeable about the region. Bookings are made via the central-offices in Wales. Vegetarian food a speciality. Highly rec, have small car for hire, can set up informed tours of the region.

Elsewhere in the region C *Palais Riad Hida*, Oulad Berhil, 40 km out of Taroudant on the P32 road to Aoulouz, T048-531044, F531026. Look out for the sign in the village

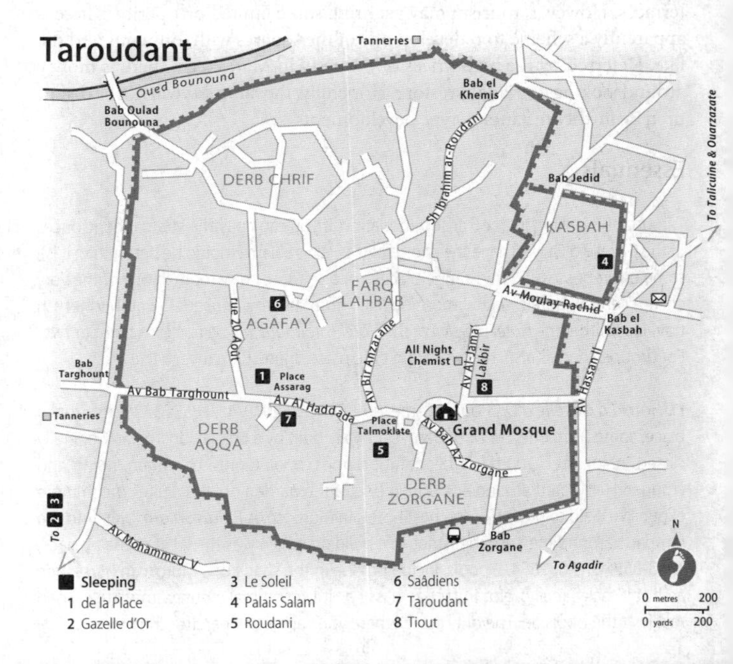

centre. Around 300dh for a double. Small establishment in a restored pacha's country residence, 10 rooms, nice grounds. Invaded by tour-groups some lunchtimes.

Eating

Expensive *La Gazelle d'Or*, route d'Amezgou, T852039. Restaurant of the hotel of the same name. Posh togs necessary. Restaurant at the *Hotel Palais Salam*, reservations via hotel reception on T852501 or numbers above. Menu at around 240dh, wine extra. In Jan 2001 this was the only place with alcohol. **Mid-range** ***Restaurant Jnane Soussia***, in a sort of tent just outside the ramparts near Bab Zorgane, T0854980. Was it necessary to put such an ugly establishment next to the ramparts? Location handy for tour buses. Overpriced Moroccan fare. Restaurant at the ***Hotel Saâdiens***. Menu and à la carte. Acceptable. Restaurant at the ***Hotel Taroudant***. Simple menu at 70dh, no alcohol for the moment. **Cheap** Quite a lot of choice on Pl Assarag. If rushed, try the restaurant of the ***Hotel Les Arcades***, basic lunch for 40dh. Rather better is the ***Restaurant el Baraka***, between the 2 squares, where lunch for 2 (chicken portion, chips and salads) will set you back 50dh.

Sport & activities

Bike hire On Pl Assarag, opposite *Hotel Taroudant*. **Hammam** Near the *Hotel Taroudant*, also off Pl Assarag. **Tennis** Try the ***Hotel Palais Salam*** for tennis.

Transport

Bus The journey to Agadir, only 80 km, can take up to 2 hrs by bus - probably better to take a grand taxi. **Marrakech** can be equally slow. For distant towns (**Casablanca**, **Marrakech** via the Tizi-n-Test, **Ouazarzate** etc), buses leave early in the morning. Buses leave from the Bab Zorgane station. Regular buses to **Agadir** (4 per day), **Casablanca** (4 per day), **Inzegane** (on the hour), **Ouarzazate** (5 per day), **Tata** (3 per week). Early morning service to Marrakech via Tizi-n-Test takes 9 hrs. **Driving** To **Agadir**, you can take the main P32 (straightforward but boring), or (for an insight into rural Morocco) a poorly surfaced minor road (P7016) along the northern side of the Oued Souss. This brings you onto the P40 from Chichaoua to the northeast of Agadir. For **Marrakech**, the quickest route is up the P40 to Chichaoua, followed by the P10 eastwards. **Taxi** Grands taxis for **Agadir** and **Inezgane**, need to change at Ould Teima.

Directory

Banks There are several ATMs, including ***Banque populaire*** and ***Société générale*** (*SGBM*) on Pl Assarag and the ***Crédit du Maroc***, opposite the *Hotel Taroudant*. Try also *BMCI* on R Bir Anzarane off Pl Talmoklate. **Medical services** Dr Ahmed ibn Jdid, T048-852032 (clinic), T853626 (home).

Taroudant to Ouarzazate, via Taliouine and Tazenakht

Colour map 2, grids C3 & C4

Basically, there are two viable road routes south over the High Atlas taking you from Taroudant to Marrakech: the western, tricky Tizi-n-Test route or the easier 4 hour drive via the Tizi-n-Tichka, which takes you down to Ouarzazate. Most people heading for the southern flanks of the Atlas will take the latter option. For those with a good head for heights, the Tizi-n-Test journey is a great option. Heading east out of Taroudant, you take the P31 to Ouarzazate. At Oulad Berrehil, where the road begins to leave the fertile **Souss Valley**, the road coming over the Tizi-n-Test intersects. The first useful settlement is, **Taliouine**, a good starting point for walking in the **Jbel Siroua**. It is also said to produce the best saffron in Morocco. The col of **Tizi n-Taghatin** marks the end of the Souss basin and the beginning of the Draâ. At **Tazenakht**, there is a carpet-makers' co-operative (Ouzguita tribal weaving available), while just before Ouarzazate is the Taghdout Dam, a place to picnic for those with a car.

If you are driving east from Taroudant on the P31, the first major settlement is **Oulad Berrehil**. Coming over the Tizi-n-Test, you meet the junction for Ouarzazate 52 km east of Taroudant.

Further along the P31, **Aoulouz**, about 30 km east of the junction to Tizi-n-Test, is a beautiful spot. There is easy access to the Oued Souss. Take the track to the right when approaching from the west, which goes right down to the water's edge. In good years there is water in the *oued*.

The road east climbs up to **Iouzioua Ounneine**, over a pass of 1,050 m with good views to the southwest. Look out for restaurant *Noukia*, better than average, a possible coffee stop.

Taliouine Taliouine is a pleasant town (usual services), improved by the presence of a magnificent kasbah to the south of the road. Petrol (*Ziz*) at the eastern end of town beyond the triumphal arches and a *Shell* in the centre, almost opposite the *Saffron Cooperative*. *Crédit Agricole* does not change travellers cheques, but has more favourable rates for currency exchange than the *Hotel Ibn Toumert*.

Sleeping and eating B *Hotel Ibn Toumert*, T048-534125, hotel.ibntaliouine@caramail.com 100 rooms shower, 2 suites bath, a/c and heating, some with view of kasbah. Breakfast 50dh, lunch menus 112-140dh, pleasant 1970s hotel, lovely surroundings. Has potential – restaurant impersonal, used by bus tours. Far cheaper are the *Hotel/Café Renaissance*, also **E** ***Auberge/Restaurant Souktana***, T048-534075, on the north side of the road, west of the road junction to *Hotel Ibn Toumert* and east of the *oued*. Small, pleasant garden surrounds it, also does camping. Recommended for good food, especially tagines, availability of guides, mules, tents for walkers etc for excursions up into the Jbel Siroua (see below). ***Hotel/Camping Siroua*** to south of road on west side of the town. ***Hotel de la Poste*** is to be avoided. **E** ***Auberge Askaoun***, T048-534017, just 1 km out of town towards Tazenakht, is a little better.

Taliouine to Tazenakht From Taliouine there is a road south to Igherm and a minor road north to Askaoun. Taliouine is recognized as a starting point for walks into the Jbel Siroua.

Between Taliouine and Tazenakht are two high passes, **Tizi-n-Taghatine** (1,886 m) and **Tizi Ikhsane** (1,650 m), with a small settlement of **Tinfat** with another imposing kasbah, midway between. The highest pass, Tizi-n-Taghatine, incorporates some of the nicest of the scenery on this route; a mixture of landforms, terracing with small trees, views on all sides, and the road, though not perfect, allows time for eyes to do a little wandering. In fact the journey is perhaps better going east to west as the snow-capped Atlas make a better backdrop, to the right and straight ahead.

Between the passes there is patchy shifting cultivation and little else. At the top of the lower pass, **Ikhsane**, there's a man with a small hut selling plain terracotta pottery. How's that for determination? Beyond Ikhsane after another very straight stretch of road is **Kourkouda**, with a few stalls with pottery and fossils, another with a few carpets, painted rams' horns and sheets of selenite, a form of calcite.

Tazenakht & beyond Tazenakht is at an important junction, though much of the town stands to the northwest of the road. Triumphal pillars announce the entrance to the town just before the junction off east to Foum Zguid. Adjacent to the arch is a petrol station with a small clean restaurant. At this junction, grands taxis and petits taxis are on the left, bus station, pharmacy on right, *Café Essaadi*, *Hotel/restaurant Senhaja*, basic rooms, very cheap, and telephone. Market Friday. *Hotel Etoile*, in the centre by the taxi stand, is a very run down motel, damp and unpleasant. *Hotel Zenaga* (T048-41032) is the only place fit to stay in, rooms vary and so do prices, hot water in evening only. The Shell petrol station is on the left by the *oued*, the triumphal arch which marks the far end of the town. Tazenakht also has a bank, a number of carpet shops, displaying wares produced by the local Ouzguita tribe - and very fine and geometrically designed they are too. There are the usual small shops for general supplies like fizzy drinks and biscuits, and a mosque.

After Tazenakht, the P32 road climbs up to Tizi-n-Bachkoum, 1,700 m. There is, at the top, a good view to the west and even a place to pull off. The inevitable group of small children could well be waiting.

Anezal stands by a large *oued* of the same name. Often tourist mini-coaches are parked at the café here, which is good for a rest and a drink.

To the right of the road between Anezal and Tiouine is a huge *oued* with tributaries which eventually lead into the barrage to the east of Ouarzazate. The road goes alongside this for 20 km, all the way to Tiouine. Here there is an old ruined fortress on the right and new buildings on the left. The road descends to cross the big Oued Iriri, just north of Tiouine. There are two junctions where roads go north to Marrakech, 178 km away over the Tizi-n-Tichka. Beyond these the road is far busier. Roadside sales on this exceedingly straight road lined with eucalyptus trees include pottery, dyed desert roses, amathyst and polished stone. The village of Taborhat is at the junction where the road goes off southeast to Zagora.

Trekking in the Jbel Siroua

Jbel Siroua is best trekked in spring and autumn

As indicated above (see Taliouine), the best starting point for Jbel Siroua treks is Taliouine. Rising to a twin-peak of 3,305 m, the Jbel Siroua is an arid, isolated region forming a sort of volcanic bridge between the High Atlas of Toubkal to the north and the Anti-Atlas to the south. As compared with the busy, even prosperous, Imilchil region, there are few trekkers for the moment. Communicating with locals can be a problem, unless you have fluent Tachelhit. Best trekked in autumn and spring, the Jbel Siroua is easily accessible from both Taroudant and Ouarzazate. From Marrakech, it is a long ride, nearly nine hours by the direct bus, depending on breakdowns and stops. Getting there from Marrakech, you could of course go for the Tizi-n-Test crossing to Taroudant, spectacular enough to make the slowness of the journey easily bearable.

Possible treks

From Taliouine, there are numerous possibilities for trekking up into the Siroua. Richard Knight in his excellent *Trekking in the Moroccan Atlas* (Hindhead: Trailblazer Publications, 2001) gives an immense amount of useful detail on a nine-day round Jbel Siroua trek. If you have less time, the *Auberge Souktana* (T048-534075, F231411) in Taliouine should be able to advise on short treks. Also try *Jnène Remane* in Taroudant, as they have excellent contacts in the region (UK contact *Naturally Morocco Ltd*, T044-07092343879, www.naturallymorocco.com). A number of European-based travel companies run treks into the Jbel Siroua, too. Another possibility might be to take a minibus from Taliouine up to Akhfamane, where many of the treks start. An irregular minibus service runs from the central *Shell* garage in Taliouine up to Akhfamane, although it is possible to walk this in about five hours. At Akhfamane, there are a rooms available and mules for hire.

Taroudant to Tata via Igherm

Colour map 2, grids C3 & C4

The landscapes on the 7025/7085/7111 route from **Taroudant** to **Tata** via **Igherm** (distance 120 km) are among most beautiful in southern Morocco. Allow plenty of time for photo-stops and perhaps a side-trip up to

Tazegzaoute. Along with the Tata to Bou Izakarn via Akka route (see below), this is a must for devotees of wilderness.

Near Taroudant: Feïja and Tioute

Heading eastwards from Taroudant on the P30, turn right onto the 7025 and pause at the small village of **Feïja**. Pisé walls crumbling amid the new building signal a rural community in full change. There are good views north over the orchards and fields of the Souss valley to High Atlas. Returning to the 7025, a few km further on the next turn off is for **Tioute**, (souk Wednesday) set in argan groves on the edge of the Souss plain, 33 km from Taroudant. Here the kasbah is easily reached by a more or less blacktop road. Again, there are superb views over the plain. A similar sort of site in Italy would be home to a monastery. Here, the old buildings have been transformed into a concrete bunker of a restaurant for tour groups. Below, in the village, you can see a strone threshing floor and the Zaouia of Sidi Abd el Kader. Normally, someone will appear to volunteer donkey rides from the Kasbah, say 30dh a head. As you arrive in Tioute, an argan oil co-operative is signed and a rather good guesthouse, **C** *Auberge Tighm*i, T048-850555, 6 simple rooms upstairs, 2 small rooms on ground floor, no air-conditioning, excellent home cooking, highly recommended for a quiet couple of days' reading and walking.

Igherm & Tazegzaoute

After Tioute, the 7025 winds upwards as the soft green of the Souss is left behind. **Igherm**, 88 km from Tata, is the first major settlement, a one-street sort of place with shops and cafés. Look out for the *Restaurant Kratrit*, an eclectic little place run by one Brahim. Note that the route southwest (7038) from Igherm to **Tafraoute** is now fully tarmacked and perfectly accessible to small hire cars (granaries to look out for on the way). The piste running northeast to Taliouine is still only for 4WD vehicles. South of Igherm, there are some very photogenic folds in the landscape in the region of Souk Khémis d'Issafen. Some 55 km south of Igherm, there is a turn off right (west) for the valley of **Tazegzaoute**, lit. 'greenery' in Tachelhit. The track, for 4WD only, although ask if the piste has been improved, will take you into a beautiful valley which has something of southwest Arabia about it. Well-equipped walkers with guide could head over the hills for Tafraoute via Tazalrhite. Back on the main 7111, there is more spectacular landscape as far as Imitek, after which the road calms for the final runs east into Tata.

Tata

The main town of the Djebel Beni region, built alongside an oasis, the rose-pink houses of Tata focus on an arcaded main street and dusty market square. The place has a definite feel of the desert garrison outpost. There are all basic facilities, banks (no ATM), the post office and basic café-restaurants. Given that within a couple of hours drive (and less) of Tata are fascinating old villages and prehistoric rock art sites, the town makes a good base, especially as a couple of its small selection of hotels are perfectly acceptable. As service stations at Akka and destinations east can run out, try to fill up in Tata before heading onwards.

For those with a morning to spare, there is a good side trip from Tata to the impressively large *ksar* of **Tazaght**. Just before Addis, and after a big village on your left, turn left (east) off the 7084 to Akka. Tazaght is just visible across several kilometres of gravelly plain traversed by tracks. Follow the piste and park up near the new pinky-red mosque and walk around ridge to right. The oldest part of the village, largely stone-built, sits atop a rocky crest, while other sections closer to the cultivated area crumble back into the earth. Look out for the original mosque which has a massive whitewashed simplicity recalling the Almoravid kouba in Marrakech. A very happy time can be had clambering round the semi-ruined houses and you might walk down to the oasis, too. Vicomte Charles de Foucauld, one of the first Europeans to travel in the Moroccan interior stayed in Tazaght with the family of his guide, the rabbi Mardochée Aby Serour. Of the ksar's once large Jewish community there would seem to be absolutely no trace.

Sleeping and eating Although used by tour-groups, the most comfortable place to stay is the **B** ***Relais des Sables***, the 'chic' mock kasbah on your left as you approach the town from the Akka/Igherm directions, T048-802301, F802300. 18 good sized a/c rooms, 42 small double rooms, all with bath; restaurant, bar, pool and private parking. Rather more central, quite homely but living perhaps on its reputation is the **D** ***Hotel de la Renaissance***, 96 Av des FAR, T048-802225. 45 rooms most with bath/WC, hot water temperamental. Perfectly acceptable food, guides to local sites show up. Other options are **F** *Hotel Sahara* and **F** *Hotel Salam*, both basic, the latter on the main arcaded street next to the chemist's. A guesthouse at Indiafen, the oasis on your left before the triumphal arches and petrol station marking Tata (as you arrive from Igherm) was being readied in winter 2002 (ask for Latifa at the *Hotel de la Renaissance*).

East from Tata

The 7084 from Tata to Tissint and its continuation, the 7148 to Foum Zguid is now fully metalled. (NB gendarmerie royale checks). Transport is by grand taxi or the daily bus, if you don't have a car. The garrison town of **Tissint** lies 70 km from Tata. Visited by French aristocrat Charles de Foucauld during his peregrinations in the 19th century, the settlement's five *ksour* were a key transit point for caravans in the lower Draâ valley. The settlement also known for its dates and its medicinal herbs. As you arrive from Tata, about 2 km before Tissint near the checkpoint, park up and take a look at the canyon and the cascade. (Is there an auberge now open?) A further 70 km from Tissint lies **Foum Zguid** (Thursday souk, basic accommodation and buses to Ouarzazate). From Foum Zguid it's 120 km to Zagora on the rough 6953 track.

Tata to Bou Izakarn via Akka, Amtoudi and Ifrane de l'Anti-Atlas

The region southwest of Tata is extremely rewarding for those interested in prehistoric rock art. You will see overlapping carvings of elegant gazelles, other beasts and spirals, also human feet, carved on large flat stones in the unlikeliest of locations – witness to the civilization resident here in a time before the desert. A good selection of sites can be covered in a long day's exploring by those with their own vehicle. For those dependent on public transport, the excellent site of **Adrar Metgourine** can be reached from **Akka** on foot. Akka lies 70 km southwest of Tata. If you want to overnight, the problem is that the settlement's one hotel, **F** *Hotel-Café Tamdoult* on the main road, is really pretty grotty. For the moment, there is no formal petrol station – the only pump is on the west (left) side of the road near the hotel. (The petrol companies have to compete with the contrabandistas, bringing petrol up from the Sahara where it is on sale more cheaply.) Akka also has cafés and shops for basic stores, with souks on Thursday and Sunday.

Prehistoric rock art at Oum el Alek

If you are really keen to visit the rock-art sites, then the best guide is Mouloud Taâret, T062-291864 (mob). He lives in Douar Touzounine, a roadside settlement a few kilometres south of Akka, handy for the rock-art site of Tamdoult, and also has a base in **Oum el Alek**, a village south of the main road a few kilometres east of Akka. A guide is practically a necessity in order to see a maximum of the carvings which tend to be located on flatish boulders on certain low ridges which run parallel, in places, to the 7084 road. The good guide may also show you the open-air sites where neolithic people worked flints. These tend to be more visible after winter rain. **NB** Do not go tramping across the gravel to the ridges in your flipflops. In winter, snakes like to sun themselves coiled up next to boulders and may be too sluggish to slither away as you approach … the nearest poison treatment centre is in Agadir.

Between Oum el Alek and Tata, there are two minor rock-art sites close to the 7084, **Oued Meskaou** (on your left, coming from Tata) and **Aman Ighriben** (on your right). The better of the two is **Oued Meskaou**. From the Tata direction, look out for the Akka 24 km post which is just a few metres after the turn-off for the site. As you come from Akka, look out for the Taroudant 234 km post, also a sign for Oued Meskaou and the *Commune rurale de Tata*. Turn off right between the concrete bollards. Park under the thorn trees near the gap between two ridges. The engravings are on the ridge tops, an interesting mix of smoothed and piqueté technique carvings, including some spirals. The chess-board designs, the so-called *bijoux berbères*, are probably recent nomad scratchings. Out in the distance, near a higher ridge line, is the oasis of **Ghans**, which has a *guelta* (pool) in rainy years.

12 km further on, **Aman Ighriben**, 12½ km from Akka, turn off near the marker 259 km to Tiznit, 246 km to Taroudant. Coming from Tata, turn off right a couple of kilometres after the Guelmim 255 km marker, just before the white markers. You should park near the palm trees some 200 m from the road. The carvings are on a low (10 m high) stoney rise close to palms and thorn bushes. The site, probably because it is so accessible, is much deteriorated, although there are still some nice gazelles.

Closer to Akka, at **Oum el Alek**, the route to the rock art is none to clear. Drive through the sandy 'streets' of the village. Beyond the houses, the military have marked out a piste on the gravel plain with occasional pairs of upright stones. The carvings are on a low rise, several hundred metres long, beyond the biggish (50 m high) hill south of the village. You will probably park below the ridge and walk along to see the carvings. There were clashes here between the Forces Armées Royales and Algerian-backed Polisario rebels in the late 1970s, and the Moroccan military still maintain a presence in the region. The site definitely merits a visit, even though the rock art has suffered from illegal 'stone quarrying' by local notables building houses. The Department of Antiquities is remote, even though the site (and others like it) is supposedly protected. Sometimes the bedouin kids see visitors clambering along the ridges. Uninformed about the importance of the carvings, they have added their own contribution to the rocks with metal implements.

For **Adrar Metgourine**, you need to turn north, right after on the first turning after roadside Akka. Like Igherm, in its day Akka was wealthy halt on the great caravan routes across the Sahara, no doubt vying in importance with Sijilmassa. After you have driven past the older settlement of Tagadirt, you will come to evidence of this in the form of the ruined Almohad-style minaret at Lala Baït Allah. Set in an oasis, the building comes as a real surprise. Does it predate the Koutoubia in Marrakech? The fact that the Almohads should have chosen to build here is evidence of Akka's importance in the trade in the trans-Saharan gold, ivory and slave trade. You should park up in the shade near here. Adrar Metgourine, a low hill which appears as a semicircle to the north, is a good 90 minutes' walk away. The prehistoric artists carefully executed their works in stones along the top of the hill, and their lines are highlighted to good effect by the setting sun. Even without the carvings, the site has its own special beauty.

Tadakousset

South of Akka, the carvings at Tamdoult near roadside Touzounine are for enthusiasts – and probably require authorization from the local Gendarmerie royale. More interesting is **Tadakousset**, a village accessed by piste running west of the 7084 from Aït Guebli (shown as Oua Belli on some maps). At this settlement, the road crossed the boulder-filled bed of a wide *oued*, which when it floods (once every 5 years) can wash away the *radier* or concrete slabs used by traffic. The track off towards Tadakousset is quite difficult in the early stages along the oued. Then a wide valley lightly wooded with acacia trees opens up and the going is easy as far as the village. There is some rock art on boulders to the right of the piste, at **Aglagal** (a couple of houses), and then, past the domed marabout of Sidi Bou Hadi, you see Tadakousset up ahead under a cliff. From here, the rock art at Tamzrart is accessible on foot with a guide. The village, however, is worth the excursion in its own right.

Foum El Hassan

Further on, the rock art at the oasis of **Foum El Hassan**, off the main road near **Icht** , has suffered. The carvings in the town centre have gone and the nearest are 4 km from the town, up the track into the mountains. You might be able to find a local guide to take you to some remoter examples. A few kilometres further on, at **Aït Herbil** , there may still be some carvings, too.

Amtoudi (aka Id Aissa)

At 55 km east of Foum El Hassan a recent metalled road heads north across the plain to Souk Tnine d'Adaï and then to the village of **Amtoudi** (26 km), marked on some maps as Agadir Id Aissa. For those without own transport Amtoudi is well worth making the effort to reach (share taxis available from Taghjijt on the 7084, and probably worth an overnight if you like a spot of walking. Because of the well preserved (and recently restored) agadir, Amtoudi is on the tourist safari circuit. Soon after you arrive, the elder who holds the key will appear to accompany you up the mule track to the top (20 minutes' steep walk, mules occasionally available). The views are magnificent. Clamber round inside, look out for the fitted stone beehives, the prehistoric carved feet at the highest point (site of some prehistoric or nomad ritual?), and the cisterns. The flat stone walls are superbly constructed to follow the line of the cliff. The agadir functioned as a guarded store for the villagers' harvest and was probably only inhabited in times of raiding.

Amtoudi has acquired a certain prosperity, in part thanks to migrant worker remittances for new building. Electricity has arrived, water is now pumped up to homes from the web – and there is even a téléboutique. If you want to stay over, the campsite down below has new French management. It originally focused on lunches for the charabanc trade, although this may change. Bunk room accommodation 30dh, hot showers available, breakfast 30dh, meals 60dh. **NB** Should there be any risk of a thunderstorm, avoid staying at campsite, as it sits below the cliff at the meeting point of two canyons. Catastrophe if there is a spate of water coming down from the plateau.

Exploring the agadirs of Amtoudi

The campsite can set you up with a guide to take you walking in the area. There is an excellent short walk up to the *gueltas* through the palm groves further up the canyon (bring your picnic and swimmies, as there's plenty of water and sun in winter). A day walk could start at the main agadir, then take you over the plateau to further ones, the best preserved of which is **Agadir Aglaoui**, an eagle's nest of a place which looks as though it should house some rapacious seigneur. After this granary, there is a difficult descent down to the oued whence you may follow through to the pools. Another energetic scramble takes you 100 m up to the top again. Head across the plateau towards the red-and-white pylon to climb back down the gorge just above the campsite. Here is yet another ruined agadir and vertiginous drops. Do not be put off by the Gaetulian squirrels scampering among the rocks.

Taghjijt & Timoulay

Back on the 7084, **Taghjijt** (Thursday market, interesting at date harvest time) is useful as a place where you can charter a grand taxi for 150dh to take you up to Amtoudi. There is also a very good breakfast café at the main junction (Gendarmerie royale checks) and the fairly comfortable **D** *Hotel Taregua*, T048-788780, meals and alcohol, should you need to stop over. As at Akka, there is no formal petrol station in Taghjijt.

Ifrane de l'Anti Atlas

At the ribbon settlement of **Timoulay Izder** (*Shell* petrol, pharmacy), you need the turn-off right onto the 7076 for **Ifrane de l'Anti Atlas** (aka Ifrane de l'Atlas Esseghir, 10km, market Saturday). This is another of those southern Moroccan villages which turned into a small town in the 1990s. There is a wide tarmacked main street, schools and services. Should you need to stay, the very basic **F** *Hotel Salam* (no phone) is on your right on the main drag as you head uphill. Park on the main street and on foot, from the square, cut through the new housing to the *oued* and the oasis gardens beyond. Try to find a local to guide you through the carefully tended olive groves and fields to the old *mellah*, or Jewish neighbourhood which once held over 500 homes. A little restoration work has been undertaken on the whitewashed synagogue (*kenissat el yahoud*), which is kept locked, however. All cult items have been removed. Jewish families still occasionally revisit the necropolis just to the north on higher ground beyond the bend in the river. While older locals have memories of Jewish families, for everyone else, Judaism is now irremediably associated with the violent apartheid policies of the State of Israel, given continuous coverage in the Moroccan (and Arab) media.

The 7076 route from Ifrane is now fully black top all the way north and comes out some 60 km further on, just east of the **Col du Kerdous**, near **Teffermit** about halfway along the Tiznit to Tafraoute road. A few kilometres north of Ifrane, there are more fortified granaries to visit. The whole area is increasingly prosperous. There is electricity, breeze-block rooms are sprouting alongside the older *pisé* homes and there are concrete water towers, too.

Bou Izakarn

Back on the main route, 14 km from Timoulay Izder, Bou Izakarn (market Friday) is a busy settlement at the junction with the Agadir to Laâyoune road. There is a *Banque populaire* on the main roundabout, pharmacy on the Goulimine road, public transport to Timoulay, Taghjijt, Goulimine and Tiznit. The **E** *Hotel Anti-Atlas*, T048-874134, 10 rooms, on the road to Goulimine, has a restaurant, small pool and garden.

Tiznit

Phone code: 048
Colour map 2, grid C2
90 km S of Agadir

Tiznit, seemingly ancient, famed for its great red-ochre pisé walls, is in fact barely 100 years old. "The town itself is a horizontal expanse of flat-roofed houses merging into one another and creating the impression of a huge pancake or rather, an omelette aux fines herbes, their mud masonry enlivened by the green patches of lovingly tended little gardens", wrote Rom Landau in the early 1950s. Although it does not have very many sights as such, Tiznit may well be worth a wander after an overnight stop. The once-famed Source Bleue, *the Blue Spring, close to the Great Mosque, is stagnant green today. On the other hand, you might pick up something silver in the Souk des Bijoutiers.*

Ins and outs

Getting there
See Transport, page 455, for further details

Coming in from north or south by bus you get off at the Pl du Mechouar, the central square, once the parade ground for the garrisons here. Both *CTM* and *SATAS* have their ticket offices here. Grands taxis stop on Av Mohammed V, close to the *Hotel CTM* and the banks. Most of the cheap hotels are situated close by. The taxi ride from Inezgane costs around 20dh.

Getting around

Historic Tiznit is a small place, easily done on foot. You may, however, wish to go to the beach near Sidi Moussa d'Aglou, 17 km out of town, where there are some troglodyte dwellings. Grands taxis from the Av Hassan II run out to Aglou village, and the coast is a couple of kilometres further on.

Background

One theory goes that Tiznit was originally founded by Fatima Tiznitia, who discovered a spring here. Another is that it derives its name from Lalla Zninia. The main town was established in 1882 by the great reforming sultan Moulay Hassan (1873-94), part of a general policy of strengthening the Alaouite Dynasty's authority in the south. He had a number of separate *ksour* enclosed within the 5 km of walls. There are 36 towers and although there are eight gates

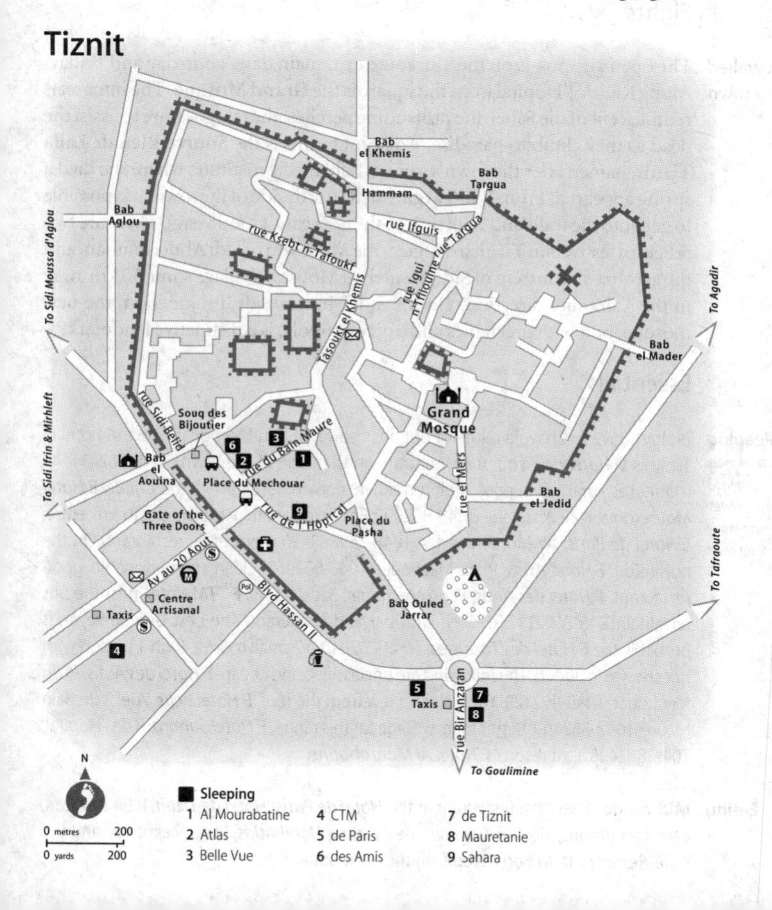

in all, the three most important are **Bab Ouled Jarrar**, **Bab el Aouina** and the **Gate of the Three Windows** – a later addition by the French.

It was at Tiznit that El Hiba, a powerful southern tribal leader, had himself proclaimed sultan in 1912, challenging the French who were extending their power. (El Hiba's father, Ma el Ainin, had already led an insurrection in 1910, rejecting the authority of the Alaouite sultan Abd el Hafiz on the basis that he was unable to resist the Christians.) In 1912, the French already controlled northeastern Morocco, the Chaouia and Casablanca. El Hiba, acting on the same basis of uniting the Muslims of Morocco to resist the infidel, organized southern resistance, declaring himself defender of the faith. A powerful confederacy seemed to be emerging, and El Hiba entered Marrakech in August 1912 unchallenged. The adventure ended in September, however, when French troops under Colonel Mangin stormed the city, easily outgunning El Hiba's tribal forces.

Today, Tiznit is an expanding town: there are new hotels on the bypass and villas on western side. It manages to retain a little something of an oasis atmosphere.The Souk des Bijoutiers, on the right between Place du Mechouar and the town walls, is still famous for its silver and cloisonné work jewellery. Driving round southern Morocco, Tiznit makes a useful lunch / service stop.

Sights

Tiznit walled town

The open air souk is on the Tafraoute exit, main days Thursday and Friday. Along Rue de l'Hôpital from the square is the **Grand Mosque**. The minaret is reminiscent of the Sahel: the protruding perches, the tale goes, are to assist the dead as they climb to paradise. Adjacent to this is the **Source Bleu de Lalla Tiznit**, named after the town's saint, a reformed prostitute: where she died a spring appeared. From **Bab Targa**, on the north side of the town, it is possible to get onto the walls and walk west to the next gate. Good views. There are two religious festivals in Tiznit in August, the Moussem of Sidi Abderrahman, and the acrobat's Moussem of Sidi Ahmed ou Moussa, a village some 50 km away in the Tafraoute direction. On the Sidi Moussa/Sidi Ifni junction, the new mosque, buff with green tiles and a green cupola, is a distinctive landmark.

Essentials

Sleeping

■ *on map, page 453*
Price codes: see inside front cover

Budget travellers have a range of options near the Pl du Mechouar. The top hotel in Tiznit is **D** ***Hotel de Tiznit***, R Bir Anzaran, on the edge of the town, T048-862411. 40 rooms, restaurant, bar, pool. A bit run down, noisy entertainment *touristique*. **E** ***Hotel Mauretanie***, R Bir Anzarane, T048-862092. Easier to park here than in the town centre. **E** ***Hotel de Paris***, Av Mohammed V, T048-862865. 20 rooms, fine restaurant. On the noisy side. **F** ***Hotel Atlas***, Pl du Mechouar, T048-862060. Clean and reasonable, good restaurant. **F** ***Hotel des Amis***, Pl du Mechouar. Satisfactory. **F** ***CTM Hotel***, near the bus terminal, T048-862211. Friendly, with bar and restaurant. The best bet, however, is probably the **F** ***Hotel des Touristes***, T048-862018. 12 small rooms, 40dh 1 person with hot shower included. The following are unclassified and cheap. **F** ***Hotel des Amis***, Pl du Mechouar, T048-862129. Fairly clean, view from the roof. **F** ***Hotel Belle Vue***, R du Bain Maure, T048-862109. Better than average for this range. **F** ***Hotel Sahara***, R de l'Hôpital, T048-862498. Last resort? **F** ***Hotel Al Mourabatine***.

Eating

Mid-range There is a restaurant at the ***Hotel de Paris***. ***Hotel de Tiznit***, R Bir Anzaran, caters for groups, alcohol. Cheaper meals at the ***Hotel Atlas***, Pl du Mechouar; and the ***Café-Restaurant du Bon Acceuil***, on the same square.

Transport

Road Most buses and grands taxis arrive at Pl du Mechouar, the focal point of the town. There are private line buses from Pl du Mechouar, including several services a day which go to **Tata, Agadir, Marrakech, Casablanca, Tafraoute, Sidi Ifni** and **Goulimine**, and on to **Laâyoune**. Buses to **Tafroaute** take 3 hrs. *CTM* bus leaves from the nearby **Bab Ouled Jarrar** at 0530 for Casablanca, via **Agadir**, **Essaouira**, **Safi** and **El Jadida**. Grands taxis leave from Pl du Mechouar: **Sidi Moussa** beach (5dh), and **Sidi Ifni** (20dh).

Directory

Around the square are a tourist information office, the *Syndicat d'Initiative, T048-869199, also hotels and cafés. Cash points and more restaurants are easily spotted on the main road outside the entrance to the square.*

Excursion from Tiznit: Sidi Moussa d'Aglou

The Atlantic can be extremely dangerous for bathing

The nearest beaches are at **Sidi Moussa d'Aglou**, 17 km northwest of Tiznit. In winter, the beach is deserted apart from a few surfers and well organised people in camping cars. In summer, however, the place is crowded, mainly with locals camping out. New homes are being built and there are seasonal restaurants. From Aglou, you can take a track some 4 km along the beach to reach a fishing village, after which there is a small troglodyte community. The campsite opens only in summer. Exceptionally cheap, it is none too secure. As well as good foot the *Café-Restaurant Ouazize* has rooms.

Tiznit to Tafraoute

Fine mountain scenery is the main feature of the 7074 road running east from Tiznit to Tafraoute. First settlement is **Assaka** after 16 km where the road winds down to the *oued*. Most of the settlement lies to the north of the road at a higher level and the mosque with its separate minaret is quite unusual. Most maps mark this as a good view – you will see why. Just beyond Assaka, across the second branch of the *oued*, is the 7057 road to Anezi, and eventually on tracks to Tanalt.

The turning to **Sidi Ahmed ou Moussa** is to the south of the road at 40 km from Tiznit. This is the home of the famous acrobats in the red pantaloons. **Tirhmi** is the next village where another route to Anezi is signed. The road then climbs up with magnificent views to the impressive Col du Kerdous (1,100 m). At km 54 from Tiznit, the **B** *Hotel Kerdous*, T048-862063, F048-600315, is an excellent address. 39 rooms, a/c, telephone, TV, restaurant has Moroccan and international dishes, two bars, panoramic terrace, shop, and secure parking. Gazing out from the col, southern Moroccan mountains give you yet another sensation of massive geological time. Photographers should note that in summer there is much heat haze right into the early afternoon, a phenomenon created by upwelling cold currents in the nearby Atlantic Ocean. After the col, the route southwards to Ifrane de l'Anti Atlas, signed just before the village of Tifermit, is now fully tarmacked. Shortly after this turn, at Tizourhane, the 7074 road swings north-east continuing towards the Ameln Valley and Tafraoute through a series of oases, some with basic services.

Tafraoute and the Ameln Valley

Phone code: 048
Colour map 2, grid C2

Located 1,200 m up in the rocky amphitheatre of the Ameln Valley, Tafraoute is a rewarding town for walkers and mountain bikers. Winter and early spring are good times to visit, when the almond trees are in blossom and the pink and ochre boulders contrast with the sharp green of the early barley and palms in the small oases, situated at intervals along the valley. Just to be part of the colour scheme, even the village houses are painted pink. For the determined, there are rewarding excursions across open country to semi-abandoned stone-built granaries.

Ins & outs

Getting there Tafraoute is accessible by bus and grand taxi. The bus ride from Agadir takes around 5 hrs, from Tiznit 3 hrs. A grand taxi from Tiznit will take about 2 hrs. **Getting around** The Vallée des Ameln is really best explored on foot or mountain bike. Aguard Oudad is 3 km south, Adaï lies 3 km southwest on the Tiznit road. Opposite the *PTT* is a place with mountain bikes for rent.

Background

Tafraoute has a most dramatic position, set in a rock amphitheatre. With a population of about 4,000, the village is the modern administrative centre and the best base for exploration. There is a large almond festival here, the **Fête des Amandes**, in January and February, and a souk on Wednesday. The town has a post office, a hospital, telephones and a *Banque Populaire*, on Place Hassan II, as well as a branch of the *BMCE* – no ATMs. Visitors looking for craft items to take home could look in at **La Maison Touareg**, Avenue Mohammed V, T048-800210. Behind its unprepossessing exterior there hides a range of carpets and leather, metal and pottery goods. 4WD and camping trips can be arranged here. It is also the only place to change money in the evening and at weekends.

Sights

Vallée des Ameln

Sometimes referred to as 'the Valley of Almonds', the Vallée des Ameln, is scattered with villages in between areas of irrigated agriculture, producing argan oil and almonds. Many of the men work elsewhere, returning for holidays or retirement. The Ameln have long been known for their involvement in the grocery trade – rather like the Djerbans of Tunisia.

Ameln Valley Circuit

The majority of the villages are precariously positioned on the south-facing slopes of Jbel El Kest. Older stone and pisé buildings, generally higher up above the agricultural land where springs emerge from the mountainside, are crumbling. Newer building, more individual two- or three-storey homes, is in reinforced concrete, with dark red rendering picked out in white.

Leave Tafraoute travelling westwards, the road by the campsite, and follow the 7074, the old road to Tiznit. There are a number of villages, **Adaï** in particular being very picturesque. The rock formations caused by weathering are most unusual, reminiscent of onion rings. After 15 km there is a crossroads, the road right is unmade and goes down to a ford and through the village of Souk el Had Tahala. Better to take the next right keeping to the surfaced road, the 7148. This way you pass a dozen or so of the villages either

on the road like **Taguenza** or high up to the left like **Annameur**. It is much more interesting to walk the upper track (a distance of say 7 km) that connects these villages. NB Both have access down to the main road.

Opposite **Asgaour** the road swings round to the right and up to Tafraoute, but it is necessary to bear left to continue the circuit along the road signed to Aït Melloul. A further 15 km of road passes more of the Ameln villages, up on your left, in particular **Oumesnate** and **Tizerht**, the former a popular call as there is a traditional house open to visitors. The French-speaking blind owner does a guided tour.

To the south of Tafraoute, just 3 km on the new road to Tiznit, is **Agard Oudad**, an interesting village built below a rock referred to as *le chapeau de Napoléon*. From here you should get a guide to show you the local artistic landscape, *les pierres bleues*. These are rocks and mountain sides, painted in various colours by the Belgian landscape artist Jean Vérame, known for his massive-scale art projects. A memorable sight, the rocks have faded a little since 1984. (Million dirham question: How many tonnes of paint were needed?).

Continue south taking the left turn on the 7075 to Souk Tlet de Tasserit, a tiny settlement. The piste to the east leads to the northern end of the gorges, while the road southwards continues for a further 5 km, becomes good grade piste for about the same distance and ends up at the southern end of the gorges. Either way, the route through the gorge threads through the oases, bypasses ancient *agadirs* and provides a fascinating, if somewhat strenuous, day. Places of interest here include ancient (and modern) Tarhat, the oasis of Tizerkine deep in the gorge and the *zaouia* at Temguilcht.

Essentials

Sleeping
■ *on map*
Price codes: see inside front cover

The better hotels often fill up early

Tafraoute does not have a huge choice of accommodation and is a popular place for walking and mountain biking. Best to phone ahead to reserve a room, especially during winter and spring breaks. **C** *Hotel Les Amandiers*, T048-800088, F800343. Once a very toney establishment, located on a rock above the town; 60 a/c rooms, TV, a restaurant, bar and well-maintained pool. Tour groups invade for lunch, otherwise a calm address. **D** *Hotel Salama*, T048-800026, F800448. Town centre, recent, comfortable, rooms with shower and WC, salon de thé. Recommended, but no heating, variable hot water and poor soundproofing. Roof terrace for breakfast. **E** *Hotel Tafraoute*, T048-800060, F800505. In the town centre near the *SOMEPI* petrol station is the best bargain, hot water, simple, clean rooms and friendly staff. **F** *Hotel Redouane*, T048-800066, close to the bridge. A bit on the grotty side. **F** *Hotel Tanger* T048-800033, opposite the *Redouane* and slightly cheaper. Basic place with hot showers, but friendly staff and good food.

Camping *Camping Les Trois Palmiers*, T048-80038, a small site located about 15 mins' walk out of town, along the Tiznit road. Reasonably equipped, has café, popular with motor caravaners. Also a few rooms for rent.

Eating
• *on map*

Hotel Les Amandiers has a reasonable restaurant and the only bar. ***Restaurant Etoile du Sud*** caters for large groups, is cheaper and often good. Cheaper still are the ***Hotel Tanger*** and the ***Café Atlas (Café Etoile d'Agadir)***, the latter with excellent value meals of local specialities. ***Snack Sportive*** is excellent value in the cheaper range.

Sport & activities

Hammam Tafraoute has a couple of hammams, both operating men's and women's sections. **Swimming** It may be possible to use the pool at the *Hotel Les Amandiers* for a small fee.

Tour operators Contact Famille Aït Sidi Brahim at *Erg Tours*, T048-221890, F229993. ***Maison Toureg*** have arranged 4WD tours in the past. May advise.

Transport **Road** Most buses from **Inezgane** and the north pass go through **Tiznit** and along the 7074. There are several buses a day from **Inezgane** and **Tiznit**, and even 1 from **Casablanca**. Grands taxis, often Landrovers, connect Tafraoute with **Tiznit**. Transport out to the villages is difficult. There are 2 buses a day, other options will be hitching, or bargaining with grand taxi drivers. 0800 bus to Inezgane takes 5 hrs.

Directory **Banks** *BMCE* and *Banque Populaire*, the latter opens only for Wed souk. **Communications** Téléboutique with internet on the main square.

Goulimine (Guelmin)

Phone code: 048
Colour map 4, grid A5

Back in the 1950s, Goulimine was practically the last place accessible to the tourist. Beyond lay the desert. Of Goulimine, the 1952 Odé guide to North Africa says that "The hirsute nomads meet here. Their gait is majestic, their gaze absent, and they wear daggers. The nearby Spanish zone of Ifni allows them to run contraband, an activity which echoes the harkas, the warrior expeditions of the past." Sidi Ifni was returned to Morocco in 1969, and the nomad 'blue men' and the camel souk of Goulimine are really for tourist purposes. Still, if you are visiting Sidi Ifni from Agadir, you can loop back up via Goulimine and Bou Izakarn.

Ins & outs

See Transport, page 459, for further details

Getting there Goulimine is on the main road south to the Saharan provinces. There are bus and grand taxi connections. Agadir is 4½ hrs from Goulimine by bus, Tiznit 2½ hrs. Coming up from the south, Laâyoune is 7 hrs by bus, and a rather faster 5 hrs by grand taxi. Goulimine is about an hour by road from Tiznit and Sidi Ifni, although note that the Sidi Ifni-Goulimine road is narrow. **Getting around** Goulimine is really a transit sort of place. However, you may want to get to the hot springs in the little oasis of Abbainou, 15 km from Goulimine off the Sidi Ifni road, or to Aït Bekkou, another oasis 10 km away from Goulimine on the Asrir road. For these you will have to hire a grand taxi, if you don't have your own transport. Around 60 km west of Goulimine is Plage Blanche, sturdy transport essential, given the state of the piste. **Tourist office**, 3 Residence Sahara, Blvd d'Agadir, T048-872545.

Background Goulimine is a regular excursion from Agadir, thanks to its Saturday morning camel souk along the Tan Tan road. The market is nowadays geared to tourist industry demands. Nomadic tribesmen ('blue men') distinguished by their indigo *boubou* robes, dance dutiful attendance. More genuine, however, are the religious festivals, or *moussems*, held in June (at Asrir) and August. From the eighth century, Goulimine was an important trading post on a route swapping Saharan salt and West African gold. From the 12th century, decline set in – apart from aforesaid camel market. Most travellers move on swifly. Look out for the ruined kasbah of **Caïd Dahman Takni**.

Excursions South and west of Goulimine, the Atlantic coast some 40 km away is referred to on the maps as **Plage Blanche**, accessible also from Sidi Ifni by the rough coastal piste. A possible stopover might be *Le Caravansérail* (contact *Maroc aventure*), BP 504, 81000 Guelmim, T/F048-873039, a hotel-restaurant and campsite run by Guy and Evy Dreumont. Accommodation ranges from nomad tents to chalets and hotel rooms (2 persons 150-300dh). Meals 50-160dh. Though they work with tour groups, there is a strong personal touch.

South of Plage Blanche, the Oued Draâ reaches the sea. On isolated places along the Saharan coast, right down to Dakhla, there are still isolated communities of nomad fisherfolk, the Chnagala or Harpooners, who fish the coast with nets and harpoons. They are not vassals to desert tribes in the way that the Imraguen of Mauritania are. Traditionally, it was the Chnagala group which collected the valuable amber from the whale corpses, which washed up on the coast near the mouth of the Oued Draâ.

Sleeping

■ on map
Price codes: see inside front cover

D ***Hotel Salam***, junction of Route de Tan Tan and Av Hassan II, T048-872057, TF872673. Friendly, 27 rooms, bar and restaurant. Sometimes block booked – phone ahead. **E** ***Hotel Tinghir***, Blvd Agadir, T048-871638, 10 rooms. **F** ***Hotel Bir Anazarene***, cheap, cold water only. **F** ***Hotel Ouedi Edhaheb***, on Pl Bir Anzarene. **F** ***Hotel La Jeunesse***, Blvd Mohammed V, opposite *Hotel L'Ere Nouvelle*. **Camping** Signposted from Pl Hassan II. Avoid.

Eating

Try ***Café March Verte***, ***Café Le Diamant Bleu***, ***Café Jour et Nuit***, with little to choose among them. The ***Café Ali Baba***, Pl Bir Anzarane, is the current in-spot.

Transport

The **grand-taxi** stop is on Pl Bir Anzarane, and the café-restaurants on Pl Hassan II; nearby is the bus stop. Express **buses** leave to **Marrakech**. Buses to **Sidi Ifni** depart at 1500, 13dh, taking 1½ hrs (taxi will cost 16dh). Several buses a day to **Tiznit** (20dh) and **Tan Tan** (28dh). Note that most *CTM* and *ONCF* buses run from outside *CTM* office in the town centre. Other buses go from the gare routière on the Bou Izakarn road, 5 mins' walk from the town centre. One night bus (*CTM*) to **Casablanca**, departs 2000, via **Tiznit** (departs 2130).

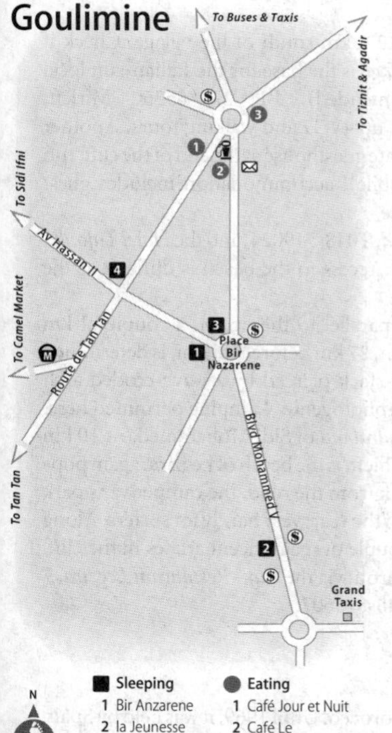

Directory

In the village there is a **bank** and **post office**. There is a **swimming pool** on the new Asrir road,10-min from town centre.

Tiznit to Sidi Ifni

Take the 7064 from the centre of Tiznit, by the large mosque, go via the small settlement of Souk el Arba du Sahel, and on to the coast with a long slow sweep down to Gourizim, a lovely small bay, stony beach, crashing Atlantic rollers. The road turns south where small fishing boats are pulled up on the shore edge at the side of the bay. From here a track runs north to Sidi Bou Ifedail and Sidi Moussa d'Aglou. It is 7 km to Mirhleft, once the border between Morocco and Spanish Sidi Ifni. Fortifications can be seen on the hill to the left, neatly cultivated land in the *oued* and one or two seasonal café/snack places on the road at the coast. For surfers, the huge Atlantic waves are the attraction. In winter, European motorcaravans can be found in large numbers.

Mirhleft is a growing, spread out sort of place. Overnight possibilities include C *Hotel de la Plage*,

Travelling in the Deep South

Generally speaking, there are no particular problems for visitors to the far south of Morocco. When setting out south of Tiznit, bear in mind, however, that the Forces Armées Royales (FAR) are very present, so avoid photographing anything that could be taken for a military installation. (If you wish to film, you should first obtain a special authorization from the Ministère de la Communication in Rabat.) There are Gendarmerie royale checkpoints, always courteous, and on the whole uninterested in foreigners driving hire cars. Although one can use mobile phones anywhere in the South, the military will take a very dim view of anyone using walkie-talkies when out desert-bashing in their top of the range 4WD. Expect no leniency.

Unleaded petrol, rare in south-central Morocco, is unobtainable in the Deep South, and sometimes pumps have only essence rather than super. (Alcohol is not on sale either, apart from in a few rare hotels.) Distances are great, so fill up whenever possible and always travel with plenty of water and some food. In cases of breakdown, almost every tiny settlement has someone who can fix a basic vehicle. Payment is always in cash – nobody takes credit cards down here, and there are few cash dispensers.

*Though the region is broadly speaking open to tourism, there are a couple of **areas still off-limits**. In the Jebl Ouarkziz, southeast of Goulimine, one can travel as far as Assa. From there on down to Zag is closed to ordinary traffic. (This is the region of Morocco closest to the separatist Polisario camps, over the frontier at Tindouf in Algeria.) Unfortunately, the handy frontier post with Mauritania, near the Moroccan town of Gueltat-Zemmour, is also closed. To get to Mauritania by road, one travels down from Dakhla in a military convoy.*

T048-719056, with 5 simple rooms, 2½ km south of the village. Check if self-catering an option. *Hotel de la Plage* is the base for the Italian-run local travel agency *Cobratours* (recommended), BP 27, 85350 Mirleft, T048-719174, F719105. They can set up 4WD and walking tours. Another possibility is a slightly eccentric **C** private guesthouse at the end of the cliff, run by Mme Molina, T061-383494 (mobile), accommodation includes guest rooms and chalets. Good cooking here.

Basic hotels include the *Hotel du Sud*, T048-719024, and the *Hotel Tafoukt*, T048-719077, prices vary seasonally. Access to the beach is difficult as the cliffs are very high.

South of Mirhleft, the 7064 runs parallel to the ocean, a couple of km inland. Sidi Mohammed Bou Abdallah, 27 km before Sidi Ifni, is determined not to be missed. An interesting sea-stack pierced by a wave-eroded arch stands in the middle of the bay – very photogenic. Camping permitted here. Nearby, also very prominent, is the *marabout* of Sidi Mohammed. At 10 km before Sidi Ifni as one comes from Mirhleft, is the beach of Legzira, again popular with surfers. Down 500 m of track from the road, the camper vans park up. There is a small hotel, open most of the year, very handy for surfers. Along the beach, erosion has produced a couple of magnificent arches in the cliff. For the hotel, contact Abdallah Sakourou, via the *Café-Restaurant Legzira*, 7 Rue Anzi, Lalla Meriem, Sidi Ifni, T048-875607.

Sidi Ifni

Phone code: 048
Colour map 2, grid A5

This is one of the strangest towns in Morocco. Until 1969, it was held by Spain and known mainly to stamp collectors, being the sort of enclave that produced variations of Spanish Saharan stamps to affirm an obscure colonial presence. Today, for much of the year, it is a quiet port town with a distinctive Iberian feel, and some unusual buildings in the art deco/neo-kasbah vein. Surfers have a number of spots nearby, while for the camper van brigade there is a newish site next to the town beach. In July and August, Sidi Ifni gets packed with returning migrant workers, so avoid this period if possible, especially as there are no waves and much mist.

Ins & outs

Getting there Sidi Ifni can be approached by the coast road directly from Tiznit, as mentioned above. Public transport runs both from Goulimine, around a 1½-hr ride away by bus or 1 hr by grand taxi and Tiznit, 2½ hrs by bus or rather less by grand taxi.

Background

Sidi Ifni was occupied by the Spanish from 1476 to 1524, and again from 1860, as a consequence of the Treaty of Tetouan. Sidi Ifni was always an enclave, surrounded by Morocco from 1860 to 1912 and from 1956 to 1969, and between 1912 and 1956 by the French Protectorate. The town had a port and an airstrip, and a role as a duty free zone. The economic survival of the town was based on the fact that the border was open to trade. In the 1960s Morocco grew tired of the continuing Spanish presence, and forced Spain into negotiations from 1966. The enclave was returned in 1969. Sidi Ifni is a wonderfully relaxing place to stay and wander for a few days, but after that its ghost town feel can get a little oppressive.

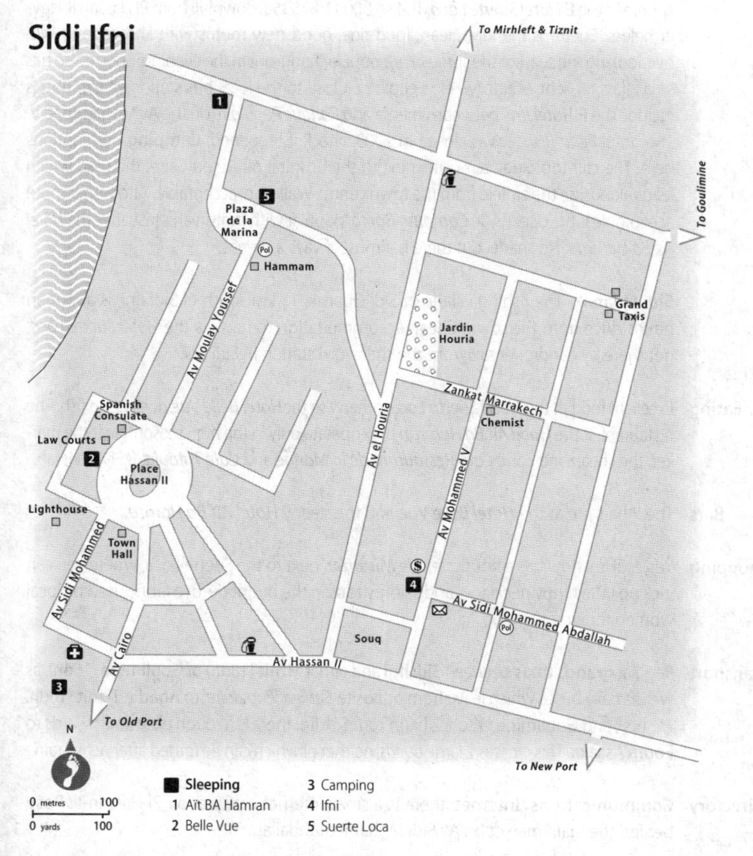

Sights Sidi Ifni does not have too much in the way of sights. Rather like Tanger, it is more of an atmosphere. The glorieta once named **Plaza de España**, now Place Hassan II, is the centre of the town. Around it can be found more or less spruce buildings with a 1930s feel: running clockwise as you face the *Hotel Belle Vue* are the former church, now home to the law courts, the very faded Spanish consulate (open one day a month), the town hall, and the discrete Royal Palace, a bijou of its kind. Past the palace and behind the police villa is a rather nice lighthouse with neo-Moorish detailing. You can walk past the hospital and campsite onto the main street of a new housing development (aerodrome on your left, the ghosts of Iberia twin-prop planes are very present). You can drop down to the beach and reach the brand new port. Offshore, the massive concrete pylon type structure was once linked to the mainland by cable. Ships would moor here and everything would be hoisted ashore. Back on land, the weekly market is held on Sunday on the old airfield. Sidi Ifni hosts a large *moussem* in June. Finally, if you have plenty of time, then one possibility, at low tide, is to walk north along the shore to the local saint's tomb or *koubba*.

Sleeping
■ *on map*
Price codes: see inside front cover

D ***Hotel Belle Vue***, 9 Pl Hassan II, T048-875072. An old building, a bit of a labyrinth with the new rooms, very pleasant terrace restaurant and bar. Ocean views. **D** ***Hotel Aït Ba Hamran***, R de la Plage, T048-875267, right next to the sea. Recent, simple rooms with shower, no breakfast. Quiet, easier to manage than the 'all New Agers together' atmosphere at the **E** ***Hotel Suerte Loca***, T048-780003, 875350, downhill from Pl Hassan II. Nevertheless, Suerte is friendly, clean, food fine, good new rooms with shower and WC, overlooking the sea. For the surfies, it's a popular hang-out in the evening. Suerte also has small flats for rent, 900dh/week, sleeping 5.Close to the local bus station, cheap hotels include the **F** ***Hotel Ifni***, between cinema and *Banque Populaire* on the Av Mohammed V. The hotel *Beau Rivage* was closed in 2003, check if reopened. **Camping** Two options here. The cliff-top older campsite, next to the hospital off Av du Caire, the road which leads alongside the airfield from the town centre. Walled in, acceptable. Altogether more acceptable is the oceanside ***Camping Barco***, popular with motorvans, just after the *Hotel Aït Ba Hamran*. No shade, but there is almost always a breeze.

Sidi Ouarsik The fishing village of Sidi Ouarsik, 17 km south of Sidi Ifni, is about an hour's drive from the town. Cheap accommodation to rent via the *Hotel Suerte Loca*, get there by Landrover taxi from the share-taxi station in Sidi Ifni.

Eating Excellent food at the ***Hotel Suerta Loca***, otherwise the***Hotel Belle Vue*** does good fish. The restaurant at the ***Hotel Aït Ba Hamran*** may operate only in the high season. Near the market, the cheap and basic ***Café-Restaurant de la Marine*** and ***Café Tafoukt***, R El Adarissah.

Bars The 2 bars are at the ***Hotel Belle Vue*** and the sleepy ***Hotel Aït Ba Hamra***.

Shopping Yes, Sidi Ifni now has a boutique, the ***Miramar***, next to the Suerte Loca, where you can pick up little hippy necklaces and skimpy tops in the bright tie-dye fabric used by local women for wraps.

Transport Regular **grands taxis** between **Sidi Ifni** and either **Tiznit** (18dh) or **Goulimine** (16dh), as well as daily buses which leave from opposite *Banque Populaire*, to **Agadir**, **Tiznit** (16dh, 2½ hrs), and **Goulimine** (13dh, 2 hrs). From Sidi Ifni there is a rough piste southwards to **Foum Assaka**. This crosses 2 large *oueds*, neither of which can be forded after heavy rain.

Directory **Communications Internet**: there is a small internet café just off Pl Hassan-II. **Post**: behind the main market on Av Sidi Mohamed Abdallah.

Sidi Ifni to Tiznit via Goulimine

Continuing the round trip, the 7129 road from Sidi Ifni to Goulimine has been much improved, winding upwards through hills (interesting side trips?) to the plain before Goulimine.

North from Goulimine to Tiznit you take the P41 to Bou Izakarn, a fast, fairly busy road with a good surface, the the P30. The highest point, shortly after Souk Tleta des Akhasass, is the Tizi Mighert, after which it is a fairly straight run into Tiznit.

Tan Tan

Phone code: 048
Colour map 4, grid A4

Tan Tan used to be the southernmost town in Morocco, before the incorporation of the Spanish Sahara into Morocco in the form of the Saharan provinces. The town is a dull administrative centre, with duty-free shops and a fishing port, where you could perhaps have a look at the fishing fleet. The blue cloth worn by the formerly nomadic inhabitants of this area is sold in the souk. There is a beach 25 km away, with some good fish cafés.

Ins & outs

Tan Tan lies over 6 hrs from Agadir by grand taxi, 3½ hrs from Laâyoune. There are bus services too, including a bus from Smara, and flights once a week from Casablanca and Laâyoune. **NB** In many small towns in the Tiznit region, 'contraband' petrol will be on sale, bought at subsidized rate in the Saharan provinces and brought north for sale in small settlements with no petrol pump.

Until 1958, there was a small Spanish 'southern protectorate' between the Oued Draâ, which marked the southern limit of the French protectorate, and the 27°C 40°C north line just south of Tarfaya. This area was returned in 1958. Spain's colony of Rio de Oro, renamed Spanish Sahara, stayed in colonial hands for almost 20 years more. Tan Tan was briefly a focus for world attention when Morocco reclaimed the Spanish-held region of the western Sahara.

Tan Tan was the starting point for the Green March into the Spanish Sahara. In October 1975, Morocco called upon the International Court of Justice in The Hague to recognize the country's claim to the Spanish colony, and in November, some 300,000 unarmed Moroccans marched upon the Sahara to reclaim the territory. This event is commemorated in numerous street names across Morocco: Avenue or Place de la Marche Verte, or, in Arabic, Chari, or Sahat Al Massira Al Khadhra. The date of the march, 6 November 1975, is also commemorated in street names, and in an illustration on the 100 dirham note. Another Saharan 'event' commemorated in street names is Bir Anzarane, a town where there was a battle between Moroccan and Polisario guerrilla forces in 1979.

Excursions

There is not a lot to see in Tan Tan itself. However, it might be worth heading for **Tantan Plage**, 25 km away in the Tarfaya direction. A hotel may be open by now, and there have been articles in the Moroccan press about a major new resort development. Birdwatchers may want to stop at **Oued Chebika** (Gendarmerie royale checkpoint), some 30 km from Tantan, still in the Tarfaya direction.

Sleeping & eating

Travellers who decide to stay have very little choice

D ***Hotel Royal***, near northern main square, T048-877186. Can be recommended, nice and quiet, rooms have bath and WC. Can be full, however, so phone ahead. **E** ***Hotel Bir Anzarane***, Blvd Hassan II, on the edge of town, T048-877834. A bit of a trek, on the opposite side of the *oued* to the town centre. **F** ***Hotel Tafoukt***, Pl de la Marche Verte, T048-877031. Cheap and clean. There are some other cheap hotels in this area. Places to eat are on the northern square (***Café Jardin*** or ***Café Séoul***) or the southern Pl de la Marche Verte – try ***Café Jour et Nuit***.

Transport **Air** There are flights from Aéroport Tan Tan, Pl Blanche, 9 km out of the town, T048-877143/877164, to **Laâyoune** and **Casablanca** (1 a week). The *Royal Air Maroc* office is on Av de la Ligue Arabe, T048-877259. From Tan Tan the onward options are to **Laâyoune**, or inland to **Smara**. **Road** There are buses, grands taxis and Landrover taxis on from Tan Tan. Several buses a day to **Goulimine** (25dh), **Tiznit** (40dh) and **Tarfaya/Laâyoune** (60dh, 4 hrs). **Taxis**: to Tan Tan port (10dh).

Directory **Banks** *BMCE*, Av Hassan II, T048-877277. ***Banque Populaire*** on the northern square.

Tarfaya

Phone code: 048
Colour map 4, grid A3

Tarfaya lies southwest of Tan Tan on a well-metalled road. A grand taxi from Laâyoune to Tarfaya (117 km, some sand drifting onto road) takes 1½ hours and costs 40dh. On the way into the town several wrecked ships are passed. The town is an oppressively quiet place, with a few old sandblown Spanish colonial buildings and the usual new constructions.

Tarfaya was Spanish from 1916 as Villa Bens, capital of the southern zone of their protectorate of Morocco from 1920 to 1958. More obscurely, between 1878 and 1895, it was a British trading post known as Port Victoria, founded by one Donald McKenzie. It was abandoned when the French proved more efficient at getting access to the Saharan trade. The post office is the most prominent building in the centre. The market is near the mosque. The **Dar Mar** is a square structure just off the beach, supposedly British. There is also an abandoned church and colonial buildings.

More excitingly, Tarfaya is a stop on an annual Rallye Aérien, recreating the heroic days of the Service Aéropostale in the 1920s and 1930s, when small, fragile planes flew the mail down from Toulouse to Dakar, via Casablanca, Port Juby (Tarfaya) and Villa Cisneros (today's Dakhla). The Aéropostale is commemorated by a monument representing a Bréguet 14 biplane of the sort used in the 1930s, and put up in 1987 for the fifth annual Rallye Toulouse – St Louis-du-Sénégal.

Tarfaya/Cap Juby was where the writer and pilot Antoine de St Exupéry was based for a few years in the late 1920s, responsible for the postal station where the planes would refuel and the pilots rest up for a night. Flying over the desert was not easy in the primitive planes of the day, and there were frequent crash-landings in the desert and encounters with unfriendly nomads, notably the fierce Rgueibet, who would take the unfortunate aviators hostage. In *Terre des hommes*, St Exupéry described the exploits of the pilots. Of Mermoz, one of the leading flyers, he wrote: "A breakdown put Mermoz in the hands of the Moors; they hesitated whether to kill him, kept him prisoner for 15 days, then sold him back. And Mermoz went back to flying over the same territories." Such was the power of the Aéropostale's mission and their motto, 'Il faut que le courrier passe' – 'The mail must get through.'

While at Cap Juby, St Exupéry found time to write a novel, *Courrier Sud*. However, he is chiefly famed for *Le Petit Prince*, the children's book about the desert adventures of an extraterrestrial small boy. No doubt the austere emptiness of the Saharan Atlantic region was to provide the resources for this work, which has puzzled several generations of kids. The flight down to Cap Juby, St Exupéry wrote, gives "an exact idea of nothingness". Some things don't change much.

Sleeping & eating There is not much in the way of facilities in Tarfaya, although there are basic cafés, which do snacks and *harira*, and a few shops. There are 2 hotels: **F** ***Hotel-Café Tarfaya***. at the end of the main street near the port; and **F** ***Hotel El Massira El Khadra***, T048-895045.

Flooding the Sahara, or by boat to Timbuktu

Though we find cause now to smile at this proposition, available knowledge at the time supported the case of the Scottish engineer Donald McKenzie. He proposed that a significant part of the Sahara be flooded with water from the Atlantic Ocean, thus allowing access by boat to the outskirts of Timbuktu. The advantages to trading would be considerable. The success of the scheme hung on the engineer's firm belief that the Sahara was mainly below sea level. This was based on the widespread deposits of salt (dried sea water?) in that area. The only major works involved cutting through the sand barrier, just a few kilometres wide, in the coastal region near present day Laâyoune. This breached, there would be no hindrance to the flooding. Whereas one can be wise after the event, more research would have revealed no land below sea level and much above 150 m. The project certainly fired the imagination of the Victorians, but it is just as well that no backers were forthcoming.

Laâyoune

Phone code: 048
Colour map 4, grid A3

Laâyoune, also spelt El Aioun, was the capital of Spanish Sahara, and continues to function as a provincial capital today. An extensive development programme has produced a city unrivalled south of Agadir. Attracted by all the activity, a population from elsewhere in Morocco has moved to Laâyoune. There is also a big military garrison. Beyond the political curiosity of seeing a post-colonial boomtown there is little to do. It is, however, a strangely calm place, and not unpleasant for a brief stay.

Ins and outs

Getting there

Laâyoune is accessible by air from Casablanca (regular flights), Agadir and Dakhla (more occasional flights), and by grand taxi and bus. There are also flights from Las Palmas in the Canaries. The bus up from Dakhla near the Mauritanian frontier takes 9 hrs, the bus down from Agadir nearly 12 hrs.

Getting around

The Hassan I Aéroport is 2 km outside the town, T048-893346/7. There are taxis into the town, although it may be necessary to wait a while. For the energetic, it is a manageable walk. The *CTM* buses arrive on Av de la Mecque, in the centre, the *ONCF* buses at the stadium a little further out. To get to Laâyoune Plage, you will have to hire a grand taxi from the taxi rank in the Colomina neighbourhood. You might even want to go to Laâyoune Port, for which there are grands taxis as well

Information

Tourist office, Ave de l'Islam, BP 471, T048-892233/75.

Background

Under the terms of a 1900 agreement, France and Spain agreed that the Sahara would be French – with the exception of Rio de Oro and Saquiet El-Hamra. On school atlases from the 1940s and earlier, you can find Spain's former Saharan colonies labelled Rio de Oro, literally 'River of Gold'. But, as one wag put it, the territories had neither water nor gold, and Spain paid scant attention to the windswept, arid expanses on the northwest coast of Africa, defined by ocean to the west and a zigzag frontier to the east.

Laâyoune was little more than a tiny settlement, where, according to the Odé guide (1952), "The Governor of Rio de Oro will show you 'his forest', composed of exactly four tamarisk trees, which, despite all his care, remain surprisingly stunted." Water was shipped in from the Canaries.

Laâyoune became capital of Spanish Sahara in 1958, and the Spanish army developed a presence, including units of the Tercio, the Spanish foreign legion. Everything changed, however, when the potential of major phosphate deposits in the Boukraâ region, to the southeast of Laâyoune, was realized. (For the uninitiated, phosphate rock is a yellowish rock, resembling limestone, rich in phosphorus thanks to the nitrogen fixing action of seaweed – and hence useful as a fertilizer base.) Although the resource had been spotted in 1947, it was not effectively exploited until the 1960s, when Spain began to invest in opencast mining and a 120 km long conveyor belt was built by Krupp to transport ore from the mines to the port 15 km south of Laâyoune. By 1974, the province was a major world producer – and the people of the Sahara and Morocco woke up to its importance.

Although Morocco retook the Sahara in 1975, there was a long and tedious campaign against the Polisario guerrilla movement, operating largely out of Algerian territory, to be fought in the early 1980s. Major public investment in urban infrastructure has turned Laâyoune into a significant town, with nearly 150,000 people from both the Saharan provinces and northern Morocco. In the 1990s the Minurso, the UN mission sent to observe the cease fire and an eventual referendum on the Saharan provinces' future, was a presence in the town – and rumoured to be costing the UN around US$4 mn per annum. But after all, peace has no price. The referendum, however, never seems to reach the point of actually happening, there being long protracted discussions over who is actually entitled to vote.

In 2000 the debate on the Sahara shifted slightly, with a new 'third way' being discussed, namely a more regional form of government for the Saharan provinces, rather like the Spanish autonomous regional system. (The first way would be full independence for some sort of Saharan statelet, the second way is maintenance of the status quo.) Given that few countries actually recognize the Polisario, especially given Morocco's intensive diplomatic efforts in Africa and Latin America, the third way offers a chance for all concerned to resolve things reasonably. The regional solution also fits well with the move towards responsive regional government in Morocco as a whole.

Sights

The main square, the Place du Mechouar, has a certain architectural interest. There are concrete canopies and exhibition space commemorating the 1975 Green March, plus the modern **Grand Mosque**. There is also a bird sanctuary, the **Colline des Oiseaux**, a calm place with some interesting species, on Rue Okba Ibn Nafi, opposite the *Hotel Parador*. The Malhfa, on Boulevard Kairouan, off Avenue de la Mecque opposite the *Hotel Massira*, is the main market area. Below the town is the lagoon, a beautiful spot, but not for swimming in. See Tour operators below for excursions.

Essentials

Sleeping Finding a place in one of the better hotels can be problematic at times, as they tend to be block-booked for official delegations. Ring ahead, otherwise you'll have to be content with a cheap hotel. **A** *Hotel Al Massira*, 12 Av de la Mecque, BP 12, T048-894225. Comfortable, 72 rooms, restaurants, bar, nightclub, tennis and pool. **A** *Hotel Parador*, R Okba Ibn Nafih, BP 189, T048-894500. Once part of the Spanish parador chain. 31 small, pleasant rooms, which you won't get to stay in until the end of the UN presence. Restaurant, popular bar, tennis, good pool. **C** ***Hotel Nagjir***, Pl Nagjir, a fork on Av de la Mecque, T048-894168. With a bar, restaurant, nightclub. **D** ***Hotel El Alya***, 193 R Kadi Ghallaoui, T048-893133. 32 rooms, restaurant, rather gloomy building requires attention, no hot water, try bargaining. Handy for the grand taxi station for destinations north. **D** ***Hotel Lakouara***, Av Hassan II, near the market, T048-893378. 40 rooms with shower and WC, in a sleepy faded establishment. Possibly Minurso in residence. **F** ***Hotel Marhaba***, Av de la Marine, T048-893249. 36 rooms, with wash basins, not very friendly, best cheap option, clean rooms, hot communal showers, roof terrace, above a café. **F** ***Hotel Rif***, T048-894369, in a square opposite R Cheikh Maalaouine, T048-894369. **Youth hostel** *Complexe Sportif*, Sakiat Alhamra,T3402. 40 beds, kitchen, 20dh.

Eating

Hotel Parador, R Okba Ibn Nafih, the ***Hotel Al Massira***, Av de la Mecque, and Pl Nagjir have good restaurants and there are several cheap ones on Av Mohammed V, and end of Av de la Marine near *Hotel Marhaba*. ***Snack Fès on Av Hassan II***, reasonable food.

Tour operators

Agence Massira Tours International, 20 Av de la Mecque, BP 85, T048-894229, who organize excursions to Tarfaya for fishing, to Laâyoune Plage and to Oasis Lemsid, and hire out Landrovers and drivers. ***Bureau du Tourisme du Sahara***, Oum Saad, T048-894224. ***Agence de Voyages Sahara***, R Kadi Ghellaoui, T048-894144. ***Royal Air Maroc***, 7 Pl Bir Anzarane, T048-894071/77.

Transport

Local **Car hire**: *Comptoir Sakia Al Hamra*, Quartier Industriel, Sahat Dchira, T048-893345. *Ouled Abdallah*, Assurance Ouled Abdallah, T048-893911. *BTS*, T048-894224.

Long distance **Air** Hassan I Aéroport is 2 km outside Laâyoune, T048-893346/7, with flights to **Casablanca** and **Agadir** (1 a day), **Tan Tan** (1 a week), **Las Palmas** (2 a week), **Dakhla** (3 a week). **Road** *CTM* buses leave from Av de la Mecque, by *Agence Massira Tours International*, services to **Boujdour/Dakhla**, **Smara/Tan Tan** and **Agadir/Marrakech**. *ONCF* services to **Agadir** and **Marrakech**, from near the stadium. Bus to **Boujdour/Dakhla** departs 0800, to Tan Tan at 1200. **Taxi** Grands taxis from the roundabout at the end of Av Hassan II, by the market, go to **Agadir** (150dh) and **Marrakech** (220dh). For grands taxis to **Tarfaya** and **Tan Tan**, go by petit taxi across the river to the *police controle* on the road out to the north, and pick one up there.

Directory

Banks *Banque Populaire*, Av Mohammed V. *BMCE*, R Mohammed Zerktouni. *Wafabank*, 5 Av Mohammed V, T048-893598. **Hammam** There are a number of hammams in Laâyoune for you to remove the dust and grime of your road journey across the desert expanses. Try the ***Hammam Samir*** in Hay El Kacem.

South into the Sahara

Laâyoune Plage & Port

To get to Laâyoune Plage, it will probably be necessary to hire a whole grand taxi, as the regular services go to the port. However, the beach itself is not very clean. It is possible to stay at the **F** *Maison des Pêcheurs* (no phone). Laâyoune Port, which no longer has ferries to the Canary Islands, is a phosphates port located 25 km from Laâyoune, 6dh by grand taxi. It is a sand-swept settlement with a few semi-operational café-restaurants, but little else.

Smara

The town of Smara lies 225 km along the new road from Tan Tan (daily bus services). There is not much to attract the traveller along this route, except a liking for long desert journeys. The settlement of **Abattekh** about 75 km from

Destination Smara – the forbidden city: a journey by Michel Vieuchange

Assisted by his brother Jean, he spent a year of study and preparation for this essential journey, essential to him, his dream. On 11 September 1930 he exchanged his European clothes for the disguising white robe, thick veil and heavy jewellery of a Berber woman, and placed his destiny in the hands of tribesmen with whom he could barely communicate. He moved into a land without government, where aggressive tribesmen fought, where a European, an infidel, was worth as much as a ransom or as little as the garments he wore. The agony of his journey ought not to be contemplated, but he accepted without question the restrictions of the enveloping garments, the overpowering heat, the numbing cold, the lice, the unpalatable water, the desperation of thirst, the irregular, unusual meals and the worst, the pain of walking on badly damaged feet unused to such demands. His guides argued and delayed him, cheated him and stole his belongings, changed their route, their minds and the price they required for their services, but he would not turn back. They bent him double and prised him into a camel's pack basket to hide him from enquiring eyes, and he urged them on. He risked three short hours in Smara on 2 November while his guides, terrified of discovery, protested, twitched and urged him away. He had succeeded. The joy was his.

The return journey was shorter but no more comfortable, as men and animals were exhausted. Michel's search for "the chance of action and the spice of danger" was over. He succumbed to dysentery and died shortly after reaching Agadir, a journey of almost 1,500 km. He was 26 years old.

Tan Tan is the best place for a coffee break. Laâyoune is 240 km to the southwest. *Royal Air Maroc* can be contacted at the airport on T048-892188 (check for internal flights).

Smara is situated in one of the most inhospitable regions of southern Morocco. It was built by Sheikh Ma el-Anin (The Blue Sultan – known for masterminding the resistance to the French and Spanish) in 1884-85 and stood astride the great caravan route to Mauritania. It was a grandiose scheme, a town built from the local black granite on a rocky prominence some 6 m higher than the rest of the stone strewn plateau. Here stood the larger kasbah with the mosque (never completed), which was based on the Mezquita in Cordoba. The circular cupola, arcades and some of the pillars survive today. There was also a library and a Koranic school (for Sheikh Ma el-Anin was a scholar), grain silos, a *hammam* and living quarters. The isolated, smaller kasbah was some 100 m away.

It was from this region that Sheikh Ma el Aïnine launched his last stand against the French, hoping to save at least the Souss and the far South from Roumi domination. He led his nomad forces north towards Fès to overthrow the sultan. The clash with French forces took place on the Tadla plain in 1910, the fighting lasted for all of June and July, the Saharan tribesmen were routed by superior French firepower. Exhausted, Ma el Aïnine fled south to Tiznit where he died in October. French vengeance was slow in coming, but terrrible: one Colonel Mouret led a raid of reprisal on Smara in 1912, destroying the town. The Tercio, the Spanish foreign legion, occupied the town in 1934.

When visited by Michel Vieuchange (see box) Smarna was deserted, the nomads of the Rio de Oro using it only as shelter as they passed by with their caravans. He visited the mosque (six bays) and a minaret (poised to send the call to prayer to the four corners of the Sahara), and the large kasbah (four high wooden doors with pointed arches and iron facings). Many of the deserted dwellings were roofless.

For the record, Ma el Aïnine's son, Mohammed el Aghdaf, was ultimately to prove worthy of his father. For 30 years, he was the Caliph of Tetouan's representative in the then Spanish province of Tarfaya. On Mohammed V's return from exile, he called a conference of all the Saharan tribes, offering allegiance to the Moroccan sultanate. France and Spain then launched attacks on Mohammed el Aghdaf and his followers, whose caravans were bombarded from the air. Right up until his death in 1960, he continued to work for national unity.

Today, as the Reguibet gradually leave behind their nomad ways, Smara is becoming an important centre. Though gradually sanding up, the oasis planted by Ma el Aïnine in the late 1890s still survives, as do the Spanish barracks, used by the FAR instead of the Tercio. Today Smara is a big settlement, with petrol, banks, post office, *hammam* and half a dozen hotels, plus restaurants/cafés on the main street, Avenue Hassan II.

Sleeping Smara's best hotel is the **E *Al Maghrib Al Arbi***, T048-899151, on Av Hassan II. Try **F *Hotel Erraha*** and **F *Hotel Atlas***, both on the same street to the right of *Al Maghrib Al Arbi* or **F** *Sakia el Houria*, also on Av Hassan II adjacent to the bus station. Another cheap possibility is the **F *Hotel Riyad***, T048-888104.

Boujdour and Dakhla

Dakhla is over 1,000 km south of Agadir and almost on the Tropic of Cancer. To continue along the coastal road, there are lorries making the journey to Dakhla, and an *ONCF* bus service leaving Laâyoune at 1200. Boujdour, 199 km south of Laâyoune, is capital of the new province of Tiris El Gharbia, and has a fishing port and beach. Dakhla, 542 km south of Laâyoune, is located on a spit with impressive beaches and cliffs. Under the Spanish, it was called Villa Cisneros. Today, it is a very minor administrative centre and a military outpost. There is ocean fishing (sea bass) and surfing.

Sleeping **C *Hotel Doumss***, 49 Av el Wallaa Dakhla. New, clean, comfortable, bar, rooms with bath/WC. **D *El Wahda***, Av el Wallaa Dakhla. New, reasonable, bargain to reduce rates, rooms with bath/WC. Basic accommodation, includes the **F *Hotel Imlil*** and **F *Sahara***, T048-897773, near the souk, both with communal facilities. Also try the **F *Pensión Atlas*** or the **F *Hotel Bahia***. **Camping** Free camping possible on beach opposite city entrance, secure. ***Moussa-Fire***, 7 km north of town at hot springs. 10dh per person.

Eating There are basic restaurants around the town, many small cafés/restaurants near souk. Best is restaurant in ***Hotel Sahara***, with good, cheap local food.

Transport Air From Aéroport Dakhla, 5 km from the town, T048-897049; direct flights to **Casablanca, Agadir** and **Laâyoune** (1 a week). The *RAM* office is on Av des PTT, T048-897050. **Road** Bus to **Agadir** departs 1200 (350dh, 18 hrs), reservation recommended. Convoys to **Mauritania** generally leave Tue and Fri.

Directory Tourist office, 1 R Tiris, T048-898228, and a travel agent, ***Dakhla Tours***, Av Mohammed V, T141. ***Bank***: *BMCE*, Av Mohammed V.

Bay of Cintra

Some 120 km from Dakhla lies the **Bay of Cintra**, a wild and remote place where ocean-going turtles and rare Monk seals can still be found. The shy seals, or 'sea wolves' as they were called, were much hunted by the Portuguese back in the 15th century for their skins and oil. Their meat was also highly appreciated by the local tribes. Today, the Monk seal is almost extinct in the Mediterranean. Even in Turkey, where they were able to reproduce in relative peace along the rocky southern coast, they are threatened by the expansion of tourism. Here on the Moroccan Atlantic, they have a last quiet refuge at the foot of the cliffs of Cintra. But for how much longer?

Travelling on to Mauritania

If you are pressed for time, it would be better to get a regular RAM flight from Casablanca to Nouakchott

From Dakhla, you may want to continue on to Mauritania by road, if you have equipped yourself with appropriate visas and a *laisser-passer* from the local police. The frontier is generally open, but you need to enquire in advance. It is necessary to travel in convoy with the Moroccan military down to the frontier post of La Gouéra (also spelt Lagouira), 370 km away (variable departure times on Tuesday and Friday). The road is new, just a little drifting sand on occasion. There will be a Moroccan gendarme or soldier in each vehicle, and you need to have supplies for two days. The Moroccan army leaves the convoy 12 km from the frontier. Here, poor quality piste begins; not to be left, however, because of the minefields. Generally speaking, because of convoy departure times from Dakhla, the frontier is reached at night. On the other side of the frontier, Mauritanian troops take over for the short run down to Nouadhibou. Make sure you have the appropriate visa and vaccinations for Mauritania. Formalities are slow at the Mauritanian border post, you will have to declare hard currency (exchange receipts requested on exit). Dirhams cannot be exchanged.

Background

472 **History**
472 Pre-Islamic times
474 The arrival of Islam
475 Tribal dynasties and religious causes: Almoravids and Almohads
475 The Merinids: from tribal to urban dynastic rule
477 Morocco and marauding Europe
477 The Alaouites and the foundations of the cherifian State
478 The 19th century: colonialism held at bay
479 The Protectorate: separate development and exploitation

482 **Modern Morocco**
482 Recent political history
484 Issues and pressures
488 Contemporary society
491 The wider picture

492 **Culture**
492 **The Moroccan people**
493 **Religion**
496 **Gender Issues**
497 **Culture of patriarchy**

499 **Architecture**
499 Prehistory
499 Roman times
499 The buildings of Islam
501 Historic médina
502 Earthern architectures
503 Fortified ports
503 Modern cities

504 **Arts and crafts**
504 Contemporary painting
506 Urban and rural crafts

507 **Language**

509 **Music**

510 **Entertainment**

511 **Sport**

512 **Land and environment**
512 **Geography**
514 **Climate**
515 **Wildlife and vegetation**
515 Habitats
516 Birdlife
516 Reptiles
516 Mammals
517 Insects
517 National Parks
517 Wildlife under threat

518 **Books**

History

The modern Kingdom of Morocco has a very particular geographic location - rather like its neighbour to the North, Spain - and this has undoubtedly been an important factor in shaping the country's history. Morocco is the westernmost country in the Muslim world, and for centuries it was 'the Land of the Farthest West', El-Maghreb El-Aqsa, to the Arabs. Despite being the closest Arab land to Europe, Morocco was the last to come under European domination. The Moroccans are highly aware of the particularities of their location, and are convinced that their history has given them a civilization which combines the virtues of the Arabs, Berbers, Andalucíans, Jews and Christians who converted to Islam.

Moroccan history can be divided into two major times: the distant pre-Islamic past, marked chiefly by Phoenicians and Romans, and the much better documented times of the Islamic dynasties - at their most brilliant during a period roughly equivalent to the European Middle Ages. From the 16th century onwards into the 19th century, the rulers of Morocco were constantly fighting back the expansionist designs of the Iberian states - and later of France - under whose rule the majority of the Cherifian Empire, as it was called by the colonisers, came from 1912 to 1956. (The last areas under colonial rule, the former Spanish Sahara, were regained in the 1970s.) The early 20th century sees the formation of the modern Moroccan State and its integration into the world system.

Pre-Islamic times

Human settlement in Morocco goes back millennia. From early times, rock carvings in the High Atlas and Sahara and objects in stone, copper and bronze have survived. Nomadic pastoralism is thought to have existed in North Africa from around 4000 BC, among a population today referred to as Libyco-Berber by historians, and thought to be part of the wider Hamito-Semitic group, which eventually sub-divided into the Egyptians in eastern North Africa, and the Berbers to the West.

The enterprising Phoenicians were to develop commercial interests in the Maghreb. Utica in Tunisia is thought to have been their first entrepôt in North Africa. Carthage (also in modern Tunisia) was founded in 814 BC, and was to develop an extensive network of trading posts along the Mediterranean and African coasts. Archaeological excavations at Russadir (Melilla) on the Mediterranean, and at Larache and Essaouira along the Atlantic coast have shown that these towns started life as Phoenician settlements. According to the Journey of Hanno, the Carthaginian expeditions undertook the careful exploration of the Mediterranean coast before proceeding southwards along the dangerous Atlantic.

Lost in the mists of ancient times is the history of the Imazighen, the Berber peoples of inland Morocco, referred to by the Romans as the Maures - hence the Latin name 'Mauritania' for the kingdom which seems to have taken shape in the fourth century BC over part of what is now Morocco. This early state may have had its capital at Volubilis, near Meknès, or possibly at Tanger or Rabat. It probably maintained close commercial links with the maritime empire of Carthage.

After the defeat and destruction of Carthage in 146 BC and the establishment of the Roman province of Africa (later to give its name to the continent), it was only natural that the empire of the Caesars develop an interest in the lands of the Maures - always a potential source of trouble. (Roman forces had had considerable trouble in putting down the revolts of the Berber kingdoms, the most difficult campaigns being in the eastern Maghreb against Jugurtha, 109-105 BC.) To establish stable rule in northwestern Africa, Augustus was to entrust Mauritania to Juba II, son of Juba I, an enemy of Julius Caesar who had committed suicide after Pompey's defeat in the civil war between Caesar and Pompey.

Quick chronology: ancient Morocco

6000-3000 BC *Neolithic era. Tumulus (Cromlech) of M'zoura, near Larache, dates from this time.*
3000 BC onwards *Proto-historic period. Bronze tools manufactured in Morocco, to judge from evidence of rock-carvings.*
Seventh century BC *First attested Phoenician presence in the form of trading posts in Morocco, notably near the sites of modern Essaouira and Larache.*
Fifth century BC *Carthage establishes trading posts on the coast.*
Fourth-third centuries BC *Kingdom of the Maures established.*
146 BC *Fall of Carthage to Rome. Northwest Africa (or Mauretania, as it is referred to by the Latin authors) comes under Roman influence.*
33 BC *King Bocchus II leaves the Kingdom of the Maures to Rome.*
24 BC *Juba II comes to the Mauretanian throne. Augustus rules in Rome.*
AD40 *Ptolomey, sone of Juba II and Cleopatra Selene, is assassinated on the orders of Emperor Caligula.*
AD42 *Northwestern Morocco becomes a Roman province as Mauretania Tingitana, with its capital at Tingi, modern Tanger.*
Third century *Christianity appears in Morocco. Rome abandons the province south of the Oued Loukkos.*
Fourth century *The elephant becomes extinct in north-western Africa.*
AD429 *The Vandals invade North Africa, but fail to establish a lasting presence in Mauretania Tingitana.*
AD533 *During the reign of Justinian, the Byzantine Empire re-establishes control of the coastal cities of Ceuta and Tanger.*

A cultured monarch, Juba II married Cleopatra Selene, daughter of Cleopatra and Mark Anthony. From 25 BC, he reigned over much of what is now Morocco. Fluent in Amazigh, Greek, Latin and Punic, he travelled constantly through his domains. He had wide-ranging interests, in the arts, sciences and medicine. His portrait in the form of a fine bronze bust was discovered during the excavation of the ancient city of Volubilis near Meknès.

Eventually, Rome was unable to tolerate the presence of the Mauritanian monarchy. The last king, Ptolomey, grandson of Anthony and Cleopatra, was put to death by the Roman emperor Gaius. The client kingdom was transformed into a Roman colony. In the early AD20s, under Claudius, Roman northwestern Africa was reorganized as two provinces, with capitals at Iol-Caesarea (Cherchell in Algeria) and Tingis, today's Tanger.

Roman administration and Latin culture were grafted onto Punic and Berber peoples. An important influence was the army (as was also the case in Roman Britain). Right down to 19 BC, there was fighting in North Africa and the army continued to extend its influence. A major Berber revolt, led by one Tacfarinas, took seven years to suppress.

Such tensions were probably generated as the Romans sought to farm areas once grazed by the nomads' flocks. Centurions were settled with grants of land. The wealth of Mauritania Tingitana was no doubt primarily agricultural, from olive and grain harvests. Army pay also brought money into the local economy. Although not as densely settled as the province of Africa (modern Tunisia), the towns had all the institutions and trappings of Romanized urban life, and were to flourish until the third century AD.

The third to eighth centuries AD are a somewhat hazy time in the history of northwestern Africa. There were a series of Amazigh insurrections, while the Romanized populations protested against the unfairly low prices of wheat, wine and olive oil supplied to the metropolis. Although Christianity became the official religion of Rome in AD313, it proved insufficient glue to hold the Empire together against the Germanic invasions. The Vandals swept down from Spain and across into the eastern Maghreb in the fifth century. Although the Byzantine Empire was to take back certain territories in the sixth century, its unity was undermined by struggles within the Church. Mauritania Tingitana was never effectively ruled again by a Roman administration.

The arrival of Islam

The key event in shaping Morocco's history was the conquest by the Muslim Arabs in the eighth century AD. Islam, the religion of the Prophet Mohammed, was born in the oases of Arabia in the seventh century AD. It gave the warring Arab tribes and oasis communities, formerly pagan, Jewish and maybe Christian, the necessary cohesion to push back the Byzantine and Sassanian Empires, exhausted by years of warfare. Mesopotamia and Syro-Palestine, along with Egypt, were quickly taken - the population of the latter, Christian heretics in the eyes of Byzantium, welcomed the invaders. The first Arab conquerors of North Africa founded Kairouan (in present-day Tunisia) in AD670, and pushed on as far as the Atlantic.

In eighth century North Africa, Islam was welcomed by the slaves - who freed themselves by becoming Muslims - and by Christian 'heretics', who saw the new religion as simpler and more tolerant than Byzantine Christianity. In 711, therefore, it was an Islamized Amazigh army which crossed the Straits of Gibraltar under Tarik Ibn Ziyed, conquering the larger part of the Iberian peninsula. Along with North Africa, the southern regions of the peninsula, referred to as Al-Andalus (whence Andalucía), were to form a strong socio-cultural area until the 15th century.

Islam, which vaunts a spirit of brotherhood within a vast community of believers, and condemns petty clan interests and local loyalties, was to prove an effective base for new states based on dynastic rule, with central governments drawing their legitimacy from their respect for the precepts of the Quran and the Hadith, the codified practice of the Prophet Mohammed.

From the arrival of Islam, Morocco's history thus becomes that of the rise and fall of dynasties, often ruling areas far wider than that of the contemporary nation state. Putting things simply, these dynasties were the Idrissids (ninth century), the Almoravids (11th century), the Almohads (12th-13th centuries), the Merinids (13th-15th centuries), the Wattasids (15th-16th centuries), the Saâdians (16th century), and finally the Alaouites, rulers of Morocco from the 17th century to the present. All these dynasties were closely linked to the development of religious life, and in most cases, sprung from politico-religious movements.

To return to the early centuries of Islamic rule in North Africa, the new religion took hold fairly slowly, as struggles between rival dynasties in the Middle East - the Ummayads and the Abbasids - divided the Islamic heartlands. The Islamic ideal was certainly not the only interest of the Arab conquerors and the governors sent out by the caliphs. Power was often exercised despotically, and exactions and repression led to a great revolt against the Arab rulers (740-780) - in the name of Islam. The revolt was of Kharijite inspiration - the Kharijites considering that they practised the most pure and egalitarian form of Islam. The Kharijites rejected the split between Sunni and Shi'a Muslims and refused to submit to the authority of the caliphs of Damascus and Baghdad. Even at the end of the struggle between Umayyads and Abbasids in AD750, and the victory of the latter, central Islamic power was slow to reassert itself in the northwestern extremities of Africa, which remained, along with the northern Sahara, independent as the Berber Kharijite Kingdom of Tahert. Then, in the mid-eighth century, an Ummayad descendant of the Prophet, fleeing the Middle East, founded the first great Muslim dynasty in 788. Idriss I founded Fès in 808, while another Ummayad prince who had taken refuge in Cordoba was to build a kingdom in Al-Andalus.

The ninth and 10th centuries saw the development of the trans-Saharan caravan trade, notably in gold. There were routes leading up into what is now Tunisia and Libya, and other, longer routes across the western regions of the Sahara. The shorter, western route finished in the Draâ Valley and the southern slopes of the Atlas. Sijilmassa, close to today's eastern Moroccan town of Rissani, was to be the capital of this trade, the mustering place from which the caravans headed onwards to the Middle East and the

Mediterranean ports. Sijilmassa was to be taken by a Shi'ite group who thanks to their control of the gold trade were able to found the Fatimid dynasty - named after Fatima, daughter of the Prophet and wife of Ali, considered by the Shi'ites as the legitimate caliph or successor of the Prophet Mohammed. This dynasty was subsequently to use Mahdiya, in Tunisia, as its springboard for the conquest of Egypt, heart of the Islamic world.

Tribal dynasties and religious causes: Almoravids and Almohads

The Saharan gold trade, in the 11th century, was to be dominated by a nomad Berber group, based in fortified religious settlements or ribat - hence their name, el-murabitoun, which transposes as Almoravid, the name of the dynasty, in English. Based in the northern Sahara, they founded a capital at Marrakech in 1062. Their empire was to expand to include much of Spain and present-day Algeria.

In the 12th century, the Almoravids were overthrown by the Almohads, el-muwahhidoun or 'unitarians', whose power base lay in the Berber tribal groupings of the High Atlas. United by their common religious cause, the Almohads took Sijilmassa, the 'gold port', and their empire expanded to include the whole of present day Morocco, Algeria and Tunisia along with Andalucía. This political unity, lasting from circa 1160 to 1260, brought cultural and economic development. The cities expanded and distinctive mosques were built, along the lines of the Koutoubia at Marrakech. Trade grew with the merchant cities of Europe. Arabic took root as the language of the urban areas.

The Almohad dynasty disintegrated towards the end of the 13th century. The ruling tribal elite lost its sense of cohesion - and the feudal Christian lands of Spain were quick to react: Seville fell to the Christians in 1248, and Granada became a sort of protectorate. The Almohad Empire split into three separate kingdoms - roughly corresponding to the independent states of today's central Maghreb. Ifrikiya (presently Tunisia) was ruled by the Hafsids, who initially ruled in the name of the Almohads; the Abdelwadids ruled from Tlemcen in modern Algeria; in Morocco, the Merinids were to establish their capital in Fès.

The Merinids: from tribal to urban dynastic rule

What made nomad tribal groups, living on the fringes of the desert or in remote mountains, seek to rule all Morocco? In the case of the Almoravids and the Almohads, it was religious doctrine which gave them motivation, while tribal solidarity provided the necessary cohesion. The Beni Merini, rulers of Morocco from the mid-13th to mid-15th centuries, were not champions of any particular religious doctrine. Nomads from the Figuig region, migrating annually to the Mlouia Basin, they appear in Moroccan history in the late 12th century, and fight alongside the Almohads in Spain. In 1212, however, after the Almohad defeat at Las Navas de Tolosa, they re-entered Morocco. The first half of the 13th century was a turbulent time, with the Merinids ruling Taza, Fès and Ksar El Kebir in the 1220s, only to be defeated by the Almohads in 1244. But they had tasted power, and wanted to rule.

In the 1250s, the Merinid forces took the main cities under Abou Yahya El Merini, and Abou Youssef Yacoub (1258-86) consolidated their rule. The 14th and 15th centuries saw the Merinids build a state centred on Fès - but more or less constantly involved in struggles with mountain tribes and neighbouring dynasties - the Tlemcen-based Zayyanids, the Hafsids farther to the east, and the Nasrids to the north in Granada. The entanglements of late-medieval dynastic politics in North Africa are tortuous, to say the least. What, then, was the importance of the Merinids?

Merinid rule saw the emergence of Fès as an important urban centre. The city consolidated its position as a centre of religious learning. Having conquered power in a land where political authority depended closely on religious credentials - as was the case for most medieval regimes - the Merinids tried to build legitimacy by sponsoring

Quick chronology: medieval and early modern Morocco

__622__ Out in Arabia, the Prophet Mohammed is forced to leave unfriendly Mecca for Médina. His hijra ('emigration') on account of his beliefs is the start of the Muslim era.
__670__ Arab general 'Uqba ibn Nafi' reaches Tunisia.
__681__ 'Uqba, the tradition says, sends his troops to conquer western North Africa.
__703__ Moussa ibn Nusayr conquers Morocco and begins the conversion of the Berbers to Islam.
__704__ Tanger falls to the Muslim armies with the help of Count Julian.
__711__ Tariq ibn Ziyad crosses the straits which today bear his name (Jabal Tariq) to begin the conquest of Iberia, which lasts until 732.
__740__ Berber revolt against central authorities in Damascus. Their heretic, kharijite, brand of Islam leads to a political break with the Arab Near East.
__786__ Idriss I, descendant of caliph Ali and the Prophet's daughter Fatima, reaches Morocco, fleeing the Abbasids of Baghdad.
__788__ Idriss becomes religious leader of the Berber tribes of the Middle Atlas.
__789__ Foundation of Fès.
__791__ Idriss I poisoned at orders of Haroun Errachid.
__803__ Idriss II on the throne.
__809__ Fès re-founded by Idriss II.
__817-18__ Hundreds of Jewish and Muslim families move to Fès from Cordoba and Kairouan.
__1048__ Abdallah ibn Yassin, a religious reformer from Sijilmassa, creates a fortified settlement or ribat, home to warriors (murabitoun) – hence the name of the dynasty he founded, the Almoravids.
__1070__ Youssouf ibn Tachfine founds Marrakech.
__1086__ The minor kings of southern Spain appeal for help to the Almoravids, who go on to beat Alfonso VI at the Battle of Sagrajas.
__1125__ One Ibn Toumert declares himself mahdi, 'the rightly guided one', at Tin Mal in the High Atlas. The purist Almohad movement is launched.
__1126__ The Almohad Abd el Mu'min ibn Ali (ruled 1130-63) takes the title of caliph. Goes on to conquer North Africa and Iberia up to the Guadalquivir.
__1143-47__ Collapse of the Almoravid Empire.
__1148-97__ Construction of major mosques, including the Koutoubia in Marrakech, the Tour Hassan in Rabat and the Giralda, Seville.
__1244-69__ Almohad Empire falls apart, having lasted barely 100 years.
__1248__ Fès falls to the Merinids. They begin the construction of Fès el Jedid.
__1269__ Fall of Marrakech marks the beginning of the Merinid era.
__1300s__ Merinid rule is at its height.
__1400s__ Internal anarchy in Morocco. Merinid collapse in 1465.
__1492__ Fall of Granada to the Catholic monarchs, Ferdinand and Isabelle.
__1509__ Spain takes Oran.
__1525-1659__ Saâdian rule.
__1578__ Battle of the Three Kings ends Portuguese threat to sultanate.
__1578-1607__ Reign of Ahmed el Mansour ed Dahabi, contemporary of Elizabeth I.
__1664__ Alaouite rule established at Fès under Moulay Rachid.
__1672-1727__ Moulay Ismaïl, contemporary of Louis XIV, rules with an iron hand.
__1757-90__ Sidi Mohammed Ben Abdallah rules a stable country.
__1817__ Corsairing is banned.

new theological foundations. Medersas, rather like the colleges of some early European universities, were founded at Fès and in other cities, providing teaching which reflected the religious mindset of the urban elite. Students, however, came from both town and country, and it may be that in attempting to build an educated group with theological and legal training, the Merinids were seeking to counter the influence of Sufi leaders in rural areas.

To an extent, the Merinids continued tribal traditions. Although there was a court and central administration in Fès, there was no civil provincial administration; regional governors came from the ruling house. However, the Merinids, unlike previous dynasties, were unable to establish their power on the basis of a single tribal element - probably because large settled communities of merchants and artisans were emerging. Thus it was that subsequent dynasties, although they had to use tribal support to achieve their initial aims, never maintained a single tribal affiliation. The European threat which emerged in the 15th century (Ceuta was occupied by the Portuguese in 1415) led to a resistance based on religious ideals, with leaders referred to as cherifs, claiming descent from the Prophet Mohammed. When the Merinids proved ineffective in fighting back the Europeans, these leaderships appeared, suitable symbols around which unity could be built due to cherifian descent. The Saâdian dynasty is an example of one such movement.

Morocco and marauding Europe

The routes of the gold caravans linking sub-Saharan Africa to North Africa meant that any Moroccan dynasty had certain importance. However, as of the 14th century, new routes opened up, reducing the importance of the Maghreb. The Mamlouks in Egypt fought back the Christian kingdoms of Nubia, Spain and Portugal began the quest for maritime routes to the 'gold coasts'. The epoch of the great discoveries began as the Portuguese explored the Atlantic coast of Africa. In 1492, Granada, the last Muslim stronghold in Andalucía, fell to Ferdinand and Isabella and Columbus sailed for America. The era of European imperialism had begun, and the Maghreb was first in the firing line as the most catholic monarchs attempted to continue the Reconquista into Africa. The two powers occupied strongpoints along the Atlantic and Mediterranean coasts (the Spanish *presidios* or garrison towns of Ceuta and Melilla date from this time). However, under Iberian powers, resources were soon to be taken up with the commercially more important development of far flung empires in the Indies and the Americas. And the Arabo-Berber peoples of North Africa (and the terrain) put up solid resistance.

In 1453, the last bastion of eastern Christianity, Constantinople, had fallen to the Ottoman Empire. Muslim resistance to the Christian powers in the western Mediterranean was led by corsairs, who called on the Ottoman sultan in Istanbul for support. By the end of the 16th century, the eastern part of the Maghreb had been divided into three vilayet or regencies: Algiers, Tunis and Tripoli. Morocco, however, remained independent, ruled by dynasties of cherifian origin, ie descendants of the Prophet Mohammed. The Saâdians (late 15th-16th century) sprang from the Sous region (Taroudant), and under Ahmed El Mansour (1578-1603) destroyed a Portuguese army, re-established (for a short while) the gold trade, developed sugar cane plantations in the Sous and re-founded Marrakech.

The Alaouites and the foundations of the cherifian State

After the decay of Saâdian power, a second cherifian dynasty, the Alaouites, originally from the oases of the Tafilalet (southeastern Morocco), came to power. The first sovereigns, Moulay Rachid (1666-72) and Moulay Ismaïl (1672-1727), a tireless builder, restored order. As Fès and Marrakech had risen against him, he created a vast new capital at Meknès: with a large palace and four new mosques, he transformed a pleasant provincial town into a regal city.

There seems to have been major political and strategic motives behind the decision to centre Alaouite authority on Meknès. It enabled the sultan to avoid identifying himself too closely with the interests of either Fès or Marrakech. Meknès was very central, and better situated for campaigning against the Middle Atlas Berbers. It was also more distant than Fès from Turkish dominated lands further east.

Above all, however, Moulay Ismaïl's authority depended on a special army corps composed of black slave troops, the Abid Bukhari. By the end of his long reign, Moulay Ismaïl had a loyal force of some 150,000 men, ever ready to deal with Ottoman encroachment from Algeria, or rebellion amongst the Sanhaja Berbers. By 1686, the sultan's authority was complete, with only remote mountain areas outside his control. The maintenance of such a strong security force required considerable resources, however, and meant resorting to rather non-Islamic forms of taxation. Such economic repression could only lead to resentment in the already defiant urban communities, notably Fès.

After a period of chaos in the 1730s, the work of Moulay Ismaïl continued under Mohammed Ben Abdallah (1757-90). Stability was restored, and the influence of Moulay Ismaïl's Abid army was ended. Many of the presidios were re-taken, including Mazagan (today's El Jadida), while Essaouira was given splendid fortifications in 1765. In 1760, the port of Anfa (today's Casablanca) was fortified, and Christian merchants were exempted from duties to encourage them to settle. Morocco came to be respected by the European powers.

Mohammed Ben Abdallah was also the first Alaouite sultan who was keen to gain the real support of the urban religious elite, the ulema. While previous sultans - and especially Moulay Ismaïl - had relied on their cherifian lineage as an ideological prop for their rule, Mohammed Ben Abdallah sought ulema support for his policies. He gained their support because of his own academic interests, and devoted time to developing scholarly activity, even initiating a reform of the curriculum at the Qaraouiyine Mosque. Thus the Moroccan State, although dependent on contingents of tribal soldiery, began to become identified with the interests and social attitudes of Morocco's city dwellers. This trend was accentuated under Mohammed Ben Abdallah's successor, Moulay Suleyman (1792-1827).

The 19th century: colonialism held at bay

In 1798, Napoleon Bonaparte led an expedition to Egypt. The lands of Islam became aware of the newly acquired technological power of European armies. Modernization was essential, despite the high financial costs. The alternative was likely to be colonial rule of some kind. The European peace of 1815 was to establish favourable conditions for colonial expansion, and France, anxious to re-establish lost prestige, looked towards North Africa. Algiers was taken in 1830, and French colonial expansion continued throughout the 19th century, with a settler population of Mediterranean origin putting down roots. European farming grew, thanks to the redistribution of land confiscated after revolts and modern land registration. New European-style cities were constructed. Although Algiers fell with little resistance, the central Maghreb was brought under French control at a terrible price to the local population.

Due to the development of French Algeria, Morocco found itself isolated from the rest of the Islamic world - and subject to severe pressure from the increasingly confident European powers. France attacked Morocco for providing shelter to the Algerian leader, the Emir Abdelkader, bombarding Tanger and Mogador (Essaouira) and defeating the Moroccan army at the Battle of Isly in 1844. Great Britain forced the Moroccans to sign a preferential trade treaty in 1856, while in 1860 a Spanish expeditionary force under one Leopoldo O'Donnell took the key northern city of Tetouan. Sultan Aberrahman was forced to accept extremely unfavourable peace terms, with customs coming under foreign control by way of an indemnity, and an ill-defined Saharan territory, the future province of Río de Oro, was ceded to Spain. The departure of Spanish troops in 1862 left Morocco considerably weakened.

A reform policy had been launched, however, under a series of bright, dynamic sultans: Abderrahman (1822-59), Mohammed IV (1859-73) and Hassan I (1873-94). Despite the latter's efforts to expand his power base with the support of the tribes of the High Atlas, further treaties were imposed by Great Britain, Spain and France. The country ran into increasing debt problems with foreign banks. The situation continued to worsen under the weak rulers who succeeded Hassan I.

Quick chronology: modern Morocco

1844 *Battle of Isly. Moroccan sultan's forces defeated by the French near Oujda.*
1880 *Conference of Madrid, while recognizing Morocco as an independent kingdom, confirms the major European powers trade interests.*
1905 *Kaiser William II visits Tanger and makes a speech proclaiming himself 'defender of Islam'.*
1907 *France uses major riots in Casablanca as a pretext for sending in troops.*
1912 *30 March. Proclamation of a French protectorate over central Morocco.*
1942 *Allied landings at Casablanca (8 November).*
1943 *Allied conference at Anfa, Casablanca.*
1947 *Sultan Mohammed V calls for independence.*
1953 *Mohammed V deposed and sent into exile, replaced by puppet ruler Mohammed Ben Arafa.*
1956 *Moroccan independence.*

At the end of the 19th century, with the vast majority of the African continent under some form of colonial rule or another, Morocco, viewed from Europe was figured as something of an exception. The fact that Morocco was not under some sort of outside rule was due in part to the fact that the European powers could not agree as to who should get such a choice piece of territory. In 1906, the Conference of Algeciras brought 12 nations together to discuss the Moroccan debt. France and Spain were nominated acting representatives of the new Bank of Morocco. In 1907, following the killing of some Europeans during unrest, France occupied the key port of Casablanca. A new sultan, Moulay Hafidh (great-uncle of the present king), was proclaimed the same year. In 1911, with Fès surrounded by insurgent tribes, he called in Algerian-based French forces to end the state of siege.

The last act came in 1912, when the Treaty of Fès, signed by France and Moulay Hafidh for Morocco, established the French Protectorate over the Cherifian Empire. A subsequent Franco-Spanish treaty split the country into a northern zone, under Spanish control, a vast central area under French rule, and a southern zone, also assigned to Spain.

The Protectorate: separate development and exploitation

The full occupation of Morocco was to be an arduous affair, with the tribes putting up heroic resistance and an area of the Rif (northern Morocco), establishing itself as an independent republic which threatened the stability of the whole protectorate system.

The French protectorate in Morocco bore the imprint of the first French resident-general, Maréchal Lyautey - and the work accomplished during his 12 year rule was to leave a long-lasting mark on the country. Lyautey, a Roman Catholic aristocrat who had seen service in Algeria, Indochina and Madagascar - and witnessed at first hand what he considered to be the errors of the colonial system - was fascinated by Morocco; as something of a monarchist, he had great respect for the sultanate, and was thus not really disposed to intervene in the new protectorate's traditional life.

Thus, the first period of French rule saw local institutions consolidated, alongside the gradual occupation of the main cities and the coastal plains. To govern the vast southern regions, the French relied on local Berber chiefs - Marrakech and its region was ruled by co-opting a local potentate, T'hami El Glaoui, for example. This meant that large scale forces did not have to be committed at a time when they were needed elsewhere.

The sultan remained ruler, although executive and legislative powers were shared with the French resident-general - and effectively only the latter could issue a dahir, a decree. Continuity was preserved: the sultan had a mini-cabinet with a grand vizier, ministers of justice and of religious affairs. Mohammed El Mokri held the post of grand vizier for the entire French period of 44 years (dying shortly after independence, aged 105).

Monarchs, battles and freedom fighters

The visitor to Morocco soon realizes that city streets draw on the same selection of names. The biggest avenue in any town will be named after ***Mohammed V*** *(1909-61). Third son of Sultan Moulay Youssef, the young Mohammed was chosen by the French to be sultan as he was thought to be more malleable. In the event, he ruled Morocco from 1927 to 1961, seeing the country to independence in 1956. His son* ***Hassan II****, ruled 1961-99, also has many streets named after him, as does* ***Prince Moulay Abdallah****, the late king's younger brother. There are also streets named for dynasties (avenue des* ***Almoravides****, des* ***Almohades****, des* ***Saâdiens****, des* ***Alaouites****) and for major monarchs (ninth century founder of Fès* ***Idriss II****, 16th century* ***Mansour Eddahbi****, 'the victorious and golden').*

In any self-respecting town, central streets also bear the names of freedom fighters and the battles of the resistance. ***Oued el Makhzen*** *was the battle in 1578 near modern Larache, where Mansour Eddahbi wiped out the invading Portuguese. The* ***Amir Abdelkader fought the French in Algeria in the 19th century, while Abdelkarim el Khattabi*** *was the leader of the Rif rebellion that set up an independent republic in northern Morocco in the 1920s. At the Battle of* ***Anoual*** *in 1921, he won a famous victory over Spanish forces. In the 1950s,* ***Mohammed Zerktouni*** *lobbed a bomb into a market much frequented by French shoppers in Marrakech, thus ensuring his commemoration on numerous major boulevards. (Imprisoned, he took his own life to avoid torture.)* ***Allal al Fassi*** *was a political leader in the struggle for independence, which was requested on* ***11 janvier 1956*** *and granted on* ***18 novembre*** *of the same year. On a more recent note, streets named* ***Al Massira al Khadra*** *('the Green March') commemorate how thousands of Moroccans flooded southwards to reclaim the Spanish Saharan provinces on* ***6 novembre 1975****. Streets named for the Battle of* ***Bir Anzarane*** *are a reminder of a major victory by Morocco's armed forces over Saharan separatists.*

But exploitation of Morocco's natural wealth marked a break with tradition: it was a capitalist venture, rather than a settler one. Banks, like the Banque de Paris et des Pays Bas, financed public and private building works, and exploited mineral concessions through the Compagnie Générale Marocaine and the Omnium Nord Africain. A major new port was constructed at Casablanca. Rabat was chosen as the capital, and other new towns were planned using the most up-to-date techniques. Working closely with the planner Léon-Henri Prost, Lyautey ensured that Morocco's traditional cities were preserved - and carefully separated from the elegant new European quarters.

It was quickly realized too that the lands controlled by the sultan's government, the bilad el-makhzen (basically the coastal plains, along with the Fès, Meknès and Oujda regions), were the most fertile - hence the term le Maroc utile, 'useful Morocco'. An increasingly dynamic European community undertook to develop the country's resources to its own advantage, helped by various tax concessions.

Infrastructure development was impressive in the French zone. In 1911, a narrow gauge railway was completed between Rabat and Casablanca. In 1956, 1,600 km of standard gauge track was in place, along with 43,000 km of road, one third of it metalled. (The Spanish zone of the protectorate had barely 500 km of road and hardly any agricultural settlers.) The European population reached 325,000 in 1951, with 5,000 people sharing the big fortunes.

But for Lyautey, Morocco was not to be a colonie de peuplement, a settler colony, like neighbouring Algeria, where the French had shattered local society with such ferocity. Great efforts were made to understand Moroccan society - the rural areas were administered by the specially trained officiers des affaires indigènes, and special government departments were created to catalogue and restore Morocco's heritage of historic buildings and crafts. Unfortunately, the knowledge of French experts often only served would-be colonists' interests - take, for example, their calculations of the amount of land necessary for a nomad family's existence.

Ultimately, however, Lyautey may have been too 'pro-Moroccan' to satisfy a growing settler lobby. The fatal moment came in 1925. The uprising in the Rif, led by the enterprising Abdelkrim El Khattabi, imperilled the two protectorates. (In July 1921, the Rif armies had captured or killed around 15,000 Spanish soldiers at the Battle of Anoual.) Maybe Lyautey was felt to have hesitated - how could things have reached a point that the tribal army of the Rif Republic, led by a Muslim scholar, actually threatened Taza and Fès? Lyautey was recalled to France, replaced by Maréchal Pétain at the head of a large army which only finally defeated the Rifans in 1926 in co-operation with Spain. Fighting to defeat rebel tribes elsewhere in Morocco continued into the early 1930s.

Hardly had Morocco been 'pacified' than a nationalist movement arose. A focal point for nationalist resentment was the so-called Berber dahir (decree) of 1933, which was basically an attempt to replace Muslim law with Berber customary law in the main Berber-speaking regions. French colonial ethnography, which had provided the reasoning behind this project, had made a fundamental miscalculation: Morocco could not be divided into Berbers versus Arabs.

The educated urban bourgeoisie demanded a reform programme in 1934, and with the Second World War, the international situation clearly shifted to favour independence. The urban elite formed the Istiqlal (Independence) Party in 1944 - with the goodwill of Sultan Mohammed V. Although closely watched by the French, the Alaouite sultan had remained a symbol and had come to be seen as an instrument of French policy, and certainly not a collaborator. The situation under which the sultan was to all intents and purposes the resident-general's unwilling puppet was viewed by the influential religious leaders as an outrage.

Tension grew in the early 1950s – under the Pacha of Marrakech, contingents of tribal horsemen converged on Rabat to demand the deposition of the sultan. In 1953 the resident-general, in violation of the protectorate treaty, deposed Mohammed V and replaced him with a harmless relative. The royal family found themselves in exile in Madagascar, which gave the nationalist movement yet another point of leverage. The sultan's return from exile was a key nationalist demand.

The situation elsewhere in the French Empire was to ensure a fast settlement of the Moroccan question. France had been defeated in Indochina in 1954, and there was a major uprising in Algeria, considered as an integral part of France by Paris. Extra problems in protectorates like Morocco and Tunisia had to be avoided. The La Celle-St Cloud agreements of November 1955 ensured a triumphal return from exile for the royal family, and independence was achieved in March 1956, with Spain renouncing its protectorate over northern Morocco at the same time. (The issue of the southern desert provinces under Spanish rule, like Río de Oro, was left to one side.)

Thus, Morocco's independence was achieved under the leadership of the country's traditional ruler. The Istiqlal Party had fostered political consciousness in the Moroccan middle classes, and a confrontation between a colonial regime and the people had developed into a conflict between colonial rulers and the Muslim ruler. The sultanate under foreign protection became an independent kingdom, with a unique position in the Arab and Mediterranean worlds.

Modern Morocco

Morocco today is a rapidly changing country whose complexities are not easily dealt with in a few pages. In political terms, the country is one of the most interesting Arab states, with a degree of openness and debate (within certain limits), rare in the Maghreb and Middle East. With a young king on the throne since July 1999, the pace of change looks set to continue, with new approaches apparent in national policy.

Recent political history

In 1943, a 'national pact' was concluded between the monarchy and the leaders of the Istiqlal (independence) party. (In June 1943, at the Anfa Conference, Franklin Roosevelt, the Sultan Mohammed V and his son, the future Hassan II, had declared the colonial system out of date, and expressed their desire to see Morocco independent once the Second World War was over.) Much of the political history of contemporary Morocco is about the shifts in the power balance between the palace and the various political groupings. The latest phase, with the left-wing opposition coming to power in 1998, referred to as *l'alternance* in the local political jargon, will be particularly interesting to watch, all the more so as Morocco is a rarity among Arab states, being a country where political opposition exists openly and where flat consensus is openly contested in the newspapers.

Independence in 1956 & after

After independence, the national pact was called into question by members of the urban elite, who thought that it would be possible to push the monarchy aside – rather as had happened in Egypt, Tunisia and Iraq – and rule the country under a one party system supported by the educated middle classes. The Istiqlal and USFP parties jockeyed for leadership; a revolt in the Rif was put down. The monarchy, however, proved remarkably durable, and after the death of Mohammed V in 1961, it built an alliance with the rural leaders which was to ensure the success of the constitutional referendum of December 1962 and the somewhat controversial parliamentary elections of April 1963.

The new monarch, Hassan II, was to prove a highly able player in the political game. The army was to play an important role as the guarantor of civil order – in particular after the Casablanca riots of March 1965. The Left lost its leader, Mehdi Ben Barka, assassinated in Paris in November 1965. As of July 1965, the King was to rule without parliament.

The 1970s

However, such a centralized system was fraught with risk, as was soon realized after two attempts on the King's life had been narrowly avoided – the Skhirat Palace attempted coup in 1971, and the attempt to shoot down the royal plane in 1972. Following these events, the King seeked to rebuild a political system which would end the monarchy's relative isolation on the political scene – and still leave considerable room for manoeuvre. The 'Moroccanization' of the remaining firms still (mainly) in French hands, launched in 1973, was part of the strategy, winning the support of the middle classes for the opportunities it offered their bright graduate offspring. Spanish-occupied Río de Oro and Saquiet el Hamza were regained in the mid-1970s: the army was to be kept busy in these new Saharan provinces, fighting the Polisario, often at bonus pay rates. A number of key players emerged to second the King on the political scene. Foremost among them from the early 1980s was Driss Basri, Minister of the Interior. The dialogue between the King and Abderrahim Bouabid, head of the left wing UNFP in the mid-1970s, was to give the opposition a chance to express itself – and represented a return to the methods used by Mohammed V after independence. In the 1990s, Parliament came to be dominated by the ruling conservative Wifak grouping and the opposition bloc, the Koutla. The early 1990s saw the King actively seeking to bring the opposition into government. Finally, in November 1997, elections were managed to produce a parliament with an opposition majority, led by the USFP (Union socialiste des forces populaires).

The 1990s: l'alternance or bringing the opposition to power

In steering things to bring the opposition into government, it is clear that Hassan II was trying to leave Morocco in good running order for his son, Crown Prince Sidi Mohammed. (Some observers have drawn parallels with the transition to democracy in neighbouring Spain in the 1970s.) By the late 1980s, the Palace was clearly aware that the political elite born of the independence struggle was running out of steam – and that the opposition criticism of the inequalities in living standards (*la fracture sociale*, in Moroccan political parlance) had very good grounds. World Bank 'remedies', strenuously applied in the 1980s and early 1990s, have only helped to impoverish a large section of the population (although the OECD would argue otherwise). Drought and poor harvests accelerated the rural exodus, swelling the poorest city districts and rendering the split between poor and wealthy all the more visible. The first opposition government of 1998 thus had a very clear remit to 'do something' – and quickly – for the poorest in Moroccan society. (Note that the Kingdom has a 60% illiteracy rate.)

Underlying the opposition's coming to power, however, was a very real fear that a large part of the *bidonville* population might be tempted by radical Islam. The middle classes have everything to lose should the country head towards an Algerian-type scenario, where thousands have died in over a decade of strife. The chaos and bloodletting just across the frontier from Oujda is felt by many to justify the sometimes strong-arm tactics of the authorities – see below regarding the bomb attacks of May 2003.

The elections of November 1997 produced no clear majority and it was not until March 1998 that the former opposition finally constituted a government led by socialist veteran Abderrahmane Youssoufi, head of the USFP and, like the king, a man in his 70s. The compromises made with the authorities earned his party the nickname of *la Gauche pastilla* (expression roughly equivalent to 'the Caviar Left' or 'Champagne socialists'). Key ministries remained in the hands of leading political figures. The much-heralded *alternance* was thus basically an attempt to give the Left hands-on experience of government.

July 1999: a new reign

The equation changedon the death of Hassan II on 23 July 1999. His eldest son, crown prince Mohammed, came to the throne as Mohammed VI. A spectacular funeral during which several hundred thousand people thronged the streets of Rabat went off without a hitch, a good sign for the new reign. New areas, in particular the need to reduce social inequality, soon figured at the top of the royal agenda. And for the first time in decades, areas of the country never visited by the reigning monarch received a royal visit. In long-ignored Tanger and the north, crowds turned out in the rain to welcome the king. In the palace, a new cohort of bright reform-minded counsellors joined the royal cabinet.

Human rights & governance

Described as "a liberal who knows how to listen to wise advice", the new king moved quickly to improve the human rights situation. Critical intellectual and one-time political prisoner Abraham Sarfaty was allowed to return, as were the families of General Oufkir (imprisoned for years before their escape to France) and assassinated left-wing politician Mehdi Ben Barka. Former political prisoners and the families of those who 'disappeared' during the repression of the 1970s and 1980s began to receive compensation payments; the house arrest of a leader of Islamist movement El Adl wal Ihsane, the ageing Cheikh Yassine, was ended. The strongest sign of all was the replacement of long-standing minister of the interior, Driss Basri. The widely detested Basri was the symbol of all that was corrupt in the *Makhzen* system. In early 2001, the International Federation of Human Rights held its annual conference in Casablanca.

Autumn 2002: the Jettou government

The Youssoufi government was much criticized for its inability to deal with deeply entrenched networks of economic influence, its constitutional legitimacy. There were no spectacular reforms. Gentle but constant improvement is felt to be the way – and given the shortage of competent personnel, probably the only one. Most Moroccans realize that the habits of decades cannot be changed overnight. The elections of 2002 provided a test for *alternance* policies. Postponed in order for the electoral rolls to be updated fairly – and to give Morocco's dinosaur-like political parties a chance to organize themselves, the actual elections were generally held to have been fair – in contrast with elections under interior minister Basri, characterized by extensive rigging and 'official' opposition parties. But only slightly over 50% of electors went to the polls, and the final results were announced a week after voting ended. With over 40 seats, the main victor was the PJD, (Parti pour la justice et le développement), which sees itself as a sort of Muslim democrat party and now effectively constitutes the opposition. To everyone's surprise, Driss Jettou, a technocrat, was appointed prime minister of a government including all major political groupings bar the PJD.

The Jettou government is set to continue the *alternance* line, continuing reforms of the civil service and taxation, security forces and justice. Whether in-depth political democratization is a possibility remains to be seen. The PJD has proved itself active in parliament and in the forthcoming local government elections (postponed to autumn 2003) Islamist parties looked set to take Casablanca, Tanger and possibly Rabat. However, in the light of events in May 2003, their success may be compromised.

14 May 2003, a Moroccan 11 September?

In early May 2003, Morocco celebrated the birth of Crown Prince Hassan. Shortly after, on 14 May, tragedy struck. The country was dumbstruck by suicide bomb attacks in the centre of Casablanca. Targets included a Jewish social club and a downtown hotel. Over 40 people were killed, all Moroccans. Police investigations soon concluded that the bombers were members of the Salafiya-Jihadiya purist Islamist movement. Several hundred arrests in Islamist circles swiftly followed. (Arrests in summer 2002 had probably already pre-empted bomb attacks, notably on American military shipping in the Straits of Gibraltar). For the Moroccans, the 14 May was truly shocking: unprovoked urban slaughter of this kind could only happen elsewhere – and notably in neighbouring Algeria. At the time of writing, the security services appeared to have the situation well under control. While the tourist industry suffered momentarily, in political terms May 14 may have deeper impact. The bombings provided the ideal pretext to crackdown on any suspected Islamist extremism. And to retain credibility, the PJD has had to make every effort to distance itself from extremist positions.

Issues and pressures

The Islamists, now clearly a part of the political equation, are not the only source of pressure on a system which needs to create conditions of well-being for all Moroccan citizens. Other issues include future of the Saharan provinces, and relations with the European Union, the North African states and international lenders. Business and the farmers, a vocal liberal-minded middle class and unemployed graduates, the Amazigh communities and shanty town dwellers all have their agenda. The Jettou government will be judged on how far it manages to satisfy such disparate groups' expectations.

Demands & expectations

The Confédération générale des entreprises marocaines (CGEM), the Moroccan employers' organization, wants a reform of the civil service, which it sees as slow and inefficient. This organization has also been highly outspoken on the issue of corruption. The liberal middle classes, though fearful of a perceived Islamist threat, would like further reforms in the official news media – and a reform of the *Moudawana*, Morocco's code on the family and marriage (see Culture, page 492). Unemployed graduates, including many with post-graduate qualifications, want jobs suited to their qualifications – and have demonstrated vigorously for this. The farming community, including modern, mechanized agro-business, wants to preserve its subsidies. The Amazigh agenda is mainly cultural. Based in the North, the High Atlas and the Souss, Amazigh activists, the so-called Berberistes, want wider recognition of their language in the education system and public life. And most. The most pressing issue is poverty, however. The shanty town dwellers and the rural poor want a decent standard of living, including access to education and health care. But in essence, it is only by reducing the terrible deprivation to which a high percentage of Morocco's population is condemned that the Jettou government can hope to avoid political instability fuelled by fundamentalist influence.

Islamist pressures

But the question of Islamic revivalist movements (*les Islamistes*) is a complex one. The King of Morocco, as a descendant of the Prophet Mohammed and Commander of the Faithful, undoubtedly occupies the religious high ground. Religious legitimacy has always formed an important part of the monarchy's power base. In 1980, at the fall of the Shah of Iran, the King is said to have remarked that the Shah had attempted to rule by the sword, but without – or rather going against – the mosque, attempting to be a secular emperor in a land where Islam has a highly organized clergy. In Morocco, the *ulema* (experts on religious matters) have maintained their influence: their councils authorize new mosque building; religious studies graduates are trained at the Kénitra School to take up jobs in the Ministry of the Interior. Under Hassan II, the monarchy's religious profile projects such as the Great Mosque at Casablanca (cost over 4 billion dirhams), and the recognition achieved by the King as a leading Islamic leader. In 1979 he became president of the Al-Quds (Jerusalem) Committee. While maintaining this public face of a monarch concerned with things Islamic, Mohammed VI is much more concerned with the practical aspects of reducing poverty and ensuring that things get done.

Simplifying heavily, there are four main strands to the Islamist movements of Morocco. Originally of Pakistani inspiration, the *Tabligh wa Da'oua* type of Islamist is an ascetic, taking the true faith to rural markets and shanty-towns. *Tablighis* may move on to join the more urban *Adl wal Ihsane*, whose main figure, Abdallah Yassine, is more of a writer producing 'intellectual propaganda' rather than a charismatic Imam Khomeini type figure. *El Adl* is active in poor areas, assisting families in difficulty. In parliament, the PJD (see earlier) is a force arguing for a more 'moral' type of government. Both *El Adl* and the PJD have been effective in organizing mass demonstrations in Casablanca. Finally, there is a shadowy, purist brand of Islamism out there, namely the Salafiya-Jihadiya movement. In 2002, Salafist groups reached the headlines after a series of bloody murders 'punishing' individuals who had strayed from the 'true' Islam. Until May 2003, the Salafists had avoided large-scale terrorist violence of the kind which proved so counter-productive in Algeria. Close links with Al Qaida are unproven, there does not appear to be a centralized national command structure. This notwithstanding, managing the Islamist movements will be a delicate task for Morocco's governments. A pious people, the Moroccans have a strong sense of the injustice of the current Middle Eastern political order, based as it is on the Zionist occupation of Palestine – including Jerusalem, Islam's third holiest city. The American occupation of Iraq has exacerbated this feeling of injustice.

The Saharan provinces

In 2003, the USA also looks set to interfere in Morocco's Saharan provinces. As part of a drive to settle minor geo-political conflicts, the Bush government would like to see a definitive settlement for the region referred to as the Spanish Sahara until 1975. After independence from France and Spain in 1956, a number of pieces of Moroccan territory remained under Spanish rule – some enclaves in the North, notably Ceuta and Melilla (still held by Spain), Sidi Ifni (retaken by Morocco in 1969), and Río de Oro, a large chunk of Saharan territory fronting onto the Atlantic. In 1974, with General Franco's ailing in Madrid, the Moroccans launched their claims to the Spanish Sahara once more. On Franco's death in 1975, Morocco and Mauritania moved into the

Sahara, and in November 1975 the Green March (*Al-Massira Al-Khadhra*) took place, with 350,000 Moroccans marching southwards into the former Spanish colony. Underlying the issue was the question of resources – the Atlantic waters off the Saharan provinces are excellent fishing grounds, and there are phosphates. And there was also a fear that neighbouring Algeria might possibly sponsor a dummy Socialist republic. (Algeria has been perceived in political discourse as a rival nation, able to dominate the Maghreb and possibly take over the whole Sahara.)

Algeria was to provide a rear base for the Polisario, an armed liberation group fighting for an independent 'Saharan' state. However, by 1987, the Moroccan army had completed seven earth ramparts to protect the Saharan provinces from armed incursion from across the frontier. In 1988, Algeria began to change its line on the Saharan issue. (In 1984, Libya had withdrawn financial help to the Polisario, and as of 1986, petrol revenues began to fall.) The Islamists had begun to appear as a major threat to the powers that be in Algiers. In February 1989, the Union du Maghreb Arabe treaty was signed at Marrakech – with North African leaders clearly agreed on the need to focus on the Islamist menace. (This only emerged in Morocco in the mid-1990s.) Morocco thus continued to invest heavily in the Sahara, developing Laâyoune and other towns. The Polisario ran out of steam – and Morocco agreed to a UN-sponsored referendum, originally to be held in 1992, on the future of the provinces.

The urgency of any referendum disappeared in the 1990s as Algeria grappled with its ongoing internal crisis. It has proved impossible to reach agreement on who should actually be allowed to vote in a Sahara referendum – or indeed on the object of the referendum. With the vast growth of Laâyoune through migration from the north, the original Sahraoui component of the population is in a minority. Although the USA would like to see a referendum-based 'settlement', the provinces seem set to remain part of Morocco, in a set-up reminiscent of the Spanish autonomous regions or the German länder.

The Union du Maghreb Arabe (UMA)

The question of the Saharan provinces cannot be dissociated from Morocco's relations with the rest of the North African or Maghreb states, namely Algeria, Tunisia, Mauritania and Libya. A United Arab Maghreb, free of outside domination, was a dream back in colonial days. In February 1947 the Committee for the Liberation of the Maghreb was set up. Just over 40 years, later, a united Maghreb seemed to be on the way to becoming reality. At Marrakech, the leaders of the five states, King Hassan II of Morocco, President Chedli Bendjedid of Algeria, President Ben Ali of Tunisia, Colonel Muammar Kaddhafi of Libya and President Ould Sidi Ahmad Al Taya of Mauritania, signed the founding act of the Union du Maghreb Arabe, whose acronym, UMA, recalls the Arabic word *umma* (community). The new union was to be presided by each nation in turn for six-month periods. In October 1990 a document was drawn up, providing for the creation of a free exchange zone before the end of 1992 and the establishment of a customs union in 1995.

Very quickly, however, the new union ran into problems. With Bendjedid removed from power in Algeria, there was a cooling of Algero-Moroccan relations. Libya proved to be a difficult member of the team, and neither Morocco nor Tunisia were keen on weather-vane diplomacy à la Kaddhafi. The security situation deteriorated rapidly in Algeria, with guerrilla warfare and appalling massacres in certain regions. Thousands of Algerians began looking to emigrate. In 1994, after a terrorist attack on a Marrakech hotel, Morocco sought to limit any risk of Islamic fundamentalist contagion and introduced a visa for Algerians – thereby depriving itself of over a million foreign visitors each year. Algeria replied by closing the frontier. In response, Morocco put its activities in the UMA on hold. While relations between Algeria, Tunisia and Libya remained generally good, there was little move to develop things at UMA level.

For the moment, the UMA is more or less stalled, although the bilateral contacts between interior ministers on the subject of Islamist terrorism may yet get the machine going. However, if it is to succeed, any relaunch of the UMA will have to be based on the settlement of Algero-Moroccan differences over the latter's Saharan provinces. Broadly speaking for Morocco commercial relations with the European Union are more crucial than a perilous project for North African political unity.

Morocco & the European Union

As of the late 1980s, Morocco opted to intensify its ties with Europe, and in 1987, the country requested membership of the EEC, perhaps more as a symbolic gesture than anything else. Although relations have been soured with Spain on occasion over the question of fishing rights, Europe and Morocco have too much in common for the two sides not to work together. Algerian gas transits over Moroccan territory on its way to the Iberian peninsula, and European companies – notably French and Spanish ones – are always on the starting blocks for major public works contracts in Morocco. The current privatization programme and the development of the Casablanca stock exchange will no doubt maintain European business interests. Morocco's credentials as a stable country, close to Europe, with a certain democratic openness, will doubtless continue to make it favourable terrain for business relocation.

Finance

The most difficult issue facing the Jettou government, however, is that of finance. The IMF recently recommended a devaluation of the dirham, while Morocco wants help servicing its debt. For the moment, widening the tax base does not seem to be a viable option, and the government is counting on privatizations to raise the money to finance its social programmes. The Jettou government has found itself with a tightrope to tread: foreign investors have to be reassured that the liberalist rigour imposed by the IMF and the European Union (including bringing the public debt down to 3% of GDP) will be respected, while the local constituency wants jobs and social services. With foreign debt repayments absorbing up to a third of the budget, there is little room for manoeuvre for a Moroccan government of whatever political colour.

The early 2000s: technocratic pragmatism

Despite the financial constraints, predictions of serious social unrest and the morose international climate, the prospects for Morocco in the early 2000s were by no means black. The poverty of the shanty towns of Casablanca is not as harsh as it was in the 1960s, and there are numerous social housing projects underway. Even the casual visitor to Morocco will be struck by the huge amount of new building. Under Mohammed VI, a lot of new energy has been released into the system. New regional governors were appointed with a remit to get things done. To take just the case of Marrakech, in just two years the medina got new sewers, paved streets and improved lighting. And in any case, the Moroccans are in many ways a patient lot, and people understand that it is impossible to achieve huge improvements overnight. People work hard and make do, and as the Marrakchi proverb puts it, "the dirham is in the dog's ass, and the dog's got rabies".

But good results will have to be shown over the next few years. Ultimately, a lot of personal prestige is at stake. Neither Palace nor government coalition want to be seen to fail. Both have invested considerable time and effort in reaching a modus vivendi. With luck, this association between monarchy and government will give Morocco a greater capacity to tackle the big issues of social justice and fair economic development. In the final analysis, a new version of the old national pact seems to be being worked out. It could be that a form of social democracy, possibly with PJD 'Muslim democrat' participation will facilitate the move towards a more limited role for the monarchy.

Europe is seen as the principal foreign partner in this venture – and the Moroccans, rightly no doubt, feel that help and understanding should be forthcoming from the economic giant to the north. Little EU finance has been made available to assist southern Mediterranean economies such as that of Morocco – compared with the funds made available for the modernization of Greece, and more recently, eastern European. Despite the growing populations of the southern Mediterranean, countries like

Morocco feel they may be neglected, while Germany directs finance and interest towards eastern Europe and the former Soviet lands.

Contemporary society

In late 1990s Morocco, institutions were being modernized, industry upgraded, the civil service reformed. Human rights were openly discussed, a critical press had emerged and was flourishing. After periods of political repression, Moroccans are proud of the changes taking place. Much is still to be done, however. Though parliamentary elections are free, open and multi-party, there are abuses. Though factories are getting their ISO 9000 certification, workers' salaries are rock bottom. Though there is a growing freedom of expression and civil liberties are respected, there are appalling and surprising exceptions. Moroccan society is in a period of change – and it can be difficult for the Moroccan to explain to the outsider the factors, both historical and social, which have led the country to where it is today.

Education & language

The state education system has been open to heavy criticism, seen by many commentators as costly and inefficient. To fast rewind to the 1950s, however, when Morocco achieved its independence, practically nothing had been done by France to extend education to its Muslim Moroccan protégés. At independence, everything had to be done practically from scratch: the overwhelming majority of Morocco's women were illiterate, and male literacy was low too. Independent Morocco had to put a comprehensive education policy together. In the enthusiastic, public-spirited late 1950s, centres for fighting illiteracy (*muharabat al umiya*) were set up. However, over 40 years later, illiteracy remains high, touching around 65% of the population over 15.

The Moroccan school system divides into nine years' basic education, followed by three years of general secondary or technical education leading to the baccalauréate. Pre-school education is split between traditional Koran schools where the sacred texts are learned by rote, and modern private kindergartens. In 1990, 71% of primary school age children were in school (**NB** only 56% of girls). How to explain this low figure?

In the countryside, girls are traditionally involved in household and agricultural tasks from an early age – all of which leaves little room for school. Considerable distances have to be travelled to school and weather conditions are often difficult. Only a small number of schools have boarding facilities for children in isolated areas. In a rural area, when a school is close by, only one girl out of 10 will complete basic schooling, and one girl out of five will complete two or three years schooling. Girls are just too important in the functioning of the rural economy to be left at school desks for long periods of time. Parental attitudes do seem to be changing, however.

Added to these factors, there is the nature of the school programmes. Education is very academic, and books and equipment are often in very short supply – or quite simply beyond the means of many families. The teaching style often favours rote learning rather than developing creative skills and a critical mind. Added to this is the language issue.

The curriculum is in Arabic, with French, Spanish and English taught as foreign languages. The Arabic used is modern standard Arabic, a version of the Arabic of the Koran modernized in lexical terms in the 19th century. This means that children with an Amazigh (Berber) language as mother tongue (about 40% of the population) are faced with a foreign language at school. Children with Moroccan Arabic as a mother tongue have to learn a new range of verb and adjectival forms, rather as if the English-speaking child had to learn to use Old English verbs with modern English vocabulary. This is basically manageable, although given translation problems, there is a severe shortage of reading material in Arabic.

A further problem comes at university. All subjects are in French, bar family and criminal law and Arabic literature, and some of the humanities. Hence parents with means put their children in bilingual primary schools with greater resources and more modern teaching methods. At secondary school level, the children with a bilingual background have much better chances of passing the bac. And after secondary school, private institutes providing training in secretarial skills, IT, management and accounting function exclusively in French.

The present system has been criticized for perpetuating Morocco's social divide, the gap between the bilingual middle classes, with their access to knowledge and wealth production, and the illiterate masses, using spoken Arabic and/or Berber in daily life. More serious still, teachers in the secondary school system sometimes fail to teach everything on the syllabus to oblige pupils to take private lessons out of school hours.

It remains then that both languages of formal instruction, standard *fus-ha* Arabic and French are foreign tongues for most Moroccan children going into primary school. No six-year-old speaks these languages as a mother tongue. But though Arabic is the official language of Morocco, nowhere is it specified that this has to be standard Arabic.

The media

Morocco has one of the liveliest mediascapes in the Arab world. The print media is particularly dynamic, as a glance at any newsvendor's pavement-spread will show. The situation was not always like this – the late 1980s saw some of the best titles closed down. Nevertheless, the present generation of critical editors owes much to the generation of the late 1970s and publications such as the leftist review *Souffles*, the sometimes stodgy but often critical *Lamalif* and the taboo-breaking *Kalima*.

The unleashing of the Moroccan print media since the early 1990s may seem surprising, given the regime's authoritarian bent. One line of thought goes that it amused the late King Hassan II to free things up, to see how far the journalists would take their criticisms. A perceptive ruler, he no doubt saw an increasingly free media as essential to the survival of the monarchy. The publication in France of French journalist Gilles Perrault's *Notre ami le Roi* in September 1990 had radically changed public perceptions of the Moroccan regime in any case. Thanks to the fax machine, this highly critical account of independent Morocco and its ruler, written from information supplied by independent human rights' organizations, probably contributed more than anything else to opening up the political climate in Morocco. The written press began to cover formerly taboo subjects, starting with analytic reporting of business issues.

In the mid-1990s, *L'Economiste* and *La Vie économique* set new standards for both reporting and layout. A number of high standard leisure magazines then appeared, accompanied by political weekly newspapers. In 2003, the key French language news outlets were *Le Journal* for raw information, weekly magazine *Tel Quel* for informed analysis and *Demain* for satire. Of the newspapers in Arabic, *Al-Ahdath al-Maghribia* and *As-Sahifa* were the most respected.

Along with the fashion features, the women's magazines like *Citadine* and *FDM (Femmes du Maroc)* began to print taboo breaking pieces on issues like sex before marriage, wife-beating and the exploitation of country girls as servants. Following the success of Ahmed Marzouki's *Tazmamart cellule 10* in 2000, an account of 17 years imprisonment in a goulag in south-east Morocco, the dailies serialized the memoirs of former political prisoners. The Establishment was rocked by revelations about USFP politicians collaborating with the military in the early 1970s to overthrow the regime. In 2002, economic magazines published seemingly well researched accounts of poor management of the royal fortune. The 'red lines' are being crossed, naturally enough in a country which endured 25 years of severe political repression. Whether the print media will continue to enjoy their present freedoms remains to be seen. Proof that there is still plenty of room for improvement is the fact that the French press, both news magazines and newspapers, continues to sell well in Morocco.

Unlike the print media, the Moroccan radio and television remain under pretty tight state control. Of the radio stations, the bilingual Tanger-based Médi Un is the most

Pilgrimage

In the 1980s, Tazmamart was a taboo word. Mentioning this name was enough to send shivers down the spines of those who knew. For Tazmamart, a nothing sort of place in the southeast Moroccan outback, was home to cruelty. The officers involved in an attempted palace coup in the early 1970s were imprisoned in a specially built goulag.

Flashback to 9 July 1971. Army cadets broke lose in the palace at Skhirat near Rabat, where King Hassan II was having his annual birthday bash. Poorly managed, the putsch failed. The king emerged from a hiding place to find tens of guests and soldiers dead. Vengeance was swift to follow. Several hundred officers were put on trial for treason; 58 of them were transferred to Tazmamart, to live out their sentences in conditions of unsuspected horror. There were two buildings of 30 cells. Each cell, 3 m long and 2½ m wide, had a cement platform for a bed and a hole in the floor for toilet waste. A tiny panel in the door and 18 holes in the wall provided ventilation. Each prisoner had a plate, a plastic jug and a five-litre water container. For the first three years, the prisoners wore the clothes they had arrived in. The food? Thirty grammes of bread, weak coffee, chick pea gruel. Fortunately, the guards changed rarely and a sort of complicity between the two sides grew, allowing a few items – medicines, a transistor radio, the occasional letter – to be smuggled in.

In the late 1970s, news of Tazmamart filtered to the outside world. Pressure from human rights groups abroad grew. In the late 1980s, the fax changed everything: people sent the latest French press reports to friends and family back in Morocco. For the country's international reputation, Tazmamart prison camp had to go. In October 1991, the survivors of this most inhumane of gaols, 28 in all, were released from their cement cages. By mutual support and a dose of religious mysticism, they had survived the cold and scorpions, madness, hunger and fear.

In October 2000, Tazmamart became a place of pilgrimage. As free men, former prisoners returned to the place of their suffering on the anniversary of their release. With them came the families of those who died there, human rights activists and journalists. The message? That in the new Morocco of Mohammed VI, the horror of Tazmamart must never happen again. Things seem to be moving in the right direction. The fact that the pilgrimage was able to go ahead to the site of a prison whose very existence was denied until 10 years ago is a sure sign of change, an indication that Morocco is now beginning to look the sinister aspects of its recent past in the face. Such was the interest aroused that Ahmed Marzouki's moving account of his time in the prison, Tazmamart Cellule 10 (Paris-Méditerranée, 2000), went into a third print-run.

popular – and is also available on the web. There are two TV channels, the rather stodgy RTM, also available on satellite, and the dynamic, formerly private second channel, 2M. A third channel is planned. There is a huge demand for quality television – hence the massive sales of satellite dishes in Morocco. Unfortunately for the RTM, it does not have direct control over its advertising revenues, making it impossible to produce quality programmes in a time of budgetary constraints. 2M does rather better – and may be returned to the private sector in the near future. The challenge is still there then for Moroccan TV professionals to produce programmes of real national and local interest. And of course, whenever there is a major international crisis, Arabic and French-language satellite channels are watched and discussed in every home and café.

Daily life Morocco's population is moving towards a 60%/30% urban rural divide. The land no longer provides the living it used to, expectations are higher, parents want their children to have some chance of an education – and this is most easily available in the towns. In the country, life is often hard, with women obliged to carry water, firewood and animal fodder over long distances.

In the cities, life is not easy either for the inhabitants of the bidonvilles. When it rains the streets fill with water. The city, however, offers more opportunities. There are plenty of people with money to buy from a street stall selling cigarettes, chewing-gum or fruit, there is occasional work on building sites and in factories and there is a chance of better housing, as government projects 'restructure' the shanty towns, bringing in water and electricity.

For the middle classes, opportunities have improved considerably, even though recruitment into government service has been cut back. There are, however, jobs in multinational companies, the banking sector and the new service economy. Compared with other Arab countries, there is a freedom in Morocco's cities. The streets, though increasingly traffic ridden, are pleasant, there are cafés, bookshops and cinemas. For those with salaries, there are car and home loans. Domestic help is available for two-career families, and there is a wide range of consumer goods. For the bright and energetic, the prospects are good – although family connections do help.

Outside the cities, life is improving, too, as even the most casual observer will notice. Mobile phones are making life easier, and electricity is arriving in isolated mountain valleys. The ONEP has undertaken major infrastructure projects to improve drinking water provision. Always a sure sign of improving living standards, there is building everywhere. The ERACs (social housing authorities) are active in all major cities, putting up huge social housing schemes. Even in quite out of the way places, much new building is in evidence, an indication that there is money in circulation and that there is a lot of work for unskilled and semi-skilled male labour. Though the official economic figures are often disappointing, Morocco's informal sector is undoubtedly extremely dynamic.

The wider picture

Morocco has changed enormously since independence. It is no longer, for the most part, a fragment of the Middle Ages anchored off the southern shores of Europe. There is, however, a striking stability and continuity in the political and social systems, looking back from the 20th-century reign of Hassan II to the reign of Hassan I. The question is whether the symbols of national unanimity – religion, the land, the people, the king – will continue to be sufficient under Mohammed VI. The palace clearly understands the divides in Moroccan society, the clans and competing family networks, the geographic and linguistic identities waiting to surface, and does its best to ensure that all groupings are able to influence events. Maybe the future of a more constitutional monarchy will be as a sort of ombudsman, arbitrating between influential groupings in society. Military intervention Algerian-style in government affairs seems unlikely. The army is only too aware of the void it would create if it were to threaten the throne.

The rural world

Moroccan rural areas will no doubt continue to depopulate. The countryside has changed hugely. In the 1960s, the caïds ran affairs, with authority over sharecroppers, shepherds and harvesters. By the 1990s, the caïds' descendants had become entrepreneurs, running mechanized farms. Seasonal workers have to get by on tiny smallholdings, or perhaps travel to cities to work as unskilled labour. Private landowners are doing well, especially in irrigated areas. The poorer parts of the countryside – the Rif and the Sous Valley – are no longer able to export their surplus labour to Europe, and drought years like 1980-84 accelerated the rural exodus to Morocco's cities.

Economy & development

In terms of the economy, Morocco has put its house in order. The rather adventurous financial policies of the 1970s are a thing of the past, and the budget deficit is now down to 1% of GDP. (It had been at 12-14% in 1982.) Debt repayments were rescheduled six times in the 1980s. Today, growth, with an average of around 5%, is above the birth rate. Nevertheless, there are some major difficulties: for sale of agricultural products, Morocco has stiff competition from Spain and Portugal; there are still large numbers of graduates coming onto the job market for whom there is no employment; and in 1998, Morocco only came 125th out of 179 countries in the UNDP human development index, a fair way behind neighbours Algeria and Tunisia.

Challenges for the 21st century But such indexes do not take into account factors like the general political climate and levels of freedom of expression. Things have moved forward considerably since the 1970s, and on the whole, the situation in the early 21st century was a positive one. Morocco, with little oil resources, benefits from any fall in the price of oil, and its proximity to Europe and an expanding internal market make it an ideal base for relocating manufacturing industry. The question over the first decade of the 21st century will be how to reduce poverty and social inequality – and so avoid the risk of Algerian-type fundamentalist destabilization and strife. To create a more socially just, open Morocco, to create an investment friendly climate, the upgrading of a slow and often poorly trained civil service will be essential. Mohammed VI and the government assembled after the elections of autumn 2002 thus face considerable challenges. A strong desire for stability and consensus should allow much to be achieved.

Culture

What makes Morocco so different from, say, Spain? In the travel brochures, it is a land peopled by men in flowing robes and camels, its cities full of winding streets, garden courtyards and banquets. It is an Islamic country – but the women (who do not feature in the brochures) are not on the whole veiled. Standing back from the bright postcards and garden courtyards, the Arab-Amazigh dichotomy, the clichés about tolerance and eternal Moroccan civilisation, what sort of a culture is this? What are its main architectural and material features? And, first of all, who are the Moroccans?

The Moroccan people

The population of Morocco was estimated in 1995 at 26.98 million. Although the crude birth rate has fallen sharply in recent years to 28 per 1,000 population, potential fertility is high. Better medical facilities and mass vaccination campaigns since the mid-1990s have improved the child survival rate. At the same time, death rates are also down to six per 1,000 and life expectancy, now 69 years on average, will no doubt improve to swell the total population. The population is fairly young on average. More than 36% of people are under the age of 15, 50% are under 20 and a mere 6% over 60.

Population distribution The coastal cities and plains are the key areas. Half the population now lives in cities, the great concentrations being in Casablanca with 2.9 mn, Rabat-Salé with 1.2 mn, Fès with 564,000 and Marrakech with 672,506, and Meknès, with 447,437 inhabitants. Areas of heavily settled land with 60-95 people per sq km are found round the Mediterranean and northern Atlantic coastal areas, notably in the Rif, Jebala, the Gharb plain and the southern Sous valley. Densities fall off rapidly as you go inland. Other than the great cities of Marrakech, Meknès and Fès, the inland regions have low population densities, averaging between 20-60 per sq km. The arid southern and eastern regions are sparsely settled with less than 20 people per sq km.

The typical Moroccan The population of contemporary Morocco is the result of a long history during which various settlers passed through the country. The earliest populations of northwestern Africa, the ancestors of today's Imazighen (Berbers) were probably of Hamitic stock stock (ie descendants of Biblical Ham, brother of Shem and Japeth). Since the Imazighen arrived, there have been numerous other inputs, including Phoenicians and Romans, and in particular the Arabs, who first occupied the region in the eighth century AD. Until the mid-20th century, there was an important Jewish community, originally part of the rural Amazigh population. This was reinforced, after the 15th century Reconquista, by highly educated and talented groups of Iberian Jews. Many Jews left Morocco after the foundation of the State of Israel in 1948. As of the late 18th century, a European population settled in the coastal towns, and was particularly numerous in the mid-20th century. There is a sub-Saharan African component to Morocco's population, originally the result of the slave trade and the preference of 17th century ruler Moulay Ismaïl for an all-black royal guard. In physical terms, then, an average roomful of Moroccans at, say, a business meeting will not look very different from Brazilian or Spanish counterparts.

There are however, certain regional types. The inhabitants of cities like Fès, Meknès and Rabat tend to be pale skinned and slightly built, and have a distinctly Iberian look. There are certain faces which to the insider look very Fassi, and others which are distinctly Amazigh – something in the shape of the face, perhaps. The older generation of Moroccans, particularly the mountain people, are shorter than their European counterparts. Life style for the urban middle classes differs little from that of southern Europeans. The rural regions, however, are vastly different, and there are still areas without electricity and other basic infrastructure, and in these regions life expectancy is lower.

Cultural focus

Moroccans differ greatly from northern Europeans in the way their lives are focused, however. The family is of primary importance, determining a person's life chances to a great degree. Family loyalty is of great importance, with the father seemingly the dominant figure – although very often wives rule the roost. Islam is a strong force, laying down the limits of what can and cannot be done. Also important to Moroccan culture is notion of *qa'ada* (tradition). The home is a private place – but strangers, when a friendship forms, are readily invited in. On the whole, however, men meet their friends in cafés, while women socialize in each others' homes.

A changing society

As society changes, Moroccan cultural attitudes are changing too. Though not yet a nation of city dwellers, Morocco's urban population is now just over 50%. Morocco's old families, and the brightest and best connected of the university-educated elite, have done very well for themselves since independence from France in 1956. (Some would say 'only too well', arguing that the Moroccan upper-middle class behaves in a colonial fashion in its own country). The second-generation urban populations have new aspirations, however, and expect some part of the national cake. And with urbanization and growing affluence come changes. Women work, criticise an essentially repressive family code, are ready to take stands against macho attitudes. At the same time, the country is seeing the expansion of purist brands of religious practice, which often imply considerable bigotry. In short, Moroccan society is subject to considerable stresses and tensions.

Religion

The people of Morocco, and of North Africa for that matter, follow Islam in the main, a religion similar to Judaism and Christianity in its philosophical content. Muslims recognize that these three revealed religions have a common basis, and Jews and Christians are referred to as *Ahl al-kitab*, 'people of the book'. Even so, there are considerable differences in ritual, public observance of religious customs and the role of religion in daily life, and when travelling in Morocco it is as well to be aware of this.

Islam is an Arabic word literally meaning 'submission to God'. As Muslims often point out, it is not just a religion, but a way of life. The main Islamic scripture is the Koran (often also spelt Quran in English), again an Arabic term meaning 'the recitation'. Islam appeared in the desert oases of western Arabia in the early seventh century AD. The isolated communities of this region were Jewish, Christian or animist, existing on oasis cultivation and the trade in beasts of burden. There was considerable inter-tribal warfare. It was in this context that the third great revealed religion was to emerge. Its prophet Mohammed, born in AD570, was a member of the aristocratic Meccan tribe of Quraysh.

The Koran Islam's holy book, the Koran divides into 114 souras or chapters, placed in order of length running from the longest to the shortest. Muslim and western scholars disagree on the nature of the Koran. For the true Muslim, it is the word of God, sent down via the Prophet Mohammed. The Koran appeared in this way in segments, some in Mecca, some after the Prophet was forced to leave Mecca for Medina in 622. The later souras tend to have a more practical content, and relate to family and inheritance law, for during the period in Medina, an embryonic Muslim community was taking shape. Western scholars, however, have opened up more critical approaches to the Koranic text and the way it was assembled. During the Prophet's lifetime, nothing was written down. After his death, fragments of the text, noted in simple script on parchment or flat bones, were assembled at the order of Abu Bakr, Mohammed's successor or *khalifa*. In fact, the Arabic script was not fully codified at the time. The language of the Koran was eventually to become the base reference point for the Arabic language. For most Muslim Arabs, the written classical form of the language can never escape this divine influence.

The Hadith The Koran does not cover all aspects of the Muslim's life – and it became apparent to early Islamic rulers that they would need another source. The *hadith*, short statements which recount what the Prophet is supposed to have said about various issues, were assembled and codified in the early days of Islam, providing crucial supplements to the main scripture.

Five pillars of Islam The practice of Islam is based on five central points, the Pillars of Islam, namely the *shahada* or profession of faith, *salat* or prayer, *sawm* or fasting during the month of Ramadhan, *zakat* or giving charity, and the *hajj* or pilgrimage to Mecca which every Muslim is supposed to accomplish at least once. The mosque is the centre of religious activity. There is no clergy in Islam, although major mosques will have an *imam* to lead prayers. In principle, the *mesjed*, a small neighbourhood mosque, will have someone chosen from the area with enough religious knowledge to conduct prayers correctly.

The ***shahada*** is the testament of faith, and involves reciting, in all sincerity, the statement, "There is no god but God, and Mohammed is the Messenger of God." A Muslim will do this at ***salat***, the prayer ritual performed five times a day, including at sunrise, midday and sunset. There are also the important Friday noon prayers, which include a sermon or *khutba*. When praying, Muslims bow and then kneel down and prostrate themselves in the direction of Mecca, indicated in a mosque by a door-sized niche in the wall called the *qibla*. The voice of the *muezzin* calling the faithful to prayer five times a day from the minaret provides Muslim cities with their characteristic soundscape. Note that a Muslim must be ritually pure to worship. This involves washing in a ritual manner, either at the *hammam* (local bathhouse) or the *midha*, the ablutions area of the mosque.

A third essential part of Islam is the giving of ***zakat*** or alms. A Muslim was supposed to give surplus revenues to the community. With time, the practice of *zakat* was codified. Today, however, zakat has largely disappeared to be replaced by modern taxation systems. The practice of *zakat al fitr*, giving alms at 'Id El Fitr, the Muslim holiday which marks the end of Ramadhan, is still current, however.

The fourth pillar of Islam is ***sawm*** or fasting during Ramadhan. The daytime month-long fast of Ramadhan is a time of contemplation, worship and piety – the Islamic equivalent of Lent. Muslims are expected to read one thirtieth of the Koran each night. Muslims who are ill or on a journey, as well as women breast-feeding are exempt from fasting. Otherwise, eating, drinking and sexual activity is only permitted at night, until "so much of the dawn appears that a white thread can be distinguished from a black one."

The ***hajj*** or pilgrimage to the holy city of Mecca in Arabia is required of all physically-able Muslims at least once in their life time. The *hajj* takes place during the month of Dhu al Hijja. The 'lesser pilgrimage' to the holy places of Islam is referred to as the *'umra*, and can be performed at any time of year. Needless to say, the journey to Mecca is not within every Muslim's financial grasp – fortunately, perhaps, as the mosques would probably be unable to cope with the millions involved, despite the extension works of recent years.

Muslim revivalists lay stress on a sixth element in their faith: ***jihad,*** which literally means struggle. The term was originally used to refer to the taking of Islam into the *dar al harb*, 'the house of war', ie the lands outside the *dar al islam*. (The fundamentalist Muslim world view is a bipolar one). It has been used to refer to the individual's struggle to be true to their faith, also to the fight against underdevelopment. Early Islam expanded rapidly through the mobilization of thousands of tribal warriors in *jihad*, taking the new religion out into Mesopotamia, Persia and the Mediterranean world. The contrast with early Christianity, essentially spread in an underground way, is marked.

On prophets & revelation

As mentioned above, Islam is a revealed religion, and God chose certain men to be **prophets**, his true representatives on Earth. In Arabic, a prophet is a *nabi*, while **Mohammed** is the messenger of God, *rasoul Allah*. The first prophet in Islam was Adam, and the last was Mohammed, 'seal of the prophets'. Major prophets are Sidna Nouh (Noah), Sidna Ibrahim (Abraham), Dawoud (David), Mousa (Moses), and 'Issa (Jesus). Yaqoub (Jacob), Youssuf (Joseph) and Ayyoub (Job) are all mentioned in the Quran. Prophets were recognised by their miracles, apart from Mohammed, who was to be the instrument via which the Quran was transmitted to humankind. Nevertheless, Mohammed's *mi'raj* or ascent to heaven on the winged horse, Al Buraq, may be considered as a sort of miracle.

The miracles performed by the prophets are not detailed in the Quran. **'Issa** (Jesus) is pictured in a particularly favourable light. While the virgin birth remains in the Quran, Issa is definitely not the son of God in Islam.

Sunna (standard Islamic practice)

The Koran and the hadith also lay down a number of other practices and customs, some of which are close to the practices of Judaism. Sexuality, provided it is within marriage, is seen as positive, and there is no category of religious personnel for whom marriage is forbidden. Sensuality and seduction, between the married couple, are encouraged, without any guilt being involved. Eating pork is out, as is drinking alcohol and gambling. In the matter of dress, habits have changed hugely in recent years. Except in certain rural areas, young women no longer automatically veil their faces, rather, a headscarf and *djellaba* is the modern version of Islamic dress for women. However, Moroccan Islam is a long way from the more extreme forms practised in Saudi Arabia, where women are forbidden from driving and are all but invisible in the public sphere. While in traditional families the women's domain is most definitely the home, Islam does not stop Moroccan women getting themselves educated and into jobs once thought of as being exclusively for men.

Fundamentalist interpretations

Literalist interpretations of the Koran would, however, lead to women to being pushed out of positions of responsibility in public life, although they would no doubt continue to operate in professions where they could work in women only institutions (hospitals, schools). Muslim fundamentalists, including the Moroccan Salafiya, claim to have the absolute monopoly on applying the letter of the Koran, in understanding the words of a book 'written' in the 7th century AD as a programme for social organization applicable in every time and every place. But as a reading of the text will show, Mohammed had no political programme: he was the vessel for the transmission of the divine word.

The sad thing about contemporary purist Islam is that it is literalist. The fundamentalist would like to see society become a carbon copy of west Arabian society as regulated by

Islamic law in Mohammed's day – with all that this included in terms of bodily mutilation as punishment. The obsession with a recreating a lost past, with the application of often obscure text, leave no room for creative thought. In a globalising world, the fundamentalist is constantly seeing and hearing things that they must consider blasphemous. They forget, however, that God in Islam is above all forgiving. Prayer always begins with the formula *bism-Illahi er Rahmane er Rahime*, 'in the name of God the Compassionate, the Merciful'.

Gender issues

Despite the changes since independence, the status of women is likely to be an increasingly hot issue over the next decade in Morocco. For the moment, Tunisia is the most advanced Muslim country in terms of legislation aimed at removing discrimination against women – and is a model often referred to by Moroccans working for women's rights. The Tunisian *Code du statut personnel*, promulgated in 1956, abolished both polygamy and *talaq* (repudiation by the male partner), a step which the Moroccan women's movement would like to see taken. The Tunisian code did not however touch the issue of Islamic inheritance rules which favour male over female descendants, although laying down strict rules for the division of property.

The Moudawana

The nature of women's status in Morocco is laid down the *Moudawana*, a code which became law in 1957. Revised in 1993, the Moudawana, like other codes in the North African states, affirms the importance of the family as the basis of society. This family is patrilinear, that is to say, takes its name from the father. Thus it is forbidden for a Muslim woman to marry a non-Muslim man. He must convert to Islam, even if this is only for form's sake, and the process is a long one. Non-Muslim women marrying Moroccans do not have to convert, however. Adoption, outlawed in the Koran, does not exist in Morocco. The marriageable age is 18 for men and 14 for women.

Much was expected of the 1993 revision of the Moudawana. Many however, considered it as a rewriting of the existing code. At the very least, however, the demands of both women and civil society had been listened to. The arguments against polygamy are many. The Moudawana does specify that if there is a risk of injustice, the judge must refuse polygamy, and Moroccan women's rights groups argue that in its essence polygamy is unjust. A similar argument runs that Islamic repudiation is also to be abolished, to be replaced by fair divorce laws, given that a *hadith* or 'saying' attributed to the prophet Mohammed runs that repudiation "is the permitted act which is most reproved by God".

A plan for change

In the late 1990s, as the result of political horse-trading, the representative of a minor political party, one Saïd Saâdi, was appointed head of the new State secretariat for family affairs and social security. Part of his brief was to look at ways to improve the socio-legal conditions of Moroccan women. A wide-range of proposals resulted, including giving women a 33 % quota of seats in the parliament, raising the minimum marriage age from 14 to 18, ending the requirement for a male guardian's permission to be given to women before marriage, banning polygamy, and reforming divorce law. As at present, Islamic repudiation is in force; the proposal was to introduce divorce by judicial decree.

In late 1999, prime minister Youssoufi in an off the cuff remark referred to the proposals as the National Action Plan for Integrating Women into the Development Process. The traditionalist press took him to task, criticizing the document for promoting 'corrupt western values'. The old guard of parties like the Istiqlal, loath to being accused of a non-Islamic stance, jumped on the anti-plan bandwagon. And so, to a storm of protest from reformists, the Saadi document was dropped. The coalition government felt it had other more pressing issues on the agenda, most notably the fight against poverty.

Justifications of conservatism

With the number of educated women increasing year by year, attitudes will no doubt change. Long established practices die hard, however, and the best thought-out family status code would have little effect without changes in mentalities. Morocco, like the rest of the Maghreb and much of southern Europe, is a macho land, and the young girls of the house are the object of jealous surveillance. Although the Koranic texts are basically clear on the principle of equality between men and women, certain *souras* and hadith stress women's weakness, the need for women to serve men, and mention the need for male protection. From a western point of view, predicated on 'universal' human rights, women are definitely second-class citizens. However, while still regulated by Islam, relations between women and men differ enormously between social classes and regional groups. And very often, in traditional areas, it is the women who seem to be the most vigilant guardians of the status quo.

Expanding women's space

However, in this system, although women rarely have direct authority, they have very definite space of their own. All is not repression – far from it. While weddings are still very often a matter of alliances between families, loving marriages certainly develop in this traditional context. Women are now present in most areas of the country's economic and professional life – and the latest government (autumn 2002) has three women ministers.

Woman are *the* force in Morocco's dynamic (and influential) NGOs as well. Women head assocations working to help single mothers, battered women, the illiterate and street children, cancer and AIDs victims. They are active in promoting micro-business programmes for women. Chabaka ('the net') brings together 200 NGOs supporting reform of the Moudawana.

Thus in the reformists' minds there is no doubt that women's status will have to change to keep up with women's responsibilities in society. The reduction of inequalities links in with the image which Morocco wishes to project for itself and for the outside world. Women's quest for new identities is a legitimate one – and probably inseparable from the evolving identity of the modern nation.

Culture of patriarchy

Despite Morocco's carefully nurtured image as one of the most tolerant, progressive Islamic nations, it remains a very conservative place in many ways. On close examination, the couplet 'tradition and modernity', a favourite in the tourist advertising, is problematic. In the late 1990s – and in particular since the accession of Mohammed VI to the throne in July 1999 – reform-minded Moroccans have been calling for change. New forces are emerging – the Islamists, the so-called Berberists, democratic pressure groups – all advocating different forms of 'progress'. How the existing dominant forces in the system, the makhzen, (roughly translatable as 'government by the palace') and the political parties will evolve will be interesting to watch. Among some observers, the survival of traditional politics into the early twenty-first century leads to gloomy talk of insurmountable cultural factors to explain the obstacles to reform. In fact, one of the great fears of the reformers is that a strongman will rise to the top, taking control of the nation's destiny. The challenge now is for the country to move from government focused on a single personality to a more open, accountable system.

Patriarchs & strongmen

One view of Moroccan political, and indeed social culture as strongly authoritarian. There are plenty examples of despots and powerful henchmen in the country's recent history. In 1894, as Sultan Hassan I lay dying, the chamberlain Ba Hmad had the weakening monarch name his youngest son, Moulay Abdelaziz, his heir. When the sultan died out in the countryside, the chamberlain kept the news quiet for days until Moulay Abdelaziz could be safely installed on the throne. From then on, Ba Hmad ruled as he saw fit, putting his relatives in key positions, removing all opposition. The young sultan was kept quiet with a range of mechanical toys and other gewgaws supplied by a former British army officer, Caïd McLean. Later, during the French protectorate, the south was ruled by the Pacha of Marrakech, Thami el Glaoui, with a similar mixture of terror and clientelism. (Gavin Maxwell gives a fine account in his *Lords of the Atlas*).

Under the late king, Hassan II, the system focused immutably on the palace, as it had done for centuries. Prime ministers were generally (but not always) rather self-effacing men. Government was dominated by a strong man, often of modest origins, heading the security apparatus in one way or another. Until 1972, General Oufkir was the regime's policeman. It was Oufkir who as minister of the Interior gave the order for the security forces to fire on unarmed demonstrators during the Casablanca riots of 1965. The abortive coup d'état at the Skhirat Palace in 1972 led to Oufkir's replacement by his shadow, Colonel Dlimi. For his effective leadership in the Saharan campaigns of the late 1970s, he was to rise to the rank of general before dying in obscure circumstances. His chief claim to fame was his role in the 'disappearance', yet to be fully explained, of key left-wing politician, Mehdi Ben Barka. The 1980s saw the emergence of Driss Basri, who as minister of the Interior operated for all the world like a Grand Vizier from some onion-domed oriental city. He started his career as a police inspector, rose to become the all powerful figure in Morocco's political life. Political opponents ran the risk of imprisonment after various forms of 'trial', torture went unmentioned. Election results were routinely falsified; with Basri's assistance, new political parties appeared as if by magic. Even potential democrats were corrupted. In short, the whole political and administrative machinery was gangrened with various forms of corruption. To universal sighs of relief, Basri was removed from office in late 1999 by the new king.

'Heads-down culture'

Morocco as run by patriarchs necessarily had a strong culture of non-criticism. With any opponent (and their family and friends) running huge risks, things could not be otherwise. 'Heads down' was the only prudent way to act (until things began to loosen up in the mid-1990s). Leftist intellectuals found themselves in a double-walled prison: the right smothered the left, and the King smothered the right. The result was a law of doing what one wanted, covering one's tracks, and making loyal allies in the positions that mattered.

Towards the end of patriarchy?

In the early 1990s, signs that political change was possible appeared. The first major breach in the patriarchal system was the new constitution of 1992, which brought in the rule that governments would be formed on the basis of a parliamentary majority. The new king, Mohammed VI has shown himself keen to reform the system. There is constant talk of 'a new concept of authority', the local administration is becoming more professional, the old guard are being replaced. The question is whether authoritarianism can be attacked while leaving the very cultural foundations of the monarchy intact. Traditionally, apparent servility went hand in hand with pumping the system for all it was worth. The rule was 'don't challenge your boss openly, screw him if you can', hardly conducive to the open, responsible management of people and institutions.

Might a new strong man emerge? Traditionally, Morocco's sultans governed alone, with the additional legitimating plus of strong religious charisma. On the downside, they ruled a land subject to frequent drought, where harvests failed provoking difficult times in town and country alike. Thus (the theory goes) in a context where power could not be shared, a strong man was essential to handle the less gratifying aspects of being ruler: putting down incipient revolts, dealing with rising opponents. And perhaps the strong man's room for action was enhance by a certain docility among the population. After all, the strong man was operating in the name of a monarch with unchallenged Islamic credentials.

So the question is really one of whether Morocco can move away from the system where one man mediated the patriarch's decisions, distributing favours and keeping the order in place. In the eyes of most Moroccans, a general or a minister with despotic powers, implementing programmes with little respect for the niceties of form is a complete dinosaur. But is there enough of a new, open political culture to replace the old system of subservience to the patriarch? Technocratic government will not be enough to create a democratic system.

On the plus side, Morocco has strong institutions. Issues of government, accountability and corruption are widely debated in the press, the constitutional reforms of the 1990s were a major step, taken by the previous monarch, in the right direction. Political patterns, methods of management and deep-rooted behaviour seem to be changing, pushed by NGOs such as Transparency Maroc. Another sign of change was a major parliamentary enquiry into corruption and mismanagement of the country's biggest state owned banks, the CIH (see box). Though prospects for a fairer system of government seem good under Mohammed VI, for those in the grinding poverty of Morocco's fourth-world countryside, this is not much consolation. And if change is too slow, many of the best and brightest will be tempted to leave.

Architecture

Morocco, as the visitor will quickly notice, has a wealth of characteristic buildings and craft forms. Though in certain areas, traditional architecture is giving way to less aesthetic – and less climatically adapted forms of buildings – there is a huge amount of interesting building to see. The Musée archéologique in Rabat has the finest collection of objects from ancient times, however.

Prehistory

The earliest traces of human settlement in Morocco go back to 800,000 BC. Towards 5000 BC, new populations, probably the ancestors of today's Berbers, are thought to have arrived. They brought with them a nomadic form of pastoralism. Morocco is particularly well endowed with early rock carvings, left behind by these nomads, which can be seen in the High Atlas (Yagour Plateau, and at Oukaïmeden) and in the Anti-Atlas, near Tafraoute, as well as in the oases of Akka and Foum Hassan. A stone circle survives at Mzoura, south-east of Asilah near Souk Tnine de Sidi el Yamami, in northwestern Morocco.

Roman times

When Rome was founded in 753 BC, the coast of Morocco was on the trade routes of Phoenician merchants. Inland areas were inhabited by a people called the Maures by the Romans – hence the name Mauritania for the Roman province covering part of what is now Morocco. No doubt the land was divided into Berber Kingdoms. From 25 BC to AD23, Juba II ruled Mauritania from Volubilis, today Morocco's best preserved Roman site, close to Meknès. Some of the finest Hellenistic and Roman bronzes extant from this site can be seen today at the Rabat archaeological museum, along with pottery and other objects from Roman times. Other visitable Roman sites, all in northwestern Morocco, include Thamusida (near Kénitra), Banasa (near Souk El Arba du Gharb) and Lixus (near Larache).

The buildings of Islam

In 682, the Arab general Okba Ibn Nafi and his army crossed the Maghreb, bringing with them a new revealed religion, Islam. This religion was to engender new architectural forms, shaped by the requirements of prayer and the Muslim urban lifestyle. The

Inside the Mosque

In all Muslim countries, mosques are built orientated towards Mecca, as the believers must pray in the direction of their holy city. In Morocco's case, this means that the orientation is east-south-east. A large mosque has four main areas: prayer halls, courtyard and colonnade, minaret, and, in all likelihood, attached ablutions facility and hammam. Most mosques will have: abthe ***qibla wall*** *(1), facing east- southeast, with a decorated niche or* ***mihrab*** *(2) in the middle, towards which the believers pray; aba colonnaded* ***prayer hall*** *(3), and a large* ***courtyard*** *(4), often with a fountain; aba* ***minaret*** *or midhana (5) from which the call to prayer is made five times a day; aban* ***entrance*** *(6), through which the non-Muslim visitor may glimpse the courtyard if there is no wooden lattice-work screen.*

On Fridays, there will often be so many people for the weekly midday prayers and accompanying sermon that latecomers, equipped with their rugs, will have to pray outside in the street.

Kasbah Mosque

After Ewert, Wisshak, 1987

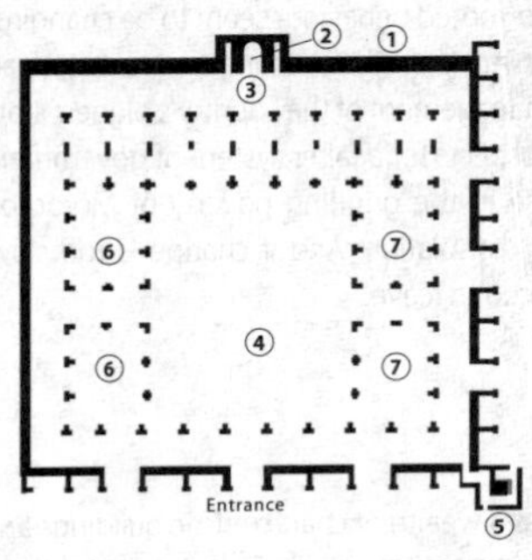

1 Qibla wall
2 Mihrab
3 "Recycled" capitals on 6 pillars around mihrab
4 Sahn
5 Minaret
6 Liwanat

key building of Islam is of course the mosque, which evolved considerably from its humble beginnings as a sort of enclosure with an adjoining low platform from which the call to prayer could be made. Mosques became spectacular buildings demonstrating the power of ruling dynasties, centring on colonnaded prayer halls and vast courtyards. The elegant towers of the minarets gave beauty and character to the skyline of the great Muslim cities.

Mosques cannot generally be visited in Morocco by the non-Muslim visitor, with some notable exceptions, including the Grande Mosquée Hassan II in Casablanca, the ruined mosque of the Chellah necropolis in Rabat, the restored Almohad mosque at Tin Mal in the High Atlas, and the so-called 'Spanish mosque', a ruin on a hilltop outside Chaouen. Minarets, visible from afar, are not always easy to photograph close by, being surrounded by narrow streets and densely built up areas.

Minarets As an essential feature of the mosque, the minaret probably developed in the late seventh century. Islam had adopted a call to prayer or *idhan* rather than bells to summon the faithful. (Bilal, an Abyssinian slave, was the first muezzin.) The first minarets, no doubt built by local Christian builders, were adapted from the square towers of Syrian churches. Moroccan minarets are generally a simple square tower, with a small 'lantern' feature on the top, from which the muezzin makes the call to prayer. Older minarets tend to feature blind horseshoe arches and a small dome on the topmost 'lantern' room. On top of the dome is an ornamental feature resembling three metal spheres on a pole, topped by a crescent. This is the *jammour*, and tourist guides have a number of entertaining explanations for this, for example, that the spheres represent the basic ingredients of bread (flour, water and salt). There are unusual exceptions to the square minaret, however, including the round tower of the Moulay Idriss Mosque, covered in green ceramic tiles with Koranic verses in white, and the octagonal minaret of the

Kasbah Mosque in Tanger. The great Almohad mosques – the Grand Mosque at Taza, Koutoubiya at Marrakech, the partially completed Tour Hassan, Rabat – are characterized by an interlinked lozenge pattern, executed in stone on their facades. (The Giralda tower of the Cathedral of Seville started life as an Almohad minaret, too – see illustrations.) One school of art history sees the proportions, arcades and decorative motifs of these buildings as setting trends, eventually to be reproduced and transformed in European Gothic architecture.

Layout & decoration

Mosques tend to have large covered prayer halls, comprising a series of narrow transepts, created by lines of arches supporting pitched roofs, generally covered with green tiles. There will be a main 'aisle' leading towards the *mihrab* (prayer niche), which indicates the direction of Mecca, and for prayer. The main nave in the traditional Moroccan mosque does not, however, have the same dimensions as the main nave of a Christian cathedral. Note that Islam does not favour representation of the human form, hence the use of highly elaborate geometric decorative motifs executed in ceramic *zellige* (mosaic), and on wood and plaster. There is no religious pictorial art. The same geometric motifs can be found in domestic architecture too. A mosque will also have an open courtyard, sometimes with a decorative fountain. Although all the usual decorative techniques can be seen, the 1990s Grande Mosquée Hassan II is an exception in layout, having just one major aisle, flanked by two narrower secondary naves.

Schools of religious science

The non-Muslim visitor can get a very good idea of Muslim sacred architecture by visiting one of the *medersas*, the colleges which were an essential part of the Moroccan Muslim education system from medieval times onward. One of the largest is the Medersa Ben Youssef in Marrakech, a 14th-century foundation entirely rebuilt in the 16th century. Like all medersas, it is essentially a hollowed out cube, the blockiness of the architecture being relieved by mesemerisingly decorative detail on every flat surface: ceramic mosaic, and densely carved stucco and cedar wood. The austere students' rooms come as something of a shock after the elaborate decoration of the courtyard. Other *medersas* can be seen in Salé (the Medersa Abou el Hassan), Meknès (the Medersa Bou Inania) and of course in that centre of Muslim theology and jurisprudence, Fès (the medersas Bou Inania, Attarine, Cherratene and es Sahrij, amongst others).

Historic médina

Perhaps the most easily photographed of the old mosques is the Koutoubiya in Marrakech (and next to it, you can see the excavated remains of an earlier mosque). However, the Koutoubiya is an exception in that it stands apart from the city. Mosques and *medersas* are generally surrounded by buildings. The visitor to Morocco quickly has to learn to navigate through the narrow streets of the médina or old towns to reach the monument or museum to be visited.

In much 19th-century European writing, the médina of the Maghreb – and of the Arab world in general – were seen as chaotic places, which although harbouring exotically clothed populations, were also home to disease and ignorance. The médina was taken as a metaphor for the backwardness of the *indigene* or native In fact, the tangled streets of the average Moroccan médina are no more disorganized than many a European medieval town. Today's visitor will immediately be struck by the external walls in *pisé* (sundried clay, gravel and lime mix). Disorientation due to narrow alleys and high walls sets in later, perhaps after leaving the main souks.

The logic of the médina

The médinas of Morocco do, however, obey a logic, satisfying architectural requirements arising from climatic and religious factors. The climate is hot in summer, but often very cold in winter. In the coastal towns, damp ocean mists roll in, while inland there are hot summer winds from the south. The city therefore has to provide protection from this climate, and networks of narrow streets are the ideal solution. Streets could be narrow as there was no wheeled transport, there being plenty of pack animals for carrying goods around. And narrow streets also ensured that precious building land within the city walls was not wasted.

For housing the Muslim family, the courtyard house was the ideal solution. This of course is an architectural model which goes back to Mesopotamia, Greece and Rome. For Islamic family life, with its insistence on gender separation in the public domain, the courtyard house provides a high level of family privacy. In densely built up cities, the roof terraces also provided a place for women to perform household tasks – and to share news and gossip. The biggest houses would have several patios, the main one having arcades on two levels. Thus extended families could be accommodated in dwellings with large open areas. Old Moroccan courtyard homes are not easily visited, however. In both Marrakech and Fès, there are houses which have been restored and altered to function as upmarket restaurants (see the late 19th century Dar Marjana in Marrakech, for example or the Palais Mnebhi in Fès). In Marrakech, however, the visitor can discover a superb concentration of Moroccan craftwork in a lovingly restored patrician house, the Maison Tiskiwin, close to the Bahia Palace. You may well be invited into ordinary homes, however, where fridges and pressure cookers are in use alongside traditional braseros in the main courtyard.

Earthen architectures

The courtyard home is the most characteristic building in Morocco's cities, discreet and anonymous to all but a neighbourhood's inhabitants from the outside, spectacularly decorated in its patrician form on the inside. There are other, more rustic, building traditions in use, however, the best known being the kasbahs and ksours of the areas south of the High Atlas, the valleys of the Dadès, the Draâ and the Ziz. Much of this traditional building in the south is in compacted earth and gravel.

Kasbahs The word kasbah probably derives from the Turkish *kasabe*, meaning small town. In contemporary North Africa, it is generally used to refer to the fortified strong point in a city. Morocco also has numerous kasbahs scattered across its territory, many erected by energetic 17th-century builder-ruler Moulay Ismaïl. (See, for example, the kasbah at Boulaouane, near Settat, and the derelict Kasbah Tadla, near Beni Mellal.)

In the southern reaches of Morocco, the term kasbah is used to denote often vast fortified villages, with spectacular tower houses often several storeys high. Good examples can be found near Ouarzazate, at Aït Benhaddou (as used in part of Orson Welles' *Sodom and Gomorrah*) and up in the High Atlas at Telouet, where a vast crumbling kasbah testifies to the power of the T'hami el Glaoui, ruler of Marrakech in the early part of the 20th century. There are a fair number of Glaoui kasbahs scattered across the southern valleys, and they tend to have decorative features of more urban inspiration than the kasbahs of the old Berber communities. There are good examples at Tamnougalt, south of Agdz in the Draâ Valley, and in the Skoura oasis (the Kasbah Amerhidl), Dadès Valley.

Ksours Ksour country is really the Ziz Valley (main towns Er Rachidia and Erfoud). The ksour sit surrounded by palm groves and walled market gardens. They house the families of the oasis dwellers, and like the kasbahs, are built in a defensive mode. Their smooth high walls, fortified with corner towers, and narrow windows enabled the inhabitants to protect their harvests. Back west again, in the mountains, the *tighremt* or *agadir*, the fortified grain store, held the same function. The ground floor was used for the animals, the first floor as a food store, and the top floor for family living space.

Spectacular though they often are, the kasbahs and ksours are under threat. This form of earth building is vulnerable to the weather, and despite its excellent qualities in terms of temperature regulation, it needs maintenance. Reinforced concrete building is now popular, perceived as 'modern'. However, in the southern regions, there is a new wave of mock kasbah architecture. The crenellations, window slits and tapering towers of the ancient earthen buildings can now be found on official buildings, hotels and electricity sub-stations. The tourist industry may yet however fuel some sort of return to traditional – and more ecological – building typologies. See for example, the kasbahs re-used as hotels, including the Aït Moro in Skoura and the Tomboctou in Tineghir.

Fortified ports

On the coasts of Morocco can be found another form of defensive architecture, the military port of early modern European inspiration. In the 15th century, both Atlantic and Mediterranean coasts were targets for the expanding Iberian powers. Ports such as Agadir, Safi, Asilah and Tanger were occupied, all the better to control the lucrative trade routes to Asia and the Americas. In the early 16th century, Portugal was still at the height of its glory as an imperial power, and elaborate fortifications were erected at Azemmour, Mazagan (today's El Jadida), Safi, Mogador (today's Essaouira) and Agadir, equipped with all the most up-to-date features of the military architecture of the day. There were monumental gateways, cannons, watchtowers and round bastions.

Citadel of El Jadida

The most spectacular example of this military architecture is the Citadel of El Jadida, held by the Portuguese until 1769. The citadel was built in 1516 on the model of the most advanced Italian military building technology of the day. Five arrow-shaped bastions jut into the ocean, to pre-empt attack from all possible angles. The thick walls would have necessitated enormous firepower to reduce them – a firepower beyond the reach of Moroccan rulers until the 18th century. The citadel as seen today was rebuilt at the beginning of the 19th century. The same ruler who took El Jadida in 1769, Sidi Mohammed Ben Abdallah, understood the importance of European military architecture. In 1764, he employed a French engineer, one Théodore Cornut, to lay out the new fortifications at Essaouira. This was to be the first example of modern urban planning on Moroccan soil.

Modern cities

The contemporary Moroccan city is very much an early 20th-century achievement, the work of two far-sighted people, Maréchal Lyautey and urban planner Henri Prost. France's first resident general in Morocco had been much impressed by Prost's plans for the re-design of Antwerp in Belgium – and was willing to give such schemes a chance in the new French protectorate. A Prost plan was characterized by a number of features that seemed particularly adaptable to the Moroccan context. Old walls were not demolished and re-used as development land, but kept as part of a buffer zone between old and new. The new areas had large open spaces planted with regular rows of trees, while a system of avenues within the city enhanced existing monumental buildings and linked in to a system of highways leading in and out of the city. The crucial point on which Prost focused was the preservation of the aesthetic face of the city, without totally cutting it off from new forms of transport and infrastructure.

Prost, like Lyautey, was all for technological innovation. However, this position was balanced with a strong social conservatism: existing hierarchies were to be kept. In Morocco, 'respect for difference' was the justification for the strict zoning between old and new quarters, rich and poor.

In Morocco, Lyautey and his experts found themselves in an enviable position. They were able to appropriate land, levy taxes and develop a land-use policy with a freedom unthinkable in France. As they drew up plans for the *villes nouvelles*, their task was made all the easier by the fact that the watchwords of the French republic – liberty, equality and fraternity – were not applied in Morocco. Equality was out of the question. Although some lip-service was paid to fraternity, liberty to participate in decisions on the country's future was reserved to the technocratic elite around the Residency General – after a show of consultation with the sultan, of course.

The uses of urbanism

Lyautey in Morocco wanted to apply the modern principles of 'the science of urbanism', and attempted to attract as many new architects as possible. With Algeria as the negative example of how the French had behaved abroad, Lyautey set out to promote a new system, the theatre of which would be the city. The crises of French and Algerian cities were to be avoided, the new urbanism was to be the showcase for the benefits of French rule. As Lyautey is reputed to have said in a famous dictum, 'a construction site means I can avoid using a battalion', 'un chantier m'évite un bataillon.'

The Moroccan notables in many cases wanted cleaner neighbourhoods with modern infrastructure – but separate from the new, impure Christian population. (Spatial segregation by religion had been a feature in many of the older Moroccan towns.) However, the new European neighbourhoods were built close enough for there to be social contact. Where British colonialism had been based essentially on a structure of police intelligence, the French *villes nouvelles* of Morocco were to allow social meeting – or so the theory went. The urban planners faced a problem of how to integrate these social requirements into development plans – the Meknès plan, in particular, was criticized for the distance between the two communities. Speculation and building styles were to be strictly controlled, while new rail systems were planned and embedded into the city's structure.

Another French creation was the Fine Arts Department to ensure the protection of the main historic monuments. Sites for protection were selected, and the ground was prepared for tourism and a new historic awareness. Both Lyautey and Prost detested the kitsch of modern Algerian neo-Moorish architecture – and the banality of French suburban building. New construction was thus to follow principles valued by Lyautey and Prost, essentially simplicity of form and a high degree of functionality. Public buildings were to have simple lines, taking on the contours of traditional Arab building. Craft techniques were used for detailing, giving a 'Moroccan style' to otherwise modern buildings. Geometric public spaces made great use of fountains and vegetation.

The Prost plans laid the basis for the development of Morocco's cities for the 20th century, creating spacious urban centres which are still agreeable today, despite vehicle pollution. (Prost could hardly have been expected to imagine the huge growth in the number of noxious diesel vehicles by the end of the 20th century.) Most importantly, a tradition of planning and architectural innovation, along with respect for architectural heritage, was established. New official building across Morocco incorporates features of traditional architecture – green-tiled roofs, stone detailing, mosaic work – in a style referred to as Neo-Makhzen. Other building is often symbolically ambitious – take, for example, the Twin Center in Casablanca, designed by Catalan architect Bofill.

Arts and crafts

Contemporary painting

In terms of painting too, Morocco has proved a considerable bed of talent, perhaps surprisingly for a country that had no tradition of representing human and animal form. However, given the proximity of Europe, easel painting soon took root after the arrival of the French protectorate. (A stay in Morocco had already been a popular source of inspiration for numerous European painters, for whom the kingdom was all exotic street scenes, cavalcades in movement, and sharp, often violent colour contrast.) A number of European artists settled in Morocco, the most important being Jacques Majorelle, 'the painter of Marrakech',

Pottery and belief

Until perhaps the 1960s, old-fashioned heavy pottery plates and dishes were in general use in Fassi homes. A study on Fassi ceramics quotes an elderly housewife recounting how her father, back in the 1930s, was insistent on eating from Fassi pottery. Said the patriarch, member of a Soufi group: "I want to eat from fakhar (traditionally made) dishes, made from the trab (clay) of Morocco, because such plates and vessels have been made with a prayer, in accordance with religion. Any foreign vessel is haram, sinful."

For great family occasions, the poorer families would rent large dishes called tabaq or mtirda. The great families did not use mokhfia dishes, but other shapes and forms. Today, these traditional forms are often recycled in less hard-wearing pottery for the tourist market, often decorated with metal or bone insets.

Pottery also accompanied the Muslim in the cemetery. A ghorraf or zlafa of water was left on top of tombs, the idea being that birds would come to drink and sing to the dead. Maybe simpler folk believed the birds to be God's messengers – and it was seen as a very worthy charitable action to leave them water to drink. Pigeons and doves were particularly appreciated, nicknamed dker Allah, *as their cooing was said to sound like the words* deker (remember) Allah.

But old-style pottery was also fragile. Oil and butter penetrated the surface, rendering the glaze fragile. Large plates were expensive, however, and would be repaired, sometimes with metal patches or occasionally staples – as was the case in Europe in the 18th century. Sometimes a small piece of pot was cemented in to replace a missing piece. This attachment to pottery shows the material value of tableware in times gone by. But it also indicates a sentimental, maybe even religious value. After all, the members of a family would have sat round a large communal dish to eat together hundreds of times, saying the words bismillah, *'in the name of God', at the start of each meal. The* hadith, *or saying of the Prophet, runs that anything you do starting with the* bismillah *will go well.*

best known for his scenes of the High Atlas, Edouard Edy-Legrand and Marianne Bertuchi. In the 1940s, a number of self-taught Moroccan painters emerged, sometimes directly imitating European styles – others, such as Moulay Ahmed Drissi, illustrating the rich heritage of oral literature. Jacques Azema produced fine frescoes – but is perhaps best known for his miniature line drawings, executed with finesse in biro.

After independence in 1956, a generation of Moroccan painters came to the fore, working in a number of registers – abstract, naïve, calligraphic. Many had received training at the fine arts schools, set up in Tetouan in 1945 and Casablanca in 1950. Unfortunately, there is as yet no museum of contemporary art, but there are frequent exhibitions in galleries in Rabat, Casablanca and Marrakech. Major abstract painters include Ahmed Cherkaoui (died 1967), Jilali Gharbaoui, Saâd Hassani, Mohammed Kacimi and Fouad Belamine. Mehdi Qotbi produces vast expanses of calligraphic signs, while Farid Belkahia works with wood, animal skins and natural pigments to produce objects and canvasses, using ancestral symbols and archetypes.

Naïve painting has an important place in the Moroccan art scene. The Galerie Frédéric Damgaard in Essaouira has enabled many local artists to exhibit and live on their work, and an 'Essaouira school' of painting has emerged, filled with movement and joyful figures. Leading figures include Abdallah El Atrach and Rashid Amerhouch. Of Morocco's self-taught naïve painters, the best known is Chaïbia, who produces raw and colourful scenes of daily life. And then there is Saladi Abbès, a native of Marrakech, creator of an ironic universe, of trees and birds, orchards and checkerboards, and strange cyclops-like creatures. Naked, both male and female, shown in Egyptian profile, their faces tapering to muzzle shape, Saladi's beings inhabit paradisiac gardens –

or fly through the air with the birds. For some say that in Morocco, when a person dies, a bowl of water is left on their tomb for the birds. Coming down to drink, they may bear the soul of the deceased away to paradise.

Urban and rural crafts

Morocco has long had a reputation as a country with a vivid and imaginative craft industry, and the visitor will not be disappointed. Collections of traditional arts and crafts from recent centuries are held at the Musée Dar Saïd in Marrakech, the Musée Dar Jamaï in Meknès and the Dar Batha in Fès. The souks of the historic cities are full of vivid pottery and carpets, the delicate tracery of wrought iron, polished thuya wood and beautifully worked leather. Basically, the traditional arts divide into two categories, rural and urban. Urban crafts are generally taken to be more refined, displaying an Andalucían influence. Rural crafts, generally from the Berber-speaking regions, have provided a rich source of inspiration for contemporary designers.

But rural and urban crafts are in many ways very different. Rural craft items – carpets and woven items such as saddle bags and tent strips, pottery, jewelry – were, and still are to a great extent, produced in very different conditions to urban items. Rural craftwork is solid, practical, made to stand up to long years of use in places of harsh climatic extremes. Carpets and pottery are made by women, jewelry and metal utensils by men. The signs and symbols used to decorate these items are generally geometric, arranged in simple, repetitive combinations to pleasing effect. Lines, dots and dashes, lozenges and squares are combined to cover surfaces made from clay, metal and wool. Sometimes these decorative forms are linked to the tribal marks tattooed on women's faces and arms. The isolation of rural communities meant that the peoples of different areas could develop very individual styles of craftwork. This is apparent in weaving, clothing and women's jewelry. But given the fact that craft-made items were subject to harsh conditions of use, few pieces can be safely said to be more than 100 years old.

Striking colour and form are often features of rural crafts. Made from thick wool, the carpets of the Middle Atlas, used both as mattresses and blankets, may have striking red and deep brown backgrounds. Carpets from the Haouz Plain (Marrakech region) also have strong orange-red backgrounds. The jewelry of southern Berber communities was once made by craftsmen Jewish by confession. It is always silver; necklaces include silver tubes and spheres, along with *tozra*, oversized orange copal beads. *Serdal*, silk headbands hung with silver coins and coral beads and *khalkhal* ankle bracelets are also worn. Simple enamel cloisoné work is another feature of southern jewelry. Pottery varies greatly from region to region, each area having very individual forms. With the spread of cheap plastic and enameled utensils, many of the local forms are disappearing.

In contrast, urban craft items are generally produced by men, often working in structured corporations. While the women folk of nomad tribes produced for their own use, men in towns were working to sell their produce. They did not, however, build up sufficient capital to develop production on a large scale. City craftsmen produced carpets, jewelry, pottery, leather items and metal ustensils. They worked the raw materials for their production. Urban jewelry is in gold, set with precious stones, and very finely worked. Pottery was enamelled and decorated with designs flowing and floral, as well as geometric. The leather workers produced footwear (*belgha*) and high quality bindings for the sacred texts. Traditional copper work included chandeliers, lamps, kettles, trays and perfume sprinklers. Wooden items were often very elaborate – and still are: witness the workshops near the Kasbah des Oudayas, Rabat. There was vogue for mosaic-type marquetry, with wooden furniture and other objects being inset with coloured woods, and precious materials such as mother-of-pearl and ivory.

There was one area of craft production (excluding the arts of cooking) in which city women were highly active: embroidery. Each region had its characteristics. *Aleuj* embroidery, said to have been introduced by Christians converted to Islam, includes gold thread. Salé embroidery is sobre and geometric, while Azzemour women embroidered mythical beasts and birds. Sadly, many of these techniques and motifs now only survive in museum collections.

It is perhaps in dress that urban crafts have best resisted change. Although most Moroccans, both women and men, dress Western style in the cities, traditional dress is alive and well. A full-blown wedding requires the bride to be displayed to guests in various costumes – the most expensive and elaborate being rented. It is deemed more fitting for Moroccan men to wear a long, hooded garment to the mosque over their ordinary clothes. A stylish caftan, a long and elegant long-sleeved gown, generally decorated with brocade motifs, is essential in a woman's wardrobe. Fashions in caftans change from season to season, with new models created by couturières like Zineb Joundy and Tami Tazy much sought after. The *jellaba* is the most common woman's garment. In the 1930s, Moroccan city women began to abandon the *haïk*, the traditional wrap, too constraining for the new ways of living. They adopted the jellaba, a man's tunic with hood, as a garment that respected the need for modesty and was practical. Today the jellaba is worn everywhere, in bright colours and synthetic fabrics, with fantasy embroidery. Things have changed since 1939, when the bourgeoisie of Fès petitioned the pasha to outlaw the wearing of the jellaba by women.

Within living memory, Morocco's cities had very locally specific forms of craft production. Today, certain craft items are mass-produced for the tourist market. And very fine production it is too. However, older items can often be found in the antique shops of Marrakech and Casablanca, where they go for very high prices. The aesthetic qualities of Moroccan craftwork are much appreciated by collectors. Unlike the rest of the Maghreb, and Egypt and the Levant, for that matter, Morocco was never occupied by the Ottomans. Craft production hence retained a certain artistic independence, evolving in great isolation in the case of the mountain areas. As in building – see the 16th-century Saâdian tombs in Marrakech, or the kasbahs of the south – a sureness in aesthetic touch is the hallmark of the best craftwork, be it a Zaïane carpet, a pair of babouches with *khanjar* motif, or a simple blue and white bowl from Fès.

Language

Who speaks what language? when? and to whom? The visitor to Morocco will quickly become aware of the range of languages spoken. Street signs and official notices are in Arabic and French, occasionally in English, people talk to each other in Arabic, Amazigh, French or even a mixture of all three.

Amazigh languages

Amazigh languages are spoken in the mountains, in scattered communities on the Atlantic plains – and in the poorer areas of the big cities. There are three main Amazigh languages: **Ta'rifit** spoken in the Rif mountains of the North, **Tamazight**, spoken in the Middle Atlas, and finally **Tachelhit**, the language of the High Atlas and the Sous Valley. While Tachelhit and Tamazight are fairly mutually comprehensible, Ta'rifit is a very different dialect. The Amazigh languages have a rich heritage of oral literature. Down in the Algerian Sahara, inscriptions in **Tamashek**, also a Amazigh language, can be seen written in Tifinagh characters. There is no great corpus of literature in Tifinagh, however. After independence, Amazigh gained a foothold in the cities as country people migrated. Although their language has no real presence in the school system, there is a new-found pride in the Amazigh identity. There are newspapers written in Amazigh using Arabic or Latin characters (*Tafoukt*, 'The Sun'), and Amazigh films and dramas circulate on video-cassette. It remains to be seen whether written forms of the Amazigh languages will gain currency, rather as the Celtic languages were revived in the British Isles.

The jeweller's craft

Jewellers must be masters of many crafts. Those in Morocco certainly are. The many types of metal and insets require great skill.

Engraved jewellery is popular. The craftsman prepares his silvered plates and moulds them to shapes . He then smears them with 'jewellers black', a preparation made from oil. When this is dried he removes with a dry tip the lines he intends to work on, and eventually the pattern emerges. He sets up his metal on a tripod called a h'mar el aoued, or 'wooden donkey', and carefully chisels where he had previously drawn. This three-dimensional work is very skilful, particularly where the work is fine and the ornament small.

Jewellers must also be masters of the art of gilding. In earlier days this process was done with veneers of thin gold leaves or powdered gold, mixed with fish glue which was then baked in a small wood fired oven. Today the gilding is done with an amalgam of powdered gold and a mercury base. This is brushed on to the base metal and then heated, leaving a small film of gold. This process is repeated many times until the desired thickness of gold has been deposited.

Enamelled jewellery is very popular. Described simply, the shape for the decoration was scraped out of the metal and the liquid enamel was poured in. An alternative method was to place the powder in the desired shape and use fire to vitrify the enamel. In the southwest of the country and in the Meknès region, jewellers still prepare their insets in their traditional way. Small enclosures are constructed with silver wires by welding them to the surface of the ornament. These circular and geometric spaces are filled with a dough of enamel paste which is then exposed to heat, care being taken not to melt the silver surround. Colours are obtained from copper (green), lead (yellow) and cobalt (blue).

Unfortunately, there is much prejudice against them in official languages. Many urban Moroccans just dismiss languages of the Amazigh group as crude country 'dialects'.

The Arabics of Morocco

Arabic is a little like German in that is has a prestigious written version, generally called **Classical Arabic** in English, and numerous spoken dialects. Spoken **Moroccan Arabic**, *al darija al maghribiya*, is learned at home and is the everyday language of the cities, the dialects of Fès and Meknès being the most prestigious. *Fusha* (pronounce fus-ha) or formal written Arabic is the language of law, religion, official government activities and political speeches. It is learned, often with some difficulty, at school. In grammatical terms, there is a considerable gap between Classical Arabic and Moroccan. In some quarters of academia, there have been calls for Moroccan Arabic to be made an official language – an unlikely possibility, since there is no standardised written form.

French & Spanish

Thus, for the time being, **French** is the language of business, science and higher education, while a mixed language, **Franco-Arabe**, is used by much of the urban educated elite on many occasions. **Spanish** – in part thanks to the availability of Spanish television – is spoken and often understood in the North. It has largely been replaced by French as the second language in the former Spanish Sahara. However, with Morocco's state schools continuing to decline and the French schools heavily oversubscribed, the Spanish schools have become very popular. With an eye to helping business interests, the Spanish government is showing signs of seeking to promote the language in Morocco, especially given Spaniards' general low level of ability when it comes to learning foreign languages.

A complex linguistic situation

The Moroccan language situation is complex – and changing. Behind the multi-lingual screen lie a range of personal attitudes and aspirations. How you get on in life is linked to your language ability, and few Moroccans have any doubt that mastery of at least one

European language is essential for access to science and technology. French is certainly still vital for achieving a useful university degree. At the same time, there is a very strong tradition of learning in Arabic, cultivated in mosques like the Qaraouiyine in Fès by generations of 'ulema (scholars). The future of the Amazigh languages will be interesting to observe. From the mid-1990s, the lunchtime TV news was broadcast in all three Amazigh languages. It remains to be seen how these languages will develop in urban areas – or whether second generation rural migrants will switch wholly to Arabic. And there is the question of whether the Amazigh languages will eventually achieve anything more than a symbolic presence in schools. After all, they are the mother-tongue of at least a third of Morocco's population. For the moment basic literacy in classical Arabic, the language of Islam, looks set to maintain its position in the education system. But there are new trends emerging. Parents with means put their children in bilingual schools as a matter of course. Written Arabic is important to many ideologically, but is of little use on a job market where technology and business skills are all.

Music

Morocco's linguistic diversity is no barrier to appreciating music and as a glance at any pirate CD and cassette stall will show, tastes are very eclectic indeed. Pirated music is very cheap too, with cassettes still popular (between 12dh and 20dh) along with CDs. Among young women, top selling cassettes are by Arab singers, like the Iraqi Kazem Essaher and Diana Haddad. The latest videos and interviews can be seen on satellite TV – Lebanese pop hits programmes are liveliest. Algerian raï music is popular too; top stars include Khaled, Mami, Cheb Zahouani, Cheb Hosni, Cheb Amro and Faudel. Local *chaâbi* music had gone out of fashion by the late 1990s, only a few of the best known singers like Stati and Jadwane, and groups like Tagada still popular. The 'politically committed' sound of the leading 1970s and 1980s groups still has its fans. You may want to buy tapes by Jil Jilala, Nass el Ghiwane or Lmachaheb. Another popular Moroccan sound is Gnaoua Jazz. Look out for tapes by the likes of Saha Koyo. Western music (*el gharbi*) is popular too, but mainly with the urban middle classes. Adolescents and students go for Bob Marley and Dr Alban, Madonna and Britney Spears, French rappers. 'Romantic' singers like Quebec's Céline Dion also have a following in Morocco.

An Andalucían taste: classical city music

There is of course a more classical taste in music. Moroccan urban music divides into a number of strands: *gharnati*, *el alat el andulsi* and *malhoun*. The latter is perhaps the most accessible form to the ear attuned to European sounds. In top bookshops you may find CD collections of these musical styles. On cassette, *malhoun* artists to look out for include the recently deceased Houcine Toulali from Meknès, Saïd Guennoun (Fès) and Mohammed Berrahal. In the late 1990s, writer Touria Hadraoui was the first woman to sing *malhoun*, and has produced a CD. In the evening, during Ramadhan, Moroccan television broadcasts music by the classical Andalusian-style orchestras. Maybe the violins and lutes, and the mix of solo and choral singing aids the digestion.

Middle Eastern divas and tenors

Also still popular in Morocco – as elsewhere in the Arab world – are the great Egyptian and Syro-Lebanese singers who had their heyday in the 1950s and 1960s. Um Kalthoum, a peasant girl from the Nile Delta who became a diva of the Arab world is popular everywhere. Her songs have probably done more for promoting classical Arabic poetry than any schoolbook. Other great names you may want to look out for from this period include Druze princess Asmahane, Mohammed Abdewahab, Farid El Atrach, the Lebanese divas Fayrouz and Sabah, Najet Es Saghira and the brown nightingale, Abdel Halim Hafez, who died tragically young of bilharzia. Concerts by singers and musicians, both Moroccan and Middle Eastern are regularly broadcast on the RTM.

Entertainment

Thus music is definitely at the heart of Moroccan good times and relaxation. A small traditional orchestra is essential to a good wedding party. Traditional women's groups, the *chikhate*, play to appreciative all male audiences during Ramadhan nights, while a small but lively minority likes a night out clubbing. While Marrakech is held to be a party city, and Tanger gets lively in summer with returning immigrant families, Casablanca has the liveliest nightlife. There are clubs for all tastes though few professional DJs. The trend in 2003? *Musique orientale*, old Arabic hits remixed or generated to suit the dance floor.

Weddings The vast majority of young Moroccans never get near a night club or a rock concert. However, they like to have a good time, as is evident if you happen to get invited to a wedding party. In its most elaborate form, weddings involve several days of festivities, and large sums are spent on ensuring that a fun is had by all (and that family status is maintained). There will be jolly henna party at which the bride will have elaborate patterns done on her hands and feet by a relative or (preferably) an expert *nakkacha*. During the actual wedding party, bride and groom sit upon twin thrones before the assembled guests and receive their best wishes. Custom has it that the bride will appear in seven different costumes, generally hired. (The general logistics of this are handled by a *neggafa*).

Religious holidays Also important as they create opportunities for gatherings of family and friends are the big religious holidays of the Muslim year. There is the Mouloud (celebration of the Prophet Mohammed's birthday, Aïd es Seghir, marking the end of Ramadhan, and Aïd el Kebir, aka Aïd el Adha, 'the Festival of the Sacrifice', two months later, when all right-minded families have a lamb to sacrifice to commemorate how Ibrahim nearly sacrificed his son, who was saved at the last minute when Allah sent a sheep as replacement. No matter how poor they are, it is absolutely vital. Of more pagan origin is the annual celebration of Achoura, a sort of Muslim Guy Fawkes day. Banging on small clay-pot drums, the kids run round the streets collecting small change to light bonfires (*el afiya*) in the street. Cheap and cheerful toys and especially firecrackers are on sale everywhere. On the actual morning of Achoura, you have licence to throw water at anyone you feel like. (Do not go out with important documents on the morning of Achoura).

Amusements ordinary and extraordinary Outside such high days and holidays, Moroccans' free time is spent in ways not dissimilar to those of their Spanish neighbours. In summer, in cities and towns, a paseo of some kind is quite the thing. In the early evening, people throng public gardens and central streets, happy to be out of crowded homes. There is not much to do, apart from eat an icecream or two, but everybody likes to look and be seen. (NB Some would say that *tberguig* or gossip is the number one free time activity).

Access to leisure pursuits depends very much on social and economic status. The children of the wealthy – the *aoulad Lyautey*, schooled in prestigious French lycées – may enjoy equitation and tennis, jetski and even occasional snow-skiing at Ifrane or abroad. Their fathers will probably be golfers, their mothers may nip over to France for a spot of shopping – or down to Essaouira for *thalassothérapie*.

With limited financial resources, the average student or employee has simpler tastes. (Remember that a primary school teacher only makes 2,500 dh a month – a relatively good salary). For a young couple, a big night out will be the cinema. Cheaper cinemas are men-only affairs, showing kung-fu epics and Hindi extravaganzas. Adolescents enjoy cards, pool and, of course, video games.

For most women, social life focuses on the visiting each other in the home, the hairdressers and the weekly outing to the *hammam*. Women in night-clubs will be wealthy or confident professional women in Casa-Rabat - or sex-workers. But right across the country, thanks to satellite TV women and the new magazines, women can experience their big city sisters' entertainments vicariously.

A finally, for the very poorest, entertainments are limited indeed. Making an early departure from a big Moroccan city, you soon become aware of the street children. You see them kipping out under arcades or gazing into nothing, a piece of cloth held to the nose. These are the *chemkara*, the glue-sniffers, those who have fallen completely through the social net. (Nabil Ayyouche's 2001 film *Ali Zaoua* is a moving portrait of street-kid life). And aware of the inequalities, others with the wherewithal to survive clutch the minimal salvation offered by fundamentalist-managed mosques.

Immoral entertainments?

In recent years, purist Salafiya Muslims have been trying to have say in how Moroccans spend their leisure. Their newspaper *El Tajdid* (Renewal) regularly condemns all sorts of activities seen as immoral. Summer 2001 saw the 'battle of the beaches' with Islamist groups squatting whole sections of shoreline in a couple of resorts, organizing sports activities and trying to impose separate bathing areas for women and men. The authorities reacted, preventing Islamist organisations' coaches from getting to the beaches. Potentially more serious was the trial of the supposedly devil-worshipping rock musicians in March 2003.

Tracked by the police for several months, 14 young amateur rock musicians were arrested and brought to trial in Casablanca. Their 'crimes' were never clear, the trial saw the young men interrogated on why they wore black T-shirts, had long hair or sang in English. Liberal-minded Casablancans moved swiftly, organizing sit-ins in front of the court building. There was a storm of protest in the press.

The prosecution's case was clearly incoherent. One theory goes that the arrests were a tit-for-tat move by fundamentalists in the judiciary, reacting to police pressure on supposedly dangerous activists. Morocco's middle class was shaken – even though the 14 rockers were soon released. But then came the Casablanca fundamentalist bomb attacks of 14 May 2003, enabling the authorities to launch a merciless crack-down on the fundamentalist milieu.

The small screen

Television, universally watched in homes and cafés, remains the great entertainment leveler. The national channel, the RTM, provides a diet of Egyptian soaps, South American soaps dubbed into standard Arabic, old Egyptian films, US films dubbed in French, Moroccan théâtre de boulevard, and the usual sports events – with pride of place given to football, along with golf and show-jumping – both royal sports. Ramadhan viewing is characterized by concerts of traditional music and the *causeries religieuses*, sermons given by leading Islamic scholars in the presence of the monarch. However, via satellite channels, Moroccans watch the world. Angry political debates on Arabic international channel Al Jazeera, films in French on 2M, have eager followings. No doubt the various erotic channels have proved an eye-opener. And of course sport is popular viewing among men, especially in cafés. International football competitions are the big draw.

Sport

Morocco of course now has its own sporting heroes. The country has been particularly successful in international athletics. In 1984, Saïd Aouita won the 5,000 metres at the Los Angeles Olympics, and went on to set five world records, ranging from the 1,500 metres to the 5,000 metres. Other Moroccan athletes went on to imitate his success, including Brahim Boutayeb, Olympic 10,000 metres champion in 1988, Khalid Skah and Hichem Guerouj. Women's sport is catching up. At the 1984 Olympics, Nawal Moutawakil unexpectedly won the 400 metres hurdles, the first major title won by an Arab woman in an international competition. Like Aouita, Moutawakil provides a model for aspiring Moroccan athletes to look up to. Events like the Marrakech marathon attract numerous participants and much media coverage.

***Koura* (football)** But football remains the number one spectator sport. At age six or seven, the little lads are out in the street or on a piece of rough ground, kicking a football around. Their heroes are the Lions of the Atlas, the national team. In 2000, Morocco had hopes that its enthusiasm for football would bring it the chance of organising the next Mondial, and construction on a major new stadium was launched. Though the bid failed, the FIFA has promised that the World Cup after Germany will be held in Africa, and Morocco is aiming to be the first African nation to host the event, possibly in cooperation with Tunisia.

Land and environment

Geography

The present-day Moroccan kingdom occupies the northwestern section of Africa. It is the African country closest to Europe, separated from Spain by the Straits of Gibraltar.

The third largest country in the Maghreb (area: 703,000 sq km; Algeria and Libya are bigger), Morocco has beautiful, diverse landscapes, from arid desert to cedar forest, snow-topped mountains and spectacular gorges, oases and olive groves. Energetic traveling in Morocco will take you across a range of habitats, generally unspoiled, often unique. (In tourism terms, this is – or perhaps will be – the country's biggest selling point).

Borders Morocco has a 1,835 km coastline from Saidia on the Algerian frontier to La Gouera on the border with Mauritania, of which a fifth lies on the Mediterranean and the rest faces the Atlantic. The main sea-ports are Nador, Tanger, Asilah, Kenitra, Mohammedia, Casablanca, El Jadida, Safi, Essaouira, Agadir, Tan-Tan, Laayoune and Dakhla. Morocco has long-standing claims to the Spanish enclave cities of Melilla and Ceuta on the Mediterranean coast. Tension with neighbouring Algeria in 1994 led to the closure of the closing of the eastern frontier. The Mauritanian frontier is generally open, although those wishing to take the land route into Mauritania are advised to check before heading for the Deep South. Military action in the Saharan provinces (Laâyoune and southwards) in the 1980s meant that much of the area was off-limits for tourism. It is possible to travel to Mauritania by land, but not back again.

Main regions Traditional regional loyalties in Morocco are largely the result of the topographic divisions of the country. Basically, without wishing to simplify too much, there are nine main regions: the Rif mountains in the North, the agriculturally rich Atlantic plains (from north to south, the Gharb, Chaouia and Abda-Doukkala), Meknès and Fès and their region, the Middle Atlas, the Haouz region of Marrakech, the High Atlas, the Sous, east of Agadir, which takes in the valley of the Oued Sous and the adjacent lands of the Anti-Atlas, the Tafilalet desert areas of eastern Morocco, and the southern desert. Racial, tribal, linguistic and historical elements give these regions distinctive flavours, among which there is both rivalry and co-operation.

Mountains The average altitude for the country as a whole is 800 m above sea level, making Morocco the most mountainous country in North Africa. Huge mountain chains running northeast to southwest dominate the relief. 100,000 sq km of the country's surface area is above 2,000 m in altitude. The High Atlas alone has over a dozen summits exceeding 4,000 m.

The limestone crescent of the **Rif mountains** rises sheer from the Mediterranean, few areas lying below 1,500 m. Highestg peak at 2,492 m is Jbel Tidighine, not far from Issaguene. Together with the outlying Jebala range, these mountains all but seal off the rest of Morocco from the Mediterranean coast. This is the best-watered range in the country. Despite much human pressure, cedars still cover the sides of the remoter mountains and pines and holm oaks cover the crests. There are even heather and ferns on the moorlands on the wetter north-facing slopes. To the south lie the Atlas Mountains in three great chains – the Middle Atlas, the High Atlas and, farthest south of the three, the Anti-Atlas.

Consisting of two separate areas, the **Middle Atlas** is in parts well wooded and fertile, having rainfall to support its forest and moorlands. Best known to visitors is the limestone **Plateau des cèdres**, lying between Khenifra. Here the valleys are thick with oaks and great stands of cedar survive. The terrain is gently undulating and there are numerous small mountain lakes. In winter, snow blocks many routes. In the eastern sector of the Middle Atlas, the land is higher, the Jbel Bou Ibane reaching 3,190 m. The terrain is very rugged, with many slopes almost precipitous. Bou Naceur is 3,343 m and Gaberaal is 3,290 m.

The great mass of the **High Atlas** extends for more than 650 km with 400 peaks over 3,000 m. It acts as a huge barrier, dividing the better-watered Atlantic and Mediterranean areas of the country from the extensive desert regions. The western part of the range, south of Marrakech, called the **High Atlas of Toubkal** after its highest peak, is popular with walkers. Here, very old rocks, resistant to erosion, rise to 4,165 m at Jbel Toubkal, the highest peak. Further east, south of Beni Mellal, north-east of Ouarzazate, lies the **High Atlas of Azilal**, a limestone massif rising to 4,071 m on the long shoulder of the Ighil M'goun. This massif is incised with deep, spectacular gorges and valleys, while some rivers have been dammed to form large lakes. Rain fed slopes have a cover of pine and juniper, much under pressure from cutting for firewood and grazing. Further east again is the **High Atlas of Imilchil**, a region of more arid mountains and chalky plateau between Imilchil and Midelt. (Highest peak: Jbel Ayyachi, 3,737 m).

The **Anti-Atlas** is another impressive range. It extends for 400 km. The highest peak, directly east of Irherm, is Adrar-n-Aklim reaching 2,531 m. There is an eastern extension, **Jbel Saghro**, with the high summits Amalou n'Mansour (2,712 m), Fengour (2,516 m) and Jbel Ougnat. At the western extremity of the range is the Atlantic Ocean. There is minimal vegetation on the mountains, compensated for by surprisingly fertile and green oases valleys, of which the most spectacular is probably the lower reaches of the Oued Ziz, south of Er Rachidia.

The **Jbel Siroua** (pronounced Sirwa) is the connection between the High and Anti-Atlas ranges. It is a vast volcanic outcrop of great height. The ancient black basaltic lava produces a rugged landscape, with deeply carved valleys radiating from the central point of 3,304 m.

The country's richest agricultural areas are the plain of the Gharb, hinterland of Kénitra, and the inland basins around Fès and Oujda. The coastal region, aligned along the Atlantic between Rabat and Essaouira and limited to the east by the High and Middle Atlas, forms a broken plateau of 210 m average height. To the east of the High Atlas and south of the Middle Atlas is the western fringe of the High Plateau, which runs in fuller form through Algeria. To the south of the Anti-Atlas is the western part of the Sahara Desert.

The chains of the Atlas Mountains, both by scale and height, tend to present problems for communications. Travellers should plan to travel over spectacular passes like the Tizi-n-Test (Marrakech – Taroudant) and Tizi-n-Tichka (Marrakech - Ouarzazate) in daylight, so as to see a maximum of scenery. Heavy snows and landslides can disrupt transport through these passes from time to time in the winter and early spring. In most years, the mountain snows have melted away by June.

Rivers

Morocco has a complex set of river systems, the majority running to the sea from the high mountain zone. In the North East, the Oued Moulouya originates in the Middle Atlas and collects the streams of the eastern Rif, before reaching the Mediterranean at Saïdia. The Rif proper is drained by a series of fast flowing streams to the Mediterranean such as the Oued Bou Frah and the Oued M'Ter, but to the south, surface water runs to the Sebou and its tributary the Ouerrha, and thence to the Atlantic near Kenitra. The Jebala region, south of Tanger, is drained by the Loukkos and its tributaries to the Atlantic coast at Larache. Coming down from the Middle Atlas, the Oum Er Rbia drains the Tadla plain before running across the Plateau des phosphates and the coastal plain to the Atlantic. The Oued Tensift drains the Haouz plain around Marrakech. In southern Morocco, two important rivers, the Sous and the Draâ, run from sources in the High Atlas towards the Atlantic. On the south-eastern side of the High Atlas, 'rivers' like the Ghéris and the Guir run southwards in occasional flood to lose themselves in the desert.

Even in the northern rivers, there are considerable variations in flow. The larger streams drawing their sources in the higher mountain areas run for most of the year, fed by snow-melt persisting as late as July. Many *oueds* elsewhere are short-lived.

Climate

As for its landscapes, Morocco has a wide range of climatic types. The northern coastal region is in the Mediterranean climatic zone. However, the classic Mediterranean pattern of mild wet winters and warm dry summers is affected by the proximity of the Atlantic: depressions move across northern Morocco from the ocean, bringing heavier and more reliable rainfall than in much of the rest of the Mediterranean basin. The Atlantic coast in the south feels the moderating influence of the ocean even in summer, thanks to the cold Canaries current.

Away from the coasts, high altitudes and the influence of the Sahara make for a complex set of micro-climates. In general, the further south and east you go, the more you feel the influence of the Sahara, including higher daytime and lower night temperatures together with greater aridity. Increasing altitude in the Atlas reduces temperatures and also means very cold nights in exposed areas, and higher risks of rain and snow in between November and March. Winters can be bitterly cold and wet throughout the Middle and High Atlas. Marrakech averages only 16°C in January, but 33°C in June. Rabat on the coast has temperatures in January of 19°C against 25°C in June.

Rain With so many people dependent on farming for a living, the rains make the difference between a good and bad year for the Moroccan economy. Though winter 2002-03 was particularly rainy, there have been periods of extreme drought, spelling disaster for rural areas. Rabat on the Atlantic coast receives an average of 530 mm of rain, while Marrakech, further south and in the foothills of the High Atlas, receives only 230 mm. In the South East, arid desert conditions prevail. Rain is often in the form of heavy showers, some with intense thunder and lightning. In the north, this can occur at any time of year. During storms there is a high risk of flash floods, with *oued* beds carrying violent spates for short periods. Be very careful of venturing into an *oued* in your four-wheel drive vehicle at such times. If you are going to be travelling to Morocco in the winter, it is as well to have waterproofs with you, as well as good shoes or boots, as it really can bucket down.

The prevailing winds are from the Atlantic Ocean and variably westerly. Occasional winds from the desert to the south, known as the *chergui*, bring high temperatures, very low relative humidity and dust storm conditions, a miserable combination for the traveller. In the Tanger area and the Strait of Gibraltar, a 'levanter' wind from the east can bring misty and cold conditions at any time of the year.

Wildlife and vegetation

All these regional variations in climate, vegetation and relief have given Morocco a diverse and interesting flora and fauna. Although the country is too densely settled to have many large mammals, birdwatchers will find much to twitch about. As pesticides are largely limited to irrigated agri-business estates, the spring flowers can be wonderful, particularly in the north. (See the various Roman sites).

Habitats

Aridlands

Semi-desert scrub is widespread, giving a green hue to wide expanses after the spring rains. In regions even less likely to receive precipitation, the vivid desert flowers appear at very infrequent intervals. On the eastern steppes, clumps of alfalfa grass help to stabilize the fragile soils and sage bush appears here too, an ungainly plant but able to withstand the wind, the cold and the drought. The soft pink flowering tamarisks hold back the sand, while handsome oleanders flower white and red in the *oueds*. Though attractive, the leaves are highly poisonous to animals.

Forests

Morocco's woodlands are both natural and human-made, ranging the mountain cedar forests of the Rif in the north to the great palm forest of the Ziz canyon south of Rachidia. On the plain north of Rabat lies the Mamora cork oak forest, much overgrazed by cattle but just about surviving. Nearby are monotonous expanses of industrially farmed eucalyptus. Natural forest is densest in the Rif – where it comprises holm oaks, juniper and great stands of cedar. On the northern, better watered slopes of the High Atlas, thick trunked junipers and bushy thuya are the main trees, surviving best where too far from human habitation to be cut for fire wood. Walnuts and poplar are the trees of the valleys, while aleppo pine survives in protected areas. In February, in the valleys south of the Atlas, the wild almond, which ought to be the national tree, produces its own breathtaking version of 'snow'.

The cedar forest

Morocco's cedar forest has much receded under human pressure. Maybe 130,000 ha of cedar forest survive, of which 74,000 ha is in the Middle Atlas. A cedar tree may grow over 50 m in height, and live for several hundred years. Mixed in with the cedar trees are pines and evergreen oaks. The cedar forest is a unique natural environment – where leopards are said to survive.

The arganeraies, the rarest woodland

Central Atlantic Morocco, from Essaouira down to Sidi Ifni, is home to the rare argan groves, until recently the most threatened of Morocco's trees. A survivor of a remote time when the region had a tropical climate, the arganier requires a unique climatic cocktail of aridity tempered by ocean mists to survive. Looking for all the world like a wild and wooly version of the olive, the arganier grows over some 650,000 ha, some of which is human-planted in groves. Goats climb into the trees to graze. Most importantly, the oil produced from the soft white heart of the argan 'almond', now internationally recognized for its therapeutic value, is one of the costliest nut oils on the market. And in the production process, no part of the fruit is wasted: the flesh can be fed to pack animals while the hard shell can be used to fuel a brasero.

Recognizing the arganier's importance, Unesco has declared the Essaouira-Agadir region a specially protected biosphere. In the same zone grow the caroubier, the red juniper and the Barbary thuya, whose large underground roots are much used in the Essaouira craft and carpentry industry.

The oases

The date palm is the miracle tree of the arid expanses of southern Morocco. Wherever there is a good supply of water, oases have sprung up. Although the oasis was originally a wholly natural environment, given the pressure on the scarce resources of the desert, it has been 'domesticated' for centuries now. Black *haratine* populations and Berbers kept cultivation going under the protection of nomad tribes. The special *khettara* underground 'canals' were created to bring melt water from the foothills to the oases. Under the protective canopy of the date palms, the ideal oasis has different layers of cultivation, including the pomegranate and crops like wheat, barley, oats and coriander. Today, the palm trees in many Moroccan oases suffer from the *bayoud* fungus. Increasingly, production of food for local consumption is abandoned and the cultivators focus solely on date production. Oases can be rewarding areas for birdwatchers.

Birdlife

Morocco has the greatest diversity of birdlife north of the Sahara with 460 species, of which 11 are threatened with extinction. The untrained eye will spot bright coloured bee-eaters and blue rollers, storks nesting on ramparts and minarets, pink flamingos and the striped hoopoes. Swifts soar and dip over Fes before settling to roost in the ramparts, while many a riad garden has a resident pair of dowdy bulbuls, 'oasis nightingales'. The trill of a *moknine* (goldfinch) can be heard coming out of shops in the souk. Of the raptors, lesser kestrels are often taken for use in obscure magic preparations.

Among the top destinations for birdwatchers are a number of coastal marsh and lagoon sites, including Kariet Arkmane and the Oued Moulouya east of Nador, the lagoon of Moulay Bouselham north of Rabat, Oualidia and Essaouira, and the Oued Massa reserve south of Agadir.

Another top birdwatching location is the Jbel Moussa, near Tanger, where the spring and autumn migrations from and to Europe can be observed. Migratory birds making use of this route to cross the narrow Strait of Gibraltar include storks and vultures, and smaller (by comparison) buzzards and eagles. Such large birds depend on soaring in the thermal currents rising from the land, and hence they opt for the shortest sea crossing possible. Smaller birds tend to migrate on a broad front, often crossing desert and Mediterranean without stopping. Some birds cover huge distances. The rare Eleonora's falcon, which nests on the Purpurine Islands off Essaouira, follows its prey, small song birds, southwards over Africa to spend the winter in Madagascar.

Another rare bird found in Morocco is the bald ibis, to be seen in the Oued Massa National Park and the reserve at Tidzi, south of Essaouira. Once widespread in central Europe, this bird survives in North Africa and the Middle East, nesting alongside the gulls and lanner falcons at Oued Massa.

Reptiles

Morocco's reptilian fauna is among the richest in the Mediterranean region. While Europe has 60 species of reptiles, Morocco has over 90. You will, however, see few lizards and even fewer snakes as many are nocturnal and most shun areas inhabited by man. In tiny shops in the souks, sad chameleons (Arabic: *bouiya*) may be seen clambering in tiny cages – or dried on skewers, no doubt for future pounding into powder to complete a special incense.

Mammals

Morocco's mammalian fauna is also very diverse, including genets, jackals, striped hyena, wild cats, fennecs, gerbils and jerboas, as well as the famed Barbary apes of the Middle Atlas. Wild boar are still common in the Rif, and the endangered Dorcas gazelle can be found in desert regions. The forests of the Middle Atlas also harbour a few elusive leopards – watch how you go. With their nocturnal habits, most of these animals are sufficiently elusive to evade casual visitors. You will, however, see a selection of animal pelts and horns at apothecaries' stalls in the médinas.

Perhaps the most easily observed of the animals are the Barbary apes (French: *magot* or *macaque de Barbarie*), to be found in the Azrou area of the Middle Atlas, and at the Cascades d'Ouzoud near Demnate, east of Marrakech. The Barbary ape can live for up to 20 years. It forages on the ground for food (leaves, roots, small insects), and has been known to enjoy yoghurt, bread and the occasional Flag beer contributed by passing picknickers.

Another observable mammal is the *anzid* or *sibsib*, known as the Barbary squirrel in English, chiefly found in the Anti-Atlas. In the Tafraoute area, you may see children at the roadside offering hapless rodents for sale. In Islam, animals have to be ritually slaughtered with the head turned towards Mecca. As the *sibsib* is said to have medicinal properties, it is licit and makes a delicious tajine.

Insects

Insects are much more easily observed than large mammals. As pesticides are far beyond the means of most farmers, there are beautiful butterflies and a multitude of moths, both in evidence when the spring flowers are in bloom. There are flies both large and small, bees, wasps and mosquitoes; these are not elusive and can at times be too attentive. Scorpions are to be found in arid areas. If bivouacking out, make sure you check your boots in the morning.

National parks

Morocco has a number of national parks, among the most important of which, internationally, is the Oued Massa National Park south of Agadir. In addition to being the haunt of the endangered bald ibis and a wide selection of water and wetland birds, it also has an interesting reptile and mammalian fauna due to its geographical position, which brings together an odd combination of tropical, Mediterranean and Saharan features. Toads, frogs, terrapins, skinks and lizards abound. The Egyptian cobra is reported in the vicinity. The National Park Authority has reintroduced the oryx, ostrich and various types of gazelle, most of which are doing rather well. There are ground squirrels and foxes too. A favourite, however, must be the Egyptian mongoose with its tufted tail. It is said to be very good in tajine.

Wildlife under threat

Most Moroccan mammals manage to evade all but the keenest visitor. Some animals are not elusive enough, however, and you will see shops offering stuffed varans, tortoises – both live and converted into banjo-like instruments – snake skin bags, and the furs of fennecs, genets and wild cats. (Leopard and lion skins are likely to have been brought up from Mali). Widely held beliefs about the efficiency of various animal parts in traditional medicine are borne out by even the most cursory glance at a medicine stall in the souk. With modern medicine out of people's ken due to poor education and cost, traditional lotions, potions and spells find a ready market, putting heavy pressure on the population of crows, owls, chameleons and other lizards. The snakes suffer even more. For the entertainments of Jemaâ el Fna, the Egyptian cobra is much favoured, as is the Puff adder. In some cases, their mouths are sewn up to ensure no-one gets a nasty bite. The ecological consequence of snake collection from the wild is a rapid growth in the rodent population, the snakes' natural snack. Saddest of all are the Barbary macaques. For the first few years of their lives as tools of the tourist trade, they are amusing and seem to enjoy life with their keepers. But on reaching early adulthood, they want to assume a position in the troop, turning aggressive and potentially dangerous in their bid to win top-place in the hierarchy. Happily, however, there are signs that Morocco is waking up to the fact that its wild species and their denizens can be maintained hand-in-hand with the development of sustainable forms of tourism.

Books

There is an abundance of material on Morocco in French, with numerous publishing houses in Casablanca and Rabat (Eddif, Le Fennec, Toubkal) bringing out essays and poetry, history and novels in that language. There is also a tradition of beaux livres, fine albums of art photography on Morocco's cities and traditions, and not always idealised either. In Morocco, booklovers will want to call in at some of the bookshops in central Rabat (*Kalila wa Dimna, Le Livre Service*) and in Maârif, Casablanca (*Le Carrefour du Livre*) to look at what's going on in Moroccan publishing. The *Maghreb Bookshop* in Bloomsbury (45 Burton St, London WC1) carries a range of Morocco-related literature. ***The Librairie Chater***, ave Mohammed V in Guéliz, Marrakech, is very good.

Arts & crafts **Ouazzani, T'hami** *La colline des potiers* Casablanca: Editions LAK International (1993). An introduction to the pottery of Safi. A superbly produced book which will no doubt become a collector's item. **Huet, K and Lamazou, T** (1988) ***Sous les toits de terre*** Casablanca: Belvisi/Publication. A superb portrait in coloured line drawings and text of life in the Vallée des Aït Bougmez.

Cities & architecture **Pochy, Y and Triki, Hamid**, ***Médersa de Marrakech*** Paris: EPA (1990). Magnificent photograph album of the Médersa Ben Youssef in Marrakech. **Revault, J, Golvin, L, et al**, ***Palais et demeures de Fès*** Paris: CNRS (1985).

Art Good bookshops in Rabat and Casablanca will also stock books on contemporary Moroccan painters like Cherkaoui, Chaïbia and Belkahia. If you are a fan of Orientalist painting any of the ACR coffee table books are well worth looking out for. See for example **Thornton, Liz** ***Les orientalistes, peintres voyageurs, 1828-1908*** Paris: ACR (1983) and ***La femme dans la peinture orientaliste*** Paris: ACT (1985).

Ethnography Morocco has attracted a good deal of scholarly interest from anthropologists based in US universities. The following could be worth a look. **Bennani-Chraïbi, Mounia** ***Soumis et rebelles, les jeunes au Maroc*** Casablanca: Editions Le Fennec (1994). Good, readable account based on interviews on what it feels to be young and aspiring in Morocco today. **Crapanzano, Vincent** ***Tuhami, story of a Moroccan*** Chicago University Press (1980). Life and times of an illiterate Moroccan tilemaker – and a great storyteller. 'Probes the limits of anthropology' says the blurb. Worth reading. **Dwyer, K** ***Moroccan Dialogues: Anthropology in Question*** Baltimore: John Hopkins University Press (1982). A classic of anthropology writing. **Mernissi, F** ***Beyond the Veil: Male/Female Dynamics in Modern Muslim Society***, London: Al Saqi. **Mernissi, F** ***The Harem Within. Tales of a Moroccan Girlhood*** New York: Bantam Books (1994). **Westermarck, E** ***Ritual and Belief in Morocco*** London: Macmillan (1926).

History **Abun-Nasr, J M** ***History of the Maghreb in the Islamic Period*** Cambridge: CUP (1987). Densely written scholarly account of the Islamic history of North Africa. **Blunt, W** ***Black Sunrise*** London: Methuen (1951). The life and times of Moulay Ismaïl, Emperor of Morocco 1646-1727. **Bovill, E W** ***The Golden Trade of the Moors*** Oxford: OUP (1968).

Novels

There is a growing amount of contemporary fiction in Arabic and French. The most translated writers include Tahar Ben Jelloun, Mohammed Choukri and Driss Chraïbi. The latter's *Le Passé simple* is an outstanding autobiographical piece of writing. You will probably easily find Paul Bowles' translations of stories by Mohammed Mrabet and Driss Ben Hamed Charhadi. Also translated are Brick Ousaïd and Abdelhak Serhane. If you read French, look out for Lotif Akalay (*Les nuits d'Azed*), Mahi Binebine, and Fouad Laroui. Rachid O. (*L'enfant ébloui, Plusieurs vies*) and Paul Smaïl (*Vivre me tue*) are both published in France, but write with a vigourous spoken-language style. Mohammed Berrada and Mohammed Zezaf are among the most highly regarded of the Arabic language novelists.

European writers working in a Moroccan background or on North African themes include: **Busi, Aldo** ***Sodomies in Elevenpoint*** London: Faber and Faber (1992). The title sets the tone. Adventures of an Italian novelist in Agadir and Taroudant. **Goytisolo, Juan** ***Makbara*** London: Serpent's Tail (1993). Surreal tale shifting between Morocco and Paris by Spain's leading writer – who resides partly in Marrakech. **Hughes, R** ***In the Lap of the Atlas*** London: Chatto & Windus (1979).

Photography

Betsch, William ***The Hakima, a tragedy in Fez*** London: Secker and Warburg (1991). A superbly atmospheric collection of photographs of contemporary Fès. Well worth looking for – a collector's item. **Rondeau, Gérard** ***Figures du Maroc*** Casablanca: Eddif (1997). Black and white portraits of Morocco's intellectuals, musicians, writers and painters. A who's who of the country's artistic life.

Travel writing

Maxwell, Gavin ***Lords of the Atlas*** London (1966). **Meakin, B** ***The Land of the Moors*** London (1901). **Ogrizek, Doré** ***L'Afrique du Nord*** Paris: Editions Odé (1952). **Potocki, Jean** ***Voyage en Turquie et en Egypte, en Hollande at au Maroc*** Paris: Fayard (1980). **Potocki, Jean** ***Voyage dans l'Empire du Maroc fait en l'année 1791*** Paris: Dédale (1997). **Secret, Dr Edmond** ***Les sept printemps de Fès*** Privately published (1990). Memoires of one of the first French doctors to work in Fès. **Vieuchange, M** ***Smara: The Forbidden City*** New York: Ecco Press (1987, reprint). A heartbreaking account of a painful and fatal journey. **Wharton, Edith** ***In Morocco*** London: Macmillan (1920). You could also look out for writing by **St Exupery, Antoine de** ***Wind, Sand and Stars*** or ***Southern Mail*** and by **Landau, Rom** writing in the 1950s and 60s, something of an apologist for the Morocco he found.

Tangerine letters

Off all Moroccan cities, Tanger generated the most interest in the world of Anglo-American and European letters. Look out for novels by **Paul Bowles**, also his translation of **Mohammed Chokri**'s *For Bread Alone*, an account of growing up poor and Moroccan in the 1960s Rif, or anything by another Bowles' protégé, **Mohammed Mrabet** (*Love for a Few Hairs*). On the atmosphere in the City of the Straits in the 1950s, sift through *The Letters of William S. Burroughs* (London: Viking Press, 1983). Try **John Hopkins** *All I wanted was company* (London: Arcadia, 1999) and **John Haylock**'s *Body of Contention* (London: Arcadia, 1999) set in an imaginary Tanger hotel in the 1960s (typical character: Rhoda, resident grande dame, who has taken a platonic interest in Abdesalam). Fans of all things Tangerine will need Paul Bowles' Photographs (Zurich: Scalo, 1994, ed Simon Bischoff). Lots of black and white views of a Morocco that was. More recent fine black and white photography of the city can be found in **Jellal Gastelli**'s *Tanger, vues choisies* (Paris: Eric Koehler, 1992). For those who read French, **Daniel Rondeau**'s *Tanger et autres Marocs* is an insider's portrait of the city (Paris: Nil Editions, 1997).

Post-beat travel writing

After the Beat Generation, Anglo-Saxon literary interest in Morocco rather died off. However, look out for **Esther Freud**'s (1992) *Hideous Kinky* (London: Penguin), a child's view of travels with a hippy mother in search of primal religious experience. (See also the recent film). For the worst of Morocco, see **Sylvia Kennedy**'s (1992) *See Ouarzazate and*

Die (London: Abacus Travel), journeys with a jaded former EFL teacher. A travelogue in which the *kif* sellers are always swarthy, the German blondes spaced out and looking for a cause for tears and confrontation. Sample sentence: "Abdul and his friends still sat at the café... shades clamped on their noses, baying about Arab dignity".

Trekking Here there is little available in English, apart from: **Dickinson, M** *Long Distance Walks in North Africa* Crowood Press (1991) and **Smith, Karl** *The Atlas Mountains, a walkers' guide* Milnthorpe: Cicerone (1989). In Morocco, you could look out for books in French, including **A Fougerolles'** *Le Haut Atlas central*. Guide alpin with many good diagrams and maps, and **Michel Peyron's** *La grande traversée de l'Atlas marocain*, (also apparently available in an English version), which describes trekking in the Toubkal region and beyond. There may be material available on ski trekking in bookshops in Marrakech or at one of the Oukaïmeden hotels.

Wildlife **Bergiers, P and Bergier, F** *A Birdwatcher's Guide to Morocco* Perry: Prion Ltd. This is a slim but useful guide to the best localities in Morocco for bird observation. Good site maps and fairly comprehensive species list. **Blamey, M and Grey-Wilson, C** *Mediterranean Wild Flowers* London: Harper Collins (1993). Beautifully illustrated and comprehensive guide to the flowers of this region. Biased towards coastal localities and not particularly easy for the non-specialist to use. Many Moroccan endemics are not described. Highly recommended nonetheless. **Cremona, J and Chote R** *The Alternative Holiday Guide to Exploring Nature in North Africa* Ashford. Difficult to obtain, but a very good general introduction to the flora and fauna of North Africa. Insufficiently detailed for the specialist, however, but good coverage of Moroccan wildlife, including that of desert regions. **Haltenorth, T and Diller, H** *Collins Field Guide to the Mammals of Africa including Madagascar* London (1980). Although continent-wide in scope, contains a considerable amount of useful data on mammals in Morocco. **Hollom, PAD, Porter, RF, Christensen, S and Willis, I** *Birds of the Middle East and North Africa* (1988). This is the definitive guide to the birds of this region but must be used in conjunction with a guide which covers birds in Europe such as **Peterson, Mountford et al's** *A Field Guide to the Birds of Britain and Europe*.

Road maps The late 1990s saw a spate of road improvement schemes across Morocco. The road maps available in 2000 had not kept pace. The **Michelin 959** was probably the most accurate, although not much cop for *pistes* (unsurfaced roads). The **Geo Center World Map**, 1:800,000 scale, is another option, although inaccurate for the region south of Azrou, for example, while the heading 'other minor roads' includes both tarmac surfaced road and difficult piste – see for example the region of the Atlas north of Skoura, El Kelaâ des Mgouna and Boumalne du Dadès. Maps identify roads by letters and numbers (P = *parcours*, ie main road, S = *route secondaire*, generally tarmac surface). Road signs, bilingual in Arabic and Latin letters, rarely show route numbers at all. Note that Morocco does not use the Arabic numerals in use in the Middle East. If you need more detailed maps, try the **Institut géographique national** (IGN), 107 R de la Boétie, Paris 75008 which may supply 1:100,000 scale maps with latitude and longitude, useful if you are working with a GPS system.

Footnotes

522 Language in Morocco

532 Glossary

536 Food and cooking glossary

537 Index

540 Shorts

541 Maps

542 Credits

543 Acknowledgements

545 Advertisers' index

548 Map symbols

549 Colour maps

Language in Morocco

Moroccan Arabic

For the English speaker, some of the sounds of Moroccan Arabic are totally alien. There is a strong glottal stop (as in the word 'bottle' when pronounced in Cockney English), generally represented by an apostrophe, and a rasping sound written here as 'kh', rather like the 'ch' of the Scots 'loch' or the Greek 'drachma'. And there is a glottal 'k' sound, which luckily often gets pronounced as the English hard 'g', and a very strongly aspirated 'h' in addition to the weak 'h'. The French 'r' sound is generally transcribed as 'gh'. Anyway, worry ye not. Moroccan acquaintances will have a fun time correcting your attempts at pronouncing Arabic. And for those with a little French and/or Spanish, the word lists after the Arabic section will be a handy reminder.

The language section here divides into three parts: Moroccan Arabic, a short section of Tachelhit Berber for the mountains (useful for reading topographic names), and a final section of French and Spanish. For Arabic and Tachelhit, the symbol ' ' is used to represent the English 'ee' sound. An apostrophe represents the glottal stop, as in the word *sa'a* (hour), for example. As mentioned above, Arabic has two sorts of 'h', and a capital H is used to represent the strongly aspirated sort.

Polite requests and saying thank you

excuse me, please – *'afek* (for calling attention politely) – عفاك
please – *min fadhlek* – من فضلك
one minute, please – *billatí* – بلاتي
(to call the the waiter) – *esh-sheríf* or *ya ma'alem* – الشريف / يامعلم
thank you – *teberkallah alík/Allah yekhallík* – تبرك الله عليك
thank you – *shukran* – شكرا

Saying hello (and goodbye)

Good morning – *sabaH el-khír* – صباح الخير
How's things? – *kí yedirkí dayir?* – كي داير ؟ كي يدير
Everything's fine – *el Hamdou lillah* (lit Praise be to God) – الحمد لله
Everything's fine – *kull shay la bas* – كل شيئ لاباس
Congratulations – *mabrouk* – مبروك
Goodbye – *bisslema* – بسلامة
Goodbye – *Allah ya'wnek* – الله يعاونك

Handy adjectives and adverbs

Like French, Moroccan Arabic has adjectives (and nouns) with feminine and masculine forms. To get the masculine form, simply knock off the final 'a'.
good – *mezyena* – مزيان
happy – *farhana* – فرحانة
beautiful – *jmíla, zwína* – جميلة
new – *jdída* – جديدة
old – *qdíma* – قديمة
cheap – *rkhíssa* – رخيسة

clean – *naqía* – نقية
full – *'amra* – عامرة
in a hurry – *zarbana* – زربانة
quickly – *dghiya dghiya* – دغية دغية
it doesn't matter – *belesh* – بلاش

Quantities

a lot – *bezaf* – بزاف
a little – *shwíya* – شوية
half – *nesf* – نصف

Numerals

one – *wahed*
two – *zouj or tnine*
three – *tlata*
four – *arba'*
five – *khamsa*
six – *setta*
seven – *saba'*
eight – *tmaniya*
nine – *ts'oud*
ten – *ashra*
eleven – *hedash*
twelve – *t'nash*
thirteen – *t'latash*
fourteen – *rb'atash*
fifteen – *kh'msatash*
sixteen – *settash*
seventeen – *sb'atash*
eighteen – *t'mentash*
nineteen – *ts'atash*
twenty – *'ashrine*
twenty-one – *wahed ou 'ashrine*
twenty-two – *tnine ou 'ashrine*
twenty-three – *tlata ou 'ashrine*
twenty-four – *'arba ou 'ashrine*
thirty – *tlatine*
forty – *'arba'ine*
fifty – *khamsine*
sixty – *sittine*
seventy – *saba'ine*
eighty – *temenine*
ninety – *t'issine*
one hundred – *miya*
two hundred – *miyatayn*
three hundred – *tlata miya*
thousand – *alf*
two thousand – *alfayn*
three thousand – *tlat alaf*
one hundred thousand – *miyat alf*

Days of the week

Monday – *nhar el itnayn* – نهار الاثنين
Tuesday – *nhar ettlata* – نهار الثلاثاء
Wednesday – *nhar el arba* – نهار الاربعاء
Thursday – *nhar el khemís* – نهار الخميس
Friday – *nhar el jema'* – نهار الجمعة
Saturday – *nhar essebt* – نهار السبت
Sunday – *nhar el had* – نهار الحد

A few expressions of time

today – *el yawm* – اليومة
yesterday – *el-bareh* – البارح

Footnotes

tomorrow – *ghedda* – غدة
day after tomorrow – *ba'da ghedda* – بعد غدة
day – *nhar* – النهار
morning – *sbah* – الصباح
midday – *letnash* – لاتناش
evening – *ashíya* – العشية
tonight/night – *el-líla/líl* – الليلة / الليل
hour – *sa'a* – ساعة
half an hour – *nes sa'a* – نصف ساعة

Miscellaneous expressions

Watch out! (as a mule comes careering down the street) – *balak! balak!*
No problem – *ma ka'in mushkil*
How much? – *bayshhal? aysh-hal ettaman?*
Free (of charge) – *fabor*
Look – *shouf* (pl *shoufou*)
OK, that's fine – *wakha*
Good luck! – *fursa sa'ída*

At the café

tea – *ettay* – التاي
weak milky coffee – *un crème* – قهوة بالحليب
half espresso, half milk – *nes nes* – نص نص
a small bottle – *gara' sghira* – قرعة صغيرة
a large bottle – *gara' kbíra* – قرعة كبيرة
a bottle of still mineral water – *gara' Sidi Ali/Sidi Harazem* – قرعة سيدي علي
a bottle of fizzy mineral water – *gara' Oulmes/Bonacqua* – قرعة اولماس
ashtray – *dfeya, cendrier* – طفاية
do you have change? – *'indak sarf/vous avez de la monnaie?* – عندك الصرف

At the restaurant

bill – *l'hseb* – لحساب
fork – *foursheta, lamtíqa* – فورشتة / لمتيقة
knife – *mous, mis* – موس
spoon – *mu'allaka* – معلقة / عاشق
glass – *ka's* (pl *kísan*) – كاس / كيسان
bowl – *zellafa* – زلافة
plate – *tobsil* – تبصيل
could you bring us some more bread – *afak tzídna khubz*– عفاك تزيدنا الخبز

Food and drink

bananas – *mouz* – موز
beef – *lham bagri* – لحم بقري
butter – *zebda* – زبدة
bread – *khobz* – خبز
chicken – *djaj* – دجاج
chips – *btata maklya, frites* – بطاطة مقلية
egg – *bíd* (sing *bída*) – بيض / بيضة

Footnotes

fruit – *fekiha* – فواكه
mandarins – *tchína* – تشينة
mutton – *lham ghenmí*– لحم غنمي
milk – *hlíb* – حليب
olive oil – *zít zítoun* – زيت زيتون
oranges – *límoun* – ليمون
rice – *rouz* – روز
tomatoes – *ma'tísha* – مطيشة
vegetables – *khudra* – خضرة
water – *ma* – ماء

At the hotel

room – *el-bít/la chambre* – البيت
bed – *tliq, farsh* – تليق / فراش
mattress – *talmíta* – طلميتة
shower – *douche* – دوش
without shower – *bila douche, sans douche* – بلا دوش
key – *es sarrout/la clef* – السروت
blanket – *ghta'/couverture* – غطاء
sheet – *izar/le drap* – ازار
corridor – *couloir* – كولوار
noise – *sda'* – صداع

At the hotel – a few requests and complaints

Can I see the room, please? – *Afak, mumkin nshouf el bít* – عفاك ممكن نشوف البيت
The water's off – *El ma maktou'a* – الماء مقطوع
There's no hot water – *El-ma skhoun ma ka'insh* – الماء سخون ماكاينش
Excuse me, are there any towels? – *Afak ka'in foutet* – عفاك كاين فوطاط
Could you bring us some towels? – *Mumkin tjíbilna foutet* – ممكن تجيب النا فوطاط
The washbasin's blocked – *El lavabo makhnouk* – الافابو مخنوقة
The window doesn't close – *Esh sherajim ma yetsidoush* – الشراجم مايتسدوش
Can you change the light bulb? – *Mumkin tebedil el bawla* – ممكن تبدل البولة
The toilet flush doesn't work – *La chasse ma tekhdemsh* – لاشاس ماخدامش
There's a lot of noise – *Ka'in sda' bezef* – كاين صداع بزاف
Can I change rooms? – *Mumkin nebedil el bít* – ممكن نبدل البيت

On the road

Where is the bus station? – *Fayn kayin maHata diyal kíran?* –
فين كاين المحطة ديال الكران
Where is the *CTM* bus station? – *Fayn kayin mHata diyal Saytayem?* –
فين كاين المحطة ديال الستيام
road – *tríq* – طريق
street – *zanqa* – زنقة
neighbourhood, also street – *derb* – درب
bridge – *qantra* – قنطرة
straight ahead – *níshan* – نيشان
to the right/left – *ila l-yemin/sh-shimal*– الى اليمن / الى اليسر
turn at the corner – *dour fil-qent* – دور في القنت
wheel – *rwída* – رويدة

Public transport

aeroplane – *tayyara* – الطيارة
bus – *tobís, Hafila* – طوبيس / حافلة
inter-city bus – *kar* (pl *kíran*) – كار / كيران
customs – *díwana* – ديوانة
express service – *sarí', mosta'jal, rapide* – سريع
luggage – *Hwayaj, bagaj* – حوايج
porter – *Hamal* – حمال
ticket – *bitaqa*, also *warqa* (lit 'paper') – ورقة
train – *qitar* – قطار
How much is the ticket? – *Aysh Hal taman diyal warqa?* – ابش حال الثمن ديال ورقة ؟
I didn't understand – *Ma fehimtiksh* – مافهمتكش
Speak slowly please – *Tekellem bishweyya min fedlek* – تكلم بشوية من فضلك
Could you write that down please? – *'Afak, uktebhu liya* – عفاك اكتب لي

Tachelhit

A few handy expressions to help you function in a village in the High Atlas, plus some topographic words to help you understand the maps. Note that Arabic and French words for numbers are generally understood.

Greetings and things

How are you? (woman/man) – *La bes darim? La bes darik?*
Fine thanks – *La bes*
Please – *Allah yarhum el welidín/'afek /mardi el welidín*
Thank you – *Barak Allaw fík*
thanks (responding to congratulations) – *el agoub alík*
Yes – *ayer, wakha*
No – *oho*

Travelling around

Is Aremd near here? – *Aremd iqarreb zeghí?*
near/far – *iqarreb/yagoug*
It's on the right/on the left – *foufessí/fozlemad*
On your right/on your left – *foufessínek/fozelmadnek*
Go straight ahead – *Zayid goud/níshen*
On foot – *Fudár*
How far is it on foot? – *Mishta nugharas aylen fudár?*
How long will it take me to get there on foot? – *Mishta el waqt ayikhsen afade adrouHagh fudár?*
30 mins/one hour/two hours – *nus sa'a/sa'a/sa'atayn*
Where is Mohammed the guide's house? – *Mani eghtilla teguemí en Mhamid le guide?*
Can you take me to Mohammed's house? – *Izd imkin aystitmellet?*
mule – *asserdoun (m), tasserdount (f)*
How much is it to rent a mule? – *Mishta izkar lekra nesserdoun?*
When does the minibus leave for Marrakech? – *Melouqt arrifough minibus ne Maraksh?*
In an hour? In two hours? – *Zeghík yan sa'a? Zeghík sa'atayn?*
How long does it take? – *Mishta fra naruh?*

In the village

Can we camp here? – *Izd imkin enkhayim ghí?*
Can we find a room to rent here? – *Izd imkin anaf kra la chambre ghí?*
How much for the night? – *Mishta iyad?*

In the shop

Please, do you have – *'afek, íz daroun*
Do you have – *kre (particle to make question)*
Can we buy – *'afek, íz imkin edsagh*
Please give me – *'afek, fkíyí*
bread – *aghroum*
eggs – *tiglay*
Sidi Ali bottled water – *amen Sidi Ali*
salt – *tisent*
meat – *tifiyí*
onions – *azelim*
potatoes – *betata*
tomatoes – *ma'tísha*
almonds – *louz*
walnuts – *guirga'a*
a little – *ímík*
a lot – *agoudí*

Expressions of time

today – *ghassa*
dawn – *zíg sbaH*
tomorrow – *azga*
day after tomorrow – *nefouzga*
next week – *símana yedísoudan*
yesterday – *idgam*

Some numbers

one – *yen*
two – *sín*
three – *krad*
four – *koz*
five – *smous*
six – *sddes*
seven – *sa*
eight – *tem*
nine – *tza*
ten – *mrawet*
eleven – *yen de mrawet*
twelve – *sín de mrawet*
twenty – *ashrínt*
one hundred – *míya*

Landscape words

Tachelhit is given first to help you identify the meanings of the terms found on the maps
adrar – mountain
afella – summit
agdal, aguedal – grazing land (also a garden in Marrakech)

agharas – path, track
aghbalou (pl *ighboula*) – spring (*taghbalout* – small spring)
aghoulid – steep slope
agrour – enclosure
aguelmane – lake
aït – lit 'the people of'
ahir (pl *iheren*) – slow flowing spring
almou – pasture
amen – water
aourir – hill
aserdoun – mule
asif – river which dries up in summer
azaghar – plateau (pl *izghwar*)
azib – shepherd's shelter
azrou – rock
douar – village
ifri – cave
ighil – arm, by extension long mountain
ighir – shoulder, rocky shoulder of mountain
ighzer – ravine
imi – mouth, hole
kerkour – cairn
moussem – annual festival
taddart – house
tagadirt – fortified granary
talat – ravine
tamda – lake
targa – irrigation channel
tighermt – fortified house
tiguimine – house
timzguida – mosque
tizi – moutain pass
taourirt – (pron tawrirt) hill
taslit – fiancée
unzar – rain

And finally, some words for beautiful: *ifulkí* (m) *tfulkí* (f)

French and Spanish

English	French	Spanish
hello	salut	hola
good morning	bonjour	buenos días
good afternoon/evening/night	bonsoir/bonne nuit	buenas tardes/noches
goodbye	au revoir/ciao	adiós/chao
see you later	à tout à l'heure	hasta luego
Pleased to meet you	enchanté	encantado
how are you?	comment allez-vous?	¿qué tal?
fine, thankyou	très bien	muy bien
yes	oui	sí

English	French	Spanish
no	non	no
please	s'il vous plaît	por favor
excuse me	s'il vous plaît/excusez-moi	con permiso
I do not understand	Je ne comprends pas	No entiendo
Speak slowly please	Parlez lentement s'il vous plaît	Hable despacio por favor
Do you speak some English? l'anglais?	Parlez-vous un peu el inglés?	¿Habla usted un poco
What is your name?	Comment vous? Appellez-vous?	¿Cómo se llama?
How do you say XX?	Comment est-ce qu'on dit XX?	¿Cómo se dice XX?
What is this called?	Comment ça s'appelle?	¿Cómo se llama esto?

Some basic vocabulary and phrases

Toilet/bathroom	les toilettes/la salle de bain	los retretes/el baño
where are the toilets?	où sont les toilettes?	¿dónde está el baño?
police/policeman	la police	la policía
hotel	hôtel, auberge	el hotel, la pensión
youth hostel	auberge de jeunesse	albergue turístico juvenil
restaurant/fast food	le restaurant/le snack	el restaurante
post office	les PTT, la poste	los correos
stamps	des timbres poste	los sellos
corner grocery	l'épicerie	la tienda
market	le marché	el mercado
bank	la banque	el banco
ATM machine	GAB guichet automatique	
bureau de change	bureau de change	la case de cambio
notes	billets de banque	los billete/
coins	pièces de monnaie	las monedas
do you have change?	est-ce que vous avez de la monnaie?	¿tiene de la moneda?
cash	du cash/du liquide	el efectivo

Meals

breakfast	petit déjeuner	desayuno
lunch	le déjeuner	el almuerzo
dinner	le dîner	la cena
meal	le repas	la comida
without meat	sans viande	sin carne
drink	la boisson	la bebida
mineral water	l'eau minérale	el agua mineral
fizzy drink	une boisson gazeuse	la gaseosa/cola
wine	le vin	el vino
beer	la bière	la cerveza
dessert	le dessert	el postre
without sugar	sans sucre	sin azúcar

Some useful adjectives

French and Spanish adjectives have masculine and feminine forms, which correspond to noun genders

English	French	Spanish
far	loin	lejos
hot	chaud	caliente (liquid) hace calor (temperature)
cold	froid	frío
That's great	C'est super	¡Qué maravilla!
beautiful	beau/belle	hermoso/hermosa

Travelling around

on the left/right	à gauche/à droite	a la izquierda/a la derecha
straight on	tout droit	derecho
first/second street	la première/deuxième rue	la primera/segunda
on the right	à droite	calle a la derecha
to walk	marcher	caminar
bus station	la gare routière	la terminal
town bus/inter city coach	le bus/le car	el bus/el autobus
city bus stop	l'arrêt (des buses)	la parada
ticket office	le guichet	la taquilla
train station (Morrocan railways)	la gare (de l'ONCF)	la estación del ferrocarril
train	le train	el tren
airport	l'aéroport	el aeropuerto
airplane	l'avion	el avión
first/second class	première/deuxième classe	primera/segunda clase
ticket (return)	le billet (aller – retour)	el billete (de ida y vuelta)
ferry/boat	le ferry/le navire	el ferry/el barco
a hire car	une voiture de location	un coche alquilado

Accommodation

room	une chambre	el cuarto, la habitación
I'd like to see the room	J'aimerais voir la chambre	Me gustaría ver el cuarto
with two beds	avec deux petits lits	con dos camas
with private bathroom	avec salle de bain	con baño
hot/cold water	de l'eau chaude/froide	agua caliente/fría
there's no hot water	il n'y a pas d'eau chaude	no hay agua caliente
noisy	bruyant	ruidoso
(there's a lot of noise)	(il y a beaucoup de bruit)	(hay mucho ruido)
to make up/clean the room	arranger/nettoyer	limpiar el cuarto la chambre
sheets/pillows	des draps/des oreillers	las sábanas/la almohadas
blankets	des couvertures	las mantas
clean/dirty towels	des serviettes propres/sales	toallas limpias/sucias
loo paper	du papier hygiénique	el papel higiénico

English	French	Spanish
Health		
chemist/all night chemist	la pharmacie/ pharmacie de garde	la farmacia
doctor	le médecin	el médico
Do you have the number of a doctor ?	Est-ce que vous avez le numéro de téléphone un médecin?	¿Por favour, tiene el número de teléfono de un médico?
emergency medical services	la SAMU	las urgencias
stomach	l'estomac	el estómago
fever/sweat	la fièvre/la sueur	la fiebre/el sudor
diarrohea	la diarrhée	la diarrea
blood	le sang	la sangre
headache	un mal de tête	un dolor de cabeza
condoms	les préservatifs	les preservativos
contraceptive pill	la pillule	la píldora anticonceptiva
period/towels	les règles	la regla/las toallas
contact lenses	les lentilles de contact	las lentes de contacto
Numbers		
one	un	uno
two	deux	dos
three	trois	tres
four	quatre	cuatro
five	cinq	cinco
six	six	seis
seven	sept	siete
eight	huit	ocho
nine	neuf	nueve
ten	dix	diez
Days of the week		
Monday	lundi	lunes
Tuesday	mardi	martes
Wednesday	mercredi	miércoles
Thursday	jeudi	jueves
Friday	vendredi	viernes
Saturday	samedi	sábado
Sunday	dimanche	domingo
Expressions of time		
today	aujourd'hui	hoy
yesterday	hier	ayer
tomorrow	demain	mañana
day	le jour	el día
morning	le matin	la mañana
midday	midi	mediodía
evening	le soir	la sera
night/tonight	la nuit/ce soir	la noche/esta noche
hour	une heure	una hora
in half an hour	dans une demie heure	después de media hora
later	plus tard	más tarde

Glossary

All terms are Arabic or French, unless marked (Amz) for Amazigh. The spellings generally used in Morocco are given. Note that 'ch' in this system is generally pronounced 'sh', and that 'ou' often represents 'w', ie 'mechoui' is pronounced 'meshwi'.

General background

A

Achoura The first day of the Muslim (or Hijra) year, a lunar month after 'Id El-Kabir, 3 months and 10 days before the Mouloud, the Prophet Mohammed's birthday.
Adrar (Amz) Mountain
Agadir (Amz) Fortified granary in the Anti-Atlas
Agdal, pl. **Aguedal** Garden
Aguelmame (Amz) Natural depression where run-off water collects.
Aghroum (Amz) Bread
Ahidous Group dance in the villages of the Middle and eastern High Atlas (Tamazight-speaking regions).
Ahouach Dance in the villages of the High and Anti-Atlas (Tachelhit-speaking regions).
Aïd (usual English spelling 'Id) Islam has two major religious holidays or 'ids, the first, the 'Id as-saghir, ends Ramadhan, the month of fasting. 'Id al-Kabir, a lunar month later, celebrated with the sacrifice of a sheep, commemorates how Allah sent down a heavenly sheep for sacrifice to Ibrahim, who was about to sacrifice his son Ismael.
Aïn Spring
Aït (Amz) 'Sons of', ie tribal grouping
Alaouite (pron. 'Alawite') The ruling dynasty in Morocco today.
Amarg (Amz) Several meanings: 1. Poetry sung by and for women; 2. Nostalgia; 3. Poetry sung by itinerant musicians.
Amghar (Amz) Broadly speaking 'leader'. Term used in many contexts in Amazigh society. An amghar may be appointed to direct the tribal council or jema'a, also to oversee access to irrigation water in a village.
Almohads (lit trans. 'Unitarians) Berber dynasty which sprang from the Atlas Mountains in the 12th century.
Almoravids First (and short lived) Muslim Berber dynasty, arose in the eleventh century.
Almou (Amz) Summer pasture in damp hollows at high altitude.
Alpinisme Mountain climbing in French.
Amazigh Singular adjective of Imazighen.
Andalucía The South of Spain, from the Arabic 'al-Andalus', the Land of the Vandals, who occupied the area before the Arabs.
Arganier The Argan Tree. A spiney, drought resistant tree. The kernels produce a high quality oil. Species unique to southwestern Morocco.
Arset Orchard – in Marrakech and the South (from the Arabic *gharasa*, to plant)
Assif (Amz) River in the High Atlas, often seasonal.
Astara (Amz) Shoulder-trembling dance performed by women.
Attarine Perfumers, as in 'Souk el Attarine'.
Azib (Amz) Seasonal mountain shelter, originally for animals.

B

Bab Gate, door.
Bahja From Marrakech.
Balgha Soft leather slippers, generally referred to in English as 'babouches'.
Bali (as in Fès el-Bali) Old – for a city area.
Baraka Divine quality inherent in all living beings. Especially present in certain chosen individuals. Holy people like the seven saints of Marrakech and Sidi Chamharouch near Jebel Toubkal have exceptional powers of baraka.
Baydhaoui From Casablanca
Bayoud Fungal infection of the palm tree which has ravaged the oases of North Africa.

Bejmet Small ceramic enamelled bricks.
Bendir Drum
Beni 'Sons of', tribal grouping.
Berber Term used by ethnographers to designate the Tamazight-speaking peoples.
Bildi From the bled, (countryside), local, indigenous, and by extension traditional. Contrasts with *roumi* (foreign, modern).
Bidonville Shanty town. From the French 'bidon', tin can, the main roofing material.
Bir Well
Bkhour Incense. Sba' bkhour, mixture of seven types of incense with strong powers.
Bled Hometown, countryside. Arabic term used in French.
Borj Tower, bastion

C

Caïd Local government official, often with considerable power.
Calèche Horse-drawn carriage.
Cercle Rural administrative unit.
Cheikhate Female dancer-musicians.
Cherif (pl. Chorfa) Descendants of the Prophet Mohammed.
Chergui Hot, dry and dusty wind blowing out of the southeast, especially in summer, raising temperatures to the 40° mark.
Chikhat Women singer dancers in the Beraber lands, performing accompanied by professional musicians (*chikh*). In Atlantic Morocco, term refers to popular women singers with a sulphurous reputation.
Chleuh French term for the inhabitants of the western High Atlas and Anti-Atlas.

D

Dar House – and by extension, the family.
Darak al-malaki The Royal Gendarmerie – highway patrols and police in rural areas.
Dayat Freshwater lake
Dechra Hamlet
Derb Street (in an old city), also neighbourhood.
Dhikr From the Arabic to remind or recall. Religious chanting invoking Allah and the Prophet, essential part of trance ceremonies.
Diffa Ceremonial banquet
Dikka In Marrakech, chanting accompanied by tambourines, often performed for Achoura.
Dir Fertile lands at the foot of the mountains, created where sediment washed down from the mountains fans out onto the plain.
Douar Village

E

Empire chérifien Term used for Morocco during the late 19th century
Erg Sand dune region of the desert.

F

Fantasia Military exercise involving charging tribal cavalry and spectacular feats by riders. Now often performed for tourists.
Fassi From Fès. Things Fassi are held to be of higher quality.
Fasqiya Pool with fountain.
Faux guide (lit. False guide) Anyone from a student hoping for a tip for showing you the town to an all-out hustler. Now heavily repressed by the *Brigade Touristique*.
Fondouk (From the Greek 'pandokeïon', hostelry) Merchants hostel in the city, now often used for craft manufacture.
Fkih, also spelt **fqih** Person learnèd in the religious sciences.

G

Gandoura Men's light-weight long summer tunic.
Gaouri European, pl goura. See also nasrani.
Gare routière Bus station
Glaoua Major tribal confederation which dominated Marrakech for the first half of the 20th century from the mountain stronghold of Telouet.
Gnaoua (from Guinea?) Mystic cult found principally in Marrakech and Essaouira.
Grand taxi Inter-city private shared taxi. Fast and sometimes dangerous.

H

Habous Land or property held under a system akin to the medieval 'morte-main', ie managed as a sort of perpetual endowment to benefit a family or a charitable cause.
Haïk Long cloth wrap for women.
Hamada Stoney plain
Hammam Bath house

Harkous Elaborate geometric henna designs on hands and feet.
Hendira Thick, wool tunic worn by men, especially in the Rif.
Herz Talisman, amulet – also called 'hjab', 'jedoual', 'ktab'.
Hizam Belt

I

Ichelhiyn (Amz) Inhabitants of the western High Atlas, Sous Valley and Anti-Atlas.
Idraren Draren (Amz) 'The Mountains of the Mountains', local name for the High Atlas.
Idrissid Early Moroccan Muslim dynasty (eighth century), founders of Fès.
Imam Essentially, the senior religious figure in a mosque.
Imazighen Lit. 'the free men'. Original Hamitic inhabitans of North Africa. There are three main Amazigh groups in Morocco, speaking respectively Ta'rifit (Znatiya) in the North, Tamazight (Middle Atlas) and Tachelhit (southern areas). The Kabyles and Chaouïa of Algeria are also Amazigh, as are the Touareg of Mali and Niger.
Imi (Amz) Gateway, mouth
Irhil (Amz) Mountain massif, also spelt Irghil.
Itouizi (Amz), **Touiza** (Ar) Co-operative labour in a mountain village.

J

Jellabah Long flowing tunic.
Jema'a Community council in the High Atlas.
Jinan sing. **Jenna** Garden. Jenna is also the Arabic for Paradise.
Jamaâ (often spelt Djam'i) Mosque. From the Arabic root 'jama'a', to gather.
Jbel (pl. Jibal) Mountain (Jeblaoui, mountain dweller).

K

Kasbah Fort, citadel
Khabiya Traditional amphora pot
Khattara Underground water channel
Khayma Tent
Kilim Flat weave carpet
Kif Hashish
Kissaria Market specializing in clothes and fabrics.
Ksar (pl. Ksour) Palace, also fortified village.
Koufic Early Arabic script, often without the dots of later Arabic writing.

L

Lalla Madame. Title of a female saint.
Lila Night. Lila ed-derdeba, nightime Gnaoua ceremony.

M

Ma'alem Master craftsman
Ma'arouf Village ritual in the High Atlas, taking the form of the sacrifice of one or more beasts, a collective meal, and the auctioning of the remaining meat.
Magana Public clock
Maghreb (lit. Land of the West, al-Gharb) North Africa, as opposed to the Machrek, (Land of the East), the Near East. (Al-Maghrib = Morocco; Al-Mamlaka al-Maghribiya = Kingdom of Morocco.)
Makhzen Term used to designate 'the authorities' in a general sense. People with power and influence close to the Palace are said to be 'makhzen'.
Maktoub Lit. 'written', used to refer to an event pre-ordained by God and therefore unavoidable. Concept helpful for overcoming grief and adversity.
Malekite The main rite of Sunni Islam in North Africa.
Maqsoura Compartment or enclosure
Marabout French term used for saint in North African context. In Arabic the term is 'wali salih' or 'sidi' (pl. sadat).
Maristan Hospital
Mechouar Royal parade ground, enclosure near the palace.
Médersa College dispensing education in the Islamic legal and religious studies.
Médina City
Mellah Jewish quarter
Merinids Major dynasty in Morocco, held sway c.1248-1420.
Mihrab Prayer niche in a mosque indicating the direction of Mecca.
Moulay Arabic honorific, 'sir', 'my lord'. Polite form of address.
Mouloud Celebration of the Prophet Mohammed's birthday.

Moussem Annual festival, of religious origin, often centred on a pilgrimage to a saint's tomb. Falling out of use in late 20th century.

N

Nasrani Christian (lit. 'follower of the man from Nazareth'), and by extension European.
Nécropole Ancient cemetery.
Neggafa (pl. 'neggafat') Women responsible for preparing the bride for her wedding.
Nekkacha (pl. 'nekkachat') Women specializing in doing henna designs on the skin.

O

Ottoman Turkey-based Muslim Empire, 13th to early 20th century.
Ouled (lit. 'Sons of') Tribal grouping.

P

Pisé Sundried earth used for building, Arabic 'toub'.
Piste Rough track, generally accessible by all but the lowest slung cars.
Politique des grands caïds French policy of indirect rule in southern Morocco based on support for dominant clans (the Glaoua and Goundafa). Practice similar to British rule through maharajahs in India.

Q

Qibla Wall of mosque facing towards Mecca.

R

Ramadhan Month of fasting in Muslim calendar.
Rays (Amz) (pl. rwayes), Lit. leader, designates poet-singers among the Chleuh. Plural indicates the whole troop of musicians.
Reg Rock desert
Roumi (lit. 'from Rome). Adjective designating things foreign or modern, especially with regard to food and recipes. Used in opposition to things 'bildi', indigenous and traditional.

S

Saâdian Dynasty ruling from Marrakech, 1554-1659.
Sabil Public fountain.
Salafiya Sometimes 'salafiya jihadiya'. Blanket term used in Morocco for various groups promoting extreme versions of Islam
Sidi Honorific. Mr, also refers to a saint.
Skalli Gilt or silver embroidery work
Sunni Mainstream Islam, as opposed to Shi'a Islam, prevalent in Iran.

T

Taghounja (Amz) Lit. wooden spoon. Ceremony to bring rain.
Tamazgha (Amz) Amazigh lands
Tamsriyt (Amz) Reception area, an upper room, often elaborately decorated in a house or kasbah, used by women and men separately for gatherings.
Targa (Amz) Irrigation ditch (Ar. 'seguia')
Tberguig Gossip
Tifinagh Oldest form of writing in Amazigh, predates the Greek alphabet by six centuries. Essentially used by the Touareg in the Sahara.
Tighremt (Amz) Fortified granary in the High Atlas.
Tit (Amz) Spring
Tizi (Amz) Col, mountain pass

U

'Ulema (sing. alim) Persons learnèd in the religious sciences
'Urf Customary law
Villes impériales French 20th century term used to designate the cities where the sultan established his temporary capital, ie Fès and Meknès, Marrakech and Rabat.

Z

Zanka Street, as opposed to 'derb', a residential street.
Zakat Islamic tithe
Zaouia Saint's shrine, a domed, building containing tomb of a wali salih (holy man).
Zellige Elaborate ceramic wall mosaics
Zenata Tribal confederation, ruled northern Morocco in late tenth century.
Zerbia Carpet
Zriba HutIndex

Food and cooking

A

Amlou Runny 'butter' from argan kernels
Arganier Tree producing an almond-like nut. The kernel of the nut produces the highly valued argan oil.
Beghir Thick pancakes often served for breakfast.
Bestila Elaborate sweet and sour pie. made of alternating layers of filo-pastry and egg, pigeon, and crushed almonds. Speciality of Fès.
Bissara Bean and pea soup, working-man's breakfast
Briouet Filo pastry envelopes, filled with crushed nuts and basted in olive oil, then dipped in honey.
Brochettes Kebabs made with tiny pieces of liver, meat and fat.

C

Chermoula Marinade sauce.
Couscous Steamed semolina made from durum wheat, heaped with meat and vegetables. Couscous may also be served with nuts, dates, raisins, sugar and milk for dessert. In the countryside, couscous is made from barley.

F

Fliou Peppermint, also used in tea preparations.

H

Harcha Thick round unleavened 'bread', popular for breakfast.
Harira Chickpea and mutton soup, especially popular when breaking the fast in Ramadhan.

K

Kaâb el-ghizal Gazelles' horns Traditional marzipan filled pastry.
Kahoua Coffee
Kefta Minced meat
Khliaâ Preserved meat (dried, boiled). Fr 'viande boucanée').

L

Likama Mint.
Luiza Verbena herbal tea.

M

Mahchi (or **mo'ammar**) Stuffed (chicken, vegetables, etc)
Mechoui Barbecued meat.
Mqali Meat dishes simmered with sauce reduced rapidly on high flame at end.
Mouhallabiya Milk pudding.

N

Na'na Mint, essential for preparing tea, also called 'likama' The best mint is produced in Meknès.

O

Orz bil-bahiya Paëlla.

Q

Qa'ida Tradition – vital to any meal prepared for guests in a Moroccan home.

R

Ra's el Hanout (lit. 'master of the shop') Special spice mix.
Roumi (lit. 'from Rome). Adjective designating things foreign or modern, especially with regard to food and recipes. Used in opposition to things 'bildi' (qv), indigenous and traditional.
Seksou (Amz) Couscous, qv.

T

Tajine Moroccan stew traditionally cooked slowly in a clay pot on a brasero.
Tajine barkouk Sweet and sour prune and mutton stew.

Z

Zitoun Olives
Zit el oud Olive oil

Index

A

Aaoua Dayat 246
accommodation 42
Adaï 456
Adrar Metgourine 449 450
Afourgan Dayat 246
Agadir 428
Agadir Aglaoui 451
Agadir Id Aissa 451
Agard Oudad 457
Agdz 392
Aghbalou 369
Aghmat 368
Agourai 234
Aguelmane Azigza 247
Aguerdn'tzek 440
Ahouli 421
Aïn Bou Kellal 280
Aïn Diab 126
Aïn Ech Chair 312
Aïn Leuh 244
air
 airlines 46
 airport tax 38
 airports 37
 international 32
 See Also under individual towns
Aït Arbi 401
Aït Baha 440
Aït Ben Haddou 390
Aït Bougmez valley 376
Aït Herbil 451
Aït Melloul 437
Aït Mohammed 405
Aït Ouaritan 404
Akermoud 157
Akka 449
Aknoul 280
Al Hoceima 217
Alaouites 477
alcohol 59
Allamghou 423
Almohads 475
Almoravid Koubba 326
Almoravids 475
Aman Ighriben 450
Amazrou 393
Amellago 406
Ameln Valley 456
Amizmiz 360
Amtoudi 451
Anergui 424
Anezal 447
Animiter 373
Annameur 457
Aoufouss 414
Aoulouz 446
Arbaa Sehoul 105
Arbaoua 111
architecture 499
art 499
 crafts 506
 painting 504
arts festivals 63
Asilah 192
Asni 360
Assaka 455
Azilal 375
Azilal High Atlas 374
Azrou 242
Azemmour 138

B

Badis 219
ballooning 64
Banasa 110
banks 31
Barrage d'El Kansera 234
Ben Slimane 112
Ben Youssef Medersa 327
Beni Mellal 136, 378
Beni Snassen Mountains 301
Berkane 300
Bhalil 272
Biougra 440
birdwatching 147, 82, 184, 437
books 72
borders 512
 with Mauritania 470
Borj Est 415
Borj Yerdi 414
Bou Izakarn 452
Bouanane 312
Bouarfa 310
Boudenib 312
Bouguedra 156
Boujad 136 379
Boujdour 469
Boulaouane 137
Boumalne du Dadès 400
bus travel 48
buses 34
business hours 37

C

Cabo Negro 210
camel trekking 64
camping 46
Cap Beddouza 148
Cap des Trois Fourches 293
Cap Malabata 183
Cap Sim 439 440
Cap Spartel 183
Cap Tafelney 439
car hire 49
car travel 34
Casablanca 116
 airport 37
 architecture 122
 bombings, 14 May 2003 41
 directory 133
 eating 129
 entertainment 130
 Médina 121
 Quartier des Habous 125
 shopping 131
 sights 121
 sleeping 127
 transport 132
Cascades d'Ouzoud 375
Cascades de Mizab 127
Casita 281 288
Cathedral Rocks 424
Caves of Hercules 183
Cèdre de Gouraud 243
Ceuta 199
 directory 204
 eating 203
 history 201
 port information 39
 sights 201
 sleeping 203
 transport 204
Chaouen 211
 directory 215
 eating 214
 sights 212
 sleeping 213
children 26
Cirque du Jaffar 422
climate 514
 when to go 19
clothing 40
 shopping 60
cost of living 32
Cotta 183
cruises 36
currency 30
customs 29
cybercafés 53

D

Dadès Gorge 400
Dakhla 469
Dar Bellarj 328
Dar Caïd Ourika 369
Dar Lahsoune 398
Dar Toundout 398
Debdou 284
Demnate 374
Diabat 160, 164
disabled travellers 26
diving 65
Draâ Valley 391
drink 59
Driouch 288
drugs 29, 41

E

East High Atlas 420
eating
 conduct 40
 restaurant price codes 56
education 488
El Aioun 284
El Hajeb 234
El Hart-n'Igouramène 405
El Jadida 140
 directory 146
 eating 145
 sights 142
 sleeping 144
El Jebha 211
El Jorf 441
El Kebab 248
El Kelaâ des Mgouna 377, 398
El Kolea 440
El Ksiba 247
El Utad 194
El-Atlal 330
email 53
emergency services 37
Er Rachidia 410
Erfoud 414
Erg Chebbi 419
Essaouira 157
 directory 167
 sights 158
 sleeping 161
etiquette 40

F

Feïja 448
ferries 35, 38
Fès 248
 directory 271
 eating 268
 Fes El Bali 256, 262
 Fes el Jedid 254
 history 249
 Qaraouiyine Mosque 261
 Seffarine 262
 sights 254
 sleeping 264
 transport 271
 vantage points 264
festivals 25, 63
Figuig 310
Fint 387

fishing 66
Folk Museum 432
food
See eating
Foum El Hassan 451
Foum Zguid 449

G

gay travellers 26
geography 512
Ghazoua 164
golf 65
Gorges de Méhéoula 143
Gorges du Dadès 401
Gorges du Todgha 404
Gorges of Ziz 411
Gouffre d'Agadir
Imoucha 439
Gouffre de Friouato 279
Goulimine 458
Goulmima 406
Grand Mosque
Agadir 432
Tanger 181
Guercif 281
guesthouses 44
guides 39

H

Hadz Aït Mezzal 440
hammams 131
health 70
Heri al Mansour 234
hiking 69
hillwalking 213
history
arrival of Islam 474
colonial rule 478
post independence 482
pre-Islamic period 472
Sahara provinces 485
tribal dynasties 475
See Also under
individual towns
holidays 62
horse riding 67
hotels 42

I

Icht 451
Ifrah Dayat 246
Ifrane de l'Anti Atlas 452
Ifrane 245
Igherm 447
Ikhsane 446
Imassine 398
Imi Mgourn 440
Imilchil 422
Imi-n-Ifri 374
Imiter 402
Imlil 365
Immouzer des Ida
Outanane 438
Immouzer du Kandar 246
Imzi 439
Inezgane 437
internet 53
Iouzioua Ounneine 446
Islam 493
architecture 499
arrival of 474
Islamic revivalist
movements 485
Islas Chafarinas 298
Isles des Purpuraires 160
Issaguen (Ketama) 215

J

Jbarna 280
Jbel Ayyachi 422
Jbel Siroua 447
Jbel Tazzeka National Park
278
Jbel Tidghine (Tidiquin) 216
Jbel Toubka 367
Jbel Yagour 370
Jemaâ el Fna 322
Jemâa-Sahi 156
Jorf el Melha 222

K

Kalah Bonita 218
Kalah Iris 219
Kariat Arkmane 292
Kasbah Amerhildl 397
Kasbah de Tamnougalt 392
Kasbah El Glaoui 403
Kasbah Hamidouch 157 168
Kasbah of Takoumit 312
Kasbah Tadla 379
Kasbah Taourirt 386
kasbahs 502
Kénitra 105
Kerrouchen 248
Ketama 215
Khemis Zemamra 156
Khemisset 234
Khénifra 380
Khouribga 136 380
Kourkouda 446
Koutoubia Mosque 324
Ksar Asrir 406
Ksar d'Akbar 418
Ksar el Kebir 111
Ksar es Seghir 183
Ksar Ouled Abd el Helim 418
Ksour circuit 418

L

La Gouéra 470
Laâyoune 465
Lac Isli 423
Lac Tislit 423
language 25, 507
in education 488
Larache 195
lesbian travellers 26
Lixus 197

M

M'Hamid 395
M'semrir 405
Ma'adid 414
malaria 71
Mamora forest 104
Mansour Edahbi Dam
386
maps 53
Marabout of Sidi Kaouki 440
Marmar Marble Factory 415
Marrakech 316
airport information 38
Almoravid Koubba 326
Ben Youssef Medersa 327
Dar Bellarj 328
directory 357
El Badi Palace 329
entertainment 351
history 317
Jemaâ el Fna 322
Koutoubia Mosque 324
Musée de Marrakech 327
Saâdian Tombs 328
shopping 351
sights 320
souks 325
tanneries 331
transport 355
Martil 210
Massa 441
Mdiq 210
Mecissi 396
media 54, 489
médina 501
Mehdiya 105
Meknès 226
directory 238
eating 236
entertainment 237
history 227
sights 230
transport 237
Melilla 293
history 293
port infromation 39
sights 294
sleeping and eating 297
transport 299
Mendoubia Gardens 180
Mendoubia Palace 180
Merdja Zerga 109
Merinids 475
Merzouga 419
Merzouga dunes 419
Meski 413
Meski Ksar 413
Mgoun , Massif du 377
Mgoun Gorges 399
M'Hamid 395
Middle Atlas 242
Midelt 420
Mischliffen 245
Missour 282
Mohammedia 134
money
ATMs/cashpoints 30
banks 31
cost of living 32
cost of travelling 32
credit cards 30
currency 30
travellers' cheques 31
Mont Aroui 288
mosques 499
entry for non-Muslims 41
Moulay Abdellah (Tit) 143
Moulay Bousselham 109
Moulay Brahim 360
Moulay Idriss 239
Moulay Ismail 233
Moulay Yacoub 272
mountains 512
Musée d'Art Contemporain de
la Ville de Tanger 181
Musée de Marrakech 327
Mzoura 194

N

Nador 288
port information 39
Nekob 396
newspapers 54, 489
Northern Rif 215

O

Old American Legation 181
Oualidia 146
Ouarzazate 385
Oued Laou 211
Oued Massa Nature Reserve
441
Oued Meskaou 450
Oued Ziz 413
Ouezzane 221
Ouirgane 360, 361
Oujda 304
directory 309
sights 305
sleeping and eating 307
transport 308
Oujda Msoun 281
Oukaïmeden 370
Ouled Teïma 441
Oulmès 369
Oum el Alek 449 450
Oumesnate 457
Oumnass 358
Ourika Valley 368
Outat Ouled el Hadj 282

Footnotes

P

Palmerie 320
parachuting 65
Paradise Beach 438
passports 28
Peñon de Alhucemas 298
Peñon de Velez de la Gomera 298
Plage des Nations 104
Plage Sidi Rahad 138
Plage Tafadna 439
Point d'Igui-n-Tama 439
population 492
post 54

R

Rabat 78
  Archaeological Museum 87
  eating 93
  entertainment 94
  history 79
  Kasbah des Oudaïas 84
  Médina 85
  shopping 95
  sights 82
  sleeping 91
  transport 97
radio 55
Ramadhan 62
Ras Kebdana 292
religion 40, 493
  arrival of Islam 474
  festivals 63
  holidays 62
  Islam 493
  Islamic architecture 499
Remlia 419
restaurants 58
Restinga Smir 210
riads 44
Rich 420
Rif, Northern 211
Rif, Southern 221
Rissani 416
road travel 34
rock art sites 449
Route de l'Unité 216

S

Saâdian Tombs 328
safety 42
Safi 148
Sahara provinces 485
Sahli 312
Saïdia 302
Salé 99
security and terrorism 41
Sefrou 273
Selouane 300
Settat 136
Setti Fatma 369
shopping 59
  See Also under individual towns
Sidi Ahmed ou Moussa 455
Sidi Bennour 156
Sidi Bou Abid Mosque 180
Sidi Bouzid 143
Sidi Harazem 272
Sidi Ifni 460
Sidi Rbat 441
Sidi Smail 156
Sidi YahiaBen Younes 306
Sijilmassa 416
Skhirat 112
skiing 67, 246
Skoura 397
sleeping 42
  mountain refuges 45
  riads 44
  youth hostels 45
Smara 469
Souira Kédima 157
Souk el Arbadu Gharb 109
Spanish Cathedral 180
Spanish enclaves 298
sport 64, 511
  ballooning 64
  diving 65
  fishing 66
  golf 65
  horse riding 67
  parachuting 65
  quad-biking 67
  skiing 67
  surfing 68, 167, 440
  swimming 68
  tennis 69
  windsurfing 68
St Andrew's Church 181
student travellers 26
surfing 68, 167, 440
swimming 68

T

Tabant 376
Tadakousset 451
Tafraoute 448, 455
Tafilalet 412
Taghazoute 438
Taghjijt 452
Tagounite 395
Taguenza 457
Taliouine 446
Tamalt 312
Tamanar 439
Tamaris Plage 138
Tamdaght 391
Tamegroute 395
Tamesloht 358
Tamri 439
Tamtatouchte 405
Tamuda 208
Tan Tan 463
Tanger 172
  airport information 38
  directory 191
  history 173
  Kasbah 178
  port information 38
  shopping 189
  sights 178
  sleeping 184
  transport 190
Taourirt 283
Taouz 419
Tarfaya 464
Taroudant 442, 447
Tata 448
Tattiouine 422
taxi 51
Taza 275
Tazegzaoute 448
Tazenakht 446
Tazezaoute 448
Tazzarine 396
telephones 54
television 54, 489
Telouet 372
Temara 112
Temsi 441
Tetouan 205
  directory 209
  eating 209
  sights 206
  sleeping 208
  transport 209
Thamusida 107
Tifeltoute 387
Tiflet 234
Timadriouine 402
time 37
Timoulay Izder 452
Tineghir 402
Tinejdad 405
Tinfat 446
Tinfou dunes 395
Tin Mal 362
Tinrheras 418
Tioumliline 243
Tioute 448
tipping 40
Tirhmi 455
Tissint 449
Tizi-n-Ichou 248
Tizi-n-Test 365
Tizi-n-Tichka 371
Tiznit 452
Todgha Gorge 397, 400
Torres de Alcalá 219
Toubkal Circuit 368
Toubkal High Atlas 358
Toubkal National Park 365
tour operators 19
tourist information 24, 39
trains
  international 36
  See Also under individual towns
transport
  air 46
  arrival 37
  bicycle 47
  bus 48
  car hire 49
  cruises 36
  domestic 46
  ferries 35
  international 32
  motorcycle 47
  off-roading 50
  road 47
  taxi 51
  trains 52
travellers' cheques 31
trekking 69, 365, 399, 424, 447

V

vaccinations 29, 71
Vallée des Oiseaux 432
Valley of Ouergha 274
vegetation 515
visas 28
Volubilis 239

W

walking 69, 365
websites 24, 71
weights and measures 37
wildlife 515
windsurfing 68
women
  status in Morocco 496
women travellers 27

Y

Youssef Ben Tachfine Dam 441
Youssoufia 137
youth hostels 45

Z

Zaâ Gorges 283
Zaër Forest 112
Zagora 393
Zaouia of Moulay Ali Cherif 418
Zaouia Tafetchna 392
Zaouiat Ahansal 424
Ziz Canyon 413
Zouala 414

Shorts

295 Abd Al-karim – rebel of the Rif
430 Agadir 1541: Portuguese merchants and a warrior dynasty
89 At the top
147 Birds in paradise
253 Building in Fès
273 Bump in the baths
342 Choosing a riàd
298 Colonial confetti: the Spanish enclaves in Morocco
468 Destination Smara – the forbidden city: a journey by Michel Vieuchange
330 El-Atlal – lamenting the past
417 Hassle and scams in Rissani
500 Inside the Mosque
152 Lamali and the invention of art pottery in Safi
102 Medersa – place of education for Islam
480 Monarchs, battles and freedom fighters
490 Pilgrimage
505 Pottery and belief
473 Quick chronology: ancient Morocco
476 Quick chronology: medieval and early modern Morocco
479 Quick chronology: modern Morocco
260 Saintly Sultan Abou Inane
131 Sample prices for basics
126 Sidi Abderrahman, the flautist
227 The 'golden age' of Moulay Ismaïl
65 The Hammam experience
252 The Fassia
465 Flooding the Sahara Timbuktu, or by boat
508 The jeweller's craft
57 Top tables
460 Travelling in the Deep South
363 Warriors from the mountains
175 With William Burroughs in Interzone

Maps

101 Abul Hassan Medersa - Salé
431 Agadir
359 Around Marrakech
139 Azzemour
327 Ben Youssef Medersa (Marrakech)
301 Beni Snassen Mountains
400 Boumalne du Dadès
118 Casablanca
124 Casablanca centre
123 Casablanca Médina
200 Ceuta
212 Chaouen
141 El Jadida
412 Er Rachidia
415 Erfoud
159 Essaouira
161 Essaouira Médina
258 Fès el Bali
255 Fès el Jedid
265 Fès Ville Nouvelle
251 Fès, three cities
311 Figuig
459 Goulimine
279 Jbel Tazzeka National Park
367 Jbel Toubkal Region
196 Larache
198 Lixus
339 Marrakech Guèliz
321 Marrakech Guèliz and Hivernage overview
336 Marrakech Jemaâ El Fna, Bab Agnaou & around
322 Marrakech Médina
341 Marrakech Northern suburbs and Palmeraie
326 Marrakech souks
228 Meknès
231 Meknès Médina
296 Melilla
86 Merinid Mausoleum at Chellah
289 Nador
386 Ouarzazate
221 Ouezzane
306 Oujda
146 Oualidia
82 Rabat
90 Rabat Médina and Ville Nouvelle
149 Safi
153 Safi centre
302 Saïdia
100 Salé
461 Sidi Ifni
456 Tafraoute
176 Tanger
180 Tanger Médina
444 Taroudant
275 Taza Médina
206 Tetouan
108 Thamusida
419 The Tafilalet oases
402 Tingehir
453 Tiznit
240 Volubilis
393 Zagora

Credits

Footprint credits
Editor: Tim Jollands
Map editor: Sarah Sorensen

Publisher: Patrick Dawson
Editorial: Alan Murphy, Sophie Blacksell, Sarah Thorowgood, Claire Boobbyer, Caroline Lascom, Felicity Laughton, Davina Rungasamy, Laura Dixon
Cartography: Robert Lunn, Claire Benison, Kevin Feeney, Zoe Franklin
Series development: Rachel Fielding
Design: Mytton Williams and Rosemary Dawson (brand)
Advertising: Debbie Wylde
Finance and administration: Sharon Hughes, Elizabeth Taylor

Photography credits
Front cover: Imagebank
Back cover: Impact Photos
Inside colour section: Ffotograff, Eye Ubiquitous, James Davis Travel Photography, Patrick Syder, Getty Images, Images Colour Library, Impact Photos, Jeremy Horner

Print
Manufactured in Italy by LegoPrint
Pulp from sustainable forests

Footprint feedback
We try as hard as we can to make each Footprint guide as up to date as possible but, of course, things always change. If you want to let us know about your experiences – good, bad or ugly – then don't delay, go to www.footprintbooks.com and send in your comments.

Publishing information
Morocco
4th edition
© Footprint Handbooks Ltd
October 2003

ISBN 1 903471 63 X
CIP DATA: A catalogue record for this book is available from the British Library

® Footprint Handbooks and the Footprint mark are a registered trademark of Footprint Handbooks Ltd

Published by Footprint
6 Riverside Court
Lower Bristol Road
Bath BA2 3DZ, UK
T +44 (0)1225 469141
F +44 (0)1225 469461
discover@footprintbooks.com
www.footprintbooks.com

Distributed in the USA by
Publishers Group West

All rights reserved. No part of this publication may be reproduced, stored in a retrieval system, or transmitted, in any form or by any means, electronic, mechanical, photocopying recording, or otherwise without the prior permission of Footprint Handbooks Ltd.

Neither the black and white nor coloured maps are intended to have any political significance.

Every effort has been made to ensure that the facts in this guidebook are accurate. However, travellers should still obtain advice from consulates, airlines etc about travel and visa requirements before travelling. The authors and publishers cannot accept responsibility for any loss, injury or inconvenience however caused.

Acknowledgements

Credit is due to numerous friends and acquaintances for their help and advice. Zoubeir Mouhli was a huge source of encouragement, providing insight on architecture and Islam. Ahmed Louarzazi, Quentin Wilbaux, Serge Meadow and Bernard Rubio provided insider's information on Marrakech, while without the advice of Jacqueline Alluchon and Jamal Boushaba the Casablanca section would be greatly lacking. Francis Russell's expert eye contemplated the mystery of the Medersa el Attarine, while David Amster, Hichem Mounir and Ismail Chemssi were unique sources of information on the houses of Fes.

Many thanks are also due to Khaled Ezzedine for looking over proofs, and to Tim Jollands for all his patience and attention to detail. Credit is also due to numerous people across Morocco who shared thoughts and ideas about the country, including AR Ben Chemsi, Abd Errahime Kassou, and Ahmed Benyahia. Some readers of an earlier edition of the guide also took time to write in with ideas and addresses picked up during their travels. Input was also provided by Maya Lemaire, Alice Baker and Vega McGuinness when inspiration flagged.

Much of the information in this guide comes from academic sources, too numerous to cite in detail here. Key sources include Abdelaziz Amine and Jean Brignon's thorough *Histoire du Maroc*, Paul McKendrick's *The North African Stones Speak*, and Jamil M Abu Nasr's *A History of the Maghrib in the Islamic Period*. On the history of the main Islamic cities, I drew on texts by Mohamed El Faiz, Roger Le Tourneau, Philippe Revault, and Hamid Triki. For Casablanca, publications by J-L Cohen and Monique Eleb were indispensable. I also derived much insight by ethnographic and other social science research by Dale Eickelman, Hassan Rachik, Mohamed Tozy and Susan Ossman.

The health section was written by **Dr Charlie Easmon** MBBS MRCP MSc Public Health DTM&H DOccMed Director of Travel Screening Services. His aid and development work has included: Raleigh International (Medical Officer in Botswana), MERLIN (in Rwanda his team set up a refugee camp for 12,000 people), Save the Children (as a consultant in Rwanda), ECHO (The European Community Humanitarian Office review of Red Cross work in Armenia, Georgia and Azerbaijan), board member of International Care and Relief and previously International Health Exchange. In addition to his time as a hospital physician, he has worked as a medical adviser to the Foreign and Commonwealth Office and as a locum consultant at the Hospital for Tropical Diseases travel clinic, London, as well as being a specialist registrar in Public Health. He now also runs Travel Screening services (www.travelscreening.co.uk) based at 1 Harley Street.

Check out...

www...

100 travel guides, 100s of destinations,
5 continents and 1 Footprint...
www.footprintbooks.com

Advertisers' index

21, 547	Exodus Travels, UK
546	GB Airways, UK
545	Putumayo World Music, USA
22	Cross Cultural Adventure, USA
173	FRS - Ferrys Rapido del Sur, Spain
20	Guerba World Travel Ltd, UK
23	Heritage Tours, USA
267	Invisible World Fez, USA
355	Menara Tours, Morocco
44	Riads au Maroc, Morocco
53	Stanfords, UK

Travel the World with Putumayo

Cairo to Casablanca: An Arabic Musical Odyssey

The music of North Africa will transport you to a romantic world filled with exotic melodies. Features Khaled, Rachid Taha and more.

Also available: Arabic Groove
Rock the kasbah with this collection of funky, contemporary music from North Africa and the Middle East.

Putumayo CDs are available in thousands of record, gift, book stores, and cafés. If you can't find a title, visit our website, www.putumayo.com or in North America, call 1-888-Putumayo (1-888-788-8629).

PUTUMAYO
World Music
Guaranteed to make you feel good!
www.putumayo.com

BRITISH AIRWAYS

More flights
To more of Morocco
(Choices, choices, choices.)

Direct flights from London to Agadir, Casablanca, Marrakech and Tangier – more flights a week to Morocco than any other carrier.
For our best fares book at ba.com
Services operated by GB Airways Ltd.

sightseeing.

exodus.co.uk

The Different Holiday

Leaders in small group Walking & Trekking, Discovery & Adventure, Biking Adventures, European Destinations, Overland Journeys, Snow and Multi Activity Holidays Worldwide.

Tel 020 8772 3822 for brochure.
e-mail: sales@exodus.co.uk

Exodus Travels Ltd ATOL

www.exodus.co.uk

Map symbols

Administration

- International border
- State/province border
- Capital city
- Other city/town

Roads and travel

- Main road
- Other road
- Jeepable track
- Footpath
- Railway with station

Water features

- River
- Lake
- Marshland
- Beach
- Ocean
- Waterfall
- Ferry

Cities and towns

- Sight
- Sleeping
- Eating
- Building
- Main through route
- Main street
- Minor street
- Pedestrianized street
- Tunnel
- One way street
- Bridge
- Steps
- Park, garden, stadium
- Fortified wall
- Airport
- Bank
- Bus station
- Metro station
- Hospital
- Market
- Museum
- Police
- Post office
- Tourist office
- Cathedral, church
- Synagogue
- Mosque
- Petrol
- Internet
- Telephone office
- Golf course
- Parking
- A Detail map
- A Related map

Topographical features

- Contours (approx), rock outcrop
- Mountain
- Mountain pass
- Escarpment
- Gorge

Other symbols

- Archaeological site
- National park/wildlife reserve
- Viewing point
- Camp site
- Refuge
- Deciduous/palm trees

Morocco

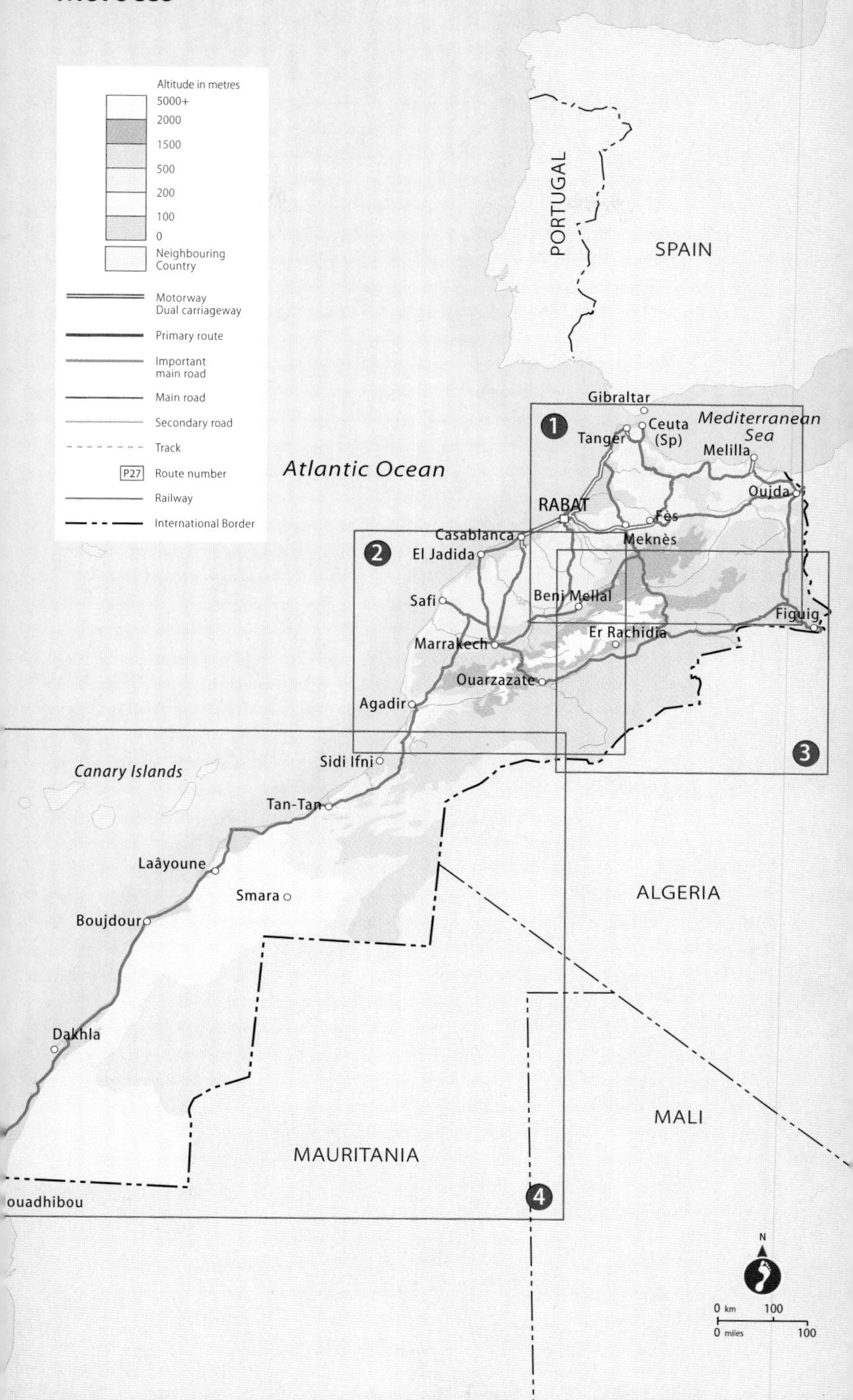

Altitude in metres
5000+
2000
1500
500
200
100
0
Neighbouring Country
Motorway
Dual carriageway
Primary route
Important main road
Main road
Secondary road
Track
P27
Route number
Railway
International Border
PORTUGAL
SPAIN
Gibraltar
Ceuta (Sp)
Tanger
Mediterranean Sea
Melilla
Atlantic Ocean
Oujda
RABAT
Fès
Casablanca
Meknès
El Jadida
Safi
Beni Mellal
Figuig
Er Rachidia
Marrakech
Ouarzazate
Agadir
Sidi Ifni
Canary Islands
Tan-Tan
Laâyoune
Smara
Boujdour
ALGERIA
Dakhla
MALI
MAURITANIA
ouadhibou
1
2
3
4
N
0 km 100
0 miles 100

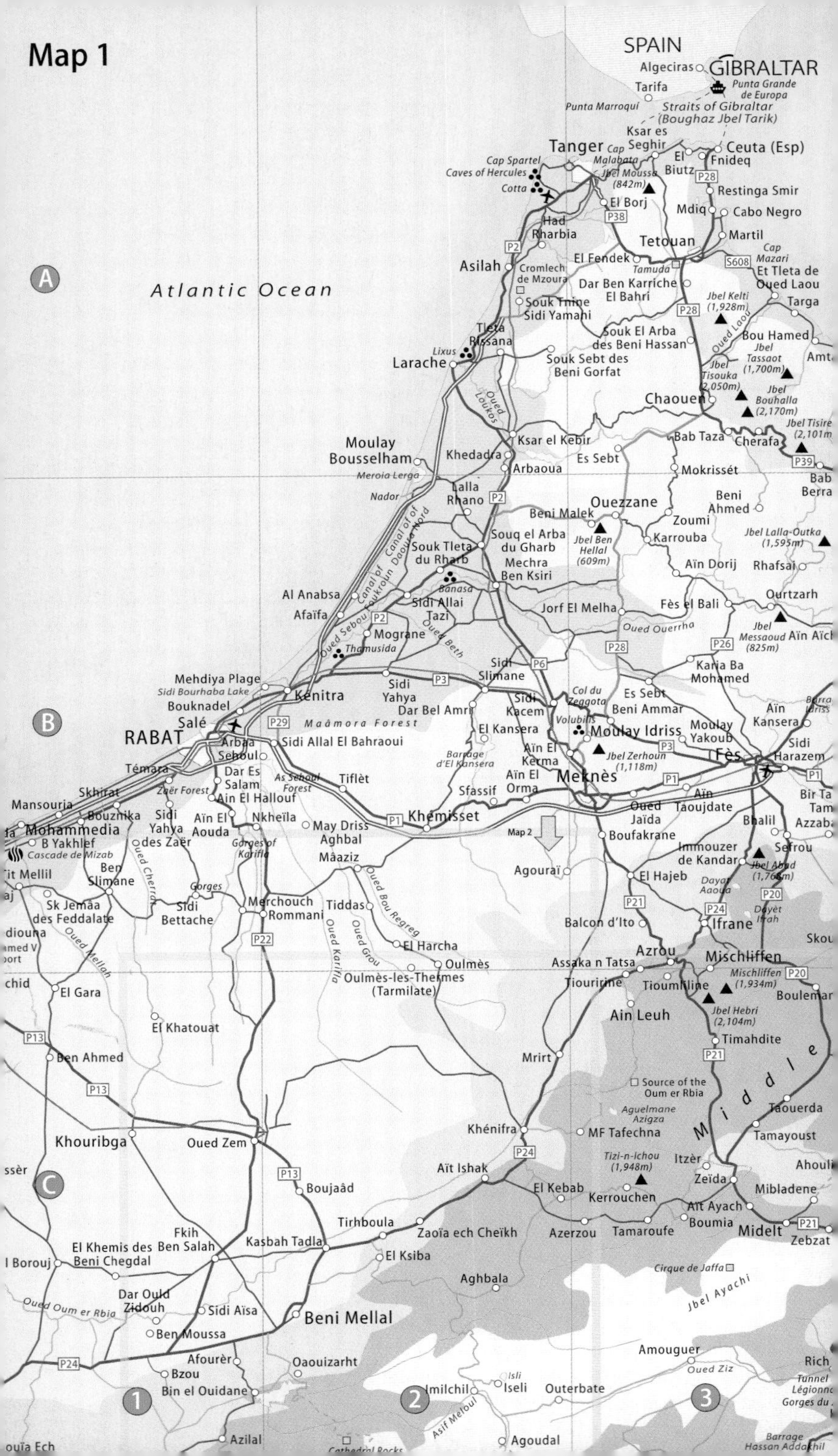
Map 1
SPAIN
Algeciras
GIBRALTAR
Tarifa
Punta Grande de Europa
Punta Marroquí
Straits of Gibraltar (Boughaz Jbel Tarik)
Ksar es Seghir
Tanger
Cap Malabata
Ceuta (Esp)
Fnideq
Cap Spartel
Caves of Hercules
Cotta
El Biutz
Jbel Moussa (842m)
P28
Restinga Smir
El Borj
Mdiq
Cabo Negro
P38
Had Rharbia
Tetouan
Martil
P2
El Fendek
Tamuda
S608
Cap Mazari
Asilah
Cromlech de Mzoura
Et Tleta de Oued Laou
Dar Ben Karriche El Bahri
A
Atlantic Ocean
Souk Tnine Sidi Yamahi
Jbel Kelti (1,928m)
Targa
Tleta Rissana
Souk El Arba des Beni Hassan
Oued Laou
Bou Hamed
Jbel Tassaot (1,700m)
Lixus
Larache
Souk Sebt des Beni Gorfat
Jbel Tisouka (2,050m)
Jbel Bouhalla (2,170m)
Oued Loukos
Chaouen
Jbel Tisirene (2,101m)
Moulay Bousselham
Ksar el Kebir
Bab Taza
Cherafa
Khedadra
Es Sebt
P39
Meroia Lerga
Arbaoua
Mokrissét
Bab Berred
Lalla Rhano
Nador
Ouezzane
Beni Ahmed
Beni Malek
Zoumi
Canal of Foukroun
Canal of Daoura Nord
Souk Tleta du Rharb
Souq el Arba du Gharb
Jbel Ben Hellal (609m)
Karrouba
Jbel Lalla-Outka (1,595m)
Mechra Ben Ksiri
Aïn Dorij
Rhafsaï
Al Anabsa
Banasa
Afaïfa
Sidi Allai Tazi
Jorf El Melha
Fès el Bali
Ourtzarh
Oued Sebou
Mograne
Oued Beth
Oued Ouerrha
Jbel Messaoud (825m)
Aïn Aïcha
Thamusida
P26
P28
Karia Ba Mohamed
Sidi Slimane
P6
Mehdiya Plage
Sidi Bourhaba Lake
Kenitra
P3
Sidi Yahya
Es Sebt Beni Ammar
Bouknadel
Sidi Kacem
Col du Zeggota
Dar Bel Amri
Aïn Kansera
Salé
B
P29
Maâmora Forest
Volubilis
Moulay Idriss
Moulay Yakoub
RABAT
El Kansera
Arbaa Sehoul
Sidi Allal El Bahraoui
P3
Sidi Harazem
Barrage d'El Kansera
Aïn El Kerma
Jbel Zerhoun (1,118m)
Fès
Témara
Dar Es Salam
As Sehoul Forest
Tiflèt
Aïn El Orma
Meknès
P1
Skhirat
Zaër Forest
Sfassif
Aïn Taoujdate
Mansouria
Ain El Hallouf
Oued Jaïda
Bouznika
Sidi Yahya des Zaër
Aïn El Aouda
Nkheïla
May Driss Aghbal
Khémisset
P1
Bhalil
Azzaba
Mohammedia
Map 2
Boufakrane
B Yakhlef
Cascade de Mizab
Gorges of Karifla
Immouzer de Kandar
Sefrou
Ben Slimane
Oued Cherrat
Mâaziz
Agouraï
Jbel Abad (1,768m)
Tit Mellil
El Hajeb
Dayat Aaoua
Gorges
P20
Sk Jemâa des Feddalate
Sidi Bettache
Merchouch
Rommani
Tiddas
Oued Bou Regreg
P21
Dayèt Ifrah
P24
Ifrane
Oued Mellah
Balcon d'Ito
P22
Oued Karifla
Oued Grou
El Harcha
Azrou
Mischliffen
Oulmès
Assaka n Tatsa
Mischliffen (1,934m)
P20
Oulmès-les-Thermes (Tarmilate)
Tiouririne
Tioumliline
Boulemane
El Gara
Jbel Hebri (2,104m)
El Khatouat
Ain Leuh
P13
Timahdite
Ben Ahmed
Mrirt
P21
Source of the Oum er Rbia
P13
Aguelmane Azigza
Middle
Taouerda
Khouribga
Oued Zem
Khénifra
MF Tafechna
Tamayoust
P24
Tizi-n-Ichou (1,948m)
Itzèr
P13
Aït Ishak
Zeïda
C
Boujaâd
El Kebab
Kerrouchen
Mibladene
Aït Ayach
Tirhboula
Boumia
Zaoïa ech Cheïkh
Azerzou
Tamaroufe
Midelt
P21
Zebzat
Fkih Ben Salah
Kasbah Tadla
El Khemis des Beni Chegdal
El Borouj
El Ksiba
Cirque de Jaffa
Aghbala
Jbel Ayachi
Dar Ould Zidouh
Oued Oum er Rbia
Sidi Aïsa
Beni Mellal
Ben Moussa
Amouguer
Afourèr
P24
Oaouizarht
Oued Ziz
Rich
Bzou
Isli
Bin el Ouidane
Imilchil
Iseli
Outerbate
Tunnel Légionnaire
Gorges du Ziz
1
2
3
Asif Melloul
Barrage Hassan Addakhil
Azilal
Cathedral Rocks
Agoudal

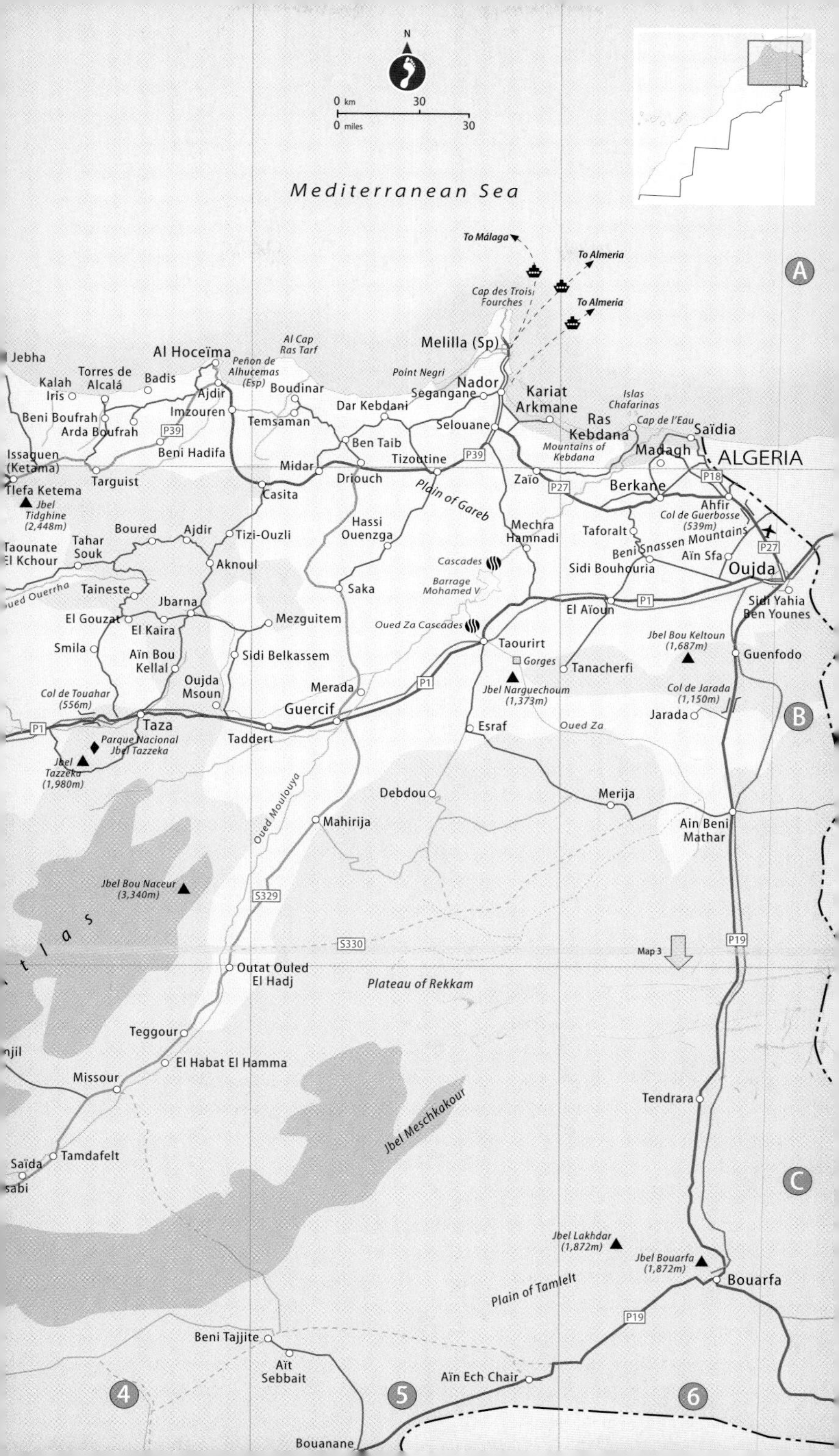

N
0 km 30
0 miles 30
Mediterranean Sea
To Málaga
To Almeria
To Almeria
Cap des Trois Fourches
A
Melilla (Sp)
Al Cap Ras Tarf
Jebha
Al Hoceïma
Peñon de Alhucemas (Esp)
Torres de Alcalá
Kalah Iris
Badis
Ajdir
Boudinar
Point Negri
Nador
Segangane
Kariat Arkmane
Islas Chafarinas
Beni Boufrah
Arda Boufrah
Imzouren
Temsaman
Dar Kebdani
Selouane
Ras Kebdana
Cap de l'Eau
Saïdia
P39
Ben Taib
Mountains of Kebdana
Madagh
ALGERIA
Issaguen (Ketama)
Beni Hadifa
Midar
Tizoutine
P39
Targuist
Driouch
Zaïo
P18
Tlefa Ketema
Casita
Plain of Gareb
P27
Berkane
Ahfir
Jbel Tidghine (2,448m)
Col de Guerbosse (539m)
Boured
Ajdir
Tizi-Ouzli
Hassi Ouenzga
Mechra Hamnadi
Taforalt
Beni Snassen Mountains
Taounate
El Kchour
Tahar Souk
P27
Aknoul
Cascades
Aïn Sfa
Sidi Bouhouria
Oujda
Oued Ouerrha
Taineste
Barrage Mohamed V
Saka
Sidi Yahia Ben Younes
Jbarna
P1
El Gouzat
Mezguitem
El Aïoun
El Kaira
Oued Za Cascades
Jbel Bou Keltoun (1,687m)
Smila
Taourirt
Aïn Bou Kellal
Sidi Belkassem
Gorges
Tanacherfi
Guenfodo
Oujda Msoun
Merada
P1
Jbel Narguechoum (1,373m)
Col de Jarada (1,150m)
Col de Touahar (556m)
Guercif
Jarada
B
P1
Taza
Esraf
Oued Za
Taddert
Parque Nacional Jbel Tazzeka
Jbel Tazzeka (1,980m)
Oued Moulouya
Debdou
Merija
Mahirija
Ain Beni Mathar
Jbel Bou Naceur (3,340m)
S329
Atlas
S330
P19
Map 3
Outat Ouled El Hadj
Plateau of Rekkam
Teggour
njil
El Habat El Hamma
Missour
Jbel Meschkakour
Tendrara
Tamdafelt
Saïda
sabi
C
Jbel Lakhdar (1,872m)
Jbel Bouarfa (1,872m)
Bouarfa
Plain of Tamlelt
P19
Beni Tajjite
Aït Sebbait
Aïn Ech Chair
4
5
6
Bouanane

Map 2

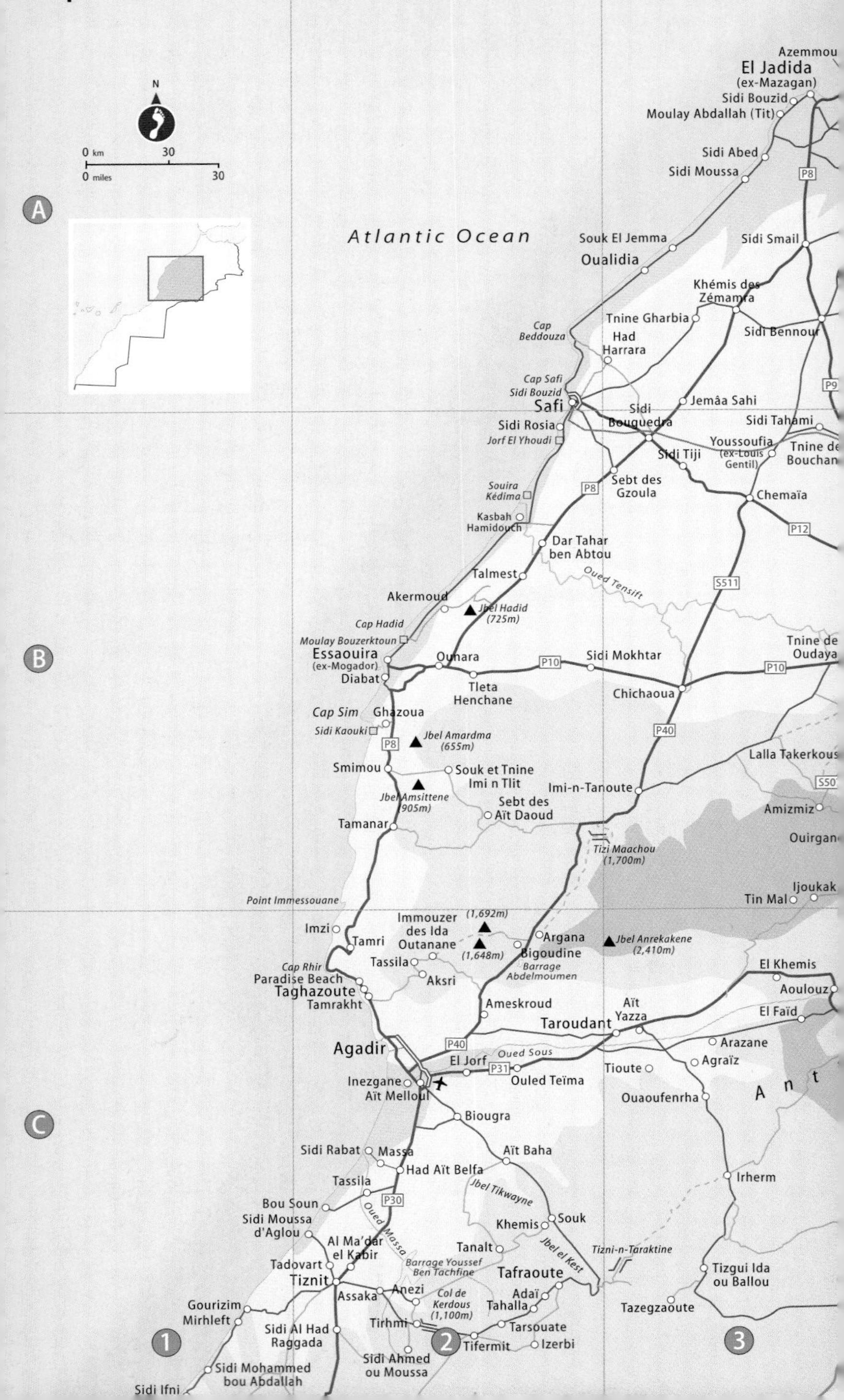
N
0 km
30
0 miles
30
A
B
C
1
2
3
Atlantic Ocean
Azemmou
El Jadida
(ex-Mazagan)
Sidi Bouzid
Moulay Abdallah (Tit)
Sidi Abed
Sidi Moussa
P8
Souk El Jemma
Oualidia
Sidi Smail
Khémis des Zémamra
Tnine Gharbia
Had Harrara
Sidi Bennour
Cap Beddouza
Cap Safi
Sidi Bouzid
Safi
Jemâa Sahi
Sidi Bouguedra
Sidi Tahami
Sidi Rosia
Jorf El Yhoudi
Youssoufia
(ex-Louis Gentil)
Tnine de Bouchan
Sidi Tiji
Sebt des Gzoula
Souira Kédima
Chemaïa
Kasbah Hamidouch
P12
Dar Tahar ben Abtou
Talmest
Oued Tensift
S511
Akermoud
Jbel Hadid
(725m)
Cap Hadid
Moulay Bouzerktoun
Essaouira
(ex-Mogador)
Diabat
Ounara
P10
Sidi Mokhtar
Tnine de Oudaya
Tleta Henchane
Chichaoua
Cap Sim
Ghazoua
Sidi Kaouki
Jbel Amardma
(655m)
P40
Lalla Takerkous
Smimou
Souk et Tnine Imi n Tlit
Imi-n-Tanoute
S50
Jbel Amsittene
(905m)
Sebt des Aït Daoud
Amizmiz
Tamanar
Ouirgan
Tizi Maachou
(1,700m)
Ijoukak
Tin Mal
Point Immessouane
Immouzer des Ida Outanane
(1,692m)
(1,648m)
Imzi
Tamri
Argana
Bigoudine
Jbel Anrekakene
(2,410m)
Tassila
Aksri
Barrage Abdelmoumen
El Khemis
Cap Rhir
Paradise Beach
Taghazoute
Tamrakht
Aoulouz
Ameskroud
Aït Yazza
El Faïd
Taroudant
Agadir
Oued Sous
Arazane
El Jorf
P31
Tioute
Agraïz
Inezgane
Aït Melloul
Ouled Teïma
Ouaoufenrha
Ant
Biougra
Sidi Rabat
Massa
Aït Baha
Had Aït Belfa
Tassila
Jbel Tikwayne
Irherm
P30
Bou Soun
Sidi Moussa d'Aglou
Oued Massa
Souk
Khemis
Al Ma'dar el Kabir
Tanalt
Jbel el Kest
Tizni-n-Taraktine
Tadovart
Barrage Youssef Ben Tachfine
Tafraoute
Tizgui Ida ou Ballou
Tiznit
Anezi
Assaka
Col de Kerdous
(1,100m)
Adaï
Tahalla
Gourizim
Mirhleft
Tazegzaoute
Sidi Al Had Raggada
Tirhmi
Tarsouate
Tifermit
Izerbi
Sidi Ahmed ou Moussa
Sidi Mohammed bou Abdallah
Sidi Ifni

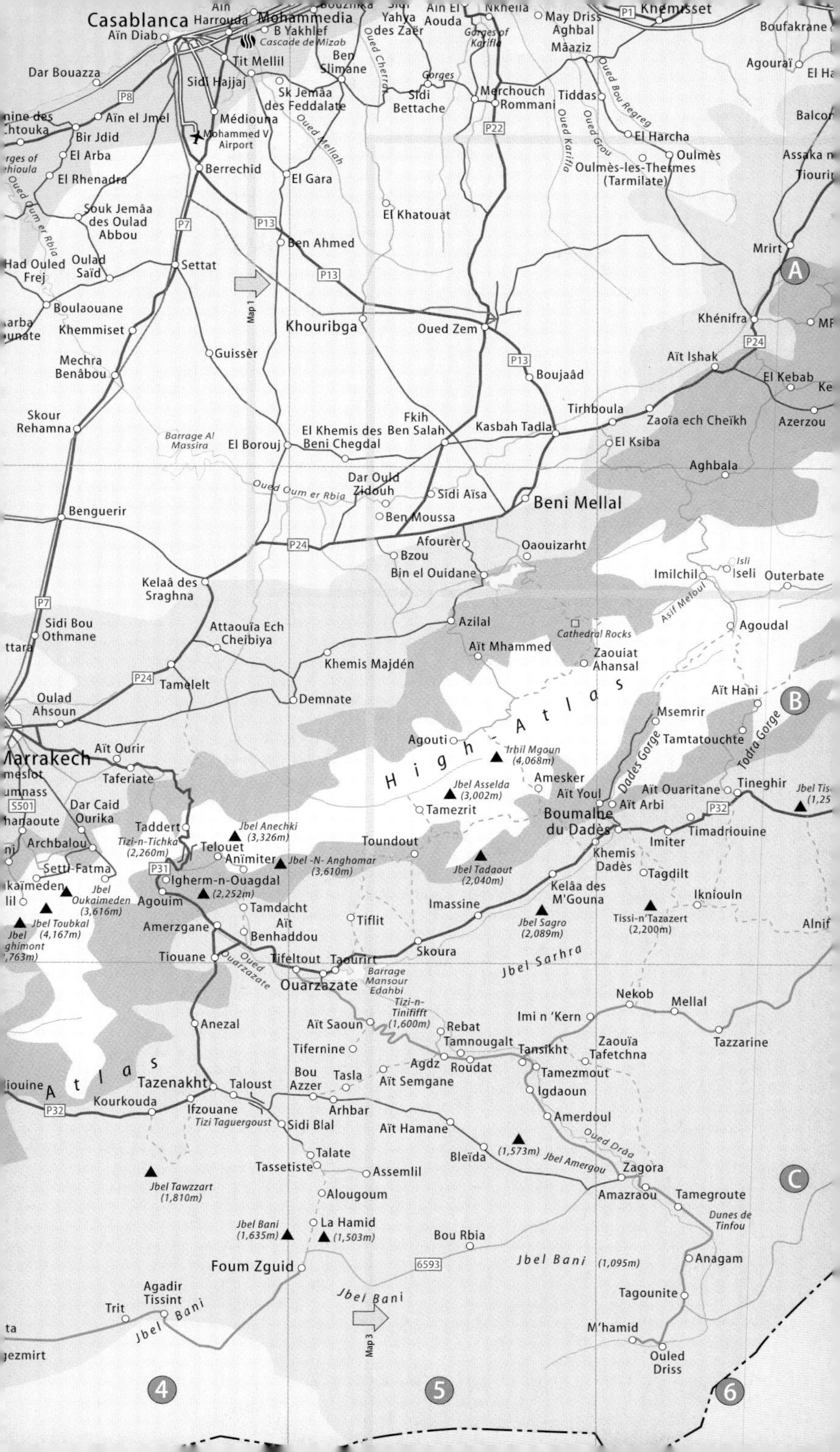
Casablanca
Aïn Diab
Harrouda
Mohammedia
B Yakhlef
Cascade de Mizab
Yahya des Zaër
Aïn El Aouda
Gorges of Karifla
May Driss Aghbal
P1
Boufakrane
Dar Bouazza
Tit Mellil
Ben Slimane
Oued Cherrat
Mâaziz
Agouraï
Sidi Hajjaj
Sk Jemâa des Feddalate
Gorges
Sidi Bettache
Merchouch
Rommani
Tiddas
Oued Bou Regreg
P8
Aïn el Jmel
Médiouna
Oued Mellah
P22
Mohammed V Airport
Oued Karifla
Oued Grou
El Harcha
Bir Jdid
El Arba
Oulmès
Oulmès-les-Thermes (Tarmilate)
Berrechid
El Rhenadra
El Gara
Oued Oum er Rbia
Souk Jemâa des Oulad Abbou
El Khatouat
P7
P13
Ben Ahmed
Had Ouled Frej
Oulad Saïd
Settat
Mrirt
A
P13
Map 1
Boulaouane
Khemmiset
Khouribga
Oued Zem
Khénifra
P24
Guissèr
Aït Ishak
P13
Mechra Benâbou
Boujaâd
El Kebab
Tirhboula
Zaoïa ech Cheïkh
Azerzou
Skour Rehamna
Fkih Ben Salah
El Khemis des Beni Chegdal
Kasbah Tadla
Barrage Al Massira
El Borouj
El Ksiba
Aghbala
Dar Ould Zidouh
Oued Oum er Rbia
Sidi Aïsa
Beni Mellal
Benguerir
Ben Moussa
Afourèr
P24
Oaouizarht
Bzou
Bin el Ouidane
Isli
Iseli
Imilchil
Outerbate
Kelaâ des Sraghna
Asif Melloul
P7
Azilal
Agoudal
Cathedral Rocks
Sidi Bou Othmane
Attaouïa Ech Cheibiya
Aït Mhammed
Zaouiat Ahansal
Khemis Majdén
P24
Tamelelt
Aït Hani
Oulad Ahsoun
Demnate
B
High - Atlas
Msemrir
Agouti
Irhil Mgoun (4,068m)
Tamtatouchte
Marrakech
Aït Ourir
Todra Gorge
Taferiate
Dades Gorge
Amesker
Jbel Asselda (3,002m)
Aït Youl
Aït Ouaritane
Tineghir
S501
Dar Caid Ourika
Aït Arbi
P32
Tamezrit
Taddert
Boumalne du Dadès
Jbel Anechki (3,326m)
Tizi-n-Tichka (2,260m)
Timadriouine
Archbalou
Telouet
Toundout
Imiter
Anïmiter
Jbel -N- Anghomar (3,610m)
Khemis Dadès
Setti-Fatma
P31
Jbel Tadaout (2,040m)
Tagdilt
Igherm-n-Ouagdal
Kelâa des M'Gouna
Jbel Oukaimeden (3,616m)
(2,252m)
Ikniouln
Agouim
Tamdacht
Imassine
Jbel Toubkal (4,167m)
Tiflit
Jbel Sagro (2,089m)
Tissi-n'Tazazert (2,200m)
Alnif
Amerzgane
Aït Benhaddou
Skoura
Tiouane
Oued Ouarzazate
Tifeltout
Taourirt
Jbel Sarhra
Barrage Mansour Edahbi
Ouarzazate
Nekob
Tizi-n-Tinififft (1,600m)
Mellal
Imi n 'Kern
Anezal
Aït Saoun
Rebat
Tazzarine
Tamnougalt
Tifernine
Tansikht
Zaouïa Tafetchna
Agdz
Roudat
Bou Azzer
Tasla
Aït Semgane
Tamezmout
Atlas
Tazenakht
Taloust
Igdaoun
P32
Kourkouda
Ifzouane
Arhbar
Amerdoul
Tizi Taguergoust
Sidi Blal
Aït Hamane
Oued Drâa
Bleïda
(1,573m)
Jbel Amergou
Talate
Zagora
Tassetiste
Assemlil
C
Jbel Tawzzart (1,810m)
Amazraou
Tamegroute
Alougoum
Dunes de Tinfou
Jbel Bani (1,635m)
La Hamid
(1,503m)
Bou Rbia
Anagam
Foum Zguid
6593
Jbel Bani
(1,095m)
Agadir Tissint
Jbel Bani
Tagounite
Trit
Jbel Bani
Map 3
M'hamid
Ouled Driss
4
5
6

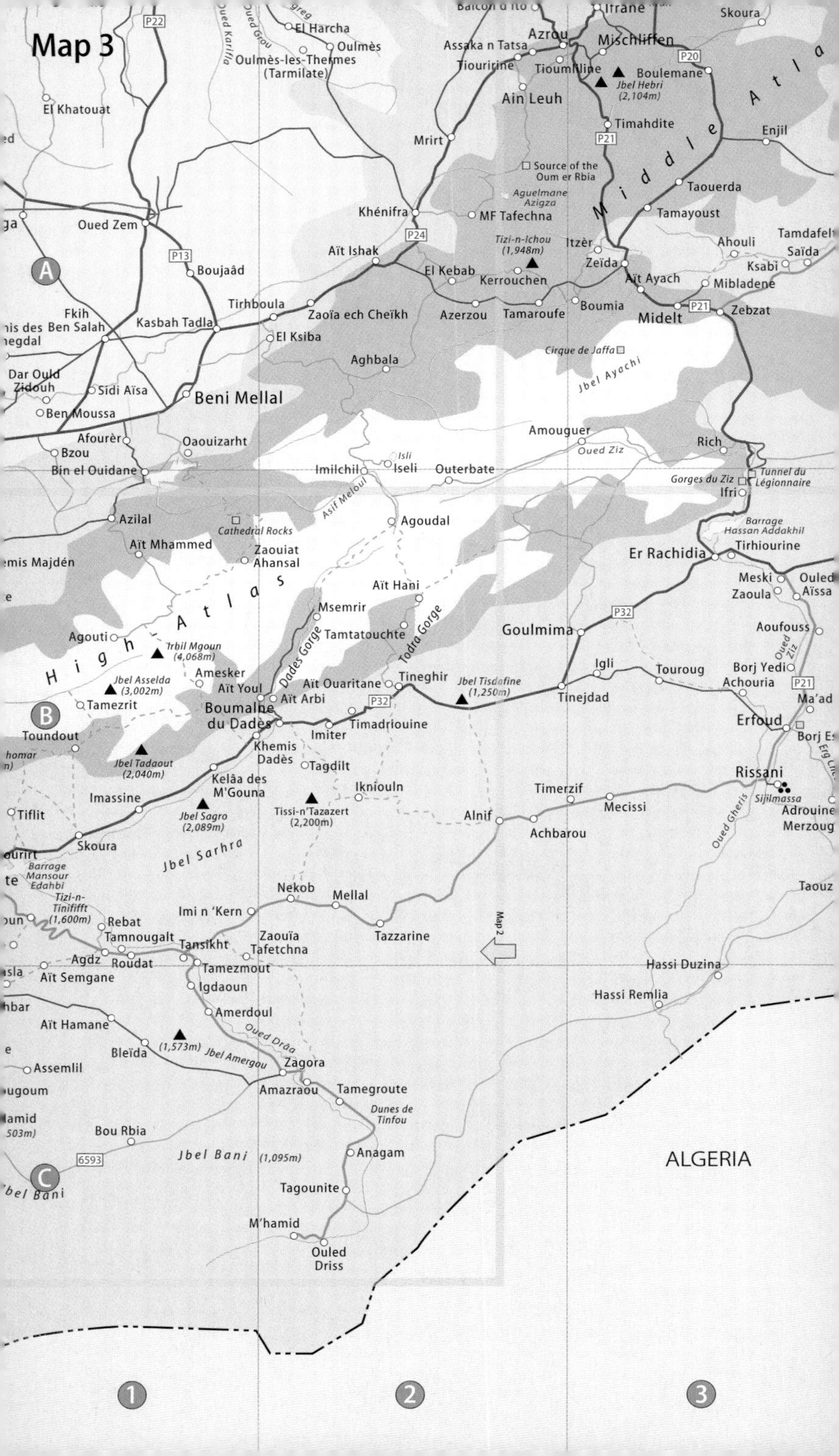
Map 3
Middle Atlas
High Atlas
ALGERIA
Azrou
Ifrane
Mischliffen
Boulemane
Jbel Hebri (2,104m)
Timahdite
Ain Leuh
Tioumliline
Tiouririne
Assaka n Tatsa
Mrirt
Khénifra
Source of the Oum er Rbia
Aguelmane Azigza
MF Tafechna
Tizi-n-Ichou (1,948m)
Itzèr
Zeïda
Aït Ayach
Midelt
Mibladene
Zebzat
Taouerda
Tamayoust
Ahouli
Enjil
Skoura
Tamdafelt
Saïda
Ksabi
El Harcha
Oulmès
Oulmès-les-Thermes (Tarmilate)
El Khatouat
Oued Zem
Boujaâd
Fkih Ben Salah
Kasbah Tadla
Tirhboula
Zaoïa ech Cheïkh
El Ksiba
Aït Ishak
El Kebab
Kerrouchen
Azerzou
Tamaroufe
Boumia
Aghbala
Cirque de Jaffa
Jbel Ayachi
Beni Mellal
Sidi Aïsa
Dar Ould Zidouh
Ben Moussa
Afourèr
Bzou
Bin el Ouidane
Oaouizarht
Imilchil
Isli
Iseli
Outerbate
Amouguer
Oued Ziz
Rich
Gorges du Ziz
Tunnel du Légionnaire
Ifri
Barrage Hassan Addakhil
Tirhiourine
Er Rachidia
Meski
Zaoula
Ouled Aïssa
Asif Melloul
Agoudal
Azilal
Cathedral Rocks
Aït Mhammed
Zaouiat Ahansal
Aït Hani
Msemrir
Tamtatouchte
Dades Gorge
Todra Gorge
Goulmima
Aoufouss
Oued Ziz
Agouti
Irhil Mgoun (4,068m)
Amesker
Aït Youl
Jbel Asselda (3,002m)
Tamezrit
Toundout
Jbel Tadaout (2,040m)
Boumalne du Dadès
Aït Ouaritane
Aït Arbi
Tineghir
Jbel Tisdafine (1,250m)
Tinejdad
Igli
Touroug
Borj Yedi
Achouria
Ma'ad
Erfoud
Timadriouine
Imiter
Khemis Dadès
Tagdilt
Kelâa des M'Gouna
Imassine
Tiflit
Skoura
Jbel Sagro (2,089m)
Tissi-n'Tazazert (2,200m)
Ikniouln
Alnif
Timerzif
Mecissi
Achbarou
Rissani
Sijilmassa
Oued Gheris
Merzoug
Taouz
Barrage Mansour Edahbi
Jbel Sarhro
Tizi-n-Tinififft (1,600m)
Rebat
Tamnougalt
Agdz
Roudat
Aït Semgane
Imi n 'Kern
Nekob
Mellal
Tazzarine
Tansikht
Zaouïa Tafetchna
Tamezmout
Igdaoun
Amerdoul
Map 2
Hassi Duzina
Hassi Remlia
Aït Hamane
Bleïda
(1,573m)
Jbel Amergou
Oued Drâa
Assemlil
Zagora
Amazraou
Tamegroute
Dunes de Tinfou
Bou Rbia
Jbel Bani
(1,095m)
Anagam
Tagounite
M'hamid
Ouled Driss
P22
P13
P24
P20
P21
P32
6593
A
B
C
1
2
3

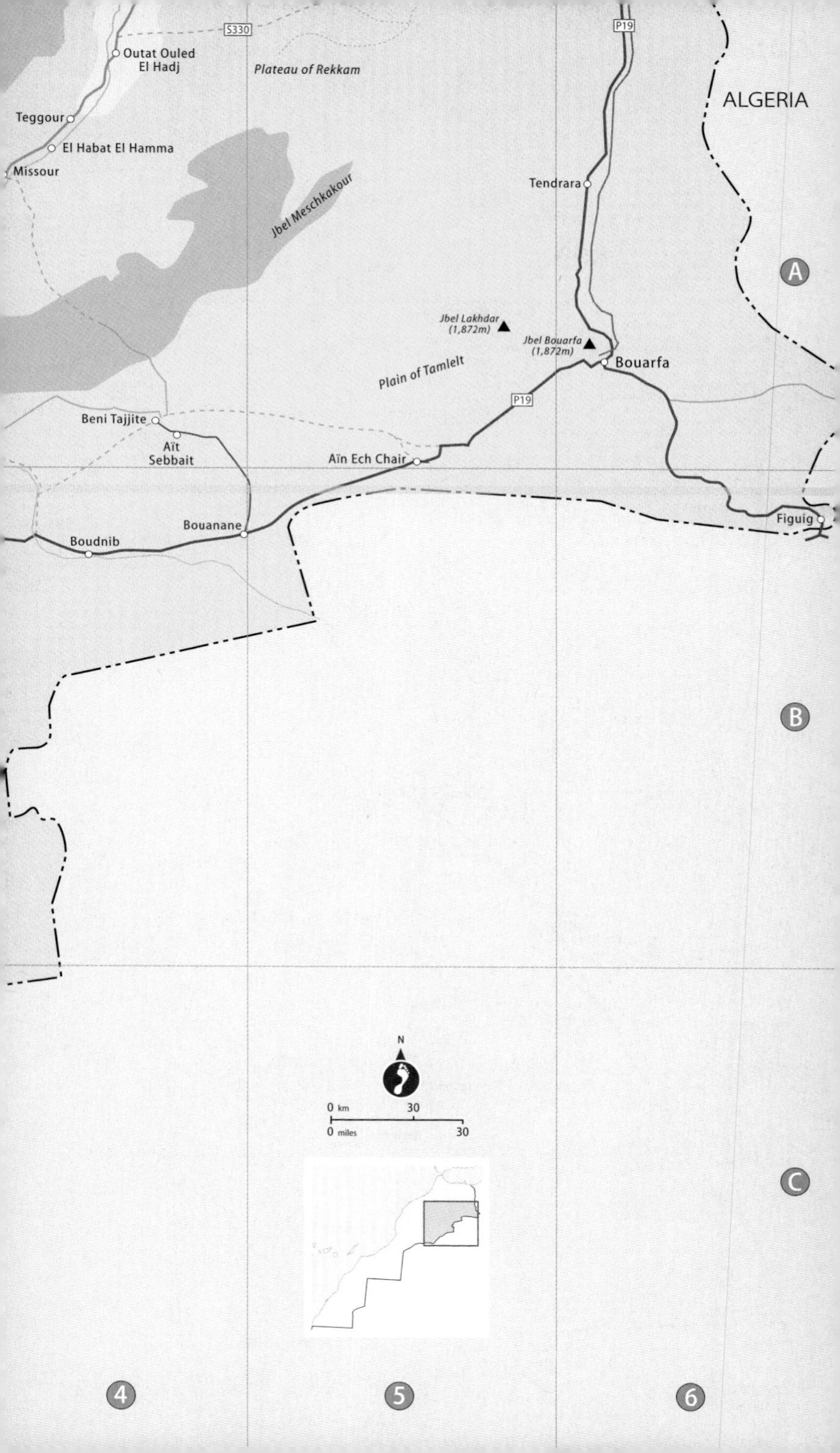

S330
Outat Ouled
El Hadj
Plateau of Rekkam
Teggour
El Habat El Hamma
Missour
Jbel Meschkakour
P19
ALGERIA
Tendrara
A
Jbel Lakhdar
(1,872m)
Jbel Bouarfa
(1,872m)
Bouarfa
Plain of Tamlelt
P19
Beni Tajjite
Aït
Sebbait
Aïn Ech Chair
Bouanane
Boudnib
Figuig
B
N
0 km
30
0 miles
30
C
4
5
6

Map 4

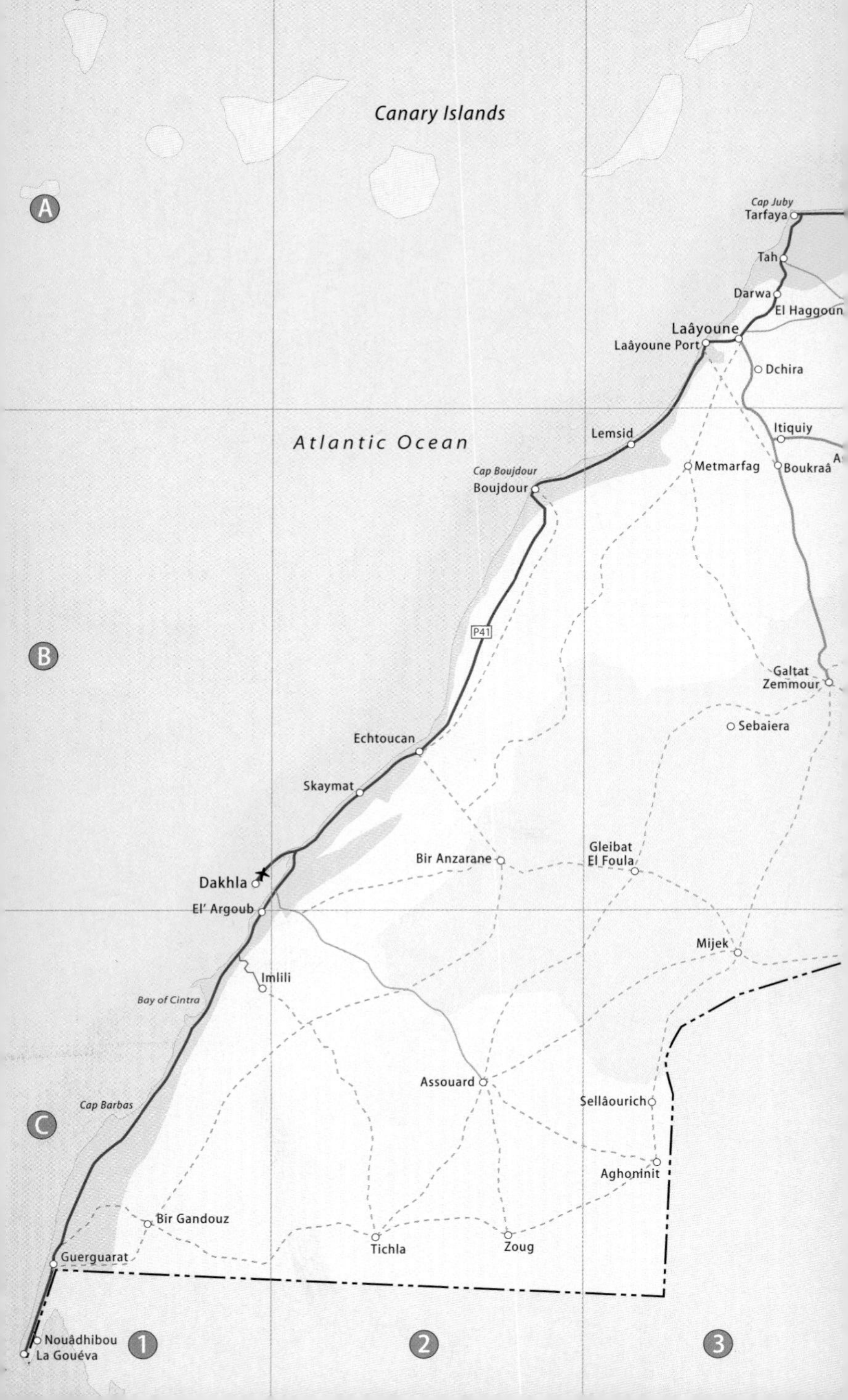

Canary Islands

Atlantic Ocean

Cap Juby
Tarfaya
Tah
Darwa
El Haggoun
Laâyoune
Laâyoune Port
Dchira
Itiquiy
Lemsid
Metmarfag
Boukraâ
Cap Boujdour
Boujdour
P41
Galtat Zemmour
Sebaiera
Echtoucan
Skaymat
Bir Anzarane
Gleibat El Foula
Dakhla
El' Argoub
Mijek
Imlili
Bay of Cintra
Assouard
Sellâourich
Cap Barbas
Aghoninit
Bir Gandouz
Guerguarat
Tichla
Zoug
Nouâdhibou
La Gouéva

A
B
C
1
2
3

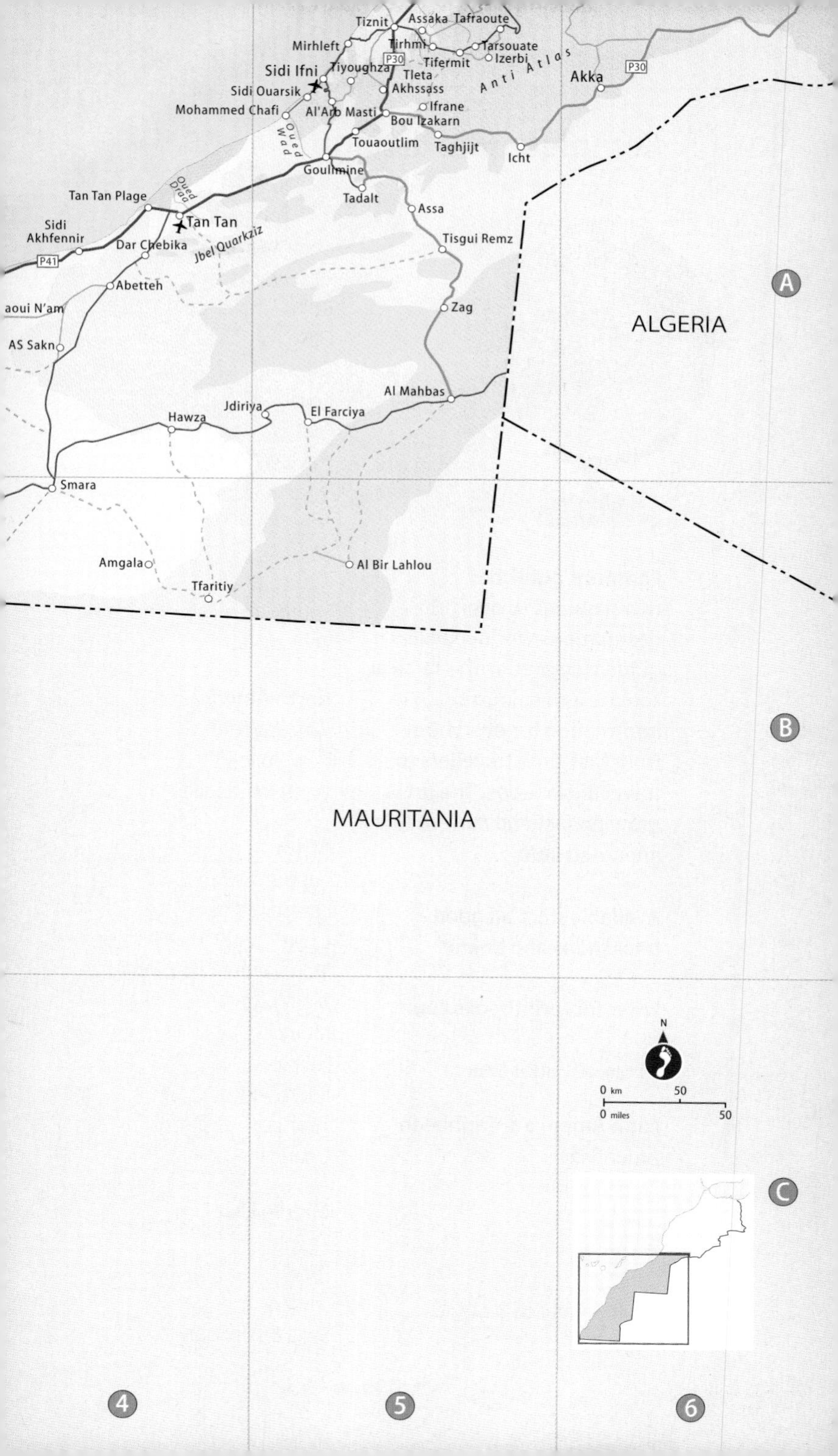

Tiznit
Assaka
Tafraoute
Mirhleft
Tirhmi
Tarsouate
P30
Tifermit
Izerbi
Sidi Ifni
Tiyoughza
Tleta
Anti Atlas
Akka
P30
Sidi Ouarsik
Akhssass
Mohammed Chafi
Al'Arb Masti
Ifrane
Bou Izakarn
Oued Wad
Touaoutlim
Taghjijt
Icht
Goulimine
Oued Draa
Tadalt
Tan Tan Plage
Assa
Tan Tan
Sidi Akhfennir
Dar Chebika
Jbel Quarkziz
Tisgui Remz
P41
Abetteh
A
aoui N'am
Zag
ALGERIA
AS Sakn
Al Mahbas
Jdiriya
Hawza
El Farciya
Smara
Amgala
Al Bir Lahlou
Tfaritiy
B
MAURITANIA
N
0 km
50
0 miles
50
C
4
5
6

Complete title listing

Footprint publishes travel guides to over 150 destinations worldwide. Each guide is packed with practical, concise and colourful information for everybody from first-time travellers to travel aficionados. The list is growing fast and current titles are noted below.

Available from all good bookshops and online

www.footprintbooks.com

(P) denotes pocket guide

Latin America & Caribbean

Argentina
Barbados (P)
Bolivia
Brazil
Caribbean Islands
Central America & Mexico
Chile
Colombia
Costa Rica
Cuba
Cusco & the Inca Trail
Dominican Republic
Ecuador & Galápagos
Guatemala
Havana (P)
Mexico
Nicaragua
Peru
Rio de Janeiro
South American Handbook
Venezuela

North America

Vancouver (P)
New York (P)
Western Canada

Africa

Cape Town (P)
East Africa
Libya
Marrakech & the High Atlas
Marrakech (P)
Morocco
Namibia
South Africa
Tunisia
Uganda

Middle East

Egypt
Israel
Jordan
Syria & Lebanon

Australasia

Australia
East Coast Australia
New Zealand
Sydney (P)
West Coast Australia

Asia

Bali
Bangkok & the Beaches
Cambodia
Goa
Hong Kong (P)
India
Indian Himalaya
Indonesia
Laos
Malaysia
Nepal
Pakistan
Rajasthan & Gujarat
Singapore
South India
Sri Lanka
Sumatra
Thailand
Tibet
Vietnam

Europe

Andalucía
Barcelona
Barcelona (P)
Berlin (P)
Bilbao (P)
Bologna (P)
Britain
Copenhagen (P)
Croatia
Dublin
Dublin (P)
Edinburgh
Edinburgh (P)
England
Glasgow
Glasgow (P)
Ireland
Lisbon (P)
London
London (P)
Madrid (P)
Naples (P)
Northern Spain
Paris (P)
Reykjavík (P)
Scotland
Scotland Highlands & Islands
Seville (P)
Spain
Tallinn (P)
Turin (P)
Turkey
Valencia (P)
Verona (P)

Also available

Traveller's Handbook (WEXAS)
Traveller's Healthbook (WEXAS)
Traveller's Internet Guide (WEXAS)

For a different view of Europe, take a Footprint

"Superstylish travel guides – perfect for short break addicts."
Harvey Nichols magazine

Discover so much more...
Listings driven, forward looking and up to date. Focuses on what's going on right now. Contemporary, stylish, and innovative approach, providing quality travel information.